A-Z GREAT BRITAIN ROAD ATLAS

Journey Route Planning maps

Southern Britain.....II-III

Northern Britain.....IV-V

Mileage Chart........2

Great Britain Road map section

Key to map pages inside front cover

Reference 3

Road Maps...........4-173

Detailed Main Route maps

London 174-181

Birmingham...........182-183

Manchester 184

City and Town centre maps

Plans of 80 principal cities and towns in Great Britain

Reference 185-186

Cities and Towns...187-214

Sea Port & Channel Tunnel plans

Principal Sea Ports in Great Britain..........215

Folkestone and Calais Terminals 276

Airport plans

Access maps to principal Airports in Great Britain
.............................216

Over 32,000 Index References

A

Abbas Combe. Som	4C 22
Abberley. Worc	4B 60
Abberley Common. Worc	4B 60
Abberton. Essx	4D 54
Abberton. Worc	5D 61
Abberwick. Nmbd	3F 121

Including cities, towns, villages, hamlets and locations 217-269

Index to Places of Interest

J

Jackfield Tile Mus. (TF8 7ND)	5A 7
Jane Austen's House Mus. (GU34 1SD)	3F 2
Jarlshof Prehistoric & Norse Settlement (ZE3 9JN)	10E 1
Jedburgh Abbey (TD8 6JQ)	3A 1
Jervaulx Abbey (HG4 4PH)	1D 9
JM Barrie's Birthplace (DD8 4BX)	3C 1

Full postcodes to easily locate over 1,700 selected places of interest on your SatNav...270-273

Motorway Junctions

M25

Junction 5
Clockwise: No exit to M26 Eastbound
Anti-clockwise: No access from M26 Westbound

Details of motorway junctions with limited interchange.....274-275

EDITION 30 2023

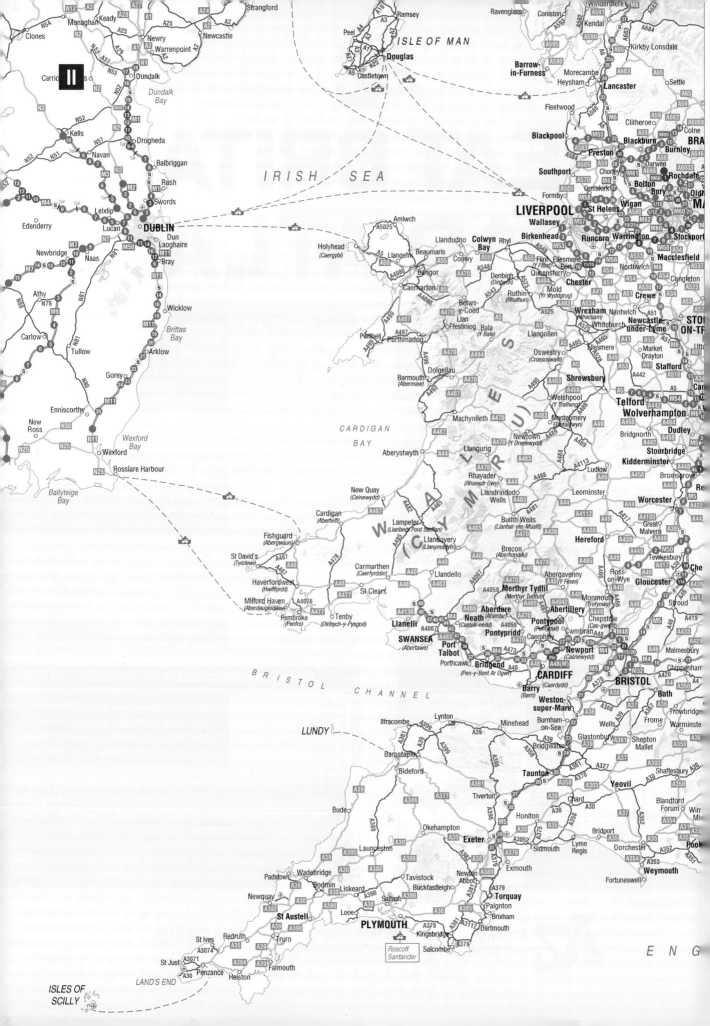

NORTH SEA

THE WASH

ENGLAND

FRANCE

ENGLISH CHANNEL

ISLE OF WIGHT

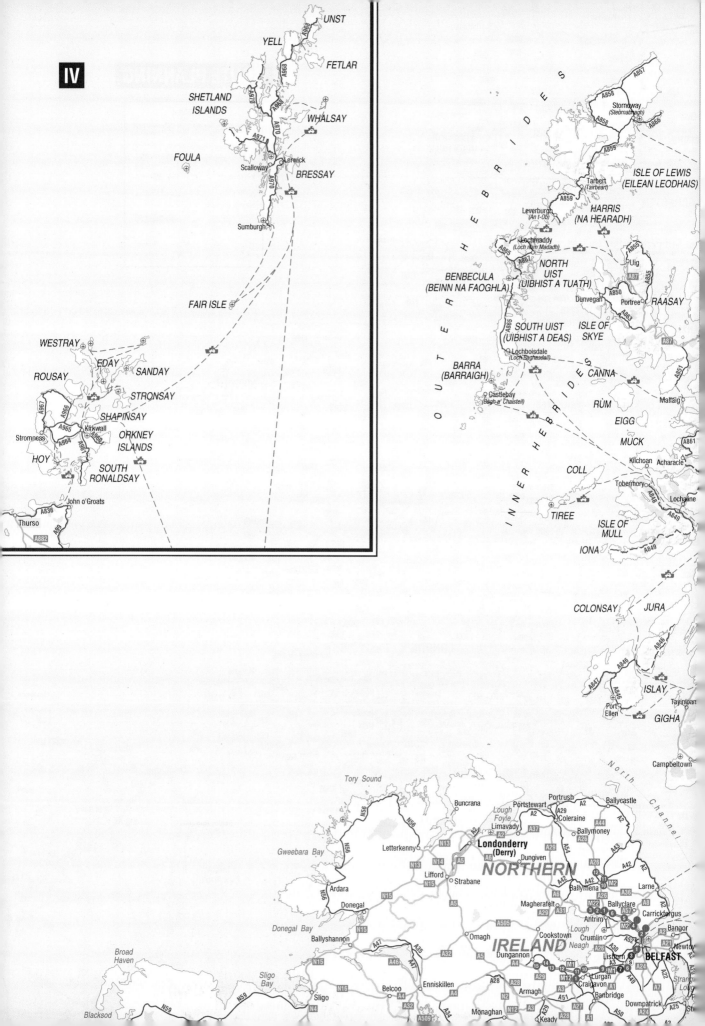

IV

UNST
YELL
FETLAR
SHETLAND
ISLANDS
WHALSAY
FOULA
Scalloway   Lerwick
BRESSAY
Sumburgh

FAIR ISLE

WESTRAY
ROUSAY   EDAY   SANDAY
STRONSAY
SHAPINSAY
Stromness   Kirkwall
HOY   ORKNEY
ISLANDS
SOUTH
RONALDSAY
John o'Groats
Thurso

OUTER HEBRIDES

Stornoway (Steòrnabhagh)
ISLE OF LEWIS
(EILEAN LEODHAIS)
Tarbert (Tairbeart)
HARRIS
(NA HEARADH)
Leverburgh (An t-Ob)
Lochmaddy (Loch nam Madadh)
Uig
BENBECULA   NORTH
(BEINN NA FAOGHLA)   UIST
(UIBHIST A TUATH)
Dunvegan   Portree   RAASAY
SOUTH UIST   ISLE OF
(UIBHIST A DEAS)   SKYE
Lochboisdale
(Loch Baghasdail)
BARRA   CANNA
(BARRAIGH)
Castlebay   RÙM   Mallaig
(Bàgh a' Chaisteil)   EIGG
MUCK
Kilchoan   Acharacle
COLL   Tobermory   Lochaline
TIREE   ISLE OF
MULL
IONA
COLONSAY   JURA
ISLAY
Port
Ellen   Tayinloan
GIGHA

Campbeltown

INNER HEBRIDES

North Channel

Tory Sound
Buncrana   Portrush   Portstewart   Ballycastle
Lough   A2
Foyle   Coleraine
Limavady   A2   Ballymoney
Letterkenny   Londonderry (Derry)
Gweebara Bay   NORTHERN
Lifford   Strabane   Dungiven   Larne
Ardara   Ballymena
Donegal   Magherafelt   Ballyclare   Carrickfergus
Antrim   Bangor
Lough   Crumlin
Donegal Bay   Neagh   BELFAST   Newto
Ballyshannon   Omagh   Cookstown   IRELAND   Lisburn
Dungannon   Lurgan
Broad   Craigavon   Stran
Haven   Lough
Sligo   Craigavon   Banbridge   Downpatrick
Bay   Belcoo   Enniskillen   Armagh   Banbridge
Sligo   Monaghan   Keady
Blacksod

NORTH SEA

SCOTLAND

Stromness · Scrabster · Thurso · John o'Groats · Wick · Tongue · Scourie · Helmsdale · Lochinver · Lairg · Bonar Bridge · Tain · Ullapool · Poolewe · Kinlochewe · Dingwall · Cromarty · Nairn · Lossiemouth · Banff · Fraserburgh · Shieldaig · Strathcarron · Achnasheen · Inverness · Elgin · Keith · Peterhead · Kyle of Lochalsh (Caol Loch Ailse) · Dufftown · Huntly · Oldmeldrum · Invermoriston · Loch Ness · Grantown-on-Spey · Inverurie · Aviemore · Peterculter · ABERDEEN · Spean Bridge · Newtonmore · Braemar · Ballater · Banchory · Fort William · Stonehaven · Invergarry · Glencoe · Pitlochry · Brechin · Montrose · Crianlarich · Dunkeld · Blairgowrie · Forfar · Arbroath · Oban · Perth · Dundee · Carnoustie · Crieff · Doune · Dunblane · Kinross · St Andrews · Glenrothes · Pittenweem · Loch Lomond · Stirling · Dunfermline · Kirkcaldy · Cowdenbeath · North Berwick · GLASGOW · Falkirk · EDINBURGH · Greenock · Clydebank · Airdrie · Livingston · Musselburgh · Dunbar · Rothesay · Paisley · Hamilton · Motherwell · Dalkeith · Eyemouth · ISLE OF BUTE · East Kilbride · Penicuik · Largs · Ardrossan · Kilmarnock · Lauder · Peebles · Galashiels · Berwick-upon-Tweed · Irvine · Troon · Biggar · Selkirk · Duns · Coldstream · Kelso · Wooler · Prestwick · Ayr · Cumnock · Hawick · Jedburgh · Brodick · Sanquhar · ISLE OF ARRAN · Alnwick · Girvan · Moffat · Amble · New Galloway · Langholm · Morpeth · Ashington · Cairnryan · Lockerbie · Blyth · Newton Stewart · Dumfries · NEWCASTLE UPON TYNE · Whitley Bay · Tynemouth · Stranraer · Annan · Hexham · Gateshead · South Shields · Castle Douglas · Corbridge · Consett · Washington · SUNDERLAND · Dalbeattie · Carlisle · Seaham · Whithorn · Kirkcudbright · Alston · Durham · Peterlee · Workington · Brampton · Bishop Auckland · HARTLEPOOL · Cockermouth · Penrith · Whitehaven · Keswick · STOCKTON-ON-TEES · Brough · Darlington · MIDDLESBROUGH · Whitby · Egremont · Barnard Castle · Ramsey · Ambleside · Windermere · Richmond · Catterick · Coniston · Ravenglass

NORTH SEA

Moray Firth · Firth of Forth · Solway Firth

Amsterdam

This chart shows the distance in miles and journey time between two cities or towns in Great Britain. Each route has been calculated using a combination of motorways, primary routes and other major roads. This is normally the quickest, though not always the shortest route.

Average journey times are calculated whilst driving at the maximum speed limit. These times are approximate and do not include traffic congestion or convenience breaks.

To find the distance and journey time between two cities or towns, follow a horizontal line and vertical column until they meet each other.

For example, the 285 mile journey from London to Penzance is approximately 4 hours and 59 minutes.

Britain

Journey times

Distance in miles

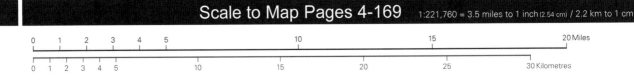

Motorway
Autoroute
Autobahn — M1

Motorway Under Construction
Autoroute en construction
Autobahn im Bau

Motorway Proposed
Autoroute prévue
Geplante Autobahn

Motorway Junctions with Numbers
Unlimited Interchange — 4
Limited Interchange — 5

Autoroute échangeur numéroté
Echangeur complet
Echangeur partiel

Autobahnanschlußstelle mit Nummer
Unbeschränkter Fahrtrichtungswechsel
Beschränkter Fahrtrichtungswechsel

Motorway Service Area (with fuel station)
with access from one carriageway only — (S)
Aire de services d'autoroute (avec station service)
accessible d'un seul côté
Rastplatz oder Raststätte (mit tankstelle)
Einbahn

Major Road Service Area (with fuel station) with 24 hour facilities
Primary Route — (S) — Class A Road — (S)
Aire de services sur route prioritaire (avec station service) Ouverte 24h sur 24
Route à grande circulation — Route de type A
Raststätte (mit tankstelle) Durchgehend geöffnet
Hauptverkehrsstraße — A- Straße

Major Road Junctions
Jonctions grands routiers — Detailed — Détaillé — Ausführlich — 4
Hauptverkehrsstraße Kreuzungen
Other — Autre — Andere

Truckstop (selection of)
Sélection d'aire pour poids lourds — (T)
Auswahl von Fernfahrerrastplatz

Primary Route
Route à grande circulation — A41
Hauptverkehrsstraße

Primary Route Junction with Number
Echangeur numéroté — 5
Hauptverkehrsstraßenkreuzung mit Nummer

Primary Route Destination
Route prioritaire, direction — DOVER
Hauptverkehrsstraße Richtung

Dual Carriageways (A & B roads)
Route à double chaussées séparées (route A & B)
Zweispurige Schnellstraße (A- und B- Straßen)

Class A Road
Route de type A — A129
A-Straße

Class B Road
Route de type B — B177
B-Straße

Narrow Major Road (passing places)
Route prioritaire étroite (possibilité de dépassement)
Schmale Hauptverkehrsstraße (mit Überholmöglichkeit)

Major Roads Under Construction
Route prioritaire en construction
Hauptverkehrsstraße im Bau

Major Roads Proposed
Route prioritaire prévue
Geplante Hauptverkehrsstraße

Gradient 1:7 (14%) & steeper
(descent in direction of arrow) — » »
Pente égale ou supérieure à 14% (dans le sens de la descente)
14% Steigung und steiler (in Pfeilrichtung)

Toll
Barrière de péage — Toll
Gebührenpflichtig

Dart Charge
www.gov.uk/pay-dartford-crossing-charge — (C)

Park & Ride
Parking avec Service Navette — P+R
Parken und Reisen

Mileage between markers
Distence en miles entre les flèches — 8
Strecke zwischen Markierungen in Meilen

Airport
Aéroport — ⊕
Flughafen

Airfield
Terrain d'aviation — +
Flugplatz

Heliport
Héliport — (H)
Hubschrauberlandeplatz

Ferry
(vehicular, sea) — Bac (véhicules, mer) — Fähre (auto, meer)
(vehicular, river) — (véhicules, rivière) — (auto, fluß)
(foot only) — (piétons) — (nur für Personen)

Railway and Station
Voie ferrée et gare
Eisenbahnlinie und Bahnhof

Level Crossing and Tunnel
Passage à niveau et tunnel
Bahnübergang und Tunnel

River or Canal
Rivière ou canal
Fluß oder Kanal

County or Unitary Authority Boundary
Limite de comté ou de division administrative
Grafschafts- oder Verwaltungsbezirksgrenze

National Boundary
Frontière nationale
Landesgrenze

Built-up Area
Agglomération
Geschlossene Ortschaft

Town, Village or Hamlet
Ville, Village ou hameau
Stadt, Dorf oder Weiler

Wooded Area
Zone boisée
Waldgebiet

Spot Height in Feet
Altitude (en pieds) — · 813
Höhe in Fuß

Relief above 400' (122m)
Relief par estompage au-dessus de 400' (122m)
Reliefschattierung über 400' (122m)

National Grid Reference (kilometres)
Coordonnées géographiques nationales (Kilomètres) — ¹00
Nationale geographische Koordinaten (Kilometer)

Page Continuation
Suite à la page indiquée — 48
Seitenfortsetzung

Area covered by Main Route map
Repartition des cartes des principaux axes routiers — MAIN ROUTE 180
Von Karten mit Hauptverkehrsstrecken

Area covered by Town Plan
Ville ayant un plan à la page indiquée — PAGE 194
Von Karten mit Stadtplänen erfaßter Bereich

Abbey, Church, Friary, Priory — †
Abbaye, église, monastère, prieuré
Abtei, Kirche, Mönchskloster, Kloster

Animal Collection
Ménagerie
Tiersammlung

Aquarium
Aquarium
Aquarium

Arboretum, Botanical Garden
Jardin Botanique
Botanischer Garten

Aviary, Bird Garden
Volière
Voliere

Battle Site and Date — 1066
Champ de bataille et date
Schlachtfeld und Datum

Blue Flag Beach
Plage Pavillon Bleu
Blaue Flagge Strand

Bridge
Pont
Brücke

Butterfly Farm
Ferme aux Papillons
Schmetterlingsfarm

Castle (open to public)
Château (ouvert au public)
Schloß / Burg (für die Öffentlichkeit zugänglich)

Castle with Garden (open to public)
Château avec parc (ouvert au public)
Schloß mit Garten (für die Öffentlichkeit zugänglich)

Cathedral — ‡
Cathédrale
Kathedrale

Cidermaker
Cidrerie (fabrication)
Apfelwein Hersteller

Country Park
Parc régional
Landschaftspark

Distillery
Distillerie
Brennerei

Farm Park, Open Farm
Park Animalier
Bauernhof Park

Fortress, Hill Fort — ✳
Château Fort
Festung

Garden (open to public)
Jardin (ouvert au public)
Garten (für die Öffentlichkeit zugänglich)

Golf Course — ⚑
Terrain de golf
Golfplatz

Historic Building (open to public)
Monument historique (ouvert au public)
Historisches Gebäude (für die Öffentlichkeit zugänglich)

Historic Building with Garden (open to public)
Monument historique avec jardin (ouvert au public)
Historisches Gebäude mit Garten (für die Öffentlichkeit zugänglich)

Horse Racecourse
Hippodrome
Pferderennbahn

Industrial Monument
Monument Industrielle
Industriedenkmal

Leisure Park, Leisure Pool
Parc d'Attraction, Loisirs Piscine
Freizeitpark, Freizeit pool

Lighthouse
Phare
Leuchtturm

Mine, Cave
Mine, Grotte
Bergwerk, Höhle

Monument
Monument
Denkmal

Motor Racing Circuit
Circuit Automobile
Automobilrennbahn

Museum, Art Gallery — M
Musée
Museum, Galerie

National Park
Parc national
Nationalpark

National Trail
Sentier national
Nationaler Weg

National Trust Property
National Trust Property
National Trust- Eigentum

Natural Attraction — ★
Attraction Naturelle
Natürliche Anziehung

Nature Reserve or Bird Sanctuary
Réserve naturelle botanique ou ornithologique
Natur- oder Vogelschutzgebiet

Nature Trail or Forest Walk
Chemin forestier, piste verte
Naturpfad oder Waldweg

Picnic Site
Lieu pour pique-nique
Picknickplatz

Place of Interest — Craft Centre •
Site, curiosité
Sehenswürdigkeit

Prehistoric Monument
Monument Préhistorique
Prähistorische Denkmal

Railway, Steam or Narrow Gauge
Chemin de fer, à vapeur ou à voie étroite
Eisenbahn, Dampf- oder Schmalspurbahn

Roman Remains
Vestiges Romains
Römische Ruinen

Theme Park
Centre de loisirs
Vergnügungspark

Tourist Information Centre
Office de Tourisme
Touristeninformationen

Viewpoint
(360 degrees) — (180 degrees)
Vue panoramique (360 degrés) — (180 degrés)
Aussichtspunkt (360 Grade) — (180 Grade)

Vineyard
Vignoble
Weinberg

Visitor Information Centre — V
Centre d'information touristique
Besucherzentrum

Wildlife Park
Réserve de faune
Wildpark

Windmill
Moulin à vent
Windmühle

Zoo or Safari Park
Parc ou réserve zoologique
Zoo oder Safari-Park

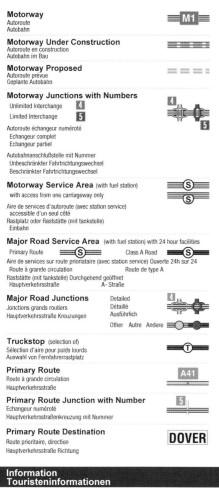

4

20

80 90 100 60

A **B** **C** **D**

ISLES OF SCILLY

Round Island

St Helen's
King Charles's Castle Piper's Hole White Island
BRYHER Lower Town Middle Town Day Mark
Cromwell's Castle Old Blockhouse Higher Town ST MARTIN'S
The Town New Grimsby Old Grimsby
Gweal Grimsby TRESCO
Maiden Bower Valhalla Ships' Figurehead Collection Tresco Abbey Halangy Down EASTERN ISLES
Mincarlo Samson Bant's Carn Crow Sound Innisidgen Burial Chamber
The Road Harry's Walls Maypole
Hugh Town Porth Hellick Down Burial Chamber
Garrison Walls Old Town ST MARY'S
ISLES OF SCILLY ISLES OF SCILLY (St Mary's)
Giant's Castle

1

North West Passage

0 10 0 10 0 50

Crim Rocks Troy Town Maze Hugh Town to Penzance 2hrs. 40mins. (Seasonal)
Annet Nag's Head Gugh
Broad Sound Smith Sound St Mary's Sound Punch Bowl
Western Rocks ST AGNES
Bishop Rock

2

90 The Isles of Scilly lie 28 miles WSW of Land's End

30 40 150

40

Navax Point Crane Islands Portreath
Godrevy Island Hell's Mouth B3301 Illogan Park Bottom
Tehidy A30 Tuckingmill Pool East Brea
The Carracks St Ives Bay S.W. Coast Path Gwithian Kehelland Treswithian CAMBORNE
Barbara Hepworth Tate Lifeboat Station Connor Downs Roseworthy Penpons Shire Horse Farm
The Carracks Hellesveor B3306 St Ives Phillack Angarrack Barripper Troon
Gurnard's Head Zennor Penbeagle Carbis Bay The Towans Copperhouse Gwinear Carnhell Green Wall Praze-an-Beeble
Carn Galver Engine House Treen Towednack Halsetown Knill's A3074 Hayle St Erth Praze B3280
Porthmeor Zennor Quoit Trencrom Hill Lelant B3302 Fraddam Leedstown Crowan B3303
Pendeen Watch Higher Morvah B3306 13 Cripplesease Lelant Downs Paradise Park St Erth Drym Releath
Levant Mine & Beam Engine 9 Maidens Stone Circle Mulfra Quoit Nancledra Canonstown A30 Townshend Nancegollan
Geevor Tin Mine Pendeen Men-an-Tol 828 Chysauster Ancient Village Relubbus Godolphin Crowntown
Trewellard Chûn Castle Ding Dong Engine House New Mill B3311 Crowlas R Hayle Trescowe Godolphin Cross Helston
Carnyorth Quoit Great Bosullow Lanyon Quoit Boswarthen Ludgvan B3309 St Hilary Rosudgeon Carleen Trew
Botallack Count House Boswens Standing Stone Holy Well Madron B3312 Trevarrack Gulval Goldsithney Germoe Ashton Lowertown
Botallack Tregeseal B3318 Newbridge Heamoor A30 Chyandour Longrock Marazion Kenneggy Downs A394 Sithney
Cape Cornwall St Just A3071 Trengwainton Trereife PENZANCE Perranuthnoe Praa Sands Breage Porthleven
The Brisons Ballowall Barrow Sancreed Drift Resr. Trewidden Newlyn St Michael's Mount Pengersick Rinsey B3304
Kelynack 736 Carn Euny Ancient Village Drift Tredavoe Paul Cudden Point Wheal Prosper Engine House Wheal Trewavas Engine Houses The Loe
LAND'S END Brane Crows-an-wra 10 Kerris Mousehole Trewavas Head Loe Bar
Whitesand Bay Escalls Boscawen-un Stone Circle B3283 Pipers Standing Stones Bird Hospital St Clement's Isle Poldhu Point Loe Pool & Bar
Sennen Cove Maen Castle Sennen B3315 St Buryan Trewoofe Lamorna Merry Maidens Stone Circle Berepper
Longships Land's End Trevescan Trevilley Tregiffian Burial Chamber Penberth MOUNT'S BAY Marconi Monument
Trevilley Telegraph Treen Cribba Head Mullion Cove Mullion Island
LAND'S END Porthcurno Penberth Penzance to Hugh Town 2hrs. 40mins. (Seasonal) Mullion Cove
Gwennap Head Porthgwarra St Levan Minack Theatre Logan Rock Vellan Head
Runnel Stone

3

30

4

20

5

10

Wolf Rock Wolf Rock

30 40 150 60

A **B** **C** **D**

CORNWALL

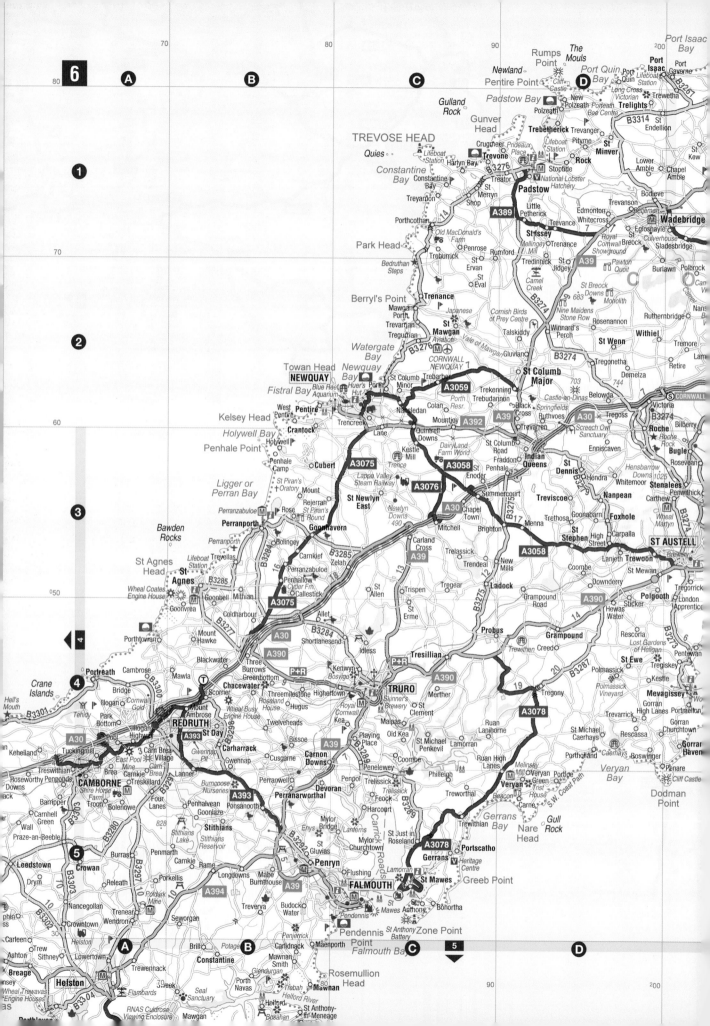

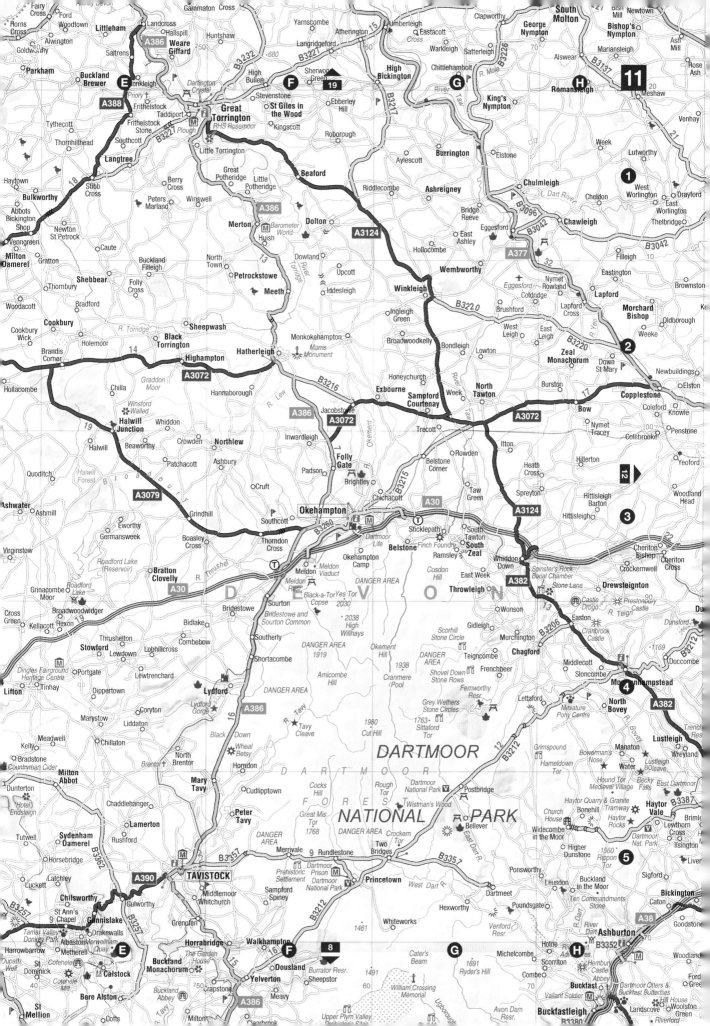

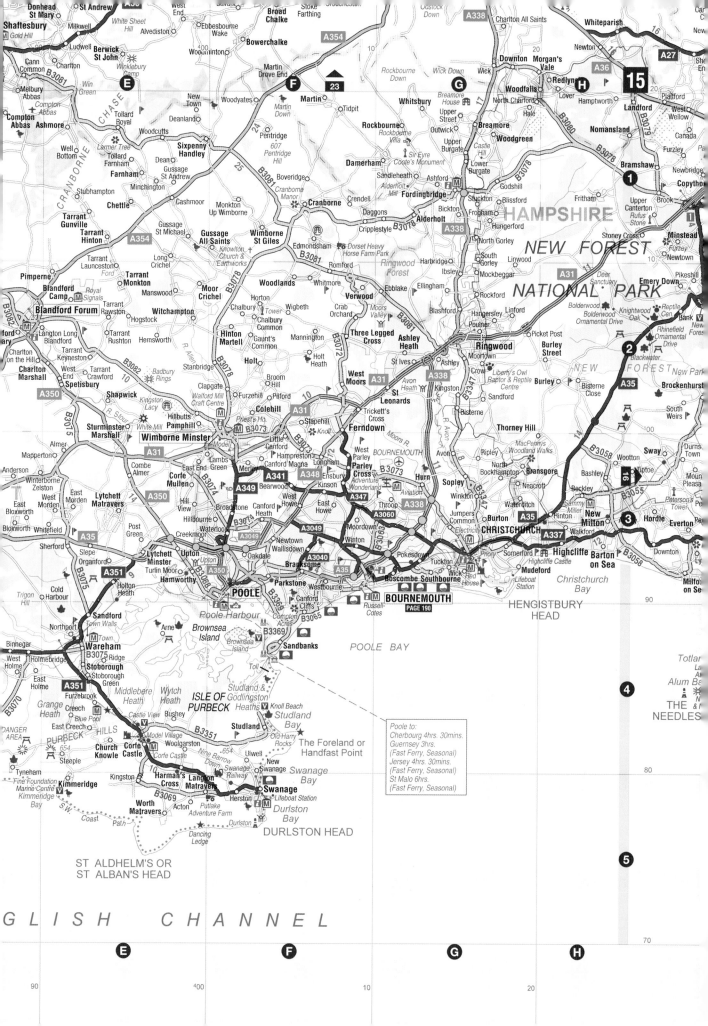

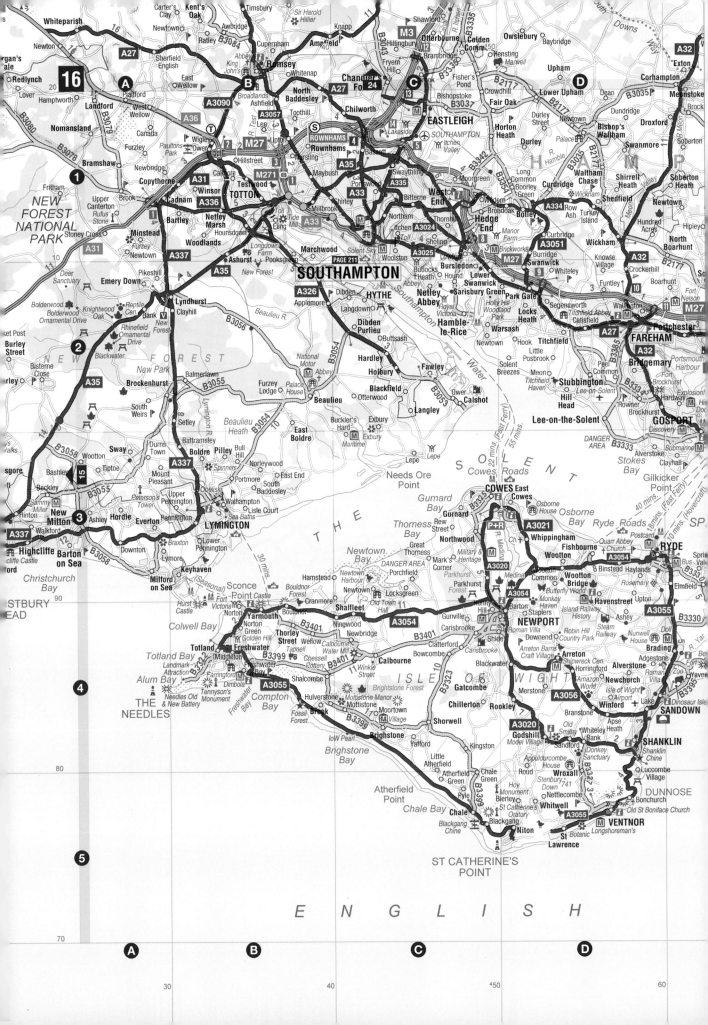

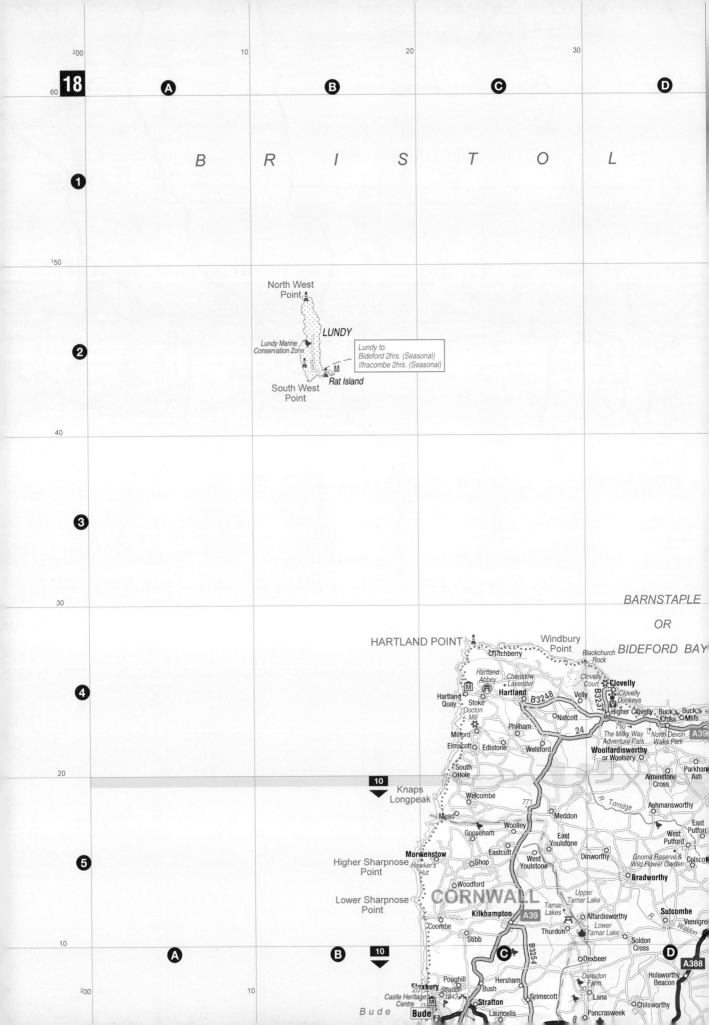

200   10   20   30

60   A   B   C   D

B   R   I   S   T   O   L

①

150

North West
Point

LUNDY

Lundy Marine
Conservation Zone

②

Lundy to:
Bideford 2hrs. (Seasonal)
Ilfracombe 2hrs. (Seasonal)

Rat Island

South West
Point

40

③

30

BARNSTAPLE

OR

HARTLAND POINT   Windbury
Point   BIDEFORD BAY

④ Titchberry   Blackchurch
Rock

Hartland
Abbey   Cheristow
Lavender   Clovelly
Court   Clovelly

M   Hartland   B3248   Velly   Clovelly Donkeys
Y
Hartland   Higher Clovelly   Buck's   Buck's
Quay   Stoke   Cross   Mills
Docton
Mill   Natcott   The Milky Way   North Devon   A39
Philham   24   Adventure Park   Wake Park
Milford   Woolfardisworthy
Elmscott   Edistone   Welsford   or Woolsery   Parkham
Ash
South   Alminstone
20   Hole   Cross   Ashmansworthy

10   Knaps   Welcome   771   R. Torridge   East
Longpeak   Putford
Meddon   West
Mead   Woolley   Putford   Gnome Reserve &
Gooseham   East   Wild Flower Garden   Colsco
Youlstone   Dinworthy
⑤ Morwenstow   Eastcott   West   Bradworthy
Higher Sharpnose   Hawker's   Shop   Youlstone
Point   Hut
Woodford   Upper   Sutcombe
Lower Sharpnose   CORNWALL   Tamar Lake   Venngre
Point   Kilkhampton   A39   Alfardisworthy   Waldon
Tamar   Lower
Coombe   Lakes   Thurdon   Tamar Lake   Soldon
Cross
10   Stibb   B3254   A388
A   B   10   C   Dexbeer   D

200   Poughill   Hersham   Dunsden   Holsworthy
Floxbury   Farm   30   Beacon
10   Stratton   Bush
Castle Heritage   1643   Grimscott   Lana   Chilsworthy
Centre   M   Stratton
Bude   Launcells   Pancrasweek

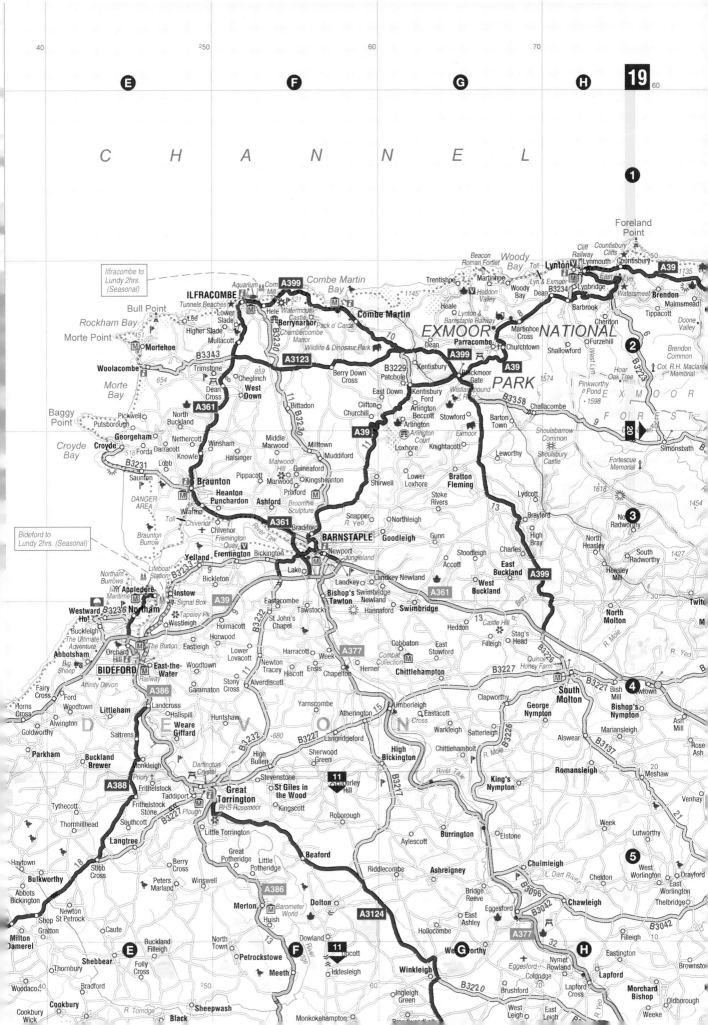

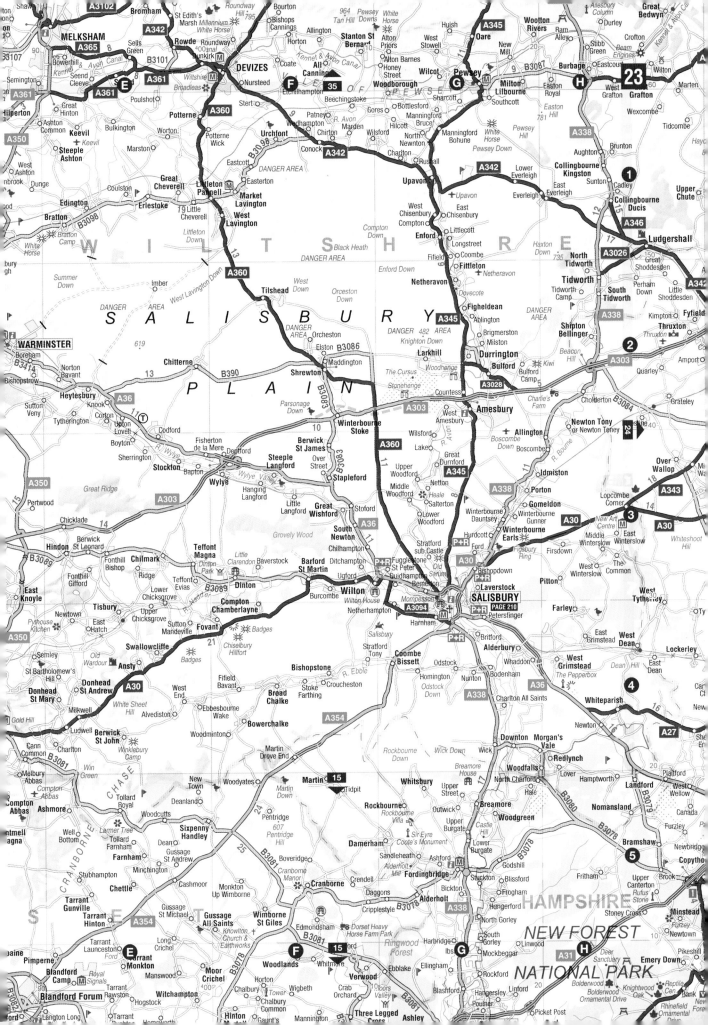

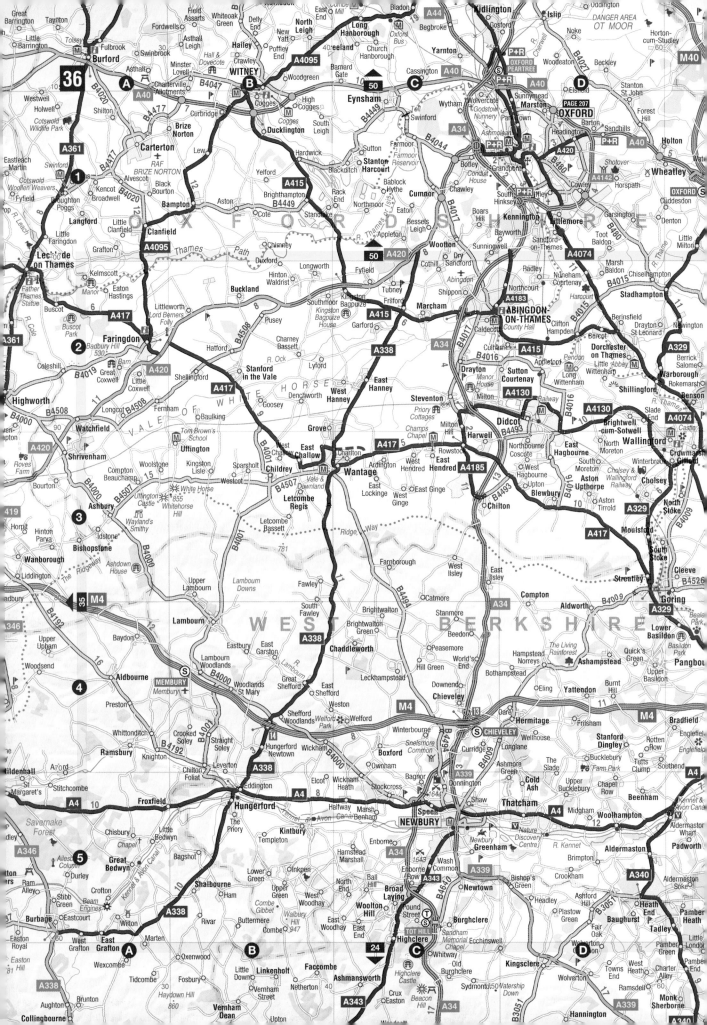

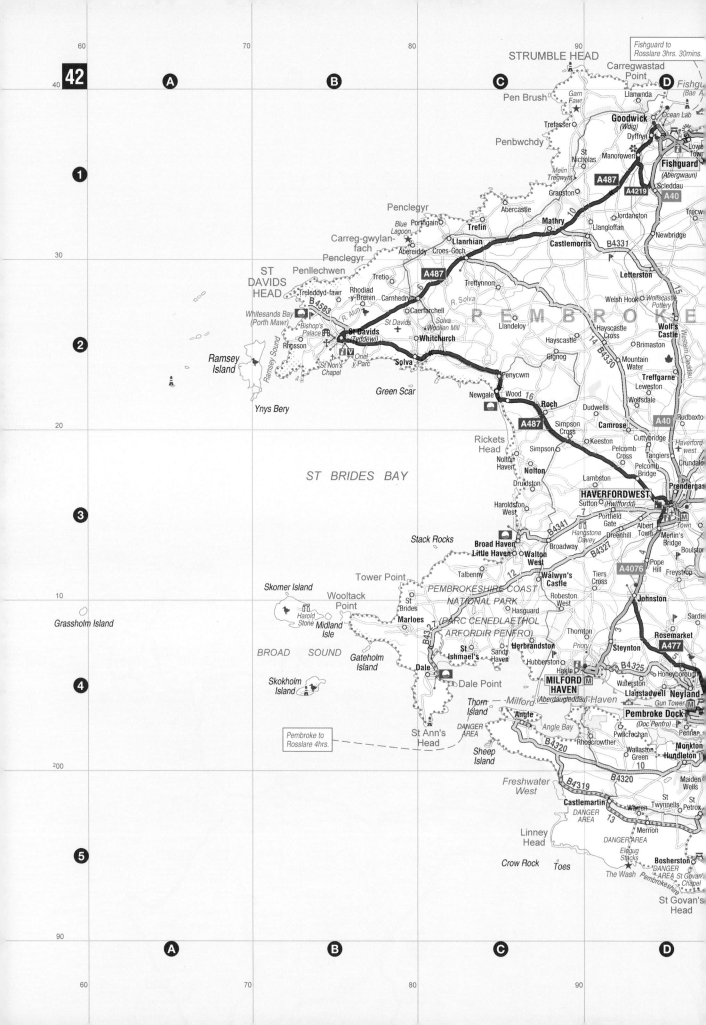

STRUMBLE HEAD

Fishguard to
Rosslare 3hrs. 30mins.

Carregwastad
Point

Pen Brush

Garn
Fawr

Llanwnda

Fishgu
(Bae A

Penbwchdy

Goodwick
(Wdig)

Ocean Lab

Trefasser

Dyffryn

Lowe
Tow

St
Nicholas

Manorowen

i

Fishguard
(Abergwaun)

Melin
Tregwynt

A487

A4219

Scleddau

A40

Trecw

Penclegyr

Grapston

Jordanston

Newbridge

Portngain

Trefin

Abercastle

Mathry

Llangloffan

Blue
Lagoon

Carreg-gwylan-
fach

Llanrhian

Croes-Goch

Castlemorris

Letterston

B4331

Abereiddy

Penclegyr

Treffynnon

PEMBROKE

15

ST
DAVIDS
HEAD

Penllechwen

Tretio

A487

Welsh Hook

Wolfscastle
Pottery

Treleddyd-fawr

Rhodiad
-y-Brenin

R. Solva

Hayscastle
Cross

Wolf's
Castle

B4583

Carnhedryn

Treffgarne

Whitesands Bay
(Porth Mawr)

R. Alun

St Davids

Caerfarchell

Solva
Woollen Mill

Hayscastle

Brimaston

14

B4330

Mountain
Water

Bishop's
Palace

St Davids
(Tyddewi)

Llandeloy

Gignog

Leweston

Wolfsdale

Rhosson

Whitchurch

i

Ramsey
Island

Ramsey Sound

St Non's
Chapel

Oriel
y Parc

Solva

Penycwm

Dudwells

A40

Rudbaxto

V

Wood

16

Roch

Simpson
Cross

Camrose

Cuttybridge

Haverford
west

Green Scar

Newgale

A487

Keeston

Pelcomb
Cross

Tangiers

Crundale

Ynys Bery

Simpson

Lambston

Pelcomb
Bridge

Rickets
Head

Nolton
Haven

Nolton

HAVERFORDWEST
(Hwlffordd)

Prendergas

20

ST BRIDES BAY

Druidston

Sutton

7

Portfield
Gate

Town

M

Haroldston
West

Dreenhill

Albert
Town

Merlin's
Bridge

Boulsto

Stack Rocks

Broad Haven

Hangstone
Davey

B4341

Broadway

B4327

Pope
Hill

Freystrop

Little Haven

Walton
West

Tower Point

Talbenny

12

Walwyn's
Castle

Tiers
Cross

A4076

Johnston

Skomer Island

Wooltack
Point

St
Brides

Robeston
West

Rosemarket

A477

Grassholm Island

Harold
Stone

Midland
Isle

Marloes

PEMBROKESHIRE COAST
NATIONAL PARK

Hasguard

Thornton

Priory

Sardis

B4321

(PARC CENEDLAETHOL
ARFORDIR PENFRO)

Herbrandston

Steynton

5

BROAD SOUND

Gateholm
Island

St
Ishmael's

Sandy
Haven

Hubberston

Honeyborough

B4325

Skokholm
Island

Dale

Hakin

MILFORD
HAVEN

M

Waterston

Llanstadwell

Neyland

Dale Point

(Aberdaugleddau)

Haven

Gun Tower

M

Pembroke to
Rosslare 4hrs.

Thorn
Island

Milford

Pembroke Dock
(Doc Penfro)

St Ann's
Head

DANGER
AREA

Angle

Angle Bay

Pwllcrochan

Pennar

Rhoscrowther

Monkton
Hundleton

Sheep
Island

B4320

Wallaston
Green

10

Freshwater
West

B4319

B4320

Maiden
Wells

Castlemartin

Warren

St
Twynnells

St
Petrox

Linney
Head

DANGER
AREA

13

Merrion

DANGER AREA

Elegug
Stacks

Bosherston

Crow Rock

Toes

The Wash

Pembrokeshire

DANGER
AREA St Govan's
Chapel

St Govan's
Head

200

90

60

70

80

90

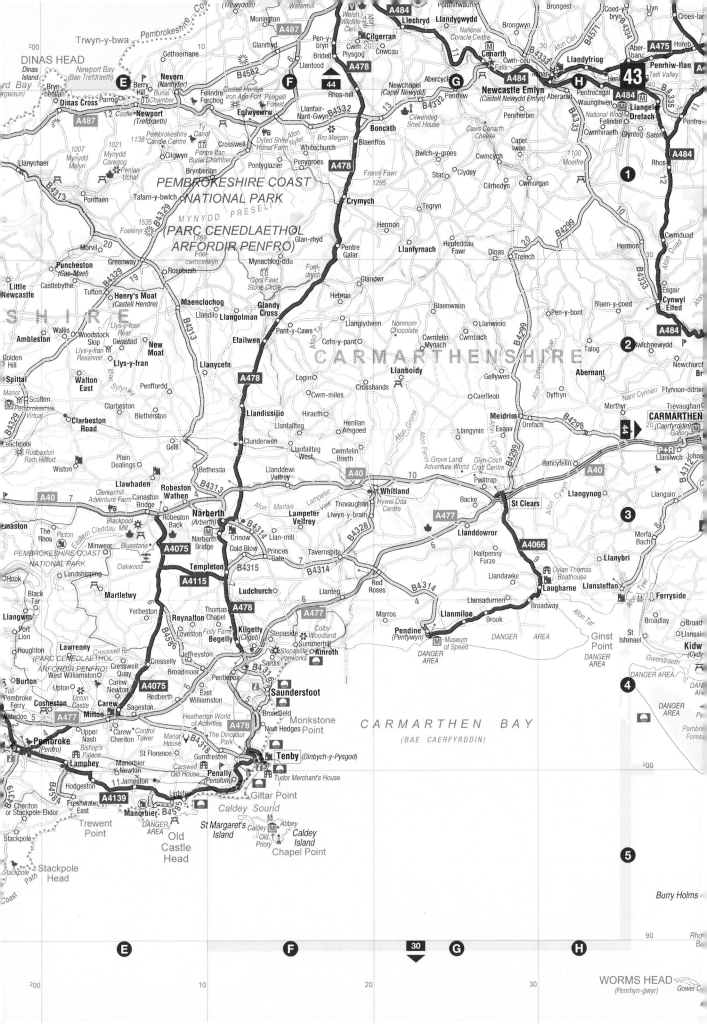

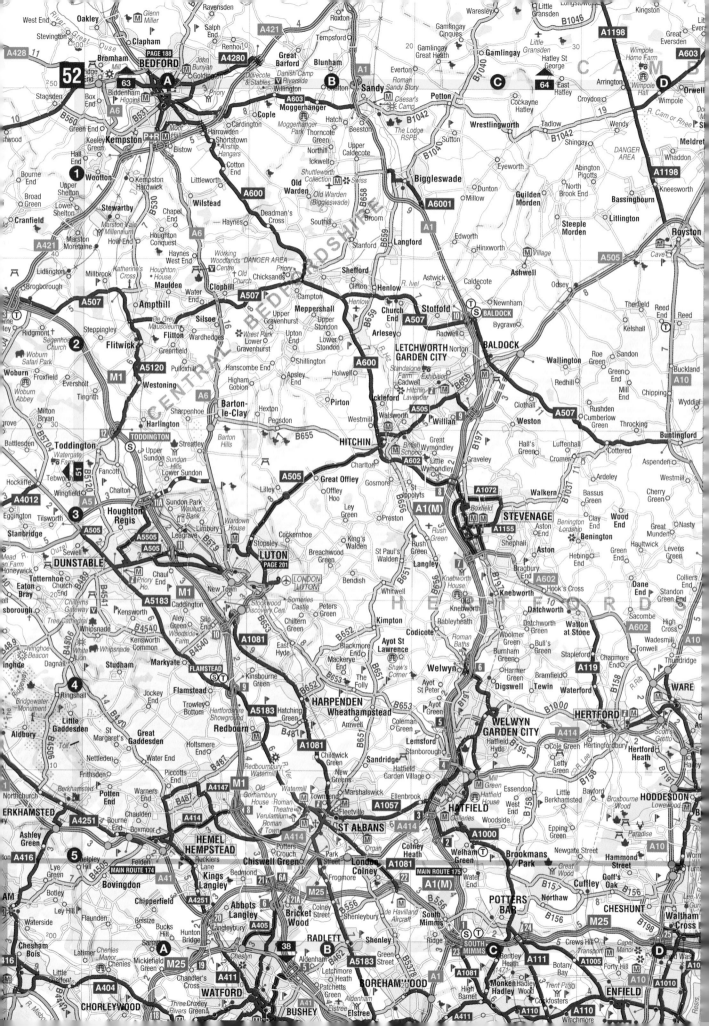

10   20   30   40

Ⓐ   Ⓑ   68   Ⓒ   Ⓓ

❶

90

❷

80

C A R D I G A N   B A Y

(B A E   C E R E D I G I O N)

❸

70

❹

Aberaeron

A482

60

Ffos-y-ffin

New Quay
(Ceinewydd)   Marine Wildlife Centre   Llwyncelyn

Maen-y-groes   Gilfachreda   Llanarth   Oakford
Cwmtudu   Cross   B4342   (Derwen Gam)
Inn   New Quay   Pen-cae   Geneva
Nanternis   Honey Farm   B4342
❺   Ynys-Lochtyn   Caerwedros   Synod Inn   Mydroilyn
Blaen   A486   (Post-Mawr)
Celyn   Llwyndafydd
Llangranog   A487
Morfa   Pontgarreg   B4338   C
Penbryn   B4334   A487   Piwmp   Talgarreg
Brynhoffnant   Pentregat   B4338
Cardigan   Tresaith
Island   Penrhiw   Capel   Bwlch-y-fadfa   Ⓓ
Rainforest   Parcllyn   Aberporth   Sarnau   Cynon
Centre   Aberporth   A486
Cardigan Island   Aberporth   B4333   Internal Fire   Tan-y-groes   B4459   B433
Cemaes Head   Coastal Farm Park   Felinwynt   (Aberporth)   Glynarthen   Brithdir
²50   44   Ⓑ   Felin   Rhydlewis   Ffostrasol   40
Allt-y-goed   Wnda   B4571   11
Pwllygranant   Cippyn   Y Ferwig   Tremain   Blaenporth   Bettws   Curlew Weavers   Hawen   Pont-Sian   12
St   Cardigan   20   Ifan   Woollen Mill   Penrhiw-   A475
Dogmaels   (Aberteifi)   Penparc   Noyadd   Beulah   Troedyraur
(Llandudoch)   A487   Pantgwyn   B4570   Trefawr   Moylgrove   Abbey

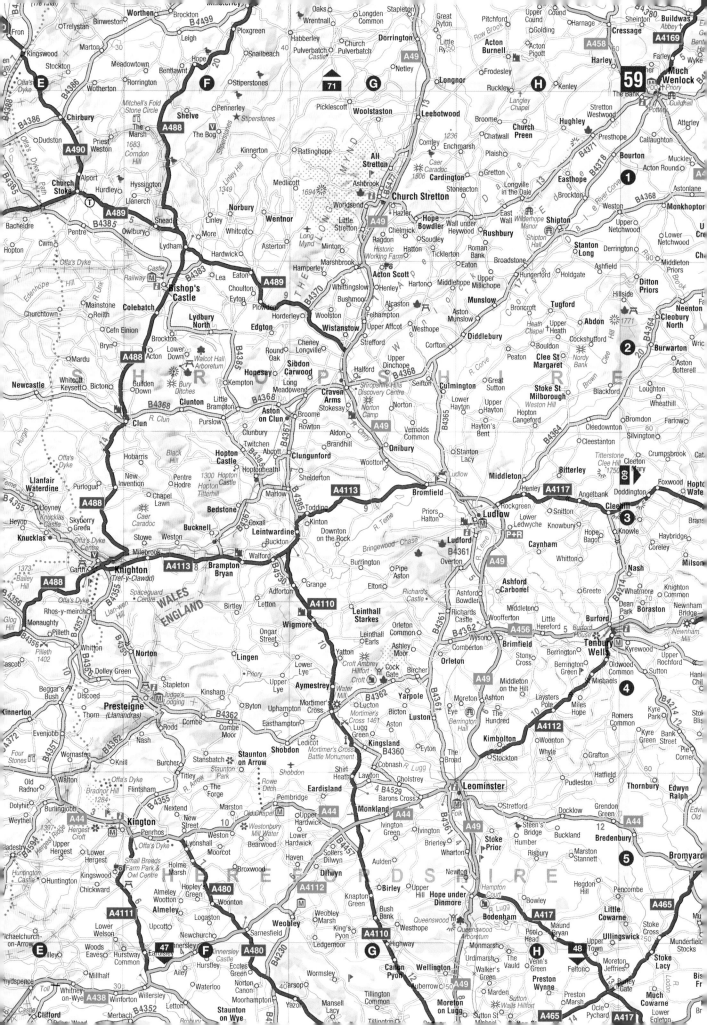

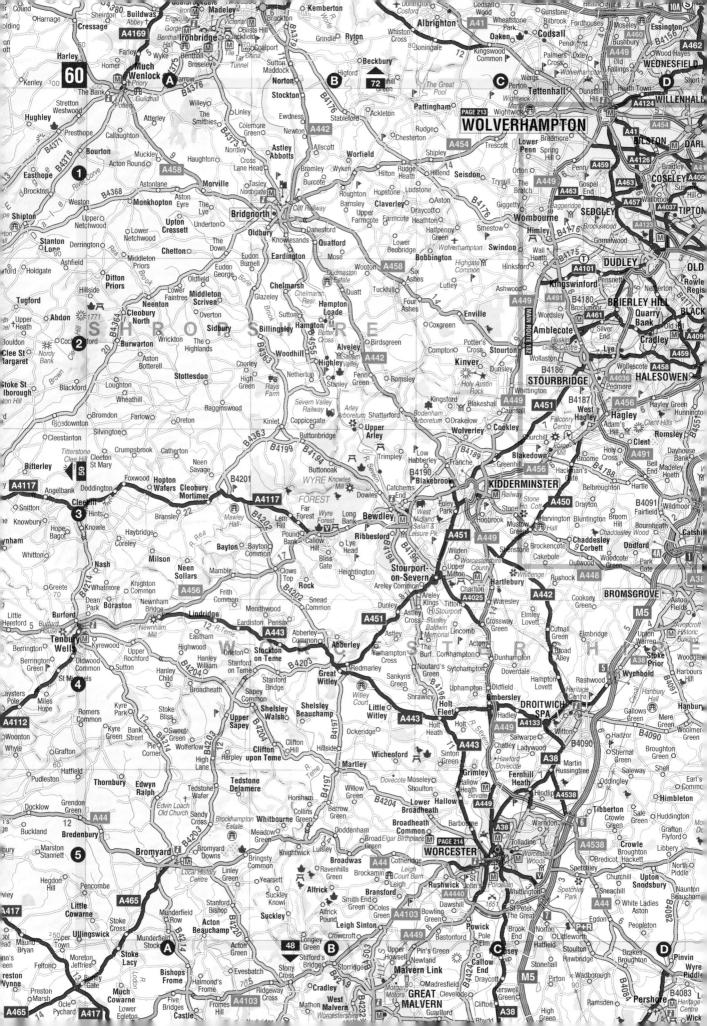

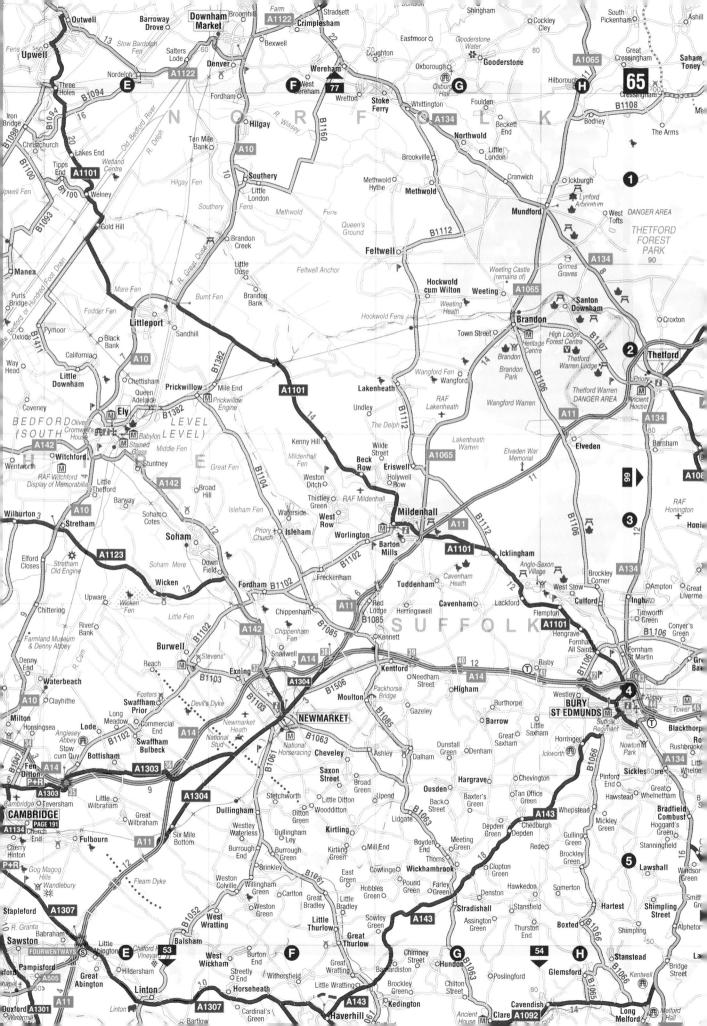

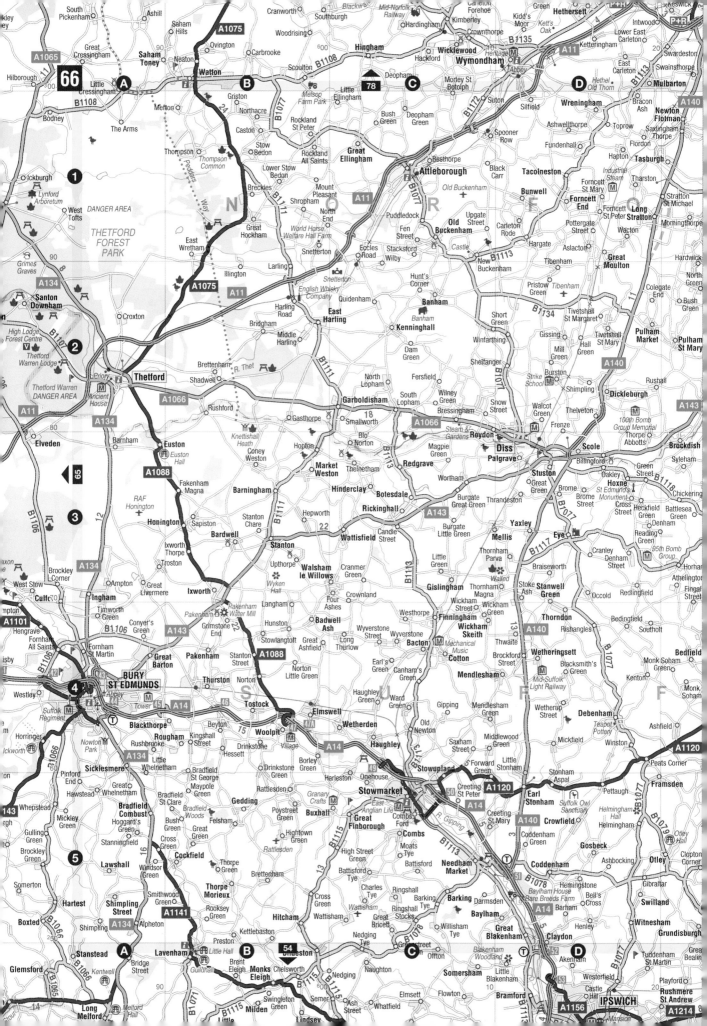

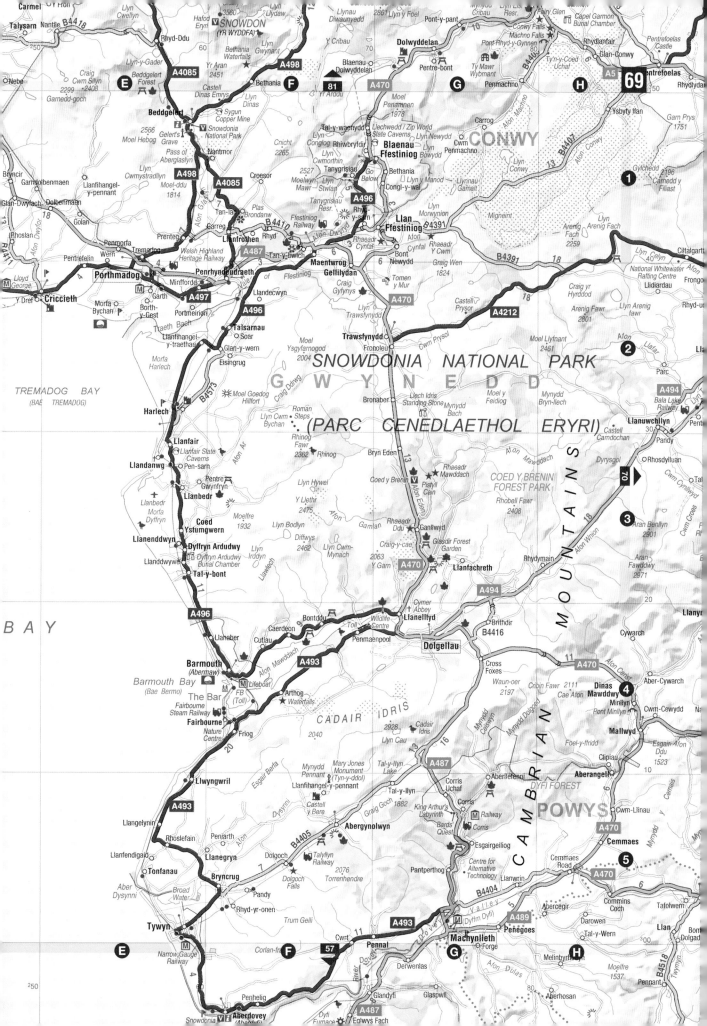

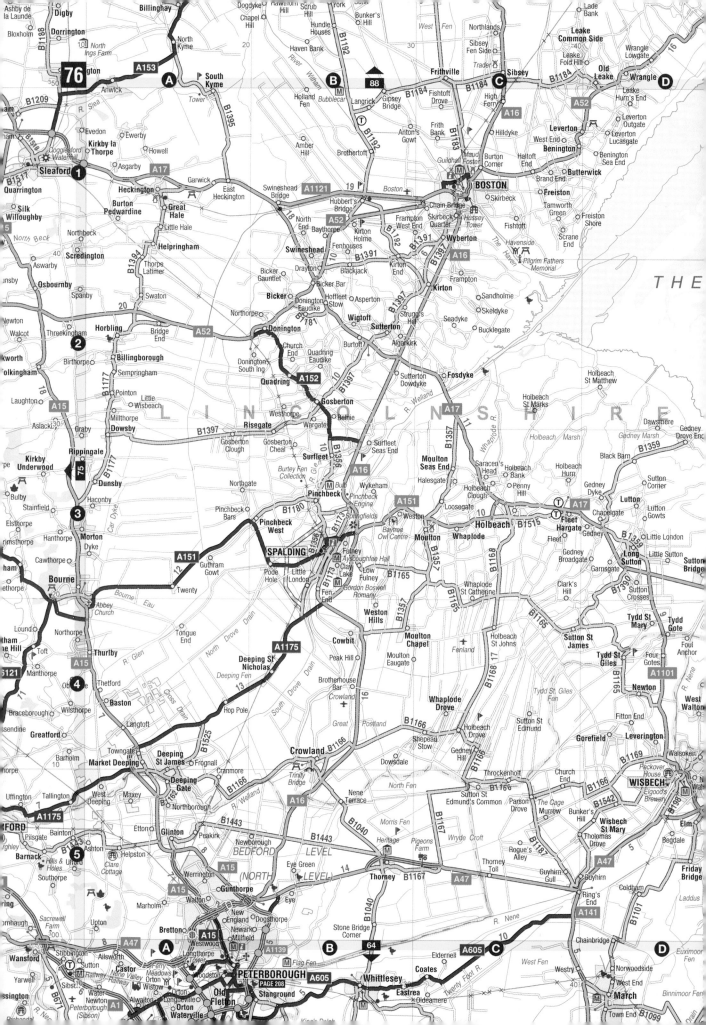

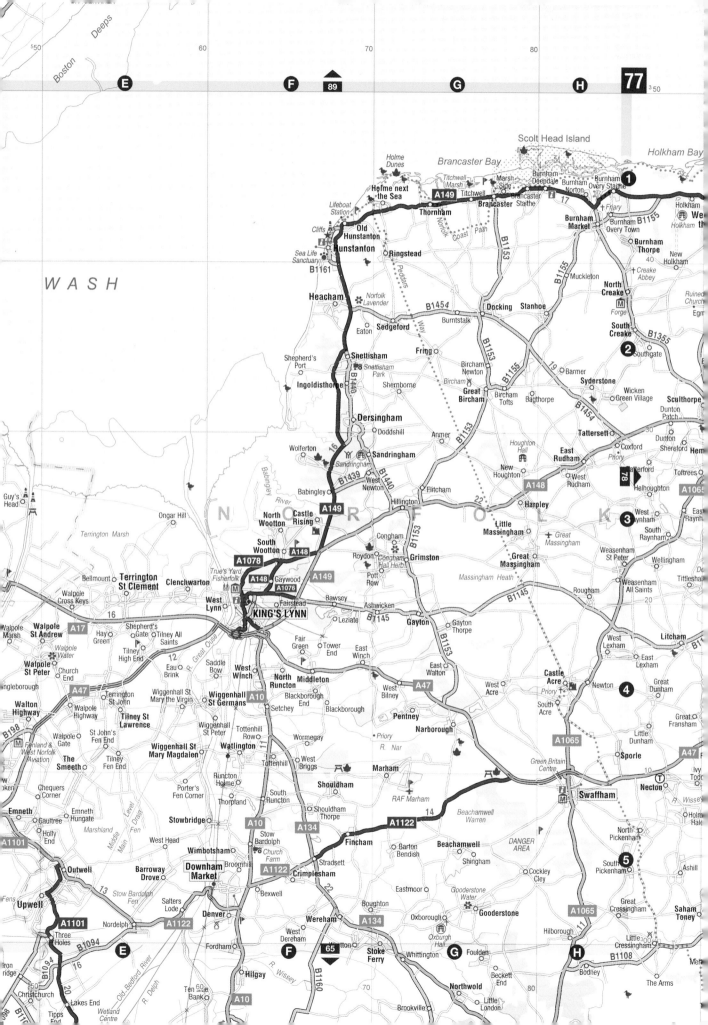

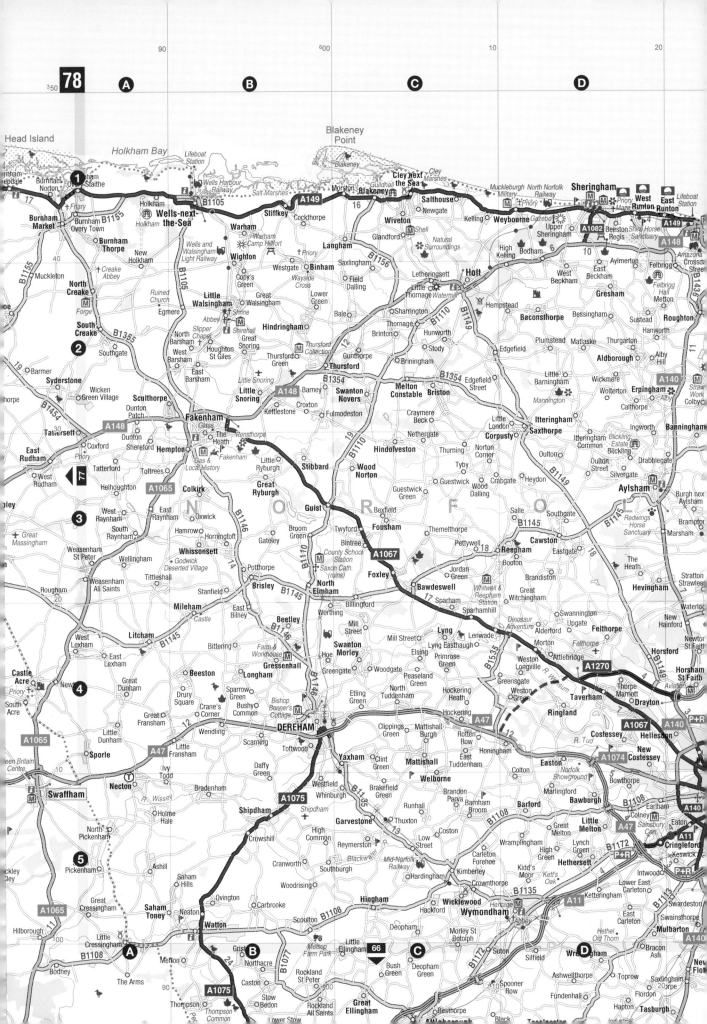

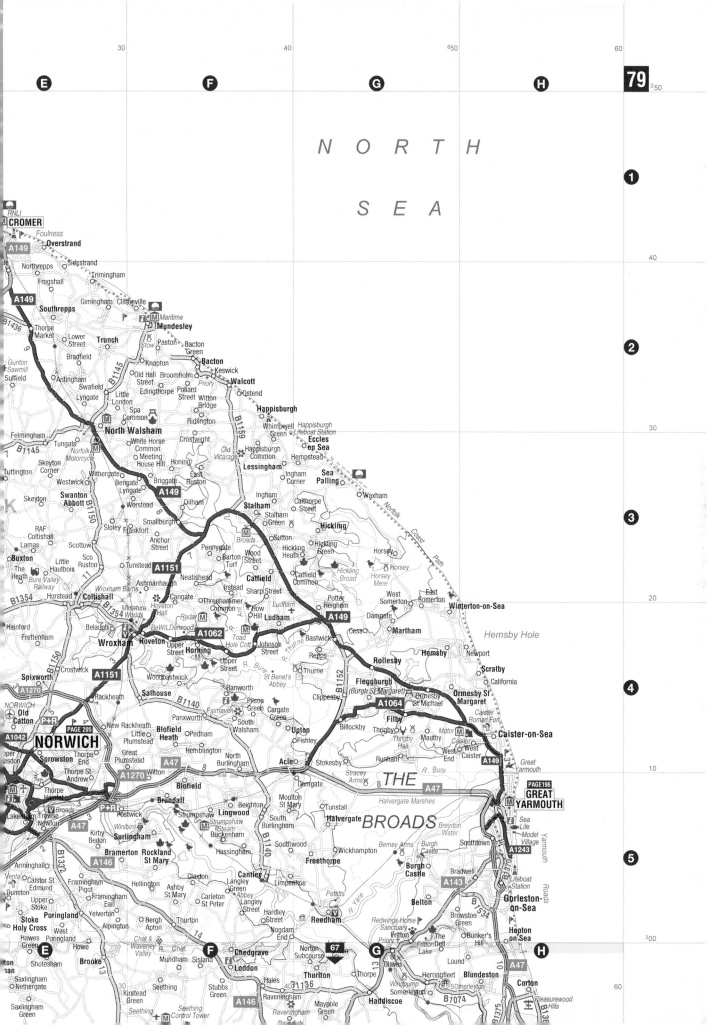

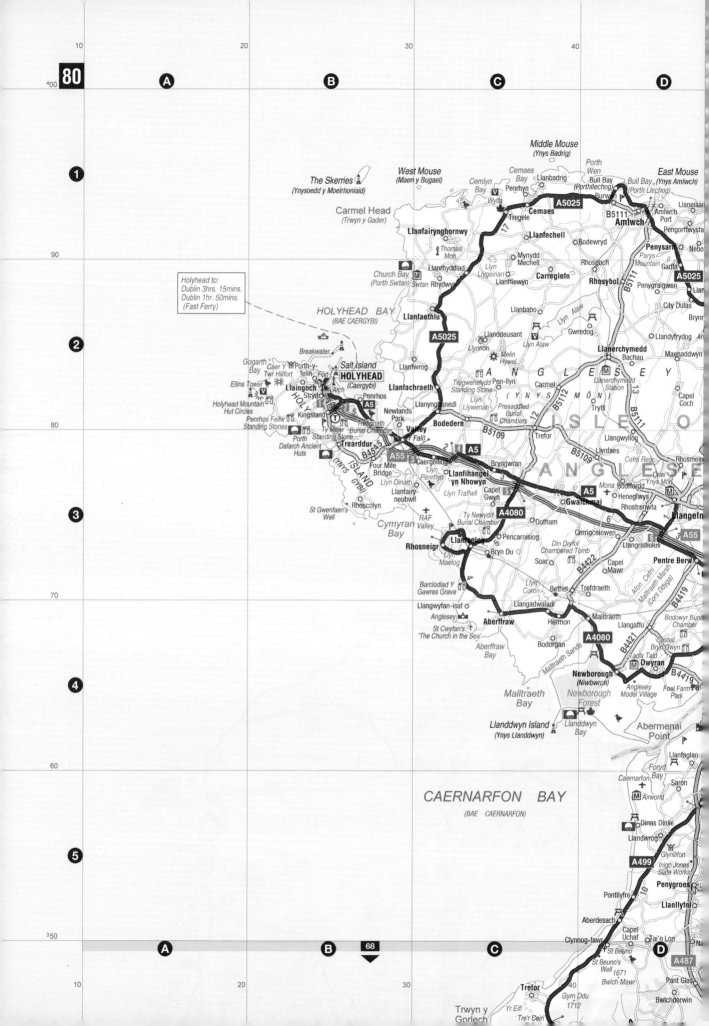

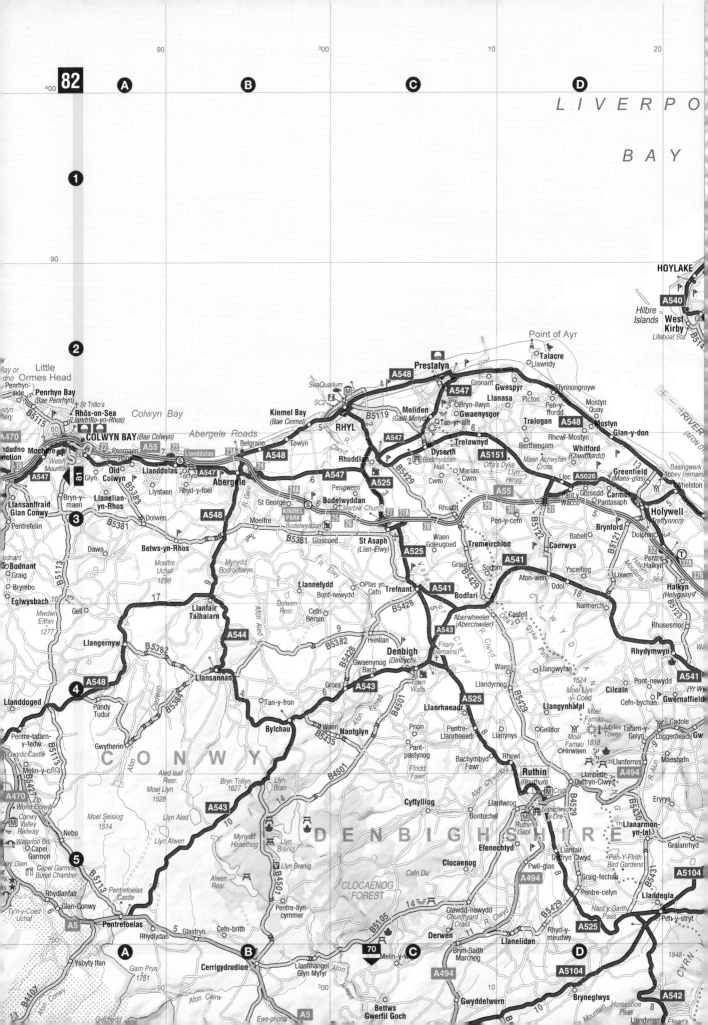

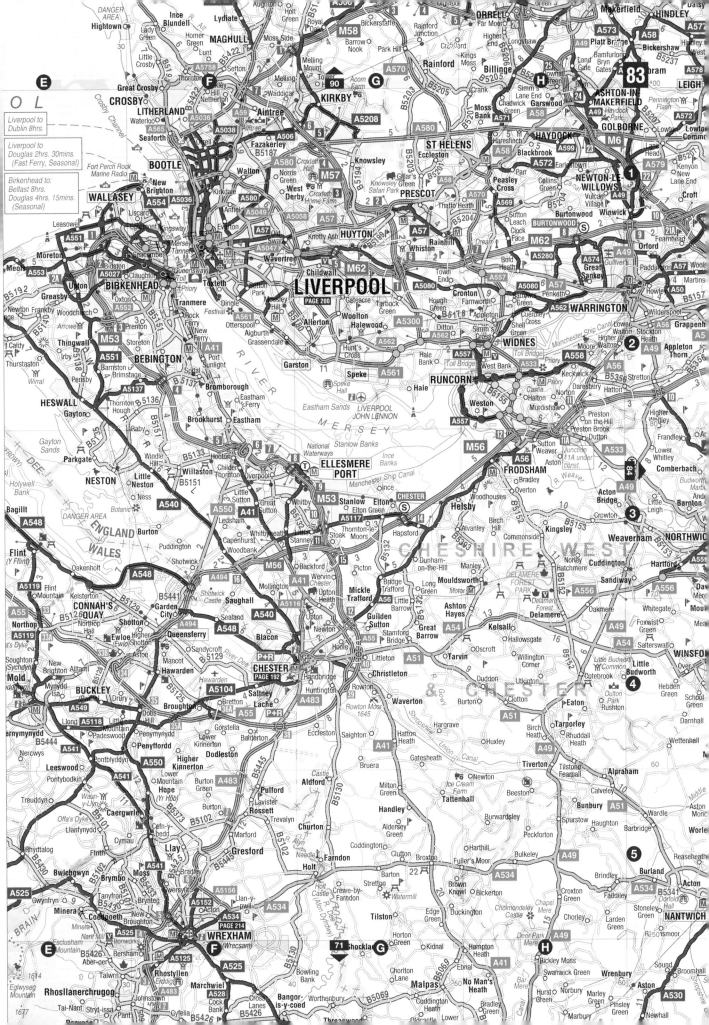

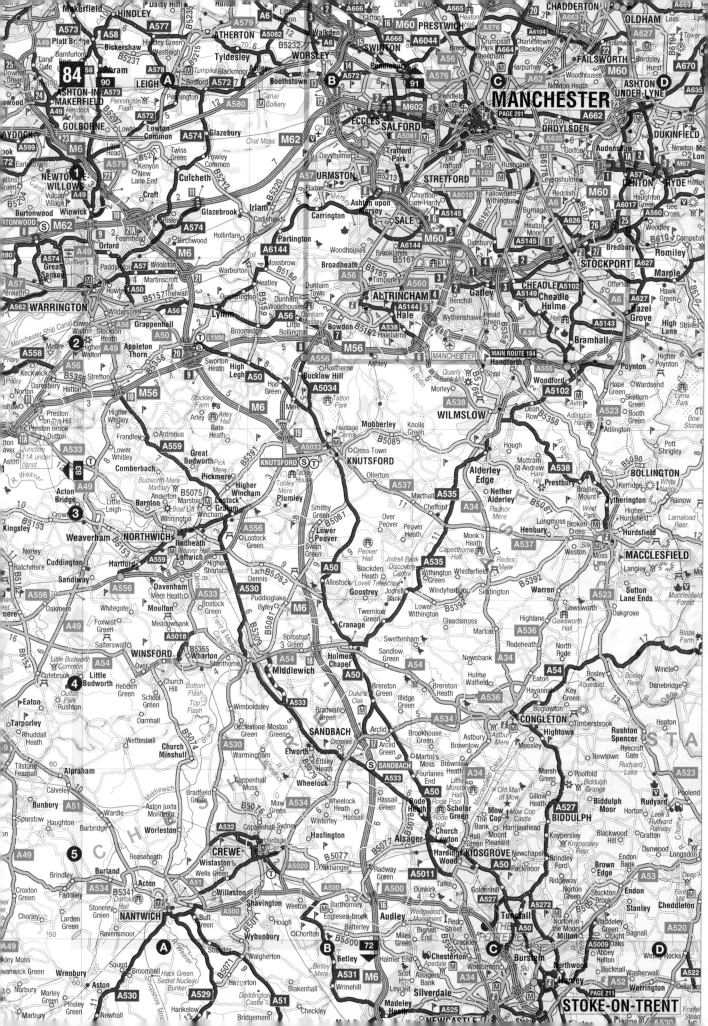

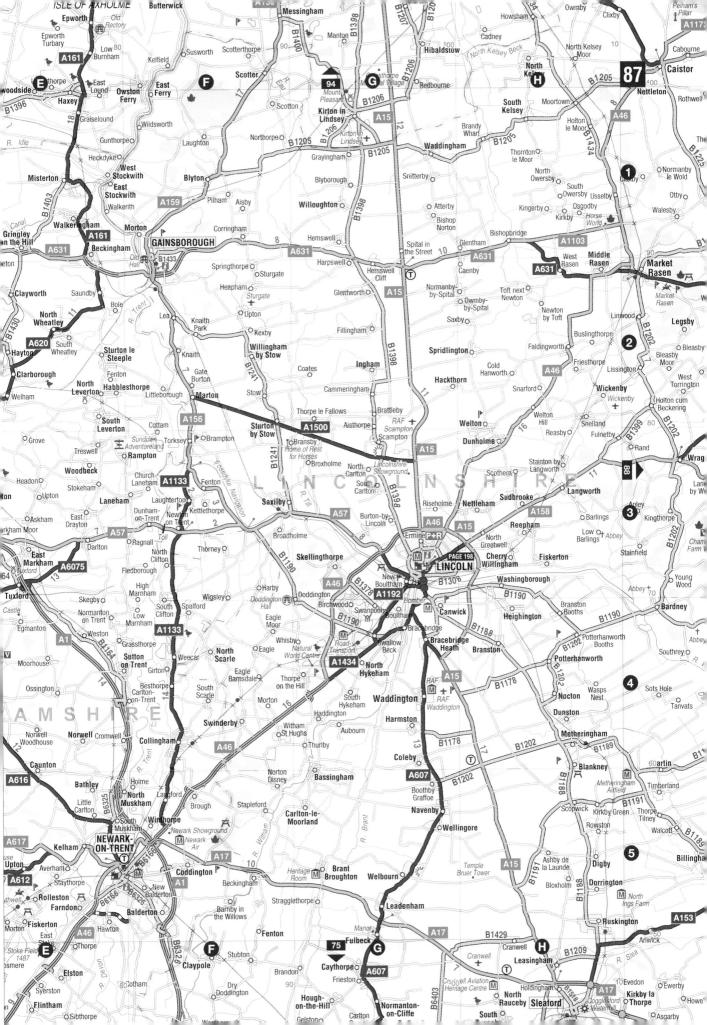

1

N O R T H

S E A

90

**Theddlethorpe
St Helen**

*Seal Sanctuary
& Wildlife Centre*

Meers
Bridge

*Lifeboat
Station*

Mablethorpe

M *Ye Olde
Curiosity*

Trusthorpe

A1104

Thorpe

Sutton on Sea

Itby
arsh

Sandilands

A1111

80

Hannah

Markby

A52

England Coast Path

Thurlby

Huttoft

Anderby

*Anderby
Creek*

M *Drainage*

3

B1449

Farlesthorpe

Mumby

M *On Your Marques*

Cumberworth

Authorpe
Row

Bonthorpe

Helsey

**Chapel St
Leonards**

Willoughby

Hogsthorpe

Sloothby

*Ashley's
Field*

A52

*Hardys
Animal Farm*

Hasthorpe

Slackholme
End

Ingoldmells

70

Addlethorpe

**Ingoldmells
Point**

Orby

*Skegness
(Ingoldmells)*

Butlin's

*Orby
Marsh*

*Water
Leisure Park*

A158

Seathorne

Winthorpe

*Natureland
Seal Sanctuary*

4

**Burgh le
Marsh**

*Church
Farm* M

*Bottons
Pleasure Beach*

SKEGNESS

*Model
Village*

Croft

A52

**Thorpe
St Peter**

Seacroft

60

Croft Marsh

*Batemans
Brewery* M *Magdalen*

**Wainfleet
St Mary**

**Wainfleet
All Saints**

Gibraltar

Key's Toft

V

*Gibraltar
Point*

5

DANGER AREA

Boston Deeps

350

Sc Head Island

Holkham Bay

*Holme
Dunes*

Brancaster Bay

Burnham

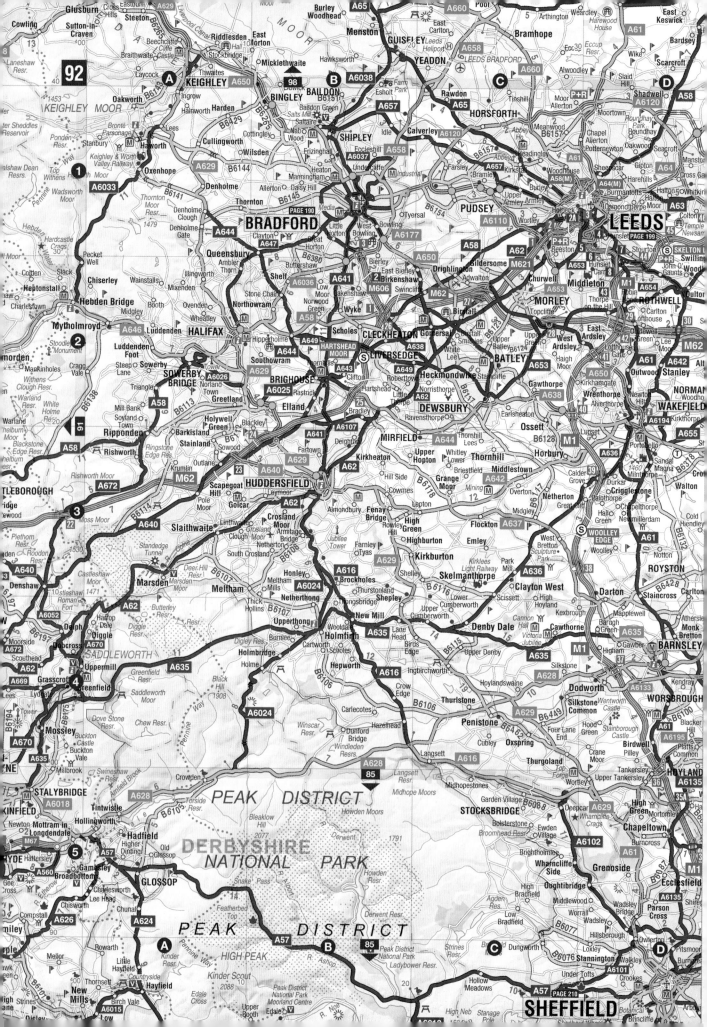

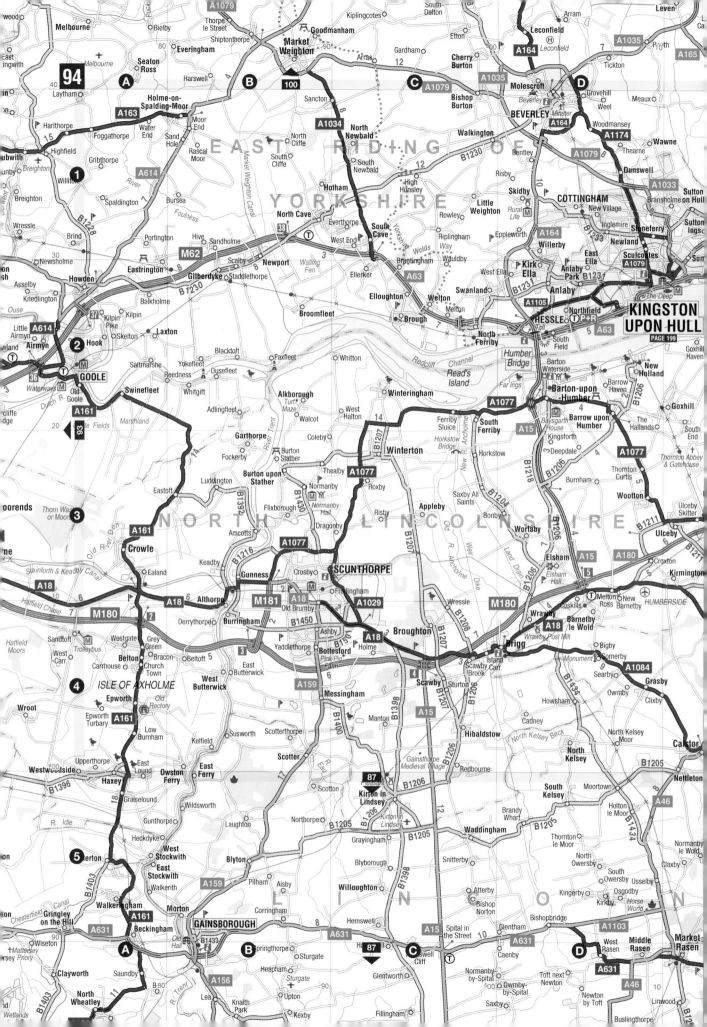

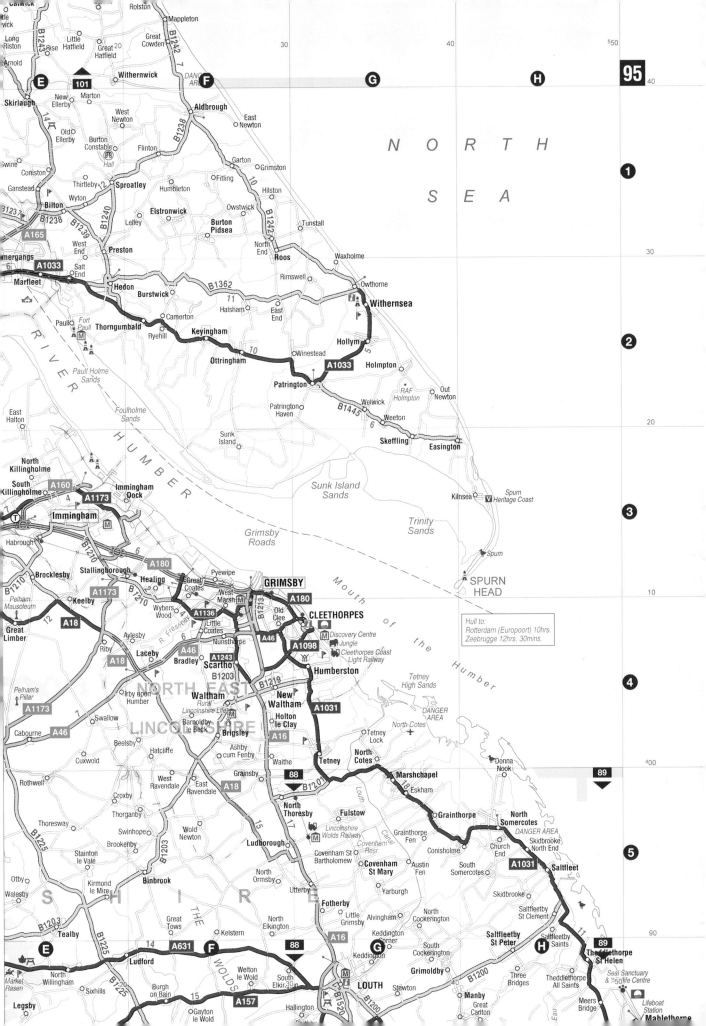

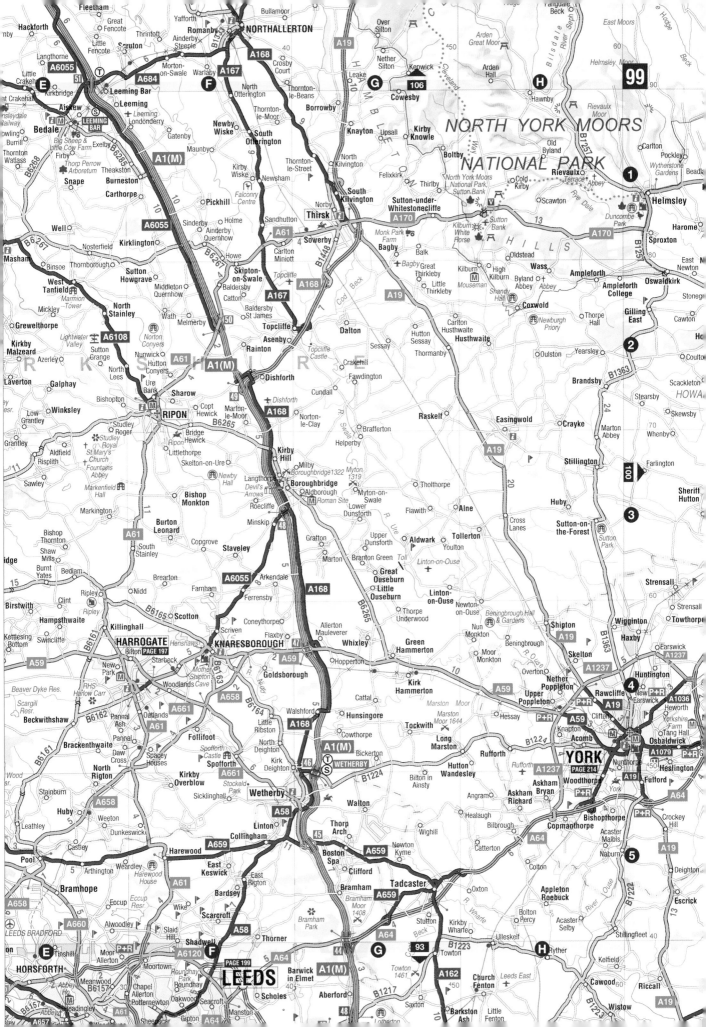

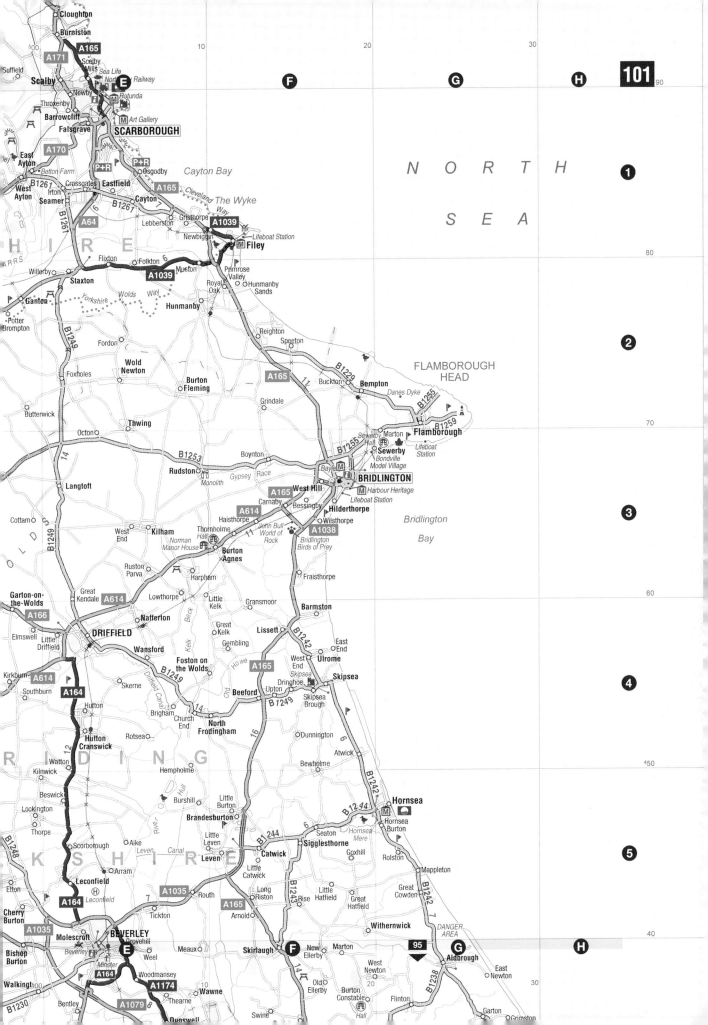

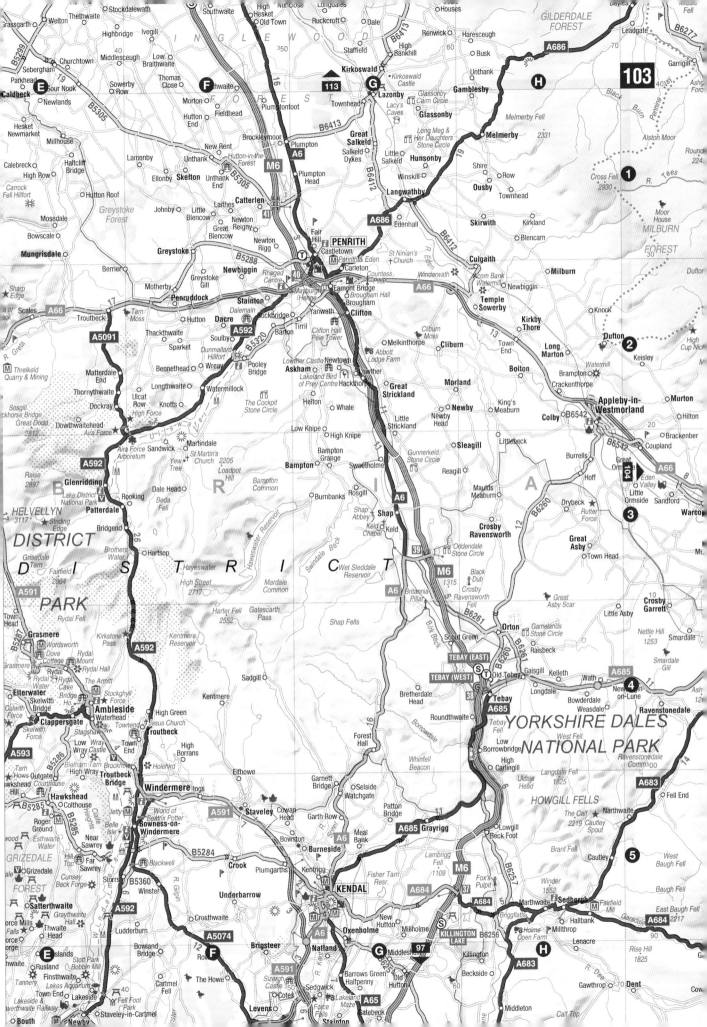

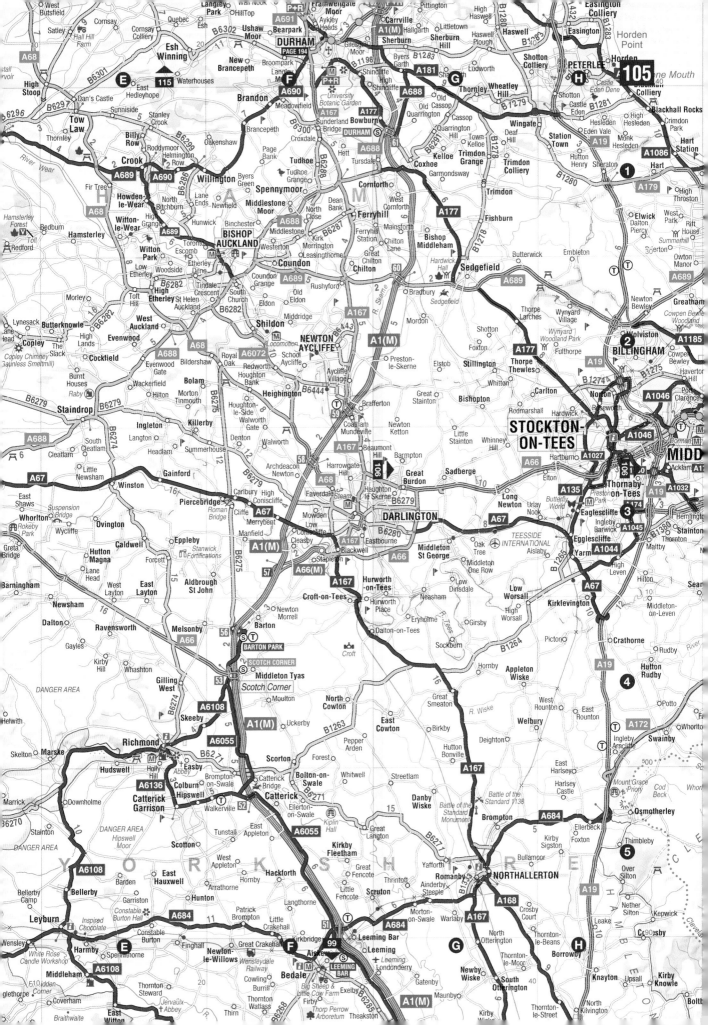

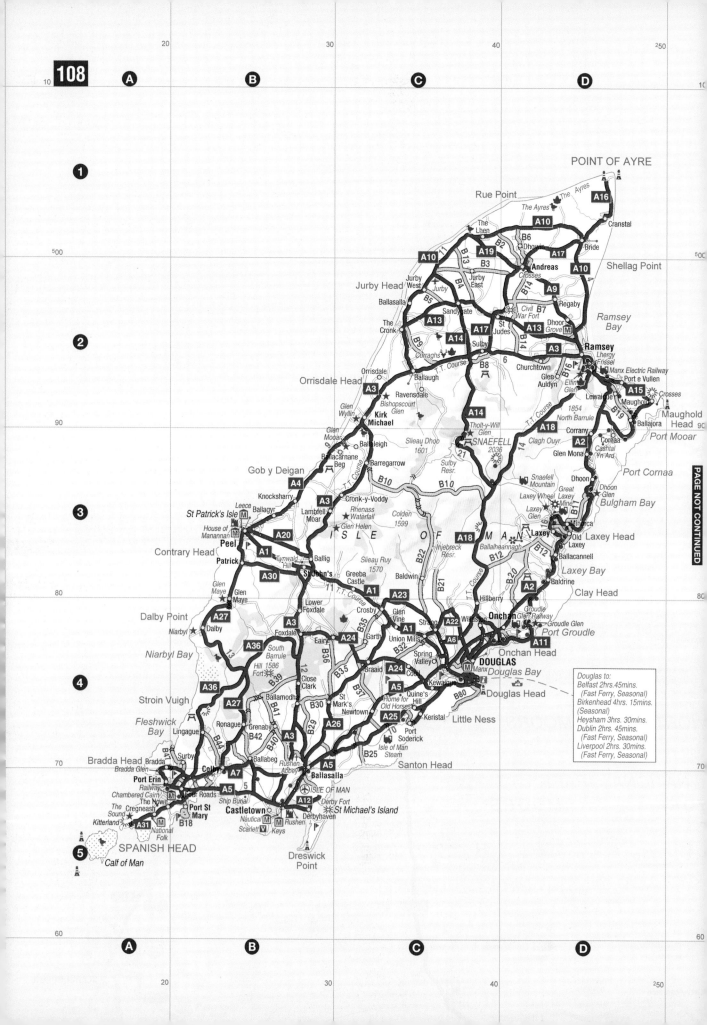

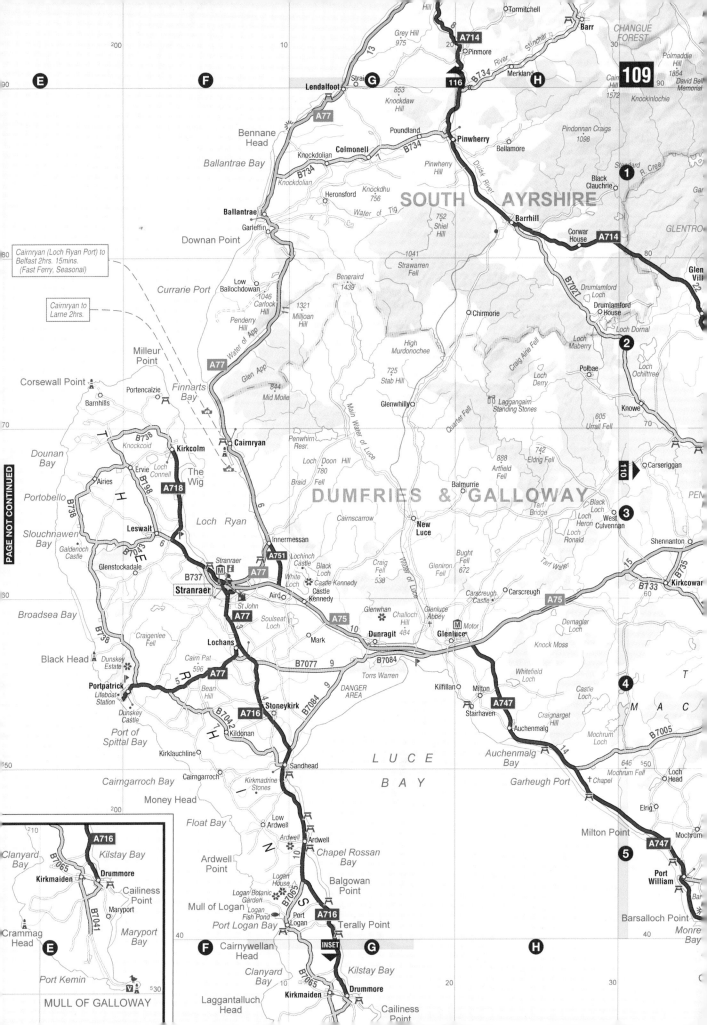

CHANGUE FOREST

Tormitchell
Barr
Polmaddie Hill 1854
David Bell Memorial
Knockinlochie

Pinmore
Grey Hill 975
Merkland
Cairn Hill 1572

A714
B734
River Stinchar

Lendalfoot
A77
Strai
853 Knockdaw Hill
116

Bennane Head
Colmonell
B734
Poundland
Pinwherry
Bellamore

Black Clauchrie
R. Cree
1

Ballantrae Bay
Knockdolian
Knockdolian
B734
Pinwherry Hill
SOUTH AYRSHIRE

Ballantrae
Garleffin
Heronsford
Knockdhu 756
Water of Tig
752 Shiel Hill
Barrhill

Downan Point
Corwar House
A714
80
GLENTRO

Currarie Port
Low Ballochdowan
1046 Carlock Hill
Beneraird 1439
Strawarren Fell
Chirmorie
Drumlamford Loch
B7021
Drumlamford House

Milleur Point
Penderry Hill
1321 Milljoan Hill
High Murdonochee
Craig Airie Fell
Loch Maberry
Loch Dornal
Glen Vill

Cairnryan (Loch Ryan Port) to Belfast 2hrs. 15mins. (Fast Ferry, Seasonal)

Cairnryan to Larne 2hrs.

Corsewall Point
Portencalzie
Finnarts Bay
844 Mid Moile
Glen App
Water of App
725 Stab Hill
Glenwhilly
Quarter Fell
Loch Derry
Polbae
Urrall Fell
Knowe
70

Barnhills

Dounan Bay
Knockcoid
B738
Kirkcolm
Cairnryan
Penwhirn Resr.
888 Artfield Fell
742 Eldrig Fell
605
Carseriggan
110

Ervie
Loch Connell
The Wig
Loch Doon Hill 780
Braid Fell
Balmurrie
Tarf Bridge
Black Loch
Loch Heron
Loch Ronald
West Culvennan
3

Airies
B798
A718
Portobello
Leswalt
Loch Ryan
Innermessan
Cairnscarrow
New Luce
Tarf Water
Shennanton
PEN

Slouchnawen Bay
B7043
Glenstockadale
A751
Lochinch Castle
Black Loch
White Loch
Castle Kennedy
Craig Fell 538
Gleniron Fell
Bught Fell 672
Carscreugh Castle
Carscreugh
A75
15
B733
Kirkcowar
60

Galdenoch Castle
Stranraer
B737
Aird
Castle Kennedy
Water of Luce
Knock Moss
Dernaglar Loch

Broadsea Bay
B738
Craigenlee Fell
St John
A77
Soulseat Loch
Mark
Glenwhan
Challoch Hill 484
Glenluce Abbey
Dunragit
Glenluce
Motor
Castle Loch
4

Black Head
Dunskey Estate
Cairn Pat 596
Lochans
B7077
9
B7084
Torrs Warren
Kilfillan
Milton
A747
Stairhaven
Auchenmalg
Whitefield Loch
B7005

Portpatrick
Lifeboat Station
A77
Bean Hill
Stoneykirk
B7084
9
DANGER AREA
Craignarget Hill
Auchenmalg Bay
646
550
Loch Head

Dunskey Castle
B7042
A716
Kildonan
Garheugh Port
Chapel
Mochrum Fell
Elrig
Mochrum

Port of Spittal Bay
Kirklauchline
Sandhead
LUCE BAY
Milton Point
A747
Port William
5

Cairngarroch Bay
Cairngarroch
Kirkmadrine Stones
Garheugh Port
Barsalloch Point
Monre Bay

Money Head
Float Bay
Low Ardwell
Ardwell
Chapel Rossan Bay
Balgowan Point

Ardwell Point
10
Logan House
Logan Botanic Garden
Logan Fish Pond
Port Logan
A716
Terally Point

Mull of Logan
Port Logan Bay
INSET

MULL OF GALLOWAY (inset)

Clanyard Bay
210
A716
Kilstay Bay
B7065
Kirkmaiden
Drummore
Cailiness Point
Maryport
B7041

Crammag Head
E
Maryport Bay
Port Kemin
V
530
MULL OF GALLOWAY

Cairnywellan Head
F
Clanyard Bay
B7065
Laggantalluch Head
Kirkmaiden
Drummore
G
Kilstay Bay
Cailiness Point
H

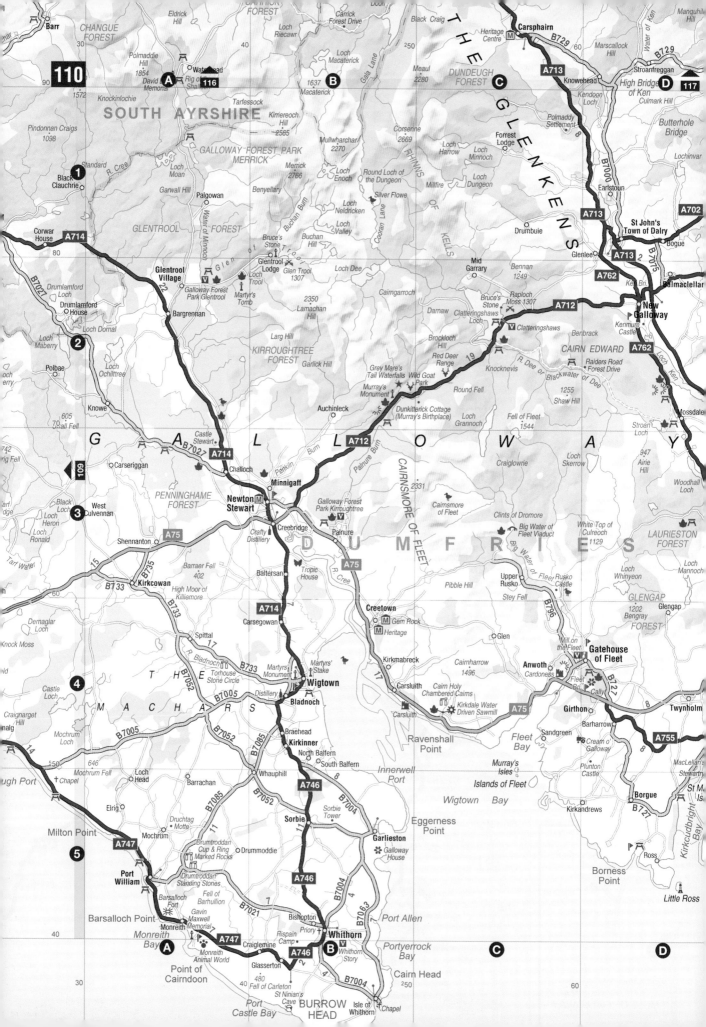

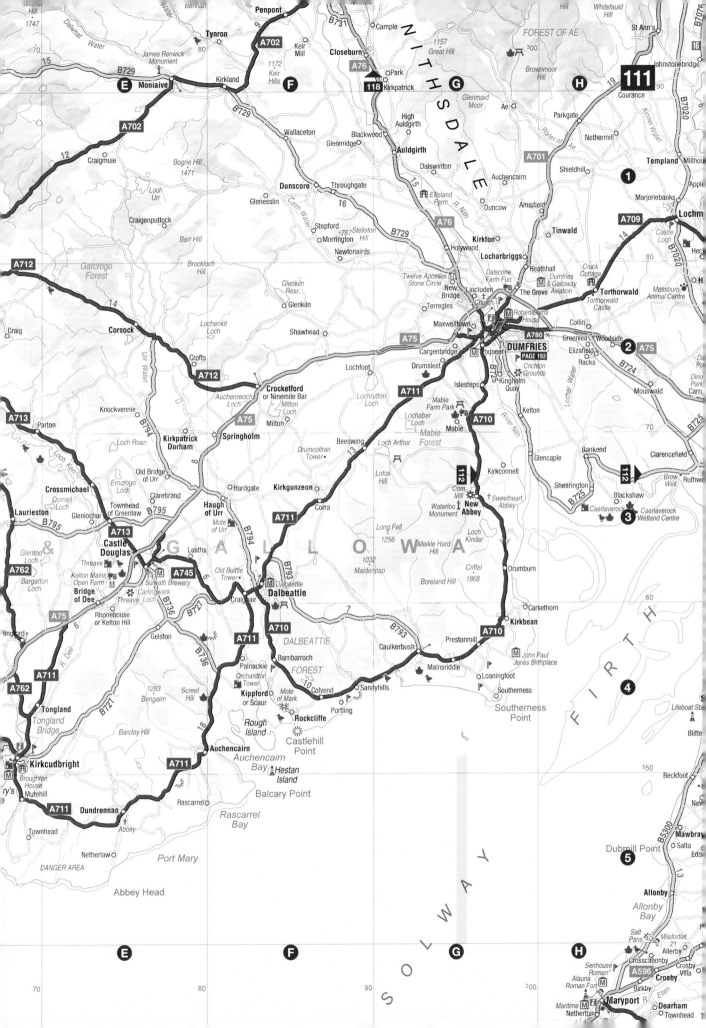

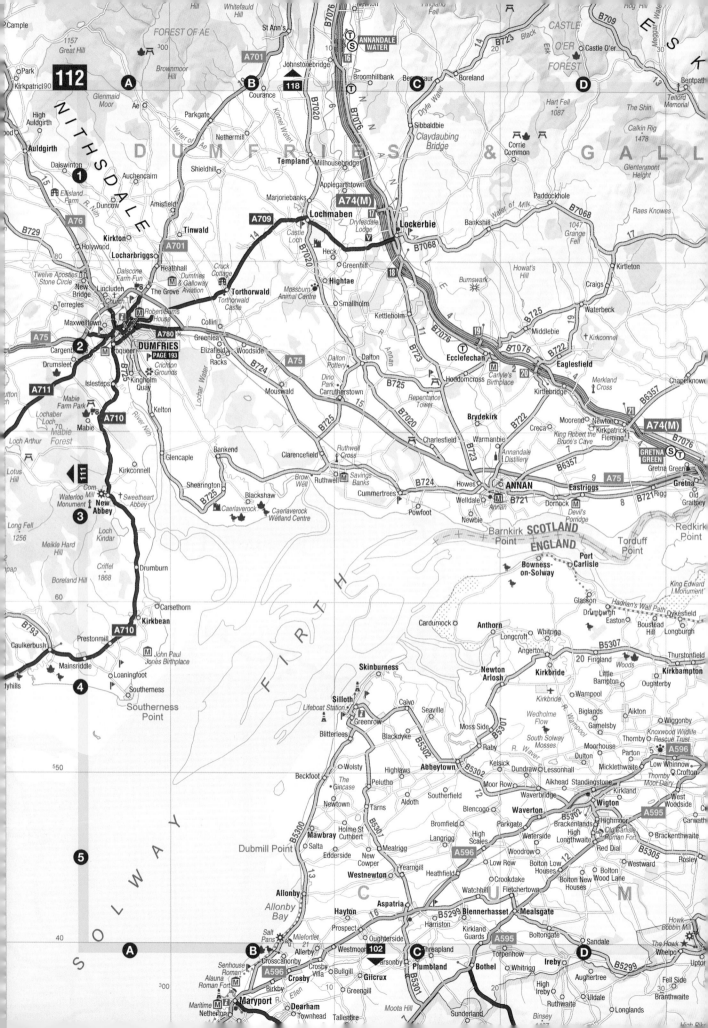

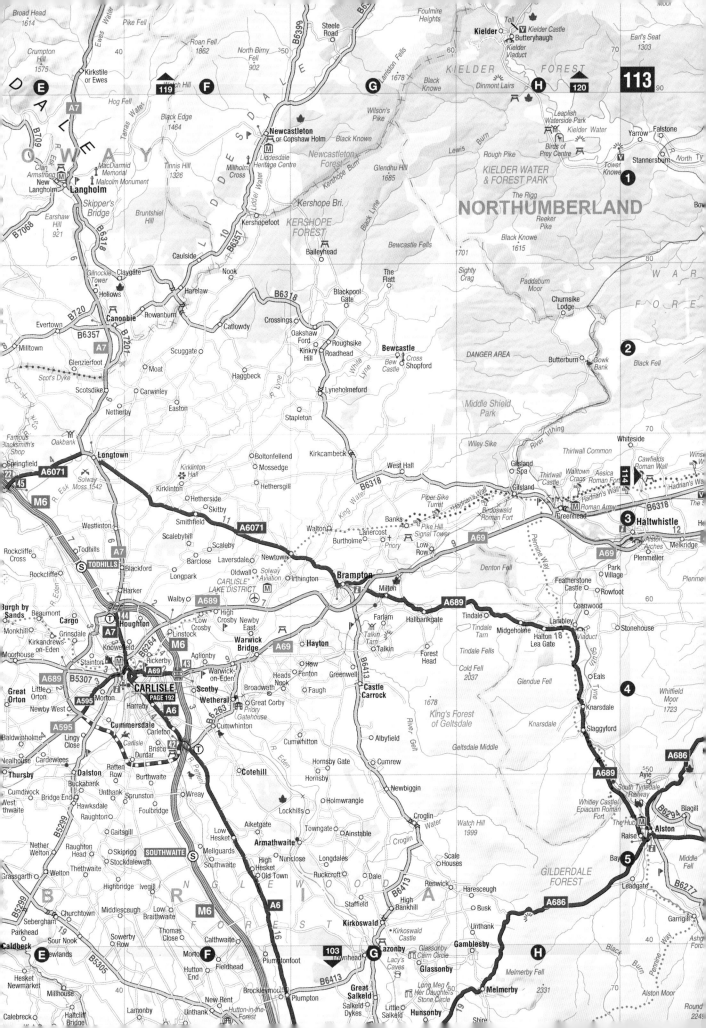

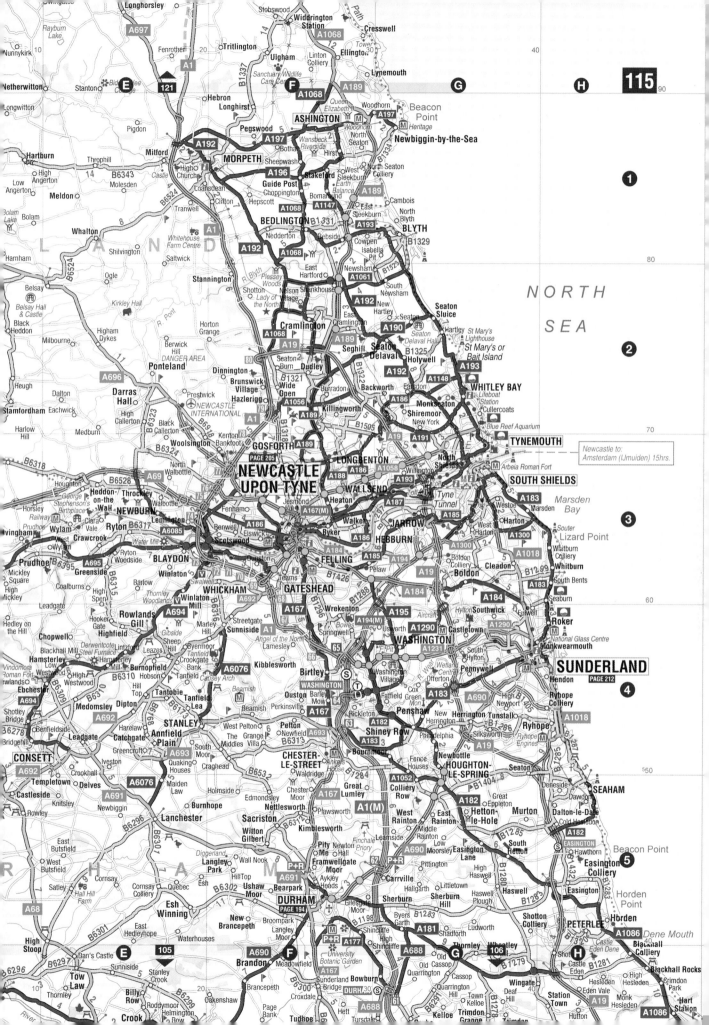

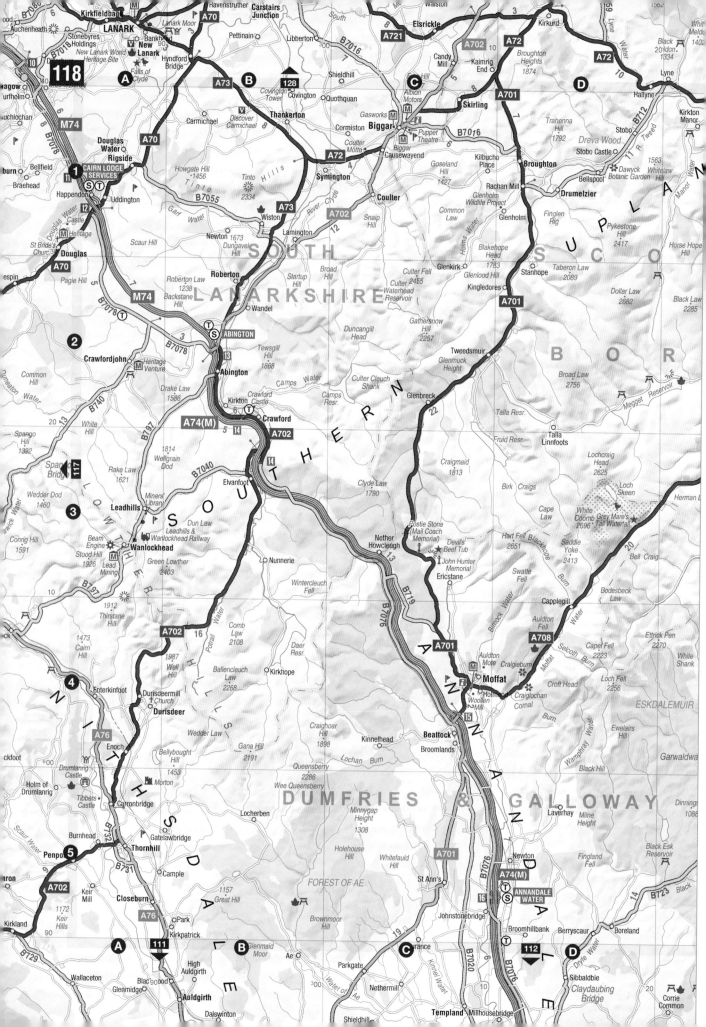

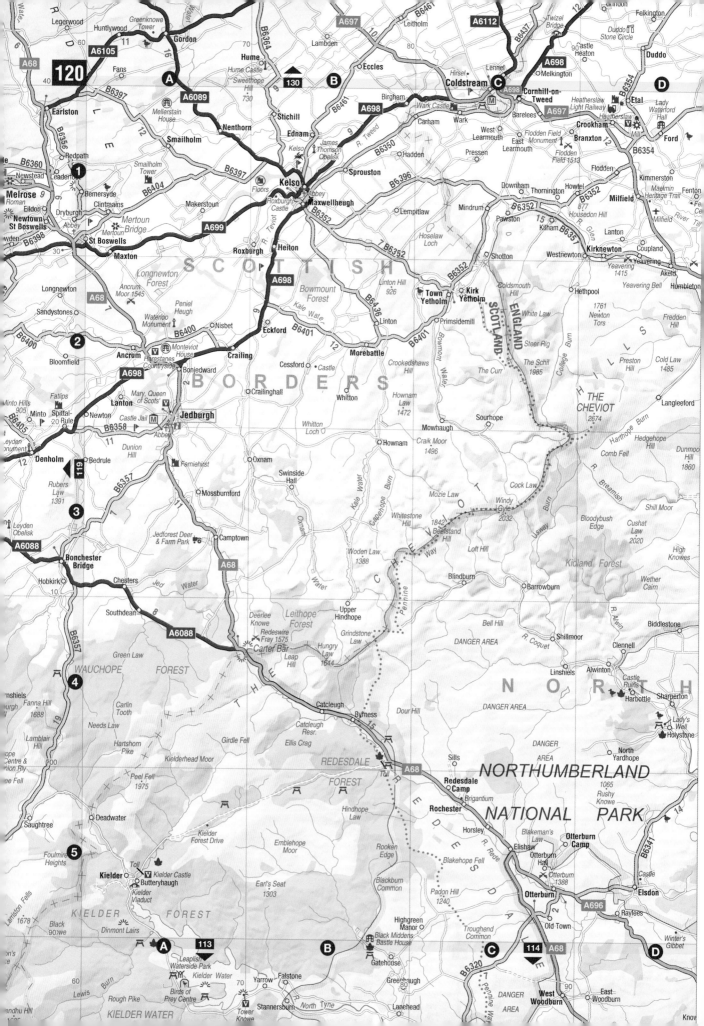

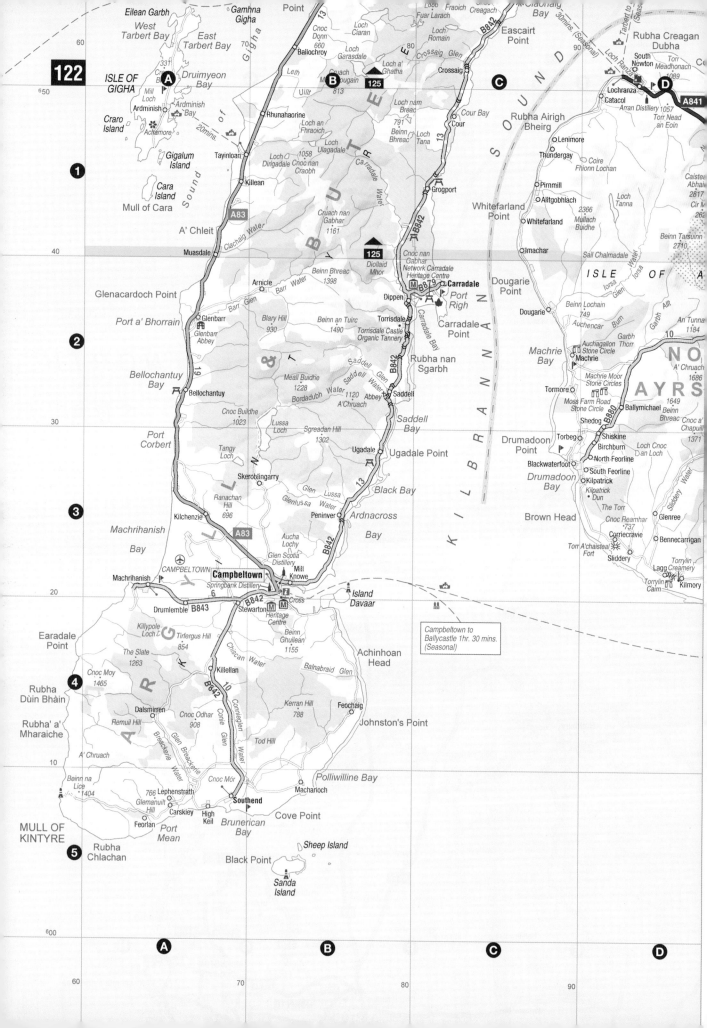

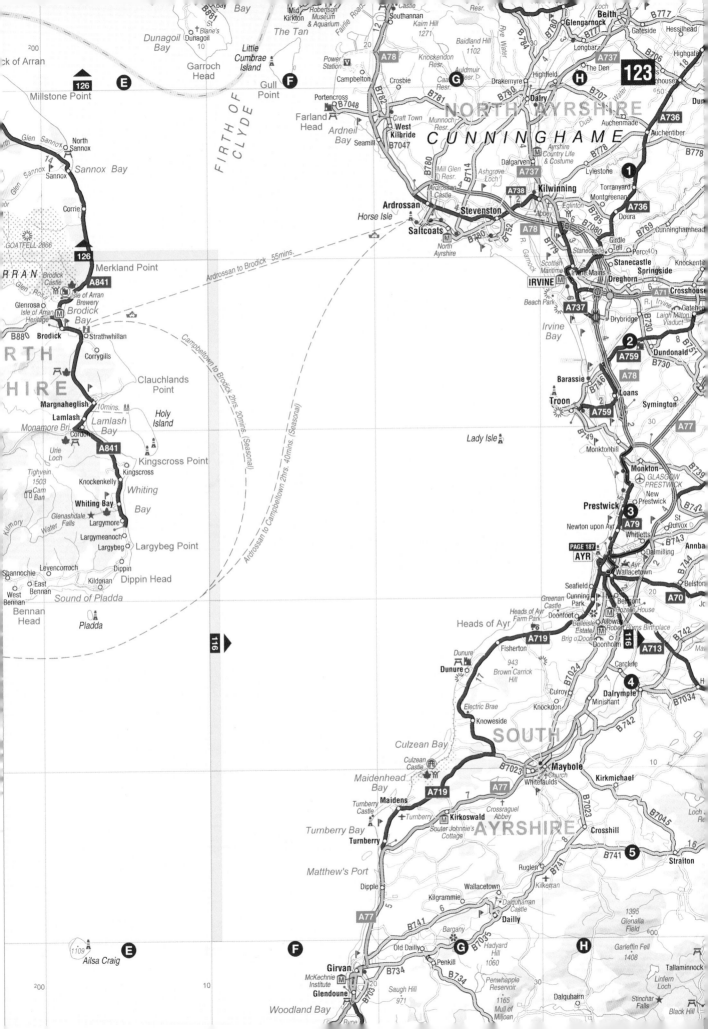

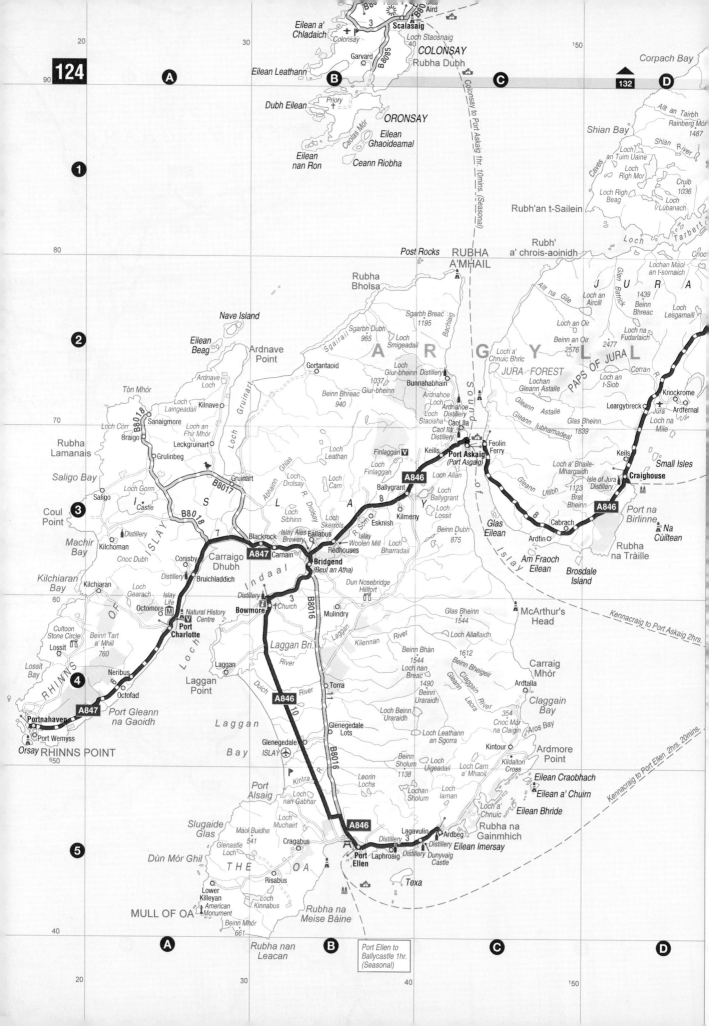

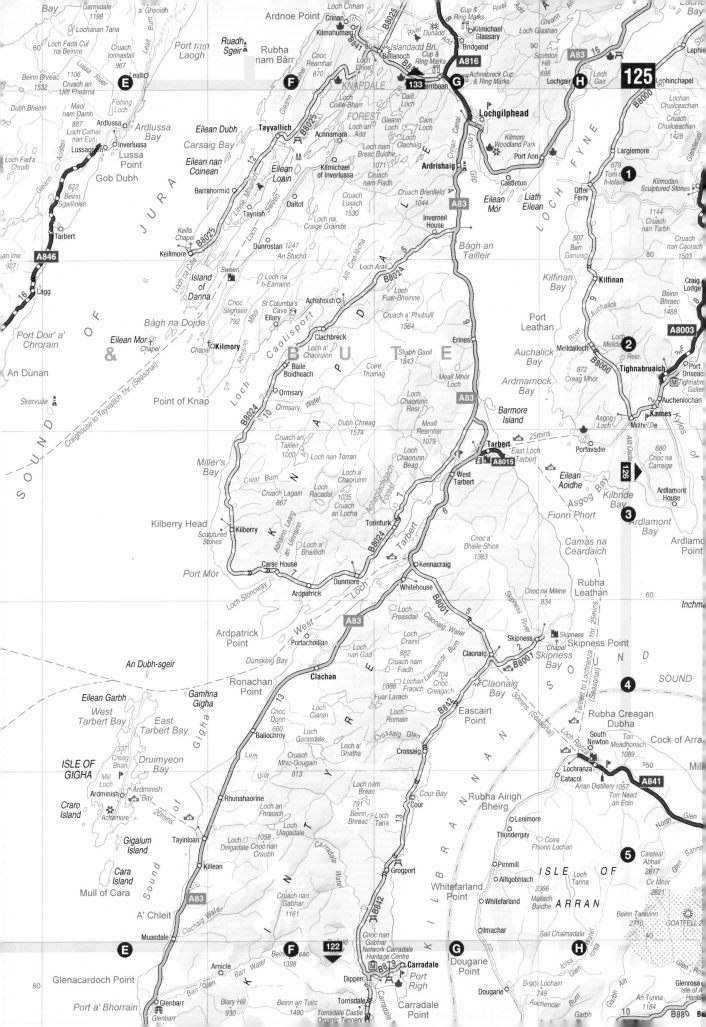

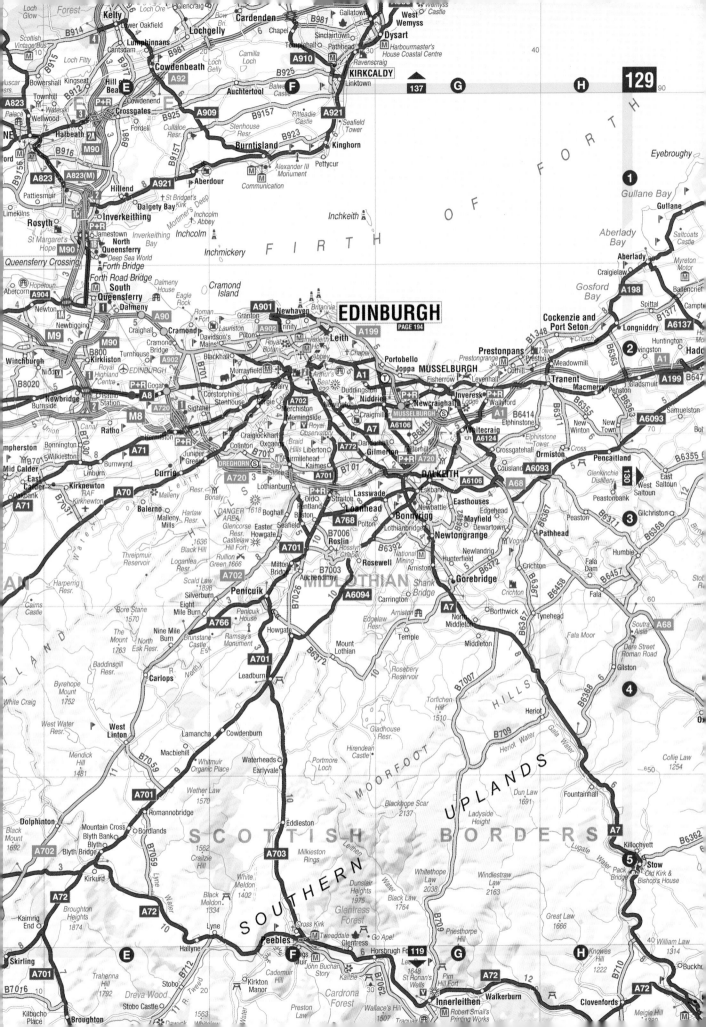

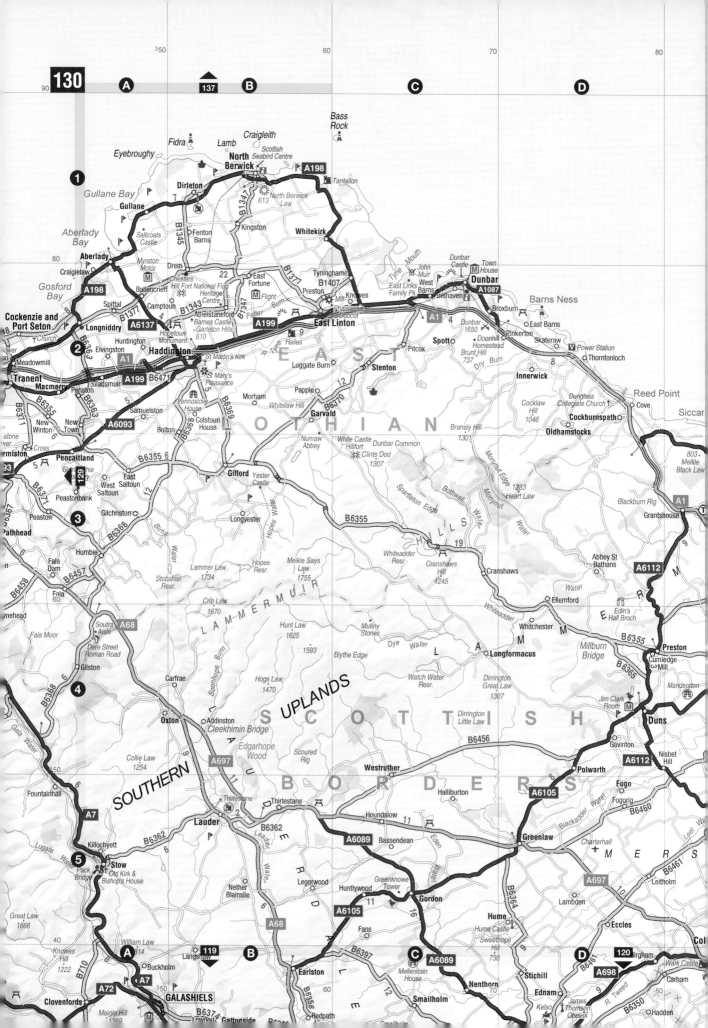

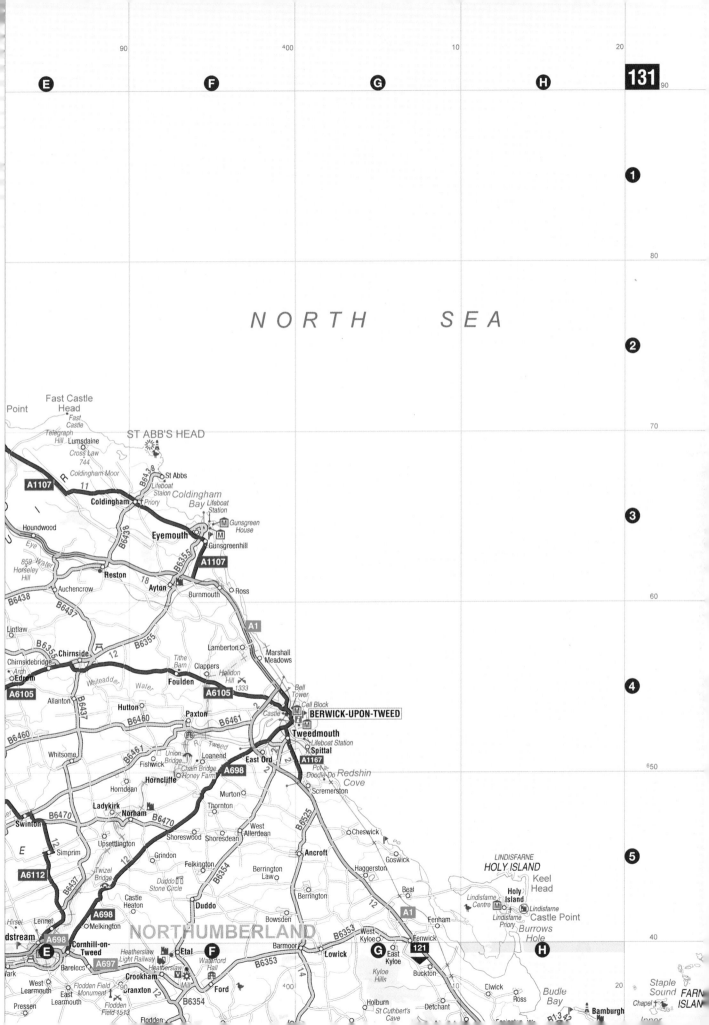

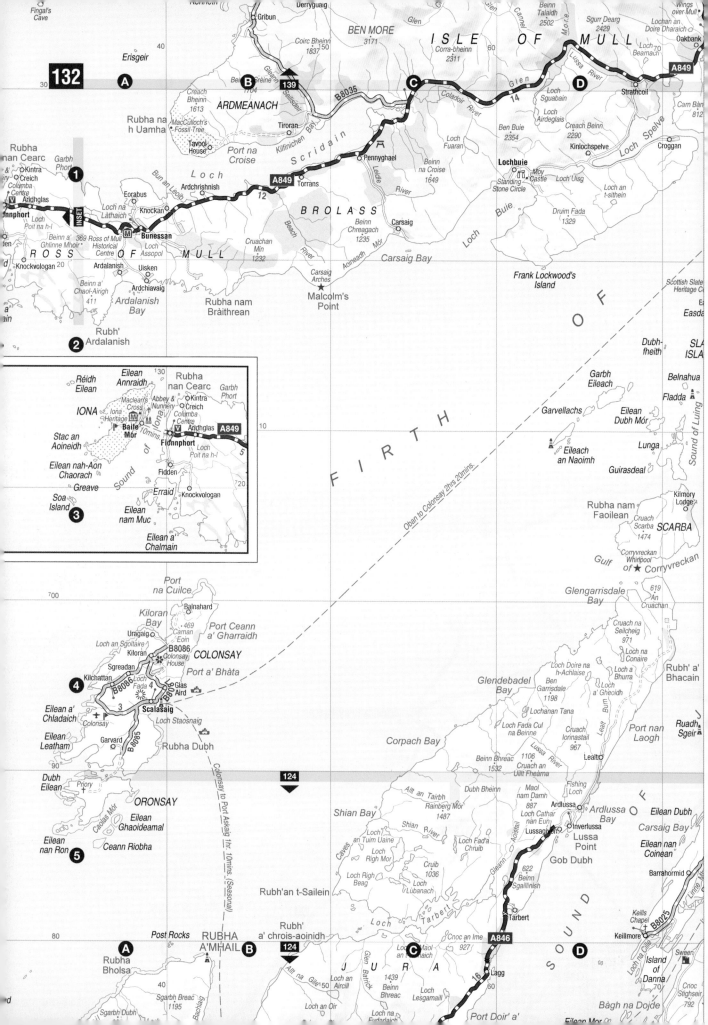

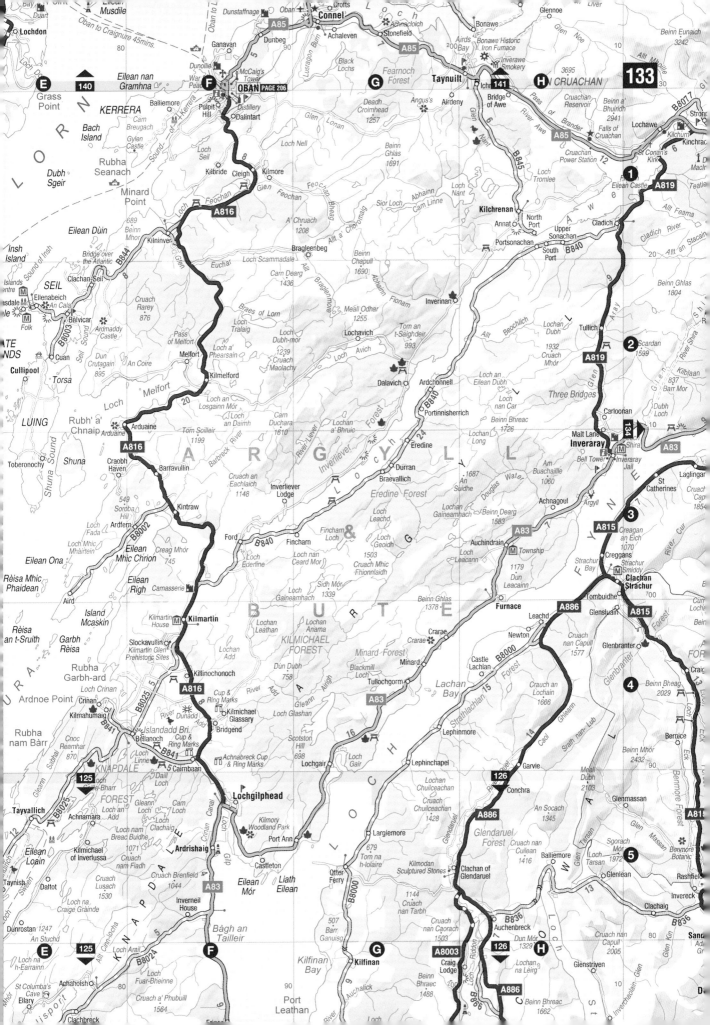

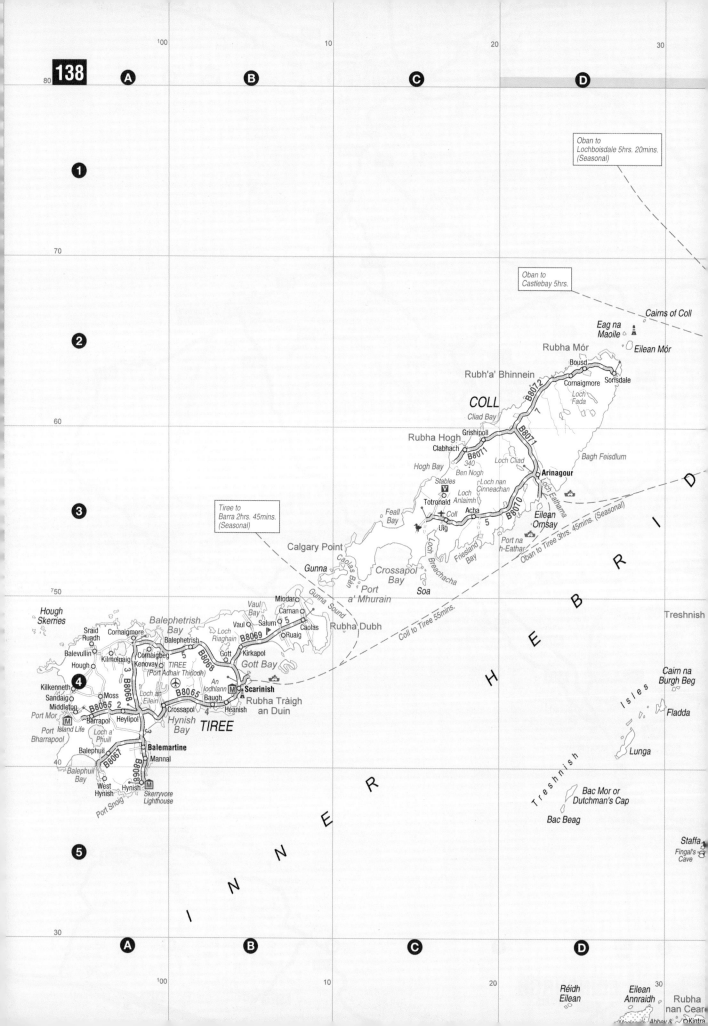

80

100   10   20   30

Ⓐ   Ⓑ   Ⓒ   Ⓓ

⓵

70

Oban to
Lochboisdale 5hrs. 20mins.
(Seasonal)

Oban to
Castlebay 5hrs.

Cairns of Coll

Eag na
Maoile
Rubha Mór   Eilean Mór

⓶   Bousd
Rubh'a' Bhinnein   Cornaigmore Sorisdale
                        B8072
COLL   7   Loch
                                Fada
Cliad Bay
60   Grishipoll   B8071
Rubha Hogh   Bagh Feisdlum
        Clabhach   B8011
Hogh Bay 340   Loch Cliad
        Ben Nogh   Arinagour
Tiree to   Stables   Loch nan
Barra 2hrs. 45mins. V   Cinneachan   Loch Eatharna
(Seasonal)   Totronald Loch   ⚓
⓷   Anlaimh   B8010   Eilean
        Feall   ✈ Coll Acha   Ornsay
        Bay   Uig   5
Calgary Point   Friesland Port na   Oban to Tiree 3hrs. 45mins. (Seasonal)
                        Bay   h-Eathar
Gunna   D
        Caolas Bàn Crossapol
Port   Bay   Soa   H
a' Mhurain   Gunna Sound   E
                                            B   Treshnish
750   Miodar   Loch Breachacha R
Hough   Vaul Carnan   Coll to Tiree 55mins. I
Skerries   Balephetrish Bay Salum 5   D
        Bay   Vaul 5 Caolas   E
Sràid   Loch   Gott Ruaig Rubha Dubh   S
Ruadh Cornaigmore Riaghain B8069   Cairn na
Balevullin   Balephetrish Kirkapol   Burgh Beg
        Kilmoluaig Cornaigbeg 5 Gott Bay
Hough   Kenovay B8068   Isles Fladda
Kilkenneth 4 TIREE An   M
Sandaig   Loch an (Port Adhair Thiridh) Iodhlann Scarinish
Middleton   Eilein B8065 Baugh Rubha Tràigh   Lunga
Port Mor B8066 2   4 Héanish an Duin
Island Life Barrapol Crossapol
Port   M   Heylipol Hynish
Bharrapool Loch a'   Bay TIREE Treshnish
        Phuill 3   Bac Mor or
Balephuil   Balemartine   Dutchman's Cap
    B8067 Mannal
40   Bac Beag
Balephuil   West M
Bay   Hynish Hynish Skerryvore
Port Snoig Lighthouse   Staffa
                        Fingal's
⓹   Cave

I   N   N   E   R

30
Ⓐ   Ⓑ   Ⓒ   Ⓓ

100   10   20   30
                    Réidh   Eilean   Rubha
                    Eilean   Annraidh nan Cearc
                        Abbey & Kintra

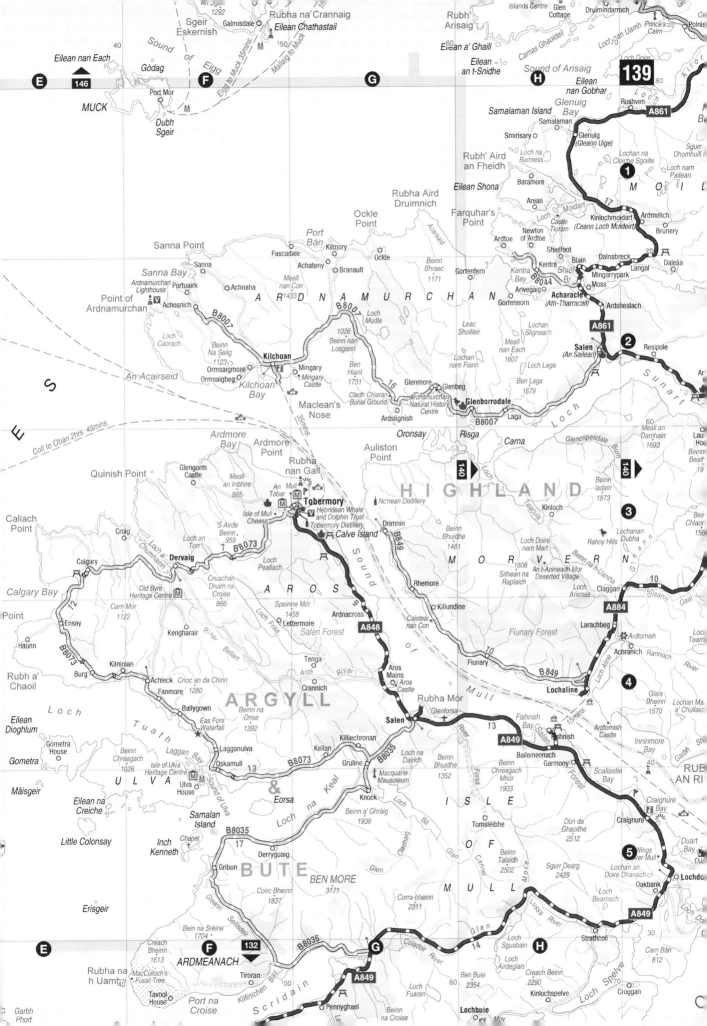

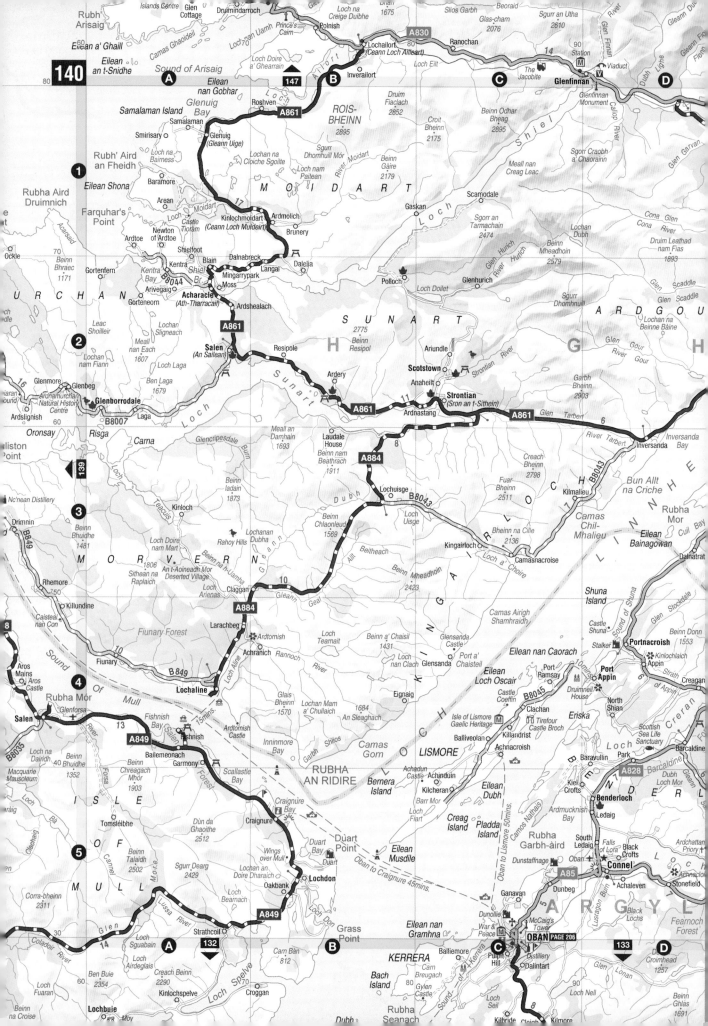

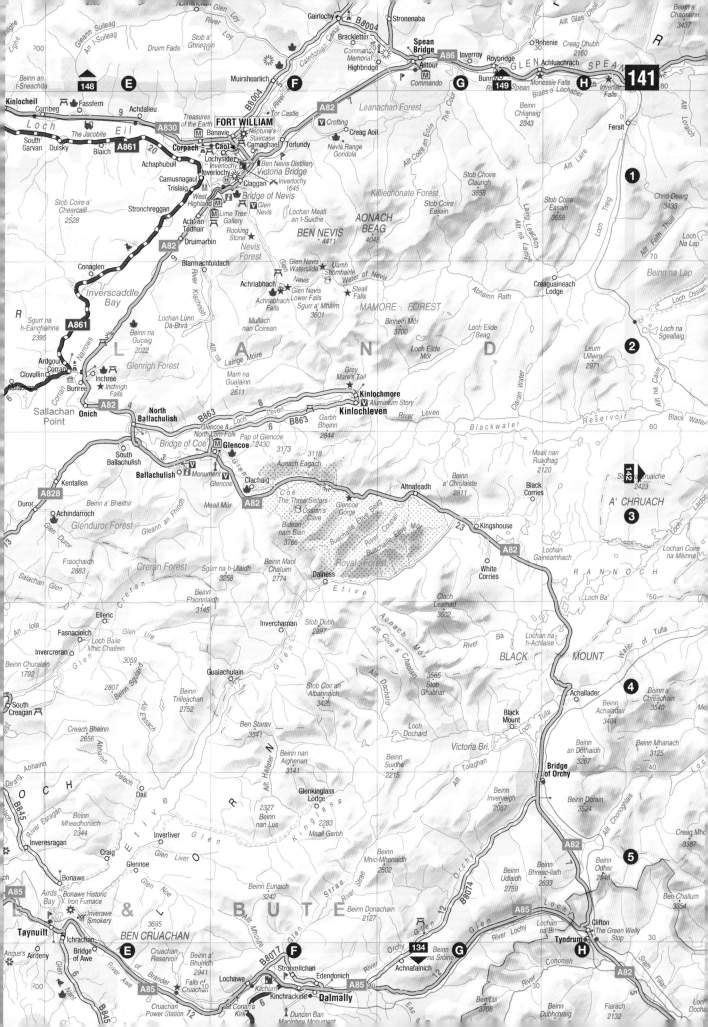

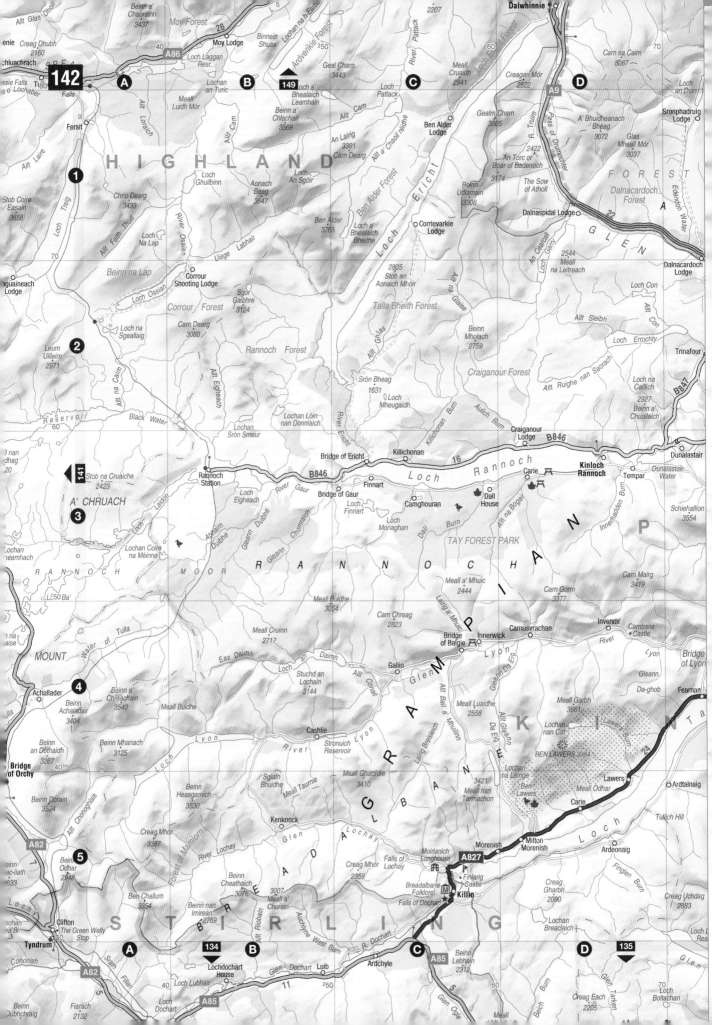

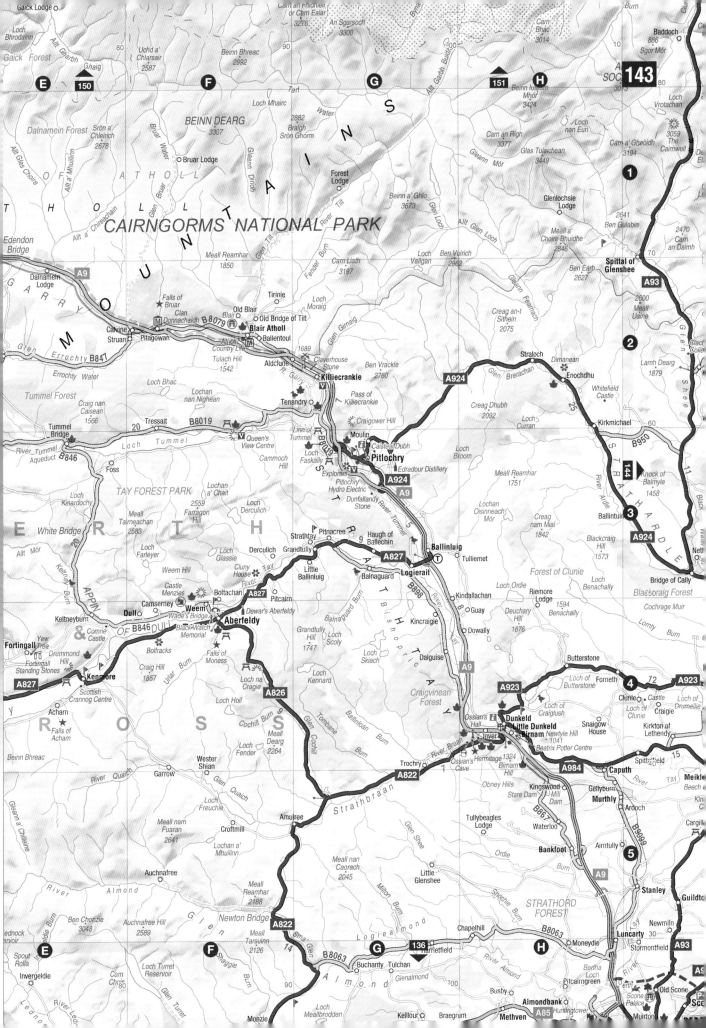

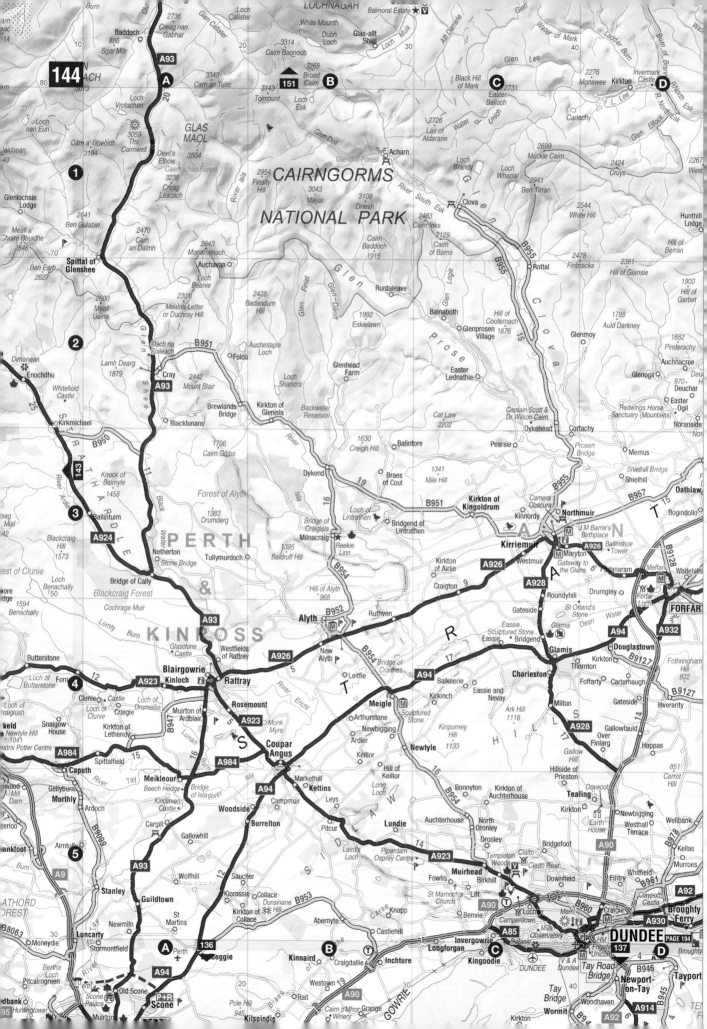

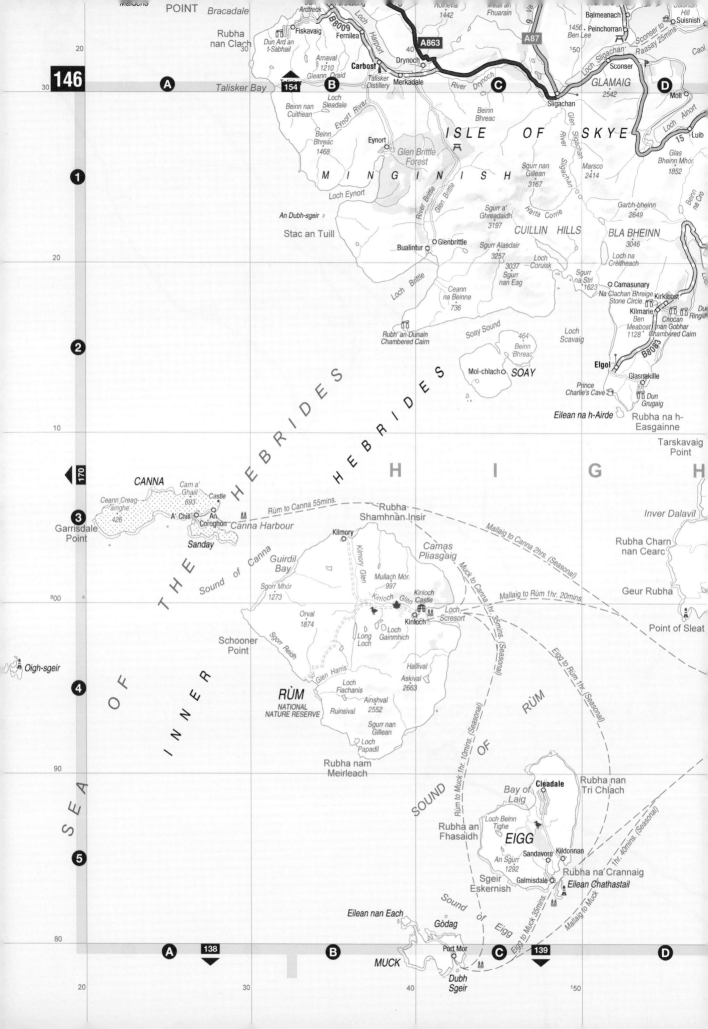

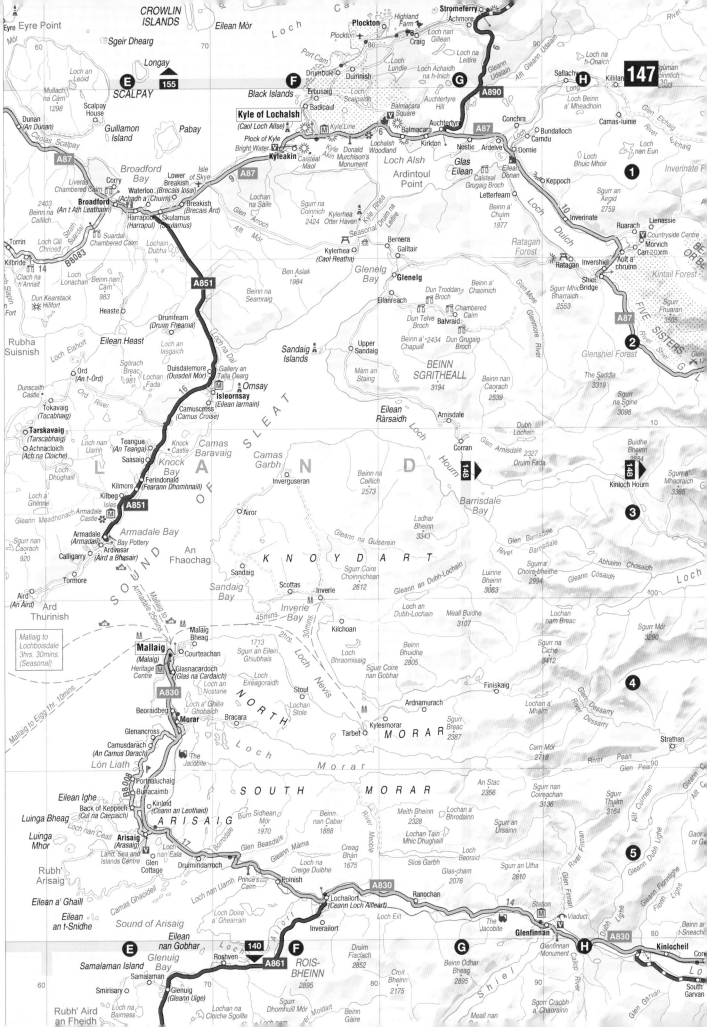

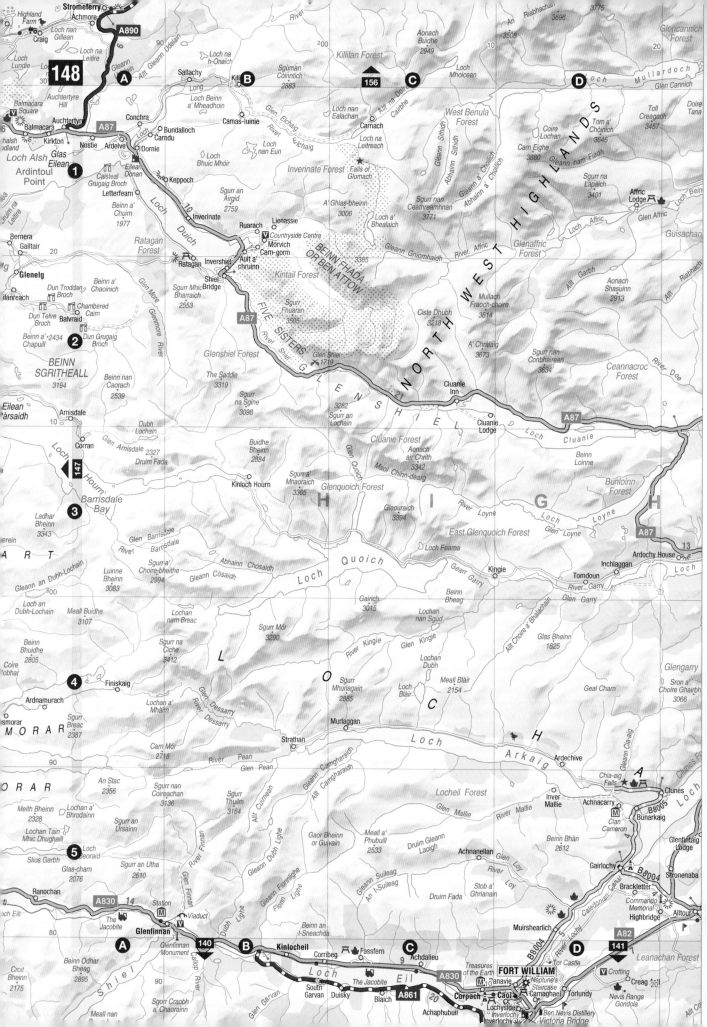

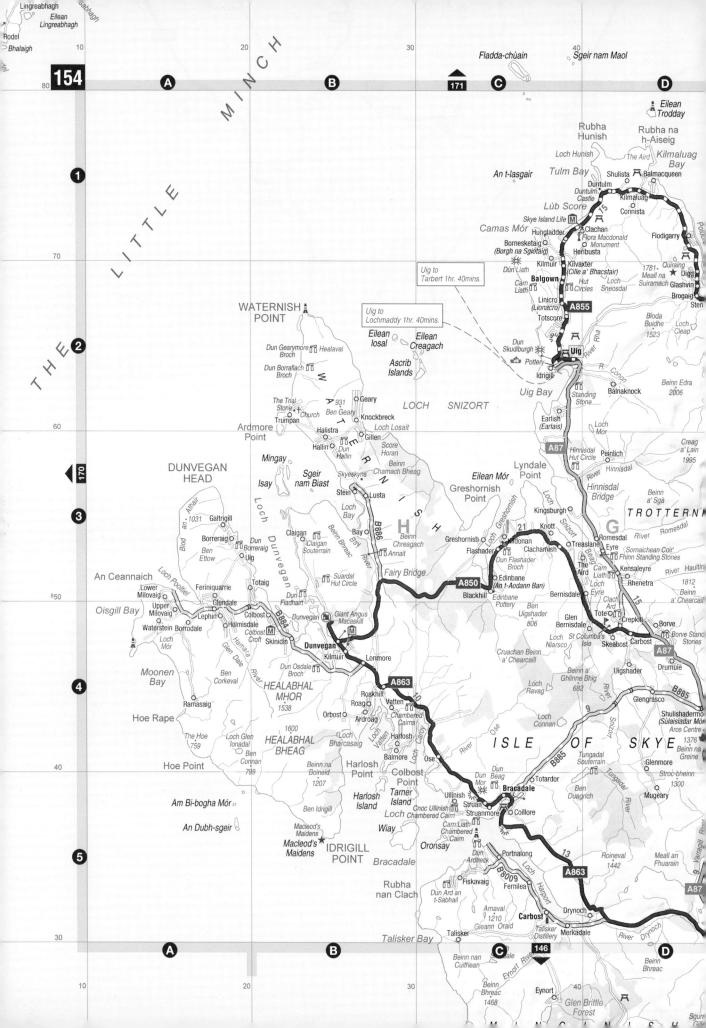

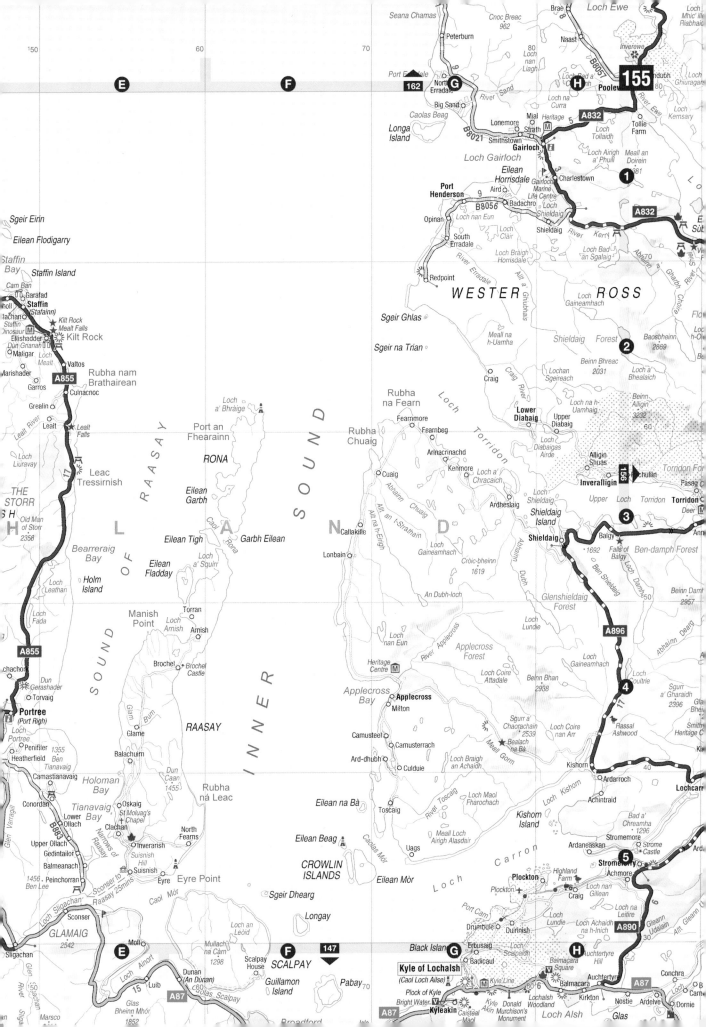

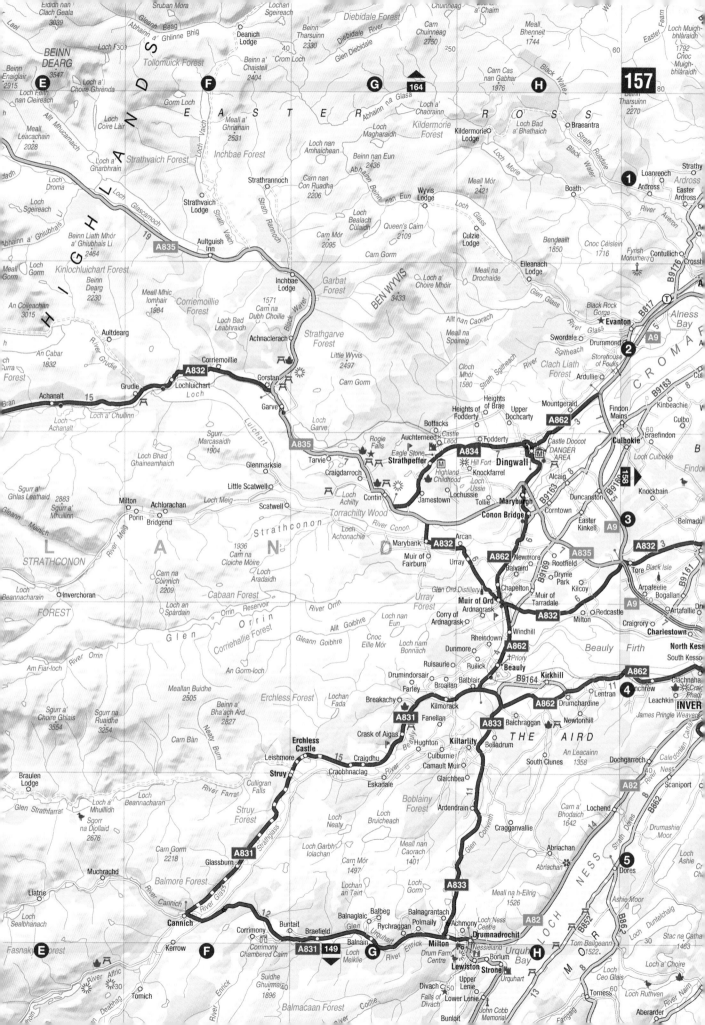

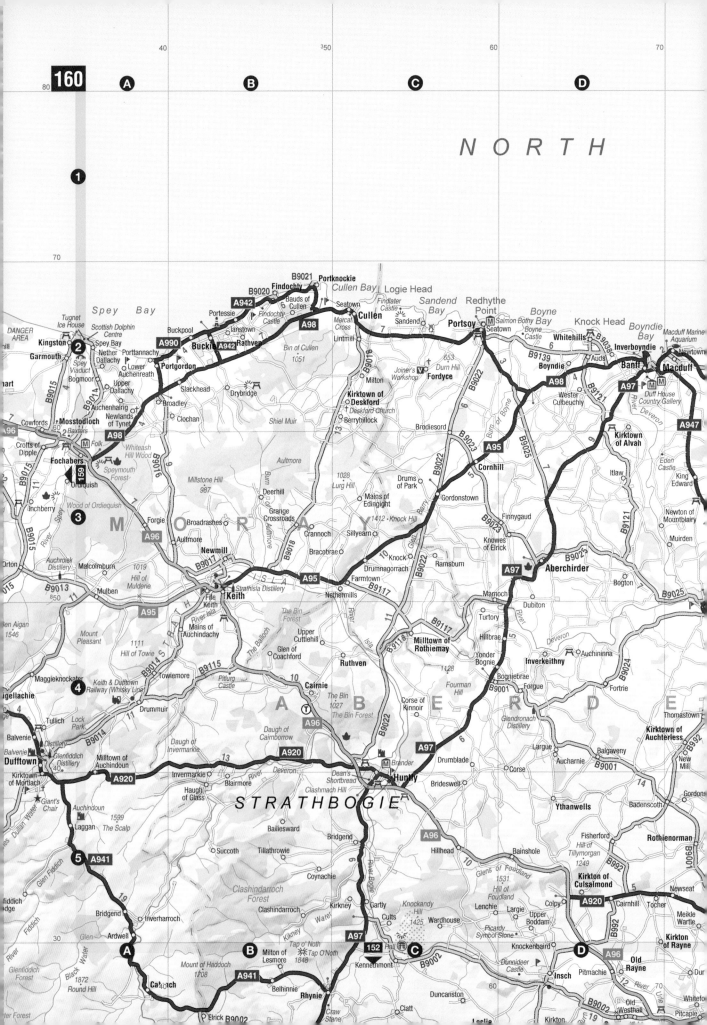

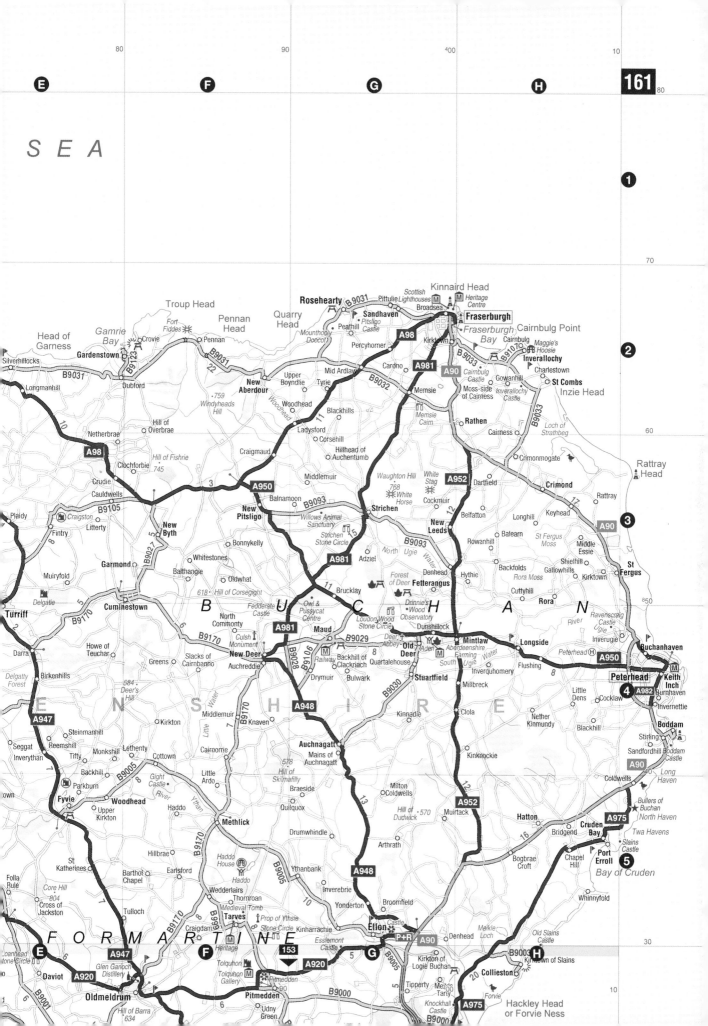

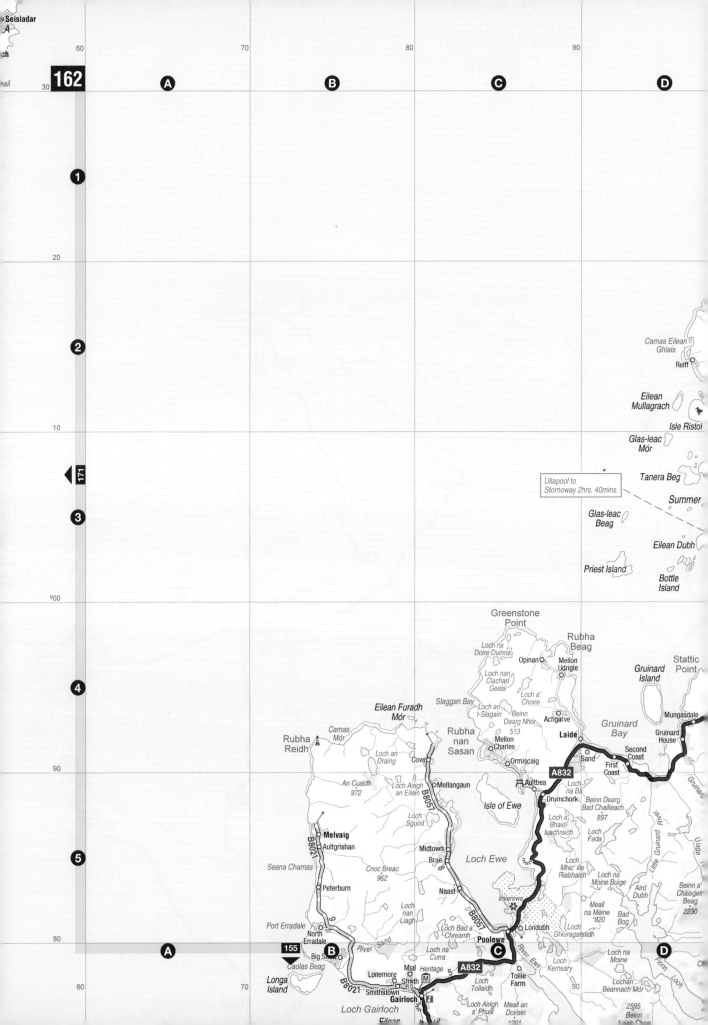

Seisiadar

171

155

60   70   80   90

30

20

10

°00

90

80

60   70   90

A   **B**   **C**   **D**

① ② ③ ④ ⑤

Camas Eilean Ghlais

Reiff

Eilean Mullagrach

Isle Ristol

Glas-leac Mór

Tanera Beg

Ullapool to Stornoway 2hrs. 40mins.

Summer

Glas-leac Beag

Eilean Dubh

Priest Island

Bottle Island

Greenstone Point

Rubha Beag

Loch na Doire Duinne

Opinan

Mellon Udrigle

Stattic Point

Gruinard Island

Mungasdale

Loch nan Clachan Geala

Loch a' Choire

Achgarve

Gruinard Bay

Gruinard House

Slaggan Bay

Loch an t-Slagain

Beinn Dearg Nhór 513

Mellon Charles

Laide

Second Coast

Eilean Furadh Mór

Rubha nan Sasan

Ormiscaig

Sand

First Coast

Camas Mór

Rubha Reidh

Cove

Aultbea

A832

Drumchork

Loch na Bà

Beinn Dearg Bad Chailleach 897

Gruinard River

Uisge

An Cuaidh 972

Loch an Draing

Mellangaun

Isle of Ewe

Loch a' Bhaid-luachraich

Loch Fada

Little Gruinard River

Loch Airigh an Eilein

B8057

Loch Sguod

Melvaig

Aultgrishan

B8021

Midtown

Brae

Loch Ewe

Loch Mhic' ille Riabhaich

Loch na Mòine Buige

Aird Dubh

Beinn a' Chàisgein Beag 2230

Seana Chamas

Cnoc Breac 962

Naast

Inverewe

Meall na Mèine *820

Bad Bog

Peterburn

Loch nan Liagh

B8057

Londubh

Loch Ghiuragarstidh

Port Erradale

North Erradale

Loch Bad a' Chreamh

Poolewe

River Ewe

Loch Kernsary

Loch na Moine

Fionn Loch

River Sand

Loch na Curra

A832

Tollie Farm

Big Sand

Caolas Beag

Mial

Strath

Heritage M

Lochan Beannach Mór

2595 Beinn

Longa Island

Lonemore

Smithstown

Gairloch

i

Loch Airigh a' Phuill

Meall an Doirein

Loch Tollaidh

B8021

Loch Gairloch

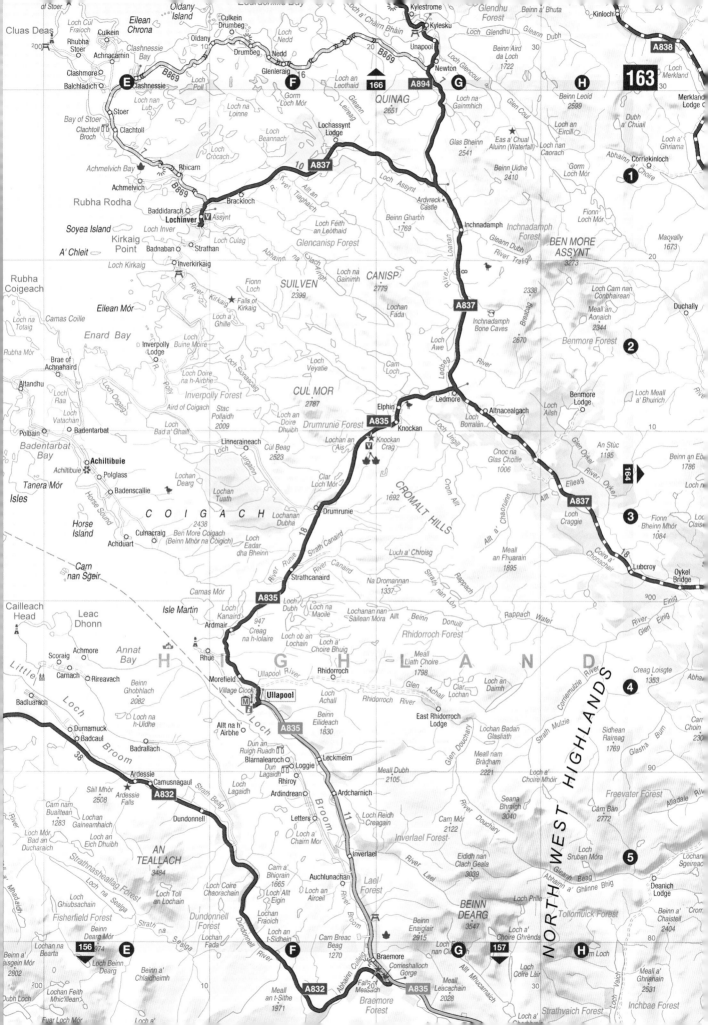

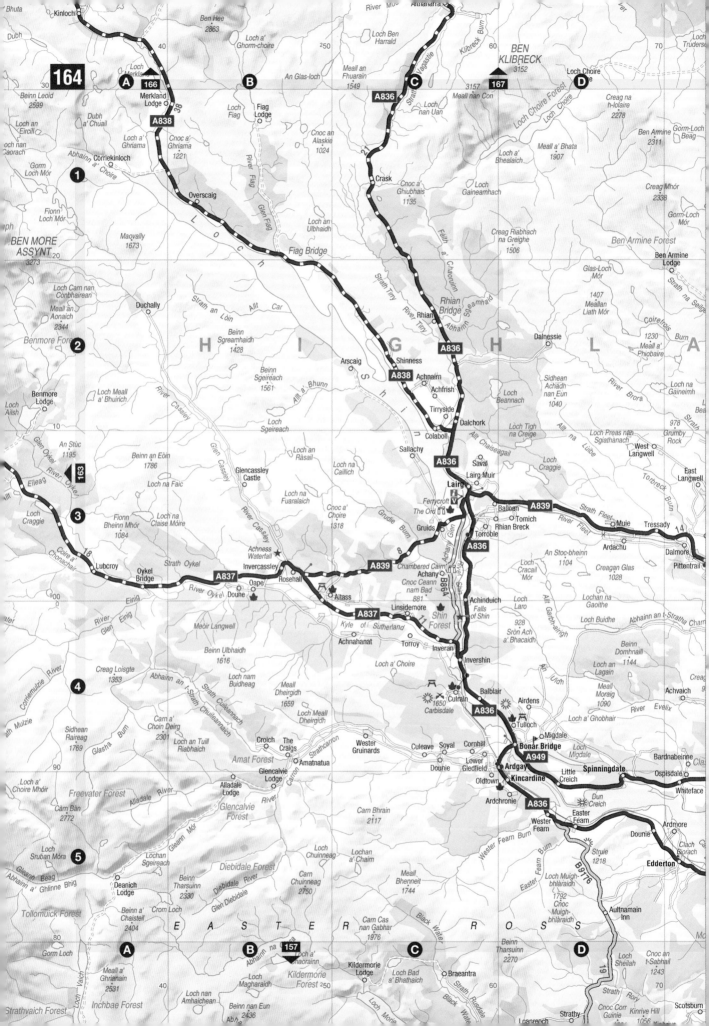

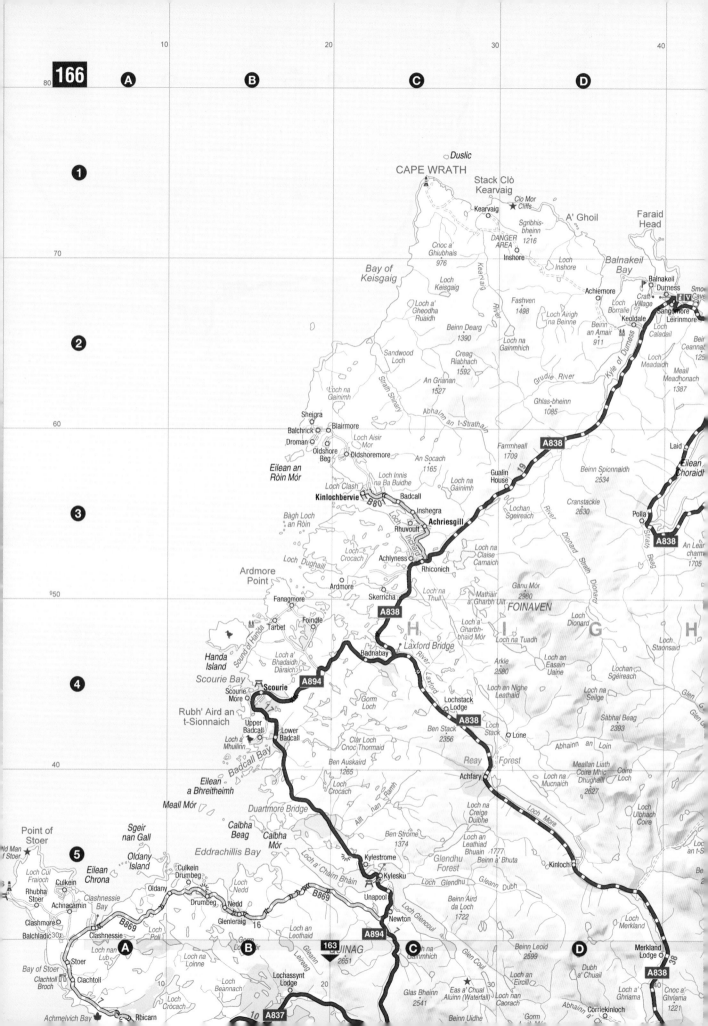

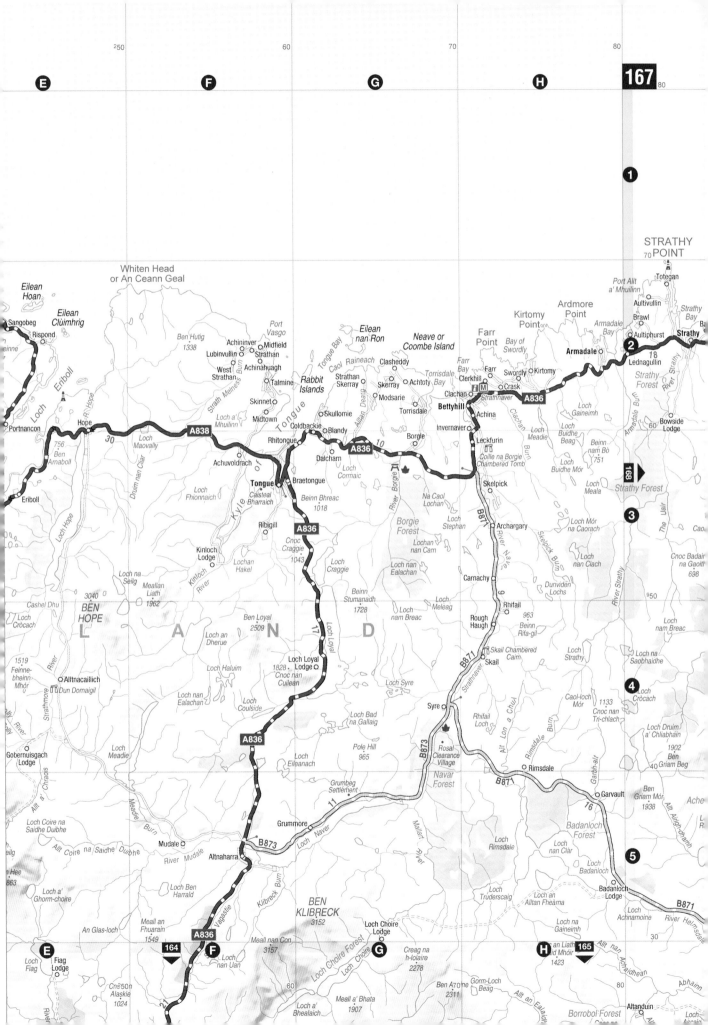

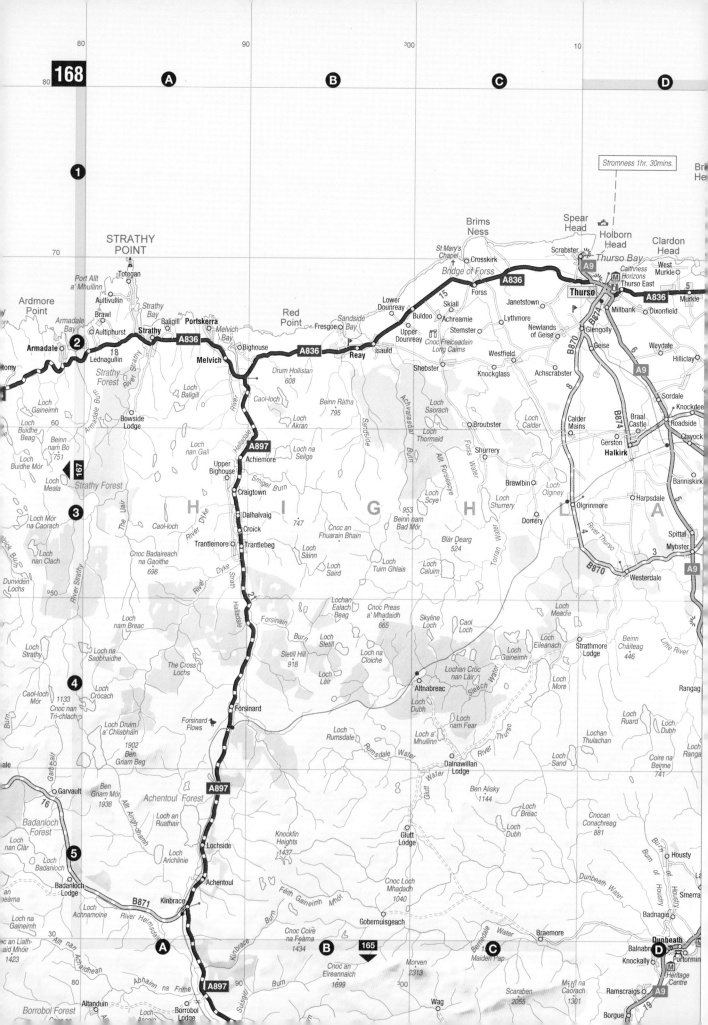

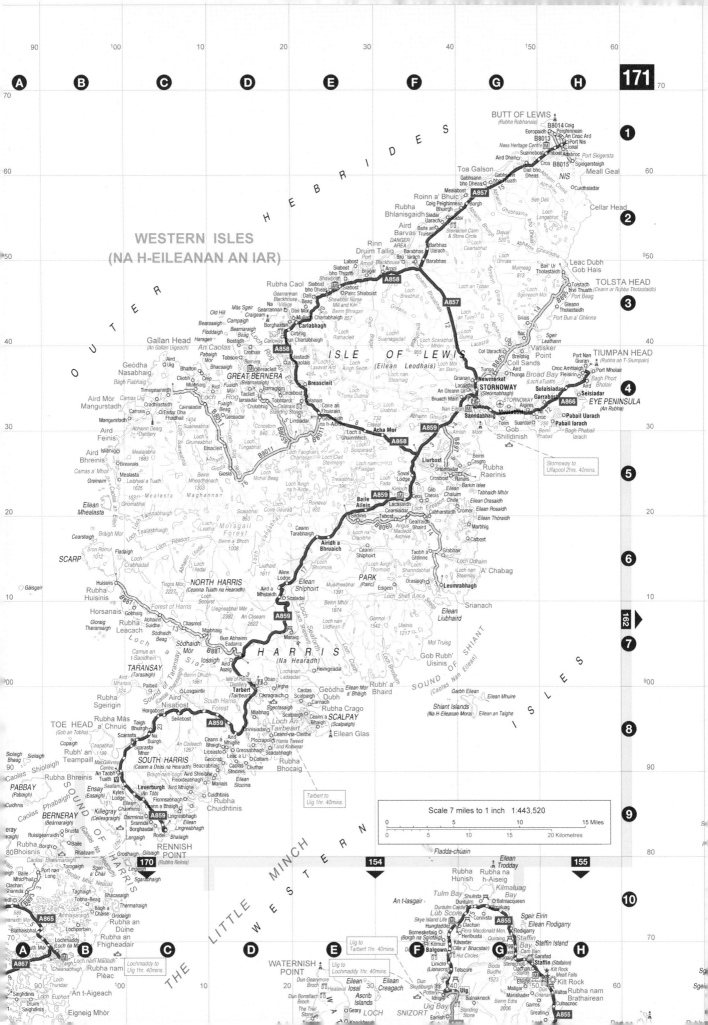

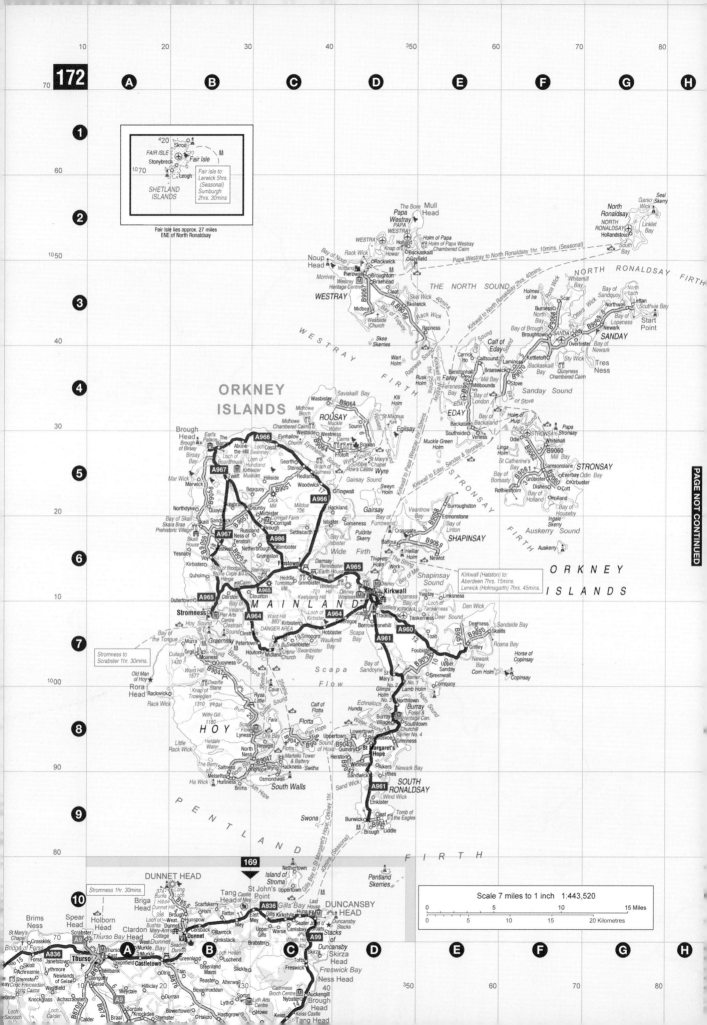

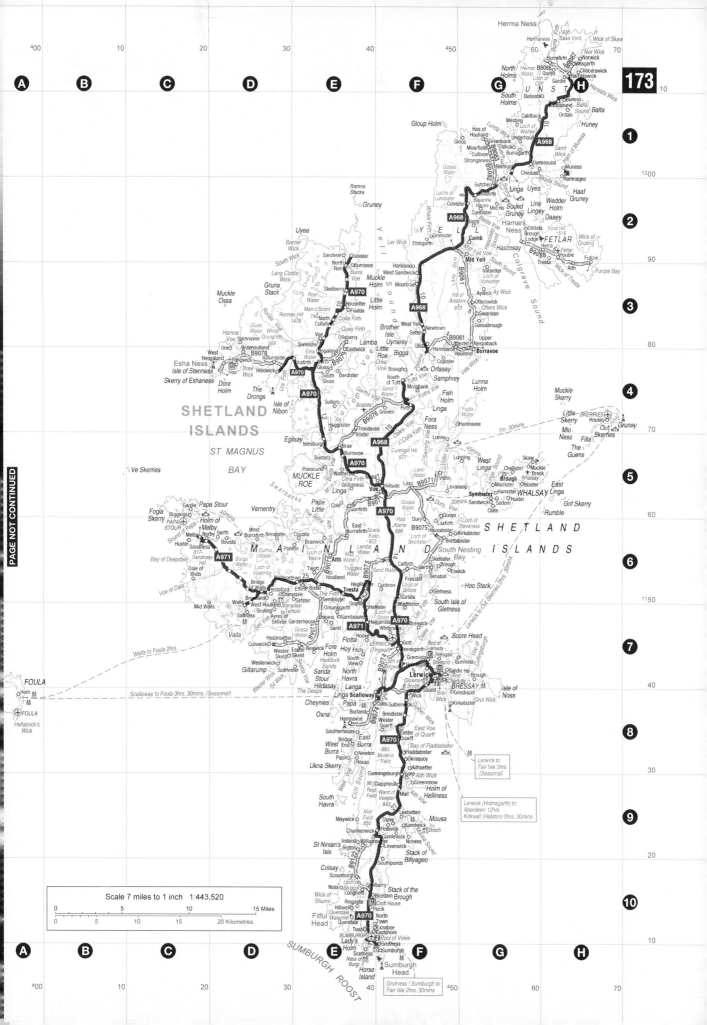

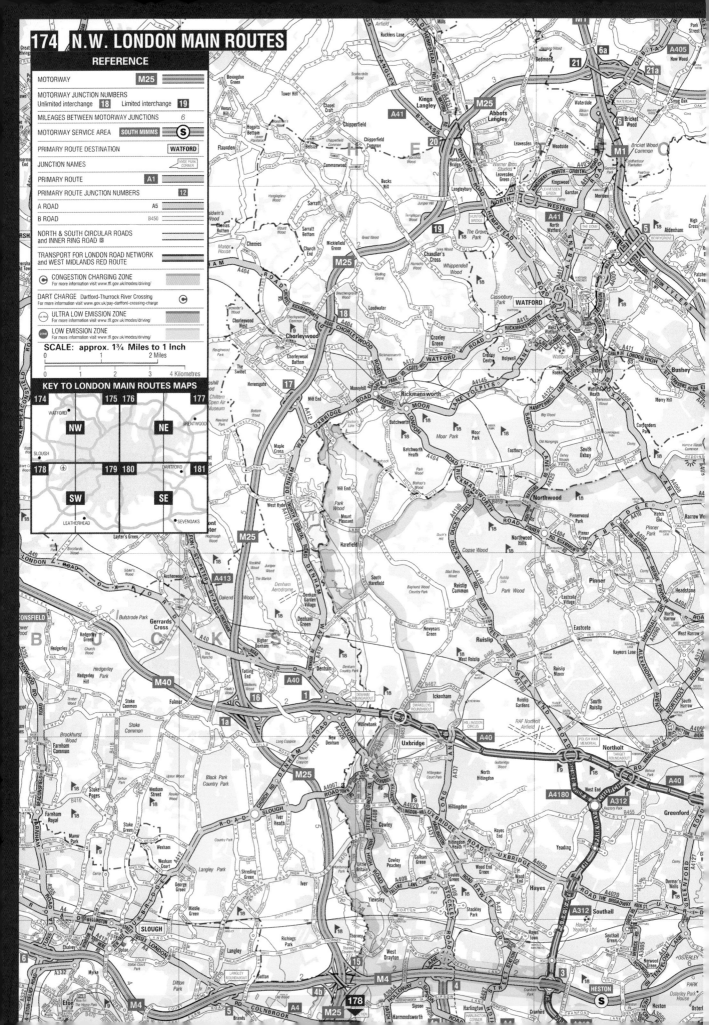

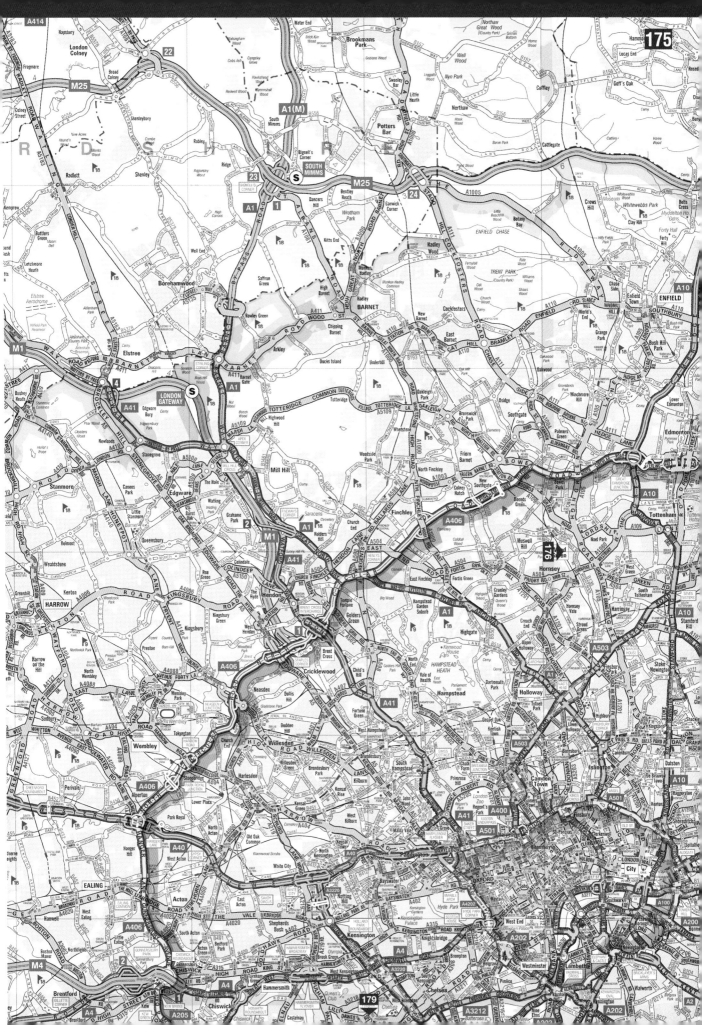

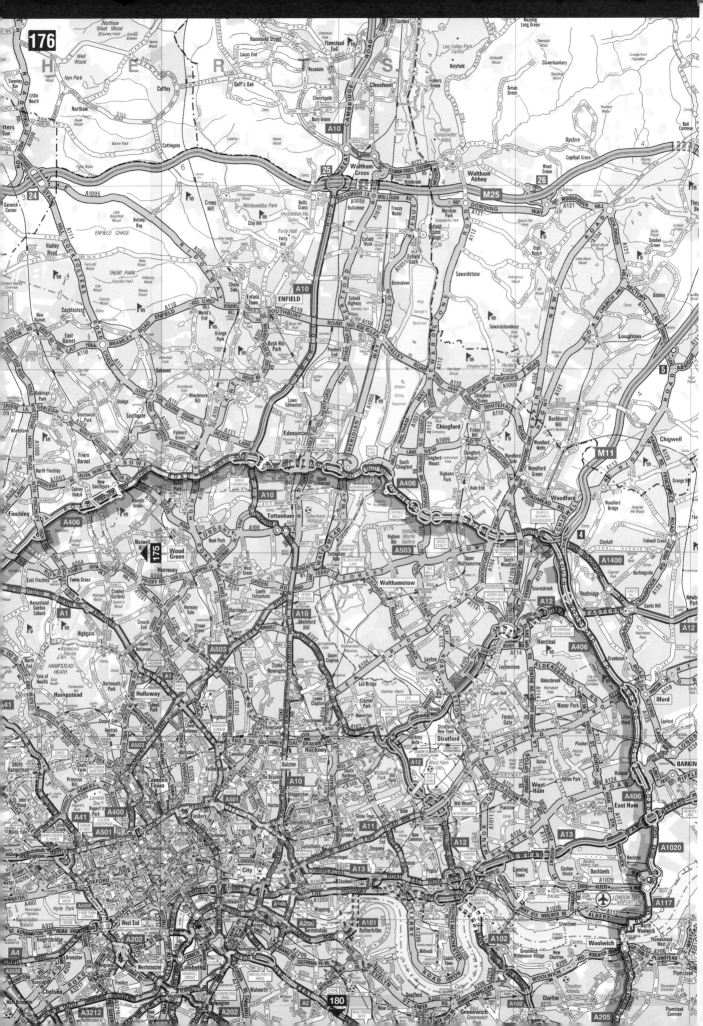

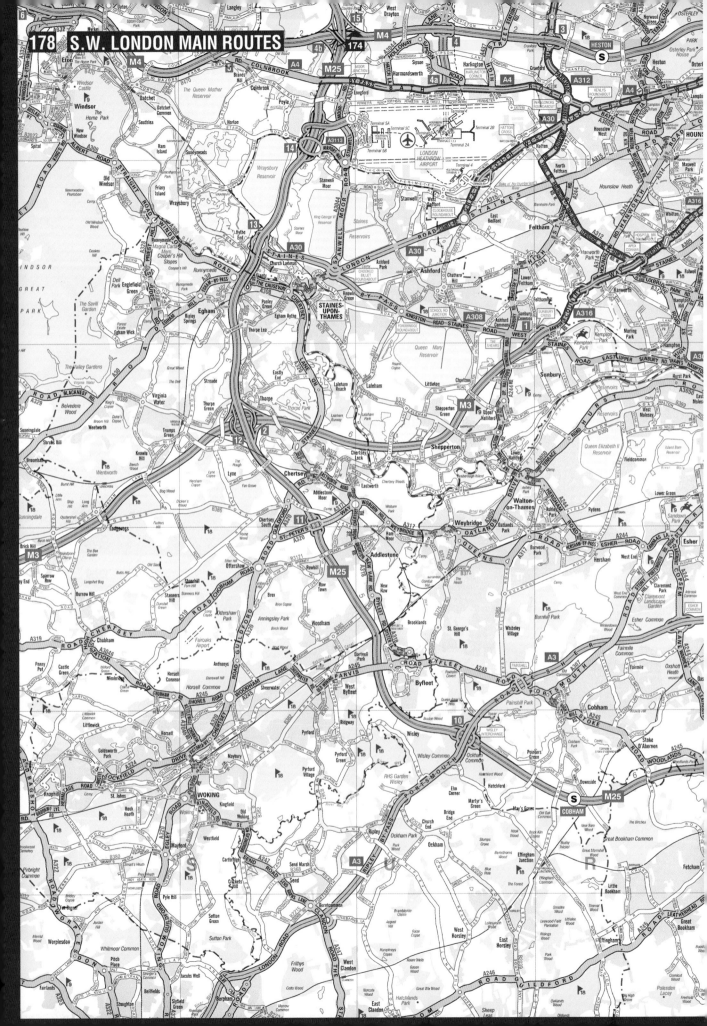

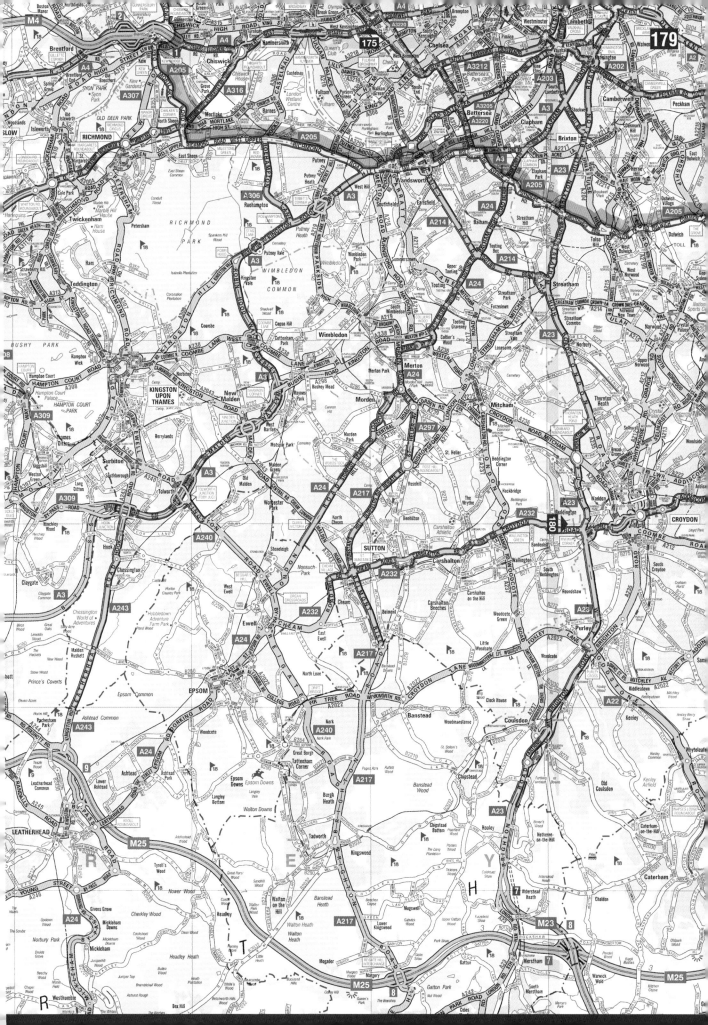

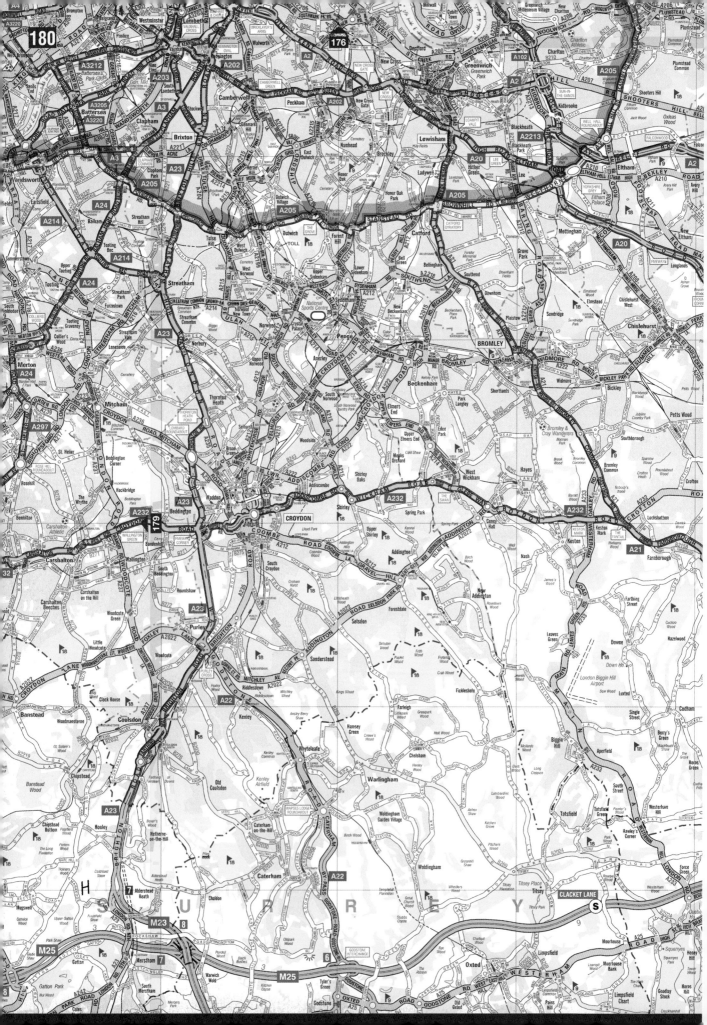

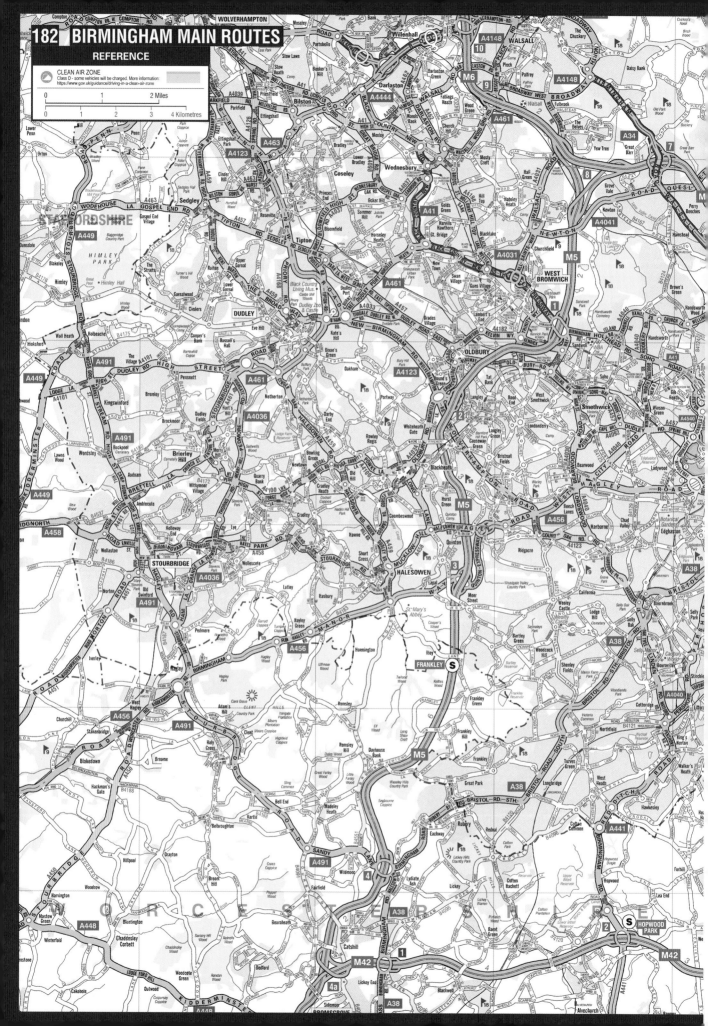

CLEAN AIR ZONE
Class D - some vehicles will be charged. More information:
https://www.gov.uk/guidance/driving-in-a-clean-air-zone

CLEAN AIR ZONE Proposed for May 2022
Class C - some vehicles will be charged. More information:
https://www.gov.uk/guidance/driving-in-a-clean-air-zone

Town Plans

Aberdeen	187
Aberystwyth	187
Ayr	187
Bath	187
Bedford	188
Birmingham	188
Blackpool	188
Bournemouth	190
Bradford	190
Brighton & Hove	189
Bristol	189
Caernarfon	190
Cambridge	191
Canterbury	190
Cardiff (Caerdydd)	191
Carlisle	192
Cheltenham	192
Chester	192
Coventry	192
Derby	193
Dover	193
Dumfries	193
Dundee	194
Durham	194
Eastbourne	195
Edinburgh	194
Exeter	195
Folkestone	195
Glasgow	196
Gloucester	196
Great Yarmouth	196
Guildford	197
Harrogate	197
Hereford	197
Inverness	198
Ipswich	198
Kilmarnock	198
Kingston upon Hull	199
Leeds	199
Leicester	200
Lincoln	198
Liverpool	200
London	202-203
Luton	201
Manchester	201
Medway Towns	204
Middlesbrough	201
Milton Keynes	204
Newcastle upon Tyne	205
Newport (Casnewydd)	205
Northampton	206
Norwich	205
Nottingham	206
Oban	206
Oxford	207
Paisley	207
Perth	207
Peterborough	208
Plymouth	208
Portsmouth	209
Preston	208
Reading	209
St Andrews	209
Salisbury	210
Sheffield	210
Shrewsbury	210
Southampton	211
Stirling	211
Stoke-on-Trent	211
Stratford-upon-Avon	212
Sunderland	212
Swansea (Abertawe)	212
Swindon	212
Taunton	213
Winchester	213
Windsor	213
Wolverhampton	213
Worcester	214
Wrexham (Wrecsam)	214
York	214

Port Plans

Harwich	215
Kingston upon Hull	215
Newcastle upon Tyne	215
Newhaven	215
Pembroke Dock (Doc Penfro)	215
Poole	215
Portsmouth	215

Airport Plans

Birmingham	216
East Midlands	216
Glasgow	216
London Gatwick	216
London Heathrow	216
London Luton	216
London Stansted	216
Manchester	216

Motorway
Autoroute
Autobahn
M1

Motorway Under Construction
Autoroute en construction
Autobahn im Bau

Motorway Proposed
Autoroute prévue
Geplante Autobahn

Motorway Junctions with Numbers
Unlimited Interchange 4
Limited Interchange 5

Autoroute échangeur numéroté
Echangeur complet
Echangeur partiel

Autobahnanschlußstelle mit Nummer
Unbeschränkter Fahrtrichtungswechsel
Beschränkter Fahrtrichtungswechsel

Primary Route
Route à grande circulation
Hauptverkehrsstraße
A41

Dual Carriageways (A & B roads)
Route à double chaussées séparées (route A & B)
Zweispurige Schnellstraße (A- und B- Straßen)

Class A Road
Route de type A
A-Straße
A129

Class B Road
Route de type B
B-Straße
B177

Major Roads Under Construction
Route prioritaire en construction
Hauptverkehrsstaße im Bau

Major Roads Proposed
Route prioritaire prévue
Geplante Hauptverkehrsstraße

Minor Roads
Route secondaire
Nebenstraße

Restricted Access
Accès réglementé
Beschränkte Zufahrt

Pedestrianized Road & Main Footway
Rue piétonne et chemin réservé aux piétons
Fußgängerstraße und Fußweg

OneWay Streets
Sens unique
Einbahnstraße

Toll
Barrière de péage
Gebührenpflichtig
TOLL

Railway & Station
Voie ferrée et gare
Eisenbahnlinie und Bahnhof

Underground / Metro & DLR Station
Station de métro et DLR
U-Bahnstation und DLR-Station
DLR

Level Crossing & Tunnel
Passage à niveau et tunnel
Bahnübergang und Tunnel

Tram Stop & One Way Tram Stop
Arrêt de tramway
Straßenbahnhaltestelle

Built-up Area
Agglomération
Geschloßene Ortschaft

Abbey, Cathedral, Priory etc
Abbaye, cathédrale, prieuré etc
Abtei, Kathedrale, Kloster usw

Airport
Aéroport
Flughafen

Bus Station
Gare routière
Bushaltestelle

Car Park (selection of)
Sélection de parkings
Auswahl von Parkplatz
P

Church
Eglise
Kirche

City Wall
Murs d'enceinte
Stadtmauer

Congestion Charging Zone
Zone de péage urbain
City-Maut Zone

Ferry (vehicular)
(foot only)

Bac (véhicules)
(piétons)

Fähre (autos)
(nur für Personen)

Golf Course
Terrain de golf
Golfplatz

Heliport
Héliport
Hubschrauberlandeplatz

Hospital
Hôpital
Krankenhaus
H

Lighthouse
Phare
Leuchtturm

Market
Marché
Markt

National Trust Property
(open)
(restricted opening)
(National Trust for Scotland)
NT
NT
NTS   NTS

National Trust Property
(ouvert)
(heures d'ouverture)
(National Trust for Scotland)

National Trust- Eigentum
(geöffnet)
(beschränkte Öffnungszeit)
(National Trust for Scotland)

Park & Ride
Parking relais
Auswahl von Parkplatz

Place of Interest
Curiosité
Sehenswürdigkeit

Police Station
Commissariat de police
Polizeirevier
▲

Post Office
Bureau de poste
Postamt
★

Shopping Area (main street & precinct)
Quartier commerçant (rue et zone principales)
Einkaufsviertel (hauptgeschäftsstraße, fußgängerzone)

Shopmobility
Shopmobility
Shopmobility

Toilet
Toilettes
Toilette

Tourist Information Centre
Syndicat d'initiative
Information

Viewpoint
Vue panoramique
Aussichtspunkt

Visitor Information Centre
Centre d'information touristique
Besucherzentrum
V

Please note: symbols have been enlarged for clarity

ABERDEEN

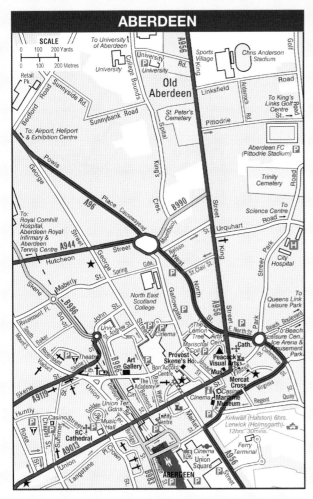

ABERYSTWYTH

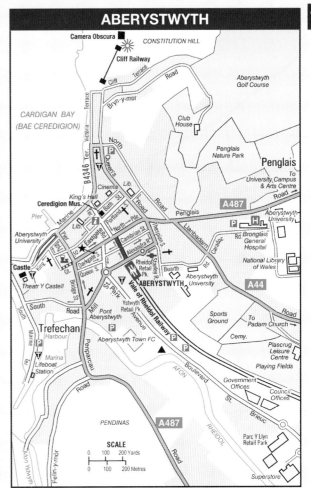

AYR

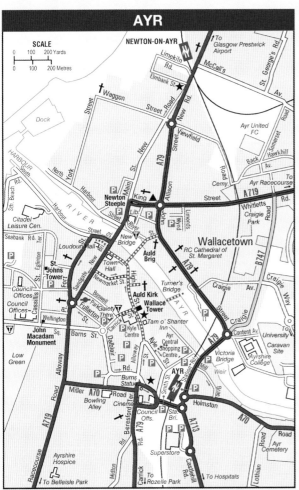

BATH

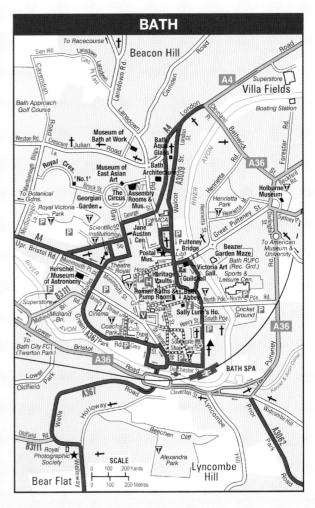

BEDFORD

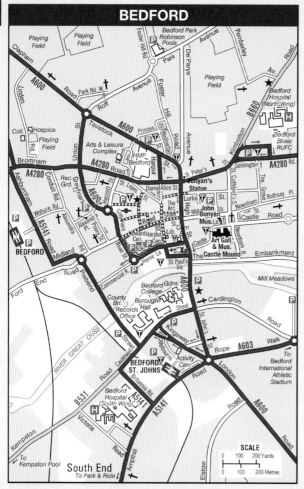

BLACKPOOL

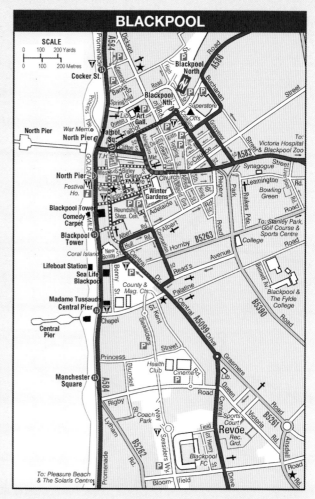

BIRMINGHAM (CITY CENTRE)

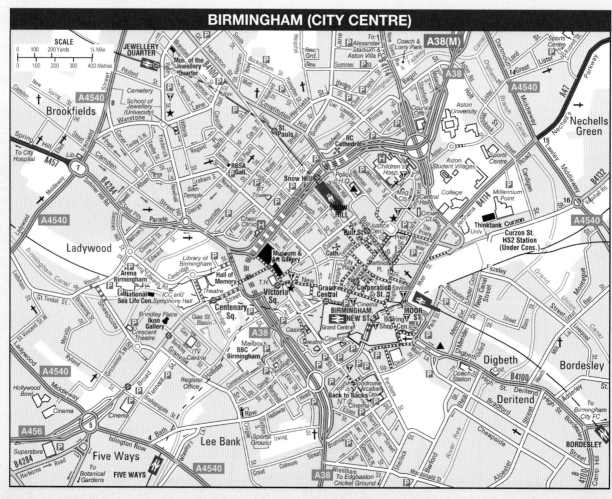

BRIGHTON and HOVE

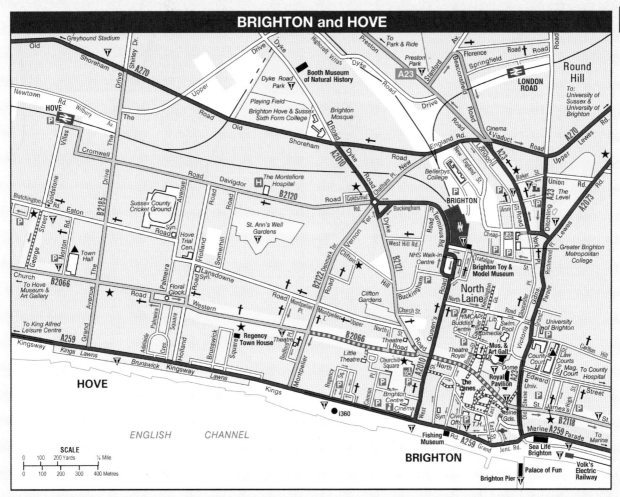

BRISTOL

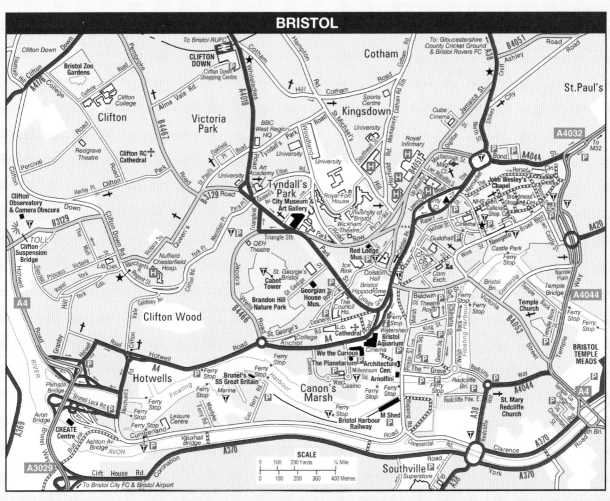

BOURNEMOUTH

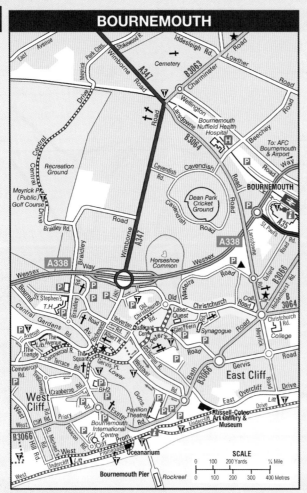

BRADFORD

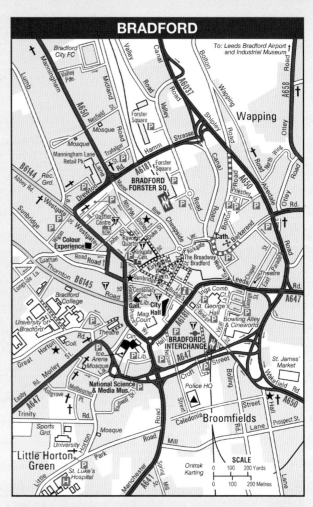

CAERNARFON

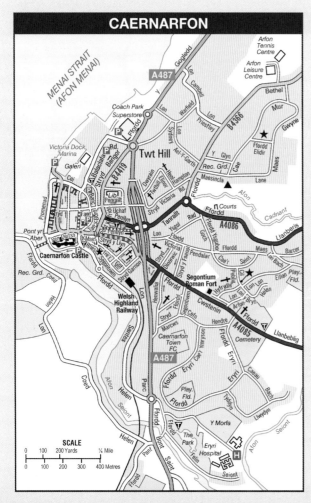

CANTERBURY

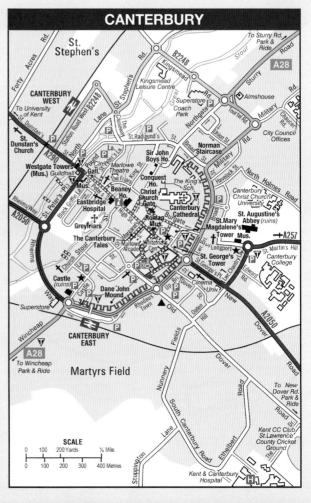

CAMBRIDGE

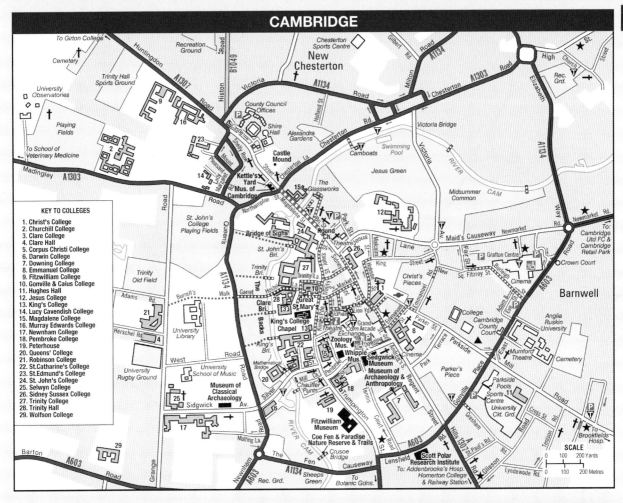

KEY TO COLLEGES
1. Christ's College
2. Churchill College
3. Clare College
4. Clare Hall
5. Corpus Christi College
6. Darwin College
7. Downing College
8. Emmanuel College
9. Fitzwilliam College
10. Gonville & Caius College
11. Hughes Hall
12. Jesus College
13. King's College
14. Lucy Cavendish College
15. Magdalene College
16. Murray Edwards College
17. Newnham College
18. Pembroke College
19. Peterhouse
20. Queens' College
21. Robinson College
22. St.Catharine's College
23. St.Edmund's College
24. St. John's College
25. Selwyn College
26. Sidney Sussex College
27. Trinity College
28. Trinity Hall
29. Wolfson College

CARDIFF (CAERDYDD)

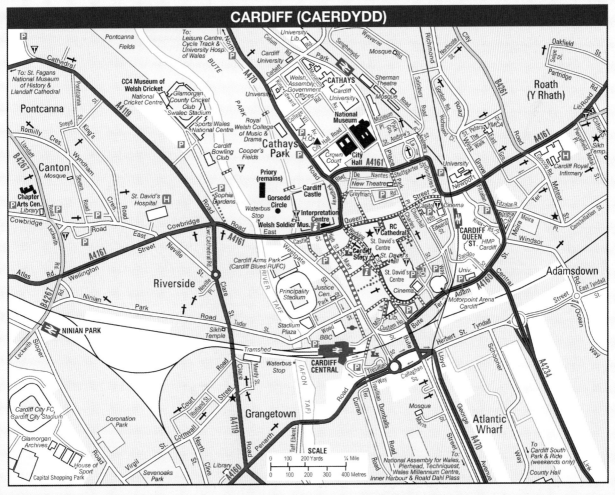

CARLISLE

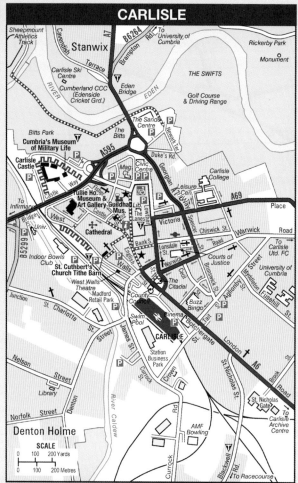

CHELTENHAM

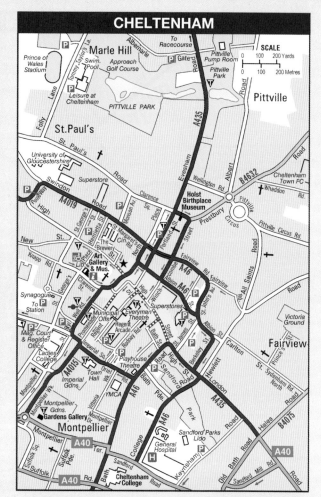

CHESTER

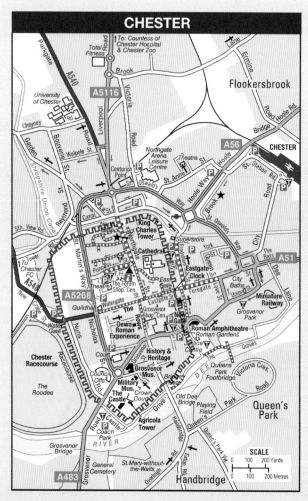

COVENTRY

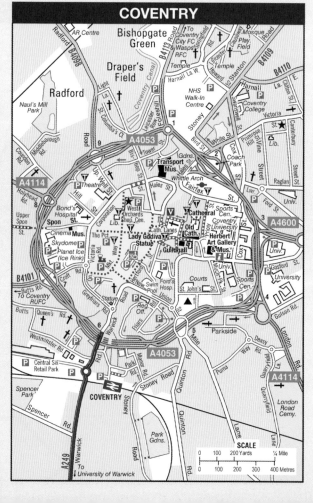

DERBY

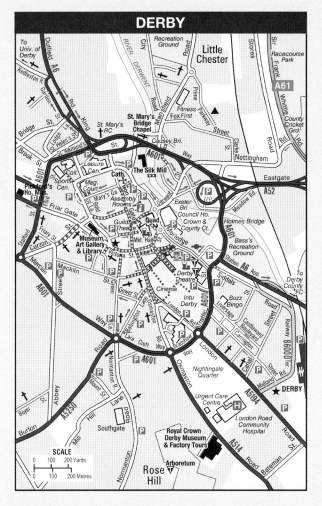

DUMFRIES

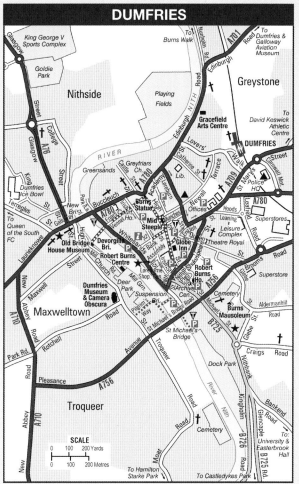

DOVER

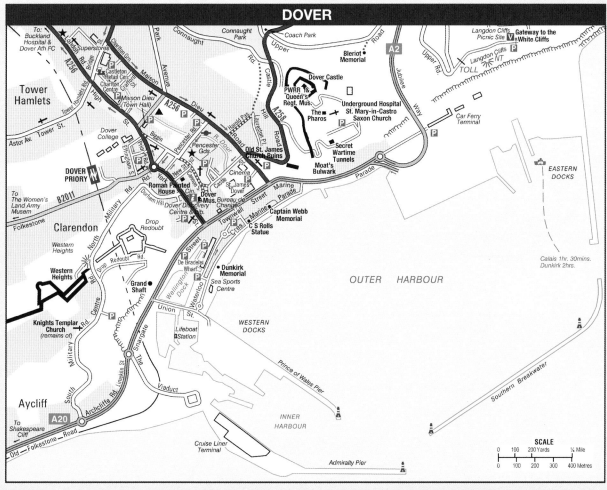

DUNDEE

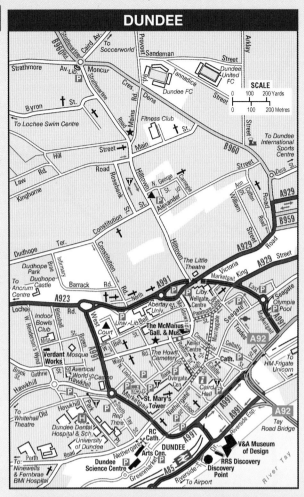

DURHAM

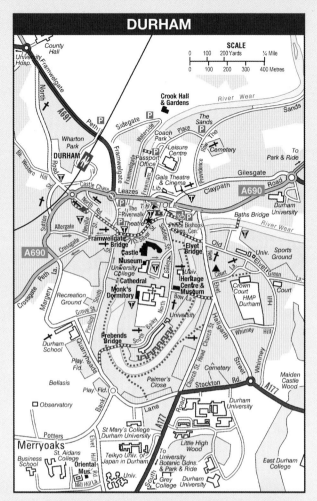

EDINBURGH

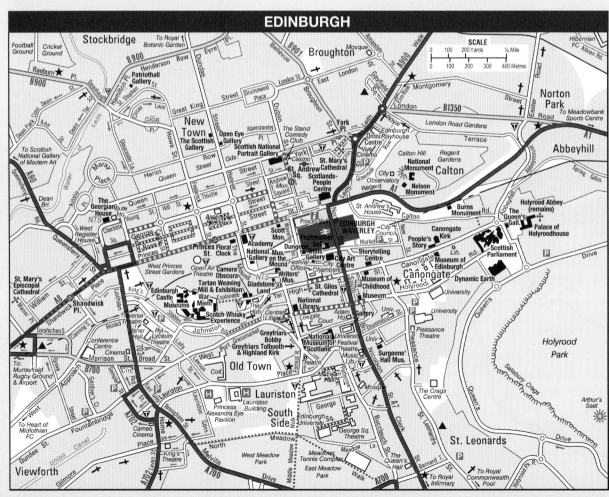

EXETER

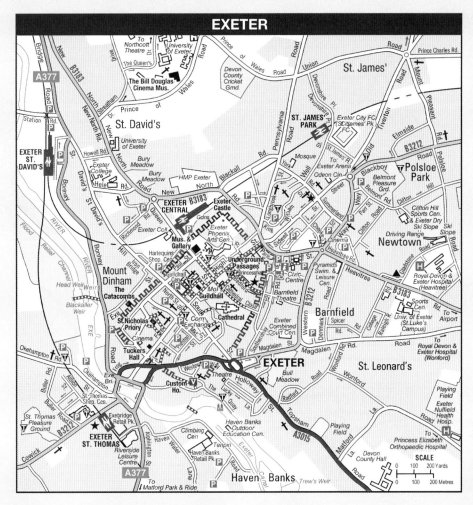

EASTBOURNE

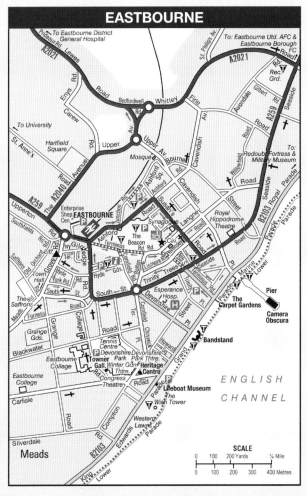

FOLKESTONE

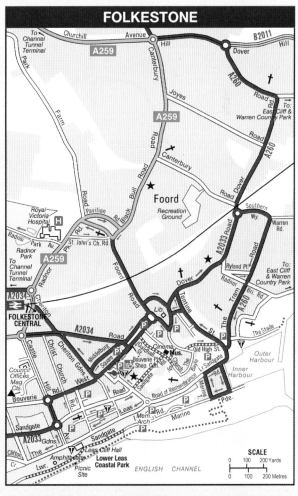

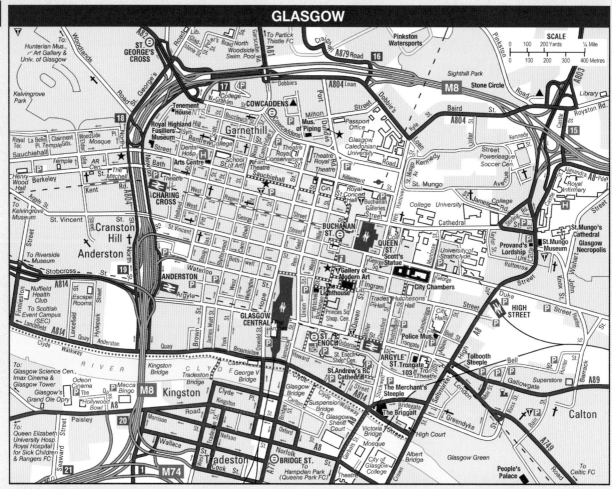

GLOUCESTER

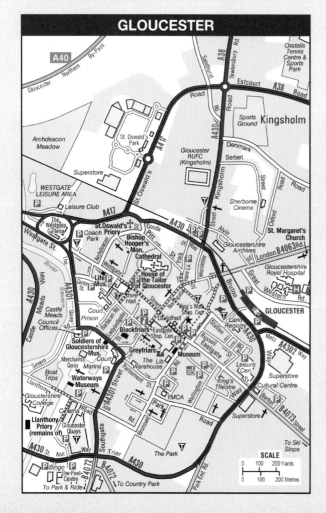

GREAT YARMOUTH

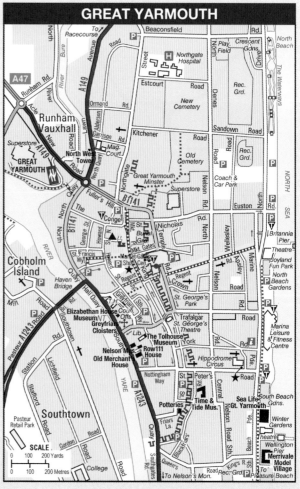

GUILDFORD

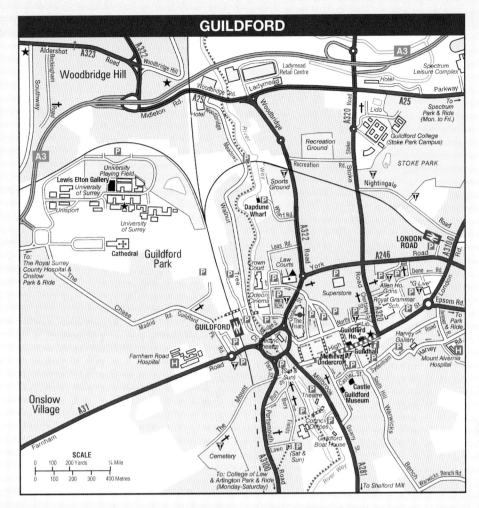

HARROGATE

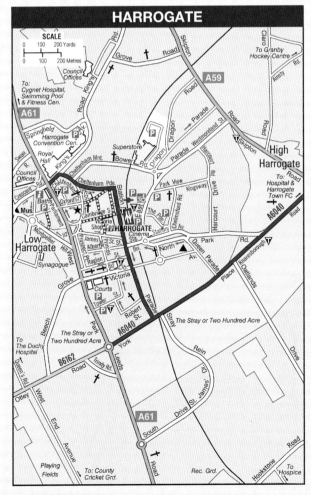

HEREFORD

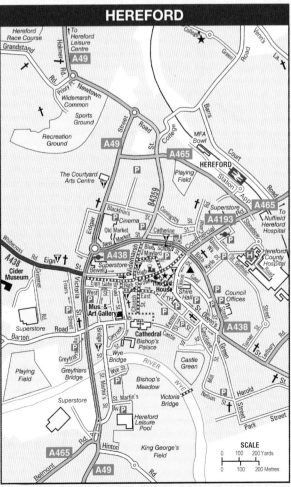

INVERNESS
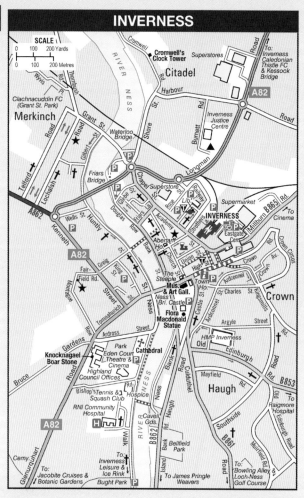

IPSWICH
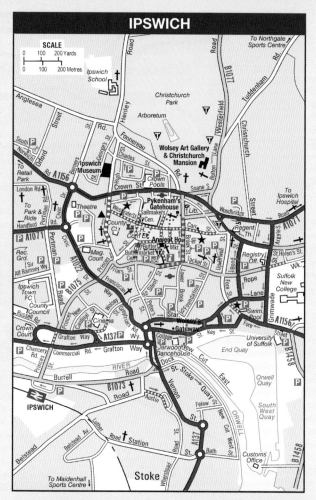

KILMARNOCK
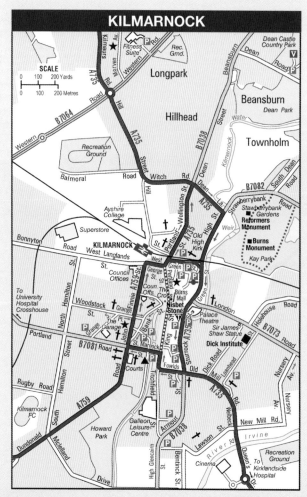

LINCOLN
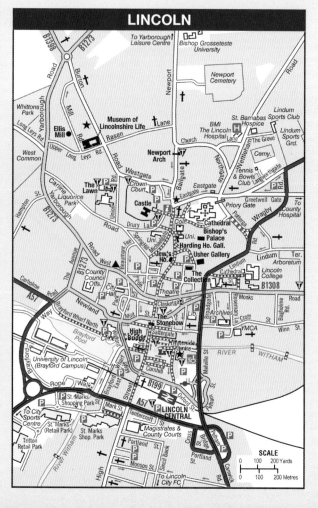

KINGSTON upon HULL

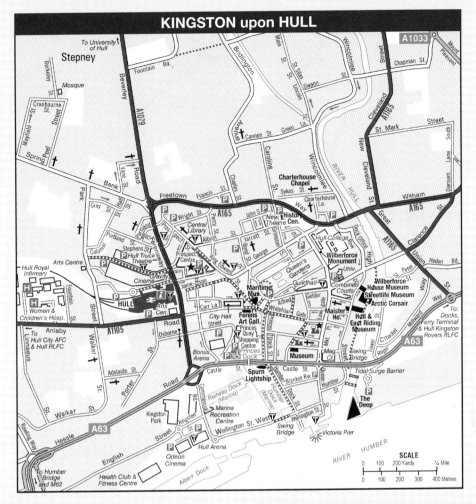

LEEDS

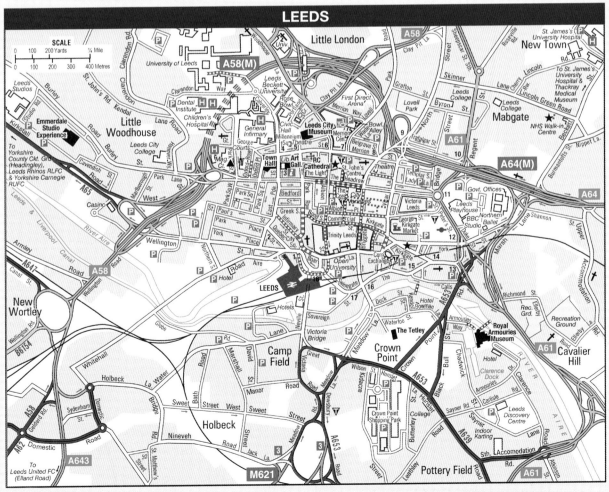

LEICESTER

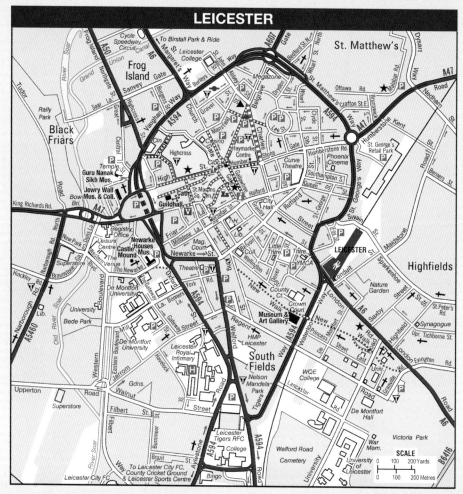

LIVERPOOL

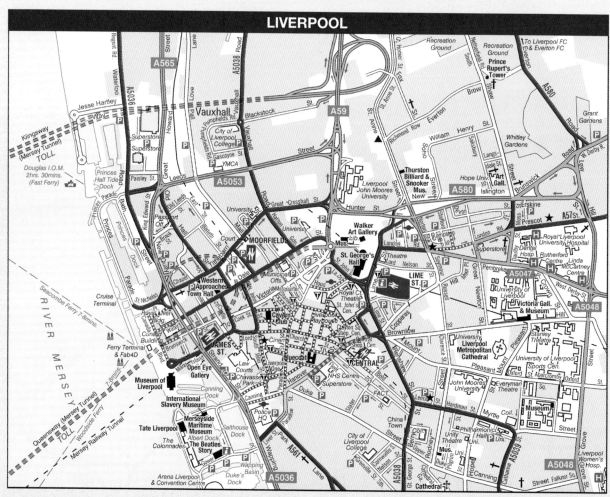

LUTON

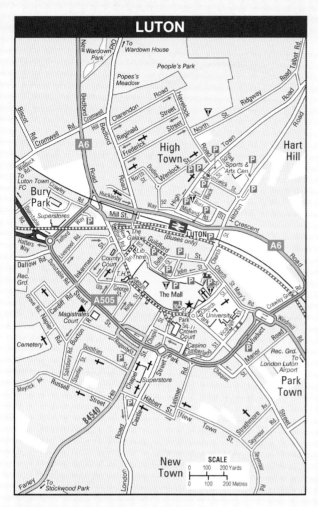

MIDDLESBROUGH

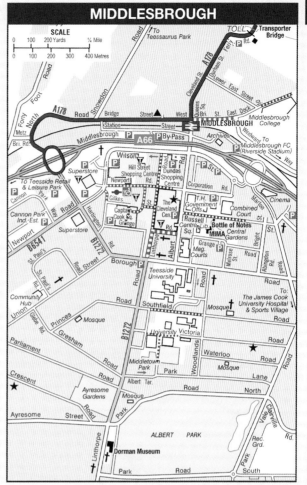

MANCHESTER (CITY CENTRE)

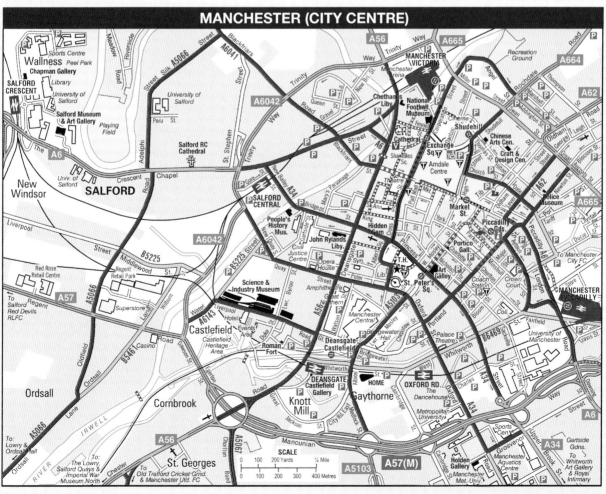

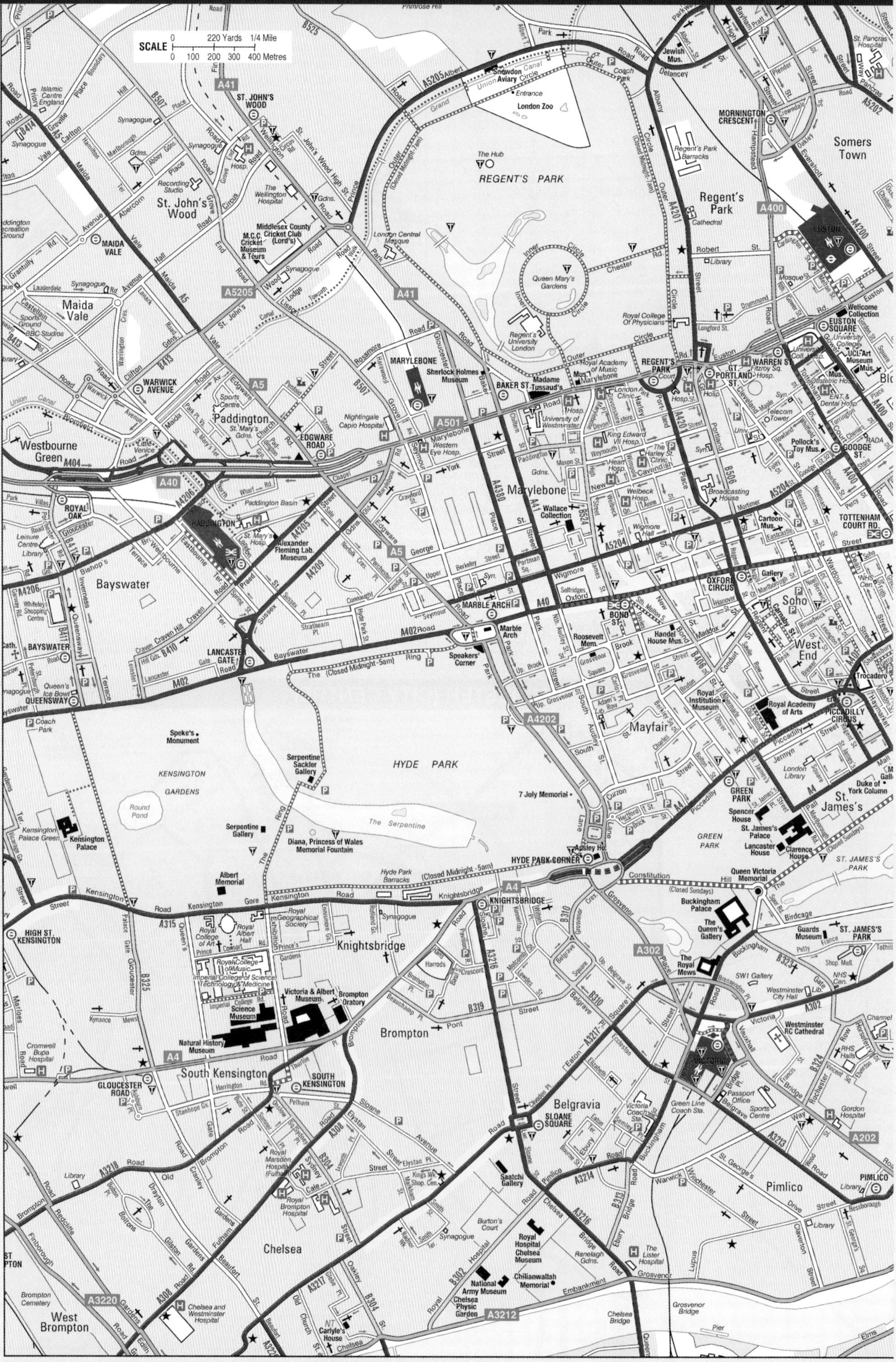

SCALE

0 220 Yards 1/4 Mile
0 100 200 300 400 Metres

REGENT'S PARK

London Zoo

The Hub

Queen Mary's Gardens

St. John's Wood

Maida Vale

WARWICK AVENUE

Paddington

Westbourne Green

Bayswater

BAYSWATER

QUEENSWAY

LANCASTER GATE

KENSINGTON GARDENS

Round Pond

Speke's Monument

Serpentine Sackler Gallery

Serpentine Gallery

HYDE PARK

The Serpentine

Diana, Princess of Wales Memorial Fountain

7 July Memorial

Kensington Palace

Kensington Palace Green

Albert Memorial

HIGH ST. KENSINGTON

Royal Albert Hall

Royal College of Art

Imperial College of Science Technology & Medicine

Science Museum

Natural History Museum

Victoria & Albert Museum

Brompton Oratory

Brompton

South Kensington

SOUTH KENSINGTON

GLOUCESTER ROAD

Cromwell Bupa Hospital

Royal Marsden Hospital (Fulham)

Royal Brompton Hospital

Chelsea

West Brompton

Brompton Cemetery

Chelsea and Westminster Hospital

Carlyle's House

National Army Museum

Chelsea Physic Garden

Chilianwallah Memorial

Royal Hospital Chelsea Museum

Saatchi Gallery

Burton's Court

Belgravia

SLOANE SQUARE

Pimlico

PIMLICO

Victoria

Westminster RC Cathedral

Passport Office

Belgrave Centre

Gordon Hospital

The Lister Hospital

Grosvenor Bridge

Chelsea Bridge

Knightsbridge

KNIGHTSBRIDGE

Harrods

Hyde Park Barracks

HYDE PARK CORNER

Apsley Ho.

Constitution Hill

GREEN PARK

Buckingham Palace

The Queen's Gallery

The Royal Mews

Queen Victoria Memorial

Guards Museum

ST. JAMES'S PARK

Westminster City Hall

Mayfair

Royal Institution Museum

Royal Academy of Arts

PICCADILLY CIRCUS

St. James's

Spencer House

St. James's Palace

Lancaster House

Clarence House

Duke of York Column

London Library

GREEN PARK

West End

Soho

Trocadero

OXFORD CIRCUS

BOND ST.

Handel House Mus.

Gallery

Selfridges Oxford

MARBLE ARCH

Marble Arch

Speakers' Corner

Roosevelt Mem.

Grosvenor Square

Marylebone

MARYLEBONE

BAKER ST.

Sherlock Holmes Museum

Madame Tussaud's

Wallace Collection

University of Westminster

Royal Academy of Music

London Central Mosque

Regent's University London

Royal College Of Physicians

Regent's Park

REGENT'S PARK

GT. PORTLAND ST.

WARREN ST.

EUSTON SQUARE

Welcome Collection

University College

UCL Art Museum

GOODGE ST.

TOTTENHAM COURT RD.

Pollock's Toy Mus.

Cartoon Mus.

Broadcasting House

Somers Town

MORNINGTON CRESCENT

Regent's Park Cathedral

Jewish Mus.

St. Pancras Hospital

EUSTON

St. John's Wood

ST. JOHN'S WOOD

M.C.C. Cricket Museum & Tours

Middlesex County Cricket Club (Lord's)

The Wellington Hospital

Synagogue

St. Mary's Hosp.

Alexander Fleming Lab. Museum

Nightingale Capio Hospital

Marylebone Western Eye Hosp.

Edgware Road

EDGWARE ROAD

Little Venice

Paddington Basin

ROYAL OAK

Whiteleys Shopping Centre

Queen's Ice Bowl

Islamic Centre England

Congestion Charging Zone

- The daily charge applies every day, 7-00am to 6-00pm, except Christmas Day (25th December).
- Payment of the daily charge allows you to drive in, around, leave and re-enter the charging zone as many times as required.
- Payment can be made in advance, or on the day of travel, or by midnight of the third day after travel. Payment after the fday of travel will incur an increased cost.
- You can pay using Auto Pay registration required), online, or using the official TfL App.
- Some vehicle types and classes are exempt, and some classes of road users can apply for a discount scheme.
- Penalty Charge for non-payment of the daily charge by midnight on the third day after the day of travel.

This information is correct at the time of publication.

Visit www.tfl.gov.uk/modes/driving for more information on London's driving zones.

MEDWAY TOWNS

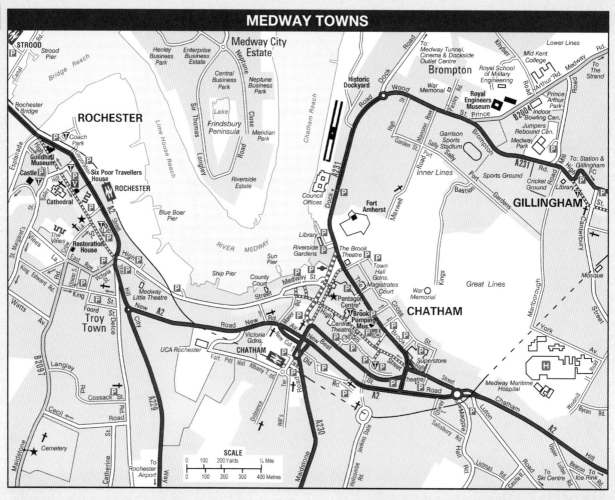

MILTON KEYNES

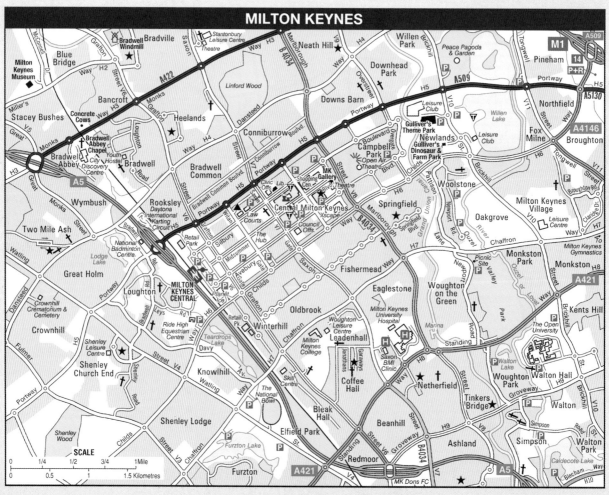

NORWICH

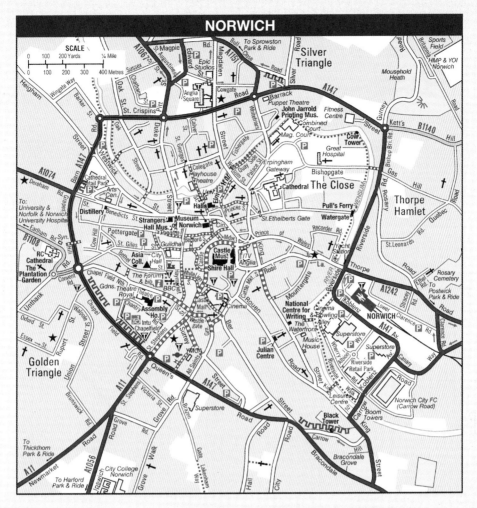

NEWCASTLE UPON TYNE

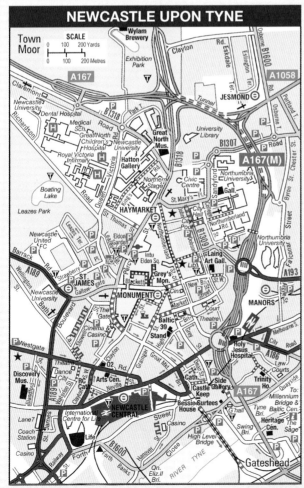

NEWPORT (CASNEWYDD)

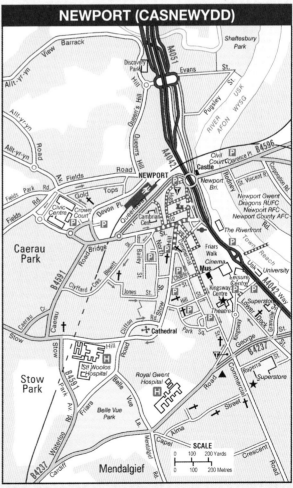

NOTTINGHAM

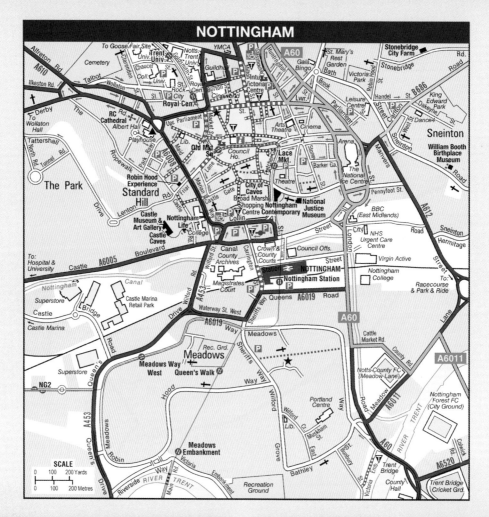

NORTHAMPTON

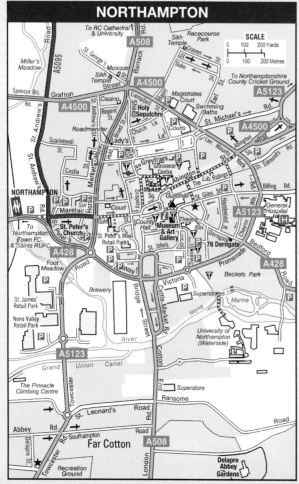

OBAN

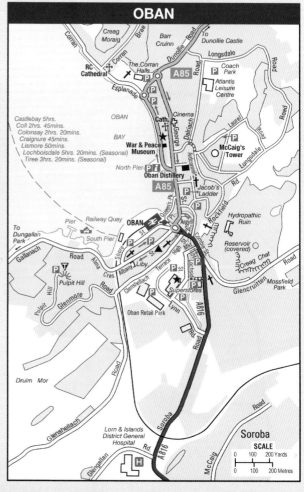

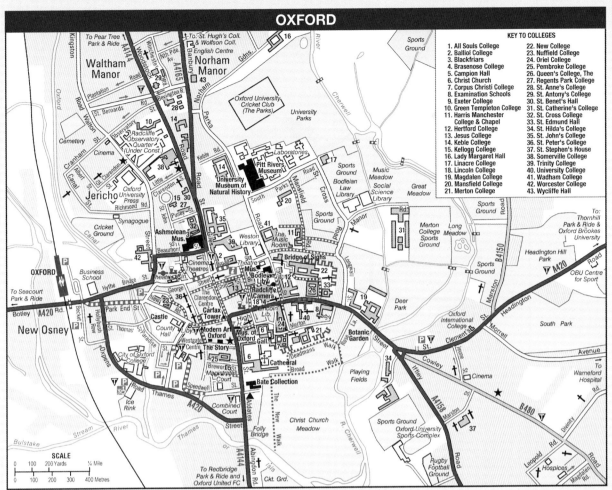

OXFORD

KEY TO COLLEGES

1. All Souls College
2. Balliol College
3. Blackfriars
4. Brasenose College
5. Campion Hall
6. Christ Church
7. Corpus Christi College
8. Examination Schools
9. Exeter College
10. Green Templeton College
11. Harris Manchester College & Chapel
12. Hertford College
13. Jesus College
14. Keble College
15. Kellogg College
16. Lady Margaret Hall
17. Linacre College
18. Lincoln College
19. Magdalen College
20. Mansfield College
21. Merton College
22. New College
23. Nuffield College
24. Oriel College
25. Pembroke College
26. Queen's College, The
27. Regents Park College
28. St. Anne's College
29. St. Antony's College
30. St. Benet's Hall
31. St. Catherine's College
32. St. Cross College
33. St. Edmund Hall
34. St. Hilda's College
35. St. John's College
36. St. Peter's College
37. St. Stephen's House
38. Somerville College
39. Trinity College
40. University College
41. Wadham College
42. Worcester College
43. Wycliffe Hall

PAISLEY

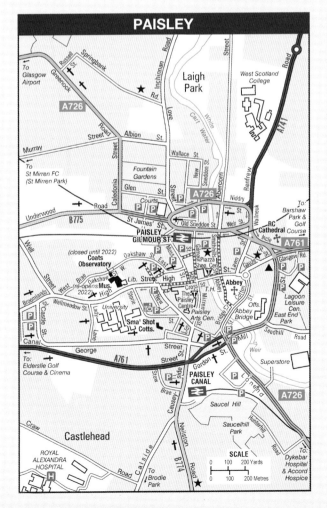

PERTH

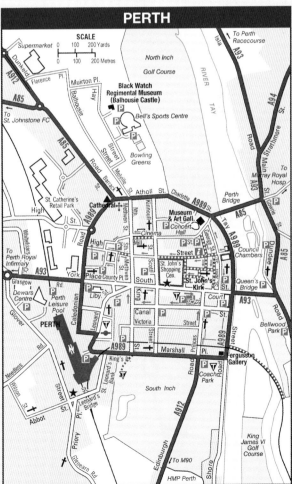

PLYMOUTH

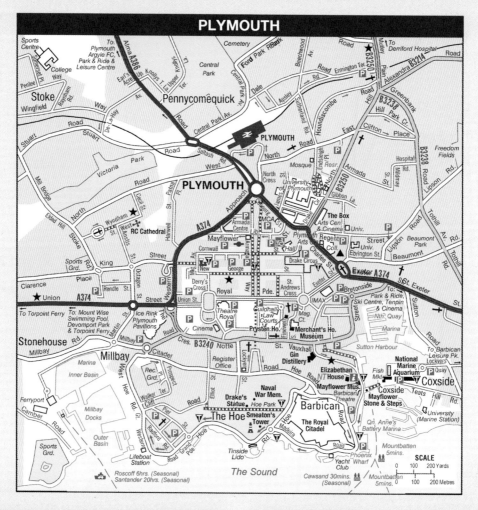

PETERBOROUGH

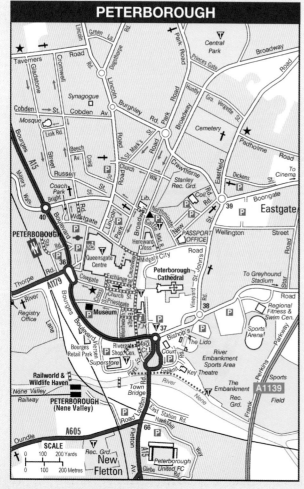

PRESTON

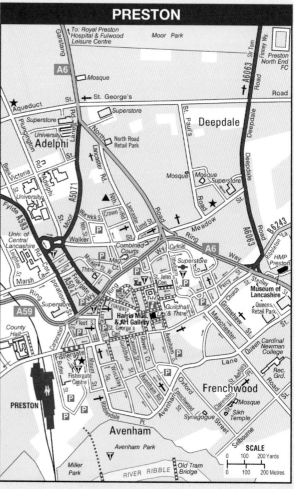

PORTSMOUTH

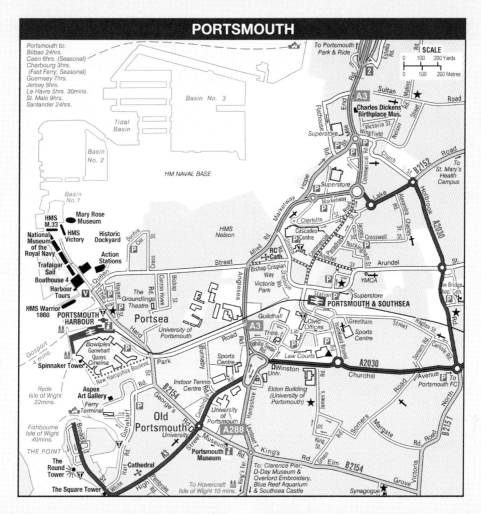

READING

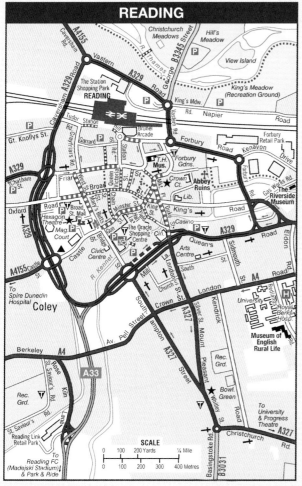

ST ANDREWS

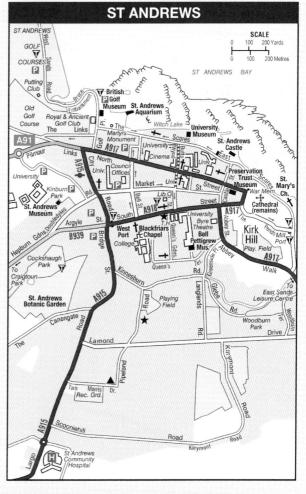

SALISBURY

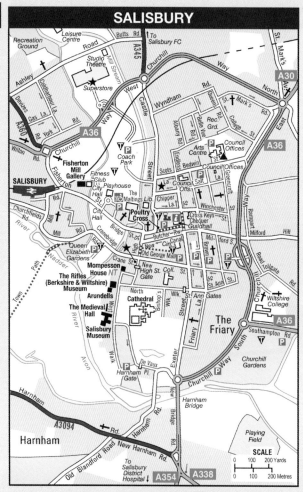

SHREWSBURY

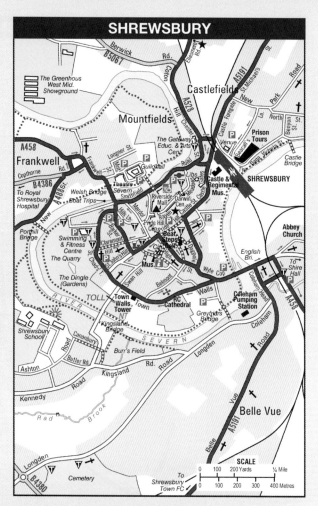

SHEFFIELD

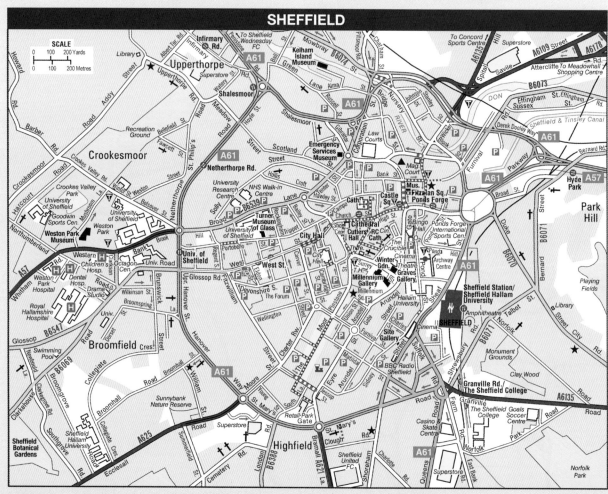

SOUTHAMPTON

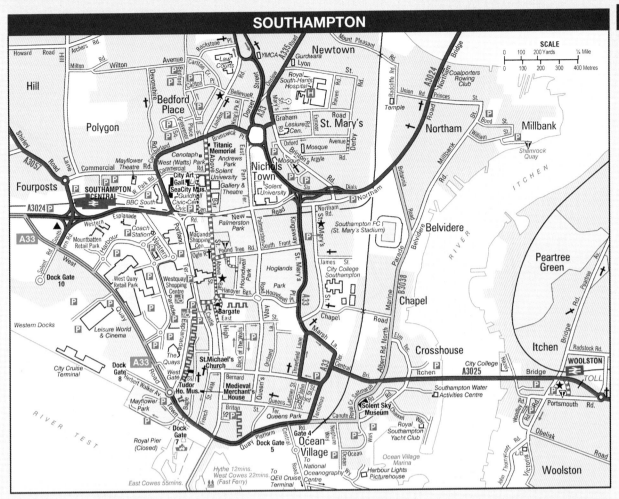

SCALE
0 100 200 Yards ¼ Mile
0 100 200 300 400 Metres

Howard Road · Archers Rd. · Rockstone Pl. · Mount Pleasant Rd. · Coalporters Rowing Club
Hill · Milton Rd. · Wilton Avenue · Bedford · Carlton Pl. · YMCA · Gurdwara · Newtown · A3024 · Princes St.
Polygon · Devonshire Rd. · Bedford Place · Bellevue R. · Dorset St. · Royal South-Hants Hospital · Lyon St. · Raven Rd. · St. Mary's · Radcliffe Rd. · Union Rd. · Bond St. · Millbank · William St.
Mayflower Theatre · Commercial Rd. · Cenotaph (West) (Watts) Park · Andrews Park · Graham Rd. · Leisure Cen. · Mosque · Argyle Rd. · Temple · Northam · Shamrock Quay
Fourposts · SOUTHAMPTON CENTRAL · City Art Gall. · SeaCity Mus. · Guildhall · Civic Cen. · Civic · BBC South · Solent University · Gallery & Theatre · Six Dials · RIVER ITCHEN
A3024 · Esplanade · Coach Station · New Palmerston Park · Northam Rd. · Britannia Rd. · Belvidere · Peartree Green
A33 · Mountbatten Retail Park · Portland · Maclands Shopping Cen. · Pound Tree Rd. · Ogle Rd. · Southampton FC (St. Mary's Stadium) · Parade · Itchen
Dock Gate 10 · West Quay Retail Park · Westquay Shopping Centre · Hoglands Park · James St. · City College Southampton · Chapel
Western Docks · Leisure World & Cinema · Quay · Bargate · Hanover Bgs. · Marsh La. · Chapel · Crosshouse · City College Itchen A3025 · Woolston TOLL
City Cruise Terminal · Dock Gate 8 · A33 · St. Michael's Church · Castle · The Wells · Orchard · Threefield Lane · Central Bri. · Albert Rd. North · B3038 · Bridge · Radstock Rd.
Tudor Ho. Mus. · West Gate · Medieval Merchant's House · Bernard St. · Queen's Ter. · Southampton Water Activities Centre · WOOLSTON · Portsmouth Rd. · Obelisk Rd.
Mayflower Park · Dock Gate 7 · Briton St. · Queens Park · Canute Rd. · Solent Sky Museum · Royal Southampton Yacht Club · Woolston
Royal Pier (Closed) · Dock Gate 5 · Ocean Village · Ocean Village Marina · Harbour Lights Picturehouse
RIVER TEST · Hythe 12mins. West Cowes 22mins. East Cowes 55mins. (Fast Ferry) · To QEII Cruise Terminal · To National Oceanography Centre

STIRLING

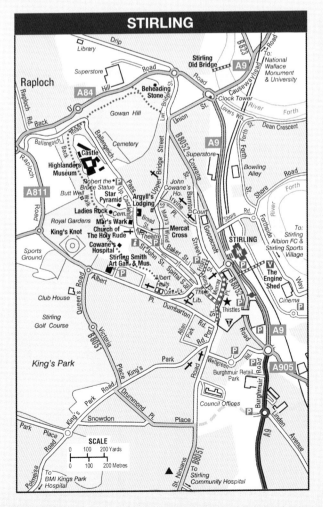

Library · Drip Rd. · B823 · To: National Wallace Monument & University · A9
Raploch · Superstore · Stirling Old Bridge · A9
A84 · Beheading Stone · Clock Tower · River Forth
Raploch Rd. · Gowan Hill · Cemetery · Dean Crescent
Ballengeich · Castle · Highlanders Museum · Robert the Bruce Statue · Butt Well · Star Pyramid · Ladies Rock · Royal Gardens · Mar's Wark · King's Knot · Church of The Holy Rude · Cowane's Hospital · Stirling Smith Art Gall. & Mus. · Argyll's Lodging · John Cowane's Ho. · Mercat Cross · STIRLING · Bowling Alley
A811 · Sports Ground · Club House · Stirling Golf Course · Albert Pl. · Albert Halls · Thistles Lib. · Thistles · The Engine Shed · Cinema · To: Stirling Albion FC & Stirling Sports Village
King's Park · Dumbarton Rd. · Allan Park · A9 · Burghmuir Retail Park · A905
King's Park · Victoria Place · Burghmuir Road · Wellgreen Pl. · Council Offices · Linden Avenue
Snowdon Place · To BMI Kings Park Hospital · To Stirling Community Hospital

SCALE
0 100 200 Yards
0 100 200 Metres

STOKE-ON-TRENT

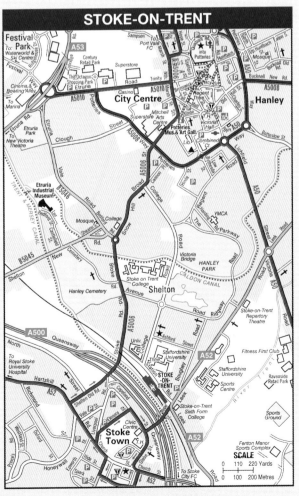

Festival Park · To: Waterworld & Ski Centre · Sampson St. · Port Vale FC · A53 · Mosque · A500
Century Retail Park · Superstore · The Octagon Shopping Park · Cinema & Bowling Alley · Etruria · City Centre · Regent Thre. · Hanley · Bucknall Old Rd. · A5008
Marina · Etruria Rd. · Mitchell Arts Centre · Potteries Mus. & Art Gall. · Victoria Hall · A50 · Bottslow St.
New Victoria Theatre · Etruria Park · Clough St. · Combined · Lib. · A5008 Way
Etruria Industrial Museum · TRENT & MERSEY CANAL · Broad St. · College · YMCA · The Parkway
Mosque · Hanley Park · CALDON CANAL
B5045 · Shelton · Stoke on Trent College · Victoria Bridge · HANLEY PARK · Stoke-on-Trent Repertory Theatre
Hanley Cemetery · Shelton · Ridgeway Rd. · A50
A500 · Queensway · North · To: Royal Stoke University Hospital · Hartshill · Univ. College · Staffordshire University · Ashford St. · Staffordshire University · Fitness First Club · A52 · Ravenside Retail Park
A52 · STOKE-ON-TRENT · Boughey Rd. · Sports Centre · Sports Ground
Shelton Old Rd. · Stoke-on-Trent Sixth Form College · A52 · Fenton Manor Sports Complex
Stoke Town · Civic Centre · T.H. · To Stoke City FC

SCALE
0 110 220 Yards
0 100 200 Metres

STRATFORD upon AVON

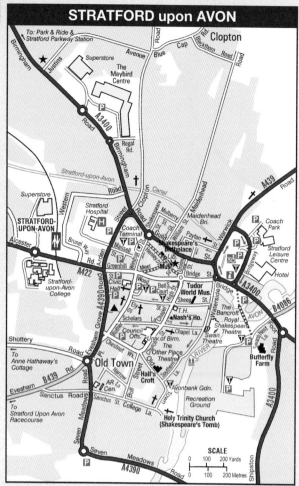

SUNDERLAND

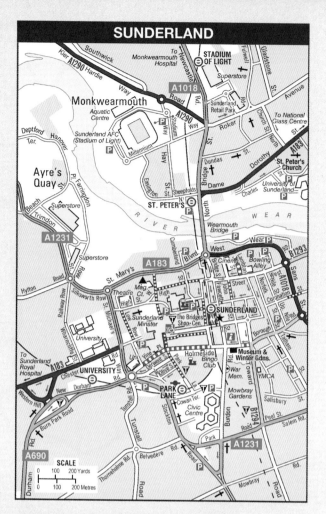

SWANSEA (ABERTAWE)

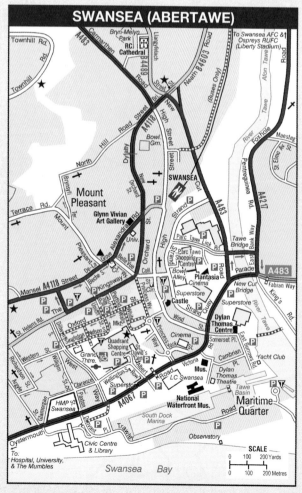

SWINDON

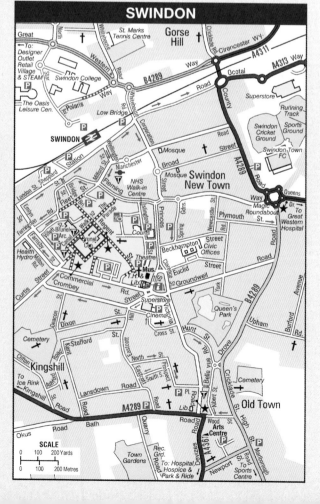

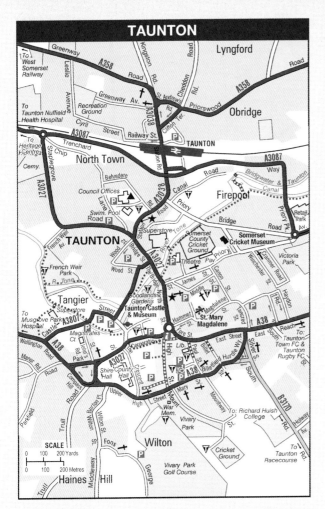

TAUNTON

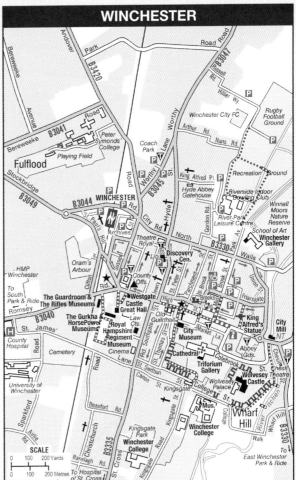

WINCHESTER

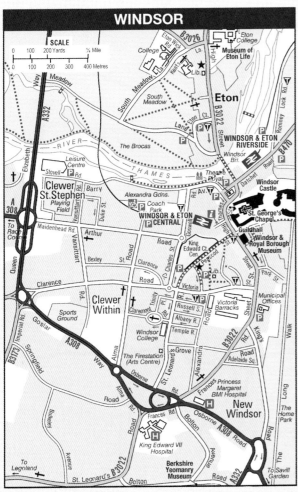

WINDSOR

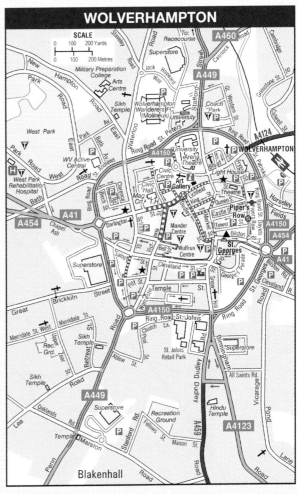

WOLVERHAMPTON

214

WORCESTER

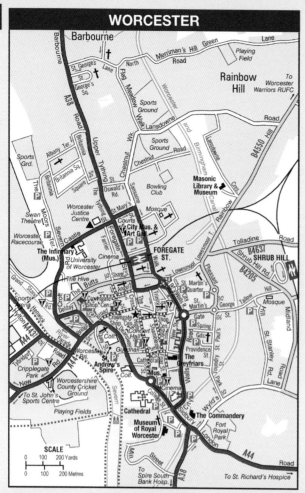

WREXHAM (WRECSAM)

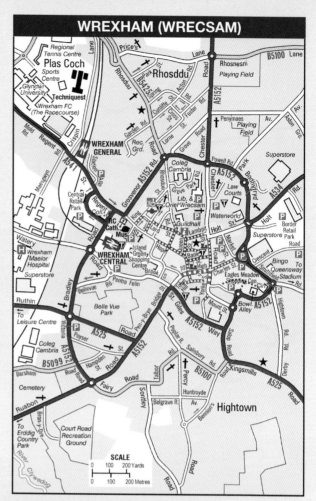

YORK

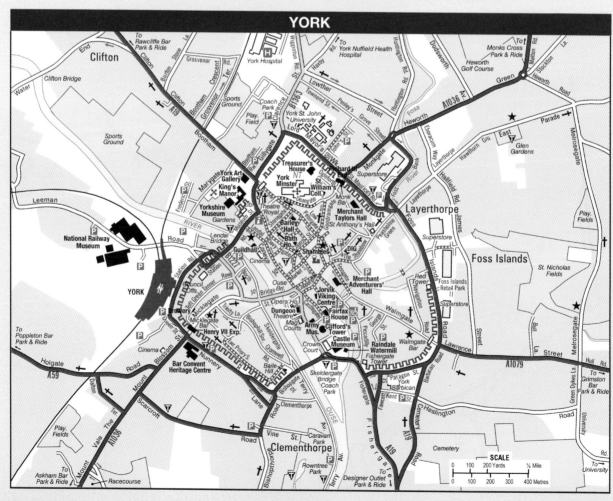

PORT PLANS

215

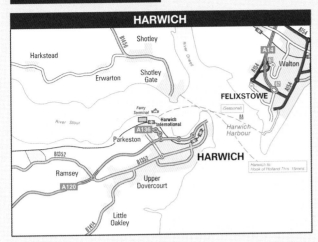

HARWICH

KINGSTON UPON HULL

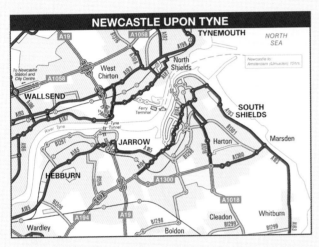

NEWCASTLE UPON TYNE

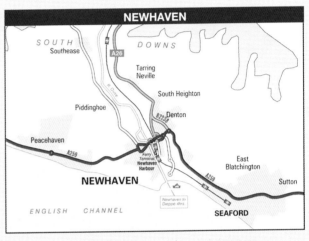

NEWHAVEN

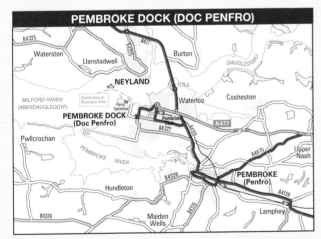

PEMBROKE DOCK (DOC PENFRO)

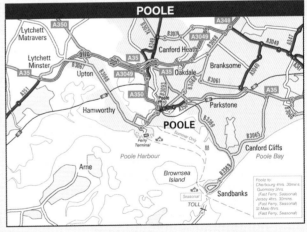

POOLE

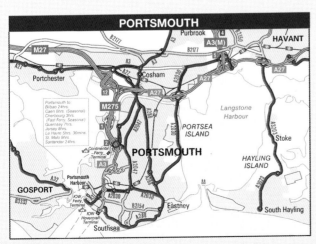

PORTSMOUTH

Other Port Plans

Please refer to Town Plans for detailed plans of the following Ports:

Dover - page 193

Plymouth - page 208

Southampton - page 211

BIRMINGHAM

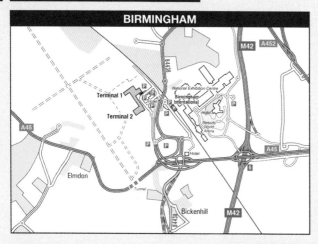

EAST MIDLANDS

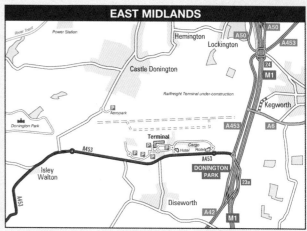

GLASGOW

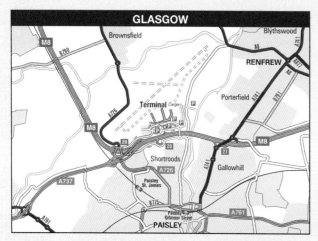

LONDON GATWICK

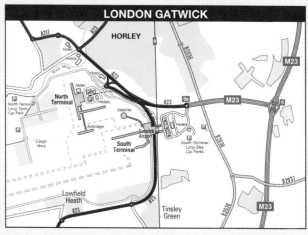

LONDON HEATHROW

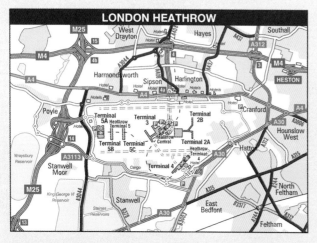

LONDON LUTON

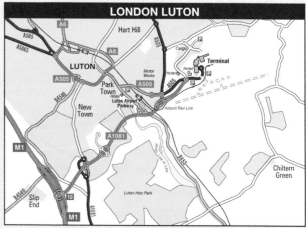

LONDON STANSTED

MANCHESTER

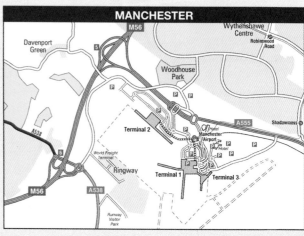

INDEX TO CITIES, TOWNS, VILLAGES, HAMLETS, LOCATIONS, AIRPORTS & PORTS

(1) A strict alphabetical order is used e.g. An Dùnan follows Andreas but precedes Andwell.

(2) The map reference given refers to the actual map square in which the town spot or built-up area is located and not to the place name.

(3) Major towns and destinations are shown in bold, i.e. **Aberdeen.** *Aber* **187** (3G **153**)
Page references for Town Plan entries are shown first.

(4) Where two or more places of the same name occur in the same County or Unitary Authority, the nearest large town is also given; e.g. Achiemore. *High* nr. Durness . . . .2D **166** indicates that Achiemore is located in square 2D on page **166** and is situated near Durness in the Unitary Authority of Highland.

(5) Only one reference is given although due to page overlaps the place may appear on more than one page.

COUNTIES and UNITARY AUTHORITIES with the abbreviations used in this index

Aberdeen : *Aber*
Aberdeenshire : *Abers*
Angus : *Ang*
Argyll & Bute : *Arg*
Bath & N E Somerset : *Bath*
Bedford : *Bed*
Blackburn with Darwen : *Bkbn*
Blackpool : *Bkpl*
Blaenau Gwent : *Blae*
Bournemouth : *Bour*
Bracknell Forest : *Brac*
Bridgend : *B'end*
Brighton & Hove : *Brig*
Bristol : *Bris*
Buckinghamshire : *Buck*
Caerphilly : *Cphy*
Cambridgeshire : *Cambs*
Cardiff : *Card*
Carmarthenshire : *Carm*
Central Bedfordshire : *C Beds*
Ceredigion : *Cdgn*
Cheshire East : *Ches E*
Cheshire West & Chester : *Ches W*
Clackmannanshire : *Clac*
Conwy : *Cnwy*
Cornwall : *Corn*
Cumbria : *Cumb*
Darlington : *Darl*
Denbighshire : *Den*
Derby : *Derb*
Derbyshire : *Derbs*
Devon : *Devn*
Dorset : *Dors*
Dumfries & Galloway : *Dum*
Dundee : *D'dee*
Durham : *Dur*
East Ayrshire : *E Ayr*
East Dunbartonshire : *E Dun*
East Lothian : *E Lot*
East Renfrewshire : *E Ren*
East Riding of Yorkshire : *E Yor*
East Sussex : *E Sus*
Edinburgh : *Edin*
Essex : *Essx*
Falkirk : *Falk*
Fife : *Fife*
Flintshire : *Flin*
Glasgow : *Glas*
Gloucestershire : *Glos*
Greater London : *G Lon*
Greater Manchester : *G Man*
Gwynedd : *Gwyn*
Halton : *Hal*
Hampshire : *Hants*
Hartlepool : *Hart*
Herefordshire : *Here*
Hertfordshire : *Herts*
Highland : *High*
Inverclyde : *Inv*
Isle of Anglesey : *IOA*
Isle of Man : *IOM*
Isle of Wight : *IOW*
Isles of Scilly : *IOS*
Kent : *Kent*
Kingston upon Hull : *Hull*
Lancashire : *Lanc*
Leicester : *Leic*
Leicestershire : *Leics*
Lincolnshire : *Linc*
Luton : *Lutn*
Medway : *Medw*
Merseyside : *Mers*
Merthyr Tydfil : *Mer T*
Middlesbrough : *Midd*
Midlothian : *Midl*
Milton Keynes : *Mil*
Monmouthshire : *Mon*
Moray : *Mor*
Neath Port Talbot : *Neat*
Newport : *Newp*
Norfolk : *Norf*
Northamptonshire : *Nptn*
North Ayrshire : *N Ayr*
North East Lincolnshire : *NE Lin*
North Lanarkshire : *N Lan*
North Lincolnshire : *N Lin*
North Somerset : *N Som*
Northumberland : *Nmbd*
North Yorkshire : *N Yor*
Nottingham : *Nott*
Nottinghamshire : *Notts*
Orkney : *Orkn*
Oxfordshire : *Oxon*
Pembrokeshire : *Pemb*
Perth & Kinross : *Per*
Peterborough : *Pet*
Plymouth : *Plym*
Poole : *Pool*
Portsmouth : *Port*
Powys : *Powy*
Reading : *Read*
Redcar & Cleveland : *Red C*
Renfrewshire : *Ren*
Rhondda Cynon Taff : *Rhon*
Rutland : *Rut*
Scottish Borders : *Bord*
Shetland : *Shet*
Shropshire : *Shrp*
Slough : *Slo*
Somerset : *Som*
Southampton : *Sotn*
South Ayrshire : *S Ayr*
Southend-on-Sea : *S'end*
South Gloucestershire : *S Glo*
South Lanarkshire : *S Lan*
South Yorkshire : *S Yor*
Staffordshire : *Staf*
Stirling : *Stir*
Stockton-on-Tees : *Stoc T*
Stoke-on-Trent : *Stoke*
Suffolk : *Suff*
Surrey : *Surr*
Swansea : *Swan*
Swindon : *Swin*
Telford & Wrekin : *Telf*
Thurrock : *Thur*
Torbay : *Torb*
Torfaen : *Torf*
Tyne & Wear : *Tyne*
Vale of Glamorgan, The : *V Glam*
Warrington : *Warr*
Warwickshire : *Warw*
West Berkshire : *W Ber*
West Dunbartonshire : *W Dun*
Western Isles : *W Isl*
West Lothian : *W Lot*
West Midlands : *W Mid*
West Sussex : *W Sus*
West Yorkshire : *W Yor*
Wiltshire : *Wilts*
Windsor & Maidenhead : *Wind*
Wokingham : *Wok*
Worcestershire : *Worc*
Wrexham : *Wrex*
York : *York*

INDEX

A

Abbas Combe. *Som* 4C **22**
Abberley. *Worc* 4B **60**
Abberley Common. *Worc* 4B **60**
Abberton. *Essx* 4D **54**
Abberton. *Worc* 5D **61**
Abberwick. *Nmbd* 3F **121**
Abbess Roding. *Essx* 4F **53**
Abbey. *Devn* 1E **13**
Abbey-cwm-hir. *Powy* 3C **58**
Abbeydale. *S Yor* 2H **85**
Abbeydale Park. *S Yor* 2H **85**
Abbey Dore. *Here* 2G **47**
Abbey Gate. *Devn* 3F **13**
Abbey Hulton. *Stoke* 1D **72**
Abbey St Bathans. *Bord* 3D **130**
Abbeystead. *Lanc* 4E **97**
Abbeytown. *Cumb* 4C **112**
Abbey Village. *Lanc* 2E **91**
Abbey Wood. *G Lon* 3F **39**
Abbots Bickington. *Devn* 1D **11**
Abbots Bromley. *Staf* 3E **73**
Abbotsbury. *Dors* 4A **14**
Abbotsham. *Devn* 4E **19**
Abbotskerswell. *Devn* 2E **9**
Abbots Langley. *Herts* 5A **52**
Abbots Leigh. *N Som* 4A **34**
Abbotsley. *Cambs* 5B **64**
Abbots Morton. *Worc* 5E **61**
Abbots Ripton. *Cambs* 3B **64**
Abbot's Salford. *Warw* 5E **61**
Abbotstone. *Hants* 3D **24**
Abbots Worthy. *Hants* 3C **24**
Abbotts Ann. *Hants* 2B **24**
Abcott. *Shrp* 3F **59**
Abdon. *Shrp* 2H **59**
Abenhall. *Glos* 4B **48**
Aber. *Cdgn* 1E **45**
Aberaeron. *Cdgn* 4D **56**
Aberafan. *Neat* 3G **31**
Aberaman. *Rhon* 5D **46**
Aberangell. *Gwyn* 4H **69**
Aberarad. *Carm* 1H **43**
Aberarder. *High* 1A **150**
Aberargie. *Per* 2D **136**
Aberarth. *Cdgn* 4D **57**
Aberavon. *Neat* 3G **31**
Aber-banc. *Cdgn* 1D **44**
Aberbargoed. *Cphy* 2E **33**
Aberbechan. *Powy* 1D **58**
Aberbeeg. *Blae* 5F **47**
Aberbowlan. *Carm* 2G **45**
Aberbran. *Powy* 3C **46**
Abercanaid. *Mer T* 5D **46**
Abercarn. *Cphy* 2F **33**
Abercastle. *Pemb* 1C **42**
Abercegir. *Powy* 5H **69**
Aberchalder. *High* 3F **149**
Aberchirder. *Abers* 3D **160**
Aberchwiler. *Den* 4C **82**
Abercorn. *W Lot* 2D **129**
Abercraf. *Powy* 4B **46**
Abercregan. *Neat* 2B **32**
Abercrombie. *Fife* 3H **137**
Abercwmboi. *Rhon* 2D **32**
Abercych. *Pemb* 1C **44**
Abercynon. *Rhon* 2D **32**
Aber-Cywarch. *Gwyn* 4A **70**
Aberdalgie. *Per* 1C **136**
Aberdar. *Rhon* 5C **46**
Aberdare. *Rhon* 5C **46**
Aberdaron. *Gwyn* 3A **68**
Aberdaugleddau. *Pemb* 4D **42**
Aberdeen. *Aber* **187** (3G **153**)
Aberdeen International Airport. *Aber* 2F **153**
Aberdesach. *Gwyn* 5D **80**
Aberdour. *Fife* 1E **129**
Aberdovey. *Gwyn* 1F **57**
Aberdulais. *Neat* 5A **46**
Aberdyfi. *Gwyn* 1F **57**
Aberedw. *Powy* 1D **46**
Abereiddy. *Pemb* 1B **42**
Abererch. *Gwyn* 2C **68**
Aberfan. *Mer T* 5D **46**
Aberfeldy. *Per* 4F **143**
Aberffraw. *IOA* 4C **80**
Aberffrwd. *Cdgn* 3F **57**
Aberford. *W Yor* 1E **93**
Aberfoyle. *Stir* 3E **135**
Abergarw. *B'end* 3C **32**
Abergarwed. *Neat* 5B **46**
Abergavenny. *Mon* 4G **47**
Abergele. *Cnwy* 3B **82**
Aber-Giâr. *Carm* 1F **45**
Abergorlech. *Carm* 2F **45**
Abergwaun. *Pemb* 1D **42**
Abergwesyn. *Powy* 5A **58**
Abergwili. *Carm* 3E **45**
Abergwynfi. *Neat* 2B **32**
Abergwyngregyn. *Gwyn* 3F **81**
Abergynolwyn. *Gwyn* 5F **69**
Aberhafesp. *Powy* 1C **58**
Aberhonddu. *Powy* 3D **46**
Aberhosan. *Powy* 1H **57**
Aberkenfig. *B'end* 3B **32**
Aberlady. *E Lot* 1A **130**
Aberlemno. *Ang* 3E **145**
Aberllefenni. *Gwyn* 5G **69**
Abermaw. *Gwyn* 4F **69**
Abermeurig. *Cdgn* 5E **57**
Aber-miwl. *Powy* 1D **58**
Abermule. *Powy* 1D **58**
Abernant. *Carm* 2H **43**
Abernant. *Rhon* 5D **46**
Abernethy. *Per* 2D **136**
Abernyte. *Per* 5B **144**
Aber-oer. *Wrex* 1E **71**
Aberpennar. *Rhon* 2D **32**
Aberporth. *Cdgn* 5B **56**
Aberriw. *Powy* 5D **70**
Abersoch. *Gwyn* 3C **68**
Abersychan. *Torf* 5F **47**
Abertawe. *Swan* **Swansea 212** (3F **31**)
Aberteifi. *Cdgn* 1B **44**
Aberthin. *V Glam* 4D **32**
Abertillery. *Blae* 5F **47**
Abertridwr. *Cphy* 3E **32**
Abertyleri. *Blae* 5F **47**
Abertysswg. *Cphy* 5E **47**
Aberuthven. *Per* 2B **136**
Aber Village. *Powy* 3E **46**
Aberwheeler. *Den* 4C **82**
Aberyscir. *Powy* 3C **46**
Aberystwyth. *Cdgn* **187** (2E **57**)
Abhainn Suidhe. *W Isl* 7C **171**
Abingdon-on-Thames. *Oxon* 2C **36**
Abinger Common. *Surr* 1C **26**
Abinger Hammer. *Surr* 1B **26**
Abington. *S Lan* 2B **118**
Abington Pigotts. *Cambs* 1D **52**
Ab Kettleby. *Leics* 3E **74**
Ab Lench. *Worc* 5E **61**
Ablington. *Glos* 5G **49**
Ablington. *Wilts* 2G **23**
Abney. *Derbs* 3F **85**
Aboyne. *Abers* 4C **152**
Abram. *G Man* 4E **90**
Abriachan. *High* 5H **157**
Abridge. *Essx* 1F **39**
Abronhill. *N Lan* 2A **128**
Abson. *S Glo* 4C **34**
Abthorpe. *Nptn* 1E **51**
Abune-the-Hill. *Orkn* 5B **172**
Aby. *Linc* 3D **88**
Acairseid. *W Isl* 8C **170**
Acaster Malbis. *York* 5H **99**
Acaster Selby. *N Yor* 5H **99**
Accott. *Devn* 3G **19**
Accrington. *Lanc* 2F **91**
Acha. *Arg* 3C **138**
Achachork. *High* 4D **155**
Achadh a' Chuirn. *High* 1E **147**
Achahoish. *Arg* 2F **125**
Achaleven. *Arg* 5D **140**
Achallader. *Arg* 4H **141**
Acha Mor. *W Isl* 5F **171**
Achanalt. *High* 2E **157**
Achandunie. *High* 1A **158**
Ach' an Todhair. *High* 1E **141**
Achany. *High* 3C **164**
Achaphubuil. *High* 1E **141**
Acharacle. *High* 2A **140**
Acharn. *Ang* 1B **144**
Acharn. *Per* 4E **143**
Acharole. *High* 3E **169**
Achateny. *High* 2G **139**
Achavanich. *High* 4D **169**
Achdalieu. *High* 1E **141**
Achduart. *High* 3E **163**
Achentoul. *High* 5A **168**
Achfary. *High* 5C **166**
Achfrish. *High* 2C **164**
Achgarve. *High* 4C **162**
Achiemore. *High*
  nr. Durness 2D **166**
  nr. Thurso 3A **168**
A' Chill. *High* 3A **146**
Achiltibuie. *High* 3E **163**
Achina. *High* 2H **167**
Achinahuagh. *High* 2F **167**
Achindarroch. *High* 3E **141**
Achinduich. *High* 3C **164**
Achinduin. *Arg* 5C **140**
Achininver. *High* 2F **167**
Achintee. *High* 4B **156**
Achintraid. *High* 5H **155**
Achleck. *Arg* 4F **139**
Achlorachan. *High* 3F **157**
Achluachrach. *High* 5E **149**
Achlyness. *High* 3C **166**
Achmelvich. *High* 1E **163**
Achmony. *High* 5H **157**
Achmore. *High*
  nr. Stromeferry 5A **156**
  nr. Ullapool 4E **163**
Achnacarnin. *High* 1E **163**
Achnacarry. *High* 5D **148**
Achnaclerach. *High* 2G **157**
Achnacloich. *High* 3D **147**
Ach na Cloiche. *High* 3D **147**
Achnaconeran. *High* 2G **149**
Achnacroish. *Arg* 4C **140**
Achnafalnich. *Arg* 1B **134**
Achnagarron. *High* 1A **158**
Achnagoul. *Arg* 3H **133**
Achnaha. *High* 2F **139**
Achnahanat. *High* 4C **164**
Achnahannet. *High* 1D **151**
Achnairn. *High* 2C **164**
Achnamara. *Arg* 1F **125**
Achnanellan. *High* 5C **148**
Achnasheen. *High* 3D **156**
Achnashellach. *High* 4C **156**
Achosnich. *High* 2F **139**
Achow. *High* 5E **169**
Achranich. *High* 4B **140**
Achreamie. *High* 2C **168**
Achriabhach. *High* 2F **141**
Achriesgill. *High* 3C **166**
Achrimsdale. *High* 3G **165**
Achscrabster. *High* 2C **168**
Achtoty. *High* 2G **167**
Achurch. *Nptn* 2H **63**
Achuvoldrach. *High* 3F **167**
Achvaich. *High* 4E **164**
Achvoan. *High* 3E **165**
Ackenthwaite. *Cumb* 1E **97**
Ackergill. *High* 3F **169**
Ackergillshore. *High* 3F **169**
Acklam. *Midd* 3B **106**
Acklam. *N Yor* 3B **100**
Ackleton. *Shrp* 1B **60**
Acklington. *Nmbd* 4G **121**
Ackton. *W Yor* 2E **93**
Ackworth Moor Top. *W Yor* 3E **93**
Acle. *Norf* 4G **79**
Acocks Green. *W Mid* 2F **61**
Acol. *Kent* 4H **41**
Acomb. *Nmbd* 3C **114**
Acomb. *York* 4H **99**
Aconbury. *Here* 2A **48**
Acre. *G Man* 4H **91**
Acre. *Lanc* 2F **91**
Acrefair. *Wrex* 1E **71**
Acrise. *Kent* 1F **29**
Acton. *Ches E* 5A **84**
Acton. *Dors* 5E **15**
Acton. *G Lon* 2C **38**
Acton. *Shrp* 2F **59**
Acton. *Staf* 1C **72**
Acton. *Suff* 1B **54**
Acton. *Worc* 4C **60**
Acton. *Wrex* 5F **83**
Acton Beauchamp. *Here* 5A **60**
Acton Bridge. *Ches W* 3H **83**
Acton Burnell. *Shrp* 5H **71**
Acton Green. *Here* 5A **60**
Acton Pigott. *Shrp* 5H **71**
Acton Round. *Shrp* 1A **60**
Acton Scott. *Shrp* 2G **59**
Acton Trussell. *Staf* 4D **72**
Acton Turville. *S Glo* 3D **34**
Adabroc. *W Isl* 1H **171**
Adam's Hill. *Worc* 3D **60**
Adbaston. *Staf* 3B **72**
Adber. *Dors* 4B **22**
Adderbury. *Oxon* 2C **50**
Adderley. *Shrp* 2A **72**
Adderstone. *Nmbd* 1F **121**
Addiewell. *W Lot* 3C **128**
Addingham. *W Yor* 5C **98**
Addington. *Buck* 3F **51**
Addington. *G Lon* 4E **39**
Addington. *Kent* 5A **40**
Addinston. *Bord* 4B **130**
Addiscombe. *G Lon* 4E **39**
Addlestone. *Surr* 4B **38**
Addlethorpe. *Linc* 4E **89**
Adeney. *Telf* 4B **72**
Adfa. *Powy* 5C **70**
Adforton. *Here* 3G **59**
Adgestone. *IOW* 4D **16**
Adisham. *Kent* 5G **41**
Adlestrop. *Glos* 3H **49**
Adlingfleet. *E Yor* 2B **94**
Adlington. *Ches E* 2D **84**
Adlington. *Lanc* 3E **90**
Admaston. *Staf* 3E **73**
Admaston. *Telf* 4A **72**
Admington. *Warw* 1H **49**
Adpar. *Cdgn* 1D **44**
Adsborough. *Som* 4F **21**
Adstock. *Buck* 2F **51**
Adstone. *Nptn* 5C **62**
Adversane. *W Sus* 3B **26**
Advie. *High* 5F **159**
Adwalton. *W Yor* 2C **92**
Adwell. *Oxon* 2E **37**
Adwick le Street. *S Yor* 4F **93**
Adwick upon Dearne. *S Yor* 4E **93**
Adziel. *Abers* 3G **161**
Ae. *Dum* 1A **112**
Affleck. *Abers* 1F **153**
Affpuddle. *Dors* 3D **14**
Affric Lodge. *High* 1D **148**
Afon-wen. *Flin* 3D **82**
Agglethorpe. *N Yor* 1C **98**
Aglionby. *Cumb* 4F **113**
Aigburth. *Mers* 2F **83**
Aiginis. *W Isl* 4G **171**
Aike. *E Yor* 5E **101**
Aikers. *Orkn* 8D **172**
Aiketgate. *Cumb* 5F **113**
Aikhead. *Cumb* 5D **112**
Aikton. *Cumb* 4D **112**
Ailey. *Here* 1G **47**
Ailsworth. *Pet* 1A **64**
Ainderby Quernhow. *N Yor* 1F **99**
Ainderby Steeple. *N Yor* 5A **106**
Aingers Green. *Essx* 3E **54**
Ainsdale. *Mers* 3B **90**
Ainsdale-on-Sea. *Mers* 3B **90**
Ainstable. *Cumb* 5G **113**
Ainsworth. *G Man* 3F **91**
Ainthorpe. *N Yor* 4E **107**
Aintree. *Mers* 1F **83**
Aird. *Arg* 3E **133**
Aird. *Dum* 3F **109**
Aird. *High*
  nr. Port Henderson 1G **155**
  nr. Tarskavaig 3D **147**
Aird. *W Isl*
  on Benbecula 3C **170**
  on Isle of Lewis 4H **171**
The Aird. *High* 3D **154**
Àird a Bhasair. *High* 3E **147**
Aird a Mhachair. *W Isl* 4C **170**
Aird a Mhulaidh. *W Isl* 6D **171**
Aird Asaig. *W Isl* 7D **171**
Aird Dhail. *W Isl* 1G **171**
Airdens. *High* 4D **164**
Airdeny. *Arg* 1G **133**
Aird Mhidhinis. *W Isl* 8C **170**
Aird Mhighe. *W Isl*
  nr. Ceann a Bhaigh 8D **171**
  nr. Fionnsabhagh 9C **171**
Aird Mhor. *W Isl*
  on Barra 8C **170**
  on South Uist 4D **170**
Airdrie. *N Lan* 3A **128**
Aird Shleibhe. *W Isl* 9D **171**
Aird Thunga. *W Isl* 4G **171**
Aird Uig. *W Isl* 4C **171**
Airedale. *W Yor* 2E **93**
Airidh a Bhruaich. *W Isl* 6E **171**
Airies. *Dum* 3E **109**
Airmyn. *E Yor* 2H **93**
Airntully. *Per* 5H **143**
Airor. *High* 3F **147**
Airth. *Falk* 1C **128**
Airton. *N Yor* 4B **98**
Aisby. *Linc*
  nr. Gainsborough 1F **87**
  nr. Grantham 2H **75**
Aisgernis. *W Isl* 6C **170**
Aish. *Devn*
  nr. Buckfastleigh 2C **8**
  nr. Totnes 3E **9**
Aisholt. *Som* 3E **21**
Aiskew. *N Yor* 1E **99**
Aislaby. *N Yor*
  nr. Pickering 1B **100**
  nr. Whitby 4F **107**
Aislaby. *Stoc T* 3B **106**
Aisthorpe. *Linc* 2G **87**

Aith. *Shet*
    on Fetlar 3H **173**
    on Mainland 6E **173**
Aithsetter. *Shet.* 8F **173**
Akeld. *Nmbd* 2D **120**
Akeley. *Buck.* 2F **51**
Akenham. *Suff.* 1E **55**
Albaston. *Corn* 5E **11**
Alberbury. *Shrp.* 4F **71**
Albert Town. *Pemb* 3D **42**
Albert Village. *Leics* 4H **73**
Albourne. *W Sus* 4D **26**
Albrighton. *Shrp*
    nr. Shrewsbury 4G **71**
    nr. Telford 5C **72**
Alburgh. *Norf.* 2E **67**
Albury. *Herts.* 3E **53**
Albury. *Surr.* 1B **26**
Albyfield. *Cumb.* 4G **113**
Alby Hill. *Norf.* 2D **78**
Alcaig. *High* 3H **157**
Alcaston. *Shrp.* 2G **59**
Alcester. *Warw* 5E **61**
Alciston. *E Sus.* 5G **27**
Alcombe. *Som* 2C **20**
Alconbury. *Cambs.* 3A **64**
Alconbury Weston. *Cambs.* 3A **64**
Aldborough. *Norf* 2D **78**
Aldborough. *N Yor.* 3G **99**
Aldbourne. *Wilts* 4A **36**
Aldbrough. *E Yor* 1F **95**
Aldbrough St John. *N Yor* 3F **105**
Aldbury. *Herts.* 4H **51**
Aldcliffe. *Lanc* 3D **96**
Aldclune. *Per.* 2G **143**
Aldeburgh. *Suff.* 5G **67**
Aldeby. *Norf.* 1G **67**
Aldenham. *Herts.* 1C **38**
Alderbury. *Wilts.* 4G **23**
Aldercar. *Derbs.* 1B **74**
Alderford. *Norf.* 4D **78**
Alderholt. *Dors.* 1G **15**
Alderley. *Glos.* 2C **34**
Alderley Edge. *Ches E.* 3C **84**
Aldermaston. *W Ber* 5D **36**
Aldermaston Soke. *Hants.* 5E **36**
Aldermaston Wharf. *W Ber* 5E **36**
Alderminster. *Warw* 1H **49**
Alder Moor. *Staf.* 3G **73**
Aldersey Green. *Ches W* 5G **83**
Aldershot. *Hants.* 1G **25**
Alderton. *Glos.* 2F **49**
Alderton. *Nptn* 1F **51**
Alderton. *Shrp.* 3G **71**
Alderton. *Suff.* 1G **55**
Alderton. *Wilts.* 3D **34**
Alderton Fields. *Glos.* 2F **49**
Alderwasley. *Derbs.* 5H **85**
Aldfield. *N Yor.* 3E **99**
Aldford. *Ches W.* 5G **83**
Aldgate. *Rut.* 5G **75**
Aldham. *Essx.* 3C **54**
Aldham. *Suff.* 1D **54**
Aldingbourne. *W Sus.* 5A **26**
Aldingham. *Cumb.* 2B **96**
Aldington. *Kent.* 2E **29**
Aldington. *Worc.* 1F **49**
Aldington Frith. *Kent.* 2E **29**
Aldochlay. *Arg* 4C **134**
Aldon. *Shrp.* 3G **59**
Aldoth. *Cumb.* 5C **112**
Aldreth. *Cambs.* 3D **64**
Aldridge. *W Mid* 5E **73**
Aldringham. *Suff.* 4G **67**
Aldsworth. *Glos.* 4G **49**
Aldsworth. *W Sus.* 2F **17**
Aldwark. *Derbs.* 5G **85**
Aldwark. *N Yor.* 3G **99**
Aldwick. *W Sus.* 3H **17**
Aldwincle. *Nptn* 2H **63**
Aldworth. *W Ber* 4D **36**
Alexandria. *W Dun.* 1E **127**
Aley. *Som.* 3E **21**
Aley Green. *C Beds.* 4A **52**
Alfardisworthy. *Devn.* 1C **10**
Alfington. *Devn.* 3E **12**
Alfold. *Surr.* 2B **26**
Alfold Bars. *W Sus.* 2B **26**
Alfold Crossways. *Surr.* 2B **26**
Alford. *Abers.* 2C **152**
Alford. *Linc.* 3D **88**
Alford. *Som.* 3B **22**
Alfreton. *Derbs* 5B **86**
Alfrick. *Worc.* 5B **60**
Alfrick Pound. *Worc.* 5B **60**
Alfriston. *E Sus.* 5G **27**
Algarkirk. *Linc.* 2B **76**
Alhampton. *Som.* 3B **22**
Aline Lodge. *W Isl* 6D **171**
Alkborough. *N Lin* 2B **94**
Alkerton. *Oxon.* 1B **50**
Alkham. *Kent.* 1G **29**
Alkington. *Shrp.* 2H **71**
Alkmonton. *Derbs.* 2F **73**
Alladale Lodge. *High.* 5B **164**
Allaleigh. *Devn.* 3E **9**
Allanbank. *N Lan* 4B **128**
Allanton. *N Lan* 4B **128**
Allanton. *Bord.* 4E **131**
Allaston. *Glos.* 5B **48**
Allbrook. *Hants.* 4C **24**
All Cannings. *Wilts.* 5F **35**
Allendale Town. *Nmbd.* 4B **114**
Allen End. *Warw* 1F **61**
Allenheads. *Nmbd.* 5B **114**
Allensford. *Dur.* 5D **115**
Allen's Green. *Herts.* 4E **53**
Allensmore. *Here.* 2H **47**
Allenton. *Derb.* 2A **74**
Aller. *Som.* 4H **21**
Allerby. *Cumb.* 1B **102**

Allercombe. *Devn.* 3D **12**
Allerford. *Som.* 2C **20**
Allerston. *N Yor.* 1C **100**
Allerthorpe. *E Yor.* 5B **100**
Allerton. *Mers.* 2G **83**
Allerton. *W Yor.* 1B **92**
Allerton Bywater. *W Yor.* 2E **93**
Allerton Mauleverer. *N Yor* 4G **99**
Allesley. *W Mid.* 2G **61**
Allestree. *Derb.* 2H **73**
Allet. *Corn.* 4B **6**
Allexton. *Leics.* 5F **75**
Allgreave. *Ches E.* 4D **84**
Allhallows. *Medw.* 3C **40**
Allhallows-on-Sea. *Medw.* 3C **40**
Alligin Shuas. *High.* 3H **155**
Allimore Green. *Staf.* 4C **72**
Allington. *Kent.* 5B **40**
Allington. *Linc.* 1F **75**
Allington. *Wilts*
    nr. Amesbury 3H **23**
    nr. Devizes 5F **35**
Allithwaite. *Cumb.* 2C **96**
Alloa. *Clac.* 4A **136**
Allonby. *Cumb.* 5B **112**
Allostock. *Ches W.* 3B **84**
Alloway. *S Ayr.* 3C **116**
Allowenshay. *Som.* 1G **13**
All Saints South Elmham. *Suff.* 2F **67**
Allscott. *Shrp.* 1B **60**
Allscott. *Telf.* 4A **72**
All Stretton. *Shrp.* 1G **59**
Allt. *Carm.* 5F **45**
Alltami. *Flin.* 4E **83**
Alltgobhlach. *N Ayr.* 5G **125**
Alltmawr. *Powy.* 1D **46**
Alltnacaillich. *High.* 4E **167**
Alltour. *High.* 5E **148**
Alltsigh. *High.* 2G **149**
Alltwalis. *Carm.* 2E **45**
Alltwen. *Neat.* 5H **45**
Alltyblaccа. *Cdgn.* 1F **45**
Allt-y-goed. *Pemb.* 1B **44**
Almeley. *Here.* 5F **59**
Almeley Wooton. *Here.* 5F **59**
Almer. *Dors.* 3E **15**
Almholme. *S Yor.* 4F **93**
Almington. *Staf.* 2B **72**
Alminstone Cross. *Devn.* 4D **18**
Almodington. *W Sus.* 3G **17**
Almondbank. *Per.* 1C **136**
Almondbury. *W Yor.* 3B **92**
Almondsbury. *S Glo* 3B **34**
Alne. *N Yor.* 3G **99**
Alness. *High.* 2A **158**
Alnessferry. *High.* 2A **158**
Alnham. *Nmbd.* 3D **121**
Alnmouth. *Nmbd.* 3G **121**
Alnwick. *Nmbd.* 3F **121**
Alphamstone. *Essx.* 2B **54**
Alpheton. *Suff.* 5A **66**
Alphington. *Devn.* 3C **12**
Alport. *Derbs.* 4G **85**
Alport. *Powy.* 1E **59**
Alpraham. *Ches E.* 5H **83**
Alresford. *Essx.* 3D **54**
Alrewas. *Staf.* 4F **73**
Alsager. *Ches E.* 5B **84**
Alsagers Bank. *Staf.* 1C **72**
Alsop en le Dale. *Derbs.* 5F **85**
Alston. *Cumb.* 5A **114**
Alston. *Devn.* 2G **13**
Alstone. *Glos.* 2E **49**
Alstone. *Som.* 2G **21**
Alstonefield. *Staf.* 5F **85**
Alston Sutton. *Som.* 1H **21**
Alswear. *Devn.* 4H **19**
Altandhu. *High.* 2D **163**
Altanduin. *High.* 1F **165**
Altarnun. *Corn.* 4C **10**
Altass. *High.* 3B **164**
Alterwall. *High.* 2E **169**
Altgaltraig. *Arg.* 2B **126**
Altham. *Lanc.* 1F **91**
Althorne. *Essx.* 1D **40**
Althorpe. *N Lin.* 4B **94**
Altnabreac. *High.* 4C **168**
Altnacealgach. *High.* 2G **163**
Altnafeadh. *High.* 3G **141**
Altnaharra. *High.* 5F **167**
Altofts. *W Yor.* 2D **93**
Alton. *Derbs.* 4A **86**
Alton. *Hants.* 3F **25**
Alton. *Staf.* 1E **73**
Alton Barnes. *Wilts.* 5G **35**
Altonhill. *E Ayr.* 1D **116**
Alton Pancras. *Dors.* 2C **14**
Alton Priors. *Wilts.* 5G **35**
Altrincham. *G Man.* 2B **84**
Altrua. *High.* 4E **149**
Alva. *Clac.* 4A **136**
Alvanley. *Ches W.* 3G **83**
Alvaston. *Derb.* 2A **74**
Alvechurch. *Worc.* 3E **61**
Alvecote. *Warw.* 5G **73**
Alvediston. *Wilts.* 4E **23**
Alveley. *Shrp.* 2B **60**
Alverdiscott. *Devn.* 4F **19**
Alverstoke. *Hants.* 3D **16**
Alverstone. *IOW.* 4D **16**
Alverthorpe. *W Yor.* 2D **92**
Alverton. *Notts.* 1E **75**
Alves. *Mor.* 2F **159**
Alvescot. *Oxon.* 5A **50**
Alveston. *S Glo.* 3B **34**
Alveston. *Warw.* 5G **61**
Alvie. *High.* 3C **150**
Alvingham. *Linc.* 1C **88**
Alvington. *Glos.* 5B **48**

Alwalton. *Cambs.* 1A **64**
Alweston. *Dors.* 1B **14**
Alwington. *Devn.* 4E **19**
Alwinton. *Nmbd.* 4D **120**
Alwoodley. *W Yor.* 5E **99**
Alyth. *Per.* 4B **144**
Amatnatua. *High.* 4B **164**
Am Baile. *W Isl.* 7C **170**
Ambaston. *Derbs.* 2B **74**
Amber Hill. *Linc.* 1B **76**
Amberley. *Glos.* 5D **48**
Amberley. *W Sus.* 4B **26**
Amble. *Nmbd.* 4G **121**
Amblecote. *W Mid.* 2C **60**
Ambergate. *Derbs.* 5H **85**
Amberley. *Glos.* 5D **48**
Amber Thorn. *W Yor.* 2A **92**
Ambleside. *Cumb.* 4E **103**
Amboth. *Pemb.* 4F **43**
Ambrosden. *Oxon.* 4E **50**
Amcotts. *N Lin.* 3B **94**
Amersham. *Buck.* 1A **38**
Amerton. *Staf.* 3D **73**
Amesbury. *Wilts.* 2G **23**
Amisfield. *Dum.* 1B **112**
Amlwch. *IOA.* 1D **80**
Amlwch Port. *IOA.* 1D **80**
Ammanford. *Carm.* 4G **45**
Amotherby. *N Yor.* 2B **100**
Ampfield. *Hants.* 4B **24**
Ampleforth. *N Yor.* 2H **99**
Ampleforth College. *N Yor* 2H **99**
Ampney Crucis. *Glos.* 5F **49**
Ampney St Mary. *Glos.* 5F **49**
Ampney St Peter. *Glos.* 5F **49**
Amport. *Hants.* 2A **24**
Ampthill. *C Beds.* 2A **52**
Ampton. *Suff.* 3A **66**
Amroth. *Pemb.* 4F **43**
Amulree. *Per.* 5G **143**
Anaheilt. *High.* 2C **140**
An Aird. *High.* 3D **147**
An Camus Darach. *High.* 4E **147**
Ancaster. *Linc.* 1G **75**
Anchor. *Shrp.* 2D **58**
Anchorsholme. *Lanc.* 5C **96**
Anchor Street. *Norf.* 3F **79**
An Coroghon. *High.* 3A **146**
Ancroft. *Nmbd.* 5G **131**
Ancrum. *Bord.* 2A **120**
Ancton. *W Sus.* 5A **26**
Anderby. *Linc.* 3E **89**
Anderby Creek. *Linc.* 3E **89**
Anderson. *Dors.* 3D **15**
Anderton. *Ches W.* 3A **84**
Andertons Mill. *Lanc.* 3D **90**
Andover. *Hants.* 2B **24**
Andover Down. *Hants.* 2B **24**
Andoversford. *Glos.* 4F **49**
Andreas. *IOM.* 2D **108**
An Dùnan. *High.* 1D **147**
Andwell. *Hants.* 1E **25**
Anelog. *Gwyn.* 3A **68**
Anfield. *Mers.* 1F **83**
Angarrack. *Corn.* 3C **4**
Angelbank. *Shrp.* 3H **59**
Angersleigh. *Som.* 1E **13**
Angerton. *Cumb.* 4D **112**
Angle. *Pemb.* 4C **42**
Angmering. *W Sus.* 5B **26**
Angmering-on-Sea. *W Sus* 5B **26**
Angram. *N Yor*
    nr. Keld 5B **104**
    nr. York 5H **99**
Anick. *Nmbd.* 3C **114**
Ankerbold. *Derbs.* 4A **86**
Ankerville. *High.* 1C **158**
Anlaby. *E Yor.* 2D **94**
Anlaby Park. *Hull* 2D **94**
An Leth Meadhanach. *W Isl* 7C **170**
Anmer. *Norf.* 3G **77**
Anmore. *Hants.* 1E **17**
Annan. *Dum.* 3D **112**
Annat. *Arg.* 1H **133**
Annat. *High.* 3A **156**
Annathill. *N Lan* 2A **128**
Anna Valley. *Hants.* 2B **24**
Annbank. *S Ayr.* 2D **116**
Annesley. *Notts.* 5C **86**
Annesley Woodhouse. *Notts.* 5C **86**
Annfield Plain. *Dur.* 4E **115**
Annscroft. *Shrp.* 5G **71**
An Sailean. *High.* 2A **140**
Ansdell. *Lanc.* 2B **90**
Ansford. *Som.* 3B **22**
Ansley. *Warw.* 1G **61**
Anslow. *Staf.* 3G **73**
Anslow Gate. *Staf.* 3F **73**
Ansteadbrook. *Surr.* 2A **26**
Anstey. *Herts.* 2E **53**
Anstey. *Leics.* 5C **74**
Anston. *S Lan.* 5D **128**
Anstruther Easter. *Fife.* 3H **137**
Anstruther Wester. *Fife.* 3H **137**
Ansty. *W Sus.* 3D **27**
Ansty. *Warw.* 2A **62**
Ansty. *Wilts.* 4E **23**
An Taobh Tuath. *W Isl.* 1E **170**
An t-Aodann Ban. *High.* 3C **154**
An t Ath Leathann. *High.* 1E **147**
An Teanga. *High.* 3E **147**
Anthill Common. *Hants.* 1E **17**
Anthorn. *Cumb.* 4C **112**
Antingham. *Norf.* 2E **79**
An t-Ôb. *W Isl.* 9C **171**
Anton's Gowt. *Linc.* 1B **76**
Antony. *Corn.* 3A **8**

An t-Òrd. *High.* 2E **147**
Antrobus. *Ches W.* 3A **84**
Anvil Corner. *Devn.* 2D **10**
Anwick. *Linc.* 5A **88**
Anwoth. *Dum.* 4C **110**
Apethorpe. *Nptn* 1H **63**
Apeton. *Staf.* 4C **72**
Apley. *Linc.* 3A **88**
Apperknowle. *Derbs.* 3A **86**
Apperley. *Glos.* 3D **48**
Apperley Dene. *Nmbd.* 4D **114**
Appersett. *N Yor.* 5B **104**
Appin. *Arg.* 4D **140**
Appleby. *N Lin.* 3C **94**
Appleby-in-Westmorland.
    Cumb. 2H **103**
Appleby Magna. *Leics.* 5H **73**
Appleby Parva. *Leics.* 5H **73**
Applecross. *High.* 4G **155**
Appledore. *Devn*
    nr. Bideford 3E **19**
    nr. Tiverton 1D **12**
Appledore. *Kent.* 3D **28**
Appledore Heath. *Kent.* 2D **28**
Appleford. *Oxon.* 2D **36**
Applegarthtown. *Dum.* 1C **112**
Applemore. *Hants.* 2B **16**
Appleshaw. *Hants.* 2B **24**
Applethwaite. *Cumb.* 2D **102**
Appleton. *Hal* 2H **83**
Appleton. *Oxon.* 5C **50**
Appleton-le-Moors. *N Yor.* 1B **100**
Appleton-le-Street. *N Yor.* 2B **100**
Appleton Roebuck. *N Yor.* 5H **99**
Appleton Thorn. *Warr.* 2A **84**
Appleton Wiske. *N Yor.* 4A **106**
Appletree. *Nptn.* 1C **50**
Appletreehall. *Bord.* 3H **119**
Appletreewick. *N Yor.* 3C **98**
Appley. *Som.* 4D **20**
Appley Bridge. *Lanc.* 3D **90**
Apse Heath. *IOW.* 4D **16**
Apsley End. *C Beds.* 2B **52**
Apuldram. *W Sus.* 2G **17**
Arabella. *High.* 1C **158**
Arasaig. *High.* 5E **147**
Arbeadie. *Abers.* 4D **152**
Arberth. *Pemb.* 3F **43**
Arbirlot. *Ang.* 4F **145**
Arborfield. *Wok.* 5F **37**
Arborfield Cross. *Wok.* 5F **37**
Arborfield Garrison. *Wok.* 5F **37**
Arbourthorne. *S Yor.* 2A **86**
Arbroath. *Ang.* 4F **145**
Arbuthnott. *Abers.* 1H **145**
Arcan. *High.* 3H **157**
Archargary. *High.* 3H **167**
Archdeacon Newton. *Darl.* 3F **105**
Archiestown. *Mor.* 4G **159**
Arclid. *Ches E.* 4B **84**
Arclid Green. *Ches E.* 4B **84**
Ardachu. *High.* 3D **164**
Ardalanish. *Arg.* 2A **132**
Ardaneaskan. *High.* 5H **155**
Ardarroch. *High.* 5H **155**
Ardbeg. *Arg*
    nr. Dunoon 1C **126**
    on Islay 5C **124**
    on Isle of Bute 3B **126**
Ardcharnich. *High.* 5F **163**
Ardchiavaig. *Arg.* 2A **132**
Ardchonnell. *Arg.* 2G **133**
Ardchrishnish. *Arg.* 1B **132**
Ardchronie. *High.* 5D **164**
Ardchullarie. *Stir.* 1E **135**
Ardchyle. *Stir.* 1E **135**
Ard-dhubh. *High.* 4G **155**
Ardeley. *Herts.* 3D **52**
Ardelve. *High.* 1A **148**
Arden. *Arg.* 1E **127**
Ardendrain. *High.* 5H **157**
Arden Hall. *N Yor.* 5C **106**
Ardens Grafton. *Warw.* 5F **61**
Ardentinny. *Arg.* 1C **126**
Ardeonaig. *Stir.* 5D **142**
Ardersier. *High.* 3B **158**
Ardery. *High.* 2B **140**
Ardessie. *High.* 5E **163**
Ardfern. *Arg.* 3F **133**
Ardfernal. *Arg.* 2D **124**
Ardfin. *Arg.* 3C **124**
Ardgartan. *Arg.* 3B **134**
Ardgay. *High.* 5D **164**
Ardglass. *Essx.* 3D **54**
Ardgour. *High.* 2E **141**
Ardheslaig. *High.* 3G **155**
Ardindrean. *High.* 5F **163**
Ardingly. *W Sus.* 3E **27**
Ardington. *Oxon.* 3C **36**
Ardlamont House. *Arg.* 3A **126**
Ardleigh. *Essx.* 3D **54**
Ardler. *Per.* 4B **144**
Ardley. *Oxon.* 3D **50**
Ardlui. *Arg.* 2C **134**
Ardlussa. *Arg.* 1E **125**
Ardmair. *High.* 4F **163**
Ardmay. *Arg.* 3B **134**
Ardminish. *Arg.* 5E **125**
Ardmolich. *High.* 1B **140**
Ardmore. *High.*
    nr. Kinlochbervie 3C **166**
    nr. Tain 5E **164**
Ardnacross. *Arg.* 4G **139**
Ardnadam. *Arg.* 1C **126**
Ardnagrask. *High.* 4H **157**
Ardnamurach. *High.* 4G **147**
Ardnarff. *High.* 5A **156**
Ardnastang. *High.* 2C **140**
Ardoch. *Per.* 5H **143**

Ardochy House. *High.* 3E **148**
Ardpatrick. *Arg.* 3F **125**
Ardrishaig. *Arg.* 1G **125**
Ardroag. *High.* 4B **154**
Ardross. *High.* 1A **158**
Ardrossan. *N Ayr.* 5D **126**
Ardshealach. *High.* 2A **140**
Ardsley. *S Yor* 4D **93**
Ardslignish. *High.* 2G **139**
Ardtalla. *Arg.* 4C **124**
Ardtalnaig. *Per.* 5E **142**
Ardtoe. *High.* 1A **140**
Arduaine. *Arg.* 2E **133**
Ardullie. *High.* 2H **157**
Ardvasar. *High.* 3E **147**
Ardvorlich. *Per.* 1F **135**
Ardwell. *Dum.* 5G **109**
Ardwell. *Mor.* 5A **160**
Arean. *High.* 1A **140**
Areley Common. *Worc.* 3C **60**
Areley Kings. *Worc.* 3C **60**
Arford. *Hants.* 3G **25**
Argoed. *Cphy.* 2E **33**
Argoed Mill. *Powy.* 4B **58**
Aridhglas. *Arg.* 2B **132**
Arinacrinachd. *High.* 3G **155**
Arinagour. *Arg.* 3D **138**
Arisaig. *High.* 5E **147**
Ariundle. *High.* 2C **140**
Arivegaig. *High.* 2A **140**
Arkendale. *N Yor.* 3F **99**
Arkesden. *Essx.* 2E **53**
Arkholme. *Lanc.* 2E **97**
Arkle Town. *N Yor.* 4D **104**
Arkley. *G Lon.* 1D **38**
Arksey. *S Yor.* 4F **93**
Arkwright Town. *Derbs.* 3B **86**
Arlecdon. *Cumb.* 3B **102**
Arlescote. *Warw.* 1B **50**
Arlesey. *C Beds.* 2B **52**
Arleston. *Telf.* 4A **72**
Arley. *Ches E.* 2A **84**
Arlingham. *Glos.* 4C **48**
Arlington. *Devn.* 2G **19**
Arlington. *E Sus.* 5G **27**
Arlington. *Glos.* 5G **49**
Arlington Beccott. *Devn.* 2G **19**
Armadail. *High.* 3E **147**
Armadale. *High*
    nr. Isleornsay 3E **147**
    nr. Strathy 2H **167**
Armadale. *W Lot.* 3C **128**
Armathwaite. *Cumb.* 5G **113**
Arminghall. *Norf.* 5E **79**
Armitage. *Staf.* 4E **73**
Armitage Bridge. *W Yor.* 3B **92**
Armley. *W Yor.* 1C **92**
The Arms. *Norf.* 1A **66**
Armscote. *Warw.* 1H **49**
Armston. *Nptn.* 2H **63**
Armthorpe. *S Yor.* 4G **93**
Arncliffe. *N Yor.* 2B **98**
Arncliffe Cote. *N Yor.* 2B **98**
Arncroach. *Fife.* 3H **137**
Arne. *Dors.* 4E **15**
Arnesby. *Leics.* 1D **62**
Arnicle. *Arg.* 2B **122**
Arnisdale. *High.* 2G **147**
Arnish. *High.* 4E **155**
Arniston. *Midl.* 3G **129**
Arnol. *W Isl.* 3F **171**
Arnold. *E Yor.* 5F **101**
Arnold. *Notts.* 1C **74**
Arnprior. *Stir.* 4F **135**
Arnside. *Cumb.* 2D **96**
Aros Mains. *Arg.* 4G **139**
Arpafeelie. *High.* 3A **158**
Arrad Foot. *Cumb* 1C **96**
Arram. *E Yor.* 5E **101**
Arrarthorne. *N Yor.* 5E **105**
Arreton. *IOW.* 4D **16**
Arrington. *Cambs.* 5C **64**
Arrochar. *Arg.* 3B **134**
Arrow. *Warw.* 5E **61**
Arscaig. *High.* 2C **164**
Artafallie. *High.* 4A **158**
Arthington. *W Yor.* 5E **99**
Arthingworth. *Nptn.* 2E **63**
Arthog. *Gwyn.* 4F **69**
Arthrath. *Abers.* 5G **161**
Arthurstone. *Per.* 4B **144**
Artington. *Surr.* 1A **26**
Arundel. *W Sus.* 5B **26**
Asby. *Cumb.* 2B **102**
Ascog. *Arg.* 3C **126**
Ascot. *Wind* 4A **38**
Ascott-under-Wychwood. *Oxon.* 4B **50**
Asenby. *N Yor.* 2F **99**
Asfordby. *Leics.* 4E **74**
Asfordby Hill. *Leics.* 4E **74**
Asgarby. *Linc.*
    nr. Horncastle 4C **88**
    nr. Sleaford 1A **76**
Ash. *Devn.* 4E **9**
Ash. *Dors.* 1D **14**
Ash. *Kent*
    nr. Sandwich 5G **41**
    nr. Swanley 4H **39**
Ash. *Som.* 4H **21**
Ash. *Surr.* 1G **25**
Ashampstead. *W Ber* 4D **36**
Ashbocking. *Suff.* 5D **66**
Ashbourne. *Derbs.* 1F **73**
Ashbrittle. *Som.* 4D **20**
Ashbrook. *Shrp.* 1G **59**
Ashburton. *Devn.* 2D **8**
Ashbury. *Devn.* 3F **11**
Ashbury. *Oxon.* 3A **36**
Ashby. *N Lin.* 4B **94**
Ashby by Partney. *Linc.* 4D **88**

Ashby cum Fenby. NE Lin 4F 95
Ashby de la Launde. Linc 5H 87
Ashby-de-la-Zouch. Leics 4A 74
Ashby Folville. Leics 4E 74
Ashby Magna. Leics 1C 62
Ashby Parva. Leics 2C 62
Ashby Puerorum. Linc 3C 88
Ashby St Ledgars. Nptn 4C 62
Ashby St Mary. Norf 5F 79
Ashchurch. Glos 2E 49
Ashcombe. Devn 5C 12
Ashcott. Som 3H 21
Ashdon. Essx 1F 53
Ashe. Hants 2D 24
Asheldham. Essx 5C 54
Ashen. Essx 1H 53
Ashendon. Buck 4F 51
Ashey. IOW 4D 16
Ashfield. Hants 1B 16
Ashfield. Here 3A 48
Ashfield. Shrp 2H 59
Ashfield. Stir 3G 135
Ashfield. Suff 4E 66
Ashfield Green. Suff 3E 67
Ashford Crossways. W Sus 3D 26
Ashford. Devn
  nr. Barnstaple 3F 19
  nr. Kingsbridge 4C 8
Ashford. Hants 1G 15
Ashford. Kent 1E 28
Ashford. Surr 3B 38
Ashford Bowdler. Shrp 3H 59
Ashford Carbonel. Shrp 3H 59
Ashford Hill. Hants 5D 36
Ashford in the Water. Derbs 4F 85
Ashgill. S Lan 5A 128
Ash Green. Warw 2H 61
Ashgrove. Mor 2G 159
Ashill. Devn 1D 12
Ashill. Norf 5A 78
Ashill. Som 1G 13
Ashingdon. Essx 1C 40
Ashington. Nmbd 1F 115
Ashington. W Sus 4C 26
Ashkirk. Bord 2G 119
Ashleworth. Glos 3D 48
Ashley. Cambs 4F 65
Ashley. Ches E 2B 84
Ashley. Dors 2G 15
Ashley. Glos 2E 35
Ashley. Hants
  nr. New Milton 3A 16
  nr. Winchester 3B 24
Ashley. Kent 1H 29
Ashley. Nptn 1E 63
Ashley. Staf 2B 72
Ashley. Wilts 5D 34
Ashley Green. Buck 5H 51
Ashley Heath. Dors 2G 15
Ashley Heath. Staf 2B 72
Ashley Moor. Here 4G 59
Ash Magna. Shrp 2H 71
Ashmanhaugh. Norf 3F 79
Ashmansworth. Hants 1C 24
Ashmansworthy. Devn 1D 10
Ashmead Green. Glos 2C 34
Ash Mill. Devn 4A 20
Ashmill. Devn 3D 11
Ashmore. Dors 1E 15
Ashmore Green. W Ber 5D 36
Ashorne. Warw 5H 61
Ashover. Derbs 4A 86
Ashow. Warw 3H 61
Ash Parva. Shrp 2H 71
Ashperton. Here 1B 48
Ashprington. Devn 3E 9
Ash Priors. Som 4E 21
Ashreigney. Devn 1G 11
Ash Street. Suff 1D 54
Ashtead. Surr 5C 38
Ash Thomas. Devn 1D 12
Ashton. Corn 4D 4
Ashton. Here 4H 59
Ashton. Inv 2D 126
Ashton. Nptn
  nr. Oundle 2H 63
  nr. Roade 1F 51
Ashton. Pet 5A 76
Ashton Common. Wilts 1D 23
Ashton Hayes. Ches W 4H 83
Ashton-in-Makerfield. G Man 1H 83
Ashton Keynes. Wilts 2F 35
Ashton under Hill. Worc 2E 49
Ashton-under-Lyne. G Man 1D 84
Ashton upon Mersey. G Man 1B 84
Ashurst. Hants 1B 16
Ashurst. Kent 2G 27
Ashurst. Lanc 4C 90
Ashurst. W Sus 4C 26
Ashurst Wood. W Sus 2F 27
Ash Vale. Surr 1G 25
Ashwater. Devn 3D 11
Ashwell. Herts 2C 52
Ashwell. Rut 4F 75
Ashwellthorpe. Norf 1D 66
Ashwick. Som 2B 22
Ashwicken. Norf 4G 77
Ashwood. Staf 2C 60
Askam in Furness. Cumb 2B 96
Askern. S Yor 3F 93
Askerswell. Dors 3A 14
Askett. Buck 5G 51
Askham. Cumb 2G 103
Askham. Notts 3E 87
Askham Bryan. York 5H 99
Askham Richard. York 5H 99
Askrigg. N Yor 5C 104
Askwith. N Yor 5D 98
Aslackby. Linc 2H 75
Aslacton. Norf 1D 66
Aslockton. Notts 1E 75

Aspatria. Cumb 5C 112
Aspenden. Herts 3D 52
Asperton. Linc 2B 76
Aspley Guise. C Beds 2H 51
Aspley Heath. C Beds 2H 51
Aspull. G Man 4E 90
Asselby. E Yor 2H 93
Assington. Suff 2C 54
Assington Green. Suff 5G 65
Astbury. Ches E 4C 84
Astcote. Nptn 5D 62
Asterby. Linc 3B 88
Asterley. Shrp 5F 71
Asterton. Shrp 1F 59
Asthall. Oxon 4A 50
Asthall Leigh. Oxon 4B 50
Astle. High 4E 165
Astley. G Man 4F 91
Astley. Shrp 4H 71
Astley. Warw 2H 61
Astley. Worc 4B 60
Astley Abbotts. Shrp 1B 60
Astley Bridge. G Man 3F 91
Astley Cross. Worc 4C 60
Aston. Ches E 1A 72
Aston. Ches W 3H 83
Aston. Derbs
  nr. Hope 2F 85
  nr. Sudbury 2F 73
Aston. Flin 4F 83
Aston. Here 4G 59
Aston. Herts 3C 52
Aston. Oxon 5B 50
Aston. Shrp
  nr. Bridgnorth 1C 60
  nr. Wem 3H 71
Aston. S Yor 2B 86
Aston. Staf 1B 72
Aston. Telf 5A 72
Aston. W Mid 1E 61
Aston. Wok 3F 37
Aston Abbotts. Buck 3G 51
Aston Botterell. Shrp 2A 60
Aston-by-Stone. Staf 2D 72
Aston Cantlow. Warw 5F 61
Aston Clinton. Buck 4G 51
Aston Crews. Here 3B 48
Aston Cross. Glos 2E 49
Aston End. Herts 3C 52
Aston Eyre. Shrp 1A 60
Aston Fields. Worc 4D 60
Aston Flamville. Leics 1B 62
Aston Ingham. Here 3B 48
Aston juxta Mondrum. Ches E 5A 84
Astonlane. Shrp 1A 60
Aston le Walls. Nptn 5B 62
Aston Magna. Glos 2G 49
Aston Munslow. Shrp 2H 59
Aston on Carrant. Glos 2E 49
Aston on Clun. Shrp 2F 59
Aston-on-Trent. Derbs 3B 74
Aston Pigott. Shrp 5F 71
Aston Rogers. Shrp 5F 71
Aston Rowant. Oxon 2F 37
Aston Sandford. Buck 5F 51
Aston Somerville. Worc 2F 49
Aston Subedge. Glos 1G 49
Aston Tirrold. Oxon 3D 36
Aston Upthorpe. Oxon 3D 36
Astrop. Nptn 2D 50
Astwick. C Beds 2C 52
Astwood. Mil 1H 51
Astwood Bank. Worc 4E 61
Aswarby. Linc 2H 75
Aswardby. Linc 3C 88
Atcham. Shrp 5H 71
Atch Lench. Worc 5E 61
Athelhampton. Dors 3C 14
Athelington. Suff 3E 66
Athelney. Som 4G 21
Athelstaneford. E Lot 2B 130
Atherfield Green. IOW 5C 16
Atherington. Devn 4F 19
Atherington. W Sus 5B 26
Athersley. S Yor 4D 92
Atherstone. Warw 1H 61
Atherstone on Stour. Warw 5G 61
Atherton. G Man 4E 91
Ath-Tharracail. High 2A 140
Atlow. Derbs 1G 73
Attadale. High 5B 156
Attenborough. Notts 2C 74
Atterby. Linc 1G 87
Atterley. Shrp 1A 60
Atterton. Leics 1A 62
Attleborough. Norf 1C 66
Attleborough. Warw 1A 62
Attlebridge. Norf 4D 78
Atwick. E Yor 4F 101
Atworth. Wilts 5D 34
Auberrow. Here 1H 47
Aubourn. Linc 4G 87
Aucharnie. Abers 4D 160
Auchattie. Abers 4D 152
Auchavan. Ang 2A 144
Auchbreck. Mor 1G 151
Auchenback. E Ren 4G 127
Auchenblae. Abers 1G 145
Auchenbrack. Dum 5G 117
Auchenbreck. Arg 1B 126
Auchencairn. Dum
  nr. Dalbeattie 4E 111
  nr. Dumfries 1A 112
Auchencarroch. W Dun 1F 127
Auchencrow. Bord 3E 131
Auchendennan. Arg 1E 127
Auchendinny. Midl 3F 129
Auchengray. S Lan 4C 128
Auchenhalrig. Mor 2A 160
Auchenheath. S Lan 5B 128
Auchenlochan. Arg 2A 126

Auchenmade. N Ayr 5E 127
Auchenmalg. Dum 4H 109
Auchentiber. N Ayr 5E 127
Auchenvennel. Arg 1D 126
Auchindrain. Arg 3H 133
Auchininna. Abers 4D 160
Auchinleck. Dum 2B 110
Auchinleck. E Ayr 2E 117
Auchinloch. N Lan 2H 127
Auchinstarry. N Lan 2A 128
Auchleven. Abers 1D 152
Auchlochan. S Lan 1H 117
Auchlunachan. High 5F 163
Auchmillan. E Ayr 2E 117
Auchmithie. Ang 4F 145
Auchmull. Ang 1E 145
Auchnacree. Ang 2D 144
Auchnafree. Per 5F 143
Auchnagallin. High 5E 159
Auchnagatt. Abers 4G 161
Aucholzie. Abers 4H 151
Auchreddie. Abers 4F 161
Auchterarder. Per 2B 136
Auchteraw. High 3F 149
Auchterderran. Fife 4E 136
Auchterhouse. Ang 5C 144
Auchtermuchty. Fife 2E 137
Auchterneed. High 3G 157
Auchtertool. Fife 4E 136
Auchtertyre. High 1G 147
Auchtubh. Stir 1E 135
Auckengill. High 2F 169
Auckley. S Yor 4G 93
Audenshaw. G Man 1D 84
Audlem. Ches E 1A 72
Audley. Staf 5B 84
Audley End. Essx 2F 53
Audmore. Staf 3C 72
Auds. Abers 2D 160
Aughertree. Cumb 1D 102
Aughton. E Yor 1H 93
Aughton. Lanc
  nr. Lancaster 3E 97
  nr. Ormskirk 4B 90
Aughton. S Yor 2B 86
Aughton. Wilts 1H 23
Aughton Park. Lanc 4C 90
Auldearn. High 3D 158
Aulden. Here 5G 59
Auldgirth. Dum 1G 111
Auldhouse. S Lan 4H 127
Ault a' chruinn. High 1B 148
Aultbea. High 5C 162
Aultdearg. High 2E 157
Aultgrishan. High 5B 162
Aultguish Inn. High 1F 157
Ault Hucknall. Derbs 4B 86
Aultibea. High 1H 165
Aultiphurst. High 2A 168
Aultivullin. High 2A 168
Aultmore. Mor 3B 160
Aultnamain Inn. High 5D 164
Aunby. Linc 4H 75
Aunsby. Linc 2H 75
Aust. S Glo 3A 34
Austerfield. S Yor 1D 86
Austin Fen. Linc 1C 88
Austrey. Warw 5G 73
Austwick. N Yor 3G 97
Authorpe. Linc 2D 88
Authorpe Row. Linc 3E 89
Avebury. Wilts 5G 35
Avebury Trusloe. Wilts 5F 35
Aveley. Thur 2G 39
Avening. Glos 2D 35
Averham. Notts 5E 87
Aveton Gifford. Devn 4C 8
Avielochan. High 2D 150
Aviemore. High 2C 150
Avington. Hants 3D 24
Avoch. High 3B 158
Avon. Hants 3G 15
Avonbridge. Falk 2C 128
Avon Dassett. Warw 5B 62
Avonmouth. Bris 4A 34
Avonwick. Devn 3D 8
Awbridge. Hants 4B 24
Awliscombe. Devn 2E 13
Awre. Glos 5C 48
Awsworth. Notts 1B 74
Axbridge. Som 1H 21
Axford. Hants 2E 24
Axford. Wilts 5H 35
Axminster. Devn 3G 13
Axmouth. Devn 3F 13
Aycliffe Village. Dur 2F 105
Aydon. Nmbd 3D 114
Aykley Heads. Dur 5F 115
Aylburton. Glos 5B 48
Aylburton Common. Glos 5B 48
Ayle. Nmbd 5A 114
Aylesbeare. Devn 3D 12
Aylesbury. Buck 4G 51
Aylesby. NE Lin 4F 95
Aylescott. Devn 1G 11
Aylesford. Kent 5B 40
Aylesham. Kent 5G 41
Aylestone. Leic 5C 74
Aylmerton. Norf 2D 78
Aylsham. Norf 3D 78
Aylton. Here 2B 48
Aylworth. Glos 3G 49
Aymestrey. Here 4G 59
Aynho. Nptn 2D 50
Ayot Green. Herts 4B 52
Ayot St Lawrence. Herts 4B 52
Ayot St Peter. Herts 4C 52
Ayr. S Ayr 187 (2C 116)
Ayres of Selivoe. Shet 7D 173
Ayreville. Torb 2E 9

Aysgarth. N Yor 1C 98
Ayshford. Devn 1D 12
Ayside. Cumb 1C 96
Ayston. Rut 5F 75
Ayton. Bord 3F 131
Aywick. Shet 3G 173
Azerley. N Yor 2E 99

B

Babbacombe. Torb 2F 9
Babbinswood. Shrp 2F 71
Babbs Green. Herts 4D 53
Babcary. Som 4A 22
Babel. Carm 2B 46
Babell. Flin 3D 82
Babingley. Norf 3F 77
Bablock Hythe. Oxon 5C 50
Babraham. Cambs 5E 65
Babworth. Notts 2D 86
Bac. W Isl 3G 171
Bachau. IOA 2D 80
Bacheldre. Powy 1E 59
Bachymbyd Fawr. Den 4C 82
Backaland. Orkn 4E 172
Backaskaill. Orkn 2D 172
Backbarrow. Cumb 1C 96
Backe. Carm 3G 43
Backfolds. Abers 3H 161
Backford. Ches W 3G 83
Backhill. Abers 5E 161
Backhill of Clackriach. Abers 4G 161
Backies. High 3F 165
Backmuir of New Gilston. Fife 3G 137
Back of Keppoch. High 5E 147
Back Street. Suff 5G 65
Backwell. N Som 5H 33
Backworth. Tyne 2G 115
Bacon End. Essx 4G 53
Baconsthorpe. Norf 2D 78
Bacton. Here 2G 47
Bacton. Norf 2F 79
Bacton. Suff 4C 66
Bacton Green. Norf 2F 79
Bacup. Lanc 2G 91
Badachonacher. High 1A 158
Badachro. High 1G 155
Badanloch Lodge. High 5H 167
Badavanich. High 3D 156
Badbury. Swin 3G 35
Badby. Nptn 5C 62
Badcall. High 3C 166
Badcaul. High 4E 163
Baddeley Green. Stoke 5D 84
Baddesley Clinton. W Mid 3G 61
Baddesley Ensor. Warw 1G 61
Baddidarach. High 1E 163
Baddoch. Abers 5F 151
Badenscallie. High 3E 163
Badenscoth. Abers 5E 160
Badentarbat. High 2E 163
Badgall. Corn 4C 10
Badgers Mount. Kent 4F 39
Badgeworth. Glos 4E 49
Badgworth. Som 1G 21
Badicaul. High 1F 147
Badingham. Suff 4F 67
Badlesmere. Kent 5E 40
Badlipster. High 4E 169
Badluarach. High 4D 162
Badminton. S Glo 3D 34
Badnaban. High 1E 163
Badnabay. High 4C 166
Badnagie. High 5D 168
Badnellan. High 3F 165
Badninish. High 4E 165
Badrallach. High 4E 163
Badsey. Worc 1F 49
Badshot Lea. Surr 2G 25
Badsworth. W Yor 3E 93
Badwell Ash. Suff 4B 66
Bae Cinmel. Cnwy 2B 82
Bae Colwyn. Cnwy 3A 82
Bae Penrhyn. Cnwy 2H 81
Bagby. N Yor 1G 99
Bag Enderby. Linc 3C 88
Bagendon. Glos 5F 49
Bagginswood. Shrp 2A 60
Bàgh a Chàise. W Isl 1E 170
Bàgh a' Chaisteil. W Isl 9B 170
Bagham. Kent 5E 41
Baghasdal. W Isl 7C 170
Bagh Mòr. W Isl 3D 170
Bagh Shiarabhagh. W Isl 8C 170
Bagillt. Flin 3E 82
Baginton. Warw 3H 61
Baglan. Neat 2A 32
Bagley. Shrp 3G 71
Bagley. Som 2H 21
Bagnall. Staf 5D 84
Bagnor. W Ber 5C 36
Bagshot. Surr 4A 38
Bagshot. Wilts 5B 36
Bagstone. S Glo 3B 34
Bagthorpe. Norf 2G 77
Bagthorpe. Notts 5B 86
Bagworth. Leics 5B 74
Bagwy Llydiart. Here 3H 47
Baildon. W Yor 1B 92
Baildon Green. W Yor 1B 92
Baile. W Isl 1E 170
Baile Ailein. W Isl 5E 171
Baile an Truiseil. W Isl 2F 171
Baile Boidheach. Arg 2F 125
Baile Glas. W Isl 3C 170
Bailemeonach. Arg 4A 140
Baile Mhanaich. W Isl 3C 170
Baile MhicPhail. W Isl 1D 170
Baile Mor. W Isl 2C 170

Baile Mòr. Arg 2A 132
Baile nan Cailleach. W Isl 3C 170
Baile Raghaill. W Isl 2C 170
Bailey Green. Hants 4E 25
Baileyhead. Cumb 1G 113
Bainsford. Falk 1B 128
Bainshole. Abers 5D 160
Bainton. E Yor 4D 100
Bainton. Oxon 3D 50
Bainton. Pet 5H 75
Baintown. Fife 3F 137
Baker Street. Thur 2H 39
Bakewell. Derbs 4G 85
Bala. Gwyn 2B 70
Y Bala. Gwyn 2B 70
Balachuirn. High 4E 155
Balbeg. High
  nr. Cannich 5G 157
  nr. Loch Ness 1G 149
Balbeggie. Per 1D 136
Balblair. High
  nr. Bonar Bridge 4C 164
  nr. Invergordon 2B 158
  nr. Inverness 4H 157
Balby. S Yor 4F 93
Balcathie. Ang 5F 145
Balchladich. High 1E 163
Balchraggan. High 4H 157
Balchrick. High 3B 166
Balcombe. W Sus 2E 27
Balcombe Lane. W Sus 2E 27
Balcurvie. Fife 3F 137
Baldersby. N Yor 2F 99
Baldersby St James. N Yor 2F 99
Balderstone. Lanc 1E 91
Balderton. Ches W 4F 83
Balderton. Notts 5F 87
Baldinnie. Fife 2G 137
Baldock. Herts 2C 52
Baldrine. IOM 3D 108
Baldslow. E Sus 4C 28
Baldwin. IOM 3C 108
Baldwinholme. Cumb 4E 113
Baldwin's Gate. Staf 2B 72
Bale. Norf 2C 78
Balearn. Abers 3H 161
Balemartine. Arg 4A 138
Balephetrish. Arg 4B 138
Balephuil. Arg 4A 138
Balerno. Edin 3E 129
Balevullin. Arg 4A 138
Balfield. Ang 2E 145
Balfour. Orkn 6D 172
Balfron. Stir 1G 127
Balgaveny. Abers 4D 160
Balgonar. Fife 4C 136
Balgowan. High 4A 150
Balgown. High 2C 154
Balgrochan. E Dun 2H 127
Balgy. High 3H 155
Balhalgardy. Abers 1E 153
Baliasta. Shet 1H 173
Baligill. High 2A 168
Balintore. High 3B 144
Balintore. Ang 1C 158
Balintraid. High 1B 158
Balk. N Yor 1G 99
Balkeerie. Ang 4C 144
Balkholme. E Yor 2A 94
Ball. Shrp 3F 71
Ballabeg. IOM 4B 108
Ballacannell. IOM 3D 108
Ballacarnane Beg. IOM 3C 108
Ballachulish. High 3E 141
Ballagyr. IOM 3B 108
Ballajora. IOM 2D 108
Ballaleigh. IOM 3C 108
Ballamodha. IOM 4B 108
Ballantrae. S Ayr 1F 109
Ballards Gore. Essx 1D 40
Ballasalla. IOM
  nr. Castletown 4B 108
  nr. Kirk Michael 2C 108
Ballater. Abers 4A 152
Ballaugh. IOM 2C 108
Ballencrieff. E Lot 2A 130
Ballencrieff Toll. W Lot 2C 128
Ballentoul. Per 2F 143
Ball Hill. Hants 5C 36
Ballidon. Derbs 5G 85
Balliemore. Arg
  nr. Dunoon 1B 126
  nr. Oban 1F 133
Ballieward. High 5E 159
Ballig. IOM 3B 108
Ballimore. Stir 2E 135
Ballingdon. Suff 1B 54
Ballinger Common. Buck 5H 51
Ballingham. Here 2A 48
Ballingry. Fife 4D 136
Ballinluig. Per 3G 143
Ballintuim. Per 3A 144
Balliveolan. Arg 4C 140
Balloan. High 3C 164
Balloch. High 4B 158
Balloch. N Lan 2A 128
Balloch. Per 2H 135
Balloch. W Dun 1E 127
Ballochan. Arg 3B 126
Ballochgoy. Arg 3B 126
Ballochmyle. E Ayr 2E 117
Balls Cross. W Sus 3A 26
Ball's Green. E Sus 2F 27

Ballygown. *Arg* 4F **139**
Ballygrant. *Arg* 3B **124**
Ballymichael. *N Ayr* 2D **122**
Balmacara. *High* 1G **147**
Balmaclellan. *Dum* 2D **110**
Balmacqueen. *High* 1D **154**
Balmaha. *Stir* 4D **134**
Balmalcolm. *Fife* 3F **137**
Balmalloch. *N Lan* 2A **128**
Balmeanach. *High* 5E **164**
Balmedie. *Abers* 2G **153**
Balmerino. *Fife* 1F **137**
Balmerlawn. *Hants* 2B **16**
Balmore. *E Dun* 2H **127**
Balmore. *High* 4B **154**
Balmullo. *Fife* 1G **137**
Balmurrie. *Dum* 3H **109**
Balnaboth. *Ang* 2C **144**
Balnabruaich. *High* 1B **158**
Balnabruich. *High* 5D **168**
Balnacoil. *High* 2F **165**
Balnacra. *High* 4B **156**
Balnacroft. *Abers* 4G **151**
Balnageith. *Mor* 3E **159**
Balnaglaic. *High* 5G **157**
Balnagrantach. *High* 5G **157**
Balnaguard. *Per* 3G **143**
Balnahard. *Arg* 4B **132**
Balnain. *High* 5G **157**
Balnakeil. *High* 2D **166**
Balnaknock. *High* 2D **154**
Balnamoon. *Abers* 3G **161**
Balnamoon. *Ang* 2E **145**
Balnapaling. *High* 2B **158**
Balornock. *Glas* 3H **127**
Balquhidder. *Stir* 1E **135**
Balsall. *W Mid* 3G **61**
Balsall Common. *W Mid* ...3G **61**
Balscote. *Oxon* 1B **50**
Balsham. *Cambs* 5E **65**
Balstonia. *Thur* 2A **40**
Baltasound. *Shet* 1H **173**
Balterley. *Staf* 5B **84**
Baltersan. *Dum* 3B **110**
Balthangie. *Abers* 3F **161**
Baltonsborough. *Som* 3A **22**
Balvaird. *High* 3H **157**
Balvaird. *Per* 2D **136**
Balvenie. *Mor* 4H **159**
Balvicar. *Arg* 2E **133**
Balvraid. *High* 2G **147**
Balvraid Lodge. *High* 5C **158**
Bamber Bridge. *Lanc* 2D **90**
Bamber's Green. *Essx* 3F **53**
Bamburgh. *Nmbd* 1F **121**
Bamford. *Derbs* 2G **85**
Bamfurlong. *G Man* 4D **90**
Bampton. *Cumb* 3G **103**
Bampton. *Devn* 4C **20**
Bampton. *Oxon* 5B **50**
Bampton Grange. *Cumb* ...3G **103**
Banavie. *High* 1F **141**
Banbury. *Oxon* 1C **50**
Bancffosfelen. *Carm* 4E **45**
Banchory. *Abers* 4D **152**
Banchory-Devenick. *Abers* ...3G **153**
Bancycapel. *Carm* 4E **45**
Bancyfelin. *Carm* 3H **43**
Banc-y-ffordd. *Carm* 2E **45**
Banff. *Abers* 2D **160**
Bangor. *Gwyn* 3E **81**
Bangor-is-y-coed. *Wrex* ...1F **71**
Bangors. *Corn* 3C **10**
Bangor's Green. *Lanc* 4B **90**
Banham. *Norf* 2C **66**
Bank. *Hants* 2A **16**
The Bank. *Ches E* 5C **84**
The Bank. *Shrp* 1A **60**
Bankend. *Dum* 3B **112**
Bankfoot. *Per* 5H **143**
Bankglen. *E Ayr* 3F **117**
Bankhead. *Aber* 2F **153**
Bankhead. *Abers* 3D **152**
Bankhead. *S Lan* 5B **128**
Bankland. *Som* 4G **21**
Bank Newton. *N Yor* 4B **98**
Banknock. *Falk* 2A **128**
Banks. *Cumb* 3G **113**
Banks. *Lanc* 2B **90**
Bankshill. *Dum* 1C **112**
Bank Street. *Worc* 4A **60**
Bank Top. *Lanc* 4D **90**
Banners Gate. *W Mid* 1E **61**
Banningham. *Norf* 3E **78**
Bannister Green. *Essx* 3G **53**
Bannockburn. *Stir* 4H **135**
Banstead. *Surr* 5D **38**
Bantham. *Devn* 4C **8**
Banton. *N Lan* 2A **128**
Banwell. *N Som* 1G **21**
Banyard's Green. *Suff* 3F **67**
Bapchild. *Kent* 4D **40**
Bapton. *Wilts* 3E **23**
Barabhas. *W Isl* 2F **171**
Barabhas Iarach. *W Isl* 3F **171**
Baramore. *High* 1A **140**
Barassie. *S Ayr* 1C **116**
Baravullin. *Arg* 4D **140**
Barbaraville. *High* 1B **158**
Barber Booth. *Derbs* 2F **85**
Barber Green. *Cumb* 1C **96**
Barbhas Uarach. *W Isl* 2F **171**
Barbieston. *S Ayr* 3D **116**
Barbon. *Cumb* 1F **97**
Barbourne. *Worc* 5C **60**
Barbridge. *Ches E* 5A **84**
Barbrook. *Devn* 2H **19**
Barby. *Nptn* 3C **62**
Barby Nortoft. *Nptn* 3C **62**
Barcaldine. *Arg* 4D **140**

Barcheston. *Warw* 2A **50**
Barclose. *Cumb* 3F **113**
Barcombe. *E Sus* 4F **27**
Barcombe Cross. *E Sus* 4F **27**
Barden. *N Yor* 5E **105**
Barden Scale. *N Yor* 4C **98**
Bardfield End Green. *Essx* ...2G **53**
Bardfield Saling. *Essx* 3G **53**
Bardister. *Shet* 4E **173**
Bardnabreine. *High* 4E **164**
Bardney. *Linc* 4A **88**
Bardon. *Leics* 4B **74**
Bardon Mill. *Nmbd* 3A **114**
Bardowie. *E Dun* 2G **127**
Bardrainney. *Inv* 2E **127**
Bardsea. *Cumb* 2C **96**
Bardsey. *W Yor* 5F **99**
Bardsley. *G Man* 4H **91**
Bardwell. *Suff* 3B **66**
Bare. *Lanc* 3D **96**
Barelees. *Nmbd* 1C **120**
Barewood. *Here* 5F **59**
Barford. *Hants* 3G **25**
Barford. *Norf* 5D **78**
Barford. *Warw* 4G **61**
Barford St John. *Oxon* 2C **50**
Barford St Martin. *Wilts* ...3F **23**
Barford St Michael. *Oxon* ...2C **50**
Barfrestone. *Kent* 5G **41**
Bargeddie. *N Lan* 3H **127**
Bargod. *Cphy* 2E **33**
Bargoed. *Cphy* 2E **33**
Bargrennan. *Dum* 2A **110**
Barham. *Cambs* 3A **64**
Barham. *Kent* 5G **41**
Barham. *Suff* 5D **66**
Barharrow. *Dum* 4D **110**
Bar Hill. *Cambs* 4C **64**
Barholm. *Linc* 4H **75**
Barkby. *Leics* 5D **74**
Barkestone-le-Vale. *Leics* ...2E **75**
Barkham. *Wok* 5F **37**
Barking. *G Lon* 2F **39**
Barking. *Suff* 5C **66**
Barkingside. *G Lon* 2F **39**
Barking Tye. *Suff* 5C **66**
Barkisland. *W Yor* 3A **92**
Barkston. *Linc* 1G **75**
Barkston Ash. *N Yor* 1E **93**
Barkway. *Herts* 2D **53**
Barlanark. *Glas* 3H **127**
Barlaston. *Staf* 2C **72**
Barlavington. *W Sus* 4A **26**
Barlborough. *Derbs* 3B **86**
Barlby. *N Yor* 1G **93**
Barlestone. *Leics* 5B **74**
Barley. *Herts* 2D **53**
Barley. *Lanc* 5H **97**
Barley Mow. *Tyne* 4F **115**
Barleythorpe. *Rut* 5F **75**
Barling. *Essx* 2D **40**
Barlings. *Linc* 3H **87**
Barlow. *Derbs* 3H **85**
Barlow. *N Yor* 2G **93**
Barlow. *Tyne* 3E **115**
Barmby Moor. *E Yor* 5B **100**
Barmby on the Marsh. *E Yor* ...2G **93**
Barmer. *Norf* 2H **77**
Barming. *Kent* 5B **40**
Barming Heath. *Kent* 5B **40**
Barmoor. *Nmbd* 1E **121**
Barmouth. *Gwyn* 4F **69**
Barmpton. *Darl* 3A **106**
Barmston. *E Yor* 4F **101**
Barmulloch. *Glas* 3H **127**
Barnack. *Pet* 5H **75**
Barnacle. *Warw* 2A **62**
Barnard Castle. *Dur* 3D **104**
Barnard Gate. *Oxon* 4C **50**
Barnardiston. *Suff* 1H **53**
Barnbarroch. *Dum* 4F **111**
Barnburgh. *S Yor* 4E **93**
Barnby. *Suff* 2G **67**
Barnby Dun. *S Yor* 4G **93**
Barnby in the Willows. *Notts* ...5F **87**
Barnby Moor. *Notts* 2D **86**
Barnes. *G Lon* 3D **38**
Barnes Street. *Kent* 1H **27**
Barnet. *G Lon* 1D **38**
Barnetby le Wold. *N Lin* ...4D **94**
Barney. *Norf* 2B **78**
Barnham. *Suff* 3A **66**
Barnham. *W Sus* 5A **26**
Barnham Broom. *Norf* 5C **78**
Barnhead. *Ang* 3F **145**
Barnhill. *D'dee* 5D **145**
Barnhill. *Mor* 3F **159**
Barnhill. *Per* 1D **136**
Barnhills. *Dum* 2E **109**
Barningham. *Dur* 3D **105**
Barningham. *Suff* 3B **66**
Barnoldby le Beck. *NE Lin* ...4F **95**
Barnoldswick. *Lanc* 5A **98**
Barns Green. *W Sus* 3C **26**
Barnsley. *Glos* 5F **49**
Barnsley. *Shrp* 1B **60**
Barnsley. *S Yor* 4D **92**
Barnstaple. *Devn* 3F **19**
Barnston. *Essx* 4G **53**
Barnston. *Mers* 2E **83**
Barnstone. *Notts* 2E **75**
Barnt Green. *Worc* 3E **61**
Barnton. *Ches W* 3A **84**
Barnwell. *Cambs* 5D **64**
Barnwell. *Nptn* 2H **63**
Barnwood. *Glos* 4D **48**
Barons Cross. *Here* 5G **59**
The Barony. *Orkn* 5B **172**
Barr. *Dum* 4G **117**
Barr. *S Ayr* 5B **116**
Barra Airport. *W Isl* 8B **170**

Barrachan. *Dum* 5A **110**
Barraglom. *W Isl* 4D **171**
Barrahormid. *Arg* 1F **125**
Barrapol. *Arg* 4A **138**
Barrasford. *Nmbd* 2C **114**
Barravullin. *Arg* 3F **133**
Barregarrow. *IOM* 3C **108**
Barrhead. *E Ren* 4G **127**
Barrhill. *S Ayr* 1H **109**
Barri. *V Glam* 5E **32**
Barrington. *Cambs* 1D **53**
Barrington. *Som* 1G **13**
Barripper. *Corn* 3D **4**
Barrmill. *N Ayr* 4E **127**
Barrock. *High* 1E **169**
Barrow. *Lanc* 1F **91**
Barrow. *Rut* 4F **75**
Barrow. *Shrp* 5A **72**
Barrow. *Som* 3C **22**
Barrow. *Suff* 4G **65**
Barroway Drove. *Norf* 5E **77**
Barrow Bridge. *G Man* 3E **91**
Barrowburn. *Nmbd* 3C **120**
Barrowby. *Linc* 2F **75**
Barrowcliff. *N Yor* 1E **101**
Barrow Common. *N Som* ...5A **34**
Barrowden. *Rut* 5G **75**
Barrowford. *Lanc* 1G **91**
Barrow Gurney. *N Som* 5A **34**
Barrow Haven. *N Lin* 2D **94**
Barrow Hill. *Derbs* 3B **86**
Barrow Nook. *Lanc* 4C **90**
Barrow's Green. *Hal* 2H **83**
Barrows Green. *Cumb* 1E **97**
Barrow Street. *Wilts* 3D **22**
Barrow upon Humber. *N Lin* ...2D **94**
Barrow upon Soar. *Leics* ...4C **74**
Barrow upon Trent. *Derbs* ...3A **74**
Barry. *Ang* 5E **145**
Barry. *V Glam* 5E **32**
Barry Island. *V Glam* 5E **32**
Barsby. *Leics* 4D **74**
Barsham. *Suff* 2F **67**
Barston. *W Mid* 3G **61**
Bartestree. *Here* 1A **48**
Barthol Chapel. *Abers* 5F **161**
Bartholomew Green. *Essx* ...3H **53**
Barthomley. *Ches E* 5B **84**
Bartley. *Hants* 1B **16**
Bartley Green. *W Mid* 2E **61**
Bartlow. *Cambs* 1F **53**
Barton. *Cambs* 5D **64**
Barton. *Ches W* 5G **83**
Barton. *Cumb* 2F **103**
Barton. *Glos* 3G **49**
Barton. *IOW* 4D **16**
Barton. *Lanc*
  nr. Ormskirk 4B **90**
  nr. Preston 1D **90**
Barton. *N Som* 1G **21**
Barton. *N Yor* 4F **105**
Barton. *Oxon* 5D **50**
Barton. *Torb* 2F **9**
Barton. *Warw* 5F **61**
Barton Bendish. *Norf* 5G **77**
Barton Gate. *Staf* 4F **73**
Barton Green. *Staf* 4F **73**
Barton Hartshorn. *Buck* ...2E **51**
Barton Hill. *N Yor* 3B **100**
Barton in Fabis. *Notts* 2C **74**
Barton in the Beans. *Leics* ...5A **74**
Barton-le-Clay. *C Beds* 2A **52**
Barton-le-Street. *N Yor* 2B **100**
Barton-le-Willows. *N Yor* ...3B **100**
Barton Mills. *Suff* 3G **65**
Barton on Sea. *Hants* 3H **15**
Barton-on-the-Heath. *Warw* ...2A **50**
Barton St David. *Som* 3A **22**
Barton Seagrave. *Nptn* 3F **63**
Barton Stacey. *Hants* 2C **24**
Barton Town. *Devn* 2G **19**
Barton Turf. *Norf* 3F **79**
Barton-Under-Needwood. *Staf* ...4F **73**
Barton-upon-Humber. *N Lin* ...2D **94**
Barton Waterside. *N Lin* ...2D **94**
Barugh Green. *S Yor* 4D **92**
Barway. *Cambs* 3E **65**
Barwell. *Leics* 1B **62**
Barwick. *Herts* 4D **53**
Barwick. *Som* 1A **14**
Barwick in Elmet. *W Yor* ...1D **93**
Baschurch. *Shrp* 3G **71**
Bascote. *Warw* 4B **62**
Basford Green. *Staf* 5D **85**
Bashall Eaves. *Lanc* 5F **97**
Bashall Town. *Lanc* 5G **97**
Bashley. *Hants* 3H **15**
Basildon. *Essx* 2B **40**
Basingstoke. *Hants* 1E **25**
Baslow. *Derbs* 3G **85**
Bason Bridge. *Som* 2G **21**
Bassaleg. *Newp* 3F **33**
Bassenthwaite. *Cumb* 1D **102**
Bassett. *Sotn* 1C **16**
Bassingbourn. *Cambs* 1D **52**
Bassingfield. *Notts* 2D **74**
Bassingham. *Linc* 4G **87**
Bassingthorpe. *Linc* 3G **75**
Bassus Green. *Herts* 3D **52**
Basta. *Shet* 2G **173**
Baston. *Linc* 4A **76**
Bastonford. *Worc* 5C **60**
Bastwick. *Norf* 4G **79**
Batchley. *Worc* 4E **61**
Batchworth. *Herts* 1B **38**
Batcombe. *Dors* 2B **14**
Batcombe. *Som* 3B **22**
Bate Heath. *Ches E* 3A **84**
Bath. *Bath* 187 (5C **34**)

Bathampton. *Bath* 5C **34**
Bathealton. *Som* 4D **20**
Batheaston. *Bath* 5C **34**
Bathford. *Bath* 5C **34**
Bathgate. *W Lot* 3C **128**
Bathley. *Notts* 5E **87**
Bathpool. *Corn* 5C **10**
Bathpool. *Som* 4F **21**
Bathville. *W Lot* 3C **128**
Bathway. *Som* 1A **22**
Batley. *W Yor* 2C **92**
Batsford. *Glos* 2G **49**
Batson. *Devn* 5D **8**
Battersby. *N Yor* 4C **106**
Battersea. *G Lon* 3D **39**
Battisborough Cross. *Devn* ...4C **8**
Battisford. *Suff* 5C **66**
Battisford Tye. *Suff* 5C **66**
Battle. *E Sus* 4B **28**
Battle. *Powy* 2D **46**
Battleborough. *Som* 1G **21**
Battledown. *Glos* 3E **49**
Battlefield. *Shrp* 4H **71**
Battlesbridge. *Essx* 1B **40**
Battlesden. *C Beds* 3H **51**
Battlesea Green. *Suff* 3E **66**
Battleton. *Som* 4C **20**
Battram. *Leics* 5B **74**
Battramsley. *Hants* 3B **16**
Batt's Corner. *Surr* 2G **25**
Bauds of Cullen. *Mor* 2B **160**
Baugh. *Arg* 4B **138**
Baughton. *Worc* 1D **49**
Baughurst. *Hants* 5D **36**
Baulking. *Oxon* 2B **36**
Baumber. *Linc* 3B **88**
Baunton. *Glos* 5F **49**
Baverstock. *Wilts* 3F **23**
Bawburgh. *Norf* 5D **78**
Bawdeswell. *Norf* 3C **78**
Bawdrip. *Som* 3G **21**
Bawdsey. *Suff* 1G **55**
Bawsey. *Norf* 4F **77**
Bawtry. *S Yor* 1D **86**
Baxenden. *Lanc* 2F **91**
Baxterley. *Warw* 1G **61**
Baxter's Green. *Suff* 5G **65**
Bay. *High* 3B **154**
Baybridge. *Hants* 4D **24**
Baybridge. *Nmbd* 4C **114**
Baycliff. *Cumb* 2B **96**
Baydon. *Wilts* 4A **36**
Bayford. *Herts* 5D **52**
Bayford. *Som* 4C **22**
Bayles. *Cumb* 5A **114**
Baylham. *Suff* 5D **66**
Baynard's Green. *Oxon* 3D **50**
Bayston Hill. *Shrp* 5G **71**
Baythorne End. *Essx* 1H **53**
Baythorpe. *Linc* 1B **76**
Bayton. *Worc* 3A **60**
Bayton Common. *Worc* 3B **60**
Bayworth. *Oxon* 5D **50**
Beach. *S Glo* 4C **34**
Beachamwell. *Norf* 5G **77**
Beachley. *Glos* 2A **34**
Beacon. *Devn* 2E **13**
Beacon End. *Essx* 3C **54**
Beacon Hill. *Surr* 3G **25**
Beacon's Bottom. *Buck* ...2F **37**
Beaconsfield. *Buck* 1A **38**
Beacrabhaic. *W Isl* 8D **171**
Beadlam. *N Yor* 1A **100**
Beadnell. *Nmbd* 2G **121**
Beaford. *Devn* 1F **11**
Beal. *Nmbd* 5G **131**
Beal. *N Yor* 2F **93**
Bealsmill. *Corn* 5D **10**
Beam Hill. *Staf* 3G **73**
Beaminster. *Dors* 2H **13**
Beamond End. *Buck* 1A **38**
Beamsley. *N Yor* 4C **98**
Bean. *Kent* 3G **39**
Beanacre. *Wilts* 5E **35**
Beanley. *Nmbd* 3E **121**
Beaquoy. *Orkn* 5C **172**
Beardwood. *Bkbn* 2E **91**
Beare Green. *Surr* 1C **26**
Bearley. *Warw* 4F **61**
Bearpark. *Dur* 5F **115**
Bearsbridge. *Nmbd* 4A **114**
Bearsden. *E Dun* 2G **127**
Bearsted. *Kent* 5B **40**
Bearstone. *Shrp* 2B **72**
Bearwood. *Pool* 3F **15**
Bearwood. *W Mid* 2E **61**
Beattock. *Dum* 4C **118**
Beauchamp Roding. *Essx* ...4F **53**
Beauchief. *S Yor* 2H **85**
Beaufort. *Blae* 4E **47**
Beaulieu. *Hants* 2B **16**
Beauly. *High* 4H **157**
Beaumaris. *IOA* 3F **81**
Beaumont. *Cumb* 4E **113**
Beaumont. *Essx* 3E **55**
Beaumont Hill. *Darl* 3F **105**
Beaumont Leys. *Leic* 5C **74**
Beausale. *Warw* 3G **61**
Beauworth. *Hants* 4D **24**
Beaworthy. *Devn* 3E **11**
Beazley End. *Essx* 3H **53**
Bebington. *Mers* 2F **83**
Bebside. *Nmbd* 1F **115**
Beccles. *Suff* 2G **67**
Becconsall. *Lanc* 2C **90**
Beckbury. *Shrp* 5B **72**
Beckenham. *G Lon* 4E **39**

Beckermet. *Cumb* 4B **102**
Beckett End. *Norf* 1G **65**
Beck Foot. *Cumb* 5H **103**
Beckfoot. *Cumb*
  nr. Broughton in Furness ...1A **96**
  nr. Seascale 4C **102**
  nr. Silloth 5B **112**
Beckford. *Worc* 2E **49**
Beckhampton. *Wilts* 5F **35**
Beck Hole. *N Yor* 4F **107**
Beckingham. *Linc* 5F **87**
Beckingham. *Notts* 1E **87**
Beckington. *Som* 1D **22**
Beckley. *E Sus* 3C **28**
Beckley. *Hants* 3H **15**
Beckley. *Oxon* 4D **50**
Beck Row. *Suff* 3F **65**
Beck Side. *Cumb*
  nr. Cartmel 1C **96**
  nr. Ulverston 1B **96**
Beckside. *Cumb* 1F **97**
Beckton. *G Lon* 2F **39**
Beckwithshaw. *N Yor* 4E **99**
Becontree. *G Lon* 2F **39**
Bedale. *N Yor* 1E **99**
Bedburn. *Dur* 1E **105**
Bedchester. *Dors* 1D **14**
Beddau. *Rhon* 3D **32**
Beddgelert. *Gwyn* 1E **69**
Beddingham. *E Sus* 5F **27**
Beddington. *G Lon* 4E **39**
Bedfield. *Suff* 4E **66**
Bedford. *Bed* 188 (1A **52**)
Bedford. *G Man* 1A **84**
Bedham. *W Sus* 3B **26**
Bedhampton. *Hants* 2F **17**
Bedingfield. *Suff* 4D **66**
Bedingham Green. *Norf* ...1E **67**
Bedlam. *N Yor* 3E **99**
Bedlar's Green. *Essx* 3F **53**
Bedlington. *Nmbd* 1F **115**
Bedlinog. *Mer T* 5D **46**
Bedminster. *Bris* 4A **34**
Bedmond. *Herts* 5A **52**
Bednall. *Staf* 4D **72**
Bedrule. *Bord* 3A **120**
Bedstone. *Shrp* 3F **59**
Bedwas. *Cphy* 3E **33**
Bedwellty. *Cphy* 5E **47**
Bedworth. *Warw* 2A **62**
Beeby. *Leics* 5D **74**
Beech. *Hants* 3E **25**
Beech. *Staf* 2C **72**
Beechcliffe. *W Yor* 5C **98**
Beech Hill. *W Ber* 5E **37**
Beechingstoke. *Wilts* 1F **23**
Beedon. *W Ber* 4C **36**
Beeford. *E Yor* 4F **101**
Beeley. *Derbs* 4G **85**
Beelsby. *NE Lin* 4F **95**
Beenham. *W Ber* 5D **36**
Beeny. *Corn* 3B **10**
Beer. *Devn* 4F **13**
Beer. *Som* 3H **21**
Beercrocombe. *Som* 4G **21**
Beer Hackett. *Dors* 1B **14**
Beesands. *Devn* 4E **9**
Beesby. *Linc* 2D **88**
Beeson. *Devn* 4E **9**
Beeston. *C Beds* 1B **52**
Beeston. *Ches W* 5H **83**
Beeston. *Norf* 4B **78**
Beeston. *Notts* 2C **74**
Beeston. *W Yor* 1C **92**
Beeston Regis. *Norf* 1D **78**
Beeswing. *Dum* 3F **111**
Beetham. *Cumb* 2D **97**
Beetham. *Som* 1F **13**
Beetley. *Norf* 4B **78**
Beffcote. *Staf* 4C **72**
Began. *Card* 3F **33**
Begbroke. *Oxon* 4C **50**
Begdale. *Cambs* 5D **76**
Begelly. *Pemb* 4F **43**
Beggar Hill. *Essx* 5G **53**
Beggar's Bush. *Powy* 4E **59**
Beggearn Huish. *Som* 3D **20**
Beguildy. *Powy* 3D **58**
Beighton. *Norf* 5F **79**
Beighton. *S Yor* 2B **86**
Beighton Hill. *Derbs* 5G **85**
Beinn Casgro. *W Isl* 5G **171**
Beith. *N Ayr* 4E **127**
Bekesbourne. *Kent* 5F **41**
Belaugh. *Norf* 4E **79**
Belbroughton. *Worc* 3D **60**
Belchalwell. *Dors* 2C **14**
Belchalwell Street. *Dors* ...2C **14**
Belchamp Otten. *Essx* 1B **54**
Belchamp St Paul. *Essx* ...1A **54**
Belchamp Walter. *Essx* 1B **54**
Belchford. *Linc* 3B **88**
Belfatton. *Abers* 3H **161**
Belford. *Nmbd* 1F **121**
Belgrano. *Cnwy* 3B **82**
Belhaven. *E Lot* 2C **130**
Belhelvie. *Abers* 2G **153**
Belhinnie. *Abers* 1B **152**
Belladrum. *High* 4H **157**
Bellamore. *S Ayr* 1H **109**
Bellanoch. *Arg* 4F **133**
Bell Busk. *N Yor* 4B **98**
Belleau. *Linc* 3D **88**
Belleheiglash. *Mor* 5F **159**
Bell End. *Worc* 3D **60**
Bellerby. *N Yor* 5E **105**
Bellerby Camp. *N Yor* 5D **105**
Belmesthorpe. *Rut* 4H **75**
Belmont. *Blkbn* 3E **91**
Belmont. *G Lon* 4D **38**
Belmont. *Shet* 1G **173**
Belnacraig. *Abers* 2A **152**
Belowda. *Corn* 2D **6**
Belper. *Derbs* 1A **74**
Belper Lane End. *Derbs* ...1A **74**
Belphin. *Denb* 3C **82**
Belsay. *Nmbd* 2E **115**
Belsford. *Devn* 3D **9**
Belsize. *Herts* 5A **52**
Belstead. *Suff* 1E **55**
Belston. *S Ayr* 2C **116**
Belstone. *Devn* 3G **11**
Belstone Corner. *Devn* 3G **11**
Belthorn. *Bkbn* 2F **91**
Beltinge. *Kent* 4F **41**
Beltoft. *N Lin* 4B **94**
Belton. *Leics* 3B **74**
Belton. *Linc* 2G **75**
Belton. *N Lin* 4A **94**
Belton. *Norf* 5G **79**
Belton-in-Rutland. *Rut* 5F **75**
Beltring. *Kent* 1A **28**
Belts of Collonach. *Abers* ...4D **152**
Belvedere. *G Lon* 3F **39**
Belvoir. *Leics* 2F **75**
Bembridge. *IOW* 4E **17**
Bemersyde. *Bord* 1H **119**
Bemerton. *Wilts* 3G **23**
Bempton. *E Yor* 2F **101**
Benacre. *Suff* 2H **67**
Ben Alder Lodge. *High* 1D **142**
Ben Armine Lodge. *High* ...2E **165**
Benbecula Airport. *W Isl* ...3C **170**
Benbuie. *Dum* 5G **117**
Benderloch. *Arg* 5D **140**
Bendish. *Herts* 3B **52**
Bendronaig Lodge. *High* ...5C **156**
Benenden. *Kent* 2C **28**
Benfieldside. *Dur* 4D **115**
Bengate. *Norf* 3F **79**
Bengeworth. *Worc* 1F **49**
Benhall Green. *Suff* 4F **67**
Benholm. *Abers* 2H **145**
Beningbrough. *N Yor* 4H **99**
Benington. *Herts* 3C **52**
Benington. *Linc* 1C **76**
Benington Sea End. *Linc* ...1D **76**
Benllech. *IOA* 2E **81**
Benmore Lodge. *High* 2H **163**
Bennacott. *Corn* 3C **10**
Bennah. *Devn* 4B **12**
Bennecarrigan. *N Ayr* 3D **122**
Bennethead. *Cumb* 2F **103**
Benniworth. *Linc* 2B **88**
Benover. *Kent* 1B **28**
Benson. *Oxon* 2E **36**
Benston. *Shet* 6F **173**
Bent. *Abers* 1F **145**
Benthall. *Shrp* 5A **72**
Bentham. *Glos* 4E **49**
Benthoul. *Aber* 3F **153**
Bentlawnt. *Shrp* 5F **71**
Bentley. *E Yor* 1D **94**
Bentley. *Hants* 2F **25**
Bentley. *Suff* 2E **55**
Bentley. *S Yor* 4F **93**
Bentley. *Warw* 1G **61**
Bentley. *W Mid* 1E **61**
Bentley Heath. *Herts* 1C **38**
Bentley Heath. *W Mid* 3F **61**
Benton. *Devn* 3G **19**
Bentpath. *Dum* 5F **119**
Bents. *W Lot* 3C **128**
Bentworth. *Hants* 2E **25**
Benvie. *D'dee* 5C **144**
Benville. *Dors* 2A **14**
Benwell. *Tyne* 3F **115**
Benwick. *Cambs* 1C **64**
Beoley. *Worc* 4E **61**
Beoraidbeg. *High* 4E **147**
Bepton. *W Sus* 4G **25**
Berden. *Essx* 3E **53**

Bellfield. *S Lan* ...1H **117**
Belliehill. *Ang* ...2E **145**
Bellingdon. *Buck* ...5H **51**
Bellingham. *Nmbd* ...1B **114**
Bellmount. *Norf* ...3E **77**
Bellochantuy. *Arg* ...2A **122**
Bellsbank. *E Ayr* ...4D **117**
Bell's Cross. *Suff* ...5D **66**
Bellshill. *N Lan* ...4A **128**
Bellshill. *Nmbd* ...1F **121**
Bellside. *N Lan* ...4B **128**
Bellspool. *Bord* ...1D **118**
Bellsquarry. *W Lot* ...3D **128**
Bells Yew Green. *E Sus* ...2H **27**
Belmaduthy. *High* ...3A **158**
Belmesthorpe. *Rut* ...4H **75**
Belmont. *Bkbn* ...3E **91**
Belmont. *Shet* ...1G **173**
Belmont. *S Ayr* ...2C **116**
Belnacraig. *Abers* ...2A **152**
Belnie. *Linc* ...2B **76**
Belowda. *Corn* ...2D **6**
Belper. *Derbs* ...1A **74**
Belper Lane End. *Derbs* ...1H **73**
Belph. *Derbs* ...3C **86**
Belsay. *Nmbd* ...2E **115**
Belsford. *Devn* ...3D **8**
Belsize. *Herts* ...5A **52**
Belstead. *Suff* ...1E **55**
Belston. *S Ayr* ...2C **116**
Belstone. *Devn* ...3G **11**
Belstone Corner. *Devn* ...3G **11**
Belthorn. *Lanc* ...2F **91**
Beltinge. *Kent* ...4F **41**
Beltoft. *N Lin* ...4B **94**
Belton. *Leics* ...3B **74**
Belton. *Linc* ...2G **75**
Belton. *Norf* ...5G **79**
Belton. *N Lin* ...4A **94**
Belton-in-Rutland. *Rut* ...5F **75**
Beltring. *Kent* ...1A **28**
Belts of Collonach. *Abers* ...4D **152**
Belvedere. *G Lon* ...3F **39**
Belvoir. *Leics* ...2F **75**
Bembridge. *IOW* ...4E **17**
Bemersyde. *Bord* ...1H **119**
Bemerton. *Wilts* ...3G **23**
Bempton. *E Yor* ...2F **101**
Benacre. *Suff* ...2H **67**
Ben Alder Lodge. *High* ...1C **142**
Ben Armine Lodge. *High* ...2E **164**
Benbecula Airport. *W Isl* ...3C **170**
Benbuie. *Dum* ...5G **117**
Benchill. *G Man* ...2C **84**
Benderloch. *Arg* ...5D **140**
Bendish. *Herts* ...3B **52**
Bendronaig Lodge. *High* ...5C **156**
Benenden. *Kent* ...2C **28**
Benfieldside. *Dur* ...4D **115**
Bengate. *Norf* ...3F **79**
Bengeworth. *Worc* ...1F **49**
Benhall Green. *Suff* ...4F **67**
Benholm. *Abers* ...2H **145**
Beningbrough. *N Yor* ...4H **99**
Benington. *Herts* ...3C **52**
Benington. *Linc* ...1C **76**
Benington Sea End. *Linc* ...1D **76**
Benllech. *IOA* ...2E **81**
Benmore Lodge. *High* ...2H **163**
Bennacott. *Corn* ...3C **10**
Bennah. *Devn* ...4B **12**
Bennecarrigan. *N Ayr* ...3D **122**
Bennethead. *Cumb* ...2F **103**
Benniworth. *Linc* ...2B **88**
Benover. *Kent* ...1B **28**
Benson. *Oxon* ...2E **36**
Benston. *Shet* ...6F **173**
Benstonhall. *Orkn* ...4E **172**
Bent. *Abers* ...1F **145**
Benthall. *Shrp* ...5A **72**
Bentham. *Glos* ...4E **49**
Bentlawnt. *Shrp* ...5F **71**
Bentley. *E Yor* ...1D **94**
Bentley. *Hants* ...2F **25**
Bentley. *S Yor* ...4F **93**
Bentley. *Suff* ...2E **54**
Bentley. *Warw* ...1G **61**
Bentley. *W Mid* ...1D **61**
Bentley Heath. *Herts* ...1D **38**
Bentley Heath. *W Mid* ...3F **61**
Bentpath. *Dum* ...5F **119**
Bents. *W Lot* ...3C **128**
Bentworth. *Hants* ...2E **25**
Benvie. *D'dee* ...5C **144**
Benville. *Dors* ...2A **14**
Benwell. *Tyne* ...3F **115**
Benwick. *Cambs* ...1C **64**
Beoley. *Worc* ...4E **61**
Beoraidbeg. *High* ...4E **147**
Bepton. *W Sus* ...1G **17**
Berden. *Essx* ...3E **53**
Bere Alston. *Devn* ...2A **8**
Bere Ferrers. *Devn* ...2A **8**
Berepper. *Corn* ...4D **4**
Bere Regis. *Dors* ...3D **14**
Bergh Apton. *Norf* ...5F **79**
Berinsfield. *Oxon* ...2D **36**
Berkeley. *Glos* ...2B **34**
Berkhamsted. *Herts* ...5H **51**
Berkley. *Som* ...2D **22**
Berkswell. *W Mid* ...3G **61**
Bermondsey. *G Lon* ...3E **39**
Bernera. *High* ...1G **147**
Bernice. *Arg* ...4A **134**
Bernisdale. *High* ...3D **154**
Berrick Salome. *Oxon* ...2E **36**
Berriedale. *High* ...1H **165**
Berrier. *Cumb* ...2E **103**
Berriew. *Powy* ...5D **70**
Berrington. *Nmbd* ...5G **131**
Berrington. *Shrp* ...5H **71**

Berrington. *Worc* ...4H **59**
Berrington Green. *Worc* ...4H **59**
Berrington Law. *Nmbd* ...5F **131**
Berrow. *Som* ...1G **21**
Berrow Green. *Worc* ...5B **60**
Berry Cross. *Devn* ...1E **11**
Berry Down Cross. *Devn* ...2F **19**
Berry Hill. *Glos* ...4A **48**
Berry Hill. *Pemb* ...1A **44**
Berryhillock. *Mor* ...2C **160**
Berrynarbor. *Devn* ...2F **19**
Berry Pomeroy. *Devn* ...2E **9**
Berryscaur. *Dum* ...5D **118**
Berry's Green. *G Lon* ...5F **39**
Bersham. *Wrex* ...1F **71**
Berthengam. *Flin* ...3D **82**
Berwick. *E Sus* ...5G **27**
Berwick Bassett. *Wilts* ...4G **35**
Berwick Hill. *Nmbd* ...2E **115**
Berwick St James. *Wilts* ...3F **23**
Berwick St John. *Wilts* ...4E **23**
Berwick St Leonard. *Wilts* ...3E **23**
Berwick-upon-Tweed.
  Nmbd ...4F **131**
Berwyn. *Den* ...1D **70**
Bescaby. *Leics* ...3F **75**
Bescar. *Lanc* ...3B **90**
Besford. *Worc* ...1E **49**
Bessacarr. *S Yor* ...4G **93**
Bessels Leigh. *Oxon* ...5C **50**
Bessingby. *E Yor* ...3F **101**
Bessingham. *Norf* ...2D **78**
Best Beech Hill. *E Sus* ...2H **27**
Besthorpe. *Norf* ...1C **66**
Besthorpe. *Notts* ...4F **87**
Bestwood Village. *Notts* ...1C **74**
Beswick. *E Yor* ...5E **101**
Betchworth. *Surr* ...5D **38**
Bethania. *Cdgn* ...4E **57**
Bethania. *Gwyn*
  nr. Blaenau Ffestiniog ...1G **69**
  nr. Caernarfon ...5F **81**
Bethel. *Gwyn*
  nr. Bala ...2B **70**
  nr. Caernarfon ...4E **81**
Bethel. *IOA* ...3C **80**
Bethersden. *Kent* ...1D **28**
Bethesda. *Gwyn* ...4F **81**
Bethesda. *Pemb* ...3E **43**
Bethlehem. *Carm* ...3G **45**
Bethnal Green. *G Lon* ...2E **39**
Betley. *Staf* ...1B **72**
Betsham. *Kent* ...3H **39**
Betteshanger. *Kent* ...5H **41**
Bettiscombe. *Dors* ...3H **13**
Bettisfield. *Wrex* ...2G **71**
Betton. *Shrp* ...2A **72**
Betton Strange. *Shrp* ...5H **71**
Bettws. *B'end* ...3C **32**
Bettws. *Newp* ...2F **33**
Bettws Bledrws. *Cdgn* ...5E **57**
Bettws Cedewain. *Powy* ...1D **58**
Bettws Gwerfil Goch. *Den* ...1C **70**
Bettws Ifan. *Cdgn* ...1D **44**
Bettws Newydd. *Mon* ...5G **47**
Bettws. *Carm* ...4G **45**
Betws Garmon. *Gwyn* ...5E **81**
Betws-y-Coed. *Cnwy* ...5G **81**
Betws-yn-Rhos. *Cnwy* ...3B **82**
Beulah. *Cdgn* ...1C **44**
Beulah. *Powy* ...5B **58**
Beul an Atha. *Arg* ...3B **124**
Bevendean. *Brig* ...5E **27**
Bevercotes. *Notts* ...3E **86**
Beverley. *E Yor* ...1D **94**
Beverston. *Glos* ...2D **34**
Bevington. *Glos* ...2B **34**
Bewaldeth. *Cumb* ...1D **102**
Bewcastle. *Cumb* ...2G **113**
Bewdley. *Worc* ...3B **60**
Bewerley. *N Yor* ...3D **98**
Bewholme. *E Yor* ...4F **101**
Bexfield. *Norf* ...3C **78**
Bexhill. *E Sus* ...5B **28**
Bexley. *G Lon* ...3F **39**
Bexleyheath. *G Lon* ...3F **39**
Bexleyhill. *W Sus* ...3A **26**
Bexwell. *Norf* ...5F **77**
Beyton. *Suff* ...4B **66**
Bhalton. *W Isl* ...4C **171**
Bhatarsaigh. *W Isl* ...9B **170**
Bibbington. *Derbs* ...3E **85**
Bibury. *Glos* ...5G **49**
Bicester. *Oxon* ...3D **50**
Bickenhall. *Som* ...1F **13**
Bickenhill. *W Mid* ...2F **61**
Bicker. *Linc* ...2B **76**
Bicker Bar. *Linc* ...2B **76**
Bicker Gauntlet. *Linc* ...2B **76**
Bickershaw. *G Man* ...4E **91**
Bickerstaffe. *Lanc* ...4C **90**
Bickerton. *Ches E* ...5H **83**
Bickerton. *Nmbd* ...4D **121**
Bickerton. *N Yor* ...4G **99**
Bickford. *Staf* ...4C **72**
Bickington. *Devn*
  nr. Barnstaple ...3F **19**
  nr. Newton Abbot ...5A **12**
Bickleigh. *Devn*
  nr. Plymouth ...2B **8**
  nr. Tiverton ...2C **12**
Bickleton. *Devn* ...3F **19**
Bickley. *N Yor* ...5G **107**
Bickley Moss. *Ches W* ...1H **71**
Bickmarsh. *Worc* ...1G **49**
Bicknacre. *Essx* ...5A **54**
Bicknoller. *Som* ...3E **20**
Bicknor. *Kent* ...5C **40**
Bickton. *Hants* ...1G **15**
Bicton. *Here* ...4G **59**

Bicton. *Shrp*
  nr. Bishop's Castle ...2E **59**
  nr. Shrewsbury ...4G **71**
Bicton Heath. *Shrp* ...4G **71**
Bidborough. *Kent* ...1G **27**
Biddenden. *Kent* ...2C **28**
Biddenden Green. *Kent* ...1C **28**
Biddenham. *Bed* ...5H **63**
Biddestone. *Wilts* ...4D **34**
Biddisham. *Som* ...1G **21**
Biddlesden. *Buck* ...1E **51**
Biddlestone. *Nmbd* ...4D **120**
Biddulph. *Staf* ...5C **84**
Biddulph Moor. *Staf* ...5D **84**
Bideford. *Devn* ...4E **19**
Bidford-on-Avon. *Warw* ...5E **61**
Bidlake. *Devn* ...4F **11**
Bidston. *Mers* ...2E **83**
Bielby. *E Yor* ...5B **100**
Bieldside. *Aber* ...3F **153**
Bierley. *IOW* ...5D **16**
Bierley. *W Yor* ...1B **92**
Bierton. *Buck* ...4G **51**
Bigbury. *Devn* ...4C **8**
Bigbury-on-Sea. *Devn* ...4C **8**
Bigby. *Linc* ...4D **94**
Biggar. *Cumb* ...3A **96**
Biggar. *S Lan* ...1C **118**
Biggin. *Derbs*
  nr. Hartington ...5F **85**
  nr. Hulland ...1G **73**
Biggin. *N Yor* ...1F **93**
Biggings. *Shet* ...5C **173**
Biggin Hill. *G Lon* ...5F **39**
Biggleswade. *C Beds* ...1B **52**
Bighouse. *High* ...2A **168**
Bighton. *Hants* ...3E **24**
Biglands. *Cumb* ...4D **112**
Bignall End. *Staf* ...5C **84**
Bignor. *W Sus* ...4A **26**
Bigrigg. *Cumb* ...3B **102**
Big Sand. *High* ...1G **155**
Bigton. *Shet* ...9E **173**
Bilberry. *Corn* ...3E **6**
Bilborough. *Nott* ...1C **74**
Bilbrook. *Som* ...2D **20**
Bilbrook. *Staf* ...5C **72**
Bilbrough. *N Yor* ...5H **99**
Bilbster. *High* ...3E **169**
Bilby. *Notts* ...2D **86**
Bildershaw. *Dur* ...2F **105**
Bildeston. *Suff* ...1C **54**
Billericay. *Essx* ...1A **40**
Billesdon. *Leics* ...5E **74**
Billesley. *Warw* ...5F **61**
Billingborough. *Linc* ...2A **76**
Billinge. *Mers* ...4D **90**
Billingford. *Norf*
  nr. Dereham ...3C **78**
  nr. Diss ...3D **66**
Billingham. *Stoc T* ...2B **106**
Billinghay. *Linc* ...5A **88**
Billingley. *S Yor* ...4E **93**
Billingshurst. *W Sus* ...3B **26**
Billingsley. *Shrp* ...2B **60**
Billington. *C Beds* ...3H **51**
Billington. *Lanc* ...1F **91**
Billington. *Staf* ...3C **72**
Billockby. *Norf* ...4G **79**
Billy Row. *Dur* ...1E **105**
Bilsborrow. *Lanc* ...5E **97**
Bilsby. *Linc* ...3D **88**
Bilsham. *W Sus* ...5A **26**
Bilsington. *Kent* ...2E **29**
Bilson Green. *Glos* ...4B **48**
Bilsthorpe. *Notts* ...4D **86**
Bilston. *Midl* ...3F **129**
Bilston. *W Mid* ...1D **60**
Bilstone. *Leics* ...5A **74**
Bilting. *Kent* ...1E **29**
Bilton. *E Yor* ...1E **95**
Bilton. *Nmbd* ...3G **121**
Bilton. *N Yor* ...4F **99**
Bilton. *Warw* ...3B **62**
Bilton in Ainsty. *N Yor* ...5G **99**
Bimbister. *Orkn* ...6C **172**
Binbrook. *Linc* ...1B **88**
Binchester. *Dur* ...1F **105**
Bincombe. *Dors* ...4B **14**
Bindal. *High* ...5G **165**
Binegar. *Som* ...2B **22**
Bines Green. *W Sus* ...4C **26**
Binfield. *Brac* ...4G **37**
Binfield Heath. *Oxon* ...4F **37**
Bingfield. *Nmbd* ...2C **114**
Bingham. *Notts* ...2E **74**
Bingham's Melcombe. *Dors* ...2C **14**
Bingley. *W Yor* ...1B **92**
Bings Heath. *Shrp* ...4H **71**
Binham. *Norf* ...2B **78**
Binley. *Hants* ...1C **24**
Binley. *W Mid* ...3A **62**
Binnegar. *Dors* ...4D **15**
Binniehill. *Falk* ...2B **128**
Binsoe. *N Yor* ...2E **99**
Binstead. *IOW* ...3D **16**
Binsted. *Hants* ...2F **25**
Binsted. *W Sus* ...5A **26**
Binton. *Warw* ...5F **61**
Bintree. *Norf* ...3C **78**
Binweston. *Shrp* ...5F **71**
Birch. *Essx* ...4C **54**
Birch. *G Man* ...4G **91**
Birchall. *Staf* ...5D **85**
Bircham Newton. *Norf* ...2G **77**
Bircham Tofts. *Norf* ...2G **77**
Birchanger. *Essx* ...3F **53**
Birchburn. *N Ayr* ...3D **122**
Birch Cross. *Staf* ...2F **73**
Bircher. *Here* ...4G **59**
Birch Green. *Essx* ...4C **54**

Birchgrove. *Card* ...3E **33**
Birchgrove. *Swan* ...3G **31**
Birch Heath. *Ches W* ...4H **83**
Birch Hill. *Ches W* ...3H **83**
Birchill. *Devn* ...2G **13**
Birchington. *Kent* ...4G **41**
Birchley Heath. *Warw* ...1G **61**
Birchmoor. *Warw* ...5G **73**
Birchmoor Green. *C Beds* ...2H **51**
Birchover. *Derbs* ...4G **85**
Birch Vale. *Derbs* ...2E **85**
Birchview. *Mor* ...5F **159**
Birchwood. *Linc* ...4G **87**
Birchwood. *Som* ...1F **13**
Birchwood. *Warr* ...1A **84**
Bircotes. *Notts* ...1D **86**
Birdbrook. *Essx* ...1H **53**
Birdham. *W Sus* ...2G **17**
Birdholme. *Derbs* ...4A **86**
Birdingbury. *Warw* ...4B **62**
Birdlip. *Glos* ...4E **49**
Birdsall. *N Yor* ...3C **100**
Birds Edge. *W Yor* ...4C **92**
Birds Green. *Essx* ...5F **53**
Birdsgreen. *Shrp* ...2B **60**
Birdsmoorgate. *Dors* ...2G **13**
Birdston. *E Dun* ...2H **127**
Birdwell. *S Yor* ...4D **92**
Birdwood. *Glos* ...4C **48**
Birgham. *Bord* ...1B **120**
Birichen. *High* ...4E **165**
Birkby. *Cumb* ...1B **102**
Birkby. *N Yor* ...4A **106**
Birkdale. *Mers* ...3B **90**
Birkenhead. *Mers* ...2F **83**
Birkenhills. *Abers* ...4E **161**
Birkenshaw. *N Lan* ...3H **127**
Birkenshaw. *W Yor* ...2C **92**
Birkhall. *Abers* ...4H **151**
Birkhill. *Ang* ...5C **144**
Birkholme. *Linc* ...3G **75**
Birkin. *N Yor* ...2F **93**
Birley. *Here* ...5G **59**
Birling. *Kent* ...4A **40**
Birling. *Nmbd* ...4G **121**
Birling Gap. *E Sus* ...5G **27**
Birlingham. *Worc* ...1E **49**
Birmingham. *W Mid* ...**188** (2E **61**)
Birmingham Airport.
  W Mid ...**216** (2F **61**)
Birnam. *Per* ...4H **143**
Birse. *Abers* ...4C **152**
Birsemore. *Abers* ...4C **152**
Birstall. *Leics* ...5C **74**
Birstall. *W Yor* ...2C **92**
Birstall Smithies. *W Yor* ...2C **92**
Birstwith. *N Yor* ...4E **99**
Birthorpe. *Linc* ...2A **76**
Birtle. *G Man* ...3G **91**
Birtley. *Here* ...4F **59**
Birtley. *Nmbd* ...2B **114**
Birtley. *Tyne* ...4F **115**
Birtsmorton. *Worc* ...2D **48**
Birts Street. *Worc* ...2C **48**
Bisbrooke. *Rut* ...1F **63**
Bisham. *Wind* ...3G **37**
Bishampton. *Worc* ...5D **61**
Bish Mill. *Devn* ...4H **19**
Bishop Auckland. *Dur* ...2F **105**
Bishopbridge. *Linc* ...1H **87**
Bishopbriggs. *E Dun* ...2H **127**
Bishop Burton. *E Yor* ...1C **94**
Bishopdown. *Wilts* ...3G **23**
Bishop Middleham. *Dur* ...1A **106**
Bishopmill. *Mor* ...2G **159**
Bishop Monkton. *N Yor* ...3F **99**
Bishop Norton. *Linc* ...1G **87**
Bishopsbourne. *Kent* ...5F **41**
Bishops Cannings. *Wilts* ...5F **35**
Bishop's Castle. *Shrp* ...2F **59**
Bishop's Caundle. *Dors* ...1B **14**
Bishop's Cleeve. *Glos* ...3E **49**
Bishop's Down. *Dors* ...1B **14**
Bishop's Frome. *Here* ...1B **48**
Bishop's Green. *Essx* ...4G **53**
Bishop's Green. *Hants* ...5D **36**
Bishop's Hull. *Som* ...4F **21**
Bishop's Itchington. *Warw* ...5A **62**
Bishops Lydeard. *Som* ...4E **21**
Bishop's Norton. *Glos* ...3D **48**
Bishop's Nympton. *Devn* ...4A **20**
Bishop's Offley. *Staf* ...3B **72**
Bishop's Stortford. *Herts* ...3E **53**
Bishop's Sutton. *Hants* ...3E **24**
Bishop's Tachbrook. *Warw* ...4H **61**
Bishop's Tawton. *Devn* ...3F **19**
Bishopsteignton. *Devn* ...5C **12**
Bishopstoke. *Hants* ...1C **16**
Bishopston. *Swan* ...4E **31**
Bishopstone. *Buck* ...4G **51**
Bishopstone. *E Sus* ...5F **27**
Bishopstone. *Here* ...1H **47**
Bishopstone. *Swin* ...3H **35**
Bishopstone. *Wilts* ...4F **23**
Bishopstrow. *Wilts* ...2D **23**
Bishop Sutton. *Bath* ...1A **22**
Bishop's Waltham. *Hants* ...1D **16**
Bishops Wood. *Staf* ...5C **72**
Bishopswood. *Som* ...1F **13**
Bishopsworth. *Bris* ...5A **34**
Bishop Thornton. *N Yor* ...3E **99**
Bishopthorpe. *York* ...5H **99**
Bishopton. *Darl* ...2A **106**
Bishopton. *Dum* ...5B **110**
Bishopton. *N Yor* ...2E **99**
Bishopton. *Ren* ...2F **127**
Bishopton. *Warw* ...5F **61**
Bishop Wilton. *E Yor* ...4B **100**
Bishton. *Newp* ...3G **33**
Bishton. *Staf* ...3E **73**
Bisley. *Glos* ...5E **49**

Bisley. *Surr* ...5A **38**
Bispham. *Bkpl* ...5C **96**
Bispham Green. *Lanc* ...3C **90**
Bissoe. *Corn* ...4B **6**
Bisterne. *Hants* ...2G **15**
Bisterne Close. *Hants* ...2H **15**
Bitchfield. *Linc* ...3G **75**
Bittadon. *Devn* ...2F **19**
Bittaford. *Devn* ...3C **8**
Bittering. *Norf* ...4B **78**
Bitterley. *Shrp* ...3H **59**
Bitterne. *Sotn* ...1C **16**
Bitteswell. *Leics* ...2C **62**
Bitton. *S Glo* ...5B **34**
Bix. *Oxon* ...3F **37**
Bixter. *Shet* ...6E **173**
Blaby. *Leics* ...1C **62**
Blackawton. *Devn* ...3E **9**
Black Bank. *Cambs* ...2E **65**
Black Barn. *Linc* ...3D **76**
Blackborough. *Devn* ...2D **12**
Blackborough. *Norf* ...4F **77**
Blackborough End. *Norf* ...4F **77**
Black Bourton. *Oxon* ...5A **50**
Blackboys. *E Sus* ...3G **27**
Blackbrook. *Derbs* ...1H **73**
Blackbrook. *Mers* ...1H **83**
Blackbrook. *Staf* ...2B **72**
Blackbrook. *Surr* ...1C **26**
Blackburn. *Abers* ...2F **153**
Blackburn. *Bkbn* ...2E **91**
Blackburn. *W Lot* ...3C **128**
Black Callerton. *Tyne* ...3E **115**
Black Carr. *Norf* ...1C **66**
Black Clauchrie. *S Ayr* ...1H **109**
Black Corries. *High* ...3G **141**
Black Crofts. *Arg* ...5D **140**
Black Cross. *Corn* ...2D **6**
Blackden Heath. *Ches E* ...3B **84**
Blackditch. *Oxon* ...5C **50**
Black Dog. *Devn* ...2B **12**
Blackdog. *Abers* ...2G **153**
Blackdown. *Dors* ...2G **13**
Blackdyke. *Cumb* ...4C **112**
Blacker Hill. *S Yor* ...4D **92**
Blackfen. *G Lon* ...3F **39**
Blackfield. *Hants* ...2C **16**
Blackford. *Cumb* ...3E **113**
Blackford. *Per* ...3A **136**
Blackford. *Shrp* ...2H **59**
Blackford. *Som*
  nr. Burnham-on-Sea ...2H **21**
  nr. Wincanton ...4B **22**
Blackfordby. *Leics* ...4H **73**
Blackgang. *IOW* ...5C **16**
Blackhall. *Edin* ...2F **129**
Blackhall. *Ren* ...3F **127**
Blackhall Colliery. *Dur* ...1B **106**
Blackhall Mill. *Tyne* ...4E **115**
Blackhall Rocks. *Dur* ...1B **106**
Blackham. *E Sus* ...2F **27**
Blackheath. *Essx* ...3D **54**
Blackheath. *G Lon* ...3E **39**
Blackheath. *Suff* ...3G **67**
Blackheath. *Surr* ...1B **26**
Blackheath. *W Mid* ...2D **61**
Black Heddon. *Nmbd* ...2D **115**
Black Hill. *Warw* ...5G **61**
Blackhill. *Abers* ...4H **161**
Blackhill. *High* ...3C **154**
Blackhills. *Abers* ...2G **161**
Blackhills. *High* ...3D **158**
Blackjack. *Linc* ...2B **76**
Blackland. *Wilts* ...5F **35**
Black Lane. *G Man* ...4F **91**
Blackleach. *Lanc* ...1C **90**
Blackley. *G Man* ...4G **91**
Blackley. *W Yor* ...3B **92**
Blacklunans. *Per* ...2A **144**
Blackmill. *B'end* ...3C **32**
Blackmoor. *G Man* ...4E **91**
Blackmoor. *Hants* ...3F **25**
Blackmoor Gate. *Devn* ...2G **19**
Blackmore. *Essx* ...5G **53**
Blackmore End. *Essx* ...2H **53**
Blackmore End. *Herts* ...4B **52**
Black Mount. *Arg* ...4G **141**
Blackness. *Falk* ...2D **128**
Blacknest. *Hants* ...2F **25**
Blackney. *Dors* ...3H **13**
Blacknoll. *Dors* ...4D **14**
Black Notley. *Essx* ...3A **54**
Blacko. *Lanc* ...5A **98**
Black Pill. *Swan* ...3F **31**
Blackpool. *Bkpl* ...**188** (1B **90**)
Blackpool. *Devn* ...4E **9**
Blackpool Corner. *Dors* ...3G **13**
Blackpool Gate. *Cumb* ...2G **113**
Blackridge. *W Lot* ...3B **128**
Blackrock. *Arg* ...3B **124**
Blackrock. *Mon* ...4F **47**
Blackrod. *G Man* ...3E **90**
Blackshaw. *Dum* ...3B **112**
Blackshaw Head. *W Yor* ...2H **91**
Blackshaw Moor. *Staf* ...5E **85**
Blacksmith's Green. *Suff* ...4D **66**
Blacksnape. *Bkbn* ...2F **91**
Blackstone. *W Sus* ...4D **26**
Black Street. *Suff* ...2H **67**
Black Tar. *Pemb* ...4D **43**
Blackthorn. *Oxon* ...4E **50**
Blackthorpe. *Suff* ...4B **66**
Blacktoft. *E Yor* ...2B **94**
Blacktop. *Aber* ...3F **153**
Black Torrington. *Devn* ...2E **11**
Blacktown. *Newp* ...3F **33**
Blackwall Tunnel. *G Lon* ...2E **39**
Blackwater. *Corn* ...4B **6**
Blackwater. *Hants* ...1G **25**
Blackwater. *IOW* ...4D **16**
Blackwater. *Som* ...1F **13**

Blackwaterfoot. N Ayr 3C 122
Blackwell. Darl 3F 105
Blackwell. Derbs
  nr. Alfreton 5B 86
  nr. Buxton 3F 85
Blackwell. Som 4D 20
Blackwell. Warw 1H 49
Blackwell. Worc 3D 61
Blackwood. Cphy 2E 33
Blackwood. Dum 1G 111
Blackwood. S Lan 5A 128
Blackwood Hill. Staf 5D 84
Blacon. Ches W 4F 83
Bladnoch. Dum 4B 110
Bladon. Oxon 4C 50
Blaenannerch. Cdgn 1C 44
Blaenau Dolwyddelan. Cnwy 5F 81
Blaenau Ffestiniog. Gwyn 1G 69
Blaenavon. Torf 5F 47
Blaenawey. Mon 4F 47
Blaen Celyn. Cdgn 5C 56
Blaen Clydach. Rhon 2C 32
Blaencwm. Rhon 2C 32
Blaendulais. Neat 5B 46
Blaenffos. Pemb 1F 43
Blaengarw. B'end 2C 32
Blaen-geuffordd. Cdgn 2F 57
Blaengwrach. Neat 5B 46
Blaengwynfi. Neat 2B 32
Blaenllechau. Rhon 2C 32
Blaenpennal. Cdgn 4F 57
Blaenplwyf. Cdgn 3E 57
Blaenporth. Cdgn 1C 44
Blaenrhondda. Rhon 5C 46
Blaenwaun. Carm 2G 43
Blaen-y-coed. Carm 2H 43
Blagdon. N Som 1A 22
Blagdon. Torb 2E 9
Blagdon Hill. Som 1F 13
Blagill. Cumb 5A 114
Blaguegate. Lanc 4C 90
Blaich. High 1E 141
Blain. High 2A 140
Blaina. Blae 5F 47
Blair Atholl. Per 2F 143
Blair Drummond. Stir 4G 135
Blairgowrie. Per 4A 144
Blairhall. Fife 1D 128
Blairingone. Per 4B 136
Blairlogie. Stir 4H 135
Blairmore. Abers 5B 160
Blairmore. Arg 1C 126
Blairmore. High 3B 166
Blairquhanan. W Dun 1F 127
Blaisdon. Glos 4C 48
Blakebrook. Worc 3C 60
Blakedown. Worc 3C 60
Blake End. Essx 3H 53
Blakemere. Here 1G 47
Blakeney. Glos 5B 48
Blakeney. Norf 1C 78
Blakenhall. Ches E 1B 72
Blakeshall. Worc 2C 60
Blakesley. Nptn 5D 62
Blanchland. Nmbd 4C 114
Blandford Camp. Dors 2E 15
Blandford Forum. Dors 2D 15
Blandford St Mary. Dors 2D 15
Bland Hill. N Yor 4E 98
Blandy. High 2G 167
Blanefield. Stir 2G 127
Blankney. Linc 4H 87
Blantyre. S Lan 4H 127
Blarmachfoldach. High 2E 141
Blarnalearoch. High 4F 163
Blashford. Hants 2G 15
Blaston. Leics 1F 63
Blatchbridge. Som 2C 22
Blathaisbhal. W Isl 1D 170
Blatherwycke. Nptn 1G 63
Blawith. Cumb 1B 96
Blaxhall. Suff 5F 67
Blaxton. S Yor 4G 93
Blaydon. Tyne 3E 115
Bleadney. Som 2H 21
Bleadon. N Som 1G 21
Blean. Kent 4F 41
Bleasby. Linc 2A 88
Bleasby. Notts 1E 74
Bleasby Moor. Linc 2A 88
Blebocraigs. Fife 2G 137
Bleddfa. Powy 4E 58
Bledington. Glos 3H 49
Bledlow. Buck 5F 51
Bledlow Ridge. Buck 2F 37
Blencarn. Cumb 1H 103
Blencogo. Cumb 5C 112
Blendworth. Hants 1F 17
Blennerhasset. Cumb 5C 112
Bletchingdon. Oxon 4D 50
Bletchingley. Surr 5E 39
Bletchley. Mil 2G 51
Bletchley. Shrp 2A 72
Bletherston. Pemb 2E 43
Bletsoe. Bed 5H 63
Blewbury. Oxon 3D 36
Blickling. Norf 3D 78
Blidworth. Notts 5C 86
Blindburn. Nmbd 3C 120
Blindcrake. Cumb 1C 102
Blindley Heath. Surr 1E 27
Blindmoor. Som 1F 13
Blisland. Corn 5B 10
Blissford. Hants 1G 15
Bliss Gate. Worc 3B 60
Blists Hill. Telf 5A 72
Blisworth. Nptn 5E 63
Blithbury. Staf 3E 73
Blitterlees. Cumb 4C 112
Blockley. Glos 2G 49
Blofield. Norf 5F 79

Blofield Heath. Norf 4F 79
Blo' Norton. Norf 3C 66
Bloomfield. Bord 2H 119
Blore. Staf 1F 73
Blount's Green. Staf 2E 73
Bloxham. Oxon 2C 50
Bloxholm. Linc 5H 87
Bloxwich. W Mid 5D 73
Bloxworth. Dors 3D 15
Blubberhouses. N Yor 4D 98
Blue Anchor. Som 2D 20
Blue Anchor. Swan 3E 31
Blue Bell Hill. Kent 4B 40
Blue Row. Essx 4D 54
Bluetown. Kent 5D 40
Blundeston. Suff 1H 67
Blunham. C Beds 5A 64
Blunsdon St Andrew. Swin 3G 35
Bluntington. Worc 3C 60
Bluntisham. Cambs 3C 64
Blunts. Corn 2H 7
Blurton. Stoke 1C 72
Blyborough. Linc 1G 87
Blyford. Suff 3G 67
Blymhill. Staf 4C 72
Blymhill Lawns. Staf 4F 73
Blyth. Nmbd 1G 115
Blyth. Notts 2D 86
Blyth. Bord 5E 129
Blyth Bank. Bord 5E 129
Blyth Bridge. Bord 5E 129
Blythburgh. Suff 3G 67
The Blythe. Staf 3E 73
Blythe Bridge. Staf 1D 72
Blythe Marsh. Staf 1D 72
Blyton. Linc 1F 87
Boarhills. Fife 2H 137
Boarhunt. Hants 2E 16
Boar's Head. G Man 4D 90
Boarshead. E Sus 2G 27
Boars Hill. Oxon 5C 50
Boarstall. Buck 4E 51
Boasley Cross. Devn 3F 11
Boath. High 1H 157
Boat of Garten. High 2D 150
Bobbing. Kent 4C 40
Bobbington. Staf 1C 60
Bobbingworth. Essx 5F 53
Bocaddon. Corn 3F 7
Bocking. Essx 3A 54
Bocking Churchstreet. Essx 3A 54
Boddam. Abers 4H 161
Boddam. Shet 10E 173
Boddington. Glos 3D 49
Bodedern. IOA 2C 80
Bodelwyddan. Den 3C 82
Bodenham. Here 5H 59
Bodenham. Wilts 4G 23
Bodewryd. IOA 1C 80
Bodfari. Den 3C 82
Bodffordd. IOA 3D 80
Bodham. Norf 1D 78
Bodiam. E Sus 3B 28
Bodicote. Oxon 2C 50
Bodieve. Corn 1D 6
Bodinnick. Corn 3F 7
Bodle Street Green. E Sus 4A 28
Bodmin. Corn 2E 7
Bodnant. Cnwy 3H 81
Bodney. Norf 1H 65
Bodorgan. IOA 4C 80
Bodrane. Corn 2G 7
Bodsham. Kent 1F 29
Boduan. Gwyn 2C 68
Bodymoor Heath. Warw 1F 61
The Bog. Shrp 1F 59
Bogallan. High 3A 158
Bogbrae Croft. Abers 5H 161
Bogend. S Ayr 1C 116
Boghall. Midl 3F 129
Boghall. W Lot 3C 128
Boghead. S Lan 5A 128
Bogindollo. Ang 3D 144
Bogmoor. Mor 2A 160
Bogniebrae. Abers 4C 160
Bognor Regis. W Sus 3H 17
Bograxie. Abers 2E 152
Bogside. N Lan 4B 128
Bogton. Abers 3D 160
Bogue. Dum 1D 110
Bohenie. High 5E 149
Bohortha. Corn 5C 6
Boirseam. W Isl 9C 171
Bokiddick. Corn 2E 7
Bolam. Dur 2E 105
Bolam. Nmbd 1D 115
Bolberry. Devn 5C 8
Bold Heath. Mers 2H 83
Boldon. Tyne 3G 115
Boldon Colliery. Tyne 3G 115
Boldre. Hants 3B 16
Boldron. Dur 3D 104
Bole. Notts 2E 87
Bolehall. Staf 5G 73
Bolehill. Derbs 5G 85
Bolenowe. Corn 5A 6
Boleside. Bord 1G 119
Bolham. Devn 1C 12
Bolham Water. Devn 1E 13
Bolingey. Corn 3B 6
Bollington. Ches E 3D 84
Bollow. Glos 4C 48
Bolney. W Sus 3D 26
Bolnhurst. Bed 5H 63
Bolshan. Derbs 2B 74
Bolsover. Derbs 3B 86
Bolsterstone. S Yor 1G 85
Bolstone. Here 2A 48
Boltachan. Per 3F 143
Boltby. N Yor 1G 99
Bolton. Cumb 2H 103
Bolton. E Lot 2B 130

Bolton. E Yor 4B 100
Bolton. G Man 4F 91
Bolton. Nmbd 3F 121
Bolton Abbey. N Yor 4C 98
Bolton-by-Bowland. Lanc 5G 97
Boltonfellend. Cumb 3F 113
Boltongate. Cumb 5D 112
Bolton Green. Lanc 3D 90
Bolton Low Houses. Cumb 5D 112
Bolton New Houses. Cumb 5D 112
Bolton-on-Swale. N Yor 5F 105
Bolton Percy. N Yor 5H 99
Bolton upon Dearne. S Yor 4E 93
Bolton Wood Lane. Cumb 5D 112
Bolventor. Corn 5B 10
Bomarsund. Nmbd 1F 115
Bomere Heath. Shrp 4G 71
Bonar Bridge. High 4D 164
Bonawe. Arg 5E 141
Bonby. N Lin 3D 94
Boncath. Pemb 1G 43
Bonchester Bridge. Bord 3H 119
Bonchurch. IOW 5D 16
Bondleigh. Devn 2G 11
Bonds. Lanc 5D 97
Bonehill. Devn 5H 11
Bonehill. Staf 5F 73
Bo'ness. Falk 1C 128
Boney Hay. Staf 4E 73
Bonhill. W Dun 2E 127
Boningale. Shrp 5C 72
Bonjedward. Bord 2A 120
Bonkle. N Lan 4B 128
Bonnington. Ang 5E 145
Bonnington. Edin 3E 129
Bonnington. Kent 2E 29
Bonnybank. Fife 3F 137
Bonnybridge. Falk 1B 128
Bonnykelly. Abers 3F 161
Bonnyrigg. Midl 3G 129
Bonnyton. Ang 5C 144
Bonnytown. Fife 2H 137
Bonsall. Derbs 5G 85
Bont. Mon 4G 47
Bontddu. Gwyn 4F 69
Bont Dolgadfan. Powy 5A 70
Y Bont-Faen. V Glam 4C 32
Bontgoch. Cdgn 2F 57
Bonthorpe. Linc 3D 89
Bont Newydd. Gwyn 1G 69
Bont-newydd. Cnwy 3C 82
Bontnewydd. Cdgn 4F 57
Bontnewydd. Gwyn 4D 81
Bontuchel. Den 5C 82
Bonvilston. V Glam 4D 32
Bon-y-maen. Swan 3F 31
Booker. Buck 2G 37
Booley. Shrp 3H 71
Boorley Green. Hants 1D 16
Boosbeck. Red C 3D 106
Boot. Cumb 4C 102
Booth. W Yor 2A 92
Boothby Graffoe. Linc 5G 87
Boothby Pagnell. Linc 2G 75
Booth of Toft. Shet 4F 173
Boothstown. G Man 4F 91
Boothville. Nptn 4E 63
Bootle. Cumb 1A 96
Bootle. Mers 1F 83
Booton. Norf 3D 78
Boot Street. Suff 1F 55
Boquhan. Stir 1G 127
Boraston. Shrp 3A 60
Borden. Kent 4C 40
Borden. W Sus 4G 25
Bordlands. Bord 5E 129
Bordley. N Yor 3B 98
Bordon. Hants 3F 25
Boreham. Essx 5A 54
Boreham. Wilts 2D 23
Boreham Street. E Sus 4A 28
Borehamwood. Herts 1C 38
Boreland. Dum 5D 118
Boreston. Devn 3D 8
Borestone Brae. Stir 4G 135
Boreton. Shrp 5H 71
Borgh. W Isl
  on Barra 8B 170
  on Benbecula 3C 170
  on Berneray 1E 170
  on Isle of Lewis 2G 171
Borghasdal. W Isl 9C 171
Borghastan. W Isl 3D 171
Borgh na Sgiotaig. High 1C 154
Borgie. High 1G 167
Borgue. Dum 5D 110
Borgue. High 1H 165
Borley. Essx 1B 54
Borley Green. Essx 1B 54
Borley Green. Suff 4B 66
Borlum. High 1H 149
Bornais. W Isl 6C 170
Boroughbridge. N Yor 3F 99
Borough Green. Kent 5H 39
Borreraig. High 3A 154
Borrobol Lodge. High 1F 165
Borrodale. High 4A 154
Borrowash. Derbs 2B 74
Borrowby. N Yor
  nr. Northallerton 1G 99
  nr. Whitby 3E 107
Borrowston. High 4F 169
Borrowstonehill. Orkn 7D 172
Borrowstoun. Falk 1C 128
Borstal. Medw 4B 40

Borth. Cdgn 2F 57
Borthwick. Midl 4G 129
Borth-y-Gest. Gwyn 2E 69
Borve. High 4D 154
Borwick. Lanc 2E 97
Bosbury. Here 1B 48
Boscastle. Corn 3A 10
Boscombe. Bour 3G 15
Boscombe. Wilts 3H 23
Boscoppa. Corn 3E 7
Bosham. W Sus 2G 17
Bosherston. Pemb 5D 42
Bosley. Ches E 4D 84
Bossall. N Yor 3B 100
Bossiney. Corn 4A 10
Bossingham. Kent 1F 29
Bossington. Som 2B 20
Bostadh. W Isl 3D 171
Bostock Green. Ches W 4A 84
Boston. Linc 1C 76
Boston Spa. W Yor 5G 99
Boswarthen. Corn 3B 4
Boswinger. Corn 4D 6
Botallack. Corn 3A 4
Botany Bay. G Lon 1D 39
Botcheston. Leics 5B 74
Botesdale. Suff 3C 66
Bothal. Nmbd 1F 115
Bothampstead. W Ber 4D 36
Bothamsall. Notts 3D 86
Bothel. Cumb 1C 102
Bothenhampton. Dors 3H 13
Bothwell. S Lan 4A 128
Botley. Buck 5H 51
Botley. Hants 1D 16
Botley. Oxon 5C 50
Botloe's Green. Glos 3C 48
Botolph Claydon. Buck 3F 51
Botolphs. W Sus 5C 26
Bottesford. Leics 2F 75
Bottesford. N Lin 4B 94
Bottisham. Cambs 4E 65
Bottlehill. Wilts 5D 34
Bottomcraig. Fife 1F 137
Bottom o' th' Moor. G Man 3E 91
Bottom. N Yor 4D 107
Botton Head. Lanc 3F 97
Bottreaux Mill. Devn 4B 20
Botus Fleming. Corn 2A 8
Bough Beech. Kent 1F 27
Boughrood. Powy 2E 47
Boughspring. Glos 2A 34
Boughton. Norf 5F 77
Boughton. Nptn 4E 63
Boughton. Notts 4D 86
Boughton Aluph. Kent 1E 29
Boughton Green. Kent 5B 40
Boughton Lees. Kent 1E 28
Boughton Malherbe. Kent 1C 28
Boughton Monchelsea. Kent 5B 40
Boughton under Blean. Kent 5E 41
Boulby. Red C 3E 107
Bouldon. IOW 4B 16
Bouldon. Shrp 2H 59
Boulmer. Nmbd 3G 121
Boulston. Pemb 3D 42
Boultham. Linc 4G 87
Boulton. Derb 2A 74
Boundary. Staf 1D 73
Bounds. Here 2B 48
Bourn. Cambs 5C 64
Bournbrook. W Mid 2E 61
Bourne. Linc 3H 75
The Bourne. Surr 2G 25
Bourne End. Bed 4H 63
Bourne End. Buck 3G 37
Bourne End. C Beds 1H 51
Bourne End. Herts 5A 52
Bournemouth. Bour 190 (3F 15)
Bournemouth Airport. Dors 3G 15
Bournes Green. Glos 5E 49
Bournes Green. S'end 2D 40
Bournheath. Worc 3D 60
Bournmoor. Dur 4G 115
Bournville. W Mid 2E 61
Bourton. Dors 3C 22
Bourton. N Som 5G 33
Bourton. Oxon 3H 35
Bourton. Shrp 1H 59
Bourton. Wilts 5F 35
Bourton on Dunsmore. Warw 3B 62
Bourton-on-the-Hill. Glos 2G 49
Bourton-on-the-Water. Glos 3G 49
Bousd. Arg 2D 138
Bousta. Shet 6D 173
Boustead Hill. Cumb 4D 112
Bouth. Cumb 1C 96
Bouthwaite. N Yor 2D 98
Boveney. Buck 3A 38
Boverton. V Glam 5C 32
Boveridge. Dors 1F 15
Bovey Tracey. Devn 5B 12
Bovingdon. Herts 5A 52
Bovingdon Green. Buck 3G 37
Bovinger. Essx 5F 53
Bovington Camp. Dors 4D 14
Bow. Devn 2H 11
Bow. Orkn 2C 104
Bow Brickhill. Mil 2H 51
Bowbridge. Glos 5D 48
Bowburn. Dur 1A 106
Bowcombe. IOW 4C 16
Bowd. Devn 4E 12
Bowden. Devn 4E 9
Bowden. Bord 1H 119
Bowden Hill. Wilts 5E 35
Bowdens. Som 4H 21
Bowderdale. Cumb 4H 103
Bowdon. G Man 2B 84

Bower. Nmbd 1A 114
Bowerchalke. Wilts 4F 23
Bowerhill. Wilts 5E 35
Bower Hinton. Som 1H 13
Bowermadden. High 2E 169
Bowers. Staf 2C 72
Bowers Gifford. Essx 2B 40
Bowershall. Fife 4C 136
Bowertower. High 2E 169
Bowes. Dur 3C 104
Bowgreave. Lanc 5D 97
Bowhousebog. N Lan 4B 128
Bowithick. Corn 4B 10
Bowland Bridge. Cumb 1D 96
Bowlees. Dur 2C 104
Bowley. Here 5H 59
Bowlhead Green. Surr 2A 26
Bowling. W Dun 2F 127
Bowling. W Yor 1B 92
Bowling Bank. Wrex 1F 71
Bowling Green. Worc 5C 60
Bowlish. Som 2B 22
Bowmanstead. Cumb 5E 102
Bowmore. Arg 4B 124
Bowness-on-Solway. Cumb 3D 112
Bowness-on-Windermere.
  Cumb 5F 103
Bow of Fife. Fife 2F 137
Bowriefauld. Ang 4E 145
Bowscale. Cumb 1E 103
Bowsden. Nmbd 5F 131
Bowside Lodge. High 2A 168
Bowston. Cumb 5F 103
Bow Street. Cdgn 2F 57
Bowthorpe. Norf 5D 78
Box. Glos 5D 48
Box. Wilts 5D 34
Boxbush. Glos 3B 48
Box End. Bed 1A 52
Boxford. Suff 1C 54
Boxford. W Ber 4C 36
Boxgrove. W Sus 5A 26
Box Hill. Wilts 5D 34
Boxley. Kent 5B 40
Boxmoor. Herts 5A 52
Box's Shop. Corn 2C 10
Boxted. Essx 2C 54
Boxted. Suff 5H 65
Boxted Cross. Essx 2D 54
Boxworth. Cambs 4C 64
Boxworth End. Cambs 4C 64
Boyden End. Suff 5G 65
Boyden Gate. Kent 4G 41
Boylestone. Derbs 2F 73
Boylestonfield. Derbs 2F 73
Boyndie. Abers 2D 160
Boynton. E Yor 3F 101
Boys Hill. Dors 1B 14
Boythorpe. Derbs 4A 86
Boyton. Corn 3D 10
Boyton. Suff 1G 55
Boyton. Wilts 3E 23
Boyton Cross. Essx 5G 53
Boyton End. Essx 2G 53
Boyton End. Suff 1H 53
Bozeat. Nptn 5G 63
Braaid. IOM 4C 108
Braal Castle. High 3D 168
Brabling Green. Suff 4E 67
Brabourne. Kent 1F 29
Brabourne Lees. Kent 1E 29
Brabster. High 2F 169
Bracadale. High 5C 154
Bracara. High 4F 147
Braceborough. Linc 4H 75
Bracebridge. Linc 4G 87
Bracebridge Heath. Linc 4G 87
Braceby. Linc 2H 75
Bracewell. Lanc 5A 98
Brackenber. Cumb 3A 104
Brackenfield. Derbs 5A 86
Brackenthwaite. Cumb 5D 112
Brackenthwaite. N Yor 4E 99
Brackla. B'end 4C 32
Brackla. High 3C 158
Bracklesham. W Sus 3G 17
Brackletter. High 5D 148
Brackley. Nptn 2D 50
Brackley Hatch. Nptn 1E 51
Brackloch. High 1F 163
Bracknell. Brac 5G 37
Braco. Per 3H 135
Bracobrae. Mor 3C 160
Bracon. N Lin 4A 94
Bracon Ash. Norf 1D 66
Bradbourne. Derbs 5G 85
Bradbury. Dur 2A 106
Bradda. IOM 4A 108
Bradden. Nptn 1E 51
Bradenham. Buck 2G 37
Bradenham. Norf 5B 78
Bradenstoke. Wilts 4F 35
Bradfield. Essx 2E 55
Bradfield. Norf 2E 79
Bradfield. W Ber 4E 36
Bradfield Combust. Suff 5A 66
Bradfield Green. Ches E 5A 84
Bradfield Heath. Essx 3E 55
Bradfield St Clare. Suff 5B 66
Bradfield St George. Suff 4B 66
Bradford. Derbs 4G 85
Bradford. Devn 2E 11
Bradford. Nmbd 1F 121
Bradford. W Yor 190 (1B 92)
Bradford Abbas. Dors 1A 14
Bradford Barton. Devn 1B 12
Bradford Leigh. Wilts 5D 34
Bradford-on-Avon. Wilts 5D 34
Bradford-on-Tone. Som 4E 21
Bradford Peverell. Dors 3B 14

Bradiford – Brompton Ralph

Bradiford. *Devn* 3F 19
Brading. *IOW* 4E 16
Bradley. *Ches W* 3H 83
Bradley. *Derbs* 1G 73
Bradley. *Glos* 2C 34
Bradley. *Hants* 2E 25
Bradley. *NE Lin* 4F 95
Bradley. *N Yor* 1C 98
Bradley. *Staf* 4C 72
Bradley. *W Mid* 1D 60
Bradley. *W Yor* 2B 92
Bradley. *Wrex* 5F 83
Bradley Cross. *Som* 1H 21
Bradley Green. *Ches W* 1H 71
Bradley Green. *Som* 3F 21
Bradley Green. *Warw* 5G 73
Bradley Green. *Worc* 4D 61
Bradley in the Moors. *Staf* 1E 73
Bradley Mount. *Ches E* 3D 84
Bradley Stoke. *S Glo* 3B 34
Bradlow. *Here* 2C 48
Bradmore. *Notts* 2C 74
Bradmore. *W Mid* 1C 60
Bradninch. *Devn* 2D 12
Bradnop. *Staf* 5E 85
Bradpole. *Dors* 3H 13
Bradshaw. *G Man* 3F 91
Bradstone. *Devn* 4D 11
Bradwall Green. *Ches E* 4B 84
Bradway. *S Yor* 2H 85
Bradwell. *Derbs* 2F 85
Bradwell. *Essx* 3B 54
Bradwell. *Mil* 2G 51
Bradwell. *Norf* 5H 79
Bradwell-on-Sea. *Essx* 5D 54
Bradwell Waterside. *Essx* 5C 54
Bradworthy. *Devn* 1D 10
Brae. *High* 5C 162
Brae. *Shet* 5E 173
Braeantra. *High* 1H 157
Braefield. *High* 5G 157
Braefindon. *High* 3A 158
Braegrum. *Per* 1C 136
Braehead. *Ang* 3F 145
Braehead. *Dum* 4B 110
Braehead. *Mor* 4G 159
Braehead. *Orkn* 3D 172
Braehead. *S Lan*
nr. Coalburn 1H 117
nr. Forth 4C 128
Braehoulland. *Shet* 4D 173
Braemar. *Abers* 4F 151
Braemore. *High*
nr. Dunbeath 5C 168
nr. Ullapool 1D 156
Brae of Achnahaird. *High* 2E 163
Brae Roy Lodge. *High* 4F 149
Braeside. *Abers* 5G 161
Braeside. *Inv* 2D 126
Braes of Coul. *Ang* 3B 144
Braeswick. *Orkn* 4F 172
Braetongue. *High* 3F 167
Braeval. *Stir* 3E 135
Braevallich. *Arg* 3G 133
Braewick. *Shet* 6E 173
Brafferton. *Darl* 2F 105
Brafferton. *N Yor* 2G 99
Brafield-on-the-Green. *Nptn* 5F 63
Bragar. *W Isl* 3E 171
Bragbury End. *Herts* 3C 52
Bragleenbeg. *Arg* 1G 133
Braichmelyn. *Gwyn* 4F 81
Braides. *Lanc* 4D 96
Braidwood. *S Lan* 5B 128
Braigo. *Arg* 3A 124
Brailsford. *Derbs* 1G 73
Braintree. *Essx* 3A 54
Braiseworth. *Suff* 3D 66
Braishfield. *Hants* 4B 24
Braithwaite. *Cumb* 2D 102
Braithwaite. *S Yor* 3G 93
Braithwaite. *W Yor* 5C 98
Braithwell. *S Yor* 1C 86
Brakefield Green. *Norf* 5C 78
Bramber. *W Sus* 4C 26
Brambridge. *Hants* 4C 24
Bramcote. *Notts* 2C 74
Bramcote. *Warw* 2B 62
Bramdean. *Hants* 4E 24
Bramerton. *Norf* 5E 79
Bramfield. *Herts* 4C 52
Bramfield. *Suff* 3F 67
Bramford. *Suff* 1E 54
Bramhall. *G Man* 2C 84
Bramham. *W Yor* 5G 99
Bramhope. *W Yor* 5E 99
Bramley. *Hants* 1E 25
Bramley. *S Yor* 1B 86
Bramley. *Surr* 1B 26
Bramley. *W Yor* 1C 92
Bramley Green. *Hants* 1E 25
Bramley Head. *N Yor* 4D 98
Bramley Vale. *Derbs* 4B 86
Bramling. *Kent* 5G 41
Brampford Speke. *Devn* 3C 12
Brampton. *Cambs* 3B 64
Brampton. *Cumb*
nr. Appleby-in-Westmorland 2H 103
nr. Carlisle 3G 113
Brampton. *Linc* 3F 87
Brampton. *Norf* 3E 78
Brampton. *S Yor* 4E 93
Brampton. *Suff* 2G 67
Brampton Abbotts. *Here* 3B 48
Brampton Ash. *Nptn* 2E 63
Brampton Bryan. *Here* 3F 59
Brampton en le Morthen. *S Yor* 2B 86
Bramshall. *Staf* 2E 73
Bramshaw. *Hants* 1A 16
Bramshill. *Hants* 5F 37
Bramshott. *Hants* 3G 25
Branault. *High* 2G 139
Brancaster. *Norf* 1G 77
Brancaster Staithe. *Norf* 1G 77
Brancepeth. *Dur* 1F 105
Branch End. *Nmbd* 3D 114
Branchill. *Mor* 3E 159
Brand End. *Linc* 1C 76
Branderburgh. *Mor* 1G 159
Brandesburton. *E Yor* 5F 101
Brandeston. *Suff* 4E 67
Brand Green. *Glos* 3C 48
Brandhill. *Shrp* 3G 59
Brandis Corner. *Devn* 2E 11
Brandish Street. *Som* 2C 20
Brandiston. *Norf* 3D 78
Brandon. *Dur* 1F 105
Brandon. *Linc* 1G 75
Brandon. *Nmbd* 3E 121
Brandon. *Suff* 2G 65
Brandon. *Warw* 3B 62
Brandon Bank. *Cambs* 2F 65
Brandon Creek. *Norf* 1F 65
Brandon Parva. *Norf* 5C 78
Brandsby. *N Yor* 2H 99
Brandy Wharf. *Linc* 1H 87
Brane. *Corn* 4B 4
Bran End. *Essx* 3G 53
Branksome. *Pool* 3F 15
Bransbury. *Hants* 2C 24
Bransby. *Linc* 3F 87
Branscombe. *Devn* 4E 13
Bransford. *Worc* 5B 60
Bransgore. *Hants* 3G 15
Bransholme. *Hull* 1E 94
Bransley. *Shrp* 3A 60
Branston. *Leics* 3F 75
Branston. *Linc* 4H 87
Branston. *Staf* 3G 73
Branston Booths. *Linc* 4H 87
Branstone. *IOW* 4D 16
Bransty. *Cumb* 3A 102
Brant Broughton. *Linc* 5G 87
Brantham. *Suff* 2E 54
Branthwaite. *Cumb*
nr. Caldbeck 1D 102
nr. Workington 2B 102
Brantingham. *E Yor* 2C 94
Branton. *Nmbd* 3E 121
Branton. *S Yor* 4G 93
Branton Green. *N Yor* 3G 99
Branxholme. *Bord* 3G 119
Branxton. *Nmbd* 1C 120
Brassington. *Derbs* 5G 85
Brasted. *Kent* 5F 39
Brasted Chart. *Kent* 5F 39
The Bratch. *Staf* 1C 60
Brathens. *Abers* 4D 152
Bratoft. *Linc* 4D 88
Brattleby. *Linc* 2G 87
Bratton. *Som* 2C 20
Bratton. *Telf* 4A 72
Bratton. *Wilts* 1E 23
Bratton Clovelly. *Devn* 3E 11
Bratton Fleming. *Devn* 3G 19
Bratton Seymour. *Som* 4B 22
Braughing. *Herts* 3D 53
Braulen Lodge. *High* 5E 157
Braunston. *Nptn* 4C 62
Braunstone Town. *Leics* 5C 74
Braunston-in-Rutland. *Rut* 5F 75
Braunton. *Devn* 3E 19
Brawby. *N Yor* 2B 100
Brawl. *High* 2A 168
Brawlbin. *High* 3C 168
Bray. *Wind* 3A 38
Braybrooke. *Nptn* 2E 63
Brayford. *Devn* 3G 19
Bray Shop. *Corn* 5D 10
Braystones. *Cumb* 4B 102
Brayton. *N Yor* 1G 93
Bray Wick. *Wind* 4G 37
Brazacott. *Corn* 3C 10
Brea. *Corn* 4A 6
Breach. *W Sus* 2F 17
Breachwood Green. *Herts* 3B 52
Breacleit. *W Isl* 4D 171
Breaden Heath. *Shrp* 2G 71
Breadsall. *Derbs* 1A 74
Breadstone. *Glos* 5C 48
Breage. *Corn* 4D 4
Breakachy. *High* 4G 157
Breakish. *High* 1E 147
Bream. *Glos* 5B 48
Breamore. *Hants* 1G 15
Bream's Meend. *Glos* 5B 48
Brean. *Som* 1F 21
Breanais. *W Isl* 5B 171
Brearton. *N Yor* 3F 99
Breascleit. *W Isl* 4E 171
Breaston. *Derbs* 2B 74
Brecais Àrd. *High* 1E 147
Brecais Iosal. *High* 1E 147
Brechfa. *Carm* 2F 45
Brechin. *Ang* 3F 145
Breckles. *Norf* 1B 66
Brecon. *Powy* 3D 46
Bredbury. *G Man* 1D 84
Brede. *E Sus* 4C 28
Bredenbury. *Here* 5A 60
Bredfield. *Suff* 5E 67
Bredgar. *Kent* 4C 40
Bredhurst. *Kent* 4B 40
Bredicot. *Worc* 5D 60
Bredon. *Worc* 2E 49
Bredon's Norton. *Worc* 2E 49
Bredwardine. *Here* 1G 47
Breedon on the Hill. *Leics* 3B 74
Breibhig. *W Isl*
on Barra 9B 170
on Isle of Lewis 4G 171
Breich. *W Lot* 3C 128
Breightmet. *G Man* 4F 91
Breighton. *E Yor* 1H 93
Breinton. *Here* 2H 47
Breinton Common. *Here* 2H 47
Breiwick. *Shet* 7F 173
Brelston Green. *Here* 3A 48
Bremhill. *Wilts* 4E 35
Brenachie. *High* 1B 158
Brenchley. *Kent* 1A 28
Brendon. *Devn* 2A 20
Brent Cross. *G Lon* 2D 38
Brent Eleigh. *Suff* 1C 54
Brentford. *G Lon* 3C 38
Brentingby. *Leics* 4E 75
Brent Knoll. *Som* 1G 21
Brent Pelham. *Herts* 2E 53
Brentwood. *Essx* 1G 39
Brenzett. *Kent* 3E 28
Brereton. *Staf* 4E 73
Brereton Cross. *Staf* 4E 73
Brereton Green. *Ches E* 4B 84
Brereton Heath. *Ches E* 4C 84
Bressingham. *Norf* 2C 66
Bretby. *Derbs* 3G 73
Bretford. *Warw* 3B 62
Bretforton. *Worc* 1F 49
Bretherdale Head. *Cumb* 4G 103
Bretherton. *Lanc* 2C 90
Brettabister. *Shet* 6F 173
Brettenham. *Norf* 2B 66
Brettenham. *Suff* 5B 66
Bretton. *Flin* 4F 83
Bretton. *Pet* 5A 76
Brewlands Bridge. *Ang* 2A 144
Brewood. *Staf* 5C 72
Briantspuddle. *Dors* 3D 14
Bricket Wood. *Herts* 5B 52
Bricklehampton. *Worc* 1E 49
Bride. *IOM* 1D 108
Bridekirk. *Cumb* 1C 102
Bridell. *Pemb* 1B 44
Bridestowe. *Devn* 4F 11
Brideswell. *Abers* 5C 160
Bridford. *Devn* 4B 12
Bridge. *Corn* 4A 6
Bridge. *Kent* 5F 41
Bridge. *Som* 2G 13
Bridge End. *Bed* 5H 63
Bridge End. *Cumb*
nr. Broughton in Furness 5D 102
nr. Dalston 5E 113
Bridge End. *Linc* 2A 76
Bridge End. *Shet* 8E 173
Bridgefoot. *Ang* 5C 144
Bridgefoot. *Cumb* 2B 102
Bridge Green. *Essx* 2E 53
Bridgehampton. *Som* 4A 22
Bridge Hewick. *N Yor* 2F 99
Bridgehill. *Dur* 4D 115
Bridgemary. *Hants* 2D 16
Bridgemere. *Ches E* 1B 72
Bridgemont. *Derbs* 2E 85
Bridgend. *Abers*
nr. Huntly 5C 160
nr. Peterhead 5H 161
Bridgend. *Ang*
nr. Brechin 2E 145
nr. Kirriemuir 4C 144
Bridgend. *Arg*
nr. Lochgilphead 4F 133
on Islay 3B 124
Bridgend. *B'end* 3C 32
Bridgend. *Cumb* 3E 103
Bridgend. *Devn* 4B 8
Bridgend. *Fife* 2F 137
Bridgend. *High* 3F 157
Bridgend. *Mor* 5A 160
Bridgend. *Per* 1D 136
Bridgend. *W Lot* 2D 128
Bridgend of Lintrathen. *Ang* 3B 144
Bridgeness. *Falk* 1D 128
Bridge of Alford. *Abers* 2C 152
Bridge of Allan. *Stir* 4G 135
Bridge of Avon. *Mor* 5F 159
Bridge of Awe. *Arg* 1H 133
Bridge of Balgie. *Per* 4C 142
Bridge of Brown. *High* 1F 151
Bridge of Cally. *Per* 3A 144
Bridge of Canny. *Abers* 4D 152
Bridge of Dee. *Dum* 3E 111
Bridge of Don. *Aber* 2G 153
Bridge of Dun. *Ang* 3F 145
Bridge of Dye. *Abers* 5D 152
Bridge of Earn. *Per* 2D 136
Bridge of Ericht. *Per* 3C 142
Bridge of Feugh. *Abers* 4E 152
Bridge of Gairn. *Abers* 4A 152
Bridge of Gaur. *Per* 3C 142
Bridge of Muchalls. *Abers* 4F 153
Bridge of Oich. *High* 3F 149
Bridge of Orchy. *Arg* 5H 141
Bridge of Walls. *Shet* 6D 173
Bridge of Weir. *Ren* 3E 127
Bridge Reeve. *Devn* 1G 11
Bridgerule. *Devn* 2C 10
Bridge Sollers. *Here* 1H 47
Bridge Street. *Suff* 1B 54
Bridge Town. *Warw* 5G 61
Bridgetown. *Devn* 2E 9
Bridgetown. *Som* 3C 20
Bridge Trafford. *Ches W* 3G 83
Bridgeyate. *S Glo* 4B 34
Bridgham. *Norf* 2B 66
Bridgnorth. *Shrp* 1B 60
Bridgtown. *Staf* 5D 73
Bridgwater. *Som* 3G 21
Bridlington. *E Yor* 3F 101
Bridport. *Dors* 3H 13
Bridstow. *Here* 3A 48
Brierfield. *Lanc* 1G 91
Brierley. *Glos* 4B 48
Brierley. *Here* 5G 59
Brierley. *S Yor* 3E 93
Brierley Hill. *W Mid* 2D 60
Brierton. *Hart* 1B 106
Briestfield. *W Yor* 3C 92
Brigg. *N Lin* 4D 94
Briggate. *Norf* 3F 79
Briggswath. *N Yor* 4F 107
Brigham. *Cumb* 1B 102
Brigham. *E Yor* 4E 101
Brighouse. *W Yor* 2B 92
Brighstone. *IOW* 4C 16
Brightgate. *Derbs* 5G 85
Brighthampton. *Oxon* 5B 50
Brightholmlee. *S Yor* 1G 85
Brightley. *Devn* 3G 11
Brightling. *E Sus* 3A 28
Brightlingsea. *Essx* 4D 54
Brighton. *Brig* 189 (5E 27)
Brighton. *Corn* 3D 6
Brighton Hill. *Hants* 2E 24
Brightons. *Falk* 2C 128
Brightwalton. *W Ber* 4C 36
Brightwalton Green. *W Ber* 4C 36
Brightwell. *Suff* 1F 55
Brightwell Baldwin. *Oxon* 2E 37
Brightwell-cum-Sotwell. *Oxon* 2D 36
Brigmerston. *Wilts* 2G 23
Brignall. *Dur* 3D 104
Brig o' Turk. *Stir* 3E 135
Brigsley. *NE Lin* 4F 95
Brigsteer. *Cumb* 1D 97
Brigstock. *Nptn* 2G 63
Brill. *Buck* 4E 51
Brill. *Corn* 4E 5
Brilley. *Here* 1F 47
Brimaston. *Pemb* 2D 42
Brimfield. *Here* 4H 59
Brimington. *Derbs* 3B 86
Brimley. *Devn* 5B 12
Brimpsfield. *Glos* 4E 49
Brimpton. *W Ber* 5D 36
Brims. *Orkn* 9B 172
Brimscombe. *Glos* 5D 48
Brimstage. *Mers* 2F 83
Brincliffe. *S Yor* 2H 85
Brind. *E Yor* 1H 93
Brindister. *Shet*
nr. West Burrafirth 6D 173
nr. West Lerwick 8F 173
Brindle. *Lanc* 2D 90
Brindley. *Ches E* 5H 83
Brindley Ford. *Stoke* 5C 84
Brineton. *Staf* 4C 72
Bringhurst. *Leics* 1F 63
Bringsty Common. *Here* 5A 60
Brington. *Cambs* 3H 63
Brinian. *Orkn* 5D 172
Briningham. *Norf* 2C 78
Brinkhill. *Linc* 3C 88
Brinkley. *Cambs* 5F 65
Brinklow. *Warw* 3B 62
Brinkworth. *Wilts* 3F 35
Brinscall. *Lanc* 2E 91
Brinscombe. *Som* 1H 21
Brinsley. *Notts* 1B 74
Brinsworth. *S Yor* 2B 86
Brinton. *Norf* 2C 78
Brisco. *Cumb* 4F 113
Brisley. *Norf* 3B 78
Brislington. *Bris* 4B 34
Brissenden Green. *Kent* 2D 28
Bristol. *Bris* 189 (4A 34)
Bristol Airport. *N Som* 5A 34
Briston. *Norf* 2C 78
Britannia. *Lanc* 2G 91
Britford. *Wilts* 4G 23
Brithdir. *Cphy* 5E 47
Brithdir. *Cdgn* 1D 44
Brithdir. *Gwyn* 4G 69
Briton Ferry. *Neat* 3G 31
Britwell Salome. *Oxon* 2E 37
Brixham. *Torb* 3F 9
Brixton. *Devn* 3B 8
Brixton. *G Lon* 3E 39
Brixton Deverill. *Wilts* 3D 22
Brixworth. *Nptn* 3E 63
Brize Norton. *Oxon* 5B 50
The Broad. *Here* 4G 59
Broad Alley. *Worc* 4C 60
Broad Blunsdon. *Swin* 2G 35
Broadbottom. *G Man* 1D 85
Broadbridge. *W Sus* 2G 17
Broadbridge Heath. *W Sus* 2C 26
Broad Campden. *Glos* 2G 49
Broad Chalke. *Wilts* 4F 23
Broadclyst. *Devn* 3C 12
Broadfield. *Inv* 2E 127
Broadfield. *Pemb* 4F 43
Broadfield. *W Sus* 2D 26
Broadford. *High* 1E 147
Broadford Bridge. *W Sus* 3B 26
Broadgate. *Cumb* 1A 96
Broad Green. *Cambs* 5F 65
Broad Green. *C Beds* 1H 51
Broad Green. *Worc*
nr. Bromsgrove 3D 61
nr. Worcester 5B 60
Broad Haven. *Pemb* 3C 42
Broadhaven. *High* 3F 169
Broad Heath. *Staf* 3C 72
Broadheath. *G Man* 2B 84
Broadheath. *Worc* 4A 60
Broadheath Common. *Worc* 5C 60
Broadhembury. *Devn* 2E 12
Broadhempston. *Devn* 2E 9
Broad Hill. *Cambs* 3E 65
Broad Hinton. *Wilts* 4G 35
Broadholme. *Derbs* 1A 74
Broadholme. *Linc* 3F 87
Broadlay. *Carm* 5D 44
Broad Laying. *Hants* 5C 36
Broadley. *Lanc* 3G 91
Broadley. *Mor* 2A 160
Broadley Common. *Essx* 5E 53
Broad Marston. *Worc* 1G 49
Broadmayne. *Dors* 4C 14
Broadmere. *Hants* 2E 24
Broadmoor. *Pemb* 4E 43
Broad Oak. *Carm* 3F 45
Broad Oak. *Cumb* 5C 102
Broad Oak. *Devn* 3D 12
Broad Oak. *Dors* 1C 14
Broad Oak. *E Sus*
nr. Hastings 4C 28
nr. Heathfield 3H 27
Broad Oak. *Here* 3H 47
Broad Oak. *Kent* 4F 41
Broadoak. *Dors* 3H 13
Broadoak. *Glos* 4B 48
Broadoak. *Hants* 1D 16
Broadrashes. *Mor* 3B 160
Broadsea. *Abers* 2G 161
Broad's Green. *Essx* 4G 53
Broadshard. *Som* 1H 13
Broadstairs. *Kent* 4H 41
Broadstone. *Pool* 3F 15
Broadstone. *Shrp* 2H 59
Broad Street. *E Sus* 4C 28
Broad Street. *Kent*
nr. Ashford 1F 29
nr. Maidstone 5C 40
Broad Street Green. *Essx* 5B 54
Broad Town. *Wilts* 4F 35
Broadwas. *Worc* 5B 60
Broadwath. *Cumb* 4F 113
Broadway. *Carm*
nr. Kidwelly 5D 45
nr. Laugharne 4G 43
Broadway. *Pemb* 3C 42
Broadway. *Som* 1G 13
Broadway. *Suff* 3F 67
Broadway. *Worc* 2F 49
Broadwell. *Glos*
nr. Cinderford 4A 48
nr. Stow-on-the-Wold 3H 49
Broadwell. *Oxon* 5A 50
Broadwell. *Warw* 4B 62
Broadwell House. *Nmbd* 4C 114
Broadwey. *Dors* 4B 14
Broadwindsor. *Dors* 2H 13
Broadwoodkelly. *Devn* 2G 11
Broadwoodwidger. *Devn* 4E 11
Broallan. *High* 4G 157
Brobury. *Here* 1G 47
Brochel. *High* 4E 155
Brockamin. *Worc* 5B 60
Brockbridge. *Hants* 1E 16
Brockdish. *Norf* 3E 66
Brockencote. *Worc* 3C 60
Brockenhurst. *Hants* 2A 16
Brocketsbrae. *S Lan* 1H 117
Brockford Street. *Suff* 4D 66
Brockhall. *Nptn* 4D 62
Brockham. *Surr* 1C 26
Brockhampton. *Glos*
nr. Bishop's Cleeve 3E 49
nr. Sevenhampton 3F 49
Brockhampton. *Here* 2A 48
Brockhill. *Bord* 2F 119
Brockholes. *W Yor* 3B 92
Brockhurst. *Hants* 2D 16
Brocklesby. *Linc* 3E 95
Brockley. *N Som* 5H 33
Brockley Corner. *Suff* 3H 65
Brockley Green. *Suff*
nr. Bury St Edmunds 1H 53
nr. Haverhill 5H 65
Brockleymoor. *Cumb* 1F 103
Brockmoor. *W Mid* 2D 60
Brockton. *Shrp*
nr. Bishop's Castle 2F 59
nr. Madeley 5B 72
nr. Much Wenlock 1H 59
nr. Pontesbury 5F 71
Brockton. *Staf* 2C 72
Brockton. *Telf* 4B 72
Brockweir. *Glos* 5A 48
Brockworth. *Glos* 4D 49
Brocton. *Staf* 4D 72
Brodick. *N Ayr* 2E 123
Brodie. *Mor* 3D 159
Brodiesord. *Abers* 3C 160
Brodsworth. *S Yor* 4F 93
Brogaig. *High* 2D 154
Brogborough. *C Beds* 2H 51
Brokenborough. *Wilts* 3E 35
Broken Cross. *Ches E* 3C 84
Bromborough. *Mers* 2F 83
Bromdon. *Shrp* 2A 60
Brome. *Suff* 3D 66
Brome Street. *Suff* 3D 66
Bromeswell. *Suff* 5F 67
Bromfield. *Cumb* 5C 112
Bromfield. *Shrp* 3G 59
Bromford. *W Mid* 1F 61
Bromham. *Bed* 5H 63
Bromham. *Wilts* 5E 35
Bromley. *G Lon* 4F 39
Bromley. *Herts* 3E 53
Bromley. *Shrp* 1B 60
Bromley Cross. *G Man* 3F 91
Bromley Green. *Kent* 2D 28
Bromley Wood. *Staf* 3F 73
Brompton. *Medw* 4B 40
Brompton. *N Yor*
nr. Northallerton 5A 106
nr. Scarborough 1D 100
Brompton. *Shrp* 5H 71
Brompton-on-Swale. *N Yor* 5F 105
Brompton Ralph. *Som* 3D 20

Brompton Regis. Som 3C 20
Bromsash. Here 3B 48
Bromsberrow. Glos 2C 48
Bromsberrow Heath. Glos 2C 48
Bromsgrove. Worc 3D 60
Bromstead Heath. Staf 4B 72
Bromyard. Here 5A 60
Bromyard Downs. Here 5A 60
Bronaber. Gwyn 2G 69
Broncroft. Shrp 2H 59
Brongest. Cdgn 1D 44
Brongwyn. Cdgn 1C 44
Bronington. Wrex 2G 71
Bronllys. Powy 2E 47
Bronnant. Cdgn 4F 57
Bronwydd Arms. Carm 3E 45
Bronydd. Powy 1F 47
Brongarth. Shrp 2E 71
Brook. Carm 4G 43
Brook. Hants
  nr. Cadnam 1A 16
  nr. Romsey 4B 24
Brook. IOW 4B 16
Brook. Kent 1E 29
Brook. Surr
  nr. Guildford 1B 26
  nr. Haslemere 2A 26
Brooke. Norf 1E 67
Brooke. Rut 5F 75
Brookenby. Linc 1B 88
Brook End. Worc 1D 48
Brookend. Glos 5B 48
Brookfield. Lanc 1D 90
Brookfield. Ren 3F 127
Brookhouse. Lanc 3E 97
Brookhouse. S Yor 2C 86
Brookhouse Green. Ches E 4C 84
Brookhouses. Staf 1D 73
Brookhurst. Mers 2F 83
Brookland. Kent 3D 28
Brooklands. G Man 1B 84
Brooklands. Shrp 1H 71
Brookmans Park. Herts 5C 52
Brooks. Powy 1D 58
Brooksby. Leics 4D 74
Brooks Green. W Sus 3C 26
Brookside. Staf 1D 73
Brook Street. Essx 1G 39
Brook Street. Kent 2D 28
Brook Street. W Sus 3E 27
Brookthorpe. Glos 4D 48
Brookville. Norf 1G 65
Brookwood. Surr 5A 38
Broom. C Beds 1B 52
Broom. Fife 3F 137
Broom. Warw 5E 61
Broome. Norf 1F 67
Broome. Shrp
  nr. Cardington 1H 59
  nr. Craven Arms 2G 59
Broome. Worc 3D 60
Broomedge. Warr 2B 84
Broomend. Abers 2E 153
Broomer's Corner. W Sus 3C 26
Broomfield. Abers 5G 161
Broomfield. Essx 4H 53
Broomfield. Kent
  nr. Herne Bay 4F 41
  nr. Maidstone 5C 40
Broomfield. Som 3F 21
Broomfleet. E Yor 2B 94
Broom Green. Norf 3B 78
Broomhall. Ches E 1A 72
Broomhall. Wind 4A 38
Broomhaugh. Nmbd 3D 114
Broom Hill. Dors 2F 15
Broom Hill. Worc 3D 60
Broomhill. High
  nr. Grantown-on-Spey 1D 151
  nr. Invergordon 1B 158
Broomhill. Norf 5F 77
Broomhill. S Yor 4E 93
Broomhillbank. Dum 5D 118
Broomholm. Norf 2F 79
Broomlands. Dum 4C 118
Broomley. Nmbd 3D 114
Broom of Moy. Mor 3E 159
Broompark. Dur 5F 115
Broom's Green. Glos 2C 48
Brora. High 3G 165
Broseley. Shrp 5A 72
Brotherhouse Bar. Linc 4B 76
Brotheridge Green. Worc 1D 48
Brotherlee. Dur 1C 104
Brothertoft. Linc 1B 76
Brotherton. N Yor 2E 93
Brotton. Red C 3D 107
Broubster. High 2C 168
Brough. Cumb 3A 104
Brough. Derbs 2F 85
Brough. E Yor 2C 94
Brough. High 1E 169
Brough. Notts 5F 87
Brough. Orkn
  nr. Finstown 6C 172
  nr. St Margaret's Hope 9D 172
Brough. Shet
  nr. Benston 6F 173
  nr. Booth of Toft 4F 173
  on Bressay 7G 173
  on Whalsay 5G 173
Broughall. Shrp 1H 71
Brougham. Cumb 2G 103
Brough Lodge. Shet 2G 173
Brough Sowerby. Cumb 3A 104
Broughton. Cambs 3B 64
Broughton. Flin 4F 83
Broughton. Hants 3B 24
Broughton. Lanc 1D 90
Broughton. Mil 2G 51
Broughton. Nptn 3F 63
Broughton. N Lin 4C 94

Broughton. N Yor
  nr. Malton 2B 100
  nr. Skipton 4B 98
Broughton. Orkn 3D 172
Broughton. Oxon 2C 50
Broughton. Bord 1D 118
Broughton. Staf 2B 72
Broughton. V Glam 4C 32
Broughton Astley. Leics 1C 62
Broughton Beck. Cumb 1B 96
Broughton Cross. Cumb 1B 102
Broughton Gifford. Wilts 5D 35
Broughton Green. Worc 4D 60
Broughton Hackett. Worc 5D 60
Broughton in Furness. Cumb 1B 96
Broughton Mills. Cumb 5D 102
Broughton Moor. Cumb 1B 102
Broughton Park. G Man 4G 91
Broughton Poggs. Oxon 5H 49
Broughtown. Orkn 3F 172
Broughty Ferry. D'dee 5D 144
Brownaber. Shet 6D 173
Brownbread Street. E Sus 4A 28
Brown Candover. Hants 3D 24
Brown Edge. Lanc 3B 90
Brown Edge. Staf 5D 84
Brownhill. Bkbn 1E 91
Brownhill. Shrp 3G 71
Brownhills. Shrp 2A 72
Brownhills. W Mid 5E 73
Brown Knowl. Ches W 5G 83
Brownlow. Ches E 4C 84
Brownlow Heath. Ches E 4C 84
Brown's Green. W Mid 1E 61
Brownshill. Glos 5D 49
Brownston. Devn 3C 8
Brownstone. Devn 2A 12
Browston Green. Norf 5G 79
Broxa. N Yor 5G 107
Broxbourne. Herts 5D 52
Broxburn. E Lot 2C 130
Broxburn. W Lot 2D 128
Broxholme. Linc 3G 87
Broxted. Essx 3F 53
Broxton. Ches W 5G 83
Broxwood. Here 5F 59
Broyle Side. E Sus 4F 27
Brù. W Isl 3F 171
Bruach Mairi. W Isl 4G 171
Bruairnis. W Isl 8C 170
Bruan. High 5F 169
Bruar Lodge. Per 1F 143
Brucehill. W Dun 2E 127
Brucklay. Abers 3G 161
Bruera. Ches W 4G 83
Bruern Abbey. Oxon 3A 50
Bruichladdich. Arg 3A 124
Bruisyard. Suff 4F 67
Bruisyard Street. Suff 4F 67
Brumby. N Lin 4B 94
Brund. Staf 4F 85
Brundall. Norf 5F 79
Brundish. Norf 1F 67
Brundish. Suff 4E 67
Brundish Street. Suff 3E 67
Brunery. High 1B 140
Brunswick Village. Tyne 2F 115
Brunthwaite. W Yor 5C 98
Bruntingthorpe. Leics 1D 62
Brunton. Fife 1F 137
Brunton. Nmbd 2G 121
Brunton. Wilts 1H 23
Brushford. Devn 2G 11
Brushford. Som 4C 20
Brusta. W Isl 1E 170
Bruton. Som 3B 22
Bryanston. Dors 2D 14
Bryant's Bottom. Buck 2G 37
Brydekirk. Dum 2C 112
Brymbo. Wrex 5E 83
Brympton D'Evercy. Som 1A 14
Bryn. Carm 5F 45
Bryn. G Man 4D 90
Bryn. Neat 2B 32
Bryn. Shrp 2F 58
Brynamman. Carm 4H 45
Brynberian. Pemb 1F 43
Brynbryddan. Neat 2A 32
Bryncae. Rhon 3C 32
Bryncethin. B'end 3C 32
Bryncir. Gwyn 1D 69
Bryncroes. Gwyn 2B 68
Bryncrug. Gwyn 5F 69
Bryn Du. IOA 3C 80
Bryn Eden. Gwyn 3G 69
Bryn Eglwys. Gwyn 4F 81
Bryneglwys. Den 1D 70
Brynford. Flin 3D 82
Bryn Gates. G Man 4D 90
Bryn Golau. Rhon 3D 32
Bryngwran. IOA 3C 80
Bryngwyn. Mon 5G 47
Bryngwyn. Powy 1E 47
Bryn-henllan. Pemb 1E 43
Brynhoffnant. Cdgn 5C 56
Bryn-llwyn. Den 2C 82
Brynllywarch. Powy 2D 58
Bryn-mawr. Gwyn 2B 68
Brynmawr. Blae 4E 47
Brynmenyn. B'end 3C 32
Brynmill. Swan 3F 31
Brynna. Rhon 3C 32
Brynrefail. Gwyn 4E 81
Brynrefail. IOA 2D 81
Brynsadler. Rhon 3D 32
Bryn-Saith Marchog. Den 5C 82
Brynsiencyn. IOA 4D 81
Brynteg. IOA 2D 81
Brynteg. Wrex 5F 83
Brynygwenyn. Mon 4G 47

Bryn-y-maen. Cnwy 3H 81
Buaile nam Bodach. W Isl 8C 170
Bualintur. High 1C 146
Bubbenhall. Warw 3A 62
Bubwith. E Yor 1H 93
Buccleuch. Bord 3F 119
Buchanan Smithy. Stir 1F 127
Buchanhaven. Abers 4H 161
Buchanty. Per 1B 136
Buchany. Stir 3G 135
Buchley. E Dun 2G 127
Buchlyvie. Stir 4E 135
Buckabank. Cumb 5E 113
Buckden. Cambs 4A 64
Buckden. N Yor 2B 98
Buckenham. Norf 5F 79
Buckerell. Devn 2E 12
Buckfast. Devn 2D 8
Buckfastleigh. Devn 2D 8
Buckhaven. Fife 4F 137
Buckholm. Bord 1G 119
Buckholt. Here 4A 48
Buckhorn Weston. Dors 4C 22
Buckhurst Hill. Essx 1F 39
Buckie. Mor 2B 160
Buckingham. Buck 2E 51
Buckland. Buck 4G 51
Buckland. Glos 2F 49
Buckland. Here 5H 59
Buckland. Herts 2D 52
Buckland. Kent 1H 29
Buckland. Oxon 2B 36
Buckland. Surr 5D 38
Buckland Brewer. Devn 4E 19
Buckland Common. Buck 5H 51
Buckland Dinham. Som 1C 22
Buckland Filleigh. Devn 2E 11
Buckland in the Moor. Devn 5H 11
Buckland Monachorum. Devn 2A 8
Buckland Newton. Dors 2B 14
Buckland Ripers. Dors 4B 14
Buckland St Mary. Som 1F 13
Buckland-tout-Saints. Devn 4D 8
Bucklebury. W Ber 4D 36
Bucklegate. Linc 2C 76
Buckleigh. Devn 4E 19
Buckler's Hard. Hants 3C 16
Bucklesham. Suff 1F 55
Buckley. Flin 4E 83
Buckley Green. Warw 4F 61
Buckley Hill. Mers 1F 83
Bucklow Hill. Ches E 2B 84
Buckminster. Leics 3F 75
Bucknall. Linc 4A 88
Bucknall. Stoke 1D 72
Bucknell. Oxon 3D 50
Bucknell. Shrp 3F 59
Buckpool. Mor 2B 160
Buck's Cross. Devn 4D 18
Bucks Green. W Sus 2B 26
Buckshaw Village. Lanc 2D 90
Bucks Hill. Herts 5A 52
Bucks Horn Oak. Hants 2G 25
Buck's Mills. Devn 4D 18
Buckton. E Yor 2F 101
Buckton. Here 3F 59
Buckton. Nmbd 1E 121
Buckton Vale. G Man 4H 91
Buckworth. Cambs 3A 64
Budby. Notts 4D 86
Bude. Corn 2C 10
Budge's Shop. Corn 3H 7
Budlake. Devn 2C 12
Budle. Nmbd 1F 121
Budleigh Salterton. Devn 4D 12
Budock Water. Corn 5B 6
Buerton. Ches E 1A 72
Buffler's Holt. Buck 2E 51
Bugbrooke. Nptn 5D 62
Buglawton. Ches E 4C 84
Bugle. Corn 3E 6
Bugthorpe. E Yor 4B 100
Buildwas. Shrp 5A 72
Builth Road. Powy 5C 58
Builth Wells. Powy 5C 58
Bulbourne. Herts 4H 51
Bulby. Linc 3H 75
Bulcote. Notts 1D 74
Buldoo. High 2B 168
Bulford. Wilts 2G 23
Bulford Camp. Wilts 2G 23
Bulkeley. Ches E 5H 83
Bulkington. Warw 2A 62
Bulkington. Wilts 1E 23
Bulkworthy. Devn 1D 11
Bullamoor. N Yor 5A 106
Bull Bay. IOA 1D 80
Bullbridge. Derbs 5A 86
Bullgill. Cumb 1B 102
Bull Hill. Hants 3B 16
Bullinghope. Here 2A 48
Bull's Green. Herts 4C 52
Bullwood. Arg 2C 126
Bulmer. Essx 1B 54
Bulmer. N Yor 3A 100
Bulmer Tye. Essx 2B 54
Bulphan. Thur 2H 39
Bulverhythe. E Sus 5B 28
Bulwark. Abers 4G 161
Bulwell. Nott 1C 74
Bulwick. Nptn 1G 63
Bumble's Green. Essx 5E 53
Bun Abhainn Eadarra. W Isl 7D 171
Bunacaimb. High 5E 147
Bun a' Mhuillinn. W Isl 7C 170
Bunarkaig. High 5D 148
Bunbury. Ches E 5H 83
Bunchrew. High 4A 158
Bundalloch. High 1A 148
Buness. Shet 1H 173

Bunessan. Arg 1A 132
Bungay. Suff 2F 67
Bunkegivie. High 2H 149
Bunker's Hill. Cambs 5D 76
Bunker's Hill. Linc 5B 88
Bunkers Hill. Linc 5B 88
Bunloit. High 1H 149
Bunnahabhain. Arg 2C 124
Bunny. Notts 3C 74
Bunoich. High 3F 149
Bunree. High 2E 141
Bunroy. High 5E 149
Buntait. High 5G 157
Buntingford. Herts 3D 52
Bunting's Green. Essx 2B 54
Bunwell. Norf 1D 66
Burbage. Derbs 3E 85
Burbage. Leics 1B 62
Burbage. Wilts 5H 35
Burcher. Here 4F 59
Burchett's Green. Wind 3G 37
Burcombe. Wilts 3F 23
Burcot. Oxon 2D 36
Burcot. Worc 3D 61
Burcote. Shrp 1B 60
Burcott. Buck 3G 51
Burcott. Som 2A 22
Burdale. N Yor 3C 100
Burdrop. Oxon 2B 50
Bures. Suff 2C 54
The Burf. Worc 4C 60
Burford. Oxon 4A 50
Burford. Shrp 4H 59
Burg. Arg 4E 139
Burgate Great Green. Suff 3C 66
Burgate Little Green. Suff 3C 66
Burgess Hill. W Sus 4E 27
Burgh. Suff 5E 67
Burgh by Sands. Cumb 4E 113
Burgh Castle. Norf 5G 79
Burghclere. Hants 5C 36
Burghead. Mor 2F 159
Burghfield. W Ber 5E 37
Burghfield Common. W Ber 5E 37
Burghfield Hill. W Ber 5E 37
Burgh Heath. Surr 5D 38
Burghill. Here 1H 47
Burgh le Marsh. Linc 4E 89
Burgh Muir. Abers 2E 153
Burgh next Aylsham. Norf 3E 78
Burgh on Bain. Linc 2B 88
Burgh St Margaret. Norf 4G 79
Burgh St Peter. Norf 1G 67
Burghwallis. S Yor 3F 93
Burham. Kent 4B 40
Buriton. Hants 4F 25
Burland. Ches E 5A 84
Burland. Shet 8E 173
Burlawn. Corn 2D 6
Burleigh. Glos 5D 48
Burleigh. Wind 4G 37
Burlescombe. Devn 1D 12
Burleston. Dors 3C 14
Burlestone. Devn 4E 9
Burley. Hants 2H 15
Burley. Rut 4F 75
Burley. W Yor 1C 92
Burleydam. Ches E 1A 72
Burley Gate. Here 1A 48
Burley in Wharfedale. W Yor 5D 98
Burley Street. Hants 2H 15
Burley Woodhead. W Yor 5D 98
Burlingjobb. Powy 5E 59
Burlington. Shrp 4B 72
Burlton. Shrp 3G 71
Burmantofts. W Yor 1D 92
Burmarsh. Kent 2F 29
Burmington. Warw 2A 50
Burn. N Yor 2F 93
Burnage. G Man 1C 84
Burnaston. Derbs 2G 73
Burnbanks. Cumb 3G 103
Burnby. E Yor 5C 100
Burncross. S Yor 1H 85
Burneside. Cumb 5G 103
Burness. Orkn 3F 172
Burneston. N Yor 1F 99
Burnett. Bath 5B 34
Burnfoot. E Ayr 4D 116
Burnfoot. Per 3B 136
Burnfoot. Bord
  nr. Hawick 3H 119
  nr. Roberton 3G 119
Burngreave. S Yor 2A 86
Burnham. Buck 2A 38
Burnham. N Lin 3D 94
Burnham Deepdale. Norf 1H 77
Burnham Green. Herts 4C 52
Burnham Market. Norf 1H 77
Burnham Norton. Norf 1H 77
Burnham-on-Crouch. Essx 1D 40
Burnham-on-Sea. Som 2G 21
Burnham Overy Staithe. Norf 1H 77
Burnham Overy Town. Norf 1H 77
Burnham Thorpe. Norf 1H 77
Burnhaven. Abers 4H 161
Burnhead. Dum 5A 118
Burnhervie. Abers 2E 153
Burnhill Green. Staf 5B 72
Burnhope. Dur 5E 115
Burnhouse. N Ayr 4E 127
Burniston. N Yor 5H 107
Burnlee. W Yor 4B 92
Burnley. Lanc 1G 91
Burnmouth. Bord 3F 131
Burn Naze. Lanc 5C 96
Burn of Cambus. Stir 3G 135
Burnopfield. Dur 4E 115
Burnsall. N Yor 3C 98
Burnside. Ang 3E 145
Burnside. E Ayr 3E 117

Burnside. Per 3D 136
Burnside. Shet 4D 173
Burnside. S Lan 4H 127
Burnside. W Lot
  nr. Broxburn 2D 129
  nr. Winchburgh 2D 128
Burntcommon. Surr 5B 38
Burnt Heath. Essx 3D 54
Burntheath. Derbs 2G 73
Burnt Hill. W Ber 4D 36
Burnt Houses. Dur 2E 105
Burntisland. Fife 1F 129
Burnton. E Ayr 4D 117
Burntstalk. Norf 2G 77
Burntwood. Staf 5E 73
Burntwood Green. Staf 5E 73
Burnt Yates. N Yor 3E 99
Burnwynd. Edin 3E 129
Burpham. Surr 5B 38
Burpham. W Sus 5B 26
Burradon. Nmbd 4D 121
Burradon. Tyne 2F 115
Burrafirth. Shet 1H 173
Burragarth. Shet 1G 173
Burras. Corn 5A 6
Burraton. Corn 3A 8
Burravoe. Shet
  nr. North Roe 3E 173
  on Mainland 5E 173
  on Yell 4G 173
Burray Village. Orkn 8D 172
Burrells. Cumb 3H 103
Burrelton. Per 5A 144
Burridge. Hants 1D 16
Burridge. Som 2G 13
Burrigill. High 5E 169
Burrill. N Yor 1E 99
Burringham. N Lin 4B 94
Burrington. Devn 1G 11
Burrington. Here 3G 59
Burrington. Som 1H 21
Burrough End. Cambs 5F 65
Burrough Green. Cambs 5F 65
Burrough on the Hill. Leics 4E 75
Burroughston. Orkn 5E 172
Burrow. Devn 4D 12
Burrow. Som 2C 20
Burrowbridge. Som 4G 21
Burrowhill. Surr 4A 38
Burry. Swan 3D 30
Burry Green. Swan 3D 30
Burry Port. Carm 5E 45
Burscough. Lanc 3C 90
Burscough Bridge. Lanc 3C 90
Bursea. E Yor 1B 94
Burshill. E Yor 5E 101
Bursledon. Hants 2C 16
Burslem. Stoke 1C 72
Burstall. Suff 1D 54
Burstock. Dors 2H 13
Burston. Devn 2H 11
Burston. Norf 2D 66
Burston. Staf 2D 72
Burstow. Surr 1E 27
Burstwick. E Yor 2F 95
Burtersett. N Yor 1A 98
Burtholme. Cumb 3G 113
Burthorpe. Suff 4G 65
Burthwaite. Cumb 5F 113
Burtle. Som 2H 21
Burtoft. Linc 2B 76
Burton. Ches W
  nr. Kelsall 4H 83
  nr. Neston 3F 83
Burton. Dors
  nr. Christchurch 3G 15
  nr. Dorchester 3B 14
Burton. Nmbd 1F 121
Burton. Pemb 4D 43
Burton. Som 2E 21
Burton. Wilts
  nr. Chippenham 4D 34
  nr. Warminster 3D 22
Burton. Wrex 5F 83
Burton Agnes. E Yor 3F 101
Burton Bradstock. Dors 4H 13
Burton-by-Lincoln. Linc 3G 87
Burton Coggles. Linc 3G 75
Burton Constable. E Yor 1E 95
Burton Corner. Linc 1C 76
Burton End. Cambs 1G 53
Burton End. Essx 3F 53
Burton Fleming. E Yor 2E 101
Burton Green. Warw 3G 61
Burton Green. Wrex 5F 83
Burton Hastings. Warw 2B 62
Burton-in-Kendal. Cumb 2E 97
Burton in Lonsdale. N Yor 2F 97
Burton Joyce. Notts 1D 74
Burton Lazars. Leics 4E 75
Burton Leonard. N Yor 3F 99
Burton on the Wolds. Leics 3C 74
Burton Overy. Leics 1D 62
Burton Pedwardine. Linc 1A 76
Burton Pidsea. E Yor 1F 95
Burton Salmon. N Yor 2E 93
Burton's Green. Essx 3B 54
Burton Stather. N Lin 3B 94
Burton upon Stather. N Lin 3B 94
Burton upon Trent. Staf 3G 73
Burton Wolds. Leics 3D 74
Burtonwood. Warr 1H 83
Burwardsley. Ches W 5H 83
Burwarton. Shrp 2A 60
Burwash. E Sus 3A 28
Burwash Common. E Sus 3H 27
Burwash Weald. E Sus 3A 28
Burwell. Cambs 4E 65
Burwell. Linc 3C 88

Burwen. IOA 1D **80**
Burwick. Orkn 9D **172**
Bury. Cambs 2B **64**
Bury. G Man 3G **91**
Bury. Som 4C **20**
Bury. W Sus 4B **26**
Burybank. Staf 2C **72**
Bury End. Worc 2F **49**
Bury Green. Herts 3E **53**
Bury St Edmunds. Suff 4H **65**
Burythorpe. N Yor 3B **100**
Busbridge. Surr 1A **26**
Busby. E Ren 4G **127**
Busby. Per 1C **136**
Buscot. Oxon 2H **35**
Bush. Corn 2C **10**
Bush Bank. Here 5G **59**
Bushbury. W Mid 5D **72**
Bushby. Leics 5D **74**
Bushey. Dors 4E **15**
Bushey. Herts 1C **38**
Bushey Heath. Herts 1C **38**
Bush Green. Norf
  nr. Attleborough 1C **66**
  nr. Harleston 2E **66**
Bush Green. Suff 5B **66**
Bushley. Worc 2D **49**
Bushley Green. Worc 2D **48**
Bushmead. Bed 4A **64**
Bushmoor. Shrp 2G **59**
Bushton. Wilts 4F **35**
Bushy Common. Norf 4B **78**
Busk. Cumb 5H **113**
Buslingthorpe. Linc 2H **87**
Bussage. Glos 5D **49**
Bussex. Som 3G **21**
Busta. Shet 5E **173**
Butcher's Cross. E Sus 3G **27**
Butcombe. N Som 5A **34**
Bute Town. Cphy 5E **46**
Butleigh. Som 3A **22**
Butleigh Wootton. Som 3A **22**
Butlers Marston. Warw 1B **50**
Butley. Suff 5F **67**
Butley High Corner. Suff 1G **55**
Butlocks Heath. Hants 2C **16**
Butterburn. Cumb 2H **113**
Buttercrambe. N Yor 4B **100**
Butterknowle. Dur 2E **105**
Butterleigh. Devn 2C **12**
Buttermere. Cumb 3C **102**
Buttermere. Wilts 5B **36**
Buttershaw. W Yor 2B **92**
Butterstone. Per 4H **143**
Butterton. Staf
  nr. Leek 5E **85**
  nr. Stoke-on-Trent 1C **72**
Butterwick. Dur 2A **106**
Butterwick. Linc 1C **76**
Butterwick. N Yor
  nr. Malton 2B **100**
  nr. Weaverthorpe 2D **101**
Butteryhaugh. Nmbd 5A **120**
Butt Green. Ches E 5A **84**
Buttington. Powy 5E **71**
Buttonbridge. Shrp 3B **60**
Buttonoak. Shrp 3B **60**
Buttsash. Hants 2C **16**
Butt's Green. Essx 5A **54**
Butt Yeats. Lanc 3E **97**
Buxhall. Suff 5C **66**
Buxted. E Sus 3F **27**
Buxton. Derbs 3E **85**
Buxton. Norf 3E **79**
Buxworth. Derbs 2E **85**
Bwcle. Flin 4E **83**
Bwlch. Powy 3E **47**
Bwlchderwin. Gwyn 1D **68**
Bwlchgwyn. Wrex 5E **83**
Bwlch-Llan. Cdgn 5E **57**
Bwlchnewydd. Carm 3D **44**
Bwlchtocyn. Gwyn 3C **68**
Bwlch-y-cibau. Powy 4D **70**
Bwlch-y-ddar. Powy 3D **70**
Bwlch-y-fadfa. Cdgn 1E **45**
Bwlch y Garreg. Powy 1C **58**
Bwlch-y-groes. Pemb 1G **43**
Bwlch-y-sarnau. Powy 3C **58**
Bybrook. Kent 1E **28**
Byermoor. Tyne 4E **115**
Byers Garth. Dur 5G **115**
Byers Green. Dur 1F **105**
Byfield. Nptn 5C **62**
Byfleet. Surr 4B **38**
Byford. Here 1G **47**
Bygrave. Herts 2C **52**
Byker. Tyne 3F **115**
Byland Abbey. N Yor 2H **99**
Bylchau. Cnwy 4B **82**
Byley. Ches W 4B **84**
Bynea. Carm 3E **31**
Byram. N Yor 2E **93**
Byrness. Nmbd 4B **120**
Bystock. Devn 4D **12**
Bythorn. Cambs 3H **63**
Byton. Here 4F **59**
Bywell. Nmbd 3D **114**
Byworth. W Sus 3A **26**

C

Cabharstadh. W Isl 6F **171**
Cabourne. Linc 4E **95**
Cabrach. Arg 3C **124**
Cabrach. Mor 1A **152**
Cabus. Lanc 5D **97**
Cadbury. Devn 2C **12**
Cadder. E Dun 2H **127**
Caddington. C Beds 4A **52**

Caddonfoot. Bord 1G **119**
Cadeby. Leics 5B **74**
Cadeby. S Yor 4F **93**
Cadeleigh. Devn 2C **12**
Cade Street. E Sus 3H **27**
Cadgwith. Corn 5E **5**
Cadham. Fife 3E **137**
Cadishead. G Man 1B **84**
Cadle. Swan 3F **31**
Cadley. Lanc 1D **90**
Cadley. Wilts
  nr. Ludgershall 1H **23**
  nr. Marlborough 5H **35**
Cadmore End. Buck 2F **37**
Cadnam. Hants 1A **16**
Cadney. N Lin 4D **94**
Cadole. Flin 4E **82**
Cadoxton-juxta-Neath. Neat 2A **32**
Cadwell. Herts 2B **52**
Cadwst. Den 2C **70**
Caeathro. Gwyn 4E **81**
Caehopkin. Powy 4B **46**
Caenby. Linc 2H **87**
Caerau. B'end 2B **32**
Caerau. Card 4E **33**
Cae'r-bont. Powy 4B **46**
Cae'r-bryn. Carm 4F **45**
Caerdeon. Gwyn 4F **69**
Caerdydd. Card 191 (4E **33**)
Caerfarchell. Pemb 2B **42**
Caerffili. Cphy 3E **33**
Caerfyrddin. Carm 4E **45**
Caergeiliog. IOA 3C **80**
Caergwrle. Flin 5F **83**
Caergybi. IOA 2B **80**
Caerlaverock. Per 2A **136**
Caerleon. Newp 2G **33**
Caerllion. Carm 2G **43**
Caerllion. Newp 2G **33**
Caernarfon. Gwyn 190 (4D **81**)
Caerphilly. Cphy 3E **33**
Caersws. Powy 1C **58**
Caerwedros. Cdgn 5C **56**
Caerwent. Mon 2H **33**
Caerwys. Flin 3D **82**
Caim. IOA 2F **81**
Caio. Carm 2G **45**
Cairinis. W Isl 2D **170**
Cairisiadar. W Isl 4C **171**
Cairiminis. W Isl 9C **171**
Cairnbaan. Arg 4F **133**
Cairnbulg. Abers 2H **161**
Cairncross. Ang 1D **145**
Cairndow. Arg 2A **134**
Cairness. Abers 2H **161**
Cairneyhill. Fife 1D **128**
Cairngarroch. Dum 5F **109**
Cairnhill. Abers 5D **160**
Cairnie. Abers 4B **160**
Cairnorrie. Abers 4F **161**
Cairnryan. Dum 3F **109**
Cairston. Orkn 6B **172**
Caister-on-Sea. Norf 4H **79**
Caistor. Linc 4E **94**
Caistor St Edmund. Norf 5E **79**
Caistron. Nmbd 4D **121**
Cakebole. Worc 3C **60**
Calais Street. Suff 1C **54**
Calanais. W Isl 4E **171**
Calbost. W Isl 6G **171**
Calbourne. IOW 4C **16**
Calceby. Linc 3C **88**
Calcot. Glos 4F **49**
Calcot Row. W Ber 4E **37**
Calcott. Kent 4F **41**
Calcott. Shrp 4G **71**
Caldback. Shet 1H **173**
Caldbeck. Cumb 1E **102**
Caldbergh. N Yor 1C **98**
Caldecote. Cambs
  nr. Cambridge 5C **64**
  nr. Peterborough 2A **64**
Caldecote. Herts 2C **52**
Caldecote. Nptn 5D **62**
Caldecote. Warw 1A **62**
Caldecott. Nptn 4G **63**
Caldecott. Oxon 2C **36**
Caldecott. Rut 1F **63**
Calderbank. N Lan 3A **128**
Calder Bridge. Cumb 4B **102**
Calderbrook. G Man 3H **91**
Caldercruix. N Lan 3B **128**
Calder Grove. W Yor 3D **92**
Calder Mains. High 3C **168**
Caldermill. S Lan 5H **127**
Calder Vale. Lanc 5E **97**
Calderwood. S Lan 4H **127**
Caldicot. Mon 3H **33**
Caldwell. Derbs 4G **73**
Caldwell. N Yor 3E **105**
Caldy. Mers 2E **83**
Calebrack. Cumb 1E **103**
Calf Heath. Staf 5D **72**
Calford Green. Suff 1G **53**
Calfsound. Orkn 4E **172**
Calgary. Arg 3E **139**
Califer. Mor 3E **159**
California. Cambs 2E **65**
California. Falk 2C **128**
California. Norf 4H **79**
California. Suff 1E **55**
Calke. Derbs 3A **74**
Callakille. High 3F **155**
Callaly. Nmbd 4E **121**
Callander. Stir 3F **135**
Callaughton. Shrp 1A **60**
Callestick. Corn 3B **6**
Calligarry. High 3E **147**
Callington. Corn 2H **7**
Callingwood. Staf 3F **73**

Callow. Here 2H **47**
Callowell. Glos 5D **48**
Callow End. Worc 1D **48**
Callow Hill. Wilts 3F **35**
Callow Hill. Worc
  nr. Bewdley 3B **60**
  nr. Redditch 4E **61**
Calmore. Hants 1B **16**
Calmsden. Glos 5F **49**
Calne. Wilts 4E **35**
Calow. Derbs 3B **86**
Calshot. Hants 2C **16**
Calstock. Corn 2A **8**
Calstone Wellington. Wilts 5F **35**
Calthorpe. Norf 2D **78**
Calthorpe Street. Norf 3G **79**
Calthwaite. Cumb 5F **113**
Calton. N Yor 4B **98**
Calton. Staf 5F **85**
Calveley. Ches E 5H **83**
Calver. Derbs 3G **85**
Calverhall. Shrp 2A **72**
Calverleigh. Devn 1C **12**
Calverley. W Yor 1C **92**
Calvert. Buck 3E **51**
Calverton. Mil 2F **51**
Calverton. Notts 1D **74**
Calvine. Per 2F **143**
Calvo. Cumb 4C **112**
Cam. Glos 2C **34**
Camaghael. High 1F **141**
Camas-luinie. High 1B **148**
Camasnacroise. High 3C **140**
Camastianavaig. High 5E **155**
Camasunary. High 2D **146**
Camault Muir. High 4H **157**
Camb. Shet 2G **173**
Camber. E Sus 4D **28**
Camberley. Surr 5G **37**
Camberwell. G Lon 3E **39**
Camblesforth. N Yor 2G **93**
Cambo. Nmbd 1D **114**
Cambois. Nmbd 1G **115**
Camborne. Corn 5A **6**
Cambourne. Cambs 5C **64**
Cambridge. Cambs 191 (5D **64**)
Cambridge. Glos 5C **48**
Cambrose. Corn 4A **6**
Cambus. Clac 4A **136**
Cambusbarron. Stir 4G **135**
Cambuskenneth. Stir 4H **135**
Cambuslang. S Lan 3H **127**
Cambusnethan. N Lan 4B **128**
Cambus o' May. Abers 4B **152**
Camden Town. G Lon 2D **39**
Cameley. Bath 1B **22**
Camelford. Corn 4B **10**
Camelon. Falk 1B **128**
Camelsdale. W Sus 3G **25**
Camer's Green. Worc 2C **48**
Camerton. Bath 1B **22**
Camerton. Cumb 1B **102**
Camerton. E Yor 2F **95**
Camghouran. Per 3C **142**
Cammachmore. Abers 4G **153**
Cammeringham. Linc 2G **87**
Camore. High 4E **165**
Campbeltown. N Ayr 4C **126**
Campbeltown. Arg 3B **122**
Campbeltown Airport. Arg 3A **122**
Cample. Dum 5A **118**
Campmuir. Per 5B **144**
Campsall. S Yor 3F **93**
Campsea Ashe. Suff 5F **67**
Camps End. Cambs 1G **53**
Campton. C Beds 2B **52**
Camptoun. E Lot 2B **130**
Camptown. Bord 3A **120**
Camrose. Pemb 2D **42**
Camserney. Per 4F **143**
Camster. High 4E **169**
Camus Croise. High 2E **147**
Camuscross. High 2E **147**
Camusdarach. High 4E **147**
Camusnagaul. High
  nr. Fort William 1E **141**
  nr. Little Loch Broom 5E **163**
Camusteel. High 4G **155**
Camusterrach. High 4G **155**
Camusvrachan. Per 4D **142**
Canada. Hants 1A **16**
Canadia. E Sus 4B **28**
Canaston Bridge. Pemb 3E **43**
Candlesby. Linc 4D **88**
Candle Street. Suff 3C **66**
Candy Mill. S Lan 5D **128**
Cane End. Oxon 4E **37**
Canewdon. Essx 1D **40**
Canford Cliffs. Pool 4F **15**
Canford Heath. Pool 3F **15**
Canford Magna. Pool 3F **15**
Cangate. Norf 3F **79**
Canham's Green. Suff 4C **66**
Canholes. Derbs 3E **85**
Canisbay. High 1F **169**
Canley. W Mid 3H **61**
Cann. Dors 4D **22**
Cann Common. Dors 4D **23**
Cannich. High 5F **157**
Cannington. Som 3F **21**
Cannock. Staf 4D **73**
Cannock Wood. Staf 4E **73**
Canonbie. Dum 2E **113**
Canon Bridge. Here 1H **47**
Canon Frome. Here 1B **48**
Canon Pyon. Here 1H **47**
Canons Ashby. Nptn 5C **62**
Canonstown. Corn 3C **4**
Canterbury. Kent 190 (5F **41**)
Cantley. Norf 5F **79**

Cantley. S Yor 4G **93**
Cantlop. Shrp 5H **71**
Canton. Card 4E **33**
Cantray. High 4B **158**
Cantraybruich. High 4B **158**
Cantraywood. High 4B **158**
Cantsdam. Fife 4D **136**
Cantsfield. Lanc 2F **97**
Canvey Island. Essx 2B **40**
Canwick. Linc 4G **87**
Canworthy Water. Corn 3C **10**
Caol. High 1F **141**
Caolas. Arg 4B **138**
Caolas. W Isl 9B **170**
Caolas Liubharsaigh. W Isl 4D **170**
Caolas Scalpaigh. W Isl 8E **171**
Caolas Stocinis. W Isl 8D **171**
Caol Ila. Arg 2C **124**
Caol Loch Ailse. High 1F **147**
Caol Reatha. High 1F **147**
Capel. Kent 1H **27**
Capel. Surr 1C **26**
Capel Bangor. Cdgn 2F **57**
Capel Betws Lleucu. Cdgn 5F **57**
Capel Coch. IOA 2D **80**
Capel Curig. Cnwy 5G **81**
Capel Cynon. Cdgn 1D **45**
Capel Dewi. Carm 3E **45**
Capel Dewi. Cdgn
  nr. Aberystwyth 2F **57**
  nr. Llandysul 1E **45**
Capel Garmon. Cnwy 5H **81**
Capel Green. Suff 1G **55**
Capel Gwyn. IOA 3C **80**
Capel Gwynfe. Carm 3H **45**
Capel Hendre. Carm 4F **45**
Capel Isaac. Carm 3F **45**
Capel Iwan. Carm 1G **43**
Capel-le-Ferne. Kent 2G **29**
Capel Llanilltern. Card 4D **32**
Capel Mawr. IOA 3D **80**
Capel Newydd. Pemb 1G **43**
Capel St Andrew. Suff 1G **55**
Capel St Mary. Suff 2D **54**
Capel Seion. Carm 4F **45**
Capel Seion. Cdgn 3F **57**
Capel Uchaf. Gwyn 1D **68**
Capel-y-ffin. Powy 2F **47**
Capenhurst. Ches W 3F **83**
Capernwray. Lanc 2E **97**
Capheaton. Nmbd 1D **114**
Cappercleuch. Bord 2E **119**
Capplegill. Dum 4D **118**
Capton. Devn 3E **9**
Capton. Som 3D **20**
Caputh. Per 5H **143**
Caradon Town. Corn 5C **10**
Carbis Bay. Corn 3C **4**
Carbost. High
  nr. Loch Harport 5C **154**
  nr. Portree 4D **154**
Carbrook. S Yor 2A **86**
Carbrooke. Norf 5B **78**
Carburton. Notts 3D **86**
Carcluie. S Ayr 3C **116**
Car Colston. Notts 1E **74**
Carcroft. S Yor 4F **93**
Cardenden. Fife 4E **136**
Cardeston. Shrp 4F **71**
Cardewlees. Cumb 4E **113**
Cardiff. Card 191 (4E **33**)
Cardiff Airport. V Glam 5D **32**
Cardigan. Cdgn 1B **44**
Cardinal's Green. Cambs 1G **53**
Cardington. Bed 1A **52**
Cardington. Shrp 1H **59**
Cardinham. Corn 2F **7**
Cardno. Abers 2G **161**
Cardow. Mor 4F **159**
Cardross. Arg 2E **127**
Cardurnock. Cumb 4C **112**
Careby. Linc 4H **75**
Careston. Ang 2E **145**
Carew. Pemb 4E **43**
Carew Cheriton. Pemb 4E **43**
Carew Newton. Pemb 4E **43**
Carey. Here 2A **48**
Carfin. N Lan 4A **128**
Carfrae. Bord 4B **130**
Cargate Green. Norf 4F **79**
Cargenbridge. Dum 2G **111**
Cargill. Per 5A **144**
Cargo. Cumb 4E **113**
Cargreen. Corn 2A **8**
Carham. Nmbd 1C **120**
Carhampton. Som 2D **20**
Carharrack. Corn 4B **6**
Carie. Per
  nr. Loch Rannach 3D **142**
  nr. Loch Tay 5D **142**
Carisbrooke. IOW 4C **16**
Cark. Cumb 2C **96**
Carkeel. Corn 2A **8**
Carlabhagh. W Isl 3E **171**
Carland Cross. Corn 3C **6**
Carlbury. Darl 3F **105**
Carlby. Linc 4H **75**
Carlecotes. S Yor 4B **92**
Carleen. Corn 4D **4**
Carlesmoor. N Yor 2D **98**
Carleton. Cumb
  nr. Carlisle 4F **113**
  nr. Egremont 4B **102**
  nr. Penrith 2G **103**
Carleton. Lanc 5C **96**
Carleton. N Yor 5B **98**
Carleton Forehoe. Norf 5C **78**
Carleton Rode. Norf 1D **66**
Carleton St Peter. Norf 5F **79**
Carlidnack. Corn 4E **5**

Carlingcott. Bath 1B **22**
Carlin How. Red C 3E **107**
Carlisle. Cumb 192 (4F **113**)
Carloonan. Arg 2H **133**
Carlops. Bord 4E **129**
Carlton. Bed 5G **63**
Carlton. Cambs 5F **65**
Carlton. Leics 5A **74**
Carlton. N Yor
  nr. Helmsley 1A **100**
  nr. Middleham 1C **98**
  nr. Selby 2G **93**
Carlton. Notts 1D **74**
Carlton. S Yor 3D **92**
Carlton. Stoc T 2A **106**
Carlton. Suff 4F **67**
Carlton. W Yor 2D **92**
Carlton Colville. Suff 1H **67**
Carlton Curlieu. Leics 1D **62**
Carlton Husthwaite. N Yor 2G **99**
Carlton in Cleveland. N Yor 4C **106**
Carlton in Lindrick. Notts 2C **86**
Carlton-le-Moorland. Linc 5G **87**
Carlton Miniott. N Yor 1F **99**
Carlton-on-Trent. Notts 4F **87**
Carlton Scroop. Linc 1G **75**
Carluke. S Lan 4B **128**
Carmarthen. Carm 4E **45**
Carmel. Carm 4F **45**
Carmel. Flin 3D **82**
Carmel. Gwyn 5D **81**
Carmel. IOA 2C **80**
Carmichael. S Lan 1B **118**
Carmunnock. Glas 4H **127**
Carmyle. Glas 3H **127**
Carmyllie. Ang 4E **145**
Carnaby. E Yor 3F **101**
Carnach. High
  nr. Lochcarron 1C **148**
  nr. Ullapool 4E **163**
Carnach. Mor 4E **159**
Carnach. W Isl 8E **171**
Carnachy. High 3H **167**
Carnain. Arg 3B **124**
Carnais. W Isl 4C **171**
Carnan. Arg 4B **138**
Carnan. W Isl 4C **170**
Carnbee. Fife 3H **137**
Carnbo. Per 3C **136**
Carn Brea Village. Corn 4A **6**
Carndu. High 1A **148**
Carne. Corn 5D **6**
Carnell. S Ayr 1D **116**
Carnforth. Lanc 2E **97**
Carn-gorm. High 1B **148**
Carnhedryn. Pemb 2C **42**
Carnhell Green. Corn 3D **4**
Carnie. Abers 3F **153**
Carnkie. Corn
  nr. Falmouth 5B **6**
  nr. Redruth 5A **6**
Carnkief. Corn 3B **6**
Carno. Powy 1B **58**
Carnock. Fife 1D **128**
Carnon Downs. Corn 4B **6**
Carnoustie. Ang 5E **145**
Carntyne. Glas 3H **127**
Carnwath. S Lan 5C **128**
Carnyorth. Corn 3A **4**
Carol Green. W Mid 3G **61**
Carpalla. Corn 3D **6**
Carperby. N Yor 1C **98**
Carradale. Arg 2C **122**
Carragraich. W Isl 8D **171**
Carrbridge. High 1D **150**
Carr Cross. Lanc 3B **90**
Carreglefn. IOA 2C **80**
Carrhouse. N Lin 4A **94**
Carrick Castle. Arg 4A **134**
Carrick Ho. Orkn 4E **172**
Carriden. Falk 1D **128**
Carrington. G Man 1B **84**
Carrington. Linc 5C **88**
Carrington. Midl 3G **129**
Carrog. Cnwy 1G **69**
Carrog. Den 1D **70**
Carron. Falk 1B **128**
Carron. Mor 4G **159**
Carronbridge. Dum 5A **118**
Carronshore. Falk 1B **128**
Carrow Hill. Mon 2H **33**
Carr Shield. Nmbd 5B **114**
Carrutherstown. Dum 2C **112**
Carr Vale. Derbs 4B **86**
Carrville. Dur 5G **115**
Carsaig. Arg 1C **132**
Carscreugh. Dum 3H **109**
Carsegowan. Dum 4B **110**
Carse House. Arg 3F **125**
Carseriggan. Dum 3A **110**
Carsethorn. Dum 4A **112**
Carshalton. G Lon 4D **39**
Carsington. Derbs 5G **85**
Carskiey. Arg 5A **122**
Carsluith. Dum 4B **110**
Carsphairn. Dum 5E **117**
Carstairs. S Lan 5C **128**
Carstairs Junction. S Lan 5C **128**
Cartbridge. Surr 5B **38**
Carterhaugh. Ang 4D **144**
Carter's Clay. Hants 4B **24**
Carterton. Oxon 5A **50**
Carterway Heads. Nmbd 4D **114**
Carthew. Corn 3E **6**
Carthorpe. N Yor 1F **99**
Cartington. Nmbd 4E **121**
Cartland. S Lan 5B **128**
Cartmel. Cumb 2C **96**
Cartmel Fell. Cumb 1D **96**
Cartworth. W Yor 4B **92**

Carwath – Chillenden

Carwath. Cumb 5E 112
Carway. Carm 5E 45
Carwinley. Cumb 2F 113
Cascob. Powy 4E 59
Cas-gwent. Mon 2A 34
Cash Feus. Fife 3E 136
Cashlie. Per 4B 142
Cashmoor. Dors 1E 15
Cas-Mael. Pemb 2E 43
Casnewydd.
Newp 205 (3G 33)
Cassington. Oxon 4C 50
Cassop. Dur 1A 106
Castell. Cnwy 4G 81
Castell. Den 4D 82
Castell Hendre. Pemb 2E 43
Castell-Nedd. Neat 2A 32
Castell Newydd Emlyn. Carm 1D 44
Castell-y-bwch. Torf 2F 33
Casterton. Cumb 2F 97
Castle. Som 2A 22
Castle Acre. Norf 4H 77
Castle Ashby. Nptn 5F 63
Castlebay. W Isl 9B 170
Castle Bolton. N Yor 5D 104
Castle Bromwich. W Mid 2F 61
Castle Bytham. Linc 4G 75
Castlebythe. Pemb 2E 43
Castle Caereinion. Powy 5D 70
Castle Camps. Cambs 1G 53
Castle Carrock. Cumb 4G 113
Castle Cary. Som 3B 22
Castlecary. N Lan 2A 128
Castle Combe. Wilts 4D 34
Castlecraig. High 2C 158
Castle Donington. Leics 3B 74
Castle Douglas. Dum 3E 111
Castle Eaton. Swin 2G 35
Castle Eden. Dur 1B 106
Castleford. W Yor 2E 93
Castle Frome. Here 1B 48
Castle Green. Surr 4A 38
Castle Green. Warw 3G 61
Castle Gresley. Derbs 4G 73
Castle Heaton. Nmbd 5F 131
Castle Hedingham. Essx 2A 54
Castle Hill. Kent 1A 28
Castle Hill. Suff 1E 55
Castlehill. Per 5B 144
Castlehill. S Lan 4B 128
Castlehill. W Dun 2E 127
Castle Kennedy. Dum 4G 109
Castle Lachlan. Arg 4H 133
Castlemartin. Pemb 5D 42
Castlemilk. Glas 4H 127
Castlemorris. Pemb 1D 42
Castlemorton. Worc 2C 48
Castle O'er. Dum 5E 119
Castle Park. N Yor 3F 107
Castlerigg. Cumb 2D 102
Castle Rising. Norf 3F 77
Castleside. Dur 5D 115
Castlethorpe. Mil 1F 51
Castleton. Abers 4F 151
Castleton. Arg 1G 125
Castleton. Derbs 2F 85
Castleton. G Man 3G 91
Castleton. Mor 1F 151
Castleton. Newp 3F 33
Castleton. N Yor 4D 107
Castleton. Per 2B 136
Castletown. Cumb 1G 103
Castletown. Dors 5B 14
Castletown. High 2D 169
Castletown. IOM 5B 108
Castletown. Tyne 4G 115
Castley. N Yor 5E 99
Caston. Norf 1B 66
Castor. Pet 1A 64
Caswell. Swan 4E 31
Catacol. N Ayr 5H 125
Catbrook. Mon 5A 48
Catchems End. Worc 3B 60
Catchgate. Dur 4E 115
Catcleugh. Nmbd 4B 120
Catcliffe. S Yor 2B 86
Catcott. Som 3G 21
Caterham. Surr 5E 39
Catfield. Norf 3F 79
Catfield Common. Norf 3F 79
Catfirth. Shet 6F 173
Catford. G Lon 3E 39
Catforth. Lanc 1C 90
Cathcart. Glas 3G 127
Cathedine. Powy 3E 47
Catherine-de-Barnes. W Mid 2F 61
Catherington. Hants 1E 17
Catherston Leweston. Dors 3G 13
Catherton. Shrp 3A 60
Catisfield. Hants 2D 16
Catlodge. High 4A 150
Catlowdy. Cumb 2F 113
Catmore. W Ber 3C 36
Caton. Devn 5A 12
Caton. Lanc 3E 97
Catrine. E Ayr 2E 117
Cat's Ash. Newp 2G 33
Catsfield. E Sus 4B 28
Catsgore. Som 4A 22
Catshill. Worc 3D 60
Cattal. N Yor 4G 99
Cattawade. Suff 2E 54
Catterall. Lanc 5E 97
Catterick. N Yor 5F 105
Catterick Bridge. N Yor 5F 105
Catterick Garrison. N Yor 5E 105
Catterlen. Cumb 1F 103
Catterline. Abers 1H 145
Catterton. N Yor 5H 99
Catteshall. Surr 1A 26
Catthorpe. Leics 3C 62
Cattistock. Dors 3A 14
Catton. Nmbd 4B 114
Catton. N Yor 2F 99
Catwick. E Yor 5F 101
Catworth. Cambs 3H 63
Caudle Green. Glos 4E 49
Caulcott. Oxon 3D 50
Cauldhame. Stir 4F 135
Cauldmill. Bord 3H 119
Cauldon. Staf 1E 73
Cauldon Lowe. Staf 1E 73
Cauldwells. Abers 3E 161
Caulkerbush. Dum 4G 111
Caulside. Dum 1F 113
Caunsall. Worc 2C 60
Caunton. Notts 4E 87
Causewayend. S Lan 1C 118
Causewayhead. Stir 4H 135
Causey Park. Nmbd 5F 121
Caute. Devn 1E 11
Cautley. Cumb 5H 103
Cavendish. Suff 1B 54
Cavendish Bridge. Leics 3B 74
Cavenham. Suff 3G 65
Caversfield. Oxon 3D 50
Caversham. Read 4F 37
Caversham Heights. Read 4F 37
Caverswall. Staf 1D 72
Cawdor. High 3C 158
Cawkwell. Linc 2B 88
Cawood. N Yor 1F 93
Cawsand. Corn 3A 8
Cawston. Norf 3D 78
Cawston. Warw 3B 62
Cawthorne. N Yor 1B 100
Cawthorne. S Yor 4C 92
Cawthorpe. Linc 3H 75
Cawton. N Yor 2A 100
Caxton. Cambs 5C 64
Caynham. Shrp 3H 59
Caythorpe. Linc 1G 75
Caythorpe. Notts 1D 74
Cayton. N Yor 1E 101
Ceallan. W Isl 3D 170
Ceann a Bhaigh. W Isl
on North Uist 2C 170
on Scalpay 8E 171
on South Harris 8D 171
Ceann a Bhàigh. W Isl 9C 171
Ceannacroc Lodge. High 2E 149
Ceann a Deas Loch Baghasdail.
W Isl 7C 170
Ceann an Leothaid. High 5E 147
Ceann a Tuath Loch Baghasdail.
W Isl 6C 170
Ceann Loch Ailleart. High 5F 147
Ceann Loch Muideirt. High 1B 140
Ceann-na-Cleithe. W Isl 8D 171
Ceann Shiphoirt. W Isl 6E 171
Ceann Tarabhaigh. W Isl 6E 171
Cearsiadar. W Isl 5F 171
Ceathramh Meadhanach.
W Isl 1D 170
Cefn Berain. Cnwy 4B 82
Cefn-brith. Cnwy 5B 82
Cefn-bryn-brain. Carm 4H 45
Cefn Bychan. Cphy 2F 33
Cefn-bychan. Flin 4D 82
Cefncaeau. Carm 3E 31
Cefn Canol. Powy 2E 71
Cefn Coch. Powy 5C 70
Cefn-coch. Powy 3D 70
Cefn-coed-y-cymmer. Mer T 5D 46
Cefn Cribwr. B'end 3B 32
Cefn-ddwysarn. Gwyn 2B 70
Cefn Einion. Shrp 2E 59
Cefneithin. Carm 4F 45
Cefn Glas. B'end 3B 32
Cefngorwydd. Powy 1C 46
Cefn Llwyd. Cdgn 2F 57
Cefn-mawr. Wrex 1E 71
Cefn-y-bedd. Flin 5F 83
Cefn-y-coed. Powy 1D 58
Cefn-y-pant. Carm 2F 43
Cegidfa. Powy 4E 70
Ceinewydd. Cdgn 5C 56
Cellan. Cdgn 1G 45
Cellardyke. Fife 3H 137
Cellarhead. Staf 1D 72
Cemaes. IOA 1C 80
Cemmaes. Powy 5H 69
Cemmaes Road. Powy 5H 69
Cenarth. Cdgn 1C 44
Cenin. Gwyn 1D 68
Ceos. W Isl 5F 171
Ceres. Fife 2G 137
Ceri. Powy 2D 58
Cerist. Powy 2B 58
Cerne Abbas. Dors 2B 14
Cerney Wick. Glos 2F 35
Cerrigceinwen. IOA 3D 80
Cerrigydrudion. Cnwy 1B 70
Cess. Norf 4G 79
Cessford. Bord 2B 120
Ceunant. Gwyn 4E 81
Chaceley. Glos 2D 48
Chacewater. Corn 4B 6
Chackmore. Buck 2E 51
Chacombe. Nptn 1C 50
Chadderton. G Man 4H 91
Chaddesden. Derb 2A 74
Chaddesden Common. Derb 2A 74
Chaddesley Corbett. Worc 3C 60
Chaddlehanger. Devn 5E 11
Chaddleworth. W Ber 4C 36
Chadlington. Oxon 3B 50
Chadshunt. Warw 5H 61
Chadstone. Nptn 5F 63
Chad Valley. W Mid 2E 61
Chadwell. Leics 3E 75
Chadwell. Shrp 4B 72
Chadwell Heath. G Lon 2F 39
Chadwell St Mary. Thur 3H 39
Chadwick End. W Mid 3G 61
Chadwick Green. Mers 1H 83
Chaffcombe. Som 1G 13
Chafford Hundred. Thur 3H 39
Chagford. Devn 4H 11
Chailey. E Sus 4E 27
Chain Bridge. Linc 1C 76
Chainbridge. Cambs 5D 76
Chainhurst. Kent 1B 28
Chalbury. Dors 2F 15
Chalbury Common. Dors 2F 15
Chaldon. Surr 5E 39
Chaldon Herring. Dors 4C 14
Chale. IOW 5C 16
Chale Green. IOW 5C 16
Chalfont Common. Buck 1B 38
Chalfont St Giles. Buck 1A 38
Chalfont St Peter. Buck 2B 38
Chalford. Glos 5D 49
Chalgrove. Oxon 2E 37
Chalk. Kent 3A 40
Chalk End. Essx 4G 53
Chalk Hill. Glos 3G 49
Challaborough. Devn 4C 8
Challacombe. Devn 2G 19
Challister. Shet 5G 173
Challoch. Dum 3A 110
Challock. Kent 5E 40
Chalton. C Beds
nr. Bedford 5A 64
nr. Luton 3A 52
Chalton. Hants 1F 17
Chalvington. E Sus 5G 27
Champany. Falk 2D 128
Chance Inn. Fife 2F 137
Chancery. Cdgn 3E 57
Chandler's Cross. Herts 1B 38
Chandler's Cross. Worc 2C 48
Chandler's Ford. Hants 4C 24
Chanlockfoot. Dum 4G 117
Channel's End. Bed 5A 64
Channel Tunnel. Kent 2F 29
Channerwick. Shet 9F 173
Chantry. Som 2C 22
Chantry. Suff 1E 55
Chapel. Cumb 1D 102
Chapel. Fife 4E 137
Chapel Allerton. Som 1H 21
Chapel Allerton. W Yor 1C 92
Chapel Amble. Corn 1D 6
Chapel Brampton. Nptn 4E 63
Chapelbridge. Cambs 1B 64
Chapel Chorlton. Staf 2C 72
Chapel Cleeve. Som 2D 20
Chapel End. C Beds 1A 52
Chapel-en-le-Frith. Derbs 2E 85
Chapelfield. Abers 2G 145
Chapelgate. Linc 3D 76
Chapel Green. Warw
nr. Coventry 2G 61
nr. Southam 4B 62
Chapel Haddlesey. N Yor 2F 93
Chapelhall. N Lan 3A 128
Chapel Hill. Abers 5H 161
Chapel Hill. Linc 5B 88
Chapel Hill. Mon 5A 48
Chapelhill. Per
nr. Glencarse 1E 136
nr. Harrietfield 5H 143
Chapelknowe. Dum 2E 112
Chapel Lawn. Shrp 3F 59
Chapel le Dale. N Yor 2G 97
Chapel Milton. Derbs 2E 85
Chapel of Garioch. Abers 1E 152
Chapel Row. W Ber 5D 36
Chapels. Cumb 1B 96
Chapel St Leonards. Linc 3E 89
Chapel Stile. Cumb 4E 102
Chapelthorpe. W Yor 3D 92
Chapelton. Ang 4F 145
Chapelton. Devn 4F 19
Chapelton. High
nr. Grantown-on-Spey 2D 150
nr. Inverness 3H 157
Chapelton. S Lan 5H 127
Chapel Town. Corn 3C 6
Chapeltown. Bkbn 3F 91
Chapeltown. Mor 1G 151
Chapeltown. S Yor 1A 86
Chapmanslade. Wilts 2D 22
Chapmans Well. Devn 3D 10
Chapmore End. Herts 4D 52
Chappel. Essx 3B 54
Chard. Som 2G 13
Chard Junction. Dors 2G 13
Chardstock. Devn 2G 13
Charfield. S Glo 2C 34
Charing. Kent 1D 28
Charing Heath. Kent 1D 28
Charing Hill. Kent 5D 40
Charingworth. Glos 2H 49
Charlbury. Oxon 4B 50
Charlcombe. Bath 5C 34
Charlcutt. Wilts 4E 35
Charlecote. Warw 5G 61
Charles. Devn 3G 19
Charlesfield. Dum 3C 112
Charleshill. Surr 2G 25
Charleston. Ang 4C 144
Charleston. Ren 3F 127
Charlestown. Aber 3G 153
Charlestown. Abers 2H 161
Charlestown. Corn 3E 7
Charlestown. Dors 5B 14
Charlestown. Fife 1D 128
Charlestown. G Man 4G 91
Charlestown. High
nr. Gairloch 1H 155
nr. Inverness 4A 158
Charlestown. W Yor 2H 91
Charlestown of Aberlour. Mor 4G 159
Charles Tye. Suff 5C 66
Charlesworth. Derbs 1E 85
Charlton. G Lon 3F 39
Charlton. Hants 2B 24
Charlton. Herts 3B 52
Charlton. Nptn 2D 50
Charlton. Nmbd 1B 114
Charlton. Oxon 3C 36
Charlton. Som
nr. Radstock 1B 22
nr. Shepton Mallet 2B 22
nr. Taunton 4F 21
Charlton. Telf 4H 71
Charlton. W Sus 1G 17
Charlton. Wilts
nr. Malmesbury 3E 35
nr. Pewsey 1G 23
nr. Shaftesbury 4E 23
Charlton. Worc
nr. Evesham 1F 49
nr. Stourport-on-Severn 3C 60
Charlton Abbots. Glos 3F 49
Charlton Adam. Som 4A 22
Charlton All Saints. Wilts 4G 23
Charlton Down. Dors 3B 14
Charlton Horethorne. Som 4B 22
Charlton Kings. Glos 3E 49
Charlton Mackrell. Som 4A 22
Charlton Marshall. Dors 2E 15
Charlton Musgrove. Som 4C 22
Charlton-on-Otmoor. Oxon 4D 50
Charlton on the Hill. Dors 2D 15
Charlwood. Hants 3E 25
Charlwood. Surr 1D 26
Charlynch. Som 3F 21
Charminster. Dors 3B 14
Charmouth. Dors 3G 13
Charndon. Buck 3E 51
Charney Bassett. Oxon 2B 36
Charnock Green. Lanc 3D 90
Charnock Richard. Lanc 3D 90
Charsfield. Suff 5E 67
The Chart. Kent 5F 39
Chart Corner. Kent 5B 40
Charter Alley. Hants 1D 24
Charterhouse. Som 1H 21
Charterville Allotments. Oxon 4B 50
Chartham. Kent 5F 41
Chartham Hatch. Kent 5F 41
Chartridge. Buck 5H 51
Chart Sutton. Kent 5B 40
Charvil. Wok 4F 37
Charwelton. Nptn 5C 62
Chase Terrace. Staf 5E 73
Chasetown. Staf 5E 73
Chastleton. Oxon 3H 49
Chasty. Devn 2D 10
Chatburn. Lanc 5G 97
Chatcull. Staf 2B 72
Chatham.
Medw
Medway Towns 204 (4B 40)
Chatham Green. Essx 4H 53
Chathill. Nmbd 2F 121
Chatley. Worc 4C 60
Chattenden. Medw 3B 40
Chatteris. Cambs 2C 64
Chattisham. Suff 1D 54
Chatton. Nmbd 2E 121
Chatwall. Shrp 1H 59
Chaulden. Herts 5A 52
Chaul End. C Beds 3A 52
Chawleigh. Devn 1H 11
Chawley. Oxon 5C 50
Chawston. Bed 5A 64
Chawton. Hants 3F 25
Chaxhill. Glos 4C 48
Cheadle. G Man 2C 84
Cheadle. Staf 1E 73
Cheadle Hulme. G Man 2C 84
Cheam. G Lon 4D 38
Cheapside. Wind 4A 38
Chearsley. Buck 4F 51
Chebsey. Staf 3C 72
Checkendon. Oxon 3E 37
Checkley. Ches E 1B 72
Checkley. Here 2A 48
Checkley. Staf 2E 73
Chedburgh. Suff 5G 65
Cheddar. Som 1H 21
Cheddington. Buck 4H 51
Cheddleton. Staf 5D 84
Cheddon Fitzpaine. Som 4F 21
Chedglow. Wilts 2E 35
Chedgrave. Norf 1F 67
Chedington. Dors 2H 13
Chediston. Suff 3F 67
Chediston Green. Suff 3F 67
Chedworth. Glos 4F 49
Chedzoy. Som 3G 21
Cheeseman's Green. Kent 2E 29
Cheetham Hill. G Man 4G 91
Cheglinch. Devn 2F 19
Cheldon. Devn 1H 11
Chelford. Ches E 3C 84
Chellaston. Derb 2A 74
Chellington. Bed 5G 63
Chelmarsh. Shrp 2B 60
Chelmick. Shrp 1G 59
Chelmondiston. Suff 2F 55
Chelmorton. Derbs 4F 85
Chelmsford. Essx 5H 53
Chelsea. G Lon 3D 38
Chelsfield. G Lon 4F 39
Chelsham. Surr 5E 39
Chelston. Som 4E 21
Chelsworth. Suff 1C 54
Cheltenham. Glos 192 (3E 49)
Chelveston. Nptn 4G 63
Chelvey. N Som 5H 33
Chelwood. Bath 5B 34
Chelwood Common. E Sus 3F 27
Chelwood Gate. E Sus 3F 27
Chelworth. Wilts 2E 35
Chelworth Lower Green. Wilts 2F 35
Chelworth Upper Green. Wilts 2F 35
Chelynch. Som 2B 22
Cheney Longville. Shrp 2G 59
Chenies. Buck 1B 38
Chepstow. Mon 2A 34
Chequerfield. W Yor 2E 93
Chequers Corner. Norf 5D 77
Cherhill. Wilts 4F 35
Cherington. Glos 2E 35
Cherington. Warw 2A 50
Cheriton. Devn 2H 19
Cheriton. Hants 4D 24
Cheriton. Kent 2G 29
Cheriton. Pemb 5D 43
Cheriton. Swan 3D 30
Cheriton Bishop. Devn 3A 12
Cheriton Cross. Devn 3A 12
Cheriton Fitzpaine. Devn 2B 12
Cherrington. Telf 3A 72
Cherrybank. Per 1D 136
Cherry Burton. E Yor 5D 101
Cherry Green. Herts 3D 52
Cherry Hinton. Cambs 5D 65
Cherry Willingham. Linc 3H 87
Chertsey. Surr 4B 38
Cheselbourne. Dors 3C 14
Chesham. Buck 5H 51
Chesham. G Man 3G 91
Chesham Bois. Buck 1A 38
Cheshunt. Herts 5D 52
Cheslyn Hay. Staf 5D 73
Chessetts Wood. Warw 3F 61
Chessington. G Lon 4C 38
Chester. Ches W 192 (4G 83)
Chesterblade. Som 2B 22
Chesterfield. Derbs 3A 86
Chesterfield. Staf 5F 73
Chesterhope. Nmbd 1B 114
Chester-le-Street. Dur 4F 115
Chester Moor. Dur 5F 115
Chesters. Bord 3A 120
Chesterton. Cambs
nr. Cambridge 4D 64
nr. Peterborough 1A 64
Chesterton. Glos 5F 49
Chesterton. Oxon 3D 50
Chesterton. Shrp 1B 60
Chesterton. Staf 1C 72
Chesterton Green. Warw 5H 61
Chesterwood. Nmbd 3B 114
Chestfield. Kent 4F 41
Cheston. Devn 3C 8
Cheswardine. Shrp 2B 72
Cheswell. Telf 4B 72
Cheswick. Nmbd 5G 131
Cheswick Green. W Mid 3F 61
Chetnole. Dors 2B 14
Chettiscombe. Devn 1C 12
Chettisham. Cambs 2E 65
Chettle. Dors 1E 15
Chetton. Shrp 1A 60
Chetwode. Buck 3E 51
Chetwynd Aston. Telf 4B 72
Cheveley. Cambs 4F 65
Chevening. Kent 5F 39
Chevington. Suff 5G 65
Chevithorne. Devn 1C 12
Chew Magna. Bath 5A 34
Chew Moor. G Man 4E 91
Chew Stoke. Bath 5A 34
Chewton Keynsham. Bath 5B 34
Chewton Mendip. Som 1A 22
Chichacott. Devn 3G 11
Chicheley. Mil 1H 51
Chichester. W Sus 2G 17
Chickerell. Dors 4B 14
Chickering. Suff 3E 66
Chicklade. Wilts 3E 23
Chicksands. C Beds 2B 52
Chickward. Here 5E 59
Chidden. Hants 1E 17
Chiddingfold. Surr 2A 26
Chiddingly. E Sus 4G 27
Chiddingstone. Kent 1G 27
Chiddingstone Causeway.
Kent 1G 27
Chiddingstone Hoath. Kent 1F 27
Chideock. Dors 3H 13
Chidgley. Som 3D 20
Chidham. W Sus 2F 17
Chieveley. W Ber 4C 36
Chignal St James. Essx 5G 53
Chignal Smealy. Essx 4G 53
Chigwell. Essx 1F 39
Chigwell Row. Essx 1F 39
Chilbolton. Hants 2B 24
Chilcomb. Hants 4D 24
Chilcombe. Dors 3A 14
Chilcompton. Som 1B 22
Chilcote. Leics 4G 73
Childer Thornton. Ches W 3F 83
Child Okeford. Dors 1D 14
Childrey. Oxon 3B 36
Child's Ercall. Shrp 3A 72
Childswickham. Worc 2F 49
Childwall. Mers 2G 83
Childwick Green. Herts 4B 52
Chilfrome. Dors 3A 14
Chilgrove. W Sus 1G 17
Chilham. Kent 5E 41
Chilhampton. Wilts 3F 23
Chilla. Devn 2E 11
Chilland. Hants 3D 24
Chillaton. Devn 4E 11
Chillenden. Kent 5G 41

Chillerton. *IOW*.............................4C **16**
Chillesford. *Suff*..........................5F **67**
Chillingham. *Nmbd*....................2E **121**
Chillington. *Devn*..........................4D **9**
Chillington. *Som*..........................1G **13**
Chilmark. *Wilts*...........................3E **23**
Chilmington Green. *Kent*..........1D **28**
Chilson. *Oxon*..............................4B **50**
Chilsworthy. *Corn*......................5E **11**
Chilsworthy. *Devn*.....................2D **10**
Chiltern Green. *C Beds*...............4B **52**
Chilthorne Domer. *Som*..............1A **14**
Chilton. *Buck*..............................4E **51**
Chilton. *Devn*..............................2B **12**
Chilton. *Dur*..............................2F **105**
Chilton. *Oxon*..............................3C **36**
Chilton Candover. *Hants*............2D **24**
Chilton Cantelo. *Som*..................4A **22**
Chilton Foliat. *Wilts*....................4B **36**
Chilton Lane. *Dur*.....................1A **106**
Chilton Polden. *Som*...................3G **21**
Chilton Street. *Suff*....................1A **54**
Chilton Trinity. *Som*....................3F **21**
Chilwell. *Notts*...........................2C **74**
Chilworth. *Hants*.........................1C **16**
Chilworth. *Surr*...........................1B **26**
Chimney. *Oxon*............................5B **50**
Chimney Street. *Suff*..................1H **53**
Chineham. *Hants*.........................1E **25**
Chingford. *G Lon*........................1E **39**
Chinley. *Derbs*............................2E **85**
Chinnor. *Oxon*.............................5F **51**
Chipley. *Som*..............................4E **20**
Chipnall. *Shrp*.............................2B **72**
Chippenham. *Cambs*...................4F **65**
Chippenham. *Wilts*......................4E **35**
Chipperfield. *Herts*.....................5A **52**
Chipping. *Herts*...........................2D **52**
Chipping. *Lanc*...........................5F **97**
Chipping Campden. *Glos*............2G **49**
Chipping Hill. *Essx*.....................4B **54**
Chipping Norton. *Oxon*...............3B **50**
Chipping Ongar. *Essx*.................5F **53**
Chipping Sodbury. *S Glo*............3C **34**
Chipping Warden. *Nptn*..............1C **50**
Chipstable. *Som*.........................4D **20**
Chipstead. *Kent*..........................5G **39**
Chipstead. *Surr*..........................5D **38**
Chirbury. *Shrp*............................1E **59**
Chirk. *Wrex*.................................2E **71**
Chirmorie. *S Ayr*......................2H **109**
Chirnside. *Bord*.........................4E **131**
Chirnsidebridge. *Bord*...............4E **131**
Chirton. *Wilts*..............................1F **23**
Chisbridge Cross. *Buck*..............3G **37**
Chisbury. *Wilts*...........................5A **36**
Chiselborough. *Som*...................1H **13**
Chiseldon. *Swin*.........................4G **35**
Chiselhampton. *Oxon*.................2D **36**
Chiserley. *W Yor*........................2A **92**
Chislehurst. *G Lon*.....................3F **39**
Chislet. *Kent*...............................4G **41**
Chiswell. *Dors*............................5B **14**
Chiswell Green. *Herts*.................5B **52**
Chiswick. *G Lon*..........................3D **38**
Chisworth. *Derbs*........................1D **85**
Chitcombe. *E Sus*.......................3C **28**
Chithurst. *W Sus*........................4G **25**
Chittering. *Cambs*......................4D **65**
Chitterley. *Devn*..........................2C **12**
Chitterne. *Wilts*...........................2E **23**
Chittlehamholt. *Devn*..................4G **19**
Chittlehampton. *Devn*.................4G **19**
Chittoe. *Wilts*.............................5E **35**
Chivelstone. *Devn*........................5D **9**
Chivenor. *Devn*............................3F **19**
Chobham. *Surr*...........................4A **38**
Cholderton. *Wilts*........................2H **23**
Cholesbury. *Buck*.......................5H **51**
Chollerford. *Nmbd*....................2C **114**
Chollerton. *Nmbd*.....................2C **114**
Cholsey. *Oxon*.............................3D **36**
Cholstrey. *Here*...........................5G **59**
Chop Gate. *N Yor*......................5C **106**
Choppington. *Nmbd*..................1F **115**
Chopwell. *Tyne*.........................4E **115**
Chorley. *Ches E*..........................5H **83**
Chorley. *Lanc*..............................3D **90**
Chorley. *Shrp*..............................2A **60**
Chorley. *Staf*...............................4E **73**
Chorleywood. *Herts*....................1B **38**
Chorlton. *Ches E*.........................5B **84**
Chorlton-cum-Hardy. *G Man*......1C **84**
Chorlton Lane. *Ches W*................1G **71**
Choulton. *Shrp*...........................2F **59**
Chrishall. *Essx*............................2E **53**
Christchurch. *Cambs*..................1D **65**
Christchurch. *Dors*......................3G **15**
Christchurch. *Glos*......................4A **48**
Christian Malford. *Wilts*...............4E **35**
Christleton. *Ches W*.....................4G **83**
Christmas Common. *Oxon*..........2F **37**
Christon. *N Som*..........................1G **21**
Christon Bank. *Nmbd*...............2G **121**
Christow. *Devn*...........................4B **12**
Chryston. *N Lan*........................2H **127**
Chuck Hatch. *E Sus*....................2F **27**
Chudleigh. *Devn*.........................5B **12**
Chudleigh Knighton. *Devn*..........5B **12**
Chulmleigh. *Devn*.......................1G **11**
Chunal. *Derbs*............................1E **85**
Church. *Lanc*...............................2F **91**
Churcham. *Glos*..........................4C **48**
Church Aston. *Telf*.......................4B **72**
Church Brampton. *Nptn*..............4E **62**
Church Broughton. *Derbs*............2G **73**
Church Corner. *Suff*....................2G **67**
Church Crookham. *Hants*............1G **25**
Churchdown. *Glos*.......................3D **49**
Church Eaton. *Staf*.......................4C **72**

Church End. *Cambs*
  nr. Cambridge......................5D **65**
  nr. Over..............................3C **64**
  nr. Sawtry............................2B **64**
  nr. Wisbech.........................5C **76**
Church End. *C Beds*
  nr. Stotfold..........................2B **52**
  nr. Totternhoe.....................3H **51**
Church End. *E Yor*.....................4E **101**
Church End. *Essx*
  nr. Braintree........................3H **53**
  nr. Great Dunmow..............3G **53**
  nr. Saffron Walden.............1F **53**
Church End. *Glos*.........................5C **48**
Church End. *Hants*......................1E **25**
Church End. *Linc*
  nr. Donington......................2B **76**
  nr. North Somercotes.........1D **88**
Church End. *Norf*........................4E **77**
Church End. *Warw*
  nr. Coleshill........................1G **61**
  nr. Nuneaton......................1G **61**
Church End. *Wilts*.......................4F **35**
Churchend. *Essx*.........................1E **40**
Church Enstone. *Oxon*................3B **50**
Church Fenton. *N Yor*...................1F **93**
Church Green. *Devn*....................3E **13**
Church Gresley. *Derbs*................4G **73**
Church Hanborough. *Oxon*..........4C **50**
Church Hill. *Ches W*.....................4A **84**
Church Hill. *Worc*........................4E **61**
Church Hougham. *Kent*...............1G **29**
Church Houses. *N Yor*...............5D **106**
Churchill. *Devn*
  nr. Axminster......................2G **13**
  nr. Barnstaple.....................2F **19**
Churchill. *N Som*.........................1H **21**
Churchill. *Oxon*...........................3A **50**
Churchill. *Worc*
  nr. Kidderminster................3C **60**
  nr. Worcester......................5D **60**
Churchinford. *Som*......................1F **13**
Church Knowle. *Dors*...................4E **15**
Church Laneham. *Notts*..............3F **87**
Church Langley. *Essx*..................5E **53**
Church Langton. *Leics*................1E **62**
Church Lawford. *Warw*................3B **62**
Church Lawton. *Ches E*...............5C **84**
Church Leigh. *Staf*......................2E **73**
Church Lench. *Worc*.....................5E **61**
Church Mayfield. *Staf*..................1F **73**
Church Minshull. *Ches E*.............4A **84**
Church Norton. *W Sus*.................3G **17**
Churchover. *Warw*.......................2C **62**
Church Preen. *Shrp*.....................1H **59**
Church Pulverbatch. *Shrp*...........5G **71**
Churchstanton. *Som*....................1E **13**
Church Stoke. *Powy*....................1E **59**
Churchstow. *Devn*........................4D **8**
Church Stowe. *Nptn*....................5D **62**
Church Street. *Kent*......................3B **40**
Church Stretton. *Shrp*..................1G **59**
Church Town. *Leics*.....................4A **74**
Church Town. *N Lin*....................4A **94**
Churchtown. *Cumb*...................5E **113**
Churchtown. *Derbs*.....................4G **85**
Churchtown. *Devn*.......................2G **19**
Churchtown. *IOM*......................2D **108**
Churchtown. *Lanc*.......................5D **97**
Churchtown. *Mers*.......................3B **90**
Churchtown. *Shrp*.......................3D **32**
Church Village. *Rhon*..................3D **32**
Church Warsop. *Notts*.................4C **86**
Church Westcote. *Glos*................3H **49**
Church Wilne. *Derbs*....................2B **74**
Churnsike Lodge. *Nmbd*...........2H **113**
Churston Ferrers. *Torb*..................3F **9**
Churt. *Surr*...................................3G **25**
Churton. *Ches W*.........................5G **83**
Churwell. *W Yor*..........................2C **92**
Chute Standen. *Wilts*...................1B **24**
Chwilog. *Gwyn*...........................2D **68**
Chwitffordd. *Flin*.........................3D **82**
Chyandour. *Corn*..........................3B **4**
Cilan Uchaf. *Gwyn*......................3B **68**
Cilcain. *Flin*.................................4D **82**
Cilcennin. *Cdgn*...........................4E **57**
Cilfrew. *Neat*................................5A **46**
Cilfynydd. *Rhon*...........................2D **32**
Cilgerran. *Pemb*..........................1B **44**
Cilgeti. *Pemb*..............................4F **43**
Cilgwyn. *Carm*.............................3H **45**
Cilgwyn. *Pemb*............................1E **43**
Ciliau Aeron. *Cdgn*......................5D **57**
Cill Amhlaidh. *W Isl*...................4C **170**
Cill Donnain. *W Isl*.....................6C **170**
Cille a' Bhacstair. *High*..............2C **154**
Cille Bhrighde. *W Isl*.................7C **170**
Cille Pheadair. *W Isl*..................7C **170**
Cilmaengwyn. *Neat*.....................5H **45**
Cilmeri. *Powy*..............................5C **58**
Cilmery. *Powy*..............................5C **58**
Cilrhedyn. *Pemb*.........................1G **43**
Cilsan. *Carm*...............................3F **45**
Ciltalgarth. *Gwyn*.......................1A **70**
Ciltwrch. *Powy*............................1E **47**
Cilybebyll. *Neat*...........................5H **45**
Cilycwm. *Carm*............................1A **46**
Cimla. *Neat*.................................2A **32**
Cinderford. *Glos*.........................4B **48**
Cinderhill. *Derbs*.........................1A **74**
Cippenham. *Slo*...........................2A **38**
Cippyn. *Pemb*..............................1B **44**
Cirbhig. *W Isl*.............................3D **171**
Cirecbost. *W Isl*.........................4D **171**
Cirencester. *Glos*.........................5F **49**
City. *Powy*....................................1E **58**
City. *V Glam*................................4C **32**
The City. *Buck*.............................2F **37**
City Airport. *G Lon*.......................2F **39**
City Centre. *Stoke*.......................1C **72**

City Dulas. *IOA*...........................2D **80**
City of London. *G Lon* **203** (2E **39**)
Clabhach. *Arg*..........................3C **138**
Clachaig. *Arg*..............................1C **126**
Clachaig. *High*
  nr. Kinlochleven...................3F **141**
  nr. Nethy Bridge...................2E **151**
Clachamish. *High*......................3C **154**
Clachan. *Arg*
  on Kintyre............................4F **125**
  on Lismore..........................4C **140**
Clachan. *High*
  nr. Bettyhill........................2H **167**
  nr. Staffin...........................2D **155**
  nr. Uig...............................1D **154**
  on Raasay..........................5E **155**
Clachan Farm. *Arg*......................2A **134**
Clachan na Luib. *W Isl*..............2D **170**
Clachan of Campsie. *E Dun*.......2H **127**
Clachan of Glendaruel. *Arg*........1A **126**
Clachan-Seil. *Arg*.......................2E **133**
Clachan Shannda. *W Isl*...........1D **170**
Clachan Strachur. *Arg*................3H **133**
Clachbreck. *Arg*..........................2F **125**
Clachnaharry. *High*.....................4A **158**
Clachtoll. *High*.........................1E **163**
Clackmannan. *Clac*....................4B **136**
Clackmannanshire Bridge.
  Clac..............................1C **128**
Clackmarras. *Mor*.......................3G **159**
Clacton-on-Sea. *Essx*...........4E **55**
Cladach a Chaolais. *W Isl*..........2C **170**
Cladach Chairinis. *W Isl*............3D **170**
Cladach Chircebost. *W Isl*..........2C **170**
Cladach Iolaraigh. *W Isl*.............1H **133**
Cladich. *Arg*................................1H **133**
Cladswell. *Worc*...........................5E **61**
Claggan. *High*
  nr. Fort William...................1F **141**
  nr. Lochaline......................3B **140**
Claigan. *High*..............................3B **154**
Clandown. *Bath*..........................1B **22**
Clanfield. *Hants*..........................1E **17**
Clanfield. *Oxon*...........................5A **50**
Clanville. *Hants*...........................2B **24**
Clanville. *Som*.............................3B **22**
Claonaig. *Arg*.............................4G **125**
Clapgate. *Dors*............................2F **15**
Clapgate. *Herts*...........................3E **53**
Clapham. *Bed*.............................5H **63**
Clapham. *Devn*...........................4B **12**
Clapham. *G Lon*......................3D **39**
Clapham. *N Yor*..........................3F **97**
Clapham. *W Sus*.........................5B **26**
Clap Hill. *Kent*............................2E **29**
Clappers. *Bord*..........................4F **131**
Clappersgate. *Cumb*.................4E **103**
Clapphoull. *Shet*.......................9F **173**
Clapton. *Som*
  nr. Crewkerne....................2H **13**
  nr. Radstock.......................1B **22**
Clapton in Gordano. *N Som*........4H **33**
Clapton-on-the-Hill. *Glos*.............4G **49**
Clapworthy. *Devn*........................4G **19**
Clara Vale. *Tyne*.......................3E **115**
Clarbeston. *Pemb*.......................2E **43**
Clarbeston Road. *Pemb*.............2E **43**
Clarborough. *Notts*.....................2E **87**
Clare. *Suff*...................................1A **54**
Clarebrand. *Dum*......................3E **111**
Clarencefield. *Dum*...................3B **112**
Clarilaw. *Bord*............................3H **119**
Clark's Green. *Surr*.....................2C **26**
Clark's Hill. *Linc*..........................3C **76**
Clarkston. *E Ren*....................4G **127**
Clasheddy. *High*........................2G **167**
Clashindarroch. *Abers*...............5B **160**
Clashmore. *High*
  nr. Dornoch........................5E **165**
  nr. Stoer...........................1E **163**
Clashnessie. *High*......................5A **166**
Clashnoir. *Mor*...........................1G **151**
Clate. *Shet*................................5G **173**
Clathick. *Per*..............................1H **135**
Clathy. *Per*..................................2B **136**
Clatt. *Abers*................................1C **152**
Clatter. *Powy*...............................1B **58**
Clatterford. *IOW*..........................4C **16**
Clatworthy. *Som*...........................3D **20**
Claughton. *Lanc*
  nr. Caton.............................3E **97**
  nr. Garstang........................5E **97**
Claughton. *Mers*.........................2E **83**
Claverdon. *Warw*.........................4F **61**
Claverham. *N Som*......................5H **33**
Clavering. *Essx*...........................2E **53**
Claverley. *Shrp*............................1B **60**
Claverton. *Bath*...........................5C **34**
Clawdd-côch. *V Glam*.................4D **32**
Clawdd-newydd. *Den*..................5C **82**
Clawson Hill. *Leics*......................3E **75**
Clawton. *Devn*.............................3D **10**
Claxby. *Linc*
  nr. Alford...........................3D **88**
  nr. Market Rasen................1A **88**
Claxton. *Norf*..............................5F **79**
Claxton. *N Yor*............................3A **100**
Claybrooke Magna. *Leics*............2B **62**
Claybrooke Parva. *Leics*..............2B **62**
Clay Common. *Suff*.....................2G **67**
Clay Coton. *Nptn*........................3C **62**
Clay Cross. *Derbs*...................4A **86**
Claydon. *Oxon*............................5B **62**
Claydon. *Suff*..............................5D **66**
Clay End. *Herts*...........................3D **52**
Claygate. *Dum*.........................2E **113**
Claygate. *Kent*.............................1B **28**
Claygate. *Surr*.............................4C **38**
Claygate Cross. *Kent*...................5H **39**
Clayhall. *Hants*............................3E **16**
Clayhanger. *Devn*........................4D **20**

Clayhanger. *W Mid*.....................5E **73**
Clayhidon. *Devn*..........................1E **13**
Clay Hill. *Bris*..............................4B **34**
Clayhill. *E Sus*.............................3C **28**
Clayhill. *Hants*............................2B **16**
Clayhithe. *Cambs*........................4E **65**
Clayholes. *Ang*..........................5E **145**
Clayock. *High*.............................3D **168**
Claypits. *Glos*..............................5C **48**
Claypole. *Linc*...............................1F **75**
Claythorpe. *Linc*..........................3D **88**
Clayton. *G Man*...........................1C **84**
Clayton. *S Yor*.............................4E **93**
Clayton. *Staf*................................1C **72**
Clayton. *W Sus*............................4E **27**
Clayton. *W Yor*............................1B **92**
Clayton Green. *Lanc*...................2D **90**
Clayton-le-Moors. *Lanc*...............1F **91**
Clayton-le-Woods. *Lanc*..............2D **90**
Clayton West. *W Yor*...................3C **92**
Clayworth. *Notts*.........................2E **87**
Cleadale. *High*...........................5C **146**
Cleadon. *Tyne*...........................3G **115**
Clearbrook. *Devn*..........................2B **8**
Clearwell. *Glos*............................5A **48**
Cleasby. *N Yor*...........................3F **105**
Cleat. *Orkn*
  nr. Braehead......................3D **172**
  nr. St Margaret's Hope........9D **172**
Cleatlam. *Dur*............................3E **105**
Cleator. *Cumb*...........................3B **102**
Cleator Moor. *Cumb*..................3B **102**
Cleckheaton. *W Yor*...............2B **92**
Cleedownton. *Shrp*......................2H **59**
Cleehill. *Shrp*..............................3H **59**
Clee St Margaret. *Shrp*...............2H **59**
Cleestanton. *Shrp*.......................3H **59**
Cleethorpes. *NE Lin*..............4G **95**
Cleeton St Mary. *Shrp*.................3A **60**
Cleeve. *N Som*............................5H **33**
Cleeve. *Oxon*..............................3E **36**
Cleeve Hill. *Glos*..........................3E **49**
Cleeve Prior. *Worc*.......................1F **49**
Clehonger. *Here*..........................2H **47**
Cleigh. *Arg*................................1F **133**
Cleish. *Per*................................4C **136**
Cleland. *N Lan*..........................4B **128**
Clench Common. *Wilts*...............5G **35**
Clenchwarton. *Norf*....................3E **77**
Clennell. *Nmbd*........................4D **120**
Clent. *Worc*.................................3D **60**
Cleobury Mortimer. *Shrp*.............3A **60**
Cleobury North. *Shrp*..................2A **60**
Clephanton. *High*.......................3C **158**
Clerkhill. *High*...........................2H **167**
Clestrain. *Orkn*..........................7C **172**
Clevancy. *Wilts*............................4F **35**
Clevedon. *N Som*....................4H **33**
Cleveley. *Oxon*............................3B **50**
Cleveleys. *Lanc*......................5C **96**
Clevelode. *Worc*..........................1D **48**
Cleverton. *Wilts*...........................3E **35**
Clewer. *Som*...............................1H **21**
Cley next the Sea. *Norf*...............1C **78**
Cliaid. *W Isl*................................8B **170**
Cliasmol. *W Isl*..........................7C **171**
Clibberswick. *Shet*....................1H **173**
Cliburn. *Cumb*...........................2G **103**
Cliddesden. *Hants*......................2E **25**
Clieves Hills. *Lanc*......................4B **90**
Cliff. *Warw*..................................1G **61**
Cliffburn. *Ang*............................4F **145**
Cliffe. *Medw*...............................3B **40**
Cliffe. *N Yor*
  nr. Darlington.....................3F **105**
  nr. Selby.............................1G **93**
Cliff End. *E Sus*...........................4C **28**
Cliffe Woods. *Medw*....................3B **40**
Clifford. *Here*...............................1F **47**
Clifford. *W Yor*............................5G **99**
Clifford Chambers. *Warw*............5F **61**
Clifford's Mesne. *Glos*................3C **48**
Cliffsend. *Kent*............................4H **41**
Clifton. *Bris*.................................4A **34**
Clifton. *C Beds*...........................2B **52**
Clifton. *Cumb*...........................2G **103**
Clifton. *Derbs*.............................1F **73**
Clifton. *Devn*..............................2F **19**
Clifton. *G Man*............................4F **91**
Clifton. *Lanc*...............................1F **90**
Clifton. *Nmbd*..........................1F **115**
Clifton. *N Yor*.............................5D **98**
Clifton. *Nott*...............................2C **74**
Clifton. *Oxon*..............................2C **50**
Clifton. *S Yor*...............................1C **86**
Clifton. *Stir*................................5H **141**
Clifton. *W Yor*.............................2B **92**
Clifton. *Worc*..............................1D **48**
Clifton. *York*...............................4H **99**
Clifton Campville. *Staf*...............4G **73**
Clifton Hampden. *Oxon*..............2D **36**
Clifton Hill. *Worc*........................4B **60**
Clifton Reynes. *Mil*.....................5G **63**
Clifton upon Dunsmore. *Warw*....3C **62**
Clifton upon Teme. *Worc*............4B **60**
Cliftonville. *Kent*..........................3H **41**
Cliftonville. *Norf*...........................2F **79**
Climping. *W Sus*.........................5A **26**
Climpy. *S Lan*...........................4C **128**
Clink. *Som*..................................2C **22**
Clint. *N Yor*.................................4E **99**
Clint Green. *Norf*.........................4C **78**
Clintmains. *Bord*......................1A **120**
Cliobh. *W Isl*.............................4C **171**
Clipiau. *Gwyn*.............................4H **69**
Clippesby. *Norf*...........................4G **79**
Clippings Green. *Norf*.................4C **78**
Clipsham. *Rut*.............................4G **75**
Clipston. *Nptn*.............................2E **62**

Clipstone. *Notts*..........................2D **74**
Clipstone. *Notts*..........................4C **86**
Clitheroe. *Lanc*.......................5G **97**
Cliuthar. *W Isl*...........................8D **171**
Clive. *Shrp*..................................3H **71**
Clivocast. *Shet*..........................1G **173**
Clixby. *Linc*.................................4D **94**
Clocaenog. *Den*..........................5C **82**
Clochan. *Mor*............................2B **160**
Clochforbie. *Abers*....................3F **161**
Clock Face. *Mers*........................1H **83**
Cloddiau. *Powy*...........................5E **70**
Cloddymoss. *Mor*......................2D **159**
Clodock. *Here*.............................3G **47**
Cloford. *Som*...............................2C **22**
Clola. *Abers*...............................4H **161**
Clophill. *C Beds*..........................2A **52**
Clopton. *Nptn*.............................2H **63**
Clopton Corner. *Suff*...................5E **66**
Clopton Green. *Suff*....................5G **65**
Closeburn. *Dum*........................5A **118**
Close Clark. *IOM*......................4B **108**
Closworth. *Som*...........................1A **14**
Clothall. *Herts*.............................2C **52**
Clotton. *Ches W*..........................4H **83**
Clough. *G Man*............................3H **91**
Clough. *W Yor*.............................3A **92**
Clough Foot. *W Yor*.....................2H **91**
Cloughton. *N Yor*......................5H **107**
Cloughton Newlands. *N Yor*......5H **107**
Clousta. *Shet*.............................6E **173**
Clouston. *Orkn*...........................6B **172**
Clova. *Abers*..............................1B **152**
Clova. *Ang*.................................1C **144**
Clovelly. *Devn*.............................4D **18**
Clovenfords. *Bord*.....................1G **119**
Clovenstone. *Abers*...................2E **153**
Clovullin. *High*...........................2E **141**
Clowne. *Derbs*............................3B **86**
Clows Top. *Worc*.........................3B **60**
Cloy. *Wrex*..................................1F **71**
Cluanie Inn. *High*......................2C **148**
Cluanie Lodge. *High*.................2C **148**
Cluddley. *Telf*..............................4A **72**
Clun. *Shrp*...................................2F **59**
Y Clun. *Neat*................................5B **46**
Clunas. *High*..............................4C **158**
Clunbury. *Shrp*............................2F **59**
Clunderwen. *Pemb*......................3F **43**
Clune. *High*................................1B **150**
Clunes. *High*...............................5E **148**
Clungunford. *Shrp*.......................3F **59**
Clunie. *Per*.................................4A **144**
Clunton. *Shrp*..............................2F **59**
Cluny. *Fife*................................4E **137**
Clutton. *Bath*...............................1B **22**
Clutton. *Ches W*..........................5G **83**
Clwt-y-bont. *Gwyn*.......................4E **81**
Clwydfagwyr. *Mer T*.....................5D **46**
Clydach. *Mon*.............................4F **47**
Clydach. *Swan*............................5G **45**
Clydach Vale. *Rhon*.....................2C **32**
Clydebank. *W Dun*................3G **127**
Clydey. *Pemb*.............................1G **43**
Clyffe Pypard. *Wilts*.....................4F **35**
Clynder. *Arg*..............................1D **126**
Clyne. *Neat*.................................5B **46**
Clynelish. *High*...........................3F **165**
Clynnog-fawr. *Gwyn*...................1D **68**
Clyro. *Powy*.................................1F **47**
Clyst Honiton. *Devn*....................3C **12**
Clyst Hydon. *Devn*......................2D **12**
Clyst St George. *Devn*.................4C **12**
Clyst St Lawrence. *Devn*.............2D **12**
Clyst St Mary. *Devn*....................3C **12**
Clyth. *High*................................5E **169**
Cnip. *W Isl*.................................4C **171**
Cnoc Amhlaigh. *W Isl*................4H **171**
Cnwcau. *Pemb*...........................1C **44**
Cnwch Coch. *Cdgn*.....................3F **57**
Coad's Green. *Corn*....................5C **10**
Coal Aston. *Derbs*.......................3A **86**
Coalbrookdale. *Telf*......................5A **72**
Coalbrookvale. *Blae*....................5E **47**
Coalburn. *S Lan*.......................1H **117**
Coalburns. *Tyne*........................3E **115**
Coalcleugh. *Nmbd*.....................5B **114**
Coaley. *Glos*...............................5C **48**
Coalford. *Abers*.........................4F **153**
Coalhall. *E Ayr*...........................3D **116**
Coalhill. *Essx*...............................1B **40**
Coalpit Heath. *S Glo*...................3B **34**
Coal Pool. *W Mid*........................5E **73**
Coalport. *Telf*...............................5B **72**
Coalsnaughton. *Clac*.................4B **136**
Coaltown of Balgonie. *Fife*.........4F **137**
Coaltown of Wemyss. *Fife*..........4F **137**
Coalville. *Leics*.......................4B **74**
Coalway. *Glos*.............................4A **48**
Coanwood. *Nmbd*.....................4H **113**
Coat. *Som*..................................4H **21**
Coatbridge. *N Lan*..................3A **128**
Coatdyke. *N Lan*.......................3A **128**
Coate. *Swin*.................................3G **35**
Coate. *Wilts*................................5F **35**
Coates. *Cambs*...........................1C **64**
Coates. *Glos*................................5E **49**
Coates. *Linc*................................2G **87**
Coates. *W Sus*...........................4A **26**
Coatham. *Red C*........................2C **106**
Coatham Mundeville. *Darl*.........2F **105**
Cobbaton. *Devn*..........................4G **19**
Coberley. *Glos*............................4E **49**
Cobhall Common. *Here*...............2H **47**
Cobham. *Kent*.............................4A **40**
Cobham. *Surr*.........................5C **38**
Cobnash. *Here*............................4G **59**
Coburg. *Devn*..............................5B **12**
Cockayne. *N Yor*.......................5D **106**
Cockayne Hatley. *C Beds*............1C **52**
Cock Bank. *Wrex*.........................1F **71**

Cock Bridge. *Abers* 3G **151**
Cockburnspath. *Bord* 2D **130**
Cock Clarks. *Essx* 5B **54**
Cockenzie and Port Seton.
  E Lot 2H **129**
Cockerham. *Lanc* 4D **96**
Cockermouth. *Cumb* 1C **102**
Cockernhoe. *Herts* 3B **52**
Cockfield. *Dur* 2E **105**
Cockfield. *Suff* 5B **66**
Cockfosters. *G Lon* 1D **39**
Cock Gate. *Here* 4G **59**
Cock Green. *Essx* 4G **53**
Cocking. *W Sus* 1G **17**
Cocking Causeway. *W Sus* ..1G **17**
Cockington. *Torb* 2E **9**
Cocklake. *Som* 2H **21**
Cocklaw. *Abers* 4H **161**
Cocklaw. *Nmbd* 2C **114**
Cockley Beck. *Cumb* 4D **102**
Cockley Cley. *Norf* 5G **77**
Cockmuir. *Abers* 3G **161**
Cockpole Green. *Wok* 3F **37**
Cockshutford. *Shrp* 2H **59**
Cockshutt. *Shrp* 3G **71**
Cockthorpe. *Norf* 1B **78**
Cockwood. *Devn* 4C **12**
Cockyard. *Derbs* 3E **85**
Cockyard. *Here* 2H **47**
Codda. *Corn* 5B **10**
Coddenham. *Suff* 5D **66**
Coddenham Green. *Suff* 5D **66**
Coddington. *Ches W* 5G **83**
Coddington. *Here* 1C **48**
Coddington. *Notts* 5F **87**
Codford. *Wilts* 3E **23**
Codicote. *Herts* 4C **52**
Codmore Hill. *W Sus* 3B **26**
Codnor. *Derbs* 1B **74**
Codrington. *S Glo* 4C **34**
Codsall. *Staf* 5C **72**
Codsall Wood. *Staf* 5C **72**
Coed Duon. *Cphy* 2E **33**
Coedely. *Rhon* 3D **32**
Coedglasson. *Powy* 4C **58**
Coedkernew. *Newp* 3F **33**
Coed Morgan. *Mon* 4G **47**
Coedpoeth. *Wrex* 5E **83**
Coedway. *Powy* 4F **71**
Coed-y-bryn. *Cdgn* 1D **44**
Coed-y-paen. *Mon* 2G **33**
Coed Ystumgwern. *Gwyn* 3E **69**
Coelbren. *Powy* 4B **46**
Coffinswell. *Devn* 2E **9**
Cofton Hackett. *Worc* 3E **61**
Cogan. *V Glam* 4E **33**
Cogenhoe. *Nptn* 4F **63**
Cogges. *Oxon* 5B **50**
Coggeshall. *Essx* 3B **54**
Coggeshall Hamlet. *Essx* 3B **54**
Coggins Mill. *E Sus* 3G **27**
Coignafearn Lodge. *High* 2A **150**
Coig Peighinnean. *W Isl* 1H **171**
Coig Peighinnean Bhuirgh.
  W Isl 2G **171**
Coilleag. *W Isl* 7C **170**
Coillemore. *High* 1A **158**
Coillore. *High* 5C **154**
Coire an Fhuarain. *W Isl* 4E **171**
Coity. *B'end* 3C **32**
Cokhay Green. *Derbs* 3G **73**
Col. *W Isl* 3G **171**
Colaboll. *High* 2C **164**
Colan. *Corn* 2C **6**
Colaton Raleigh. *Devn* 4D **12**
Colbost. *High* 4B **154**
Colburn. *N Yor* 5E **105**
Colby. *Cumb* 2H **103**
Colby. *IOM* 4B **108**
Colby. *Norf* 2E **78**
Colchester. *Essx* 3D **54**
Cold Ash. *W Ber* 5D **36**
Cold Ashby. *Nptn* 3D **62**
Cold Ashton. *S Glo* 4C **34**
Cold Aston. *Glos* 4G **49**
Coldbackie. *High* 3G **167**
Cold Blow. *Pemb* 3F **43**
Cold Brayfield. *Mil* 5G **63**
Cold Cotes. *N Yor* 2G **97**
Coldean. *Brig* 5E **27**
Coldeast. *Devn* 5B **12**
Colden. *W Yor* 2H **91**
Colden Common. *Hants* 4C **24**
Coldfair Green. *Suff* 4G **67**
Coldham. *Cambs* 5D **76**
Coldham. *Staf* 5C **72**
Cold Hanworth. *Linc* 2H **87**
Cold Harbour. *Dors* 3E **15**
Coldharbour. *Corn* 4B **6**
Coldharbour. *Glos* 5A **48**
Coldharbour. *Kent* 5G **39**
Coldharbour. *Surr* 1C **26**
Cold Hatton. *Telf* 3A **72**
Cold Hatton Heath. *Telf* 3A **72**
Cold Hesledon. *Dur* 5H **115**
Cold Hiendley. *W Yor* 3D **92**
Cold Higham. *Nptn* 5D **62**
Coldingham. *Bord* 3F **131**
Cold Kirby. *N Yor* 1H **99**
Coldmeece. *Staf* 2C **72**
Cold Northcott. *Corn* 4C **10**
Cold Norton. *Essx* 5B **54**
Cold Overton. *Leics* 4F **75**
Coldrain. *Per* 3C **136**
Coldred. *Kent* 1G **29**
Coldridge. *Devn* 2G **11**
Cold Row. *Lanc* 5C **96**
Coldstream. *Bord* 5E **131**
Coldwaltham. *W Sus* 4B **26**
Coldwell. *Here* 2H **47**
Coldwells. *Abers* 5H **161**

Coldwells Croft. *Abers* 1C **152**
Cole. *Shet* 5E **173**
Cole. *Som* 3B **22**
Colebatch. *Shrp* 2F **59**
Colebrook. *Devn* 2D **12**
Colebrooke. *Devn* 3A **12**
Coleburn. *Mor* 3G **159**
Coleby. *Linc* 4G **87**
Coleby. *N Lin* 3B **94**
Cole End. *Warw* 2G **61**
Coleford. *Devn* 2A **12**
Coleford. *Glos* 4A **48**
Coleford. *Som* 2B **22**
Colegate End. *Norf* 2D **66**
Cole Green. *Herts* 4C **52**
Cole Henley. *Hants* 1C **24**
Colehill. *Dors* 2F **15**
Coleman Green. *Herts* 4B **52**
Coleman's Hatch. *E Sus* 2F **27**
Colemere. *Shrp* 2G **71**
Colemore. *Hants* 3F **25**
Colemore Green. *Shrp* 1B **60**
Coleorton. *Leics* 4B **74**
Colerne. *Wilts* 4D **34**
Colesbourne. *Glos* 4F **49**
Colesden. *Bed* 5A **64**
Coles Green. *Worc* 5B **60**
Coleshill. *Buck* 1A **38**
Coleshill. *Oxon* 2H **35**
Coleshill. *Warw* 2G **61**
Colestocks. *Devn* 2D **12**
Colethrop. *Glos* 4D **48**
Coley. *Bath* 1A **22**
Colgate. *W Sus* 2D **26**
Colinsburgh. *Fife* 3G **137**
Colinton. *Edin* 3F **129**
Colintraive. *Arg* 2B **126**
Colkirk. *Norf* 3B **78**
Collace. *Per* 5B **144**
Collam. *W Isl* 8D **171**
Collaton. *Devn* 5D **8**
Collaton St Mary. *Torb* 2E **9**
College of Roseisle. *Mor* 2F **159**
Collessie. *Fife* 2E **137**
Collier Row. *G Lon* 1F **39**
Colliers End. *Herts* 3D **52**
Collier Street. *Kent* 1B **28**
Colliery Row. *Tyne* 5G **115**
Colliston. *Ang* 4F **145**
Colliton. *Devn* 2D **12**
Collydean. *Fife* 3E **137**
Collyweston. *Nptn* 5G **75**
Colmonell. *S Ayr* 1G **109**
Colmworth. *Bed* 5A **64**
Colnbrook. *Slo* 3B **38**
Colne. *Cambs* 3C **64**
Colne. *Lanc* 5A **98**
Colne Engaine. *Essx* 2B **54**
Colney. *Norf* 5D **78**
Colney Heath. *Herts* 5C **52**
Colney Street. *Herts* 5B **52**
Coln Rogers. *Glos* 5F **49**
Coln St Aldwyns. *Glos* 5G **49**
Coln St Dennis. *Glos* 4F **49**
Colpitts Grange. *Nmbd* 4C **114**
Colpy. *Abers* 5D **160**
Colscott. *Devn* 1D **10**
Colsterdale. *N Yor* 1D **98**
Colsterworth. *Linc* 3G **75**
Colston Bassett. *Notts* 2E **74**
Colstoun House. *E Lot* 2B **130**
Coltfield. *Mor* 2F **159**
Colthouse. *Cumb* 5E **103**
Coltishall. *Norf* 4E **79**
Coltness. *N Lan* 4B **128**
Colton. *Cumb* 1C **96**
Colton. *Norf* 5D **78**
Colton. *N Yor* 5H **99**
Colton. *Staf* 3E **73**
Colton. *W Yor* 1D **92**
Colt's Hill. *Kent* 1H **27**
Col Uarach. *W Isl* 4G **171**
Colvend. *Dum* 4F **111**
Colvister. *Shet* 2G **173**
Colwall. *Here* 1C **48**
Colwall Green. *Here* 1C **48**
Colwell. *Nmbd* 2C **114**
Colwich. *Staf* 3E **73**
Colwick. *Notts* 1D **74**
Colwinston. *V Glam* 4C **32**
Colworth. *W Sus* 5A **26**
Colwyn Bay. *Cnwy* 3A **82**
Colyford. *Devn* 3F **13**
Colyton. *Devn* 3F **13**
Combe. *Devn* 2E **11**
Combe. *Here* 4F **59**
Combe. *Oxon* 4C **50**
Combe. *W Ber* 5B **36**
Combe Almer. *Dors* 3E **15**
Combebow. *Devn* 4E **11**
Combe Fishacre. *Devn* 2E **9**
Combe Florey. *Som* 3E **21**
Combe Hay. *Bath* 1C **22**
Combeinteignhead. *Devn* 5C **12**
Combe Martin. *Devn* 2F **19**
Combe Moor. *Here* 4F **59**
Combe Raleigh. *Devn* 2E **13**
Comberbach. *Ches W* 3A **84**
Comberford. *Staf* 5F **73**
Comberton. *Cambs* 5C **64**

Comberton. *Here* 4G **59**
Combe St Nicholas. *Som* 1G **13**
Combpyne. *Devn* 3F **13**
Combridge. *Staf* 2E **73**
Combrook. *Warw* 5H **61**
Combs. *Derbs* 3E **85**
Combs. *Suff* 5C **66**
Combs Ford. *Suff* 5C **66**
Combwich. *Som* 2F **21**
Comers. *Abers* 3D **152**
Comhampton. *Worc* 4C **60**
Comins Coch. *Cdgn* 2F **57**
Comley. *Shrp* 1G **59**
Commercial End. *Cambs* 4E **65**
Commins. *Powy* 3D **70**
Commins Coch. *Powy* 5H **69**
The Common. *Wilts*
  nr. Salisbury 3H **23**
  nr. Swindon 3F **35**
Commondale. *N Yor* 3D **106**
Common End. *Cumb* 2B **102**
Common Hill. *Here* 2A **48**
Common Moor. *Corn* 2G **7**
Common Side. *Derbs* 3H **85**
Commonside. *Derbs* 1G **73**
Compass. *Som* 3F **21**
Compstall. *G Man* 1D **84**
Compton. *Devn* 2E **9**
Compton. *Hants* 4C **24**
Compton. *Staf* 2C **60**
Compton. *Surr* 1A **26**
Compton. *W Ber* 4D **36**
Compton. *W Sus* 1F **17**
Compton. *Wilts* 1G **23**
Compton Abbas. *Dors* 1D **15**
Compton Abdale. *Glos* 4F **49**
Compton Bassett. *Wilts* 4F **35**
Compton Beauchamp. *Oxon* .3A **36**
Compton Bishop. *Som* 1G **21**
Compton Chamberlayne.
  Wilts 4F **23**
Compton Dando. *Bath* 5B **34**
Compton Dundon. *Som* 3H **21**
Compton Greenfield. *S Glo* ...3A **34**
Compton Martin. *Bath* 1A **22**
Compton Pauncefoot. *Som* ...4B **22**
Compton Valence. *Dors* 3A **14**
Comrie. *Fife* 1D **128**
Comrie. *Per* 1G **135**
Conaglen. *High* 2E **141**
Conchra. *Arg* 1B **126**
Conchra. *High* 1A **148**
Conder Green. *Lanc* 4D **96**
Conderton. *Worc* 2E **49**
Condicote. *Glos* 3G **49**
Condorrat. *N Lan* 2A **128**
Condover. *Shrp* 5G **71**
Coneyhurst. *W Sus* 3C **26**
Coneysthorpe. *N Yor* 2B **100**
Coneythorpe. *N Yor* 4F **99**
Coney Weston. *Suff* 3B **66**
Conford. *Hants* 3G **25**
Congdon's Shop. *Corn* 5C **10**
Congerstone. *Leics* 5A **74**
Congham. *Norf* 3G **77**
Congleton. *Ches E* 4C **84**
Congl-y-wal. *Gwyn* 1G **69**
Congresbury. *N Som* 5H **33**
Congreve. *Staf* 4D **72**
Conham. *S Glo* 4B **34**
Conicaval. *Mor* 3D **159**
Coningsby. *Linc* 5B **88**
Conington. *Cambs*
  nr. Fenstanton 4C **64**
  nr. Sawtry 2A **64**
Conisbrough. *S Yor* 1C **86**
Conisby. *Arg* 3A **124**
Conisholme. *Linc* 1D **88**
Coniston. *Cumb* 5E **102**
Coniston. *E Yor* 1E **95**
Coniston Cold. *N Yor* 4B **98**
Conistone. *N Yor* 3B **98**
Connah's Quay. *Flin* 3E **83**
Connel. *Arg* 5D **140**
Connel Park. *E Ayr* 3F **117**
Connista. *High* 1D **154**
Connor Downs. *Corn* 3C **4**
Conock. *Wilts* 1F **23**
Conon Bridge. *High* 3H **157**
Cononley. *N Yor* 5B **98**
Cononsyth. *Ang* 4E **145**
Conordan. *High* 5E **155**
Consall. *Staf* 1D **73**
Consett. *Dur* 4E **115**
Constable Burton. *N Yor* 5E **105**
Constantine. *Corn* 4E **5**
Constantine Bay. *Corn* 1C **6**
Contin. *High* 3G **157**
Contullich. *High* 1A **158**
Conwy. *Cnwy* 3G **81**
Conyer. *Kent* 4D **40**
Conyer's Green. *Suff* 4A **66**
Cooden. *E Sus* 5B **28**
Cooil. *IOM* 4C **108**
Cookbury. *Devn* 2E **11**
Cookbury Wick. *Devn* 2D **11**
Cookham. *Wind* 3G **37**
Cookham Dean. *Wind* 3G **37**
Cookham Rise. *Wind* 3G **37**
Cookhill. *Worc* 5E **61**
Cookley. *Suff* 3F **67**
Cookley. *Worc* 2C **60**
Cookley Green. *Oxon* 2E **37**
Cookney. *Abers* 4F **153**
Cooksbridge. *E Sus* 4F **27**
Cooksey Green. *Worc* 4D **60**
Cookshill. *Staf* 1D **72**
Cooksmill Green. *Essx* 5G **53**
Coolham. *W Sus* 3C **26**
Cooling. *Medw* 3B **40**
Cooling Street. *Medw* 3B **40**

Coombe. *Corn*
  nr. Bude 1C **10**
  nr. St Austell 3D **6**
  nr. Truro 4C **6**
Coombe. *Devn*
  nr. Sidmouth 3E **12**
  nr. Teignmouth 5C **12**
Coombe. *Glos* 2C **34**
Coombe. *Hants* 4E **25**
Coombe Bissett. *Wilts* 4G **23**
Coombe Hill. *Glos* 3D **49**
Coombe Keynes. *Dors* 4D **14**
Coombes. *W Sus* 5C **26**
Coopersale. *Essx* 5E **53**
Coopersale Street. *Essx* 5E **53**
Cooper's Corner. *Kent* 1F **27**
Cooper Street. *Kent* 5H **41**
Cootham. *W Sus* 4B **26**
Copalder Corner. *Cambs* 1C **64**
Copdock. *Suff* 1E **54**
Copford. *Essx* 3C **54**
Copford Green. *Essx* 3C **54**
Copgrove. *N Yor* 3F **99**
Copister. *Shet* 4F **173**
Cople. *Bed* 1B **52**
Copley. *Dur* 2D **105**
Coplow Dale. *Derbs* 3F **85**
Copmanthorpe. *York* 5H **99**
Copp. *Lanc* 1C **90**
Coppathorne. *Corn* 2C **10**
Coppenhall. *Ches E* 5B **84**
Coppenhall. *Staf* 4D **72**
Coppenhall Moss. *Ches E* 5B **84**
Copperhouse. *Corn* 3C **4**
Coppicegate. *Shrp* 2B **60**
Coppingford. *Cambs* 2A **64**
Copplestone. *Devn* 2A **12**
Coppull. *Lanc* 3D **90**
Coppull Moor. *Lanc* 3D **90**
Copsale. *W Sus* 3C **26**
Copshaw Holm. *Bord* 1F **113**
Copster Green. *Lanc* 1E **91**
Copston Magna. *Warw* 2B **62**
Copt Green. *Warw* 4F **61**
Copthall Green. *Essx* 5E **53**
Copt Heath. *W Mid* 3F **61**
Copt Hewick. *N Yor* 2F **99**
Copthill. *Dur* 5B **114**
Copthorne. *W Sus* 1E **27**
Coptiviney. *Shrp* 2G **71**
Copy's Green. *Norf* 2B **78**
Copythorne. *Hants* 1B **16**
Corbridge. *Nmbd* 3C **114**
Corby. *Nptn* 2F **63**
Corby Glen. *Linc* 3G **75**
Cordon. *N Ayr* 2E **123**
Coreley. *Shrp* 3A **60**
Corfe. *Som* 1F **13**
Corfe Castle. *Dors* 4E **15**
Corfe Mullen. *Dors* 3E **15**
Corfton. *Shrp* 2G **59**
Corgarff. *Abers* 3G **151**
Corhampton. *Hants* 4E **24**
Corlae. *Dum* 5F **117**
Corlannau. *Neat* 2A **32**
Corley. *Warw* 2H **61**
Corley Ash. *Warw* 2G **61**
Corley Moor. *Warw* 2G **61**
Cormiston. *S Lan* 1C **118**
Cornaa. *IOM* 3D **108**
Cornaigbeg. *Arg* 4A **138**
Cornaigmore. *Arg*
  on Coll 2D **138**
  on Tiree 4A **138**
Corner Row. *Lanc* 1C **90**
Corney. *Cumb* 5C **102**
Cornforth. *Dur* 1A **106**
Cornhill. *Abers* 3C **160**
Cornhill. *High* 4C **164**
Cornhill-on-Tweed. *Nmbd* 1C **120**
Cornholme. *W Yor* 2H **91**
Cornish Hall End. *Essx* 2G **53**
Cornquoy. *Orkn* 7E **172**
Cornriggs. *Dur* 5B **114**
Cornsay. *Dur* 5E **115**
Cornsay Colliery. *Dur* 5E **115**
Corntown. *High* 3H **157**
Corntown. *V Glam* 4C **32**
Cornwall Airport Newquay.
  Corn 2C **6**
Cornwell. *Oxon* 3A **50**
Cornwood. *Devn* 3C **8**
Cornworthy. *Devn* 3E **9**
Corpach. *High* 1E **141**
Corpusty. *Norf* 3D **78**
Corra. *Dum* 3F **111**
Corran. *High*
  nr. Arnisdale 2E **141**
  nr. Fort William 3A **148**
Corrany. *IOM* 3D **108**
Corribeg. *High* 1D **141**
Corrie. *N Ayr* 5H **126**
Corrie Common. *Dum* 1D **112**
Corriecravie. *N Ayr* 3D **122**
Corriekinloch. *High* 1A **164**
Corriemoillie. *High* 2F **157**
Corrievarkie Lodge. *Per* 1C **142**
Corrievorrie. *High* 1B **150**
Corrigall. *Orkn* 6C **172**
Corrimony. *High* 5F **157**
Corringham. *Linc* 1F **87**
Corringham. *Thur* 2B **40**
Corris. *Gwyn* 5G **69**
Corris Uchaf. *Gwyn* 5G **69**
Corrour Shooting Lodge.
  High 2B **142**
Corry. *High* 1E **147**
Corrybrough. *High* 1C **150**
Corrygills. *N Ayr* 2E **123**
Corry of Ardnagrask. *High* 4H **157**

Corsback. *High*
  nr. Dunnet 1E **169**
  nr. Halkirk 3E **169**
Corscombe. *Dors* 2A **14**
Corse. *Abers* 4D **160**
Corse. *Glos* 3C **48**
Corsehill. *Abers* 3G **161**
Corse Lawn. *Worc* 2D **48**
Corse of Kinnoir. *Abers* 4C **160**
Corsham. *Wilts* 4D **34**
Corsley. *Wilts* 2D **22**
Corsley Heath. *Wilts* 2D **22**
Corsock. *Dum* 2E **111**
Corston. *Bath* 5B **34**
Corston. *Wilts* 3E **35**
Corstorphine. *Edin* 2F **129**
Cortachy. *Ang* 3C **144**
Corton. *Suff* 1H **67**
Corton. *Wilts* 2E **23**
Corton Denham. *Som* 4B **22**
Corwar House. *S Ayr* 1H **109**
Corwen. *Den* 1C **70**
Coryates. *Dors* 4B **14**
Coryton. *Devn* 4E **11**
Coryton. *Thur* 2B **40**
Cosby. *Leics* 1C **62**
Coscote. *Oxon* 3D **36**
Coseley. *W Mid* 1D **60**
Cosgrove. *Nptn* 1F **51**
Cosham. *Port* 2E **17**
Cosheston. *Pemb* 4E **43**
Coskills. *N Lin* 3D **94**
Cosmeston. *V Glam* 5E **33**
Cossall. *Notts* 1B **74**
Cossington. *Leics* 4D **74**
Cossington. *Som* 2G **21**
Costa. *Orkn* 5C **172**
Costessey. *Norf* 4D **78**
Costock. *Notts* 3C **74**
Coston. *Leics* 3F **75**
Coston. *Norf* 5C **78**
Cote. *Oxon* 5B **50**
Cotebrook. *Ches W* 4H **83**
Cotehill. *Cumb* 4F **113**
Cotes. *Cumb* 1D **97**
Cotes. *Leics* 3C **74**
Cotes. *Staf* 2C **72**
Cotesbach. *Leics* 2C **62**
Cotes Heath. *Staf* 2C **72**
Cotford St Luke. *Som* 4E **21**
Cotgrave. *Notts* 2D **74**
Cothal. *Abers* 2F **153**
Cotham. *Notts* 1E **75**
Cothelstone. *Som* 3E **21**
Cotheridge. *Worc* 5B **60**
Cotherstone. *Dur* 3D **104**
Cothill. *Oxon* 2C **36**
Cotland. *Mon* 5A **48**
Cotleigh. *Devn* 2F **13**
Cotmanhay. *Derbs* 1B **74**
Coton. *Cambs* 5D **64**
Coton. *Nptn* 3D **62**
Coton. *Staf*
  nr. Gnosall 3C **72**
  nr. Stone 2D **73**
  nr. Tamworth 5F **73**
Coton Clanford. *Staf* 3C **72**
Coton Hayes. *Staf* 2D **73**
Coton Hill. *Shrp* 4G **71**
Coton in the Clay. *Staf* 3F **73**
Coton in the Elms. *Derbs* 4G **73**
Cotonwood. *Shrp* 2H **71**
Cotonwood. *Staf* 3C **72**
Cott. *Devn* 2D **9**
Cott. *Orkn* 5F **172**
Cottam. *E Yor* 3D **101**
Cottam. *Lanc* 1D **90**
Cottam. *Notts* 3F **87**
Cottartown. *High* 5E **159**
Cottarville. *Nptn* 4E **63**
Cottenham. *Cambs* 4D **64**
Cotterdale. *N Yor* 5B **104**
Cottered. *Herts* 3D **52**
Cotterstock. *Nptn* 1H **63**
Cottesbrooke. *Nptn* 3E **62**
Cottesmore. *Rut* 4G **75**
Cotteylands. *Devn* 1C **12**
Cottingham. *E Yor* 1D **94**
Cottingham. *Nptn* 1F **63**
Cottingley. *W Yor* 1B **92**
Cottisford. *Oxon* 2D **50**
Cotton. *Staf* 1E **73**
Cotton. *Suff* 4C **66**
Cotton End. *Bed* 1A **52**
Cottown. *Abers* 4F **161**
Cotts. *Devn* 2A **8**
Cotwalton. *Staf* 2D **72**
Couch's Mill. *Corn* 3F **7**
Coughton. *Here* 3A **48**
Coughton. *Warw* 4E **61**
Coulags. *High* 4B **156**
Coulby Newham. *Midd* 3C **106**
Coulderton. *Cumb* 4A **102**
Coulin Lodge. *High* 3C **156**
Coull. *Abers* 3C **152**
Coulport. *Arg* 1D **126**
Coulsdon. *G Lon* 5D **39**
Coulston. *Wilts* 1E **23**
Coulter. *S Lan* 1C **118**
Coultings. *Som* 2F **21**
Coulton. *N Yor* 2A **100**
Cound. *Shrp* 5H **71**
Coundon. *Dur* 2F **105**
Coundon Grange. *Dur* 2F **105**
Countersett. *N Yor* 1B **98**
Countess. *Wilts* 2G **23**
Countess Cross. *Essx* 2B **54**
Countesthorpe. *Leics* 1C **62**
Countisbury. *Devn* 2H **19**
Coupar Angus. *Per* 4B **144**
Coupe Green. *Lanc* 2D **90**

Coupland – Cuan

Coupland. Cumb 3A 104
Coupland. Nmbd 1D 120
Cour. Arg 5G 125
Courance. Dum 5C 118
Court-at-Street. Kent 2E 29
Courteachan. High 4E 147
Courteenhall. Nptn 5E 63
Court Henry. Carm 3F 45
Courtsend. Essx 1E 41
Courtway. Som 3F 21
Cousland. Midl 3G 129
Cousley Wood. E Sus 2A 28
Coustonn. Arg 2B 126
Cove. Arg 1D 126
Cove. Devn 1C 12
Cove. Hants 1G 25
Cove. High 4C 162
Cove. Bord 2D 130
Cove Bay. Aber 3G 153
Covehithe. Suff 2H 67
Coven. Staf 5D 72
Coveney. Cambs 2D 65
Covenham St Bartholomew. Linc 1C 88
Covenham St Mary. Linc 1C 88
Coven Heath. Staf 5D 72
Coventry. W Mid 192 (3H 61)
Coverack. Corn 5E 5
Coverham. N Yor 1D 98
Covesea. Mor 1F 159
Covingham. Swin 3G 35
Covington. Cambs 3H 63
Covington. S Lan 1B 118
Cowan Bridge. Lanc 2F 97
Cowan Head. Cumb 5F 103
Cowbar. Red C 3E 107
Cowbeech. E Sus 4H 27
Cowbit. Linc 4B 76
Cowbridge. V Glam 4C 32
Cowden. Kent 1F 27
Cowdenbeath. Fife 4D 136
Cowdenburn. Bord 4F 129
Cowdenend. Fife 4D 136
Cowers Lane. Derbs 1H 73
Cowes. IOW 3C 16
Cowesby. N Yor 1G 99
Cowfold. W Sus 3D 26
Cowfords. Mor 2H 159
Cowgill. Cumb 1G 97
Cowie. Abers 5F 153
Cowie. Stir 1B 128
Cowlam. E Yor 3D 100
Cowley. Devn 3C 12
Cowley. Glos 4E 49
Cowley. G Lon 2B 38
Cowley. Oxon 5D 50
Cowley. Staf 4C 72
Cowleymoor. Devn 1C 12
Cowling. Lanc 3D 90
Cowling. N Yor
nr. Bedale 1E 99
nr. Glusburn 5B 98
Cowlinge. Suff 5G 65
Cowmes. W Yor 3B 92
Cowpe. Lanc 2G 91
Cowpen. Nmbd 1F 115
Cowpen Bewley. Stoc T 2B 106
Cowplain. Hants 1E 17
Cowshill. Dur 5B 114
Cowslip Green. N Som 5H 33
Cowstrandburn. Fife 4C 136
Cowthorpe. N Yor 4G 99
Coxall. Here 3F 59
Coxbank. Ches E 1A 72
Coxbench. Derbs 1A 74
Cox Common. Suff 2G 67
Coxford. Norf 3H 77
Cox Green. Surr 2B 26
Cox Green. Tyne 4G 115
Coxgreen. Staf 2C 60
Coxheath. Kent 5B 40
Coxhoe. Dur 1A 106
Coxley. Som 2A 22
Coxwold. N Yor 2H 99
Coychurch. B'end 3C 32
Coylton. S Ayr 3D 116
Coylumbridge. High 2D 150
Coynach. Abers 3B 152
Coynachie. Abers 5B 160
Coytrahen. B'end 3B 32
Crabbs Cross. Worc 4E 61
Crabgate. Norf 3C 78
Crab Orchard. Dors 2F 15
Crabtree. W Sus 3D 26
Crabtree Green. Wrex 1F 71
Crackaig. High 2G 165
Crackenthorpe. Cumb 2H 103
Crackington Haven. Corn 3B 10
Crackley. Staf 5C 84
Crackley. Warw 3G 61
Crackleybank. Shrp 4B 72
Crackpot. N Yor 5C 104
Cracoe. N Yor 3B 98
Craddock. Devn 1D 12
Cradhlastadh. W Isl 4C 171
Cradley. Here 1C 48
Cradley. W Mid 2D 60
Cradoc. Powy 2D 46
Crafthole. Corn 3H 7
Crafton. Buck 4G 51
Cragabus. Arg 5B 124
Crag Foot. Lanc 2D 97
Craggan. High 1E 151
Cragganmore. Mor 5F 159
Cragganvallie. High 5H 157
Craggie. High 2F 165
Craggiemore. High 5B 158
Cragg Vale. W Yor 2A 92
Craghead. Dur 4F 115
Crai. Powy 3B 46
Craichie. Ang 4E 145
Craig. Arg 5E 141
Craig. Dum 2D 111
Craig. High
nr. Achnashellach 4C 156
nr. Lower Diabaig 2G 155
nr. Stromeferry 5H 155
Craiganour Lodge. Per 3D 142
Craigbrack. Arg 4A 134
Craig-Cefn-Parc. Swan 5G 45
Craigdallie. Per 1E 137
Craigdam. Abers 5F 161
Craigdarroch. E Ayr 4F 117
Craigdarroch. High 3G 157
Craigdhu. High 4G 157
Craigearn. Abers 2E 152
Craigellachie. Mor 4G 159
Craigend. Per 1D 136
Craigendoran. Arg 1E 126
Craigends. Ren 3F 127
Craigenputtock. Dum 1E 111
Craigens. E Ayr 3E 117
Craighall. Edin 2E 129
Craighead. Fife 2H 137
Craighouse. Arg 3D 124
Craigie. Abers 2G 153
Craigie. D'dee 5D 144
Craigie. Per
nr. Blairgowrie 4A 144
nr. Perth 1D 136
Craigie. S Ayr 1D 116
Craigielaw. E Lot 2A 130
Craiglemine. Dum 5B 110
Craig-llwyn. Shrp 3E 71
Craiglockhart. Edin 2F 129
Craig Lodge. Arg 2B 126
Craigmalloch. E Ayr 5D 117
Craigmaud. Abers 3F 161
Craigmill. Stir 4H 135
Craigmillar. Edin 2F 129
Craigmore. Arg 3C 126
Craigmuie. Dum 1E 111
Craignair. Dum 3F 111
Craignant. Shrp 2E 71
Craigneuk. N Lan
nr. Airdrie 3A 128
nr. Motherwell 4A 128
Craignure. Arg 5B 140
Craigo. Ang 2F 145
Craigrory. High 4A 158
Craigrothie. Fife 2F 137
Craigs. Dum 2D 112
The Craigs. High 4B 164
Craigshill. W Lot 3D 128
Craigton. Aber 3F 153
Craigton. Abers 3E 152
Craigton. Ang
nr. Carnoustie 5E 145
nr. Kirriemuir 3C 144
Craigton. High 4A 158
Craigtown. High 3A 168
Craig-y-Duke. Neat 5H 45
Craig-y-nos. Powy 4B 46
Craik. Bord 4F 119
Crail. Fife 3H 137
Crailing. Bord 2A 120
Crailinghall. Bord 2A 120
Crakehill. N Yor 2G 99
Crakemarsh. Staf 2E 73
Crambe. N Yor 3B 100
Crambeck. N Yor 3B 100
Cramlington. Nmbd 2F 115
Cramond. Edin 2E 129
Cramond Bridge. Edin 2E 129
Cranage. Ches E 4B 84
Cranberry. Staf 2C 72
Cranborne. Dors 1F 15
Cranbourne. Brac 3A 38
Cranbrook. Devn 3D 12
Cranbrook. Kent 2B 28
Cranbrook Common. Kent 2B 28
Crane Moor. S Yor 4D 92
Crane's Corner. Norf 4B 78
Cranfield. C Beds 1H 51
Cranford. G Lon 3C 38
Cranford St Andrew. Nptn 3G 63
Cranford St John. Nptn 3G 63
Cranham. Glos 4D 49
Cranham. G Lon 2G 39
Crank. Mers 1H 83
Cranleigh. Surr 2B 26
Cranley. Suff 3D 66
Cranloch. Mor 3G 159
Cranmer Green. Suff 3C 66
Cranmore. IOW 3C 16
Cranmore. Linc 5A 76
Crannich. Arg 4G 139
Crannoch. Mor 3B 160
Cranoe. Leics 1E 63
Cransford. Suff 4F 67
Cranshaws. Bord 3C 130
Cranstal. IOM 1D 108
Crantock. Corn 2B 6
Cranwell. Linc 1H 75
Cranwich. Norf 1G 65
Cranworth. Norf 5B 78
Craobh Haven. Arg 3E 133
Craobhnaclag. High 4G 157
Crapstone. Devn 2B 8
Crarae. Arg 4G 133
Crask. High
nr. Bettyhill 2H 167
nr. Lairg 1C 164
Crask of Aigas. High 4G 157
Craster. Nmbd 2G 121
Craswall. Here 2F 47
Cratfield. Suff 3F 67
Crathes. Abers 4E 153
Crathie. Abers 4G 151
Crathie. High 4H 149
Crathorne. N Yor 4B 106
Craven Arms. Shrp 2G 59
Crawcrook. Tyne 3E 115
Crawford. Lanc 4C 90
Crawford. S Lan 2B 118
Crawforddyke. S Lan 4B 128
Crawfordjohn. S Lan 2A 118
Crawick. Dum 3G 117
Crawley. Devn 2F 13
Crawley. Hants 3C 24
Crawley. Oxon 4B 50
Crawley. W Sus 2D 26
Crawley Down. W Sus 2E 27
Crawley End. Essx 1E 53
Crawley Side. Dur 5C 114
Crawshawbooth. Lanc 2G 91
Crawton. Abers 5F 153
Cray. N Yor 2B 98
Cray. Per 2A 144
Crayford. G Lon 3G 39
Crayke. N Yor 2H 99
Craymere Beck. Norf 2C 78
Crays Hill. Essx 1B 40
Cray's Pond. Oxon 3E 37
Crazies Hill. Wok 3F 37
Creacombe. Devn 1B 12
Creagan. Arg 4D 140
Creag Aoil. High 1F 141
Creag Ghoraidh. W Isl 4C 170
Creaguaineach Lodge. High 2H 141
Creamore Bank. Shrp 2H 71
Creaton. Nptn 3E 62
Creca. Dum 2D 112
Credenhill. Here 1H 47
Crediton. Devn 2B 12
Creebridge. Dum 3B 110
Creech. Dors 4E 15
Creech Heathfield. Som 4F 21
Creech St Michael. Som 4F 21
Creed. Corn 4D 6
Creekmoor. Pool 3E 15
Creekmouth. G Lon 2F 39
Creeting St Mary. Suff 5C 66
Creeting St Peter. Suff 5C 66
Creeton. Linc 3H 75
Creetown. Dum 4B 110
Creggans. Arg 3H 133
Cregneash. IOM 5A 108
Cregrina. Powy 5D 58
Creich. Arg 2B 132
Creich. Fife 1F 137
Creighton. Staf 2E 73
Creigiau. Card 3D 32
Cremyll. Corn 3A 8
Crendell. Dors 1F 15
Crepkill. High 4D 154
Cressage. Shrp 5H 71
Cressbrook. Derbs 3F 85
Cresselly. Pemb 4E 43
Cressing. Essx 3A 54
Cresswell. Nmbd 5G 121
Cresswell. Staf 2D 73
Cresswell Quay. Pemb 4E 43
Creswell. Derbs 3C 86
Creswell Green. Staf 4E 73
Cretingham. Suff 4E 67
Crewe. Ches E 5B 84
Crewe-by-Farndon. Ches W 5G 83
Crewgreen. Powy 4F 71
Crewkerne. Som 2H 13
Crews Hill. G Lon 5D 52
Crewton. Derb 2A 74
Crianlarich. Stir 1C 134
Cribbs Causeway. S Glo 3A 34
Cribyn. Cdgn 5E 57
Criccieth. Gwyn 2D 69
Crich. Derbs 5A 86
Crichton. Midl 3G 129
Crick. Mon 2H 33
Crick. Nptn 3C 62
Crickadarn. Powy 1D 46
Cricket Hill. Hants 5G 37
Cricket Malherbie. Som 1G 13
Cricket St Thomas. Som 2G 13
Crickham. Som 2H 21
Crickheath. Shrp 3E 71
Crickhowell. Powy 4F 47
Cricklade. Wilts 2G 35
Cricklewood. G Lon 2D 38
Cridling Stubbs. N Yor 2F 93
Crieff. Per 1A 136
Criftins. Shrp 2F 71
Criggion. Powy 4E 71
Crigglestone. W Yor 3D 92
Crimchard. Som 2G 13
Crimdon Park. Dur 1B 106
Crimond. Abers 3H 161
Crimonmogate. Abers 3H 161
Crimplesham. Norf 5F 77
Crimscote. Warw 1H 49
Crinan. Arg 4E 133
Cringleford. Norf 5D 78
Crinow. Pemb 3F 43
Cripplesease. Corn 3C 4
Cripplestyle. Dors 1F 15
Cripp's Corner. E Sus 3B 28
Croanford. Corn 5A 10
Crockenhill. Kent 4G 39
Crocker End. Oxon 3F 37
Crockerhill. Hants 2D 16
Crockernwell. Devn 3A 12
Crocker's Ash. Here 4A 48
Crockerton. Wilts 2D 22
Crocketford. Dum 2F 111
Crockey Hill. York 5A 100
Crockham Hill. Kent 5F 39
Crockhurst Street. Kent 1H 27
Crockleford Heath. Essx 3D 54
Croeserw. Neat 2B 32
Croes-Goch. Pemb 1C 42
Croes Hywel. Mon 4G 47
Croes-lan. Cdgn 1D 45
Croesor. Gwyn 1F 69
Croesoswallt. Shrp 3E 71
Croesyceiliog. Carm 4E 45
Croesyceiliog. Torf 2G 33
Croes-y-mwyalch. Torf 2G 33
Croesywaun. Gwyn 5E 81
Croford. Som 4E 20
Croft. Leics 1C 62
Croft. Linc 4E 89
Croft. Warr 1A 84
Croftamie. Stir 1F 127
Croftfoot. Glas 3G 127
Croftmill. Per 5F 143
Crofton. Cumb 4E 112
Crofton. W Yor 3D 93
Crofton. Wilts 5A 36
Croft-on-Tees. N Yor 4F 105
Crofts. Dum 2E 111
Crofts of Benachielt. High 5D 169
Crofts of Dipple. Mor 3H 159
Crofty. Swan 3E 31
Croggan. Arg 1E 132
Croglin. Cumb 5G 113
Croich. High 4B 164
Croick. High 3A 168
Croig. Arg 3E 139
Cromarty. High 2B 158
Crombie. Fife 1D 128
Cromdale. High 1E 151
Cromer. Herts 3C 52
Cromer. Norf 1E 78
Cromford. Derbs 5G 85
Cromhall. S Glo 2B 34
Cromor. W Isl 5G 171
Cromra. High 5H 149
Cromwell. Notts 4E 87
Cronberry. E Ayr 2F 117
Crondall. Hants 2F 25
The Cronk. IOM 2C 108
Cronk-y-Voddy. IOM 3C 108
Cronton. Mers 2G 83
Crook. Cumb 5F 103
Crook. Dur 1E 105
Crookdake. Cumb 5C 112
Crooke. G Man 4D 90
Crookedholm. E Ayr 1D 116
Crooked Soley. Wilts 4B 36
Crookes. S Yor 2H 85
Crookgate Bank. Dur 4E 115
Crookhall. Dur 4E 115
Crookham. Nmbd 1D 120
Crookham. W Ber 5D 36
Crookham Village. Hants 1F 25
Crooklands. Cumb 1E 97
Crook of Devon. Per 3C 136
Crookston. Glas 3G 127
Cropredy. Oxon 1C 50
Cropston. Leics 4C 74
Cropthorne. Worc 1E 49
Cropton. N Yor 1B 100
Cropwell Bishop. Notts 2D 74
Cropwell Butler. Notts 2D 74
Cros. W Isl 1H 171
Crosbie. N Ayr 4D 126
Crosbost. W Isl 5F 171
Crosby. Cumb 1B 102
Crosby. IOM 4C 108
Crosby. Mers 1F 83
Crosby. N Lin 3B 94
Crosby Court. N Yor 5A 106
Crosby Garrett. Cumb 4A 104
Crosby Ravensworth. Cumb 3H 103
Crosby Villa. Cumb 1B 102
Croscombe. Som 2A 22
Crosland Moor. W Yor 3B 92
Cross. Som 1H 21
Crossaig. Arg 4G 125
Crossapol. Arg 4A 138
Cross Ash. Mon 4H 47
Cross-at-Hand. Kent 1B 28
Crossbush. W Sus 5B 26
Crosscanonby. Cumb 1B 102
Crossdale Street. Norf 2E 79
Cross End. Essx 2B 54
Crossens. Mers 2B 90
Crossford. Fife 1D 128
Crossford. S Lan 5B 128
Cross Foxes. Gwyn 4G 69
Crossgate. Orkn 6D 172
Crossgate. Staf 2D 72
Crossgatehall. E Lot 3G 129
Cross Gates. W Yor 1D 92
Crossgates. Fife 1E 129
Crossgates. N Yor 1E 101
Crossgates. Powy 4C 58
Crossgill. Lanc 3E 97
Cross Green. Devn 4D 11
Cross Green. Staf 5D 72
Cross Green. Suff
nr. Cockfield 5A 66
nr. Hitcham 5B 66
Cross Hands. Carm 4F 45
Crosshands. Carm 2F 43
Crosshands. E Ayr 1D 117
Cross Hill. Derbs 1B 74
Cross Hill. Glos 2A 34
Crosshill. E Ayr 2D 117
Crosshill. Fife 4D 136
Crosshill. S Ayr 4C 116
Cross Hills. N Yor 5C 98
Crosshills. High 1A 158
Cross Holme. N Yor 5C 106
Crosshouse. E Ayr 1C 116
Cross Houses. Shrp 5H 71
Crossings. Cumb 2G 113
Cross in Hand. E Sus 3G 27
Cross Inn. Cdgn
nr. Aberaeron 4E 57
nr. New Quay 5C 56
Cross Inn. Rhon 3D 32
Crosskeys. Cphy 2F 33
Crosskirk. High 2C 168
Crosslands. Cumb 1C 96
Cross Lane Head. Shrp 1B 60
Cross Lanes. Corn 4D 5
Cross Lanes. Dur 3D 104
Cross Lanes. N Yor 3H 99
Cross Lanes. Wrex 1F 71
Crosslanes. Shrp 4F 71
Crosslee. Ren 3F 127
Crossmichael. Dum 3E 111
Crossmoor. Lanc 1C 90
Cross Oak. Powy 3E 46
Cross of Jackston. Abers 5E 161
Cross o' th' Hands. Derbs 1G 73
Crossroads. Abers
nr. Aberdeen 3G 153
nr. Banchory 4E 153
Crossroads. E Ayr 1D 116
Cross Side. Devn 4B 20
Cross Street. Suff 3D 66
Crosston. Ang 3E 145
Cross Town. Ches E 3B 84
Crossway. Mon 4H 47
Crossway. Powy 5C 58
Crossway Green. Mon 2A 34
Crossway Green. Worc 4C 60
Crossways. Dors 4C 14
Crosswell. Pemb 1F 43
Crosswood. Cdgn 3F 57
Crosthwaite. Cumb 5F 103
Croston. Lanc 3C 90
Crostwick. Norf 4E 79
Crostwight. Norf 3F 79
Crothair. W Isl 4D 171
Crouch. Kent 5H 39
Croucheston. Wilts 4F 23
Crouch Hill. Dors 1C 14
Croughton. Nptn 2D 50
Crovie. Abers 2F 161
Crow. Hants 2G 15
Crowan. Corn 3D 4
Crowborough. E Sus 2G 27
Crowcombe. Som 3E 21
Crowcroft. Worc 5B 60
Crowdecote. Derbs 4F 85
Crowden. Derbs 1E 85
Crowden. Devn 3E 11
Crowdhill. Hants 1C 16
Crowdon. N Yor 5G 107
Crow Edge. S Yor 4B 92
Crow End. Cambs 5C 64
Crowfield. Nptn 1E 50
Crowfield. Suff 5D 66
Crow Green. Essx 1G 39
Crow Hill. Here 3B 48
Crowhurst. E Sus 4B 28
Crowhurst. Surr 1E 27
Crowhurst Lane End. Surr 1E 27
Crowland. Linc 4B 76
Crowland. Suff 3C 66
Crowlas. Corn 3C 4
Crowle. N Lin 3A 94
Crowle. Worc 5D 60
Crowle Green. Worc 5D 60
Crowmarsh Gifford. Oxon 3E 36
Crown Corner. Suff 3E 67
Crownthorpe. Norf 5C 78
Crowntown. Corn 3D 4
Crows-an-wra. Corn 4A 4
Crowshill. Norf 5B 78
Crowthorne. Brac 5G 37
Crowton. Ches W 3H 83
Croxall. Staf 4F 73
Croxby. Linc 1A 88
Croxdale. Dur 1F 105
Croxden. Staf 2E 73
Croxley Green. Herts 1B 38
Croxton. Cambs 4B 64
Croxton. Norf
nr. Fakenham 2B 78
nr. Thetford 2A 66
Croxton. N Lin 3D 94
Croxton. Staf 2B 72
Croxtonbank. Staf 2B 72
Croxton Green. Ches E 5H 83
Croxton Kerrial. Leics 3F 75
Croy. High 4B 158
Croy. N Lan 2A 128
Croyde. Devn 3E 19
Croydon. Cambs 1D 52
Croydon. G Lon 4E 39
Crubenbeg. High 4A 150
Crubenmore Lodge. High 4A 150
Cruckmeole. Shrp 5G 71
Cruckton. Shrp 4G 71
Cruden Bay. Abers 5H 161
Crudgington. Telf 4A 72
Crudie. Abers 3E 161
Crudwell. Wilts 2E 35
Cruft. Devn 3F 11
Crug. Powy 3D 58
Crughywel. Powy 4F 47
Crugmeer. Corn 1D 6
Crugybar. Carm 2G 45
Crug-y-byddar. Powy 2D 58
Crulabhig. W Isl 4D 171
Crumlin. Cphy 2F 33
Crumpsall. G Man 4G 91
Crumpsbrook. Shrp 3A 60
Crundale. Kent 1E 29
Crundale. Pemb 3D 42
Cruwys Morchard. Devn 1B 12
Crux Easton. Hants 1C 24
Cruxton. Dors 3B 14
Crwbin. Carm 4E 45
Cryers Hill. Buck 2G 37
Crymych. Pemb 1F 43
Crynant. Neat 5A 46
Crystal Palace. G Lon 3E 39
Cuaich. High 5A 150
Cuaig. High 3G 155
Cuan. Arg 2E 133

Cubbington – Didsbury

Cubbington. *Warw* 4H 61
Cubert. *Corn* 3B 6
Cubley. *S Yor* 4C 92
Cubley Common. *Derbs* 2F 73
Cublington. *Buck* 3G 51
Cublington. *Here* 2G 47
Cuckfield. *W Sus* 3E 27
Cucklington. *Som* 4C 22
Cuckney. *Notts* 3C 86
Cuckron. *Shet* 6F 173
Cuddesdon. *Oxon* 5E 50
Cuddington. *Buck* 4F 51
Cuddington. *Ches W* 3A 84
Cuddington Heath. *Ches W* 1G 71
Cuddy Hill. *Lanc* 1C 90
Cudham. *G Lon* 5F 39
Cudlipptown. *Devn* 5F 11
Cudworth. *Som* 1G 13
Cudworth. *S Yor* 4D 93
Cudworth. *Surr* 1D 26
Cuerdley Cross. *Warr* 2H 83
Cuffley. *Herts* 5D 52
Cuidhir. *W Isl* 8B 170
Cuidhsiadar. *W Isl* 2H 171
Cuidhtinis. *W Isl* 9C 171
Culbo. *High* 2A 158
Culbokie. *High* 3A 158
Culburnie. *High* 4G 157
Culcabock. *High* 4A 158
Culcharry. *High* 3C 158
Culcheth. *Warr* 1A 84
Culduie. *High* 4G 155
Culeave. *High* 4C 164
Culford. *Suff* 3H 65
Culgaith. *Cumb* 2H 103
Culham. *Oxon* 2D 36
Culkein. *High* 1E 163
Culkein Drumbeg. *High* 5B 166
Culkerton. *Glos* 2E 35
Cullen. *Mor* 2C 160
Cullercoats. *Tyne* 2G 115
Cullicudden. *High* 2A 158
Cullingworth. *W Yor* 1A 92
Cullipool. *Arg* 2E 133
Cullivoe. *Shet* 1G 173
Culloch. *Per* 2G 135
Culloden. *High* 4B 158
Cullompton. *Devn* 2D 12
Culm Davy. *Devn* 1E 13
Culmington. *Shrp* 2G 59
Culmstock. *Devn* 1E 12
Cul na Caepaich. *High* 5E 147
Culnacnoc. *High* 2E 155
Culnacraig. *High* 3E 163
Culrain. *High* 4C 164
Culross. *Fife* 1C 128
Culroy. *S Ayr* 3C 116
Culswick. *Shet* 7D 173
Cults. *Aber* 3F 153
Cults. *Abers* 5C 160
Cults. *Fife* 3F 137
Cultybraggan Camp. *Per* 1G 135
Culver. *Devn* 3B 12
Culverlane. *Devn* 2D 8
Culverstone Green. *Kent* 4H 39
Culverthorpe. *Linc* 1H 75
Culworth. *Nptn* 1D 50
Culzie Lodge. *High* 1H 157
Cumberlow Green. *Herts* 2D 52
Cumbernauld. *N Lan* 2A 128
Cumbernauld Village. *N Lan* 2A 128
Cumberworth. *Linc* 3E 89
Cumdivock. *Cumb* 5E 113
Cuminestown. *Abers* 3F 161
Cumledge Mill. *Bord* 4D 130
Cumlewick. *Shet* 9F 173
Cummersdale. *Cumb* 4E 113
Cummertrees. *Dum* 3C 112
Cummingstown. *Mor* 2F 159
Cumnock. *E Ayr* 2E 117
Cumnor. *Oxon* 5C 50
Cumrew. *Cumb* 4G 113
Cumwhinton. *Cumb* 4F 113
Cumwhitton. *Cumb* 4G 113
Cundall. *N Yor* 2G 99
Cunninghamhead. *N Ayr* 5E 127
Cunning Park. *S Ayr* 3C 116
Cunningsburgh. *Shet* 9F 173
Cunnister. *Shet* 2G 173
Cupar. *Fife* 2F 137
Cupar Muir. *Fife* 2F 137
Cupernham. *Hants* 4B 24
Curbar. *Derbs* 3G 85
Curborough. *Staf* 4F 73
Curbridge. *Hants* 1D 16
Curbridge. *Oxon* 5B 50
Curdridge. *Hants* 1D 16
Curdworth. *Warw* 1F 61
Curland. *Som* 1F 13
Curland Common. *Som* 1F 13
Curridge. *W Ber* 4C 36
Currie. *Edin* 3E 129
Curry Mallet. *Som* 4G 21
Curry Rivel. *Som* 4G 21
Curtisden Green. *Kent* 1B 28
Curtisknowle. *Devn* 3D 8
Cury. *Corn* 4D 5
Cusgarne. *Corn* 4B 6
Cusop. *Here* 1F 47
Cusworth. *S Yor* 4F 93
Cutcombe. *Som* 3C 20
Cuthill. *E Lot* 2G 129
Cutiau. *Gwyn* 4F 69
Cutlers Green. *Essx* 2F 53
Cutmadoc. *Corn* 2E 7
Cutnall Green. *Worc* 4C 60
Cutsdean. *Glos* 2F 49
Cutthorpe. *Derbs* 3H 85
Cuttiford's Door. *Som* 1G 13
Cuttivett. *Corn* 2H 7
Cutts. *Shet* 8E 173
Cuttybridge. *Pemb* 3D 42
Cuttyhill. *Abers* 3H 161
Cuxham. *Oxon* 2E 37
Cuxton. *Medw* 4B 40
Cuxwold. *Linc* 4E 95
Cwm. *Blae* 5E 47
Cwm. *Den* 3C 82
Cwm. *Powy* 1E 59
Cwmafan. *Neat* 2A 32
Cwmaman. *Rhon* 2C 32
Cwmann. *Carm* 1F 45
Cwmbach. *Carm* 2G 43
Cwmbach. *Powy* 2E 47
Cwmbach. *Rhon* 5D 46
Cwmbach Llechrhyd. *Powy* 5C 58
Cwmbelan. *Powy* 2B 58
Cwmbran. *Torf* 2F 33
Cwmbrwyno. *Cdgn* 2G 57
Cwm Capel. *Carm* 5E 45
Cwmcarn. *Cphy* 2F 33
Cwmcarvan. *Mon* 5H 47
Cwm-celyn. *Blae* 5F 47
Cwmcerdinen. *Swan* 5G 45
Cwm-Cewydd. *Gwyn* 4A 70
Cwm-cou. *Cdgn* 1C 44
Cwmcych. *Pemb* 1G 43
Cwmdare. *Rhon* 5C 46
Cwmdu. *Carm* 2G 45
Cwmdu. *Powy* 3E 47
Cwmduad. *Carm* 2D 45
Cwm Dulais. *Swan* 5G 45
Cwmerfyn. *Cdgn* 2F 57
Cwmfelin. *B'end* 3B 32
Cwmfelin Boeth. *Carm* 3F 43
Cwmfelinfach. *Cphy* 2E 33
Cwmfelin Mynach. *Carm* 2G 43
Cwmffrwd. *Carm* 4E 45
Cwmgiedd. *Powy* 4A 46
Cwmgors. *Neat* 4H 45
Cwmgwili. *Carm* 4F 45
Cwmgwrach. *Neat* 5B 46
Cwmhiraeth. *Carm* 1H 43
Cwmifor. *Carm* 3G 45
Cwmisfael. *Carm* 4E 45
Cwm-Llinau. *Powy* 5H 69
Cwmllynfell. *Neat* 4H 45
Cwm-mawr. *Carm* 4F 45
Cwm-miles. *Carm* 2F 43
Cwmorgan. *Carm* 1G 43
Cwmparc. *Rhon* 2C 32
Cwm Penmachno. *Cnwy* 1G 69
Cwmpennar. *Rhon* 5D 46
Cwm Plysgog. *Pemb* 1B 44
Cwmrhos. *Powy* 3E 47
Cwmsychpant. *Cdgn* 1E 45
Cwmsyfiog. *Cphy* 5E 47
Cwmsymlog. *Cdgn* 2F 57
Cwmtillery. *Blae* 5F 47
Cwm-twrch Isaf. *Powy* 5A 46
Cwm-twrch Uchaf. *Powy* 4A 46
Cwmwysg. *Powy* 3B 46
Cwm-y-glo. *Gwyn* 4E 81
Cwmyoy. *Mon* 3G 47
Cwmystwyth. *Cdgn* 3G 57
Cwrt. *Gwyn* 5F 69
Cwrtnewydd. *Cdgn* 1E 45
Cwrt-y-Cadno. *Carm* 1G 45
Cydweli. *Carm* 5E 45
Cyffylliog. *Den* 5C 82
Cymau. *Flin* 5E 83
Cymer. *Neat* 2B 32
Cymmer. *Neat* 2B 32
Cymmer. *Rhon* 2D 32
Cyncoed. *Card* 3E 33
Cynghordy. *Carm* 2B 46
Cynheidre. *Carm* 5E 45
Cynonville. *Neat* 2B 32
Cynwyd. *Den* 1C 70
Cynwyl Elfed. *Carm* 3D 44
Cywarch. *Gwyn* 4A 70

D

Dacre. *Cumb* 2F 103
Dacre. *N Yor* 3D 98
Dacre Banks. *N Yor* 3D 98
Daddry Shield. *Dur* 1B 104
Dadford. *Buck* 2E 51
Dadlington. *Leics* 1B 62
Dafen. *Carm* 5F 45
Daffy Green. *Norf* 5B 78
Dagdale. *Staf* 2E 73
Dagenham. *G Lon* 2F 39
Daggons. *Dors* 1G 15
Daglingworth. *Glos* 5E 49
Dagnall. *Buck* 4H 51
Dagtail End. *Worc* 4E 61
Dail. *Arg* 5E 141
Dail Beag. *W Isl* 3E 171
Dail bho Dheas. *W Isl* 1G 171
Dailly. *S Ayr* 4B 116
Dail Mor. *W Isl* 3E 171
Dairsie. *Fife* 2G 137
Daisy Bank. *W Mid* 1E 61
Daisy Hill. *G Man* 4E 91
Daisy Hill. *W Yor* 1B 92
Dalabrog. *W Isl* 6C 170
Dalavich. *Arg* 2G 133
Dalbeattie. *Dum* 3F 111
Dalblair. *E Ayr* 3F 117
Dalbury. *Derbs* 2G 73
Dalby. *IOM* 4B 108
Dalby Wolds. *Leics* 3D 74
Dalchalm. *High* 3G 165
Dalcharn. *High* 3G 167
Dalchork. *High* 2C 164
Dalchreichart. *High* 2E 149
Dalchruin. *Per* 2G 135
Dalcross. *High* 4B 158
Dalderby. *Linc* 4B 88
Dale. *Cumb* 5G 113
Dale. *Pemb* 4C 42
Dale Abbey. *Derbs* 2B 74
Dalebank. *Derbs* 4A 86
Dale Bottom. *Cumb* 2D 102
Dale Head. *Cumb* 3F 103
Dalehouse. *N Yor* 3E 107
Dalelia. *High* 2B 140
Dale of Walls. *Shet* 6C 173
Dalgarven. *N Ayr* 5D 126
Dalgety Bay. *Fife* 1E 129
Dalginross. *Per* 1G 135
Dalguise. *Per* 4G 143
Dalhalvaig. *High* 3A 168
Dalham. *Suff* 4G 65
Dalintart. *Arg* 1F 133
Dalkeith. *Midl* 3G 129
Dallas. *Mor* 3F 159
Dalleagles. *E Ayr* 3E 117
Dall House. *Per* 3C 142
Dallinghoo. *Suff* 5E 67
Dallington. *E Sus* 4A 28
Dallow. *N Yor* 2D 98
Dalmally. *Arg* 1A 134
Dalmarnock. *Glas* 3H 127
Dalmellington. *E Ayr* 4D 117
Dalmeny. *Edin* 2E 129
Dalmigavie. *High* 2B 150
Dalmilling. *S Ayr* 2C 116
Dalmore. *High*
nr. Alness 2A 158
nr. Rogart 3E 164
Dalmuir. *W Dun* 2F 127
Dalmunach. *Mor* 4G 159
Dalnabreck. *High* 2B 140
Dalnacardoch Lodge. *Per* 1E 142
Dalnamein Lodge. *Per* 2E 143
Dalnaspidal Lodge. *Per* 1D 142
Dalnatrat. *High* 3D 140
Dalnavie. *High* 1A 158
Dalnawillan Lodge. *High* 4C 168
Dalness. *High* 3F 141
Dalnessie. *High* 2D 164
Dalqueich. *Per* 3C 136
Dalquhairn. *S Ayr* 5C 116
Dalreavoch. *High* 3E 165
Dalreoch. *Per* 2C 136
Dalry. *Edin* 2F 129
Dalry. *N Ayr* 5D 126
Dalrymple. *E Ayr* 3C 116
Dalscote. *Nptn* 5D 62
Dalserf. *S Lan* 4B 128
Dalsmirren. *Arg* 4A 122
Dalston. *Cumb* 4E 113
Dalswinton. *Dum* 1G 111
Dalton. *Dum* 2C 112
Dalton. *Lanc* 4C 90
Dalton. *Nmbd*
nr. Hexham 4C 114
nr. Ponteland 2E 115
Dalton. *N Yor*
nr. Richmond 4E 105
nr. Thirsk 2G 99
Dalton. *S Lan* 4H 127
Dalton. *S Yor* 1B 86
Dalton-in-Furness. *Cumb* 2B 96
Dalton-le-Dale. *Dur* 5H 115
Dalton Magna. *S Yor* 1B 86
Dalton-on-Tees. *N Yor* 4F 105
Dalton Piercy. *Hart* 1B 106
Daltot. *Arg* 1F 125
Dalvey. *High* 5F 159
Dalwhinnie. *High* 5A 150
Dalwood. *Devn* 2F 13
Damerham. *Hants* 1G 15
Damgate. *Norf*
nr. Acle 5G 79
nr. Martham 4G 79
Dam Green. *Norf* 2C 66
Damhead. *Mor* 3E 159
Danaway. *Kent* 4C 40
Danbury. *Essx* 5A 54
Danby. *N Yor* 4E 107
Danby Botton. *N Yor* 4D 107
Danby Wiske. *N Yor* 5A 106
Danderhall. *Midl* 3G 129
Danebank. *Ches E* 2D 85
Danebridge. *Ches E* 4D 84
Dane End. *Herts* 3D 52
Danehill. *E Sus* 3F 27
Danesford. *Shrp* 1B 60
Daneshill. *Hants* 1E 25
Danesmoor. *Derbs* 4B 86
Danestone. *Aber* 2G 153
Dangerous Corner. *Lanc* 3D 90
Daniel's Water. *Kent* 1D 28
Dan's Castle. *Dur* 1E 105
Danzey Green. *Warw* 4F 61
Dapple Heath. *Staf* 3E 73
Daren. *Powy* 4F 47
Darenth. *Kent* 3G 39
Daresbury. *Hal* 2H 83
Darfield. *S Yor* 4E 93
Dargate. *Kent* 4E 41
Dargill. *Per* 2A 136
Darite. *Corn* 2G 7
Darlaston. *W Mid* 1D 61
Darley. *N Yor* 4E 98
Darley Abbey. *Derb* 2H 73
Darley Bridge. *Derbs* 4G 85
Darley Dale. *Derbs* 4G 85
Darley Head. *N Yor* 4D 98
Darlingscott. *Warw* 1H 49
Darlington. *Darl* 3F 105
Darliston. *Shrp* 2H 71
Darlton. *Notts* 3E 87
Darmsden. *Suff* 5C 66
Darnall. *S Yor* 2A 86
Darnford. *Abers* 4E 153
Darnford. *Staf* 5F 73
Darnhall. *Ches W* 4A 84
Darnick. *Bord* 1H 119
Darowen. *Powy* 5H 69
Darra. *Abers* 4E 161
Darracott. *Devn* 3E 19
Darras Hall. *Nmbd* 2E 115
Darrington. *W Yor* 2E 93
Darrow Green. *Norf* 2E 67
Darsham. *Suff* 4G 67
Dartfield. *Abers* 3H 161
Dartford. *Kent* 3G 39
Dartford-Thurrock River Crossing.
Kent 3G 39
Dartington. *Devn* 2D 9
Dartmeet. *Devn* 5G 11
Dartmouth. *Devn* 3E 9
Darton. *S Yor* 3D 92
Darvel. *E Ayr* 1E 117
Darwen. *Bkbn* 2E 91
Dassels. *Herts* 3D 53
Datchet. *Wind* 3A 38
Datchworth. *Herts* 4C 52
Datchworth Green. *Herts* 4C 52
Daubhill. *G Man* 4F 91
Dauntsey. *Wilts* 3E 35
Dauntsey Green. *Wilts* 3E 35
Dauntsey Lock. *Wilts* 3E 35
Dava. *Mor* 5E 159
Davenham. *Ches W* 3A 84
Daventry. *Nptn* 4C 62
Davidson's Mains. *Edin* 2F 129
Davidston. *High* 2B 158
Davidstow. *Corn* 4B 10
David's Well. *Powy* 3C 58
Davington. *Dum* 4E 119
Daviot. *Abers* 1E 153
Daviot. *High* 5B 158
Davyhulme. *G Man* 1B 84
Daw Cross. *N Yor* 4E 99
Dawdon. *Dur* 5H 115
Dawesgreen. *Surr* 1D 26
Dawley. *Telf* 5A 72
Dawlish. *Devn* 5C 12
Dawlish Warren. *Devn* 5C 12
Dawn. *Cnwy* 3A 82
Daws Heath. *Essx* 2C 40
Dawshill. *Worc* 5C 60
Daw's House. *Corn* 4D 10
Dawsmere. *Linc* 2D 76
Dayhills. *Staf* 2D 72
Dayhouse Bank. *Worc* 3D 60
Daylesford. *Glos* 3H 49
Daywall. *Shrp* 2E 71
Ddol. *Flin* 3D 82
Ddol Cownwy. *Powy* 4C 70
Deadman's Cross. *C Beds* 1B 52
Deadwater. *Nmbd* 5A 120
Deaf Hill. *Dur* 1A 106
Deal. *Kent* 5H 41
Dean. *Cumb* 2B 102
Dean. *Devn*
nr. Combe Martin 2G 19
nr. Lynton 2H 19
Dean. *Dors* 1E 15
Dean. *Hants*
nr. Bishop's Waltham 1D 16
nr. Winchester 3C 24
Dean. *Oxon* 3B 50
Dean. *Som* 2B 22
Dean Bank. *Dur* 1F 105
Deanburnhaugh. *Bord* 3F 119
Dean Cross. *Devn* 2F 19
Deane. *Hants* 1D 24
Deanich Lodge. *High* 5A 164
Deanland. *Dors* 1E 15
Deanlane End. *W Sus* 1F 17
Dean Park. *Shrp* 4A 60
Dean Prior. *Devn* 2D 8
Dean Row. *Ches E* 2C 84
Deans. *W Lot* 3D 128
Deanscales. *Cumb* 2B 102
Deanshanger. *Nptn* 1F 51
Deanston. *Stir* 3G 135
Dearham. *Cumb* 1B 102
Dearne Valley. *S Yor* 4D 93
Debach. *Suff* 5E 67
Debden. *Essx* 2F 53
Debden Green. *Essx*
nr. Loughton 1F 39
nr. Saffron Walden 2F 53
Debenham. *Suff* 4D 66
Dechmont. *W Lot* 2D 128
Deddington. *Oxon* 2C 50
Dedham. *Essx* 2D 54
Dedham Heath. *Essx* 2D 54
Deebank. *Abers* 4D 152
Deene. *Nptn* 1G 63
Deenethorpe. *Nptn* 1G 63
Deepcar. *S Yor* 1G 85
Deepcut. *Surr* 5A 38
Deepdale. *Cumb* 1G 97
Deepdale. *N Lin* 3D 94
Deepdale. *N Yor* 2A 98
Deeping Gate. *Pet* 5A 76
Deeping St James. *Linc* 4A 76
Deeping St Nicholas. *Linc* 4B 76
Deerhill. *Mor* 3B 160
Deerhurst. *Glos* 3D 48
Deerhurst Walton. *Glos* 3D 49
Deerness. *Orkn* 7E 172
Defford. *Worc* 1E 49
Defynnog. *Powy* 3C 46
Deganwy. *Cnwy* 3G 81
Deighton. *N Yor* 4A 106
Deighton. *W Yor* 3B 92
Deighton. *York* 5A 100
Deiniolen. *Gwyn* 4E 81
Delabole. *Corn* 4A 10
Delamere. *Ches W* 4H 83
Delfour. *High* 3C 150
The Dell. *Suff* 1G 67
Delliefure. *High* 5E 159
Delly End. *Oxon* 4B 50
Delny. *High* 1B 158
Delph. *G Man* 4H 91
Delves. *Dur* 5E 115
The Delves. *W Mid* 1E 61
Delvin End. *Essx* 2A 54
Dembleby. *Linc* 2H 75
Demelza. *Corn* 2D 6
The Den. *N Ayr* 4E 127
Denaby Main. *S Yor* 1B 86
Denbeath. *Fife* 4F 137
Denbigh. *Den* 4C 82
Denbury. *Devn* 2E 9
Denby. *Derbs* 1A 74
Denby Common. *Derbs* 1B 74
Denby Dale. *W Yor* 4C 92
Denchworth. *Oxon* 2B 36
Dendron. *Cumb* 2B 96
Deneside. *Dur* 5H 115
Denford. *Nptn* 3G 63
Dengie. *Essx* 5C 54
Denham. *Buck* 2B 38
Denham. *Suff*
nr. Bury St Edmunds 4G 65
nr. Eye 3D 66
Denham Green. *Buck* 2B 38
Denham Street. *Suff* 3D 66
Denhead. *Abers*
nr. Ellon 5G 161
nr. Strichen 3G 161
Denhead. *Fife* 2G 137
Denholm. *Bord* 3H 119
Denholme. *W Yor* 1A 92
Denholme Clough. *W Yor* 1A 92
Denholme Gate. *W Yor* 1A 92
Denio. *Gwyn* 2C 68
Denmead. *Hants* 1E 17
Dennington. *Suff* 4E 67
Denny. *Falk* 1B 128
Denny End. *Cambs* 4D 65
Dennyloanhead. *Falk* 1B 128
Den of Lindores. *Fife* 2E 137
Denshaw. *G Man* 3H 91
Denside. *Abers* 4F 153
Densole. *Kent* 1G 29
Denston. *Suff* 5G 65
Denstone. *Staf* 1F 73
Denstroude. *Kent* 4F 41
Dent. *Cumb* 1G 97
Denton. *Cambs* 2A 64
Denton. *Darl* 3F 105
Denton. *E Sus* 5F 27
Denton. *G Man* 1D 84
Denton. *Kent* 1G 29
Denton. *Linc* 2F 75
Denton. *Norf* 2E 67
Denton. *Nptn* 5F 63
Denton. *N Yor* 5D 98
Denton. *Oxon* 5D 50
Denver. *Norf* 5F 77
Denwick. *Nmbd* 3G 121
Deopham. *Norf* 5C 78
Deopham Green. *Norf* 1C 66
Depden. *Suff* 5G 65
Depden Green. *Suff* 5G 65
Deptford. *G Lon* 3E 39
Deptford. *Wilts* 3F 23
Derby. *Derb* 193 (2A 74)
Derbyhaven. *IOM* 5B 108
Derculich. *Per* 3F 143
Dereham. *Norf* 4B 78
Deri. *Cphy* 5E 47
Derril. *Devn* 2D 10
Derringstone. *Kent* 1G 29
Derrington. *Shrp* 1A 60
Derrington. *Staf* 3C 72
Derriton. *Devn* 2D 10
Derryguaig. *Arg* 5F 139
Derry Hill. *Wilts* 4E 35
Derrythorpe. *N Lin* 4B 94
Dersingham. *Norf* 2F 77
Dervaig. *Arg* 3F 139
Derwen. *Den* 5C 82
Derwen Gam. *Cdgn* 5D 56
Derwenlas. *Powy* 1G 57
Desborough. *Nptn* 2F 63
Desford. *Leics* 5B 74
Detchant. *Nmbd* 1E 121
Dethick. *Derbs* 5H 85
Detling. *Kent* 5B 40
Deuchar. *Ang* 2D 144
Deuddwr. *Powy* 4E 71
Devauden. *Mon* 2H 33
Devil's Bridge. *Cdgn* 3G 57
Devitts Green. *Warw* 1G 61
Devizes. *Wilts* 5F 35
Devonport. *Plym* 3A 8
Devonside. *Clac* 4B 136
Devoran. *Corn* 5B 6
Dewartown. *Midl* 3G 129
Dewlish. *Dors* 3C 14
Dewsall Court. *Here* 2H 47
Dewsbury. *W Yor* 2C 92
Dexbeer. *Devn* 2C 10
Dhoon. *IOM* 3D 108
Dhoor. *IOM* 2D 108
Dhowin. *IOM* 1D 108
Dial Green. *W Sus* 3A 26
Dial Post. *W Sus* 4C 26
Dibberford. *Dors* 2H 13
Dibden. *Hants* 2C 16
Dibden Purlieu. *Hants* 2C 16
Dickleburgh. *Norf* 2D 66
Didbrook. *Glos* 2F 49
Didcot. *Oxon* 2D 36
Diddington. *Cambs* 4A 64
Diddlebury. *Shrp* 2H 59
Didley. *Here* 2H 47
Didling. *W Sus* 1G 17
Didmarton. *Glos* 3D 34
Didsbury. *G Man* 1C 84

Didworthy. *Devn* 2C **8**
Digby. *Linc* 5H **87**
Digg. *High* 2D **154**
Diggle. *G Man* 4A **92**
Digmoor. *Lanc* 4C **90**
Digswell. *Herts* 4C **52**
Dihewyd. *Cdgn* 5D **57**
Dilham. *Norf* 3F **79**
Dilhorne. *Staf* 1D **72**
Dillarburn. *S Lan* 5B **128**
Dillington. *Cambs* 4A **64**
Dilston. *Nmbd* 3C **114**
Dilton Marsh. *Wilts* 2D **22**
Dilwyn. *Here* 5G **59**
Dimmer. *Som* 3B **22**
Dimple. *G Man* 3F **91**
Dinas. *Carm* 1G **43**
Dinas. *Gwyn*
　nr. Caernarfon 5D **81**
　nr. Tudweiliog 2B **68**
Dinas Cross. *Pemb* 1E **43**
Dinas Dinlle. *Gwyn* 5D **80**
Dinas Mawddwy. *Gwyn* 4A **70**
Dinas Powys. *V Glam* 4E **33**
Dinbych. *Den* 4C **82**
Dinbych-y-Pysgod.
　Pemb 4F **43**
Dinckley. *Lanc* 1E **91**
Dinder. *Som* 2A **22**
Dinedor. *Here* 2A **48**
Dinedor Cross. *Here* 2A **48**
Dingestow. *Mon* 4H **47**
Dingle. *Mers* 2F **83**
Dingleden. *Kent* 2C **28**
Dingleton. *Bord* 1H **119**
Dingley. *Nptn* 2E **63**
Dingwall. *High* 3H **157**
Dinmael. *Cnwy* 1C **70**
Dinnet. *Abers* 4B **152**
Dinnington. *Som* 1H **13**
Dinnington. *S Yor* 2C **86**
Dinnington. *Tyne* 2F **115**
Dinorwig. *Gwyn* 4E **81**
Dinton. *Buck* 4F **51**
Dinton. *Wilts* 3F **23**
Dinworthy. *Devn* 1D **10**
Dipley. *Hants* 1F **25**
Dippen. *Arg* 2B **122**
Dippenhall. *Surr* 2G **25**
Dippertown. *Devn* 4E **11**
Dippin. *N Ayr* 3E **123**
Dipple. *S Ayr* 4B **116**
Diptford. *Devn* 3D **8**
Dipton. *Dur* 4E **115**
Dirleton. *E Lot* 1B **130**
Dirt Pot. *Nmbd* 5B **114**
Discoed. *Powy* 4E **59**
Diseworth. *Leics* 3B **74**
Dishes. *Orkn* 5F **172**
Dishforth. *N Yor* 2F **99**
Disley. *Ches E* 2D **85**
Diss. *Norf* 3D **66**
Disserth. *Powy* 5C **58**
Distington. *Cumb* 2B **102**
Ditchampton. *Wilts* 3F **23**
Ditcheat. *Som* 3B **22**
Ditchingham. *Norf* 1F **67**
Ditchling. *E Sus* 4E **27**
Ditteridge. *Wilts* 5D **34**
Dittisham. *Devn* 3E **9**
Ditton. *Hal* 2G **83**
Ditton. *Kent* 5B **40**
Ditton Green. *Cambs* 5F **65**
Ditton Priors. *Shrp* 2A **60**
Divach. *High* 1G **149**
Dixonfield. *High* 2D **168**
Dixton. *Glos* 2E **49**
Dixton. *Mon* 4A **48**
Dizzard. *Corn* 3B **10**
Dobcross. *G Man* 4H **91**
Dobs Hill. *Flin* 4F **83**
Dobson's Bridge. *Shrp* 2G **71**
Dobwalls. *Corn* 2G **7**
Doccombe. *Devn* 4A **12**
Dochgarroch. *High* 4A **158**
Docking. *Norf* 2G **77**
Docklow. *Here* 5H **59**
Dockray. *Cumb* 2E **103**
Doc Penfro.
　Pemb ....**215 (4D 42)**
Dodbrooke. *Devn* 4D **8**
Doddenham. *Worc* 5B **60**
Doddinghurst. *Essx* 1G **39**
Doddington. *Cambs* 1C **64**
Doddington. *Kent* 5D **40**
Doddington. *Linc* 3G **87**
Doddington. *Nmbd* 1D **121**
Doddington. *Shrp* 3A **60**
Doddiscombsleigh. *Devn* ...4B **12**
Doddshill. *Norf* 2G **77**
Dodford. *Nptn* 4D **62**
Dodford. *Worc* 3D **60**
Dodington. *Som* 2E **21**
Dodington. *S Glo* 3C **34**
Dodleston. *Ches W* 4F **83**
Dods Leigh. *Staf* 2E **73**
Dodworth. *S Yor* 4D **92**
Doe Lea. *Derbs* 4B **86**
Dogdyke. *Linc* 5B **88**
Dogmersfield. *Hants* 1F **25**
Dogsthorpe. *Pet* 5B **76**
Dog Village. *Devn* 3C **12**
Dolanog. *Powy* 4C **70**
Dolau. *Powy* 4D **58**
Dolau. *Rhon* 3D **32**
Dolbenmaen. *Gwyn* 1E **69**
Doley. *Staf* 3B **72**
Dol-fâch. *Powy* 5B **70**
Dolfach. *Powy* 3B **58**
Dolfor. *Powy* 2D **58**
Dolgarrog. *Cnwy* 4G **81**

Dolgellau. *Gwyn* 4G **69**
Dolgoch. *Gwyn* 5F **69**
Dol-gran. *Carm* 2E **45**
Dolhelfa. *Powy* 3B **58**
Doll. *High* 3F **165**
Dollar. *Clac* 4B **136**
Dolley Green. *Powy* 4E **59**
Dollwen. *Cdgn* 2F **57**
Dolphin. *Flin* 3D **82**
Dolphinholme. *Lanc* 4E **97**
Dolphinton. *S Lan* 5E **129**
Dolton. *Devn* 1F **11**
Dolwen. *Cnwy* 3A **82**
Dolwyddelan. *Cnwy* 5G **81**
Dol-y-Bont. *Cdgn* 2F **57**
Dolyhir. *Powy* 5E **59**
Domgay. *Powy* 4E **71**
Doncaster. *S Yor* 4F **93**
Doncaster Sheffield Airport.
　S Yor 1D **86**
Donhead St Andrew. *Wilts* ...4E **23**
Donhead St Mary. *Wilts* 4E **23**
Doniford. *Som* 2D **20**
Donington. *Linc* 2B **76**
Donington. *Shrp* 5C **72**
Donington Eaudike. *Linc* 2B **76**
Donington le Heath. *Leics* 4B **74**
Donington on Bain. *Linc* 2B **88**
Donington South Ing. *Linc* ...2B **76**
Donisthorpe. *Leics* 4H **73**
Donkey Street. *Kent* 2F **29**
Donkey Town. *Surr* 4A **38**
Donna Nook. *Linc* 1D **88**
Donnington. *Glos* 3G **49**
Donnington. *Here* 2C **48**
Donnington. *Shrp* 5H **71**
Donnington. *Telf* 4B **72**
Donnington. *W Ber* 5C **36**
Donnington. *W Sus* 2G **17**
Donyatt. *Som* 1G **13**
Doomsday Green. *W Sus* 3C **26**
Doonfoot. *S Ayr* 3C **116**
Doonholm. *S Ayr* 3C **116**
Dorback Lodge. *High* 2E **151**
Dorchester. *Dors* 3B **14**
Dorchester on Thames.
　Oxon 2D **36**
Dordon. *Warw* 5G **73**
Dore. *S Yor* 2H **85**
Dores. *High* 5H **157**
Dorking. *Surr* 1C **26**
Dorking Tye. *Suff* 2C **54**
Dormansland. *Surr* 1F **27**
Dormans Park. *Surr* 1E **27**
Dormanstown. *Red C* 2C **106**
Dormington. *Here* 1A **48**
Dormston. *Worc* 5D **61**
Dorn. *Glos* 2H **49**
Dorney. *Buck* 3A **38**
Dornie. *High* 1A **148**
Dornoch. *High* 5E **165**
Dornock. *Dum* 3D **112**
Dorrery. *High* 3C **168**
Dorridge. *W Mid* 3F **61**
Dorrington. *Linc* 5H **87**
Dorrington. *Shrp* 5G **71**
Dorsington. *Warw* 1G **49**
Dorstone. *Here* 1G **47**
Dorton. *Buck* 4E **51**
Dosthill. *Staf* 5G **73**
Dotham. *IOA* 3C **80**
Dottery. *Dors* 3H **13**
Doublebois. *Corn* 2F **7**
Dougarie. *N Ayr* 2C **122**
Doughton. *Glos* 2D **35**
Douglas. *IOM* 4C **108**
Douglas. *S Lan* 1H **117**
Douglastown. *Ang* 4D **144**
Douglas Water. *S Lan* 1A **118**
Doulting. *Som* 2B **22**
Dounby. *Orkn* 5B **172**
Doune. *High*
　nr. Kingussie 2C **150**
　nr. Lairg 3B **164**
Doune. *Stir* 3G **135**
Dounie. *High*
　nr. Bonar Bridge 4C **164**
　nr. Tain 5D **164**
Dounreay, Upper & Lower.
　High 2B **168**
Doura. *N Ayr* 5E **127**
Dousland. *Devn* 2B **8**
Dovaston. *Shrp* 3F **71**
Dove Holes. *Derbs* 3E **85**
Dovenby. *Cumb* 1B **102**
Dover. *Kent* ....**193 (1H 29)**
Dovercourt. *Essx* 2F **55**
Doverdale. *Worc* 4C **60**
Doveridge. *Derbs* 2F **73**
Doversgreen. *Surr* 1D **26**
Dowally. *Per* 4H **143**
Dowbridge. *Lanc* 1C **90**
Dowdeswell. *Glos* 4F **49**
Dowlais. *Mer T* 5D **46**
Dowland. *Devn* 1F **11**
Dowlands. *Devn* 3F **13**
Dowles. *Worc* 3B **60**
Dowlesgreen. *Wok* 5G **37**
Dowlish Wake. *Som* 1G **13**
The Down. *Shrp* 1A **60**
Downall Green. *Mers* 4D **90**
Down Ampney. *Glos* 2G **35**
Downderry. *Corn*
　nr. Looe 3H **7**
　nr. St Austell 3D **6**
Downe. *G Lon* 4F **39**
Downend. *IOW* 4D **16**
Downend. *S Glo* 4B **34**
Downend. *W Ber* 4C **36**
Down Field. *Cambs* 3F **65**
Downfield. *D'dee* 5C **144**

Downgate. *Corn*
　nr. Kelly Bray 5D **10**
　nr. Upton Cross 5C **10**
Downham. *Essx* 1B **40**
Downham. *Lanc* 5G **97**
Downham. *Nmbd* 1C **120**
Downham Market. *Norf* 5F **77**
Down Hatherley. *Glos* 3D **48**
Downhead. *Som*
　nr. Frome 2B **22**
　nr. Yeovil 4A **22**
Downholland Cross. *Lanc* 4B **90**
Downholme. *N Yor* 5E **105**
Downies. *Abers* 4G **153**
Downley. *Buck* 2G **37**
Down St Mary. *Devn* 2H **11**
Downside. *Som*
　nr. Chilcompton 1B **22**
　nr. Shepton Mallet 2B **22**
Downside. *Surr* 5C **38**
Down Thomas. *Devn* 3B **8**
Downton. *Hants* 3A **16**
Downton. *Wilts* 4G **23**
Downton on the Rock. *Here* ...3G **59**
Dowsby. *Linc* 3A **76**
Dowsdale. *Linc* 4B **76**
Dowthwaitehead. *Cumb* 2E **103**
Doxey. *Staf* 3D **72**
Doxford. *Nmbd* 2F **121**
Doynton. *S Glo* 4C **34**
Drabblegate. *Norf* 3E **78**
Draethen. *Cphy* 3F **33**
Draffan. *S Lan* 5A **128**
Dragonby. *N Lin* 3C **94**
Dragon's Green. *W Sus* 3C **26**
Drakelow. *Worc* 2C **60**
Drakemyre. *N Ayr* 4D **126**
Drakes Broughton. *Worc* 1E **49**
Drakes Cross. *Worc* 3E **61**
Drakewalls. *Corn* 5E **11**
Draughton. *Nptn* 3E **63**
Draughton. *N Yor* 4C **98**
Drax. *N Yor* 2G **93**
Draycot. *Oxon* 5E **51**
Draycote. *Warw* 3B **62**
Draycot Foliat. *Swin* 4G **35**
Draycott. *Derbs* 2B **74**
Draycott. *Glos* 2G **49**
Draycott. *Shrp* 1C **60**
Draycott. *Som*
　nr. Cheddar 1H **21**
　nr. Yeovil 4A **22**
Draycott. *Worc* 1D **48**
Draycott in the Clay. *Staf* 3F **73**
Draycott in the Moors. *Staf* ...1D **73**
Drayford. *Devn* 1A **12**
Drayton. *Leics* 1F **63**
Drayton. *Linc* 2B **76**
Drayton. *Norf* 4D **78**
Drayton. *Nptn* 4C **62**
Drayton. *Oxon*
　nr. Abingdon 2C **36**
　nr. Banbury 1C **50**
Drayton. *Port* 2E **17**
Drayton. *Som* 4H **21**
Drayton. *Warw* 5F **61**
Drayton. *Worc* 3D **60**
Drayton Bassett. *Staf* 5F **73**
Drayton Beauchamp. *Buck* ...4H **51**
Drayton Parslow. *Buck* 3G **51**
Drayton St Leonard. *Oxon* ...2D **36**
Drebley. *N Yor* 4C **98**
Dreenhill. *Pemb* 3D **42**
Y Dref. *Gwyn* 2D **69**
Drefach. *Carm*
　nr. Meidrim 4F **45**
　nr. Newcastle Emlyn 2D **44**
　nr. Tumble 2G **43**
Drefach. *Cdgn* 1E **45**
Dreghorn. *N Ayr* 1C **116**
Drellingore. *Kent* 1G **29**
Drem. *E Lot* 2B **130**
Dreumasdal. *W Isl* 5C **170**
Drewsteignton. *Devn* 3H **11**
Driby. *Linc* 3C **88**
Driffield. *E Yor* 4E **101**
Driffield. *Glos* 2F **35**
Drift. *Corn* 4B **4**
Drigg. *Cumb* 5B **102**
Drighlington. *W Yor* 2C **92**
Drimnin. *High* 3G **139**
Drimpton. *Dors* 2H **13**
Dringhoe. *E Yor* 4F **101**
Drinisiadar. *W Isl* 8D **171**
Drinkstone. *Suff* 4B **66**
Drinkstone Green. *Suff* 4B **66**
Drointon. *Staf* 3E **73**
Droitwich Spa. *Worc* 4C **60**
Droman. *High* 3B **166**
Dron. *Per* 2D **136**
Dronfield. *Derbs* 3A **86**
Dronfield Woodhouse. *Derbs* ...3H **85**
Drongan. *E Ayr* 3D **116**
Dronley. *Ang* 5C **144**
Droop. *Dors* 2C **14**
Drope. *V Glam* 4E **32**
Droxford. *Hants* 1E **16**
Droylsden. *G Man* 1C **84**
Druggers End. *Worc* 2C **48**
Druid. *Den* 1C **70**
Druid's Heath. *W Mid* 5E **73**
Druidston. *Pemb* 3C **42**
Druim. *High* 3D **158**
Druimarbin. *High* 1E **141**
Druim Fhearna. *High* 2E **147**
Druimindarroch. *High* 5E **147**
Druim Saighdinis. *W Isl* 2D **170**
Drum. *Per* 3C **136**
Drumbeg. *High* 5B **166**
Drumblade. *Abers* 4C **160**

Drumbuie. *Dum* 1C **110**
Drumbuie. *High* 5G **155**
Drumburgh. *Cumb* 4D **112**
Drumburn. *Dum* 3A **112**
Drumchapel. *Glas* 2G **127**
Drumchardine. *High* 4H **157**
Drumchork. *High* 5C **162**
Drumclog. *S Lan* 1F **117**
Drumeldrie. *Fife* 3G **137**
Drumelzier. *Bord* 1D **118**
Drumfearn. *High* 2E **147**
Drumgask. *High* 4A **150**
Drumgelloch. *N Lan* 3A **128**
Drumgley. *Ang* 3D **144**
Drumguish. *High* 4B **150**
Drumin. *Mor* 5F **159**
Drumindorsair. *High* 4G **157**
Drumlasie. *Abers* 3D **152**
Drumlemble. *Arg* 4A **122**
Drumlithie. *Abers* 5E **153**
Drummoddie. *Dum* 5A **110**
Drummond. *High* 2A **158**
Drummore. *Dum* 5E **109**
Drummuir. *Mor* 4A **160**
Drumnadrochit. *High* 5H **157**
Drumnagorrach. *Mor* 3C **160**
Drumoak. *Abers* 4E **153**
Drumrunie. *High* 3F **163**
Drumry. *W Dun* 2G **127**
Drums. *Abers* 1G **153**
Drumsleet. *Dum* 2G **111**
Drumsmittal. *High* 4A **158**
Drums of Park. *Abers* 3C **160**
Drumsturdy. *Ang* 5D **145**
Drumtochty Castle. *Abers* ...5D **152**
Drumuie. *High* 4D **154**
Drumuillie. *High* 1D **150**
Drumvaich. *Stir* 3F **135**
Drumwhindle. *Abers* 5G **161**
Drunkendub. *Ang* 4F **145**
Drury. *Flin* 4E **83**
Drury Square. *Norf* 4B **78**
Drybeck. *Cumb* 3H **103**
Drybridge. *Mor* 2B **160**
Drybridge. *N Ayr* 1C **116**
Drybrook. *Glos* 4B **48**
Drybrook. *Here* 4A **48**
Dryburgh. *Bord* 1H **119**
Dry Doddington. *Linc* 1F **75**
Dry Drayton. *Cambs* 4C **64**
Drymen. *Stir* 1F **127**
Drymuir. *Abers* 4G **161**
Drynachan Lodge. *High* 5C **158**
Drynie Park. *High* 3H **157**
Drynoch. *High* 5D **154**
Dry Sandford. *Oxon* 5C **50**
Dryslwyn. *Carm* 3F **45**
Dry Street. *Essx* 2A **40**
Dryton. *Shrp* 5H **71**
Dubford. *Abers* 2E **161**
Dubiton. *Abers* 3D **160**
Dubton. *Ang* 3E **145**
Duchally. *High* 2A **164**
Duck End. *Essx* 3G **53**
Duckington. *Ches W* 5G **83**
Ducklington. *Oxon* 5B **50**
Duckmanton. *Derbs* 3B **86**
Duck Street. *Hants* 2B **24**
Dudbridge. *Glos* 5D **48**
Duddenhoe End. *Essx* 2E **53**
Duddingston. *Edin* 2F **129**
Duddington. *Nptn* 5G **75**
Duddleswell. *E Sus* 3F **27**
Duddo. *Nmbd* 5F **131**
Duddon. *Ches W* 4H **83**
Duddon Bridge. *Cumb* 1A **96**
Dudleston. *Shrp* 2F **71**
Dudleston Heath. *Shrp* 2F **71**
Dudley. *Tyne* 2F **115**
Dudley. *W Mid* 2D **60**
Dudston. *Shrp* 1E **59**
Dudwells. *Pemb* 2D **42**
Duffield. *Derbs* 1H **73**
Duffryn. *Neat* 2B **32**
Dufftown. *Mor* 4H **159**
Duffus. *Mor* 2F **159**
Dufton. *Cumb* 2H **103**
Duggleby. *N Yor* 3C **100**
Duirinish. *High* 5G **155**
Duisdalemore. *High* 2E **147**
Duisdeil Mór. *High* 2E **147**
Duisky. *High* 1E **141**
Dukesfield. *Nmbd* 4C **114**
Dukestown. *Blae* 5E **47**
Dukinfield. *G Man* 1D **84**
Dulas. *IOA* 2D **81**
Dulcote. *Som* 2A **22**
Dulford. *Devn* 2D **12**
Dull. *Per* 4F **143**
Dullatur. *N Lan* 2A **128**
Dullingham. *Cambs* 5F **65**
Dullingham Ley. *Cambs* 5F **65**
Dulnain Bridge. *High* 1D **151**
Duloe. *Bed* 4A **64**
Duloe. *Corn* 3G **7**
Dulverton. *Som* 4C **20**
Dulwich. *G Lon* 3E **39**
Dumbarton. *W Dun* 2F **127**
Dumbleton. *Glos* 2F **49**
Dumfries. *Dum* ....**193 (2A 112)**
Dumgoyne. *Stir* 1G **127**
Dummer. *Hants* 2D **24**
Dumpford. *W Sus* 4G **25**
Dun. *Ang* 2F **145**
Dunagoil. *Arg* 4B **126**
Dunalastair. *Per* 3E **142**
Dunan. *High* 1D **147**
Dunball. *Som* 2G **21**

Dunbar. *E Lot* 2C **130**
Dunbeath. *High* 5D **168**
Dunbeg. *Arg* 5C **140**
Dunblane. *Stir* 3G **135**
Dunbog. *Fife* 2E **137**
Dunbridge. *Hants* 4B **24**
Duncanston. *Abers* 1C **152**
Duncanston. *High* 3H **157**
Dun Charlabhaigh. *W Isl* 3D **171**
Dunchideock. *Devn* 4B **12**
Dunchurch. *Warw* 3B **62**
Duncote. *Nptn* 5D **62**
Duncow. *Dum* 1A **112**
Duncrievie. *Per* 3D **136**
Duncton. *W Sus* 4A **26**
Dundee. *D'dee* ....**194 (5D 144)**
Dundee Airport. *D'dee* 1F **137**
Dundon. *Som* 3H **21**
Dundonald. *S Ayr* 1C **116**
Dundonnell. *High* 5E **163**
Dundraw. *Cumb* 5D **112**
Dundreggan. *High* 2F **149**
Dundrennan. *Dum* 5E **111**
Dundridge. *Hants* 1D **16**
Dundry. *N Som* 5A **34**
Dunecht. *Abers* 3E **153**
Dunfermline. *Fife* 1D **129**
Dunford Bridge. *S Yor* 4B **92**
Dungate. *Kent* 5D **40**
Dunge. *Wilts* 1D **23**
Dungeness. *Kent* 4E **29**
Dungworth. *S Yor* 2G **85**
Dunham-on-the-Hill. *Ches W* ...3G **83**
Dunham-on-Trent. *Notts* 3F **87**
Dunhampton. *Worc* 4C **60**
Dunham Town. *G Man* 2B **84**
Dunham Woodhouses. *G Man* ...2B **84**
Dunholme. *Linc* 3H **87**
Dunino. *Fife* 2H **137**
Dunipace. *Falk* 1B **128**
Dunira. *Per* 1G **135**
Dunkeld. *Per* 4H **143**
Dunkerton. *Bath* 1C **22**
Dunkeswell. *Devn* 2E **13**
Dunkeswick. *N Yor* 5F **99**
Dunkirk. *Kent* 5E **41**
Dunkirk. *S Glo* 3C **34**
Dunkirk. *Staf* 5C **84**
Dunkirk. *Wilts* 5E **35**
Dunk's Green. *Kent* 5H **39**
Dunlappie. *Ang* 2E **145**
Dunley. *Hants* 1C **24**
Dunley. *Worc* 4B **60**
Dunlichity Lodge. *High* 5A **158**
Dunlop. *E Ayr* 5F **127**
Dunmaglass Lodge. *High* 1H **149**
Dunmore. *Arg* 3F **125**
Dunmore. *Falk* 1B **128**
Dunmore. *High* 4H **157**
Dunnet. *High* 1E **169**
Dunnichen. *Ang* 4E **145**
Dunning. *Per* 2C **136**
Dunnington. *E Yor* 4F **101**
Dunnington. *Warw* 5E **61**
Dunnington. *York* 4A **100**
Dunningwell. *Cumb* 1A **96**
Dunnockshaw. *Lanc* 2G **91**
Dunoon. *Arg* 2C **126**
Dunphail. *Mor* 4E **159**
Dunragit. *Dum* 4G **109**
Dunrostan. *Arg* 1F **125**
Duns. *Bord* 4D **130**
Dunsby. *Linc* 3A **76**
Dunscar. *G Man* 3F **91**
Dunscore. *Dum* 1F **111**
Dunscroft. *S Yor* 4G **93**
Dunsdale. *Red C* 3D **106**
Dunsden Green. *Oxon* 4F **37**
Dunsfold. *Surr* 2B **26**
Dunsford. *Devn* 4B **12**
Dunshalt. *Fife* 2E **137**
Dunshillock. *Abers* 4G **161**
Dunsley. *N Yor* 3F **107**
Dunsley. *Staf* 2C **60**
Dunsmore. *Buck* 5G **51**
Dunsop Bridge. *Lanc* 4F **97**
Dunstable. *C Beds* 3A **52**
Dunstal. *Staf* 3E **73**
Dunstall. *Staf* 3F **73**
Dunstall Green. *Suff* 4G **65**
Dunstall Hill. *W Mid* 5D **72**
Dunstan. *Nmbd* 3G **121**
Dunster. *Som* 2C **20**
Duns Tew. *Oxon* 3C **50**
Dunston. *Linc* 4H **87**
Dunston. *Norf* 5E **79**
Dunston. *Staf* 4D **72**
Dunston. *Tyne* 3F **115**
Dunstone. *Devn* 3B **8**
Dunston Heath. *Staf* 4D **72**
Dunsville. *S Yor* 4G **93**
Dunswell. *E Yor* 1D **94**
Dunsyre. *S Lan* 5D **128**
Dunterton. *Devn* 5D **11**
Duntisbourne Abbots. *Glos* ...5E **49**
Duntisbourne Leer. *Glos* 5E **49**
Duntisbourne Rouse. *Glos* ...5E **49**
Duntish. *Dors* 2B **14**
Duntocher. *W Dun* 2F **127**
Dunton. *Buck* 3G **51**
Dunton. *C Beds* 1C **52**
Dunton. *Norf* 2A **78**
Dunton Bassett. *Leics* 1C **62**
Dunton Green. *Kent* 5G **39**
Dunton Patch. *Norf* 2A **78**
Duntulm. *High* 1D **154**
Dinure. *S Ayr* 3B **116**
Dunvant. *Swan* 3E **31**
Dunvegan. *High* 4B **154**
Dunwich. *Suff* 3G **67**
Dunwood. *Staf* 5D **84**

Durdar – Edington

Durdar. Cumb 4F 113
Durgates. E Sus 2H 27
Durham. Dur 194 (5F 115)
Durham Tees Valley Airport.
Darl 3A 106
Durisdeer. Dum 4A 118
Durisdeermill. Dum 4A 118
Durkar. W Yor 3D 92
Durleigh. Som 3F 21
Durley. Hants 1D 16
Durley. Wilts 5H 35
Durley Street. Hants 1D 16
Durlow Common. Here 2B 48
Durnamuck. High 4E 163
Durness. High 2E 166
Durno. Abers 1E 152
Durns Town. Hants 3A 16
Duror. High 3D 141
Durran. Arg 3G 133
Durran. High 2D 169
Durrant Green. Kent 2C 28
Durrants. Hants 1F 17
Durrington. W Sus 5C 26
Durrington. Wilts 2G 23
Dursley. Glos 2C 34
Dursley Cross. Glos 4B 48
Durston. Som 4F 21
Durweston. Dors 2D 14
Dury. Shet 6F 173
Duston. Nptn 4E 63
Duthil. High 1D 150
Dutlas. Powy 3E 58
Duton Hill. Essx 3G 53
Dutson. Corn 4D 10
Dutton. Ches W 3H 83
Duxford. Cambs 1E 53
Duxford. Oxon 2B 36
Dwygyfylchi. Cnwy 3G 81
Dwyran. IOA 4D 80
Dyce. Aber 2F 153
Dyffryn. B'end 2B 32
Dyffryn. Carm 2H 43
Dyffryn. Pemb 1D 42
Dyffryn. V Glam 4D 32
Dyffryn Ardudwy. Gwyn 3E 69
Dyffryn Castell. Cdgn 2G 57
Dyffryn Ceidrych. Carm 3H 45
Dyffryn Cellwen. Neat 5B 46
Dyke. Linc 3A 76
Dyke. Mor 3D 159
Dykehead. Ang 2C 144
Dykehead. N Lan 3B 128
Dykehead. Stir 4E 135
Dykend. Ang 3B 144
Dykesfield. Cumb 4E 112
Dylife. Powy 1A 58
Dymchurch. Kent 3F 29
Dymock. Glos 2C 48
Dyrham. S Glo 4C 34
Dysart. Fife 4F 137
Dyserth. Den 3C 82

E

Eachwick. Nmbd 2E 115
Eadar Dha Fhadhail. W Isl 4C 171
Eagland Hill. Lanc 5D 96
Eagle. Linc 4F 87
Eagle Barnsdale. Linc 4F 87
Eagle Moor. Linc 4F 87
Eaglescliffe. Stoc T 3B 106
Eaglesfield. Cumb 2B 102
Eaglesfield. Dum 2D 112
Eaglesham. E Ren 4G 127
Eaglethorpe. Nptn 1H 63
Eagley. G Man 3F 91
Eairy. IOM 4B 108
Eakley Lanes. Mil 5F 63
Eakring. Notts 4D 86
Ealand. N Lin 3A 94
Ealing. G Lon 2C 38
Eallabus. Arg 3B 124
Eals. Nmbd 4H 113
Eamont Bridge. Cumb 2G 103
Earby. Lanc 5B 98
Earcroft. Bkbn 2E 91
Eardington. Shrp 1B 60
Eardisland. Here 5G 59
Eardisley. Here 1G 47
Eardiston. Shrp 3F 71
Eardiston. Worc 4A 60
Earith. Cambs 3C 64
Earlais. High 2C 154
Earle. Nmbd 2D 121
Earlesfield. Linc 2G 75
Earlestown. Mers 1H 83
Earley. Wok 4F 37
Earlham. Norf 5D 78
Earlish. High 2C 154
Earls Barton. Nptn 4F 63
Earls Colne. Essx 3B 54
Earls Common. Worc 5D 60
Earl's Croome. Worc 1D 48
Earlsdon. W Mid 3H 61
Earlsferry. Fife 3G 137
Earlsford. Abers 5F 161
Earl's Green. Suff 4C 66
Earlsheaton. W Yor 2C 92
Earl Shilton. Leics 1B 62
Earl Soham. Suff 4E 67
Earl Sterndale. Derbs 4E 85
Earlston. E Ayr 1D 116
Earlston. Bord 1H 119
Earl Stonham. Suff 5D 66
Earlstoun. Dum 1D 110
Earlswood. Mon 2H 33
Earlswood. Warw 3F 61
Earlyvale. Bord 4F 129
Earnley. W Sus 3G 17
Earsairidh. W Isl 9C 170
Earsdon. Tyne 2G 115
Earsham. Norf 2F 67
Earsham Street. Suff 3E 67
Earswick. York 4A 100
Eartham. W Sus 5A 26
Earthcott Green. S Glo 3B 34
Easby. N Yor
nr. Great Ayton 4C 106
nr. Richmond 4E 105
Easdale. Arg 2E 133
Easebourne. W Sus 4G 25
Easenhall. Warw 3B 62
Eashing. Surr 1A 26
Easington. Buck 4E 51
Easington. Dur 5H 115
Easington. E Yor 3G 95
Easington. Nmbd 1F 121
Easington. Oxon
nr. Banbury 2C 50
nr. Watlington 2E 37
Easington. Red C 3E 107
Easington Colliery. Dur 5H 115
Easington Lane. Tyne 5G 115
Easingwold. N Yor 2H 99
Eassie. Ang 4C 144
Eassie and Nevay. Ang 4C 144
East Aberthaw. V Glam 5D 32
Eastacombe. Devn 4F 19
Eastacott. Devn 4G 19
East Allington. Devn 4D 8
East Anstey. Devn 4B 20
East Anton. Hants 2B 24
East Appleton. N Yor 5F 105
East Ardsley. W Yor 2D 92
East Ashley. Devn 1G 11
East Ashling. W Sus 2G 17
East Aston. Hants 2C 24
East Ayton. N Yor 1D 101
East Barkwith. Linc 2A 88
East Barnby. N Yor 3F 107
East Barnet. G Lon 1D 39
East Barns. E Lot 2D 130
East Barsham. Norf 2B 78
East Beach. W Sus 3G 17
East Beckham. Norf 2D 78
East Bedfont. G Lon 3B 38
East Bennan. N Ayr 3D 123
East Bergholt. Suff 2D 54
East Bierley. W Yor 2C 92
East Bilney. Norf 4B 78
East Blatchington. E Sus 5F 27
East Bloxworth. Dors 3D 15
East Boldre. Hants 2B 16
East Bolton. Nmbd 3F 121
Eastbourne. Darl 3F 105
Eastbourne. E Sus 195 (5H 27)
East Brent. Som 1G 21
East Bridge. Suff 4G 67
East Bridgford. Notts 1D 74
East Briscoe. Dur 3C 104
East Buckland. Devn
nr. Barnstaple 3G 19
nr. Thurlestone 4C 8
East Budleigh. Devn 4D 12
Eastburn. W Yor 5C 98
East Burnham. Buck 2A 38
East Burrafirth. Shet 6E 173
East Burton. Dors 4D 14
Eastbury. Herts 1B 38
Eastbury. W Ber 4B 36
East Butsfield. Dur 5E 115
East Butterleigh. Devn 2C 12
East Butterwick. N Lin 4B 94
Eastby. N Yor 4C 98
East Calder. W Lot 3D 129
East Carleton. Norf 5D 78
East Carlton. Nptn 2F 63
East Carlton. W Yor 5E 98
East Chaldon. Dors 4C 14
East Challow. Oxon 3B 36
East Charleton. Devn 4D 8
East Chelborough. Dors 2A 14
East Chiltington. E Sus 4E 27
East Chinnock. Som 1H 13
East Chisenbury. Wilts 1G 23
Eastchurch. Kent 3D 40
East Clandon. Surr 5B 38
East Claydon. Buck 3F 51
East Clevedon. N Som 4H 33
East Clyne. High 3F 165
East Clyth. High 5E 169
East Coker. Som 1A 14
East Combe. Som 3E 21
Eastcombe. Glos 5D 49
East Common. N Yor 1G 93
East Compton. Som 2B 22
East Cornworthy. Devn 3E 9
Eastcote. G Lon 2C 38
Eastcote. Nptn 5D 62
Eastcote. W Mid 3F 61
Eastcott. Corn 1C 10
Eastcott. Wilts 1F 23
East Cottingwith. E Yor 5B 100
Eastcourt. Wilts
nr. Pewsey 5H 35
nr. Tetbury 2E 35
East Cowes. IOW 3D 16
East Cowick. E Yor 2G 93
East Cowton. N Yor 4A 106
East Cramlington. Nmbd 2F 115
East Cranmore. Som 2B 22
East Creech. Dors 4E 15
East Croachy. High 1A 150
East Dean. E Sus 5G 27
East Dean. Glos 3B 48
East Dean. Hants 4A 24
East Dean. W Sus 4A 26
East Down. Devn 2G 19
East Drayton. Notts 3E 87
East Dundry. N Som 5A 34
East Ella. Hull 2D 94
East End. Cambs 3C 64
East End. Dors 3E 15
East End. E Yor
nr. Ulrome 4F 101
nr. Withernsea 2F 95
East End. Hants
nr. Lymington 3B 16
nr. Newbury 5C 36
East End. Herts 3E 53
East End. Kent
nr. Minster 3D 40
nr. Tenterden 2C 28
East End. N Som 4H 33
East End. Oxon 4B 50
East End. Som 1A 22
East End. Suff 2E 54
Easter Ardross. High 1A 158
Easter Balgedie. Per 3D 136
Easter Balmoral. Abers 4G 151
Easter Brae. High 2A 158
Easter Buckieburn. Stir 1A 128
Easter Compton. S Glo 3A 34
Easter Fearn. High 5D 164
Easter Galcantray. High 4C 158
Eastergate. W Sus 5A 26
Easterhouse. Glas 3H 127
Easter Howgate. Midl 3F 129
Easter Kinkell. High 3H 157
Easter Lednathie. Ang 2C 144
Easter Ogil. Ang 2D 144
Easter Ord. Abers 3F 153
Easter Quarff. Shet 8F 173
Easter Rhynd. Per 2D 136
Easter Skeld. Shet 7E 173
Easter Suddie. High 3A 158
Easterton. Wilts 1F 23
Eastertown. Som 1G 21
Easter Tulloch. Abers 1G 145
East Everleigh. Wilts 1H 23
East Farleigh. Kent 5B 40
East Farndon. Nptn 2E 62
East Ferry. Linc 1F 87
Eastfield. N Lan
nr. Caldercruix 3B 128
nr. Harthill 3B 128
Eastfield. N Yor 1E 101
Eastfield. S Lan 3H 127
Eastfield Hall. Nmbd 4G 121
East Fortune. E Lot 2B 130
East Garforth. W Yor 1E 93
East Garston. W Ber 4B 36
Eastgate. Dur 1C 104
Eastgate. Norf 3D 78
East Ginge. Oxon 3C 36
East Gores. Essx 3B 54
East Goscote. Leics 4D 74
East Grafton. Wilts 5A 36
East Green. Suff 5F 65
East Grimstead. Wilts 4H 23
East Grinstead. W Sus 2E 27
East Guldeford. E Sus 3D 28
East Haddon. Nptn 4D 62
East Hagbourne. Oxon 3D 36
East Halton. N Lin 2E 95
East Ham. G Lon 2F 39
Eastham. Mers 2F 83
Eastham. Worc 4A 60
Eastham Ferry. Mers 2F 83
Easthampstead. Brac 5G 37
Easthampton. Here 4G 59
East Hanney. Oxon 2C 36
East Hanningfield. Essx 5A 54
East Hardwick. W Yor 3E 93
East Harling. Norf 2B 66
East Harlsey. N Yor 5B 106
East Harptree. Bath 1A 22
East Hartford. Nmbd 2F 115
East Harting. W Sus 1G 17
East Hatch. Wilts 4E 23
East Hatley. Cambs 5B 64
Easthaugh. Norf 4C 78
East Hauxwell. N Yor 5E 105
East Haven. Ang 5E 145
Eastheath. Wok 5G 37
East Heckington. Linc 1A 76
East Hedleyhope. Dur 5E 115
East Helmsdale. High 2H 165
East Hendred. Oxon 3C 36
East Heslerton. N Yor 2D 100
East Hoathly. E Sus 4G 27
East Holme. Dors 4D 15
Easthope. Shrp 1H 59
Easthorpe. Essx 3C 54
Easthorpe. Leics 2F 75
East Horrington. Som 2A 22
East Horsley. Surr 5B 38
East Horton. Nmbd 1E 121
Easthouses. Midl 3G 129
East Howe. Bour 3F 15
East Huntspill. Som 2G 21
East Hyde. C Beds 4B 52
East Ilsley. W Ber 3C 36
Eastington. Devn 2H 11
Eastington. Glos
nr. Northleach 4G 49
nr. Stonehouse 5C 48
East Keal. Linc 4C 88
East Kennett. Wilts 5G 35
East Keswick. W Yor 5F 99
East Kilbride. S Lan 4H 127
East Kirkby. Linc 4C 88
East Knapton. N Yor 2C 100
East Knighton. Dors 4D 14
East Knowstone. Devn 4B 20
East Knoyle. Wilts 3D 23
East Kyloe. Nmbd 1E 121
East Lambrook. Som 1H 13
East Langdon. Kent 1H 29
East Langton. Leics 1E 63
East Langwell. High 3E 164
East Lavant. W Sus 2G 17
East Lavington. W Sus 4A 26
East Layton. N Yor 4E 105
Eastleach Martin. Glos 5H 49
Eastleach Turville. Glos 5G 49
East Leake. Notts 3C 74
East Learmouth. Nmbd 1C 120
East Leigh. Devn
nr. Crediton 2G 11
nr. Modbury 3C 8
Eastleigh. Devn 4E 19
Eastleigh. Hants 1C 16
East Lexham. Norf 4A 78
East Lilburn. Nmbd 2E 121
Eastling. Kent 5D 40
East Linton. E Lot 2B 130
East Liss. Hants 4F 25
East Lockinge. Oxon 3C 36
East Looe. Corn 3G 7
East Lound. N Lin 1E 87
East Lulworth. Dors 4D 14
East Lutton. N Yor 3D 100
East Lydford. Som 3A 22
East Lyng. Som 4G 21
East Mains. Abers 4D 152
East Malling. Kent 5B 40
East Marden. W Sus 1G 17
East Markham. Notts 3E 87
East Marton. N Yor 4B 98
East Meon. Hants 4E 25
East Mersea. Essx 4D 54
East Mey. High 1F 169
East Midlands Airport.
Leics 216 (3B 74)
East Molesey. Surr 4C 38
Eastmoor. Norf 5G 77
East Morden. Dors 3E 15
East Morton. W Yor 5D 98
East Ness. N Yor 2A 100
East Newton. E Yor 1F 95
East Newton. N Yor 2A 100
Eastney. Port 3E 17
Eastnor. Here 2C 48
East Norton. Leics 5E 75
East Nynehead. Som 4E 21
East Oakley. Hants 1D 24
Eastoft. N Lin 3B 94
East Ogwell. Devn 5B 12
Easton. Cambs 3A 64
Easton. Cumb
nr. Burgh by Sands 4D 112
nr. Longtown 2F 113
Easton. Devn 4H 11
Easton. Dors 5B 14
Easton. Hants 3D 24
Easton. Linc 3G 75
Easton. Norf 4D 78
Easton. Som 2A 22
Easton. Suff 5E 67
Easton. Wilts 4D 35
Easton Grey. Wilts 3D 35
Easton-in-Gordano. N Som 4A 34
Easton Maudit. Nptn 5F 63
Easton on the Hill. Nptn 5H 75
Easton Royal. Wilts 5H 35
East Orchard. Dors 1D 14
East Ord. Nmbd 4F 131
East Panson. Devn 3D 10
East Peckham. Kent 1A 28
East Pennard. Som 3A 22
East Perry. Cambs 4A 64
East Pitcorthie. Fife 3H 137
East Portlemouth. Devn 5D 8
East Prawle. Devn 5D 9
East Preston. W Sus 5B 26
East Putford. Devn 1D 10
East Quantoxhead. Som 2E 21
East Rainton. Tyne 5G 115
East Ravendale. NE Lin 1B 88
East Raynham. Norf 3A 78
Eastrea. Cambs 1B 64
East Rhidorroch Lodge. High 4G 163
Eastriggs. Dum 3D 112
East Rigton. W Yor 5F 99
Eastrington. E Yor 2A 94
East Rounton. N Yor 4B 106
East Row. N Yor 3F 107
East Rudham. Norf 3H 77
East Runton. Norf 1D 78
East Ruston. Norf 3F 79
Eastry. Kent 5H 41
East Saltoun. E Lot 3A 130
East Shaws. Dur 3D 105
East Shefford. W Ber 4B 36
Eastshore. Shet 10E 173
East Sleekburn. Nmbd 1F 115
East Somerton. Norf 4G 79
East Stockwith. Linc 1E 87
East Stoke. Dors 4D 14
East Stoke. Notts 1E 75
East Stoke. Som 1H 13
East Stour. Dors 4D 22
East Stourmouth. Kent 4G 41
East Stowford. Devn 4G 19
East Stratton. Hants 2D 24
East Studdal. Kent 1H 29
East Taphouse. Corn 2F 7
East-the-Water. Devn 4E 19
East Thirston. Nmbd 5F 121
East Tilbury. Thur 3A 40
East Tisted. Hants 3F 25
East Torrington. Linc 2A 88
East Tuddenham. Norf 4C 78
East Tytherley. Hants 4A 24
East Tytherton. Wilts 4E 35
East Village. Devn 2B 12
Eastville. Linc 5D 88
East Wall. Shrp 1H 59
East Walton. Norf 4G 77
East Week. Devn 3G 11
Eastwell. Leics 3E 75
East Wellow. Hants 4B 24
East Wemyss. Fife 4F 137
East Whitburn. W Lot 3C 128
Eastwick. Herts 4E 53
Eastwick. Shet 4E 173
East Williamston. Pemb 4E 43
East Winch. Norf 4F 77
East Winterslow. Wilts 3H 23
East Wittering. W Sus 3F 17
East Witton. N Yor 1D 98
Eastwood. Notts 1B 74
Eastwood. S'end 2C 40
East Woodburn. Nmbd 1C 114
Eastwood End. Cambs 1D 64
East Woodhay. Hants 5C 36
East Woodlands. Som 2C 22
East Worldham. Hants 3F 25
East Worlington. Devn 1A 12
East Wretham. Norf 1B 66
East Youlstone. Devn 1C 10
Eathorpe. Warw 4A 62
Eaton. Ches E 4C 84
Eaton. Ches W 4H 83
Eaton. Leics 3E 75
Eaton. Norf
nr. Heacham 2F 77
nr. Norwich 5E 78
Eaton. Notts 3E 86
Eaton. Oxon 5C 50
Eaton. Shrp
nr. Bishop's Castle 2F 59
nr. Church Stretton 2H 59
Eaton Bishop. Here 2H 47
Eaton Bray. C Beds 3H 51
Eaton Constantine. Shrp 5H 71
Eaton Hastings. Oxon 2A 36
Eaton Socon. Cambs 5A 64
Eaton upon Tern. Shrp 3A 72
Eau Brink. Norf 4E 77
Eaves Green. W Mid 2G 61
Ebberley Hill. Devn 1F 11
Ebberston. N Yor 1C 100
Ebbesbourne Wake. Wilts 4E 23
Ebblake. Dors 2G 15
Ebbsfleet. Kent 3H 39
Ebbw Vale. Blae 5E 47
Ebchester. Dur 4E 115
Ebernoe. W Sus 3A 26
Ebford. Devn 4C 12
Ebley. Glos 5D 48
Ebnal. Ches W 1G 71
Ebrington. Glos 1G 49
Ecchinswell. Hants 1D 24
Ecclefechan. Dum 2C 112
Eccles. G Man 1B 84
Eccles. Kent 4B 40
Eccles. Bord 5D 130
Ecclesall. S Yor 2H 85
Ecclesfield. S Yor 1A 86
Eccles Green. Here 1G 47
Eccleshall. Staf 3C 72
Eccleshill. W Yor 1B 92
Ecclesmachan. W Lot 2D 128
Eccles on Sea. Norf 3G 79
Eccles Road. Norf 1C 66
Eccleston. Ches W 4G 83
Eccleston. Lanc 3D 90
Eccleston. Mers 1G 83
Eccup. W Yor 5E 99
Echt. Abers 3E 153
Eckford. Bord 2B 120
Eckington. Derbs 3B 86
Eckington. Worc 1E 49
Ecton. Nptn 4F 63
Edale. Derbs 2F 85
Eday Airport. Orkn 4E 172
Edburton. W Sus 4D 26
Edderside. Cumb 5C 112
Edderton. High 5E 164
Eddington. Kent 4F 41
Eddington. W Ber 5B 36
Eddleston. Bord 5F 129
Eddlewood. S Lan 4A 128
Edenbridge. Kent 1F 27
Edendonich. Arg 1A 134
Edenfield. Lanc 3F 91
Edenhall. Cumb 1G 103
Edenham. Linc 3H 75
Edensor. Derbs 3G 85
Edentaggart. Arg 4C 134
Edenthorpe. S Yor 4G 93
Eden Vale. Dur 1B 106
Edern. Gwyn 2B 68
Edgarley. Som 3A 22
Edgbaston. W Mid 2E 61
Edgcott. Buck 3E 51
Edgcott. Som 3B 20
Edge. Glos 5D 48
Edge. Shrp 5F 71
Edgebolton. Shrp 3H 71
Edge End. Glos 4A 48
Edgefield. Norf 2C 78
Edgefield Street. Norf 2C 78
Edge Green. Ches W 5G 83
Edgehead. Midl 3G 129
Edgeley. Shrp 1H 71
Edgeside. Lanc 2G 91
Edgeworth. Glos 5E 49
Edgiock. Worc 4E 61
Edgmond. Telf 4B 72
Edgmond Marsh. Telf 3B 72
Edgton. Shrp 2F 59
Edgware. G Lon 1C 38
Edgworth. Bkbn 3F 91
Edinbane. High 3C 154
Edinburgh. Edin 194 (2F 129)
Edinburgh Airport. Edin 2E 129
Edingale. Staf 4G 73
Edingley. Notts 5D 86
Edingthorpe. Norf 2F 79
Edington. Som 3G 21
Edington. Wilts 1E 23

Edingworth. *Som* ...1G 21
Edistone. *Devn* ...4C 18
Edithmead. *Som* ...2G 21
Edith Weston. *Rut* ...5G 75
Edlesborough. *Buck* ...4H 51
Edlingham. *Nmbd* ...4F 121
Edlington. *Linc* ...3B 88
Edmondsham. *Dors* ...1F 15
Edmondsley. *Dur* ...5F 115
Edmondthorpe. *Leics* ...4F 75
Edmonstone. *Orkn* ...5E 172
Edmonton. *Corn* ...1D 6
Edmonton. *G Lon* ...1E 39
Edmundbyers. *Dur* ...4D 114
Ednam. *Bord* ...1B 120
Ednaston. *Derbs* ...1G 73
Edney Common. *Essx* ...5G 53
Edrom. *Bord* ...4E 131
Edstaston. *Shrp* ...2H 71
Edstone. *Warw* ...4F 61
Edwalton. *Notts* ...2C 74
Edwardstone. *Suff* ...1C 54
Edwardsville. *Mer T* ...2D 32
Edwinsford. *Carm* ...2G 45
Edwinstowe. *Notts* ...4D 86
Edworth. *C Beds* ...1C 52
Edwyn Ralph. *Here* ...5A 60
Edzell. *Ang* ...2F 145
Efail-fach. *Neat* ...2A 32
Efail Isaf. *Rhon* ...3D 32
Efailnewydd. *Gwyn* ...2C 68
Efail-rhyd. *Powy* ...3D 70
Efailwen. *Carm* ...2F 43
Efenechtyd. *Den* ...5D 82
Effingham. *Surr* ...5C 38
Effingham Common. *Surr* ...5C 38
Effirth. *Shet* ...6E 173
Efflinch. *Staf* ...4F 73
Efford. *Devn* ...2B 12
Efstigarth. *Shet* ...2F 173
Egbury. *Hants* ...1C 24
Egdon. *Worc* ...5D 60
Egerton. *G Man* ...3F 91
Egerton. *Kent* ...1D 28
Egerton Forstal. *Kent* ...1C 28
Eggborough. *N Yor* ...2F 93
Eggbuckland. *Plym* ...3A 8
Eggesford. *Devn* ...1G 11
Eggington. *C Beds* ...3H 51
Egginton. *Derbs* ...3G 73
Egglescliffe. *Stoc T* ...3B 106
Eggleston. *Dur* ...2C 104
Egham. *Surr* ...3B 38
Egham Hythe. *Surr* ...3B 38
Egleton. *Rut* ...5F 75
Eglingham. *Nmbd* ...3F 121
Egloshayle. *Corn* ...5A 10
Egloskerry. *Corn* ...4C 10
Eglwysbach. *Cnwy* ...3H 81
Eglwys-Brewis. *V Glam* ...5D 32
Eglwys Fach. *Cdgn* ...1F 57
Eglwyswrw. *Pemb* ...1F 43
Egmanton. *Notts* ...4E 87
Egmere. *Norf* ...2B 78
Egremont. *Cumb* ...3B 102
Egremont. *Mers* ...1F 83
Egton. *N Yor* ...4F 107
Egton Bridge. *N Yor* ...4F 107
Egypt. *Buck* ...2A 38
Egypt. *Hants* ...2C 24
Eight Ash Green. *Essx* ...3C 54
Eight Mile Burn. *Midl* ...4E 129
Eignaig. *High* ...4B 140
Eilanreach. *High* ...2G 147
Eildon. *Bord* ...1H 119
Eileanach Lodge. *High* ...2H 157
Eilean Fhlodaigh. *W Isl* ...3D 170
Eilean Iarmain. *High* ...2F 147
Einacleit. *W Isl* ...5D 171
Eisgein. *W Isl* ...6F 171
Eisingrug. *Gwyn* ...2F 69
Elan Village. *Powy* ...4B 58
Elberton. *S Glo* ...3B 34
Elbridge. *W Sus* ...5A 26
Elburton. *Plym* ...3B 8
Elcho. *Per* ...1D 136
Elcombe. *Swin* ...3G 35
Elcot. *W Ber* ...5B 36
Eldernell. *Cambs* ...1C 64
Eldersfield. *Worc* ...2D 48
Elderslie. *Ren* ...3F 127
Elder Street. *Essx* ...2F 53
Eldon. *Dur* ...2F 105
Eldroth. *N Yor* ...3G 97
Eldwick. *W Yor* ...5D 98
Elfhowe. *Cumb* ...5F 103
Elford. *Nmbd* ...1F 121
Elford. *Staf* ...4F 73
Elford Closes. *Cambs* ...3D 65
Elgin. *Mor* ...2G 159
Elgol. *High* ...2D 146
Elham. *Kent* ...1F 29
Elie. *Fife* ...3G 137
Eling. *Hants* ...1B 16
Eling. *W Ber* ...4D 36
Elishaw. *Nmbd* ...5C 120
Elizafield. *Dum* ...2B 112
Elkesley. *Notts* ...3D 86
Elkington. *Nptn* ...3D 62
Elkins Green. *Essx* ...5G 53
Elkstone. *Glos* ...4E 49
Ellan. *High* ...1C 150
Elland. *W Yor* ...2B 92
Ellary. *Arg* ...2F 125
Ellastone. *Staf* ...1F 73
Ellbridge. *Corn* ...2A 8
Ellel. *Lanc* ...4D 97
Ellemford. *Bord* ...3D 130
Ellenabeich. *Arg* ...2E 133
Ellenborough. *Cumb* ...1B 102

Ellenbrook. *Herts* ...5C 52
Ellenhall. *Staf* ...3C 72
Ellen's Green. *Surr* ...2B 26
Ellerbeck. *N Yor* ...5B 106
Ellerburn. *N Yor* ...1C 100
Ellerby. *N Yor* ...3E 107
Ellerdine. *Telf* ...3A 72
Ellerdine Heath. *Telf* ...3A 72
Ellerhayes. *Devn* ...2C 12
Elleric. *Arg* ...4E 141
Ellerker. *E Yor* ...2C 94
Ellerton. *E Yor* ...1H 93
Ellerton. *Shrp* ...3B 72
Ellerton-on-Swale. *N Yor* ...5F 105
Ellesborough. *Buck* ...5G 51
Ellesmere. *Shrp* ...2G 71
Ellesmere Port. *Ches W* ...3G 83
Ellingham. *Hants* ...2G 15
Ellingham. *Norf* ...1F 67
Ellingham. *Nmbd* ...2F 121
Ellingstring. *N Yor* ...1D 98
Ellington. *Cambs* ...3A 64
Ellington. *Nmbd* ...5G 121
Ellington Thorpe. *Cambs* ...3A 64
Elliot. *Ang* ...5F 145
Ellisfield. *Hants* ...2E 25
Ellishadder. *High* ...2E 155
Ellistown. *Leics* ...4B 74
Ellon. *Abers* ...5G 161
Ellonby. *Cumb* ...1F 103
Ellough. *Suff* ...2G 67
Elloughton. *E Yor* ...2C 94
Ellwood. *Glos* ...5A 48
Elm. *Cambs* ...5D 76
Elmbridge. *Glos* ...4D 48
Elmbridge. *Worc* ...4D 60
Elmdon. *Essx* ...2E 53
Elmdon. *W Mid* ...2F 61
Elmdon Heath. *W Mid* ...2F 61
Elmesthorpe. *Leics* ...1B 62
Elmfield. *IOW* ...3E 16
Elm Hill. *Dors* ...4D 22
Elmhurst. *Staf* ...4F 73
Elmley Castle. *Worc* ...1E 49
Elmley Lovett. *Worc* ...4C 60
Elmore. *Glos* ...4C 48
Elmore Back. *Glos* ...4C 48
Elm Park. *G Lon* ...2G 39
Elmscott. *Devn* ...4C 18
Elmsett. *Suff* ...1D 54
Elmstead. *Essx* ...3D 54
Elmstead Heath. *Essx* ...3D 54
Elmstead Market. *Essx* ...3D 54
Elmsted. *Kent* ...1F 29
Elmstone. *Kent* ...4G 41
Elmstone Hardwicke. *Glos* ...3E 49
Elmswell. *E Yor* ...4D 101
Elmswell. *Suff* ...4B 66
Elmton. *Derbs* ...3C 86
Elphin. *High* ...2G 163
Elphinstone. *E Lot* ...2G 129
Elrick. *Abers* ...3F 153
Elrick. *Mor* ...1B 152
Elrig. *Dum* ...5A 110
Elsdon. *Nmbd* ...5D 120
Elsecar. *S Yor* ...1A 86
Elsenham. *Essx* ...3F 53
Elsfield. *Oxon* ...4D 50
Elsham. *N Lin* ...3D 94
Elsing. *Norf* ...4C 78
Elslack. *N Yor* ...5B 98
Elsrickle. *S Lan* ...5D 128
Elstead. *Surr* ...1A 26
Elsted. *W Sus* ...1G 17
Elsted Marsh. *W Sus* ...4G 25
Elsthorpe. *Linc* ...3H 75
Elstob. *Dur* ...2A 106
Elston. *Devn* ...2A 12
Elston. *Lanc* ...1E 90
Elston. *Notts* ...1E 75
Elston. *Wilts* ...2F 23
Elstone. *Devn* ...1G 11
Elstow. *Bed* ...1A 52
Elstree. *Herts* ...1C 38
Elstronwick. *E Yor* ...1F 95
Elswick. *Lanc* ...1C 90
Elswick. *Tyne* ...3F 115
Elsworth. *Cambs* ...4C 64
Elterwater. *Cumb* ...4E 103
Eltham. *G Lon* ...3F 39
Eltisley. *Cambs* ...5B 64
Elton. *Cambs* ...1H 63
Elton. *Ches W* ...3G 83
Elton. *Derbs* ...4G 85
Elton. *Glos* ...4C 48
Elton. *G Man* ...3F 91
Elton. *Here* ...3G 59
Elton. *Notts* ...2E 75
Elton. *Stoc T* ...3B 106
Elton Green. *Ches W* ...3G 83
Elvanfoot. *S Lan* ...3B 118
Elvaston. *Derbs* ...2B 74
Elveden. *Suff* ...3H 65
Elvetham Heath. *Hants* ...1F 25
Elvingston. *E Lot* ...2A 130
Elvington. *Kent* ...5G 41
Elvington. *York* ...5B 100
Elwick. *Hart* ...1B 106
Elwick. *Nmbd* ...1F 121
Elworth. *Ches E* ...4B 84
Elworthy. *Dors* ...4A 14
Elworthy. *Som* ...3D 20
Ely. *Cambs* ...2E 65
Ely. *Card* ...4E 33
Emberton. *Mil* ...1G 51
Embleton. *Cumb* ...1C 102
Embleton. *Hart* ...2B 106
Embleton. *Nmbd* ...2G 121
Embo. *High* ...4F 165
Emborough. *Som* ...1B 22

Embo Street. *High* ...4F 165
Embsay. *N Yor* ...4C 98
Emery Down. *Hants* ...2A 16
Emley. *W Yor* ...3C 92
Emmbrook. *Wok* ...5F 37
Emmer Green. *Read* ...4F 37
Emmington. *Oxon* ...5F 51
Emneth. *Norf* ...5D 77
Emneth Hungate. *Norf* ...5E 77
Empingham. *Rut* ...5G 75
Empshott. *Hants* ...3F 25
Emsworth. *Hants* ...2F 17
Enborne. *W Ber* ...5C 36
Enborne Row. *W Ber* ...5C 36
Enchmarsh. *Shrp* ...1H 59
Enderby. *Leics* ...1C 62
Endmoor. *Cumb* ...1E 97
Endon. *Staf* ...5D 84
Endon Bank. *Staf* ...5D 84
Enfield. *G Lon* ...1E 39
Enfield Wash. *G Lon* ...1E 39
Enford. *Wilts* ...1G 23
Engine Common. *S Glo* ...3B 34
Englefield. *W Ber* ...4E 37
Englefield Green. *Surr* ...3A 38
Englesea-brook. *Ches E* ...5B 84
English Bicknor. *Glos* ...4A 48
Englishcombe. *Bath* ...5C 34
English Frankton. *Shrp* ...3G 71
Enham Alamein. *Hants* ...2B 24
Enmore. *Som* ...3F 21
Ennerdale Bridge. *Cumb* ...3B 102
Enniscaven. *Corn* ...3D 6
Enoch. *Dum* ...4A 118
Enochdhu. *Per* ...2H 143
Ensay. *Arg* ...4E 139
Ensbury. *Bour* ...3F 15
Ensdon. *Shrp* ...4G 71
Ensis. *Devn* ...4F 19
Enson. *Staf* ...3D 72
Enstone. *Oxon* ...3B 50
Enterkinfoot. *Dum* ...4A 118
Enville. *Staf* ...2C 60
Eolaigearraidh. *W Isl* ...8C 170
Eorabus. *Arg* ...1A 132
Eoropaidh. *W Isl* ...1H 171
Epney. *Glos* ...4C 48
Epperstone. *Notts* ...1D 74
Epping. *Essx* ...5E 53
Epping Green. *Essx* ...5E 53
Epping Green. *Herts* ...5C 52
Epping Upland. *Essx* ...5E 53
Eppleby. *N Yor* ...3E 105
Eppleworth. *E Yor* ...1D 94
Epsom. *Surr* ...4D 38
Epwell. *Oxon* ...1B 50
Epworth. *N Lin* ...4A 94
Epworth Turbary. *N Lin* ...4A 94
Erbistock. *Wrex* ...1F 71
Erbusaig. *High* ...1F 147
Erchless Castle. *High* ...4G 157
Erdington. *W Mid* ...1F 61
Eredine. *Arg* ...3G 133
Eriboll. *High* ...3E 167
Ericstane. *Dum* ...3C 118
Eridge Green. *E Sus* ...2G 27
Erines. *Arg* ...2G 125
Eriswell. *Suff* ...3G 65
Erith. *G Lon* ...3G 39
Erlestoke. *Wilts* ...1E 23
Ermine. *Linc* ...4C 78
Ermington. *Devn* ...3C 8
Ernesettle. *Plym* ...3A 8
Erpingham. *Norf* ...2D 78
Erriott Wood. *Kent* ...5D 40
Errogie. *High* ...1H 149
Errol. *Per* ...1E 137
Errol Station. *Per* ...1E 137
Erskine. *Ren* ...2F 127
Erskine Bridge. *Ren* ...2F 127
Ervie. *Dum* ...3F 109
Erwarton. *Suff* ...2F 55
Erwood. *Powy* ...1D 46
Eryholme. *N Yor* ...4A 106
Eryrys. *Den* ...5E 82
Escalls. *Corn* ...4A 4
Escomb. *Dur* ...1E 105
Escrick. *N Yor* ...5A 100
Esgair. *Carm*
  nr. Carmarthen ...3D 45
  nr. St Clears ...3G 43
Esgairgeiliog. *Powy* ...5G 69
Esh. *Dur* ...5E 115
Esher. *Surr* ...4C 38
Esholt. *W Yor* ...5D 98
Eshott. *Nmbd* ...5G 121
Eshton. *N Yor* ...4B 98
Esh Winning. *Dur* ...5E 115
Eskadale. *High* ...5G 157
Eskbank. *Midl* ...3G 129
Eskdale Green. *Cumb* ...4C 102
Eskdalemuir. *Dum* ...5E 119
Eskham. *Linc* ...1C 88
Esknish. *Arg* ...3B 124
Esk Valley. *N Yor* ...4F 107
Eslington Hall. *Nmbd* ...3E 121
Esprick. *Lanc* ...1C 90
Essendine. *Rut* ...4H 75
Essendon. *Herts* ...5C 52
Essich. *High* ...5A 158
Essington. *Staf* ...5D 72
Eston. *Red C* ...3C 106
Estover. *Plym* ...3B 8
Eswick. *Shet* ...6F 173
Etal. *Nmbd* ...1D 120
Etchilhampton. *Wilts* ...5F 35
Etchingham. *E Sus* ...3B 28
Etchinghill. *Kent* ...2F 29
Etchinghill. *Staf* ...4E 73
Etherley Dene. *Dur* ...2E 105
Ethie Haven. *Ang* ...4F 145

Etling Green. *Norf* ...4C 78
Etloe. *Glos* ...5B 48
Eton. *Wind* ...3A 38
Eton Wick. *Wind* ...3A 38
Etteridge. *High* ...4A 150
Ettersgill. *Dur* ...2B 104
Ettiley Heath. *Ches E* ...4B 84
Ettington. *Warw* ...1A 50
Etton. *E Yor* ...5D 101
Etton. *Pet* ...5A 76
Ettrick. *Bord* ...3E 119
Ettrickbridge. *Bord* ...2F 119
Etwall. *Derbs* ...2G 73
Eudon Burnell. *Shrp* ...2B 60
Eudon George. *Shrp* ...2A 60
Euston. *Suff* ...3A 66
Euxton. *Lanc* ...3D 90
Evanstown. *B'end* ...3C 32
Evanton. *High* ...2A 158
Evedon. *Linc* ...1H 75
Evelix. *High* ...4E 165
Evendine. *Here* ...1C 48
Evenjobb. *Powy* ...4E 59
Evenley. *Nptn* ...2D 50
Evenlode. *Glos* ...3H 49
Even Swindon. *Swin* ...3G 35
Evenwood. *Dur* ...2E 105
Evenwood Gate. *Dur* ...2E 105
Everbay. *Orkn* ...5F 172
Evercreech. *Som* ...3B 22
Everdon. *Nptn* ...5C 62
Everingham. *E Yor* ...5C 100
Everleigh. *Wilts* ...1H 23
Everley. *N Yor* ...1D 100
Eversholt. *C Beds* ...2H 51
Evershot. *Dors* ...2A 14
Eversley. *Hants* ...5F 37
Eversley Centre. *Hants* ...5F 37
Eversley Cross. *Hants* ...5F 37
Everthorpe. *E Yor* ...1C 94
Everton. *C Beds* ...5B 64
Everton. *Hants* ...3A 16
Everton. *Mers* ...1F 83
Everton. *Notts* ...1D 86
Evertown. *Dum* ...2E 113
Evesbatch. *Here* ...1B 48
Evesham. *Worc* ...1F 49
Evington. *Leic* ...5D 74
Ewden Village. *S Yor* ...1G 85
Ewdness. *Shrp* ...1B 60
Ewell. *Surr* ...4D 38
Ewell Minnis. *Kent* ...1G 29
Ewelme. *Oxon* ...2E 37
Ewen. *Glos* ...2F 35
Ewenny. *V Glam* ...4C 32
Ewerby. *Linc* ...1A 76
Ewes. *Dum* ...5F 119
Ewesley. *Nmbd* ...5E 121
Ewhurst. *Surr* ...1B 26
Ewhurst Green. *E Sus* ...3B 28
Ewhurst Green. *Surr* ...2B 26
Ewlo. *Flin* ...4E 83
Ewloe. *Flin* ...4E 83
Ewood Bridge. *Lanc* ...2F 91
Eworthy. *Devn* ...3E 11
Ewshot. *Hants* ...1G 25
Ewyas Harold. *Here* ...3G 47
Exbourne. *Devn* ...2G 11
Exbury. *Hants* ...2C 16
Exceat. *E Sus* ...5G 27
Exebridge. *Som* ...4C 20
Exelby. *N Yor* ...1E 99
Exeter. *Devn* ...195 (3C 12)
Exeter Airport. *Devn* ...3D 12
Exford. *Som* ...3B 20
Exfords Green. *Shrp* ...5G 71
Exhall. *Warw* ...5F 61
Exlade Street. *Oxon* ...3E 37
Exminster. *Devn* ...4C 12
Exmouth. *Devn* ...4D 12
Exnaboe. *Shet* ...10E 173
Exning. *Suff* ...4F 65
Exton. *Devn* ...4C 12
Exton. *Hants* ...4E 24
Exton. *Rut* ...4F 75
Exton. *Som* ...3C 20
Exwick. *Devn* ...3C 12
Eyam. *Derbs* ...3G 85
Eydon. *Nptn* ...5C 62
Eye. *Here* ...4G 59
Eye. *Pet* ...5B 76
Eye. *Suff* ...3D 66
Eye Green. *Pet* ...5B 76
Eyemouth. *Bord* ...3F 131
Eyeworth. *C Beds* ...1C 52
Eyhorne Street. *Kent* ...5C 40
Eyke. *Suff* ...5F 67
Eynesbury. *Cambs* ...5A 64
Eynort. *High* ...1B 146
Eynsford. *Kent* ...4G 39
Eynsham. *Oxon* ...5C 50
Eyre. *High*
  on Isle of Skye ...3D 154
  on Raasay ...5E 155
Eythorne. *Kent* ...1G 29
Eyton. *Here* ...4G 59
Eyton. *Shrp*
  nr. Bishop's Castle ...2F 59
  nr. Shrewsbury ...4F 71
Eyton. *Wrex* ...1F 71
Eyton on Severn. *Shrp* ...5H 71
Eyton upon the Weald Moors.
  Telf ...4A 72

F

Faccombe. *Hants* ...1B 24
Faceby. *N Yor* ...4B 106
Faddiley. *Ches E* ...5H 83
Fadmoor. *N Yor* ...1A 100

Fagwyr. *Swan* ...5G 45
Faichem. *High* ...3E 149
Faifley. *W Dun* ...2G 127
Fail. *S Ayr* ...2D 116
Failand. *N Som* ...4A 34
Failford. *S Ayr* ...2D 116
Failsworth. *G Man* ...4H 91
Fairbourne. *Gwyn* ...4F 69
Fairbourne Heath. *Kent* ...5C 40
Fairburn. *N Yor* ...2E 93
Fairfield. *Derbs* ...3E 85
Fairfield. *Kent* ...3D 28
Fairfield. *Worc*
  nr. Bromsgrove ...3D 60
  nr. Evesham ...1F 49
Fairford. *Glos* ...5G 49
Fair Green. *Norf* ...4F 77
Fair Hill. *Cumb* ...1G 103
Fairhill. *S Lan* ...4A 128
Fair Isle Airport. *Shet* ...1B 172
Fairlands. *Surr* ...5A 38
Fairlie. *N Ayr* ...4D 126
Fairlight. *E Sus* ...4C 28
Fairlight Cove. *E Sus* ...4C 28
Fairmile. *Devn* ...3D 12
Fairmile. *Surr* ...4C 38
Fairmilehead. *Edin* ...3F 129
Fair Oak. *Devn* ...1D 12
Fair Oak. *Hants*
  nr. Eastleigh ...1C 16
  nr. Kingsclere ...5D 36
Fairoak. *Staf* ...2B 72
Fair Oak Green. *Hants* ...5E 37
Fairseat. *Kent* ...4H 39
Fairstead. *Essx* ...4A 54
Fairstead. *Norf* ...4F 77
Fairwarp. *E Sus* ...3F 27
Fairwater. *Card* ...4E 33
Fairy Cross. *Devn* ...4E 19
Fakenham. *Norf* ...2B 78
Fakenham Magna. *Suff* ...3B 66
Fala. *Midl* ...3H 129
Fala Dam. *Midl* ...3H 129
Falcon. *Here* ...2B 48
Faldingworth. *Linc* ...2H 87
Falfield. *S Glo* ...2B 34
Y Fali. *IOA* ...3B 80
Falkenham. *Suff* ...2F 55
Falkirk. *Falk* ...1B 128
Falkland. *Fife* ...3E 137
Fallin. *Stir* ...4H 135
Fallowfield. *G Man* ...1C 84
Falmer. *E Sus* ...5E 27
Falmouth. *Corn* ...5C 6
Falsgrave. *N Yor* ...1E 101
Falstone. *Nmbd* ...1A 114
Fanagmore. *High* ...4B 166
Fancott. *C Beds* ...3A 52
Fanellan. *High* ...4G 157
Fangdale Beck. *N Yor* ...5C 106
Fangfoss. *E Yor* ...4B 100
Fankerton. *Falk* ...1A 128
Fanmore. *Arg* ...4F 139
Fanner's Green. *Essx* ...4G 53
Fannich Lodge. *High* ...2E 156
Fans. *Bord* ...5C 130
Far Cotton. *Nptn* ...5E 63
Fareham. *Hants* ...2D 16
Farewell. *Staf* ...4E 73
Far Forest. *Worc* ...3B 60
Farforth. *Linc* ...3C 88
Far Green. *Glos* ...5C 48
Far Hoarcross. *Staf* ...3F 73
Faringdon. *Oxon* ...2A 36
Farington. *Lanc* ...2D 90
Farlam. *Cumb* ...4G 113
Farleigh. *N Som* ...5H 33
Farleigh. *Surr* ...4E 39
Farleigh Hungerford. *Som* ...1D 22
Farleigh Wallop. *Hants* ...2E 24
Farleigh Wick. *Wilts* ...5D 34
Farlesthorpe. *Linc* ...3D 88
Farleton. *Cumb* ...1E 97
Farleton. *Lanc* ...3E 97
Farley. *High* ...4G 157
Farley. *Shrp*
  nr. Shrewsbury ...5F 71
  nr. Telford ...5A 72
Farley. *Staf* ...1E 73
Farley. *Wilts* ...4H 23
Farley Green. *Suff* ...5G 65
Farley Green. *Surr* ...1B 26
Farley Hill. *Wok* ...5F 37
Farley's End. *Glos* ...4C 48
Farlington. *N Yor* ...3A 100
Farlington. *Port* ...2E 17
Farlow. *Shrp* ...2A 60
Farmborough. *Bath* ...5B 34
Farmcote. *Glos* ...3F 49
Farmcote. *Shrp* ...1B 60
Farmington. *Glos* ...4G 49
Far Moor. *G Man* ...4D 90
Farmoor. *Oxon* ...5C 50
Farmtown. *Mor* ...3C 160
Farnah Green. *Derbs* ...1H 73
Farnborough. *G Lon* ...4F 39
Farnborough. *Hants* ...1G 25
Farnborough. *Warw* ...1C 50
Farnborough. *W Ber* ...3C 36
Farncombe. *Surr* ...1A 26
Farndish. *Bed* ...4G 63
Farndon. *Ches W* ...5G 83
Farndon. *Notts* ...5E 87
Farnell. *Ang* ...3F 145
Farnham. *Dors* ...1E 15
Farnham. *Essx* ...3E 53
Farnham. *N Yor* ...3F 99
Farnham. *Suff* ...4F 67
Farnham. *Surr* ...2G 25
Farnham Common. *Buck* ...2A 38

Farnham Green – Four Marks

Farnham Green. *Essx* 3E **53**
Farnham Royal. *Buck* 2A **38**
Farnhill. *N Yor* 5C **98**
Farningham. *Kent* 4G **39**
Farnley. *N Yor* 5E **98**
Farnley Tyas. *W Yor* 3B **92**
Farnsfield. *Notts* 5D **86**
Farnworth. *G Man* 4F **91**
Farnworth. *Hal* 2H **83**
Far Oakridge. *Glos* 5E **49**
Farr. *High*
  nr. Bettyhill 2H **167**
  nr. Inverness 5A **158**
  nr. Kingussie 3C **150**
Farraline. *High* 1H **149**
Farringdon. *Devn* 3D **12**
Farrington. *Dors* 1D **14**
Farrington Gurney. *Bath* 1B **22**
Far Sawrey. *Cumb* 5E **103**
Farsley. *W Yor* 1C **92**
Farthinghoe. *Nptn* 2D **50**
Farthingstone. *Nptn* 5D **62**
Farthorpe. *Linc* 3B **88**
Fartown. *W Yor* 3B **92**
Farway. *Devn* 3E **13**
Fasag. *High* 3A **156**
Fascadale. *High* 1G **139**
Fasnacloich. *Arg* 4E **141**
Fassfern. *High* 1E **141**
Fatfield. *Tyne* 4G **115**
Faugh. *Cumb* 4G **113**
Fauld. *Staf* 3F **73**
Fauldhouse. *W Lot* 3C **128**
Faulkbourne. *Essx* 4A **54**
Faulkland. *Som* 1C **22**
Fauls. *Shrp* 2H **71**
Faverdale. *Darl* 3F **105**
Faversham. *Kent* 4E **40**
Fawdington. *N Yor* 2G **99**
Fawfieldhead. *Staf* 4E **85**
Fawkham Green. *Kent* 4G **39**
Fawler. *Oxon* 4B **50**
Fawley. *Buck* 3F **37**
Fawley. *Hants* 2C **16**
Fawley. *W Ber* 3B **36**
Fawley Chapel. *Here* 3A **48**
Fawton. *Corn* 2F **7**
Faxfleet. *E Yor* 2B **94**
Faygate. *W Sus* 2D **26**
Fazakerley. *Mers* 1F **83**
Fazeley. *Staf* 5F **73**
Feagour. *High* 4H **149**
Fearann Dhomhnaill. *High* 3E **147**
Fearby. *N Yor* 1D **98**
Fearn. *High* 1C **158**
Fearnan. *Per* 4E **142**
Fearnbeg. *High* 3G **155**
Fearnhead. *Warr* 1A **84**
Fearnmore. *High* 2G **155**
Featherstone. *Staf* 5D **72**
Featherstone. *W Yor* 2E **93**
Featherstone Castle. *Nmbd* 3H **113**
Feckenham. *Worc* 4E **61**
Feering. *Essx* 3B **54**
Feetham. *N Yor* 5C **104**
Feizor. *N Yor* 3G **97**
Felbridge. *Surr* 2E **27**
Felbrigg. *Norf* 2E **78**
Felcourt. *Surr* 1E **27**
Felden. *Herts* 5A **52**
Felhampton. *Shrp* 2G **59**
Felindre. *Carm*
  nr. Llandeilo 3F **45**
  nr. Llandovery 2G **45**
  nr. Newcastle Emlyn 2D **44**
Felindre. *Powy* 2D **58**
Felindre. *Swan* 5G **45**
Felindre Farchog. *Pemb* 1F **43**
Felinfach. *Cdgn* 5E **57**
Felinfach. *Powy* 2D **46**
Felinfoel. *Carm* 5F **45**
Felingwmisaf. *Carm* 3F **45**
Felingwmuchaf. *Carm* 3F **45**
Y Felinheli. *Gwyn* 4E **81**
Felin Newydd. *Powy*
  nr. Newtown 5C **70**
  nr. Oswestry 3E **70**
Felin Wnda. *Cdgn* 1D **44**
Felinwynt. *Cdgn* 5B **56**
Felixkirk. *N Yor* 1G **99**
Felixstowe. *Suff* 2F **55**
Felixstowe Ferry. *Suff* 2G **55**
Felkington. *Nmbd* 5F **131**
Fell End. *Cumb* 5A **104**
Felling. *Tyne* 3F **115**
Fell Side. *Cumb* 1E **102**
Felmersham. *Bed* 5G **63**
Felmingham. *Norf* 3E **79**
Felpham. *W Sus* 3H **17**
Felsham. *Suff* 5B **66**
Felsted. *Essx* 3G **53**
Feltham. *G Lon* 3C **38**
Felthamhill. *Surr* 3B **38**
Felthorpe. *Norf* 4D **78**
Felton. *Here* 1A **48**
Felton. *N Som* 5A **34**
Felton. *Nmbd* 4F **121**
Felton Butler. *Shrp* 4F **71**
Feltwell. *Norf* 1G **65**
Fenay Bridge. *W Yor* 3B **92**
Fence. *Lanc* 1G **91**
Fence Houses. *Tyne* 4G **115**
Fencott. *Oxon* 4D **50**
Fen Ditton. *Cambs* 4D **65**
Fen Drayton. *Cambs* 4C **64**
Fen End. *Linc* 3B **76**
Fen End. *W Mid* 3G **61**
Fenham. *Nmbd* 5G **131**
Fenham. *Tyne* 3F **115**
Fenhouses. *Linc* 1B **76**
Feniscowles. *Bkbn* 2E **91**
Feniton. *Devn* 3D **12**
Fenn Green. *Shrp* 2B **60**
Y Fenni. *Mon* 4G **47**
Fenn's Bank. *Wrex* 2H **71**
Fenn Street. *Medw* 3B **40**
Fenny Bentley. *Derbs* 5F **85**
Fenny Bridges. *Devn* 3E **12**
Fenny Compton. *Warw* 5B **62**
Fenny Drayton. *Leics* 1H **61**
Fenny Stratford. *Mil* 2G **51**
Fenrother. *Nmbd* 5F **121**
Fenstanton. *Cambs* 4C **64**
Fen Street. *Norf* 1C **66**
Fenton. *Cambs* 3C **64**
Fenton. *Cumb* 4G **113**
Fenton. *Linc*
  nr. Caythorpe 5F **87**
  nr. Saxilby 3F **87**
Fenton. *Nmbd* 1D **120**
Fenton. *Notts* 2E **87**
Fenton. *Stoke* 1C **72**
Fentonadle. *Corn* 5A **10**
Fenton Barns. *E Lot* 1B **130**
Fenwick. *E Ayr* 5F **127**
Fenwick. *Nmbd*
  nr. Berwick-upon-Tweed 5G **131**
  nr. Hexham 2D **114**
Fenwick. *S Yor* 3F **93**
Feochaig. *Arg* 4B **122**
Feock. *Corn* 5C **6**
Feolin Ferry. *Arg* 3C **124**
Feorlan. *Arg* 5A **122**
Ferindonald. *High* 3E **147**
Feriniquarrie. *High* 3A **154**
Fern. *Ang* 2D **145**
Ferndale. *Rhon* 2C **32**
Ferndown. *Dors* 2F **15**
Ferness. *High* 4D **158**
Fernham. *Oxon* 2A **36**
Fernhill. *W Sus* 1E **27**
Fernhill Heath. *Worc* 5C **60**
Fernhurst. *W Sus* 4G **25**
Fernieflatt. *Abers* 1H **145**
Ferniegair. *S Lan* 4A **128**
Fernilea. *High* 5C **154**
Fernilee. *Derbs* 3E **85**
Ferrensby. *N Yor* 3F **99**
Ferriby Sluice. *N Lin* 2C **94**
Ferring. *W Sus* 5B **26**
Ferrybridge. *W Yor* 2E **93**
Ferryden. *Ang* 3G **145**
Ferry Hill. *Cambs* 2C **64**
Ferryhill. *Aber* 3G **153**
Ferryhill. *Dur* 1F **105**
Ferryhill Station. *Dur* 1A **106**
Ferryside. *Carm* 4D **44**
Ferryton. *High* 2A **158**
Fersfield. *Norf* 2C **66**
Fersit. *High* 1A **142**
Y Ferwig. *Cdgn* 1B **44**
Feshiebridge. *High* 3C **150**
Fetcham. *Surr* 5C **38**
Fetterangus. *Abers* 3G **161**
Fettercairn. *Abers* 1F **145**
Fewcott. *Oxon* 3D **50**
Fewston. *N Yor* 4D **98**
Ffairfach. *Carm* 3G **45**
Ffair Rhos. *Cdgn* 4G **57**
Ffaldybrenin. *Carm* 1G **45**
Ffarmers. *Carm* 1G **45**
Ffawyddog. *Powy* 4F **47**
Y Fflint. *Flin* 3E **83**
Ffodun. *Powy* 5E **71**
Ffont-y-gari. *V Glam* 5D **32**
Y Ffor. *Gwyn* 2C **68**
Fforest. *Carm* 5F **45**
Fforest-fach. *Swan* 3F **31**
Fforest Goch. *Neat* 5H **45**
Ffostrasol. *Cdgn* 1D **44**
Ffos-y-ffin. *Cdgn* 4D **56**
Ffrith. *Flin* 5E **83**
Ffwl-y-mwn. *V Glam* 5D **32**
Ffynnon-ddrain. *Carm* 3E **45**
Ffynnongroyw. *Flin* 2D **82**
Ffynnon Gynydd. *Powy* 1E **47**
Ffynnon-oer. *Cdgn* 5E **57**
Fiag Lodge. *High* 1B **164**
Fidden. *Arg* 2B **132**
Fiddington. *Glos* 2E **49**
Fiddington. *Som* 2F **21**
Fiddleford. *Dors* 1D **14**
Fiddlers Hamlet. *Essx* 5E **53**
Field. *Staf* 2E **73**
Field Assarts. *Oxon* 4B **50**
Field Broughton. *Cumb* 1C **96**
Field Dalling. *Norf* 2C **78**
Field Head. *Leics* 5B **74**
Fieldhead. *Cumb* 1F **103**
Fifehead Magdalen. *Dors* 4C **22**
Fifehead Neville. *Dors* 1C **14**
Fifehead St Quintin. *Dors* 1C **14**
Fife Keith. *Mor* 3B **160**
Fifield. *Oxon* 4H **49**
Fifield. *Wilts* 1G **23**
Fifield. *Wind* 3A **38**
Fifield Bavant. *Wilts* 4F **23**
Figheldean. *Wilts* 2G **23**
Filby. *Norf* 4G **79**
Filey. *N Yor* 1F **101**
Filford. *Dors* 3H **13**
Filgrave. *Mil* 1G **51**
Filkins. *Oxon* 5H **49**
Filleigh. *Devn*
  nr. Crediton 1H **11**
  nr. South Molton 4G **19**
Fillingham. *Linc* 2G **87**
Fillongley. *Warw* 2G **61**
Filton. *S Glo* 4B **34**
Fimber. *E Yor* 3C **100**
Finavon. *Ang* 3D **145**
Fincham. *Norf* 5F **77**
Finchampstead. *Wok* 5F **37**
Fincharn. *Arg* 3G **133**
Finchdean. *Hants* 1F **17**
Finchingfield. *Essx* 2G **53**
Finchley. *G Lon* 1D **38**
Findern. *Derbs* 2H **73**
Findhorn. *Mor* 2E **159**
Findhorn Bridge. *High* 1C **150**
Findochty. *Mor* 2B **160**
Findo Gask. *Per* 1C **136**
Findon. *Abers* 4G **153**
Findon. *W Sus* 5C **26**
Findon Mains. *High* 2A **158**
Findon Valley. *W Sus* 5C **26**
Finedon. *Nptn* 3G **63**
Fingal Street. *Suff* 3E **66**
Fingest. *Buck* 2F **37**
Finghall. *N Yor* 1D **98**
Fingland. *Cumb* 4D **112**
Fingland. *Dum* 3G **117**
Finglesham. *Kent* 5H **41**
Fingringhoe. *Essx* 3D **54**
Finiskaig. *High* 4A **148**
Finmere. *Oxon* 2E **51**
Finnart. *Per* 3C **142**
Finningham. *Suff* 4C **66**
Finningley. *S Yor* 1D **86**
Finnygaud. *Abers* 3D **160**
Finsbury. *G Lon* 2E **39**
Finstall. *Worc* 4D **61**
Finsthwaite. *Cumb* 1C **96**
Finstock. *Oxon* 4B **50**
Finstown. *Orkn* 6C **172**
Fintry. *Abers* 3E **161**
Fintry. *D'dee* 5D **144**
Fintry. *Stir* 1H **127**
Finwood. *Warw* 4F **61**
Finzean. *Abers* 4D **152**
Fionnphort. *Arg* 2B **132**
Fionnsabhagh. *W Isl* 9C **171**
Firbeck. *S Yor* 2C **86**
Firby. *N Yor*
  nr. Bedale 1E **99**
  nr. Malton 3B **100**
Firgrove. *G Man* 3H **91**
Firle. *E Sus* 5F **27**
Firsby. *Linc* 4D **88**
Firsdown. *Wilts* 3H **23**
First Coast. *High* 4D **162**
Firth. *Shet* 4F **173**
Fir Tree. *Dur* 1E **105**
Fishbourne. *IOW* 3D **16**
Fishbourne. *W Sus* 2G **17**
Fishburn. *Dur* 1A **106**
Fishcross. *Clac* 4A **136**
Fisherford. *Abers* 5D **160**
Fisherrow. *E Lot* 2G **129**
Fisher's Pond. *Hants* 4C **24**
Fisher's Row. *Lanc* 5D **96**
Fisherstreet. *W Sus* 2A **26**
Fisherton. *High* 3B **158**
Fisherton. *S Ayr* 3B **116**
Fisherton de la Mere. *Wilts* 3E **23**
Fishguard. *Pemb* 1D **42**
Fishlake. *S Yor* 3G **93**
Fishley. *Norf* 4G **79**
Fishnish. *Arg* 4A **140**
Fishpond Bottom. *Dors* 3G **13**
Fishponds. *Bris* 4B **34**
Fishpool. *Glos* 3B **48**
Fishpool. *G Man* 3G **91**
Fishpools. *Powy* 4D **58**
Fishtoft. *Linc* 1C **76**
Fishtoft Drove. *Linc* 1C **76**
Fishwick. *Bord* 4F **131**
Fiskavaig. *High* 5C **154**
Fiskerton. *Linc* 3H **87**
Fiskerton. *Notts* 5E **87**
Fitch. *Shet* 7E **173**
Fitling. *E Yor* 1F **95**
Fittleton. *Wilts* 2G **23**
Fittleworth. *W Sus* 4B **26**
Fitton End. *Cambs* 4D **76**
Fitz. *Shrp* 4G **71**
Fitzhead. *Som* 4E **20**
Fitzwilliam. *W Yor* 3E **93**
Fiunary. *High* 4A **140**
Five Ash Down. *E Sus* 3F **27**
Five Ashes. *E Sus* 3G **27**
Five Bells. *Som* 2D **20**
Five Bridges. *Here* 1B **48**
Fivehead. *Som* 4G **21**
Fivelanes. *Corn* 4C **10**
Five Oak Green. *Kent* 1H **27**
Five Oaks. *W Sus* 3B **26**
Five Roads. *Carm* 5E **45**
Five Ways. *Warw* 3G **61**
Flack's Green. *Essx* 4A **54**
Flackwell Heath. *Buck* 3G **37**
Fladbury. *Worc* 1E **49**
Fladda. *Shet* 3E **173**
Fladdabister. *Shet* 8F **173**
Flagg. *Derbs* 4F **85**
Flamborough. *E Yor* 2G **101**
Flamstead. *Herts* 4A **52**
Flansham. *W Sus* 5A **26**
Flasby. *N Yor* 4B **98**
Flash. *Staf* 4E **85**
Flashader. *High* 3C **154**
The Flatt. *Cumb* 2G **113**
Flaunden. *Herts* 5A **52**
Flawborough. *Notts* 1E **75**
Flawith. *N Yor* 3G **99**
Flax Bourton. *N Som* 5A **34**
Flaxby. *N Yor* 4F **99**
Flaxholme. *Derbs* 1H **73**
Flaxley. *Glos* 4B **48**
Flaxley Green. *Staf* 4E **73**
Flaxpool. *Som* 3E **21**
Flaxton. *N Yor* 3A **100**
Fleck. *Shet* 10E **173**
Fleckney. *Leics* 1D **62**
Flecknoe. *Warw* 4C **62**
Fledborough. *Notts* 3F **87**
Fleet. *Dors* 4B **14**
Fleet. *Hants*
  nr. Farnborough 1G **25**
Fleet. *Hants*
  nr. South Hayling 2F **17**
Fleet. *Linc* 3C **76**
Fleet Hargate. *Linc* 3C **76**
Fleetville. *Herts* 5B **52**
Fleetwood. *Lanc* 5C **96**
Fleggburgh. *Norf* 4G **79**
Fleisirin. *W Isl* 4H **171**
Flemingston. *V Glam* 5D **32**
Flemington. *S Lan*
  nr. Glasgow 3H **127**
  nr. Strathaven 5A **128**
Flempton. *Suff* 4H **65**
Fleoideabhagh. *W Isl* 9C **171**
Fletcher's Green. *Kent* 1G **27**
Fletchertown. *Cumb* 5D **112**
Fletching. *E Sus* 3F **27**
Fleuchary. *High* 4E **165**
Flexbury. *Corn* 2C **10**
Flexford. *Surr* 1A **26**
Flimby. *Cumb* 1B **102**
Flimwell. *E Sus* 2B **28**
Flint. *Flin* 3E **83**
Flintham. *Notts* 1E **75**
Flint Mountain. *Flin* 3E **83**
Flinton. *E Yor* 1F **95**
Flintsham. *Here* 5F **59**
Flishinghurst. *Kent* 2B **28**
Flitcham. *Norf* 3G **77**
Flitton. *C Beds* 2A **52**
Flitwick. *C Beds* 2A **52**
Flixborough. *N Lin* 3B **94**
Flixton. *G Man* 1B **84**
Flixton. *N Yor* 2E **101**
Flixton. *Suff* 2F **67**
Flockton. *W Yor* 3C **92**
Flodden. *Nmbd* 1D **120**
Flodigarry. *High* 1D **154**
Flood's Ferry. *Cambs* 1C **64**
Flookburgh. *Cumb* 2C **96**
Flordon. *Norf* 1D **66**
Flore. *Nptn* 4D **62**
Flotterton. *Nmbd* 4D **121**
Flowton. *Suff* 1D **54**
Flushing. *Abers* 4H **161**
Flushing. *Corn* 5C **6**
Fluxton. *Devn* 3D **12**
Flyford Flavell. *Worc* 5D **61**
Fobbing. *Thur* 2B **40**
Fochabers. *Mor* 3H **159**
Fochriw. *Cphy* 5E **46**
Fockerby. *N Lin* 3B **94**
Fodderty. *High* 3H **157**
Foddington. *Som* 4A **22**
Foel. *Powy* 4B **70**
Foffarty. *Ang* 4D **144**
Foggathorpe. *E Yor* 1A **94**
Fogo. *Bord* 5D **130**
Fogorig. *Bord* 5D **130**
Foindle. *High* 4B **166**
Folda. *Ang* 2A **144**
Fole. *Staf* 2E **73**
Foleshill. *W Mid* 2A **62**
Foley Park. *Worc* 3C **60**
Folke. *Dors* 1B **14**
Folkestone. *Kent* **195** (2G **29**)
Folkingham. *Linc* 2H **75**
Folkington. *E Sus* 5G **27**
Folksworth. *Cambs* 2A **64**
Folkton. *N Yor* 2E **101**
Folla Rule. *Abers* 5E **161**
Follifoot. *N Yor* 4F **99**
The Folly. *Herts* 4B **52**
Folly Cross. *Devn* 2E **11**
Folly Gate. *Devn* 3F **11**
Fonmon. *V Glam* 5D **32**
Fonthill Bishop. *Wilts* 3E **23**
Fonthill Gifford. *Wilts* 3E **23**
Fontmell Magna. *Dors* 1D **14**
Fontwell. *W Sus* 5A **26**
Font-y-gary. *V Glam* 5D **32**
Foodieash. *Fife* 2F **137**
Foolow. *Derbs* 3F **85**
Footdee. *Aber* 3G **153**
Footherley. *Staf* 5F **73**
Foots Cray. *G Lon* 3F **39**
Forbestown. *Abers* 2A **152**
Force Forge. *Cumb* 5E **103**
Force Mills. *Cumb* 5E **103**
Forcett. *N Yor* 3E **105**
Ford. *Arg* 3F **133**
Ford. *Buck* 5F **51**
Ford. *Derbs* 2B **86**
Ford. *Devn*
  nr. Bideford 4E **19**
  nr. Holbeton 3C **8**
  nr. Salcombe 4D **9**
Ford. *Glos* 3F **49**
Ford. *Nmbd* 1D **120**
Ford. *Plym* 3A **8**
Ford. *Shrp* 4G **71**
Ford. *Som*
  nr. Wells 1A **22**
  nr. Wiveliscombe 4D **20**
Ford. *Staf* 5E **85**
Ford. *W Sus* 5B **26**
Ford. *Wilts*
  nr. Chippenham 4D **34**
  nr. Salisbury 3G **23**
Forda. *Devn* 3E **19**
Ford Barton. *Devn* 1C **12**
Fordcombe. *Kent* 1G **27**
Fordell. *Fife* 1E **129**
Forden. *Powy* 5E **71**
Ford End. *Essx* 4G **53**
Forder Green. *Devn* 2D **9**
Ford Green. *Lanc* 5D **97**
Fordham. *Cambs* 3F **65**
Fordham. *Essx* 3C **54**
Fordham. *Norf* 1F **65**
Fordham Heath. *Essx* 3C **54**
Ford Heath. *Shrp* 4G **71**
Fordhouses. *W Mid* 5D **72**
Fordie. *Per* 1G **135**
Fordingbridge. *Hants* 1G **15**
Fordington. *Linc* 3D **88**
Fordon. *E Yor* 2E **101**
Fordoun. *Abers* 1G **145**
Ford Street. *Essx* 3C **54**
Ford Street. *Som* 1E **13**
Fordton. *Devn* 3B **12**
Fordwells. *Oxon* 4B **50**
Fordwich. *Kent* 5F **41**
Fordyce. *Abers* 2C **160**
Forebridge. *Staf* 3D **72**
Foremark. *Derbs* 3H **73**
Forest. *N Yor* 4F **105**
Forestburn Gate. *Nmbd* 5E **121**
Foresterseat. *Mor* 3F **159**
Forest Green. *Glos* 2D **34**
Forest Green. *Surr* 1C **26**
Forest Hall. *Cumb* 4G **103**
Forest Head. *Cumb* 4G **113**
Forest Hill. *Oxon* 5D **50**
Forest-in-Teesdale. *Dur* 2B **104**
Forest Lodge. *Per* 1G **143**
Forest Mill. *Clac* 4B **136**
Forest Row. *E Sus* 2F **27**
Forestside. *W Sus* 1F **17**
Forest Town. *Notts* 4C **86**
Forfar. *Ang* 3D **144**
Forgandenny. *Per* 2C **136**
Forge. *Powy* 1G **57**
The Forge. *Here* 5F **59**
Forge Side. *Torf* 5F **47**
Forgewood. *N Lan* 4A **128**
Forgie. *Mor* 3A **160**
Forgue. *Abers* 4D **160**
Formby. *Mers* 4B **90**
Forncett End. *Norf* 1D **66**
Forncett St Mary. *Norf* 1D **66**
Forncett St Peter. *Norf* 1D **66**
Forneth. *Per* 4H **143**
Fornham All Saints. *Suff* 4H **65**
Fornham St Martin. *Suff* 4A **66**
Forres. *Mor* 3E **159**
Forrestfield. *N Lan* 3B **128**
Forrest Lodge. *Dum* 1C **110**
Forsbrook. *Staf* 1D **72**
Forse. *High* 5E **169**
Forsinard. *High* 4A **168**
Forss. *High* 2C **168**
The Forstal. *Kent* 2E **29**
Forston. *Dors* 3B **14**
Fort Augustus. *High* 3F **149**
Forteviot. *Per* 2C **136**
Fort George. *High* 3B **158**
Forth. *S Lan* 4C **128**
Forthampton. *Glos* 2D **48**
Forthay. *Glos* 2C **34**
Fortingall. *Per* 4E **143**
Fort Matilda. *Inv* 2D **126**
Forton. *Hants* 2C **24**
Forton. *Lanc* 4D **97**
Forton. *Shrp* 4G **71**
Forton. *Som* 2G **13**
Forton. *Staf* 3B **72**
Forton Heath. *Shrp* 4G **71**
Fortrie. *Abers* 4D **160**
Fortrose. *High* 3B **158**
Fortuneswell. *Dors* 5B **14**
Fort William. *High* 1F **141**
Forty Green. *Buck* 1A **38**
Forty Hill. *G Lon* 1E **39**
Forward Green. *Suff* 5C **66**
Fosbury. *Wilts* 1B **24**
Foscot. *Oxon* 3H **49**
Fosdyke. *Linc* 2C **76**
Foss. *Per* 3E **143**
Fossebridge. *Glos* 4F **49**
Foster Street. *Essx* 5E **53**
Foston. *Derbs* 2F **73**
Foston. *Leics* 1D **62**
Foston. *Linc* 1F **75**
Foston. *N Yor* 3A **100**
Foston on the Wolds. *E Yor* 4F **101**
Fotherby. *Linc* 1C **88**
Fothergill. *Cumb* 1B **102**
Fotheringhay. *Nptn* 1H **63**
Foubister. *Orkn* 7E **172**
Foula Airport. *Shet* 8A **173**
Foul Anchor. *Cambs* 4D **76**
Foulbridge. *Cumb* 5F **113**
Foulden. *Norf* 1G **65**
Foulden. *Bord* 4F **131**
Foul Mile. *E Sus* 4H **27**
Foulridge. *Lanc* 5A **98**
Foulsham. *Norf* 3C **78**
Fountainhall. *Bord* 5H **129**
The Four Alls. *Shrp* 2A **72**
Four Ashes. *Staf*
  nr. Cannock 5D **72**
  nr. Kinver 2C **60**
Four Ashes. *Suff* 3C **66**
Four Crosses. *Powy*
  nr. Llanerfyl 5C **70**
  nr. Llanymynech 4E **71**
Four Crosses. *Staf* 5D **72**
Four Elms. *Kent* 1F **27**
Four Forks. *Som* 3F **21**
Four Gotes. *Cambs* 4D **76**
Four Lane End. *S Yor* 4C **92**
Four Lane Ends. *Lanc* 4E **97**
Four Lanes. *Corn* 5A **6**
Fourlanes End. *Ches E* 5C **84**
Four Marks. *Hants* 3E **25**

Four Mile Bridge. *IOA*.....3B 80
Four Oaks. *E Sus*.....3C 28
Four Oaks. *Glos*.....3B 48
Four Oaks. *W Mid*.....2G 61
Four Roads. *Carm*.....5E 45
Four Roads. *IOM*.....5B 108
Fourstones. *Nmbd*.....3B 114
Four Throws. *Kent*.....3B 28
Fovant. *Wilts*.....4F 23
Foveran. *Abers*.....1G 153
Fowey. *Corn*.....3F 7
Fowlershill. *Aber*.....2G 153
Fowley Common. *Warr*.....1A 84
Fowlis. *Ang*.....5C 144
Fowlis Wester. *Per*.....1B 136
Fowlmere. *Cambs*.....1E 53
Fownhope. *Here*.....2A 48
Fox Corner. *Surr*.....5A 38
Foxcote. *Glos*.....4F 49
Foxcote. *Som*.....1C 22
Foxdale. *IOM*.....4B 108
Foxearth. *Essx*.....1B 54
Foxfield. *Cumb*.....1B 96
Foxham. *Wilts*.....4E 35
Fox Hatch. *Essx*.....1G 39
Foxhole. *Corn*.....3D 6
Foxholes. *N Yor*.....2E 101
Foxhunt Green. *E Sus*.....4G 27
Fox Lane. *Hants*.....1G 25
Foxley. *Norf*.....3C 78
Foxley. *Nptn*.....5D 62
Foxley. *Wilts*.....3D 35
Foxlydiate. *Worc*.....4E 61
Fox Street. *Essx*.....3D 54
Foxt. *Staf*.....1E 73
Foxton. *Cambs*.....1E 53
Foxton. *Dur*.....2A 106
Foxton. *Leics*.....2D 62
Foxton. *N Yor*.....5B 106
Foxup. *N Yor*.....2A 98
Foxwist Green. *Ches W*.....4A 84
Foxwood. *Shrp*.....3A 60
Foy. *Here*.....3A 48
Foyers. *High*.....1G 149
Foynesfield. *High*.....3C 158
Fraddam. *Corn*.....3C 4
Fraddon. *Corn*.....3D 6
Fradley. *Staf*.....4F 73
Fradley South. *Staf*.....4F 73
Fradswell. *Staf*.....2D 73
Fraisthorpe. *E Yor*.....3F 101
Framfield. *E Sus*.....3F 27
Framingham Earl. *Norf*.....5E 79
Framingham Pigot. *Norf*.....5E 79
Framlingham. *Suff*.....4E 67
Frampton. *Dors*.....3B 14
Frampton. *Linc*.....2C 76
Frampton Cotterell. *S Glo*.....3B 34
Frampton Mansell. *Glos*.....5E 49
Frampton on Severn. *Glos*.....5C 48
Frampton West End. *Linc*.....1B 76
Framsden. *Suff*.....5D 66
Framwellgate Moor. *Dur*.....5F 115
Franche. *Worc*.....3C 60
Frandley. *Ches W*.....3A 84
Frankby. *Mers*.....2E 83
Frankfort. *Norf*.....3F 79
Frankley. *Worc*.....2D 61
Frank's Bridge. *Powy*.....5D 58
Frankton. *Warw*.....3B 62
Frankwell. *Shrp*.....4G 71
Frant. *E Sus*.....2G 27
Fraserburgh. *Abers*.....2G 161
Frating Green. *Essx*.....3D 54
Fratton. *Port*.....2E 17
Freathy. *Corn*.....3A 8
Freckenham. *Suff*.....3F 65
Freckleton. *Lanc*.....2C 90
Freeby. *Leics*.....3F 75
Freefolk Priors. *Hants*.....2C 24
Freehay. *Staf*.....1E 73
Freeland. *Oxon*.....4C 50
Freester. *Shet*.....6F 173
Freethorpe. *Norf*.....5G 79
Freiston. *Linc*.....1C 76
Freiston Shore. *Linc*.....1C 76
Fremington. *Devn*.....3F 19
Fremington. *N Yor*.....5D 104
Frenchay. *S Glo*.....4B 34
Frenchbeer. *Devn*.....4G 11
Frenich. *Stir*.....3D 134
Frensham. *Surr*.....2G 25
Frenze. *Norf*.....2D 66
Fresgoe. *High*.....2B 168
Freshfield. *Mers*.....4A 90
Freshford. *Bath*.....5C 34
Freshwater. *IOW*.....4B 16
Freshwater Bay. *IOW*.....4B 16
Freshwater East. *Pemb*.....5E 43
Fressingfield. *Suff*.....3E 67
Freston. *Suff*.....2E 55
Freswick. *High*.....2F 169
Fretherne. *Glos*.....5C 48
Frettenham. *Norf*.....4E 79
Freuchie. *Fife*.....3E 137
Freystrop. *Pemb*.....3D 42
Friar's Gate. *E Sus*.....2F 27
Friar Waddon. *Dors*.....4B 14
Friday Bridge. *Cambs*.....5D 76
Friday Street. *E Sus*.....5H 27
Friday Street. *Surr*.....1C 26
Fridaythorpe. *E Yor*.....4C 100
Friden. *Derbs*.....4F 85
Friern Barnet. *G Lon*.....1D 39
Friesthorpe. *Linc*.....2H 87
Frieston. *Linc*.....1G 75
Frieth. *Buck*.....2F 37
Friezeland. *Notts*.....5B 86
Frilford. *Oxon*.....2C 36
Frilsham. *W Ber*.....4D 36
Frimley. *Surr*.....1G 25

Frimley Green. *Surr*.....1G 25
Frindsbury. *Medw*.....4B 40
Fring. *Norf*.....2G 77
Fringford. *Oxon*.....3E 50
Frinsted. *Kent*.....5C 40
Frinton-on-Sea. *Essx*.....4F 55
Friockheim. *Ang*.....4E 145
Friog. *Gwyn*.....4F 69
Frisby. *Leics*.....5E 74
Frisby on the Wreake.
.....4D 74
Friskney. *Linc*.....5D 88
Friskney Eaudyke. *Linc*.....5D 88
Friston. *E Sus*.....5G 27
Friston. *Suff*.....4G 67
Fritchley. *Derbs*.....5A 86
Fritham. *Hants*.....1H 15
Frith Bank. *Linc*.....1C 76
Frith Common. *Worc*.....4A 60
Frithelstock. *Devn*.....1E 11
Frithelstock Stone. *Devn*.....1E 11
Frithsden. *Herts*.....5A 52
Frithville. *Linc*.....5C 88
Frittenden. *Kent*.....1C 28
Frittiscombe. *Devn*.....4E 9
Fritton. *Norf*
    nr. Great Yarmouth.....5G 79
    nr. Long Stratton.....1E 67
Fritwell. *Oxon*.....3D 50
Frizinghall. *W Yor*.....1B 92
Frizington. *Cumb*.....3B 102
Frobost. *W Isl*.....6C 170
Frocester. *Glos*.....5C 48
Frochas. *Powy*.....5D 70
Frodesley. *Shrp*.....5H 71
Frodingham. *N Lin*.....3C 94
Frodsham. *Ches W*.....3H 83
Froggatt. *Derbs*.....3G 85
Froghall. *Staf*.....1E 73
Frogham. *Hants*.....1G 15
Frogham. *Kent*.....5G 41
Frogmore. *Devn*.....4D 8
Frogmore. *Hants*.....5G 37
Frogmore. *Herts*.....5B 52
Frognall. *Linc*.....4A 76
Frogshall. *Norf*.....2E 79
Frogwell. *Corn*.....2H 7
Frolesworth. *Leics*.....1C 62
Frome. *Som*.....2C 22
Fromefield. *Som*.....2C 22
Frome St Quintin. *Dors*.....2A 14
Fromes Hill. *Here*.....1B 48
Fron. *Gwyn*.....2C 68
Fron. *Powy*
    nr. Llandrindod Wells.....4C 58
    nr. Newtown.....1D 58
    nr. Welshpool.....5E 71
Y Fron. *Gwyn*.....5E 81
Froncysyllte. *Wrex*.....1E 71
Frongoch. *Gwyn*.....2B 70
Fron Isaf. *Wrex*.....1E 71
Fronoleu. *Gwyn*.....2G 69
Frosterley. *Dur*.....1D 104
Frotoft. *Orkn*.....5D 172
Froxfield. *C Beds*.....2H 51
Froxfield. *Wilts*.....5A 36
Froxfield Green. *Hants*.....4F 25
Fryern Hill. *Hants*.....4C 24
Fryerning. *Essx*.....5G 53
Fryton. *N Yor*.....2A 100
Fugglestone St Peter. *Wilts*.....3G 23
Fulbeck. *Linc*.....5G 87
Fulbourn. *Cambs*.....5E 65
Fulbrook. *Oxon*.....4A 50
Fulflood. *Hants*.....3C 24
Fulford. *Som*.....4F 21
Fulford. *Staf*.....2D 72
Fulford. *York*.....5A 100
Fulham. *G Lon*.....3D 38
Fulking. *W Sus*.....4D 26
Fuller's Moor. *Ches W*.....5G 83
Fuller Street. *Essx*.....4H 53
Fullerton. *Hants*.....3B 24
Fulletby. *Linc*.....3B 88
Full Sutton. *E Yor*.....4B 100
Fullwood. *E Ayr*.....4F 127
Fulmer. *Buck*.....2A 38
Fulmodeston. *Norf*.....2B 78
Fulnetby. *Linc*.....3H 87
Fulney. *Linc*.....3B 76
Fulstow. *Linc*.....1C 88
Fulthorpe. *Stoc T*.....2B 106
Fulwell. *Tyne*.....4G 115
Fulwood. *Lanc*.....1D 90
Fulwood. *Notts*.....5B 86
Fulwood. *Som*.....1F 13
Fulwood. *S Yor*.....2G 85
Fundenhall. *Norf*.....1D 66
Funtington. *W Sus*.....2G 17
Funtley. *Hants*.....2D 16
Funzie. *Shet*.....2H 173
Furley. *Devn*.....2F 13
Furnace. *Arg*.....3H 133
Furnace. *Carm*.....5F 45
Furnace. *Here*.....1F 57
Furner's Green. *E Sus*.....3F 27
Furness Vale. *Derbs*.....2E 85
Furneux Pelham. *Herts*.....3E 53
Furzebrook. *Dors*.....4E 15
Furzehill. *Devn*.....2H 19
Furzehill. *Dors*.....2F 15
Furzeley Corner. *Hants*.....1E 17
Furzey Lodge. *Hants*.....2B 16
Furzley. *Hants*.....1A 16
Fyfield. *Essx*.....5F 53
Fyfield. *Glos*.....5H 49
Fyfield. *Hants*.....2A 24
Fyfield. *Oxon*.....2C 36
Fyfield. *Wilts*.....5G 35
The Fylde. *Lanc*.....1B 90
Fylingthorpe. *N Yor*.....4G 107

Fyning. *W Sus*.....4G 25
Fyvie. *Abers*.....5E 161

G

Gabhsann bho Dheas. *W Isl*.....2G 171
Gabhsann bho Thuath. *W Isl*.....2G 171
Gabroc Hill. *E Ayr*.....4F 127
Gadbrook. *Surr*.....1D 26
Gaddesby. *Leics*.....4D 74
Gadfa. *IOA*.....2D 80
Gadgirth. *S Ayr*.....2D 116
Gaer. *Powy*.....3E 47
Gaerwen. *IOA*.....3D 81
Gagingwell. *Oxon*.....3C 50
Gaick Lodge. *High*.....5B 150
Gailey. *Staf*.....4D 72
Gainford. *Dur*.....3E 105
Gainsborough. *Linc*.....1F 87
Gainsborough. *Suff*.....1E 55
Gainsford End. *Essx*.....2H 53
Gairletter. *Arg*.....1C 126
Gairloch. *Abers*.....3E 153
Gairloch. *High*.....1H 155
Gairlochy. *High*.....5D 148
Gairney Bank. *Per*.....4D 136
Gairnshiel Lodge. *Abers*.....3G 151
Gaisgill. *Cumb*.....4H 103
Gaitsgill. *Cumb*.....5E 113
Galashiels. *Bord*.....1G 119
Galgate. *Lanc*.....4D 97
Galhampton. *Som*.....4B 22
Gallatown. *Fife*.....4E 137
Galley Common. *Warw*.....1H 61
Galleyend. *Essx*.....5H 53
Galleywood. *Essx*.....5H 53
Gallin. *Per*.....4C 142
Gallowfauld. *Ang*.....4D 144
Gallowhill. *Per*.....5A 144
Gallowhill. *Ren*.....3F 127
Gallowhills. *Abers*.....3H 161
Gallows Green. *Staf*.....1E 73
Gallows Green. *Worc*.....4D 60
Gallowstree Common. *Oxon*.....3E 37
Galltair. *High*.....1G 147
Gallt Melyd. *Den*.....2C 82
Galmington. *Som*.....4F 21
Galmisdale. *High*.....5C 146
Galmpton. *Devn*.....4C 8
Galmpton. *Torb*.....3E 9
Galmpton Warborough. *Torb*.....3E 9
Galphay. *N Yor*.....2E 99
Galston. *E Ayr*.....1D 117
Galton. *Dors*.....4C 14
Galtrigill. *High*.....3A 154
Gamblesby. *Cumb*.....1H 103
Gamelsby. *Cumb*.....4D 112
Gamesley. *Derbs*.....1E 85
Gamlingay. *Cambs*.....5B 64
Gamlingay Cinques. *Cambs*.....5B 64
Gamlingay Great Heath. *Cambs*.....5B 64
Gammaton. *Devn*.....4E 19
Gammersgill. *N Yor*.....1C 98
Gamston. *Notts*
    nr. Nottingham.....2D 74
    nr. Retford.....3E 86
Ganarew. *Here*.....4A 48
Ganavan. *Arg*.....5C 140
Ganborough. *Glos*.....3G 49
Gang. *Corn*.....2H 7
Ganllwyd. *Gwyn*.....3G 69
Gannochy. *Ang*.....1E 145
Gannochy. *Per*.....1D 136
Gansclet. *High*.....4F 169
Ganstead. *E Yor*.....1E 95
Ganthorpe. *N Yor*.....2A 100
Ganton. *N Yor*.....2D 101
Gants Hill. *G Lon*.....2F 39
Gappah. *Devn*.....5B 12
Garafad. *High*.....2D 155
Garboldisham. *Norf*.....2C 66
Garden City. *Flin*.....4F 83
Gardeners Green. *Wok*.....5G 37
Gardenstown. *Abers*.....2E 161
Garden Village. *S Yor*.....1G 85
Garden Village. *Swan*.....3E 31
Garderhouse. *Shet*.....7E 173
Gardham. *E Yor*.....5D 100
Gardie. *Shet*
    on Papa Stour.....5C 173
    on Unst.....1H 173
Gardie Ho. *Shet*.....7F 173
Gare Hill. *Wilts*.....2C 22
Garelochhead. *Arg*.....4B 134
Garford. *Oxon*.....2C 36
Garforth. *W Yor*.....1E 93
Gargrave. *N Yor*.....4B 98
Gargunnock. *Stir*.....4G 135
Garleffin. *S Ayr*.....1F 109
Garlieston. *Dum*.....5B 110
Garlinge Green. *Kent*.....5F 41
Garlogie. *Abers*.....3E 153
Garmelow. *Staf*.....3B 72
Garmond. *Abers*.....3F 161
Garmondsway. *Dur*.....1A 106
Garmony. *Arg*.....4A 140
Garmouth. *Mor*.....2H 159
Garmston. *Shrp*.....5A 72
Garnant. *Carm*.....4G 45
Garndiffaith. *Torf*.....5F 47
Garndolbenmaen. *Gwyn*.....1D 69
Garnett Bridge. *Cumb*.....5G 103
Garnfadryn. *Gwyn*.....2B 68
Garnkirk. *N Lan*.....3H 127
Garnlydan. *Blae*.....4E 47
Garnsgate. *Linc*.....3D 76
Garnswllt. *Swan*.....5G 45
Garn yr Erw. *Torf*.....4F 47
Garrabost. *W Isl*.....4H 171
Garrallan. *E Ayr*.....3E 117

Garras. *Corn*.....4E 5
Garreg. *Gwyn*.....1F 69
Garrigill. *Cumb*.....5A 114
Garriston. *N Yor*.....5E 105
Garroogie Lodge. *High*.....2H 149
Garros. *High*.....2D 155
Garrow. *Per*.....4F 143
Garsdale. *Cumb*.....1G 97
Garsdale Head. *Cumb*.....5A 104
Garsdon. *Wilts*.....3E 35
Garshall Green. *Staf*.....2D 72
Garsington. *Oxon*.....5D 50
Garstang. *Lanc*.....5D 97
Garston. *Mers*.....2G 83
Garswood. *Mers*.....1H 83
Gartcosh. *N Lan*.....3H 127
Garth. *B'end*.....2B 32
Garth. *Cdgn*.....2F 57
Garth. *Gwyn*.....2E 69
Garth. *IOM*.....4C 108
Garth. *Powy*
    nr. Builth Wells.....1C 46
    nr. Knighton.....3E 59
Garth. *Shet*
    nr. Sandness.....6D 173
    nr. Skellister.....6F 173
Garth. *Wrex*.....1E 71
Garthamlock. *Glas*.....3H 127
Garthbrengy. *Powy*.....2D 46
Gartheli. *Cdgn*.....5E 57
Garthmyl. *Powy*.....1D 58
Garthorpe. *Leics*.....3F 75
Garthorpe. *N Lin*.....3B 94
Garth Owen. *Powy*.....1D 58
Garth Place. *Cphy*.....3E 33
Garth Row. *Cumb*.....5G 103
Gartly. *Abers*.....5C 160
Gartmore. *Stir*.....4E 135
Gartness. *N Lan*.....3A 128
Gartness. *Stir*.....1G 127
Gartocharn. *W Dun*.....1F 127
Garton. *E Yor*.....1F 95
Garton-on-the-Wolds. *E Yor*.....4D 101
Gartsherrie. *N Lan*.....3A 128
Gartymore. *High*.....2H 165
Garvald. *E Lot*.....2B 130
Garvamore. *High*.....4H 149
Garvard. *Arg*.....4A 132
Garvault. *High*.....5H 167
Garve. *High*.....2F 157
Garvestone. *Norf*.....5C 78
Garvie. *Arg*.....4H 133
Garvock. *Abers*.....1G 145
Garvock. *Inv*.....2D 126
Garway. *Here*.....3H 47
Garway Common. *Here*.....3H 47
Garway Hill. *Here*.....3H 47
Garwick. *Linc*.....1A 76
Gaskan. *High*.....1C 140
Gasper. *Wilts*.....3C 22
Gastard. *Wilts*.....5D 35
Gasthorpe. *Norf*.....2B 66
Gatcombe. *IOW*.....4C 16
Gateacre. *Mers*.....2G 83
Gatebeck. *Cumb*.....1E 97
Gate Burton. *Linc*.....2F 87
Gateforth. *N Yor*.....2F 93
Gatehead. *E Ayr*.....1C 116
Gate Helmsley. *N Yor*.....4A 100
Gatehouse. *Nmbd*.....1A 114
Gatehouse of Fleet. *Dum*.....4D 110
Gatelawbridge. *Dum*.....5B 118
Gateley. *Norf*.....3B 78
Gatenby. *N Yor*.....1F 99
Gatesgarth. *Cumb*.....3C 102
Gateshead. *Tyne*.....3F 115
Gatesheath. *Ches W*.....4G 83
Gateside. *Ang*
    nr. Forfar.....4D 144
    nr. Kirriemuir.....4C 144
Gateside. *Fife*.....3D 136
Gateside. *N Ayr*.....4E 127
Gathurst. *G Man*.....4D 90
Gatley. *G Man*.....2C 84
Gatton. *Surr*.....5D 39
Gattonside. *Bord*.....1H 119
Gatwick Airport. *W Sus*.....216 (1D 27)
Gaufron. *Powy*.....4B 58
Gaulby. *Leics*.....5D 74
Gauldry. *Fife*.....1F 137
Gaultree. *Norf*.....5D 77
Gaunt's Common. *Dors*.....2F 15
Gaunt's Earthcott. *S Glo*.....3B 34
Gautby. *Linc*.....3A 88
Gavinton. *Bord*.....4D 130
Gawber. *S Yor*.....4D 92
Gawcott. *Buck*.....2E 51
Gawsworth. *Ches E*.....4C 84
Gawthorpe. *W Yor*.....2C 92
Gawthrop. *Cumb*.....1F 97
Gawthwaite. *Cumb*.....1B 96
Gay Bowers. *Essx*.....5A 54
Gaydon. *Warw*.....5A 62
Gayfield. *Orkn*.....2D 172
Gayhurst. *Mil*.....1G 51
Gayle. *N Yor*.....1A 98
Gayles. *N Yor*.....4E 105
Gay Street. *W Sus*.....3B 26
Gayton. *Mers*.....2E 83
Gayton. *Norf*.....4G 77
Gayton. *Nptn*.....5E 62
Gayton. *Staf*.....3D 73
Gayton le Marsh. *Linc*.....2D 88
Gayton le Wold. *Linc*.....2B 88
Gayton Thorpe. *Norf*.....4G 77
Gaywood. *Norf*.....3F 77
Gazeley. *Suff*.....4G 65
Geanies. *High*.....1C 158
Gearraidh Bhaltos. *W Isl*.....4D 171
Gearraidh Bhaird. *W Isl*.....6F 171
Gearraidh ma Monadh. *W Isl*.....7C 170

Gearraidh na h-Aibhne. *W Isl*.....4E 171
Geary. *High*.....2B 154
Geddes. *High*.....3C 158
Gedding. *Suff*.....5B 66
Geddington. *Nptn*.....2F 63
Gedintailor. *High*.....5E 155
Gedling. *Notts*.....1D 74
Gedney. *Linc*.....3D 76
Gedney Broadgate. *Linc*.....3D 76
Gedney Drove End. *Linc*.....3D 76
Gedney Dyke. *Linc*.....3D 76
Gedney Hill. *Linc*.....4C 76
Gee Cross. *G Man*.....1D 84
Geeston. *Rut*.....5G 75
Geilston. *Arg*.....2E 127
Geirinis. *W Isl*.....4C 170
Geise. *High*.....2D 168
Geisiadar. *W Isl*.....4D 171
Gelder Shiel. *Abers*.....5G 151
Geldeston. *Norf*.....1F 67
Gell. *Cnwy*.....4A 82
Gelli. *Pemb*.....3E 43
Gelli. *Rhon*.....2C 32
Gellifor. *Den*.....4D 82
Gelligaer. *Cphy*.....2E 33
Y Gelli Gandryll. *Powy*.....1F 47
Gellilydan. *Gwyn*.....2F 69
Gellinudd. *Neat*.....5H 45
Gellyburn. *Per*.....5H 143
Gellywen. *Carm*.....2G 43
Gelston. *Dum*.....4E 111
Gelston. *Linc*.....1G 75
Gembling. *E Yor*.....4F 101
Geneva. *Cdgn*.....5D 56
Gentleshaw. *Staf*.....4E 73
Geocrab. *W Isl*.....8D 171
George Green. *Buck*.....2A 38
Georgeham. *Devn*.....3E 19
George Nympton. *Devn*.....4H 19
Georgetown. *Blae*.....5E 47
Georgetown. *Ren*.....3F 127
Georth. *Orkn*.....5C 172
Gerlan. *Gwyn*.....4F 81
Germansweek. *Devn*.....3E 11
Germoe. *Corn*.....4C 4
Gerrans. *Corn*.....5C 6
Gerrard's Bromley. *Staf*.....2B 72
Gerrards Cross. *Buck*.....2A 38
Gerston. *High*.....3D 168
Gestingthorpe. *Essx*.....2B 54
Gethsemane. *Pemb*.....1A 44
Geuffordd. *Powy*.....4E 70
Gibraltar. *Buck*.....4F 51
Gibraltar. *Linc*.....5E 89
Gibraltar. *Suff*.....5D 66
Gibsmere. *Notts*.....1E 74
Giddeahall. *Wilts*.....4D 34
Gidea Park. *G Lon*.....2G 39
Gidleigh. *Devn*.....4G 11
Giffnock. *E Ren*.....4G 127
Gifford. *E Lot*.....3B 130
Giffordtown. *Fife*.....2E 137
Giggetty. *Staf*.....1C 60
Giggleswick. *N Yor*.....3H 97
Gilberdyke. *E Yor*.....2B 94
Gilbert's End. *Worc*.....1D 48
Gilbert's Green. *Warw*.....3F 61
Gilchriston. *E Lot*.....3A 130
Gilcrux. *Cumb*.....1C 102
Gildersome. *W Yor*.....2C 92
Gildingwells. *S Yor*.....2C 86
Gilesgate Moor. *Dur*.....5F 115
Gileston. *V Glam*.....5D 32
Gilfach. *Cphy*.....2E 33
Gilfach Goch. *Rhon*.....3C 32
Gilfachreda. *Cdgn*.....5D 56
Gilgarran. *Cumb*.....2B 102
Gillamoor. *N Yor*.....5D 107
Gillan. *Corn*.....4E 5
Gillar's Green. *Mers*.....1G 83
Gillen. *High*.....3B 154
Gilling East. *N Yor*.....2A 100
Gillingham. *Dors*.....4D 22
Gillingham.
    Medw
    .....Medway Towns 204 (4B 40)
Gillingham. *Norf*.....1G 67
Gilling West. *N Yor*.....4E 105
Gillock. *High*.....3E 169
Gillow Heath. *Staf*.....5C 84
Gills. *High*.....1F 169
Gilmanscleuch. *Bord*.....2F 119
Gilmerton. *Edin*.....3F 129
Gilmerton. *Per*.....1A 136
Gilmonby. *Dur*.....3C 104
Gilmorton. *Leics*.....2C 62
Gilsland. *Nmbd*.....3H 113
Gilsland Spa. *Cumb*.....3H 113
Gilston. *Bord*.....4H 129
Giltbrook. *Notts*.....1B 74
Gilwern. *Mon*.....4F 47
Gimingham. *Norf*.....2E 79
Giosla. *W Isl*.....4D 171
Gipping. *Suff*.....4C 66
Gipsey Bridge. *Linc*.....1B 76
Gipton. *W Yor*.....1D 92
Girdle Toll. *N Ayr*.....5E 127
Girlsta. *Shet*.....6F 173
Girsby. *N Yor*.....4A 106
Girthon. *Dum*.....4D 110
Girton. *Cambs*.....4D 64
Girton. *Notts*.....4F 87
Girvan. *S Ayr*.....5A 116
Gisburn. *Lanc*.....5H 97
Gisleham. *Suff*.....2H 67
Gislingham. *Suff*.....3C 66
Gissing. *Norf*.....2D 66
Gittisham. *Devn*.....3E 13
Gladestry. *Powy*.....5E 59

Gladsmuir. E Lot 2A 130
Glaichbea. High 5H 157
Glais. Swan 5H 45
Glaisdale. N Yor 4E 107
Glame. High 4E 155
Glamis. Ang 4C 144
Glanaman. Carm 4G 45
Glan-Conwy. Cnwy 5H 81
Glandford. Norf 1C 78
Glan Duar. Carm 1F 45
Glandwr. Blae 5F 47
Glandwr. Pemb 2F 43
Glan-Dwyfach. Gwyn 1D 69
Glandy Cross. Carm 2F 43
Glandyfi. Cdgn 1F 57
Glangrwyney. Powy 4F 47
Glanmule. Powy 1D 58
Glan-rhyd. Pemb 1F 43
Glan-rhyd. Powy 5A 46
Glanrhyd. Gwyn 2B 68
Glanrhyd. Pemb 1B 44
Glanton. Nmbd 3E 121
Glanton Pyke. Nmbd 3E 121
Glanvilles Wootton. Dors 2B 14
Glan-y-don. Flin 3D 82
Glan-y-nant. Powy 2B 58
Glan-yr-afon. Gwyn 1C 70
Glan-yr-afon. IOA 2F 81
Glan-yr-afon. Powy 5C 70
Glan-y-wern. Gwyn 2F 69
Glapthorn. Nptn 1H 63
Glapwell. Derbs 4B 86
Glas Aird. Arg 4A 132
Glasbury. Powy 2E 47
Glaschoil. High 5E 159
Glascoed. Den 3B 82
Glascoed. Mon 5G 47
Glascote. Staf 5G 73
Glascwm. Powy 5D 58
Glasfryn. Cnwy 5B 82
Glasgow. Glas 196 (3G 127)
Glasgow Airport. Ren 216 (3F 127)
Glasgow Prestwick Airport.
S Ayr 2C 116
Glashvin. High 2D 154
Glasinfryn. Gwyn 4E 81
Glas na Cardaich. High 4E 147
Glasnacardoch. High 4E 147
Glasnakille. High 2D 146
Glaspwll. Cdgn 1G 57
Glassburn. High 5F 157
Glassenbury. Kent 2B 28
Glasserton. Dum 5B 110
Glassford. S Lan 5A 128
Glassgreen. Mor 2G 159
Glasshouse. Glos 3C 48
Glasshouses. N Yor 3D 98
Glasson. Cumb 3D 112
Glasson. Lanc 4D 96
Glassonby. Cumb 1G 103
Glasterlaw. Ang 3E 145
Glaston. Rut 5F 75
Glastonbury. Som 3H 21
Glatton. Cambs 2A 64
Glazebrook. Warr 1A 84
Glazebury. Warr 1A 84
Glazeley. Shrp 2B 60
Gleadless. S Yor 2A 86
Gleadsmoss. Ches E 4C 84
Gleann Dail bho Dheas. W Isl ... 7C 170
Gleann Tholastaidh. W Isl 3H 171
Gleann Uige. High 1A 140
Gleaston. Cumb 2B 96
Glecknabae. Arg 3B 126
Gledrid. Shrp 2E 71
Gleiniant. Powy 1B 58
Glemsford. Suff 1B 54
Glen. Dum 4C 110
Glenancross. High 4E 147
Glen Auldyn. IOM 2D 108
Glenbarr. Arg 2A 122
Glenbeg. High 2G 139
Glen Bernisdale. High 4D 154
Glenbervie. Abers 5E 153
Glenboig. N Lan 3A 128
Glenborrodale. High 2A 140
Glenbranter. Arg 4A 134
Glenbreck. Bord 2C 118
Glenbrein Lodge. High 2G 149
Glenbrittle. High 1C 146
Glenbuchat Lodge. Abers 2H 151
Glenbuck. E Ayr 2G 117
Glenburn. Ren 3F 127
Glencalvie Lodge. High 5B 164
Glencaple. Dum 3A 112
Glencarron Lodge. High 3C 156
Glencarse. Per 1D 136
Glencassley Castle. High 3B 164
Glencat. Abers 4C 152
Glencoe. High 3F 141
Glen Cottage. High 5E 147
Glencraig. Fife 4D 136
Glendale. High 4A 154
Glendevon. Per 3B 136
Glendoebeg. High 3G 149
Glendoick. Per 1E 136
Glendoune. S Ayr 5A 116
Glenduckie. Fife 2E 137
Gleneagles. Per 3B 136
Glenegedale. Arg 4B 124
Glenegedale Lots. Arg 4B 124
Glenelg. High 2G 147
Glenernie. Mor 4E 159
Glenesslin. Dum 1F 111
Glenfarg. Per 2D 136
Glenfarquhar Lodge. Abers 5E 152
Glenferness Mains. High 4D 158
Glenfeshie Lodge. High 4C 150
Glenfiddich Lodge. Mor 5H 159
Glenfield. Leics 5C 74

Glenfinnan. High 5B 148
Glenfintaig Lodge. High 5E 148
Glenfoot. Per 2D 136
Glenfyne Lodge. Arg 2B 134
Glengarnock. N Ayr 4E 126
Glengap. Dum 4D 110
Glengarrasco. High 4D 154
Glengolly. High 2D 168
Glengorm Castle. Arg 3F 139
Glengrasco. High 4D 154
Glenhead Farm. Ang 2B 144
Glenholm. Bord 1D 118
Glenhurich. High 2C 140
Glenkerry. Bord 3E 119
Glenkiln. Dum 2F 111
Glenkindie. Abers 2B 152
Glenkinglass Lodge. Arg 5F 141
Glenkirk. Bord 2C 118
Glenlean. Arg 1B 126
Glenlee. Dum 1D 110
Glenleraig. High 5B 166
Glenlichorn. Per 2G 135
Glenlivet. Mor 1F 151
Glenlochar. Dum 3E 111
Glenlochsie Lodge. Per 1H 143
Glenluce. Dum 4G 109
Glenmarksie. High 3F 157
Glenmassan. Arg 1C 126
Glenmavis. N Lan 3A 128
Glen Maye. IOM 4B 108
Glenmazeran Lodge. High 1B 150
Glenmidge. Dum 1F 111
Glen Mona. IOM 3D 108
Glenmore. High
nr. Glenborrodale 2G 139
nr. Kingussie 3D 151
on Isle of Skye 4D 154
Glenmoy. Ang 2D 144
Glennoe. Arg 5E 141
Glen of Coachford. Abers 4B 160
Glenogil. Ang 2D 144
Glen Parva. Leics 1C 62
Glenprosen Village. Ang 2C 144
Glenree. N Ayr 3D 122
Glenridding. Cumb 3E 103
Glenrosa. N Ayr 2E 123
Glenrothes. Fife 3E 137
Glensanda. Abers 4C 140
Glensaugh. Abers 1F 145
Glenshero Lodge. High 4H 149
Glensluain. Arg 4H 133
Glenstockadale. Dum 3F 109
Glenstriven. Arg 2B 126
Glen Tanar House. Abers 4B 152
Glentham. Linc 1H 87
Glenton. Abers 1D 152
Glentress. Bord 1E 119
Glentromie Lodge. High 4B 150
Glen Trool Lodge. Dum 1B 110
Glentrool Village. Dum 2A 110
Glentruim House. High 4A 150
Glentworth. Linc 2G 87
Glenuig. High 1A 140
Glen Village. Falk 2B 128
Glen Vine. IOM 4C 108
Glenwhilly. Dum 2G 109
Glenzierfoot. Dum 2E 113
Glespin. S Lan 2H 117
Gletness. Shet 6F 173
Glewstone. Here 3A 48
Glib Cheois. W Isl 5F 171
Glinton. Pet 5A 76
Glooston. Leics 1E 63
Glossop. Derbs 1E 85
Gloster Hill. Nmbd 4G 121
Gloucester. Glos 196 (4D 48)
Gloucestershire Airport. Glos ... 3D 49
Gloup. Shet 1G 173
Glusburn. N Yor 5C 98
Glutt Lodge. High 5B 168
Glutton Bridge. Derbs 4E 85
Gluvian. Corn 2D 6
Glympton. Oxon 3C 50
Glyn. Cnwy 3A 82
Glynarthen. Cdgn 1D 44
Glynbrochan. Powy 2B 58
Glyn Ceiriog. Wrex 2E 70
Glyncoch. Rhon 2D 32
Glyncorrwg. Neat 2B 32
Glynde. E Sus 5F 27
Glyndebourne. E Sus 4F 27
Glyndyfrdwy. Den 1D 70
Glyn Ebwy. Blae 5E 47
Glynllan. B'end 3C 32
Glyn-neath. Neat 5B 46
Glynogwr. B'end 3C 32
Glyntaff. Rhon 3D 32
Glyntawe. Powy 4B 46
Glynteg. Carm 2D 44
Gnosall. Staf 3C 72
Gnosall Heath. Staf 3C 72
Goadby. Leics 1E 63
Goadby Marwood. Leics 3E 75
Goatacre. Wilts 4F 35
Goathill. Dors 1B 14
Goathland. N Yor 4F 107
Goathurst. Som 3F 21
Goathurst Common. Kent 5F 39
Goat Lees. Kent 1E 28
Gobernuisgach Lodge. High 4E 167
Gobernuisgeach. High 5B 168
Gobhaig. W Isl 7C 171
Gobowen. Shrp 2F 71
Godalming. Surr 1A 26
Goddard's Corner. Suff 4E 67
Goddard's Green. Kent
nr. Benenden 2C 28
nr. Cranbrook 2B 28
Goddards' Green. W Sus 3D 27
Godford Cross. Devn 2E 13
Godleybrook. Staf 1D 73

Godmanchester. Cambs 3B 64
Godmanstone. Dors 3B 14
Godmersham. Kent 5E 41
Godolphin Cross. Corn 3D 4
Godre'r-graig. Neat 5A 46
Godshill. Hants 1G 15
Godshill. IOW 4D 16
Godstone. Staf 2E 73
Godstone. Surr 5E 39
Goetre. Mon 5G 47
Goff's Oak. Herts 5D 52
Gogar. Edin 2E 129
Goginan. Cdgn 2F 57
Golan. Gwyn 1E 69
Golant. Corn 3F 7
Golberdon. Corn 5D 10
Golborne. G Man 1A 84
Golcar. W Yor 3A 92
Goldcliff. Newp 3G 33
Golden Cross. E Sus 4G 27
Golden Green. Kent 1H 27
Golden Grove. Carm 4F 45
Golden Grove. N Yor 4F 107
Goldenhill. Stoke 5C 84
Golden Pot. Hants 2F 25
Golden Valley. Glos 3E 49
Golders Green. G Lon 2D 38
Goldhanger. Essx 5C 54
Gold Hill. Norf 1E 65
Golding. Shrp 5H 71
Goldington. Bed 5H 63
Goldsborough. N Yor
nr. Harrogate 4F 99
nr. Whitby 3F 107
Goldsithney. Corn 3C 4
Goldstone. Kent 4G 41
Goldstone. Shrp 3B 72
Goldthorpe. S Yor 4E 93
Goldworthy. Devn 4D 19
Golfa. Powy 3D 70
Gollanfield. High 3C 158
Gollinglith Foot. N Yor 1D 98
Golsoncott. Som 3D 20
Golspie. High 4F 165
Gomeldon. Wilts 3G 23
Gomersal. W Yor 2C 92
Gometra House. Arg 4E 139
Gomshall. Surr 1B 26
Gonalston. Notts 1D 74
Gonerby Hill Foot. Linc 2G 75
Gonfirth. Shet 5E 173
Good Easter. Essx 4G 53
Gooderstone. Norf 5G 77
Goodleigh. Devn 3G 19
Goodmanham. E Yor 5C 100
Goodmayes. G Lon 2F 39
Goodnestone. Kent
nr. Aylesham 5G 41
nr. Faversham 4E 41
Goodrich. Here 4A 48
Goodrington. Torb 3E 9
Goodshaw. Lanc 2G 91
Goodshaw Fold. Lanc 2G 91
Goodstone. Devn 5A 12
Goodwick. Pemb 1D 42
Goodworth Clatford. Hants 2B 24
Goole. E Yor 2H 93
Goom's Hill. Worc 5E 61
Goonabarn. Corn 3D 6
Goonbell. Corn 4B 6
Goonhavern. Corn 3B 6
Goonlaze. Corn 5B 6
Goonvrea. Corn 4B 6
Goose Green. Cumb 1E 97
Goose Green. S Glo 3C 34
Gooseham. Corn 1C 10
Goosewell. Plym 3B 8
Goosey. Oxon 2B 36
Goosnargh. Lanc 1D 90
Goostrey. Ches E 3B 84
Gorcott Hill. Warw 4E 61
Gord. Shet 9F 173
Gordon. Bord 5C 130
Gordonbush. High 3F 165
Gordonstown. Abers
nr. Cornhill 3C 160
nr. Fyvie 5E 160
Gorebridge. Midl 3G 129
Gorefield. Cambs 4D 76
Gores. Wilts 1G 23
Gorgie. Edin 2F 129
Goring. Oxon 3E 36
Goring-by-Sea. W Sus 5C 26
Goring Heath. Oxon 4E 37
Gorleston-on-Sea. Norf 5H 79
Gornalwood. W Mid 1D 60
Gorran Churchtown. Corn 4D 6
Gorran Haven. Corn 4E 6
Gorran High Lanes. Corn 4D 6
Gors. Cdgn 3F 57
Gorsedd. Flin 3D 82
Gorseinon. Swan 3E 31
Gorseness. Orkn 6D 172
Gorseybank. Derbs 5G 85
Gorsgoch. Cdgn 5D 57
Gorslas. Carm 4F 45
Gorsley. Glos 3B 48
Gorsley Common. Here 3B 48
Gorstan. High 2F 157
Gorstella. Ches W 4F 83
Gorsty Common. Here 2H 47
Gorsty Hill. Staf 3F 73
Gortantaoid. Arg 2B 124
Gorteneorn. High 2A 140
Gorton. G Man 1C 84
Gosbeck. Suff 5D 66
Gosberton. Linc 2B 76
Gosberton Cheal. Linc 3B 76
Gosberton Clough. Linc 3A 76

Goseley Dale. Derbs 3H 73
Gosfield. Essx 3A 54
Gosford. Oxon 4D 50
Gosforth. Cumb 4B 102
Gosforth. Tyne 3F 115
Gosmore. Herts 3B 52
Gospel End. Staf 1C 60
Gosport. Hants 3E 16
Gossabrough. Shet 3G 173
Gossington. Glos 5C 48
Gossops Green. W Sus 2D 26
Goswick. Nmbd 5G 131
Gotham. Notts 2C 74
Gotherington. Glos 3E 49
Gott. Arg 4B 138
Gott. Shet 7F 173
Goulceby. Linc 3B 88
Gourdon. Abers 1H 145
Gourock. Inv 2D 126
Govan. Glas 3G 127
Govanhill. Glas 3G 127
Goverton. Notts 1E 74
Goveton. Devn 4D 8
Govilon. Mon 4F 47
Gowanhill. Abers 2H 161
Gowdall. E Yor 2G 93
Gowerton. Swan 3E 31
Gowkhall. Fife 1D 128
Gowthorpe. E Yor 4B 100
Goxhill. E Yor 5F 101
Goxhill. N Lin 2E 94
Goxhill Haven. N Lin 2E 94
Goytre. Neat 3A 32
Grabhair. W Isl 6F 171
Graby. Linc 3H 75
Graffham. W Sus 4A 26
Grafham. Cambs 4A 64
Grafham. Surr 1B 26
Grafton. Here 2H 47
Grafton. N Yor 3G 99
Grafton. Oxon 5A 50
Grafton. Shrp 4G 71
Grafton. Worc
nr. Evesham 2E 49
nr. Leominster 4H 59
Grafton Flyford. Worc 5D 60
Grafton Regis. Nptn 1F 51
Grafton Underwood. Nptn 2G 63
Grafty Green. Kent 1C 28
Graianrhyd. Den 5E 82
Graig. Carm 5E 45
Graig. Cnwy 3H 81
Graig. Den 3C 82
Graig-fechan. Den 5D 82
Graig Penllyn. V Glam 4C 32
Grain. Medw 3C 40
Grainsby. Linc 1B 88
Grainthorpe. Linc 1C 88
Grainthorpe Fen. Linc 1C 88
Graiselound. N Lin 1E 87
Gramasdail. W Isl 3D 170
Grampound. Corn 4D 6
Grampound Road. Corn 3D 6
Granborough. Buck 3F 51
Granby. Notts 2E 75
Grandborough. Warw 4B 62
Grandpont. Oxon 5D 50
Grandtully. Per 3G 143
Grange. Cumb 3D 102
Grange. E Ayr 1D 116
Grange. Here 3G 59
Grange. Mers 2E 82
Grange. Per 1E 137
The Grange. N Yor 5C 106
Grange Crossroads. Mor 3B 160
Grange Hill. Essx 1F 39
Grangemill. Derbs 5G 85
Grange Moor. W Yor 3C 92
Grangemouth. Falk 1C 128
Grange of Lindores. Fife 2E 137
Grange-over-Sands. Cumb 2D 96
Grangepans. Falk 1D 128
Grangetown. Card 4E 33
Grangetown. Red C 2C 106
Grange Villa. Dur 4F 115
Granish. High 2C 150
Gransmoor. E Yor 4F 101
Granston. Pemb 1C 42
Grantchester. Cambs 5D 64
Grantham. Linc 2G 75
Grantley. N Yor 3E 99
Grantlodge. Abers 2E 152
Granton. Edin 2F 129
Grantown-on-Spey. High 1E 151
Grantshouse. Bord 3E 130
Grappenhall. Warr 2A 84
Grasby. Linc 4D 94
Grasmere. Cumb 4E 103
Grasscroft. G Man 4H 91
Grassendale. Mers 2F 83
Grassgarth. Cumb 5E 113
Grassholme. Dur 2C 104
Grassington. N Yor 3C 98
Grassmoor. Derbs 4B 86
Grassthorpe. Notts 4E 87
Grateley. Hants 2A 24
Gratton. Devn 1D 11
Gratton. Staf 5D 84
Gratwich. Staf 2E 73
Graveley. Cambs 4B 64
Graveley. Herts 3C 52
Gravelhill. Shrp 4G 71
Gravel Hole. G Man 4H 91
Gravelly Hill. W Mid 1F 61
Graven. Shet 4F 173
Graveney. Kent 4E 41
Gravesend. Kent 3H 39
Grayingham. Linc 1G 87
Grayrigg. Cumb 5G 103
Grays. Thur 3H 39

Grayshott. Hants 3G 25
Grayson Green. Cumb 2A 102
Grayswood. Surr 2A 26
Graythorp. Hart 2C 106
Grazeley. Wok 5E 37
Grealin. High 2E 155
Greasbrough. S Yor 1B 86
Greasby. Mers 2E 83
Great Abington. Cambs 1F 53
Great Addington. Nptn 3G 63
Great Alne. Warw 5F 61
Great Altcar. Lanc 4B 90
Great Amwell. Herts 4D 52
Great Asby. Cumb 3H 103
Great Ashfield. Suff 4B 66
Great Ayton. N Yor 3C 106
Great Baddow. Essx 5H 53
Great Bardfield. Essx 2G 53
Great Barford. Bed 5A 64
Great Barr. W Mid 1E 61
Great Barrington. Glos 4H 49
Great Barrow. Ches W 4G 83
Great Barton. Suff 4A 66
Great Barugh. N Yor 2B 100
Great Bavington. Nmbd 1C 114
Great Bealings. Suff 1F 55
Great Bedwyn. Wilts 5A 36
Great Bentley. Essx 3E 54
Great Billing. Nptn 4F 63
Great Bircham. Norf 2G 77
Great Blakenham. Suff 5D 66
Great Blencow. Cumb 1F 103
Great Bolas. Telf 3A 72
Great Bookham. Surr 5C 38
Great Bosullow. Corn 3B 4
Great Bourton. Oxon 1C 50
Great Bowden. Leics 2E 63
Great Bradley. Suff 5F 65
Great Braxted. Essx 4B 54
Great Bricett. Suff 5C 66
Great Brickhill. Buck 2H 51
Great Bridgeford. Staf 3C 72
Great Brington. Nptn 4D 62
Great Bromley. Essx 3D 54
Great Broughton. Cumb 1B 102
Great Broughton. N Yor 4C 106
Great Budworth. Ches W 3A 84
Great Burdon. Darl 3A 106
Great Burstead. Essx 1A 40
Great Busby. N Yor 4C 106
Great Canfield. Essx 4F 53
Great Carlton. Linc 2D 88
Great Casterton. Rut 5G 75
Great Chalfield. Wilts 5D 34
Great Chart. Kent 1D 28
Great Chatwell. Staf 4B 72
Great Chesterford. Essx 1F 53
Great Cheverell. Wilts 1E 23
Great Chilton. Dur 1F 105
Great Chishill. Cambs 2E 53
Great Clacton. Essx 4E 55
Great Cliff. W Yor 3D 92
Great Clifton. Cumb 2B 102
Great Coates. NE Lin 3F 95
Great Comberton. Worc 1E 49
Great Corby. Cumb 4F 113
Great Cornard. Suff 1B 54
Great Cowden. E Yor 5G 101
Great Coxwell. Oxon 2A 36
Great Crakehall. N Yor 5F 105
Great Cransley. Nptn 3F 63
Great Cressingham. Norf 5A 78
Great Crosby. Mers 4B 90
Great Cubley. Derbs 2F 73
Great Dalby. Leics 4E 75
Great Doddington. Nptn 4F 63
Great Doward. Here 4A 48
Great Dunham. Norf 4A 78
Great Dunmow. Essx 3G 53
Great Durnford. Wilts 3G 23
Great Easton. Essx 3G 53
Great Easton. Leics 1F 63
Great Eccleston. Lanc 5D 96
Great Edstone. N Yor 1B 100
Great Ellingham. Norf 1C 66
Great Elm. Som 2C 22
Great Eppleton. Tyne 5G 115
Great Eversden. Cambs 5C 64
Great Fencote. N Yor 5F 105
Great Finborough. Suff 5C 66
Greatford. Linc 4H 75
Great Fransham. Norf 4A 78
Great Gaddesden. Herts 4A 52
Great Gate. Staf 1E 73
Great Gidding. Cambs 2A 64
Great Givendale. E Yor 4C 100
Great Glemham. Suff 4F 67
Great Glen. Leics 1D 62
Great Gonerby. Linc 2F 75
Great Gransden. Cambs 5B 64
Great Green. Norf 2E 67
Great Green. Suff
nr. Lavenham 5B 66
nr. Palgrave 3D 66
Great Habton. N Yor 2B 100
Great Hale. Linc 1A 76
Great Hallingbury. Essx 4F 53
Greatham. Hants 3F 25
Greatham. Hart 2B 106
Greatham. W Sus 4B 26
Great Hampden. Buck 5G 51
Great Harrowden. Nptn 3F 63
Great Harwood. Lanc 1F 91
Great Haseley. Oxon 5E 51
Great Hatfield. E Yor 5F 101
Great Haywood. Staf 3D 73
Great Heath. W Mid 2H 61
Great Heck. N Yor 2F 93
Great Henny. Essx 2B 54
Great Hinton. Wilts 1E 23
Great Hockham. Norf 1B 66

Great Holland. Essx........4F 55
Great Horkesley. Essx.......2C 54
Great Hormead. Herts......2E 53
Great Horton. W Yor........1B 92
Great Horwood. Buck.......2F 51
Great Houghton. Nptn......5E 63
Great Houghton. S Yor......4E 93
Great Hucklow. Derbs......3F 85
Great Kelk. E Yor..........4F 101
Great Kendale. E Yor.......3E 101
Great Kimble. Buck.........5G 51
Great Kingshill. Buck.......2G 37
Great Langdale. Cumb......4D 102
Great Langton. N Yor.......5F 105
Great Leighs. Essx.........4H 53
Great Limber. Linc.........4E 95
Great Linford. Mil..........1G 51
Great Livermere. Suff.......3A 66
Great Longstone. Derbs.....3G 85
Great Lumley. Dur.........5F 115
Great Lyth. Shrp...........5G 71
Great Malvern. Worc......1C 48
Great Maplestead. Essx.....2B 54
Great Marton. Bkpl........1B 90
Great Massingham. Norf....3G 77
Great Melton. Norf........5D 78
Great Milton. Oxon........5E 51
Great Missenden. Buck.....5G 51
Great Mitton. Lanc.........1F 91
Great Mongeham. Kent.....5H 41
Great Moulton. Norf.......1D 66
Great Munden. Herts.......3D 52
Great Musgrave. Cumb......3A 104
Great Ness. Shrp...........4F 71
Great Notley. Essx.........3H 53
Great Oak. Mon............5G 47
Great Oakley. Essx.........3E 55
Great Oakley. Nptn.........2F 63
Great Offley. Herts.........3B 52
Great Ormside. Cumb.......3A 104
Great Orton. Cumb.........4E 113
Great Ouseburn. N Yor.....3G 99
Great Oxendon. Nptn.......2E 63
Great Oxney Green. Essx....5G 53
Great Parndon. Essx........5E 53
Great Paxton. Cambs.......4B 64
Great Plumpton. Lanc......1B 90
Great Plumstead. Norf......4F 79
Great Ponton. Linc.........2G 75
Great Potheridge. Devn.....1F 11
Great Preston. W Yor.......2E 93
Great Raveley. Cambs.......2B 64
Great Rissington. Glos......4G 49
Great Rollright. Oxon.......2B 50
Great Ryburgh. Norf........3B 78
Great Ryle. Nmbd..........3E 121
Great Ryton. Shrp..........5G 71
Great Saling. Essx..........3H 53
Great Salkeld. Cumb.......1G 103
Great Sampford. Essx.......2G 53
Great Sankey. Warr.......2H 83
Great Saredon. Staf........5D 72
Great Saxham. Suff.........4G 65
Great Shefford. W Ber......4B 36
Great Shelford. Cambs......5D 64
Great Shoddesden. Hants...2A 24
Great Smeaton. N Yor......4A 106
Great Snoring. Norf........2B 78
Great Somerford. Wilts.....3E 35
Great Stainton. Darl.......2A 106
Great Stambridge. Essx.....1C 40
Great Staughton. Cambs....4A 64
Great Steeping. Linc.......4D 88
Great Stonar. Kent.........5H 41
Greatstone-on-Sea. Kent....3E 29
Great Strickland. Cumb.....2G 103
Great Stukeley. Cambs......3B 64
Great Sturton. Linc.........3B 88
Great Sutton. Ches W.......3F 83
Great Sutton. Shrp.........2H 59
Great Swinburne. Nmbd.....2C 114
Great Tew. Oxon...........3B 50
Great Tey. Essx............3B 54
Great Thirkleby. N Yor.....2G 99
Great Thorness. IOW.......3C 16
Great Thurlow. Suff........5F 65
Great Torr. Devn...........4C 8
Great Torrington. Devn.....1E 11
Great Tosson. Nmbd........4E 121
Great Totham North. Essx...4B 54
Great Totham South. Essx...4B 54
Great Tows. Linc..........1B 88
Great Urswick. Cumb.......2B 96
Great Wakering. Essx.......2D 40
Great Waldingfield. Suff.....1C 54
Great Walsingham. Norf.....2B 78
Great Waltham. Essx........4G 53
Great Warley. Essx.........1G 39
Great Washbourne. Glos....2E 49
Great Wenham. Suff........2D 54
Great Whelnetham. Suff.....5A 66
Great Whittington. Nmbd...2D 114
Great Wigborough. Essx....4C 54
Great Wilbraham. Cambs....5E 65
Great Wilne. Derbs.........2B 74
Great Wishford. Wilts.......3F 23
Great Witchingham. Norf....3D 78
Great Witcombe. Glos.......4E 49
Great Witley. Worc.........4B 60
Great Wolford. Warw.......2H 49
Greatworth. Nptn..........1D 50
Great Wratting. Suff........1G 53
Great Wyrley. Staf........5D 73
Great Wytheford. Shrp......4H 71
Great Yarmouth. Norf......196 (5H 79)
Great Yeldham. Essx........2A 54
Grebby. Linc..............4D 88
Greeba Castle. IOM........3C 108
The Green. Cumb...........1A 96
The Green. Wilts...........3D 22

Greenbank. Shet...........1G 173
Greenbottom. Corn.........4B 6
Greenburn. W Lot.........3C 128
Greencroft. Dur...........4E 115
Greendown. Som...........1A 22
Green End. Bed
 nr. Bedford.............1A 52
 nr. Little Staughton......4A 64
Green End. Herts
 nr. Buntingford..........2D 52
 nr. Stevenage............3D 52
Green End. N Yor..........4F 107
Green End. Warw...........2G 61
Greenfield. Arg...........4B 134
Greenfield. C Beds.........2A 52
Greenfield. Flin...........3D 82
Greenfield. G Man..........4H 91
Greenfield. Oxon..........2F 37
Greenfoot. N Lan..........3A 128
Greenford. G Lon.........2C 38
Greengairs. N Lan.........2A 128
Greengate. Norf...........4C 78
Greengill. Cumb...........1C 102
Greenhalgh. Lanc..........1C 90
Greenham. Dors...........2H 13
Greenham. Som............4D 20
Greenham. W Ber..........5C 36
Green Hammerton. N Yor...4G 99
Greenhaugh. Nmbd........1A 114
Greenhead. Nmbd.........3H 113
Green Heath. Staf.........4D 73
Greenhill. Dum...........2C 112
Greenhill. Falk...........2B 128
Greenhill. Kent...........4F 41
Greenhill. S Yor..........2H 85
Greenhill. Worc...........3C 60
Greenhills. N Ayr.........4E 127
Greenhithe. Kent.........3G 39
Greenholm. E Ayr.........1E 117
Greenhow Hill. N Yor......3D 98
Greenigoe. Orkn..........7D 172
Greenland. High..........2E 169
Greenland Mains. High.....2E 169
Greenlands. Worc.........4E 61
Green Lane. Shrp.........3A 72
Green Lane. Worc.........4E 61
Greenlaw. Bord...........5D 130
Greenlea. Dum...........2B 112
Greenloaning. Per.........3H 135
Greenmount. G Man.......3F 91
Greenmow. Shet..........9F 173
Greenock. Inv..........2D 126
Greenock Mains. E Ayr.....2F 117
Greenodd. Cumb..........1C 96
Green Ore. Som..........1A 22
Greenrow. Cumb.........4C 112
Greens. Abers...........4F 161
Greensgate. Norf.........4D 78
Greenside. Tyne..........3E 115
Greensidehill. Nmbd.......3D 121
Greens Norton. Nptn......1E 51
Greenstead Green. Essx....3B 54
Greensted Green. Essx.....5F 53
Green Street. Herts.......1C 38
Green Street. Suff.........3D 66
Green Street Green. G Lon..4F 39
Green Street Green. Kent...3G 39
Greenstreet Green. Suff....1D 54
Green Tye. Herts..........4E 53
Greenwall. Orkn..........7E 172
Greenway. Pemb..........1E 43
Greenway. V Glam.........4D 32
Greenwell. Cumb..........4G 113
Greenwich. G Lon.......3E 39
Greet. Glos..............2F 49
Greete. Shrp............3H 59
Greetham. Linc...........3C 88
Greetham. Rut...........4G 75
Greetland. W Yor.........2A 92
Gregson Lane. Lanc.......2D 90
Grein. W Isl.............8B 170
Greinetobht. W Isl........1D 170
Greinton. Som...........3H 21
Gremista. Shet...........7F 173
Grenaby. IOM............4B 108
Grendon. Nptn...........4F 63
Grendon. Warw...........1G 61
Grendon Common. Warw....1G 61
Grendon Green. Here......5H 59
Grendon Underwood. Buck..3E 51
Grenofen. Devn...........5E 11
Greosabhagh. W Isl.......8D 171
Gresford. Wrex...........5F 83
Gresham. Norf...........2D 78
Greshornish. High........3C 154
Gressenhall. Norf.........4B 78
Gressingham. Lanc........3E 97
Greta Bridge. Dur.........3D 105
Gretna. Dum.............3E 112
Gretna Green. Dum........3E 112
Gretton. Glos............2F 49
Gretton. Nptn............1G 63
Gretton. Shrp...........1H 59
Grewelthorpe. N Yor......2E 99
Greygarth. N Yor.........2D 98
Grey Green. N Lin.........4A 94
Greylake. Som...........3G 21
Greysouthen. Cumb.......2B 102
Greystoke. Cumb.........1F 103
Greystoke Gill. Cumb......2F 103
Greystone. Ang..........4E 145
Greystones. S Yor........2H 85
Greywell. Hants..........1F 25
Griais. W Isl............3G 171
Grianan. W Isl...........4G 171
Gribthorpe. E Yor.........1A 94
Gribun. Arg.............5F 139
Griff. Warw.............2A 62
Griffithstown. Torf.......2F 33

Griffydam. Leics..........4B 74
Griggs Green. Hants.......3G 25
Grimbister. Orkn..........6C 172
Grimeford Village. Lanc....3E 90
Grimeston. Orkn..........6C 172
Grimethorpe. S Yor........4E 93
Griminis. W Isl
 on Benbecula............3C 170
 on North Uist...........1C 170
Grimister. Shet...........2F 173
Grimley. Worc............4C 60
Grimness. Orkn...........8D 172
Grimoldby. Linc...........2C 88
Grimpo. Shrp............3F 71
Grimsargh. Lanc..........1D 90
Grimscote. Nptn..........5D 62
Grimscott. Corn..........2C 10
Grimshaw. Bkbn..........2F 91
Grimshaw Green. Lanc.....3C 90
Grimsthorpe. Linc.........3H 75
Grimston. E Yor..........1F 95
Grimston. Leics...........3D 74
Grimston. Norf...........3G 77
Grimston. York...........4A 100
Grimstone. Dors..........3B 14
Grimstone End. Suff.......4B 66
Grinacombe Moor. Devn....3E 11
Grindale. E Yor...........2F 101
Grindhill. Devn...........3E 11
Grindiscol. Shet..........8F 173
Grindle. Shrp............5B 72
Grindleford. Derbs........3G 85
Grindleton. Lanc.........5G 97
Grindley. Staf...........3E 73
Grindley Brook. Shrp......1H 71
Grindlow. Derbs..........3F 85
Grindon. Nmbd...........5F 131
Grindon. Staf...........5E 85
Gringley on the Hill. Notts..1E 87
Grinsdale. Cumb.........4E 113
Grinshill. Shrp..........3H 71
Grinton. N Yor...........5D 104
Griomsiadar. W Isl........5G 171
Grishipoll. Arg..........3C 138
Gristhorpe. N Yor........1E 101
Griston. Norf............1B 66
Gritley. Orkn............7E 172
Grittenham. Wilts........3F 35
Grittleton. Wilts.........3D 34
Grizebeck. Cumb.........1B 96
Grizedale. Cumb.........5E 103
Grobister. Orkn..........5F 172
Grobsness. Shet.........5E 173
Groby. Leics............5C 74
Groes. Cnwy............4C 82
Groes. Neat............3A 32
Groes-faen. Rhon.........3D 32
Groesffordd. Gwyn........2B 68
Groesffordd. Powy........3D 46
Groeslon. Gwyn..........5D 81
Groes-lwyd. Powy........4E 70
Groes-wen. Cphy.........3E 33
Grogport. Arg...........5G 125
Groigearraidh. W Isl......4C 170
Gromford. Suff..........5F 67
Gronant. Flin............2C 82
Groombridge. E Sus.......2G 27
Grosmont. Mon..........3H 47
Grosmont. N Yor.........4F 107
Groton. Suff............1C 54
Grove. Dors.............5B 14
Grove. Kent.............4G 41
Grove. Notts............3E 87
Grove. Oxon............2B 36
The Grove. Dum..........2A 112
The Grove. Worc.........1D 48
Grovehill. E Yor.........1D 94
Grove Park. G Lon........3F 39
Grovesend. Swan.........5F 45
Grub Street. Staf.........3B 72
Grudie. High............2F 157
Gruids. High............3C 164
Gruinard House. High.....4D 162
Gruinart. Arg...........3A 124
Grulinbeg. Arg..........3A 124
Gruline. Arg............4G 139
Grummore. High.........5G 167
Grundisburgh. Suff.......5E 66
Gruting. Shet...........7D 173
Grutness. Shet..........10F 173
Gualachulain. High.......4F 141
Gualin House. High.......3D 166
Guardbridge. Fife.........2G 137
Guarlford. Worc.........1D 48
Guay. Per..............4H 143
Gubblecote. Herts........4H 51
Guestling Green. E Sus....4C 28
Guestling Thorn. E Sus....4C 28
Guestwick. Norf.........3C 78
Guestwick Green. Norf....3C 78
Guide. Bkbn............2F 91
Guide Post. Nmbd........1F 115
Guilden Down. Shrp......2F 59
Guilden Morden. Cambs...1C 52
Guilden Sutton. Ches W...4G 83
Guildford. Surr.......197 (1A 26)
Guildtown. Per..........5A 144
Guilsborough. Nptn.......3D 62
Guilsfield. Powy.........4E 70
Guineaford. Devn........3F 19
Guisborough. Red C.....3D 106
Guiseley. W Yor.........5D 98
Guist. Norf............3B 78
Guiting Power. Glos......3F 49
Gulberwick. Shet.........8F 173
Gullane. E Lot..........1A 130
Gulling Green. Suff.......5H 65
Gulval. Corn............3B 4

Gulworthy. Devn.........5E 11
Gumfreston. Pemb........4F 43
Gumley. Leics...........1D 62
Gunby. E Yor............1H 93
Gunby. Linc............3G 75
Gundleton. Hants........3E 24
Gun Green. Kent.........2B 28
Gun Hill. E Sus..........4G 27
Gunn. Devn.............3G 19
Gunnerside. N Yor.......5C 104
Gunnerton. Nmbd.......2C 114
Gunness. N Lin..........3B 94
Gunnislake. Corn........5E 11
Gunnista. Shet..........7F 173
Gunsgreenhill. Bord.......3F 131
Gunstone. Staf..........5C 72
Gunthorpe. Norf.........2C 78
Gunthorpe. N Lin.........1F 87
Gunthorpe. Notts........1D 74
Gunthorpe. Pet..........5A 76
Gunville. IOW...........4C 16
Gupworthy. Som.........3C 20
Gurnard. IOW...........3C 16
Gurney Slade. Som.......2B 22
Gurnos. Powy...........5A 46
Gussage All Saints. Dors...1F 15
Gussage St Andrew. Dors...1E 15
Gussage St Michael. Dors...1E 15
Guston. Kent............1H 29
Gutcher. Shet...........2G 173
Guthram Gowt. Linc......3A 76
Guthrie. Ang............3E 145
Guyhirn. Cambs.........5D 76
Guyhirn Gull. Cambs......5C 76
Guy's Head. Linc.........3D 77
Guy's Marsh. Dors........4D 22
Guyzance. Nmbd.........4G 121
Gwaelod-y-garth. Card....3E 32
Gwaenynog Bach. Den.....4C 82
Gwaenysgor. Flin.........2C 82
Gwalchmai. IOA.........3C 80
Gwastad. Pemb..........2E 43
Gwaun-Cae-Gurwen. Neat...4H 45
Gwbert. Cdgn...........1B 44
Gweek. Corn............4E 5
Gwehelog. Mon..........5G 47
Gwenddwr. Powy.........1D 46
Gwennap. Corn..........4B 6
Gwenter. Corn...........5E 5
Gwernaffield. Flin........4E 82
Gwernesney. Mon........5H 47
Gwernogle. Carm........2F 45
Gwern-y-go. Powy........1E 58
Gwernymynydd. Flin......4E 82
Gwersyllt. Wrex.........5F 83
Gwespyr. Flin...........2D 82
Gwinear. Corn..........3C 4
Gwithian. Corn..........2C 4
Gwredog. IOA...........2D 80
Gwyddelwern. Den.......1C 70
Gwyddgrug. Carm........2E 45
Gwynfryn. Wrex.........5E 83
Gwystre. Powy..........4C 58
Gwytherin. Cnwy........4A 82
Gyfelia. Wrex...........1F 71
Gyffin. Cnwy............3G 81

H

Haa of Houlland. Shet.......1G 173
Habberley. Shrp..........5G 71
Habblesthorpe. Notts.....2E 87
Habergham. Lanc........1G 91
Habin. W Sus............4G 25
Habrough. NE Lin........3E 95
Haceby. Linc............2H 75
Hacheston. Suff.........5F 67
Hackenthorpe. S Yor......2B 86
Hackford. Norf..........5C 78
Hackforth. N Yor.........5F 105
Hackland. Orkn..........5C 172
Hackleton. Nptn.........5F 63
Hackman's Gate. Worc....3C 60
Hackness. N Yor.........5G 107
Hackness. Orkn..........8C 172
Hackney. G Lon.........2E 39
Hackthorn. Linc.........2G 87
Hackthorpe. Cumb........2G 103
Haclait. W Isl...........4D 170
Haconby. Linc...........3A 76
Hadden. Bord...........1B 120
Haddenham. Buck........5F 51
Haddenham. Cambs.......3D 64
Haddenham End Field. Cambs...3D 64
Haddington. E Lot........2B 130
Haddington. Linc.........4G 87
Haddiscoe. Norf.........1G 67
Haddo. Abers............5F 161
Haddon. Cambs..........1A 64
Hademore. Staf..........5F 73
Hadfield. Derbs..........1E 85
Hadham Cross. Herts......4E 53
Hadham Ford. Herts......3E 53
Hadleigh. Essx..........2C 40
Hadleigh. Suff...........1D 54
Hadleigh Heath. Suff......1C 54
Hadley. Telf............4A 72
Hadley. Worc............4C 60
Hadley End. Staf.........3F 73
Hadley Wood. G Lon......1D 38
Hadlow. Kent...........1H 27
Hadlow Down. E Sus......3G 27
Hadnall. Shrp...........3H 71
Hadstock. Essx..........1F 53
Hadston. Nmbd..........4G 121
Hady. Derbs............3A 86
Hadzor. Worc...........4D 60
Haffenden Quarter. Kent...1C 28
Haggate. Lanc...........1G 91
Haggbeck. Cumb.........2F 113

Haggersta. Shet..........7E 173
Haggerston. Nmbd........5G 131
Haggrister. Shet.........4E 173
Hagley. Here............1A 48
Hagley. Worc...........2D 60
Hagnaby. Linc..........4C 88
Hagworthingham. Linc....4C 88
Haigh. G Man...........4E 90
Haigh Moor. W Yor......2C 92
Haighton Green. Lanc.....1D 90
Haile. Cumb............4B 102
Hailes. Glos............2F 49
Hailey. Herts...........4D 52
Hailey. Oxon............4B 50
Hailsham. E Sus.......5G 27
Hail Weston. Cambs.......4A 64
Hainault. G Lon..........1F 39
Hainford. Norf...........4E 78
Hainton. Linc...........2A 88
Hainworth. W Yor........1A 92
Haisthorpe. E Yor........3F 101
Hakin. Pemb............4C 42
Halam. Notts...........5D 86
Hales. Glos.............2F 49
Hales. Norf.............1F 67
Hales. Staf.............2B 72
Halesgate. Linc.........3C 76
Hales Green. Derbs.......1F 73
Halesowen. W Mid......2D 60
Hale Street. Kent........1A 28
Halesworth. Suff.........3F 67
Halewood. Mers.........2G 83
Halford. Shrp...........2G 59
Halford. Warw...........1A 50
Halfpenny. Cumb.........1E 97
Halfpenny Furze. Carm....3G 43
Halfpenny Green. Staf.....1C 60
Halfway. Carm
 nr. Llandeilo............2G 45
 nr. Llandovery..........2B 46
Halfway. S Yor..........2B 86
Halfway. W Ber.........5C 36
Halfway House. Shrp......4F 71
Halfway Houses. Kent.....3D 40
Halgabron. Corn.........4A 10
Halifax. W Yor..........2A 92
Halistra. High..........3B 154
Halket. E Ayr...........4F 127
Halkirk. High...........3D 168
Halkyn. Flin............3E 82
Hall. E Ren.............4F 127
Hallam Fields. Derbs......1B 74
Halland. E Sus..........4G 27
The Hallands. N Lin.......2D 94
Hallaton. Leics..........1E 63
Hallatrow. Bath..........1B 22
Hallbank. Cumb.........5H 103
Hallbankgate. Cumb......4G 113
Hall Dunnerdale. Cumb....5D 102
Hallen. S Glo...........3A 34
Hall End. Bed...........1A 52
Hallgarth. Dur..........5G 115
Hall Green. Ches E.......5C 84
Hall Green. Norf.........2D 66
Hall Green. W Mid........2F 61
Hall Green. Wrex.........1G 71
Halliburton. Bord........5C 130
Hallin. High............3B 154
Halling. Medw..........4B 40
Hallington. Linc.........2C 88
Hallington. Nmbd........2C 114
Halloughton. Notts.......5D 86
Hallow. Worc...........5C 60
Hallow Heath. Worc......5C 60
Hallowsgate. Ches W......4H 83
Hallsands. Devn.........5E 9
Hall's Green. Herts.......3C 52
Hallspill. Devn..........4E 19
Hallthwaites. Cumb.......1A 96
Hall Waberthwaite. Cumb...5C 102
Hallwood Green. Glos......2B 48
Hallworthy. Corn.........4B 10
Hallyne. Bord...........5E 129
Halmer End. Staf.........1C 72
Halmond's Frome. Here....1B 48
Halmore. Glos...........5B 48
Halnaker. W Sus.........5A 26
Halsall. Lanc...........3B 90
Halse. Nptn............1D 50
Halse. Som.............4E 21
Halsetown. Corn.........3C 4
Halsham. E Yor..........2F 95
Halsinger. Devn.........3F 19
Halstead. Essx.........2B 54
Halstead. Kent..........4F 39
Halstead. Leics.........5E 75
Halstock. Dors..........2A 14
Halsway. Som...........3E 21
Haltcliff Bridge. Cumb.....1E 103
Haltham. Linc...........4B 88
Haltoft End. Linc.........1C 76
Halton. Buck............5G 51
Halton. Hal.............2H 83
Halton. Lanc............3E 97
Halton. Nmbd...........3C 114
Halton. W Yor...........1D 92
Halton. Wrex............2F 71
Halton East. N Yor........4C 98
Halton Fenside. Linc......4D 88
Halton Gill. N Yor........2A 98
Halton Holegate. Linc.....4D 88

Halton Lea Gate – Heapham

Halton Lea Gate. Nmbd 4H 113
Halton Moor. W Yor 1D 92
Halton Shields. Nmbd 3D 114
Halton West. N Yor 4H 97
Haltwhistle. Nmbd 3A 114
Halvergate. Norf 5G 79
Halwell. Devn 3D 9
Halwill. Devn 3E 11
Halwill Junction. Devn 3E 11
Ham. Devn 2F 13
Ham. Glos 2B 34
Ham. G Lon 3C 38
Ham. High 1E 169
Ham. Kent 5H 41
Ham. Plym 3A 8
Ham. Shet 8A 173
Ham. Som
nr. Ilminster 1F 13
nr. Taunton 4F 21
nr. Wellington 4E 21
Ham. Wilts 5B 36
Hambleden. Buck 3F 37
Hambledon. Hants 1E 17
Hambledon. Surr 2A 26
Hamble-le-Rice. Hants 2C 16
Hambleton. Lanc 5C 96
Hambleton. N Yor 1F 93
Hambridge. Som 4G 21
Hambrook. S Glo 4B 34
Hambrook. W Sus 2F 17
Ham Common. Dors 4D 22
Hameringham. Linc 4C 88
Hamerton. Cambs 3A 64
Ham Green. Here 1C 48
Ham Green. Kent 4C 40
Ham Green. N Som 4A 34
Ham Green. Worc 4E 61
Ham Hill. Kent 4A 40
Hamilton. Leic 5D 74
Hamilton. S Lan 4A 128
Hamister. Shet 5G 173
Hammer. W Sus 3G 25
Hammersmith. G Lon 3D 38
Hammerwich. Staf 5E 73
Hammerwood. E Sus 2F 27
Hammill. Kent 5G 41
Hammond Street. Herts 5D 52
Hammoon. Dors 1D 14
Hamnavoe. Shet
nr. Braehoulland 3D 173
nr. Burland 8E 173
nr. Lunna 4F 173
on Yell 3F 173
Hamp. Som 3G 21
Hampden Park. E Sus 5G 27
Hampen. Glos 4F 49
Hamperden End. Essx 2F 53
Hamperley. Shrp 2G 59
Hampnett. Glos 4F 49
Hampole. S Yor 3F 93
Hampreston. Dors 3F 15
Hampstead. G Lon 2D 38
Hampstead Norreys. W Ber 4D 36
Hampsthwaite. N Yor 4E 99
Hampton. Devn 3F 13
Hampton. G Lon 3C 38
Hampton. Kent 4F 41
Hampton. Shrp 2B 60
Hampton. Swin 2G 35
Hampton. Worc 1F 49
Hampton Bishop. Here 2A 48
Hampton Fields. Glos 2D 35
Hampton Hargate. Pet 1A 64
Hampton Heath. Ches W 1H 71
Hampton in Arden. W Mid 2G 61
Hampton Loade. Shrp 2B 60
Hampton Lovett. Worc 4C 60
Hampton Lucy. Warw 5G 61
Hampton Magna. Warw 4G 61
Hampton on the Hill. Warw 4G 61
Hampton Poyle. Oxon 4D 50
Hampton Wick. G Lon 4C 38
Hamptworth. Wilts 1H 15
Hamrow. Norf 3B 78
Hamsey. E Sus 4F 27
Hamsey Green. Surr 5E 39
Hamstall Ridware. Staf 4F 73
Hamstead. IOW 3C 16
Hamstead. W Mid 1E 61
Hamstead Marshall. W Ber 5C 36
Hamsterley. Dur
nr. Consett 4E 115
nr. Wolsingham 1E 105
Hamsterley Mill. Dur 4E 115
Ham Street. Som 3A 22
Hamstreet. Kent 2E 28
Hamworthy. Pool 3E 15
Hanbury. Staf 3F 73
Hanbury. Worc 4D 60
Hanbury Woodend. Staf 3F 73
Hanby. Linc 2H 75
Hanchurch. Staf 1C 72
Hand and Pen. Devn 3D 12
Handbridge. Ches W 4G 83
Handcross. W Sus 2D 26
Handforth. Ches E 2C 84
Handley. Ches W 5G 83
Handley. Derbs 4A 86
Handsacre. Staf 4E 73
Handsworth. S Yor 2B 86
Handsworth. W Mid 1E 61
Handy Cross. Buck 2G 37
Hanford. Dors 1D 14
Hanford. Stoke 1C 72
Hangersley. Hants 2G 15
Hanging Houghton. Nptn 3E 63
Hanging Langford. Wilts 3F 23
Hangleton. Brig 5D 26
Hangleton. W Sus 5B 26
Hanham. S Glo 4B 34
Hanham Green. S Glo 4B 34
Hankelow. Ches E 1A 72
Hankerton. Wilts 2E 35
Hankham. E Sus 5H 27
Hanley. Stoke 211 (1C 72)
Hanley Castle. Worc 1D 48
Hanley Childe. Worc 4A 60
Hanley Swan. Worc 1D 48
Hanley William. Worc 4A 60
Hanlith. N Yor 3B 98
Hanmer. Wrex 2G 71
Hannaborough. Devn 2F 11
Hannaford. Devn 4G 19
Hannah. Linc 3E 89
Hannington. Hants 1D 24
Hannington. Nptn 3F 63
Hannington. Swin 2G 35
Hannington Wick. Swin 2G 35
Hanscombe End. C Beds 2B 52
Hanslope. Mil 1G 51
Hanthorpe. Linc 3H 75
Hanwell. G Lon 2C 38
Hanwell. Oxon 1C 50
Hanwood. Shrp 5G 71
Hanworth. G Lon 3C 38
Hanworth. Norf 2D 78
Happas. Ang 4D 144
Happendon. S Lan 1A 118
Happisburgh. Norf 2F 79
Happisburgh Common. Norf 3F 79
Hapsford. Ches W 3G 83
Hapton. Lanc 1F 91
Hapton. Norf 1D 66
Harberton. Devn 3D 9
Harbertonford. Devn 3D 9
Harbledown. Kent 5F 41
Harborne. W Mid 2E 61
Harborough Magna. Warw 3B 62
Harbottle. Nmbd 4D 120
Harbourneford. Devn 2D 8
Harbours Hill. Worc 4D 60
Harbridge. Hants 1G 15
Harbury. Warw 4A 62
Harby. Leics 2E 75
Harby. Notts 3F 87
Harcombe. Devn 3E 13
Harcombe Bottom. Devn 3G 13
Harcourt. Corn 5C 6
Harden. W Yor 1A 92
Hardenhuish. Wilts 4E 35
Hardgate. Abers 3E 153
Hardgate. Dum 3F 111
Hardham. W Sus 4B 26
Hardingham. Norf 5C 78
Hardingstone. Nptn 5E 63
Hardings Wood. Staf 5C 84
Hardington. Som 1C 22
Hardington Mandeville. Som 1A 14
Hardington Marsh. Som 2A 14
Hardington Moor. Som 1A 14
Hardley. Hants 2C 16
Hardley Street. Norf 5F 79
Hardmead. Mil 1H 51
Hardraw. N Yor 5B 104
Hardstoft. Derbs 4B 86
Hardway. Hants 2E 16
Hardway. Som 3C 22
Hardwick. Buck 4G 51
Hardwick. Cambs 5C 64
Hardwick. Norf 2E 66
Hardwick. Nptn 4F 63
Hardwick. Oxon
nr. Bicester 3D 50
nr. Witney 5B 50
Hardwick. Shrp 1F 59
Hardwick. S Yor 2B 86
Hardwick. Stoc T 2B 106
Hardwick. W Mid 1E 61
Hardwicke. Glos
nr. Cheltenham 3E 49
nr. Gloucester 4C 48
Hardwicke. Here 1F 47
Hardwick Village. Notts 3D 86
Hardy's Green. Essx 3C 54
Hare. Som 1F 13
Hareby. Linc 4C 88
Hareden. Lanc 4F 97
Harefield. G Lon 1B 38
Hare Green. Essx 3D 54
Hare Hatch. Wok 4G 37
Harehill. Derbs 2F 73
Harehills. W Yor 1D 92
Harehope. Nmbd 2E 121
Harelaw. Dum 2F 113
Harelaw. Dur 4E 115
Hareplain. Kent 2C 28
Haresceugh. Cumb 5H 113
Harescombe. Glos 4D 48
Haresfield. Glos 4D 48
Haresfinch. Mers 1H 83
Hareshaw. N Lan 3B 128
Hare Street. Essx 5E 53
Hare Street. Herts 3D 53
Harewood. W Yor 5F 99
Harewood End. Here 3A 48
Harford. Devn 3C 8
Hargate. Norf 1D 66
Hargatewall. Derbs 3F 85
Hargrave. Ches W 4G 83
Hargrave. Nptn 3H 63
Hargrave. Suff 5G 65
Harker. Cumb 3E 113
Harkland. Shet 3F 173
Harkstead. Suff 2E 55
Harlaston. Staf 4G 73
Harlaxton. Linc 2F 75
Harlech. Gwyn 2E 69
Harlequin. Notts 2D 74
Harlescott. Shrp 4H 71
Harleston. Devn 4D 9
Harleston. Norf 2E 67
Harleston. Suff 4C 66
Harlestone. Nptn 4E 62
Harley. Shrp 5H 71
Harley. S Yor 1A 86
Harling Road. Norf 2B 66
Harlington. C Beds 2A 52
Harlington. G Lon 3B 38
Harlington. S Yor 4E 93
Harlosh. High 4B 154
Harlow. Essx 4E 53
Harlow Hill. Nmbd 3D 115
Harlsey Castle. N Yor 5B 106
Harlthorpe. E Yor 1H 93
Harlton. Cambs 5C 64
Harlyn Bay. Corn 1C 6
Harman's Cross. Dors 4E 15
Harmby. N Yor 1D 98
Harmer Green. Herts 4C 52
Harmer Hill. Shrp 3G 71
Harmondsworth. G Lon 3B 38
Harmston. Linc 4G 87
Harnage. Shrp 5H 71
Harnham. Nmbd 1D 115
Harnham. Wilts 4G 23
Harnhill. Glos 5F 49
Harold Hill. G Lon 1G 39
Haroldston West. Pemb 3C 42
Haroldswick. Shet 1H 173
Harold Wood. G Lon 1G 39
Harome. N Yor 1A 100
Harpenden. Herts 4B 52
Harpford. Devn 3D 12
Harpham. E Yor 3E 101
Harpley. Norf 3G 77
Harpley. Worc 4A 60
Harpole. Nptn 4D 62
Harpsdale. High 3D 168
Harpsden. Oxon 3F 37
Harpswell. Linc 2G 87
Harpurhey. G Man 4G 91
Harpur Hill. Derbs 3E 85
Harraby. Cumb 4F 113
Harracott. Devn 4F 19
Harrapool. High 1E 147
Harrapul. High 1E 147
Harrietfield. Per 1B 136
Harrietsham. Kent 5C 40
Harrington. Cumb 2A 102
Harrington. Linc 3C 88
Harrington. Nptn 2E 63
Harringworth. Nptn 1G 63
Harriseahead. Staf 5C 84
Harriston. Cumb 5C 112
Harrogate. N Yor 197 (4F 99)
Harrold. Bed 5G 63
Harrop Dale. G Man 4A 92
Harrow. G Lon 2C 38
Harrowbarrow. Corn 2H 7
Harrowden. Bed 1A 52
Harrowgate Hill. Darl 3F 105
Harrow on the Hill. G Lon 2C 38
Harrow Weald. G Lon 1C 38
Harry Stoke. S Glo 4B 34
Harston. Cambs 5D 64
Harston. Leics 2F 75
Harswell. E Yor 5C 100
Hart. Hart 1B 106
Hartburn. Nmbd 1D 115
Hartburn. Stoc T 3B 106
Hartest. Suff 5H 65
Hartfield. E Sus 2F 27
Hartford. Cambs 3B 64
Hartford. Ches W 3A 84
Hartford. Som 4C 20
Hartford Bridge. Hants 1F 25
Hartford End. Essx 4G 53
Harthill. Ches W 5H 83
Harthill. N Lan 3C 128
Harthill. S Yor 2B 86
Hartington. Derbs 4F 85
Hartland. Devn 4C 18
Hartland Quay. Devn 4C 18
Hartle. Worc 3D 60
Hartlebury. Worc 3C 60
Hartlepool. Hart 1C 106
Hartley. Cumb 4A 104
Hartley. Kent
nr. Cranbrook 2B 28
nr. Dartford 4H 39
Hartley. Nmbd 2G 115
Hartley Green. Staf 3D 73
Hartley Mauditt. Hants 3F 25
Hartley Wespall. Hants 1E 25
Hartley Wintney. Hants 1F 25
Hartlip. Kent 4C 40
Hartmount Holdings. High 1B 158
Hartoft End. N Yor 5E 107
Harton. N Yor 3B 100
Harton. Shrp 2G 59
Harton. Tyne 3G 115
Hartpury. Glos 3D 48
Hartshead. W Yor 2B 92
Hartshill. Warw 1H 61
Hartshorne. Derbs 3H 73
Hartsop. Cumb 3F 103
Hart Station. Hart 1B 106
Hartswell. Som 4D 20
Hartwell. Nptn 5E 63
Hartwood. Lanc 3D 90
Hartwood. N Lan 4B 128
Harvel. Kent 4A 40
Harvington. Worc
nr. Evesham 1F 49
nr. Kidderminster 3C 60
Harwell. Oxon 3C 36
Harwich. Essx 215 (2F 55)
Harwood. Dur 1B 104
Harwood. G Man 3F 91
Harwood Dale. N Yor 5G 107
Harworth. Notts 1D 86
Hascombe. Surr 2A 26
Haselbech. Nptn 3E 62
Haselbury Plucknett. Som 1H 13
Haseley. Warw 4G 61
Hasfield. Glos 3D 48
Hasguard. Pemb 4C 42
Haskayne. Lanc 4B 90
Hasketon. Suff 5E 67
Hasland. Derbs 4A 86
Haslemere. Surr 2A 26
Haslingden. Lanc 2F 91
Haslingfield. Cambs 5D 64
Haslington. Ches E 5B 84
Hassall. Ches E 5B 84
Hassall Green. Ches E 5B 84
Hassell Street. Kent 1E 29
Hassendean. Bord 2H 119
Hassingham. Norf 5F 79
Hassness. Cumb 3C 102
Hassocks. W Sus 4E 27
Hassop. Derbs 3G 85
Haster. High 3F 169
Hasthorpe. Linc 4D 89
Hastigrow. High 2E 169
Hastingleigh. Kent 1E 29
Hastings. E Sus 5C 28
Hastingwood. Essx 5E 53
Hastoe. Herts 5H 51
Haston. Shrp 3H 71
Haswell. Dur 5G 115
Haswell Plough. Dur 5G 115
Hatch. C Beds 1B 52
Hatch Beauchamp. Som 4G 21
Hatch End. G Lon 1C 38
Hatch Green. Som 1G 13
Hatching Green. Herts 4B 52
Hatchmere. Ches W 3H 83
Hatch Warren. Hants 2E 24
Hatcliffe. NE Lin 4F 95
Hatfield. Here 5H 59
Hatfield. Herts 5C 52
Hatfield. S Yor 4G 93
Hatfield. Worc 5C 60
Hatfield Broad Oak. Essx 4F 53
Hatfield Garden Village. Herts 5C 52
Hatfield Heath. Essx 4F 53
Hatfield Hyde. Herts 4C 52
Hatfield Peverel. Essx 4A 54
Hatfield Woodhouse. S Yor 4G 93
Hatford. Oxon 2B 36
Hatherden. Hants 1B 24
Hatherleigh. Devn 2F 11
Hathern. Leics 3B 74
Hatherop. Glos 5G 49
Hathersage. Derbs 2G 85
Hathersage Booths. Derbs 2G 85
Hatherton. Ches E 1A 72
Hatherton. Staf 4D 72
Hatley St George. Cambs 5B 64
Hatt. Corn 2H 7
Hattersley. G Man 1D 85
Hattingley. Hants 3E 25
Hatton. Abers 5H 161
Hatton. Derbs 2G 73
Hatton. G Lon 3B 38
Hatton. Linc 3A 88
Hatton. Shrp 1G 59
Hatton. Warr 2A 84
Hatton. Warw 4G 61
Hattoncrook. Abers 1F 153
Hatton Heath. Ches W 4G 83
Hatton of Fintray. Abers 2F 153
Haugh. E Ayr 2D 117
Haugh. Linc 3D 88
Haugham. Linc 2C 88
Haugh Head. Nmbd 2E 121
Haughley. Suff 4C 66
Haughley Green. Suff 4C 66
Haugh of Ballechin. Per 3G 143
Haugh of Glass. Mor 5B 160
Haugh of Urr. Dum 3F 111
Haughton. Ches E 5H 83
Haughton. Notts 3D 86
Haughton. Shrp
nr. Bridgnorth 1A 60
nr. Oswestry 3F 71
nr. Shifnal 5B 72
nr. Shrewsbury 4H 71
Haughton. Staf 3C 72
Haughton Green. G Man 1D 84
Haughton le Skerne. Darl 3A 106
Haultwick. Herts 3D 52
Haunn. Arg 4E 139
Haunn. W Isl 7C 170
Haunton. Staf 4G 73
Hauxton. Cambs 5D 64
Havannah. Ches E 4C 84
Havant. Hants 2F 17
Haven. Here 5G 59
The Haven. W Sus 2B 26
Haven Bank. Linc 5B 88
Havenstreet. IOW 3D 16
Havercroft. W Yor 3D 93
Haverfordwest. Pemb 3D 42
Haverhill. Suff 1G 53
Haverigg. Cumb 2A 96
Havering-Atte-Bower. G Lon 1G 39
Havering's Grove. Essx 1A 40
Haversham. Mil 1G 51
Haverthwaite. Cumb 1C 96
Haverton Hill. Stoc T 2B 106
Havyatt. Som 3A 22
Hawarden. Flin 4F 83
Hawbridge. Worc 1E 49
Hawcoat. Cumb 2B 96
Hawcross. Glos 2C 48
Hawen. Cdgn 1D 44
Hawes. N Yor 1A 98
Hawes Green. Norf 1E 67
Hawick. Bord 3H 119
Hawkchurch. Devn 2G 13
Hawkedon. Suff 5G 65
Hawkenbury. Kent 1C 28
Hawkeridge. Wilts 1D 22
Hawkerland. Devn 4D 12
Hawkesbury. S Glo 3C 34
Hawkesbury. Warw 2A 62
Hawkesbury Upton. S Glo 3C 34
Hawkes End. W Mid 2G 61
Hawk Green. G Man 2D 84
Hawkhurst. Kent 2B 28
Hawkhurst Common. E Sus 4G 27
Hawkinge. Kent 1G 29
Hawkley. Hants 4F 25
Hawkridge. Som 3B 20
Hawksdale. Cumb 5E 113
Hawkshaw. G Man 3F 91
Hawkshead. Cumb 5E 103
Hawkshead Hill. Cumb 5E 103
Hawkswick. N Yor 2B 98
Hawksworth. Notts 1E 75
Hawksworth. W Yor 5D 98
Hawkwell. Essx 1C 40
Hawley. Hants 1G 25
Hawley. Kent 3G 39
Hawling. Glos 3F 49
Hawnby. N Yor 1H 99
Haworth. W Yor 1A 92
Hawstead. Suff 5A 66
Hawthorn. Dur 5H 115
Hawthorn Hill. Brac 4G 37
Hawthorn Hill. Linc 5B 88
Hawthorpe. Linc 3H 75
Hawton. Notts 5E 87
Haxby. York 4A 100
Haxey. N Lin 1E 87
Haybridge. Shrp 3A 60
Haybridge. Som 2A 22
Haydock. Mers 1H 83
Haydon. Bath 1B 22
Haydon. Dors 1B 14
Haydon. Som 4F 21
Haydon Bridge. Nmbd 3B 114
Haydon Wick. Swin 3G 35
Haye. Corn 2H 7
Hayes. G Lon
nr. Bromley 4F 39
Hayes. G Lon
nr. Uxbridge 2B 38
Hayfield. Derbs 2E 85
Hay Green. Norf 4E 77
Hayhill. E Ayr 3D 116
Haylands. IOW 3D 16
Hayle. Corn 3C 4
Hayley Green. W Mid 2D 60
Hayling Island. Hants 3F 17
Hayne. Devn 2B 12
Haynes. C Beds 1A 52
Haynes West End. C Beds 1A 52
Hay-on-Wye. Powy 1F 47
Hayscastle. Pemb 2C 42
Hayscastle Cross. Pemb 2D 42
Hayshead. Ang 4F 145
Hay Street. Herts 3D 53
Hayton. Aber 3G 153
Hayton. Cumb
nr. Aspatria 5C 112
nr. Brampton 4G 113
Hayton. E Yor 5C 100
Hayton. Notts 2E 87
Hayton's Bent. Shrp 2H 59
Haytor Vale. Devn 5A 12
Haytown. Devn 1D 11
Haywards Heath. W Sus 3E 27
Haywood. S Lan 4C 128
Hazelbank. S Lan 5B 128
Hazelbury Bryan. Dors 2C 14
Hazeleigh. Essx 5B 54
Hazeley. Hants 1F 25
Hazel Grove. G Man 2D 84
Hazelhead. S Yor 4B 92
Hazelslade. Staf 4E 73
Hazel Street. Kent 2A 28
Hazelton Walls. Fife 1F 137
Hazelwood. Derbs 1H 73
Hazlemere. Buck 2G 37
Hazler. Shrp 1G 59
Hazlerigg. Tyne 2F 115
Hazles. Staf 1E 73
Hazleton. Glos 4F 49
Hazon. Nmbd 4F 121
Heacham. Norf 2F 77
Headbourne Worthy. Hants 3C 24
Headcorn. Kent 1C 28
Headingley. W Yor 1C 92
Headington. Oxon 5D 50
Headlam. Dur 3E 105
Headless Cross. Worc 4E 61
Headley. Hants
nr. Haslemere 3G 25
nr. Kingsclere 5D 36
Headley. Surr 5D 38
Headley Down. Hants 3G 25
Headley Heath. Worc 3E 61
Headley Park. Bris 5A 34
Head of Muir. Falk 1B 128
Headon. Notts 3E 87
Heads Nook. Cumb 4F 113
Heage. Derbs 5A 86
Healaugh. N Yor
nr. Grinton 5D 104
nr. York 5H 99
Heald Green. G Man 2C 84
Heale. Devn 2G 19
Healey. G Man 3G 91
Healey. Nmbd 4D 114
Healey. N Yor 1D 98
Healeyfield. Dur 5D 114
Healing. NE Lin 3F 95
Heamoor. Corn 3B 4
Heanish. Arg 4B 138
Heanor. Derbs 1B 74
Heanton Punchardon. Devn 3F 19
Heapham. Linc 2F 87

Heartsease – Hillside

Heartsease. Powy 4D 58
Heasley Mill. Devn 3H 19
Heaste. High 2E 147
Heath. Derbs 4B 86
The Heath. Norf
nr. Buxton 3E 79
nr. Fakenham 3B 78
nr. Hevingham 3D 78
The Heath. Staf 2E 73
The Heath. Suff 2E 55
Heath and Reach. C Beds 3H 51
Heath Common. W Sus 4C 26
Heathcote. Derbs 4F 85
Heath Cross. Devn 3H 11
Heathencote. Nptn 1F 51
Heath End. Hants 5D 36
Heath End. Leics 3A 74
Heath End. W Mid 5E 73
Heather. Leics 4A 74
Heatherfield. High 4D 155
Heatherton. Derb 2H 73
Heathfield. Cambs 1E 53
Heathfield. Cumb 5C 112
Heathfield. Devn 5B 12
Heathfield. E Sus 3G 27
Heathfield. Ren 3E 126
Heathfield. Som
nr. Lydeard St Lawrence 3E 21
nr. Norton Fitzwarren 4E 21
Heath Green. Worc 3E 61
Heathhall. Dum 2A 112
Heath Hayes. Staf 4E 73
Heath Hill. Shrp 4B 72
Heath House. Som 2H 21
Heathrow Airport. G Lon 216 (3B 38)
Heathstock. Devn 2F 13
Heathton. Shrp 1C 60
Heathtop. Derbs 2G 73
Heath Town. W Mid 1D 60
Heatley. Staf 3E 73
Heatley. Warr 2B 84
Heaton. Lanc 3D 96
Heaton. Staf 4D 84
Heaton. Tyne 3F 115
Heaton. W Yor 1B 92
Heaton Moor. G Man 1C 84
Heaton's Bridge. Lanc 3C 90
Heaverham. Kent 5G 39
Heavitree. Devn 3C 12
Hebburn. Tyne 3G 115
Hebden. N Yor 3C 98
Hebden Bridge. W Yor 2H 91
Hebden Green. Ches W 4A 84
Hebing End. Herts 3D 52
Hebron. Carm 2F 43
Hebron. Nmbd 1E 115
Heck. Dum 1B 112
Heckdyke. Notts 1E 87
Heckfield. Hants 5F 37
Heckfield Green. Suff 3D 66
Heckfordbridge. Essx 3C 54
Heckington. Linc 1A 76
Heckmondwike. W Yor 2C 92
Heddington. Wilts 5E 35
Heddle. Orkn 6C 172
Heddon. Devn 4G 19
Heddon-on-the-Wall. Nmbd 3E 115
Hedenham. Norf 1F 67
Hedge End. Hants 1C 16
Hedgerley. Buck 2A 38
Hedging. Som 4G 21
Hedley on the Hill. Nmbd 4D 115
Hednesford. Staf 4E 73
Hedon. E Yor 2E 95
Hegdon Hill. Here 5H 59
Heglibister. Shet 6E 173
Heighington. Darl 2F 105
Heighington. Linc 4H 87
Heightington. Worc 3B 60
Heights of Brae. High 2H 157
Heights of Fodderty. High 2H 157
Heights of Kinlochewe. High 2C 156
Heiton. Bord 1B 120
Hele. Devn
nr. Exeter 2C 12
nr. Holsworthy 3D 10
nr. Ilfracombe 2F 19
Hele. Torb 2F 9
Helensburgh. Arg 1D 126
Helford. Corn 4E 5
Helhoughton. Norf 3A 78
Helions Bumpstead. Essx 1G 53
Helland. Corn 5A 10
Helland. Som 4G 21
Hellandbridge. Corn 5A 10
Hellesdon. Norf 4E 78
Hellesveor. Corn 2C 4
Hellidon. Nptn 5C 62
Hellifield. N Yor 4A 98
Hellingly. E Sus 4G 27
Hellington. Norf 5F 79
Hellister. Shet 7E 173
Helmdon. Nptn 1D 50
Helmingham. Suff 5D 66
Helmington Row. Dur 1E 105
Helmsdale. High 2H 165
Helmshore. Lanc 2F 91
Helmsley. N Yor 1A 100
Helperby. N Yor 3G 99
Helperthorpe. N Yor 2D 100
Helpringham. Linc 1A 76
Helpston. Pet 5A 76
Helsby. Ches W 3G 83
Helsey. Linc 3E 89
Helston. Corn 4D 4
Helstone. Corn 4A 10
Helton. Cumb 2G 103
Helwith. N Yor 4D 105
Helwith Bridge. N Yor 3H 97
Helygain. Flin 3E 82
The Hem. Shrp 5B 72
Hemblington. Norf 4F 79
Hemel Hempstead. Herts 5A 52
Hemerdon. Devn 3B 8
Hemingbrough. N Yor 1G 93
Hemingby. Linc 3B 88
Hemingfield. S Yor 4D 93
Hemingford Abbots. Cambs 3B 64
Hemingford Grey. Cambs 3B 64
Hemingstone. Suff 5D 66
Hemington. Leics 3B 74
Hemington. Nptn 2H 63
Hemington. Som 1C 22
Hemley. Suff 1F 55
Hemlington. Midd 3B 106
Hempholme. E Yor 4E 101
Hempnall. Norf 1E 67
Hempnall Green. Norf 1E 67
Hempriggs. High 4F 169
Hemp's Green. Essx 3C 54
Hempstead. Essx 2G 53
Hempstead. Medw 4B 40
Hempstead. Norf
nr. Holt 2D 78
nr. Stalham 3G 79
Hempsted. Glos 4D 48
Hempton. Norf 3B 78
Hempton. Oxon 2C 50
Hemsby. Norf 4G 79
Hemswell. Linc 1G 87
Hemswell Cliff. Linc 2G 87
Hemsworth. Dors 2E 15
Hemsworth. W Yor 3E 93
Hemyock. Devn 1E 13
Henallt. Carm 3E 45
Henbury. Bris 4A 34
Henbury. Ches E 3C 84
Hendomen. Powy 1E 58
Hendon. G Lon 2D 38
Hendon. Tyne 4H 115
Hendra. Corn 3D 6
Hendre. B'end 3C 32
Hendreforgan. Rhon 3C 32
Hendy. Carm 5F 45
Heneglwys. IOA 3D 80
Henfeddau Fawr. Pemb 1G 43
Henfield. S Glo 4B 34
Henfield. W Sus 4D 26
Henford. Devn 3D 10
Hengoed. Cphy 2E 33
Hengoed. Shrp 2E 71
Hengrave. Suff 4H 65
Henham. Essx 3F 53
Heniarth. Powy 5D 70
Henlade. Som 4F 21
Henley. Dors 2B 14
Henley. Shrp
nr. Church Stretton 2G 59
nr. Ludlow 3H 59
Henley. Som 3H 21
Henley. Suff 5D 66
Henley. W Sus 4G 25
Henley Down. E Sus 4B 28
Henley-in-Arden. Warw 4F 61
Henley-on-Thames. Oxon 3F 37
Henley Street. Kent 4A 40
Henllan. Cdgn 1D 44
Henllan. Den 4C 82
Henllan. Mon 3F 47
Henllan Amgoed. Carm 3F 43
Henllys. Torf 2F 33
Henlow. C Beds 2B 52
Hennock. Devn 4B 12
Henny Street. Essx 2B 54
Henryd. Cnwy 3G 81
Henry's Moat. Pemb 2E 43
Hensall. N Yor 2F 93
Henshaw. Nmbd 3A 114
Hensingham. Cumb 3A 102
Henstead. Suff 2G 67
Hensting. Hants 4C 24
Henstridge. Som 1C 14
Henstridge Ash. Som 4C 22
Henstridge Bowden. Som 4B 22
Henstridge Marsh. Som 4C 22
Henton. Oxon 5F 51
Henton. Som 2H 21
Henwood. Corn 5C 10
Heogan. Shet 7F 173
Heolgerrig. Mer T 5D 46
Heol Senni. Powy 3C 46
Heol-y-Cyw. B'end 3C 32
Hepburn. Nmbd 2E 121
Hepple. Nmbd 4D 121
Hepscott. Nmbd 1F 115
Heptonstall. W Yor 2H 91
Hepworth. Suff 3B 66
Hepworth. W Yor 4B 92
Herbrandston. Pemb 4C 42
Hereford. Here 197 (2A 48)
Heribusta. High 1D 154
Heriot. Bord 4H 129
Hermiston. Edin 2E 129
Hermitage. Dors 2B 14
Hermitage. Bord 5H 119
Hermitage. W Ber 4D 36
Hermitage. W Sus 2F 17
Hermon. Carm
nr. Llandeilo 3G 45
nr. Newcastle Emlyn 2D 44
Hermon. IOA 4C 80
Hermon. Pemb 1G 43
Herne. Kent 4F 41
Herne Bay. Kent 4F 41
Herne Common. Kent 4F 41
Herne Pound. Kent 5A 40
Herner. Devn 4F 19
Hernhill. Kent 4E 41
Herodsfoot. Corn 2G 7
Heronden. Kent 5G 41
Herongate. Essx 1H 39
Heronsford. S Ayr 1G 109
Heronsgate. Herts 1B 38
Heron's Ghyll. E Sus 3F 27
Herra. Shet 2H 173
Herriard. Hants 2E 25
Herringfleet. Suff 1G 67
Herringswell. Suff 4G 65
Herrington. Tyne 4G 115
Hersden. Kent 4G 41
Hersham. Corn 2C 10
Hersham. Surr 4C 38
Herstmonceux. E Sus 4H 27
Herston. Dors 5F 15
Herston. Orkn 8D 172
Hertford. Herts 4D 52
Hertford Heath. Herts 4D 52
Hertingfordbury. Herts 4D 52
Hesketh. Lanc 2C 90
Hesketh Bank. Lanc 2C 90
Hesketh Lane. Lanc 5F 97
Hesket Newmarket. Cumb 1E 103
Heskin Green. Lanc 3D 90
Hesleden. Dur 1B 106
Hesleyside. Nmbd 1B 114
Heslington. York 4A 100
Hessay. York 4H 99
Hessenford. Corn 3H 7
Hessett. Suff 4B 66
Hessilhead. N Ayr 4E 127
Hessle. E Yor 2D 94
Hestaford. Shet 6D 173
Hest Bank. Lanc 3D 96
Hester's Way. Glos 3E 49
Hestinsetter. Shet 7D 173
Heston. G Lon 3C 38
Hestwall. Orkn 6B 172
Heswall. Mers 2E 83
Hethe. Oxon 3D 50
Hethelpit Cross. Glos 3C 48
Hethersett. Norf 5D 78
Hethersgill. Cumb 3F 113
Hetherside. Cumb 3F 113
Hethpool. Nmbd 2C 120
Hett. Dur 1F 105
Hetton. N Yor 4B 98
Hetton-le-Hole. Tyne 5G 115
Hetton Steads. Nmbd 1E 121
Heugh. Nmbd 2D 115
Heugh-head. Abers 2A 152
Heveningham. Suff 3F 67
Hever. Kent 1F 27
Heversham. Cumb 1D 97
Hevingham. Norf 3D 78
Hewas Water. Corn 4D 6
Hewelsfield. Glos 5A 48
Hewish. N Som 5H 33
Hewish. Som 2H 13
Hewood. Dors 2G 13
Heworth. York 4A 100
Hexham. Nmbd 3C 114
Hextable. Kent 3G 39
Hexton. Herts 2B 52
Hexworthy. Devn 5G 11
Heybridge. Essx
nr. Brentwood 1H 39
nr. Maldon 5B 54
Heybridge Basin. Essx 5B 54
Heybrook Bay. Devn 4A 8
Heydon. Cambs 1E 53
Heydon. Norf 3D 78
Heydour. Linc 2H 75
Heylipol. Arg 4A 138
Heyop. Powy 3E 59
Heysham. Lanc 3D 96
Heyshott. W Sus 1G 17
Heytesbury. Wilts 2E 23
Heythrop. Oxon 3B 50
Heywood. G Man 3G 91
Heywood. Wilts 1D 22
Hibaldstow. N Lin 4C 94
Hickleton. S Yor 4E 93
Hickling. Norf 3G 79
Hickling. Notts 3D 74
Hickling Green. Norf 3G 79
Hickling Heath. Norf 3G 79
Hickstead. W Sus 3D 26
Hidcote Bartrim. Glos 1G 49
Hidcote Boyce. Glos 1G 49
Higford. Shrp 5B 72
High Ackworth. W Yor 3E 93
Higham. Derbs 5A 86
Higham. Kent 3B 40
Higham. Lanc 1G 91
Higham. S Yor 4D 92
Higham. Suff
nr. Ipswich 2D 54
nr. Newmarket 4G 65
Higham Dykes. Nmbd 2E 115
Higham Ferrers. Nptn 4G 63
Higham Gobion. C Beds 2B 52
Higham on the Hill. Leics 1A 62
Highampton. Devn 2E 11
Higham Wood. Kent 1H 27
High Angerton. Nmbd 1D 115
High Auldgirth. Dum 1G 111
High Bankhill. Cumb 5G 113
High Banton. N Lan 1A 128
High Barnet. G Lon 1D 38
High Beech. Essx 1F 39
High Bentham. N Yor 3F 97
High Bickington. Devn 4G 19
High Biggins. Cumb 2E 97
High Birkwith. N Yor 2G 97
High Blantyre. S Lan 4H 127
High Bonnybridge. Falk 2B 128
High Borrans. Cumb 4F 103
High Bradfield. S Yor 1G 85
High Bray. Devn 3G 19
Highbridge. Cumb 5E 113
Highbridge. High 5E 148
Highbridge. Som 2G 21
Highbrook. W Sus 2E 27
High Brooms. Kent 1G 27
High Bullen. Devn 4F 19
Highburton. W Yor 3B 92
Highbury. Som 2B 22
High Buston. Nmbd 4G 121
High Callerton. Nmbd 2E 115
High Carlingill. Cumb 4H 103
High Catton. E Yor 4B 100
High Church. Nmbd 1E 115
Highclere. Hants 5C 36
Highcliffe. Dors 3H 15
High Cogges. Oxon 5B 50
High Common. Norf 5B 78
High Coniscliffe. Darl 3F 105
High Crosby. Cumb 4F 113
High Cross. Hants 4F 25
High Cross. Herts 4D 52
High Easter. Essx 4G 53
High Eggborough. N Yor 2F 93
High Ellington. N Yor 1D 98
Higher Alham. Som 2B 22
Higher Ansty. Dors 2C 14
Higher Ashton. Devn 4B 12
Higher Ballam. Lanc 1B 90
Higher Bartle. Lanc 1D 90
Higher Bockhampton. Dors 3C 14
Higher Bojewyan. Corn 3A 4
High Ercall. Telf 4H 71
Higher Cheriton. Devn 2E 12
Higher Clovelly. Devn 4D 18
Higher Compton. Plym 3A 8
Higher Dean. Devn 2D 8
Higher Dinting. Derbs 1E 85
Higher Dunstone. Devn 5H 11
Higher End. G Man 4D 90
Higherford. Lanc 5A 98
Higher Gabwell. Devn 2F 9
Higher Halstock Leigh. Dors 2A 14
Higher Heysham. Lanc 3D 96
Higher Hurdsfield. Ches E 3D 84
Higher Kingcombe. Dors 3A 14
Higher Kinnerton. Flin 4F 83
Higher Melcombe. Dors 2C 14
Higher Penwortham. Lanc 2D 90
Higher Porthpean. Corn 3E 7
Higher Poynton. Ches E 2D 84
Higher Shotton. Flin 4F 83
Higher Shurlach. Ches W 3A 84
Higher Slade. Devn 2F 19
Higher Tale. Devn 2D 12
Higher Town. IOS 1B 4
Higher Town. Som 2C 20
Highertown. Corn 4C 6
Higher Vexford. Som 3E 20
Higher Walton. Lanc 2D 90
Higher Walton. Warr 2H 83
Higher Whatcombe. Dors 2D 14
Higher Wheelton. Lanc 2E 90
Higher Whiteleigh. Corn 3C 10
Higher Whitley. Ches W 2A 84
Higher Wincham. Ches W 3A 84
Higher Wraxall. Dors 2A 14
Higher Wych. Ches W 1G 71
Higher Yalberton. Torb 3E 9
High Etherley. Dur 2E 105
High Ferry. Linc 1C 76
Highfield. E Yor 1H 93
Highfield. N Ayr 4E 126
Highfield. Tyne 4E 115
Highfields Caldecote. Cambs 5C 64
High Gallowhill. E Dun 2H 127
High Garrett. Essx 3A 54
Highgate. G Lon 2D 39
Highgate. N Ayr 4E 127
Highgate. Powy 1D 58
High Grange. Dur 1E 105
High Green. Cumb 4F 103
High Green. Norf 5D 78
High Green. Shrp 2B 60
High Green. S Yor 1H 85
High Green. W Yor 3B 92
High Green. Worc 1D 49
Highgreen Manor. Nmbd 5C 120
High Halden. Kent 2C 28
High Halstow. Medw 3B 40
High Ham. Som 3H 21
High Harrington. Cumb 2B 102
High Haswell. Dur 5G 115
High Hatton. Shrp 3A 72
High Hawsker. N Yor 4G 107
High Hesket. Cumb 5F 113
High Hesleden. Dur 1B 106
High Hoyland. S Yor 3C 92
High Hunsley. E Yor 1C 94
High Hurstwood. E Sus 3F 27
High Hutton. N Yor 3B 100
High Ireby. Cumb 1D 102
High Keil. Arg 5A 122
High Kelling. Norf 2D 78
High Kilburn. N Yor 2H 99
High Knipe. Cumb 3G 103
High Lands. Dur 2E 105
The Highlands. Shrp 2A 60
High Lane. G Man 2D 84
High Lane. Worc 4A 60
Highlane. Ches E 4C 84
Highlane. Derbs 2B 86
High Laver. Essx 5F 53
Highlaws. Cumb 5C 112
Highleadon. Glos 3C 48
High Legh. Ches E 2B 84
Highleigh. W Sus 3G 17
High Leven. Stoc T 3B 106
Highley. Shrp 2B 60
High Littleton. Bath 1B 22
High Longthwaite. Cumb 5D 112
High Lorton. Cumb 2C 102
High Marishes. N Yor 2C 100
High Marnham. Notts 3F 87
High Melton. S Yor 4F 93
High Mickley. Nmbd 3D 115
High Moor. Lanc 3D 90
Highmoor. Cumb 5D 112
Highmoor. Oxon 3F 37
Highmoor Cross. Oxon 3F 37
Highmoor Hill. Mon 3H 33
Highnam. Glos 4C 48
High Newport. Tyne 4G 115
High Newton. Cumb 1D 96
High Newton-by-the-Sea. Nmbd 2G 121
High Nibthwaite. Cumb 1B 96
High Offley. Staf 3B 72
High Ongar. Essx 5F 53
High Onn. Staf 4C 72
High Orchard. Glos 4D 48
High Park. Mers 3B 90
High Roding. Essx 4G 53
High Row. Cumb 1E 103
High Salvington. W Sus 5C 26
High Scales. Cumb 5C 112
High Shaw. N Yor 5B 104
High Shincliffe. Dur 5F 115
High Side. Cumb 1D 102
High Spen. Tyne 3E 115
Highsted. Kent 4D 40
High Stoop. Dur 5E 115
High Street. Corn 3D 6
High Street. Suff
nr. Aldeburgh 5G 67
nr. Bungay 2F 67
nr. Yoxford 3G 67
High Street Green. Suff 5C 66
Highstreet Green. Essx 2A 54
Highstreet Green. Surr 2A 26
Hightae. Dum 2B 112
High Throston. Hart 1B 106
High Town. Staf 4D 73
Hightown. Ches E 4C 84
Hightown. Mers 4A 90
Hightown Green. Suff 5B 66
High Toynton. Linc 4B 88
High Trewhitt. Nmbd 4E 121
High Valleyfield. Fife 1D 128
Highway. Here 1H 47
Highweek. Devn 5B 12
High Westwood. Dur 4E 115
Highwood. Staf 2E 73
Highwood. Worc 4A 60
High Worsall. N Yor 4A 106
Highworth. Swin 2H 35
High Wray. Cumb 5E 103
High Wych. Herts 4E 53
High Wycombe. Buck 2G 37
Hilborough. Norf 5H 77
Hilcott. Wilts 1G 23
Hildenborough. Kent 1G 27
Hildersham. Cambs 1F 53
Hilderstone. Staf 2D 72
Hilderthorpe. E Yor 3F 101
Hilfield. Dors 2B 14
Hilgay. Norf 1F 65
Hill. S Glo 2B 34
Hill. Warw 4B 62
Hill. Worc 1E 49
The Hill. Cumb 1A 96
Hillam. N Yor 2F 93
Hillbeck. Cumb 3A 104
Hillberry. IOM 4C 108
Hillborough. Kent 4G 41
Hillbourne. Pool 3F 15
Hillbrae. Abers
nr. Aberchirder 4D 160
nr. Inverurie 1E 153
nr. Methlick 5F 161
Hill Brow. Hants 4F 25
Hillbutts. Dors 2E 15
Hillclifflane. Derbs 1G 73
Hillcommon. Som 4E 21
Hill Deverill. Wilts 2D 22
Hilldyke. Linc 1C 76
Hill End. Dur 1D 104
Hill End. Fife 4C 136
Hill End. N Yor 4C 98
Hillend. Fife 1E 129
Hillend. N Lan 3B 128
Hillend. Shrp 1C 60
Hillend. Swan 3D 30
Hillersland. Glos 4A 48
Hillerton. Devn 3H 11
Hillesden. Buck 3E 51
Hillesley. Glos 3C 34
Hillfarrance. Som 4E 21
Hill Gate. Here 3H 47
Hill Green. Essx 2E 53
Hill Green. W Ber 4C 36
Hill Head. Hants 2D 16
Hillhead. Abers 5C 160
Hillhead. Devn 3F 9
Hillhead. S Ayr 3D 116
Hillhead of Auchentumb. Abers 3G 161
Hilliard's Cross. Staf 4F 73
Hilliclay. High 2D 168
Hillingdon. G Lon 2B 38
Hillington. Glas 3G 127
Hillington. Norf 3G 77
Hillmorton. Warw 3C 62
Hill of Beath. Fife 4D 136
Hill of Fearn. High 1C 158
Hill of Fiddes. Abers 1G 153
Hill of Keillor. Ang 4B 144
Hill of Overbrae. Abers 2F 161
Hill Ridware. Staf 4E 73
Hillsborough. S Yor 1H 85
Hill Side. W Yor 3B 92
Hillside. Abers 4G 153
Hillside. Ang 2G 145
Hillside. Devn 2D 8
Hillside. Mers 3B 90
Hillside. Orkn 5C 172
Hillside. Shet 5F 173

Hillside – Howley

Hillside. Shrp 2A 60
Hillside. Worc 4B 60
Hillside of Prieston. Ang 5C 144
Hill Somersal. Derbs 2F 73
Hillstown. Derbs 4B 86
Hillstreet. Hants 1B 16
Hillswick. Shet 4D 173
Hill Top. Dur
nr. Barnard Castle 2C 104
nr. Durham 5F 115
nr. Stanley 4E 115
Hill View. Dors 3E 15
Hillwell. Shet 10E 173
Hill Wootton. Warw 4H 61
Hillyland. Per 1C 136
Hilmarton. Wilts 4F 35
Hilperton. Wilts 1D 22
Hilperton Marsh. Wilts 1D 22
Hilsea. Port 2E 17
Hilston. E Yor 1F 95
Hiltingbury. Hants 4C 24
Hilton. Cambs 4B 64
Hilton. Cumb 2A 104
Hilton. Derbs 2G 73
Hilton. Dors 2C 14
Hilton. Dur 2E 105
Hilton. High 5E 165
Hilton. Shrp 1B 60
Hilton. Staf 5E 73
Hilton. Stoc T 3B 106
Hilton of Cadboll. High 1C 158
Himbleton. Worc 5D 60
Himley. Staf 1C 60
Hincaster. Cumb 1E 97
Hinchwick. Glos 3G 49
Hinckley. Leics 1B 62
Hinderclay. Suff 3C 66
Hinderwell. N Yor 3E 107
Hindford. Shrp 2F 71
Hindhead. Surr 3G 25
Hindley. G Man 4E 90
Hindley. Nmbd 4D 114
Hindley Green. G Man 4E 91
Hindlip. Worc 5C 60
Hindolveston. Norf 3C 78
Hindon. Wilts 3E 23
Hindringham. Norf 2B 78
Hingham. Norf 5C 78
Hinksford. Staf 2C 60
Hinstock. Shrp 3A 72
Hintlesham. Suff 1D 54
Hinton. Hants 3H 15
Hinton. Here 2G 47
Hinton. Nptn 5C 62
Hinton. Shrp 5G 71
Hinton. S Glo 4C 34
Hinton Ampner. Hants 4D 24
Hinton Blewett. Bath 1A 22
Hinton Charterhouse. Bath 1C 22
Hinton-in-the-Hedges. Nptn 2D 50
Hinton Martell. Dors 2F 15
Hinton on the Green. Worc 1F 49
Hinton Parva. Swin 3H 35
Hinton St George. Som 1H 13
Hinton St Mary. Dors 1C 14
Hinton Waldrist. Oxon 2B 36
Hints. Shrp 3A 60
Hints. Staf 5F 73
Hinwick. Bed 4G 63
Hinxhill. Kent 1E 29
Hinxton. Cambs 1E 53
Hinxworth. Herts 1C 52
Hipley. Hants 1E 16
Hipperholme. W Yor 2B 92
Hipsburn. Nmbd 3G 121
Hipswell. N Yor 5E 105
Hiraeth. Carm 2F 43
Hirn. Abers 3E 153
Hirnant. Powy 3C 70
Hirst. N Lan 3B 128
Hirst. Nmbd 1F 115
Hirst Courtney. N Yor 2G 93
Hirwaen. Den 4D 82
Hirwaun. Rhon 5C 46
Hiscott. Devn 4F 19
Histon. Cambs 4D 64
Hitcham. Suff 5B 66
Hitchin. Herts 3B 52
Hittisleigh. Devn 3H 11
Hittisleigh Barton. Devn 3H 11
Hive. E Yor 1B 94
Hixon. Staf 3E 73
Hoaden. Kent 5G 41
Hoar Cross. Staf 3F 73
Hoarwithy. Here 3A 48
Hoath. Kent 4G 41
Yr Hôb. Flin 5F 83
Hobarris. Shrp 3F 59
Hobbister. Orkn 7C 172
Hobbles Green. Suff 5G 65
Hobbs Cross. Essx 1F 39
Hobkirk. Bord 3H 119
Hobson. Dur 4E 115
Hoby. Leics 4D 74
Hockering. Norf 4C 78
Hockering Heath. Norf 4C 78
Hockerton. Notts 5E 86
Hockley. Essx 1C 40
Hockley. Staf 5G 73
Hockley. W Mid 3G 61
Hockley Heath. W Mid 3F 61
Hockliffe. C Beds 3H 51
Hockwold cum Wilton. Norf 2G 65
Hockworthy. Devn 1D 12
Hoddesdon. Herts 5D 52
Hoddlesden. Bkbn 2F 91
Hoddomcross. Dum 2C 112
Hodgeston. Pemb 5E 43
Hodley. Powy 1D 58
Hodnet. Shrp 3A 72
Hodsoll Street. Kent 4H 39
Hodson. Swin 3G 35
Hodthorpe. Derbs 3C 86
Hoe. Norf 4B 78
The Hoe. Plym 3A 8
Hoe Gate. Hants 1E 17
Hoff. Cumb 3H 103
Hoffleet Stow. Linc 2B 76
Hogaland. Shet 4E 173
Hogben's Hill. Kent 5E 41
Hoggard's Green. Suff 5A 66
Hoggeston. Buck 3G 51
Hoggrill's End. Warw 1G 61
Hogha Gearraidh. W Isl 1C 170
Hoghton. Lanc 2E 90
Hoghton Bottoms. Lanc 2E 91
Hognaston. Derbs 5G 85
Hogsthorpe. Linc 3E 89
Hogstock. Dors 2E 15
Holbeach. Linc 3C 76
Holbeach Bank. Linc 3C 76
Holbeach Clough. Linc 3C 76
Holbeach Drove. Linc 4C 76
Holbeach Hurn. Linc 3C 76
Holbeach St Johns. Linc 4C 76
Holbeach St Marks. Linc 2C 76
Holbeach St Matthew. Linc 2D 76
Holbeck. Notts 3C 86
Holbeck. W Yor 1C 92
Holbeck Woodhouse. Notts 3C 86
Holberrow Green. Worc 5E 61
Holbeton. Devn 3C 8
Holborn. G Lon 2E 39
Holbrook. Derbs 1A 74
Holbrook. S Yor 2B 86
Holbrook. Suff 2E 55
Holburn. Nmbd 1E 121
Holbury. Hants 2C 16
Holcombe. Devn 5C 12
Holcombe. G Man 3F 91
Holcombe. Som 2B 22
Holcombe Brook. G Man 3F 91
Holcombe Rogus. Devn 1D 12
Holcot. Nptn 4E 63
Holden. Lanc 5G 97
Holdenby. Nptn 4D 62
Holder's Green. Essx 3G 53
Holdgate. Shrp 2H 59
Holdingham. Linc 1H 75
Holditch. Dors 2G 13
Holemoor. Devn 2E 11
Hole Street. W Sus 4C 26
Holford. Som 2E 21
Holker. Cumb 2C 96
Holkham. Norf 1A 78
Hollacombe. Devn 2D 11
Holland. Orkn
on Papa Westray 2D 172
on Stronsay 5F 172
Holland Fen. Linc 1B 76
Holland Lees. Lanc 4D 90
Holland-on-Sea. Essx 4F 55
Holland Park. W Mid 5E 73
Hollandstoun. Orkn 2G 172
Hollesley. Suff 1G 55
Hollinfare. Warr 1A 84
Hollingbourne. Kent 5C 40
Hollingbury. Brig 5E 27
Hollingdon. Buck 3G 51
Hollingrove. E Sus 3A 28
Hollington. Derbs 2G 73
Hollington. E Sus 4B 28
Hollington. Staf 2E 73
Hollington Grove. Derbs 2G 73
Hollingwood B3 86
Hollingworth. G Man 1E 85
Hollins. Derbs 3H 85
Hollins. G Man
nr. Bury 4G 91
nr. Middleton 4G 91
Hollinsclough. Staf 4E 85
Hollinswood. Telf 5B 72
Hollinthorpe. W Yor 1D 93
Hollinwood. G Man 4H 91
Hollinwood. Shrp 2H 71
Hollocombe. Devn 1G 11
Holloway. Derbs 5H 85
Hollowell. Nptn 3D 62
Hollow Meadows. S Yor 2G 85
Hollows. Dum 2E 113
Hollybush. Cphy 5E 47
Hollybush. E Ayr 3C 116
Hollybush. Worc 2C 48
Holly End. Norf 5D 77
Holly Hill. N Yor 4E 105
Hollyhurst. Shrp 1H 71
Hollym. E Yor 2G 95
Hollywood. Worc 3E 61
Holmacott. Devn 4F 19
Holmbridge. W Yor 4B 92
Holmbury St Mary. Surr 1C 26
Holmbush. Corn 3E 7
Holmcroft. Staf 3D 72
Holme. Cambs 2A 64
Holme. Cumb 2E 97
Holme. N Lin 4C 94
Holme. N Yor 1F 99
Holme. Notts 5F 87
Holme. W Yor 4B 92
Holmebridge. Dors 4D 15
Holme Chapel. Lanc 2G 91
Holme Hale. Norf 5A 78
Holme Lacy. Here 2A 48
Holme Marsh. Here 5F 59
Holmend. Dum 4C 118
Holme next the Sea. Norf 1G 77
Holme-on-Spalding-Moor. E Yor 1B 94
Holme on the Wolds. E Yor 5D 100
Holme Pierrepont. Notts 2D 74
Holmer. Here 1A 48
Holmer Green. Buck 1A 38
Holmes. Lanc 3C 90
Holme St Cuthbert. Cumb 5C 112
Holmes Chapel. Ches E 4B 84
Holmesfield. Derbs 3H 85
Holmeswood. Lanc 3C 90
Holmewood. Derbs 4B 86
Holmfirth. W Yor 4B 92
Holmhead. E Ayr 2E 117
Holmisdale. High 4A 154
Holm of Drumlanrig. Dum 5H 117
Holmpton. E Yor 2G 95
Holmrook. Cumb 5B 102
Holmsgarth. Shet 7F 173
Holmside. Dur 5F 115
Holmwrangle. Cumb 5G 113
Holne. Devn 2D 8
Holsworthy. Devn 2D 10
Holsworthy Beacon. Devn 2D 10
Holt. Dors 2F 15
Holt. Norf 2C 78
Holt. Wilts 5D 34
Holt. Worc 4C 60
Holt. Wrex 5G 83
Holtby. York 4A 100
Holt End. Hants 3E 25
Holt End. Worc 4E 61
Holt Fleet. Worc 4C 60
Holt Green. Lanc 4B 90
Holt Heath. Dors 2F 15
Holt Heath. Worc 4C 60
Holton. Oxon 5D 50
Holton. Som 4B 22
Holton. Suff 3F 67
Holton cum Beckering. Linc 2A 88
Holton Heath. Dors 3E 15
Holton le Clay. Linc 4F 95
Holton le Moor. Linc 1H 87
Holton St Mary. Suff 2D 54
Holt Pound. Hants 2G 25
Holtsmere End. Herts 4A 52
Holtye. E Sus 2F 27
Holwell. Dors 1C 14
Holwell. Herts 2B 52
Holwell. Leics 3E 75
Holwell. Oxon 5H 49
Holwell. Som 2C 22
Holwick. Dur 2C 104
Holworth. Dors 4C 14
Holybourne. Hants 2F 25
Holy City. Devn 2G 13
Holy Cross. Worc 3D 60
Holyfield. Essx 5D 53
Holyhead. IOA 2B 80
Holy Island. Nmbd 5H 131
Holymoorside. Derbs 4H 85
Holyport. Wind 4G 37
Holystone. Nmbd 4D 120
Holytown. N Lan 3A 128
Holywell. Cambs 3C 64
Holywell. Corn 3B 6
Holywell. Dors 2A 14
Holywell. Flin 3D 82
Holywell. Glos 2C 34
Holywell. Nmbd 2G 115
Holywell. Warw 4F 61
Holywell Green. W Yor 3A 92
Holywell Lake. Som 4E 20
Holywell Row. Suff 3G 65
Holywood. Dum 1G 111
Homer. Shrp 5A 72
Homer Green. Mers 4B 90
Homersfield. Suff 2E 67
Hom Green. Here 3A 48
Homington. Wilts 4G 23
Honeyborough. Pemb 4D 42
Honeybourne. Worc 1G 49
Honeychurch. Devn 2G 11
Honeydon. Bed 5A 64
Honey Hill. Kent 4F 41
Honey Street. Wilts 5G 35
Honey Tye. Suff 2C 54
Honeywick. C Beds 3H 51
Honiley. Warw 3G 61
Honing. Norf 3F 79
Honingham. Norf 4D 78
Honington. Linc 1G 75
Honington. Suff 3B 66
Honington. Warw 1A 50
Honiton. Devn 2E 13
Honley. W Yor 3B 92
Honnington. Telf 4B 72
Hoo. Suff 5E 67
Hoobrook. Worc 3C 60
Hood Green. S Yor 4D 92
Hooe. E Sus 5A 28
Hooe. Plym 3B 8
Hooe Common. E Sus 4A 28
Hoo Green. Ches E 2B 84
Hoohill. Bkpl 1B 90
Hook. Cambs 1D 64
Hook. E Yor 2A 94
Hook. G Lon 4C 38
Hook. Hants
nr. Basingstoke 1F 25
nr. Fareham 2D 16
Hook. Pemb 3D 43
Hook. Wilts 3F 35
Hook-a-Gate. Shrp 5G 71
Hook Bank. Worc 1D 48
Hooke. Dors 2A 14
Hooker Gate. Tyne 4E 115
Hookgate. Staf 2B 72
Hook Green. Kent
nr. Lamberhurst 2A 28
nr. Meopham 4H 39
nr. Southfleet 3H 39
Hook Norton. Oxon 2B 50
Hook's Cross. Herts 3C 52
Hook Street. Glos 2B 34
Hookway. Devn 3B 12
Hookwood. Surr 1D 26
Hoole. Ches W 4G 83
Hooley. Surr 5D 39
Hooley Bridge. G Man 3G 91
Hooley Brow. G Man 3G 91
Hoo St Werburgh. Medw 3B 40
Hooton. Ches W 3F 83
Hooton Levitt. S Yor 1C 86
Hooton Pagnell. S Yor 4E 93
Hooton Roberts. S Yor 1B 86
Hoove. Shet 7E 173
Hope. Derbs 2F 85
Hope. Flin 5F 83
Hope. High 2E 167
Hope. Powy 5E 71
Hope. Shrp 5F 71
Hope. Staf 5F 85
Hope Bagot. Shrp 3H 59
Hope Bowdler. Shrp 1G 59
Hopedale. Staf 5F 85
Hope Green. Ches E 2D 84
Hopeman. Mor 2F 159
Hope Mansell. Here 4B 48
Hopesay. Shrp 2F 59
Hope's Green. Essx 2B 40
Hopetown. W Yor 2D 93
Hope under Dinmore. Here 5H 59
Hopley's Green. Here 5F 59
Hopperton. N Yor 4G 99
Hop Pole. Linc 4A 76
Hopstone. Shrp 1B 60
Hopton. Derbs 5G 85
Hopton. Powy 1E 59
Hopton. Shrp
nr. Oswestry 3F 71
nr. Wem 3H 71
Hopton. Staf 3D 72
Hopton. Suff 3B 66
Hopton Cangeford. Shrp 2H 59
Hopton Castle. Shrp 3F 59
Hopton Heath. Staf 3D 72
Hoptonheath. Shrp 3F 59
Hopton on Sea. Norf 5H 79
Hopton Wafers. Shrp 3A 60
Hopwas. Staf 5F 73
Hopwood. Worc 3E 61
Horam. E Sus 4G 27
Horbling. Linc 2A 76
Horbury. W Yor 3C 92
Horcott. Glos 5G 49
Horden. Dur 5H 115
Horderley. Shrp 2G 59
Hordle. Hants 3A 16
Hordley. Shrp 2F 71
Horeb. Carm
nr. Brechfa 3F 45
nr. Llanelli 5E 45
Horeb. Cdgn 1D 45
Horfield. Bris 4A 34
Horgabost. W Isl 8C 171
Horham. Suff 3E 66
Horkstow. N Lin 3C 94
Horley. Oxon 1C 50
Horley. Surr 1D 27
Horn Ash. Dors 2G 13
Hornblotton Green. Som 3A 22
Hornby. Lanc 3E 97
Hornby. N Yor
nr. Appleton Wiske 4A 106
nr. Catterick Garrison 5F 105
Horncastle. Linc 4B 88
Hornchurch. G Lon 2G 39
Horncliffe. Nmbd 5F 131
Horndean. Hants 1F 17
Horndean. Bord 5E 131
Horndon. Devn 4F 11
Horndon on the Hill. Thur 2A 40
Horne. Surr 1E 27
Horner. Som 2C 20
Horning. Norf 4F 79
Horninghold. Leics 1F 63
Horninglow. Staf 3G 73
Horningsea. Cambs 4D 65
Horningsham. Wilts 2D 22
Horningtoft. Norf 3B 78
Hornsbury. Som 1G 13
Hornsby. Cumb 4G 113
Hornsbygate. Cumb 4G 113
Horns Corner. Kent 3B 28
Horns Cross. Devn 4D 19
Hornsea. E Yor 5G 101
Hornsea Burton. E Yor 5G 101
Hornsey. G Lon 2E 39
Hornton. Oxon 1B 50
Horpit. Swin 3H 35
Horrabridge. Devn 2B 8
Horringer. Suff 4H 65
Horringford. IOW 4D 16
Horrocks Fold. G Man 3F 91
Horrocksford. Lanc 5G 97
Horsbrugh Ford. Bord 1E 119
Horsebridge. Devn 5E 11
Horsebridge. Hants 3B 24
Horsebrook. Staf 4C 72
Horsecastle. N Som 5H 33
Horsehay. Telf 5A 72
Horseheath. Cambs 1G 53
Horsehouse. N Yor 1C 98
Horsell. Surr 5A 38
Horseman's Green. Wrex 1G 71
Horsenden. Buck 5F 51
Horseway. Cambs 2D 64
Horsey. Norf 3G 79
Horsey. Som 3G 21
Horsford. Norf 4D 78
Horsforth. W Yor 1C 92
Horsham. W Sus 2C 26
Horsham. Worc 5B 60
Horsham St Faith. Norf 4E 78
Horsington. Linc 4A 88
Horsington. Som 4C 22
Horsley. Derbs 1A 74
Horsley. Glos 2D 34
Horsley. Nmbd
nr. Prudhoe 3D 115
nr. Rochester 5C 120
Horsley Cross. Essx 3E 54
Horsleycross Street. Essx 3E 54
Horsleyhill. Bord 3H 119
Horsleyhope. Dur 5D 114
Horsley Woodhouse. Derbs 1A 74
Horsmonden. Kent 1A 28
Horspath. Oxon 5D 50
Horstead. Norf 4E 79
Horsted Keynes. W Sus 3E 27
Horton. Buck 4H 51
Horton. Dors 2F 15
Horton. Lanc 4A 98
Horton. Nptn 5F 63
Horton. Shrp 2G 71
Horton. Som 1G 13
Horton. S Glo 3C 34
Horton. Staf 5D 84
Horton. Swan 4D 30
Horton. Wilts 5F 35
Horton. Wind 3B 38
Horton Cross. Som 1G 13
Horton-cum-Studley. Oxon 4D 50
Horton Grange. Nmbd 2F 115
Horton Green. Ches W 1G 71
Horton Heath. Hants 1C 16
Horton in Ribblesdale. N Yor 2H 97
Horton Kirby. Kent 4G 39
Hortonwood. Telf 4A 72
Horwich. G Man 3E 91
Horwich End. Derbs 2E 85
Horwood. Devn 4F 19
Hoscar. Lanc 3C 90
Hose. Leics 3E 75
Hosh. Per 1A 136
Hosta. W Isl 1C 170
Hoswick. Shet 9F 173
Hotham. E Yor 1B 94
Hothfield. Kent 1D 28
Hoton. Leics 3C 74
Houbie. Shet 2H 173
Hough. Arg 4A 138
Hough. Ches E
nr. Crewe 5B 84
nr. Wilmslow 3C 84
Hougham. Linc 1F 75
Hough Green. Hal 2G 83
Hough-on-the-Hill. Linc 1G 75
Houghton. Cambs 3B 64
Houghton. Cumb 4F 113
Houghton. Hants 3B 24
Houghton. Nmbd 3E 115
Houghton. Pemb 4D 43
Houghton. W Sus 4B 26
Houghton Bank. Darl 2F 105
Houghton Conquest. C Beds 1A 52
Houghton Green. E Sus 3D 28
Houghton-le-Side. Darl 2F 105
Houghton-le-Spring. Tyne 4G 115
Houghton on the Hill. Leics 5D 74
Houghton Regis. C Beds 3A 52
Houghton St Giles. Norf 2B 78
Houlland. Shet
on Mainland 6E 173
on Yell 4G 173
Houlsyke. N Yor 4E 107
Houlton. Warw 3C 62
Hound. Hants 2C 16
Hound Green. Hants 1F 25
Houndslow. Bord 5C 130
Houndsmoor. Som 4E 21
Houndwood. Bord 3E 131
Hounsdown. Hants 1B 16
Hounslow. G Lon 3C 38
Housabister. Shet 6F 173
Housay. Shet 4H 173
Househill. High 3C 158
Housetter. Shet 3E 173
Houss. Shet 8E 173
Houston. Ren 3F 127
Housty. High 5D 168
Houton. Orkn 7C 172
Hove. Brig 189 (5D 27)
Hoveringham. Notts 1D 74
Hoveton. Norf 4F 79
Hovingham. N Yor 2A 100
How. Cumb 4G 113
How Caple. Here 2B 48
Howden. E Yor 2H 93
Howden-le-Wear. Dur 1E 105
Howe. High 2F 169
Howe. Norf 5E 79
Howe. N Yor 1F 99
The Howe. Cumb 1D 96
The Howe. IOM 5A 108
Howe Green. Essx 5H 53
Howe Green. Warw 2H 61
Howegreen. Essx 5B 54
Howell. Linc 1A 76
How End. C Beds 1A 52
Howe of Teuchar. Abers 4E 161
Howes. Dum 3C 112
Howe Street. Essx
nr. Chelmsford 4G 53
nr. Finchingfield 2G 53
Howey. Powy 5C 58
Howgate. Midl 4F 129
Howgill. Lanc 5H 97
Howgill. N Yor 4C 98
How Green. Kent 1F 27
How Hill. Norf 4F 79
Howick. Nmbd 3G 121
Howle. Telf 3A 72
Howle Hill. Here 3B 48
Howleigh. Som 1F 13
Howlett End. Essx 2F 53
Howley. Som 2F 13
Howley. Warr 2A 84

Hownam. *Bord*	3B **120**
Howsham. *N Lin*	4D **94**
Howsham. *N Yor*	3B **100**
Howtel. *Nmbd*	1C **120**
Howt Green. *Kent*	4C **40**
Howton. *Here*	3H **47**
Howwood. *Ren*	3E **127**
Hoxne. *Suff*	3D **66**
Hoylake. *Mers*	2E **82**
Hoyland. *S Yor*	4D **92**
Hoylandswaine. *S Yor*	4C **92**
Hoyle. *W Sus*	4A **26**
Hubberholme. *N Yor*	2B **98**
Hubberston. *Pemb*	4C **42**
Hubbert's Bridge. *Linc*	1B **76**
Huby. *N Yor*	
nr. Harrogate	5E **99**
nr. York	3H **99**
Hucclecote. *Glos*	4D **48**
Hucking. *Kent*	5C **40**
Hucknall. *Notts*	1C **74**
Huddersfield. *W Yor*	3B **92**
Huddington. *Worc*	5D **60**
Huddlesford. *Staf*	5F **73**
Hudswell. *N Yor*	4E **105**
Huggate. *E Yor*	4C **100**
Hugglescote. *Leics*	4B **74**
Hughenden Valley. *Buck*	2G **37**
Hughley. *Shrp*	1H **59**
Hughton. *High*	4G **157**
Hugh Town. *IOS*	1B **4**
Hugus. *Corn*	4B **6**
Huish. *Devn*	1F **11**
Huish. *Wilts*	5G **35**
Huish Champflower. *Som*	4D **20**
Huish Episcopi. *Som*	4H **21**
Huisinis. *W Isl*	6B **171**
Hulcote. *Nptn*	1F **51**
Hulcott. *Buck*	4G **51**
Hulham. *Devn*	4D **12**
Hull. *Hull*	**199** (2E **94**)
Hulland. *Derbs*	1G **73**
Hulland Moss. *Derbs*	1G **73**
Hulland Ward. *Derbs*	1G **73**
Hullavington. *Wilts*	3D **35**
Hullbridge. *Essx*	1C **40**
Hulme. *G Man*	1C **84**
Hulme. *Staf*	1D **72**
Hulme End. *Staf*	5F **85**
Hulme Walfield. *Ches E*	4C **84**
Hulverstone. *IOW*	4B **16**
Hulver Street. *Suff*	2G **67**
Humber. *Devn*	5C **12**
Humber. *Here*	5H **59**
Humber Bridge. *N Lin*	2D **94**
Humberside Airport. *N Lin*	3D **94**
Humberston. *NE Lin*	4G **95**
Humberstone. *Leic*	5D **74**
Humbie. *E Lot*	3A **130**
Humbleton. *E Yor*	1F **95**
Humbleton. *Nmbd*	2D **121**
Humby. *Linc*	2H **75**
Hume. *Bord*	5D **130**
Humshaugh. *Nmbd*	2C **114**
Huna. *High*	1F **169**
Huncoat. *Lanc*	1F **91**
Huncote. *Leics*	1C **62**
Hundall. *Derbs*	3A **86**
Hunderthwaite. *Dur*	2C **104**
Hundleby. *Linc*	4C **88**
Hundle Houses. *Linc*	5B **88**
Hundleton. *Pemb*	4D **42**
Hundon. *Suff*	1H **53**
The Hundred. *Here*	4H **59**
Hundred Acres. *Hants*	1D **16**
Hundred House. *Powy*	5D **58**
Hungarton. *Leics*	5D **74**
Hungerford. *Hants*	1G **15**
Hungerford. *Shrp*	2H **59**
Hungerford. *Som*	2D **20**
Hungerford. *W Ber*	5B **36**
Hungerford Newtown. *W Ber*	4B **36**
Hunger Hill. *G Man*	4E **91**
Hungerton. *Linc*	2F **75**
Hungladder. *High*	1C **154**
Hungryhatton. *Shrp*	3A **72**
Hunmanby. *N Yor*	2E **101**
Hunmanby Sands. *N Yor*	2F **101**
Hunningham. *Warw*	4A **62**
Hunnington. *Worc*	2D **60**
Hunny Hill. *IOW*	4C **16**
Hunsdon. *Herts*	4E **53**
Hunsdonbury. *Herts*	4E **53**
Hunsingore. *N Yor*	4G **99**
Hunslet. *W Yor*	1D **92**
Hunslet Carr. *W Yor*	1D **92**
Hunsonby. *Cumb*	1G **103**
Hunspow. *High*	1E **169**
Hunstanton. *Norf*	1F **77**
Hunstanworth. *Dur*	5C **114**
Hunston. *Suff*	4B **66**
Hunston. *W Sus*	2G **17**
Hunstrete. *Bath*	5B **34**
Hunt End. *Worc*	4E **61**
Hunterfield. *Midl*	3G **129**
Hunters Forstal. *Kent*	4F **41**
Hunter's Quay. *Arg*	2C **126**
Huntham. *Som*	4G **21**
Hunthill Lodge. *Ang*	1D **144**
Huntingdon. *Cambs*	3B **64**
Huntingfield. *Suff*	3F **67**
Huntingford. *Wilts*	4D **22**
Huntington. *Ches W*	4G **83**
Huntington. *E Lot*	2A **130**
Huntington. *Here*	5E **59**
Huntington. *Staf*	4D **72**
Huntington. *Telf*	5A **72**
Huntington. *York*	4A **100**
Huntingtower. *Per*	1C **136**
Huntley. *Glos*	4C **48**
Huntley. *Staf*	1E **73**

Huntly. *Abers*	5C **160**
Huntlywood. *Bord*	5C **130**
Hunton. *Hants*	3C **24**
Hunton. *Kent*	1B **28**
Hunton. *N Yor*	5E **105**
Hunton Bridge. *Herts*	1B **38**
Hunt's Corner. *Norf*	2C **66**
Huntscott. *Som*	2C **20**
Hunt's Cross. *Mers*	2G **83**
Hunts Green. *Warw*	1F **61**
Huntsham. *Devn*	4D **20**
Huntshaw. *Devn*	4F **19**
Huntspill. *Som*	2G **21**
Huntstile. *Som*	3F **21**
Huntworth. *Som*	3G **21**
Hunwick. *Dur*	1E **105**
Hunworth. *Norf*	2C **78**
Hurcott. *Som*	
nr. Ilminster	1G **13**
nr. Somerton	4A **22**
Hurdcott. *Wilts*	3G **23**
Hurdley. *Powy*	1E **59**
Hurdsfield. *Ches E*	3D **84**
Hurlet. *Glas*	3G **127**
Hurley. *Warw*	1G **61**
Hurley. *Wind*	3G **37**
Hurlford. *E Ayr*	1D **116**
Hurliness. *Orkn*	9B **172**
Hurlston Green. *Lanc*	3C **90**
Hurn. *Dors*	3G **15**
Hursey. *Dors*	2H **13**
Hursley. *Hants*	4C **24**
Hurst. *G Man*	4H **91**
Hurst. *N Yor*	4D **104**
Hurst. *Som*	1H **13**
Hurst. *Wok*	4F **37**
Hurstbourne Priors. *Hants*	2C **24**
Hurstbourne Tarrant. *Hants*	1B **24**
Hurst Green. *Ches E*	1H **71**
Hurst Green. *E Sus*	3B **28**
Hurst Green. *Essx*	4D **54**
Hurst Green. *Lanc*	1E **91**
Hurst Green. *Surr*	5E **39**
Hurstley. *Here*	1G **47**
Hurstpierpoint. *W Sus*	4D **27**
Hurstway Common. *Here*	1G **47**
Hurst Wickham. *W Sus*	4D **27**
Hurstwood. *Lanc*	1G **91**
Hurtmore. *Surr*	1A **26**
Hurworth-on-Tees. *Darl*	3A **106**
Hurworth Place. *Darl*	4F **105**
Hury. *Dur*	3C **104**
Husbands Bosworth. *Leics*	2D **62**
Husborne Crawley. *C Beds*	2H **51**
Husthwaite. *N Yor*	2H **99**
Hutcherleigh. *Devn*	3D **9**
Hut Green. *N Yor*	2F **93**
Huthwaite. *Notts*	5B **86**
Huttoft. *Linc*	3E **89**
Hutton. *Cumb*	2F **103**
Hutton. *E Yor*	4E **101**
Hutton. *Essx*	1H **39**
Hutton. *Lanc*	2C **90**
Hutton. *N Som*	1G **21**
Hutton. *Bord*	4F **131**
Hutton Bonville. *N Yor*	4A **106**
Hutton Buscel. *N Yor*	1D **100**
Hutton Conyers. *N Yor*	2F **99**
Hutton Cranswick. *E Yor*	4E **101**
Hutton End. *Cumb*	1F **103**
Hutton Gate. *Red C*	3C **106**
Hutton Henry. *Dur*	1B **106**
Hutton-le-Hole. *N Yor*	1B **100**
Hutton Magna. *Dur*	3E **105**
Hutton Mulgrave. *N Yor*	4F **107**
Hutton Roof. *Cumb*	
nr. Kirkby Lonsdale	2E **97**
nr. Penrith	1E **103**
Hutton Rudby. *N Yor*	4B **106**
Huttons Ambo. *N Yor*	3B **100**
Hutton Sessay. *N Yor*	2G **99**
Hutton Village. *Red C*	3D **106**
Hutton Wandesley. *N Yor*	4H **99**
Huxham. *Devn*	3C **12**
Huxham Green. *Som*	3A **22**
Huxley. *Ches W*	4H **83**
Huxter. *Shet*	
on Mainland	6C **173**
on Whalsay	5G **173**
Huyton. *Mers*	1G **83**
Hwlffordd. *Pemb*	3D **42**
Hycemoor. *Cumb*	1A **96**
Hyde. *Glos*	
nr. Stroud	5D **49**
nr. Winchcombe	3F **49**
Hyde. *G Man*	1D **84**
Hyde Heath. *Buck*	5H **51**
Hyde Lea. *Staf*	4D **72**
Hyde Park. *S Yor*	4F **93**
Hydestile. *Surr*	1A **26**
Hyndford Bridge. *S Lan*	5C **128**
Hynish. *Arg*	5A **138**
Hyssington. *Powy*	1F **59**
Hythe. *Hants*	2C **16**
Hythe. *Kent*	2F **29**
Hythe End. *Wind*	3B **38**
Hythie. *Abers*	3H **161**
Hyton. *Cumb*	1A **96**

I

Ianstown. *Mor*	2B **160**
Iarsiadar. *W Isl*	4D **171**
Ibberton. *Dors*	2C **14**
Ible. *Derbs*	5G **85**
Ibrox. *Glas*	3G **127**
Ibsley. *Hants*	2G **15**
Ibstock. *Leics*	4B **74**
Ibstone. *Buck*	2F **37**
Ibthorpe. *Hants*	1B **24**

Iburndale. *N Yor*	4F **107**
Ibworth. *Hants*	1D **24**
Icelton. *N Som*	5G **33**
Ichrachan. *Arg*	5E **141**
Ickburgh. *Norf*	1H **65**
Ickenham. *G Lon*	2B **38**
Ickenthwaite. *Cumb*	1C **96**
Ickford. *Buck*	5E **51**
Ickham. *Kent*	5G **41**
Ickleford. *Herts*	2B **52**
Icklesham. *E Sus*	4C **28**
Ickleton. *Cambs*	1E **53**
Icklingham. *Suff*	3G **65**
Ickwell. *C Beds*	1B **52**
Icomb. *Glos*	3H **49**
Idbury. *Oxon*	4H **49**
Iddesleigh. *Devn*	2F **11**
Ide. *Devn*	3B **12**
Ideford. *Devn*	5B **12**
Ide Hill. *Kent*	5F **39**
Iden. *E Sus*	3D **28**
Iden Green. *Kent*	
nr. Benenden	2C **28**
nr. Goudhurst	2B **28**
Idle. *W Yor*	1B **92**
Idless. *Corn*	4C **6**
Idlicote. *Warw*	1A **50**
Idmiston. *Wilts*	3G **23**
Idole. *Carm*	4E **45**
Idridgehay. *Derbs*	1G **73**
Idrigill. *High*	2C **154**
Idstone. *Oxon*	3A **36**
Iffley. *Oxon*	5D **50**
Ifield. *W Sus*	2D **26**
Ifieldwood. *W Sus*	2D **26**
Ifold. *W Sus*	2B **26**
Iford. *E Sus*	5F **27**
Ifton Heath. *Shrp*	2F **71**
Ightfield. *Shrp*	2H **71**
Ightham. *Kent*	5G **39**
Iken. *Suff*	5G **67**
Ilam. *Staf*	5F **85**
Ilchester. *Som*	4A **22**
Ilderton. *Nmbd*	2E **121**
Ilford. *G Lon*	2F **39**
Ilford. *Som*	1G **13**
Ilfracombe. *Devn*	2F **19**
Ilkeston. *Derbs*	1B **74**
Ilketshall St Andrew. *Suff*	2F **67**
Ilketshall St Lawrence. *Suff*	2F **67**
Ilketshall St Margaret. *Suff*	2F **67**
Ilkley. *W Yor*	5D **98**
Illand. *Corn*	5C **10**
Illey. *W Mid*	2D **61**
Illidge Green. *Ches E*	4B **84**
Illington. *Norf*	2B **66**
Illingworth. *W Yor*	2A **92**
Illogan. *Corn*	4A **6**
Illogan Highway. *Corn*	4A **6**
Illston on the Hill. *Leics*	1E **62**
Ilmer. *Buck*	5F **51**
Ilmington. *Warw*	1H **49**
Ilminster. *Som*	1G **13**
Ilsington. *Devn*	5A **12**
Ilsington. *Dors*	3C **14**
Ilston. *Swan*	3E **31**
Ilton. *N Yor*	2D **98**
Ilton. *Som*	1G **13**
Imachar. *N Ayr*	5G **125**
Imber. *Wilts*	2E **23**
Immingham. *NE Lin*	3E **95**
Immingham Dock. *NE Lin*	3F **95**
Impington. *Cambs*	4D **64**
Ince. *Ches W*	3G **83**
Ince Blundell. *Mers*	4B **90**
Ince-in-Makerfield. *G Man*	4D **90**
Inchbae Lodge. *High*	2G **157**
Inchbare. *Ang*	2F **145**
Inchberry. *Mor*	3H **159**
Inchbraoch. *Ang*	3G **145**
Inchbrook. *Glos*	5D **48**
Incheril. *High*	2C **156**
Inchinnan. *Ren*	3F **127**
Inchlaggan. *High*	3D **148**
Inchmichael. *Per*	1E **137**
Inchnadamph. *High*	1G **163**
Inchree. *High*	2E **141**
Inchture. *Per*	1E **137**
Inchyra. *Per*	1D **136**
Indian Queens. *Corn*	3D **6**
Ingatestone. *Essx*	1H **39**
Ingbirchworth. *S Yor*	4C **92**
Ingestre. *Staf*	3D **73**
Ingham. *Linc*	2G **87**
Ingham. *Norf*	3F **79**
Ingham. *Suff*	3A **66**
Ingham Corner. *Norf*	3F **79**
Ingleborough. *Norf*	4D **76**
Ingleby. *Derbs*	3H **73**
Ingleby Arncliffe. *N Yor*	4B **106**
Ingleby Barwick. *Stoc T*	3B **106**
Ingleby Greenhow. *N Yor*	4C **106**
Ingleigh Green. *Devn*	2G **11**
Inglemire. *Hull*	1D **94**
Inglesbatch. *Bath*	5C **34**
Ingleton. *Dur*	2E **105**
Ingleton. *N Yor*	2F **97**
Inglewhite. *Lanc*	5E **97**
Ingoe. *Nmbd*	2D **114**
Ingol. *Lanc*	1D **90**
Ingoldisthorpe. *Norf*	2F **77**
Ingoldmells. *Linc*	4E **89**
Ingoldsby. *Linc*	2H **75**
Ingon. *Warw*	5G **61**
Ingram. *Nmbd*	3E **121**
Ingrave. *Essx*	1H **39**
Ingrow. *W Yor*	1A **92**
Ings. *Cumb*	5F **103**
Ingst. *S Glo*	3A **34**
Ingthorpe. *Rut*	5G **75**
Ingworth. *Norf*	3D **78**

Inkberrow. *Worc*	5E **61**
Inkford. *Worc*	3E **61**
Inkpen. *W Ber*	5B **36**
Inkstack. *High*	1E **169**
Innellan. *Arg*	3C **126**
Inner Hope. *Devn*	5C **8**
Innerleith. *Fife*	2E **137**
Innerleithen. *Bord*	1F **119**
Innerleven. *Fife*	3F **137**
Innermessan. *Dum*	3F **109**
Innerwick. *E Lot*	2D **130**
Innerwick. *Per*	4C **142**
Innsworth. *Glos*	3D **48**
Insch. *Abers*	1D **152**
Insh. *High*	3C **150**
Inshegra. *High*	3C **166**
Inshore. *High*	1D **166**
Inskip. *Lanc*	1C **90**
Instow. *Devn*	3E **19**
Intwood. *Norf*	5D **78**
Inver. *Abers*	4G **151**
Inver. *High*	5F **165**
Inver. *Per*	4H **143**
Inverailort. *High*	5F **147**
Inveralligin. *High*	3H **155**
Inverallochy. *Abers*	2H **161**
Inveramsay. *Abers*	1E **153**
Inveran. *High*	4C **164**
Inveraray. *Arg*	3H **133**
Inverarish. *High*	5E **155**
Inverarity. *Ang*	4D **144**
Inverarnan. *Stir*	2C **134**
Inverarnie. *High*	5A **158**
Inverbeg. *Arg*	4C **134**
Inverbervie. *Abers*	1H **145**
Inverboyndie. *Abers*	2D **160**
Invercassley. *High*	3B **164**
Invercharnan. *High*	4F **141**
Inverchoran. *High*	3E **157**
Invercreran. *Arg*	4E **141**
Inverdruie. *High*	2D **150**
Inverebrie. *Abers*	5G **161**
Invereck. *Arg*	1C **126**
Inveresk. *E Lot*	2G **129**
Inveresragan. *Arg*	5D **141**
Inverey. *Abers*	5E **151**
Inverfarigaig. *High*	1H **149**
Invergarry. *High*	3F **149**
Invergeldie. *Per*	1G **135**
Invergordon. *High*	2B **158**
Invergowrie. *Per*	5C **144**
Inverguseran. *High*	3F **147**
Inverharroch. *Mor*	5A **160**
Inverie. *High*	3F **147**
Inverinan. *Arg*	2G **133**
Inverinate. *High*	1B **148**
Inverkeilor. *Ang*	4F **145**
Inverkeithing. *Fife*	1E **129**
Inverkeithny. *Abers*	4D **160**
Inverkip. *Inv*	2D **126**
Inverkirkaig. *High*	2E **163**
Inverlael. *High*	5F **163**
Inverliever Lodge. *Arg*	3F **133**
Inverliver. *Arg*	5E **141**
Inverlochlarig. *Stir*	2D **134**
Inverlochy. *High*	1F **141**
Inverlussa. *Arg*	1E **125**
Inver Mallie. *High*	5D **148**
Invermarkie. *Abers*	5B **160**
Invermoriston. *High*	2G **149**
Invernaver. *High*	2H **167**
Inverneil House. *Arg*	1G **125**
Inverness. *High*	**198** (4A **158**)
Inverness Airport. *High*	3B **158**
Invernettie. *Abers*	4H **161**
Inverpolly Lodge. *High*	2E **163**
Inverquharity. *Ang*	3D **144**
Inverquhomery. *Abers*	4H **161**
Inverroy. *High*	5E **149**
Inversanda. *High*	3D **140**
Invershiel. *High*	2B **148**
Invershin. *High*	4C **164**
Invershore. *High*	5E **169**
Inversnaid. *Stir*	3C **134**
Inverugie. *Abers*	4H **161**
Inveruglas. *Arg*	3C **134**
Inverurie. *Abers*	1E **153**
Invervar. *Per*	4D **142**
Inverythan. *Abers*	4E **161**
Inwardleigh. *Devn*	3F **11**
Inworth. *Essx*	4B **54**
Iochdar. *W Isl*	4C **170**
Iping. *W Sus*	4G **25**
Ipplepen. *Devn*	2E **9**
Ipsden. *Oxon*	3E **37**
Ipstones. *Staf*	1E **73**
Ipswich. *Suff*	**198** (1E **55**)
Irby. *Mers*	2E **83**
Irby in the Marsh. *Linc*	4D **88**
Irby upon Humber. *NE Lin*	4E **95**
Irchester. *Nptn*	4G **63**
Ireby. *Cumb*	1D **102**
Ireby. *Lanc*	2F **97**
Ireland. *Shet*	9E **173**
Ireleth. *Cumb*	2B **96**
Ireshopeburn. *Dur*	1B **104**
Ireton Wood. *Derbs*	1G **73**
Irlam. *G Man*	1B **84**
Irnham. *Linc*	3H **75**
Iron Acton. *S Glo*	3B **34**
Iron Bridge. *Cambs*	1D **65**
Ironbridge. *Telf*	5A **72**
Iron Cross. *Warw*	5E **61**
Ironville. *Derbs*	5B **86**
Irstead. *Norf*	3F **79**
Irthington. *Cumb*	3F **113**
Irthlingborough. *Nptn*	3G **63**
Irton. *N Yor*	1E **101**
Irvine. *N Ayr*	1C **116**
Irvine Mains. *N Ayr*	1C **116**
Isabella Pit. *Nmbd*	1G **115**
Isauld. *High*	2B **168**

Isbister. *Orkn*	6C **172**
Isbister. *Shet*	
on Mainland	2E **173**
on Whalsay	5G **173**
Isfield. *E Sus*	4F **27**
Isham. *Nptn*	3F **63**
Island Carr. *N Lin*	4C **94**
Islay Airport. *Arg*	4B **124**
Isle Abbotts. *Som*	4G **21**
Isle Brewers. *Som*	4G **21**
Isleham. *Cambs*	3F **65**
Isle of Man Airport. *IOM*	5B **108**
Isle of Thanet. *Kent*	4H **41**
Isle of Whithorn. *Dum*	5B **110**
Isle of Wight. *IOW*	4C **16**
Isleornsay. *High*	2F **147**
Islesburgh. *Shet*	5E **173**
Isles of Scilly Airport. *IOS*	1B **4**
Islesteps. *Dum*	2A **112**
Isleworth. *G Lon*	3C **38**
Isley Walton. *Leics*	3B **74**
Islibhig. *W Isl*	5B **171**
Islington. *G Lon*	2E **39**
Islington. *Telf*	3B **72**
Islip. *Nptn*	3G **63**
Islip. *Oxon*	4D **50**
Isombridge. *Telf*	4A **72**
Istead Rise. *Kent*	4H **39**
Itchen. *Sotn*	1C **16**
Itchen Abbas. *Hants*	3D **24**
Itchenor. *W Sus*	2F **17**
Itchen Stoke. *Hants*	3D **24**
Itchingfield. *W Sus*	3C **26**
Itchington. *S Glo*	3B **34**
Itlaw. *Abers*	3D **160**
Itteringham. *Norf*	2D **78**
Itteringham Common. *Norf*	3D **78**
Itton. *Devn*	3G **11**
Itton Common. *Mon*	2H **33**
Ivegill. *Cumb*	5F **113**
Ivelet. *N Yor*	5C **104**
Iverchaolain. *Arg*	2B **126**
Iver Heath. *Buck*	2B **38**
Iveston. *Dur*	4E **115**
Ivetsey Bank. *Staf*	4C **72**
Ivinghoe. *Buck*	4H **51**
Ivinghoe Aston. *Buck*	4H **51**
Ivington. *Here*	5G **59**
Ivington Green. *Here*	5G **59**
Ivybridge. *Devn*	3C **8**
Ivychurch. *Kent*	3E **29**
Ivy Hatch. *Kent*	5G **39**
Ivy Todd. *Norf*	5A **78**
Iwade. *Kent*	4D **40**
Iwerne Courtney. *Dors*	1D **14**
Iwerne Minster. *Dors*	1D **14**
Ixworth. *Suff*	3B **66**
Ixworth Thorpe. *Suff*	3B **66**

J

Jackfield. *Shrp*	5A **72**
Jack Hill. *N Yor*	4D **98**
Jacksdale. *Notts*	5B **86**
Jackton. *S Lan*	4G **127**
Jacobstow. *Corn*	3B **10**
Jacobstowe. *Devn*	2F **11**
Jacobs Well. *Surr*	5A **38**
Jameston. *Pemb*	5E **43**
Jamestown. *Dum*	5F **119**
Jamestown. *Fife*	1E **129**
Jamestown. *High*	3G **157**
Jamestown. *W Dun*	1E **127**
Janetstown. *High*	
nr. Thurso	2C **168**
nr. Wick	3F **169**
Jarrow. *Tyne*	3G **115**
Jarvis Brook. *E Sus*	3G **27**
Jasper's Green. *Essx*	3H **53**
Jaywick. *Essx*	4E **55**
Jedburgh. *Bord*	2A **120**
Jeffreyston. *Pemb*	4E **43**
Jemimaville. *High*	2B **158**
Jenkins Park. *High*	3F **149**
Jersey Marine. *Neat*	3G **31**
Jesmond. *Tyne*	3F **115**
Jevington. *E Sus*	5G **27**
Jingle Street. *Mon*	4H **47**
Jockey End. *Herts*	4A **52**
Jodrell Bank. *Ches E*	3B **84**
Johnby. *Cumb*	1F **103**
John O'Gaunts. *W Yor*	2D **92**
John o' Groats. *High*	1F **169**
John's Cross. *E Sus*	3B **28**
Johnshaven. *Abers*	2G **145**
Johnson Street. *Norf*	4F **79**
Johnston. *Pemb*	3D **42**
Johnstone. *Ren*	3F **127**
Johnstonebridge. *Dum*	5C **118**
Johnstown. *Carm*	4E **45**
Johnstown. *Wrex*	1F **71**
Joppa. *Edin*	2G **129**
Joppa. *S Ayr*	3D **116**
Jordan Green. *Norf*	3C **78**
Jordans. *Buck*	1A **38**
Jordanston. *Pemb*	1D **42**
Jump. *S Yor*	4D **93**
Jumpers Common. *Dors*	3G **15**
Juniper. *Nmbd*	4C **114**
Juniper Green. *Edin*	3E **129**
Jurby East. *IOM*	2C **108**
Jurby West. *IOM*	2C **108**
Jury's Gap. *E Sus*	4D **28**

K

Kaber. *Cumb*	3A **104**
Kaimend. *S Lan*	5C **128**
Kaimes. *Edin*	3F **129**

Kaimrig End – Kintillo

Kaimrig End. Bord 5D 129
Kames. Arg 2A 126
Kames. E Ayr 2F 117
Kea. Corn 4C 6
Keadby. N Lin 3B 94
Keal Cotes. Linc 4C 88
Kearsley. G Man 4F 91
Kearsney. Kent 1G 29
Kearstwick. Cumb 1F 97
Kearton. N Yor 5C 104
Kearvaig. High 1C 166
Keasden. N Yor 3G 97
Keason. Corn 2H 7
Keckwick. Hal 2H 83
Keddington. Linc 2C 88
Keddington Corner. Linc 2C 88
Kedington. Suff 1H 53
Kedleston. Derbs 1H 73
Kedlock Feus. Fife 2F 137
Keekle. Cumb 3B 102
Keelby. Linc 3E 95
Keele. Staf 1C 72
Keeley Green. Bed 1A 52
Keeston. Pemb 3D 42
Keevil. Wilts 1E 23
Kegworth. Leics 3B 74
Kehelland. Corn 2D 4
Keig. Abers 2D 152
Keighley. W Yor 5C 98
Keilarsbrae. Clac 4A 136
Keillmore. Arg 1E 125
Keillor. Per 4B 144
Keillour. Per 1B 136
Keills. Arg 3C 124
Keiloch. Abers 4F 151
Keils. Arg 3D 124
Keinton Mandeville. Som 3A 22
Keir Mill. Dum 5A 118
Keirsleywell Row. Nmbd 4A 114
Keisby. Linc 3H 75
Keisley. Cumb 2A 104
Keiss. High 2F 169
Keith. Mor 3B 160
Keith Inch. Abers 4H 161
Kelbrook. Lanc 5B 98
Kelby. Linc 1H 75
Keld. Cumb 3G 103
Keld. N Yor 4B 104
Keldholme. N Yor 1B 100
Kelfield. N Lin 4B 94
Kelfield. N Yor 1F 93
Kelham. Notts 5E 87
Kellacott. Devn 4E 11
Kellan. Arg 4G 139
Kellas. Ang 5D 144
Kellas. Mor 3F 159
Kellaton. Devn 5E 9
Kelleth. Cumb 4H 103
Kelling. Norf 1C 78
Kellingley. N Yor 2F 93
Kellington. N Yor 2F 93
Kelloe. Dur 1A 106
Kelloholm. Dum 3G 117
Kells. Cumb 3A 102
Kelly. Devn 4D 11
Kelly Bray. Corn 5D 10
Kelmarsh. Nptn 3E 63
Kelmscott. Oxon 2H 35
Kelsale. Suff 4F 67
Kelsall. Ches W 4H 83
Kelshall. Herts 2D 52
Kelsick. Cumb 4C 112
Kelso. Bord 1B 120
Kelstedge. Derbs 4H 85
Kelstern. Linc 1B 88
Kelsterton. Flin 3E 83
Kelston. Bath 5C 34
Keltneyburn. Per 4E 143
Kelton. Dum 2A 112
Kelton Hill. Dum 4E 111
Kelty. Fife 4D 136
Kelvedon. Essx 4B 54
Kelvedon Hatch. Essx 1G 39
Kelvinside. Glas 3G 127
Kelynack. Corn 3A 4
Kemback. Fife 2G 137
Kemberton. Shrp 5B 72
Kemble. Glos 2E 35
Kemerton. Worc 2E 49
Kemeys Commander. Mon 5G 47
Kemnay. Abers 2E 153
Kempe's Corner. Kent 1E 29
Kempley. Glos 3B 48
Kempley Green. Glos 3B 48
Kempsey. Worc 1D 48
Kempsford. Glos 2G 35
Kemps Green. Warw 3F 61
Kempshott. Hants 2E 24
Kempston. Bed 1A 52
Kempston Hardwick. Bed 1A 52
Kempton. Shrp 2F 59
Kemp Town. Brig 5E 27
Kemsing. Kent 5G 39
Kemsley. Kent 4D 40
Kenardington. Kent 2D 28
Kenchester. Here 1H 47
Kencot. Oxon 5A 50
Kendal. Cumb 5G 103
Kendleshire. S Glo 4B 34
Kendray. S Yor 4D 92
Kenfig. B'end 3B 32
Kenfig Hill. B'end 3B 32
Kengharair. Arg 4F 139
Kenilworth. Warw 3G 61
Kenknock. Stir 5B 142
Kenley. G Lon 5E 39
Kenley. Shrp 5H 71
Kenmore. High 3G 155
Kenmore. Per 4E 143
Kenn. Devn 4C 12
Kenn. N Som 5H 33
Kennacraig. Arg 3G 125
Kenneggy Downs. Corn 4C 4
Kennerleigh. Devn 2B 12
Kennet. Clac 4B 136
Kennethmont. Abers 1C 152
Kennett. Cambs 4G 65
Kennford. Devn 4C 12
Kenninghall. Norf 2C 66
Kennington. Kent 1E 28
Kennington. Oxon 5D 50
Kennoway. Fife 3F 137
Kennyhill. Suff 3F 65
Kennythorpe. N Yor 3B 100
Kenovay. Arg 4A 138
Kensaleyre. High 3D 154
Kensington. G Lon 3D 38
Kenstone. Shrp 3H 71
Kensworth. C Beds 4A 52
Kensworth Common. C Beds 4A 52
Kentallen. High 3E 141
Kentchurch. Here 3H 47
Kentford. Suff 4G 65
Kentisbeare. Devn 2D 12
Kentisbury. Devn 2G 19
Kentisbury Ford. Devn 2G 19
Kentmere. Cumb 4F 103
Kenton. Devn 4C 12
Kenton. G Lon 2C 38
Kenton. Suff 4D 66
Kenton Bankfoot. Tyne 3F 115
Kentra. High 2A 140
Kentrigg. Cumb 5G 103
Kents Bank. Cumb 2C 96
Kent's Green. Glos 3C 48
Kent's Oak. Hants 4B 24
Kent Street. E Sus 4B 28
Kent Street. Kent 5A 40
Kent Street. W Sus 3D 26
Kenwick. Shrp 2G 71
Kenwyn. Corn 4C 6
Kenyon. Warr 1A 84
Keoldale. High 2D 166
Keppoch. High 1B 148
Kepwick. N Yor 5B 106
Keresley. W Mid 2H 61
Keresley Newland. Warw 2H 61
Keristal. IOM 4C 108
Kerne Bridge. Here 4A 48
Kerridge. Ches E 3D 84
Kerris. Corn 4B 4
Kerrow. High 5F 157
Kerry. Powy 2D 58
Kerrycroy. Arg 3C 126
Kerry's Gate. Here 2G 47
Kersall. Notts 4E 86
Kersbrook. Devn 4D 12
Kerse. Ren 4E 127
Kersey. Suff 1D 54
Kershopefoot. Cumb 1F 113
Kersoe. Worc 1E 49
Kerswell. Devn 2D 12
Kerswell Green. Worc 1D 48
Kesgrave. Suff 1F 55
Kessingland. Suff 2H 67
Kessingland Beach. Suff 2H 67
Kestle. Corn 4D 6
Kestle Mill. Corn 3C 6
Keston. G Lon 4F 39
Keswick. Cumb 2D 102
Keswick. Norf
nr. North Walsham 2F 79
nr. Norwich 5E 78
Ketsby. Linc 3C 88
Kettering. Nptn 3F 63
Ketteringham. Norf 5D 78
Kettins. Per 5B 144
Kettlebaston. Suff 5B 66
Kettlebridge. Fife 3F 137
Kettlebrook. Staf 5G 73
Kettleburgh. Suff 4E 67
Kettleholm. Dum 2C 112
Kettleness. N Yor 3F 107
Kettleshulme. Ches E 3D 85
Kettlesing. N Yor 4E 98
Kettlesing Bottom. N Yor 4E 99
Kettlestone. Norf 2B 78
Kettlethorpe. Linc 3F 87
Kettletoft. Orkn 4F 172
Kettlewell. N Yor 2B 98
Ketton. Rut 5G 75
Kew. G Lon 3C 38
Kewaigue. IOM 4C 108
Kewstoke. N Som 5G 33
Kexbrough. S Yor 4C 92
Kexby. Linc 2F 87
Kexby. York 4B 100
Keyford. Som 2C 22
Key Green. Ches E 4C 84
Key Green. N Yor 4F 107
Keyham. Leics 5D 74
Keyhaven. Hants 3B 16
Keyhead. Abers 3H 161
Keyingham. E Yor 2F 95
Keymer. W Sus 4E 27
Keynsham. Bath 5B 34
Keysoe. Bed 4H 63
Keysoe Row. Bed 4H 63
Key's Toft. Linc 5D 89
Keyston. Cambs 3H 63
Key Street. Kent 4C 40
Keyworth. Notts 2D 74
Kibblesworth. Tyne 4F 115
Kibworth Beauchamp. Leics 1D 62
Kibworth Harcourt. Leics 1D 62
Kidbrooke. G Lon 3F 39
Kidburngill. Cumb 2B 102
Kiddemore Green. Staf 5C 72
Kidderminster. Worc 3C 60
Kiddington. Oxon 3C 50
Kidd's Moor. Norf 5D 78
Kidlington. Oxon 4C 50
Kidmore End. Oxon 4E 37
Kidnal. Ches W 1G 71
Kidsgrove. Staf 5C 84
Kidstones. N Yor 1B 98
Kidwelly. Carm 5E 45
Kiel Crofts. Arg 5D 140
Kielder. Nmbd 5A 120
Kilbagie. Fife 4B 136
Kilbarchan. Ren 3F 127
Kilbeg. High 3E 147
Kilberry. Arg 3F 125
Kilbirnie. N Ayr 4E 126
Kilbride. Arg 1F 133
Kilbride. High 1D 147
Kilbucho Place. Bord 1C 118
Kilburn. Derbs 1A 74
Kilburn. G Lon 2D 38
Kilburn. N Yor 2H 99
Kilby. Leics 1D 62
Kilchattan. Arg 4A 132
Kilchattan Bay. Arg 4C 126
Kilchenzie. Arg 3A 122
Kilcheran. Arg 5C 140
Kilchiaran. Arg 3A 124
Kilchoan. High
nr. Inverie 4F 147
nr. Tobermory 2F 139
Kilchoman. Arg 3A 124
Kilchrenan. Arg 1H 133
Kilconquhar. Fife 3G 137
Kilcot. Glos 3B 48
Kilcoy. High 3H 157
Kilcreggan. Arg 1D 126
Kildale. N Yor 4D 106
Kildary. High 1B 158
Kildermorie Lodge. High 1H 157
Kildonan. Dum 4F 109
Kildonan. High
nr. Helmsdale 1G 165
on Isle of Skye 3C 154
Kildonan. N Ayr 3E 123
Kildonnan. High 5C 146
Kildrummy. Abers 2B 152
Kildwick. N Yor 5C 98
Kilfillan. Dum 4H 109
Kilfinan. Arg 2H 125
Kilfinnan. High 4E 149
Kilgetty. Pemb 4F 43
Kilgour. Fife 3E 136
Kilgrammie. S Ayr 4B 116
Kilham. E Yor 3E 101
Kilham. Nmbd 1C 120
Kilkenneth. Arg 4A 138
Kilkhampton. Corn 1C 10
Killamarsh. Derbs 2B 86
Killandrist. Arg 4C 140
Killay. Swan 3F 31
Killean. Arg 5E 125
Killearn. Stir 1G 127
Killellan. Arg 4A 122
Killen. High 3A 158
Killerby. Darl 3E 105
Killichonan. Per 3C 142
Killiechronan. Arg 4G 139
Killiecrankie. Per 2G 143
Killilan. High 5B 156
Killimster. High 3F 169
Killin. Stir 5C 142
Killinghall. N Yor 4E 99
Killington. Cumb 1F 97
Killingworth. Tyne 2F 115
Killin Lodge. High 3H 149
Killinochonoch. Arg 4F 133
Killochyett. Bord 5A 130
Killundine. High 4G 139
Kilmacolm. Inv 3E 127
Kilmahog. Stir 3F 135
Kilmahumaig. Arg 4E 133
Kilmalieu. High 3C 140
Kilmaluag. High 1D 154
Kilmany. Fife 1F 137
Kilmarie. High 2D 146
Kilmarnock. E Ayr 198 (1D 116)
Kilmaron. Fife 2F 137
Kilmartin. Arg 4F 133
Kilmaurs. E Ayr 5F 127
Kilmelford. Arg 2F 133
Kilmeny. Arg 3B 124
Kilmersdon. Som 1B 22
Kilmeston. Hants 4D 24
Kilmichael Glassary. Arg 4F 133
Kilmichael of Inverlussa. Arg 1F 125
Kilmington. Devn 3F 13
Kilmington. Wilts 3C 22
Kilmoluaig. Arg 4A 138
Kilmorack. High 4G 157
Kilmore. Arg 1F 133
Kilmore. High 3E 147
Kilmory. Arg 2F 125
Kilmory. High
nr. Kilchoan 1G 139
on Rùm 3B 146
Kilmory. N Ayr 3D 122
Kilmory Lodge. Arg 3E 132
Kilmote. High 2G 165
Kilmuir. High
nr. Dunvegan 4B 154
nr. Invergordon 1B 158
nr. Inverness 4A 158
nr. Uig 1C 154
Kilmun. Arg 1C 126
Kilnave. Arg 2A 124
Kilncadzow. S Lan 5B 128
Kilndown. Kent 2B 28
Kiln Green. Here 4B 48
Kiln Green. Wok 4G 37
Kilnhill. Cumb 1D 102
Kilnhurst. S Yor 1B 86
Kilninian. Arg 4E 139
Kilninver. Arg 1F 133
Kiln Pit Hill. Nmbd 4D 114
Kilnsea. E Yor 3H 95
Kilnsey. N Yor 3B 98
Kilnwick. E Yor 5D 101
Kiloran. Arg 4A 132
Kilpatrick. N Ayr 3D 122
Kilpeck. Here 2H 47
Kilpin. E Yor 2A 94
Kilpin Pike. E Yor 2A 94
Kilrenny. Fife 3H 137
Kilsby. Nptn 3C 62
Kilspindie. Per 1E 136
Kilsyth. N Lan 2A 128
Kiltarlity. High 4H 157
Kilton. Som 2E 21
Kilton Thorpe. Red C 3D 107
Kilvaxter. High 2C 154
Kilve. Som 2E 21
Kilvington. Notts 1F 75
Kilwinning. N Ayr 5D 126
Kimberley. Norf 5C 78
Kimberley. Notts 1B 74
Kimblesworth. Dur 5F 115
Kimble Wick. Buck 5G 51
Kimbolton. Cambs 4H 63
Kimbolton. Here 4H 59
Kimcote. Leics 2C 62
Kimmeridge. Dors 5E 15
Kimmerston. Nmbd 1D 120
Kimpton. Hants 2A 24
Kimpton. Herts 4B 52
Kinbeachie. High 2A 158
Kinbrace. High 5A 168
Kinbuck. Stir 3G 135
Kincaple. Fife 2G 137
Kincardine. Fife 1C 128
Kincardine. High 5D 164
Kincardine Bridge. Falk 1C 128
Kincardine O'Neil. Abers 4C 152
Kinchrackine. Arg 1A 134
Kincorth. Aber 3G 153
Kincraig. High 3C 150
Kincraigie. Per 4G 143
Kindallachan. Per 3G 143
Kineton. Glos 3F 49
Kineton. Warw 5H 61
Kinfauns. Per 1D 136
Kingairloch. High 3C 140
Kingarth. Arg 4B 126
Kingcoed. Mon 5H 47
King Edward. Abers 3E 160
Kingerby. Linc 1H 87
Kingham. Oxon 3A 50
Kingholm Quay. Dum 2A 112
Kinghorn. Fife 1F 129
Kingie. High 3D 148
Kinglassie. Fife 4E 137
Kingledores. Bord 2D 118
King o' Muirs. Clac 4A 136
Kingoodie. Per 1F 137
King's Acre. Here 1H 47
Kingsand. Corn 3A 8
Kingsash. Buck 5G 51
Kingsbarns. Fife 2H 137
Kingsbridge. Devn 4D 8
Kingsbridge. Som 3C 20
King's Bromley. Staf 4F 73
Kingsburgh. High 3C 154
Kingsbury. G Lon 2C 38
Kingsbury. Warw 1G 61
Kingsbury Episcopi. Som 4H 21
Kings Caple. Here 3A 48
Kingscavil. W Lot 2D 128
Kingsclere. Hants 1D 24
King's Cliffe. Nptn 1H 63
Kings Clipstone. Notts 4D 86
Kingscote. Glos 2D 34
Kingscott. Devn 1F 11
Kings Coughton. Warw 5E 61
Kingscross. N Ayr 3E 123
Kingsdon. Som 4A 22
Kingsdown. Kent 1H 29
Kingsdown. Swin 3G 35
Kingsdown. Wilts 5D 34
Kingseat. Fife 4D 136
Kingsey. Buck 5F 51
Kingsfold. Lanc 2D 90
Kingsfold. W Sus 2C 26
Kingsford. E Ayr 5F 127
Kingsford. Worc 2C 60
Kingsforth. N Lin 3D 94
Kingsgate. Kent 3H 41
King's Green. Glos 2C 48
Kingshall Street. Suff 4B 66
Kingsheanton. Devn 3F 19
King's Heath. W Mid 2E 61
Kings Hill. Kent 5A 40
Kingsholm. Glos 4D 48
Kingshouse. High 3G 141
Kingshouse. Stir 1E 135
Kingshurst. W Mid 2F 61
Kingskerswell. Devn 2E 9
Kingskettle. Fife 3F 137
Kingsland. Here 4G 59
Kingsland. IOA 2B 80
Kings Langley. Herts 5A 52
Kingsley. Ches W 3H 83
Kingsley. Hants 3F 25
Kingsley. Staf 1E 73
Kingsley Green. W Sus 3G 25
Kingsley Holt. Staf 1E 73
King's Lynn. Norf 3F 77
King's Meaburn. Cumb 2H 103
Kings Moss. Mers 4D 90
Kings Muir. Bord 1E 119
Kingsmuir. Ang 4D 145
Kingsmuir. Fife 3H 137
King's Newnham. Warw 3B 62
King's Newton. Derbs 3A 74
Kingsnorth. Kent 2E 28
Kingsnorth. Medw 3C 40
King's Norton. Leics 5D 74
Kings Norton. W Mid 3E 61
King's Nympton. Devn 1G 11
King's Pyon. Here 5G 59
Kings Ripton. Cambs 3B 64
King's Somborne. Hants 3B 24
King's Stag. Dors 1C 14
King's Stanley. Glos 5D 48
King's Sutton. Nptn 2C 50
Kingstanding. W Mid 1E 61
Kingsteignton. Devn 5B 12
Kingsteps. High 3D 158
King Sterndale. Derbs 3E 85
King's Thorn. Here 2A 48
Kingsthorpe. Nptn 4E 63
Kingston. Cambs 5C 64
Kingston. Devn 4C 8
Kingston. Dors
nr. Sturminster Newton 2C 14
nr. Swanage 5E 15
Kingston. E Lot 1B 130
Kingston. Hants 2G 15
Kingston. IOW 4C 16
Kingston. Kent 5F 41
Kingston. Mor 2H 159
Kingston. W Sus 5B 26
Kingston Bagpuize. Oxon 2C 36
Kingston Blount. Oxon 2F 37
Kingston by Sea. W Sus 5D 26
Kingston Deverill. Wilts 3D 22
Kingstone. Here 2H 47
Kingstone. Som 1G 13
Kingstone. Staf 3E 73
Kingston Lisle. Oxon 3B 36
Kingston Maurward. Dors 3C 14
Kingston near Lewes. E Sus 5E 27
Kingston on Soar. Notts 3C 74
Kingston Russell. Dors 3A 14
Kingston St Mary. Som 4F 21
Kingston Seymour. N Som 5H 33
Kingston Stert. Oxon 5F 51
Kingston upon Hull.
Hull 199 (2E 94)
Kingston upon Thames. G Lon 4C 38
King's Walden. Herts 3B 52
Kingswear. Devn 3E 9
Kingswells. Aber 3F 153
Kingswinford. W Mid 2C 60
Kingswood. Buck 4E 51
Kingswood. Glos 2C 34
Kingswood. Here 5E 59
Kingswood. Kent 5C 40
Kingswood. Per 5H 143
Kingswood. Powy 5E 71
Kingswood. Som 3E 20
Kingswood. S Glo 4B 34
Kingswood. Surr 5D 38
Kingswood. Warw 3F 61
Kingswood Common. Staf 5C 72
Kings Worthy. Hants 3C 24
Kingthorpe. Linc 3A 88
Kington. Here 5E 59
Kington. S Glo 2B 34
Kington. Worc 5D 61
Kington Langley. Wilts 4E 35
Kington Magna. Dors 4C 22
Kington St Michael. Wilts 4E 35
Kingussie. High 3B 150
Kingweston. Som 3A 22
Kinharrachie. Abers 5G 161
Kinhrive. High 1A 158
Kinkell Bridge. Per 2B 136
Kinknockie. Abers 4H 161
Kinkry Hill. Cumb 2G 113
Kinlet. Shrp 2B 60
Kinloch. High
nr. Lochaline 3A 140
nr. Loch More 5D 166
on Rùm 4B 146
Kinloch. Per 4A 144
Kinlochard. Stir 3D 134
Kinlochbervie. High 3C 166
Kinlocheil. High 1D 140
Kinlochewe. High 2C 156
Kinloch Hourn. High 3B 148
Kinloch Laggan. High 5H 149
Kinlochleven. High 2F 141
Kinloch Lodge. High 3F 167
Kinlochmoidart. High 1B 140
Kinlochmore. High 2F 141
Kinloch Rannoch. Per 3D 142
Kinlochspelve. Arg 1D 132
Kinloid. High 5E 147
Kinloss. Mor 2E 159
Kinmel Bay. Cnwy 2B 82
Kinmuck. Abers 2F 153
Kinnadie. Abers 4G 161
Kinnaird. Per 1E 137
Kinneff. Abers 1H 145
Kinnelhead. Dum 4C 118
Kinnell. Ang 3F 145
Kinnerley. Shrp 3F 71
Kinnernie. Abers 3E 152
Kinnersley. Here 1G 47
Kinnersley. Worc 1D 48
Kinnerton. Powy 4E 59
Kinnerton. Shrp 1F 59
Kinnesswood. Per 3D 136
Kinninvie. Dur 2D 104
Kinnordy. Ang 3C 144
Kinoulton. Notts 2D 74
Kinross. Per 3D 136
Kinrossie. Per 5A 144
Kinsbourne Green. Herts 4B 52
Kinsey Heath. Ches E 1A 72
Kinsham. Here 4F 59
Kinsham. Worc 2E 49
Kinsley. W Yor 3E 93
Kinson. Bour 3F 15
Kintbury. W Ber 5B 36
Kintessack. Mor 2E 159
Kintillo. Per 2D 136

Kinton. *Here*......................................3G **59**
Kinton. *Shrp*.....................................4F **71**
Kintore. *Abers*................................2E **153**
Kintour. *Arg*.....................................4C **124**
Kintra. *Arg*.......................................2B **132**
Kintraw. *Arg*....................................3F **133**
Kinveachy. *High*..............................2D **150**
Kinver. *Staf*......................................2C **60**
Kinwarton. *Warw*.............................5F **61**
Kiplingcotes. *E Yor*........................5D **100**
Kippax. *W Yor*...................................1E **93**
Kippen. *Stir*.....................................4F **135**
Kippford. *Dum*.................................4F **111**
Kipping's Cross. *Kent*......................1H **27**
Kirbister. *Orkn*
  nr. Hobbister.............................7C **172**
  nr. Quholm...............................6B **172**
Kirbuster. *Orkn*...............................5F **172**
Kirby Bedon. *Norf*............................5E **79**
Kirby Bellars. *Leics*.........................4E **74**
Kirby Cane. *Norf*...............................1F **67**
Kirby Cross. *Essx*.............................3F **55**
Kirby Fields. *Leics*...........................5C **74**
Kirby Green. *Norf*..............................1F **67**
Kirby Grindalythe. *N Yor*..............3D **100**
Kirby Hill. *N Yor*
  nr. Richmond...........................4E **105**
  nr. Ripon...................................3F **99**
Kirby Knowle. *N Yor*..........................1G **99**
Kirby-le-Soken. *Essx*.......................3F **55**
Kirby Misperton. *N Yor*.................2B **100**
Kirby Muxloe. *Leics*.........................5C **74**
Kirby Sigston. *N Yor*......................5B **106**
Kirby Underdale. *E Yor*..................4C **100**
Kirby Wiske. *N Yor*............................1F **99**
Kirdford. *W Sus*................................3B **26**
Kirk. *High*......................................3E **169**
Kirkabister. *Shet*
  on Bressay...............................8F **173**
  on Mainland..............................6F **173**
Kirkandrews. *Dum*..........................5D **110**
Kirkandrews-on-Eden. *Cumb*......4E **113**
Kirkapol. *Arg*...................................4B **138**
Kirkbampton. *Cumb*......................4E **112**
Kirkbean. *Dum*...............................4A **112**
Kirk Bramwith. *S Yor*.......................3G **93**
Kirkbride. *Cumb*..............................4D **112**
Kirkbridge. *N Yor*...........................5F **105**
Kirkbuddo. *Ang*..............................4E **145**
Kirkburn. *E Yor*..............................4D **101**
Kirkburton. *W Yor*............................3B **92**
Kirkby. *Linc*.....................................1H **87**
Kirkby. *Mers*..................................1G **83**
Kirkby. *N Yor*..................................4C **106**
Kirkby Fenside. *Linc*.......................4C **88**
Kirkby Fleetham. *N Yor*.................5F **105**
Kirkby Green. *Linc*.........................5H **87**
Kirkby-in-Ashfield. *Notts*..............5C **86**
Kirkby-in-Furness. *Cumb*..............1B **96**
Kirkby la Thorpe. *Linc*...................1A **76**
Kirkby Lonsdale. *Cumb*..................2F **97**
Kirkby Malham. *N Yor*.....................3A **98**
Kirkby Mallory. *Leics*.......................5B **74**
Kirkby Malzeard. *N Yor*..................2E **99**
Kirkby Mills. *N Yor*.........................1B **100**
Kirkbymoorside. *N Yor*..................1A **100**
Kirkby on Bain. *Linc*........................4B **88**
Kirkby Overblow. *N Yor*....................5F **99**
Kirkby Stephen. *Cumb*..................4A **104**
Kirkby Thore. *Cumb*.......................2H **103**
Kirkby Underwood. *Linc*.................3H **75**
Kirkby Wharfe. *N Yor*.......................5H **99**
Kirkcaldy. *Fife*..............................4E **137**
Kirkcambeck. *Cumb*.......................3G **113**
Kirkcolm. *Dum*................................3F **109**
Kirkconnel. *Dum*.............................3G **117**
Kirkconnell. *Dum*...........................3A **112**
Kirkcowan. *Dum*..............................3A **110**
Kirkcudbright. *Dum*........................4D **111**
Kirkdale. *Mers*..................................1F **83**
Kirk Deighton. *N Yor*.......................4F **99**
Kirk Ella. *E Yor*................................2D **94**
Kirkfieldbank. *S Lan*......................5B **128**
Kirkforthar Feus. *Fife*....................3E **137**
Kirkgunzeon. *Dum*.........................3F **111**
Kirk Hallam. *Derbs*.........................1B **74**
Kirkham. *Lanc*..................................1C **90**
Kirkham. *N Yor*...............................3B **100**
Kirkhamgate. *W Yor*.........................2C **92**
Kirk Hammerton. *N Yor*...................4G **99**
Kirkharle. *Nmbd*.............................1D **114**
Kirkheaton. *Nmbd*.........................2D **114**
Kirkheaton. *W Yor*............................3B **92**
Kirkhill. *Ang*....................................2F **145**
Kirkhill. *High*...................................4H **157**
Kirkhope. *S Lan*...............................4B **118**
Kirkhouse. *Bord*..............................1F **119**
Kirkibost. *High*...............................2D **146**
Kirkinch. *Ang*..................................4C **144**
Kirkinner. *Dum*...............................4B **110**
Kirkintilloch. *E Dun*.....................2H **127**
Kirk Ireton. *Derbs*............................5G **85**
Kirkland. *Dum*
  nr. Cleator Moor.......................3B **102**
  nr. Penrith................................1H **103**
  nr. Wigton.................................5D **112**
Kirkland. *Dum*
  nr. Kirkconnel...........................3G **117**
  nr. Moniaive.............................5H **117**
Kirkland Guards. *Cumb*..................5C **112**
Kirk Langley. *Derbs*.........................2G **73**
Kirklauchline. *Dum*........................4F **109**
Kirkleatham. *Red C*.......................2C **106**
Kirklevington. *Stoc T*......................4B **106**
Kirkley. *Suff*.....................................1H **67**
Kirklington. *N Yor*............................1F **99**
Kirklington. *Notts*...........................5D **86**
Kirklinton. *Cumb*............................3F **113**
Kirkliston. *Edin*..............................2E **129**
Kirkmabreck. *Dum*..........................4B **110**
Kirkmaiden. *Dum*............................5E **109**

Kirk Merrington. *Dur*.....................1F **105**
Kirkmichael. *IOM*..........................2C **108**
Kirkmichael. *Per*............................2H **143**
Kirkmichael. *S Ayr*.........................4C **116**
Kirkmuirhill. *S Lan*........................5A **128**
Kirknewton. *Nmbd*........................1D **120**
Kirknewton. *W Lot*.........................3E **129**
Kirkney. *Abers*.................................5C **160**
Kirk of Shotts. *N Lan*....................3B **128**
Kirkoswald. *Cumb*..........................5G **113**
Kirkoswald. *S Ayr*...........................4B **116**
Kirkpatrick. *Dum*............................5B **118**
Kirkpatrick Durham. *Dum*..............2E **111**
Kirkpatrick-Fleming. *Dum*............2D **112**
Kirk Sandall. *S Yor*........................4G **93**
Kirksanton. *Cumb*...........................1A **96**
Kirk Smeaton. *N Yor*........................3F **93**
Kirkstall. *W Yor*...............................1C **92**
Kirkstile. *Dum*................................5F **119**
Kirkstyle. *High*...............................1F **169**
Kirkthorpe. *W Yor*............................2D **92**
Kirkton. *Abers*
  nr. Alford.................................2D **152**
  nr. Insch...................................1D **152**
  nr. Turriff.................................4F **161**
Kirkton. *Ang*
  nr. Dundee...............................5D **144**
  nr. Forfar..................................4D **144**
  nr. Tarfside..............................5B **152**
Kirkton. *Dum*..................................1A **112**
Kirkton. *Fife*....................................1F **137**
Kirkton. *High*
  nr. Golspie..............................4E **165**
  nr. Kyle of Lochalsh.................1G **147**
  nr. Lochcarron........................4B **156**
Kirkton. *Bord*..................................3H **119**
Kirkton. *S Lan*.................................2B **118**
Kirktonhill. *W Dun*.........................2E **127**
Kirkton Manor. *Bord*.....................1E **118**
Kirkton of Airlie. *Ang*....................3C **144**
Kirkton of Auchterhouse. *Ang*.....5C **144**
Kirkton of Bourtie. *Abers*...............1F **153**
Kirkton of Collace. *Per*..................5A **144**
Kirkton of Craig. *Ang*....................3G **145**
Kirkton of Culsalmond. *Abers*......5D **160**
Kirkton of Durris. *Abers*...............4E **153**
Kirkton of Glenbuchat. *Abers*......2A **152**
Kirkton of Glenisla. *Ang*...............2B **144**
Kirkton of Kingoldrum. *Ang*..........3C **144**
Kirkton of Largo. *Fife*...................3G **137**
Kirkton of Lethendy. *Per*...............4A **144**
Kirkton of Logie Buchan.
  Abers......................................1G **153**
Kirkton of Maryculter. *Abers*.........4F **153**
Kirkton of Menmuir. *Ang*..............2E **145**
Kirkton of Monikie. *Ang*................5E **145**
Kirkton of Oyne. *Abers*..................1D **152**
Kirkton of Rayne. *Abers*................5D **160**
Kirkton of Skene. *Abers*.................3F **153**
Kirktown. *Abers*
  nr. Fraserburgh.......................2G **161**
  nr. Peterhead...........................3H **161**
Kirktown of Alvah. *Abers*..............2D **160**
Kirktown of Auchterless.
  Abers......................................4E **160**
Kirktown of Deskford. *Mor*............2C **160**
Kirktown of Fetteresso. *Abers*......5F **153**
Kirktown of Mortlach. *Mor*............5H **159**
Kirktown of Slains. *Abers*.............1H **153**
Kirkurd. *Bord*..................................5E **129**
Kirkwall. *Orkn*................................6D **172**
Kirkwall Airport. *Orkn*...................7D **172**
Kirkwhelpington. *Nmbd*................1C **114**
Kirk Yetholm. *Bord*........................2C **120**
Kirmington. *N Lin*...........................3E **94**
Kirmond le Mire. *Linc*....................1A **88**
Kirn. *Arg*..2C **126**
Kirriemuir. *Ang*...............................3C **144**
Kirstead Green. *Norf*.......................1E **67**
Kirtlebridge. *Dum*..........................2D **112**
Kirtleton. *Dum*................................2D **112**
Kirtling. *Cambs*..............................5F **65**
Kirtling Green. *Cambs*....................5F **65**
Kirtlington. *Oxon*............................4D **50**
Kirtomy. *High*.................................2H **167**
Kirton. *Linc*.....................................2C **76**
Kirton. *Notts*....................................4D **86**
Kirton. *Suff*......................................2F **55**
Kirton End. *Linc*...............................1B **76**
Kirton Holme. *Linc*..........................1B **76**
Kirton in Lindsey. *N Lin*..................1G **87**
Kishorn. *High*.................................4H **155**
Kislingbury. *Nptn*...........................5D **62**
Kites Hardwick. *Warw*......................4B **62**
Kittisford. *Som*................................4D **20**
Kittle. *Swan*.....................................4E **31**
Kittybrewster. *Aber*........................3G **153**
Kitwood. *Hants*...............................3E **25**
Kivernoll. *Here*................................2H **47**
Kiveton Park. *S Yor*.........................2B **86**
Knaith. *Linc*.....................................2F **87**
Knaith Park. *Linc*.............................2F **87**
Knaphill. *Surr*.................................5A **38**
Knapp. *Hants*..................................4C **24**
Knapp. *Per*......................................5B **144**
Knapp. *Som*....................................4G **21**
Knapperfield. *High*.........................3E **169**
Knapton. *Norf*..................................2F **79**
Knapton. *York*..................................4H **99**
Knapton Green. *Here*.......................5G **59**
Knapwell. *Cambs*............................4C **64**
Knaresborough. *N Yor*...................4F **99**
Knarsdale. *Nmbd*..........................4H **113**
Knatts Valley. *Kent*.........................4G **39**
Knaven. *Abers*.................................4F **161**
Knayton. *N Yor*................................1G **99**
Knebworth. *Herts*............................3C **52**
Knedlington. *E Yor*..........................2H **93**
Kneesall. *Notts*...............................4E **86**
Kneesworth. *Cambs*.......................1D **52**
Kneeton. *Notts*................................1E **74**

Knelston. *Swan*..............................4D **30**
Knenhall. *Staf*.................................2D **72**
Knightacott. *Devn*...........................3G **19**
Knightcote. *Warw*...........................5B **62**
Knightcott. *N Som*...........................1G **21**
Knightley. *Staf*................................3C **72**
Knightley Dale. *Staf*.......................3C **72**
Knightlow Hill. *Warw*......................3B **62**
Knighton. *Devn*..................................4B **8**
Knighton. *Dors*...............................1B **14**
Knighton. *Leic*.................................5C **74**
Knighton. *Powy*...............................3E **59**
Knighton. *Som*.................................2E **21**
Knighton. *Staf*
  nr. Eccleshall...........................3B **72**
  nr. Woore..................................1B **72**
Knighton. *Wilts*...............................4A **36**
Knighton. *Worc*................................5E **61**
Knighton Common. *Worc*...............3A **60**
Knight's End. *Cambs*.......................1D **64**
Knightswood. *Glas*.........................3G **127**
Knightwick. *Worc*.............................5B **60**
Knill. *Here*.......................................4E **59**
Knipton. *Leics*.................................2F **75**
Knitsley. *Dur*..................................5E **115**
Kniveton. *Derbs*..............................5G **85**
Knock. *Arg*......................................5G **139**
Knock. *Cumb*..................................2H **103**
Knock. *Mor*......................................3C **160**
Knockally. *High*..............................5D **168**
Knockan. *Arg*...................................1B **132**
Knockan. *High*................................2G **163**
Knockandhu. *Mor*...........................1G **151**
Knockando. *Mor*.............................4F **159**
Knockarthur. *High*.........................3E **165**
Knockbain. *High*.............................3A **158**
Knockbreck. *High*...........................2B **154**
Knockdee. *High*...............................2D **168**
Knockdolian. *S Ayr*........................1G **109**
Knockdon. *S Ayr*.............................3C **116**
Knockdown. *Glos*...............................3D **34**
Knockenbaird. *Abers*.....................1D **152**
Knockenkelly. *N Ayr*........................3E **123**
Knockentiber. *E Ayr*.......................1C **116**
Knockfarrel. *High*...........................3H **157**
Knockglass. *High*...........................2C **168**
Knockholt. *Kent*..............................5F **39**
Knockholt Pound. *Kent*...................5F **39**
Knockie Lodge. *High*......................2G **149**
Knockin. *Shrp*..................................3F **71**
Knockinlaw. *E Ayr*..........................1D **116**
Knockinnon. *High*..........................5D **169**
Knockrome. *Arg*..............................2D **124**
Knocksharry. *IOM*..........................3B **108**
Knockshinnoch. *E Ayr*...................3D **116**
Knockvennie. *Dum*.........................2E **111**
Knockvologan. *Arg*.........................3B **132**
Knodishall. *Suff*..............................4G **67**
Knole. *Som*......................................4H **21**
Knollbury. *Mon*................................3H **33**
Knolls Green. *Ches E*......................3C **84**
Knolton. *Wrex*..................................2F **71**
Knook. *Wilts*....................................2E **23**
Knossington. *Leics*.........................5F **75**
Knott. *High*.....................................3C **154**
Knott End-on-Sea. *Lanc*................5C **96**
Knotting. *Bed*.................................4H **63**
Knotting Green. *Bed*.......................4H **63**
Knottingley. *W Yor*.......................2E **93**
Knotts. *Cumb*..................................2F **103**
Knotty Ash. *Mers*.............................1G **83**
Knotty Green. *Buck*........................1A **38**
Knowbury. *Shrp*...............................3H **59**
Knowe. *Dum*....................................2A **110**
Knowefield. *Cumb*..........................4F **113**
Knowehead. *Dum*...........................5F **117**
Knowes. *E Lot*.................................2C **130**
Knowesgate. *Nmbd*........................1C **114**
Knoweside. *S Ayr*............................3B **116**
Knowes of Elrick. *Abers*.................3D **160**
Knowle. *Bris*....................................4B **34**
Knowle. *Devn*
  nr. Braunton............................3E **19**
  nr. Budleigh Salterton............4D **12**
  nr. Crediton.............................2A **12**
Knowle. *Shrp*...................................3H **59**
Knowle. *W Mid*................................3F **61**
Knowle Green. *Lanc*.........................1E **91**
Knowle St Giles. *Som*......................1G **13**
Knowlesands. *Shrp*.........................1B **60**
Knowle Village. *Hants*.....................2D **16**
Knowl Hill. *Wind*.............................4G **37**
Knowlton. *Kent*...............................5G **41**
Knowsley. *Mers*...............................1G **83**
Knowstone. *Devn*.............................4B **20**
Knucklas. *Powy*...............................3E **59**
Knuston. *Nptn*.................................4G **63**
Knutsford. *Ches E*.........................3B **84**
Knypersley. *Staf*.............................5C **84**
Krumlin. *W Yor*................................3A **92**
Kuggar. *Corn*.......................................5E **5**
Kyleakin. *High*................................1F **147**
Kyle of Lochalsh. *High*...................1F **147**
Kylerhea. *High*................................1F **147**
Kylesku. *High*.................................5C **166**
Kyles Lodge. *W Isl*.........................1E **170**
Kylesmorar. *High*............................4F **147**
Kylestrome. *High*...........................5C **166**
Kymin. *Mon*....................................4A **48**
Kynaston. *Here*................................2B **48**
Kynaston. *Shrp*................................3F **71**
Kynnersley. *Telf*...............................4A **72**
Kyre Green. *Worc*.............................4A **60**
Kyre Park. *Worc*...............................4A **60**
Kyrewood. *Worc*...............................4A **60**

L

Labost. *W Isl*...................................3E **171**
Lacasaidh. *W Isl*.............................5F **171**

Lacasdail. *W Isl*.............................4G **171**
Laceby. *NE Lin*.................................4F **95**
Lacey Green. *Buck*..........................5G **51**
Lach Dennis. *Ches W*......................3B **84**
Lache. *Ches W*.................................4F **83**
Lackford. *Suff*..................................3G **65**
Lacock. *Wilts*..................................5E **35**
Ladbroke. *Warw*...............................5B **62**
Laddingford. *Kent*..........................1A **28**
Lade Bank. *Linc*..............................5C **88**
Ladock. *Corn*.....................................3C **6**
Lady. *Orkn*......................................3F **172**
Ladybank. *Fife*................................2E **137**
Ladycross. *Corn*..............................4D **10**
Lady Green. *Mers*............................4B **90**
Lady Hall. *Cumb*..............................1A **96**
Ladykirk. *Bord*...............................5E **131**
Ladysford. *Abers*...........................2G **161**
Ladywood. *W Mid*...........................2E **61**
Ladywood. *Worc*..............................4C **60**
Laga. *High*......................................2A **140**
Lagavulin. *Arg*...............................5C **124**
Lagg. *Arg*..2D **125**
Lagg. *N Ayr*....................................3D **122**
Laggan. *Arg*....................................4A **124**
Laggan. *High*
  nr. Fort Augustus....................4E **149**
  nr. Newtonmore......................4A **150**
Laggan. *Mor*...................................5H **159**
Lagganlia. *High*..............................3C **150**
Lagganulva. *Arg*.............................4F **139**
Laglingarten. *Arg*...........................3A **134**
Lagness. *W Sus*...............................2G **17**
Laid. *High*.......................................3E **166**
Laide. *High*.....................................4C **162**
Laigh Fenwick. *E Ayr*......................5F **127**
Laindon. *Essx*..................................2A **40**
Lairg. *High*......................................3C **164**
Lairg Muir. *High*.............................3C **164**
Laithes. *Cumb*................................1F **103**
Laithkirk. *Dur*.................................2C **104**
Lake. *Devn*..3F **19**
Lake. *IOW*..4D **16**
Lake. *Wilts*..3G **23**
Lakenham. *Norf*...............................5E **79**
Lakenheath. *Suff*.............................2G **65**
Lakesend. *Norf*................................1E **65**
Lakeside. *Cumb*................................1C **96**
Laleham. *Surr*..................................4B **38**
Laleston. *B'end*...............................3B **32**
Lamancha. *Bord*.............................4F **129**
Lamarsh. *Essx*.................................2B **54**
Lamas. *Norf*....................................3E **79**
Lamb Corner. *Essx*..........................2D **54**
Lambden. *Bord*..............................5D **130**
Lamberhead Green. *G Man*.............4D **90**
Lamberhurst. *Kent*.........................2A **28**
Lamberhurst Quarter. *Kent*............2A **28**
Lamberton. *Bord*............................4F **131**
Lambeth. *G Lon*...........................3E **39**
Lambfell Moar. *IOM*.......................3B **108**
Lambhill. *Glas*...............................3G **127**
Lambley. *Nmbd*..............................4H **113**
Lambley. *Notts*.................................1D **74**
Lambourn. *W Ber*............................4B **36**
Lambourne End. *Essx*......................1F **39**
Lambourn Woodlands. *W Ber*........4B **36**
Lambs Green. *Dors*..........................3E **15**
Lambs Green. *W Sus*.......................2D **26**
Lambston. *Pemb*.............................3D **42**
Lamellion. *Corn*...............................2G **7**
Lamerton. *Devn*...............................5E **11**
Lamesley. *Tyne*..............................4F **115**
Laminess. *Orkn*...............................4F **172**
Lamington. *High*............................1B **158**
Lamington. *S Lan*..........................1B **118**
Lamlash. *N Ayr*................................2E **123**
Lamonby. *Cumb*.............................1F **103**
Lamorick. *Corn*..................................2E **7**
Lamorna. *Corn*....................................4B **4**
Lamorran. *Corn*.................................4C **6**
Lampeter. *Cdgn*................................1F **45**
Lampeter Velfrey. *Pemb*...................3F **43**
Lamphey. *Pemb*................................4E **43**
Lamplugh. *Cumb*............................2B **102**
Lamport. *Nptn*.................................3E **63**
Lamyatt. *Som*..................................3B **22**
Lana. *Devn*
  nr. Ashwater............................2D **10**
  nr. Holsworthy........................2D **10**
Lanark. *S Lan*..................................5B **128**
Lanarth. *Corn*.....................................4E **5**
Lancaster. *Lanc*..........................3D **97**
Lanchester. *Dur*.............................5E **115**
Lancing. *W Sus*............................5C **26**
Landbeach. *Cambs*.........................4D **65**
Landcross. *Devn*..............................4E **19**
Landerberry. *Abers*........................3E **153**
Landford. *Wilts*...............................1A **16**
Land Gate. *G Man*............................4D **90**
Landhallow. *High*...........................5D **169**
Landimore. *Swan*.............................3D **30**
Landkey. *Devn*..................................3F **19**
Landkey Newland. *Devn*...................3F **19**
Landore. *Swan*.................................3F **31**
Landport. *Port*..................................2E **17**
Landrake. *Corn*..................................2H **7**
Landscove. *Devn*................................2D **9**
Land's End Airport. *Corn*...................4A **4**
Landshipping. *Pemb*.......................3E **43**
Landulph. *Corn*..................................2A **8**
Landywood. *Staf*..............................5D **73**
Lane. *Corn*...2C **6**
Laneast. *Corn*..................................4C **10**
Lane Bottom. *Lanc*...........................1G **91**
Lane End. *Buck*.................................2G **37**
Lane End. *Cumb*..............................5B **102**
Lane End. *Hants*...............................4D **24**
Lane End. *IOW*.................................4E **17**
Lane End. *Wilts*................................2D **22**
Lane Ends. *Derbs*.............................2G **73**
Lane Ends. *Dur*................................1E **105**

Lane Ends. *Lanc*.............................4G **97**
Laneham. *Notts*...............................3F **87**
Lane Head. *Dur*
  nr. Hutton Magna....................3E **105**
  nr. Woodland...........................2D **105**
Lane Head. *G Man*...........................1A **84**
Lane Head. *W Yor*.............................4B **92**
Lanehead. *Dur*................................5B **114**
Lanehead. *Nmbd*............................1A **114**
Lane Heads. *Lanc*............................1C **90**
Lanercost. *Cumb*...........................3G **113**
Laneshaw Bridge. *Lanc*..................5B **98**
Laney Green. *Staf*............................5D **72**
Langais. *W Isl*................................2D **170**
Langal. *High*...................................2B **140**
Langar. *Notts*...................................2E **74**
Langbank. *Ren*................................2E **127**
Langbar. *N Yor*.................................4C **98**
Langburnshiels. *Bord*....................4H **119**
Langcliffe. *N Yor*..............................3H **97**
Langdon. *Corn*.................................4C **10**
Langdon Beck. *Dur*.........................1B **104**
Langdon Cross. *Corn*.......................4D **10**
Langdon Hills. *Essx*.........................2A **40**
Langdown. *Hants*.............................2C **16**
Langdyke. *Fife*................................3F **137**
Langenhoe. *Essx*..............................4D **54**
Langford. *C Beds*............................1B **52**
Langford. *Devn*................................2D **12**
Langford. *Essx*.................................5B **54**
Langford. *Notts*...............................5F **87**
Langford. *Oxon*................................5H **49**
Langford. *Som*...................................4F **21**
Langford Budville. *Som*..................4E **20**
Langham. *Dors*................................4C **22**
Langham. *Essx*.................................2D **54**
Langham. *Norf*.................................1C **78**
Langham. *Rut*..................................4F **75**
Langham. *Suff*.................................4B **66**
Langho. *Lanc*...................................1F **91**
Langholm. *Dum*..............................1E **113**
Langland. *Swan*...............................4F **31**
Langleeford. *Nmbd*.......................2D **120**
Langley. *Ches E*................................3D **84**
Langley. *Derbs*.................................1B **74**
Langley. *Essx*...................................2E **53**
Langley. *Glos*....................................3F **49**
Langley. *Hants*..................................2C **16**
Langley. *Herts*..................................3C **52**
Langley. *Kent*....................................5C **40**
Langley. *Nmbd*...............................3B **114**
Langley. *Slo*.....................................3B **38**
Langley. *Warw*..................................4F **61**
Langley. *W Sus*.................................4G **25**
Langley Burrell. *Wilts*......................4E **35**
Langleybury. *Herts*..........................5A **52**
Langley Common. *Derbs*..................2G **73**
Langley Green. *Derbs*.......................2G **73**
Langley Green. *Norf*.........................5F **79**
Langley Green. *Warw*........................4F **61**
Langley Green. *W Sus*......................2D **26**
Langley Heath. *Kent*.........................5C **40**
Langley Marsh. *Som*.........................4D **20**
Langley Moor. *Dur*..........................5F **115**
Langley Park. *Dur*..........................5F **115**
Langley Street. *Norf*.........................5F **79**
Langney. *E Sus*................................5H **27**
Langold. *Notts*.................................2C **86**
Langore. *Corn*.................................4C **10**
Langport. *Som*..................................4H **21**
Langrick. *Linc*...................................1B **76**
Langridge. *Bath*...............................5C **34**
Langridgeford. *Devn*........................4F **19**
Langrigg. *Cumb*.............................5C **112**
Langrish. *Hants*...............................4F **25**
Langsett. *S Yor*.................................4C **92**
Langshaw. *Bord*.............................1H **119**
Langstone. *Hants*............................2F **17**
Langthorne. *N Yor*..........................5F **105**
Langthorpe. *N Yor*............................3F **99**
Langthwaite. *N Yor*........................4D **104**
Langtoft. *E Yor*................................3E **101**
Langtoft. *Linc*..................................4A **76**
Langton. *Dur*..................................3E **105**
Langton. *Linc*
  nr. Horncastle.........................4B **88**
  nr. Spilsby................................3C **88**
Langton. *N Yor*...............................3B **100**
Langton by Wragby. *Linc*................3A **88**
Langton Green. *Kent*.......................2G **27**
Langton Herring. *Dors*......................4B **14**
Langton Long Blandford. *Dors*........2D **15**
Langton Matravers. *Dors*...............5E **15**
Langtree. *Devn*................................1E **11**
Langwathby. *Cumb*........................1G **103**
Langwith. *Derbs*...............................3C **86**
Langworth. *Linc*..............................3H **87**
Lanivet. *Corn*.....................................2E **7**
Lanjeth. *Corn*....................................3D **6**
Lank. *Corn*......................................5A **10**
Lanlivery. *Corn*..................................3E **7**
Lanner. *Corn*.......................................5B **6**
Lanreath. *Corn*..................................3F **7**
Lansallos. *Corn*..................................3F **7**
Lansdown. *Bath*..............................5C **34**
Lansdown. *Glos*...............................3E **49**
Lanteglos Highway. *Corn*..................3F **7**
Lanton. *Nmbd*................................1D **120**
Lanton. *Bord*..................................2A **120**
Lapford. *Devn*..................................2H **11**
Lapford Cross. *Devn*.........................2H **11**
Laphroaig. *Arg*...............................5B **124**
Lapley. *Staf*......................................4C **72**
Lapworth. *Warw*...............................3F **61**
Larachbeg. *High*.............................4A **140**
Larbert. *Falk*..................................1B **128**
Larden Green. *Ches E*.......................5H **83**
Larel. *High*......................................3D **169**
Largie. *Abers*..................................5D **160**

Largiemore. *Arg*............................1H **125**
Largoward. *Fife*..........................3G **137**
Largs. *N Ayr*..............................4D **126**
Largue. *Abers*..............................4D **160**
Largybeg. *N Ayr*.........................3E **123**
Largymeanoch. *N Ayr*.................3E **123**
Largymore. *N Ayr*........................3E **123**
Larkfield. *Inv*..............................2D **126**
Larkfield. *Kent*.............................5B **40**
Larkhall. *Bath*................................5C **34**
Larkhall. *S Lan*.........................4A **128**
Larkhill. *Wilts*...............................2G **23**
Larling. *Norf*..................................2B **66**
Larport. *Here*..................................2A **48**
Lartington. *Dur*...........................3D **104**
Lary. *Abers*...................................3H **151**
Lasham. *Hants*..............................2E **25**
Lashenden. *Kent*............................1C **28**
Lasswade. *Midl*...........................3G **129**
Lastingham. *N Yor*......................5E **107**
Latchford. *Herts*............................3D **53**
Latchford. *Oxon*............................5E **51**
Latchingdon. *Essx*.........................5B **54**
Latchley. *Corn*...............................5E **11**
Latchmere Green. *Hants*.............1E **25**
Lathbury. *Mil*..................................1G **51**
Latheron. *High*............................5D **169**
Latheronwheel. *High*..................5D **169**
Lathom. *Lanc*.................................4C **90**
Lathones. *Fife*..............................3G **137**
Latimer. *Buck*................................1B **38**
Latteridge. *S Glo*...........................3B **34**
Lattiford. *Som*................................4B **22**
Latton. *Wilts*..................................2F **35**
Laudale House. *High*....................3B **140**
Lauder. *Bord*................................5B **130**
Laugharne. *Carm*..........................3H **43**
Laughterton. *Linc*..........................3F **87**
Laughton. *E Sus*............................4G **27**
Laughton. *Leics*.............................2D **62**
Laughton. *Linc*
  nr. Gainsborough 1F **87**
  nr. Grantham 2H **75**
Laughton Common. *S Yor*............2C **86**
Laughton en le Morthen. *S Yor*...2C **86**
Launcells. *Corn*.............................2C **10**
Launceston. *Corn*..........................4D **10**
Launcherley. *Som*..........................2A **22**
Launton. *Oxon*...............................3E **50**
Laurencekirk. *Abers*....................1G **145**
Laurieston. *Dum*..........................3D **111**
Laurieston. *Falk*..........................2C **128**
Lavendon. *Mil*................................5G **63**
Lavenham. *Suff*..............................1C **54**
Laverhay. *Dum*.............................5D **118**
Laversdale. *Cumb*........................3F **113**
Laverstock. *Wilts*...........................3G **23**
Laverstoke. *Hants*..........................2C **24**
Laverton. *Glos*...............................2F **49**
Laverton. *N Yor*............................2E **99**
Laverton. *Som*...............................1C **22**
Lavister. *Wrex*................................5F **83**
Law. *S Lan*...................................4B **128**
Lawers. *Per*.................................5D **142**
Lawford. *Essx*................................2D **54**
Lawhitton. *Corn*............................4D **10**
Lawkland. *N Yor*............................3G **97**
Lawley. *Telf*...................................5A **72**
Lawnhead. *Staf*..............................3C **72**
Lawrenny. *Pemb*...........................4E **43**
Lawshall. *Suff*................................5A **66**
Lawton. *Here*..................................5G **59**
Laxey. *IOM*...................................3D **108**
Laxfield. *Suff*.................................3E **67**
Laxfirth. *Shet*...............................6F **173**
Laxo. *Shet*..................................5F **173**
Laxton. *E Yor*.................................2A **94**
Laxton. *Nptn*..................................1G **63**
Laxton. *Notts*.................................4E **86**
Laycock. *W Yor*.............................5C **98**
Layer Breton. *Essx*.........................4C **54**
Layer-de-la-Haye. *Essx*.................3C **54**
Layer Marney. *Essx*........................4C **54**
Laymore. *Dors*...............................2G **13**
Laysters Pole. *Here*.......................4H **59**
Layter's Green. *Buck*......................1A **38**
Laytham. *E Yor*...............................1H **93**
Lazenby. *Red C*.............................3C **106**
Lazonby. *Cumb*............................1G **103**
Lea. *Derbs*....................................5H **85**
Lea. *Here*.......................................3B **48**
Lea. *Linc*.......................................2F **87**
Lea. *Shrp*
  nr. Bishop's Castle 2F **59**
  nr. Shrewsbury 5G **71**
Lea. *Wilts*......................................3E **35**
Leabrooks. *Derbs*...........................5B **86**
Leac a Li. *W Isl*...........................8D **171**
Leachkin. *High*.............................4A **158**
Leachpool. *Pemb*...........................3D **42**
Leadburn. *Midl*............................4F **129**
Leadenham. *Linc*..........................5G **87**
Leaden Roding. *Essx*......................4F **53**
Leaderfoot. *Bord*...........................1H **119**
Leadgate. *Cumb*.........................5A **114**
Leadgate. *Dur*.............................4E **115**
Leadgate. *Nmbd*.........................4E **115**
Leadhills. *S Lan*...........................3A **118**
Leadingcross Green. *Kent*.............5C **40**
Lea End. *Worc*................................3E **61**
Leafield. *Oxon*................................4B **50**
Leagrave. *Lutn*...............................3A **52**
Lea Hall. *W Mid*.............................2F **61**
Lea Heath. *Staf*..............................3E **73**
Leake. *N Yor*................................5B **106**
Leake Common Side. *Linc*............5C **88**
Leake Fold Hill. *Linc*.....................5D **88**
Leake Hurn's End. *Linc*.................1D **76**
Lealholm. *N Yor*...........................4E **107**
Lealt. *Arg*....................................4D **132**

Lealt. *High*....................................2E **155**
Leam. *Derbs*...................................3G **85**
Lea Marston. *Warw*........................1G **61**
Leamington Hastings. *Warw*.........4B **62**
Leamington Spa, Royal.
  Warw......................................4H **61**
Leamonsley. *Staf*...........................5F **73**
Leamside. *Dur*.............................5G **115**
Leargybreck. *Arg*.........................2D **124**
Lease Rigg. *N Yor*.......................4F **107**
Leasgill. *Cumb*..............................1D **97**
Leasingham. *Linc*.........................1H **75**
Leasingthorne. *Dur*.....................1F **105**
Leasowe. *Mers*...............................1E **83**
Leatherhead. *Surr*......................5C **38**
Leathley. *N Yor*..............................5E **99**
Leaths. *Dum*................................3E **111**
Leaton. *Shrp*..................................4G **71**
Leaton. *Telf*....................................4A **72**
Lea Town. *Lanc*..............................1C **90**
Leavenheath. *Suff*..........................2C **54**
Leavening. *N Yor*.........................3B **100**
Leaves Green. *G Lon*......................4F **39**
Lea Yeat. *Cumb*.............................1G **97**
Leazes. *Dur*.................................4E **115**
Lebberston. *N Yor*.......................1E **101**
Lechlade on Thames. *Glos*............2H **35**
Leck. *Lanc*......................................2F **97**
Leckford. *Hants*..............................3B **24**
Leckfurin. *High*............................3H **167**
Leckgruinart. *Arg*.........................3A **124**
Leckhampstead. *Buck*....................2F **51**
Leckhampstead. *W Ber*.................4C **36**
Leckhampton. *Glos*........................4E **49**
Leckmelm. *High*..........................4F **163**
Leckwith. *V Glam*..........................4E **33**
Leconfield. *E Yor*..........................5E **101**
Ledaig. *Arg*..................................5D **140**
Ledburn. *Buck*...............................3H **51**
Ledbury. *Here*.................................2C **48**
Ledgemoor. *Here*............................5G **59**
Ledgowan. *High*..........................3D **156**
Ledicot. *Here*.................................4G **59**
Ledmore. *High*.............................2G **163**
Lednabirichen. *High*.....................4E **165**
Lednagullin. *High*........................2A **168**
Ledsham. *Ches W*..........................3F **83**
Ledsham. *W Yor*.............................2E **93**
Ledston. *W Yor*...............................2E **93**
Ledstone. *Devn*................................4D **8**
Ledwell. *Oxon*................................3C **50**
Lee. *Devn*
  nr. Ilfracombe 2E **19**
  nr. South Molton 4B **20**
Lee. *G Lon*.....................................3E **39**
Lee. *Hants*......................................1B **16**
Lee. *Lanc*.......................................4E **97**
Lee. *Shrp*..2G **71**
The Lee. *Buck*................................5H **51**
Leeans. *Shet*................................7E **173**
Leebotten. *Shet*..........................9F **173**
Leebotwood. *Shrp*..........................1G **59**
Lee Brockhurst. *Shrp*....................3H **71**
Leece. *Cumb*..................................3B **96**
Leechpool. *Mon*.............................3A **34**
Lee Clump. *Buck*...........................5H **51**
Leeds. *Kent*....................................5C **40**
Leeds. *W Yor*...............**199** (1C **92**)
Leeds Bradford Airport. *W Yor*.....5E **99**
Leedstown. *Corn*.............................3D **4**
Leegomery. *Telf*.............................4A **72**
Lee Head. *Derbs*............................1E **85**
Leek. *Staf*...................................5D **85**
Leekbrook. *Staf*.............................5D **85**
Leek Wootton. *Warw*......................4G **61**
Lee Mill. *Devn*.................................3B **8**
Leeming. *N Yor*..............................1E **99**
Leeming Bar. *N Yor*.....................5F **105**
Lee Moor. *Devn*.............................2B **8**
Lee Moor. *W Yor*............................2D **92**
Lee-on-the-Solent. *Hants*..............2D **16**
Lees. *Derbs*....................................2G **73**
Lees. *G Man*...................................4H **91**
Lees. *W Yor*....................................1A **92**
The Lees. *Kent*................................5E **40**
Leeswood. *Flin*...............................4E **83**
Leetown. *Per*................................1E **136**
Leftwich. *Ches W*...........................3A **84**
Legbourne. *Linc*.............................2C **88**
Legburthwaite. *Cumb*.................3E **102**
Legerwood. *Bord*.........................5B **130**
Legsby. *Linc*...................................2A **88**
Leicester. *Leic*.............**200** (5C **74**)
Leicester Forest East. *Leics*...........5C **74**
Leigh. *Dors*....................................2B **14**
Leigh. *G Man*..............................4E **91**
Leigh. *Kent*.....................................1G **27**
Leigh. *Shrp*.....................................5F **71**
Leigh. *Surr*.....................................1D **26**
Leigh. *Wilts*....................................2F **35**
Leigh. *Worc*....................................5B **60**
The Leigh. *Glos*..............................3D **48**
Leigham. *Plym*.................................3B **8**
Leigh Beck. *Essx*............................2C **40**
Leigh Common. *Som*......................4C **22**
Leigh Delamere. *Wilts*...................4D **35**
Leigh Green. *Kent*..........................2D **28**
Leighland Chapel. *Som*..................3D **20**
Leigh-on-Sea. *S'end*.......................2C **40**
Leigh Park. *Hants*..........................2F **17**
Leigh Sinton. *Worc*........................5B **60**
Leighterton. *Glos*...........................2D **34**
Leighton. *N Yor*.............................2D **98**
Leighton. *Powy*..............................5E **71**
Leighton. *Shrp*...............................5A **72**
Leighton. *Som*................................2C **22**
Leighton Bromswold. *Cambs*........3A **64**
Leighton Buzzard. *C Beds*.........3H **51**
Leigh-upon-Mendip. *Som*..............2B **22**
Leinthall Earls. *Here*......................4G **59**

Leinthall Starkes. *Here*...................4G **59**
Leintwardine. *Here*.........................3G **59**
Leire. *Leics*.....................................1C **62**
Leirinmore. *High*..........................2E **166**
Leishmore. *High*...........................4G **157**
Leiston. *Suff*..................................4G **67**
Leitfie. *Per*.....................................4B **144**
Leith. *Edin*.....................................2F **129**
Leitholm. *Bord*.............................5D **130**
Lelant. *Corn*.....................................3C **4**
Lelant Downs. *Corn*.........................3C **4**
Lelley. *E Yor*...................................1F **95**
Lem Hill. *Shrp*................................3B **60**
Lemington. *Tyne*..........................3E **115**
Lempitlaw. *Bord*...........................1B **120**
Lemsford. *Herts*.............................4C **52**
Lenchwick. *Worc*............................1F **49**
Lendalfoot. *S Ayr*.........................5C **116**
Lendrick. *Stir*................................3E **135**
Lenham. *Kent*.................................5C **40**
Lenham Heath. *Kent*......................1D **28**
Lennel. *Bord*................................5E **131**
Lenton. *Linc*...................................2H **75**
Lentran. *High*...............................4H **157**
Lenwade. *Norf*...............................4C **78**
Lenzie. *E Dun*...........................2H **127**
Leochel Cushnie. *Abers*..............2C **152**
Leogh. *Shet*..................................1B **172**
Leominster. *Here*........................5G **59**
Leonard Stanley. *Glos*....................5D **48**
Lepe. *Hants*....................................3C **16**
Lephenstrath. *Arg*.........................5A **122**
Lephin. *High*................................4A **154**
Lephinchapel. *Arg*........................4G **133**
Lephinmore. *Arg*..........................4G **133**
Leppington. *N Yor*.......................3B **100**
Lepton. *W Yor*................................3C **92**
Lerryn. *Corn*..................................3F **7**
Lerwick. *Shet*...............................7F **173**
Lerwick (Tingwall) Airport.
  Shet......................................7F **173**
Lesbury. *Nmbd*............................3G **121**
Leslie. *Abers*................................1C **152**
Leslie. *Fife*...................................3E **137**
Lesmahagow. *S Lan*.....................1H **117**
Lesnewth. *Corn*...............................3B **10**
Lessingham. *Norf*...........................3F **79**
Lessonhall. *Cumb*.........................4D **112**
Leswalt. *Dum*...............................3F **109**
Letchmore Heath. *Herts*.................1C **38**
Letchworth Garden City.
  Herts......................................2C **52**
Letcombe Bassett. *Oxon*................3B **36**
Letcombe Regis. *Oxon*...................3B **36**
Letham. *Ang*................................4E **145**
Letham. *Falk*................................1B **128**
Letham. *Fife*.................................2F **137**
Lethanhill. *E Ayr*..........................3D **116**
Lethenty. *Abers*............................4F **161**
Letheringham. *Suff*........................5E **67**
Letheringsett. *Norf*.........................2C **78**
Lettaford. *Devn*..............................4H **11**
Lettan. *Orkn*...............................3G **172**
Letter. *Abers*................................2E **153**
Letterewe. *High*...........................1B **156**
Letterfearn. *High*.........................1A **148**
Lettermore. *Arg*.............................4F **139**
Letters. *High*...............................5F **163**
Letterston. *Pemb*...........................2D **42**
Letton. *Here*
  nr. Kington 1G **47**
  nr. Leintwardine........................3F **59**
Letty Green. *Herts*..........................4C **52**
Letwell. *S Yor*................................2C **86**
Leuchars. *Fife*................................1G **137**
Leumrabhagh. *W Isl*....................6F **171**
Leusdon. *Devn*................................5H **11**
Levaneap. *Shet*...........................5F **173**
Levedale. *Staf*................................4C **72**
Leven. *E Yor*.................................5F **101**
Leven. *Fife*...................................3F **137**
Levencorroch. *N Ayr*....................3E **123**
Levenhall. *E Lot*...........................2G **129**
Levens. *Cumb*................................1D **97**
Levens Green. *Herts*.......................3D **52**
Levenshulme. *G Man*......................1C **84**
Levenwick. *Shet*...........................9F **173**
Leverburgh. *W Isl*.........................9C **171**
Leverington. *Cambs*......................4D **76**
Leverton. *Linc*................................1D **76**
Leverton. *W Ber*.............................4B **36**
Leverton Lucasgate. *Linc*...............1D **76**
Leverton Outgate. *Linc*..................1D **76**
Levington. *Suff*...............................2F **55**
Levisham. *N Yor*..........................5F **107**
Levishie. *High*.............................2G **149**
Lew. *Oxon*......................................5B **50**
Lewaigue. *IOM*............................2D **108**
Lewannick. *Corn*............................4C **10**
Lewdown. *Devn*..............................4E **11**
Lewes. *E Sus*..............................5F **27**
Leweston. *Pemb*.............................2D **42**
Lewisham. *G Lon*.......................3E **39**
Lewiston. *High*.............................1H **149**
Lewistown. *B'end*...........................3C **32**
Lewknor. *Oxon*...............................2F **37**
Leworthy. *Devn*
  nr. Barnstaple 3G **19**
  nr. Holsworthy.........................2D **10**
Lewson Street. *Kent*......................4D **40**
Lewthorn Cross. *Devn*...................5A **12**
Lewtrenchard. *Devn*........................4E **11**
Ley. *Corn*..2F **7**
Leybourne. *Kent*.............................5A **40**
Leyburn. *N Yor*............................5E **105**
Leycett. *Staf*..................................1B **72**
Leyfields. *Staf*................................5G **73**

Ley Green. *Herts*.............................3B **52**
Ley Hill. *Buck*................................5H **51**
Leyland. *Lanc*.............................2D **90**
Leylodge. *Abers*.............................2E **153**
Leymoor. *W Yor*.............................3B **92**
Leys. *Per*......................................5B **144**
Leysdown-on-Sea. *Kent*..................3E **41**
Leysmill. *Ang*................................4F **145**
Leyton. *G Lon*.............................2E **39**
Leytonstone. *G Lon*........................2F **39**
Lezant. *Corn*..................................5D **10**
Leziate. *Norf*..................................4F **77**
Lhanbryde. *Mor*...........................2G **159**
The Lhen. *IOM*.............................1C **108**
Liatrie. *High*.................................5E **157**
Libanus. *Powy*................................3C **46**
Libberton. *S Lan*..........................5C **128**
Libbery. *Worc*................................5D **60**
Liberton. *Edin*..............................3F **129**
Liceasto. *W Isl*.............................8D **171**
Lichfield. *Staf*.............................5F **73**
Lickey. *Worc*...................................3D **61**
Lickey End. *Worc*............................3D **60**
Lickfold. *W Sus*..............................3A **26**
Liddaton. *Devn*...............................4E **11**
Liddington. *Swin*.............................3H **35**
Liddle. *Orkn*.................................9D **172**
Lidgate. *Suff*..................................5G **65**
Lidgett. *Notts*.................................4D **86**
Lidham Hill. *E Sus*..........................4C **28**
Lidlington. *C Beds*..........................2H **51**
Lidsey. *W Sus*.................................5A **26**
Lidstone. *Oxon*...............................3B **50**
Lienassie. *High*..............................1B **148**
Liff. *Ang*.......................................5C **144**
Lifford. *W Mid*................................2E **61**
Lifton. *Devn*....................................4D **11**
Liftondown. *Devn*...........................4D **10**
Lighthorne. *Warw*...........................5H **61**
Light Oaks. *Stoke*...........................5D **84**
Lightwater. *Surr*.............................4A **38**
Lightwood. *Staf*..............................1E **73**
Lightwood. *Stoke*...........................1D **72**
Lightwood Green. *Ches E*.............1A **72**
Lightwood Green. *Wrex*.................1F **71**
Lilbourne. *Nptn*...............................3C **62**
Lilburn Tower. *Nmbd*....................2E **121**
Lilleshall. *Telf*................................4B **72**
Lilley. *Herts*...................................3B **52**
Lilliesleaf. *Bord*.............................2H **119**
Lillingstone Dayrell. *Buck*.............2F **51**
Lillingstone Lovell. *Buck*................1F **51**
Lillington. *Dors*...............................1B **14**
Lilstock. *Som*.................................2E **21**
Lilybank. *Inv*.................................2E **126**
Lilyhurst. *Shrp*................................4B **72**
Limbrick. *Lanc*...............................3E **90**
Limbury. *Lutn*.................................3A **52**
Limekilnburn. *S Lan*....................4A **128**
Limekilns. *Fife*..............................1D **129**
Limerigg. *Falk*...............................2B **128**
Limestone Brae. *Nmbd*.................5A **114**
Lime Street. *Worc*...........................2D **48**
Limington. *Som*..............................4A **22**
Limpenhoe. *Norf*.............................5F **79**
Limpley Stoke. *Wilts*......................5C **34**
Limpsfield. *Surr*.............................5F **39**
Limpsfield Chart. *Surr*...................5F **39**
Linburn. *W Lot*.............................3E **129**
Linby. *Notts*...................................5C **86**
Linchmere. *W Sus*..........................3G **25**
Lincluden. *Dum*............................2A **112**
Lincoln. *Linc*...............**198** (3G **87**)
Lincomb. *Worc*................................4C **60**
Lindale. *Cumb*...............................1D **96**
Lindal in Furness. *Cumb*................2B **96**
Lindean. *Bord*...............................1G **119**
Linden. *Glos*...................................4D **48**
Lindfield. *W Sus*............................3E **27**
Lindford. *Hants*..............................3G **25**
Lindores. *Fife*...............................2E **137**
Lindridge. *Worc*.............................4A **60**
Lindsell. *Essx*.................................3G **53**
Lindsey. *Suff*...................................1C **54**
Lindsey Tye. *Suff*...........................1C **54**
Linford. *Hants*................................2G **15**
Linford. *Thur*..................................3A **40**
Lingague. *IOM*.............................4B **108**
Lingdale. *Red C*...........................3D **106**
Lingen. *Here*...................................4F **59**
Lingfield. *Surr*................................1E **27**
Lingreabhagh. *W Isl*....................9C **171**
Lingwood. *Norf*..............................5F **79**
Lingy Close. *Cumb*......................4E **113**
Linicro. *High*................................2C **154**
Linkend. *Worc*................................2D **48**
Linkenholt. *Hants*...........................1B **24**
Linkinhorne. *Corn*..........................5D **10**
Linklater. *Orkn*............................9D **172**
Linksness. *Orkn*...........................6E **172**
Linktown. *Fife*...............................4E **137**
Linkwood. *Mor*..............................2G **159**
Linley. *Shrp*
  nr. Bishop's Castle 1F **59**
  nr. Bridgnorth 1A **60**
Linley Green. *Here*.........................5A **60**
Linlithgow. *W Lot*......................2C **128**
Linlithgow Bridge. *Falk*.................2C **128**
Linneraineach. *High*.....................3F **163**
Linshiels. *Nmbd*...........................4C **120**
Linsiadar. *W Isl*............................4E **171**
Linsidemore. *High*........................4C **164**
Linslade. *C Beds*............................3H **51**
Linstead Parva. *Suff*......................3F **67**
Linstock. *Cumb*............................4F **113**
Linthwaite. *W Yor*..........................3B **92**
Lintlaw. *Bord*................................4E **131**
Lintmill. *Mor*..................................2C **160**
Linton. *Cambs*................................1F **53**
Linton. *Derbs*.................................4G **73**

Linton. *Here*....................................3B **48**
Linton. *Kent*....................................1B **28**
Linton. *N Yor*..................................3B **98**
Linton. *Bord*.................................2B **120**
Linton. *W Yor*.................................5F **99**
Linton Colliery. *Nmbd*..................5G **121**
Linton Hill. *Here*.............................3B **48**
Linton-on-Ouse. *N Yor*...................3G **99**
Lintzford. *Dur*...............................4E **115**
Lintzgarth. *Dur*.............................5C **114**
Linwood. *Hants*..............................2G **15**
Linwood. *Linc*.................................2A **88**
Linwood. *Ren*.............................3F **127**
Lionacleit. *W Isl*............................4C **170**
Lionacro. *W Isl*..............................2C **154**
Lionacuidhe. *W Isl*........................4C **170**
Lional. *W Isl*.................................1H **171**
Liphook. *Hants*...............................3G **25**
Lipley. *Shrp*....................................2B **72**
Lipyeate. *Som*................................1B **22**
Liquo. *N Lan*................................4B **128**
Liscard. *Mers*.................................1F **83**
Liscombe. *Som*...............................3B **20**
Liskeard. *Corn*..................................2G **7**
Lisle Court. *Hants*...........................3B **16**
Liss. *Hants*.....................................4F **25**
Lissett. *E Yor*................................4F **101**
Liss Forest. *Hants*..........................4F **25**
Lissington. *Linc*..............................2A **88**
Liston. *Essx*....................................1B **54**
Lisvane. *Card*.................................3E **33**
Liswerry. *Newp*...............................3G **33**
Litcham. *Norf*.................................4A **78**
Litchard. *B'end*...............................3C **32**
Litchborough. *Nptn*........................5D **62**
Litchfield. *Hants*.............................1C **24**
Litherland. *Mers*.........................1F **83**
Litlington. *Cambs*...........................1D **52**
Litlington. *E Sus*.............................5G **27**
Littlemill. *Nmbd*...........................3G **121**
Litterty. *Abers*...............................3E **161**
Little Abington. *Cambs*..................1F **53**
Little Addington. *Nptn*...................3G **63**
Little Airmyn. *N Yor*.......................2H **93**
Little Alne. *Warw*...........................4F **61**
Little Ardo. *Abers*..........................5F **161**
Little Asby. *Cumb*.........................4H **103**
Little Aston. *Staf*............................5E **73**
Little Atherfield. *IOW*.....................4C **16**
Little Ayton. *N Yor*.......................3C **106**
Little Baddow. *Essx*........................5A **54**
Little Badminton. *S Glo*..................3D **34**
Little Ballinluig. *Per*......................3G **143**
Little Bampton. *Cumb*..................4D **112**
Little Bardfield. *Essx*......................2G **53**
Little Barford. *Bed*..........................5A **64**
Little Barningham. *Norf*.................2D **78**
Little Barrington. *Glos*....................4H **49**
Little Barrow. *Ches W*....................4G **83**
Little Barugh. *N Yor*.....................2B **100**
Little Bavington. *Nmbd*................2C **114**
Little Bealings. *Suff*.......................1F **55**
Littlebeck. *Cumb*..........................3H **103**
Little Bedwyn. *Wilts*.......................5A **36**
Little Bentley. *Essx*.........................3E **54**
Little Berkhamsted. *Herts*..............5C **52**
Little Billing. *Nptn*.........................4F **63**
Little Billington. *C Beds*.................3H **51**
Little Birch. *Here*............................2A **48**
Little Bispham. *Bkpl*......................5C **96**
Little Blakenham. *Suff*...................1E **54**
Little Blencow. *Cumb*...................1F **103**
Little Bognor. *W Sus*......................3B **26**
Little Bolas. *Shrp*...........................3A **72**
Little Bollington. *Ches E*................2B **84**
Little Bookham. *Surr*......................5C **38**
Littleborough. *Devn*.......................1B **12**
Littleborough. *G Man*.................3H **91**
Littleborough. *Notts*.......................2F **87**
Littlebourne. *Kent*..........................5G **41**
Little Bourton. *Oxon*......................1C **50**
Little Bowden. *Leics*.......................2E **63**
Little Bradley. *Suff*.........................5F **65**
Little Brampton. *Shrp*....................2F **59**
Little Brechin. *Ang*......................2E **145**
Littlebredy. *Dors*............................4A **14**
Little Brickhill. *Mil*.........................2H **51**
Little Bridgeford. *Staf*....................3C **72**
Little Brington. *Nptn*......................4D **62**
Little Bromley. *Essx*.......................3D **54**
Little Broughton. *Cumb*................1B **102**
Little Budworth. *Ches W*..............4H **83**
Little Burstead. *Essx*......................1A **40**
Little Burton. *E Yor*......................5F **101**
Littlebury. *Essx*..............................2F **53**
Littlebury Green. *Essx*....................2E **53**
Little Bytham. *Linc*........................4H **75**
Little Canfield. *Essx*.......................3F **53**
Little Canford. *Dors*.......................3F **15**
Little Carlton. *Linc*........................2C **88**
Little Carlton. *Notts*.......................5E **87**
Little Casterton. *Rut*.......................5H **75**
Little Catwick. *E Yor*.....................5F **101**
Little Catworth. *Cambs*.................3A **64**
Little Cawthorpe. *Linc*...................2C **88**
Little Chalfont. *Buck*......................1A **38**
Little Chart. *Kent*...........................1D **28**
Little Chesterford. *Essx*..................1F **53**
Little Cheverell. *Wilts*.....................1E **23**
Little Chishill. *Cambs*....................2E **53**
Little Clacton. *Essx*........................4E **55**
Little Clanfield. *Oxon*.....................5A **50**
Little Clifton. *Cumb*......................2B **102**
Little Coates. *NE Lin*......................4F **95**
Little Comberton. *Worc*..................1E **49**
Little Common. *E Sus*....................5B **28**
Little Compton. *Warw*....................2A **50**
Little Cornard. *Suff*........................2B **54**
Littlecote. *Buck*..............................3G **51**
Littlecott. *Wilts*...............................1G **23**
Little Cowarne. *Here*......................5A **60**

Little Coxwell. Oxon....2A 36
Little Crakehall. N Yor....5F 105
Little Crawley. Mil....1H 51
Little Creich. High....5D 164
Little Cressingham. Norf....5A 78
Little Crosby. Mers....4B 90
Little Crosthwaite. Cumb....2D 102
Little Cubley. Derbs....2F 73
Little Dalby. Leics....4E 75
Little Dawley. Telf....5A 72
Littledean. Glos....4B 48
Little Dens. Abers....4H 161
Little Dewchurch. Here....2A 48
Little Ditton. Cambs....5F 65
Little Down. Hants....1B 24
Little Downham. Cambs....2E 65
Little Drayton. Shrp....2A 72
Little Driffield. E Yor....4E 101
Little Dunham. Norf....4A 78
Little Dunkeld. Per....4H 143
Little Dunmow. Essx....3G 53
Little Easton. Essx....3G 53
Little Eaton. Derbs....1A 74
Little Eccleston. Lanc....5D 96
Little Ellingham. Norf....1C 66
Little Elm. Som....2C 22
Little End. Essx....5F 53
Little Everdon. Nptn....5C 62
Little Eversden. Cambs....5C 64
Little Faringdon. Oxon....5H 49
Little Fencote. N Yor....5F 105
Little Fenton. N Yor....1F 93
Littleferry. High....4F 165
Little Fransham. Norf....4B 78
Little Gaddesden. Herts....4H 51
Little Garway. Here....3H 47
Little Gidding. Cambs....2A 64
Little Glemham. Suff....5F 67
Little Glenshee. Per....5G 143
Little Gransden. Cambs....5B 64
Little Green. Suff....3C 66
Little Green. Wrex....1G 71
Little Grimsby. Linc....1C 88
Little Habton. N Yor....2B 100
Little Hadham. Herts....3E 53
Little Hale. Linc....1A 76
Little Hallingbury. Essx....4E 53
Littleham. Devn
  nr. Bideford....4E 19
  nr. Exmouth....4D 12
Little Hampden. Buck....5G 51
Littlehampton. W Sus....5B 26
Little Haresfield. Glos....5D 48
Little Harrowden. Nptn....3F 63
Little Haseley. Oxon....5E 51
Little Hatfield. E Yor....5F 101
Little Hautbois. Norf....3E 79
Little Haven. Pemb....3C 42
Little Hay. Staf....5F 73
Little Hayfield. Derbs....2E 85
Little Haywood. Staf....3E 73
Little Heath. W Mid....2H 61
Little Heck. N Yor....2F 93
Littlehempston. Devn....2E 9
Little Herbert's. Glos....4E 49
Little Hereford. Here....4H 59
Little Horkesley. Essx....2C 54
Little Hormead. Herts....3D 53
Little Horsted. E Sus....4F 27
Little Horton. W Yor....1B 92
Little Horwood. Buck....2F 51
Little Houghton. Nptn....5F 63
Little Houghton. S Yor....4E 93
Littlehoughton. Nmbd....3G 121
Little Hucklow. Derbs....3F 85
Little Hulton. G Man....4F 91
Little Irchester. Nptn....4G 63
Little Kelk. E Yor....3E 101
Little Kimble. Buck....5G 51
Little Kineton. Warw....5H 61
Little Kingshill. Buck....2G 37
Little Langdale. Cumb....4E 102
Little Langford. Wilts....3F 23
Little Laver. Essx....5F 53
Little Lawford. Warw....3B 62
Little Leigh. Ches W....3A 84
Little Leighs. Essx....4H 53
Little Lever. E Yor....5E 101
Little Lever. G Man....4F 91
Little Linford. Mil....1G 51
Little London. Buck....4E 51
Little London. E Sus....4G 27
Little London. Hants
  nr. Andover....2B 24
  nr. Basingstoke....1E 24
Little London. Linc
  nr. Long Sutton....3D 76
  nr. Spalding....3B 76
Little London. Norf
  nr. North Walsham....2E 79
  nr. Northwold....1G 65
  nr. Saxthorpe....2D 78
  nr. Southery....1F 65
Little London. Powy....2C 58
Little Longstone. Derbs....3F 85
Little Malvern. Worc....1C 48
Little Maplestead. Essx....2B 54
Little Marcle. Here....2B 48
Little Marlow. Buck....3G 37
Little Massingham. Norf....3G 77
Little Melton. Norf....5D 78
Little Mill. Mon....5G 47
Littlemill. Abers....4H 151
Littlemill. E Ayr....3D 116
Littlemill. High....4D 158
Little Milton. Oxon....5E 50
Little Missenden. Buck....1A 38
Littlemoor. Derbs....4A 86
Littlemoor. Dors....4B 14
Littlemore. Oxon....5D 50
Little Mountain. Flin....4E 83

Little Musgrave. Cumb....3A 104
Little Ness. Shrp....4G 71
Little Neston. Ches W....3E 83
Little Newcastle. Pemb....2D 43
Little Newsham. Dur....3E 105
Little Oakley. Essx....3F 55
Little Oakley. Nptn....2F 63
Little Onn. Staf....4C 72
Little Ormside. Cumb....3A 104
Little Orton. Cumb....4E 113
Little Orton. Leics....5H 73
Little Ouse. Cambs....2F 65
Little Ouseburn. N Yor....3G 99
Littleover. Derb....2H 73
Little Packington. Warw....2G 61
Little Paxton. Cambs....4A 64
Little Petherick. Corn....1D 6
Little Plumpton. Lanc....1B 90
Little Plumstead. Norf....4F 79
Little Ponton. Linc....2G 75
Littleport. Cambs....2E 65
Little Posbrook. Hants....2D 16
Little Potheridge. Devn....1F 11
Little Preston. Nptn....5C 62
Little Raveley. Cambs....3B 64
Little Reynoldston. Swan....4D 31
Little Ribston. N Yor....4F 99
Little Rissington. Glos....4G 49
Little Rogart. High....3E 165
Little Rollright. Oxon....2A 50
Little Ryburgh. Norf....3B 78
Little Ryle. Nmbd....3E 121
Little Ryton. Shrp....5G 71
Little Salkeld. Cumb....1G 103
Little Sampford. Essx....2G 53
Little Sandhurst. Brac....5G 37
Little Saredon. Staf....5D 72
Little Saxham. Suff....4G 65
Little Scatwell. High....3F 157
Little Shelford. Cambs....5D 64
Little Shoddesden. Hants....2A 24
Little Singleton. Lanc....1B 90
Little Smeaton. N Yor....3F 93
Little Snoring. Norf....2B 78
Little Sodbury. S Glo....3C 34
Little Somborne. Hants....3B 24
Little Somerford. Wilts....3E 35
Little Soudley. Shrp....3B 72
Little Stainforth. N Yor....3H 97
Little Stainton. Darl....3A 106
Little Stanney. Ches W....3G 83
Little Staughton. Bed....4A 64
Little Steeping. Linc....4D 88
Littlester. Shet....3G 173
Little Stoke. Staf....2D 72
Littlestone-on-Sea. Kent....3E 29
Little Stretton. Leics....5D 74
Little Stretton. Shrp....1G 59
Little Strickland. Cumb....3G 103
Little Stukeley. Cambs....3B 64
Little Sugnall. Staf....2C 72
Little Sutton. Ches W....3F 83
Little Sutton. Linc....3D 76
Little Swinburne. Nmbd....2C 114
Little Tew. Oxon....3B 50
Little Tey. Essx....3B 54
Little Thetford. Cambs....3E 65
Little Thirkleby. N Yor....2G 99
Little Thornage. Norf....2C 78
Little Thornton. Lanc....5C 96
Little Thorpe. W Yor....2B 92
Little Thurlow. Suff....5F 65
Little Thurrock. Thur....3H 39
Littleton. Ches W....4G 83
Littleton. Hants....3C 24
Littleton. Som....3H 21
Littleton. Surr
  nr. Guildford....1A 26
  nr. Staines....4B 38
Littleton Drew. Wilts....3D 34
Littleton Pannell. Wilts....1F 23
Littleton-upon-Severn. S Glo....3A 34
Little Torbull. High....4E 165
Little Torrington. Devn....1E 11
Little Totham. Essx....4B 54
Little Town. Cumb....3D 102
Little Town. Lanc....1E 91
Littletown. Dur....5G 115
Littletown. High....5E 165
Little Twycross. Leics....5H 73
Little Urswick. Cumb....2B 96
Little Wakering. Essx....2D 40
Little Walden. Essx....1F 53
Little Waldingfield. Suff....1C 54
Little Walsingham. Norf....2B 78
Little Waltham. Essx....4H 53
Little Warley. Essx....1H 39
Little Weighton. E Yor....1C 94
Little Wenham. Suff....2D 54
Little Wenlock. Telf....5A 72
Little Whelnetham. Suff....4A 66
Little Whittingham Green.
  Suff....3E 67
Littlewick Green. Wind....4G 37
Little Wilbraham. Cambs....5E 65
Littlewindsor. Dors....2H 13
Little Wisbeach. Linc....2A 76
Little Witcombe. Glos....4E 49
Little Witley. Worc....4B 60
Little Wittenham. Oxon....2D 36
Little Wolford. Warw....2A 50
Littleworth. Bed....1A 52
Littleworth. Glos....2G 49
Littleworth. Oxon....2B 36
Littleworth. Staf
  nr. Cannock....4E 73
  nr. Eccleshall....3B 72
  nr. Stafford....3D 72

Littleworth. W Sus....3C 26
Littleworth. Worc
  nr. Redditch....4D 61
  nr. Worcester....5C 60
Little Wratting. Suff....1G 53
Little Wymondley. Herts....3C 52
Little Wyrley. Staf....5E 73
Little Yeldham. Essx....2A 54
Littley Green. Essx....4G 53
Litton. Derbs....3F 85
Litton. N Yor....2B 98
Litton. Som....1A 22
Litton Cheney. Dors....3A 14
Liurbost. W Isl....5F 171
Liverpool. Mers....200 (1F 83)
Liverpool John Lennon Airport.
  Mers....2G 83
Liversedge. W Yor....2B 92
Liverton. Devn....5B 12
Liverton. Red C....3E 107
Liverton Mines. Red C....3E 107
Livingston. W Lot....3D 128
Livingston Village. W Lot....3D 128
Lixwm. Flin....3D 82
Lizard. Corn....5E 5
Llaingoch. IOA....2B 80
Llaithddu. Powy....2C 58
Llampha. V Glam....4C 32
Llan. Powy....5A 70
Llanaber. Gwyn....4F 69
Llanaelhaearn. Gwyn....1C 68
Llanaeron. Cdgn....4D 57
Llanafan. Cdgn....3F 57
Llanafan-fawr. Powy....5B 58
Llanafan-fechan. Powy....5B 58
Llanallgo. IOA....2D 81
Llanandras. Powy....4F 59
Llananno. Powy....3C 58
Llanarmon. Gwyn....2D 68
Llanarmon Dyffryn Ceiriog.
  Wrex....2D 70
Llanarmon-yn-Ial. Den....5D 82
Llanarth. Cdgn....5D 56
Llanarth. Mon....4G 47
Llanarthne. Carm....3F 45
Llanasa. Flin....2D 82
Llanbabo. IOA....2C 80
Llanbadarn Fawr. Cdgn....2F 57
Llanbadarn Fynydd. Powy....3D 58
Llanbadarn-y-garreg. Powy....1E 46
Llanbadoc. Mon....5G 47
Llanbadrig. IOA....1C 80
Llanbeder. Newp....2G 33
Llanbedr. Gwyn....3E 69
Llanbedr. Powy
  nr. Crickhowell....3F 47
  nr. Hay-on-Wye....1E 47
Llanbedr-Dyffryn-Clwyd. Den....5D 82
Llanbedrgoch. IOA....2E 81
Llanbedrog. Gwyn....2C 68
Llanbedr Pont Steffan. Cdgn....1F 45
Llanbedr-y-cennin. Cnwy....4G 81
Llanberis. Gwyn....4E 81
Llanbethery. V Glam....5D 32
Llanbister. Powy....3D 58
Llanblethian. V Glam....4C 32
Llanboidy. Carm....2G 43
Llanbradach. Cphy....2E 33
Llanbrynmair. Powy....5A 70
Llanbydderi. V Glam....5D 32
Llancadle. V Glam....5D 32
Llancarfan. V Glam....4D 32
Llancatal. V Glam....5D 32
Llancayo. Mon....5G 47
Llancloudy. Here....3H 47
Llancoch. Powy....3E 58
Llancynfelyn. Cdgn....1F 57
Llandaff. Card....4E 33
Llandanwg. Gwyn....3E 69
Llandarcy. Neat....3G 31
Llandawke. Carm....3G 43
Llanddaniel Fab. IOA....3D 81
Llanddarog. Carm....4F 45
Llanddeiniol. Cdgn....3E 57
Llanddeiniolen. Gwyn....4E 81
Llandderfel. Gwyn....2B 70
Llanddeusant. Carm....3A 46
Llanddeusant. IOA....2C 80
Llanddew. Powy....2D 46
Llanddewi. Swan....4D 30
Llanddewi Brefi. Cdgn....5F 57
Llanddewi'r Cwm. Powy....1D 46
Llanddewi Rhydderch. Mon....4G 47
Llanddewi Velfrey. Pemb....3F 43
Llanddewi Ystradenni. Powy....4D 58
Llanddoged. Cnwy....4H 81
Llanddona. IOA....3E 81
Llanddowror. Carm....3G 43
Llanddulas. Cnwy....3B 82
Llanddwywe. Gwyn....3E 69
Llanddyfnan. IOA....3D 81
Llandecwyn. Gwyn....2F 69
Llandefaelog Fach. Powy....2D 46
Llandefaelog-tre'r-graig.
  Powy....2E 47
Llandefalle. Powy....2E 46
Llandegfan. IOA....3E 81
Llandegla. Den....5D 82
Llandegley. Powy....4D 58
Llandegveth. Mon....2G 33
Llandeilo. Carm....3G 45
Llandeilo Graban. Powy....1D 46
Llandeilo'r Fan. Powy....2B 46
Llandeloy. Pemb....2C 42
Llandenny. Mon....5H 47
Llandevaud. Newp....2H 33
Llandevenny. Mon....3H 33
Llandilo. Pemb....2F 43
Llandinabo. Here....3A 48
Llandinam. Powy....2C 58
Llandissilio. Pemb....2F 43

Llandogo. Mon....5A 48
Llandough. V Glam
  nr. Cowbridge....4C 32
  nr. Penarth....4E 33
Llandovery. Carm....2A 46
Llandow. V Glam....4C 32
Llandre. Cdgn....2F 57
Llandrillo. Den....2C 70
Llandrillo-yn-Rhos. Cnwy....2H 81
Llandrindod. Powy....4C 58
Llandrindod Wells. Powy....4C 58
Llandrinio. Powy....4E 71
Llandudno. Cnwy....2G 81
Llandudno Junction. Cnwy....3G 81
Llandudoch. Pemb....1B 44
Llandw. V Glam....4C 32
Llandwrog. Gwyn....5D 80
Llandybie. Carm....4G 45
Llandyfaelog. Carm....4E 45
Llandyfan. Carm....4G 45
Llandyfriog. Cdgn....1D 44
Llandyfrydog. IOA....2D 80
Llandygai. Gwyn....3F 81
Llandygwydd. Cdgn....1C 44
Llandynan. Den....1D 70
Llandyrnog. Den....4D 82
Llandysilio. Powy....4E 71
Llandyssil. Powy....1D 58
Llandysul. Cdgn....1E 45
Llanedeyrn. Card....3F 33
Llaneglwys. Powy....2D 46
Llanegryn. Gwyn....5F 69
Llanegwad. Carm....3F 45
Llaneilian. IOA....1D 80
Llanelian-yn-Rhos. Cnwy....3A 82
Llanelidan. Den....5D 82
Llanelieu. Powy....2E 47
Llanellen. Mon....4G 47
Llanelli. Carm....3E 31
Llanelltyd. Gwyn....4G 69
Llanelly. Mon....4F 47
Llanelly Hill. Mon....4F 47
Llanelwedd. Powy....5C 58
Llan-Elwy. Den....3C 82
Llanenddwyn. Gwyn....3E 69
Llanengan. Gwyn....3B 68
Llanerch. Powy....1F 59
Llanerchymedd. IOA....2D 80
Llanerfyl. Powy....5C 70
Llaneuddog. IOA....2D 80
Llanfachraeth. IOA....2C 80
Llanfachreth. Gwyn....3G 69
Llanfaelog. IOA....3C 80
Llanfaelrhys. Gwyn....3B 68
Llanfaenor. Mon....4H 47
Llanfaes. IOA....3F 81
Llanfaes. Powy....3D 46
Llanfaethlu. IOA....2C 80
Llanfaglan. Gwyn....4D 80
Llanfair. Gwyn....3E 69
Llanfair. Here....1F 47
Llanfair Caereinion. Powy....5D 70
Llanfair Clydogau. Cdgn....5F 57
Llanfair Dyffryn Clwyd. Den....5D 82
Llanfairfechan. Cnwy....3F 81
Llanfair-Nant-Gwyn. Pemb....1F 43
Llanfair Pwllgwyngyll. IOA....3E 81
Llanfair Talhaiarn. Cnwy....3B 82
Llanfair Waterdine. Shrp....3E 59
Llanfair-ym-Muallt. Powy....5C 58
Llanfairyneubwll. IOA....3C 80
Llanfairynghornwy. IOA....1C 80
Llanfallteg. Carm....3F 43
Llanfallteg West. Carm....3F 43
Llanfaredd. Powy....5C 58
Llanfarian. Cdgn....3E 57
Llanfechain. Powy....3D 70
Llanfechell. IOA....1C 80
Llanfendigaid. Gwyn....5E 69
Llanferres. Den....4D 82
Llan Ffestiniog. Gwyn....1G 69
Llanfflewyn. IOA....2C 80
Llanfihangel-ar-Arth. Carm....2E 45
Llanfihangel Glyn Myfyr. Cnwy....1B 70
Llanfihangel Nant Bran. Powy....2C 46
Llanfihangel-Nant-Melan.
  Powy....5D 58
Llanfihangel near Rogiet. Mon....3H 33
Llanfihangel Rhydithon. Powy....4D 58
Llanfihangel Tai-y-llyn. Powy....3E 46
Llanfihangel-uwch-Gwili. Carm....3E 45
Llanfihangel-y-Creuddyn. Cdgn....3F 57
Llanfihangel-yng-Ngwynfa.
  Powy....4C 70
Llanfihangel yn Nhowyn. IOA....3C 80
Llanfihangel-y-pennant. Gwyn
  nr. Golan....1E 69
  nr. Tywyn....5F 69
Llanfihangel-y-traethau. Gwyn....2E 69
Llanfilo. Powy....2E 46
Llanfleiddan. V Glam....4C 32
Llanfoist. Mon....4F 47
Llanfor. Gwyn....2B 70
Llanfrechfa. Torf....2G 33
Llanfrothen. Gwyn....1F 69
Llanfrynach. Powy....3D 46
Llanfwrog. Den....5D 82
Llanfwrog. IOA....2C 80
Llanfyllin. Powy....4D 70
Llanfynydd. Carm....3F 45
Llanfynydd. Flin....5E 83
Llanfyrnach. Pemb....1G 43
Llangadfan. Powy....4C 70
Llangadog. Carm
  nr. Llandovery....3H 45
  nr. Llanelli....5E 45
Llangadwaladr. IOA....4C 80
Llangadwaladr. Powy....2D 70
Llangaffo. IOA....4D 80
Llangain. Carm....4D 45
Llangammarch Wells. Powy....1C 46

Llangan. V Glam....4C 32
Llangarron. Here....3A 48
Llangasty-Talyllyn. Powy....3E 47
Llangathen. Carm....3F 45
Llangattock. Powy....4F 47
Llangattock Lingoed. Mon....3G 47
Llangattock-Vibon-Avel. Mon....4H 47
Llangedwyn. Powy....3D 70
Llangefni. IOA....3D 80
Llangeinor. B'end....3C 32
Llangeitho. Cdgn....5F 57
Llangeler. Carm....2D 44
Llangelynin. Gwyn....5E 69
Llangendeirne. Carm....4E 45
Llangennech. Carm....5F 45
Llangennith. Swan....3D 30
Llangenny. Powy....4F 47
Llangernyw. Cnwy....4A 82
Llangian. Gwyn....3B 68
Llangiwg. Neat....5H 45
Llangloffan. Pemb....1D 42
Llanglydwen. Carm....2F 43
Llangoed. IOA....3F 81
Llangoedmor. Cdgn....1B 44
Llangollen. Den....1E 70
Llangolman. Pemb....2F 43
Llangorse. Powy....3E 47
Llangorwen. Cdgn....2F 57
Llangovan. Mon....5H 47
Llangower. Gwyn....2B 70
Llangranog. Cdgn....5C 56
Llangristiolus. IOA....3D 80
Llangrove. Here....4A 48
Llangua. Mon....3G 47
Llangunllo. Powy....3E 58
Llangunnor. Carm....4E 45
Llangurig. Powy....3B 58
Llangwm. Cnwy....1B 70
Llangwm. Mon....5H 47
Llangwm. Pemb....4D 43
Llangwm-isaf. Mon....5H 47
Llangwnnadl. Gwyn....2B 68
Llangwyfan. Den....4D 82
Llangwyfan-isaf. IOA....4C 80
Llangwyllog. IOA....3D 80
Llangwyryfon. Cdgn....3F 57
Llangybi. Cdgn....5F 57
Llangybi. Gwyn....1D 68
Llangybi. Mon....2G 33
Llangyfelach. Swan....3F 31
Llangynhafal. Den....4D 82
Llangynidr. Powy....4E 47
Llangynin. Carm....3G 43
Llangynog. Carm....3H 43
Llangynog. Powy....3C 70
Llangynwyd. B'end....3B 32
Llanhamlach. Powy....3D 46
Llanharan. Rhon....3D 32
Llanharry. Rhon....3D 32
Llanhennock. Mon....2G 33
Llanhilleth. Blae....5F 47
Llanidloes. Powy....2B 58
Llaniestyn. Gwyn....2B 68
Llanigon. Powy....1F 47
Llanilar. Cdgn....3F 57
Llanilid. Rhon....3C 32
Llanilltud Fawr. V Glam....5C 32
Llanishen. Card....3E 33
Llanishen. Mon....5H 47
Llanllawddog. Carm....3E 45
Llanllechid. Gwyn....4F 81
Llanllowell. Mon....2G 33
Llanllugan. Powy....5C 70
Llanllwch. Carm....4D 45
Llanllwchaiarn. Powy....1D 58
Llanllwni. Carm....2E 45
Llanllyfni. Gwyn....5D 80
Llanmadoc. Swan....3D 30
Llanmaes. V Glam....5C 32
Llanmartin. Newp....3G 33
Llanmerwig. Powy....1D 58
Llanmihangel. V Glam....4C 32
Llan-mill. Pemb....3F 43
Llanmiloe. Carm....4G 43
Llanmorlais. Swan....3E 31
Llannefydd. Cnwy....3B 82
Llan-non. Cdgn....4E 57
Llannon. Carm....5F 45
Llannor. Gwyn....2C 68
Llanover. Mon....5G 47
Llanpumsaint. Carm....3E 45
Llanrhaeadr. Den....4C 82
Llanrhaeadr-ym-Mochnant.
  Powy....3D 70
Llanrhian. Pemb....1C 42
Llanrhidian. Swan....3D 31
Llanrhos. Cnwy....2G 81
Llanrhyddlad. IOA....2C 80
Llanrhystud. Cdgn....4E 57
Llanrothal. Here....4H 47
Llanrug. Gwyn....4E 81
Llanrumney. Card....3F 33
Llanrwst. Cnwy....4G 81
Llansadurnen. Carm....3G 43
Llansadwrn. Carm....2G 45
Llansadwrn. IOA....3E 81
Llansaint. Carm....5D 45
Llansamlet. Swan....3F 31
Llansanffraid Glan Conwy.
  Cnwy....3H 81
Llansannan. Cnwy....4B 82
Llansannor. V Glam....4C 32
Llansantffraed. Cdgn....4E 57
Llansantffraed. Powy....3E 46
Llansantffraed Cwmdeuddwr.
  Powy....4B 58
Llansantffraed-in-Elwel. Powy....5C 58
Llansantffraid-ym-Mechain.
  Powy....3E 70
Llansawel. Carm....2G 45
Llansawel. Neat....3G 31

Llansilin. Powy 3E 70
Llansoy. Mon 5H 47
Llanspyddid. Powy 3D 46
Llanstadwell. Pemb 4D 42
Llansteffan. Carm 4D 44
Llanstephan. Powy 1E 46
Llanteg. Pemb 3F 43
Llanthony. Mon 3F 47
Llantilio Crossenny. Mon 4G 47
Llantilio Pertholey. Mon 4G 47
Llantood. Pemb 1B 44
Llantrisant. Mon 2G 33
Llantrisant. Rhon 3D 32
Llantrithyd. V Glam 4D 32
Llantwit Fardre. Rhon 3D 32
Llantwit Major. V Glam 5C 32
Llanuwchllyn. Gwyn 2A 70
Llanvaches. Newp 2H 33
Llanvair Discoed. Mon 2H 33
Llanvapley. Mon 4G 47
Llanvetherine. Mon 4G 47
Llanveynoe. Here 2G 47
Llanvihangel Crucorney.
    Mon 3G 47
Llanvihangel Gobion. Mon 5G 47
Llanvihangel Ystern-Llewern.
    Mon 4H 47
Llanwarne. Here 3A 48
Llanwddyn. Powy 4C 70
Llanwenarth. Mon 4F 47
Llanwenog. Cdgn 1E 45
Llanwern. Newp 3G 33
Llanwinio. Carm 2G 43
Llanwnda. Gwyn 5D 80
Llanwnda. Pemb 1D 42
Llanwnnen. Cdgn 1F 45
Llanwnog. Powy 1C 58
Llanwrda. Carm 2H 45
Llanwrin. Powy 5G 69
Llanwrthwl. Powy 4B 58
Llanwrtyd. Powy 1B 46
Llanwrtyd Wells. Powy 1B 46
Llanwyddelan. Powy 5C 70
Llanyblodwel. Shrp 3E 71
Llanybri. Carm 3H 43
Llanybydder. Carm 1F 45
Llanycefn. Pemb 2E 43
Llanychaer. Pemb 1D 43
Llanycil. Gwyn 2B 70
Llanymawddwy. Gwyn 4B 70
Llanymddyfri. Carm 2A 46
Llanymynech. Powy 3E 71
Llanynghenedl. IOA 2C 80
Llanynys. Den 4D 82
Llan-y-pwll. Wrex 5F 83
Llanyrafon. Torf 2G 33
Llanystumdwy. Gwyn 2D 68
Llanywern. Powy 3E 46
Llawhaden. Pemb 3E 43
Llawndy. Flin 2D 82
Llawnt. Shrp 2E 71
Llawr Dref. Gwyn 3B 68
Llawryglyn. Powy 1B 58
Llay. Wrex 5F 83
Llechfaen. Powy 3D 46
Llechryd. Cphy 5E 46
Llechryd. Cdgn 1C 44
Llechrydau. Wrex 2E 71
Lledrod. Cdgn 3F 57
Llethrid. Swan 3E 31
Llidiad-Nenog. Carm 2F 45
Llidiardau. Gwyn 2A 70
Llidiart y Parc. Den 1D 70
Llithfaen. Gwyn 1C 68
Lloc. Flin 3D 82
Llong. Flin 4E 83
Llowes. Powy 1E 47
Lloyney. Powy 3E 59
Llundain-fach. Cdgn 5E 57
Llwydcoed. Rhon 5C 46
Llwyncelyn. Cdgn 5D 56
Llwyncelyn. Swan 5G 45
Llwyndafydd. Cdgn 5C 56
Llwynderw. Powy 5E 70
Llwyn-du. Mon 4F 47
Llwyngwril. Gwyn 5E 69
Llwynhendy. Carm 3E 31
Llwynmawr. Wrex 2E 71
Llwyn-on Village. Mer T 4D 46
Llwyn-têg. Carm 5F 45
Llwyn-y-brain. Carm 3F 43
Llwynygog. Powy 1A 58
Llwyn-y-groes. Cdgn 5E 57
Llwynypia. Rhon 2C 32
Llynclys. Shrp 3E 71
Llynfaes. IOA 3D 80
Llysfaen. Cnwy 3A 82
Llyswen. Powy 2E 47
Llysworney. V Glam 4C 32
Llys-y-fran. Pemb 2E 43
Llywel. Powy 2B 46
Llywernog. Cdgn 2G 57
Loan. Falk 2C 128
Loanend. Nmbd 4F 131
Loanhead. Midl 3F 129
Loaningfoot. Dum 4A 112
Loanreoch. High 1A 158
Loans. S Ayr 1C 116
Loansdean. Nmbd 1E 115
Lobb. Devn 3E 19
Lobhillcross. Devn 4E 11
Lochaber. Mor 3E 159
Loch a Charnain. W Isl 4D 170
Loch a Ghainmhich. W Isl 5E 171
Lochailort. High 5F 147
Lochaline. High 4A 140
Lochans. Dum 4F 109
Locharbriggs. Dum 1A 112

Lochardil. High 4A 158
Lochassynt Lodge. High 1F 163
Lochavich. Arg 2G 133
Lochawe. Arg 1A 134
Loch Baghasdail. W Isl 7C 170
Lochboisdale. W Isl 7C 170
Lochbuie. Arg 1D 132
Loch Choire Lodge. High 5G 167
Lochdochart House. Stir 1D 134
Lochdon. Arg 5B 140
Lochearnhead. Stir 1E 135
Lochee. D'dee 5C 144
Lochend. High
    nr. Inverness 5H 157
    nr. Thurso 2E 169
Lochend. Falk 2A 128
Locherben. Dum 5B 118
Loch Euphort. W Isl 2D 170
Lochfoot. Dum 2F 111
Lochgair. Arg 4G 133
Lochgarthside. High 2H 149
Lochgelly. Fife 4D 136
Lochgilphead. Arg 1G 125
Lochgoilhead. Arg 3A 134
Loch Head. Dum 5A 110
Lochhill. Mor 2G 159
Lochindorb Lodge. High 5D 158
Lochinver. High 1E 163
Lochlane. Per 1H 135
Loch Lomond. Arg 3C 134
Loch Loyal Lodge. High 4G 167
Lochluichart. High 2F 157
Lochmaben. Dum 1B 112
Lochmaddy. W Isl 2E 170
Loch nam Madadh. W Isl 2E 170
Lochore. Fife 4D 136
Lochportain. W Isl 1E 170
Lochranza. N Ayr 4H 125
Loch Sgioport. W Isl 5D 170
Lochside. Abers 2G 145
Lochside. High
    nr. Achentoul 5A 168
    nr. Nairn 3C 158
Lochslin. High 5F 165
Lochstack Lodge. High 4C 166
Lochton. Abers 4E 153
Lochty. Fife 3H 137
Lochuisge. High 3B 140
Lochussie. High 3G 157
Lochwinnoch. Ren 4E 127
Lochyside. High 1F 141
Lockengate. Corn 2E 7
Lockerbie. Dum 1C 112
Lockeridge. Wilts 5G 35
Lockerley. Hants 4A 24
Lockhills. Cumb 5G 113
Locking. N Som 1G 21
Lockington. E Yor 5D 101
Lockington. Leics 3B 74
Lockleywood. Shrp 3A 72
Locksgreen. IOW 3C 16
Locks Heath. Hants 2D 16
Lockton. N Yor 5F 107
Loddington. Leics 5E 75
Loddington. Nptn 3F 63
Loddiswell. Devn 4D 8
Loddon. Norf 1F 67
Lode. Cambs 4E 65
Loders. Dors 3H 13
Lodsworth. W Sus 3A 26
Lofthouse. High 2D 98
Lofthouse. W Yor 2D 92
Lofthouse Gate. W Yor 2D 92
Loftus. Red C 3E 107
Logan. E Ayr 2E 117
Loganlea. W Lot 3C 128
Logaston. Here 5F 59
Loggerheads. Den 4D 82
Loggerheads. Staf 2B 72
Logie. High 4F 163
Logie. Ang 2F 145
Logie. Fife 1G 137
Logie. Mor 3E 159
Logie Coldstone. Abers 3B 152
Logie Pert. Ang 2F 145
Logierait. Per 3G 143
Login. Carm 2F 43
Lolworth. Cambs 4C 64
Lonbain. High 3F 155
Londesborough. E Yor 5C 100
London. G Lon 202-203 (2E 39)
London Apprentice. Corn 3E 6
London Ashford Airport.
    Kent 3E 29
London City Airport. G Lon 2F 39
London Colney. Herts 5B 52
Londonderry. N Yor 1F 99
London Gatwick Airport.
    W Sus 216 (1D 26)
London Heathrow Airport.
    G Lon 216 (3B 38)
London Luton Airport.
    Lutn 216 (3B 52)
London Southend Airport.
    Essx 2C 40
London Stansted Airport.
    Essx 216 (3F 53)
Londonthorpe. Linc 2G 75
Londubh. High 5C 162
Lone. High 4D 166
Lonemore. High
    nr. Dornoch 5E 165
    nr. Gairloch 1G 155
Long Ashton. N Som 4A 34
Long Bank. Worc 3B 60
Longbar. N Ayr 4E 127
Long Bennington. Linc 1F 75
Longbenton. Tyne 3F 115
Longborough. Glos 3G 49
Long Bredy. Dors 3A 14
Longbridge. Warw 4G 61

Longbridge. W Mid 3E 61
Longbridge Deverill. Wilts 2D 22
Long Buckby. Nptn 4D 62
Long Buckby Wharf. Nptn 4D 62
Longburgh. Cumb 4E 112
Longburton. Dors 1B 14
Long Clawson. Leics 3E 74
Longcliffe. Derbs 5G 85
Long Common. Hants 1D 16
Long Compton. Staf 3C 72
Long Compton. Warw 2A 50
Longcot. Oxon 2A 36
Long Crendon. Buck 5E 51
Long Crichel. Dors 1E 15
Longcroft. Cumb 4D 112
Longcroft. Falk 2A 128
Longcross. Surr 4A 38
Longdale. Cumb 4H 103
Longdales. Cumb 5G 113
Longden. Shrp 5G 71
Longden Common. Shrp 5G 71
Long Ditton. Surr 4C 38
Longdon. Staf 4E 73
Longdon. Worc 2D 48
Longdon Green. Staf 4E 73
Longdon on Tern. Telf 4A 72
Longdown. Devn 3B 12
Longdowns. Corn 5B 6
Long Drax. N Yor 2G 93
Long Duckmanton. Derbs 3B 86
Long Eaton. Derbs 2B 74
Longfield. Kent 4H 39
Longfield. Shet 10E 173
Longfield Hill. Kent 4H 39
Longford. Derbs 2G 73
Longford. Glos 3D 48
Longford. G Lon 3B 38
Longford. Shrp 2A 72
Longford. Telf 4B 72
Longford. W Mid 2A 62
Longforgan. Per 5C 144
Longformacus. Bord 4C 130
Longframlington. Nmbd 4F 121
Long Gardens. Essx 2B 54
Long Green. Ches W 3G 83
Long Green. Worc 2D 48
Longham. Dors 3F 15
Longham. Norf 4B 78
Long Hanborough. Oxon 4C 50
Longhedge. Wilts 2D 22
Longhill. Abers 3H 161
Longhirst. Nmbd 1F 115
Longhope. Glos 4B 48
Longhope. Orkn 8C 172
Longhorsley. Nmbd 5F 121
Longhoughton. Nmbd 3G 121
Long Itchington. Warw 4B 62
Longlands. Cumb 1D 102
Long Lane. Telf 4A 72
Longlane. Derbs 2G 73
Longlane. W Ber 4C 36
Long Lawford. Warw 3B 62
Longley Green. Worc 5B 60
Long Load. Som 4H 21
Longmanhill. Abers 2E 161
Long Marston. Herts 4G 51
Long Marston. N Yor 4H 99
Long Marston. Warw 1G 49
Long Marton. Cumb 2H 103
Long Meadow. Cambs 4E 65
Long Meadowend. Shrp 2G 59
Long Melford. Suff 1B 54
Longmoor Camp. Hants 3F 25
Longmorn. Mor 3G 159
Longmoss. Ches E 3C 84
Long Newnton. Glos 2E 35
Long Newton. Stoc T 3A 106
Longnewton. Bord 2H 119
Longney. Glos 4C 48
Longniddry. E Lot 2H 129
Longnor. Shrp 5G 71
Longnor. Staf
    nr. Leek 4E 85
    nr. Stafford 4C 72
Longparish. Hants 2C 24
Longpark. Cumb 3F 113
Long Preston. N Yor 4H 97
Longridge. Lanc 1E 90
Longridge. Staf 4D 72
Longridge. W Lot 3C 128
Longriggend. N Lan 2B 128
Long Riston. E Yor 5F 101
Longrock. Corn 3C 4
Longsdon. Staf 5D 84
Longshaw. G Man 4D 90
Longshaw. Staf 1E 73
Longside. Abers 4H 161
Longslow. Shrp 2A 72
Longstanton. Cambs 4C 64
Longstock. Hants 3B 24
Longstowe. Cambs 5C 64
Long Stratton. Norf 1D 66
Long Street. Mil 1F 51
Longstreet. Wilts 1G 23
Long Sutton. Hants 2F 25
Long Sutton. Linc 3D 76
Long Sutton. Som 4H 21
Longthorpe. Pet 1A 64
Long Thurlow. Suff 4C 66
Longthwaite. Cumb 2F 103
Longton. Lanc 2C 90
Longton. Stoke 1D 72
Longtown. Cumb 3E 113
Longtown. Here 3G 47
Longville in the Dale. Shrp 1H 59
Long Whatton. Leics 3B 74
Longwick. Buck 5F 51
Long Wittenham. Oxon 2D 36
Longwitton. Nmbd 1D 115
Longworth. Oxon 2B 36

Longyester. E Lot 3B 130
Lonmore. High 4B 154
Looe. Corn 3G 7
Loose. Kent 5B 40
Loosegate. Linc 3C 76
Loosley Row. Buck 5G 51
Lopcombe Corner. Wilts 3A 24
Lopen. Som 1H 13
Loppington. Shrp 3G 71
Lorbottle. Nmbd 4E 121
Lordington. W Sus 2F 17
Loscoe. Derbs 1B 74
Loscombe. Dors 3A 14
Losgaintir. W Isl 8C 171
Lossiemouth. Mor 2G 159
Lossit. Arg 4A 124
Lostock Gralam. Ches W 3A 84
Lostock Green. Ches W 3A 84
Lostock Hall. Lanc 2D 90
Lostock Junction. G Man 4E 91
Lostwithiel. Corn 3F 7
Lothbeg. High 2G 165
Lothersdale. N Yor 5B 98
Lothianbridge. Midl 3G 129
Lothianburn. Midl 3F 129
Lothmore. High 2G 165
Lottisham. Som 3A 22
Loudwater. Buck 1A 38
Loughborough. Leics 4C 74
Loughor. Swan 3E 31
Loughton. Essx 1F 39
Loughton. Mil 2G 51
Loughton. Shrp 2A 60
Lound. Linc 4H 75
Lound. Notts 2D 86
Lound. Suff 1H 67
Lount. Leics 4A 74
Louth. Linc 2C 88
Love Clough. Lanc 2G 91
Lovedean. Hants 1E 17
Lover. Wilts 4H 23
Loversall. S Yor 1C 86
Loves Green. Essx 5G 53
Loveston. Pemb 4E 43
Lovington. Som 3A 22
Low Ackworth. W Yor 3E 93
Low Angerton. Nmbd 1D 115
Low Ardwell. Dum 5F 109
Low Ballochdowan. S Ayr 2F 109
Lowbands. Glos 2C 48
Low Barlings. Linc 3H 87
Low Bell End. N Yor 5E 107
Low Bentham. N Yor 3F 97
Low Borrowbridge. Cumb 4H 103
Low Bradfield. S Yor 1G 85
Low Bradley. N Yor 5C 98
Low Braithwaite. Cumb 5F 113
Low Brunton. Nmbd 2C 114
Low Burnham. N Lin 4A 94
Lowca. Cumb 2A 102
Low Catton. E Yor 4B 100
Low Coniscliffe. Darl 3F 105
Low Coylton. S Ayr 3D 116
Low Crosby. Cumb 4F 113
Low Dalby. N Yor 1C 100
Lowdham. Notts 1D 74
Low Dinsdale. Darl 3A 106
Lowe. Shrp 2H 71
Low Ellington. N Yor 1E 98
Lower Amble. Corn 1D 6
Lower Ansty. Dors 2C 14
Lower Arboll. High 5F 165
Lower Arncott. Oxon 4E 50
Lower Ashton. Devn 4B 12
Lower Assendon. Oxon 3F 37
Lower Auchenreath. Mor 2A 160
Lower Badcall. High 4B 166
Lower Ballam. Lanc 1B 90
Lower Basildon. W Ber 4E 36
Lower Beeding. W Sus 3D 26
Lower Benefield. Nptn 2G 63
Lower Bentley. Worc 4D 61
Lower Beobridge. Shrp 1B 60
Lower Bockhampton. Dors 3C 14
Lower Boddington. Nptn 5B 62
Lower Bordean. Hants 4E 25
Lower Brailes. Warw 2B 50
Lower Breakish. High 1E 147
Lower Broadheath. Worc 5C 60
Lower Brynamman. Neat 4H 45
Lower Bullingham. Here 2A 48
Lower Bullington. Hants 2C 24
Lower Burgate. Hants 1G 15
Lower Catesby. Nptn 5C 62
Lower Chapel. Powy 2D 46
Lower Cheriton. Devn 2E 12
Lower Chicksgrove. Wilts 3E 23
Lower Chute. Wilts 1B 24
Lower Clopton. Warw 5F 61
Lower Common. Hants 2E 25
Lower Crossings. Derbs 2E 85
Lower Cumberworth. W Yor ...4C 92
Lower Darwen. Bkbn 2E 91
Lower Dean. Bed 4H 63
Lower Dean. Devn 2D 8
Lower Diabaig. High 2G 155
Lower Dicker. E Sus 4G 27
Lower Dounreay. High 2B 168
Lower Down. Shrp 2F 59
Lower Dunsforth. N Yor 3G 99
Lower East Carleton. Norf 5D 78
Lower Egleton. Here 1B 48
Lower Ellastone. Staf 1F 73
Lower End. Nptn 4F 63
Lower Everleigh. Wilts 1G 23
Lower Eype. Dors 3H 13
Lower Failand. N Som 4A 34
Lower Faintree. Shrp 2A 60
Lower Farringdon. Hants 3F 25
Lower Foxdale. IOM 4B 108

Lower Frankton. Shrp 2F 71
Lower Froyle. Hants 2F 25
Lower Gabwell. Devn 2F 9
Lower Gledfield. High 4C 164
Lower Godney. Som 2H 21
Lower Gravenhurst. C Beds 2B 52
Lower Green. Essx 2E 53
Lower Green. Norf 2B 78
Lower Green. W Ber 5B 36
Lower Halstow. Kent 4C 40
Lower Hardres. Kent 5F 41
Lower Hardwick. Here 5G 59
Lower Hartshay. Derbs 5A 86
Lower Hawthwaite. Cumb 1B 96
Lower Haysden. Kent 1G 27
Lower Hayton. Shrp 2H 59
Lower Hergest. Here 5E 59
Lower Heyford. Oxon 3C 50
Lower Heysham. Lanc 3D 96
Lower Higham. Kent 3B 40
Lower Holbrook. Suff 2E 55
Lower Holditch. Dors 2G 13
Lower Hordley. Shrp 3F 71
Lower Horncroft. W Sus 4B 26
Lower Horsebridge. E Sus 4G 27
Lower Kilcott. Glos 3C 34
Lower Killeyan. Arg 5A 124
Lower Kingcombe. Dors 3A 14
Lower Kingswood. Surr 5D 38
Lower Kinnerton. Ches W 4F 83
Lower Langford. N Som 5H 33
Lower Largo. Fife 3G 137
Lower Layham. Suff 1D 54
Lower Ledwyche. Shrp 3H 59
Lower Leigh. Staf 2E 73
Lower Lemington. Glos 2H 49
Lower Lenie. High 1H 149
Lower Ley. Glos 4C 48
Lower Llanfadog. Powy 4B 58
Lower Lode. Glos 2D 49
Lower Lovacott. Devn 4F 19
Lower Loxhore. Devn 3G 19
Lower Loxley. Staf 2E 73
Lower Lydbrook. Glos 4A 48
Lower Lye. Here 4G 59
Lower Machen. Newp 3F 33
Lower Maes-coed. Here 2G 47
Lower Meend. Glos 5A 48
Lower Midway. Derbs 3H 73
Lower Milovaig. High 3A 154
Lower Moor. Worc 1E 49
Lower Morton. S Glo 2B 34
Lower Mountain. Flin 5F 83
Lower Nazeing. Essx 5D 53
Lower Netchwood. Shrp 1A 60
Lower Nyland. Dors 4C 22
Lower Oakfield. Fife 4D 136
Lower Oddington. Glos 3H 49
Lower Ollach. High 5E 155
Lower Penarth. V Glam 5E 33
Lower Penn. Staf 1C 60
Lower Pennington. Hants 3B 16
Lower Peover. Ches W 3B 84
Lower Pilsley. Derbs 4B 86
Lower Pitkerrie. High 1C 158
Lower Place. G Man 3H 91
Lower Quinton. Warw 1G 49
Lower Rainham. Medw 4C 40
Lower Raydon. Suff 2D 54
Lower Seagry. Wilts 3E 35
Lower Shelton. C Beds 1H 51
Lower Shiplake. Oxon 4F 37
Lower Shuckburgh. Warw 4B 62
Lower Sketty. Swan 3F 31
Lower Slade. Devn 2F 19
Lower Slaughter. Glos 3G 49
Lower Soudley. Glos 4B 48
Lower Stanton St Quintin.
    Wilts 3E 35
Lower Stoke. Medw 3C 40
Lower Stondon. C Beds 2B 52
Lower Stonnall. Staf 5E 73
Lower Stow Bedon. Norf 1B 66
Lower Street. Norf 2E 79
Lower Strensham. Worc 1E 49
Lower Sundon. C Beds 3A 52
Lower Swanwick. Hants 2C 16
Lower Swell. Glos 3G 49
Lower Tale. Devn 2D 12
Lower Tean. Staf 2E 73
Lower Thurlton. Norf 1G 67
Lower Thurnham. Lanc 4D 96
Lower Thurvaston. Derbs 2G 73
Lower Town. Here 1B 48
Lower Town. IOS 1B 4
Lower Town. Pemb 1D 42
Lowertown. Corn 4D 4
Lowertown. Orkn 8D 172
Lower Tysoe. Warw 1B 50
Lower Upham. Hants 1D 16
Lower Upnor. Medw 3B 40
Lower Vexford. Som 3E 20
Lower Walton. Warr 2A 84
Lower Wear. Devn 4C 12
Lower Weare. Som 1H 21
Lower Welson. Here 5E 59
Lower Whatcombe. Dors 2D 14
Lower Whitley. Ches W 3A 84
Lower Wield. Hants 2E 25
Lower Withington. Ches E 4C 84
Lower Woodend. Buck 3G 37
Lower Woodford. Wilts 3G 23
Lower Wraxall. Dors 2A 14
Lower Wych. Ches W 1G 71
Lower Wyche. Worc 1C 48
Lowesby. Leics 5D 74
Lowestoft. Suff 1H 67
Loweswater. Cumb 2C 102
Low Etherley. Dur 2E 105
Lowfield Heath. W Sus 1D 26
Lowford. Hants 1C 16

Low Fulney. *Linc* 3B **76**
Low Gate. *Nmbd*.................3C **114**
Lowgill. *Cumb*.................5H **103**
Lowgill. *Lanc* 3F **97**
Low Grantley. *N Yor* 2E **99**
Low Green. *N Yor* 4E **98**
Low Habberley. *Worc* 3C **60**
Low Ham. *Som* 4H **21**
Low Hameringham. *Linc* 4C **88**
Low Hawsker. *N Yor* 4G **107**
Low Hesket. *Cumb* 5F **113**
Low Hesleyhurst. *Nmbd*.................5E **121**
Lowick. *Cumb*.................1B **96**
Lowick. *Nptn*.................2G **63**
Lowick. *Nmbd*.................1E **121**
Lowick Bridge. *Cumb*.................1B **96**
Lowick Green. *Cumb*.................1B **96**
Low Knipe. *Cumb*.................2G **103**
Low Leighton. *Derbs*.................2E **85**
Low Lorton. *Cumb*.................2C **102**
Low Marishes. *N Yor*.................2C **100**
Low Marnham. *Notts*.................4F **87**
Low Mill. *N Yor*.................5D **106**
Low Moor. *Lanc*.................5G **97**
Low Moor. *W Yor*.................2B **92**
Low Moorsley. *Tyne*.................5G **115**
Low Newton-by-the-Sea.
  Nmbd.................2G **121**
Lownie Moor. *Ang*.................4D **145**
Lowood. *Bord*.................1H **119**
Low Row. *Cumb*
  nr. Brampton.................3G **113**
  nr. Wigton.................5C **112**
Low Row. *N Yor*.................5C **104**
Lowsonford. *Warw*.................4F **61**
Low Street. *Norf*.................5C **78**
Lowther. *Cumb*.................2G **103**
Lowthorpe. *E Yor*.................3E **101**
Lowton. *Devn*.................2G **11**
Lowton. *G Man*.................1A **84**
Lowton. *Som*.................1E **13**
Lowton Common.
  G Man.................1A **84**
Low Torry. *Fife*.................1D **128**
Low Toynton. *Linc*.................3B **88**
Low Valleyfield. *Fife*.................1C **128**
Low Westwood. *Dur*.................4E **115**
Low Whinnow. *Cumb*.................4E **112**
Low Wood. *Cumb*.................1C **96**
Low Worsall. *N Yor*.................4A **106**
Low Wray. *Cumb*.................4E **103**
Loxbeare. *Devn*.................1C **12**
Loxhill. *Surr*.................2B **26**
Loxhore. *Devn*.................3G **19**
Loxley. *S Yor*.................2H **85**
Loxley. *Warw*.................5G **61**
Loxley Green. *Staf*.................2E **73**
Loxton. *N Som*.................1G **21**
Loxwood. *W Sus*.................2B **26**
Lubcroy. *High*.................3A **164**
Lubenham. *Leics*.................2E **62**
Lubinvullin. *High*.................2F **167**
Luccombe. *Som*.................2C **20**
Luccombe Village. *IOW*.................4D **16**
Lucker. *Nmbd*.................1F **121**
Luckett. *Corn*.................5D **11**
Luckington. *Wilts*.................3D **34**
Lucklawhill. *Fife*.................1G **137**
Luckwell Bridge. *Som*.................3C **20**
Lucton. *Here*.................4G **59**
Ludag. *W Isl*.................7C **170**
Ludborough. *Linc*.................1B **88**
Ludchurch. *Pemb*.................3F **43**
Luddenden. *W Yor*.................2A **92**
Luddenden Foot. *W Yor*.................2A **92**
Luddenham. *Kent*.................4D **40**
Ludderburn. *Cumb*.................5F **103**
Luddesdown. *Kent*.................4A **40**
Luddington. *N Lin*.................3B **94**
Luddington. *Warw*.................5F **61**
Luddington in the Brook.
  Nptn.................2A **64**
Ludford. *Linc*.................2A **88**
Ludford. *Shrp*.................3H **59**
Ludgershall. *Buck*.................4E **51**
Ludgershall. *Wilts*.................1A **24**
Ludgvan. *Corn*.................3C **4**
Ludham. *Norf*.................4F **79**
Ludlow. *Shrp*.................3H **59**
Ludstone. *Shrp*.................1C **60**
Ludwell. *Wilts*.................4E **23**
Ludworth. *Dur*.................5G **115**
Luffenhall. *Herts*.................3C **52**
Luffincott. *Devn*.................3D **10**
Lugar. *E Ayr*.................2E **117**
Luggate Burn. *E Lot*.................2C **130**
Lugg Green. *Here*.................4G **59**
Luggiebank. *N Lan*.................2A **128**
Lugton. *E Ayr*.................4F **127**
Lugwardine. *Here*.................1A **48**
Luib. *High*.................1D **146**
Luib. *Stir*.................1D **135**
Lulham. *Here*.................1H **47**
Lullington. *Derbs*.................4G **73**
Lullington. *E Sus*.................5G **27**
Lullington. *Som*.................1C **22**
Lulsgate Bottom. *N Som*.................5A **34**
Lulsley. *Worc*.................5B **60**
Lulworth Camp. *Dors*.................4D **14**
Lumb. *Lanc*.................2G **91**
Lumby. *N Yor*.................1E **93**
Lumphanan. *Abers*.................3C **152**
Lumphinnans. *Fife*.................4D **136**
Lumsdaine. *Bord*.................3E **131**
Lumsden. *Abers*.................1B **152**
Lunan. *Ang*.................3F **145**
Lunanhead. *Ang*.................3D **145**
Luncarty. *Per*.................1C **136**
Lund. *E Yor*.................5D **100**
Lund. *N Yor*.................1G **93**
Lundie. *Ang*.................5B **144**

Lundin Links. *Fife*.................3G **137**
Lundy Green. *Norf*.................1E **67**
Lunna. *Shet*.................5F **173**
Lunning. *Shet*.................5G **173**
Lunnon. *Swan*.................4E **31**
Lunsford. *Kent*.................5A **40**
Lunsford's Cross. *E Sus*.................4B **28**
Lunt. *Mers*.................4B **90**
Luppitt. *Devn*.................2E **13**
Lupridge. *Devn*.................3D **8**
Lupset. *W Yor*.................3D **92**
Lupton. *Cumb*.................1E **97**
Lurgashall. *W Sus*.................3A **26**
Lurley. *Devn*.................1C **12**
Lusby. *Linc*.................4C **88**
Luscombe. *Devn*.................3D **9**
Luson. *Devn*.................4C **8**
Luss. *Arg*.................4C **134**
Lussagiven. *Arg*.................1E **125**
Lusta. *High*.................3B **154**
Lustleigh. *Devn*.................4A **12**
Luston. *Here*.................4G **59**
Luthermuir. *Abers*.................2F **145**
Luthrie. *Fife*.................2F **137**
Lutley. *Staf*.................2C **60**
Luton. *Devn*
  nr. Honiton.................2D **12**
  nr. Teignmouth.................5C **12**
Luton. *Lutn*.................**201** (3A **52**)
Luton Airport. *Lutn*.................**216** (3B **52**)
Lutterworth. *Leics*.................2C **62**
Lutton. *Devn*
  nr. Ivybridge.................3B **8**
  nr. South Brent.................2C **8**
Lutton. *Linc*.................3D **76**
Lutton. *Nptn*.................2A **64**
Lutton Gowts. *Linc*.................3D **76**
Lutworthy. *Devn*.................1A **12**
Luxborough. *Som*.................3C **20**
Luxley. *Glos*.................3B **48**
Luxulyan. *Corn*.................3E **7**
Lybster. *High*.................5E **169**
Lydbury North. *Shrp*.................2F **59**
Lydcott. *Devn*.................3G **19**
Lydd. *Kent*.................3E **29**
Lydd Airport. *Kent*.................3E **29**
Lydden. *Kent*
  nr. Dover.................1G **29**
  nr. Margate.................4H **41**
Lyddington. *Rut*.................1F **63**
Lydd-on-Sea. *Kent*.................3E **29**
Lydeard St Lawrence.
  Som.................3E **21**
Lyde Green. *Hants*.................1F **25**
Lydford. *Devn*.................4F **11**
Lydford Fair Place. *Som*.................3A **22**
Lydgate. *G Man*.................4H **91**
Lydgate. *W Yor*.................2H **91**
Lydham. *Shrp*.................1F **59**
Lydiard Millicent. *Wilts*.................3F **35**
Lydiate. *Mers*.................4B **90**
Lydiate Ash. *Worc*.................3D **61**
Lydlinch. *Dors*.................1C **14**
Lydmarsh. *Som*.................2G **13**
Lydney. *Glos*.................5B **48**
Lydstep. *Pemb*.................5E **43**
Lye. *W Mid*.................2D **60**
The Lye. *Shrp*.................1A **60**
Lye Green. *Buck*.................5H **51**
Lye Green. *E Sus*.................2G **27**
Lye Head. *Worc*.................3B **60**
Lyford. *Oxon*.................2B **36**
Lyham. *Nmbd*.................1E **121**
Lylestone. *N Ayr*.................5E **127**
Lymbridge Green. *Kent*.................1F **29**
Lyme Regis. *Dors*.................3G **13**
Lyminge. *Kent*.................1F **29**
Lymington. *Hants*.................3A **16**
Lyminster. *W Sus*.................5B **26**
Lymm. *Warr*.................2A **84**
Lymore. *Hants*.................3A **16**
Lympne. *Kent*.................2F **29**
Lympsham. *Som*.................1G **21**
Lympstone. *Devn*.................4C **12**
Lynaberack Lodge. *High*.................4B **150**
Lynbridge. *Devn*.................2H **19**
Lynch. *Som*.................2C **20**
Lynchat. *High*.................3B **150**
Lynch Green. *Norf*.................5D **78**
Lyndhurst. *Hants*.................2B **16**
Lyndon. *Rut*.................5G **75**
Lyne. *Bord*.................5F **129**
Lyne. *Surr*.................4B **38**
Lyneal. *Shrp*.................2G **71**
Lyne Down. *Here*.................2B **48**
Lyneham. *Oxon*.................3A **50**
Lyneham. *Wilts*.................4F **35**
Lyneholmeford. *Cumb*.................2G **113**
Lynemouth. *Nmbd*.................5G **121**
Lyne of Gorthleck. *High*.................1H **149**
Lyne of Skene. *Abers*.................2E **153**
Lynesack. *Dur*.................2D **105**
Lyness. *Orkn*.................8C **172**
Lyng. *Norf*.................4C **78**
Lyngate. *Norf*
  nr. North Walsham.................2E **79**
  nr. Worstead.................3F **79**
Lynmouth. *Devn*.................2H **19**
Lynn. *Staf*.................5E **73**
Lynn. *Telf*.................4B **72**
Lynsted. *Kent*.................4D **40**
Lynstone. *Corn*.................2C **10**
Lynton. *Devn*.................2H **19**
Lynwilg. *High*.................2C **150**
Lyon's Gate. *Dors*.................2B **14**
Lyonshall. *Here*.................5F **59**
Lytchett Matravers. *Dors*.................3E **15**
Lytchett Minster. *Dors*.................3E **15**
Lyth. *High*.................2E **169**
Lytham. *Lanc*.................2B **90**
Lytham St Anne's. *Lanc*.................2B **90**

Lythe. *N Yor*.................3F **107**
Lythes. *Orkn*.................9D **172**
Lythmore. *High*.................2C **168**

M

Mabe Burnthouse. *Corn*.................5B **6**
Mabie. *Dum*.................2A **112**
Mablethorpe. *Linc*.................2E **89**
Macbiehill. *Bord*.................4E **129**
Macclesfield. *Ches E*.................3D **84**
Macclesfield Forest. *Ches E*.................3D **84**
Macduff. *Abers*.................2E **160**
Machan. *S Lan*.................4A **128**
Macharioch. *Arg*.................5B **122**
Machen. *Cphy*.................3F **33**
Machrie. *N Ayr*.................2C **122**
Machrihanish. *Arg*.................3A **122**
Machroes. *Gwyn*.................3C **68**
Machynlleth. *Powy*.................5G **69**
Mackerye End. *Herts*.................4B **52**
Mackworth. *Derb*.................2H **73**
Macmerry. *E Lot*.................2H **129**
Madderty. *Per*.................1B **136**
Maddington. *Wilts*.................2F **23**
Maddiston. *Falk*.................2C **128**
Madehurst. *W Sus*.................4A **26**
Madeley. *Staf*.................1B **72**
Madeley. *Telf*.................5A **72**
Madeley Heath. *Staf*.................1B **72**
Madeley Heath. *Worc*.................3D **60**
Madford. *Devn*.................1E **13**
Madingley. *Cambs*.................4C **64**
Madley. *Here*.................2H **47**
Madresfield. *Worc*.................1D **48**
Madron. *Corn*.................3B **4**
Maenaddwyn. *IOA*.................2D **80**
Maenclochog. *Pemb*.................2E **43**
Maendy. *V Glam*.................4D **32**
Maenporth. *Corn*.................4E **5**
Maentwrog. *Gwyn*.................1F **69**
Maen-y-groes. *Cdgn*.................5C **56**
Maer. *Staf*.................2B **72**
Maerdy. *Carm*.................3G **45**
Maerdy. *Cnwy*.................1C **70**
Maerdy. *Rhon*.................2C **32**
Maesbrook. *Shrp*.................3F **71**
Maesbury. *Shrp*.................3F **71**
Maesbury Marsh. *Shrp*.................3F **71**
Maes-glas. *Flin*.................3D **82**
Maesgwyn-Isaf. *Powy*.................4D **70**
Maeshafn. *Den*.................4E **82**
Maes Llyn. *Cdgn*.................1D **44**
Maesmynis. *Powy*.................1D **46**
Maesteg. *B'end*.................2B **32**
Maestir. *Cdgn*.................1F **45**
Maesybont. *Carm*.................4F **45**
Maescrugiau. *Carm*.................1E **45**
Maesycwmmer. *Cphy*.................2E **33**
Maesyrhandir. *Powy*.................1C **58**
Magdalen Laver. *Essx*.................5F **53**
Maggieknockater. *Mor*.................4H **159**
Magham Down. *E Sus*.................4H **27**
Maghull. *Mers*.................4B **90**
Magna Park. *Leics*.................2C **62**
Magor. *Mon*.................3H **33**
Magpie Green. *Suff*.................3C **66**
Magwyr. *Mon*.................3H **33**
Maidenbower. *W Sus*.................2D **27**
Maiden Bradley. *Wilts*.................3D **22**
Maidencombe. *Torb*.................2F **9**
Maidenhayne. *Devn*.................3F **13**
Maidenhead. *Wind*.................3G **37**
Maiden Law. *Dur*.................5E **115**
Maiden Newton. *Dors*.................3A **14**
Maidens. *S Ayr*.................4B **116**
Maiden's Green. *Brac*.................4G **37**
Maidensgrove. *Oxon*.................3F **37**
Maidenwell. *Corn*.................5B **10**
Maidenwell. *Linc*.................3C **88**
Maiden Wells. *Pemb*.................5D **42**
Maidford. *Nptn*.................5D **62**
Maids Moreton. *Buck*.................2F **51**
Maidstone. *Kent*.................5B **40**
Maidwell. *Nptn*.................3E **63**
Mail. *Shet*.................9F **173**
Maindee. *Newp*.................3G **33**
Mainsforth. *Dur*.................1A **106**
Mains of Auchindachy. *Mor*.................4B **160**
Mains of Auchnagatt. *Abers*.................4G **161**
Mains of Drum. *Abers*.................4F **153**
Mains of Edingight. *Mor*.................3C **160**
Mainsriddle. *Dum*.................4G **111**
Mainstone. *Shrp*.................2E **59**
Maisemore. *Glos*.................3D **48**
Major's Green. *Worc*.................3F **61**
Makeney. *Derbs*.................1A **74**
Makerstoun. *Bord*.................1A **120**
Malacleit. *W Isl*.................1C **170**
Malaig. *High*.................4E **147**
Malaig Bheag. *High*.................4E **147**
Malborough. *Devn*.................5D **8**
Malcoff. *Derbs*.................2E **85**
Malcolmburn. *Mor*.................3A **160**
Malden Rushett. *G Lon*.................4C **38**
Maldon. *Essx*.................5B **54**
Malham. *N Yor*.................3B **98**
Maligar. *High*.................2D **155**
Malinslee. *Telf*.................5A **72**
Mallaig. *High*.................4E **147**
Malleny Mills. *Edin*.................3E **129**
Mallows Green. *Essx*.................3E **53**
Malltraeth. *IOA*.................4D **80**
Mallwyd. *Gwyn*.................4A **70**
Malmesbury. *Wilts*.................3E **35**
Malmsmead. *Devn*.................2A **20**
Malpas. *Ches W*.................1G **71**
Malpas. *Corn*.................4C **6**
Malpas. *Newp*.................2G **33**
Malswick. *Glos*.................3C **48**

Maltby. *S Yor*.................1C **86**
Maltby. *Stoc T*.................3B **106**
Maltby le Marsh. *Linc*.................2D **88**
Malt Lane. *Arg*.................3H **133**
Malton. *N Yor*.................2B **100**
Malvern Link. *Worc*.................1C **48**
Malvern Wells. *Worc*.................1C **48**
Mamble. *Worc*.................3A **60**
Mamhilad. *Mon*.................5G **47**
Manaccan. *Corn*.................4E **5**
Manafon. *Powy*.................5D **70**
Manais. *W Isl*.................9D **171**
Manaton. *Devn*.................4A **12**
Manby. *Linc*.................2C **88**
Manchester. *G Man*.................**201** (1C **84**)
Manchester Airport.
  G Man.................**216** (2C **84**)
Mancot. *Flin*.................4F **83**
Manea. *Cambs*.................2D **65**
Maney. *W Mid*.................1F **61**
Manfield. *N Yor*.................3F **105**
Mangotsfield. *S Glo*.................4B **34**
Mangurstadh. *W Isl*.................4C **171**
Mankinholes. *W Yor*.................2H **91**
Manley. *Ches W*.................3H **83**
Manmoel. *Cphy*.................5E **47**
Mannal. *Arg*.................4A **138**
Mannerston. *Falk*.................2D **128**
Manningford Bohune. *Wilts*.................1G **23**
Manningford Bruce. *Wilts*.................1G **23**
Manningham. *W Yor*.................1B **92**
Mannings Heath. *W Sus*.................3D **26**
Mannington. *Dors*.................2F **15**
Manningtree. *Essx*.................2E **54**
Mannofield. *Aber*.................3G **153**
Manorbier. *Pemb*.................5E **43**
Manorbier Newton. *Pemb*.................5E **43**
Manordeilo. *Carm*.................3G **45**
Manorowen. *Pemb*.................1D **42**
Manor Park. *G Lon*.................2F **39**
Mansell Gamage. *Here*.................1G **47**
Mansell Lacy. *Here*.................1H **47**
Mansergh. *Cumb*.................1F **97**
Mansewood. *Glas*.................3G **127**
Mansfield. *E Ayr*.................3F **117**
Mansfield. *Notts*.................4C **86**
Mansfield Woodhouse. *Notts*.................4C **86**
Mansriggs. *Cumb*.................1B **96**
Manston. *Dors*.................1D **14**
Manston. *Kent*.................4H **41**
Manston. *W Yor*.................1D **92**
Manswood. *Dors*.................2E **15**
Manthorpe. *Linc*
  nr. Bourne.................4H **75**
  nr. Grantham.................2G **75**
Manton. *N Lin*.................4C **94**
Manton. *Notts*.................3C **86**
Manton. *Rut*.................5F **75**
Manton. *Wilts*.................5G **35**
Manuden. *Essx*.................3E **53**
Maperton. *Som*.................4B **22**
Maplebeck. *Notts*.................4E **86**
Maple Cross. *Herts*.................1B **38**
Mapledurham. *Oxon*.................4E **37**
Mapledurwell. *Hants*.................1E **25**
Maplehurst. *W Sus*.................3C **26**
Maplescombe. *Kent*.................4G **39**
Mapleton. *Derbs*.................1F **73**
Mapperley. *Derbs*.................1B **74**
Mapperley. *Nott*.................1C **74**
Mapperley Park. *Nott*.................1C **74**
Mapperton. *Dors*
  nr. Beaminster.................3A **14**
  nr. Poole.................3E **15**
Mappleborough Green. *Warw*.................4E **61**
Mappleton. *E Yor*.................5G **101**
Mappiewell. *S Yor*.................4D **92**
Mappowder. *Dors*.................2C **14**
Maraig. *W Isl*.................7E **171**
Marazion. *Corn*.................3C **4**
Marbhig. *W Isl*.................6G **171**
Marbury. *Ches E*.................1H **71**
March. *Cambs*.................1D **64**
Marcham. *Oxon*.................2C **36**
Marchamley. *Shrp*.................3H **71**
Marchington. *Staf*.................2F **73**
Marchington Woodlands. *Staf*.................3F **73**
Marchwiel. *Wrex*.................1F **71**
Marchwood. *Hants*.................1B **16**
Marcross. *V Glam*.................5C **32**
Marden. *Here*.................1A **48**
Marden. *Kent*.................1B **28**
Marden. *Wilts*.................1F **23**
Marden Beech. *Kent*.................1B **28**
Marden Thorn. *Kent*.................1B **28**
Mardu. *Shrp*.................2E **59**
Mardy. *Mon*.................4G **47**
Marefield. *Leics*.................5E **75**
Mareham le Fen. *Linc*.................4B **88**
Mareham on the Hill. *Linc*.................4B **88**
Marehay. *Derbs*.................1B **74**
Marehill. *W Sus*.................4B **26**
Maresfield. *E Sus*.................3F **27**
Marfleet. *Hull*.................2E **95**
Marford. *Wrex*.................5F **83**
Margam. *Neat*.................3A **32**
Margaret Marsh. *Dors*.................1D **14**
Margaret Roding. *Essx*.................4F **53**
Margaretting. *Essx*.................5G **53**
Margaretting Tye. *Essx*.................5G **53**
Margate. *Kent*.................3H **41**
Margnaheglish. *N Ayr*.................2E **123**
Margrove Park. *Red C*.................3D **106**
Marham. *Norf*.................5G **77**
Marhamchurch. *Corn*.................2C **10**
Marholm. *Pet*.................5A **76**
Marian Cwm. *Den*.................3C **82**
Mariandyrys. *IOA*.................2F **81**
Marian-glas. *IOA*.................2E **81**

Mariansleigh. *Devn*.................4H **19**
Marian-y-de. *Gwyn*.................2C **68**
Marian-y-mor. *Gwyn*.................2C **68**
Marine Town. *Kent*.................3D **40**
Marishader. *High*.................2D **155**
Marjoriebanks. *Dum*.................1B **112**
Mark. *Dum*.................4G **109**
Mark. *Som*.................2G **21**
Markbeech. *Kent*.................1F **27**
Markby. *Linc*.................3D **89**
Mark Causeway. *Som*.................2G **21**
Mark Cross. *E Sus*.................2G **27**
Markeaton. *Derb*.................2H **73**
Market Bosworth. *Leics*.................5B **74**
Market Deeping. *Linc*.................4A **76**
Market Drayton. *Shrp*.................2A **72**
Market End. *Warw*.................2H **61**
Market Harborough. *Leics*.................2E **63**
Markethill. *Per*.................5B **144**
Market Lavington. *Wilts*.................1F **23**
Market Overton. *Rut*.................4F **75**
Market Rasen. *Linc*.................2A **88**
Market Stainton. *Linc*.................2B **88**
Market Weighton. *E Yor*.................5C **100**
Market Weston. *Suff*.................3B **66**
Markfield. *Leics*.................4B **74**
Markham. *Cphy*.................5E **47**
Markinch. *Fife*.................3E **137**
Markington. *N Yor*.................3E **99**
Marksbury. *Bath*.................5B **34**
Mark's Corner. *IOW*.................3C **16**
Marks Tey. *Essx*.................3C **54**
Markwell. *Corn*.................3H **7**
Markyate. *Herts*.................4A **52**
Marlborough. *Wilts*.................5G **35**
Marlcliff. *Warw*.................5E **61**
Maldon. *Devn*.................2E **9**
Marle Green. *E Sus*.................4G **27**
Marlesford. *Suff*.................5F **67**
Marley Green. *Ches E*.................1H **71**
Marley Hill. *Tyne*.................4F **115**
Marlingford. *Norf*.................5D **78**
Mar Lodge. *Abers*.................5E **151**
Marloes. *Pemb*.................4B **42**
Marlow. *Buck*.................3G **37**
Marlow. *Here*.................3F **59**
Marlow Bottom. *Buck*.................3G **37**
Marlow Common. *Buck*.................3G **37**
Marlpit Hill. *Kent*.................1F **27**
Marlpits. *E Sus*.................3F **27**
Marlpool. *Derbs*.................1B **74**
Marnhull. *Dors*.................1C **14**
Marnoch. *Abers*.................3C **160**
Marnock. *N Lan*.................3A **128**
Marple. *G Man*.................2D **84**
Marr. *S Yor*.................4F **93**
Marrel. *High*.................2H **165**
Marrick. *N Yor*.................5D **105**
Marrister. *Shet*.................5G **173**
Marros. *Carm*.................4G **43**
Marsden. *Tyne*.................3G **115**
Marsden. *W Yor*.................3A **92**
Marsett. *N Yor*.................1B **98**
Marsh. *Buck*.................5G **51**
Marsh. *Devn*.................1F **13**
The Marsh. *Powy*.................1F **59**
The Marsh. *Shrp*.................3A **72**
Marshall Meadows. *Nmbd*.................4F **131**
Marshalsea. *Dors*.................2G **13**
Marshalswick. *Herts*.................5B **52**
Marsham. *Norf*.................3D **78**
Marshaw. *Lanc*.................4E **97**
Marsh Baldon. *Oxon*.................2D **36**
Marsh Benham. *W Ber*.................5C **36**
Marshborough. *Kent*.................5H **41**
Marshbrook. *Shrp*.................2G **59**
Marshchapel. *Linc*.................1C **88**
Marshfield. *Newp*.................3F **33**
Marshfield. *S Glo*.................4C **34**
Marshgate. *Corn*.................3B **10**
Marsh Gibbon. *Buck*.................3E **51**
Marsh Green. *Devn*.................3D **12**
Marsh Green. *Kent*.................1F **27**
Marsh Green. *Staf*.................5C **84**
Marsh Green. *Telf*.................4A **72**
Marsh Lane. *Derbs*.................3B **86**
Marsh Side. *Norf*.................1G **77**
Marshside. *Kent*.................4G **41**
Marshside. *Mers*.................3B **90**
Marsh Street. *Som*.................2C **20**
Marshwood. *Dors*.................3G **13**
Marske. *N Yor*.................4E **105**
Marske-by-the-Sea. *Red C*.................2D **106**
Marston. *Ches W*.................3A **84**
Marston. *Here*.................5F **59**
Marston. *Linc*.................1F **75**
Marston. *Oxon*.................5D **50**
Marston. *Staf*
  nr. Stafford.................3D **72**
  nr. Wheaton Aston.................4C **72**
Marston. *Warw*.................1G **61**
Marston. *Wilts*.................1E **23**
Marston Doles. *Warw*.................5B **62**
Marston Green. *W Mid*.................2F **61**
Marston Hill. *Glos*.................2G **35**
Marston Jabbett. *Warw*.................2A **62**
Marston Magna. *Som*.................4A **22**
Marston Meysey. *Wilts*.................2G **35**
Marston Montgomery. *Derbs*.................2F **73**
Marston Moretaine. *C Beds*.................1H **51**
Marston on Dove. *Derbs*.................3G **73**
Marston St Lawrence. *Nptn*.................1D **50**
Marston Stannett. *Here*.................5H **59**
Marston Trussell. *Nptn*.................2D **62**
Marstow. *Here*.................4A **48**
Marsworth. *Buck*.................4H **51**
Marten. *Wilts*.................1A **24**
Marthall. *Ches E*.................3C **84**
Martham. *Norf*.................4G **79**
Marthwaite. *Cumb*.................5H **103**
Martin. *Hants*.................1F **15**

Martin – Milltimber

Martin. Kent 1H 29
Martin. Linc
nr. Horncastle 4B 88
nr. Metheringham 5A 88
Martindale. Cumb 3F 103
Martin Dales. Linc 4A 88
Martin Drove End. Hants 4F 23
Martinhoe. Devn 2G 19
Martinhoe Cross. Devn 2G 19
Martin Hussingtree. Worc 4C 60
Martin Mill. Kent 1H 29
Martinscroft. Warr 2A 84
Martin's Moss. Ches E 4C 84
Martinstown. Dors 4B 14
Martlesham. Suff 1F 55
Martlesham Heath. Suff 1F 55
Martletwy. Pemb 3E 43
Martley. Worc 4B 60
Martock. Som 1H 13
Marton. Ches E 4C 84
Marton. Cumb 2B 96
Marton. E Yor
nr. Bridlington 3G 101
nr. Hull 1E 95
Marton. Linc 2F 87
Marton. Midd 3C 106
Marton. N Yor
nr. Boroughbridge 3G 99
nr. Pickering 1B 100
Marton. Shrp
nr. Myddle 3G 71
nr. Worthen 5E 71
Marton. Warw 4B 62
Marton Abbey. N Yor 3H 99
Marton-le-Moor. N Yor 2F 99
Martyr's Green. Surr 5B 38
Martyr Worthy. Hants 3D 24
Marwick. Orkn 5B 172
Marwood. Devn 3F 19
Marybank. High
nr. Dingwall 3G 157
nr. Invergordon 1B 158
Maryburgh. High 3H 157
Maryfield. Corn 3A 8
Maryhill. Glas 3G 127
Marykirk. Abers 2F 145
Marylebone. G Lon 2D 39
Marylebone. G Man 4D 90
Marypark. Mor 5F 159
Maryport. Cumb 1B 102
Maryport. Dum 5E 109
Marystow. Devn 4E 11
Mary Tavy. Devn 5F 11
Maryton. Ang
nr. Kirriemuir 3C 144
nr. Montrose 3F 145
Marywell. Abers 4C 152
Marywell. Ang 4F 145
Masham. N Yor 1E 98
Mashbury. Essx 4G 53
Masongill. N Yor 2F 97
Masons Lodge. Abers 3F 153
Mastin Moor. Derbs 3B 86
Mastrick. Aber 3G 153
Matching. Essx 4F 53
Matching Green. Essx 4F 53
Matching Tye. Essx 4F 53
Matfen. Nmbd 2D 114
Matfield. Kent 1A 28
Mathern. Mon 2A 34
Mathon. Here 1C 48
Mathry. Pemb 1C 42
Matlaske. Norf 2D 78
Matlock. Derbs 5G 85
Matlock Bath. Derbs 5G 85
Matterdale End. Cumb 2E 103
Mattersey. Notts 2D 86
Mattersey Thorpe. Notts 2D 86
Mattingley. Hants 1F 25
Mattishall. Norf 4C 78
Mattishall Burgh. Norf 4C 78
Mauchline. E Ayr 2D 117
Maud. Abers 4G 161
Maudlin. Corn 2E 7
Maugersbury. Glos 3G 49
Maughold. IOM 2D 108
Maulden. C Beds 2A 52
Maulds Meaburn. Cumb 3H 103
Maunby. N Yor 1F 99
Maund Bryan. Here 5H 59
Mautby. Norf 4G 79
Mavesyn Ridware. Staf 4E 73
Mavis Enderby. Linc 4C 88
Mawbray. Cumb 5B 112
Mawdesley. Lanc 3C 90
Mawdlam. B'end 3B 32
Mawgan. Corn 4E 5
Mawgan Porth. Corn 2C 6
Maw Green. Ches E 5B 84
Mawla. Corn 4B 6
Mawnan. Corn 4E 5
Mawnan Smith. Corn 4E 5
Mawsley Village. Nptn 3E 63
Mawthorpe. Linc 3D 88
Maxey. Pet 5A 76
Maxstoke. Warw 2G 61
Maxted Street. Kent 1F 29
Maxton. Kent 1G 29
Maxton. Bord 1A 120
Maxwellheugh. Bord 1B 120
Maxwelltown. Dum 2A 112
Maxworthy. Corn 3C 10
Mayals. Swan 4F 31
Maybole. S Ayr 3C 116
Maybush. Sotn 1B 16
Mayes Green. Surr 2C 26
Mayfield. E Sus 3G 27
Mayfield. Midl 3G 129
Mayfield. Per 1C 136
Mayfield. Staf 1F 73
Mayford. Surr 5A 38
Mayhill. Swan 3F 31
Mayland. Essx 5C 54
Maylandsea. Essx 5C 54
Maynard's Green. E Sus 4G 27
Maypole. IOS 1B 4
Maypole. Kent 4G 41
Maypole. Mon 4H 47
Maypole Green. Norf 1G 67
Maypole Green. Suff 5B 66
Maywick. Shet 9E 173
Mead. Devn 1C 10
Meadgate. Bath 1B 22
Meadle. Buck 5G 51
Meadowbank. Ches W 4A 84
Meadowfield. Dur 1F 105
Meadow Green. Here 5B 60
Meadowmill. E Lot 2H 129
Meadows. Nott 2C 74
Meadowtown. Shrp 5F 71
Meadwell. Devn 4E 11
Meaford. Staf 2C 72
Mealabost. W Isl
nr. Borgh 2G 171
nr. Stornoway 4G 171
Mealasta. W Isl 5B 171
Meal Bank. Cumb 5G 103
Mealrigg. Cumb 5C 112
Mealsgate. Cumb 5D 112
Meanwood. W Yor 1C 92
Mearbeck. N Yor 3H 97
Meare. Som 2H 21
Meare Green. Som
nr. Curry Mallet 4F 21
nr. Stoke St Gregory 4G 21
Mears Ashby. Nptn 4F 63
Measham. Leics 4H 73
Meath Green. Surr 1D 27
Meathop. Cumb 1D 96
Meaux. E Yor 1D 94
Meavy. Devn 2B 8
Medbourne. Leics 1E 63
Medburn. Nmbd 2E 115
Meddon. Devn 1C 10
Meden Vale. Notts 4C 86
Medlam. Linc 5C 88
Medlicott. Shrp 1G 59
Medmenham. Buck 3G 37
Medomsley. Dur 4E 115
Medstead. Hants 3E 25
Medway Towns. Medw 204 (4B 40)
Meerbrook. Staf 4D 85
Meer End. W Mid 3G 61
Meers Bridge. Linc 2D 89
Meesden. Herts 2E 53
Meeson. Telf 3A 72
Meeth. Devn 2F 11
Meeting Green. Suff 5G 65
Meeting House Hill. Norf 3F 79
Meidrim. Carm 2G 43
Meifod. Powy 4D 70
Meigle. Per 4B 144
Meikle Earnock. S Lan 4A 128
Meikle Kilchattan Butts. Arg 4B 126
Meikleour. Per 5A 144
Meikle Tarty. Abers 1G 153
Meikle Wartle. Abers 5E 160
Meinciau. Carm 4E 45
Meir. Stoke 1D 72
Meir Heath. Staf 1D 72
Melbourn. Cambs 1D 53
Melbourne. Derbs 3A 74
Melbourne. E Yor 5B 100
Melbury Abbas. Dors 4D 23
Melbury Bubb. Dors 2A 14
Melbury Osmond. Dors 2A 14
Melbury Sampford. Dors 2A 14
Melby. Shet 6C 173
Melchbourne. Bed 4H 63
Melcombe Bingham. Dors 2C 14
Melcombe Regis. Dors 4B 14
Meldon. Devn 3F 11
Meldon. Nmbd 1E 115
Meldreth. Cambs 1D 53
Melfort. Arg 2F 133
Melgarve. High 4G 149
Meliden. Den 2C 82
Melinbyrhedyn. Powy 1H 57
Melincourt. Neat 5B 46
Melin-y-coed. Cnwy 4H 81
Melin-y-ddol. Powy 5C 70
Melin-y-wig. Den 1C 70
Melkington. Nmbd 5E 131
Melkinthorpe. Cumb 2G 103
Melkridge. Nmbd 3A 114
Melksham. Wilts 5E 35
Mellangaun. High 5C 162
Melldalloch. Arg 2H 125
Mellguards. Cumb 5F 113
Melling. Lanc 2E 97
Melling. Mers 4B 90
Melling Mount. Mers 4C 90
Mellis. Suff 3C 66
Mellon Charles. High 4C 162
Mellon Udrigle. High 4C 162
Mellor. G Man 2D 85
Mellor. Lanc 1E 91
Mellor Brook. Lanc 1E 91
Mells. Som 2C 22
Melmerby. Cumb 1H 103
Melmerby. N Yor
nr. Middleham 1C 98
nr. Ripon 2F 99
Melplash. Dors 3H 13
Melrose. Bord 1H 119
Melsetter. Orkn 9B 172
Melsonby. N Yor 4E 105
Meltham. W Yor 3B 92
Meltham Mills. W Yor 3B 92
Melton. E Yor 2C 94
Melton. Suff 5E 67
Meltonby. E Yor 4B 100
Melton Constable. Norf 2C 78
Melton Mowbray. Leics 4E 75
Melton Ross. N Lin 3D 94
Melvaig. High 5B 162
Melverley. Shrp 4F 71
Melverley Green. Shrp 4F 71
Melvich. High 2A 168
Membury. Devn 2F 13
Memsie. Abers 2G 161
Memus. Ang 3D 144
Menabilly. Corn 3E 7
Menai Bridge. IOA 3E 81
Mendham. Suff 2E 67
Mendlesham. Suff 4D 66
Mendlesham Green. Suff 4C 66
Menethorpe. N Yor 3B 100
Menheniot. Corn 2G 7
Menithwood. Worc 4B 60
Menna. Corn 3D 6
Mennock. Dum 4H 117
Menston. W Yor 5D 98
Menstrie. Clac 4H 135
Menthorpe. N Yor 1H 93
Mentmore. Buck 4H 51
Meole Brace. Shrp 4G 71
Meols. Mers 1E 83
Meon. Hants 2D 16
Meonstoke. Hants 1E 16
Meopham. Kent 4H 39
Meopham Green. Kent 4H 39
Meopham Station. Kent 4H 39
Mepal. Cambs 2D 64
Meppershall. C Beds 2B 52
Merbach. Here 1G 47
Mercaston. Derbs 1G 73
Merchiston. Edin 2F 129
Mere. Ches E 2B 84
Mere. Wilts 3D 22
Mere Brow. Lanc 3C 90
Mereclough. Lanc 1G 91
Mere Green. W Mid 1F 61
Mere Green. Worc 4D 60
Mere Heath. Ches W 3A 84
Mereside. Bkpl 1B 90
Meretown. Staf 3B 72
Mereworth. Kent 5A 40
Meriden. W Mid 2G 61
Merkadale. High 5C 154
Merkland. S Ayr 5B 116
Merkland Lodge. High 1A 164
Merley. Pool 3F 15
Merlin's Bridge. Pemb 3D 42
Merridge. Som 3F 21
Merrington. Shrp 3G 71
Merrion. Pemb 5D 42
Merriott. Som 1H 13
Merrivale. Devn 5F 11
Merrow. Surr 5B 38
Merrybent. Darl 3F 105
Merry Lees. Leics 5B 74
Merrymeet. Corn 2G 7
Mersham. Kent 2E 29
Merstham. Surr 5D 39
Merston. W Sus 2G 17
Merstone. IOW 4D 16
Merther. Corn 4C 6
Merthyr. Carm 3D 44
Merthyr Cynog. Powy 2C 46
Merthyr Dyfan. V Glam 4E 32
Merthyr Mawr. B'end 4B 32
Merthyr Tudful. Mer T 5D 46
Merthyr Tydfil. Mer T 5D 46
Merthyr Vale. Mer T 2D 32
Merton. Devn 1F 11
Merton. G Lon 4D 38
Merton. Norf 1B 66
Merton. Oxon 4D 50
Meshaw. Devn 1A 12
Messing. Essx 4B 54
Messingham. N Lin 4B 94
Metcombe. Devn 3D 12
Metfield. Suff 2E 67
Metherell. Corn 2A 8
Metheringham. Linc 4H 87
Methil. Fife 4F 137
Methilhill. Fife 4F 137
Methley. W Yor 2D 93
Methley Junction. W Yor 2D 93
Methlick. Abers 5F 161
Methven. Per 1C 136
Methwold. Norf 1G 65
Methwold Hythe. Norf 1G 65
Mettingham. Suff 2F 67
Metton. Norf 2D 78
Mevagissey. Corn 4E 6
Mexborough. S Yor 4E 93
Mey. High 1E 169
Meysey Hampton. Glos 2G 35
Miabhag. W Isl 8D 171
Miabhaig. W Isl
nr. Cliasmol 7C 171
nr. Timsgearraidh 4C 171
Mial. High 1G 155
Michaelchurch. Here 3A 48
Michaelchurch Escley. Here 2G 47
Michaelchurch-on-Arrow. Powy 5E 59
Michaelston-le-Pit. V Glam 4E 33
Michaelston-y-Fedw. Newp 3F 33
Michaelstow. Corn 5A 10
Michelcombe. Devn 2C 8
Micheldever. Hants 3D 24
Micheldever Station. Hants 2D 24
Michelmersh. Hants 4B 24
Mickfield. Suff 4D 66
Micklebring. S Yor 1C 86
Mickleby. N Yor 3F 107
Micklefield. W Yor 1E 93
Micklefield Green. Herts 1B 38
Mickleham. Surr 5C 38
Mickleover. Derb 2H 73
Micklethwaite. Cumb 4D 112
Micklethwaite. W Yor 5D 98
Mickleton. Dur 2C 104
Mickleton. Glos 1G 49
Mickletown. W Yor 2D 93
Mickle Trafford. Ches W 4G 83
Mickley. N Yor 2E 99
Mickley Green. Suff 5H 65
Mickley Square. Nmbd 3D 115
Mid Ardlaw. Abers 2G 161
Midbea. Orkn 3D 172
Mid Beltie. Abers 3D 152
Mid Calder. W Lot 3D 129
Mid Clyth. High 5E 169
Middle Assendon. Oxon 3F 37
Middle Aston. Oxon 3C 50
Middle Barton. Oxon 3C 50
Middlebie. Dum 2D 112
Middle Chinnock. Som 1H 13
Middle Claydon. Buck 3F 51
Middlecliffe. S Yor 4E 93
Middlecott. Devn 4H 11
Middle Drums. Ang 3E 145
Middle Duntisbourne. Glos 5E 49
Middle Essie. Abers 3H 161
Middleforth Green. Lanc 2D 90
Middleham. N Yor 1D 98
Middle Handley. Derbs 3B 86
Middle Harling. Norf 2B 66
Middlehope. Shrp 2G 59
Middle Littleton. Worc 1F 49
Middle Maes-coed. Here 2G 47
Middlemarsh. Dors 2B 14
Middle Marwood. Devn 3F 19
Middle Mayfield. Staf 1F 73
Middlemoor. Devn 5E 11
Middlemuir. Abers
nr. New Deer 4F 161
nr. Strichen 3G 161
Middle Rainton. Tyne 5G 115
Middle Rasen. Linc 2H 87
The Middles. Dur 4F 115
Middlesbrough. Midd 201 (3B 106)
Middlesceugh. Cumb 5E 113
Middleshaw. Cumb 1E 97
Middlesmoor. N Yor 2C 98
Middlestone. Dur 1F 105
Middlestone Moor. Dur 1F 105
Middle Stoughton. Som 2H 21
Middlestown. W Yor 3C 92
Middle Street. Glos 5C 48
Middle Taphouse. Corn 2F 7
Middleton. Ang 4E 145
Middleton. Arg 4A 138
Middleton. Cumb 1F 97
Middleton. Derbs
nr. Bakewell 4F 85
nr. Wirksworth 5G 85
Middleton. Essx 2B 54
Middleton. G Man 4G 91
Middleton. Hants 2C 24
Middleton. Hart 1C 106
Middleton. Here 4H 59
Middleton. IOW 4B 16
Middleton. Lanc 4D 96
Middleton. Midl 4G 129
Middleton. Norf 4F 77
Middleton. Nptn 2F 63
Middleton. Nmbd
nr. Belford 1F 121
nr. Morpeth 1D 114
Middleton. N Yor
nr. Ilkley 5D 98
nr. Pickering 1B 100
Middleton. Per 3D 136
Middleton. Shrp
nr. Ludlow 3H 59
nr. Oswestry 3F 71
Middleton. Suff 4G 67
Middleton. Swan 4D 30
Middleton. Warw 1F 61
Middleton. W Yor 2C 92
Middleton Cheney. Nptn 1D 50
Middleton Green. Staf 2D 73
Middleton-in-Teesdale. Dur 2C 104
Middleton One Row. Darl 3A 106
Middleton-on-Leven. N Yor 4B 106
Middleton-on-Sea. W Sus 5A 26
Middleton on the Hill. Here 4H 59
Middleton-on-the-Wolds. E Yor 5D 100
Middleton Priors. Shrp 1A 60
Middleton Quernhow. N Yor 2F 99
Middleton St George. Darl 3A 106
Middleton Scriven. Shrp 2A 60
Middleton Stoney. Oxon 3D 50
Middleton Tyas. N Yor 4F 105
Middle Town. IOS 1B 4
Middletown. Cumb 4A 102
Middletown. Powy 4F 71
Middle Tysoe. Warw 1B 50
Middle Wallop. Hants 3A 24
Middlewich. Ches E 4B 84
Middle Winterslow. Wilts 3H 23
Middlewood. Corn 5C 10
Middlewood. S Yor 1H 85
Middle Woodford. Wilts 3G 23
Middlewood Green. Suff 4C 66
Middleyard. Glos 5D 48
Middlezoy. Som 3G 21
Middridge. Dur 2F 105
Midelney. Som 4H 21
Midfield. High 2F 167
Midford. Bath 5C 34
Mid Garrary. Dum 2C 110
Midge Hall. Lanc 2D 90
Midgeholme. Cumb 4H 113
Midgham. W Ber 5D 36
Midgley. W Yor
nr. Halifax 2A 92
nr. Horbury 3C 92
Mid Ho. Shet 2G 173
Midhopestones. S Yor 1G 85
Midhurst. W Sus 4G 25
Mid Kirkton. N Ayr 4C 126
Mid Lambrook. Som 1H 13
Midland. Orkn 7C 172
Mid Lavant. W Sus 2G 17
Midlem. Bord 2H 119
Midney. Som 4A 22
Midsomer Norton. Bath 1B 22
Midton. Inv 2D 126
Midtown. High
nr. Poolewe 5C 162
nr. Tongue 2F 167
Midville. Linc 5C 88
Mid Walls. Shet 7C 173
Mid Yell. Shet 2G 173
Migdale. High 4D 164
Migvie. Abers 3B 152
Milborne Port. Som 1B 14
Milborne St Andrew. Dors 3D 14
Milborne Wick. Som 4B 22
Milbourne. Nmbd 2E 115
Milbourne. Wilts 3E 35
Milburn. Cumb 2H 103
Milbury Heath. S Glo 2B 34
Milby. N Yor 3G 99
Milcombe. Oxon 2C 50
Milden. Suff 1C 54
Mildenhall. Suff 3G 65
Mildenhall. Wilts 5H 35
Milebrook. Powy 3F 59
Milebush. Kent 1B 28
Mile End. Cambs 2F 65
Mile End. Essx 3C 54
Mileham. Norf 4B 78
Mile Oak. Brig 5D 26
Miles Green. Staf 5C 84
Miles Hope. Here 4H 59
Milesmark. Fife 1D 128
Mile Town. Kent 3D 40
Milfield. Nmbd 1D 120
Milford. Derbs 1A 74
Milford. Devn 4C 18
Milford. Powy 1C 58
Milford. Staf 3D 72
Milford. Surr 1A 26
Milford Haven. Pemb 4D 42
Milford on Sea. Hants 3A 16
Milkwall. Glos 5A 48
Milkwell. Wilts 4E 23
Milland. W Sus 4G 25
Mill Bank. W Yor 2A 92
Millbank. High 2D 168
Millbeck. Cumb 2D 102
Millbounds. Orkn 4E 172
Millbreck. Abers 4H 161
Millbridge. Surr 2G 25
Millbrook. C Beds 2A 52
Millbrook. Corn 3A 8
Millbrook. G Man 1D 85
Millbrook. Sotn 1B 16
Mill Common. Suff 2G 67
Mill Corner. E Sus 3C 28
Milldale. Staf 5F 85
Millden Lodge. Ang 1E 145
Milldens. Ang 3E 145
Millearn. Per 2B 136
Mill End. Buck 3F 37
Mill End. Cambs 5F 65
Mill End. Glos 4G 49
Mill End. Herts 2D 52
Millend. Glos 2C 34
Millerhill. Midl 3G 129
Miller's Dale. Derbs 3F 85
Millers Green. Derbs 5G 85
Millerston. Glas 3H 127
Millfield. Abers 4B 152
Millfield. Pet 5A 76
Millgate. Lanc 3G 91
Mill Green. Essx 5G 53
Mill Green. Norf 2D 66
Mill Green. Shrp 3A 72
Mill Green. Staf 3E 73
Mill Green. Suff 1C 54
Millhalf. Here 1F 47
Millhall. E Ren 4G 127
Millhayes. Devn
nr. Honiton 2F 13
nr. Wellington 1E 13
Millhead. Lanc 2D 97
Millheugh. S Lan 4A 128
Mill Hill. Bkbn 2E 91
Mill Hill. G Lon 1D 38
Millholme. Cumb 5G 103
Millhouse. Arg 2A 126
Millhouse. Cumb 1E 103
Millhousebridge. Dum 1C 112
Millhouses. S Yor 2H 85
Millikenpark. Ren 3F 127
Millington. E Yor 4C 100
Millington Green. Derbs 1G 73
Mill Knowe. Arg 3B 122
Mill Lane. Hants 1F 25
Millmeece. Staf 2C 72
Mill of Craigievar. Abers 2C 152
Mill of Fintray. Abers 2F 153
Mill of Haldane. W Dun 1F 127
Millom. Cumb 1A 96
Millow. C Beds 1C 52
Millpool. Corn 5B 10
Millport. N Ayr 4C 126
Mill Side. Cumb 1D 96
Mill Street. Norf
nr. Lyng 4C 78
nr. Swanton Morley 4C 78
Millthorpe. Derbs 3H 85
Millthorpe. Linc 2A 76
Millthrop. Cumb 5H 103
Milltimber. Aber 3F 153

Milltown – Murrell Green

Milltown. Abers
nr. Corgarff 3G 151
nr. Lumsden 2B 152
Milltown. Corn 3F 7
Milltown. Derbs 4A 86
Milltown. Devn 3F 19
Milltown. Dum 2E 113
Milltown of Aberdalgie. Per 1C 136
Milltown of Auchindoun. Mor 4A 160
Milltown of Campfield. Abers 3D 152
Milltown of Edinvillie. Mor 4G 159
Milltown of Rothiemay. Mor 4C 160
Milltown of Towie. Abers 2B 152
Milnacraig. Ang 3B 144
Milnathort. Per 3D 136
Milngavie. E Dun 2G 127
Milnholm. Stir 1A 128
Milnrow. G Man 3H 91
Milnthorpe. Cumb 1D 97
Milnthorpe. W Yor 3D 92
Milson. Shrp 3A 60
Milstead. Kent 5D 40
Milston. Wilts 2G 23
Milthorpe. Nptn 1D 50
Milton. Ang 4C 144
Milton. Cambs 4D 65
Milton. Cumb
nr. Brampton 3G 113
nr. Crooklands 1E 97
Milton. Derbs 3H 73
Milton. Dum
nr. Crocketford 2F 111
nr. Glenluce 4H 109
Milton. Glas 3G 127
Milton. High
nr. Achnasheen 3F 157
nr. Applecross 4G 155
nr. Drumnadrochit 5G 157
nr. Invergordon 1B 158
nr. Inverness 4H 157
nr. Wick 3F 169
Milton. Mor
nr. Cullen 2C 160
nr. Tomintoul 2F 151
Milton. N Som 5G 33
Milton. Notts 3E 86
Milton. Oxon
nr. Bloxham 2C 50
nr. Didcot 2C 36
Milton. Pemb 4E 43
Milton. Port 3E 17
Milton. Som 4H 21
Milton. S Ayr 2D 116
Milton. Stir
nr. Aberfoyle 3E 135
nr. Drymen 4D 134
Milton. Stoke 5D 84
Milton. W Dun 2F 127
Milton Abbas. Dors 2D 14
Milton Abbot. Devn 5E 11
Milton Auchlossan. Abers 3C 152
Milton Bridge. Midl 3F 129
Milton Bryan. C Beds 2H 51
Milton Clevedon. Som 3B 22
Milton Coldwells. Abers 5G 161
Milton Combe. Devn 2A 8
Milton Common. Oxon 5E 51
Milton Damerel. Devn 1D 11
Miltonduff. Mor 2F 159
Milton End. Glos 5G 49
Milton Ernest. Bed 5H 63
Milton Green. Ches W 5G 83
Milton Hill. Devn 5C 12
Milton Hill. Oxon 2C 36
Milton Keynes. Mil 204 (2G 51)
Milton Keynes Village. Mil 2G 51
Milton Lilbourne. Wilts 5G 35
Milton Malsor. Nptn 5E 63
Milton Morenish. Per 5D 142
Milton of Auchinhove. Abers 3C 152
Milton of Balgonie. Fife 3F 137
Milton of Barras. Abers 1H 145
Milton of Campsie. E Dun 2H 127
Milton of Cultoquhey. Per 1A 136
Milton of Cushnie. Abers 2C 152
Milton of Finavon. Ang 3D 145
Milton of Gollanfield. High 3B 158
Milton of Lesmore. Abers 1B 152
Milton of Leys. High 4A 158
Milton of Tullich. Abers 4A 152
Milton on Stour. Dors 4C 22
Milton Regis. Kent 4C 40
Milton Street. E Sus 5G 27
Milton-under-Wychwood.
Oxon 4A 50
Milverton. Som 4E 20
Milverton. Warw 4H 61
Milwich. Staf 2D 72
Mimbridge. Surr 4A 38
Minard. Arg 4G 133
Minchington. Dors 1E 15
Minchinhampton. Glos 5D 48
Mindrum. Nmbd 1C 120
Minehead. Som 2C 20
Minera. Wrex 5E 83
Minety. Wilts 2F 35
Minffordd. Gwyn 2E 69
Mingarrypark. High 2A 140
Mingary. High 2G 139
Mingearraidh. W Isl 6C 170
Miningsby. Linc 4C 88
Minions. Corn 5C 10
Minishant. S Ayr 3C 116
Minllyn. Gwyn 4A 70
Minnigaff. Dum 3B 110
Minorca. IOM 3D 108
Minskip. N Yor 3F 99
Minstead. Hants 1A 16
Minsted. W Sus 4G 25
Minster. Kent
nr. Ramsgate 4H 41
Minster. Kent
nr. Sheerness 3D 40
Minsteracres. Nmbd 4D 114
Minsterley. Shrp 5F 71
Minster Lovell. Oxon 4B 50
Minsterworth. Glos 4C 48
Minterne Magna. Dors 2B 14
Minterne Parva. Dors 2B 14
Minting. Linc 3A 88
Mintlaw. Abers 4H 161
Minto. Bord 2H 119
Minton. Shrp 1G 59
Minwear. Pemb 3E 43
Minworth. W Mid 1F 61
Miodar. Arg 4B 138
Mirbister. Orkn 5C 172
Mirehouse. Cumb 3A 102
Mireland. High 2F 169
Mirfield. W Yor 3C 92
Miserden. Glos 5E 49
Miskin. Rhon 3D 32
Misson. Notts 1D 86
Misterton. Leics 2C 62
Misterton. Notts 1E 87
Misterton. Som 2H 13
Mistley. Essx 2E 54
Mistley Heath. Essx 2E 55
Mitcham. G Lon 4D 39
Mitcheldean. Glos 4B 48
Mitchell. Corn 3C 6
Mitchel Troy. Mon 4H 47
Mitcheltroy Common. Mon 5H 47
Mitford. Nmbd 1E 115
Mithian. Corn 3B 6
Mitton. Staf 4C 72
Mixbury. Oxon 2E 50
Mixenden. W Yor 2A 92
Mixon. Staf 5E 85
Moaness. Orkn 7B 172
Moarfield. Shet 1G 173
Moat. Cumb 2F 113
Moats Tye. Suff 5C 66
Mobberley. Ches E 3B 84
Mobberley. Staf 1E 73
Moccas. Here 1G 47
Mochdre. Cnwy 3H 81
Mochdre. Powy 2C 58
Mochrum. Dum 5A 110
Mockbeggar. Hants 2G 15
Mockerkin. Cumb 2B 102
Modbury. Devn 3C 8
Moddershall. Staf 2D 72
Modsarie. High 2G 167
Moelfre. Cnwy 3B 82
Moelfre. IOA 2E 81
Moelfre. Powy 3D 70
Moffat. Dum 4C 118
Moggerhanger. C Beds 1B 52
Mogworthy. Devn 1B 12
Moira. Leics 4H 73
Molash. Kent 5E 41
Mol-chlach. High 2C 146
Mold. Flin 4E 83
Molehill Green. Essx 3F 53
Molescroft. E Yor 5E 101
Molesden. Nmbd 1E 115
Molesworth. Cambs 3H 63
Moll. High 1D 146
Molland. Devn 4B 20
Mollington. Ches W 3F 83
Mollington. Oxon 1C 50
Mollinsburn. N Lan 2A 128
Monachty. Cdgn 4E 57
Monachyle. Stir 2D 135
Monar Lodge. High 4E 156
Monaughty. Powy 4E 59
Monewden. Suff 5E 67
Moneydie. Per 1C 136
Moneyrow Green. Wind 4G 37
Moniaive. Dum 5G 117
Monifieth. Ang 5E 145
Monikie. Ang 5E 145
Monimail. Fife 2E 137
Monington. Pemb 1B 44
Monk Bretton. S Yor 4D 92
Monken Hadley. G Lon 1D 38
Monk Fryston. N Yor 2F 93
Monk Hesleden. Dur 1B 106
Monkhide. Here 1B 48
Monkhill. Cumb 4E 113
Monkhopton. Shrp 1A 60
Monkland. Here 5G 59
Monkleigh. Devn 4E 19
Monknash. V Glam 4C 32
Monkokehampton. Devn 2F 11
Monkseaton. Tyne 2G 115
Monks Eleigh. Suff 1C 54
Monk's Gate. W Sus 3D 26
Monk's Heath. Ches E 3C 84
Monk Sherborne. Hants 1E 24
Monkshill. Abers 4E 161
Monksilver. Som 3D 20
Monks Kirby. Warw 2B 62
Monk Soham. Suff 4E 66
Monk Soham Green. Suff 4E 66
Monkspath. W Mid 3F 61
Monks Risborough. Buck 5G 51
Monksthorpe. Linc 4D 88
Monk Street. Essx 3G 53
Monkswood. Mon 5G 47
Monkton. Devn 2E 13
Monkton. Kent 4G 41
Monkton. Pemb 4D 42
Monkton. S Ayr 2C 116
Monkton Combe. Bath 5C 34
Monkton Deverill. Wilts 3D 22
Monkton Farleigh. Wilts 5D 34
Monkton Heathfield. Som 4F 21
Monktonhill. S Ayr 2C 116
Monkton Up Wimborne. Dors 1F 15
Monkton Wyld. Dors 3G 13
Monkwearmouth. Tyne 4G 115
Monkwood. Dors 3H 13
Monkwood. Hants 3E 25
Monmarsh. Here 1A 48
Monmouth. Mon 4A 48
Monnington on Wye. Here 1G 47
Monreith. Dum 5A 110
Montacute. Som 1H 13
Montford. Arg 3C 126
Montford. Shrp 4G 71
Montford Bridge. Shrp 4G 71
Montgarrie. Abers 2C 152
Montgarswood. E Ayr 2E 117
Montgomery. Powy 1E 58
Montgreenan. N Ayr 5E 127
Montrave. Fife 3F 137
Montrose. Ang 3G 145
Monxton. Hants 2B 24
Monyash. Derbs 4F 85
Monymusk. Abers 2D 152
Monzie. Per 1A 136
Moodiesburn. N Lan 2H 127
Moon's Green. Kent 3C 28
Moonzie. Fife 2F 137
Moor. Som 1H 13
The Moor. Kent 3B 28
Moor Allerton. W Yor 1C 92
Moorbath. Dors 3H 13
Moorbrae. Shet 3F 173
Moorby. Linc 4B 88
Moorcot. Here 5F 59
Moor Crichel. Dors 2E 15
Moor Cross. Devn 3C 8
Moordown. Bour 3F 15
Moore. Hal 2H 83
Moor End. E Yor 1B 94
Moorend. Dum 2D 112
Moorend. Glos
nr. Dursley 5C 48
nr. Gloucester 4D 48
Moorends. S Yor 3G 93
Moorgate. S Yor 1B 86
Moor Green. Wilts 5D 34
Moorgreen. Hants 1C 16
Moorgreen. Notts 1B 74
Moorhaigh. Notts 4C 86
Moorhall. Derbs 3H 85
Moorhampton. Here 1G 47
Moorhouse. Cumb
nr. Carlisle 4E 113
nr. Wigton 4D 112
Moorhouse. Notts 4E 87
Moorhouse. Surr 5F 39
Moorhouses. Linc 5B 88
Moorland. Som 3G 21
Moorlinch. Som 3H 21
Moor Monkton. N Yor 4H 99
Moor of Granary. Mor 3E 159
Moor Row. Cumb
nr. Whitehaven 3B 102
nr. Wigton 5D 112
Moorsholm. Red C 3D 107
Moorside. Dors 1C 14
Moorside. G Man 4H 91
Moortown. Devn 3D 10
Moortown. Hants 2G 15
Moortown. IOW 4C 16
Moortown. Linc 1H 87
Moortown. Telf 4A 72
Moortown. W Yor 1D 92
Morangie. High 5E 165
Morar. High 4E 147
Morborne. Cambs 1A 64
Morchard Bishop. Devn 2A 12
Morcombelake. Dors 3H 13
Morcott. Rut 5G 75
Morda. Shrp 3E 71
Morden. G Lon 4D 38
Mordiford. Here 2A 48
Mordon. Dur 2A 106
More. Shrp 1F 59
Morebath. Devn 4C 20
Morebattle. Bord 2B 120
Morecambe. Lanc 3D 96
Morefield. High 4F 163
Moreleigh. Devn 3D 8
Morenish. Per 5C 142
Moresby Parks. Cumb 3A 102
Morestead. Hants 4D 24
Moreton. Dors 4D 14
Moreton. Essx 5F 53
Moreton. Here 4H 59
Moreton. Mers 1E 83
Moreton. Oxon 5E 51
Moreton. Staf 4B 72
Moreton Corbet. Shrp 3H 71
Moretonhampstead. Devn 4A 12
Moreton-in-Marsh. Glos 2H 49
Moreton Jeffries. Here 1B 48
Moreton Morrell. Warw 5H 61
Moreton on Lugg. Here 1A 48
Moreton Pinkney. Nptn 1D 50
Moreton Say. Shrp 2A 72
Moreton Valence. Glos 5C 48
Morfa. Cdgn 5C 56
Morfa Bach. Carm 4D 44
Morfa Bychan. Gwyn 2E 69
Morfa Glas. Neat 5B 46
Morfa Nefyn. Gwyn 1B 68
Morganstown. Card 3E 33
Morgan's Vale. Wilts 4G 23
Morham. E Lot 2B 130
Moriah. Cdgn 3F 57
Morland. Cumb 2G 103
Morley. Ches E 2C 84
Morley. Derbs 1A 74
Morley. Dur 2E 105
Morley. W Yor 2C 92
Morley St Botolph. Norf 1C 66
Morningside. Edin 2F 129
Morningside. N Lan 4B 128
Morningthorpe. Norf 1E 66
Morpeth. Nmbd 1F 115
Morrey. Staf 4F 73
Morridge Side. Staf 5E 85
Morridge Top. Staf 4E 85
Morrington. Dum 1F 111
Morris Green. Essx 2H 53
Morriston. Swan 3F 31
Morston. Norf 1C 78
Mortehoe. Devn 2E 19
Morthen. S Yor 2B 86
Mortimer. W Ber 5E 37
Mortimer's Cross. Here 4G 59
Mortimer West End. Hants 5E 37
Mortomley. S Yor 1H 85
Morton. Cumb
nr. Calthwaite 1F 103
nr. Carlisle 4E 113
Morton. Derbs 4B 86
Morton. Linc
nr. Bourne 3H 75
nr. Gainsborough 1F 87
nr. Lincoln 4F 87
Morton. Norf 4D 78
Morton. Notts 5E 87
Morton. Shrp 3E 71
Morton. S Glo 2B 34
Morton Bagot. Warw 4F 61
Morton Mill. Shrp 3H 71
Morton-on-Swale. N Yor 5A 106
Morton Tinmouth. Dur 2E 105
Morvah. Corn 3B 4
Morval. Corn 3G 7
Morvich. High
nr. Golspie 3E 165
nr. Shiel Bridge 1B 148
Morvil. Pemb 1E 43
Morville. Shrp 1A 60
Morwenstow. Corn 1C 10
Morwick. Nmbd 4G 121
Mosborough. S Yor 2B 86
Moscow. E Ayr 5F 127
Mose. Shrp 1B 60
Mosedale. Cumb 1E 103
Moseley. W Mid
nr. Birmingham 2E 61
nr. Wolverhampton 5D 72
Moseley. Worc 5C 60
Moss. Arg 4A 138
Moss. High 2A 140
Moss. S Yor 3F 93
Moss. Wrex 5F 83
Mossatt. Abers 2B 152
Moss Bank. Mers 1H 83
Mossbank. Shet 4F 173
Mossblown. S Ayr 2D 116
Mossbrow. G Man 2B 84
Mossburnford. Bord 3A 120
Mossdale. Dum 2D 110
Mossedge. Cumb 3F 113
Mossend. N Lan 3A 128
Mossgate. Staf 2D 72
Moss Lane. Ches E 3D 84
Mossley. Ches E 4C 84
Mossley. G Man 4H 91
Mossley Hill. Mers 2F 83
Moss of Barmuckity. Mor 2G 159
Mosspark. Glas 3G 127
Mosspaul. Bord 5G 119
Moss Side. Cumb 4C 112
Moss Side. G Man 1C 84
Moss Side. Lanc
nr. Blackpool 1B 90
nr. Preston 2D 90
Moss Side. Mers 4B 90
Moss-side. High 3C 158
Moss-side of Cairness. Abers 2H 161
Mosstodloch. Mor 2H 159
Mosswood. Nmbd 4D 114
Mossy Lea. Lanc 3D 90
Mosterton. Dors 2H 13
Moston. Shrp 3H 71
Moston Green. Ches E 4B 84
Mostyn. Flin 2D 82
Mostyn Quay. Flin 2D 82
Motcombe. Dors 4D 22
Mothecombe. Devn 4C 8
Motherby. Cumb 2F 103
Motherwell. N Lan 4A 128
Mottingham. G Lon 3F 39
Mottisfont. Hants 4B 24
Mottistone. IOW 4C 16
Mottram in Longdendale.
G Man 1D 85
Mottram St Andrew. Ches E 3C 84
Mott's Mill. E Sus 2G 27
Mouldsworth. Ches W 3H 83
Moulin. Per 3G 143
Moulsecoomb. Brig 5E 27
Moulsford. Oxon 3D 36
Moulsoe. Mil 1H 51
Moulton. Ches W 4A 84
Moulton. Linc 3C 76
Moulton. Nptn 4E 63
Moulton. N Yor 4F 105
Moulton. Suff 4F 65
Moulton. V Glam 4D 32
Moulton Chapel. Linc 4B 76
Moulton Eaugate. Linc 4C 76
Moulton St Mary. Norf 5F 79
Moulton Seas End. Linc 3C 76
Mount. Corn
nr. Bodmin 2F 7
nr. Newquay 3B 6
Mountain Ash. Rhon 2D 32
Mountain Cross. Bord 5E 129
Mountain Street. Kent 5E 41
Mountain Water. Pemb 2D 42
Mount Ambrose. Corn 4B 6
Mountbenger. Bord 2F 119
Mountblow. W Dun 2F 127
Mount Bures. Essx 2C 54
Mountfield. E Sus 3B 28
Mountgerald. High 2H 157
Mount Hawke. Corn 4B 6
Mount High. High 2A 158
Mountjoy. Corn 2C 6
Mount Lothian. Midl 4F 129
Mountnessing. Essx 1H 39
Mounton. Mon 2A 34
Mount Pleasant. Buck 2E 51
Mount Pleasant. Ches E 5C 84
Mount Pleasant. Derbs
nr. Derby 1H 73
nr. Swadlincote 4G 73
Mount Pleasant. E Sus 4F 27
Mount Pleasant. Hants 3A 16
Mount Pleasant. Norf 1B 66
Mount Skippett. Oxon 4B 50
Mountsorrel. Leics 4C 74
Mount Stuart. Arg 4C 126
Mousehole. Corn 4B 4
Mouswald. Dum 2B 112
Mow Cop. Ches E 5C 84
Mowden. Darl 3F 105
Mowhaugh. Bord 2C 120
Mowmacre Hill. Leic 5C 74
Mowsley. Leics 2D 62
Moy. High 5B 158
Moylgrove. Pemb 1B 44
Moy Lodge. High 5G 149
Muasdale. Arg 5E 125
Muchalls. Abers 4G 153
Much Birch. Here 2A 48
Much Cowarne. Here 1B 48
Much Dewchurch. Here 2H 47
Muchelney. Som 4H 21
Muchelney Ham. Som 4H 21
Much Hadham. Herts 4E 53
Much Hoole. Lanc 2C 90
Muchlarnick. Corn 3G 7
Much Marcle. Here 2B 48
Muchrachd. High 5E 157
Much Wenlock. Shrp 5A 72
Mucking. Thur 2A 40
Muckle Breck. Shet 5G 173
Muckleford. Dors 3B 14
Mucklestone. Staf 2B 72
Muckleton. Norf 2H 77
Muckleton. Shrp 3H 71
Muckley. Shrp 1A 60
Muckley Corner. Staf 5E 73
Muckton. Linc 2C 88
Mudale. High 5F 167
Muddiford. Devn 3F 19
Mudeford. Dors 3G 15
Mudford. Som 1A 14
Mudgley. Som 2H 21
Mugdock. Stir 2G 127
Mugeary. High 5D 154
Muggington. Derbs 1G 73
Muggintonlane End. Derbs 1G 73
Muggleswick. Dur 4D 114
Mugswell. Surr 5D 38
Muie. High 3D 164
Muirden. Abers 3E 160
Muirdrum. Ang 5E 145
Muiredge. Per 1E 137
Muirend. Glas 3G 127
Muirhead. Ang 5C 144
Muirhead. Fife 3E 137
Muirhead. N Lan 3H 127
Muirhouses. Falk 1D 128
Muirkirk. E Ayr 2F 117
Muir of Alford. Abers 2C 152
Muir of Fairburn. High 3G 157
Muir of Fowlis. Abers 2C 152
Muir of Miltonduff. Mor 3F 159
Muir of Ord. High 3H 157
Muir of Tarradale. High 3H 157
Muirshearlich. High 5D 148
Muirtack. Abers 5G 161
Muirton. High 2B 158
Muirton. Per 1D 136
Muirton of Ardblair. Per 4A 144
Muirtown. Per 2B 136
Muiryfold. Abers 3E 161
Muker. N Yor 5C 104
Mulbarton. Norf 5D 78
Mulben. Mor 3A 160
Mulindry. Arg 4B 124
Mulla. Shet 5F 173
Mullach Charlabhaigh. W Isl 3E 171
Mullacott. Devn 2F 19
Mullion. Corn 5D 5
Mullion Cove. Corn 5D 4
Mumbles. Swan 4F 31
Mumby. Linc 3E 89
Munderfield Row. Here 5A 60
Munderfield Stocks. Here 5A 60
Mundesley. Norf 2F 79
Mundford. Norf 1H 65
Mundham. Norf 1F 67
Mundon. Essx 5B 54
Munerigie. High 3E 149
Muness. Shet 1H 173
Mungasdale. High 4D 162
Mungrisdale. Cumb 1E 103
Munlochy. High 3A 158
Munsley. Here 1B 48
Munslow. Shrp 2H 59
Murchington. Devn 4G 11
Murcot. Worc 1F 49
Murcott. Oxon 4D 50
Murdishaw. Hal 2H 83
Murieston. W Lot 3D 128
Murkle. High 2D 168
Murlaggan. High 4C 148
Murra. Orkn 7B 172
The Murray. S Lan 4H 127
Murrayfield. Edin 2F 129
Murrell Green. Hants 1F 25

Murroes – Newton

Murroes. Ang 5D 144
Murrow. Cambs 5C 76
Mursley. Buck 3G 51
Murthly. Per 5H 143
Murton. Cumb 2A 104
Murton. Dur 5G 115
Murton. Nmbd 5F 131
Murton. Swan 4E 31
Murton. York 4A 100
Musbury. Devn 3F 13
Muscoates. N Yor 1A 100
Muscott. Nptn 4D 62
Musselburgh. E Lot 2G 129
Muston. Leics 2F 75
Muston. N Yor 2E 101
Mustow Green. Worc 3C 60
Muswell Hill. G Lon 2D 39
Mutehill. Dum 5D 111
Mutford. Suff 2G 67
Muthill. Per 2A 136
Mutterton. Devn 2D 12
Muxton. Telf 4B 72
Mwmbwls. Swan 4F 31
Mybster. High 3D 168
Myddfai. Carm 2A 46
Myddle. Shrp 3G 71
Mydroilyn. Cdgn 5D 56
Myerscough. Lanc 1C 90
Mylor Bridge. Corn 5C 6
Mylor Churchtown. Corn 5C 6
Mynachlog-ddu. Pemb 1F 43
Mynydd-bach. Mon 2H 33
Mynydd Isa. Flin 4E 83
Mynyddislwyn. Cphy 2E 33
Mynydd Llandegai. Gwyn 4F 81
Mynydd Mechell. IOA 1C 80
Mynydd-y-briw. Powy 3D 70
Mynyddygarreg. Carm 5E 45
Mynytho. Gwyn 2C 68
Myrebird. Abers 4E 153
Myrelandhorn. High 3E 169
Mytchett. Surr 1G 25
The Mythe. Glos 2D 49
Mytholmroyd. W Yor 2A 92
Myton-on-Swale. N Yor 3G 99
Mytton. Shrp 4G 71

N

Naast. High 5C 162
Na Buirgh. W Isl 8C 171
Naburn. York 5H 99
Nab Wood. W Yor 1B 92
Nackington. Kent 5F 41
Nacton. Suff 1F 55
Nafferton. E Yor 4E 101
Na Gearrannan. W Isl 3D 171
Nailbridge. Glos 4B 48
Nailsbourne. Som 4F 21
Nailsea. N Som 4H 33
Nailstone. Leics 5B 74
Nailsworth. Glos 2D 34
Nairn. High 3C 158
Nalderswood. Surr 1D 26
Nancegollan. Corn 3D 4
Nancledra. Corn 3B 4
Nangreaves. G Man 3G 91
Nanhyfer. Pemb 1E 43
Nannerch. Flin 4D 82
Nanpantan. Leics 4C 74
Nanpean. Corn 3D 6
Nanstedan C2 6
Nanstallon. Corn 2E 7
Nant-ddu. Powy 4D 46
Nanternis. Cdgn 5C 56
Nantgaredig. Carm 3E 45
Nantgarw. Rhon 3E 33
Nant Glas. Powy 4B 58
Nantglyn. Den 4C 82
Nantgwyn. Powy 3B 58
Nantlle. Gwyn 5E 81
Nantmawr. Shrp 3E 71
Nantmel. Powy 4C 58
Nantmor. Gwyn 1F 69
Nant Peris. Gwyn 5F 81
Nantwich. Ches E 5A 84
Nant-y-bai. Carm 1A 46
Nant-y-bwch. Blae 4E 47
Nant-y-Derry. Mon 5G 47
Nant-y-dugoed. Powy 4B 70
Nant-y-felin. Cnwy 3F 81
Nantyffyllon. B'end 2B 32
Nantyglo. Blae 4E 47
Nant-y-meichiaid. Powy 4D 70
Nant-y-moel. B'end 2C 32
Nant-y-pandy. Cnwy 3F 81
Naphill. Buck 2G 37
Nappa. N Yor 4A 98
Napton on the Hill. Warw 4B 62
Narberth. Pemb 3F 43
Narberth Bridge. Pemb 3F 43
Narborough. Leics 1C 62
Narborough. Norf 4G 77
Narkurs. Corn 3H 7
The Narth. Mon 5A 48
Narthwaite. Cumb 5A 104
Nasareth. Gwyn 5D 80
Naseby. Nptn 3D 62
Nash. Buck 2F 51
Nash. Here 4F 59
Nash. Kent 5G 41
Nash. Newp 3G 33
Nash. Shrp 3A 60
Nash Lee. Buck 5G 51
Nassington. Nptn 1H 63
Nasty. Herts 3D 52
Natcott. Devn 4C 18
Nateby. Cumb 4A 104
Nateby. Lanc 5D 96
Nately Scures. Hants 1F 25
Natland. Cumb 1E 97
Naughton. Suff 1D 54
Naunton. Glos 3G 49
Naunton. Worc 2D 49
Naunton Beauchamp. Worc 5D 60
Navenby. Linc 5G 87
Navestock. Essx 1G 39
Navestock Side. Essx 1G 39
Navidale. High 2H 165
Nawton. N Yor 1A 100
Nayland. Suff 2C 54
Nazeing. Essx 5E 53
Neacroft. Hants 3G 15
Nealhouse. Cumb 4E 113
Neal's Green. Warw 2H 61
Near Sawrey. Cumb 5E 103
Neasden. G Lon 2D 38
Neasham. Darl 3A 106
Neath. Neat 2A 32
Neath Abbey. Neat 3G 31
Neatishead. Norf 3F 79
Neaton. Norf 5B 78
Nebo. Cdgn 4E 57
Nebo. Cnwy 5H 81
Nebo. Gwyn 5D 81
Nebo. IOA 1D 80
Necton. Norf 5A 78
Nedd. High 5B 166
Nedderton. Nmbd 1F 115
Nedging. Suff 1D 54
Nedging Tye. Suff 1D 54
Needham. Norf 2E 67
Needham Market. Suff 5C 66
Needham Street. Suff 4G 65
Needingworth. Cambs 3C 64
Needwood. Staf 3F 73
Neen Savage. Shrp 3A 60
Neen Sollars. Shrp 3A 60
Neenton. Shrp 2A 60
Nefyn. Gwyn 1C 68
Neilston. E Ren 4F 127
Neithrop. Oxon 1C 50
Nelly Andrews Green. Powy 5E 71
Nelson. Cphy 2E 32
Nelson. Lanc 1G 91
Nelson Village. Nmbd 2F 115
Nemphlar. S Lan 5B 128
Nempnett Thrubwell. Bath 5A 34
Nene Terrace. Linc 5B 76
Nenthall. Cumb 5A 114
Nenthead. Cumb 5A 114
Nenthorn. Bord 1A 120
Nercwys. Flin 4E 83
Neribus. Arg 4A 124
Nerston. S Lan 4H 127
Nesbit. Nmbd 1D 121
Nesfield. N Yor 5C 98
Ness. Ches W 3F 83
Nesscliffe. Shrp 4F 71
Ness of Tenston. Orkn 6B 172
Neston. Ches W 3E 83
Neston. Wilts 5D 34
Nethanfoot. S Lan 5B 128
Nether Alderley. Ches E 3C 84
Netheravon. Wilts 2G 23
Nether Blainslie. Bord 5B 130
Netherbrae. Abers 3E 161
Netherbrough. Orkn 6C 172
Nether Broughton. Leics 3D 74
Netherburn. S Lan 5B 128
Nether Burrow. Lanc 2F 97
Netherbury. Dors 3H 13
Netherby. Cumb 2E 113
Nether Careston. Ang 3E 145
Nether Cerne. Dors 3B 14
Nether Compton. Dors 1A 14
Nethercote. Glos 3G 49
Nethercote. Warw 4C 62
Nethercott. Devn 3E 19
Nethercott. Oxon 3C 50
Nether Dallachy. Mor 2A 160
Nether Durdie. Per 1E 136
Nether End. Derbs 3G 85
Netherend. Glos 5A 48
Nether Exe. Devn 2C 12
Netherfield. E Sus 4B 28
Netherfield. Notts 1D 74
Nethergate. Norf 3C 78
Netherhampton. Wilts 4G 23
Nether Handley. Derbs 3B 86
Nether Haugh. S Yor 1B 86
Nether Heage. Derbs 5A 86
Nether Heyford. Nptn 5D 62
Netherhouses. Cumb 1B 96
Nether Howcleugh. S Lan 3C 118
Nether Kellet. Lanc 3E 97
Nether Kinmundy. Abers 4H 161
Netherland Green. Staf 2F 73
Nether Langwith. Notts 3C 86
Netherlaw. Dum 5E 111
Netherley. Abers 4F 153
Nethermill. Dum 1B 112
Nethermills. Mor 3C 160
Nether Moor. Derbs 4A 86
Nether Padley. Derbs 3G 85
Netherplace. E Ren 4G 127
Nether Poppleton. York 4H 99
Netherseal. Derbs 4G 73
Nether Silton. N Yor 5B 106
Nether Stowey. Som 3E 21
Nether Street. Essx 4F 53
Netherstreet. Wilts 5E 35
Netherthird. E Ayr 3E 117
Netherthong. W Yor 4B 92
Netherton. Ang 3E 145
Netherton. Cumb 1B 102
Netherton. Devn 5B 12
Netherton. Hants 1B 24
Netherton. Here 3A 48
Netherton. Mers 1F 83
Netherton. N Lan 4A 128
Netherton. Nmbd 4D 121
Netherton. Per 3A 144
Netherton. Shrp 2B 60
Netherton. Stir 2G 127
Netherton. W Mid 2D 60
Netherton. W Yor
nr. Armitage Bridge 3B 92
nr. Horbury 3C 92
Netherton. Worc 1E 49
Nethertown. Cumb 4A 102
Nethertown. High 1F 169
Nethertown. Staf 4F 73
Nether Urquhart. Fife 3D 136
Nether Wallop. Hants 3B 24
Nether Wasdale. Cumb 4C 102
Nether Welton. Cumb 5E 113
Nether Westcote. Glos 3H 49
Nether Whitacre. Warw 1G 61
Nether Winchendon. Buck 4F 51
Netherwitton. Nmbd 5F 121
Nether Worton. Oxon 2C 50
Nethy Bridge. High 1E 151
Netley. Shrp 5G 71
Netley Abbey. Hants 2C 16
Netley Marsh. Hants 1B 16
Nettlebed. Oxon 3F 37
Nettlebridge. Som 2B 22
Nettlecombe. Dors 3A 14
Nettlecombe. IOW 5D 16
Nettleden. Herts 4A 52
Nettleham. Linc 3H 87
Nettlestead. Kent 5A 40
Nettlestead Green. Kent 5A 40
Nettlestone. IOW 3E 16
Nettlesworth. Dur 5F 115
Nettleton. Linc 4E 94
Nettleton. Wilts 4D 34
Netton. Devn 4B 8
Netton. Wilts 3G 23
Neuadd. Powy 5C 70
The Neuk. Abers 4E 153
Nevendon. Essx 1B 40
Nevern. Pemb 1E 43
New Abbey. Dum 3A 112
New Aberdour. Abers 2F 161
New Addington. G Lon 4E 39
Newall. W Yor 5E 98
New Alresford. Hants 3D 24
New Alyth. Per 4B 144
Newark. Orkn 3G 172
Newark. Pet 5B 76
Newark-on-Trent. Notts 5E 87
New Arley. Warw 2G 61
Newarthill. N Lan 4A 128
New Ash Green. Kent 4H 39
New Balderton. Notts 5F 87
New Barn. Kent 4H 39
New Barnetby. N Lin 3D 94
Newbattle. Midl 3G 129
New Bewick. Nmbd 2E 121
Newbie. Dum 3C 112
Newbiggin. Cumb
nr. Appleby 2H 103
nr. Barrow-in-Furness 3B 96
nr. Cumrew 5G 113
nr. Penrith 2F 103
nr. Seascale 5B 102
Newbiggin. Dur
nr. Consett 5E 115
nr. Holwick 2C 104
Newbiggin. Nmbd 5C 114
Newbiggin. N Yor
nr. Askrigg 5C 104
nr. Filey 1F 101
nr. Thoralby 1B 98
Newbiggin-by-the-Sea. Nmbd 1G 115
Newbigging. Ang
nr. Monikie 5D 145
nr. Newtyle 4B 144
nr. Tealing 5D 144
Newbigging. Edin 2E 129
Newbigging. S Lan 5D 128
Newbiggin-on-Lune. Cumb 4A 104
Newbold. Derbs 3A 86
Newbold. Leics 4B 74
Newbold on Avon. Warw 3B 62
Newbold on Stour. Warw 1H 49
Newbold Pacey. Warw 5G 61
Newbold Verdon. Leics 5B 74
New Bolingbroke. Linc 5C 88
Newborough. IOA 4D 80
Newborough. Pet 5B 76
Newborough. Staf 3F 73
Newbottle. Nptn 2D 50
Newbottle. Tyne 4G 115
New Boultham. Linc 3G 87
Newbourne. Suff 1F 55
New Brancepeth. Dur 5F 115
New Bridge. Dum 2G 111
Newbridge. Cphy 2F 33
Newbridge. Cdgn 5E 57
Newbridge. Corn 3B 4
Newbridge. Edin 2E 129
Newbridge. Hants 1A 16
Newbridge. IOW 4C 16
Newbridge. N Yor 1C 100
Newbridge. Pemb 1D 42
Newbridge. Wrex 1E 71
Newbridge Green. Worc 2D 48
Newbridge-on-Usk. Mon 2G 33
Newbridge on Wye. Powy 5C 58
New Brighton. Flin 4E 83
New Brighton. Hants 2F 17
New Brighton. Mers 1F 83
New Brinsley. Notts 5B 86
Newbrough. Nmbd 3B 114
New Broughton. Wrex 5F 83
New Buckenham. Norf 1C 66
Newbuildings. Devn 2A 12
Newburgh. Abers 1G 153
Newburgh. Fife 2E 137
Newburgh. Lanc 3C 90
Newburn. Tyne 3E 115
Newbury. W Ber 5C 36
Newbury. Wilts 2D 22
Newby. Cumb 2G 103
Newby. N Yor
nr. Ingleton 2G 97
nr. Scarborough 1E 101
nr. Stokesley 3C 106
Newby Bridge. Cumb 1C 96
Newby Cote. N Yor 2G 97
Newby East. Cumb 4F 113
Newby Head. Cumb 2G 103
New Byth. Abers 3F 161
Newby West. Cumb 4E 113
Newby Wiske. N Yor 1F 99
Newcastle. B'end 3B 32
Newcastle. Mon 4H 47
Newcastle. Shrp 2E 59
Newcastle Emlyn. Carm 1D 44
Newcastle International Airport. Tyne 2E 115
Newcastleton. Bord 1F 113
Newcastle-under-Lyme. Staf 1C 72
Newcastle upon Tyne. Tyne 205 (3F 115)
Newchapel. Pemb 1G 43
Newchapel. Powy 2B 58
Newchapel. Staf 5C 84
Newchapel. Surr 1E 27
New Cheriton. Hants 4D 24
Newchurch. Carm 3D 45
Newchurch. Here 5F 59
Newchurch. IOW 4D 16
Newchurch. Kent 2E 29
Newchurch. Lanc 2G 91
Newchurch. Mon 2H 33
Newchurch. Powy 5E 58
Newchurch. Staf 3F 73
Newchurch in Pendle. Lanc 1G 91
New Costessey. Norf 4D 78
Newcott. Devn 2F 13
New Cowper. Cumb 5C 112
Newcraighall. Edin 2G 129
New Crofton. W Yor 3D 93
New Cross. Cdgn 3F 57
New Cross. Som 1H 13
New Cumnock. E Ayr 3F 117
New Deer. Abers 4F 161
New Denham. Buck 2B 38
Newdigate. Surr 1C 26
New Duston. Nptn 4E 62
New Earswick. York 4A 100
New Edlington. S Yor 1C 86
New Elgin. Mor 2G 159
New Ellerby. E Yor 1E 95
Newell Green. Brac 4G 37
New Eltham. G Lon 3F 39
New End. Warw 4F 61
New End. Worc 5E 61
Newenden. Kent 3C 28
New England. Essx 1H 53
New England. Pet 5A 76
Newent. Glos 3C 48
New Ferry. Mers 2F 83
Newfield. Dur
nr. Chester-le-Street 4F 115
nr. Willington 1F 105
Newfound. Hants 1D 24
New Fryston. W Yor 2E 93
Newgale. Pemb 2C 42
New Galloway. Dum 2D 110
Newgate. Norf 1C 78
Newgate Street. Herts 5D 52
New Greens. Herts 5B 52
New Grimsby. IOS 1A 4
New Hainford. Norf 4E 78
Newhall. Ches E 1A 72
Newhall. Derbs 3G 73
Newham. Nmbd 2F 121
New Hartley. Nmbd 2G 115
Newhaven. Derbs 4F 85
Newhaven. E Sus 215 (5F 27)
Newhaven. Edin 2F 129
New Haw. Surr 4B 38
New Hedges. Pemb 4F 43
New Herrington. Tyne 4G 115
Newhey. G Man 3H 91
New Holkham. Norf 2A 78
New Holland. N Lin 2D 94
Newholm. N Yor 3F 107
New Houghton. Derbs 4C 86
New Houghton. Norf 3G 77
Newhouse. N Lan 3A 128
New Houses. N Yor 2H 97
New Hutton. Cumb 5G 103
New Hythe. Kent 5B 40
Newick. E Sus 3F 27
Newingreen. Kent 2F 29
Newington. Edin 2F 129
Newington. Kent
nr. Folkestone 2F 29
nr. Sittingbourne 4C 40
Newington. Notts 1D 86
Newington. Oxon 2E 36
Newington Bagpath. Glos 2D 34
New Inn. Carm 2E 45
New Inn. Mon 5H 47
New Inn. N Yor 2H 97
New Inn. Torf 2G 33
New Invention. Shrp 3E 59
New Kelso. High 4B 156
New Lanark. S Lan 5B 128
Newland. Glos 5A 48
Newland. Hull 1D 94
Newland. N Yor 2G 93
Newland. Som 3B 20
Newland. Worc 1C 48
Newlandrig. Midl 3G 129
Newlands. Cumb 1E 103
Newlands. High 4B 158
Newlands. Nmbd 4D 115
Newlands. Staf 3E 73
Newlands of Geise. High 2C 168
Newlands of Tynet. Mor 2A 160
Newlands Park. IOA 2B 80
New Lane. Lanc 3C 90
New Lane End. Warr 1A 84
New Langholm. Dum 1E 113
New Leake. Linc 5D 88
New Leeds. Abers 3G 161
New Lenton. Nott 2C 74
New Longton. Lanc 2D 90
Newlot. Orkn 6E 172
New Luce. Dum 3G 109
Newlyn. Corn 4B 4
Newmachar. Abers 2F 153
Newmains. N Lan 4B 128
New Mains of Ury. Abers 5F 153
New Malden. G Lon 4D 38
Newman's Green. Suff 1B 54
Newmarket. Suff 4F 65
Newmarket. W Isl 4G 171
New Marske. Red C 2D 106
New Marton. Shrp 2F 71
New Micklefield. W Yor 1E 93
New Mill. Abers 4E 160
New Mill. Corn 3B 4
New Mill. Herts 4H 51
New Mill. W Yor 4B 92
New Mill. Wilts 5G 35
Newmill. Mor 3B 160
Newmill. Bord 3G 119
Newmillerdam. W Yor 3D 92
New Mills. Corn 3C 6
New Mills. Derbs 2E 85
New Mills. Mon 5A 48
New Mills. Powy 5C 70
Newmills. Fife 1D 128
Newmills. High 2A 158
Newmiln. Per 5A 144
Newmilns. E Ayr 1E 117
New Milton. Hants 3H 15
New Mistley. Essx 2E 54
New Moat. Pemb 2E 43
Newmore. High
nr. Dingwall 3H 157
nr. Invergordon 1A 158
Newnham. Cambs 5D 64
Newnham. Glos 4B 48
Newnham. Hants 1F 25
Newnham. Herts 2C 52
Newnham. Kent 5D 40
Newnham. Nptn 5C 62
Newnham. Warw 4F 61
Newnham Bridge. Worc 4A 60
New Ollerton. Notts 4D 86
New Oscott. W Mid 1E 61
New Park. N Yor 4E 99
Newpark. Fife 2G 137
New Pitsligo. Abers 3F 161
New Polzeath. Corn 1D 6
Newport. Corn 4D 10
Newport. Devn 3F 19
Newport. E Yor 1B 94
Newport. Essx 2F 53
Newport. Glos 2B 34
Newport. High 1H 165
Newport. IOW 4D 16
Newport. Newp 205 (3G 33)
Newport. Norf 4H 79
Newport. Pemb 1E 43
Newport. Som 4G 21
Newport. Telf 4B 72
Newport-on-Tay. Fife 1G 137
Newport Pagnell. Mil 1G 51
Newpound Common. W Sus 3B 26
New Prestwick. S Ayr 2C 116
New Quay. Cdgn 5C 56
Newquay. Corn 2C 6
Newquay Cornwall Airport. Corn 2C 6
New Rackheath. Norf 4E 79
New Radnor. Powy 4E 58
New Rent. Cumb 1F 103
New Ridley. Nmbd 4D 114
New Romney. Kent 3E 29
New Rossington. S Yor 1D 86
New Row. Cdgn 3G 57
New Sauchie. Clac 4A 136
Newsbank. Ches E 4C 84
Newseat. Abers 5E 160
Newsham. Lanc 1D 90
Newsham. Nmbd 2G 115
Newsham. N Yor
nr. Richmond 3E 105
nr. Thirsk 1F 99
New Sharlston. W Yor 2D 93
Newsholme. E Yor 2H 93
Newsholme. Lanc 4H 97
New Shoreston. Nmbd 1F 121
New Springs. G Man 4D 90
Newstead. Notts 5C 86
Newstead. Bord 1H 119
New Stevenston. N Lan 4A 128
New Street. Here 5F 59
Newstreet Lane. Shrp 2A 72
New Swanage. Dors 4F 15
New Swannington. Leics 4B 74
Newthorpe. N Yor 1E 93
Newthorpe. Notts 1B 74
Newton. Arg 4H 133
Newton. B'end 4B 32
Newton. Cambs
nr. Cambridge 1E 53
nr. Wisbech 4D 76
Newton. Ches W
nr. Chester 4G 83
nr. Tattenhall 5H 83
Newton. Cumb 2B 96
Newton. Derbs 5B 86
Newton. Dors 1C 14

Newton. *Dum*
  nr. Annan 2D 112
  nr. Moffat 5D 118
Newton. *G Man* 1D 84
Newton. *Here*
  nr. Ewyas Harold 2G 47
  nr. Leominster 5H 59
Newton. *High*
  nr. Cromarty 2B 158
  nr. Inverness 4B 158
  nr. Kylestrome 5C 166
  nr. Wick 4F 169
Newton. *Lanc*
  nr. Blackpool 1B 90
  nr. Carnforth 2E 97
  nr. Clitheroe 4F 97
Newton. *Linc* 2H 75
Newton. *Mers* 2E 83
Newton. *Mor* 2F 159
Newton. *Norf* 4H 77
Newton. *Nptn* 2F 63
Newton. *Nmbd* 3D 114
Newton. *Notts* 1D 74
Newton. *Bord* 2A 120
Newton. *Shet* 8E 173
Newton. *Shrp*
  nr. Bridgnorth 1B 60
  nr. Wem 2G 71
Newton. *Som* 3E 20
Newton. *S Lan*
  nr. Glasgow 3H 127
  nr. Lanark 1B 118
Newton. *Staf* 3E 73
Newton. *Suff* 1C 54
Newton. *Swan* 4F 31
Newton. *Warw* 3C 62
Newton. *W Lot* 2D 129
Newton. *Wilts* 4H 23
Newton Abbot. *Devn* 5B 12
Newtonairds. *Dum* 1F 111
Newton Arlosh. *Cumb* 4D 112
Newton Aycliffe. *Dur* 2F 105
Newton Bewley. *Hart* 2B 106
Newton Blossomville. *Mil* 5G 63
Newton Bromswold. *Nptn* 4G 63
Newton Burgoland. *Leics* 5A 74
Newton by Toft. *Linc* 2H 87
Newton Ferrers. *Devn* 4B 8
Newton Flotman. *Norf* 1E 66
Newtongrange. *Midl* 3G 129
Newton Green. *Mon* 2A 34
Newton Hall. *Dur* 5F 115
Newton Hall. *Nmbd* 3D 114
Newton Harcourt. *Leics* 1D 62
Newton Heath. *G Man* 4G 91
Newton Hill. *W Yor* 2D 92
Newtonhill. *Abers* 4G 153
Newtonhill. *High* 4H 157
Newton Ketton. *Darl* 2A 106
Newton Kyme. *N Yor* 5G 99
Newton-le-Willows. *Mers* . 1H 83
Newton-le-Willows. *N Yor* 1E 98
Newton Longville. *Buck* 2G 51
Newton Mearns. *E Ren* 4G 127
Newtonmore. *High* 4B 150
Newton Morrell. *N Yor* 4F 105
Newton Mulgrave. *N Yor* 3E 107
Newton of Ardtoe. *High* 1A 140
Newton of Balcanquhal.
  Per 2D 136
Newton of Beltrees. *Ren* 4E 127
Newton of Falkland. *Fife* 3E 137
Newton of Mountblairy.
  Abers 3D 160
Newton of Pitcairns. *Per* 2C 136
Newton-on-Ouse. *N Yor* 4H 99
Newton-on-Rawcliffe. *N Yor* .. 5F 107
Newton on the Hill. *Shrp* 3G 71
Newton-on-the-Moor.
  Nmbd 4F 121
Newton on Trent. *Linc* 3F 87
Newton Poppleford. *Devn* 4D 12
Newton Purcell. *Oxon* 2E 51
Newton Regis. *Warw* 5G 73
Newton Reigny. *Cumb* 1F 103
Newton Rigg. *Cumb* 1F 103
Newton St Cyres. *Devn* 3B 12
Newton St Faith. *Norf* 4E 78
Newton St Loe. *Bath* 5C 34
Newton St Petrock. *Devn* 1E 11
Newton Solney. *Derbs* 3G 73
Newton Stacey. *Hants* 2C 24
Newton Stewart. *Dum* 3B 110
Newton Toney. *Wilts* 2H 23
Newton Tony. *Wilts* 2H 23
Newton Tracey. *Devn* 4F 19
Newton under Roseberry.
  Red C 3C 106
Newton upon Ayr. *S Ayr* 2C 116
Newton upon Derwent.
  E Yor 5B 100
Newton Valence. *Hants* 3F 25
Newton-with-Scales. *Lanc* 1C 90
New Town. *Dors* 1E 15
New Town. *E Lot* 2H 129
New Town. *Lutn* 3A 52
New Town. *W Yor* 2E 93
Newtown. *Abers* 2E 160
Newtown. *Cambs* 4H 63
Newtown. *Corn* 5C 10
Newtown. *Cumb*
  nr. Aspatria 5B 112
  nr. Brampton 3G 113
  nr. Penrith 2G 103
Newtown. *Derbs* 2D 85
Newtown. *Devn* 4A 20
Newtown. *Devn* 2H 13
Newtown. *Falk* 1C 128
Newtown. *Glos*
  nr. Lydney 5B 48
  nr. Tewkesbury 2E 49

Newtown. *Hants*
  nr. Bishop's Waltham 1D 16
  nr. Liphook 3G 25
  nr. Lyndhurst 1A 16
  nr. Newbury 5C 36
  nr. Romsey 4B 24
  nr. Warsash 2C 16
  nr. Wickham 1E 16
Newtown. *Here*
  nr. Little Dewchurch 2A 48
  nr. Stretton Grandison 1B 48
Newtown. *High* 3F 149
Newtown. *IOM* 4C 108
Newtown. *IOW* 3C 16
Newtown. *Lanc* 3D 90
Newtown. *Nmbd*
  nr. Rothbury 4E 121
  nr. Wooler 2E 121
Newtown. *Pool* 3F 15
Newtown. *Powy* 1D 58
Newtown. *Rhon* 2D 32
Newtown. *Shet* 3F 173
Newtown. *Shrp* 2G 71
Newtown. *Som* 1F 13
Newtown. *Staf*
  nr. Biddulph 4D 84
  nr. Cannock 5D 73
  nr. Longnor 4E 85
Newtown. *Wilts* 4E 23
Newtown-in-St Martin. *Corn* .. 4E 5
Newtown Linford. *Leics* 5C 74
Newtown St Boswells.
  Bord 1H 119
Newtown Unthank. *Leics* 5B 74
New Tredegar. *Cphy* 5E 47
Newtyle. *Ang* 4B 144
New Village. *E Yor* 1D 94
New Village. *S Yor* 4F 93
New Walsoken. *Cambs* 5D 76
New Waltham. *NE Lin* 4F 95
New Winton. *E Lot* 2H 129
New World. *Cambs* 1C 64
New Yatt. *Oxon* 4B 50
Newyears Green. *G Lon* 2B 38
New York. *Linc* 5B 88
New York. *Tyne* 2G 115
Nextend. *Here* 5F 59
Neyland. *Pemb* 4D 42
Nib Heath. *Shrp* 4G 71
Nicholashayne. *Devn* 1E 12
Nicholaston. *Swan* 4E 31
Nidd. *N Yor* 3F 99
Niddrie. *Edin* 2G 129
Niddry. *W Lot* 2D 129
Nigg. *Aber* 3G 153
Nigg. *High* 1C 158
Nigg Ferry. *High* 2B 158
Nightcott. *Som* 4B 20
Nimmer. *Som* 1G 13
Nine Ashes. *Essx* 5F 53
Ninebanks. *Nmbd* 4A 114
Nine Elms. *Swin* 3G 35
Ninemile Bar. *Dum* 2F 111
Nine Mile Burn. *Midl* 4E 129
Ninfield. *E Sus* 4B 28
Ningwood. *IOW* 4C 16
Nisbet. *Bord* 2A 120
Nisbet Hill. *Bord* 4D 130
Niton. *IOW* 5D 16
Nitshill. *Glas* 3G 127
Niwbwrch. *IOA* 4D 80
Noak Hill. *G Lon* 1G 39
Nobold. *Shrp* 4G 71
Nobottle. *Nptn* 4D 62
Nocton. *Linc* 4H 87
Nogdam End. *Norf* 5F 79
Noke. *Oxon* 4D 50
Nolton. *Pemb* 3C 42
Nolton Haven. *Pemb* 3C 42
No Man's Heath. *Ches W* 1H 71
No Man's Heath. *Warw* 5G 73
Nomansland. *Devn* 1B 12
Nomansland. *Wilts* 1A 16
Noneley. *Shrp* 3G 71
Noness. *Shet* 9F 173
Nonikiln. *High* 1A 158
Nonington. *Kent* 5G 41
Nook. *Cumb*
  nr. Longtown 2F 113
  nr. Milnthorpe 1E 97
Noranside. *Ang* 2D 144
Norbreck. *Bkpl* 5C 96
Norbridge. *Here* 1C 48
Norbury. *Ches E* 1H 71
Norbury. *Derbs* 1F 73
Norbury. *Shrp* 1F 59
Norbury. *Staf* 3B 72
Norby. *N Yor* 1G 99
Norby. *Shet* 6C 173
Norcross. *Lanc* 5C 96
Nordelph. *Norf* 5E 77
Norden. *G Man* 3G 91
Nordley. *Shrp* 1A 60
Norham. *Nmbd* 5F 131
Norland Town. *W Yor* 2A 92
Norley. *Ches W* 3H 83
Norleywood. *Hants* 3B 16
Normanby. *N Lin* 3B 94
Normanby. *N Yor* 1B 100
Normanby. *Red C* 3C 106
Normanby-by-Spital. *Linc* 2H 87
Normanby le Wold. *Linc* 1A 88
Norman Cross. *Cambs* 1A 64
Normandy. *Surr* 5A 38
Norman's Bay. *E Sus* 5A 28
Norman's Green. *Devn* 2D 12
Normanton. *Derb* 2H 73
Normanton. *Leics* 1F 75
Normanton. *Notts* 5E 86
Normanton. *W Yor* 2D 93
Normanton le Heath. *Leics* ... 4A 74

Normanton-on-Cliffe. *Linc* ... 1G 75
Normanton on Soar. *Notts* 3C 74
Normanton-on-the-Wolds.
  Notts 2D 74
Normanton on Trent. *Notts* ... 4E 87
Normoss. *Lanc* 1B 90
Norrington Common. *Wilts* 5D 35
Norris Green. *Mers* 1F 83
Norris Hill. *Leics* 4H 73
Norristhorpe. *W Yor* 2C 92
Northacre. *Norf* 1B 66
Northall. *Buck* 3H 51
Northallerton. *N Yor* 5A 106
Northam. *Devn* 4E 19
Northam. *Sotn* 1C 16
Northampton. *Nptn* 206 (4E 63)
North Anston. *S Yor* 2C 86
North Ascot. *Brac* 4A 38
North Aston. *Oxon* 3C 50
Northaw. *Herts* 5C 52
North Baddesley. *Hants* 4B 24
North Balfern. *Dum* 4B 110
North Ballachulish. *High* 2E 141
North Barrow. *Som* 4B 22
North Barsham. *Norf* 2B 78
Northbeck. *Linc* 1H 75
North Benfleet. *Essx* 2B 40
North Bersted. *W Sus* 5A 26
North Berwick. *E Lot* 1B 130
North Bitchburn. *Dur* 1E 105
North Blyth. *Nmbd* 1G 115
North Boarhunt. *Hants* 1E 16
North Bockhampton.
  Dors 3G 15
Northborough. *Pet* 5A 76
Northbourne. *Kent* 5H 41
Northbourne. *Oxon* 3D 36
North Bovey. *Devn* 4H 11
North Bowood. *Dors* 3H 13
North Bradley. *Wilts* 1D 22
North Brentor. *Devn* 4E 11
North Brewham. *Som* 3C 22
Northbrook. *Oxon* 3C 50
North Brook End. *Cambs* 1C 52
North Broomhill. *Nmbd* 4G 121
North Buckland. *Devn* 2E 19
North Burlingham. *Norf* 4F 79
North Cadbury. *Som* 4B 22
North Carlton. *Linc* 3G 87
North Cave. *E Yor* 1B 94
North Cerney. *Glos* 5F 49
North Chailey. *E Sus* 3E 27
Northchapel. *W Sus* 3A 26
North Charford. *Hants* 1G 15
North Charlton. *Nmbd* 2F 121
North Cheriton. *Som* 4B 22
North Chideock. *Dors* 3H 13
North Cliffe. *E Yor* 1B 94
North Clifton. *Notts* 3F 87
North Close. *Dur* 1F 105
North Cockerington. *Linc* 1C 88
North Coker. *Som* 1A 14
North Collafirth. *Shet* 3E 173
North Common. *E Sus* 3E 27
North Commonty. *Abers* 4F 161
North Coombe. *Devn* 1B 12
North Cornelly. *B'end* 3B 32
North Cotes. *Linc* 4G 95
Northcott. *Devn*
  nr. Boyton 3D 10
  nr. Culmstock 1D 12
Northcourt. *Oxon* 2D 36
North Cove. *Suff* 2G 67
North Cowton. *N Yor* 4F 105
North Craigo. *Ang* 2F 145
North Crawley. *Mil* 1H 51
North Cray. *G Lon* 3F 39
North Creake. *Norf* 2A 78
North Curry. *Som* 4G 21
North Dalton. *E Yor* 4D 100
North Deighton. *N Yor* 4F 99
North Dronley. *Ang* 5C 144
North Duffield. *N Yor* 1G 93
Northdyke. *Orkn* 5B 172
Northedge. *Derbs* 4A 86
North Elkington. *Linc* 1B 88
North Elmham. *Norf* 3B 78
North Elmsall. *W Yor* 3E 93
North End. *E Yor* 1F 95
North End. *Essx*
  nr. Great Dunmow 4G 53
  nr. Great Yeldham 2A 54
North End. *Hants* 5C 36
North End. *Leics* 4D 74
North End. *Linc* 1B 76
North End. *Norf* 1B 66
North End. *N Som* 5H 33
North End. *Port* 2E 17
North End. *W Sus* 5C 26
North End. *Wilts* 2F 35
Northend. *Buck* 2F 37
Northend. *Warw* 5A 62
North Erradale. *High* 5B 162
North Evington. *Leic* 5D 74
North Fambridge. *Essx* 1C 40
North Fearns. *High* 5E 155
North Featherstone. *W Yor* ... 2E 93
North Ferriby. *E Yor* 2C 94
Northfield. *Aber* 3F 153
Northfield. *E Yor* 2D 94
Northfield. *Som* 3F 21
Northfield. *W Mid* 3E 61
Northfleet. *Kent* 3H 39
North Frodingham. *E Yor* 4F 101
Northgate. *Linc* 3A 76
North Gluss. *Shet* 4E 173
North Gorley. *Hants* 1G 15
North Green. *Norf* 2E 66

North Green. *Suff*
  nr. Framlingham 4F 67
  nr. Halesworth 3F 67
  nr. Saxmundham 4F 67
North Greetwell. *Linc* 3H 87
North Grimston. *N Yor* 3C 100
North Halling. *Medw* 4B 40
North Hayling. *Hants* 2F 17
North Hazelrigg. *Nmbd* 1E 121
North Heasley. *Devn* 3H 19
North Heath. *W Sus* 3B 26
North Hill. *Corn* 5C 10
North Holmwood. *Surr* 1C 26
North Huish. *Devn* 3D 8
North Hykeham. *Linc* 4G 87
Northiam. *E Sus* 3C 28
Northill. *C Beds* 1B 52
Northington. *Hants* 3D 24
North Kelsey. *Linc* 4D 94
North Kelsey Moor. *Linc* 4D 94
North Kessock. *High* 4A 158
North Killingholme. *N Lin* ... 3E 95
North Kilvington. *N Yor* 1G 99
North Kilworth. *Leics* 2D 62
North Kyme. *Linc* 5A 88
North Lancing. *W Sus* 5C 26
Northlands. *Linc* 5C 88
Northleach. *Glos* 4G 49
North Lee. *Buck* 5G 51
North Lees. *N Yor* 2E 99
North Leigh. *Kent* 1F 29
North Leigh. *Oxon* 4B 50
Northleigh. *Devn*
  nr. Barnstaple 3G 19
  nr. Honiton 3E 13
North Leverton. *Notts* 2E 87
Northlew. *Devn* 3F 11
North Littleton. *Worc* 1F 49
North Lopham. *Norf* 2C 66
North Luffenham. *Rut* 5G 75
North Marden. *W Sus* 1G 17
North Marston. *Buck* 3F 51
North Middleton. *Midl* 4G 129
North Middleton. *Nmbd* 2E 121
North Molton. *Devn* 4H 19
North Moor. *N Yor* 1D 100
Northmoor. *Oxon* 5C 50
Northmoor Green. *Som* 3G 21
North Moreton. *Oxon* 3D 36
Northmuir. *Ang* 3C 144
North Mundham. *W Sus* 2G 17
North Murie. *Per* 1E 137
North Muskham. *Notts* 5E 87
North Ness. *Orkn* 8C 172
North Newbald. *E Yor* 1C 94
North Newington. *Oxon* 2C 50
North Newnton. *Wilts* 1G 23
North Newton. *Som* 3F 21
Northney. *Hants* 2F 17
North Nibley. *Glos* 2C 34
North Oakley. *Hants* 1D 24
North Ockendon. *G Lon* 2G 39
Northolt. *G Lon* 2C 38
Northop. *Flin* 4E 83
Northop Hall. *Flin* 4E 83
North Ormesby. *Midd* 3C 106
North Ormsby. *Linc* 1B 88
Northorpe. *Linc*
  nr. Bourne 4H 75
  nr. Donington 2B 76
  nr. Gainsborough 1F 87
North Otterington. *N Yor* 1F 99
Northover. *Som*
  nr. Glastonbury 3H 21
  nr. Yeovil 4A 22
North Owersby. *Linc* 1H 87
Northowram. *W Yor* 2B 92
North Perrott. *Som* 2H 13
North Petherton. *Som* 3F 21
North Petherwin. *Corn* 4C 10
North Pickenham. *Norf* 5A 78
North Piddle. *Worc* 5D 60
North Poorton. *Dors* 3A 14
North Port. *Arg* 1H 133
Northport. *Dors* 4E 15
North Queensferry. *Fife* 1E 129
North Radworthy. *Devn* 3A 20
North Rauceby. *Linc* 1H 75
Northrepps. *Norf* 2E 79
North Rigton. *N Yor* 5E 99
North Rode. *Ches E* 4C 84
North Roe. *Shet* 3E 173
North Ronaldsay Airport.
  Orkn 2G 172
North Row. *Cumb* 1D 102
North Runcton. *Norf* 4F 77
North Sannox. *N Ayr* 5B 126
North Scale. *Cumb* 2A 96
North Scarle. *Linc* 4F 87
North Seaton. *Nmbd* 1F 115
North Seaton Colliery. *Nmbd* . 1F 115
North Sheen. *G Lon* 3C 38
North Shields. *Tyne* 3G 115
North Shoebury. *S'end* 2D 40
North Shore. *Bkpl* 1B 90
North Side. *Cumb* 2B 102
North Skelton. *Red C* 3D 106
North Somercotes. *Linc* 1D 88
North Stainley. *N Yor* 2E 99
North Stainmore. *Cumb* 3B 104
North Stifford. *Thur* 2H 39
North Stoke. *Bath* 5C 34
North Stoke. *Oxon* 3E 36
North Stoke. *W Sus* 4B 26
Northstowe. *Cambs* 4D 64
North Street. *Hants* 3E 25
North Street. *Kent* 5E 40
North Street. *Medw* 3C 40
North Street. *W Ber* 4E 37
North Sunderland. *Nmbd* 1G 121

North Tamerton. *Corn* 3D 10
North Tawton. *Devn* 2G 11
North Thoresby. *Linc* 1B 88
North Tidworth. *Wilts* 2H 23
North Town. *Devn* 2F 11
North Town. *Shet* 10E 173
Northtown. *Orkn* 8D 172
North Tuddenham. *Norf* 4C 78
North Walbottle. *Tyne* 3E 115
Northwall. *Orkn* 3G 172
North Walney. *Cumb* 3A 96
North Walsham. *Norf* 2E 79
North Waltham. *Hants* 2D 24
North Warnborough. *Hants* 1F 25
North Water Bridge. *Ang* 2F 145
North Watten. *High* 3E 169
Northway. *Glos* 2E 49
Northway. *Swan* 4E 31
North Weald Bassett. *Essx* ... 5F 53
North Weston. *N Som* 4H 33
North Weston. *Oxon* 5E 51
North Wheatley. *Notts* 2E 87
North Whilborough. *Devn* 2E 9
Northwich. *Ches W* 3A 84
North Wick. *Bath* 5A 34
Northwick. *Som* 2G 21
Northwick. *S Glo* 3A 34
North Widcombe. *Bath* 1A 22
North Willingham. *Linc* 2A 88
North Wingfield. *Derbs* .. 4B 86
North Witham. *Linc* 3G 75
Northwold. *Norf* 1G 65
Northwood. *Derbs* 4G 85
Northwood. *G Lon* 1B 38
Northwood. *IOW* 3C 16
Northwood. *Kent* 4H 41
Northwood. *Shrp* 2G 71
Northwood. *Stoke* 1C 72
Northwood Green. *Glos* 4C 48
North Wootton. *Dors* 1B 14
North Wootton. *Norf* 3F 77
North Wootton. *Som* 2A 22
North Wraxall. *Wilts* 4D 34
North Wroughton. *Swin* 3G 35
North Yardhope. *Nmbd* 4D 120
Norton. *Devn* 3E 9
Norton. *Glos* 3D 48
Norton. *Hal* 2H 83
Norton. *Herts* 2C 52
Norton. *IOW* 4B 16
Norton. *Mon* 3H 47
Norton. *Nptn* 4D 62
Norton. *Notts* 3C 86
Norton. *Powy* 4F 59
Norton. *Shrp*
  nr. Ludlow 2G 59
  nr. Madeley 5B 72
  nr. Shrewsbury 5H 71
Norton. *S Yor*
  nr. Askern 3F 93
  nr. Sheffield 2A 86
Norton. *Stoc T* 2B 106
Norton. *Suff* 4B 66
Norton. *Swan* 4F 31
Norton. *W Sus*
  nr. Selsey 3G 17
  nr. Westergate 5A 26
Norton. *Wilts* 3D 35
Norton. *Worc*
  nr. Evesham 1F 49
  nr. Worcester 5C 60
Norton Bavant. *Wilts* 2E 23
Norton Bridge. *Staf* 2C 72
Norton Canes. *Staf* 5E 73
Norton Canon. *Here* 1G 47
Norton Corner. *Norf* 3C 78
Norton Disney. *Linc* 5F 87
Norton East. *Staf* 5E 73
Norton Ferris. *Wilts* 3C 22
Norton Fitzwarren. *Som* 4F 21
Norton Green. *IOW* 4B 16
Norton Green. *Stoke* 5D 84
Norton Hawkfield. *Bath* 5A 34
Norton Heath. *Essx* 5F 53
Norton in Hales. *Shrp* 2B 72
Norton in the Moors. *Stoke* .. 5C 84
Norton-Juxta-Twycross. *Leics* .. 5H 73
Norton-le-Clay. *N Yor* 2G 99
Norton Lindsey. *Warw* 4G 61
Norton Little Green. *Suff* ... 4B 66
Norton Malreward. *Bath* 5B 34
Norton Mandeville. *Essx* 5F 53
Norton-on-Derwent. *N Yor* 2B 100
Norton St Philip. *Som* 1C 22
Norton Subcourse. *Norf* 1G 67
Norton sub Hamdon. *Som* 1H 13
Norton Woodseats. *S Yor* 2A 86
Norwell. *Notts* 4E 87
Norwell Woodhouse. *Notts* 4E 87
Norwich. *Norf* 205 (5E 79)
Norwich Airport. *Norf* 4E 79
Norwick. *Shet* 1H 173
Norwood. *Derbs* 2B 86
Norwood Green. *W Yor* 2B 92
Norwood Hill. *Surr* 1D 26
Norwood Park. *Som* 3A 22
Norwoodside. *Cambs* 1D 64
Noseley. *Leics* 1E 63
Noss. *Shet* 10E 173
Noss Mayo. *Devn* 4B 8
Nosterfield. *N Yor* 1E 99
Nostie. *High* 1A 148
Notgrove. *Glos* 3G 49
Nottage. *B'end* 4B 32
Nottingham. *Nott* 206 (1C 74)
Notton. *Dors* 3B 14
Notton. *W Yor* 3D 92
Notton. *Wilts* 5E 35
Nounsley. *Essx* 4A 54
Noutard's Green. *Worc* 4B 60

Nox – Paddington

Nox. Shrp 4G 71
Noyadd Trefawr. Cdgn 1C 44
Nuffield. Oxon 3E 37
Nunburnholme. E Yor 5C 100
Nuncargate. Notts 5C 86
Nunclose. Cumb 5F 113
Nuneaton. Warw 1A 62
Nuneham Courtenay. Oxon 2D 36
Nun Monkton. N Yor 4H 99
Nunnerie. S Lan 3B 118
Nunney. Som 2C 22
Nunnington. N Yor 2A 100
Nunnykirk. Nmbd 5E 121
Nunsthorpe. NE Lin 4F 95
Nunthorpe. Midd 3C 106
Nunthorpe. York 4H 99
Nunton. Wilts 4G 23
Nunwick. Nmbd 2B 114
Nunwick. N Yor 2F 99
Nupend. Glos 5C 48
Nursling. Hants 1B 16
Nursted. Hants 4F 25
Nursteed. Wilts 5F 35
Nurston. V Glam 5D 32
Nutbourne. W Sus
nr. Chichester 2F 17
nr. Pulborough 4B 26
Nutfield. Surr 5E 39
Nuthall. Notts 1C 74
Nuthampstead. Herts 2E 53
Nuthurst. Warw 3F 61
Nuthurst. W Sus 3C 26
Nutley. E Sus 3F 27
Nuttall. G Man 3F 91
Nutwell. S Yor 4G 93
Nybster. High 2F 169
Nyetimber. W Sus 3G 17
Nyewood. W Sus 4G 25
Nymet Rowland. Devn 2H 11
Nymet Tracey. Devn 2H 11
Nympsfield. Glos 5D 48
Nynehead. Som 4E 21
Nyton. W Sus 5A 26

O

Oadby. Leics 5D 74
Oad Street. Kent 4C 40
Oakamoor. Staf 1E 73
Oakbank. Arg 5B 140
Oakbank. W Lot 3D 129
Oakdale. Cphy 2E 33
Oakdale. Pool 3F 15
Oake. Som 4E 21
Oaken. Staf 5C 72
Oakenclough. Lanc 5E 97
Oakengates. Telf 4A 72
Oakenholt. Flin 3E 83
Oakenshaw. Dur 1F 105
Oakenshaw. W Yor 2B 92
Oakerthorpe. Derbs 5A 86
Oakford. Cdgn 5D 56
Oakford. Devn 4C 20
Oakfordbridge. Devn 4C 20
Oakgrove. Ches E 4D 84
Oakham. Rut 5F 75
Oakhanger. Ches E 5B 84
Oakhanger. Hants 3F 25
Oakhill. Som 2B 22
Oakington. Cambs 4D 64
Oaklands. Powy 5C 58
Oakle Street. Glos 4C 48
Oakley. Bed 5H 63
Oakley. Buck 4E 51
Oakley. Fife 1D 128
Oakley. Hants 1D 24
Oakley. Suff 3D 66
Oakley Green. Wind 3A 38
Oakley Park. Powy 2B 58
Oakmere. Ches W 4H 83
Oakridge Lynch. Glos 5E 49
Oaks. Shrp 5G 71
Oaksey. Wilts 2E 35
Oaks Green. Derbs 2F 73
Oakshaw Ford. Cumb 2G 113
Oakshott. Hants 4F 25
Oakthorpe. Leics 4H 73
Oak Tree. Darl 3A 106
Oakwood. Derb 2A 74
Oakwood. W Yor 1D 92
Oakwoodhill. Surr 2C 26
Oakworth. W Yor 1A 92
Oape. High 3B 164
Oare. Kent 4E 40
Oare. Som 2B 20
Oare. W Ber 4D 36
Oare. Wilts 5G 35
Oareford. Som 2B 20
Oasby. Linc 2H 75
Oath. Som 4G 21
Oathlaw. Ang 3D 145
Oatlands. N Yor 4F 99
Oban. Arg 206 (1F 133)
Oban. W Isl 7D 171
Oborne. Dors 1B 14
Obsdale. High 2A 158
Obthorpe. Linc 4H 75
Occlestone Green. Ches W 4A 84
Occold. Suff 3D 66
Ochiltree. E Ayr 2E 117
Ochtermuthill. Per 2H 135
Ochtertyre. Per 1H 135
Ockbrook. Derbs 2B 74
Ockeridge. Worc 4B 60
Ockham. Surr 5B 38
Ockle. High 1G 139
Ockley. Surr 1C 26
Ocle Pychard. Here 1A 48
Octofad. Arg 4A 124
Octomore. Arg 4A 124
Octon. E Yor 3E 101
Odcombe. Som 1A 14
Odd Down. Bath 5C 34
Oddingley. Worc 5D 60
Oddington. Oxon 4D 50
Oddsta. Shet 2G 173
Odell. Bed 5G 63
Odie. Orkn 5F 172
Odiham. Hants 1F 25
Odsey. Cambs 2C 52
Odstock. Wilts 4G 23
Odstone. Leics 5A 74
Offchurch. Warw 4A 62
Offenham. Worc 1F 49
Offenham Cross. Worc 1F 49
Offerton. G Man 2D 84
Offerton. Tyne 4G 115
Offham. E Sus 4E 27
Offham. Kent 5A 40
Offham. W Sus 5B 26
Offleyhay. Staf 3C 72
Offley Hoo. Herts 3B 52
Offleymarsh. Staf 3B 72
Offord Cluny. Cambs 4B 64
Offord D'Arcy. Cambs 4B 64
Offton. Suff 1D 54
Offwell. Devn 3E 13
Ogbourne Maizey. Wilts 4G 35
Ogbourne St Andrew. Wilts 4G 35
Ogbourne St George. Wilts 4H 35
Ogden. G Man 3H 91
Ogle. Nmbd 2E 115
Ogmore. V Glam 4B 32
Ogmore-by-Sea. V Glam 4B 32
Ogmore Vale. B'end 2C 32
Okeford Fitzpaine. Dors 1D 14
Okehampton. Devn 3F 11
Okehampton Camp. Devn 3F 11
Okraquoy. Shet 8F 173
Okus. Swin 3G 35
Old. Nptn 3E 63
Old Aberdeen. Aber 3G 153
Old Alresford. Hants 3D 24
Oldany. High 5B 166
Old Arley. Warw 1G 61
Old Basford. Nott 1C 74
Old Basing. Hants 1E 25
Oldberrow. Warw 4F 61
Old Bewick. Nmbd 2E 121
Old Bexley. G Lon 3F 39
Old Blair. Per 2F 143
Old Bolingbroke. Linc 4C 88
Oldborough. Devn 2A 12
Old Brampton. Derbs 3H 85
Old Bridge of Tilt. Per 2F 143
Old Bridge of Urr. Dum 3E 111
Old Brumby. N Lin 4B 94
Old Buckenham. Norf 1C 66
Old Burghclere. Hants 1C 24
Oldbury. Shrp 1B 60
Oldbury. Warw 1H 61
Oldbury. W Mid 2D 61
Oldbury-on-Severn. S Glo 2B 34
Oldbury on the Hill. Glos 3D 34
Old Byland. N Yor 1H 99
Old Cassop. Dur 1A 106
Oldcastle. Mon 3G 47
Oldcastle Heath. Ches W 1G 71
Old Catton. Norf 4E 79
Old Clee. NE Lin 4F 95
Old Cleeve. Som 2D 20
Old Colwyn. Cnwy 3A 82
Oldcotes. Notts 2C 86
Old Coulsdon. G Lon 5E 39
Old Dailly. S Ayr 5B 116
Old Dalby. Leics 3D 74
Old Dam. Derbs 3F 85
Old Deer. Abers 4G 161
Old Dilton. Wilts 2D 22
Old Down. S Glo 3B 34
Oldeamere. Cambs 1C 64
Old Edlington. S Yor 1C 86
Old Eldon. Dur 2F 105
Old Ellerby. E Yor 1E 95
Old Fallings. W Mid 5D 72
Oldfallow. Staf 4D 73
Old Felixstowe. Suff 2G 55
Oldfield. Shrp 2A 60
Oldfield. Worc 4C 60
Old Fletton. Pet 1A 64
Oldford. Som 1C 22
Old Forge. Here 4A 48
Old Glossop. Derbs 1E 85
Old Goole. E Yor 2H 93
Old Gore. Here 3B 48
Old Graitney. Dum 3E 112
Old Grimsby. IOS 1A 4
Oldhall. High 3E 169
Old Hall Street. Norf 2F 79
Oldham. G Man 4H 91
Oldhamstocks. E Lot 2D 130
Old Heathfield. E Sus 3G 27
Old Hill. W Mid 2D 60
Old Hunstanton. Norf 1F 77
Oldhurst. Cambs 3B 64
Old Hutton. Cumb 1E 97
Old Kea. Corn 4C 6
Old Kilpatrick. W Dun 2F 127
Old Kinnernie. Abers 3E 152
Old Knebworth. Herts 3C 52
Oldland. S Glo 4B 34
Old Laxey. IOM 3D 108
Old Leake. Linc 5D 88
Old Lenton. Nott 2C 74
Old Llanberis. Gwyn 5F 81
Old Malton. N Yor 2B 100
Oldmeldrum. Abers 1F 153
Old Micklefield. W Yor 1E 93
Old Mill. Corn 5D 10
Oldmixon. N Som 1G 21
Old Monkland. N Lan 3A 128
Old Newton. Suff 4C 66
Old Park. Telf 5A 72
Old Pentland. Midl 3F 129
Old Philpstoun. W Lot 2D 128
Old Quarrington. Dur 1A 106
Old Radnor. Powy 5E 59
Old Rayne. Abers 1D 152
Oldridge. Devn 3B 12
Old Romney. Kent 3E 29
Old Scone. Per 1D 136
Oldshore Beg. High 3B 166
Oldshoremore. High 3C 166
Old Snydale. W Yor 2E 93
Old Sodbury. S Glo 3C 34
Old Somerby. Linc 2G 75
Old Spital. Dur 3C 104
Oldstead. N Yor 1H 99
Old Stratford. Nptn 1F 51
Old Swan. Mers 1F 83
Old Swarland. Nmbd 4F 121
Old Tebay. Cumb 4H 103
Old Town. Cumb 5F 113
Old Town. E Sus 5G 27
Old Town. IOS 1B 4
Old Town. Nmbd 5C 120
Oldtown. High 5C 164
Old Trafford. G Man 1C 84
Old Tupton. Derbs 4A 86
Oldwall. Cumb 3F 113
Oldwalls. Swan 3D 31
Old Warden. C Beds 1B 52
Oldways End. Som 4B 20
Old Westhall. Abers 1D 152
Old Weston. Cambs 3H 63
Oldwhat. Abers 3F 161
Old Windsor. Wind 3A 38
Old Wives Lees. Kent 5E 41
Old Woking. Surr 5B 38
Oldwood Common. Worc 4H 59
Old Woodstock. Oxon 4C 50
Olgrinmore. High 3C 168
Oliver's Battery. Hants 4C 24
Ollaberry. Shet 3E 173
Ollerton. Ches E 3B 84
Ollerton. Notts 4D 86
Ollerton. Shrp 3A 72
Olmarch. Cdgn 5F 57
Olmstead Green. Cambs 1G 53
Olney. Mil 5F 63
Olrig. High 2D 169
Olton. W Mid 2F 61
Olveston. S Glo 3B 34
Ombersley. Worc 4C 60
Ompton. Notts 4D 86
Omunsgarth. Shet 7E 173
Onchan. IOM 4D 108
Onecote. Staf 5E 85
Onehouse. Suff 5C 66
Onen. Mon 4H 47
Ongar Hill. Norf 3E 77
Ongar Street. Here 4F 59
Onibury. Shrp 3G 59
Onich. High 2E 141
Onllwyn. Neat 4B 46
Onneley. Staf 1B 72
Onslow Green. Essx 4G 53
Onslow Village. Surr 1A 26
Onthank. E Ayr 1D 116
Openwoodgate. Derbs 1A 74
Opinan. High
nr. Gairloch 1G 155
nr. Laide 4C 162
Orasaigh. W Isl 6F 171
Orbost. High 4B 154
Orby. Linc 4D 89
Orchard Hill. Devn 4E 19
Orchard Portman. Som 4F 21
Orcheston. Wilts 2F 23
Orcop. Here 3H 47
Orcop Hill. Here 3H 47
Ord. High 2E 147
Ordale. Shet 1H 173
Ordhead. Abers 2D 152
Ordie. Abers 3B 152
Ordiquish. Mor 3H 159
Ordley. Nmbd 4C 114
Ordsall. Notts 3E 86
Ore. E Sus 4C 28
Oreton. Shrp 2A 60
Orford. Suff 1H 55
Orford. Warr 1A 84
Organford. Dors 3E 15
Orgil. Orkn 7B 172
Orgreave. Staf 4F 73
Oridge Street. Glos 3C 48
Orlestone. Kent 2D 28
Orleton. Here 4G 59
Orleton. Worc 4A 60
Orleton Common. Here 4G 59
Orlingbury. Nptn 3F 63
Ormacleit. W Isl 5C 170
Ormathwaite. Cumb 2D 102
Ormesby. Red C 3C 106
Ormesby St Margaret. Norf 4G 79
Ormesby St Michael. Norf 4G 79
Ormiscaig. High 4C 162
Ormiston. E Lot 3H 129
Ormsaigbeg. High 2F 139
Ormsaigmore. High 2F 139
Ormsary. Arg 2F 125
Ormsgill. Cumb 2A 96
Ormskirk. Lanc 4C 90
Orphir. Orkn 7C 172
Orpington. G Lon 4F 39
Orrell. G Man 4D 90
Orrell. Mers 1F 83
Orrisdale. IOM 2C 108
Orsett. Thur 2H 39
Orslow. Staf 4C 72
Orston. Notts 1E 75
Orthwaite. Cumb 1D 102
Orton. Cumb 4H 103
Orton. Mor 3H 159
Orton. Nptn 3F 63
Orton. Staf 1C 60
Orton Longueville. Pet 1A 64
Orton-on-the-Hill. Leics 5H 73
Orton Waterville. Pet 1A 64
Orton Wistow. Pet 1A 64
Orwell. Cambs 5C 64
Osbaldeston. Lanc 1E 91
Osbaldwick. York 4A 100
Osbaston. Leics 5B 74
Osbaston. Shrp 3F 71
Osbournby. Linc 2H 75
Osclay. High 5E 169
Oscroft. Ches W 4H 83
Ose. High 4C 154
Osgathorpe. Leics 4B 74
Osgodby. Linc 1H 87
Osgodby. N Yor
nr. Scarborough 1E 101
nr. Selby 1G 93
Oskaig. High 5E 155
Oskamull. Arg 5F 139
Osleston. Derbs 2G 73
Osmaston. Derb 2A 74
Osmaston. Derbs 1G 73
Osmington. Dors 4C 14
Osmington Mills. Dors 4C 14
Osmondthorpe. W Yor 1D 92
Osmondwall. Orkn 9C 172
Osmotherley. N Yor 5B 106
Osnaburgh. Fife 2G 137
Ospisdale. High 5E 164
Ospringe. Kent 4E 40
Ossett. W Yor 2C 92
Ossington. Notts 4E 87
Ostend. Essx 1D 40
Ostend. Norf 2F 79
Osterley. G Lon 3C 38
Oswaldkirk. N Yor 2A 100
Oswaldtwistle. Lanc 2F 91
Oswestry. Shrp 3E 71
Otby. Linc 1A 88
Otford. Kent 5G 39
Otham. Kent 5B 40
Otherton. Staf 4D 72
Othery. Som 3G 21
Otley. Suff 5E 66
Otley. W Yor 5E 98
Otterbourne. Hants 4C 24
Otterburn. Nmbd 5C 120
Otterburn. N Yor 4A 98
Otterburn Camp. Nmbd 5C 120
Otterburn Hall. Nmbd 5C 120
Otter Ferry. Arg 1H 125
Otterford. Som 1F 13
Otterham. Corn 3B 10
Otterhampton. Som 2F 21
Otterham Quay. Medw 4C 40
Ottershaw. Surr 4B 38
Otterspool. Mers 2F 83
Otterswick. Shet 3G 173
Otterton. Devn 4D 12
Otterwood. Hants 2C 16
Ottery St Mary. Devn 3D 12
Ottinge. Kent 1F 29
Ottringham. E Yor 2F 95
Oughterby. Cumb 4D 112
Oughtershaw. N Yor 1A 98
Oughterside. Cumb 5C 112
Oughtibridge. S Yor 1H 85
Oughtrington. Warr 2A 84
Oulston. N Yor 2H 99
Oulton. Cumb 4D 112
Oulton. Norf 3D 78
Oulton. Staf
nr. Gnosall Heath 3B 72
nr. Stone 2D 72
Oulton. Suff 1H 67
Oulton. W Yor 2D 92
Oulton Broad. Suff 1H 67
Oulton Street. Norf 3D 78
Oundle. Nptn 2H 63
Ousby. Cumb 1H 103
Ousdale. High 2H 165
Ousden. Suff 5G 65
Ousefleet. E Yor 2B 94
Ouston. Dur 4F 115
Ouston. Nmbd
nr. Bearsbridge 4A 114
nr. Stamfordham 2D 114
Outer Hope. Devn 4C 8
Outertown. Orkn 6B 172
Outgate. Cumb 5E 103
Outhgill. Cumb 4A 104
Outlands. Staf 2B 72
Outlane. W Yor 3A 92
Out Newton. E Yor 2G 95
Out Rawcliffe. Lanc 5D 96
Outwell. Norf 5E 77
Outwick. Hants 1G 15
Outwood. Surr 1E 27
Outwood. W Yor 2D 92
Outwood. Worc 3D 60
Outwoods. Leics 4B 74
Outwoods. Staf 4B 72
Ouzlewell Green. W Yor 2D 92
Ovenden. W Yor 2A 92
Over. Cambs 3C 64
Over. Ches W 4A 84
Over. Glos 4D 48
Over. S Glo 3A 34
Overbister. Orkn 3F 172
Over Burrows. Derbs 2G 73
Overbury. Worc 2E 49
Overcombe. Dors 4B 14
Over Compton. Dors 1A 14
Over End. Cambs 1H 63
Over Finlarg. Ang 4D 144
Over Green. Warw 1F 61
Overgreen. Derbs 3H 85
Over Haddon. Derbs 4G 85
Over Hulton. G Man 4E 91
Over Kellet. Lanc 2E 97
Over Kiddington. Oxon 3C 50
Overleigh. Som 3H 21
Overley. Staf 4F 73
Over Monnow. Mon 4A 48
Over Norton. Oxon 3B 50
Over Peover. Ches E 3B 84
Overpool. Ches W 3F 83
Overscaig. High 1B 164
Overseal. Derbs 4G 73
Over Silton. N Yor 5B 106
Oversland. Kent 5E 41
Overstone. Nptn 4F 63
Over Stowey. Som 3E 21
Overstrand. Norf 1E 79
Over Stratton. Som 1H 13
Over Street. Wilts 3F 23
Overthorpe. Nptn 1C 50
Overton. Aber 2F 153
Overton. Ches W 3H 83
Overton. Hants 2D 24
Overton. High 5E 169
Overton. Lanc 4D 96
Overton. N Yor 4H 99
Overton. Shrp
nr. Bridgnorth 2A 60
nr. Ludlow 3H 59
Overton. Swan 4D 30
Overton. W Yor 3C 92
Overton. Wrex 1F 71
Overtown. Lanc 2F 97
Overtown. N Lan 4B 128
Overtown. Swin 4G 35
Over Wallop. Hants 3A 24
Over Whitacre. Warw 1G 61
Over Worton. Oxon 3C 50
Oving. Buck 3F 51
Oving. W Sus 5A 26
Ovingdean. Brig 5E 27
Ovingham. Nmbd 3D 115
Ovington. Dur 3E 105
Ovington. Essx 1A 54
Ovington. Hants 3D 24
Ovington. Norf 5B 78
Ovington. Nmbd 3D 114
Owen's Bank. Staf 3G 73
Ower. Hants
nr. Holbury 2C 16
nr. Totton 1B 16
Owermoigne. Dors 4C 14
Owlbury. Shrp 1F 59
Owler Bar. Derbs 3G 85
Owlerton. S Yor 1H 85
Owlsmoor. Brac 5G 37
Owlswick. Buck 5F 51
Owmby. Linc 4D 94
Owmby-by-Spital. Linc 2H 87
Ownham. W Ber 4C 36
Owrytn. Wrex 1F 71
Owslebury. Hants 4D 24
Owston. Leics 5E 75
Owston. S Yor 3F 93
Owston Ferry. N Lin 4B 94
Owstwick. E Yor 1F 95
Owthorne. E Yor 2G 95
Owthorpe. Notts 2D 74
Owton Manor. Hart 2B 106
Oxborough. Norf 5G 77
Oxbridge. Dors 3H 13
Oxcombe. Linc 3C 88
Oxen End. Essx 3G 53
Oxenhall. Glos 3C 48
Oxenholme. Cumb 5G 103
Oxenhope. W Yor 1A 92
Oxen Park. Cumb 1C 96
Oxenpill. Som 2H 21
Oxenton. Glos 2E 49
Oxenwood. Wilts 1B 24
Oxford. Oxon 207 (5D 50)
Oxgangs. Edin 3F 129
Oxhey. Herts 1C 38
Oxhill. Warw 1B 50
Oxley. W Mid 5D 72
Oxley Green. Essx 4C 54
Oxley's Green. E Sus 3A 28
Oxlode. Cambs 2D 65
Oxnam. Bord 3B 120
Oxshott. Surr 4C 38
Oxspring. S Yor 4C 92
Oxted. Surr 5E 39
Oxton. Mers 2F 83
Oxton. N Yor 5H 99
Oxton. Notts 5D 86
Oxton. Bord 4A 130
Oxwich. Swan 4D 31
Oxwich Green. Swan 4D 31
Oxwick. Norf 3B 78
Oykel Bridge. High 3A 164
Oyne. Abers 1D 152
Oystermouth. Swan 4F 31
Ozleworth. Glos 2C 34

P

Pabail Iarach. W Isl 4H 171
Pabail Uarach. W Isl 4H 171
Pachesham Park. Surr 5C 38
Packers Hill. Dors 1C 14
Packington. Leics 4A 74
Packmoor. Stoke 5C 84
Packmores. Warw 4G 61
Packwood. W Mid 3F 61
Packwood Gullet. W Mid 3F 61
Padanaram. Ang 3D 144
Padbury. Buck 2F 51
Paddington. G Lon 2D 38
Paddington. Warr 2A 84

Paddlesworth. *Kent*................2F **29**
Paddock. *Kent*........................5D **40**
Paddockhole. *Dum*.................1D **112**
Paddock Wood. *Kent*............1A **28**
Paddolgreen. *Shrp*.................2H **71**
Padeswood. *Flin*.....................4E **83**
Padiham. *Lanc*.....................1F **91**
Padside. *N Yor*.......................4D **98**
Padson. *Devn*........................3F **11**
Padstow. *Corn*.........................1D **6**
Padworth. *W Ber*...................5E **36**
Page Bank. *Dur*......................1F **105**
Pagham. *W Sus*......................3G **17**
Paglesham Churchend. *Essx*....1D **40**
Paglesham Eastend. *Essx*.......1D **40**
Paibeil. *W Isl*
     on North Uist................2C **170**
     on Taransay.................8C **171**
Paiblesgearraidh. *W Isl*.........2C **170**
Paignton. *Torb*.......................2E **9**
Pailton. *Warw*........................2B **62**
Paine's Corner. *E Sus*.............3H **27**
Painleyhill. *Staf*.....................2E **73**
Painscastle. *Powy*...................1E **47**
Painshawfield. *Nmbd*.............3D **113**
Painsthorpe. *E Yor*.................4C **100**
Painswick. *Glos*......................5D **48**
Painter's Forstal. *Kent*...........5D **40**
Painthorpe. *W Yor*..................3D **92**
Pairc Shiaboist. *W Isl*.............3E **171**
Paisley. *Ren*.................**207** (3F **127**)
Pakefield. *Suff*........................1H **67**
Pakenham. *Suff*......................4B **66**
Pale. *Gwyn*.............................2B **70**
Palehouse Common. *E Sus*....4F **27**
Palestine. *Hants*....................2A **24**
Paley Street. *Wind*.................4G **37**
Palgowan. *Dum*......................1A **110**
Palgrave. *Suff*.........................3D **66**
Pallington. *Dors*......................3C **14**
Palmarsh. *Kent*......................2F **29**
Palmer Moor. *Derbs*...............2F **73**
Palmers Cross. *W Mid*............5C **72**
Palmerstown. *V Glam*.............5E **33**
Palnackie. *Dum*......................4F **111**
Palnure. *Dum*.........................3B **110**
Palterton. *Derbs*.....................4B **86**
Pamber End. *Hants*.................1E **24**
Pamber Green. *Hants*..............1E **24**
Pamber Heath. *Hants*..............5E **36**
Pamington. *Glos*.....................2E **49**
Pamphill. *Dors*.......................2E **15**
Pampisford. *Cambs*.................1E **53**
Panborough. *Som*...................2H **21**
Panbride. *Ang*........................5E **145**
Pancrasweek. *Devn*................2C **10**
Pandy. *Gwyn*
     nr. Bala...........................2A **70**
     nr. Tywyn.........................5F **69**
Pandy. *Mon*............................3G **47**
Pandy. *Powy*..........................5B **70**
Pandy. *Wrex*..........................2D **70**
Pandy Tudur. *Cnwy*................4A **82**
Panfield. *Essx*........................3H **53**
Pangbourne. *W Ber*................4E **37**
Pannal. *N Yor*........................4F **99**
Pannal Ash. *N Yor*..................4E **99**
Pannanich. *Abers*...................4A **152**
Pant. *Shrp*.............................3E **71**
Pant. *Wrex*.............................1E **71**
Pantasaph. *Flin*......................3D **82**
Pant Glas. *Gwyn*....................1D **68**
Pant-glas. *Shrp*......................2E **71**
Pantgwyn. *Carm*....................3F **45**
Pantgwyn. *Cdgn*.....................1C **44**
Pant-lasau. *Swan*...................5G **45**
Panton. *Linc*..........................3A **88**
Pant-pastynog. *Den*................4C **82**
Pantperthog. *Gwyn*................5G **69**
Pant-teg. *Carm*.......................3E **45**
Pant-y-Caws. *Carm*.................2F **43**
Pant-y-dwr. *Powy*....................3B **58**
Pant-y-ffridd. *Powy*.................5D **70**
Pantyffynnon. *Carm*................4G **45**
Pant-y-llyn. *Carm*...................4G **45**
Pant-yr-awel. *B'end*.................3C **32**
Pant y Wacco. *Flin*..................3D **82**
Panxworth. *Norf*.....................4F **79**
Papa Stour Airport. *Shet*.......6C **173**
Papa Westray Airport.
     Orkn................................2D **172**
Papcastle. *Cumb*....................1C **102**
Papigoe. *High*........................3F **169**
Papil. *Shet*.............................8E **173**
Papple. *E Lot*.........................2B **130**
Papplewick. *Notts*..................5C **86**
Papworth Everard. *Cambs*........4B **64**
Papworth St Agnes. *Cambs*.....4B **64**
Par. *Corn*................................3E **7**
Paramour Street. *Kent*............4G **41**
Parbold. *Lanc*.........................3C **90**
Parbrook. *Som*.......................3A **22**
Parbrook. *W Sus*.....................3B **26**
Parc. *Gwyn*............................2A **70**
Parcllyn. *Cdgn*.......................5B **56**
Parc-Seymour. *Newp*...............2H **33**
Pardown. *Hants*.....................2D **24**
Pardshaw. *Cumb*....................2B **102**
Parham. *Suff*..........................4F **67**
Park. *Abers*............................4E **153**
Park. *Arg*...............................4D **140**
Park. *Dum*..............................5B **118**
Park Bottom. *Corn*..................4A **6**
Parkburn. *Abers*.....................5E **161**
Park Corner. *E Sus*..................2G **27**
Park Corner. *Oxon*..................3E **37**
Park End. *Nmbd*.....................2B **114**
Parkend. *Glos*........................5B **48**
Parkeston. *Essx*......................2F **55**
Parkfield. *Corn*.......................2H **7**

Park Gate. *Hants*....................2D **16**
Park Gate. *Worc*.....................3D **60**
Parkgate. *Ches W*...................3E **83**
Parkgate. *Cumb*.....................5D **112**
Parkgate. *Dum*.......................1B **112**
Parkgate. *Surr*.......................1D **26**
Parkhall. *W Dun*....................2F **127**
Parkham. *Devn*......................4D **19**
Parkham Ash. *Devn*................4D **18**
Parkhead. *Cumb*....................5E **113**
Parkhead. *Glas*......................3H **127**
Park Hill. *Mers*.......................4C **90**
Parkhouse. *Mon*.....................5A **48**
Parkhurst. *IOW*......................3C **16**
Park Lane. *G Man*...................4F **91**
Park Lane. *Staf*......................5C **72**
Park Mill. *W Yor*.....................3C **92**
Parkmill. *Swan*......................4E **31**
Parkneuk. *Abers*....................1G **145**
Parkside. *N Lan*......................4B **128**
Parkstone. *Pool*......................3F **15**
Park Street. *Herts*...................5B **52**
Park Street. *W Sus*..................2C **26**
Park Town. *Oxon*.....................5D **50**
Park Village. *Nmbd*................3H **113**
Parkway. *Here*........................2C **48**
Parley Cross. *Dors*..................3F **15**
Parmoor. *Buck*.......................3F **37**
Parr. *Mers*..............................1H **83**
Parracombe. *Devn*..................2G **19**
Parrog. *Pemb*.........................1E **43**
Parsonage Green. *Essx*...........4H **53**
Parsonby. *Cumb*....................1C **102**
Parson Cross. *S Yor*................1H **85**
Parson Drove. *Cambs*.............5C **76**
Partick. *Glas*..........................3G **127**
Partington. *G Man*.................1B **84**
Partney. *Linc*.........................4D **88**
Parton. *Cumb*
     nr. Whitehaven...............2A **102**
     nr. Wigton......................4D **112**
Parton. *Dum*..........................2D **111**
Partridge Green. *W Sus*...........4C **26**
Parwich. *Derbs*.......................5F **85**
Passenham. *Nptn*..................2F **51**
Passfield. *Hants*.....................3G **25**
Passingford Bridge. *Essx*.........1G **39**
Paston. *Norf*...........................2F **79**
Pasturefields. *Staf*..................3D **73**
Patchacott. *Devn*....................3E **11**
Patcham. *Brig*........................5E **27**
Patchetts Green. *Herts*...........1C **38**
Patching. *W Sus*.....................5B **26**
Patchole. *Devn*.......................2G **19**
Patchway. *S Glo*.....................3B **34**
Pateley Bridge. *N Yor*..............3D **98**
Pathe. *Som*............................3G **21**
Pathfinder Village. *Devn*.........3B **12**
Pathhead. *Abers*.....................2G **145**
Pathhead. *E Ayr*.....................3F **117**
Pathhead. *Fife*........................4E **137**
Pathhead. *Midl*......................3G **129**
Pathlow. *Warw*.......................5F **61**
Path of Condie. *Per*.................2C **136**
Pathstruie. *Per*......................2C **136**
Patmore Heath. *Herts*.............3E **53**
Patna. *E Ayr*..........................3D **116**
Patney. *Wilts*.........................1F **23**
Patrick. *IOM*..........................3B **108**
Patrick Brompton. *N Yor*.........5F **105**
Patrington. *E Yor*...................2G **95**
Patrington Haven. *E Yor*..........2G **95**
Patrixbourne. *Kent*.................5F **41**
Patterdale. *Cumb*...................3E **103**
Pattiesmuir. *Fife*....................1D **129**
Pattingham. *Staf*...................1C **60**
Pattishall. *Nptn*.....................5D **62**
Pattiswick. *Essx*.....................3B **54**
Patton Bridge. *Cumb*..............5G **103**
Paul. *Corn*...............................4B **4**
Paulerspury. *Nptn*..................1F **51**
Paull. *E Yor*............................2E **95**
Paulton. *Bath*........................1B **22**
Pauperhaugh. *Nmbd*..............5F **121**
Pave Lane. *Telf*......................4B **72**
Pavenham. *Bed*......................5G **63**
Pawlett. *Som*.........................2F **21**
Pawston. *Nmbd*......................1C **120**
Paxford. *Glos*.........................2G **49**
Paxton. *Bord*.........................4F **131**
Payhembury. *Devn*.................2D **12**
Paythorne. *Lanc*.....................4H **97**
Payton. *Devn*.........................4E **20**
Peacehaven. *E Sus*...............5F **27**
Peak Dale. *Derbs*....................3E **85**
Peak Forest. *Derbs*.................3F **85**
Peak Hill. *Linc*.......................4B **76**
Peakirk. *Pet*...........................5A **76**
Pearsie. *Ang*..........................3C **144**
Peasedown St John. *Bath*........1C **22**
Peaseland Green. *Norf*............4D **78**
Peasemore. *W Ber*..................4C **36**
Peasenhall. *Suff*.....................4F **67**
Pease Pottage. *W Sus*.............2D **26**
Peaslake. *Surr*.......................1B **26**
Peasley Cross. *Mers*...............1H **83**
Peasmarsh. *E Sus*...................3C **28**
Peasmarsh. *Som*....................1G **13**
Peasmarsh. *Surr*.....................1A **26**
Peaston. *E Lot*........................3H **129**
Peastonbank. *E Lot*.................3H **129**
Peathill. *Abers*.......................2G **161**
Peat Inn. *Fife*.........................3G **137**
Peatling Magna. *Leics*.............1C **62**
Peatling Parva. *Leics*...............2C **62**
Peaton. *Shrp*..........................2H **59**
Peaton. *Shrp*..........................2H **59**
Peats Corner. *Suff*...................4D **66**
Pebmarsh. *Essx*.....................2B **54**
Pebworth. *Worc*......................1G **49**
Pecket Well. *W Yor*..................2H **91**

Peckforton. *Ches E*..................5H **83**
Peckham Bush. *Kent*..............5A **40**
Peckleton. *Leics*......................5B **74**
Pedair-ffordd. *Powy*................3D **70**
Pedham. *Norf*.........................4F **79**
Pedlinge. *Kent*........................2F **29**
Pedmore. *W Mid*.....................2D **60**
Pedwell. *Som*.........................3H **21**
Peebles. *Bord*........................5F **129**
Peel. *IOM*...............................3B **108**
Peel. *Bord*..............................1G **119**
Peel Common. *Hants*..............2D **16**
Peening Quarter. *Kent*............3C **28**
Peggs Green. *Leics*..................4B **74**
Pegsdon. *C Beds*....................2B **52**
Pegswood. *Nmbd*...................1F **115**
Peinchorran. *High*..................5E **155**
Peinlich. *High*........................3D **154**
Pelaw. *Tyne*...........................3F **115**
Pelcomb Bridge. *Pemb*...........3D **42**
Pelcomb Cross. *Pemb*.............3D **42**
Peldon. *Essx*..........................4C **54**
Pelsall. *W Mid*......................5E **73**
Pelton. *Dur*............................4F **115**
Pelutho. *Cumb*.......................5C **112**
Pelynt. *Corn*............................3G **7**
Pemberton. *Carm*...................5E **45**
Pembrey. *Carm*......................5E **45**
Pembridge. *Here*....................5F **59**
Pembroke. *Pemb*...................4D **43**
Pembroke Dock. *Pemb*...**215** (4D **42**)
Pembroke Ferry. *Pemb*............4D **42**
Pembury. *Kent*.......................1H **27**
Penallt. *Mon*..........................4A **48**
Penally. *Pemb*........................5F **43**
Penalt. *Here*...........................3A **48**
Penalum. *Pemb*.....................5F **43**
Penare. *Corn*............................4D **6**
Penarth. *V Glam*..................4E **33**
Penbeagle. *Corn*......................3C **4**
Penberth. *Corn*........................4B **4**
Pen-bont Rhydybeddau. *Cdgn*...2F **57**
Penbryn. *Cdgn*.......................5B **56**
Pencader. *Carm*......................2E **45**
Pen-cae. *Cdgn*........................5D **56**
Pencaenewydd. *Gwyn*.............1D **68**
Pencaerau. *Neat*.....................3G **31**
Pencaitland. *E Lot*..................3H **129**
Pencarnisiog. *IOA*..................3C **80**
Pencarreg. *Carm*....................1F **45**
Pencarrow. *Corn*.....................4B **10**
Pencelli. *Powy*........................3D **46**
Pen-clawdd. *Swan*..................3E **31**
Pencoed. *B'end*.......................3C **32**
Pencombe. *Here*.....................5H **59**
Pencraig. *Here*.......................3A **48**
Pencraig. *Powy*......................3C **70**
Pendeen. *Corn*.........................3A **4**
Pendeford. *W Mid*...................5C **72**
Penderyn. *Rhon*.....................5C **46**
Pendine. *Carm*.......................4G **43**
Pendlebury. *G Man*..............4F **91**
Pendleton. *G Man*...................1C **84**
Pendleton. *Lanc*.....................1F **91**
Pendock. *Worc*.......................2C **48**
Pendoggett. *Corn*...................5A **10**
Pendomer. *Som*......................1A **14**
Pendoylan. *V Glam*..................4D **32**
Pendre. *B'end*.........................3C **32**
Penegoes. *Powy*.....................5G **69**
Penelewey. *Corn*......................4C **6**
Penffordd. *Pemb*....................2E **43**
Penffordd-Lâs. *Powy*...............1A **58**
Penfro. *Pemb*.........................4D **43**
Pengam. *Cphy*........................2E **33**
Pengam. *Card*.........................4F **33**
Penge. *G Lon*.......................4E **39**
Pengelly. *Corn*.......................4A **10**
Pengenffordd. *Powy*...............2E **47**
Pengersick. *Corn*......................4C **4**
Pengorffwysfa. *IOA*................1D **80**
Pengover Green. *Corn*...............2G **7**
Pengwern. *Den*......................3C **82**
Penhale. *Corn*
     nr. Mullion.......................5D **5**
     nr. St Austell..................3D **6**
Penhale Camp. *Corn*................3B **6**
Penhallow. *Corn*.....................3B **6**
Penhalvean. *Corn*...................5B **6**
Penhelig. *Gwyn*.....................1F **57**
Penhill. *Swin*..........................3G **35**
Penhow. *Newp*.......................2H **33**
Penhurst. *E Sus*......................4A **28**
Peniarth. *Gwyn*......................5F **69**
Penicuik. *Midl*......................3F **129**
Peniel. *Carm*..........................3E **45**
Penifiler. *High*........................4D **155**
Peninver. *Arg*.........................3B **122**
Penisa'r Waun. *Gwyn*..............4E **81**
Penistone. *S Yor*.....................4C **92**
Penketh. *Warr*........................2H **83**
Penkill. *S Ayr*.........................5B **116**
Penkridge. *Staf*......................4D **72**
Penley. *Wrex*..........................2G **71**
Penllech. *Gwyn*......................2B **68**
Penllergaer. *Swan*..................3F **31**
Pen-llyn. *IOA*.........................2C **80**
Penmachno. *Cnwy*..................5G **81**
Penmaen. *Swan*.....................4E **31**
Penmaenmawr. *Cnwy*.............3F **81**
Penmaenpool. *Gwyn*...............4F **69**
Penmaen Rhos. *Cnwy*.............3A **82**
Pen-marc. *V Glam*...................5D **32**
Penmark. *V Glam*....................5D **32**
Penmarth. *Corn*.......................5B **6**
Penmon. *IOA*.........................2F **81**
Penmorfa. *Gwyn*.....................1E **69**
Penmynydd. *IOA*....................3E **81**
Penn. *Buck*............................1A **38**
Penn. *Dors*.............................3G **13**
Penn. *W Mid*..........................1C **60**

Pennal. *Gwyn*........................5G **69**
Pennan. *Abers*.......................2F **161**
Pennant. *Cdgn*.......................4E **57**
Pennant. *Den*.........................2C **70**
Pennant. *Powy*.......................3B **70**
Pennant Melangell. *Powy*........3D **70**
Pennar. *Pemb*........................4D **42**
Pennard. *Swan*......................4E **31**
Pennerley. *Shrp*.....................1F **59**
Pennington. *Cumb*.................2B **96**
Pennington. *G Man*................1A **84**
Pennington. *Hants*.................3B **16**
Pennorth. *Powy*......................3E **46**
Penn Street. *Buck*...................1A **38**
Pennsylvania. *Devn*.................3C **12**
Pennsylvania. *S Glo*................4C **34**
Penny Bridge. *Cumb*...............1C **96**
Pennycross. *Plym*.....................3A **8**
Pennygate. *Norf*.....................3F **79**
Pennyghael. *Arg*....................1C **132**
Penny Hill. *Linc*......................3C **76**
Pennylands. *Lanc*...................4C **90**
Pennymoor. *Devn*...................1B **12**
Pennyvenie. *E Ayr*...................4D **117**
Pennywell. *Tyne*.....................4G **115**
Penparc. *Cdgn*........................1C **44**
Penparcau. *Cdgn*....................2E **57**
Pen-pedair-heol. *Cphy*.............2E **33**
Penperlleni. *Mon*...................5G **47**
Penpillick. *Corn*.......................3E **7**
Penpol. *Corn*............................5C **6**
Penpoll. *Corn*...........................3F **7**
Penponds. *Corn*.......................3D **4**
Penpont. *Corn*.........................5A **10**
Penpont. *Dum*.......................5H **117**
Penpont. *Powy*.......................3C **46**
Penprysg. *B'end*.....................3C **32**
Penquit. *Devn*..........................3C **8**
Penrherber. *Carm*...................1G **43**
Penrhiw. *Pemb*.......................1C **44**
Penrhiwceiber. *Rhon*...............2D **32**
Pen-Rhiw-fawr. *Neat*...............4H **45**
Penrhiw-llan. *Cdgn*.................1D **44**
Penrhiw-pal. *Cdgn*..................1D **44**
Penrhos. *Gwyn*......................2C **68**
Penrhos. *Here*.........................5F **59**
Penrhos. *IOA*..........................2B **80**
Penrhos. *Mon*........................4H **47**
Penrhos. *Powy*.......................4B **46**
Penrhos Garnedd. *Gwyn*.........3E **81**
Penrhyn. *IOA*.........................1C **80**
Penrhyn Bay. *Cnwy*................2H **81**
Penrhyn-coch. *Cdgn*...............2F **57**
Penrhyndeudraeth. *Gwyn*.......2F **69**
Penrhyn-side. *Cnwy*................2H **81**
Penrice. *Swan*........................4D **31**
Penrith. *Cumb*....................2G **103**
Penrose. *Corn*..........................1C **6**
Penruddock. *Cumb*................2F **103**
Penryn. *Corn*...........................5B **6**
Penzance. *Corn*....................3B **4**
Peopleton. *Worc*....................5D **60**
Peover Heath. *Ches E*..............3B **84**
Peper Harow. *Surr*..................1A **26**
Peplow. *Shrp*.........................3A **72**
Pepper Arden. *N Yor*...............4F **105**
Perceton. *N Ayr*......................5E **127**
Percyhorner. *Abers*.................2G **161**
Perham Down. *Wilts*...............2A **24**
Periton. *Som*..........................2C **20**
Perkinsville. *Dur*....................4F **115**
Perlethorpe. *Notts*..................3D **86**
Perranarworthal. *Corn*.............5B **6**
Perranporth. *Corn*....................3B **6**
Perranuthnoe. *Corn*..................4C **4**
Perranwell. *Corn*.....................5B **6**
Perranzabuloe. *Corn*................3B **6**
Perrott's Brook. *Glos*...............5F **49**
Perry. *W Mid*.........................1E **61**
Perry Barr. *W Mid*...................1E **61**
Perry Crofts. *Staf*...................5G **73**
Perry Green. *Essx*...................3B **54**
Perry Green. *Herts*..................4E **53**
Perry Green. *Wilts*..................3E **35**
Perry Street. *Kent*...................3H **39**
Perry Street. *Som*....................2G **13**
Perrywood. *Kent*.....................5E **41**
Pershall. *Staf*.........................3C **72**
Pershore. *Worc*......................1E **49**
Pertenhall. *Bed*......................4H **63**
Perth. *Per*....................**207** (1D **136**)
Perthy. *Shrp*...........................2F **71**
Perton. *Staf*...........................1C **60**
Pertwood. *Wilts*.....................3D **23**
Peterborough. *Pet*......**208** (1A **64**)
Peterburn. *High*.....................5B **162**
Peterchurch. *Here*...................2G **47**
Peterculter. *Aber*....................3F **153**
Peterhead. *Abers*.................4H **161**
Peterlee. *Dur*.........................5H **115**
Petersfield. *Hants*................4F **25**
Petersfinger. *Wilts*..................4G **23**
Peters Green. *Herts*.................4B **52**
Peters Marland. *Devn*..............1E **11**
Peterstone Wentlooge.
     Newp.............................3F **33**
Peterston-super-Ely.
     V Glam..........................4D **32**
Peterstow. *Here*.....................3A **48**
Peters Village. *Kent*................4B **40**
Peter Tavy. *Devn*....................5F **11**
Petertown. *Orkn*....................7C **172**
Petham. *Kent*.........................5F **41**
Petherwin Gate. *Corn*..............4C **10**
Petrockstowe. *Devn*................2F **11**
Petsoe End. *Mil*.....................1G **51**
Pett. *E Sus*.............................4C **28**
Pettaugh. *Suff*.......................5D **66**
Pett Bottom. *Kent*...................5F **41**
Petteridge. *Kent*.....................1A **28**
Pettinain. *S Lan*......................5C **128**

Pettistree – Prescot

Pettistree. Suff 5E 67
Petton. Devn 4D 20
Petton. Shrp 3G 71
Petts Wood. G Lon 4F 39
Pettycur. Fife 1F 129
Pettywell. Norf 3C 78
Petworth. W Sus 3A 26
Pevensey. E Sus 5H 27
Pevensey Bay. E Sus 5A 28
Pewsey. Wilts 5G 35
Pheasants Hill. Buck 3F 37
Philadelphia. Tyne 4G 115
Philham. Devn 4C 18
Philiphaugh. Bord 2G 119
Phillack. Corn 3C 4
Philleigh. Corn 5C 6
Philpstoun. W Lot 2D 128
Phocle Green. Here 3B 48
Phoenix Green. Hants 1F 25
Pibsbury. Som 4H 21
Pibwrlwyd. Carm 4E 45
Pica. Cumb 2B 102
Piccadilly. Warw 1G 61
Piccadilly Corner. Norf 2E 67
Piccotts End. Herts 5A 52
Pickering. N Yor 1B 100
Picket Piece. Hants 2B 24
Picket Post. Hants 2G 15
Pickford. W Mid 2G 61
Pickhill. N Yor 1F 99
Picklenash. Glos 3C 48
Picklescott. Shrp 1G 59
Pickletillem. Fife 1G 137
Pickmere. Ches E 3A 84
Pickstock. Telf 3B 72
Pickwell. Devn 2E 19
Pickwell. Leics 4E 75
Pickworth. Linc 2H 75
Pickworth. Rut 4G 75
Picton. Ches W 3G 83
Picton. Flin 2D 82
Picton. N Yor 4B 106
Pict's Hill. Som 4H 21
Piddinghoe. E Sus 5F 27
Piddington. Buck 2G 37
Piddington. Nptn 5F 63
Piddington. Oxon 4E 51
Piddlehinton. Dors 3C 14
Piddletrenthide. Dors 2C 14
Pidley. Cambs 3C 64
Pidney. Dors 2C 14
Pie Corner. Here 4A 60
Piercebridge. Darl 3F 105
Pierowall. Orkn 3D 172
Pigdon. Nmbd 1E 115
Pightley. Som 3F 21
Pikehall. Derbs 5F 85
Pikeshill. Hants 2A 16
Pilford. Dors 2F 15
Pilgrims Hatch. Essx 1G 39
Pilham. Linc 1F 87
Pill. N Som 4A 34
The Pill. Mon 3H 33
Pillaton. Corn 2H 7
Pillaton. Staf 4D 72
Pillerton Hersey. Warw 1B 50
Pillerton Priors. Warw 1A 50
Pilleth. Powy 4E 59
Pilley. Hants 3B 16
Pilley. S Yor 4D 92
Pillgwenlly. Newp 3G 33
Pilling. Lanc 5D 96
Pilling Lane. Lanc 5C 96
Pillowell. Glos 5B 48
Pillwell. Dors 1C 14
Pilning. S Glo 3A 34
Pilsbury. Derbs 4F 85
Pilsdon. Dors 3H 13
Pilsgate. Pet 5H 75
Pilsley. Derbs
nr. Bakewell 3G 85
nr. Clay Cross 4B 86
Pilson Green. Norf 4F 79
Piltdown. E Sus 3F 27
Pilton. Edin 2F 129
Pilton. Nptn 2H 63
Pilton. Rut 5G 75
Pilton. Som 2A 22
Pilton Green. Swan 4D 30
Pimperne. Dors 2E 15
Pinchbeck. Linc 3B 76
Pinchbeck Bars. Linc 3A 76
Pinchbeck West. Linc 3B 76
Pinfold. Lanc 3B 90
Pinford End. Suff 5H 65
Pinged. Carm 5E 45
Pinhoe. Devn 3C 12
Pinkerton. E Lot 2D 130
Pinkneys Green. Wind 3G 37
Pinley. W Mid 3A 62
Pinley Green. Warw 4G 61
Pinmill. Suff 2F 55
Pinmore. S Ayr 5B 116
Pinner. G Lon 2C 38
Pins Green. Worc 1C 48
Pinsley Green. Ches E 1H 71
Pinvin. Worc 1E 49
Pinwherry. S Ayr 1G 109
Pinxton. Derbs 5B 86
Pipe and Lyde. Here 1A 48
Pipe Aston. Here 3G 59
Pipe Gate. Shrp 1B 72
Pipehill. Staf 5E 73
Piperhill. High 3C 158
Pipe Ridware. Staf 4E 73
Pipers Pool. Corn 4C 10
Pipewell. Nptn 2F 63
Pippacott. Devn 3F 19
Pipton. Powy 2E 47
Pirbright. Surr 5A 38
Pirnmill. N Ayr 5G 125
Pirton. Herts 2B 52
Pirton. Worc 1D 49
Pisgah. Stir 3G 135
Pishill. Oxon 3F 37
Pistyll. Gwyn 1C 68
Pitagowan. Per 2F 143
Pitcairn. Per 3F 143
Pitcairngreen. Per 1C 136
Pitcalnie. High 1C 158
Pitcaple. Abers 1E 152
Pitchcombe. Glos 5D 48
Pitchcott. Buck 3F 51
Pitchford. Shrp 5H 71
Pitch Green. Buck 5F 51
Pitch Place. Surr 5A 38
Pitcombe. Som 3B 22
Pitcox. E Lot 2C 130
Pitcur. Per 5B 144
Pitfichie. Abers 2D 152
Pitgrudy. High 4E 165
Pitkennedy. Ang 3E 145
Pitlessie. Fife 3F 137
Pitlochry. Per 3G 143
Pitmachie. Abers 1D 152
Pitmaduthy. High 1B 158
Pitmedden. Abers 1F 153
Pitminster. Som 1F 13
Pitnacree. Per 3G 143
Pitney. Som 4H 21
Pitroddie. Per 1E 136
Pitscottie. Fife 2G 137
Pitsea. Essx 2B 40
Pitsford. Nptn 4E 63
Pitsford Hill. Som 3E 20
Pitsmoor. S Yor 2A 86
Pitstone. Buck 4H 51
Pitt. Hants 4C 24
Pitt Court. Glos 2C 34
Pittentrail. High 3E 164
Pittenweem. Fife 3H 137
Pittington. Dur 5G 115
Pitton. Swan 4D 30
Pitton. Wilts 3H 23
Pittswood. Kent 1H 27
Pittulie. Abers 2G 161
Pittville. Glos 3E 49
Pitversie. Per 2D 136
Pity Me. Dur 5F 115
Pityme. Corn 1D 6
Pixey Green. Suff 3E 67
Pixley. Here 2B 48
Place Newton. N Yor 2C 100
Plaidy. Abers 3E 161
Plaidy. Corn 3G 7
Plain Dealings. Pemb 3E 43
Plains. N Lan 3A 128
Plainsfield. Som 3E 21
Plaish. Shrp 1H 59
Plaistow. Here 2B 48
Plaistow. W Sus 2B 26
Plaitford. Wilts 1A 16
Plastow Green. Hants 5D 36
Plas yn Cefn. Den 3C 82
The Platt. E Sus 2G 27
Platt Bridge. G Man 4E 90
Platt Lane. Shrp 2H 71
Platts Common. S Yor 4D 92
Platt's Heath. Kent 5C 40
Plawsworth. Dur 5F 115
Plaxtol. Kent 5H 39
Playden. E Sus 3D 28
Playford. Suff 1F 55
Play Hatch. Oxon 4F 37
Playing Place. Corn 4C 6
Playley Green. Glos 2C 48
Plealey. Shrp 5G 71
Plean. Stir 1B 128
Pleasington. Bkbn 2E 91
Pleasley. Derbs 4C 86
Pledgdon Green. Essx 3F 53
Plenmeller. Nmbd 3A 114
Pleshey. Essx 4G 53
Plockton. High 5H 155
Plocrapol. W Isl 8D 171
Ploughfield. Here 1G 47
Plowden. Shrp 2F 59
Ploxgreen. Shrp 5F 71
Pluckley. Kent 1D 28
Plucks Gutter. Kent 4G 41
Plumbland. Cumb 1C 102
Plumgarths. Cumb 5F 103
Plumley. Ches E 3B 84
Plummers Plain. W Sus 3D 26
Plumpton. Cumb 1F 103
Plumpton. E Sus 4E 27
Plumpton. Nptn 1D 50
Plumpton Foot. Cumb 1F 103
Plumpton Green. E Sus 4E 27
Plumpton Head. Cumb 1G 103
Plumstead. G Lon 3F 39
Plumstead. Norf 2D 78
Plumtree. Notts 2D 74
Plumtree Park. Notts 2D 74
Plungar. Leics 2E 75
Plush. Dors 2C 14
Plushabridge. Corn 5D 10
Plwmp. Cdgn 5C 56
Plymouth. Plym 208 (3A 8)
Plympton. Plym 3B 8
Plymstock. Plym 3B 8
Plymtree. Devn 2D 12
Pockley. N Yor 1A 100
Pocklington. E Yor 5C 100
Pode Hole. Linc 3B 76
Podimore. Som 4A 22
Podington. Bed 4G 63
Podmore. Staf 2B 72
Poffley End. Oxon 4B 50
Point Clear. Essx 4D 54
Pointon. Linc 2A 76
Pokesdown. Bour 3G 15
Polbae. Dum 2H 109
Polbain. High 3E 163
Polbathic. Corn 3H 7
Polbeth. W Lot 3D 128
Polbrock. Corn 2E 6
Polchar. High 3C 150
Polebrook. Nptn 2H 63
Pole Elm. Worc 1D 48
Polegate. E Sus 5G 27
Pole Moor. W Yor 3A 92
Poles. High 4E 165
Polesworth. Warw 5G 73
Polglass. High 3E 163
Polgooth. Corn 3D 6
Poling. W Sus 5B 26
Poling Corner. W Sus 5B 26
Polio. High 1B 158
Polkerris. Corn 3E 7
Polla. High 3D 166
Pollard Street. Norf 2F 79
Pollicott. Buck 4F 51
Pollington. E Yor 3G 93
Polloch. High 2B 140
Pollok. Glas 3G 127
Pollokshaws. Glas 3G 127
Pollokshields. Glas 3G 127
Polmaily. High 5G 157
Polmassick. Corn 4D 6
Polmont. Falk 2C 128
Polnessan. E Ayr 3D 116
Polnish. High 5F 147
Polperro. Corn 3G 7
Polruan. Corn 3F 7
Polscoe. Corn 2F 7
Polsham. Som 2A 22
Polskeoch. Dum 4F 117
Polstead. Suff 2C 54
Polstead Heath. Suff 1C 54
Poltesco. Corn 5E 5
Poltimore. Devn 3C 12
Polton. Midl 3F 129
Polwarth. Bord 4D 130
Polyphant. Corn 4C 10
Polzeath. Corn 1D 6
Ponde. Powy 2E 46
Pondersbridge. Cambs 1B 64
Ponders End. G Lon 1E 39
Pond Street. Essx 2E 53
Pondtail. Hants 1G 25
Ponsanooth. Corn 5B 6
Ponsongath. Corn 5E 5
Ponsworthy. Devn 5H 11
Pontamman. Carm 4G 45
Pontantwn. Carm 4E 45
Pontardawe. Neat 5H 45
Pontarddulais. Swan 5F 45
Pontarfynach. Cdgn 3G 57
Pont-ar-gothi. Carm 3F 45
Pont ar Hydfer. Powy 3B 46
Pontarllechau. Carm 3H 45
Pontarsais. Carm 3E 45
Pontblyddyn. Flin 4E 83
Pontbren Llwyd. Rhon 5C 46
Pont-Cyfyng. Cnwy 5G 81
Pontdolgoch. Powy 1C 58
Pontefract. W Yor 2E 93
Ponteland. Nmbd 2E 115
Ponterwyd. Cdgn 2G 57
Pontesbury. Shrp 5G 71
Pontesford. Shrp 5G 71
Pontfadog. Wrex 2E 71
Pont-Faen. Shrp 2E 71
Pont-faen. Powy 2C 46
Pontfaen. Pemb 1E 43
Pontgarreg. Cdgn 5C 56
Pont-Henri. Carm 5E 45
Ponthir. Torf 2G 33
Ponthirwaun. Cdgn 1C 44
Pont-iets. Carm 5E 45
Pontllanfraith. Cphy 2E 33
Pontlliw. Swan 5G 45
Pont Llogel. Powy 4C 70
Pontllyfni. Gwyn 5D 80
Pontlottyn. Cphy 5E 46
Pontneddfechan. Powy 5C 46
Pont-newydd. Carm 5E 45
Pont-newydd. Flin 4D 82
Pontnewydd. Torf 2F 33
Ponton. Shet 6E 173
Pont Pen-y-benglog. Gwyn 4F 81
Pontrhydfendigaid. Cdgn 4G 57
Pont Rhyd-y-cyff. B'end 3B 32
Pontrhydyfen. Neat 2A 32
Pont-rhyd-y-groes. Cdgn 3G 57
Pontrhydyrun. Torf 2F 33
Pont-Rhythallt. Gwyn 4E 81
Pontrilas. Here 3G 47
Pontrilas Road. Here 3G 47
Pontrobert. Powy 4D 70
Pont-rug. Gwyn 4E 81
Ponts Green. E Sus 4A 28
Pontshill. Here 3B 48
Pont-Sian. Cdgn 1E 45
Pontsticill. Mer T 4D 46
Pont-Walby. Neat 5B 46
Pontwelly. Carm 2E 45
Pontwgan. Cnwy 3G 81
Pontyates. Carm 5E 45
Pontyberem. Carm 4F 45
Pontybodkin. Flin 5E 83
Pontyclun. Rhon 3D 32
Pontycymer. B'end 2C 32
Pontyglazier. Pemb 1F 43
Pontygwaith. Rhon 2D 32
Pont-y-pant. Cnwy 5G 81
Pontypool. Torf 2F 33
Pontypridd. Rhon 3D 32
Pontypwl. Torf 2F 33
Pontywaun. Cphy 2F 33
Pooksgreen. Hants 1B 16
Pool. Corn 4A 6
Pool. W Yor 5E 99
Poole. N Yor 2E 93
Poole. Pool 215 (3F 15)
Poole. Som 4E 21
Poole Keynes. Glos 2E 35
Poolend. Staf 5D 84
Poolewe. High 5C 162
Pooley Bridge. Cumb 2F 103
Poolfold. Staf 5C 84
Pool Head. Here 5H 59
Pool Hey. Lanc 3B 90
Poolhill. Glos 3C 48
Poolmill. Here 3A 48
Pool o' Muckhart. Clac 3C 136
Pool Quay. Powy 4E 71
Poolsbrook. Derbs 3B 86
Pool Street. Essx 2A 54
Pootings. Kent 1F 27
Pope Hill. Pemb 3D 42
Pope's Hill. Glos 4B 48
Popeswood. Brac 5G 37
Popham. Hants 2D 24
Poplar. G Lon 2E 39
Popley. Hants 1E 25
Porchfield. IOW 3C 16
Porin. High 3F 157
Poringland. Norf 5E 79
Porkellis. Corn 5A 6
Porlock. Som 2B 20
Porlock Weir. Som 2B 20
Portachoillan. Arg 4F 125
Port Adhair Bheinn na Faoghla.
W Isl 3C 170
Port Adhair Thirlodh. Arg 4B 138
Port Ann. Arg 1H 125
Port Appin. Arg 4D 140
Port Asgaig. Arg 3C 124
Port Askaig. Arg 3C 124
Portavadie. Arg 3H 125
Port Bannatyne. Arg 3B 126
Portbury. N Som 4A 34
Port Carlisle. Cumb 3D 112
Port Charlotte. Arg 4A 124
Portchester. Hants 2E 16
Port Clarence. Stoc T 2B 106
Port Driseach. Arg 2A 126
Port Dundas. Glas 3G 127
Port Ellen. Arg 5B 124
Port Elphinstone. Abers 1E 153
Portencalzie. Dum 2F 109
Portencross. N Ayr 5C 126
Port Erin. IOM 5A 108
Port Erroll. Abers 5H 161
Porter's Fen Corner. Norf 5E 77
Portesham. Dors 4B 14
Portessie. Mor 2B 160
Port e Vullen. IOM 2D 108
Port-Eynon. Swan 4D 30
Portfield. Som 4H 21
Portfield Gate. Pemb 3D 42
Portgate. Devn 4E 11
Port Gaverne. Corn 4A 10
Port Glasgow. Inv 2E 127
Portgordon. Mor 2A 160
Portgower. High 2H 165
Porth. Corn 2C 6
Porth. Rhon 2D 32
Porthaethwy. IOA 3E 81
Porthallow. Corn
nr. Looe 3G 7
nr. St Keverne 4E 5
Porthcawl. B'end 4B 32
Porthceri. V Glam 5D 32
Porthcothan. Corn 1C 6
Porthcurno. Corn 4A 4
Port Henderson. High 1G 155
Porthgain. Pemb 1C 42
Porthgwarra. Corn 4A 4
Porthill. Shrp 4G 71
Porthkerry. V Glam 5D 32
Porthleven. Corn 4D 4
Porthllechog. IOA 1D 80
Porthmadog. Gwyn 2E 69
Porthmeor. Corn 3B 4
Porth Navas. Corn 4E 5
Portholland. Corn 4D 6
Porthoustock. Corn 4F 5
Porthtowan. Corn 4A 6
Porth Tywyn. Carm 5E 45
Porth-y-felin. IOA 2B 80
Porthyrhyd. Carm
nr. Carmarthen 4F 45
nr. Llandovery 2H 45
Porth-y-waen. Shrp 3E 71
Portincaple. Arg 4B 134
Portington. E Yor 1A 94
Portinnisherrich. Arg 2G 133
Portinscale. Cumb 2D 102
Port Isaac. Corn 1D 6
Portishead. N Som 4H 33
Portknockie. Mor 2B 160
Port Lamont. Arg 2B 126
Portlethen. Abers 4G 153
Portlethen Village. Abers 4G 153
Portling. Dum 4F 111
Port Lion. Pemb 4D 43
Portloe. Corn 5D 6
Port Logan. Dum 5F 109
Portmahomack. High 5G 165
Portmead. Swan 3F 31
Portmeirion. Gwyn 2E 69
Portmellon. Corn 4E 6
Port Mholair. W Isl 4H 171
Port Mor. High 1F 139
Portmore. Hants 3B 16
Port Mulgrave. N Yor 3E 107
Portnacroish. Arg 4D 140
Portnahaven. Arg 4A 124
Portnalong. High 5C 154
Portnaluchaig. High 5E 147
Portnancon. High 2E 167
Port Nan Giuran. W Isl 4H 171
Port nan Long. W Isl 1D 170
Port Nis. W Isl 1H 171
Portobello. Edin 2G 129
Portobello. W Yor 3D 92
Port of Menteith. Stir 3E 135
Porton. Wilts 3G 23
Portormin. High 5D 168
Portpatrick. Dum 4F 109
Port Quin. Corn 1D 6
Port Ramsay. Arg 4C 140
Portreath. Corn 4A 6
Portree. High 4D 155
Port Righ. High 4D 155
Port St Mary. IOM 5B 108
Portscatho. Corn 5C 6
Portsea. Port 2E 17
Port Seton. E Lot 2H 129
Portskerra. High 2A 168
Portskewett. Mon 3A 34
Portslade-by-Sea. Brig 5D 26
Portsmouth. Port 209 (2E 17)
Portsmouth. W Yor 2H 91
Port Soderick. IOM 4C 108
Port Solent. Port 2E 17
Portsonachan. Arg 1H 133
Portsoy. Abers 2C 160
Port Sunlight. Mers 2F 83
Portswood. Sotn 1C 16
Port Talbot. Neat 3A 32
Porttannachy. Mor 2A 160
Port Tennant. Swan 3F 31
Portuairk. High 2F 139
Portway. Here 1H 47
Portway. Worc 3E 61
Port Wemyss. Arg 4A 124
Port William. Dum 5A 110
Portwrinkle. Corn 3H 7
Poslingford. Suff 1A 54
Postbridge. Devn 5G 11
Postcombe. Oxon 2F 37
Post Green. Dors 3E 15
Postling. Kent 2F 29
Postlip. Glos 3F 49
Post-Mawr. Cdgn 5D 56
Postwick. Norf 5E 79
Potarch. Abers 4D 152
Potsgrove. C Beds 3H 51
Potten End. Herts 5A 52
Potter Brompton. N Yor 2D 101
Pottergate Street. Norf 1D 66
Potterhanworth. Linc 4H 87
Potterhanworth Booths.
Linc 4H 87
Potter Heigham. Norf 4G 79
Potter Hill. Leics 3E 75
The Potteries. Stoke 1C 72
Potterne. Wilts 1E 23
Potterne Wick. Wilts 1F 23
Potternewton. W Yor 1D 92
Potters Bar. Herts 5C 52
Potters Brook. Lanc 4D 97
Potter's Cross. Staf 2C 60
Potters Crouch. Herts 5B 52
Potter Somersal. Derbs 2F 73
Potterspury. Nptn 1F 51
Potter Street. Essx 5E 53
Potterton. Abers 2G 153
Potthorpe. Norf 3B 78
Pottle Street. Wilts 2D 22
Potto. N Yor 4B 106
Potton. C Beds 1C 52
Pott Row. Norf 3G 77
Pott Shrigley. Ches E 3D 84
Poughill. Corn 2C 10
Poughill. Devn 2B 12
Poulner. Hants 2G 15
Poulshot. Wilts 1E 23
Poulton. Glos 5G 49
Poulton-le-Fylde. Lanc 1B 90
Pound Bank. Worc 3B 60
Poundbury. Dors 3B 14
Poundfield. E Sus 2G 27
Poundgate. E Sus 3F 27
Pound Green. E Sus 3G 27
Pound Green. Suff 5G 65
Pound Hill. W Sus 2D 27
Poundland. S Ayr 1G 109
Poundon. Buck 3E 51
Poundsgate. Devn 5H 11
Poundstock. Corn 3C 10
Pound Street. Hants 5C 36
Pounsley. E Sus 3G 27
Powburn. Nmbd 3E 121
Powderham. Devn 4C 12
Powerstock. Dors 3A 14
Powfoot. Dum 3C 112
Powick. Worc 5C 60
Powmill. Per 4C 136
Poxwell. Dors 4C 14
Poyle. Slo 3B 38
Poynings. W Sus 4D 26
Poyntington. Dors 4B 22
Poynton. Ches E 2D 84
Poynton. Telf 4H 71
Poynton Green. Telf 4H 71
Poystreet Green. Suff 5B 66
Praa Sands. Corn 4C 4
Pratt's Bottom. G Lon 4F 39
Praze-an-Beeble. Corn 3D 4
Prees. Shrp 2H 71
Preesall. Lanc 5C 96
Preesall Park. Lanc 5C 96
Prees Green. Shrp 2H 71
Prees Higher Heath. Shrp 2H 71
Prendergast. Pemb 3D 42
Prendwick. Nmbd 3E 121
Pren-gwyn. Cdgn 1E 45
Prenteg. Gwyn 1E 69
Prenton. Mers 2F 83
Prescot. Mers 1G 83

Prescott. *Devn* 1D 12
Prescott. *Shrp* 3G 71
Preshute. *Wilts* 5G 35
Pressen. *Nmbd* 1C 120
Prestatyn. *Den* 2C 82
Prestbury. *Ches E* 3D 84
Prestbury. *Glos* 3E 49
Presteigne. *Powy* 4F 59
Presthope. *Shrp* 1H 59
Prestleigh. *Som* 2B 22
Preston. *Brig* 5E 27
Preston. *Devn* 5B 12
Preston. *Dors* 4C 14
Preston. *E Lot*
  nr. East Linton 2B 130
  nr. Prestonpans 2G 129
Preston. *E Yor* 1E 95
Preston. *Glos* 5F 49
Preston. *Herts* 3B 52
Preston. *Kent*
  nr. Canterbury 4G 41
  nr. Faversham 4E 41
Preston. *Lanc* 208 (2D 90)
Preston. *Nmbd* 2F 121
Preston. *Rut* 5F 75
Preston. *Bord* 4D 130
Preston. *Shrp* 4H 71
Preston. *Suff* 5B 66
Preston. *Wilts*
  nr. Aldbourne 4A 36
  nr. Lyneham 4F 35
Preston Bagot. *Warw* 4F 61
Preston Bissett. *Buck* 3E 51
Preston Bowyer. *Som* 4E 21
Preston Brockhurst. *Shrp* 3H 71
Preston Brook. *Hal* 2H 83
Preston Candover. *Hants* 2E 24
Preston Capes. *Nptn* 5C 62
Preston Cross. *Glos* 2B 48
Preston Gubbals. *Shrp* 4G 71
Preston-le-Skerne. *Dur* 2A 106
Preston Marsh. *Here* 1A 48
Prestonmill. *Dum* 4A 112
Preston on Stour. *Warw* 1H 49
Preston on the Hill. *Hal* 2H 83
Preston on Wye. *Here* 1G 47
Prestonpans. *E Lot* 2G 129
Preston Plucknett. *Som* 1A 14
Preston-under-Scar. *N Yor* 5D 104
Preston upon the Weald Moors.
  Telf 4A 72
Preston Wynne. *Here* 1A 48
Prestwich. *G Man* 4G 91
Prestwick. *Nmbd* 2E 115
Prestwick. *S Ayr* 2C 116
Prestwold. *Leics* 3C 74
Prestwood. *Buck* 5G 51
Prestwood. *Staf* 1F 73
Price Town. *B'end* 2C 32
Prickwillow. *Cambs* 2E 65
Priddy. *Som* 1A 22
Priestcliffe. *Derbs* 3F 85
Priesthill. *Glas* 3G 127
Priest Hutton. *Lanc* 2E 97
Priestland. *E Ayr* 1E 117
Priest Weston. *Shrp* 1E 59
Priestwood. *Brac* 4G 37
Priestwood. *Kent* 4A 40
Primethorpe. *Leics* 1C 62
Primrose Green. *Norf* 4C 78
Primrose Hill. *Glos* 5B 48
Primrose Hill. *Lanc* 4B 90
Primrose Valley. *N Yor* 2F 101
Primsidemill. *Bord* 2C 120
Princes Gate. *Pemb* 3F 43
Princes Risborough.
  Buck 5G 51
Princethorpe. *Warw* 3B 62
Princetown. *Devn* 5F 11
Prinsted. *W Sus* 2F 17
Prion. *Den* 4C 82
Prior Muir. *Fife* 2H 137
Prior's Frome. *Here* 2A 48
Priors Halton. *Shrp* 3G 59
Priors Hardwick. *Warw* 5B 62
Priorslee. *Telf* 4B 72
Priors Marston. *Warw* 5B 62
Prior's Norton. *Glos* 3D 48
The Priory. *W Ber* 5B 36
Priory Wood. *Here* 1F 47
Priston. *Bath* 5B 34
Pristow Green. *Norf* 2D 66
Prittlewell. *S'end* 2C 40
Privett. *Hants* 4E 25
Prixford. *Devn* 3F 19
Probus. *Corn* 4C 6
Prospect. *Cumb* 5C 112
Prospect Village. *Staf* 4E 73
Provanmill. *Glas* 3H 127
Prudhoe. *Nmbd* 3D 115
Publow. *Bath* 5B 34
Puckeridge. *Herts* 3D 53
Puckington. *Som* 1G 13
Pucklechurch. *S Glo* 4B 34
Puckrup. *Glos* 2D 49
Puddinglake. *Ches W* 4B 84
Puddington. *Ches W* 3F 83
Puddington. *Devn* 1B 12
Puddlebrook. *Glos* 4B 48
Puddledock. *Norf* 1C 66
Puddletown. *Dors* 3C 14
Pudleston. *Here* 5H 59
Pudsey. *W Yor* 1C 92
Pulborough. *W Sus* 4B 26
Puleston. *Telf* 3B 72
Pulford. *Ches W* 5F 83
Pulham. *Dors* 2C 14
Pulham Market. *Norf* 2D 66
Pulham St Mary. *Norf* 2E 66
Pulley. *Shrp* 5G 71
Pulloxhill. *C Beds* 2A 52

Pulpit Hill. *Arg* 1F 133
Pulverbatch. *Shrp* 5G 71
Pumpherston. *W Lot* 3D 128
Pumsaint. *Carm* 1G 45
Puncheston. *Pemb* 2E 43
Puncknowle. *Dors* 4A 14
Punnett's Town. *E Sus* 3H 27
Purbrook. *Hants* 2E 17
Purfleet-on-Thames. *Thur* 3G 39
Puriton. *Som* 2G 21
Purleigh. *Essx* 5B 54
Purley. *G Lon* 4E 39
Purley on Thames. *W Ber* 4E 37
Purlogue. *Shrp* 3E 59
Purl's Bridge. *Cambs* 2D 65
Purse Caundle. *Dors* 1B 14
Purslow. *Shrp* 2F 59
Purston Jaglin. *W Yor* 3E 93
Purtington. *Som* 2G 13
Purton. *Glos*
  nr. Lydney 5B 48
  nr. Sharpness 5B 48
Purton. *Wilts* 3F 35
Purton Stoke. *Wilts* 2F 35
Pury End. *Nptn* 1F 51
Pusey. *Oxon* 2B 36
Putley. *Here* 2B 48
Putney. *G Lon* 3D 38
Putsborough. *Devn* 2E 19
Puttenham. *Herts* 4G 51
Puttenham. *Surr* 1A 26
Puttock End. *Essx* 1B 54
Puttock's End. *Essx* 4F 53
Puxey. *Dors* 1C 14
Puxton. *N Som* 5H 33
Pwll. *Carm* 5E 45
Pwll. *Powy* 5D 70
Pwllcrochan. *Pemb* 4D 42
Pwll-glas. *Den* 5D 82
Pwllgloyw. *Powy* 2D 46
Pwllheli. *Gwyn* 2C 68
Pwllmeyric. *Mon* 2A 34
Pwlltrap. *Carm* 3G 43
Pwll-y-glaw. *Neat* 2A 32
Pyecombe. *W Sus* 4D 27
Pye Corner. *Herts* 4E 53
Pye Corner. *Newp* 3G 33
Pye Green. *Staf* 4D 73
Pyewipe. *NE Lin* 3F 95
Pyle. *B'end* 3B 32
Pyle. *IOW* 5C 16
Pyle Hill. *Surr* 5A 38
Pylle. *Som* 3B 22
Pymoor. *Cambs* 2D 65
Pymore. *Dors* 3H 13
Pyrford. *Surr* 5B 38
Pyrford Village. *Surr* 5B 38
Pyrton. *Oxon* 2E 37
Pytchley. *Nptn* 3F 63
Pyworthy. *Devn* 2D 10

Q

Quabbs. *Shrp* 2E 58
Quadring. *Linc* 2B 76
Quadring Eaudike. *Linc* 2B 76
Quainton. *Buck* 3F 51
Quaking Houses. *Dur* 4E 115
Quarley. *Hants* 2A 24
Quarndon. *Derbs* 1H 73
Quarrendon. *Buck* 4G 51
Quarrier's Village. *Inv* 3E 127
Quarrington. *Linc* 1H 75
Quarrington Hill. *Dur* 1A 106
The Quarry. *Glos* 2C 34
Quarry Bank. *W Mid* 2D 60
Quarrywood. *Mor* 2F 159
Quartalehouse. *Abers* 4G 161
Quarter. *N Ayr* 3C 126
Quarter. *S Lan* 4A 128
Quatford. *Shrp* 1B 60
Quatt. *Shrp* 2B 60
Quebec. *Dur* 5E 115
Quedgeley. *Glos* 4D 48
Queen Adelaide. *Cambs* 2E 65
Queenborough. *Kent* 3D 40
Queen Camel. *Som* 4A 22
Queen Charlton. *Bath* 5B 34
Queen Dart. *Devn* 1B 12
Queenhill. *Worc* 2D 48
Queen Oak. *Dors* 3C 22
Queensbury. *W Yor* 1B 92
Queensferry. *Flin* 4F 83
Queensferry Crossing.
  Edin 2E 129
Queenstown. *Bkpl* 1B 90
Queen Street. *Kent* 1A 28
Queenzieburn. *N Lan* 2H 127
Quemerford. *Wilts* 5F 35
Quendale. *Shet* 10E 173
Quendon. *Essx* 2F 53
Queniborough. *Leics* 4D 74
Quenington. *Glos* 5G 49
Quernmore. *Lanc* 3E 97
Quethiock. *Corn* 2H 7
Quholm. *Orkn* 6B 172
Quick's Green. *W Ber* 4D 36
Quidenham. *Norf* 2C 66
Quidhampton. *Hants* 1D 24
Quidhampton. *Wilts* 3G 23
Quilquox. *Abers* 5G 161
Quina Brook. *Shrp* 2H 71
Quindry. *Orkn* 8D 172
Quine's Hill. *IOM* 4C 108
Quinton. *Nptn* 5E 63
Quinton. *W Mid* 2D 61
Quintrell Downs. *Corn* 2C 6
Quixhill. *Staf* 1F 73
Quoditch. *Devn* 3E 11
Quorn. *Leics* 4C 74

Quorndon. *Leics* 4C 74
Quothquan. *S Lan* 1B 118
Quoyloo. *Orkn* 5B 172
Quoyness. *Orkn* 7B 172
Quoys. *Shet*
  on Mainland 5F 173
  on Unst 1H 173

R

Rableyheath. *Herts* 4C 52
Raby. *Cumb* 4C 112
Raby. *Mers* 3F 83
Rachan Mill. *Bord* 1D 118
Rachub. *Gwyn* 4F 81
Rack End. *Oxon* 5C 50
Rackenford. *Devn* 1B 12
Rackham. *W Sus* 4B 26
Rackheath. *Norf* 4E 79
Racks. *Dum* 2B 112
Rackwick. *Orkn*
  on Hoy 8B 172
  on Westray 3U 172
Radbourne. *Derbs* 2G 73
Radcliffe. *G Man* 4F 91
Radcliffe. *Nmbd* 4G 121
Radcliffe on Trent. *Notts* 2D 74
Radclive. *Buck* 2E 51
Radernie. *Fife* 3G 137
Radfall. *Kent* 4F 41
Radford. *Bath* 1B 22
Radford. *Nott* 1C 74
Radford. *Oxon* 3C 50
Radford. *W Mid* 2H 61
Radford. *Worc* 5E 61
Radford Semele. *Warw* 4H 61
Radipole. *Dors* 4B 14
Radlett. *Herts* 1C 38
Radley. *Oxon* 2D 36
Radnage. *Buck* 2F 37
Radstock. *Bath* 1B 22
Radstone. *Nptn* 1D 50
Radway. *Warw* 1B 50
Radway Green. *Ches E* 5B 84
Radwell. *Bed* 5H 63
Radwell. *Herts* 2C 52
Radwinter. *Essx* 2G 53
Radyr. *Cardf* 3E 33
RAF Coltishall. *Norf* 3E 79
Rafford. *Mor* 3E 159
Ragdale. *Leics* 4D 74
Ragdon. *Shrp* 1G 59
Ragged Appleshaw. *Hants* 2B 24
Raggra. *Arg* 4F 169
Raglan. *Mon* 5H 47
Ragnall. *Notts* 3F 87
Raigbeg. *High* 1C 150
Rainford. *Mers* 4C 90
Rainford Junction. *Mers* 4C 90
Rainham. *G Lon* 2G 39
Rainham. *Medw* 4C 40
Rainhill. *Mers* 1G 83
Rainow. *Ches E* 3D 84
Rainton. *N Yor* 2F 99
Rainworth. *Notts* 5C 86
Raisbeck. *Cumb* 4H 103
Raise. *Cumb* 5A 114
Rait. *Per* 1E 137
Raithby. *Linc* 2C 88
Raithby by Spilsby. *Linc* 4C 88
Raithwaite. *N Yor* 3F 107
Rake. *W Sus* 4G 25
Rake End. *Staf* 4E 73
Rakeway. *Staf* 1E 73
Rakewood. *G Man* 3H 91
Ralia. *High* 4B 150
Ram Alley. *Wilts* 5H 35
Ramasaig. *High* 4A 154
Rame. *Corn*
  nr. Millbrook 4A 8
  nr. Penryn 5B 6
Ram Lane. *Kent* 1D 28
Ramnageo. *Shet* 1H 173
Rampisham. *Dors* 2A 14
Rampside. *Cumb* 3B 96
Rampton. *Cambs* 4D 64
Rampton. *Notts* 3E 87
Ramsbottom. *G Man* 3F 91
Ramsburn. *Mor* 3C 160
Ramsbury. *Wilts* 4A 36
Ramscraigs. *High* 1H 165
Ramsdean. *Hants* 4F 25
Ramsdell. *Hants* 1D 24
Ramsden. *Oxon* 4B 50
Ramsden. *Worc* 1E 49
Ramsden Bellhouse. *Essx* 1B 40
Ramsden Heath. *Essx* 1B 40
Ramsey. *Cambs* 2B 64
Ramsey. *Essx* 2F 55
Ramsey. *IOM* 2D 108
Ramsey Forty Foot. *Cambs* 2C 64
Ramsey Heights. *Cambs* 2B 64
Ramsey Island. *Essx* 5C 54
Ramsey Mereside. *Cambs* 2B 64
Ramsey St Mary's. *Cambs* 2B 64
Ramsgate. *Kent* 4H 41
Ramsgill. *N Yor* 2D 98
Ramshaw. *Dur* 5C 114
Ramshorn. *Staf* 1E 73
Ramsley. *Devn* 3G 11
Ramsnest Common. *Surr* 2A 26
Ramstone. *Abers* 2D 152
Ranais. *W Isl* 5G 171
Ranby. *Linc* 3B 88
Ranby. *Notts* 2D 86
Rand. *Linc* 3A 88
Randwick. *Glos* 5D 48
Ranfurly. *Ren* 3E 127
Rangag. *High* 4D 169
Rangemore. *Staf* 3F 73

Rangeworthy. *S Glo* 3B 34
Rankinston. *E Ayr* 3D 116
Rank's Green. *Essx* 4H 53
Ranmore Common. *Surr* 5C 38
Rannoch Station. *Per* 3B 142
Ranochan. *High* 5G 147
Ranskill. *Notts* 2D 86
Ranton. *Staf* 3C 72
Ranton Green. *Staf* 3C 72
Ranworth. *Norf* 4F 79
Raploch. *Stir* 4G 135
Rapness. *Orkn* 3E 172
Rapps. *Som* 1G 13
Rascal Moor. *E Yor* 1B 94
Rascarrel. *Dum* 5E 111
Rashfield. *Arg* 1C 126
Rashwood. *Worc* 4D 60
Raskelf. *N Yor* 2G 99
Rassau. *Blae* 4E 47
Rastrick. *W Yor* 2B 92
Ratagan. *High* 2B 148
Ratby. *Leics* 5C 74
Ratcliffe Culey. *Leics* 1H 61
Ratcliffe on Soar. *Notts* 3B 74
Ratcliffe on the Wreake. *Leics* 4D 74
Rathen. *Abers* 2H 161
Rathillet. *Fife* 1F 137
Rathmell. *N Yor* 3H 97
Ratho. *Edin* 2E 129
Ratho Station. *Edin* 2E 129
Rathven. *Mor* 2B 160
Ratley. *Hants* 4B 24
Ratley. *Warw* 1B 50
Ratlinghope. *Shrp* 1G 59
Rattar. *High* 1E 169
Ratten Row. *Cumb* 5E 113
Ratten Row. *Lanc* 5D 96
Rattery. *Devn* 2D 8
Rattlesden. *Suff* 5B 66
Ratton Village. *E Sus* 5G 27
Rattray. *Abers* 3H 161
Rattray. *Per* 4A 144
Raughton. *Cumb* 5E 113
Raughton Head. *Cumb* 5E 113
Raunds. *Nptn* 3G 63
Ravenfield. *S Yor* 1B 86
Ravenfield Common. *S Yor* 1B 86
Ravenglass. *Cumb* 5B 102
Raveningham. *Norf* 1F 67
Ravenscar. *N Yor* 4G 107
Ravensdale. *IOM* 2C 108
Ravensden. *Bed* 5H 63
Ravenseat. *N Yor* 4B 104
Ravenshead. *Notts* 5C 86
Ravensmoor. *Ches E* 5A 84
Ravensthorpe. *Nptn* 3D 62
Ravensthorpe. *W Yor* 2C 92
Ravenstone. *Leics* 4B 74
Ravenstone. *Mil* 5F 63
Ravenstonedale. *Cumb* 4A 104
Ravenstown. *Cumb* 2C 96
Ravenstruther. *S Lan* 5C 128
Ravensworth. *N Yor* 4E 105
Raw. *N Yor* 4G 107
Rawcliffe. *E Yor* 2G 93
Rawcliffe. *York* 4H 99
Rawcliffe Bridge. *E Yor* 2G 93
Rawdon. *W Yor* 1C 92
Rawgreen. *Nmbd* 4C 114
Rawmarsh. *S Yor* 1B 86
Rawnsley. *Staf* 4E 73
Rawreth. *Essx* 1B 40
Rawridge. *Devn* 2F 13
Rawson Green. *Derbs* 1A 74
Rawtenstall. *Lanc* 2G 91
Raydon. *Suff* 2D 54
Raylees. *Nmbd* 5D 120
Rayleigh. *Essx* 1C 40
Raymond's Hill. *Devn* 3G 13
Rayne. *Essx* 3H 53
Rayners Lane. *G Lon* 2C 38
Reach. *Cambs* 4E 65
Read. *Lanc* 1F 91
Reading. *Read* 209 (4F 37)
Reading Green. *Suff* 3D 66
Reading Street. *Kent* 2D 28
Readymoney. *Corn* 3F 7
Reagill. *Cumb* 3H 103
Rearquhar. *High* 4E 165
Rearsby. *Leics* 4D 74
Reasby. *Linc* 3H 87
Reaseheath. *Ches E* 5A 84
Reaster. *High* 2E 169
Reawick. *Shet* 7E 173
Reay. *High* 2B 168
Rechullin. *High* 3A 156
Reculver. *Kent* 4G 41
Redberth. *Pemb* 4E 43
Redbourn. *Herts* 4B 52
Redbourne. *N Lin* 4C 94
Redbrook. *Glos* 5A 48
Redbrook. *Wrex* 1H 71
Redburn. *High* 4D 158
Redburn. *Nmbd* 3A 114
Redcar. *Red C* 2D 106
Redcastle. *High* 4H 157
Redcliff Bay. *N Som* 4H 33
Red Dial. *Cumb* 5D 112
Redding. *Falk* 2C 128
Reddingmuirhead. *Falk* 2C 128
The Reddings. *Glos* 3E 49
Reddish. *G Man* 1C 84
Redditch. *Worc* 4E 61
Rede. *Suff* 5H 65
Redenhall. *Norf* 2E 67
Redesdale Camp. *Nmbd* 5C 120
Redesmouth. *Nmbd* 1B 114
Redford. *Ang* 4E 145
Redford. *Dur* 1D 105
Redford. *W Sus* 4G 25

Redfordgreen. *Bord* 3F 119
Redgate. *Corn* 2G 7
Redgrave. *Suff* 3C 66
Red Hill. *Warw* 5F 61
Red Hill. *W Yor* 2E 93
Redhill. *Herts* 2C 52
Redhill. *N Som* 5A 34
Redhill. *Shrp* 4B 72
Redhill. *Surr* 5D 39
Redhouses. *Arg* 3B 124
Redisham. *Suff* 2G 67
Redland. *Bris* 4A 34
Redland. *Orkn* 5C 172
Redlingfield. *Suff* 3D 66
Red Lodge. *Suff* 3F 65
Redlynch. *Som* 3C 22
Redlynch. *Wilts* 4H 23
Redmain. *Cumb* 1C 102
Redmarley. *Worc* 4B 60
Redmarley D'Abitot. *Glos* 2C 48
Redmarshall. *Stoc T* 2A 106
Redmile. *Leics* 2E 75
Redmire. *N Yor* 5D 104
Rednal. *Shrp* 3F 71
Redpath. *Bord* 1H 119
Redpoint. *High* 2G 155
Red Post. *Corn* 2C 10
Red Rock. *G Man* 4D 90
Red Roses. *Carm* 3G 43
Red Row. *Nmbd* 5G 121
Redruth. *Corn* 4B 6
Red Street. *Staf* 5C 84
Redvales. *G Man* 4G 91
Red Wharf Bay. *IOA* 2E 81
Redwick. *Newp* 3H 33
Redwick. *S Glo* 3A 34
Redworth. *Darl* 2F 105
Reed. *Herts* 2D 52
Reed End. *Herts* 2D 52
Reedham. *Linc* 5B 88
Reedham. *Norf* 5G 79
Reedness. *E Yor* 2B 94
Reeds Beck. *Linc* 4B 88
Reemshill. *Abers* 4E 161
Reepham. *Linc* 3H 87
Reepham. *Norf* 3C 78
Reeth. *N Yor* 5D 104
Regaby. *IOM* 2D 108
Regil. *N Som* 5A 34
Regoul. *High* 3C 158
Reiff. *High* 2D 162
Reigate. *Surr* 5D 38
Reighton. *N Yor* 2F 101
Reilth. *Shrp* 2E 59
Reinigeadal. *W Isl* 7E 171
Reisque. *Abers* 2F 153
Reiss. *High* 3F 169
Rejerrah. *Corn* 3B 6
Releath. *Corn* 5A 6
Relubbus. *Corn* 3C 4
Relugas. *Mor* 4D 159
Remenham. *Wok* 3F 37
Remenham Hill. *Wok* 3F 37
Rempstone. *Notts* 3C 74
Rendcomb. *Glos* 5F 49
Rendham. *Suff* 4F 67
Rendlesham. *Suff* 5F 67
Renfrew. *Ren* 3G 127
Renhold. *Bed* 5H 63
Renishaw. *Derbs* 3B 86
Rennington. *Nmbd* 3G 121
Renton. *W Dun* 2E 127
Renwick. *Cumb* 5G 113
Repps. *Norf* 4G 79
Repton. *Derbs* 3H 73
Rescassa. *Corn* 4D 6
Rescobie. *Ang* 3E 145
Rescorla. *Corn*
  nr. Penwithick 3E 7
  nr. Sticker 4D 6
Resipole. *High* 2B 140
Resolfen. *Neat* 5B 46
Resolis. *High* 2A 158
Resolven. *Neat* 5B 46
Rest and be thankful. *Arg* 3B 134
Reston. *Bord* 3E 131
Restrop. *Wilts* 3F 35
Retford. *Notts* 2E 86
Retire. *Corn* 2E 6
Rettendon. *Essx* 1B 40
Revesby. *Linc* 4B 88
Rew. *Devn* 5D 8
Rewe. *Devn* 3C 12
Rew Street. *IOW* 3C 16
Rexon. *Devn* 4E 11
Reybridge. *Wilts* 5E 35
Reydon. *Suff* 3H 67
Reymerston. *Norf* 5C 78
Reynalton. *Pemb* 4E 43
Reynoldston. *Swan* 4D 31
Rezare. *Corn* 5D 10
Rhadyr. *Mon* 5G 47
Rhaeadr Gwy. *Powy* 4B 58
Rhandirmwyn. *Carm* 1A 46
Rhayader. *Powy* 4B 58
Rheindown. *High* 4H 157
Rhemore. *High* 3G 139
Rhenetra. *High* 3D 154
Rhewl. *Den*
  nr. Llangollen 1D 70
  nr. Ruthin 4D 82
Rhewl. *Shrp* 2F 71
Rhewl-Mostyn. *Flin* 2D 82
Rhian. *High* 2C 164
Rhian Breck. *High* 3C 164
Rhicarn. *High* 1E 163
Rhiconich. *High* 3C 166
Rhicullen. *High* 1A 158
Rhidorroch. *High* 4F 163
Rhifail. *High* 4H 167

Rhigos – Rumford

Rhigos. Rhon 5C **46**
Rhilochan. High 3E **165**
Rhiroy. High 5F **163**
Rhitongue. High 3G **167**
Rhiw. Gwyn 3B **68**
Rhiwabon. Wrex 1F **71**
Rhiwbina. Card 3E **33**
Rhiwbryfdir. Gwyn 1F **69**
Rhiwderin. Newp 3F **33**
Rhiwlas. Gwyn
nr. Bala 2B **70**
nr. Bangor 4E **81**
Rhiwlas. Powy 2D **70**
Rhodes. G Man 4G **91**
Rhodesia. Notts 2C **86**
Rhodes Minnis. Kent 1F **29**
Rhodiad-y-Brenin. Pemb 2B **42**
Rhondda. Rhon 2C **32**
Rhonehouse. Dum 4E **111**
Rhoose. V Glam 5D **32**
Rhos. Carm 2D **45**
Rhos. Neat 5H **45**
The Rhos. Pemb 3E **43**
Rhosaman. Carm 4H **45**
Rhoscefnhir. IOA 3E **81**
Rhoscolyn. IOA 3B **80**
Rhos Common. Powy 4E **71**
Rhoscrowther. Pemb 4D **42**
Rhos-ddu. Gwyn 2B **68**
Rhosdylluan. Gwyn 3A **70**
Rhosesmor. Flin 4E **82**
Rhos-fawr. Gwyn 2C **68**
Rhosgadfan. Gwyn 5E **81**
Rhosgoch. IOA 2D **80**
Rhosgoch. Powy 1E **47**
Rhos Haminiog. Cdgn 4E **57**
Rhos-hill. Pemb 1B **44**
Rhoshirwaun. Gwyn 3A **68**
Rhoslan. Gwyn 1D **69**
Rhoslefain. Gwyn 5E **69**
Rhosllanerchrugog. Wrex 1E **71**
Rhôs Lligwy. IOA 2D **81**
Rhosmaen. Carm 3G **45**
Rhosmeirch. IOA 3D **80**
Rhosneigr. IOA 3C **80**
Rhôs-on-Sea. Cnwy 2H **81**
Rhossili. Swan 4D **30**
Rhosson. Pemb 2B **42**
Rhostrenwfa. IOA 3D **80**
Rhostryfan. Gwyn 5D **81**
Rhostyllen. Wrex 1F **71**
Rhoswiel. Shrp 2E **71**
Rhosybol. IOA 2D **80**
Rhos-y-brithdir. Powy 3D **70**
Rhos-y-garth. Cdgn 3F **57**
Rhos-y-gwaliau. Gwyn 2B **70**
Rhos-y-llan. Gwyn 2B **68**
Rhos-y-meirch. Powy 4E **59**
Rhu. Arg 1D **126**
Rhualt. Den 3C **82**
Rhubha Stoer. High 1E **163**
Rhubodach. Arg 2B **126**
Rhuddall Heath. Ches W 4H **83**
Rhuddlan. Cdgn 1E **45**
Rhuddlan. Den 3C **82**
Rhue. High 4E **163**
Rhulen. Powy 1E **47**
Rhunahaorine. Arg 5F **125**
Rhuthun. Den 5D **82**
Rhuvoult. High 3C **166**
Y Rhws. V Glam 5D **32**
Rhyd. Gwyn 1F **69**
Rhydaman. Carm 4G **45**
Rhydargaeau. Carm 3E **45**
Rhydcymerau. Carm 2F **45**
Rhydd. Worc 1D **48**
Rhyd-Ddu. Gwyn 5E **81**
Rhydding. Neat 3G **31**
Rhydfudr. Cdgn 4E **57**
Rhydlanfair. Cnwy 5H **81**
Rhydlewis. Cdgn 1D **44**
Rhydlios. Gwyn 2A **68**
Rhydlydan. Cnwy 5A **82**
Rhyd-meirionydd. Cdgn 2F **57**
Rhydowen. Cdgn 1E **45**
Rhyd-Rosser. Cdgn 4E **57**
Rhydspence. Here 1F **47**
Rhydtalog. Flin 5E **83**
Rhyd-uchaf. Gwyn 2B **70**
Rhydwyn. IOA 2C **80**
Rhyd-y-clafdy. Gwyn 2C **68**
Rhydycroesau. Powy 2E **71**
Rhydyfelin. Cdgn 3E **57**
Rhydyfelin. Rhon 3D **32**
Rhyd-y-foel. Cnwy 3B **82**
Rhyd-y-fro. Neat 5H **45**
Rhydymain. Gwyn 3H **69**
Rhyd-y-meudwy. Den 5D **82**
Rhydymwyn. Flin 4E **82**
Rhyd-yr-onen. Gwyn 5F **69**
Rhyd-y-sarn. Gwyn 1F **69**
Rhyl. Den 2C **82**
Rhymney. Cphy 5E **46**
Rhymni. Cphy 5E **46**
Rhynd. Per 1D **136**
Rhynie. Abers 1B **152**
Ribbesford. Worc 3B **60**
Ribbleton. Lanc 1D **90**
Ribby. Lanc 1C **90**
Ribchester. Lanc 1E **91**
Riber. Derbs 5H **85**
Ribigill. High 3F **167**
Riby. Linc 4E **95**
Riccall. N Yor 1G **93**
Riccarton. E Ayr 1D **116**
Richards Castle. Here 4G **59**
Richborough Port. Kent 4H **41**
Richings Park. Buck 3B **38**
Richmond. G Lon 3C **38**
Richmond. N Yor 4E **105**
Rickarton. Abers 5F **153**
Rickerby. Cumb 4F **113**
Rickerscote. Staf 3D **72**
Rickford. N Som 1H **21**
Rickham. Devn 5D **8**
Rickinghall. Suff 3C **66**
Rickleton. Tyne 4F **115**
Rickling. Essx 2E **53**
Rickling Green. Essx 3F **53**
Rickmansworth. Herts 1B **38**
Riddings. Derbs 5B **86**
Riddlecombe. Devn 1G **11**
Riddlesden. W Yor 5C **98**
Ridge. Dors 4E **15**
Ridge. Herts 5C **52**
Ridge. Wilts 3E **23**
Ridgebourne. Powy 4C **58**
Ridge Lane. Warw 1G **61**
Ridgeway. Derbs
nr. Alfreton 5A **86**
nr. Sheffield 2B **86**
Ridgeway. Staf 5C **84**
Ridgeway Cross. Here 1C **48**
Ridgeway Moor. Derbs 2B **86**
Ridgewell. Essx 1H **53**
Ridgewood. E Sus 3F **27**
Ridgmont. C Beds 2H **51**
Ridgwardine. Shrp 2A **72**
Riding Mill. Nmbd 3D **114**
Ridley. Kent 4H **39**
Ridley. Nmbd 3A **114**
Ridlington. Norf 2F **79**
Ridlington. Rut 5F **75**
Ridsdale. Nmbd 1C **114**
Riemore Lodge. Per 4H **143**
Rievaulx. N Yor 1H **99**
Rift House. Hart 1B **106**
Rigg. Dum 3D **112**
Riggend. N Lan 2A **128**
Rigsby. Linc 3D **88**
Rigside. S Lan 1A **118**
Riley Green. Lanc 2E **90**
Rileyhill. Staf 4F **73**
Rilla Mill. Corn 5C **10**
Rillington. N Yor 2C **100**
Rimington. Lanc 5H **97**
Rimpton. Som 4B **22**
Rimsdale. High 4H **167**
Rimswell. E Yor 2G **95**
Ringasta. Shet 10E **173**
Ringford. Dum 4D **111**
Ringing Hill. Leics 4B **74**
Ringinglow. S Yor 2G **85**
Ringland. Norf 4D **78**
Ringlestone. Kent 5C **40**
Ringmer. E Sus 4F **27**
Ringmore. Devn
nr. Kingsbridge 4C **8**
nr. Teignmouth 5C **12**
Ring o' Bells. Lanc 3C **90**
Ring's End. Cambs 5C **76**
Ringsfield. Suff 2G **67**
Ringsfield Corner. Suff 2G **67**
Ringshall. Buck 4H **51**
Ringshall. Suff 5C **66**
Ringshall Stocks. Suff 5C **66**
Ringstead. Norf 1G **77**
Ringstead. Nptn 3G **63**
Ringwood. Hants 2G **15**
Ringwould. Kent 1H **29**
Rinmore. Abers 2B **152**
Rinnigill. Orkn 8C **172**
Rinsey. Corn 4C **4**
Riof. W Isl 4D **171**
Ripe. E Sus 4G **27**
Ripley. Derbs 5B **86**
Ripley. Hants 3G **15**
Ripley. N Yor 3E **99**
Ripley. Surr 5B **38**
Riplingham. E Yor 1C **94**
Ripon. N Yor 2F **99**
Rippingale. Linc 3H **75**
Ripple. Kent 1H **29**
Ripple. Worc 2D **48**
Ripponden. W Yor 3A **92**
Rireavach. High 4E **163**
Risabus. Arg 5B **124**
Risbury. Here 5H **59**
Risby. E Yor 1D **94**
Risby. N Lin 3C **94**
Risby. Suff 4G **65**
Risca. Cphy 2F **33**
Rise. E Yor 5F **101**
Riseden. E Sus 2H **27**
Riseden. Kent 2B **28**
Rise End. Derbs 5G **85**
Risegate. Linc 3B **76**
Riseholme. Linc 3G **87**
Riseley. Bed 4H **63**
Riseley. Wok 5F **37**
Rishangles. Suff 4D **66**
Rishton. Lanc 1F **91**
Rishworth. W Yor 3A **92**
Risley. Derbs 2B **74**
Risley. Warr 1A **84**
Risplith. N Yor 3E **99**
Rispond. High 2E **167**
Rivar. Wilts 5B **36**
Rivenhall. Essx 4B **54**
Rivenhall End. Essx 4B **54**
River. Kent 1G **29**
River. W Sus 3A **26**
River Bank. Cambs 4E **65**
Riverhead. Kent 5G **39**
Rivington. Lanc 3E **91**
Roach Bridge. Lanc 2D **90**
Roachill. Devn 4B **20**
Roade. Nptn 5E **63**
Road Green. Norf 1E **67**
Roadhead. Cumb 2G **113**
Roadmeetings. S Lan 5B **128**
Roadside. High 2D **168**
Roadside of Catterline. Abers 1H **145**
Roadside of Kinneff. Abers 1H **145**
Roadwater. Som 3D **20**
Road Weedon. Nptn 5D **62**
Roag. High 4B **154**
Roa Island. Cumb 3B **96**
Roath. Card 4E **33**
Roberton. Bord 3G **119**
Roberton. S Lan 2B **118**
Robertsbridge. E Sus 3B **28**
Robertstown. Mor 4G **159**
Robertstown. Rhon 5C **46**
Roberttown. W Yor 2B **92**
Robeston Back. Pemb 3E **43**
Robeston Wathen. Pemb 3E **43**
Robeston West. Pemb 4C **42**
Robin Hood. Lanc 3D **90**
Robin Hood. W Yor 2D **92**
Robinhood End. Essx 2H **53**
Robin Hood's Bay. N Yor 4G **107**
Roborough. Devn
nr. Great Torrington 1F **11**
nr. Plymouth 2B **8**
Rob Roy's House. Arg 2A **134**
Roby Mill. Lanc 4D **90**
Rocester. Staf 2F **73**
Roch. Pemb 2C **42**
Rochdale. G Man 3G **91**
Roche. Corn 2D **6**
Rochester.
Medw
.... **Medway Towns 204** (4B **40**)
Rochester. Nmbd 5C **120**
Rochford. Essx 1C **40**
Rock. Corn 1D **6**
Rock. Nmbd 2G **121**
Rock. W Sus 4C **26**
Rock. Worc 3B **60**
Rockbeare. Devn 3D **12**
Rockbourne. Hants 1G **15**
Rockcliffe. Cumb 3E **113**
Rockcliffe. Dum 4F **111**
Rockcliffe Cross. Cumb 3E **113**
Rock Ferry. Mers 2F **83**
Rockfield. High 5G **165**
Rockfield. Mon 4H **47**
Rockford. Hants 2G **15**
Rockgreen. Shrp 3H **59**
Rockhampton. S Glo 2B **34**
Rockhead. Corn 4A **10**
Rockingham. Nptn 1F **63**
Rockland All Saints. Norf 1B **66**
Rockland St Mary. Norf 5F **79**
Rockland St Peter. Norf 1B **66**
Rockley. Wilts 4G **35**
Rockwell End. Buck 3F **37**
Rockwell Green. Som 1E **13**
Rodborough. Glos 5D **48**
Rodbourne. Wilts 3E **35**
Rodd. Here 4F **59**
Roddam. Nmbd 2E **121**
Rodden. Dors 4B **14**
Roddenloft. E Ayr 2D **117**
Roddymoor. Dur 1E **105**
Rode. Som 1D **22**
Rode Heath. Ches E 5C **84**
Rodeheath. Ches E 4C **84**
Rodel. W Isl 9C **171**
Roden. Telf 4H **71**
Rodhuish. Som 3D **20**
Rodington. Telf 4H **71**
Rodington Heath. Telf 4H **71**
Rodley. Glos 4C **48**
Rodmarton. Glos 2E **35**
Rodmell. E Sus 5F **27**
Rodmersham. Kent 4D **40**
Rodmersham Green. Kent 4D **40**
Rodney Stoke. Som 2H **21**
Rodsley. Derbs 1G **73**
Rodway. Som 3F **21**
Rodway. Telf 4A **72**
Rodwell. Dors 5B **14**
Roecliffe. N Yor 3F **99**
Roe Green. Herts 2D **52**
Roehampton. G Lon 3D **38**
Roesound. Shet 5E **173**
Roffey. W Sus 2C **26**
Rogart. High 3E **165**
Rogate. W Sus 4G **25**
Roger Ground. Cumb 5E **103**
Rogerstone. Newp 3F **33**
Rogiet. Mon 3H **33**
Rogue's Alley. Cambs 5C **76**
Roke. Oxon 2E **37**
Rokemarsh. Oxon 2E **36**
Roker. Tyne 4H **115**
Rollesby. Norf 4G **79**
Rolleston. Leics 5E **75**
Rolleston. Notts 5E **87**
Rolleston on Dove. Staf 3G **73**
Rolston. E Yor 5G **101**
Rolvenden. Kent 2C **28**
Rolvenden Layne. Kent 2C **28**
Romaldkirk. Dur 2C **104**
Roman Bank. Shrp 1H **59**
Romanby. N Yor 5A **106**
Romannobridge. Bord 5E **129**
Romansleigh. Devn 4H **19**
Romers Common. Worc 4H **59**
Romesdal. High 3D **154**
Romford. Dors 2F **15**
Romford. G Lon 2G **39**
Romiley. G Man 1D **84**
Romsey. Hants 4B **24**
Romsley. Shrp 2B **60**
Romsley. Worc 3D **60**
Ronague. IOM 4B **108**
Ronaldsvoe. Orkn 8D **172**
Rookby. Cumb 3B **104**
Rookhope. Dur 5C **114**
Rooking. Cumb 3F **103**
Rookley. IOW 4D **16**
Rooks Bridge. Som 1G **21**
Rooksey Green. Suff 5B **66**
Rook's Nest. Som 3D **20**
Rookwood. W Sus 3F **17**
Roos. E Yor 1F **95**
Roosebeck. Cumb 3B **96**
Roosecote. Cumb 3B **96**
Rootfield. High 3H **157**
Rootham's Green. Bed 5A **64**
Rootpark. S Lan 4C **128**
Ropley. Hants 3E **25**
Ropley Dean. Hants 3E **25**
Ropsley. Linc 2G **75**
Rora. Abers 3H **161**
Rorandle. Abers 2D **152**
Rorrington. Shrp 5F **71**
Rose. Corn 3B **6**
Roseacre. Lanc 1C **90**
Rose Ash. Devn 4A **20**
Rosebank. S Lan 5B **128**
Rosebush. Pemb 2E **43**
Rosedale Abbey. N Yor 5E **107**
Roseden. Nmbd 2E **121**
Rose Green. Essx 3B **54**
Rose Green. Suff 1C **54**
Rosehall. High 3B **164**
Rosehearty. Abers 2G **161**
Rose Hill. E Sus 4F **27**
Rose Hill. Lanc 1G **91**
Rosehill. Shrp
nr. Market Drayton 2A **72**
nr. Shrewsbury 4G **71**
Roseisle. Mor 2F **159**
Rosemarket. Pemb 4D **42**
Rosemarkie. High 3B **158**
Rosemary Lane. Devn 1E **13**
Rosemount. Per 4A **144**
Rosenannon. Corn 2D **6**
Roser's Cross. E Sus 3G **27**
Rosevean. Corn 3E **6**
Rosewell. Midl 3F **129**
Roseworth. Stoc T 2B **106**
Roseworthy. Corn 3D **4**
Rosgill. Cumb 3G **103**
Roshven. High 1B **140**
Roskhill. High 4B **154**
Roskorwell. Corn 4E **5**
Rosley. Cumb 5E **113**
Roslin. Midl 3F **129**
Rosliston. Derbs 4G **73**
Rosneath. Arg 1D **126**
Ross. Dum 5D **110**
Ross. Nmbd 1F **121**
Ross. Per 1G **135**
Ross. Bord 3F **131**
Rossendale. Lanc 2F **91**
Rossett. Wrex 5F **83**
Rossington. S Yor 1D **86**
Rosskeen. High 2A **158**
Rossland. Ren 2F **127**
Ross-on-Wye. Here 3B **48**
Roster. High 5E **169**
Rostherne. Ches E 2B **84**
Rostholme. S Yor 4F **93**
Rosthwaite. Cumb 3D **102**
Roston. Derbs 1F **73**
Rosudgeon. Corn 4C **4**
Rosyth. Fife 1E **129**
Rothbury. Nmbd 4E **121**
Rotherby. Leics 4D **74**
Rotherfield. E Sus 3G **27**
Rotherfield Greys. Oxon 3F **37**
Rotherfield Peppard. Oxon 3F **37**
Rotherham. S Yor 1B **86**
Rothersthorpe. Nptn 5E **62**
Rotherwick. Hants 1F **25**
Rothes. Mor 4G **159**
Rothesay. Arg 3B **126**
Rothienorman. Abers 5E **160**
Rothiesholm. Orkn 5F **172**
Rothley. Leics 4C **74**
Rothley. Nmbd 1D **114**
Rothwell. Linc 1A **88**
Rothwell. Nptn 2F **63**
Rothwell. W Yor 2D **92**
Rotsea. E Yor 4E **101**
Rottal. Ang 2C **144**
Rotten End. Suff 4F **67**
Rotten Row. Norf 4C **78**
Rotten Row. W Ber 4D **36**
Rotten Row. W Mid 3F **61**
Rottingdean. Brig 5E **27**
Rottington. Cumb 3A **102**
Roud. IOW 4D **16**
Rougham. Norf 3H **77**
Rougham. Suff 4B **66**
Rough Close. Staf 2D **72**
Rough Common. Kent 5F **41**
Roughcote. Staf 1D **72**
Rough Haugh. High 4H **167**
Rough Hay. Staf 3G **73**
Roughlee. Lanc 5H **97**
Roughley. W Mid 1F **61**
Roughsike. Cumb 2G **113**
Roughton. Linc 4B **88**
Roughton. Norf 2E **78**
Roughton. Shrp 1B **60**
Roundbush Green. Essx 4F **53**
Roundham. Som 2H **13**
Roundhay. W Yor 1D **92**
Round Hill. Torb 2E **9**
Roundhurst. W Sus 2A **26**
Round Maple. Suff 1C **54**
Round Oak. Shrp 2F **59**
Roundstreet Common. W Sus 3B **26**
Roundthwaite. Cumb 4H **103**
Roundway. Wilts 5F **35**
Roundyhill. Ang 3C **144**
Rousdon. Devn 3F **13**
Rousham. Oxon 3C **50**
Rous Lench. Worc 5E **61**
Routh. E Yor 5E **101**
Rout's Green. Buck 2F **37**
Row. Corn 5A **10**
Row. Cumb
nr. Kendal 1D **96**
nr. Penrith 1H **103**
The Row. Lanc 2D **96**
Rowanburn. Dum 2F **113**
Rowanhill. Abers 3H **161**
Rowardennan. Stir 4C **134**
Rowarth. Derbs 2E **85**
Row Ash. Hants 1D **16**
Rowberrow. Som 1H **21**
Rowde. Wilts 5E **35**
Rowden. Devn 3G **11**
Rowen. Cnwy 3G **81**
Rowfoot. Nmbd 3H **113**
Row Green. Essx 3H **53**
Row Heath. Essx 4E **55**
Rowhedge. Essx 3D **54**
Rowhook. W Sus 2C **26**
Rowington. Warw 4G **61**
Rowland. Derbs 3G **85**
Rowlands Castle. Hants 1F **17**
Rowlands Gill. Tyne 4E **115**
Rowledge. Hants 2G **25**
Rowley. Dur 5D **115**
Rowley. E Yor 1C **94**
Rowley. Shrp 5F **71**
Rowley Hill. W Yor 3B **92**
Rowley Regis. W Mid 2D **60**
Rowlstone. Here 3G **47**
Rowly. Surr 1B **26**
Rowner. Hants 2D **16**
Rowney Green. Worc 3E **61**
Rownhams. Hants 1B **16**
Rowrah. Cumb 3B **102**
Rowsham. Buck 4G **51**
Rowsley. Derbs 4G **85**
Rowstock. Oxon 3C **36**
Rowston. Linc 5H **87**
Rowthorne. Derbs 4B **86**
Rowton. Ches W 4G **83**
Rowton. Shrp
nr. Ludlow 2G **59**
nr. Shrewsbury 4F **71**
Rowton. Telf 4A **72**
Row Town. Surr 4B **38**
Roxburgh. Bord 1B **120**
Roxby. N Lin 3C **94**
Roxby. N Yor 3E **107**
Roxton. Bed 5A **64**
Roxwell. Essx 5G **53**
Royal Leamington Spa.
Warw 4H **61**
Royal Oak. Darl 2F **105**
Royal Oak. Lanc 4C **90**
Royal Oak. N Yor 2F **101**
Royal's Green. Ches E 1A **72**
Royal Sutton Coldfield.
W Mid 1F **61**
Royal Tunbridge Wells. Kent 2G **27**
Royal Wootton Bassett. Wilts 3F **35**
Roybridge. High 5E **149**
Roydon. Essx 4E **53**
Roydon. Norf
nr. Diss 2C **66**
nr. King's Lynn 3G **77**
Roydon Hamlet. Essx 5E **53**
Royston. Herts 1D **52**
Royston. S Yor 3D **92**
Royston Water. Som 1F **13**
Royton. G Man 4H **91**
Ruabon. Wrex 1F **71**
Ruaig. Arg 4B **138**
Ruan High Lanes. Corn 5D **6**
Ruan Lanihorne. Corn 4C **6**
Ruan Major. Corn 5E **5**
Ruan Minor. Corn 5E **5**
Ruarach. High 1B **148**
Ruardean. Glos 4B **48**
Ruardean Hill. Glos 4B **48**
Ruardean Woodside. Glos 4B **48**
Rubery. Worc 3D **61**
Ruchazie. Glas 3H **127**
Ruckcroft. Cumb 5G **113**
Ruckinge. Kent 2E **29**
Ruckland. Linc 3C **88**
Rucklers Lane. Herts 5A **52**
Ruckley. Shrp 5H **71**
Rudbaxton. Pemb 2D **42**
Rudby. N Yor 4B **106**
Ruddington. Notts 2C **74**
Rudford. Glos 3C **48**
Rudge. Shrp 1C **60**
Rudge. Wilts 1D **22**
Rudge Heath. Shrp 1B **60**
Rudgeway. S Glo 3B **34**
Rudgwick. W Sus 2B **26**
Rudhall. Here 3B **48**
Rudheath. Ches W 3A **84**
Rudley Green. Essx 5B **54**
Rudloe. Wilts 4D **34**
Rudry. Cphy 3F **33**
Rudston. E Yor 3E **101**
Rudyard. Staf 5D **84**
Rufford. Lanc 3C **90**
Rufforth. York 4H **99**
Rugby. Warw 3C **62**
Rugeley. Staf 4E **73**
Ruglen. S Ayr 4B **116**
Ruilick. High 4H **157**
Ruisaurie. High 4G **157**
Ruishton. Som 4F **21**
Ruisigearraidh. W Isl 1E **170**
Ruislip. G Lon 2B **38**
Ruislip Common. G Lon 2B **38**
Rumbling Bridge. Per 4C **136**
Rumburgh. Suff 2F **67**
Rumford. Corn 1C **6**

Rumford. Falk 2C 128
Rumney. Card 4F 33
Rumwell. Som 4E 21
Runcorn. Hal 2H 83
Runcton. W Sus 2G 17
Runcton Holme. Norf 5F 77
Rundlestone. Devn 5F 11
Runfold. Surr 2G 25
Runhall. Norf 5C 78
Runham. Norf 4G 79
Runnington. Som 4E 20
Runshaw Moor. Lanc 3D 90
Runswick. N Yor 3F 107
Runtaleave. Ang 2B 144
Runwell. Essx 1B 40
Ruscombe. Wok 4F 37
Rushall. Here 2B 48
Rushall. Norf 2D 66
Rushall. W Mid 5E 73
Rushall. Wilts 1G 23
Rushbrooke. Suff 4A 66
Rushbury. Shrp 1H 59
Rushden. Herts 2D 52
Rushden. Nptn 4G 63
Rushenden. Kent 3D 40
Rushford. Devn 5E 11
Rushford. Norf 2B 66
Rush Green. Herts 3C 52
Rushlake Green. E Sus 4H 27
Rushmere. Suff 2G 67
Rushmere St Andrew. Suff 1F 55
Rushmoor. Surr 2G 25
Rushock. Worc 3C 60
Rusholme. G Man 1C 84
Rushton. Ches W 4H 83
Rushton. Nptn 2F 63
Rushton. Shrp 5A 72
Rushton Spencer. Staf 4D 84
Rushwick. Worc 5C 60
Rushyford. Dur 2F 105
Ruskie. Stir 3F 135
Ruskington. Linc 5H 87
Rusland. Cumb 1C 96
Rusper. W Sus 2D 26
Ruspidge. Glos 4B 48
Russell's Water. Oxon 3F 37
Russel's Green. Suff 3E 67
Russ Hill. Surr 1D 26
Russland. Orkn 6C 172
Rusthall. Kent 2G 27
Rustington. W Sus 5B 26
Ruston. N Yor 1D 100
Ruston Parva. E Yor 3E 101
Ruswarp. N Yor 4F 107
Rutherglen. S Lan 3H 127
Ruthernbridge. Corn 2E 6
Ruthin. Den 5D 82
Ruthin. V Glam 4C 32
Ruthrieston. Abers 3G 153
Ruthven. Abers 4C 160
Ruthven. Ang 4B 144
Ruthven. High
  nr. Inverness 5C 158
  nr. Kingussie 4B 150
Ruthvoes. Corn 2D 6
Ruthwaite. Cumb 1D 102
Ruthwell. Dum 3C 112
Ruxton Green. Here 4A 48
Ruyton-XI-Towns. Shrp 3F 71
Ryal. Nmbd 2D 114
Ryall. Dors 3H 13
Ryall. Worc 1D 48
Ryarsh. Kent 5A 40
Rychraggan. High 5G 157
Rydal. Cumb 4E 103
Ryde. IOW 3D 16
Rye. E Sus 3D 28
Ryecroft Gate. Staf 4D 84
Ryeford. Here 3B 48
Rye Foreign. E Sus 3D 28
Rye Harbour. E Sus 4D 28
Ryehill. E Yor 2F 95
Rye Street. Worc 2C 48
Ryhall. Rut 4H 75
Ryhill. W Yor 3D 93
Ryhope. Tyne 4H 115
Ryhope Colliery. Tyne 4H 115
Rylands. Notts 2C 74
Rylstone. N Yor 4B 98
Ryme Intrinseca. Dors 1A 14
Ryther. N Yor 1F 93
Ryton. Glos 2C 48
Ryton. N Yor 2B 100
Ryton. Shrp 5B 72
Ryton. Tyne 3E 115
Ryton. Warw 2B 62
Ryton-on-Dunsmore. Warw 3A 62
Ryton Woodside. Tyne 3E 115

S

Saasaig. High 3E 147
Sabden. Lanc 1F 91
Sacombe. Herts 4D 52
Sacriston. Dur 5F 115
Sadberge. Darl 3A 106
Saddell. Arg 2B 122
Saddington. Leics 1D 62
Saddle Bow. Norf 4F 77
Saddlescombe. W Sus 4D 26
Saddleworth. G Man 4H 91
Sadgill. Cumb 4F 103
Saffron Walden. Essx 2F 53
Sageston. Pemb 4E 43
Saham Hills. Norf 5B 78
Saham Toney. Norf 5A 78
Saighdinis. W Isl 2D 170
Saighton. Ches W 4G 83
Sain Dunwyd. V Glam 5C 32
Sain Hilari. V Glam 4D 32

St Abbs. Bord 3F 131
St Agnes. Corn 3B 6
St Albans. Herts 5B 52
St Allen. Corn 3C 6
St Andrews. Fife 209 (2H 137)
St Andrews Major. V Glam 4E 33
St Anne's. Lanc 2B 90
St Ann's. Dum 5C 118
St Ann's Chapel. Corn 5E 11
St Ann's Chapel. Devn 4C 8
St Anthony. Corn 5C 6
St Anthony-in-Meneage. Corn 4E 5
St Arvans. Mon 2A 34
St Asaph. Den 3C 82
Sain Tathan. V Glam 5D 32
St Athan. V Glam 5D 32
St Austell. Corn 3E 6
St Bartholomew's Hill. Wilts 4E 23
St Bees. Cumb 3A 102
St Blazey. Corn 3E 7
St Blazey Gate. Corn 3E 7
St Boswells. Bord 1H 119
St Breock. Corn 1D 6
St Breward. Corn 5A 10
St Briavels. Glos 5A 48
St Brides. Pemb 3B 42
St Brides Major. V Glam 4B 32
St Bride's Netherwent. Mon 3H 33
St Bride's-super-Ely. V Glam 4D 32
St Brides Wentlooge. Newp 3F 33
St Budeaux. Plym 3A 8
Saintbury. Glos 2G 49
St Buryan. Corn 4B 4
St Catherine. Bath 4C 34
St Catherines. Arg 3A 134
St Clears. Carm 3G 43
St Cleer. Corn 2G 7
St Clement. Corn 4C 6
St Clether. Corn 4C 10
St Colmac. Arg 3B 126
St Columb Major. Corn 2D 6
St Columb Minor. Corn 2C 6
St Columb Road. Corn 3D 6
St Combs. Abers 2H 161
St Cross. Hants 4C 24
St Cross South Elmham. Suff 2E 67
St Cyrus. Abers 2G 145
St David's. Per 1B 136
St David's. Pemb 2B 42
St Day. Corn 4B 6
St Dennis. Corn 3D 6
St Dogmaels. Pemb 1B 44
St Dominick. Corn 2H 7
St Donat's. V Glam 5C 32
St Edith's Marsh. Wilts 5E 35
St Endellion. Corn 1D 6
St Enoder. Corn 3C 6
St Erme. Corn 4C 6
St Erney. Corn 3H 7
St Erth. Corn 3C 4
St Erth Praze. Corn 3C 4
St Ervan. Corn 1C 6
St Eval. Corn 2C 6
St Ewe. Corn 4D 6
St Fagans. Card 4E 32
St Fergus. Abers 3H 161
St Fillans. Per 1F 135
St Florence. Pemb 4E 43
St Gennys. Corn 3B 10
St George. Cnwy 3B 82
St George's. N Som 5G 33
St Georges. V Glam 4D 32
St George's Hill. Surr 4B 38
St Germans. Corn 3H 7
St Giles in the Wood. Devn 1F 11
St Giles on the Heath. Devn 3D 10
St Giles's Hill. Hants 4C 24
St Gluvias. Corn 5B 6
St Harmon. Powy 3B 58
St Helena. Warw 5G 73
St Helen Auckland. Dur 2E 105
St Helen's. E Sus 4C 28
St Helen's. IOW 4E 17
St Helens. Cumb 1B 102
St Helens. IOW 4E 17
St Helens. Mers 1H 83
St Hilary. Corn 3C 4
St Hilary. V Glam 4D 32
Saint Hill. Devn 2D 12
Saint Hill. W Sus 2E 27
St Illtyd. Blae 5F 47
St Ippolyts. Herts 3B 52
St Ishmael. Carm 5D 44
St Ishmael's. Pemb 4C 42
St Issey. Corn 1D 6
St Ive. Corn 2H 7
St Ives. Cambs 3C 64
St Ives. Corn 2C 4
St Ives. Dors 2G 15
St James' End. Nptn 4E 62
St James South Elmham. Suff 2F 67
St Jidgey. Corn 2D 6
St John. Corn 3A 8
St John's. IOM 3B 108
St John's. Worc 5C 60
St John's Chapel. Devn 4F 19
St John's Chapel. Dur 1B 104
St John's Fen End. Norf 4E 77
St John's Town of Dalry. Dum 1D 110
St Judes. IOM 2C 108
St Just. Corn 3A 4
St Just in Roseland. Corn 5C 6
St Katherines. Abers 5E 161
St Keverne. Corn 4E 5
St Kew. Corn 5A 10
St Kew Highway. Corn 5A 10
St Keyne. Corn 2G 7
St Lawrence. Corn 2G 7
St Lawrence. Essx 5C 54
St Lawrence. IOW 5D 16
St Leonards. Buck 5H 51
St Leonards. Dors 2G 15

St Leonards. E Sus 5B 28
St Levan. Corn 4A 4
St Lythans. V Glam 4E 32
St Mabyn. Corn 5A 10
St Madoes. Per 1D 136
St Margaret's. Herts 4A 52
St Margaret's. Wilts 5H 35
St Margarets. Here 2G 47
St Margarets. Herts 4D 53
St Margaret's at Cliffe. Kent 1H 29
St Margaret's Hope. Orkn 8D 172
St Margaret South Elmham.
  Suff 2F 67
St Mark's. IOM 4B 108
St Martin. Corn
  nr. Helston 4E 5
  nr. Looe 3G 7
St Martin's. Shrp 2F 71
St Martins. Per 5A 144
St Mary Bourne. Hants 1C 24
St Mary Church. V Glam 4D 32
St Marychurch. Torb 2F 9
St Mary Cray. G Lon 4F 39
St Mary Hill. V Glam 4C 32
St Mary Hoo. Medw 3C 40
St Mary in the Marsh. Kent 3E 29
St Mary's. Orkn 7D 172
St Mary's Airport. IOS 1B 4
St Mary's Bay. Kent 3E 29
St Marys Platt. Kent 5H 39
St Maughan's Green. Mon 4H 47
St Mawes. Corn 5C 6
St Mawgan. Corn 2C 6
St Mellion. Corn 2H 7
St Mellons. Card 3F 33
St Merryn. Corn 1C 6
St Mewan. Corn 3D 6
St Michael Caerhays. Corn 4D 6
St Michael Penkevil. Corn 4C 6
St Michaels. Kent 2C 28
St Michaels. Torb 3E 9
St Michaels. Worc 4H 59
St Michael's on Wyre. Lanc 5D 96
St Michael South Elmham.
  Suff 2F 67
St Minver. Corn 1D 6
St Monans. Fife 3H 137
St Neot. Corn 2F 7
St Neots. Cambs 4A 64
St Newlyn East. Corn 3C 6
St Nicholas. Pemb 1C 42
St Nicholas. V Glam 4D 32
St Nicholas at Wade. Kent 4G 41
St Nicholas South Elmham.
  Suff 2F 67
St Ninians. Stir 4G 135
St Olaves. Norf 1G 67
St Osyth. Essx 4E 54
St Osyth Heath. Essx 4E 55
St Owen's Cross. Here 3A 48
St Paul's Cray. G Lon 4F 39
St Paul's Walden. Herts 3B 52
St Peter's. Kent 4H 41
St Peter The Great. Worc 5C 60
St Petrox. Pemb 5D 42
St Pinnock. Corn 2G 7
St Quivox. S Ayr 2C 116
St Ruan. Corn 5E 5
St Stephen. Corn 3D 6
St Stephens. Corn
  nr. Launceston 4D 10
  nr. Saltash 3A 8
St Teath. Corn 4A 10
St Thomas. Devn 3C 12
St Thomas. Swan 3F 31
St Tudy. Corn 5A 10
St Twynnells. Pemb 5D 42
St Veep. Corn 3F 7
St Vigeans. Ang 4F 145
St Wenn. Corn 2D 6
St Weonards. Here 3H 47
St Winnolls. Corn 3H 7
St Winnow. Corn 3F 7
Salcombe. Devn 5D 8
Salcombe Regis. Devn 4E 13
Salcott. Essx 4C 54
Sale. G Man 1B 84
Saleby. Linc 3D 88
Sale Green. Worc 5D 60
Salehurst. E Sus 3B 28
Salem. Carm 3G 45
Salem. Cdgn 2F 57
Salen. Arg 4G 139
Salen. High 2A 140
Salesbury. Lanc 1E 91
Saleway. Worc 5D 60
Salford. C Beds 2H 51
Salford.
  G Man .... Manchester 201 (1C 84)
Salford. Oxon 3A 50
Salford Priors. Warw 5E 61
Salfords. Surr 1D 27
Salhouse. Norf 4F 79
Saligo. Arg 3A 124
Saline. Fife 4C 136
Salisbury. Wilts 210 (3G 23)
Salkeld Dykes. Cumb 1G 103
Sallachan. High 2D 141
Sallachy. High
  nr. Lairg 3C 164
  nr. Stromeferry 5B 156
Salle. Norf 3D 78
Salmonby. Linc 3C 88
Salmond's Muir. Ang 5E 145
Salperton. Glos 3F 49
Salph End. Bed 5H 63
Salsburgh. N Lan 3B 128
Salt. Staf 3D 72
Salta. Cumb 5B 112
Saltaire. W Yor 1B 92

Saltash. Corn 3A 8
Saltburn. High 2B 158
Saltburn-by-the-Sea. Red C 2D 106
Saltby. Leics 3F 75
Saltcoats. Cumb 5B 102
Saltcoats. N Ayr 5D 126
Saltdean. Brig 5E 27
Salt End. E Yor 2E 95
Salter. Lanc 3F 97
Salterforth. Lanc 5A 98
Salters Lode. Norf 5E 77
Salterswall. Ches W 4A 84
Salterton. Wilts 3G 23
Saltfleet. Linc 1D 88
Saltfleetby All Saints. Linc 1D 88
Saltfleetby St Clements. Linc 1D 88
Saltfleetby St Peter. Linc 2D 88
Saltford. Bath 5B 34
Salthouse. Norf 1C 78
Saltmarshe. E Yor 2A 94
Saltness. Orkn 9B 172
Saltness. Shet 7D 173
Saltney. Flin 4F 83
Salton. N Yor 2B 100
Saltrens. Devn 4E 19
Saltwick. Nmbd 2E 115
Saltwood. Kent 2F 29
Salum. Arg 4B 138
Salwarpe. Worc 4C 60
Salwayash. Dors 3H 13
Samalaman. High 1A 140
Sambourne. Warw 4E 61
Sambourne. Wilts 2D 22
Sambrook. Telf 3B 72
Samhia. W Isl 2C 170
Samlesbury. Lanc 1D 90
Samlesbury Bottoms. Lanc 2E 90
Sampford Arundel. Som 1E 12
Sampford Brett. Som 2D 20
Sampford Courtenay. Devn 2G 11
Sampford Peverell. Devn 1D 12
Sampford Spiney. Devn 5F 11
Samsonslane. Orkn 5F 172
Samuelston. E Lot 2A 130
Sanaigmore. Arg 2A 124
Sancreed. Corn 4B 4
Sancton. E Yor 1C 94
Sand. High 4D 162
Sand. Shet 7E 173
Sand. Som 2H 21
Sandaig. Arg 4A 138
Sandaig. High 3F 147
Sandale. Cumb 5D 112
Sandal Magna. W Yor 3D 92
Sandavore. High 5C 146
Sanday Airport. Orkn 3F 172
Sandbach. Ches E 4B 84
Sandbank. Arg 1C 126
Sandbanks. Pool 4F 15
Sandend. Abers 2C 160
Sanderstead. G Lon 4E 39
Sandfields. Neat 3G 31
Sandford. Cumb 3A 104
Sandford. Devn 2B 12
Sandford. Dors 4E 15
Sandford. Hants 2G 15
Sandford. IOW 4D 16
Sandford. N Som 1H 21
Sandford. Shrp
  nr. Oswestry 3F 71
  nr. Whitchurch 2H 71
Sandford. S Lan 5A 128
Sandfordhill. Abers 4H 161
Sandford-on-Thames. Oxon 5D 50
Sandford Orcas. Dors 4B 22
Sandford St Martin. Oxon 3C 50
Sandgate. Kent 2F 29
Sandgreen. Dum 4C 110
Sandhaven. Abers 2G 161
Sandhead. Dum 4F 109
Sandhill. Cambs 2E 65
Sandhills. Dors 1B 14
Sandhills. Oxon 5D 50
Sandhills. Surr 2A 26
Sand Hole. E Yor 1B 94
Sandholme. E Yor 1B 94
Sandholme. Linc 2C 76
Sandhurst. Brac 5G 37
Sandhurst. Glos 3D 48
Sandhurst. Kent 3B 28
Sandhurst Cross. Kent 3B 28
Sand Hutton. N Yor 4A 100
Sandhutton. N Yor 1F 99
Sandiacre. Derbs 2B 74
Sandilands. Linc 2E 89
Sandiway. Ches W 3A 84
Sandleheath. Hants 1G 15
Sandling. Kent 5B 40
Sandlow Green. Ches E 4B 84
Sandness. Shet 6C 173
Sandon. Essx 5H 53
Sandon. Herts 2D 52
Sandon. Staf 3D 72
Sandonbank. Staf 3D 72
Sandown. IOW 4D 16
Sandplace. Corn 3G 7
Sandridge. Herts 4B 52
Sandringham. Norf 3F 77
The Sands. Surr 2G 25
Sandsend. N Yor 3F 107
Sandside. Cumb 2D 96
Sandsound. Shet 7E 173
Sandtoft. N Lin 4H 93
Sandvoe. Shet 2E 173
Sandway. Kent 5C 40
Sandwich. Kent 5H 41
Sandwick. Cumb 3F 103
Sandwick. Orkn
  on Mainland 6B 172
  on South Ronaldsay 9D 172

Sandwick. Shet
  on Mainland 9F 173
  on Whalsay 5G 173
Sandwith. Cumb 3A 102
Sandy. Carm 5E 45
Sandy. C Beds 1B 52
Sandy Bank. Linc 5B 88
Sandycroft. Flin 4F 83
Sandy Cross. Here 5A 60
Sandygate. Devn 5B 12
Sandygate. IOM 2C 108
Sandy Haven. Pemb 4C 42
Sandyhills. Dum 4F 111
Sandylands. Lanc 3D 96
Sandy Lane. Wilts 5E 35
Sandylane. Swan 4E 31
Sandystones. Bord 2H 119
Sandyway. Here 3H 47
Sangobeg. High 2E 167
Sangomore. High 2E 166
Sankyn's Green. Worc 4B 60
Sanna. High 2F 139
Sanndabhaig. W Isl
  on Isle of Lewis 4G 171
  on South Uist 4D 170
Sannox. N Ayr 5B 126
Sanquhar. Dum 3G 117
Santon. Cumb 4B 102
Santon Bridge. Cumb 4C 102
Santon Downham. Suff 2H 65
Sapcote. Leics 1B 62
Sapey Common. Here 4B 60
Sapiston. Suff 3B 66
Sapley. Cambs 3B 64
Sapperton. Derbs 2F 73
Sapperton. Glos 5E 49
Sapperton. Linc 2H 75
Saracen's Head. Linc 3C 76
Sarclet. High 4F 169
Sardis. Carm 5F 45
Sardis. Pemb
  nr. Milford Haven 4D 42
  nr. Tenby 4F 43
Sarisbury Green. Hants 2D 16
Sarn. B'end 3C 32
Sarn. Powy 1E 58
Sarnau. Carm 3E 45
Sarnau. Cdgn 5C 56
Sarnau. Gwyn 2B 70
Sarnau. Powy
  nr. Brecon 2D 46
  nr. Welshpool 4E 71
Sarn Bach. Gwyn 3C 68
Sarnesfield. Here 5F 59
Sarn Meyllteyrn. Gwyn 2B 68
Saron. Carm
  nr. Ammanford 4G 45
  nr. Newcastle Emlyn 2D 45
Saron. Gwyn
  nr. Bethel 4E 81
  nr. Bontnewydd 5D 80
Sarratt. Herts 1B 38
Sarre. Kent 4G 41
Sarsden. Oxon 3A 50
Satley. Dur 5E 115
Satron. N Yor 5C 104
Satterleigh. Devn 4G 19
Satterthwaite. Cumb 5E 103
Satwell. Oxon 3F 37
Sauchen. Abers 2D 152
Saucher. Per 5A 144
Saughall. Ches W 3F 83
Saughtree. Bord 5H 119
Saul. Glos 5C 48
Saundby. Notts 2E 87
Saundersfoot. Pemb 4F 43
Saunderton. Buck 5F 51
Saunderton Lee. Buck 2G 37
Saunton. Devn 3E 19
Sausthorpe. Linc 4C 88
Saval. High 3C 164
Saverley Green. Staf 2D 72
Sawbridge. Warw 4C 62
Sawbridgeworth. Herts 4E 53
Sawdon. N Yor 1D 100
Sawley. Derbs 2B 74
Sawley. Lanc 5G 97
Sawley. N Yor 3E 99
Sawston. Cambs 1E 53
Sawtry. Cambs 2A 64
Saxby. Leics 3F 75
Saxby. Linc 2H 87
Saxby All Saints. N Lin 3C 94
Saxelby. Leics 3D 74
Saxelbye. Leics 3D 74
Saxham Street. Suff 4C 66
Saxilby. Linc 3F 87
Saxlingham. Norf 2C 78
Saxlingham Green. Norf 1E 67
Saxlingham Nethergate. Norf 1E 67
Saxlingham Thorpe. Norf 1E 66
Saxmundham. Suff 4F 67
Saxondale. Notts 1D 74
Saxon Street. Cambs 5F 65
Saxtead. Suff 4E 67
Saxtead Green. Suff 4E 67
Saxthorpe. Norf 2D 78
Saxton. N Yor 1E 93
Sayers Common. W Sus 4D 26
Scackleton. N Yor 2A 100
Scadabhagh. W Isl 8D 171
Scaftworth. Notts 1D 86
Scagglethorpe. N Yor 2C 100
Scaitcliffe. Lanc 2F 91
Scaladal. W Isl 6D 171
Scalasaig. Arg 4A 132
Scalby. E Yor 2B 94
Scalby. N Yor 5H 107
Scalby Mills. N Yor 5H 107
Scaldwell. Nptn 3E 63
Scaleby. Cumb 3F 113

Scaleby Hill. Cumb...................3F **113**
Scale Houses. Cumb...................5G **113**
Scales. Cumb
  nr. Barrow-in-Furness......2B **96**
  nr. Keswick......................2E **103**
Scalford. Leics..........................3E **75**
Scaling. N Yor..........................3E **107**
Scaling Dam. Red C...................3E **107**
Scalloway. Shet........................8F **173**
Scalpaigh. W Isl.......................8E **171**
Scalpay House. High..................1E **147**
Scamblesby. Linc......................3B **88**
Scamodale. High......................1C **140**
Scampston. N Yor.....................2C **100**
Scampton. Linc........................3G **87**
Scaniport. High.........................5A **158**
Scapa. Orkn.............................7D **172**
Scapegoat Hill. W Yor................3A **92**
Scar. Orkn...............................3F **172**
Scarasta. W Isl.........................8C **171**
Scarborough. N Yor...................1E **101**
Scarcliffe. Derbs.......................4B **86**
Scarcroft. W Yor.......................5F **99**
Scardroy. High.........................3E **156**
Scarfskerry. High......................1E **169**
Scargill. Dur...........................3D **104**
Scarinish. Arg..........................4B **138**
Scarisbrick. Lanc.......................3B **90**
Scarning. Norf..........................4B **78**
Scarrington. Notts.....................1E **75**
Scarth Hill. Lanc.......................4C **90**
Scartho. NE Lin........................4F **95**
Scarvister. Shet.......................7E **173**
Scatness. Shet.......................10E **173**
Scatwell. High........................3F **157**
Scaur. Dum..............................4F **111**
Scawby. N Lin..........................4C **94**
Scawby Brook. N Lin..................4C **94**
Scawsby. S Yor........................4F **93**
Scawton. N Yor........................1H **99**
Scaynes Hill. W Sus..................3E **27**
Scethrog. Powy........................3E **46**
Scholar Green. Ches E...............5C **84**
Scholes. G Man.......................4D **90**
Scholes. W Yor
  nr. Bradford....................2B **92**
  nr. Holmfirth...................4B **92**
  nr. Leeds........................1D **93**
Scholey Hill. W Yor...................2D **93**
School Aycliffe. Darl..................2F **105**
School Green. Ches W...............4A **84**
School Green. Essx...................2H **53**
Scissett. W Yor........................3C **92**
Scleddau. Pemb.......................1D **42**
Scofton. Notts.........................2D **86**
Scole. Norf..............................3D **66**
Scolpaig. W Isl........................1C **170**
Scolton. Pemb..........................2D **43**
Scone. Per..............................1D **136**
Sconser. High..........................5E **155**
Scoonie. Fife...........................3F **137**
Scopwick. Linc.........................5H **87**
Scoraig. High...........................4E **163**
Scorborough. E Yor....................5E **101**
Scorrier. Corn...........................4B **6**
Scorriton. Devn.........................2D **8**
Scorton. Lanc...........................5E **97**
Scorton. N Yor..........................4F **105**
Sco Ruston. Norf.......................3E **79**
Scotbheinn. W Isl.....................3D **170**
Scotby. Cumb...........................4F **113**
Scotch Corner. N Yor...............4F **105**
Scotforth. Lanc.........................3D **97**
Scot Hay. Staf..........................1C **72**
Scothern. Linc..........................3H **87**
Scotland End. Oxon....................2B **50**
Scotlandwell. Per.......................3D **136**
Scot Lane End. G Man................4E **91**
Scotsburn. High........................1B **158**
Scotsburn. Mor..........................2G **159**
Scotsdike. Cumb.......................2E **113**
Scot's Gap. Nmbd......................1D **114**
Scotstoun. Glas.........................3G **127**
Scotstown. High........................2C **140**
Scotswood. Tyne.......................3F **115**
Scottas. High............................3F **147**
Scotter. Linc.............................4B **94**
Scotterthorpe. Linc.....................4B **94**
Scottlethorpe. Linc.....................3H **75**
Scotton. Linc............................1F **87**
Scotton. N Yor
  nr. Catterick Garrison.....5E **105**
  nr. Harrogate..................4F **99**
Scottow. Norf............................3E **79**
Scoulton. Norf...........................5B **78**
Scounslow Green. Staf...............3E **73**
Scourie. High............................4B **166**
Scourie More. High.....................4B **166**
Scousburgh. Shet....................10E **173**
Scout Green. Cumb.....................4G **103**
Scouthead. G Man......................4H **91**
Scrabster. High..........................1C **168**
Scrafield. Linc...........................4C **88**
Scrainwood. Nmbd.....................4D **121**
Scrane End. Linc........................1C **76**
Scraptoft. Leics.........................5D **74**
Scratby. Norf.............................4H **79**
Scrayingham. N Yor....................3B **100**
Scredington. Linc......................1H **75**
Scremby. Linc...........................4D **88**
Scremerston. Nmbd....................5G **131**
Screveton. Notts.......................1E **75**
Scrivelsby. Linc.........................4B **88**
Scriven. N Yor...........................4F **99**
Scronkey. Lanc..........................5D **96**
Scrooby. Notts..........................1D **86**
Scropton. Derbs.........................2F **73**
Scrub Hill. Linc..........................5B **88**
Scruton. N Yor...........................5F **105**
Scuggate. Cumb........................2F **113**
Sculamus. High.........................1E **147**

Sculcoates. Hull.......................1D **94**
Sculthorpe. Norf........................2B **78**
Scunthorpe. N Lin......................3B **94**
Scurlage. Swan.........................4D **30**
Sea. Som................................1G **13**
Seaborough. Dors......................2H **13**
Seabridge. Staf..........................1C **72**
Seabrook. Kent..........................2F **29**
Seaburn. Tyne...........................3H **115**
Seacombe. Mers.......................1F **83**
Seacroft. Linc...........................4E **89**
Seacroft. W Yor..........................1D **92**
Seadyke. Linc............................2C **76**
Seafield. High............................5G **165**
Seafield. Midl.............................3F **129**
Seafield. S Ayr...........................2C **116**
Seafield. W Lot.........................3D **128**
Seaford. E Sus.........................5F **27**
Seaforth. Mers...........................1F **83**
Seagrave. Leics.........................4D **74**
Seaham. Dur...........................5H **115**
Seahouses. Nmbd.....................1G **121**
Seal. Kent.................................5G **39**
Sealand. Flin.............................4F **83**
Seale. Surr...............................2G **25**
Seamer. N Yor
  nr. Scarborough...............1E **101**
  nr. Stokesley...................3B **106**
Seamill. N Ayr............................5D **126**
Sea Mills. Bris............................4A **34**
Sea Palling. Norf........................3G **79**
Searby. Linc..............................4D **94**
Seasalter. Kent..........................4E **41**
Seascale. Cumb........................4B **102**
Seaside. Per.............................1E **137**
Seater. High..............................1F **169**
Seathorne. Linc.........................4E **89**
Seathwaite. Cumb
  nr. Buttermere.................3D **102**
  nr. Ulpha.......................5D **102**
Seatle. Cumb.............................1C **96**
Seatoller. Cumb.........................3D **102**
Seaton. Corn.............................3H **7**
Seaton. Cumb............................1B **102**
Seaton. Devn.............................3F **13**
Seaton. Dur...............................4G **115**
Seaton. E Yor.............................5F **101**
Seaton. Nmbd............................2G **115**
Seaton. Rut................................1G **63**
Seaton Burn. Tyne......................2F **115**
Seaton Carew. Hart.....................2C **106**
Seaton Delaval. Nmbd.................2G **115**
Seaton Junction. Devn.................3F **13**
Seaton Ross. E Yor.....................5B **100**
Seaton Sluice. Nmbd...................2G **115**
Seatown. Abers..........................2C **160**
Seatown. Dors............................3H **13**
Seatown. Mor
  nr. Cullen.......................2C **160**
  nr. Lossiemouth...............1G **159**
Seave Green. N Yor.....................4C **106**
Seaview. IOW.............................3E **17**
Seaville. Cumb...........................4C **112**
Seavington St Mary. Som.............1H **13**
Seavington St Michael. Som..........1H **13**
Seawick. Essx............................4E **55**
Sebastopol. Torf.........................2F **33**
Sebergham. Cumb......................5E **113**
Seckington. Warw.......................5G **73**
Second Coast. High.....................4D **162**
Sedbergh. Cumb.........................5H **103**
Sedbury. Glos............................2A **34**
Sedbusk. N Yor..........................5B **104**
Sedgeberrow. Worc.....................2F **49**
Sedgebrook. Linc........................2F **75**
Sedgefield. Dur...........................2A **106**
Sedgeford. Norf...........................2G **77**
Sedgehill. Wilts..........................4D **22**
Sedgley. W Mid.........................1D **60**
Sedgwick. Cumb.........................1E **97**
Sedlescombe. E Sus.....................4B **28**
Seend. Wilts...............................5E **35**
Seend Cleeve. Wilts.....................5E **35**
Seer Green. Buck.........................1A **38**
Seething. Norf.............................1F **67**
Sefster. Shet...............................6E **173**
Sefton. Mers...............................4B **90**
Sefton Park. Mers.........................2F **83**
Segensworth. Hants......................2D **16**
Seggat. Abers..............................4E **161**
Seghill. Nmbd..............................2F **115**
Seifton. Shrp................................2G **59**
Seighford. Staf.............................3C **72**
Seilebost. W Isl.............................8C **171**
Seisdon. Staf...............................1C **60**
Seisiadar. W Isl...........................4H **171**
Selattyn. Shrp.............................2E **71**
Selborne. Hants...........................3F **25**
Selby. N Yor...............................1G **93**
Selham. W Sus............................3A **26**
Selkirk. Bord................................2G **119**
Sellack. Here................................3A **48**
Sellafirth. Shet.............................2G **173**
Sellick's Green. Som......................1F **13**
Sellindge. Kent.............................2F **29**
Selling. Kent.................................5E **41**
Sells Green. Wilts.........................5E **35**
Selly Oak. W Mid..........................2E **61**
Selmeston. E Sus.........................5G **27**
Selsdon. G Lon.............................4E **39**
Selsey. W Sus..............................3G **17**
Selsfield Common. W Sus.............2E **27**
Selside. Cumb.............................5G **103**
Selside. N Yor..............................2G **97**
Selsley. Glos................................5D **48**
Selsted. Kent...............................1G **29**
Selston. Notts...............................5B **86**
Selworthy. Som.............................2C **20**
Semblister. Shet...........................6E **173**
Semer. Suff..................................1D **54**
Semington. Wilts..........................5D **35**

Semley. Wilts..............................4D **23**
Sempringham. Linc......................2A **76**
Send. Surr..................................5B **38**
Send Marsh. Surr.........................5B **38**
Senghenydd. Cphy.......................2E **32**
Sennen. Corn...............................4A **4**
Sennen Cove. Corn........................4A **4**
Sennybridge. Powy.......................3C **46**
Serlby. Notts.................................2D **86**
Sessay. N Yor...............................2G **99**
Setchey. Norf................................4F **77**
Setley. Hants................................2B **16**
Setter. Shet..................................3F **173**
Settiscarth. Orkn...........................6C **172**
Settle. N Yor.................................3H **97**
Settrington. N Yor..........................2C **100**
Seven Ash. Som...........................3E **21**
Sevenhampton. Glos.....................3F **49**
Sevenhampton. Swin.....................2H **35**
Sevenoaks. Kent.........................5G **39**
Sevenoaks Weald. Kent.................5G **39**
Seven Sisters. Neat.......................5B **46**
Seven Springs. Glos......................4E **49**
Severn Beach. S Glo.....................3A **34**
Severn Stoke. Worc.......................1D **48**
Sevington. Kent.............................1E **29**
Sewards End. Essx........................2F **53**
Sewardstone. Essx........................1E **39**
Sewell. C Beds..............................3H **51**
Sewerby. E Yor..............................3G **101**
Seworgan. Corn.............................5B **6**
Sewstern. Leics..............................3F **75**
Sgallairidh. W Isl...........................9B **170**
Sgarasta Mhor. W Isl......................8C **171**
Sgiogarstaigh. W Isl.......................1H **171**
Sgreadan. Arg...............................4A **132**
Shabbington. Buck.........................5E **51**
Shackerley. Shrp...........................5C **72**
Shackerstone. Leics.......................5A **74**
Shackleford. Surr...........................1A **26**
Shadforth. Dur...............................5G **115**
Shadingfield. Suff...........................2G **67**
Shadoxhurst. Kent..........................2D **28**
Shadsworth. Bkbn..........................2F **91**
Shadwell. Norf...............................2B **66**
Shadwell. W Yor.............................1D **92**
Shaftesbury. Dors..........................4D **22**
Shafton. S Yor................................3D **93**
Shafton Two Gates. S Yor...............3D **93**
Shaggs. Dors.................................4D **14**
Shakesfield. Glos...........................2B **48**
Shalbourne. Wilts..........................5B **36**
Shalcombe. IOW............................4B **16**
Shalden. Hants..............................2E **25**
Shaldon. Devn...............................5C **12**
Shalfleet. IOW...............................4C **16**
Shalford. Essx................................3H **53**
Shalford. Surr................................1B **26**
Shalford Green. Essx.......................3H **53**
Shallowford. Devn...........................2H **19**
Shallowford. Staf.............................3C **72**
Shalmsford Street. Kent...................5E **41**
Shalstone. Buck..............................2E **51**
Shamley Green. Surr........................1B **26**
Shandon. Arg..................................1D **126**
Shandwick. High.............................1C **158**
Shangton. Leics..............................1E **62**
Shankhouse. Nmbd.........................2F **115**
Shanklin. IOW...............................4D **16**
Shannochie. N Ayr...........................3D **123**
Shap. Cumb....................................3G **103**
Shapwick. Dors...............................2E **15**
Shapwick. Som................................3H **21**
Sharcott. Wilts.................................1G **23**
Shardlow. Derbs..............................2B **74**
Shareshill. Staf................................5D **72**
Sharlston. W Yor.............................3D **93**
Sharlston Common. W Yor.............3D **93**
Sharnal Street. Medw......................3B **40**
Sharnbrook. Bed.............................5G **63**
Sharneyford. Lanc...........................2G **91**
Sharnford. Leics..............................1B **62**
Sharnhill Green. Dors.......................2C **14**
Sharoe Green. Lanc.........................1D **90**
Sharow. N Yor.................................2F **99**
Sharpenhoe. C Beds........................2A **52**
Sharperton. Nmbd...........................4D **120**
Sharpness. Glos..............................5B **48**
Sharp Street. Norf...........................3F **79**
Sharpthorne. W Sus........................2E **27**
Sharrington. Norf.............................2C **78**
Shatterford. Worc.............................2B **60**
Shatton. Derbs.................................2F **85**
Shaugh Prior. Devn...........................2B **8**
Shavington. Ches E.........................5B **84**
Shaw. G Man...............................4H **91**
Shaw. W Ber...................................5C **36**
Shaw. Wilts....................................5D **35**
Shawbirch. Telf...............................4A **72**
Shawbury. Shrp...............................3H **71**
Shawell. Leics.................................2C **62**
Shawford. Hants..............................4C **24**
Shawforth. Lanc...............................2G **91**
Shaw Green. Lanc............................3D **90**
Shawhead. Dum...............................2F **111**
Shaw Mills. N Yor.............................3E **99**
Shawwood. E Ayr.............................2E **117**
Shearington. Dum............................3B **112**
Shearsby. Leics...............................1D **62**
Shearston. Som................................3F **21**
Shebbear. Devn................................2E **11**
Shebdon. Staf..................................3B **72**
Shebster. High.................................2C **168**
Sheddocksley. Aber........................3F **153**
Shedfield. Hants...............................1D **16**
Shedog. N Ayr..................................2D **122**
Sheen. Staf......................................4F **85**
Sheepbridge. Derbs..........................3A **86**
Sheep Hill. Dur.................................4E **115**
Sheepscar. W Yor.............................1D **92**
Sheepscombe. Glos..........................4D **49**

Sheepstor. Devn...............................2B **8**
Sheepwash. Devn..............................2E **11**
Sheepwash. Nmbd............................1F **115**
Sheepway. N Som.............................4H **33**
Sheepy Magna. Leics........................5H **73**
Sheepy Parva. Leics.........................5H **73**
Sheering. Essx..................................4F **53**
Sheerness. Kent..............................3D **40**
Sheerwater. Surr...............................4B **38**
Sheet. Hants.....................................4F **25**
Sheffield. S Yor..................210 (2A **86**)
Sheffield Bottom. W Ber....................5E **37**
Sheffield Green. E Sus.......................3F **27**
Shefford. C Beds...............................2B **52**
Shefford Woodlands. W Ber..............4B **36**
Sheigra. High....................................2B **166**
Sheinton. Shrp...................................5A **72**
Shelderton. Shrp...............................3G **59**
Sheldon. Derbs..................................4F **85**
Sheldon. Devn...................................2E **12**
Sheldon. W Mid.................................2F **61**
Sheldwich. Kent................................5E **40**
Sheldwich Lees. Kent.........................5E **40**
Shelf. W Yor.....................................2B **92**
Shelfanger. Norf................................2D **66**
Shelfield. Warw.................................4F **61**
Shelfield. W Mid................................5E **73**
Shelford. Notts..................................1D **74**
Shelford. Warw..................................2B **62**
Shell. Worc.......................................5D **60**
Shelley. Suff.....................................2D **54**
Shelley. W Yor...................................3C **92**
Shell Green. Hal................................2H **83**
Shellingford. Oxon............................2B **36**
Shellow Bowells. Essx.......................5G **53**
Shelsley Beauchamp. Worc...............4B **60**
Shelsley Walsh. Worc........................4B **60**
Shelthorpe. Leics...............................4C **74**
Shelton. Bed.....................................4H **63**
Shelton. Norf.....................................1E **67**
Shelton. Notts...................................1E **75**
Shelton. Shrp....................................4G **71**
Shelton Green. Norf...........................1E **67**
Shelton Lock. Derb............................2A **74**
Shelve. Shrp.....................................1F **59**
Shelwick. Here..................................1A **48**
Shelwick Green. Here........................1A **48**
Shenfield. Essx.................................1H **39**
Shenington. Oxon..............................1B **50**
Shenley. Herts..................................5B **52**
Shenley Brook End. Mil.....................2G **51**
Shenleybury. Herts...........................5B **52**
Shenley Church End. Mil...................2G **51**
Shenmore. Here................................2H **47**
Shennanton. Dum.............................3A **110**
Shenstone. Staf................................5F **73**
Shenstone. Worc..............................3C **60**
Shenstone Woodend. Staf................5F **73**
Shenton. Leics..................................5A **74**
Shenval. Mor....................................1G **151**
Shepeau Stow. Linc..........................4C **76**
Shephall. Herts.................................3C **52**
Shepherd's Bush. G Lon....................2D **38**
Shepherd's Gate. Norf.......................4E **77**
Shepherd's Green. Oxon...................3F **37**
Shepherd's Port. Norf........................2F **77**
Shepherdswell. Kent.........................1G **29**
Shepley. W Yor................................4B **92**
Sheppardstown. High.......................4D **169**
Shepperdine. S Glo..........................2B **34**
Shepperton. Surr..............................4B **38**
Shepreth. Cambs.............................1D **53**
Shepshed. Leics............................4B **74**
Shepton Beauchamp. Som...............1H **13**
Shepton Mallet. Som.........................2B **22**
Shepton Montague. Som....................3B **22**
Shepway. Kent.................................5B **40**
Sheraton. Dur..................................1B **106**
Sherborne. Dors...............................1B **14**
Sherborne. Glos...............................4G **49**
Sherborne. Som...............................1A **22**
Sherborne Causeway. Dors..............4D **22**
Sherborne St John. Hants.................1E **24**
Sherbourne. Warw............................4G **61**
Sherburn. Dur..................................5G **115**
Sherburn. N Yor...............................2D **100**
Sherburn Hill. Dur............................5G **115**
Sherburn in Elmet. N Yor..................1E **93**
Shere. Surr......................................1B **26**
Shereford. Norf................................3A **78**
Sherfield English. Hants....................4A **24**
Sherfield on Loddon. Hants...............1E **25**
Sherford. Devn.................................4D **9**
Sherford. Dors.................................3E **15**
Sheriffhales. Shrp............................4B **72**
Sheriff Hutton. N Yor.........................3A **100**
Sheriffston. Mor...............................2G **159**
Sheringham. Norf.............................1D **78**
Sherington. Mil................................1G **51**
Shermanbury. W Sus........................4D **26**
Shernal Green. Worc.........................4D **60**
Shernborne. Norf..............................2G **77**
Sherrington. Wilts.............................3E **23**
Sherston. Wilts.................................3D **34**
Sherwood. Nott................................1C **74**
Sherwood Green. Devn......................4F **19**
Shettleston. Glas..............................3H **127**
Shevington. G Man...........................4D **90**
Shevington Moor. G Man...................3D **90**
Shevington Vale. G Man....................4D **90**
Sheviock. Corn.................................3H **7**
Shide. IOW......................................4C **16**
Shiel Bridge. High.............................2B **148**
Shieldaig. High
  nr. Charlestown................1H **155**
  nr. Torridon....................3H **155**
Shieldhill. Falk.................................2B **128**
Shieldhill. S Lan...............................5D **128**
Shieldmuir. N Lan.............................4A **128**
Shielfoot. High.................................1A **140**

Shielhill. Abers................................3H **161**
Shielhill. Ang..................................3D **144**
Shifnal. Shrp....................................5B **72**
Shilbottle. Nmbd...............................4G **121**
Shilbottle Grange. Nmbd...................4G **121**
Shildon. Dur...................................2F **105**
Shillford. E Ren.................................4F **127**
Shillingford. Devn.............................4C **20**
Shillingford. Oxon.............................2D **36**
Shillingford St George. Devn..............4C **12**
Shillingstone. Dors...........................1D **14**
Shillington. C Beds...........................2B **52**
Shillmoor. Nmbd...............................4C **120**
Shilton. Oxon...................................5A **50**
Shilton. Warw..................................2B **62**
Shilvinghampton. Dors......................4B **14**
Shilvington. Nmbd............................1E **115**
Shimpling. Norf................................2D **66**
Shimpling. Suff................................5A **66**
Shimpling Street. Suff.......................5A **66**
Shincliffe. Dur.................................5F **115**
Shiney Row. Tyne.............................4G **115**
Shinfield. Wok................................5F **37**
Shingay. Cambs...............................1D **52**
Shingham. Norf................................5G **77**
Shingle Street. Suff...........................1G **55**
Shinner's Bridge. Devn........................2D **9**
Shinness. High.................................2C **164**
Shipbourne. Kent.............................5G **39**
Shipdham. Norf................................5B **78**
Shipham. Som.................................1H **21**
Shiphay. Torb....................................2E **9**
Shiplake. Oxon.................................4F **37**
Shipley. Derbs.................................1B **74**
Shipley. Nmbd.................................3F **121**
Shipley. Shrp...................................1C **60**
Shipley. W Sus................................3C **26**
Shipley. W Yor................................1B **92**
Shipley Bridge. Surr..........................1E **27**
Shipmeadow. Suff............................2F **67**
Shippon. Oxon.................................2C **36**
Shipston-on-Stour. Warw..................1A **50**
Shipton. Buck...................................3F **51**
Shipton. Glos...................................4F **49**
Shipton. N Yor.................................4H **99**
Shipton. Shrp...................................1H **59**
Shipton Bellinger. Hants....................2H **23**
Shipton Gorge. Dors.........................3H **13**
Shipton Green. W Sus.......................3G **17**
Shipton Moyne. Glos.........................3D **35**
Shipton-on-Cherwell. Oxon...............4C **50**
Shiptonthorpe. E Yor.........................5C **100**
Shipton-under-Wychwood.
  Oxon............................4A **50**
Shirburn. Oxon.................................2E **37**
Shirdley Hill. Lanc.............................3B **90**
Shire. Cumb....................................1H **103**
Shirebrook. Derbs..........................4C **86**
Shiregreen. S Yor.............................1A **86**
Shirehampton. Bris...........................4A **34**
Shiremoor. Tyne...............................2G **115**
Shirenewton. Mon............................2H **33**
Shireoaks. Notts..............................2C **86**
Shires Mill. Fife...............................1D **128**
Shirkoak. Kent.................................2D **28**
Shirland. Derbs................................5A **86**
Shirley. Derbs..................................1G **73**
Shirley. Sotn....................................1B **16**
Shirley. W Mid..................................3F **61**
Shirleywich. Staf..............................3D **73**
Shirl Heath. Here..............................5G **59**
Shirrell Heath. Hants.........................1D **16**
Shirwell. Devn..................................3F **19**
Shiskine. N Ayr................................3D **122**
Shobdon. Here..................................4F **59**
Shobnall. Staf...................................3G **73**
Shobrooke. Devn..............................2B **12**
Shoby. Leics.....................................3D **74**
Shocklach. Ches W............................1G **71**
Shoeburyness. S'end........................2D **40**
Sholden. Kent..................................5H **41**
Sholing. Sotn...................................1C **16**
Sholver. G Man................................4H **91**
Shoot Hill. Shrp................................4G **71**
Shop. Corn
  nr. Bude.........................1C **10**
  nr. Padstow....................1C **6**
Shop. Devn......................................1D **11**
Shopford. Cumb...............................2G **113**
Shoreditch. G Lon..........................2E **39**
Shoreditch. Som..............................4F **21**
Shoregill. Cumb...............................4A **104**
Shoreham. Kent...............................4G **39**
Shoreham-by-Sea. W Sus...............5D **26**
Shoresdean. Nmbd...........................5F **131**
Shoreswood. Nmbd..........................5F **131**
Shorncote. Glos...............................2F **35**
Shorne. Kent...................................3A **40**
Shorne Ridgeway. Kent.....................3A **40**
Shortacombe. Devn.........................4F **11**
Shortbridge. E Sus...........................3F **27**
Shortgate. E Sus..............................4F **27**
Short Green. Norf.............................2C **66**
Shorthampton. Oxon........................3B **50**
Shortlanesend. Corn.........................4C **6**
Shorton. Torb...................................2E **9**
Shortstown. Bed..............................1A **52**
Shortwood. S Glo.............................4B **34**
Shorwell. IOW..................................4C **16**
Shoscombe. Bath..............................1C **22**
Shotesham. Norf..............................1E **67**
Shotgate. Essx.................................1B **40**
Shotley. Suff...................................2F **55**
Shotley Bridge. Dur..........................4D **115**
Shotleyfield. Nmbd...........................4D **114**
Shotley Gate. Suff............................2F **55**
Shottenden. Kent.............................5E **41**

Shottermill. Surr ...3G 25
Shottery. Warw ...5F 61
Shotteswell. Warw ...1C 50
Shottisham. Suff ...1G 55
Shottle. Derbs ...1H 73
Shotton. Dur
  nr. Peterlee ...1B 106
  nr. Sedgefield ...2A 106
Shotton. Flin ...4F 83
Shotton. Nmbd
  nr. Morpeth ...2F 115
  nr. Town Yetholm ...1C 120
Shotton Colliery. Dur ...5G 115
Shotts. N Lan ...3B 128
Shotwick. Ches W ...3F 83
Shouldham. Norf ...5F 77
Shouldham Thorpe. Norf ...5F 77
Shoulton. Worc ...5C 60
Shrawardine. Shrp ...4G 71
Shrawley. Worc ...4C 60
Shreding Green. Buck ...2B 38
Shrewley. Warw ...4G 61
Shrewsbury. Shrp ...210 (4G 71)
Shrewton. Wilts ...2F 23
Shripney. W Sus ...5A 26
Shrivenham. Oxon ...3H 35
Shropham. Norf ...1B 66
Shroton. Dors ...1D 14
Shrub End. Essx ...3C 54
Shucknall. Here ...1A 48
Shudy Camps. Cambs ...1G 53
Shulishadermor. High ...4D 155
Shulista. High ...1D 154
Shurdington. Glos ...4E 49
Shurlock Row. Wind ...4G 37
Shurrery. High ...3C 168
Shurton. Som ...2F 21
Shustoke. Warw ...1G 61
Shute. Devn
  nr. Axminster ...3F 13
  nr. Crediton ...2B 12
Shutford. Oxon ...1B 50
Shut Heath. Staf ...3C 72
Shuthonger. Glos ...2D 49
Shutlanehead. Staf ...1C 72
Shutlanger. Nptn ...1F 51
Shutt Green. Staf ...5C 72
Shuttington. Warw ...5G 73
Shuttlewood. Derbs ...3B 86
Shuttleworth. G Man ...3G 91
Siabost. W Isl ...3E 171
Siabost bho Dheas. W Isl ...3E 171
Siabost bho Thuath. W Isl ...3E 171
Siadar. W Isl ...2F 171
Siadar Uarach. W Isl ...2F 171
Sibbaldbie. Dum ...1C 112
Sibbertoft. Nptn ...2D 62
Sibdon Carwood. Shrp ...2G 59
Sibertswold. Kent ...1G 29
Sibford Ferris. Oxon ...2B 50
Sibford Gower. Oxon ...2B 50
Sible Hedingham. Essx ...2A 54
Sibsey. Linc ...5C 88
Sibsey Fen Side. Linc ...5C 88
Sibson. Cambs ...1H 63
Sibson. Leics ...5A 74
Sibster. High ...3F 169
Sibthorpe. Notts ...1E 75
Sibton. Suff ...4F 67
Sicklesmere. Suff ...4A 66
Sicklinghall. N Yor ...5F 99
Sid. Devn ...4E 13
Sidbury. Devn ...3E 13
Sidbury. Shrp ...2A 60
Sidcot. N Som ...1H 21
Sidcup. G Lon ...3F 39
Siddick. Cumb ...1B 102
Siddington. Ches E ...3C 84
Siddington. Glos ...2F 35
Side of the Moor. G Man ...3F 91
Sidestrand. Norf ...2E 79
Sidford. Devn ...3E 13
Sidlesham. W Sus ...3G 17
Sidley. E Sus ...5B 28
Sidlow. Surr ...1D 26
Sidmouth. Devn ...4E 13
Sigford. Devn ...5A 12
Sigglesthorne. E Yor ...5F 101
Sighthill. Edin ...2E 129
Sigingstone. V Glam ...4C 32
Signet. Oxon ...4H 49
Silchester. Hants ...5E 37
Sildinis. W Isl ...6E 171
Sileby. Leics ...4D 74
Silecroft. Cumb ...1A 96
Silfield. Norf ...1D 66
Silian. Cdgn ...5E 57
Silkstone. S Yor ...4C 92
Silkstone Common. S Yor ...4C 92
Silksworth. Tyne ...4G 115
Silk Willoughby. Linc ...1H 75
Silloth. Cumb ...4C 112
Sills. Nmbd ...4C 120
Sillyearn. Mor ...3C 160
Silpho. N Yor ...5G 107
Silsden. W Yor ...5C 98
Silsoe. C Beds ...2A 52
Silverbank. Abers ...4E 152
Silverburn. Midl ...3F 129
Silverdale. Lanc ...2D 96
Silverdale. Staf ...1C 72
Silverdale Green. Lanc ...2D 96
Silver End. Essx ...4B 54
Silver End. W Mid ...2D 60
Silvergate. Norf ...3D 78
Silver Green. Norf ...1E 67
Silverhillocks. Abers ...2E 161
Silverley's Green. Suff ...3E 67
Silverstone. Nptn ...1E 51
Silverton. Devn ...2C 12
Silverton. W Dun ...2F 127

Silvington. Shrp ...3A 60
Simm's Cross. Hal ...2H 83
Simm's Lane End. Mers ...4D 90
Simonburn. Nmbd ...2B 114
Simonsbath. Som ...3A 20
Simonstone. Lanc ...1F 91
Simprim. Bord ...5E 131
Simpson. Pemb ...3C 42
Simpson Cross. Pemb ...3C 42
Sinclairston. E Ayr ...3D 116
Sinclairtown. Fife ...4E 137
Sinderby. N Yor ...1F 99
Sinderhope. Nmbd ...4B 114
Sindlesham. Wok ...5F 37
Sinfin. Derb ...2H 73
Singleborough. Buck ...2F 51
Singleton. Kent ...1D 28
Singleton. Lanc ...1B 90
Singleton. W Sus ...1G 17
Singlewell. Kent ...3A 40
Sinkhurst Green. Kent ...1C 28
Sinnahard. Abers ...2B 152
Sinnington. N Yor ...1B 100
Sinton Green. Worc ...4C 60
Sipson. G Lon ...3B 38
Sirhowy. Blae ...4E 47
Sisland. Norf ...1F 67
Sissinghurst. Kent ...2B 28
Siston. S Glo ...4B 34
Sithney. Corn ...4D 4
Sittingbourne. Kent ...4D 40
Six Ashes. Staf ...2B 60
Six Bells. Blae ...5F 47
Six Hills. Leics ...3D 74
Sixhills. Linc ...2A 88
Six Mile Bottom. Cambs ...5E 65
Sixpenny Handley. Dors ...1E 15
Sizewell. Suff ...4G 67
Skail. High ...4H 167
Skaill. Orkn ...6B 172
Skaills. Orkn ...7E 172
Skares. E Ayr ...3E 117
Skateraw. E Lot ...2D 130
Skaw. Shet ...5G 173
Skeabost. High ...4D 154
Skeabrae. Orkn ...5B 172
Skeeby. N Yor ...4E 105
Skeffington. Leics ...5E 75
Skeffling. E Yor ...3G 95
Skegby. Notts
  nr. Mansfield ...4B 86
  nr. Tuxford ...3E 87
Skegness. Linc ...4E 89
Skelberry. Shet
  nr. Boddam ...10E 173
  nr. Housetter ...3E 173
Skelbo. High ...4E 165
Skelbo Street. High ...4E 165
Skelbrooke. S Yor ...3F 93
Skeldyke. Linc ...2C 76
Skelfhill. Bord ...4G 119
Skellingthorpe. Linc ...3G 87
Skellister. Shet ...6F 173
Skellorn Green. Ches E ...2D 84
Skellow. S Yor ...3F 93
Skelmanthorpe. W Yor ...3C 92
Skelmersdale. Lanc ...4C 90
Skelmorlie. N Ayr ...3C 126
Skelpick. High ...3H 167
Skelton. Cumb ...1F 103
Skelton. E Yor ...2A 94
Skelton. N Yor
  nr. Richmond ...4D 105
  nr. Ripon ...3F 99
Skelton. Red C ...3D 106
Skelton. York ...4H 99
Skelton Green. Red C ...3D 106
Skelwick. Orkn ...3D 172
Skelwith Bridge. Cumb ...4E 103
Skendleby. Linc ...4D 88
Skendleby Psalter. Linc ...3D 88
Skenfrith. Mon ...3H 47
Skerne. E Yor ...4E 101
Skeroblingarry. Arg ...3B 122
Skerray. High ...2G 167
Skerricha. High ...3C 166
Skerries Airport. Shet ...4H 173
Skerton. Lanc ...3D 97
Sketchley. Leics ...1B 62
Sketty. Swan ...3F 31
Skewen. Neat ...3G 31
Skewsby. N Yor ...2A 100
Skeyton. Norf ...3E 79
Skeyton Corner. Norf ...3E 79
Skiall. High ...2C 168
Skidbrooke. Linc ...1D 88
Skidbrooke North End. Linc ...1D 88
Skidby. E Yor ...1D 94
Skilgate. Som ...4C 20
Skillington. Linc ...3F 75
Skinburness. Cumb ...4C 112
Skinflats. Falk ...1C 128
Skinidin. High ...4B 154
Skinnet. High ...2F 167
Skinningrove. Red C ...3E 107
Skipness. Arg ...4G 125
Skippool. Lanc ...5C 96
Skiprigg. Cumb ...5E 113
Skipsea. E Yor ...4F 101
Skipsea Brough. E Yor ...4F 101
Skipton. N Yor ...4B 98
Skipton-on-Swale. N Yor ...2F 99
Skipwith. N Yor ...1G 93
Skirbeck. Linc ...1C 76
Skirbeck Quarter. Linc ...1C 76
Skirlaugh. E Yor ...1E 95
Skirling. Bord ...1C 118
Skirmett. Buck ...2F 37
Skirpenbeck. E Yor ...4B 100
Skirwith. Cumb ...1H 103
Skirwith. N Yor ...2G 97

Skirza. High ...2F 169
Skitby. Cumb ...3F 113
Skitham. Lanc ...5D 96
Skittle Green. Buck ...5F 51
Skroo. Shet ...1B 172
Skulamus. High ...1E 147
Skullomie. High ...2G 167
Skyborry Green. Shrp ...3E 59
Skye Green. Essx ...3B 54
Skye of Curr. High ...1D 151
Slack. W Yor ...2H 91
The Slack. Dur ...2E 105
Slackhall. Derbs ...2E 85
Slack Head. Cumb ...2D 97
Slackhead. Mor ...2B 160
Slackholme End. Linc ...3E 89
Slad. Glos ...5D 48
The Slade. W Ber ...5D 36
Slade End. Oxon ...2D 36
Slade Field. Cambs ...2C 64
Slade Green. G Lon ...3G 39
Slade Heath. Staf ...5D 72
Slade Hooton. S Yor ...2C 86
Sladesbridge. Corn ...5A 10
Slaggyford. Nmbd ...4H 113
Slaidburn. Lanc ...4G 97
Slaid Hill. W Yor ...5F 99
Slaithwaite. W Yor ...3A 92
Slaley. Derbs ...5G 85
Slaley. Nmbd ...4C 114
Slamannan. Falk ...2B 128
Slapton. Buck ...3H 51
Slapton. Devn ...4E 9
Slapton. Nptn ...1E 51
Slattocks. G Man ...4G 91
Slaugham. W Sus ...3D 26
Slaughterbridge. Corn ...4B 10
Slaughterford. Wilts ...4D 34
Slawston. Leics ...1E 63
Sleaford. Hants ...3G 25
Sleaford. Linc ...1H 75
Sleagill. Cumb ...3G 103
Sleap. Shrp ...3G 71
Sledmere. E Yor ...3D 100
Sleightholme. Dur ...3C 104
Sleights. N Yor ...4F 107
Slepe. Dors ...3E 15
Slickly. High ...2E 169
Sliddery. N Ayr ...3D 122
Sligachan. High ...1C 146
Slimbridge. Glos ...5C 48
Slindon. Staf ...2C 72
Slindon. W Sus ...5A 26
Slinfold. W Sus ...2C 26
Slingsby. N Yor ...2A 100
Slip End. C Beds ...4A 52
Slipton. Nptn ...3G 63
Slitting Mill. Staf ...4E 73
Slochd. High ...1C 150
Slockavullin. Arg ...4F 133
Sloley. Norf ...3E 79
Sloncombe. Devn ...4H 11
Sloothby. Linc ...3D 89
Slough. Slo ...3A 38
Slough Green. Som ...4F 21
Slough Green. W Sus ...3D 27
Sluggan. High ...1C 150
Slyne. Lanc ...3D 97
Smailholm. Bord ...1A 120
Smallbridge. G Man ...3H 91
Smallbrook. Devn ...3B 12
Smallburgh. Norf ...3F 79
Smallburn. Abers ...2F 117
Smalldale. Derbs ...3E 85
Small Dole. W Sus ...4D 26
Smalley. Derbs ...1B 74
Smallfield. Surr ...1E 27
Small Heath. W Mid ...2E 61
Smallholm. Dum ...2C 112
Small Hythe. Kent ...2C 28
Smallrice. Staf ...2D 72
Smallridge. Devn ...2G 13
Smallwood Hey. Lanc ...5C 96
Smallworth. Norf ...2C 66
Smannell. Hants ...2B 24
Smardale. Cumb ...4A 104
Smarden. Kent ...1C 28
Smarden Bell. Kent ...1C 28
Smart's Hill. Kent ...1G 27
Smeatharpe. Devn ...1F 13
Smeeth. Kent ...2E 29
The Smeeth. Norf ...4E 77
Smeeton Westerby. Leics ...1D 62
Smeircleit. W Isl ...7C 170
Smerral. High ...5D 168
Smestow. Staf ...1C 60
Smethwick. W Mid ...2E 61
Smirisary. High ...1A 140
Smisby. Derbs ...4H 73
Smitham Hill. Bath ...1A 22
Smith End Green. Worc ...5B 60
Smithfield. Cumb ...3F 113
Smith Green. Lanc ...4D 97
The Smithies. Shrp ...1A 60
Smithincott. Devn ...1D 12
Smith's Green. Essx ...3F 53
Smithstown. High ...1G 155
Smithton. High ...4B 158
Smithwood Green. Suff ...5B 66
Smithy Bridge. G Man ...3H 91
Smithy Green. Ches E ...3B 84
Smithy Lane Ends. Lanc ...3C 90
Smockington. Leics ...2B 62
Smoogro. Orkn ...7C 172
Smythe's Green. Essx ...4C 54
Snaigow House. Per ...4H 143
Snailbeach. Shrp ...5F 71
Snailwell. Cambs ...4F 65
Snainton. N Yor ...1D 100

Snaith. E Yor ...2G 93
Snape. N Yor ...1E 99
Snape. Suff ...5F 67
Snape Green. Lanc ...3B 90
Snapper. Devn ...3F 19
Snarestone. Leics ...5H 73
Snarford. Linc ...2H 87
Snargate. Kent ...3D 28
Snave. Kent ...3E 28
Sneachill. Worc ...5D 60
Snead. Powy ...1F 59
Snead Common. Worc ...4B 60
Sneaton. N Yor ...4F 107
Sneatonthorpe. N Yor ...4G 107
Snelland. Linc ...2H 87
Snelston. Derbs ...1F 73
Snetterton. Norf ...1B 66
Snettisham. Norf ...2F 77
Snibston. Leics ...4B 74
Sniseabhal. W Isl ...5C 170
Snitter. Nmbd ...4E 121
Snitterby. Linc ...1G 87
Snitterfield. Warw ...5G 61
Snitton. Shrp ...3H 59
Snodhill. Here ...1G 47
Snodland. Kent ...4B 40
Snods Edge. Nmbd ...4D 114
Snowshill. Glos ...2F 49
Snow Street. Norf ...2C 66
Snydale. W Yor ...2E 93
Soake. Hants ...1E 17
Soar. Carm ...3G 45
Soar. Devn ...5D 8
Soar. Gwyn ...2C 69
Soar. IOA ...3C 80
Soar. Powy ...2C 46
Soberton. Hants ...1E 16
Soberton Heath. Hants ...1E 16
Sockbridge. Cumb ...2G 103
Sockburn. Darl ...4A 106
Sodom. Den ...3C 82
Sodom. Shet ...5G 173
Soham. Cambs ...3E 65
Soham Cotes. Cambs ...3E 65
Solas. W Isl ...1D 170
Soldon Cross. Devn ...1D 10
Soldridge. Hants ...3E 25
Solent Breezes. Hants ...2D 16
Sole Street. Kent
  nr. Meopham ...4A 40
  nr. Waltham ...1E 29
Solihull. W Mid ...2F 61
Sollers Dilwyn. Here ...5G 59
Sollers Hope. Here ...2B 48
Sollom. Lanc ...3C 90
Solva. Pemb ...2B 42
Somerby. Leics ...4E 75
Somerby. Linc ...4D 94
Somercotes. Derbs ...5B 86
Somerford. Dors ...3G 15
Somerford. Staf ...5C 72
Somerford Keynes. Glos ...2F 35
Somerley. W Sus ...3G 17
Somerleyton. Suff ...1G 67
Somersal Herbert. Derbs ...2F 73
Somersby. Linc ...3C 88
Somersham. Cambs ...3C 64
Somersham. Suff ...1D 54
Somerton. Oxon ...3C 50
Somerton. Som ...4H 21
Somerton. Suff ...5H 65
Sompting. W Sus ...5C 26
Sonning. Wok ...4F 37
Sonning Common. Oxon ...3F 37
Sonning Eye. Oxon ...4F 37
Sookholme. Notts ...4C 86
Sopley. Hants ...3G 15
Sopworth. Wilts ...3D 34
Sorbie. Dum ...5B 110
Sordale. High ...2D 168
Sorisdale. Arg ...2D 138
Sorn. E Ayr ...2E 117
Sornhill. E Ayr ...1E 117
Sortat. High ...2E 169
Sotby. Linc ...3B 88
Sots Hole. Linc ...4A 88
Sotterley. Suff ...2G 67
Soudley. Shrp
  nr. Church Stretton ...1G 59
  nr. Market Drayton ...3B 72
Soughton. Flin ...4E 83
Soulbury. Buck ...3G 51
Soulby. Cumb
  nr. Appleby ...3A 104
  nr. Penrith ...2F 103
Souldern. Oxon ...2D 50
Souldrop. Bed ...4G 63
Sound. Ches E ...1A 72
Sound. Shet
  nr. Lerwick ...7F 173
  nr. Tresta ...6E 173
Soundwell. S Glo ...4B 34
Sourhope. Bord ...2C 120
Sourin. Orkn ...4D 172
Sour Nook. Cumb ...5E 113
Sourton. Devn ...3F 11
Soutergate. Cumb ...1B 96
South Acre. Norf ...4H 77
Southall. G Lon ...3C 38
South Allington. Devn ...5D 9
South Alloa. Falk ...4A 136
Southam. Glos ...3E 49
Southam. Warw ...4B 62
Southampton. Sotn ...211 (1C 16)
Southampton Airport. Hants ...1C 16
Southannan. N Ayr ...4D 126
South Anston. S Yor ...2C 86
South Ascot. Wind ...4A 38
South Baddesley. Hants ...3B 16
South Balfern. Dum ...4B 110
South Ballachulish. High ...3E 141

South Bank. Red C ...2C 106
South Barrow. Som ...4B 22
South Benfleet. Essx ...2B 40
South Bents. Tyne ...3H 115
South Bersted. W Sus ...5A 26
Southborough. Kent ...1G 27
Southbourne. Bour ...3G 15
Southbourne. W Sus ...2F 17
South Bowood. Dors ...3H 13
South Brent. Devn ...3C 8
South Brewham. Som ...3C 22
South Broomage. Falk ...1B 128
South Broomhill. Nmbd ...5G 121
Southburgh. Norf ...5B 78
South Burlingham. Norf ...5F 79
Southburn. E Yor ...4D 101
South Cadbury. Som ...4B 22
South Carlton. Linc ...3G 87
South Cave. E Yor ...1C 94
South Cerney. Glos ...2F 35
South Chailey. E Sus ...4E 27
South Chard. Som ...2G 13
South Charlton. Nmbd ...2F 121
South Cheriton. Som ...4B 22
South Church. Dur ...2F 105
Southchurch. S'end ...2D 40
South Cleatlam. Dur ...3E 105
South Cliffe. E Yor ...1B 94
South Clifton. Notts ...3F 87
South Clunes. High ...4H 157
South Cockerington. Linc ...2C 88
South Common. Devn ...2G 13
South Cornelly. B'end ...3B 32
Southcott. Devn
  nr. Great Torrington ...1E 11
  nr. Okehampton ...3F 11
Southcott. Wilts ...1G 23
Southcourt. Buck ...4G 51
South Cove. Suff ...2G 67
South Creagan. Arg ...4D 141
South Creake. Norf ...2A 78
South Crosland. W Yor ...3B 92
South Croxton. Leics ...4D 74
South Dalton. E Yor ...5D 100
South Darenth. Kent ...4G 39
Southdean. Bord ...4A 120
Southdown. Bath ...5C 34
South Duffield. N Yor ...1G 93
Southease. E Sus ...5F 27
South Elkington. Linc ...2B 88
South Elmsall. W Yor ...3E 93
South End. Cumb ...3B 96
South End. N Lin ...2E 94
Southend. Arg ...5A 122
Southend. Glos ...2C 34
Southend. W Ber ...4D 36
Southend Airport. Essx ...2C 40
Southend-on-Sea. S'end ...2C 40
Southerfield. Cumb ...5C 112
Southerhouse. Shet ...8E 173
Southerly. Devn ...4F 11
Southernden. Kent ...1C 28
Southerndown. V Glam ...4B 32
Southerness. Dum ...4A 112
South Erradale. High ...1G 155
Southerton. Devn ...3D 12
Southery. Norf ...1F 65
Southey Green. Essx ...2A 54
South Fambridge. Essx ...1C 40
South Fawley. W Ber ...3B 36
South Feorline. N Ayr ...3D 122
South Ferriby. N Lin ...2C 94
South Field. E Yor ...2D 94
Southfleet. Kent ...3H 39
South Garvan. High ...1D 141
Southgate. G Lon ...1E 39
Southgate. Norf
  nr. Aylsham ...3D 78
  nr. Fakenham ...2A 78
Southgate. Swan ...4E 31
South Gluss. Shet ...4E 173
South Godstone. Surr ...1E 27
South Gorley. Hants ...1G 15
South Green. Essx
  nr. Billericay ...1A 40
  nr. Colchester ...4D 54
South Green. Kent ...4C 40
South Hanningfield. Essx ...1B 40
South Harting. W Sus ...1F 17
South Hayling. Hants ...3F 17
South Hazelrigg. Nmbd ...1E 121
South Heath. Buck ...5H 51
South Heath. Essx ...4E 54
South Heighton. E Sus ...5F 27
South Hetton. Dur ...5G 115
South Hiendley. W Yor ...3D 93
South Hill. Corn ...5D 10
South Hill. Som ...4H 21
South Hinksey. Oxon ...5D 50
South Hole. Devn ...4C 18
South Holme. N Yor ...2B 100
South Holmwood. Surr ...1C 26
South Hornchurch. G Lon ...2G 39
South Huish. Devn ...4C 8
South Hykeham. Linc ...4G 87
South Hylton. Tyne ...4G 115
Southill. C Beds ...1B 52
Southington. Hants ...2D 24
South Kelsey. Linc ...1H 87
South Kessock. High ...4A 158
South Killingholme. N Lin ...3E 95
South Kilvington. N Yor ...1G 99
South Kilworth. Leics ...2D 62
South Kirkby. W Yor ...3E 93
South Kirkton. Abers ...3E 153
South Knighton. Devn ...5B 12
South Kyme. Linc ...1A 76
South Lancing. W Sus ...5C 26
South Ledaig. Arg ...5D 140
South Leigh. Oxon ...5B 50

Southleigh. Devn....3F 13
South Leverton. Notts....2E 87
South Littleton. Worc....1F 49
South Lopham. Norf....2C 66
South Luffenham. Rut....5G 75
South Malling. E Sus....4F 27
South Marston. Swin....3G 35
South Middleton. Nmbd....2D 121
South Milford. N Yor....1E 93
South Milton. Devn....4D 8
South Mimms. Herts....5C 52
Southminster. Essx....1D 40
South Molton. Devn....4H 19
South Moor. Dur....4E 115
Southmoor. Oxon....2B 36
South Moreton. Oxon....3D 36
South Mundham. W Sus....2G 17
South Muskham. Notts....5E 87
South Newbald. E Yor....1C 94
South Newington. Oxon....2C 50
South Newsham. Nmbd....2G 115
South Newton. N Ayr....4H 125
South Newton. Wilts....3F 23
South Normanton. Derbs....5B 86
South Norwood. G Lon....4E 39
South Nutfield. Surr....1E 27
South Ockendon. Thur....2G 39
Southoe. Cambs....4A 64
Southolt. Suff....4D 66
South Ormsby. Linc....3C 88
Southorpe. Pet....5H 75
South Otterington. N Yor....1F 99
South Owersby. Linc....1H 87
Southowram. W Yor....2B 92
South Oxhey. Herts....1C 38
South Perrott. Dors....2H 13
South Petherton. Som....1H 13
South Petherwin. Corn....4D 10
South Pickenham. Norf....5A 78
South Pool. Devn....4D 9
South Poorton. Dors....3A 14
South Port. Arg....1H 133
Southport. Mers....3B 90
Southpunds. Shet....10F 173
South Queensferry. Edin....2E 129
South Radworthy. Devn....3A 20
South Rauceby. Linc....1H 75
South Raynham. Norf....3A 78
Southrepps. Norf....2E 79
South Reston. Linc....2D 88
Southrey. Linc....4A 88
Southrop. Glos....5G 49
Southrope. Hants....2E 25
South Runcton. Norf....5F 77
South Scarle. Notts....4F 87
Southsea. Port....3E 17
South Shields. Tyne....3G 115
South Shore. Bkpl....1B 90
Southside. Orkn....5E 172
South Somercotes. Linc....1D 88
South Stainley. N Yor....3F 99
South Stainmore. Cumb....3B 104
South Stifford. Thur....3G 39
South Stoke. Bath....5C 34
South Stoke. Oxon....3D 36
South Stoke. W Sus....5B 26
South Street. E Sus....4E 27
South Street. Kent
   nr. Faversham....5E 41
   nr. Whitstable....4F 41
South Tawton. Devn....3G 11
South Thoresby. Linc....3D 88
South Tidworth. Wilts....2H 23
South Town. Devn....4C 12
South Town. Hants....3E 25
Southtown. Norf....5H 79
Southtown. Orkn....8D 172
South View. Shet....7E 173
Southwaite. Cumb....5F 113
South Walsham. Norf....4F 79
South Warnborough. Hants....2F 25
Southwater. W Sus....3C 26
Southwater Street. W Sus....3C 26
Southway. Som....2A 22
South Weald. Essx....1G 39
South Weirs. Hants....2A 16
Southwell. Dors....5B 14
Southwell. Notts....5E 86
South Weston. Oxon....2F 37
South Wheatley. Corn....3C 10
South Wheatley. Notts....2E 87
Southwick. Hants....2E 17
Southwick. Nptn....1H 63
Southwick. Tyne....4G 115
Southwick. W Sus....5D 26
Southwick. Wilts....1D 22
South Widcombe. Bath....1A 22
South Wigston. Leics....1C 62
South Willingham. Linc....2A 88
South Wingfield. Derbs....5A 86
South Witham. Linc....4G 75
Southwold. Suff....3H 67
South Wonston. Hants....3C 24
Southwood. Norf....5F 79
Southwood. Som....3A 22
South Woodham Ferrers.
   Essx....1C 40
South Wootton. Norf....3F 77
South Wraxall. Wilts....5D 34
South Zeal. Devn....3G 11
Soval Lodge. W Isl....5F 171
Sowerby. N Yor....1G 99
Sowerby. W Yor....2A 92
Sowerby Bridge. W Yor....2A 92
Sowerby Row. Cumb....5E 113
Sower Carr. Lanc....5C 96
Sowley Green. Suff....5G 65
Sowood. W Yor....3A 92
Sowton. Devn....3C 12
Soyal. High....4C 164
Soyland Town. W Yor....2A 92

Spacey Houses. N Yor....4F 99
Spa Common. Norf....2E 79
Spalding. Linc....3B 76
Spaldington. E Yor....1A 94
Spaldwick. Cambs....3A 64
Spalford. Notts....4F 87
Spanby. Linc....2H 75
Sparham. Norf....4C 78
Sparhamhill. Norf....4C 78
Spark Bridge. Cumb....1C 96
Sparket. Cumb....2F 103
Sparkford. Som....4B 22
Sparkwell. Devn....3B 8
Sparrow Green. Norf....4B 78
Sparrowpit. Derbs....2E 85
Sparrow's Green. E Sus....2H 27
Sparsholt. Hants....3C 24
Sparsholt. Oxon....3B 36
Spartylea. Nmbd....5B 114
Spath. Staf....2E 73
Spaunton. N Yor....1B 100
Spaxton. Som....3F 21
Spean Bridge. High....5E 149
Spear Hill. W Sus....4C 26
Speen. Buck....2G 37
Speen. W Ber....5C 36
Speeton. N Yor....2F 101
Speke. Mers....2G 83
Speldhurst. Kent....1G 27
Spellbrook. Herts....4E 53
Spelsbury. Oxon....3B 50
Spencers Wood. Wok....5F 37
Spennithorne. N Yor....1D 98
Spennymoor. Dur....1F 105
Spernall. Warw....4E 61
Spetchley. Worc....5C 60
Spetisbury. Dors....2E 15
Spexhall. Suff....2F 67
Speybank. High....3C 150
Spey Bay. Mor....2A 160
Speybridge. High....1E 151
Speyview. Mor....4G 159
Spilsby. Linc....4D 88
Spindlestone. Nmbd....1F 121
Spinkhill. Derbs....3B 86
Spinney Hills. Leic....5D 74
Spinningdale. High....5D 164
Spital. Mers....2F 83
Spitalhill. Derbs....1F 73
Spital in the Street. Linc....1G 87
Spithurst. E Sus....4F 27
Spittal. Dum....4A 110
Spittal. E Lot....2A 130
Spittal. High....3D 168
Spittal. Nmbd....4G 131
Spittal. Pemb....2D 43
Spittalfield. Per....4A 144
Spittal of Glenmuick. Abers....5H 151
Spittal of Glenshee. Per....1A 144
Spittal-on-Rule. Bord....2H 119
Spixworth. Norf....4E 79
Splatt. Corn....4C 10
Spofforth. N Yor....4F 99
Spon End. W Mid....3H 61
Spooner Row. Norf....1C 66
Sporle. Norf....4H 77
Spott. E Lot....2C 130
Spratton. Nptn....3E 62
Spreakley. Surr....2G 25
Spreyton. Devn....3H 11
Spridlington. Linc....2H 87
Springburn. Glas....3H 127
Springfield. Dum....3E 113
Springfield. Fife....2F 137
Springfield. High....2A 158
Springfield. W Mid....2E 61
Spring Hill. W Mid....1C 60
Springhill. Staf....5D 73
Springholm. Dum....3F 111
Springside. N Ayr....1C 116
Springthorpe. Linc....2F 87
Spring Vale. IOW....3E 16
Spring Valley. IOM....4C 108
Sproatley. E Yor....1E 95
Sproston Green. Ches W....4B 84
Sprotbrough. S Yor....4F 93
Sproughton. Suff....1E 54
Sprowston. Norf....4E 79
Sproxton. Leics....3F 75
Sproxton. N Yor....1A 100
Sprunston. Cumb....5F 113
Spurstow. Ches E....5H 83
Squires Gate. Bkpl....1B 90
Sraid Ruadh. Arg....4A 138
Srannda. W Isl....9C 171
Sron an t-Sithein. High....2C 140
Sronphadruig Lodge. Per....1E 142
Sruth Mor. W Isl....2E 170
Stableford. Shrp....1B 60
Stackhouse. N Yor....3H 97
Stackpole. Pemb....5D 43
Stackpole Elidor. Pemb....5D 43
Stacksford. Norf....1C 66
Stacksteads. Lanc....2G 91
Staddiscombe. Plym....3B 8
Staddlethorpe. E Yor....2B 94
Staddon. Devn....2D 10
Stadhampton. Oxon....2E 36
Stadhlaigearraidh. W Isl....5C 170
Stafainn. High....2D 155
Staffield. Cumb....5G 113
Staffin. High....2D 155
Stafford. Staf....3D 72
Stafford Park. Telf....5B 72
Stagsden. Bed....1H 51
Stag's Head. Devn....4G 19
Stainburn. Cumb....2B 102

Stainburn. N Yor....5E 99
Stainby. Linc....3G 75
Staincliffe. W Yor....2C 92
Staincross. S Yor....3D 92
Staindrop. Dur....2E 105
Staines-upon-Thames. Surr....3B 38
Stainfield. Linc
   nr. Bourne....3H 75
   nr. Lincoln....3A 88
Stainforth. N Yor....3H 97
Stainforth. S Yor....3G 93
Staining. Lanc....1B 90
Stainland. W Yor....3A 92
Stainsacre. N Yor....4G 107
Stainton. Cumb
   nr. Carlisle....4E 113
   nr. Kendal....1E 97
   nr. Penrith....2F 103
Stainton. Dur....3D 104
Stainton. Midd....3B 106
Stainton. N Yor....5E 105
Stainton. S Yor....1C 86
Stainton by Langworth. Linc....3H 87
Staintondale. N Yor....5G 107
Stainton le Vale. Linc....1A 88
Stainton with Adgarley. Cumb....2B 96
Stair. Cumb....2D 102
Stair. E Ayr....2D 116
Stairhaven. Dum....4H 109
Staithes. N Yor....3E 107
Stakeford. Nmbd....1F 115
Stake Pool. Lanc....5D 96
Stakes. Hants....2E 17
Stalbridge. Dors....1C 14
Stalbridge Weston. Dors....1C 14
Stalham. Norf....3F 79
Stalham Green. Norf....3F 79
Stalisfield Green. Kent....5D 40
Stallen. Dors....1B 14
Stallingborough. NE Lin....3F 95
Stalling Busk. N Yor....1B 98
Stallington. Staf....2D 72
Stalmine. Lanc....5C 96
Stalybridge. G Man....1D 84
Stambourne. Essx....2H 53
Stamford. Linc....5H 75
Stamford. Nmbd....3G 121
Stamford Bridge. Ches W....4G 83
Stamford Bridge. E Yor....4B 100
Stamfordham. Nmbd....2D 115
Stamperland. E Ren....4G 127
Stanah. Lanc....5C 96
Stanborough. Herts....4C 52
Stanbridge. C Beds....3H 51
Stanbridge. Dors....2F 15
Stanbury. W Yor....1A 92
Stand. N Lan....3A 128
Standburn. Falk....2C 128
Standeford. Staf....5D 72
Standen. Kent....1C 28
Standen Street. Kent....2C 28
Standerwick. Som....1D 22
Standford. Hants....3G 25
Standford Bridge. Telf....3B 72
Standingstone. Cumb....5D 112
Standish. Glos....5D 48
Standish. G Man....3D 90
Standish Lower Ground.
   G Man....4D 90
Standlake. Oxon....5B 50
Standon. Hants....4C 24
Standon. Herts....3D 53
Standon. Staf....2C 72
Standon Green End. Herts....4D 52
Stane. N Lan....4B 128
Stanecastle. N Ayr....1C 116
Stanfield. Norf....3B 78
Stanfield. Suff....5G 65
Stanford. C Beds....1B 52
Stanford. Kent....2F 29
Stanford Bishop. Here....5A 60
Stanford Bridge. Worc....4B 60
Stanford Dingley. W Ber....4D 36
Stanford in the Vale. Oxon....2B 36
Stanford-le-Hope. Thur....2A 40
Stanford on Avon. Nptn....3C 62
Stanford on Soar. Notts....3C 74
Stanford on Teme. Worc....4B 60
Stanford Rivers. Essx....5F 53
Stanfree. Derbs....3B 86
Stanghow. Red C....3D 107
Stanground. Pet....1B 64
Stanhoe. Norf....2H 77
Stanhope. Dur....1C 104
Stanhope. Bord....2D 118
Stanion. Nptn....2G 63
Stanley. Derbs....1B 74
Stanley. Dur....4E 115
Stanley. Per....5A 144
Stanley. Shrp....2B 60
Stanley. Staf....5D 84
Stanley. W Yor....2D 92
Stanley Common. Derbs....1B 74
Stanley Crook. Dur....1E 105
Stanley Hill. Here....1B 48
Stanlow. Ches W....3G 83
Stanmer. Brig....5E 27
Stanmore. G Lon....1C 38
Stanmore. Hants....4C 24
Stanmore. W Ber....4C 36
Stannersburn. Nmbd....1A 114
Stanningfield. Suff....5A 66
Stannington. Nmbd....2F 115
Stannington. S Yor....2H 85
Stansbatch. Here....4F 59
Stansfield. Suff....5G 65
Stanstead. Suff....1B 54
Stanstead Abbotts. Herts....4D 53
Stansted. Kent....4H 39
Stansted Airport. Essx....216 (3F 53)
Stansted Mountfitchet. Essx....3F 53

Stanthorne. Ches W....4A 84
Stanton. Derbs....4G 73
Stanton. Glos....2F 49
Stanton. Nmbd....5F 121
Stanton. Staf....1F 73
Stanton. Suff....3B 66
Stanton by Bridge. Derbs....3A 74
Stanton-by-Dale. Derbs....2B 74
Stanton Chare. Suff....3B 66
Stanton Drew. Bath....5A 34
Stanton Fitzwarren. Swin....2G 35
Stanton Harcourt. Oxon....5C 50
Stanton Hill. Notts....4B 86
Stanton in Peak. Derbs....4G 85
Stanton Lacy. Shrp....3G 59
Stanton Long. Shrp....1H 59
Stanton-on-the-Wolds. Notts....2D 74
Stanton Prior. Bath....5B 34
Stanton St Bernard. Wilts....5F 35
Stanton St John. Oxon....5D 50
Stanton St Quintin. Wilts....4E 35
Stanton Street. Suff....4B 66
Stanton under Bardon. Leics....4B 74
Stanton upon Hine Heath. Shrp....3H 71
Stanton Wick. Bath....5B 34
Stanwardine in the Fields. Shrp....3G 71
Stanwardine in the Wood. Shrp....3G 71
Stanway. Essx....3C 54
Stanway. Glos....2F 49
Stanwell. Surr....3B 38
Stanwell Green. Suff....3D 66
Stanwell Moor. Surr....3B 38
Stanwick. Nptn....3G 63
Stanydale. Shet....6D 173
Staoinebrig. W Isl....5C 170
Stape. N Yor....5E 107
Stapehill. Dors....2F 15
Stapeley. Ches E....1A 72
Stapenhill. Staf....3G 73
Staple. Kent....5G 41
Staple Cross. Devn....4D 20
Staplecross. E Sus....3B 28
Staplefield. W Sus....3D 27
Staple Fitzpaine. Som....1F 13
Stapleford. Cambs....5D 64
Stapleford. Herts....4D 52
Stapleford. Leics....4F 75
Stapleford. Linc....5F 87
Stapleford. Notts....2B 74
Stapleford. Wilts....3F 23
Stapleford Abbotts. Essx....1G 39
Stapleford Tawney. Essx....1G 39
Staplegrove. Som....4F 21
Staplehay. Som....4F 21
Staple Hill. S Glo....4B 34
Staplehurst. Kent....1B 28
Staplers. IOW....4D 16
Stapleton. Bris....4B 34
Stapleton. Cumb....2G 113
Stapleton. Here....4F 59
Stapleton. Leics....1B 62
Stapleton. N Yor....3F 105
Stapleton. Shrp....5G 71
Stapleton. Som....4H 21
Stapley. Som....1E 13
Staploe. Bed....4A 64
Staplow. Here....1B 48
Star. Fife....3F 137
Starbeck. N Yor....4F 99
Starbotton. N Yor....2B 98
Starcross. Devn....4C 12
Stareton. Warw....3H 61
Starkholmes. Derbs....5H 85
Starling. G Man....3F 91
Starling's Green. Essx....2E 53
Starston. Norf....2E 67
Start. Devn....4E 9
Startforth. Dur....3D 104
Start Hill. Essx....3F 53
Startley. Wilts....3E 35
Stathe. Som....4G 21
Stathern. Leics....2E 75
Station Town. Dur....1B 106
Staughton Green. Cambs....4A 64
Staughton Highway. Cambs....4A 64
Staunton. Glos
   nr. Cheltenham....3C 48
   nr. Monmouth....4A 48
Staunton in the Vale. Notts....1F 75
Staunton on Arrow. Here....4F 59
Staunton on Wye. Here....1G 47
Staveley. Cumb....5F 103
Staveley. Derbs....3B 86
Staveley. N Yor....3F 99
Staveley-in-Cartmel. Cumb....1C 96
Staverton. Devn....2D 9
Staverton. Glos....3D 49
Staverton. Nptn....4C 62
Staverton. Wilts....5D 34
Stawell. Som....3G 21
Stawley. Som....4D 20
Staxigoe. High....3F 169
Staxton. N Yor....2E 101
Staylittle. Powy....1A 58
Staynall. Lanc....5C 96
Staythorpe. Notts....5E 87
Stean. N Yor....2C 98
Stearsby. N Yor....2A 100
Steart. Som....2F 21
Stebbing. Essx....3G 53
Stebbing Green. Essx....3G 53
Stedham. W Sus....4G 25
Steel. Nmbd....4C 114
Steel Cross. E Sus....2G 27
Steele Road. Bord....5H 119
Steel Heath. Shrp....2H 71
Steen's Bridge. Here....5H 59
Steep. Hants....4F 25
Steep Lane. W Yor....2A 92

Steeple. Dors....4E 15
Steeple. Essx....5C 54
Steeple Ashton. Wilts....1E 23
Steeple Aston. Oxon....3C 50
Steeple Barton. Oxon....3C 50
Steeple Bumpstead. Essx....1G 53
Steeple Claydon. Buck....3E 51
Steeple Gidding. Cambs....2A 64
Steeple Langford. Wilts....3F 23
Steeple Morden. Cambs....1C 52
Steeton. W Yor....5C 98
Stein. High....3B 154
Steinmanhill. Abers....4E 161
Stelling Minnis. Kent....1F 29
Stembridge. Som....4H 21
Stemster. High
   nr. Halkirk....2D 169
   nr. Westfield....2C 168
Stenalees. Corn....3E 6
Stenhill. Devn....1D 12
Stenhouse. Edin....2F 129
Stenhousemuir. Falk....1B 128
Stenigot. Linc....2B 88
Stenscholl. High....2D 155
Stenso. Orkn....5C 172
Stenson. Derbs....3H 73
Stenson Fields. Derbs....2H 73
Stenton. E Lot....2C 130
Stenwith. Linc....2F 75
Steòrnabhagh. W Isl....4G 171
Stepaside. Pemb....4F 43
Stepford. Dum....1F 111
Stepney. G Lon....2E 39
Steppingley. C Beds....2A 52
Stepps. N Lan....3H 127
Sternfield. Suff....4F 67
Sterndale Moor. Derbs....4F 85
Stert. Wilts....1F 23
Stetchworth. Cambs....5F 65
Stevenage. Herts....3C 52
Stevenston. N Ayr....5D 126
Stevenstone. Devn....1F 11
Steventon. Hants....2D 24
Steventon. Oxon....2C 36
Steventon End. Essx....1F 53
Stevington. Bed....5G 63
Stewartby. Bed....1A 52
Stewarton. Arg....4A 122
Stewarton. E Ayr....5F 127
Stewkley. Buck....3G 51
Stewkley Dean. Buck....3G 51
Stewley. Som....1G 13
Stewton. Linc....2C 88
Steyning. W Sus....4C 26
Steynton. Pemb....4D 42
Stibb. Corn....1C 10
Stibbard. Norf....3B 78
Stibb Cross. Devn....1E 11
Stibb Green. Wilts....5H 35
Stibbington. Cambs....1H 63
Stichill. Bord....1B 120
Sticker. Corn....3D 6
Stickford. Linc....4C 88
Sticklepath. Devn....3G 11
Sticklinch. Som....3A 22
Stickling Green. Essx....2E 53
Stickney. Linc....5C 88
Stiffkey. Norf....1B 78
Stifford's Bridge. Here....1C 48
Stileway. Som....2H 21
Stillingfleet. N Yor....5H 99
Stillington. N Yor....3H 99
Stillington. Stoc T....2A 106
Stilton. Cambs....2A 64
Stinchcombe. Glos....2C 34
Stinsford. Dors....3C 14
Stiperstones. Shrp....5F 71
Stirchley. Telf....5B 72
Stirchley. W Mid....2E 61
Stirling. Abers....4H 161
Stirling. Stir....211 (4G 135)
Stirton. N Yor....4B 98
Stisted. Essx....3A 54
Stitchcombe. Wilts....5H 35
Stithians. Corn....5B 6
Stittenham. High....1A 158
Stivichall. W Mid....3H 61
Stixwould. Linc....4A 88
Stoak. Ches W....3G 83
Stobo. Bord....1D 118
Stobo Castle. Bord....1D 118
Stoborough. Dors....4E 15
Stoborough Green. Dors....4E 15
Stobs Castle. Bord....4H 119
Stobswood. Nmbd....5G 121
Stock. Essx....1A 40
Stockbridge. Hants....3B 24
Stockbridge. W Yor....5C 98
Stockbury. Kent....4C 40
Stockcross. W Ber....5C 36
Stockdalewath. Cumb....5E 113
Stocker's Head. Kent....5D 40
Stockerston. Leics....1F 63
Stock Green. Worc....5D 61
Stocking. Here....2B 48
Stockingford. Warw....1H 61
Stocking Green. Essx....2F 53
Stocking Pelham. Herts....3E 53
Stockland. Devn....2F 13
Stockland Bristol. Som....2F 21
Stockleigh English. Devn....2B 12
Stockleigh Pomeroy. Devn....2B 12
Stockley. Wilts....5F 35
Stocklinch. Som....1G 13
Stockport. G Man....2C 84
The Stocks. Kent....3D 28
Stocksbridge. S Yor....1G 85
Stocksfield. Nmbd....3D 114
Stockstreet. Essx....3B 54
Stockton. Here....4H 59
Stockton. Norf....1F 67

Stockton – Swaythling

Stockton. Shrp
nr. Bridgnorth 1B 60
nr. Chirbury 5E 71
Stockton. Telf 4B 72
Stockton. Warw 4B 62
Stockton. Wilts 3E 23
Stockton Brook. Staf 5D 84
Stockton Cross. Here 4H 59
Stockton Heath. Warr 2A 84
Stockton-on-Tees. Stoc T 3B 106
Stockton on Teme. Worc 4B 60
Stockton-on-the-Forest. York 4A 100
Stockwell Heath. Staf 3E 73
Stock Wood. Worc 5E 61
Stockwood. Bris 5B 34
Stodmarsh. Kent 4G 41
Stody. Norf 2C 78
Stoer. High 1E 163
Stoford. Som 1A 14
Stoford. Wilts 3F 23
Stogumber. Som 3D 20
Stogursey. Som 2F 21
Stoke. Devn 4C 18
Stoke. Hants
nr. Andover 1C 24
nr. South Hayling 2F 17
Stoke. Medw 3C 40
Stoke. W Mid 3A 62
Stoke Abbott. Dors 2H 13
Stoke Albany. Nptn 2F 63
Stoke Ash. Suff 3D 66
Stoke Bardolph. Notts 1D 74
Stoke Bliss. Worc 4A 60
Stoke Bruerne. Nptn 1F 51
Stoke by Clare. Suff 1H 53
Stoke-by-Nayland. Suff 2C 54
Stoke Canon. Devn 3C 12
Stoke Charity. Hants 3C 24
Stoke Climsland. Corn 5D 10
Stoke Cross. Here 5A 60
Stoke D'Abernon. Surr 5C 38
Stoke Doyle. Nptn 2H 63
Stoke Dry. Rut 1F 63
Stoke Edith. Here 1B 48
Stoke Farthing. Wilts 4F 23
Stoke Ferry. Norf 5G 77
Stoke Fleming. Devn 4E 9
Stokeford. Dors 4D 14
Stoke Gabriel. Devn 3E 9
Stoke Gifford. S Glo 4B 34
Stoke Golding. Leics 1A 62
Stoke Goldington. Mil 1G 51
Stokeham. Notts 3E 87
Stoke Hammond. Buck 3G 51
Stoke Heath. Shrp 3A 72
Stoke Holy Cross. Norf 5E 79
Stokeinteignhead. Devn 5C 12
Stoke Lacy. Here 1B 48
Stoke Lyne. Oxon 3D 50
Stoke Mandeville. Buck 4G 51
Stokenchurch. Buck 2F 37
Stoke Newington. G Lon 2E 39
Stokenham. Devn 4E 9
Stoke on Tern. Shrp 3A 72
Stoke-on-Trent. Stoke 211 (1C 72)
Stoke Orchard. Glos 3E 49
Stoke Pero. Som 2B 20
Stoke Poges. Buck 2A 38
Stoke Prior. Here 5H 59
Stoke Prior. Worc 4D 60
Stoke Rivers. Devn 3G 19
Stoke Rochford. Linc 3G 75
Stoke Row. Oxon 3E 37
Stoke St Gregory. Som 4G 21
Stoke St Mary. Som 4F 21
Stoke St Michael. Som 2B 22
Stoke St Milborough. Shrp 2H 59
Stokesay. Shrp 2G 59
Stokesby. Norf 4G 79
Stokesley. N Yor 4C 106
Stoke sub Hamdon. Som 1H 13
Stoke Talmage. Oxon 2E 37
Stoke Town. Stoke 211 (1C 72)
Stoke Trister. Som 4C 22
Stoke Wake. Dors 2C 14
Stolford. Som 2F 21
Stondon Massey. Essx 5F 53
Stone. Buck 4F 51
Stone. Glos 2B 34
Stone. Kent 3G 39
Stone. Som 3A 22
Stone. Staf 2D 72
Stone. Worc 3C 60
Stonea. Cambs 1D 64
Stoneacton. Shrp 1H 59
Stone Allerton. Som 1H 21
Ston Easton. Som 1B 22
Stonebridge. N Som 1G 21
Stonebridge. Surr 1C 26
Stone Bridge Corner. Pet 5B 76
Stonebroom. Derbs 5B 86
Stonebyres Holdings. S Lan 5B 128
Stone Chair. W Yor 2B 92
Stone Cross. E Sus 5H 27
Stone Cross. Kent 2G 27
Stone-edge Batch. N Som 4H 33
Stoneferry. Hull 1D 94
Stonefield. Arg 5D 140
Stonefield. S Lan 4H 127
Stonegate. E Sus 3A 28
Stonegate. N Yor 4E 107
Stonegrave. N Yor 2A 100
Stonehall. Worc 1D 49
Stonehaugh. Nmbd 2A 114
Stonehaven. Abers 5F 153
Stone Heath. Staf 2D 72
Stone Hill. Kent 2E 29
Stone House. Cumb 1G 97
Stonehouse. Glos 5D 48
Stonehouse. Nmbd 4H 113
Stonehouse. S Lan 5A 128
Stone in Oxney. Kent 3D 28
Stoneleigh. Warw 3H 61
Stoneley Green. Ches E 5A 84
Stonely. Cambs 4A 64
Stonepits. Worc 5E 61
Stoner Hill. Hants 4F 25
Stonesby. Leics 3F 75
Stonesfield. Oxon 4B 50
Stones Green. Essx 3E 55
Stone Street. Kent 5G 39
Stone Street. Suff
nr. Boxford 2C 54
nr. Halesworth 2F 67
Stonethwaite. Cumb 3D 102
Stoneyburn. W Lot 3C 128
Stoney Cross. Hants 1A 16
Stoneyford. Devn 2D 12
Stoneygate. Leic 5D 74
Stoneyhills. Essx 1D 40
Stoneykirk. Dum 4F 109
Stoney Middleton. Derbs 3G 85
Stoney Stanton. Leics 1B 62
Stoney Stoke. Som 3C 22
Stoney Stratton. Som 3B 22
Stoney Stretton. Shrp 5F 71
Stoneywood. Aber 2F 153
Stonham Aspal. Suff 5D 66
Stonnall. Staf 5E 73
Stonor. Oxon 3F 37
Stonton Wyville. Leics 1E 63
Stonybreck. Shet 1B 172
Stony Cross. Devn 4F 19
Stony Cross. Here
nr. Great Malvern 1C 48
nr. Leominster 4H 59
Stony Houghton. Derbs 4B 86
Stony Stratford. Mil 1F 51
Stoodleigh. Devn
nr. Barnstaple 3G 19
nr. Tiverton 1C 12
Stopham. W Sus 4B 26
Stopsley. Lutn 3B 52
Stoptide. Corn 1D 6
Storeton. Mers 2F 83
Stormontfield. Per 1D 136
Stornoway. W Isl 4G 171
Stornoway Airport. W Isl 4G 171
Storridge. Here 1C 48
Storrington. W Sus 4B 26
Storrs. Cumb 5E 103
Storth. Cumb 1D 97
Storwood. E Yor 5B 100
Stotfield. Mor 1G 159
Stotfold. C Beds 2C 52
Stottesdon. Shrp 2A 60
Stoughton. Leics 5D 74
Stoughton. Surr 5A 38
Stoughton. W Sus 1G 17
Stoul. High 4F 147
Stoulton. Worc 1E 49
Stourbridge. W Mid 2C 60
Stourpaine. Dors 2D 14
Stourport-on-Severn. Worc 3C 60
Stour Provost. Dors 4C 22
Stour Row. Dors 4D 22
Stourton. Staf 2C 60
Stourton. Warw 2A 50
Stourton. W Yor 1D 92
Stourton. Wilts 3C 22
Stourton Caundle. Dors 1C 14
Stove. Orkn 4F 172
Stove. Shet 9F 173
Stoven. Suff 2G 67
Stow. Linc
nr. Billingborough 2H 75
nr. Gainsborough 2F 87
Stow. Bord 5A 130
Stow Bardolph. Norf 5F 77
Stow Bedon. Norf 1B 66
Stowbridge. Norf 5F 77
Stow cum Quy. Cambs 4E 65
Stowe. Glos 5A 48
Stowe. Shrp 3F 59
Stowe. Staf 4F 73
Stowe-by-Chartley. Staf 3E 73
Stowell. Som 4B 22
Stowey. Bath 1A 22
Stowford. Devn
nr. Colaton Raleigh 4D 12
nr. Combe Martin 2G 19
nr. Tavistock 4E 11
Stowlangtoft. Suff 4B 66
Stow Longa. Cambs 3A 64
Stow Maries. Essx 1C 40
Stowmarket. Suff 5C 66
Stow-on-the-Wold. Glos 3G 49
Stowting. Kent 1F 29
Stowupland. Suff 5C 66
Straad. Arg 3B 126
Strachan. Abers 4D 152
Stradbroke. Suff 3E 67
Stradishall. Suff 5G 65
Stradsett. Norf 5F 77
Stragglethorpe. Linc 5G 87
Stragglethorpe. Notts 2D 74
Straid. S Ayr 5A 116
Straight Soley. Wilts 4B 36
Straiton. Midl 3F 129
Straiton. S Ayr 4C 116
Straloch. Per 2H 143
Stramshall. Staf 2E 73
Strang. IOM 4C 108
Strangford. Here 3A 48
Stranraer. Dum 3F 109
Strata Florida. Cdgn 4G 57
Stratfield Mortimer. W Ber 5E 37
Stratfield Saye. Hants 5E 37
Stratfield Turgis. Hants 1E 25
Stratford. G Lon 2E 39
Stratford. Worc 2D 49
Stratford St Andrew. Suff 4F 67
Stratford St Mary. Suff 2D 54
Stratford sub Castle. Wilts 3G 23
Stratford Tony. Wilts 4F 23
Stratford-upon-Avon. Warw 212 (5G 61)
Strath. High
nr. Gairloch 1G 155
nr. Wick 3E 169
Strathan. High
nr. Fort William 4B 148
nr. Lochinver 1E 163
nr. Tongue 2F 167
Strathan Skerray. High 2G 167
Strathaven. S Lan 5A 128
Strathblane. Stir 2G 127
Strathcanaird. High 3F 163
Strathcarron. High 4B 156
Strathcoil. Arg 5A 140
Strathdon. Abers 2A 152
Strathkinness. Fife 2G 137
Strathmashie House. High 4H 149
Strathmiglo. Fife 2E 136
Strathmore Lodge. High 4D 168
Strathpeffer. High 3G 157
Strathrannoch. High 1F 157
Strathtay. Per 3G 143
Strathvaich Lodge. High 1F 157
Strathwhillan. N Ayr 2E 123
Strathy. High
nr. Invergordon 1A 158
nr. Melvich 2A 168
Strathyre. Stir 2E 135
Stratton. Corn 2C 10
Stratton. Dors 3B 14
Stratton. Glos 5F 49
Stratton Audley. Oxon 3E 50
Stratton-on-the-Fosse. Som 1B 22
Stratton St Margaret. Swin 3G 35
Stratton St Michael. Norf 1E 66
Stratton Strawless. Norf 3E 78
Stravithie. Fife 2H 137
Stream. Som 3D 20
Streat. E Sus 4E 27
Streatham. G Lon 3E 39
Streatley. C Beds 3A 52
Streatley. W Ber 3D 36
Street. Corn 3C 10
Street. Lanc 4E 97
Street. N Yor 4E 107
Street. Som
nr. Chard 2G 13
Street. Som
nr. Glastonbury 3H 21
Street Ash. Som 1F 13
Street Dinas. Shrp 2F 71
Street End. Kent 5F 41
Street End. W Sus 3G 17
Streetgate. Tyne 4F 115
Streethay. Staf 4F 73
Streethouse. W Yor 2D 93
Streetlam. N Yor 5A 106
Street Lane. Derbs 1A 74
Streetly. W Mid 1E 61
Streetly End. Cambs 1G 53
Street on the Fosse. Som 3B 22
Strefford. Shrp 2G 59
Strelley. Notts 1C 74
Strensall. York 3A 100
Strensall Camp. York 4A 100
Stretcholt. Som 2F 21
Strete. Devn 4E 9
Stretford. G Man 1C 84
Stretford. Here 5H 59
Strethall. Essx 2E 53
Stretham. Cambs 3E 65
Stretton. Ches W 5G 83
Stretton. Derbs 4A 86
Stretton. Rut 4G 75
Stretton. Staf
nr. Brewood 4C 72
nr. Burton upon Trent 3G 73
Stretton. Warr 2A 84
Stretton en le Field. Leics 4H 73
Stretton Grandison. Here 1B 48
Stretton Heath. Shrp 4F 71
Stretton-on-Dunsmore. Warw 3B 62
Stretton-on-Fosse. Warw 2H 49
Stretton Sugwas. Here 1H 47
Stretton under Fosse. Warw 2B 62
Stretton Westwood. Shrp 1H 59
Strichen. Abers 3G 161
Strines. G Man 2D 84
Stringston. Som 2E 21
Strixton. Nptn 4G 63
Stroanfreggan. Dum 5F 117
Stroat. Glos 2A 34
Stromeferry. High 5A 156
Stromemore. High 5A 156
Stromness. Orkn 7B 172
Stronachie. Per 3C 136
Stronachlachar. Stir 2D 134
Stronchreggan. High 1E 141
Strone. Arg 1C 126
Strone. High
nr. Drumnadrochit 1H 149
nr. Kingussie 3B 150
Stronenaba. High 5E 148
Stronganess. Shet 1G 173
Stronmilchan. Arg 1A 134
Stronsay Airport. Orkn 5F 172
Strontian. High 2C 140
Strood. Kent 2C 28
Strood. Medw 4B 40
Strood Green. Surr 1D 26
Strood Green. W Sus
nr. Billingshurst 3B 26
nr. Horsham 2C 26
Strothers Dale. Nmbd 4C 114
Stroud. Glos 5D 48
Stroud. Hants 4F 25
Stroud Green. Essx 1C 40
Stroxton. Linc 2G 75
Struan. High 5C 154
Struan. Per 2F 143
Struanmore. High 5C 154
Strubby. Linc 2D 88
Strugg's Hill. Linc 2B 76
Strumpshaw. Norf 5F 79
Strutherhill. S Lan 4A 128
Struy. High 5G 157
Stryd. IOA 2B 80
Stryt-issa. Wrex 1E 71
Stuartfield. Abers 4G 161
Stubbington. Hants 2D 16
Stubbins. Lanc 3F 91
Stubble Green. Cumb 5B 102
Stubb's Cross. Kent 2D 28
Stubbs Green. Norf 1F 67
Stubhampton. Dors 1E 15
Stubton. Linc 1F 75
Stubwood. Staf 2E 73
Stuckton. Hants 1G 15
Studham. C Beds 4A 52
Studland. Dors 4F 15
Studley. Warw 4E 61
Studley. Wilts 4E 35
Studley Roger. N Yor 2E 99
Stuntney. Cambs 3E 65
Stunts Green. E Sus 4H 27
Sturbridge. Staf 2C 72
Sturgate. Linc 2F 87
Sturmer. Essx 1G 53
Sturminster Marshall. Dors 2E 15
Sturminster Newton. Dors 1C 14
Sturry. Kent 4F 41
Sturton. N Lin 4C 94
Sturton by Stow. Linc 2F 87
Sturton le Steeple. Notts 2E 87
Stuston. Suff 3D 66
Stutton. N Yor 5G 99
Stutton. Suff 2E 55
Styal. Ches E 2C 84
Stydd. Lanc 1E 91
Styrrup. Notts 1D 86
Suainebost. W Isl 1H 171
Suardail. W Isl 4G 171
Succoth. Abers 5B 160
Succoth. Arg 3B 134
Suckley. Worc 5B 60
Suckley Knowl. Worc 5B 60
Sudborough. Nptn 2G 63
Sudbourne. Suff 5G 67
Sudbrook. Linc 1G 75
Sudbrook. Mon 3A 34
Sudbrooke. Linc 3H 87
Sudbury. Derbs 2F 73
Sudbury. Suff 1B 54
Sudgrove. Glos 5E 49
Suffield. Norf 2E 79
Suffield. N Yor 5G 107
Sugnall. Staf 2B 72
Sugwas Pool. Here 1H 47
Suisnish. High 5E 155
Sulaisiadar. W Isl 4H 171
Sùlaisiadar Mòr. High 4D 155
Sulby. IOM 2C 108
Sulgrave. Nptn 1D 50
Sulham. W Ber 4E 37
Sulhamstead. W Ber 5E 37
Sullington. W Sus 4B 26
Sullom. Shet 4E 173
Sully. V Glam 5E 33
Sumburgh. Shet 10F 173
Sumburgh Airport. Shet 10E 173
Summer Bridge. N Yor 3E 98
Summercourt. Corn 3C 6
Summergangs. Hull 1E 94
Summer Hill. W Mid 1D 60
Summerhill. Aber 3G 153
Summerhill. Pemb 4F 43
Summerhouse. Darl 3F 105
Summersdale. W Sus 2G 17
Summerseat. G Man 3F 91
Summit. G Man 3H 91
Sunbury. Surr 4C 38
Sunderland. Cumb 1C 102
Sunderland. Lanc 4D 96
Sunderland. Tyne 212 (4G 115)
Sunderland Bridge. Dur 1F 105
Sundon Park. Lutn 3A 52
Sundridge. Kent 5F 39
Sunk Island. E Yor 3F 95
Sunningdale. Wind 4A 38
Sunninghill. Wind 4A 38
Sunningwell. Oxon 5C 50
Sunniside. Dur 1E 105
Sunniside. Tyne 4F 115
Sunny Bank. Cumb 5D 102
Sunny Hill. Derb 2H 73
Sunnyhurst. Bkbn 2E 91
Sunnylaw. Stir 4G 135
Sunnymead. Oxon 5D 50
Sunnyside. S Yor 1B 86
Sunnyside. W Sus 2E 27
Sunton. Wilts 1H 23
Surbiton. G Lon 4C 38
Surby. IOM 4B 108
Surfleet. Linc 3B 76
Surfleet Seas End. Linc 3B 76
Surlingham. Norf 5F 79
Surrex. Essx 3B 54
Sustead. Norf 2D 78
Susworth. Linc 4B 94
Sutcombe. Devn 1D 10
Suton. Norf 1C 66
Sutors of Cromarty. High 2C 158
Sutterby. Linc 3C 88
Sutterton. Linc 2B 76
Sutterton Dowdyke. Linc 2B 76
Sutton. Buck 3B 38
Sutton. Cambs 3D 64
Sutton. C Beds 1C 52
Sutton. E Sus 5F 27
Sutton. G Lon 4D 38
Sutton. Kent 1H 29
Sutton. Norf 3F 79
Sutton. Notts 2E 75
Sutton. Oxon 5C 50
Sutton. Pemb 3D 42
Sutton. Pet 1H 63
Sutton. Shrp
nr. Bridgnorth 2B 60
nr. Market Drayton 2A 72
nr. Oswestry 3F 71
nr. Shrewsbury 4H 71
Sutton. Som 3B 22
Sutton. S Yor 3F 93
Sutton. Staf 3B 72
Sutton. Suff 1G 55
Sutton. W Sus 4A 26
Sutton. Worc 4A 60
Sutton Abinger. Surr 1C 26
Sutton at Hone. Kent 3G 39
Sutton Bassett. Nptn 1E 63
Sutton Benger. Wilts 4E 35
Sutton Bingham. Som 1A 14
Sutton Bonington. Notts 3C 74
Sutton Bridge. Linc 3D 76
Sutton Cheney. Leics 5B 74
Sutton Coldfield, Royal. W Mid 1F 61
Sutton Corner. Linc 3D 76
Sutton Courtenay. Oxon 2D 36
Sutton Crosses. Linc 3D 76
Sutton cum Lound. Notts 2D 86
Sutton Gault. Cambs 3D 64
Sutton Grange. N Yor 2E 99
Sutton Green. Surr 5B 38
Sutton Howgrave. N Yor 2F 99
Sutton in Ashfield. Notts 5B 86
Sutton-in-Craven. N Yor 5C 98
Sutton Ings. Hull 1E 94
Sutton in the Elms. Leics 1C 62
Sutton Lane Ends. Ches E 3D 84
Sutton Leach. Mers 1H 83
Sutton Maddock. Shrp 5B 72
Sutton Mallet. Som 3G 21
Sutton Mandeville. Wilts 4E 23
Sutton Montis. Som 4B 22
Sutton on Hull. Hull 1E 94
Sutton on Sea. Linc 2E 89
Sutton-on-the-Forest. N Yor 3H 99
Sutton on the Hill. Derbs 2G 73
Sutton on Trent. Notts 4E 87
Sutton Poyntz. Dors 4C 14
Sutton St Edmund. Linc 4C 76
Sutton St Edmund's Common. Linc 5C 76
Sutton St James. Linc 4C 76
Sutton St Michael. Here 1A 48
Sutton St Nicholas. Here 1A 48
Sutton Scarsdale. Derbs 4B 86
Sutton Scotney. Hants 3C 24
Sutton-under-Brailes. Warw 2B 50
Sutton-under-Whitestonecliffe. N Yor 1G 99
Sutton upon Derwent. E Yor 5B 100
Sutton Valence. Kent 1C 28
Sutton Veny. Wilts 2E 23
Sutton Waldron. Dors 1D 14
Sutton Weaver. Ches W 3H 83
Swaby. Linc 3C 88
Swadlincote. Derbs 4G 73
Swaffham. Norf 5H 77
Swaffham Bulbeck. Cambs 4E 65
Swaffham Prior. Cambs 4E 65
Swafield. Norf 2E 79
Swainby. N Yor 4B 106
Swainshill. Here 1H 47
Swainsthorpe. Norf 5E 78
Swainswick. Bath 5C 34
Swalcliffe. Oxon 2B 50
Swalecliffe. Kent 4F 41
Swallow. Linc 4E 95
Swallow Beck. Linc 4G 87
Swallowcliffe. Wilts 4E 23
Swallowfield. Wok 5F 37
Swallownest. S Yor 2B 86
Swampton. Hants 1C 24
Swanage. Dors 5F 15
Swanbister. Orkn 7C 172
Swanbourne. Buck 3G 51
Swanbridge. V Glam 5E 33
Swan Green. Ches W 3B 84
Swanland. E Yor 2C 94
Swanley. Kent 4G 39
Swanmore. Hants 1D 16
Swannington. Leics 4B 74
Swannington. Norf 4D 78
Swanpool. Linc 4G 87
Swanscombe. Kent 3H 39
Swansea. Swan 212 (3F 31)
Swan Street. Essx 3B 54
Swanton Abbott. Norf 3E 79
Swanton Morley. Norf 4C 78
Swanton Novers. Norf 2C 78
Swanton Street. Kent 5C 40
Swanwick. Derbs 5B 86
Swanwick. Hants 2D 16
Swanwick Green. Ches E 1H 71
Swarby. Linc 1H 75
Swardeston. Norf 5E 78
Swarister. Shet 3G 173
Swarkestone. Derbs 3A 74
Swarland. Nmbd 4F 121
Swarraton. Hants 3D 24
Swartha. W Yor 5C 98
Swarthmoor. Cumb 2B 96
Swaton. Linc 2A 76
Swavesey. Cambs 4C 64
Sway. Hants 3A 16
Swayfield. Linc 3G 75
Swaythling. Sotn 1C 16

Sweet Green. Worc....4A 60
Sweetham. Devn....3B 12
Sweetholme. Cumb....3G 103
Sweets. Corn....3B 10
Sweetshouse. Corn....2E 7
Swefling. Suff....4F 67
Swell. Som....4G 21
Swepstone. Leics....4A 74
Swerford. Oxon....2B 50
Swettenham. Ches E....4C 84
Swetton. N Yor....2D 98
Swffryd. Blae....2F 33
Swiftsden. E Sus....3B 28
Swilland. Suff....5D 66
Swillington. W Yor....1D 93
Swimbridge. Devn....4G 19
Swimbridge Newland. Devn....3G 19
Swinbrook. Oxon....4A 50
Swincliffe. N Yor....4E 99
Swincliffe. W Yor....2C 92
Swinderby. Linc....4F 87
Swindon. Glos....3E 49
Swindon. Nmbd....5D 121
Swindon. Staf....1C 60
Swindon. Swin....212 (3G 35)
Swine. E Yor....1E 95
Swinefleet. E Yor....2A 94
Swineford. S Glo....5B 34
Swineshead. Bed....4H 63
Swineshead. Linc....1B 76
Swineshead Bridge. Linc....1B 76
Swiney. High....5E 169
Swinford. Leics....3C 62
Swinford. Oxon....5C 50
Swingate. Notts....1C 74
Swingbrow. Cambs....2C 64
Swingfield Minnis. Kent....1G 29
Swingfield Street. Kent....1G 29
Swingleton Green. Suff....1C 54
Swinhill. S Lan....5A 128
Swinhoe. Nmbd....2G 121
Swinhope. Linc....1B 88
Swinister. Shet....3E 173
Swinithwaite. N Yor....1C 98
Swinmore Common. Here....1B 48
Swinscoe. Staf....1F 73
Swinside Hall. Bord....3B 120
Swinstead. Linc....3H 75
Swinton. G Man....4F 91
Swinton. N Yor
nr. Malton....2B 100
nr. Masham....2E 98
Swinton. Bord....5E 131
Swinton. S Yor....1B 86
Swithland. Leics....4C 74
Swordale. High....2H 157
Swordly. High....2H 167
Sworton Heath. Ches E....2A 84
Swyddffynnon. Cdgn....4F 57
Swynnerton. Staf....2C 72
Swyre. Dors....4A 14
Sycharth. Powy....3E 70
Sychdyn. Flin....4E 83
Sychnant. Powy....3B 58
Sychtyn. Powy....5B 70
Syde. Glos....4E 49
Sydenham. G Lon....3E 39
Sydenham. Oxon....5F 51
Sydenham. Som....3G 21
Sydenham Damerel. Devn....5E 11
Syderstone. Norf....2H 77
Sydling St Nicholas. Dors....3B 14
Sydmonton. Hants....1C 24
Sydney. Ches E....5B 84
Syerston. Notts....1E 75
Syke. G Man....3G 91
Sykehouse. S Yor....3G 93
Sykes. Lanc....4F 97
Syleham. Suff....3E 66
Sylen. Carm....5F 45
Sylfaen. Powy....5D 70
Symbister. Shet....5G 173
Symington. S Ayr....1C 116
Symington. S Lan....1B 118
Symondsbury. Dors....3H 13
Symonds Yat. Here....4A 48
Synod Inn. Cdgn....5D 56
Syre. High....4G 167
Syreford. Glos....3F 49
Syresham. Nptn....1E 51
Syston. Leics....4D 74
Syston. Linc....1G 75
Sytchampton. Worc....4C 60
Sywell. Nptn....4F 63

T

Tabost. W Isl
nr. Cearsiadar....6F 171
nr. Suainebost....1H 171
Tachbrook Mallory. Warw....4H 61
Tackley. Oxon....3C 50
Tacleit. W Isl....4D 171
Tacolneston. Norf....1D 66
Tadcaster. N Yor....5G 99
Taddington. Derbs....3F 85
Taddington. Glos....2F 49
Taddiport. Devn....1E 11
Tadley. Hants....5E 36
Tadlow. Cambs....1C 52
Tadmarton. Oxon....2B 50
Tadwick. Bath....4C 34
Tadworth. Surr....5D 38
Tafarnaubach. Blae....4E 46
Tafarn-y-bwlch. Pemb....1E 43
Tafarn-y-Gelyn. Den....4D 82
Taff's Well. Rhon....3E 33
Tafolwern. Powy....5A 70
Tai-bach. Powy....3D 70
Taibach. Neat....3A 32

Taigh a Ghearraidh. W Isl....1C 170
Taigh Bhuirgh. W Isl....8C 171
Tain. High
nr. Invergordon....5E 165
nr. Thurso....2E 169
Tai-Nant. Wrex....1E 71
Tai'n Lon. Gwyn....5D 80
Tairbeart. W Isl....8D 171
Tairgwaith. Neat....4H 45
Takeley. Essx....3F 53
Takeley Street. Essx....3F 53
Talachddu. Powy....2D 46
Talacre. Flin....2D 82
Talardd. Gwyn....3A 70
Talaton. Devn....3D 12
Talbenny. Pemb....3C 42
Talbot Green. Rhon....3D 32
Taleford. Devn....3D 12
Talerddig. Powy....5B 70
Talgarreg. Cdgn....5D 56
Talgarth. Powy....2E 47
Talisker. High....5C 154
Talke. Staf....5C 84
Talkin. Cumb....4G 113
Talladale. High....1B 156
Talla Linnfoots. Bord....2D 118
Tallaminnock. S Ayr....5C 116
Tallarn Green. Wrex....1G 71
Tallentire. Cumb....1C 102
Talley. Carm....2G 45
Tallington. Linc....5H 75
Talmine. High....2F 167
Talog. Carm....2H 43
Talsarn. Carm....3A 46
Talsarn. Cdgn....5E 57
Talsarnau. Gwyn....2F 69
Talskiddy. Corn....2D 6
Talwrn. IOA....3D 81
Talwrn. Wrex....1E 71
Tal-y-Bont. Cnwy....4G 81
Tal-y-bont. Cdgn....2F 57
Tal-y-bont. Gwyn
nr. Bangor....3F 81
nr. Barmouth....3E 69
Talybont-on-Usk. Powy....3E 46
Tal-y-cafn. Cnwy....3G 81
Tal-y-coed. Mon....4H 47
Tal-y-llyn. Gwyn....5G 69
Talyllyn. Powy....3E 46
Talysarn. Gwyn....5D 81
Tal-y-waenydd. Gwyn....1F 69
Talywain. Torf....5F 47
Tal-y-Wern. Powy....5H 69
Tamerton Foliot. Plym....2A 8
Tamworth. Staf....5G 73
Tamworth Green. Linc....1C 76
Tandlehill. Ren....3F 127
Tandridge. Surr....5E 39
Tanerdy. Carm....3E 45
Tanfield. Dur....4E 115
Tanfield Lea. Dur....4E 115
Tangasdal. W Isl....8B 170
Tang Hall. York....4A 100
Tangiers. Pemb....3D 42
Tangley. Hants....1B 24
Tangmere. W Sus....5A 26
Tangwick. Shet....4D 173
Tankerness. Orkn....7E 172
Tankersley. S Yor....1H 85
Tankerton. Kent....4F 41
Tan-lan. Cnwy....4G 81
Tan-lan. Gwyn....1F 69
Tannach. High....4F 169
Tannadice. Ang....3D 145
Tanner's Green. Worc....3E 61
Tannington. Suff....4E 67
Tannochside. N Lan....3A 128
Tan Office Green. Suff....5G 65
Tansley. Derbs....5H 85
Tansley Knoll. Derbs....4H 85
Tansor. Nptn....1H 63
Tantobie. Dur....4E 115
Tanton. N Yor....3C 106
Tanvats. Linc....4A 88
Tanworth-in-Arden. Warw....3F 61
Tan-y-bwlch. Gwyn....1F 69
Tan-y-fron. Cnwy....4B 82
Tanyfron. Wrex....5E 83
Tangyrisiau. Gwyn....1F 69
Tan-y-groes. Cdgn....1C 44
Tan-y-pistyll. Powy....3C 70
Tan-yr-allt. Den....2C 82
Taobh a Chaolais. W Isl....7C 170
Taobh a Deas Loch Aineort.
W Isl....6C 170
Taobh a Ghlinne. W Isl....6F 171
Taobh a Tuath Loch Aineort.
W Isl....6C 170
Taplow. Buck....2A 38
Tapton. Derbs....3A 86
Tarbert. Arg
on Jura....1E 125
on Kintyre....3G 125
Tarbert. W Isl....8D 171
Tarbet. Arg....3C 134
Tarbet. High
nr. Mallaig....4F 147
nr. Scourie....4B 166
Tarbock Green. Mers....2G 83
Tarbolton. S Ayr....2D 116
Tarbrax. S Lan....4D 128
Tardebigge. Worc....4D 61
Tarfside. Ang....1D 145
Tarland. Abers....3B 152
Tarleton. Lanc....2C 90
Tarlogie. High....5E 165
Tarlscough. Lanc....3C 90
Tarlton. Glos....2E 35
Tarnbrook. Lanc....4E 97
Tarnock. Som....1G 21
Tarns. Cumb....5C 112

Tarporley. Ches W....4H 83
Tarpots. Essx....2B 40
Tarr. Som....3E 20
Tarrant Crawford. Dors....2E 15
Tarrant Gunville. Dors....1E 15
Tarrant Hinton. Dors....1E 15
Tarrant Keyneston. Dors....2E 15
Tarrant Launceston. Dors....2E 15
Tarrant Monkton. Dors....2E 15
Tarrant Rawston. Dors....2E 15
Tarrant Rushton. Dors....2E 15
Tarrel. High....5F 165
Tarrington. Here....1B 48
Tarsappie. Per....1D 136
Tarscabhaig. High....3D 147
Tarskavaig. High....3D 147
Tarves. Abers....5F 161
Tarvie. High....3G 157
Tarvin. Ches W....4G 83
Tasburgh. Norf....1E 66
Tasley. Shrp....1A 60
Taston. Oxon....3B 50
Tatenhill. Staf....3G 73
Tathall End. Mil....1G 51
Tatham. Lanc....3F 97
Tathwell. Linc....2C 88
Tating End. Buck....2B 38
Tatsfield. Surr....5F 39
Tattenhall. Ches W....5G 83
Tatterford. Norf....3A 78
Tattersett. Norf....2H 77
Tattershall. Linc....5B 88
Tattershall Bridge. Linc....5A 88
Tattershall Thorpe. Linc....5B 88
Tattingstone. Suff....2E 55
Tattingstone White Horse. Suff....2E 55
Tattle Bank. Warw....4F 61
Tatworth. Som....2G 13
Taunton. Som....213 (4F 21)
Taverham. Norf....4D 78
Taverners Green. Essx....4F 53
Tavernspite. Pemb....3F 43
Tavistock. Devn....5E 11
Tavool House. Arg....1B 132
Taw Green. Devn....3G 11
Tawstock. Devn....4F 19
Taxal. Derbs....2E 85
Tayinloan. Arg....5E 125
Taynish. Arg....1F 125
Taynton. Glos....3C 48
Taynton. Oxon....4H 49
Taynuilt. Arg....5E 141
Tayport. Fife....1G 137
Tay Road Bridge. D'dee....1G 137
Tayvallich. Arg....1F 125
Tealby. Linc....1A 88
Tealing. Ang....5D 144
Teams. Tyne....3F 115
Teangue. High....3E 147
Teanna Mhachair. W Isl....2C 170
Tebay. Cumb....4H 103
Tebworth. C Beds....3H 51
Tedburn St Mary. Devn....3B 12
Teddington. Glos....2E 49
Teddington. G Lon....3C 38
Tedsmore. Shrp....3F 71
Tedstone Delamere. Here....5A 60
Tedstone Wafer. Here....5A 60
Teesport. Red C....2C 106
Teesside. Stoc T....2C 106
Teeton. Nptn....3D 62
Teffont Evias. Wilts....3E 23
Teffont Magna. Wilts....3E 23
Tegryn. Pemb....1G 43
Teigh. Rut....4F 75
Teigncombe. Devn....4G 11
Teigngrace. Devn....5B 12
Teignmouth. Devn....5C 12
Telford. Telf....4A 72
Telham. E Sus....4B 28
Tellisford. Som....1D 22
Telscombe. E Sus....5F 27
Telscombe Cliffs. E Sus....5E 27
Tempar. Per....3D 142
Templand. Dum....1B 112
Temple. Corn....5B 10
Temple. Glas....3G 127
Temple. Midl....4G 129
Temple Balsall. W Mid....3G 61
Temple Bar. Carm....4F 45
Temple Bar. Cdgn....5E 57
Temple Cloud. Bath....1B 22
Templecombe. Som....4C 22
Temple Ewell. Kent....1G 29
Temple Grafton. Warw....5F 61
Temple Guiting. Glos....3F 49
Templehall. Fife....4E 137
Temple Hirst. N Yor....2G 93
Temple Normanton. Derbs....4B 86
Temple Sowerby. Cumb....2H 103
Templeton. Devn....1B 12
Templeton. Pemb....3F 43
Templeton. W Ber....5B 36
Templetown. Dur....5E 115
Tempsford. C Beds....5A 64
Tenandry. Per....2G 143
Tenbury Wells. Worc....4H 59
Tenby. Pemb....4F 43
Tendring. Essx....3E 55
Tendring Green. Essx....3E 55
Tenga. Arg....4G 139
Ten Mile Bank. Norf....1F 65
Tenterden. Kent....2C 28
Terfyn. Cnwy....3B 82
Terhill. Som....3E 21
Terling. Essx....4A 54
Ternhill. Shrp....2A 72
Terregles. Dum....2G 111
Terrick. Buck....5G 51
Terrington. N Yor....2A 100

Terrington St Clement. Norf....3E 77
Terrington St John. Norf....4E 77
Terry's Green. Warw....3F 61
Teston. Kent....5B 40
Testwood. Hants....1B 16
Tetbury. Glos....2D 35
Tetbury Upton. Glos....2D 35
Tetchill. Shrp....2F 71
Tetcott. Devn....3D 10
Tetford. Linc....3C 88
Tetney. Linc....4G 95
Tetney Lock. Linc....4G 95
Tetsworth. Oxon....5E 51
Tettenhall. W Mid....5C 72
Teversal. Notts....4B 86
Teversham. Cambs....5D 65
Teviothead. Bord....4G 119
Tewel. Abers....5F 153
Tewin. Herts....4C 52
Tewkesbury. Glos....2D 49
Teynham. Kent....4D 40
Teynham Street. Kent....4D 40
Thackthwaite. Cumb....2F 103
Thakeham. W Sus....4C 26
Thame. Oxon....5F 51
Thames Ditton. Surr....4C 38
Thames Haven. Thur....2B 40
Thamesmead. G Lon....2F 39
Thamesport. Medw....3C 40
Thanington Without. Kent....5F 41
Thankerton. S Lan....1B 118
Tharston. Norf....1D 66
Thatcham. W Ber....5D 36
Thatto Heath. Mers....1H 83
Thaxted. Essx....2G 53
Theakston. N Yor....1F 99
Thealby. N Lin....3B 94
Theale. Som....2H 21
Theale. W Ber....4E 37
Thearne. E Yor....1D 94
Theberton. Suff....4G 67
Theddingworth. Leics....2D 62
Theddlethorpe All Saints. Linc....2D 88
Theddlethorpe St Helen. Linc....2D 89
Thelbridge Barton. Devn....1A 12
Thelnetham. Suff....3C 66
Thelveton. Norf....2D 66
Thelwall. Warr....2A 84
Themelthorpe. Norf....3C 78
Thenford. Nptn....1D 50
Therfield. Herts....2D 52
Thetford. Linc....4A 76
Thetford. Norf....2A 66
Thethwaite. Cumb....5E 113
Theydon Bois. Essx....1F 39
Thick Hollins. W Yor....3B 92
Thickwood. Wilts....4D 34
Thimbleby. Linc....4B 88
Thimbleby. N Yor....5B 106
Thingwall. Mers....2E 83
Thirlby. N Yor....1G 99
Thirlestane. Bord....5B 130
Thirn. N Yor....1E 98
Thirsk. N Yor....1G 99
Thirtleby. E Yor....1E 95
Thistleton. Lanc....1C 90
Thistleton. Rut....4G 75
Thistley Green. Suff....3F 65
Thixendale. N Yor....3C 100
Thockrington. Nmbd....2C 114
Tholomas Drove. Cambs....5D 76
Tholthorpe. N Yor....3G 99
Thomas Chapel. Pemb....4F 43
Thomas Close. Cumb....5F 113
Thomastown. Abers....4E 160
Thomastown. Rhon....3D 32
Thompson. Norf....1B 66
Thomshill. Mor....3G 159
Thong. Kent....3A 40
Thongsbridge. W Yor....4B 92
Thoralby. N Yor....1C 98
Thoresby. Notts....3D 86
Thoresway. Linc....1A 88
Thorganby. Linc....1B 88
Thorganby. N Yor....5A 100
Thorgill. N Yor....5E 107
Thorington. Suff....3G 67
Thorington Street. Suff....2D 54
Thorlby. N Yor....4B 98
Thorley. Herts....4E 53
Thorley Street. Herts....4E 53
Thorley Street. IOW....4B 16
Thormanby. N Yor....2G 99
Thorn. Powy....4E 59
Thornaby-on-Tees. Stoc T....3B 106
Thornage. Norf....2C 78
Thornborough. Buck....2F 51
Thornborough. N Yor....2E 99
Thornbury. Devn....2E 11
Thornbury. Here....5A 60
Thornbury. S Glo....2B 34
Thornby. Cumb....4D 112
Thornby. Nptn....3D 62
Thorncliffe. Staf....5E 85
Thorncombe. Dors....2G 13
Thorncombe Street. Surr....1A 26
Thorncote Green. C Beds....1B 52
Thorndon. Suff....4D 66
Thorndon Cross. Devn....3F 11
Thorne. S Yor....3G 93
Thornehillhead. Devn....1E 11
Thorner. W Yor....5F 99
Thorne St Margaret. Som....4D 20
Thorney. Notts....3F 87
Thorney. Pet....5B 76
Thorney. Som....4H 21
Thorney Hill. Hants....3G 15
Thorney Toll. Cambs....5C 76
Thornfalcon. Som....4F 21
Thornford. Dors....1B 14
Thorngrafton. Nmbd....3A 114

Thorngrove. Som....3G 21
Thorngumbald. E Yor....2F 95
Thornham. Norf....1G 77
Thornham Magna. Suff....3D 66
Thornham Parva. Suff....3D 66
Thornhaugh. Pet....5H 75
Thornhill. Cphy....3E 33
Thornhill. Cumb....4B 102
Thornhill. Derbs....2F 85
Thornhill. Dum....5A 118
Thornhill. Sotn....1C 16
Thornhill. Stir....4F 135
Thornhill. W Yor....3C 92
Thornhill Lees. W Yor....3C 92
Thornhills. W Yor....2B 92
Thornholme. E Yor....3F 101
Thornicombe. Dors....2D 14
Thornington. Nmbd....1C 120
Thornley. Dur
nr. Durham....1A 106
nr. Tow Law....1E 105
Thornley Gate. Nmbd....4B 114
Thornliebank. E Ren....3G 127
Thornroan. Abers....5F 161
Thorns. Suff....5G 65
Thornsett. Derbs....2E 85
Thornthwaite. Cumb....2D 102
Thornthwaite. N Yor....4D 98
Thornton. Ang....4C 144
Thornton. Buck....2F 51
Thornton. E Yor....5B 100
Thornton. Fife....4E 137
Thornton. Lanc....5C 96
Thornton. Leics....5B 74
Thornton. Linc....4B 88
Thornton. Mers....4B 90
Thornton. Midd....3B 106
Thornton. Nmbd....5F 131
Thornton. Pemb....4D 42
Thornton. W Yor....1A 92
Thornton Curtis. N Lin....3D 94
Thorntonhall. S Lan....4G 127
Thornton Heath. G Lon....4E 39
Thornton Hough. Mers....2F 83
Thornton-in-Craven. N Yor....5B 98
Thornton in Lonsdale. N Yor....2F 97
Thornton-le-Beans. N Yor....5A 106
Thornton-le-Clay. N Yor....3A 100
Thornton-le-Dale. N Yor....1C 100
Thornton le Moor. Linc....1H 87
Thornton-le-Moor. N Yor....1F 99
Thornton-le-Moors. Ches W....3G 83
Thornton-le-Street. N Yor....1G 99
Thorntonloch. E Lot....2D 130
Thornton Rust. N Yor....1B 98
Thornton Steward. N Yor....1D 98
Thornton Watlass. N Yor....1E 99
Thornwood Common. Essx....5E 53
Thornythwaite. Cumb....2E 103
Thoroton. Notts....1E 75
Thorp Arch. W Yor....5G 99
Thorpe. Derbs....5F 85
Thorpe. E Yor....5D 101
Thorpe. Linc....2D 89
Thorpe. Norf....1G 67
Thorpe. N Yor....3C 98
Thorpe. Notts....1E 75
Thorpe. Surr....4B 38
Thorpe Abbotts. Norf....3D 66
Thorpe Acre. Leics....3C 74
Thorpe Arnold. Leics....3E 75
Thorpe Audlin. W Yor....3E 93
Thorpe Bassett. N Yor....2C 100
Thorpe Bay. S'end....2D 40
Thorpe by Water. Rut....1F 63
Thorpe Common. S Yor....1A 86
Thorpe Common. Suff....2F 55
Thorpe Constantine. Staf....5G 73
Thorpe End. Norf....4E 79
Thorpe Fendike. Linc....4D 88
Thorpe Green. Essx....3E 55
Thorpe Green. Suff....5B 66
Thorpe Hamlet. Norf....5E 79
Thorpe Hesley. S Yor....1A 86
Thorpe in Balne. S Yor....3F 93
Thorpe in the Fallows. Linc....2G 87
Thorpe Langton. Leics....1E 63
Thorpe Larches. Dur....2A 106
Thorpe Latimer. Linc....1A 76
Thorpe-le-Soken. Essx....3E 55
Thorpe le Street. E Yor....5C 100
Thorpe Malsor. Nptn....3F 63
Thorpe Mandeville. Nptn....1D 50
Thorpe Market. Norf....2E 79
Thorpe Marriott. Norf....4D 78
Thorpe Morieux. Suff....5B 66
Thorpeness. Suff....5G 67
Thorpe on the Hill. Linc....4G 87
Thorpe on the Hill. W Yor....2D 92
Thorpe St Andrew. Norf....5E 79
Thorpe St Peter. Linc....4D 89
Thorpe Salvin. S Yor....2C 86
Thorpe Satchville. Leics....4E 75
Thorpe Thewles. Stoc T....2A 106
Thorpe Tilney. Linc....5A 88
Thorpe Underwood. N Yor....4G 99
Thorpe Waterville. Nptn....2H 63
Thorpe Willoughby. N Yor....1F 93
Thorpland. Norf....5F 77
Thorrington. Essx....3D 54
Thorverton. Devn....2C 12
Thrandeston. Suff....3D 66
Thrapston. Nptn....3G 63
Thrashbush. N Lan....3A 128
Threapland. Cumb....1C 102
Threapland. N Yor....3B 98
Threapwood. Ches W....1G 71
Threapwood. Staf....1E 73
Three Ashes. Here....3A 48
Three Bridges. Linc....2D 88

Three Bridges – Trenance

Three Bridges. *W Sus* 2D **27**
Three Burrows. *Corn* 4B **6**
Three Chimneys. *Kent* 2C **28**
Three Cocks. *Powy* 2E **47**
Three Crosses. *Swan* 3E **31**
Three Cups Corner. *E Sus* 3H **27**
Threehammer Common. *Norf* 3F **79**
Three Holes. *Norf* 5E **77**
Threekingham. *Linc* 2H **75**
Three Leg Cross. *E Sus* 2A **28**
Three Legged Cross. *Dors* 2F **15**
Three Mile Cross. *Wok* 5F **37**
Threemilestone. *Corn* 4B **6**
Three Oaks. *E Sus* 4C **28**
Threlkeld. *Cumb* 2E **102**
Threshfield. *N Yor* 3B **98**
Thrigby. *Norf* 4G **79**
Thringarth. *Dur* 2C **104**
Thringstone. *Leics* 4B **74**
Thrintoft. *N Yor* 5A **106**
Thriplow. *Cambs* 1E **53**
Throckenholt. *Linc* 5C **76**
Throcking. *Herts* 2D **52**
Throckley. *Tyne* 3E **115**
Throckmorton. *Worc* 1E **49**
Throop. *Bour* 3G **15**
Throphill. *Nmbd* 1E **115**
Thropton. *Nmbd* 4E **121**
Throsk. *Stir* 4A **136**
Througham. *Glos* 5E **49**
Throughgate. *Dum* 1F **111**
Throwleigh. *Devn* 3G **11**
Throwley. *Kent* 5D **40**
Throwley Forstal. *Kent* 5D **40**
Throxenby. *N Yor* 1E **101**
Thrumpton. *Notts* 2C **74**
Thrumster. *High* 4F **169**
Thrunton. *Nmbd* 3E **121**
Thrupp. *Glos* 5D **48**
Thrupp. *Oxon* 4C **50**
Thrushelton. *Devn* 4E **11**
Thrushgill. *Lanc* 3F **97**
Thrussington. *Leics* 4D **74**
Thruxton. *Hants* 2A **24**
Thruxton. *Here* 2H **47**
Thrybergh. *S Yor* 1B **86**
Thulston. *Derbs* 2B **74**
Thundergay. *N Ayr* 5G **125**
Thundersley. *Essx* 2B **40**
Thundridge. *Herts* 4D **52**
Thurcaston. *Leics* 4C **74**
Thurcroft. *S Yor* 2B **86**
Thurdon. *Corn* 1C **10**
Thurgarton. *Norf* 2D **78**
Thurgarton. *Notts* 1D **74**
Thurgoland. *S Yor* 4C **92**
Thurlaston. *Leics* 1C **62**
Thurlaston. *Warw* 3B **62**
Thurlbear. *Som* 4F **21**
Thurlby. *Linc*
nr. Alford 3D **89**
nr. Baston 4A **76**
nr. Lincoln 4G **87**
Thurleigh. *Bed* 5H **63**
Thurlestone. *Devn* 4C **8**
Thurloxton. *Som* 3F **21**
Thurlstone. *S Yor* 4C **92**
Thurlton. *Norf* 1G **67**
Thurmaston. *Leics* 5D **74**
Thurnby. *Leics* 5D **74**
Thurne. *Norf* 4G **79**
Thurnham. *Kent* 5C **40**
Thurning. *Norf* 3C **78**
Thurning. *Nptn* 2H **63**
Thurnscoe. *S Yor* 4E **93**
Thursby. *Cumb* 4E **113**
Thursford. *Norf* 2B **78**
Thursford Green. *Norf* 2B **78**
Thursley. *Surr* 2A **26**
Thurso. *High* 2D **168**
Thurso East. *High* 2D **168**
Thurstaston. *Mers* 2E **83**
Thurston. *Suff* 4B **66**
Thurston End. *Suff* 5G **65**
Thurstonfield. *Cumb* 4E **112**
Thurstonland. *W Yor* 3B **92**
Thurton. *Norf* 5F **79**
Thurvaston. *Derbs*
nr. Ashbourne 2F **73**
nr. Derby 2G **73**
Thuxton. *Norf* 5C **78**
Thwaite. *Dur* 3D **104**
Thwaite. *N Yor* 5B **104**
Thwaite. *Suff* 4D **66**
Thwaite Head. *Cumb* 5E **103**
Thwaites. *W Yor* 5C **98**
Thwaite St Mary. *Norf* 1F **67**
Thwing. *E Yor* 2E **101**
Tibbermore. *Per* 1C **136**
Tibberton. *Glos* 3C **48**
Tibberton. *Telf* 3A **72**
Tibberton. *Worc* 5D **60**
Tibenham. *Norf* 2D **66**
Tibshelf. *Derbs* 4B **86**
Tibthorpe. *E Yor* 4D **100**
Ticehurst. *E Sus* 2A **28**
Tichborne. *Hants* 3D **24**
Tickencote. *Rut* 5G **75**
Tickenham. *N Som* 4H **33**
Tickhill. *S Yor* 1C **86**
Ticklerton. *Shrp* 1G **59**
Ticknall. *Derbs* 3A **74**
Tickton. *E Yor* 5E **101**
Tidbury Green. *W Mid* 3F **61**
Tidcombe. *Wilts* 1A **24**
Tiddington. *Oxon* 5E **51**
Tiddington. *Warw* 5G **61**
Tiddleywink. *Wilts* 4D **34**
Tidebrook. *E Sus* 3H **27**
Tideford. *Corn* 3H **7**
Tideford Cross. *Corn* 2H **7**
Tidenham. *Glos* 2A **34**
Tideswell. *Derbs* 3F **85**
Tidmarsh. *W Ber* 4E **37**
Tidmington. *Warw* 2A **50**
Tidpit. *Hants* 1F **15**
Tidworth. *Wilts* 2H **23**
Tidworth Camp. *Wilts* 2H **23**
Tiers Cross. *Pemb* 3D **42**
Tiffield. *Nptn* 5D **62**
Tifty. *Abers* 4E **161**
Tigerton. *Ang* 2E **145**
Tighnabruaich. *Arg* 2A **126**
Tigley. *Devn* 2D **8**
Tilbrook. *Cambs* 4H **63**
Tilbury. *Thur* 3H **39**
Tilbury Green. *Essx* 1H **53**
Tilbury Juxta Clare. *Essx* 1A **54**
Tile Hill. *W Mid* 3G **61**
Tilehurst. *Read* 4E **37**
Tilford. *Surr* 2G **25**
Tilgate Forest Row. *W Sus* 2D **26**
Tillathrowie. *Abers* 5B **160**
Tillers Green. *Glos* 2B **48**
Tillery. *Abers* 1G **153**
Tilley. *Shrp* 3H **71**
Tillicoultry. *Clac* 4B **136**
Tillingham. *Essx* 5C **54**
Tillington. *Here* 1H **47**
Tillington. *W Sus* 3A **26**
Tillington Common. *Here* 1H **47**
Tillybirloch. *Abers* 3D **152**
Tillyfourie. *Abers* 2D **152**
Tilmanstone. *Kent* 5H **41**
Tilney All Saints. *Norf* 4E **77**
Tilney Fen End. *Norf* 4E **77**
Tilney High End. *Norf* 4E **77**
Tilney St Lawrence. *Norf* 4E **77**
Tilshead. *Wilts* 2F **23**
Tilstock. *Shrp* 2H **71**
Tilston. *Ches W* 5G **83**
Tilstone Fearnall. *Ches W* 4H **83**
Tilsworth. *C Beds* 3H **51**
Tilton on the Hill. *Leics* 5E **75**
Tiltups End. *Glos* 2D **34**
Timberland. *Linc* 5A **88**
Timbersbrook. *Ches E* 4C **84**
Timberscombe. *Som* 2C **20**
Timble. *N Yor* 4D **98**
Timperley. *G Man* 2B **84**
Timsbury. *Bath* 1B **22**
Timsbury. *Hants* 4B **24**
Timsgearraidh. *W Isl* 4C **171**
Timworth Green. *Suff* 4A **66**
Tincleton. *Dors* 3C **14**
Tindale. *Cumb* 4H **113**
Tindale Crescent. *Dur* 2F **105**
Tingewick. *Buck* 2E **51**
Tingrith. *C Beds* 2A **52**
Tingwall. *Orkn* 5D **172**
Tinhay. *Devn* 4D **11**
Tinshill. *W Yor* 1C **92**
Tinsley. *S Yor* 1B **86**
Tinsley Green. *W Sus* 2D **27**
Tintagel. *Corn* 4A **10**
Tintern. *Mon* 5A **48**
Tintinhull. *Som* 1H **13**
Tintwistle. *Derbs* 1E **85**
Tinwald. *Dum* 1B **112**
Tinwell. *Rut* 5H **75**
Tippacott. *Devn* 2A **20**
Tipperty. *Abers* 1G **153**
Tipps End. *Cambs* 1E **65**
Tiptoe. *Hants* 3A **16**
Tipton. *W Mid* 1D **60**
Tipton St John. *Devn* 3D **12**
Tiptree. *Essx* 4B **54**
Tiptree Heath. *Essx* 4B **54**
Tirabad. *Powy* 1B **46**
Tircoed Forest Village. *Swan* 5G **45**
Tiree Airport. *Arg* 4B **138**
Tirinie. *Per* 2F **143**
Tirley. *Glos* 3D **48**
Tiroran. *Arg* 1B **132**
Tir-Phil. *Cphy* 5E **47**
Tirril. *Cumb* 2G **103**
Tirryside. *High* 2C **164**
Tir-y-dail. *Carm* 4G **45**
Tisbury. *Wilts* 4E **23**
Tisman's Common. *W Sus* 2B **26**
Tissington. *Derbs* 5F **85**
Titchberry. *Devn* 4C **18**
Titchfield. *Hants* 2D **16**
Titchmarsh. *Nptn* 3H **63**
Titchwell. *Norf* 1G **77**
Tithby. *Notts* 2D **74**
Titley. *Here* 5F **59**
Titlington. *Nmbd* 3E **121**
Titsey. *Surr* 5F **39**
Titson. *Corn* 2C **10**
Tittensor. *Staf* 2C **72**
Tittleshall. *Norf* 3A **78**
Titton. *Worc* 4C **60**
Tiverton. *Ches W* 4H **83**
Tiverton. *Devn* 1C **12**
Tivetshall St Margaret. *Norf* 2D **66**
Tivetshall St Mary. *Norf* 2D **66**
Tivington. *Som* 2C **20**
Tixall. *Staf* 3D **73**
Tixover. *Rut* 5G **75**
Toab. *Orkn* 7E **172**
Toab. *Shet* 10E **173**
Toadmoor. *Derbs* 5A **86**
Tobermory. *Arg* 3G **139**
Toberonochy. *Arg* 3E **133**
Tobha Beag. *W Isl* 5C **170**
Tobha-Beag. *W Isl* 1E **170**
Tobha Mor. *W Isl* 5C **170**
Tobhtarol. *W Isl* 4D **171**
Tobson. *W Isl* 4D **171**
Tocabhaig. *High* 2E **147**
Tocher. *Abers* 5D **160**
Tockenham. *Wilts* 4F **35**
Tockenham Wick. *Wilts* 3F **35**
Tockholes. *Bkbn* 2E **91**
Tockington. *S Glo* 3B **34**
Tockwith. *N Yor* 4G **99**
Todber. *Dors* 4D **22**
Todding. *Here* 3G **59**
Toddington. *C Beds* 3A **52**
Toddington. *Glos* 2F **49**
Todenham. *Glos* 2H **49**
Todhills. *Cumb* 3E **113**
Todmorden. *W Yor* 2H **91**
Todwick. *S Yor* 2B **86**
Toft. *Cambs* 5C **64**
Toft. *Linc* 4H **75**
Toft Hill. *Dur* 2E **105**
Toft Monks. *Norf* 1G **67**
Toft next Newton. *Linc* 2H **87**
Toftrees. *Norf* 3A **78**
Tofts. *High* 2F **169**
Toftwood. *Norf* 4B **78**
Togston. *Nmbd* 4G **121**
Tokavaig. *High* 2E **147**
Tokers Green. *Oxon* 4F **37**
Tolastadh a Chaolais. *W Isl* 4D **171**
Tolladine. *Worc* 5C **60**
Tolland. *Som* 3E **20**
Tollard Farnham. *Dors* 1E **15**
Tollard Royal. *Wilts* 1E **15**
Toll Bar. *S Yor* 4F **93**
Toller Fratrum. *Dors* 3A **14**
Toller Porcorum. *Dors* 3A **14**
Tollerton. *N Yor* 3H **99**
Tollerton. *Notts* 2D **74**
Toller Whelme. *Dors* 2A **14**
Tollesbury. *Essx* 4C **54**
Tolleshunt D'Arcy. *Essx* 4C **54**
Tolleshunt Knights. *Essx* 4C **54**
Tolleshunt Major. *Essx* 4C **54**
Tollie. *High* 3H **157**
Tollie Farm. *High* 1A **156**
Tolm. *W Isl* 4G **171**
Tolpuddle. *Dors* 3C **14**
Tolstadh bho Thuath. *W Isl* 3H **171**
Tolworth. *G Lon* 4C **38**
Tomachlaggan. *Mor* 1F **151**
Tomaknock. *Per* 1A **136**
Tomatin. *High* 1C **150**
Tombuidhe. *Arg* 3H **133**
Tomdoun. *High* 3D **148**
Tomich. *High*
nr. Cannich 1F **149**
nr. Invergordon 1B **158**
nr. Lairg 3D **164**
Tomintoul. *Mor* 2F **151**
Tomnavoulin. *Mor* 1G **151**
Tomsléibhe. *Arg* 5A **140**
Ton. *Mon* 2G **33**
Tonbridge. *Kent* 1G **27**
Tondu. *B'end* 3B **32**
Tonedale. *Som* 4E **21**
Tonfanau. *Gwyn* 5E **69**
Tong. *Shrp* 5B **72**
Tonge. *Leics* 3B **74**
Tong Forge. *Shrp* 5B **72**
Tongham. *Surr* 2G **25**
Tongland. *Dum* 4D **111**
Tong Norton. *Shrp* 5B **72**
Tongue. *High* 3F **167**
Tongue End. *Linc* 4A **76**
Tongwynlais. *Card* 3E **33**
Tonmawr. *Neat* 2B **32**
Tonna. *Neat* 2A **32**
Tonnau. *Neat* 2A **32**
Ton Pentre. *Rhon* 2C **32**
Ton-Teg. *Rhon* 3D **32**
Tonwell. *Herts* 4D **52**
Tonypandy. *Rhon* 2C **32**
Tonyrefail. *Rhon* 3D **32**
Toot Baldon. *Oxon* 5D **50**
Toot Hill. *Essx* 5F **53**
Toothill. *Hants* 1B **16**
Topcliffe. *N Yor* 2G **99**
Topcliffe. *W Yor* 2C **92**
Topcroft. *Norf* 1E **67**
Topcroft Street. *Norf* 1E **67**
Toppesfield. *Essx* 2H **53**
Toppings. *G Man* 3F **91**
Toprow. *Norf* 1D **66**
Topsham. *Devn* 4C **12**
Torbay. *Torb* 2F **9**
Torbeg. *N Ayr* 3C **122**
Torbothie. *N Lan* 4B **128**
Torbryan. *Devn* 2E **9**
Torcross. *Devn* 4E **9**
Tore. *High* 3A **158**
Torgyle. *High* 2F **149**
Torinturk. *Arg* 3G **125**
Torksey. *Linc* 3F **87**
Torlum. *W Isl* 3C **170**
Torlundy. *High* 1F **141**
Tormarton. *S Glo* 4C **34**
Tormitchell. *S Ayr* 5B **116**
Tormore. *High* 3E **147**
Tormore. *N Ayr* 2C **122**
Tornagrain. *High* 4B **158**
Tornaveen. *Abers* 3D **152**
Torness. *High* 1H **149**
Toronto. *Dur* 1E **105**
Torpenhow. *Cumb* 1D **102**
Torphichen. *W Lot* 2C **128**
Torphins. *Abers* 3D **152**
Torpoint. *Corn* 3A **8**
Torquay. *Torb* 2F **9**
Torr. *Devn* 3B **8**
Torra. *Arg* 4B **124**
Torran. *High* 4E **155**
Torrance. *E Dun* 2H **127**
Torrans. *Arg* 1B **132**
Torranyard. *N Ayr* 5E **127**
Torre. *Som* 3D **20**
Torre. *Torb* 2F **9**
Torridon. *High* 3B **156**
Torrin. *High* 1D **147**
Torrisdale. *Arg* 2B **122**
Torrisdale. *High* 2G **167**
Torrish. *High* 2G **165**
Torrisholme. *Lanc* 3D **96**
Torroble. *High* 3C **164**
Torroy. *High* 4C **164**
Torry. *Aber* 3G **153**
Torryburn. *Fife* 1D **128**
Torthorwald. *Dum* 2B **112**
Tortington. *W Sus* 5B **26**
Tortworth. *S Glo* 2C **34**
Torvaig. *High* 4D **155**
Torver. *Cumb* 5D **102**
Torwood. *Falk* 1B **128**
Torworth. *Notts* 2D **86**
Toscaig. *High* 5G **155**
Toseland. *Cambs* 4B **64**
Tosside. *N Yor* 4G **97**
Tostock. *Suff* 4B **66**
Totaig. *High* 3A **154**
Totardor. *High* 5C **154**
Tote. *High* 4D **154**
Totegan. *High* 2A **168**
Tothill. *Linc* 2D **88**
Totland. *IOW* 4B **16**
Totley. *S Yor* 3H **85**
Totnell. *Dors* 2B **14**
Totnes. *Devn* 2E **9**
Toton. *Notts* 2B **74**
Totronald. *Arg* 3C **138**
Totscore. *High* 2C **154**
Tottenham. *G Lon* 1E **39**
Tottenhill. *Norf* 4F **77**
Tottenhill Row. *Norf* 4F **77**
Totteridge. *G Lon* 1D **38**
Totternhoe. *C Beds* 3H **51**
Tottington. *G Man* 3F **91**
Totton. *Hants* 1B **16**
Touchen-end. *Wind* 4G **37**
Toulvaddie. *High* 5F **165**
The Towans. *Corn* 3C **4**
Toward. *Arg* 3C **126**
Towcester. *Nptn* 1E **51**
Towednack. *Corn* 3B **4**
Tower End. *Norf* 4F **77**
Tower Hill. *Mers* 4C **90**
Tower Hill. *W Sus* 3C **26**
Towersey. *Oxon* 5F **51**
Towie. *Abers* 2B **152**
Towiemore. *Mor* 4A **160**
Tow Law. *Dur* 1E **105**
The Town. *IOS* 1A **4**
Town End. *Cambs* 1D **64**
Town End. *Cumb*
nr. Ambleside 4F **103**
nr. Kirkby Thore 2H **103**
nr. Lindale 1D **96**
nr. Newby Bridge 1C **96**
Town End. *Mers* 2G **83**
Townend. *W Dun* 2F **127**
Townfield. *Dur* 5C **114**
Towngate. *Cumb* 5G **113**
Towngate. *Linc* 4A **76**
Town Green. *Lanc* 4C **90**
Town Head. *Cumb*
nr. Grasmere 4E **103**
nr. Great Asby 3H **103**
Townhead. *Cumb*
nr. Lazonby 1G **103**
nr. Maryport 1B **102**
nr. Ousby 1H **103**
Townhead. *Dum* 5D **111**
Townhead of Greenlaw. *Dum* 3E **111**
Townhill. *Fife* 1E **129**
Townhill. *Swan* 3F **31**
Town Kelloe. *Dur* 1A **106**
Town Littleworth. *E Sus* 4F **27**
Town Row. *E Sus* 2G **27**
Towns End. *Hants* 1D **24**
Townsend. *Herts* 5B **52**
Townshend. *Corn* 3C **4**
Town Street. *Suff* 2G **65**
Town Yetholm. *Bord* 2C **120**
Towthorpe. *E Yor* 3D **100**
Towthorpe. *York* 4A **100**
Towton. *N Yor* 1E **93**
Towyn. *Cnwy* 3B **82**
Toxteth. *Mers* 2F **83**
Toynton All Saints. *Linc* 4C **88**
Toynton Fen Side. *Linc* 4C **88**
Toynton St Peter. *Linc* 4D **88**
Toy's Hill. *Kent* 5F **39**
Trabboch. *E Ayr* 2D **116**
Traboe. *Corn* 4E **5**
Tradespark. *High* 3C **158**
Tradespark. *Orkn* 7D **172**
Trafford Park. *G Man* 1B **84**
Trallong. *Powy* 3C **46**
Y Trallwng. *Powy* 5E **70**
Tranent. *E Lot* 2H **129**
Tranmere. *Mers* 2F **83**
Trantlebeg. *High* 3A **168**
Trantlemore. *High* 3A **168**
Tranwell. *Nmbd* 1E **115**
Trapp. *Carm* 4G **45**
Traquair. *Bord* 1F **119**
Trash Green. *W Ber* 5E **37**
Trawden. *Lanc* 1H **91**
Trawscoed. *Powy* 2D **46**
Trawsfynydd. *Gwyn* 2G **69**
Trawsgoed. *Cdgn* 3F **57**
Treaddow. *Here* 3A **48**
Trealaw. *Rhon* 2D **32**
Treales. *Lanc* 1C **90**
Trearddur. *IOA* 3B **80**
Treaslane. *High* 3C **154**
Treator. *Corn* 1D **6**
Trebanog. *Rhon* 2D **32**
Trebanos. *Neat* 5H **45**
Trebarber. *Corn* 2C **6**
Trebartha. *Corn* 5C **10**
Trebarwith. *Corn* 4A **10**
Trebetherick. *Corn* 1D **6**
Treborough. *Som* 3D **20**
Trebudannon. *Corn* 2C **6**
Trebullett. *Corn* 5D **10**
Treburley. *Corn* 5D **10**
Treburrick. *Corn* 1C **6**
Trebyan. *Corn* 2E **7**
Trecastle. *Powy* 3B **46**
Trecenydd. *Cphy* 3E **33**
Trecott. *Devn* 2G **11**
Trecwn. *Pemb* 1D **42**
Trecynon. *Rhon* 5C **46**
Tredaule. *Corn* 4C **10**
Tredavoe. *Corn* 4B **4**
Tredegar. *Blae* 5E **47**
Trederwen. *Powy* 4E **71**
Tredington. *Glos* 3E **49**
Tredington. *Warw* 1A **50**
Tredinnick. *Corn*
nr. Bodmin 2F **7**
nr. Looe 3G **7**
nr. Padstow 1D **6**
Tredogan. *V Glam* 5D **32**
Tredomen. *Powy* 2E **46**
Tredunnock. *Mon* 2G **33**
Tredustan. *Powy* 2E **47**
Treen. *Corn*
nr. Land's End 4A **4**
nr. St Ives 3B **4**
Treeton. *S Yor* 2B **86**
Trefaldwyn. *Powy* 1E **58**
Trefasser. *Pemb* 1C **42**
Trefdraeth. *IOA* 3D **80**
Trefdraeth. *Pemb* 1E **43**
Trefecca. *Powy* 2E **47**
Trefechan. *Mer T* 5D **46**
Trefeglwys. *Powy* 1B **58**
Trefenter. *Cdgn* 4F **57**
Treffgarne. *Pemb* 2D **42**
Treffynnon. *Flin* 3D **82**
Treffynnon. *Pemb* 2C **42**
Trefil. *Blae* 4E **46**
Trefilan. *Cdgn* 5E **57**
Trefin. *Pemb* 1C **42**
Treflach. *Shrp* 3E **71**
Trefnant. *Den* 3C **82**
Trefonen. *Shrp* 3E **71**
Trefor. *Gwyn* 1C **68**
Trefor. *IOA* 2C **80**
Treforest. *Rhon* 3D **32**
Trefrew. *Corn* 4B **10**
Trefriw. *Cnwy* 4G **81**
Tref-y-Clawdd. *Powy* 3E **59**
Trefynwy. *Mon* 4A **48**
Tregada. *Corn* 4D **10**
Tregadillett. *Corn* 4C **10**
Tregare. *Mon* 4H **47**
Tregarne. *Corn* 4E **5**
Tregaron. *Cdgn* 5F **57**
Tregarth. *Gwyn* 4F **81**
Tregear. *Corn* 3C **6**
Tregeare. *Corn* 4C **10**
Tregeiriog. *Wrex* 2D **70**
Tregele. *IOA* 1C **80**
Tregeseal. *Corn* 3A **4**
Tregiskey. *Corn* 4E **6**
Tregole. *Corn* 3B **10**
Tregolwyn. *V Glam* 4C **32**
Tregonetha. *Corn* 2D **6**
Tregonhawke. *Corn* 3A **8**
Tregony. *Corn* 4D **6**
Tregoodwell. *Corn* 4B **10**
Tregorrick. *Corn* 3E **6**
Tregoss. *Corn* 2D **6**
Tregowris. *Corn* 4E **5**
Tregoyd. *Powy* 2E **47**
Tregrehan Mills. *Corn* 3E **7**
Tre-groes. *Cdgn* 1E **45**
Tregullon. *Corn* 2E **7**
Tregurrian. *Corn* 2C **6**
Tregynon. *Powy* 1C **58**
Trehafod. *Rhon* 2D **32**
Trehan. *Corn* 3A **8**
Treharris. *Mer T* 2D **32**
Treherbert. *Rhon* 2C **32**
Trehunist. *Corn* 2H **7**
Trekenner. *Corn* 5D **10**
Trekenning. *Corn* 2D **6**
Treknow. *Corn* 4A **10**
Trelales. *B'end* 3B **32**
Trelan. *Corn* 5E **5**
Trelash. *Corn* 3B **10**
Trelassick. *Corn* 3C **6**
Trelawnyd. *Flin* 3C **82**
Trelech. *Carm* 1G **43**
Treleddyd-fawr. *Pemb* 2B **42**
Trelewis. *Mer T* 2E **32**
Treligga. *Corn* 4A **10**
Trelights. *Corn* 1D **6**
Trelill. *Corn* 5A **10**
Trelissick. *Corn* 5C **6**
Trellech. *Mon* 5A **48**
Trelleck Grange. *Mon* 5H **47**
Trelogan. *Flin* 2D **82**
Trelystan. *Powy* 5E **71**
Tremadog. *Gwyn* 1E **69**
Tremail. *Corn* 4B **10**
Tremain. *Cdgn* 1C **44**
Tremaine. *Corn* 4C **10**
Tremar. *Corn* 2G **7**
Trematon. *Corn* 3H **7**
Tremeirchion. *Den* 3C **82**
Tremore. *Corn* 2E **6**
Tremorfa. *Card* 4F **33**
Trenance. *Corn*
nr. Newquay 2C **6**
nr. Padstow 1D **6**

Trenarren – Upper Poppleton

Trenarren. Corn 4E 7
Trench. Telf 4A 72
Trencreek. Corn 2C 6
Trendeal. Corn 3C 6
Trenear. Corn 5A 6
Treneglos. Corn 4C 10
Trenewan. Corn 3F 7
Trengune. Corn 3B 10
Trent. Dors 1A 14
Trentham. Stoke 1C 72
Trentishoe. Devn 2G 19
Trentlock. Derbs 2B 74
Treoes. V Glam 4C 32
Treorchy. Rhon 2C 32
Treorci. Rhon 2C 32
Tre'r-ddol. Cdgn 1F 57
Tre'r llai. Powy 5E 71
Trerulefoot. Corn 3H 7
Tresaith. Cdgn 5B 56
Trescott. Staf 1C 60
Trescowe. Corn 3C 4
Tresham. Glos 2C 34
Tresigin. V Glam 4C 32
Tresillian. Corn 4C 6
Tresimwn. V Glam 4D 32
Tresinney. Corn 4B 10
Treskillard. Corn 5A 6
Treskinnick Cross. Corn 3C 10
Tresmeer. Corn 4C 10
Tresparrett. Corn 3B 10
Tresparrett Posts. Corn 3B 10
Tressady. High 3D 164
Tressait. Per 2F 143
Tresta. Shet
  on Fetlar 2H 173
  on Mainland 6E 173
Treswell. Notts 3E 87
Treswithian. Corn 3D 4
Tre Taliesin. Cdgn 1F 57
Trethomas. Cphy 3E 33
Trethosa. Corn 3D 6
Trethurgy. Corn 3E 7
Tretio. Pemb 2B 42
Tretire. Here 3A 48
Tretower. Powy 3E 47
Treuddyn. Flin 5E 83
Trevadlock. Corn 5C 10
Trevalga. Corn 4A 10
Trevalyn. Wrex 5F 83
Trevance. Corn 1D 6
Trevanger. Corn 1D 6
Trevanson. Corn 1D 6
Trevarrack. Corn 3B 4
Trevarren. Corn 2D 6
Trevarrian. Corn 2C 6
Trevarrick. Corn 4D 6
Trevaughan. Carm
  nr. Carmarthen 3E 45
  nr. Whitland 3F 43
Treveighan. Corn 5A 10
Trevellas. Corn 3B 6
Trevelmond. Corn 2G 7
Treverva. Corn 5B 6
Trevescan. Corn 4A 4
Trevethin. Torf 5F 47
Trevia. Corn 4A 10
Trevigro. Corn 2H 7
Trevilley. Corn 4A 4
Treviscoe. Corn 3D 6
Trevivian. Corn 4B 10
Trevone. Corn 1C 6
Trevor. Wrex 1E 71
Trevor Uchaf. Den 1E 71
Trew. Corn 4D 4
Trewalder. Corn 4A 10
Trewarlett. Corn 4D 10
Trewarmett. Corn 4A 10
Trewassa. Corn 4B 10
Treween. Corn 4C 10
Trewellard. Corn 3A 4
Trewen. Corn 4C 10
Trewennack. Corn 4D 5
Trewern. Powy 4E 71
Trewetha. Corn 5A 10
Trewidland. Corn 3G 7
Trewint. Corn 3B 10
Trewithian. Corn 5C 6
Trewoofe. Corn 4B 4
Trewoon. Corn 3D 6
Treworthal. Corn 5C 6
Treyarnon. Corn 1C 6
Treyford. W Sus 1G 17
Triangle. Staf 5E 73
Triangle. W Yor 2A 92
Trickett's Cross. Dors 2F 15
Trimdon. Dur 1A 106
Trimdon Colliery. Dur 1A 106
Trimdon Grange. Dur 1A 106
Trimingham. Norf 2E 79
Trimley Lower Street. Suff 2F 55
Trimley St Martin. Suff 2F 55
Trimley St Mary. Suff 2F 55
Trimpley. Worc 3B 60
Trimsaran. Carm 5E 45
Trimstone. Devn 2F 19
Trinafour. Per 2E 143
Trinant. Cphy 2F 33
Tring. Herts 4H 51
Trinity. Ang 2F 145
Trinity. Edin 2F 129
Trisant. Cdgn 3G 57
Triscombe. Som 3E 21
Trislaig. High 1E 141
Trispen. Corn 3C 6
Tritlington. Nmbd 5G 121
Trochry. Per 4G 143
Troedrhiwdalar. Powy 5B 58
Troedrhiwfuwch. Cphy 5E 47
Troedrhiw-gwair. Blae 5E 47
Troedyraur. Cdgn 1D 44
Troedyrhiw. Mer T 5D 46
Trondavoe. Shet 4E 173
Troon. Corn 5A 6
Troon. S Ayr 1C 116
Troqueer. Dum 2A 112
Troston. Suff 3A 66
Trottiscliffe. Kent 4H 39
Trotton. W Sus 4G 25
Troutbeck. Cumb
  nr. Ambleside 4F 103
  nr. Penrith 2E 103
Troutbeck Bridge. Cumb 4F 103
Troway. Derbs 3A 86
Trowbridge. Wilts 1D 22
Trowell. Notts 2B 74
Trowle Common. Wilts 1D 22
Trowley Bottom. Herts 4A 52
Trowse Newton. Norf 5E 79
Trudoxhill. Som 2C 22
Trull. Som 4F 21
Trumaisgearraidh. W Isl 1D 170
Trumpan. High 2B 154
Trumpet. Here 2B 48
Trumpington. Cambs 5D 64
Trumps Green. Surr 4A 38
Trunch. Norf 2E 79
Trunnah. Lanc 5C 96
Truro. Corn 4C 6
Trusham. Devn 4B 12
Trusley. Derbs 2G 73
Trusthorpe. Linc 2E 89
Tryfil. IOA 2D 80
Trysull. Staf 1C 60
Tubney. Oxon 2C 36
Tuckenhay. Devn 3E 9
Tuckhill. Shrp 2B 60
Tuckingmill. Corn 4A 6
Tuckton. Bour 3G 15
Tuddenham. Suff 3G 65
Tuddenham St Martin. Suff 1E 55
Tudeley. Kent 1H 27
Tudhoe. Dur 1F 105
Tudhoe Grange. Dur 1F 105
Tudorville. Here 3A 48
Tudweiliog. Gwyn 2B 68
Tuesley. Surr 1A 26
Tufton. Hants 2C 24
Tufton. Pemb 2E 43
Tugby. Leics 5E 75
Tugford. Shrp 2H 59
Tughall. Nmbd 2G 121
Tulchan. Per 1B 136
Tullibardine. Per 2B 136
Tullibody. Clac 4A 136
Tullich. Arg 2H 133
Tullich. High
  nr. Lochcarron 4B 156
  nr. Tain 1C 158
Tullich. Mor 4H 159
Tullich Muir. High 1B 158
Tulliemet. Per 3G 143
Tulloch. Abers 5F 161
Tulloch. High
  nr. Bonar Bridge 4D 164
  nr. Fort William 5F 149
  nr. Grantown-on-Spey 2D 151
Tulloch. Per 1C 136
Tullochgorm. Arg 4G 133
Tullybeagles Lodge. Per 5H 143
Tullymurdoch. Per 3B 144
Tullynessle. Abers 2C 152
Tumble. Carm 4F 45
Tumbler's Green. Essx 3B 54
Tumby. Linc 4B 88
Tumby Woodside. Linc 5B 88
Tummel Bridge. Per 3E 143
Tunbridge Wells, Royal. Kent 2G 27
Tunga. W Isl 4G 171
Tungate. Norf 3E 79
Tunley. Bath 1B 22
Tunstall. E Yor 1G 95
Tunstall. Kent 4C 40
Tunstall. Lanc 2F 97
Tunstall. Norf 5G 79
Tunstall. N Yor 5F 105
Tunstall. Staf 3B 72
Tunstall. Stoke 5C 84
Tunstall. Suff 5F 67
Tunstall. Tyne 4G 115
Tunstead. Derbs 3F 85
Tunstead. Norf 3E 79
Tunstead Milton. Derbs 2E 85
Tunworth. Hants 2E 25
Tupsley. Here 1A 48
Tupton. Derbs 4A 86
Turfholm. S Lan 1H 117
Turfmoor. Devn 2F 13
Turgis Green. Hants 1E 25
Turkdean. Glos 4G 49
Turkey Island. Hants 1D 16
Tur Langton. Leics 1E 62
Turleigh. Wilts 5D 34
Turlin Moor. Pool 3E 15
Turnastone. Here 2G 47
Turnberry. S Ayr 4B 116
Turnchapel. Plym 3A 8
Turnditch. Derbs 1G 73
Turners Hill. W Sus 2E 27
Turners Puddle. Dors 3D 14
Turnford. Herts 5D 52
Turnhouse. Edin 2E 129
Turnworth. Dors 2D 14
Turriff. Abers 4E 161
Tursdale. Dur 1A 106
Turton Bottoms. Bkbn 3F 91
Turtory. Mor 4C 160
Turves Green. W Mid 3E 61
Turvey. Bed 5G 63
Turville. Buck 2F 37
Turville Heath. Buck 2F 37
Turweston. Buck 2E 50
Tushielaw. Bord 3F 119
Tutbury. Staf 3G 73
Tutnall. Worc 3D 61
Tutshill. Glos 2A 34
Tuttington. Norf 3E 79
Tutts Clump. W Ber 4D 36
Tutwell. Corn 5D 11
Tuxford. Notts 3E 87
Twatt. Orkn 5B 172
Twatt. Shet 6E 173
Twechar. E Dun 2H 127
Tweedale. Telf 5B 72
Tweedbank. Bord 1H 119
Tweedmouth. Nmbd 4F 131
Tweedsmuir. Bord 2C 118
Twelveheads. Corn 4B 6
Twemlow Green. Ches E 4B 84
Twenty. Linc 3A 76
Twerton. Bath 5C 34
Twickenham. G Lon 3C 38
Twigworth. Glos 3D 48
Twineham. W Sus 4D 26
Twinhoe. Bath 1C 22
Twinstead. Essx 2B 54
Twinstead Green. Essx 2B 54
Twiss Green. Warr 1A 84
Twiston. Lanc 5H 97
Twitchen. Devn 3A 20
Twitchen. Shrp 3F 59
Two Bridges. Devn 5G 11
Two Bridges. Glos 5B 48
Two Dales. Derbs 4G 85
Two Gates. Staf 5G 73
Two Mile Oak. Devn 2E 9
Twycross. Leics 5H 73
Twyford. Buck 3E 51
Twyford. Derbs 3H 73
Twyford. Dors 1D 14
Twyford. Hants 4C 24
Twyford. Leics 4E 75
Twyford. Norf 3C 78
Twyford. Wok 4F 37
Twyford Common. Here 2A 48
Twynholm. Dum 4D 110
Twyning. Glos 2D 49
Twyning Green. Glos 2E 49
Twynllanan. Carm 3A 46
Twyn-y-Sheriff. Mon 5H 47
Twywell. Nptn 3G 63
Tyberton. Here 2G 47
Tyburn. W Mid 1F 61
Tyby. Norf 3C 78
Tycroes. Carm 4G 45
Tycrwyn. Powy 4D 70
Tyddewi. Pemb 2B 42
Tydd Gote. Linc 4D 76
Tydd St Giles. Cambs 4D 76
Tydd St Mary. Linc 4D 76
Tye. Hants 2F 17
Tye Green. Essx
  nr. Bishop's Stortford 3F 53
  nr. Braintree 3A 54
  nr. Saffron Walden 2F 53
Tyersal. W Yor 1B 92
Ty Issa. Powy 2D 70
Tyldesley. G Man 4E 91
Tyler Hill. Kent 4F 41
Tyler's Green. Essx 5F 53
Tylers Green. Buck 2G 37
Tylorstown. Rhon 2D 32
Tylwch. Powy 2B 58
Y Tymbl. Carm 4F 45
Ty-nant. Cnwy 1B 70
Tyndrum. Stir 5H 141
Tyneham. Dors 4D 15
Tynehead. Midl 4G 129
Tynemouth. Tyne 3G 115
Tyneside. Tyne 3F 115
Tyne Tunnel. Tyne 3G 115
Tynewydd. Rhon 2C 32
Tyninghame. E Lot 2C 130
Tynron. Dum 5H 117
Ty'n-y-bryn. Rhon 3D 32
Tyn-y-celyn. Wrex 2D 70
Tyn-y-cwm. Swan 5G 45
Tyn-y-ffridd. Powy 2D 70
Tynygongl. IOA 2E 81
Tynygraig. Cdgn 4F 57
Ty'n-y-groes. Cnwy 3G 81
Ty'n-yr-eithin. Cdgn 4F 57
Tyn-y-rhyd. Powy 4C 70
Tyn-y-wern. Powy 3C 70
Tyrie. Abers 2G 161
Tyringham. Mil 1G 51
Tythecott. Devn 1E 11
Tythegston. B'end 4B 32
Tytherington. Ches E 3D 84
Tytherington. Som 2C 22
Tytherington. S Glo 3B 34
Tytherington. Wilts 2E 23
Tytherleigh. Devn 2G 13
Tywardreath. Corn 3E 7
Tywardreath Highway. Corn 3E 7
Tywyn. Cnwy 3G 81
Tywyn. Gwyn 5E 69

U

Uachdar. W Isl 3D 170
Uags. High 5G 155
Ubbeston Green. Suff 3F 67
Ubley. Bath 1A 22
Uckerby. N Yor 4F 105
Uckfield. E Sus 3F 27
Uckinghall. Worc 2D 48
Uckington. Glos 3E 49
Uckington. Shrp 5H 71
Uddingston. S Lan 3H 127
Uddington. S Lan 1A 118
Udimore. E Sus 4C 28
Udny Green. Abers 1F 153
Udny Station. Abers 1G 153
Udston. S Lan 4H 127
Udstonhead. S Lan 5A 128
Uffcott. Wilts 4G 35
Uffculme. Devn 1D 12
Uffington. Linc 5H 75
Uffington. Oxon 3B 36
Uffington. Shrp 4H 71
Ufford. Pet 5H 75
Ufford. Suff 5E 67
Ufton. Warw 4A 62
Ufton Nervet. W Ber 5E 37
Ugadale. Arg 3B 122
Ugborough. Devn 3C 8
Ugford. Wilts 3F 23
Uggeshall. Suff 2G 67
Ugglebarnby. N Yor 4F 107
Ugley. Essx 3F 53
Ugley Green. Essx 3F 53
Ugthorpe. N Yor 3E 107
Uidh. W Isl 9B 170
Uig. Arg 3C 138
Uig. High
  nr. Balgown 2C 154
  nr. Dunvegan 3A 154
Uigshader. High 4D 154
Uisken. Arg 2A 132
Ulbster. High 4F 169
Ulcat Row. Cumb 2F 103
Ulceby. Linc 3D 88
Ulceby. N Lin 3E 94
Ulceby Skitter. N Lin 3E 94
Ulcombe. Kent 1C 28
Uldale. Cumb 1D 102
Uley. Glos 2C 34
Ulgham. Nmbd 5G 121
Ullapool. High 4F 163
Ullenhall. Warw 4F 61
Ulleskelf. N Yor 1F 93
Ullesthorpe. Leics 2C 62
Ulley. S Yor 2B 86
Ullingswick. Here 5H 59
Ullinish. High 5C 154
Ullock. Cumb 2B 102
Ulpha. Cumb 5C 102
Ulrome. E Yor 4F 101
Ulsta. Shet 3F 173
Ulting. Essx 5B 54
Ulva House. Arg 5F 139
Ulverston. Cumb 2B 96
Ulwell. Dors 4F 15
Umberleigh. Devn 4G 19
Unapool. High 5C 166
Underbarrow. Cumb 5F 103
Undercliffe. W Yor 1B 92
Underdale. Shrp 4H 71
Underhoull. Shet 1G 173
Underriver. Kent 5G 39
Under Tofts. S Yor 2H 85
Underton. Shrp 1A 60
Underwood. Newp 3G 33
Underwood. Notts 5B 86
Underwood. Plym 3B 8
Undley. Suff 2F 65
Undy. Mon 3H 33
Union Mills. IOM 4C 108
Union Street. E Sus 2B 28
Unstone. Derbs 3A 86
Unstone Green. Derbs 3A 86
Unthank. Cumb
  nr. Carlisle 5E 113
  nr. Gamblesby 5H 113
  nr. Penrith 1F 103
Unthank End. Cumb 1F 103
Upavon. Wilts 1G 23
Up Cerne. Dors 2B 14
Upchurch. Kent 4C 40
Upcott. Devn 2F 11
Upcott. Here 5F 59
Upend. Cambs 5F 65
Up Exe. Devn 2C 12
Upgate. Norf 4D 78
Upgate Street. Norf 1C 66
Uphall. Dors 2A 14
Uphall. W Lot 2D 128
Uphall Station. W Lot 2D 128
Upham. Devn 2B 12
Upham. Hants 4D 24
Uphampton. Here 4F 59
Uphampton. Worc 4C 60
Up Hatherley. Glos 3E 49
Uphill. N Som 1G 21
Up Holland. Lanc 4D 90
Uplawmoor. E Ren 4F 127
Upleadon. Glos 3C 48
Upleatham. Red C 3D 106
Uplees. Kent 4D 40
Uploders. Dors 3A 14
Uplowman. Devn 1D 12
Uplyme. Devn 3G 13
Up Marden. W Sus 1F 17
Upminster. G Lon 2G 39
Up Nately. Hants 1E 25
Upottery. Devn 2F 13
Uppat. High 3F 165
Upper Affcot. Shrp 2G 59
Upper Arley. Worc 2B 60
Upper Armley. W Yor 1C 92
Upper Arncott. Oxon 4E 50
Upper Astrop. Nptn 2D 50
Upper Badcall. High 4B 166
Upper Bangor. Gwyn 3E 81
Upper Basildon. W Ber 4D 36
Upper Batley. W Yor 2C 92
Upper Beeding. W Sus 4C 26
Upper Benefield. Nptn 2G 63
Upper Bentley. Worc 4D 61
Upper Bighouse. High 3A 168
Upper Boddam. Abers 5D 160
Upper Boddington. Nptn 5B 62
Upper Bogside. Mor 3G 159
Upper Booth. Derbs 2F 85
Upper Borth. Cdgn 2F 57
Upper Boyndlie. Abers 2G 161
Upper Brailes. Warw 1B 50
Upper Breinton. Here 1H 47
Upper Broughton. Notts 3D 74
Upper Brynamman. Carm 4H 45
Upper Bucklebury. W Ber 5D 36
Upper Bullington. Hants 2C 24
Upper Burgate. Hants 1G 15
Upper Caldecote. C Beds 1B 52
Upper Canterton. Hants 1A 16
Upper Catesby. Nptn 5C 62
Upper Chapel. Powy 1D 46
Upper Cheddon. Som 4F 21
Upper Chicksgrove. Wilts 4E 23
Upper Church Village. Rhon 3D 32
Upper Chute. Wilts 1A 24
Upper Clatford. Hants 2B 24
Upper Coberley. Glos 4E 49
Upper Coedcae. Torf 5F 47
Upper Cound. Shrp 5H 71
Upper Cudworth. S Yor 4D 93
Upper Cumberworth. W Yor 4C 92
Upper Cuttlehill. Abers 4B 160
Upper Cwmbran. Torf 2F 33
Upper Dallachy. Mor 2A 160
Upper Dean. Bed 4H 63
Upper Denby. W Yor 4C 92
Upper Derraid. High 5E 159
Upper Diabaig. High 2H 155
Upper Dicker. E Sus 5G 27
Upper Dinchope. Shrp 2G 59
Upper Dochcarty. High 2H 157
Upper Dounreay. High 2B 168
Upper Dovercourt. Essx 2F 55
Upper Dunsforth. N Yor 3G 99
Upper Dunsley. Herts 4H 51
Upper Eastern Green.
  W Mid 2G 61
Upper Elkstone. Staf 5E 85
Upper Ellastone. Staf 1F 73
Upper End. Derbs 3E 85
Upper Enham. Hants 2B 24
Upper Farmcote. Shrp 1B 60
Upper Farringdon. Hants 3F 25
Upper Framilode. Glos 4C 48
Upper Froyle. Hants 2F 25
Upper Gills. High 1F 169
Upper Glenfintaig. High 5E 149
Upper Godney. Som 2H 21
Upper Gravenhurst. C Beds 2B 52
Upper Green. Essx 2E 53
Upper Green. W Ber 5B 36
Upper Green. W Yor 2C 92
Upper Grove Common.
  Here 3A 48
Upper Hackney. Derbs 4G 85
Upper Hale. Surr 2G 25
Upper Halliford. Surr 4B 38
Upper Halling. Medw 4A 40
Upper Hambleton. Rut 5G 75
Upper Hardres Court. Kent 5F 41
Upper Hardwick. Here 5G 59
Upper Hartfield. E Sus 2F 27
Upper Haugh. S Yor 1B 86
Upper Hayton. Shrp 2H 59
Upper Heath. Shrp 2H 59
Upper Hellesdon. Norf 4E 78
Upper Helmsley. N Yor 4A 100
Upper Hengoed. Shrp 2E 71
Upper Hergest. Here 5E 59
Upper Heyford. Nptn 5D 62
Upper Heyford. Oxon 3C 50
Upper Hill. Here 5G 59
Upper Hindhope. Bord 4B 120
Upper Hopton. W Yor 3B 92
Upper Howsell. Worc 1C 48
Upper Hulme. Staf 4E 85
Upper Inglesham. Swin 2H 35
Upper Kilcott. S Glo 3C 34
Upper Killay. Swan 3E 31
Upper Kirkton. Abers 5E 161
Upper Kirkton. N Ayr 4C 126
Upper Knockando. Mor 4F 159
Upper Knockchoilum. High 2G 149
Upper Lambourn. W Ber 3B 36
Upper Langford. N Som 1H 21
Upper Langwith. Derbs 4C 86
Upper Largo. Fife 3G 137
Upper Latheron. High 5D 169
Upper Layham. Suff 1D 54
Upper Leigh. Staf 2E 73
Upper Lenie. High 1H 149
Upper Lochton. Abers 4D 152
Upper Longdon. Staf 4E 73
Upper Longwood. Shrp 5A 72
Upper Lybster. High 5E 169
Upper Lydbrook. Glos 4B 48
Upper Lye. Here 4F 59
Upper Maes-coed. Here 2G 47
Upper Midway. Derbs 3G 73
Uppermill. G Man 4H 91
Upper Millichope. Shrp 2H 59
Upper Milovaig. High 4A 154
Upper Minety. Wilts 2F 35
Upper Mitton. Worc 3C 60
Upper Nash. Pemb 4E 43
Upper Neepaback. Shet 3G 173
Upper Netchwood. Shrp 1A 60
Upper Nobut. Staf 2E 73
Upper North Dean. Buck 2G 37
Upper Norwood. W Sus 4A 26
Upper Nyland. Dors 4C 22
Upper Oddington. Glos 3H 49
Upper Ollach. High 5E 155
Upper Outwoods. Staf 3G 73
Upper Padley. Derbs 3G 85
Upper Pennington. Hants 3B 16
Upper Poppleton. York 4H 99

Upper Quinton. *Warw*	1G **49**	Upton Snodsbury. *Worc*	5D **60**	Waen. *Den*		Walterston. *V Glam*	4D **32**

Place	Grid
Upper Quinton. *Warw*	1G **49**
Upper Rissington. *Glos.*	4H **49**
Upper Rochford. *Worc.*	4A **60**
Upper Rusko. *Dum.*	3C **110**
Upper Sandaig. *High*	2F **147**
Upper Sanday. *Orkn*	7E **172**
Upper Sapey. *Here*	4A **60**
Upper Seagry. *Wilts*	3E **35**
Upper Shelton. *C Beds*	1H **51**
Upper Sheringham. *Norf*	1D **78**
Upper Skelmorlie. *N Ayr*	3C **126**
Upper Slaughter. *Glos*	3G **49**
Upper Sonachan. *Arg*	1H **133**
Upper Soudley. *Glos*	4B **48**
Upper Staploe. *Bed*	5A **64**
Upper Stoke. *Norf*	5E **79**
Upper Stondon. *C Beds*	2B **52**
Upper Stowe. *Nptn*	5D **62**
Upper Street. *Hants*	1G **15**
Upper Street. *Norf*	
nr. Horning	4F **79**
nr. Hoveton	4F **79**
Upper Street. *Suff.*	2E **55**
Upper Strensham. *Worc.*	2E **49**
Upper Studley. *Wilts*	1D **22**
Upper Sundon. *C Beds*	3A **52**
Upper Swell. *Glos*	3G **49**
Upper Tankersley. *S Yor*	1H **85**
Upper Tean. *Staf*	2E **73**
Upperthong. *W Yor*	4B **92**
Upperthorpe. *N Lin*	4A **94**
Upper Thurnham. *Lanc*	4D **96**
Upper Tillyrie. *Per*	3D **136**
Upperton. *W Sus*	3A **26**
Upper Tooting. *G Lon*	3D **39**
Upper Town. *Derbs*	
nr. Bonsall	5G **85**
nr. Hognaston	5G **85**
Upper Town. *Here*	1A **48**
Upper Town. *N Som*	5A **34**
Uppertown. *Derbs*	4H **85**
Uppertown. *High*	1F **169**
Uppertown. *Nmbd*	2B **114**
Uppertown. *Orkn*	8D **172**
Upper Tysoe. *Warw*	1B **50**
Upper Upham. *Wilts*	4H **35**
Upper Upnor. *Medw*	3B **40**
Upper Urquhart. *Fife*	3D **136**
Upper Wardington. *Oxon*	1C **50**
Upper Weald. *Mil*	2F **51**
Upper Weedon. *Nptn*	5D **62**
Upper Wellingham. *E Sus*	4F **27**
Upper Whiston. *S Yor*	2B **86**
Upper Wield. *Hants*	3E **25**
Upper Winchendon. *Buck*	4F **51**
Upperwood. *Derbs*	5G **85**
Upper Woodford. *Wilts*	3G **23**
Upper Wootton. *Hants*	1D **24**
Upper Wraxall. *Wilts*	4D **34**
Upper Wyche. *Worc*	1C **48**
Uppincott. *Devn*	2B **12**
Uppingham. *Rut*	1F **63**
Uppington. *Shrp*	5A **72**
Upsall. *N Yor*	1G **99**
Upsettlington. *Bord*	5E **131**
Upshire. *Essx*	5E **53**
Up Somborne. *Hants*	3B **24**
Upstreet. *Kent*	4G **41**
Up Sydling. *Dors*	2B **14**
Upthorpe. *Suff*	3B **66**
Upton. *Buck*	4F **51**
Upton. *Cambs*	3A **64**
Upton. *Ches W*	4G **83**
Upton. *Corn*	
nr. Bude	2C **10**
nr. Liskeard	5C **10**
Upton. *Cumb*	1E **102**
Upton. *Devn*	
nr. Honiton	2D **12**
nr. Kingsbridge	4D **8**
Upton. *Dors*	
nr. Poole	3E **15**
nr. Weymouth	4C **14**
Upton. *E Yor*	4F **101**
Upton. *Hants*	
nr. Andover	1B **24**
nr. Southampton	1B **16**
Upton. *IOW*	3D **16**
Upton. *Leics*	1A **62**
Upton. *Linc*	2F **87**
Upton. *Mers*	2E **83**
Upton. *Norf*	4F **79**
Upton. *Nptn*	4E **62**
Upton. *Notts*	
nr. Retford	3E **87**
nr. Southwell	5E **87**
Upton. *Oxon*	3D **36**
Upton. *Pemb*	4E **43**
Upton. *Pet*	5A **76**
Upton. *Slo*	3A **38**
Upton. *Som*	
nr. Somerton	4H **21**
nr. Wiveliscombe	4C **20**
Upton. *Warw*	5F **61**
Upton. *W Yor*	3E **93**
Upton. *Wilts*	3D **22**
Upton Bishop. *Here.*	3B **48**
Upton Cheyney. *S Glo*	5B **34**
Upton Cressett. *Shrp*	1A **60**
Upton Crews. *Here*	3B **48**
Upton Cross. *Corn.*	5C **10**
Upton End. *C Beds*	2B **52**
Upton Grey. *Hants*	2E **25**
Upton Heath. *Ches W*	4G **83**
Upton Hellions. *Devn.*	2B **12**
Upton Lovell. *Wilts*	2E **23**
Upton Magna. *Shrp*	4H **71**
Upton Noble. *Som.*	3C **22**
Upton Pyne. *Devn*	3C **12**
Upton St Leonards. *Glos.*	4D **48**
Upton Scudamore. *Wilts*	2D **22**
Upton upon Severn. *Worc*	1D **48**
Upton Warren. *Worc*	4D **60**
Upwaltham. *W Sus*	4A **26**
Upware. *Cambs*	3E **65**
Upwell. *Norf*	5E **77**
Upwey. *Dors*	4B **14**
Upwick Green. *Herts*	3E **53**
Upwood. *Cambs*	2B **64**
Urafirth. *Shet*	4E **173**
Uragaig. *Arg*	4A **132**
Urchany. *High*	4C **158**
Urchfont. *Wilts*	1F **23**
Urdimarsh. *Here*	1A **48**
Ure. *Shet*	4D **173**
Ure Bank. *N Yor*	2F **99**
Urgha. *W Isl*	8D **171**
Urlay Nook. *Stoc T*	3B **106**
Urmston. *G Man*	1B **84**
Urquhart. *Mor*	2G **159**
Urra. *N Yor*	4C **106**
Urray. *High*	3H **157**
Usan. *Ang*	3G **145**
Ushaw Moor. *Dur*	5F **115**
Usk. *Mon*	5G **47**
Usselby. *Linc*	1H **87**
Usworth. *Tyne*	4G **115**
Utkinton. *Ches W*	4H **83**
Uton. *Devn*	3B **12**
Utterby. *Linc*	1C **88**
Uttoxeter. *Staf*	2E **73**
Uwchmynydd. *Gwyn*	3A **68**
Uxbridge. *G Lon*	2B **38**
Uyeasound. *Shet*	1G **173**
Uzmaston. *Pemb*	3D **42**

V

Place	Grid
Valley. *IOA*	3B **80**
Valley End. *Surr*	4A **38**
Valley Truckle. *Corn*	4B **10**
Valsgarth. *Shet*	1H **173**
Valtos. *High*	2E **155**
Van. *Powy*	2B **58**
Vange. *Essx*	2B **40**
Varteg. *Torf*	5F **47**
Vatsetter. *Shet*	3G **173**
Vatten. *High*	4B **154**
Vaul. *Arg*	4B **138**
The Vauld. *Here*	1A **48**
Vaynor. *Mer T*	4D **46**
Veensgarth. *Shet*	7F **173**
Velindre. *Powy*	2E **47**
Vellow. *Som*	3D **20**
Velly. *Devn*	4C **18**
Veness. *Orkn*	5E **172**
Venhay. *Devn*	1A **12**
Venn. *Devn*	4D **8**
Venngreen. *Devn*	1D **11**
Vennington. *Shrp*	5F **71**
Venn Ottery. *Devn*	3D **12**
Venn's Green. *Here*	1A **48**
Venny Tedburn. *Devn*	3B **12**
Venterdon. *Corn*	5D **10**
Ventnor. *IOW*	5D **16**
Vernham Dean. *Hants*	1B **24**
Vernham Street. *Hants*	1B **24**
Vernolds Common. *Shrp*	2G **59**
Verwood. *Dors*	2F **15**
Veryan. *Corn*	5D **6**
Veryan Green. *Corn.*	5D **6**
Vicarage. *Devn*	4F **13**
Vickerstown. *Cumb.*	3A **96**
Victoria. *Corn*	2D **6**
Vidlin. *Shet*	5F **173**
Viewpark. *N Lan*	3A **128**
Vigo. *W Mid*	5E **73**
Vigo Village. *Kent.*	4H **39**
Vinehall Street. *E Sus*	3B **28**
Vine's Cross. *E Sus.*	4G **27**
Viney Hill. *Glos.*	5B **48**
Virginia Water. *Surr*	4A **38**
Virginstow. *Devn.*	3D **11**
Vobster. *Som*	2C **22**
Voe. *Shet*	
nr. Hillside	5F **173**
nr. Swinister	3E **173**
Vole. *Som*	2G **21**
Vowchurch. *Here*	2G **47**
Voxter. *Shet*	4E **173**
Voy. *Orkn*	6B **172**
Vulcan Village. *Mers*	1H **83**

W

Place	Grid
Waberthwaite. *Cumb*	5C **102**
Wackerfield. *Dur*	2E **105**
Wacton. *Norf.*	1D **66**
Wadbister. *Shet*	7F **173**
Wadborough. *Worc*	1E **49**
Wadbrook. *Devn*	2G **13**
Waddesdon. *Buck*	4F **51**
Waddeton. *Devn*	3E **9**
Waddicar. *Mers*	1F **83**
Waddingham. *Linc*	1G **87**
Waddington. *Lanc*	5G **97**
Waddington. *Linc*	4G **87**
Waddon. *Devn*	5B **12**
Wadebridge. *Corn*	1D **6**
Wadeford. *Som.*	1G **13**
Wadenhoe. *Nptn*	2H **63**
Wadesmill. *Herts*	4D **52**
Wadhurst. *E Sus*	2H **27**
Wadshelf. *Derbs*	3H **85**
Wadsley. *S Yor*	1H **85**
Wadsley Bridge. *S Yor*	1H **85**
Wadswick. *Wilts*	5D **34**
Wadwick. *Hants.*	1C **24**
Wadworth. *S Yor*	1C **86**
Waen. *Den*	
nr. Llandyrnog	4D **82**
nr. Nantglyn	4B **82**
Waen. *Powy*	1B **58**
Waen Fach. *Powy*	4E **70**
Waen Goleugoed. *Den*	3C **82**
Wag. *High*	1H **165**
Wainfleet All Saints. *Linc*	5D **89**
Wainfleet Bank. *Linc.*	5D **89**
Wainfleet St Mary. *Linc.*	5D **89**
Wainhouse Corner. *Corn*	3B **10**
Wainscott. *Medw.*	3B **40**
Wainstalls. *W Yor*	2A **92**
Waitby. *Cumb*	4A **104**
Waithe. *Linc.*	4F **95**
Wakefield. *W Yor*	2D **92**
Wakerley. *Nptn*	1G **63**
Wakes Colne. *Essx*	3B **54**
Walberswick. *Suff.*	3G **67**
Walberton. *W Sus.*	5A **26**
Walbottle. *Tyne.*	3E **115**
Walby. *Cumb*	3F **113**
Walcombe. *Som*	2A **22**
Walcot. *Linc.*	2H **75**
Walcot. *N Lin*	2B **94**
Walcot. *Swin*	3G **35**
Walcot. *Telf.*	4H **71**
Walcot. *Warw*	5F **61**
Walcote. *Leics*	2C **62**
Walcot Green. *Norf*	2D **66**
Walcott. *Linc.*	5A **88**
Walcott. *Norf.*	2F **79**
Walden. *N Yor*	1C **98**
Walden Head. *N Yor*	1B **98**
Walden Stubbs. *N Yor*	3F **93**
Walderslade. *Medw*	4B **40**
Walderton. *W Sus.*	1F **17**
Walditch. *Dors*	3H **13**
Waldley. *Derbs*	2F **73**
Waldridge. *Dur.*	4F **115**
Waldringfield. *Suff.*	1F **55**
Waldron. *E Sus.*	4G **27**
Wales. *S Yor*	2B **86**
Walesby. *Linc*	1A **88**
Walesby. *Notts.*	3D **86**
Walford. *Here*	
nr. Leintwardine	3F **59**
nr. Ross-on-Wye	3A **48**
Walford. *Shrp*	3G **71**
Walford. *Staf.*	2C **72**
Walford Heath. *Shrp*	4G **71**
Walgherton. *Ches E*	1A **72**
Walgrave. *Nptn*	3F **63**
Walhampton. *Hants*	3B **16**
Walkden. *G Man*	4F **91**
Walker. *Tyne.*	3F **115**
Walkerburn. *Bord*	1F **119**
Walker Fold. *Lanc.*	5F **97**
Walkeringham. *Notts*	1E **87**
Walkerith. *Linc.*	1E **87**
Walkern. *Herts*	3C **52**
Walker's Green. *Here.*	1A **48**
Walkerton. *Fife*	3E **137**
Walkerville. *N Yor*	5F **105**
Walkford. *Dors*	3H **15**
Walkhampton. *Devn*	2B **8**
Walkington. *E Yor*	1C **94**
Walkley. *S Yor*	2H **85**
Walk Mill. *Lanc.*	1G **91**
Wall. *Corn*	3D **4**
Wall. *Nmbd*	3C **114**
Wall. *Staf.*	5F **73**
Wallaceton. *Dum*	1F **111**
Wallacetown. *Shet*	6E **173**
Wallacetown. *S Ayr*	
nr. Ayr	2C **116**
nr. Dailly	4B **116**
Wallands Park. *E Sus.*	4F **27**
Wallasey. *Mers.*	1E **83**
Wallaston Green. *Pemb.*	4D **42**
Wallbrook. *W Mid*	1D **60**
Wallcrouch. *E Sus.*	2A **28**
Wall End. *Cumb*	1B **96**
Wallend. *Medw.*	3C **40**
Wall Heath. *W Mid*	2C **60**
Wallingford. *Oxon*	3E **36**
Wallington. *G Lon*	4D **39**
Wallington. *Hants.*	2D **16**
Wallington. *Herts*	2C **52**
Wallis. *Pemb.*	2E **43**
Wallisdown. *Bour.*	3F **15**
Walliswood. *Surr.*	2C **26**
Wall Nook. *Dur*	5F **115**
Walls. *Shet*	7D **173**
Wallsend. *Tyne.*	3G **115**
Wallsworth. *Glos.*	3D **48**
Wall under Heywood. *Shrp.*	1H **59**
Wallyford. *E Lot*	2G **129**
Walmer. *Kent.*	5H **41**
Walmer Bridge. *Lanc.*	2C **90**
Walmersley. *G Man.*	3G **91**
Walmley. *W Mid*	1F **61**
Walnut Grove. *Per.*	1D **136**
Walpole. *Suff*	3F **67**
Walpole Cross Keys. *Norf*	4E **77**
Walpole Gate. *Norf*	4E **77**
Walpole Highway. *Norf.*	4E **77**
Walpole Marsh. *Norf.*	4D **77**
Walpole St Andrew. *Norf.*	4E **77**
Walpole St Peter. *Norf*	4E **77**
Walsall. *W Mid*	1E **61**
Walsall Wood. *W Mid*	5E **73**
Walsden. *W Yor*	2H **91**
Walsgrave on Sowe. *W Mid*	2A **62**
Walsham le Willows. *Suff.*	3C **66**
Walshaw. *G Man.*	3F **91**
Walshford. *N Yor*	4G **99**
Walsoken. *Norf.*	4D **76**
Walston. *S Lan*	5D **128**
Walsworth. *Herts*	2B **52**
Walter's Ash. *Buck*	2G **37**
Waltham. *Kent.*	1F **29**
Waltham. *NE Lin*	4F **95**
Waltham Abbey. *Essx*	5D **53**
Waltham Chase. *Hants.*	1D **16**
Waltham Cross. *Herts.*	5D **52**
Waltham on the Wolds. *Leics.*	3F **75**
Waltham St Lawrence. *Wind.*	4G **37**
Waltham's Cross. *Essx*	2G **53**
Walthamstow. *G Lon.*	2E **39**
Walton. *Cumb.*	3G **113**
Walton. *Derbs.*	4A **86**
Walton. *Leics.*	2C **62**
Walton. *Mers.*	1F **83**
Walton. *Mil.*	2G **51**
Walton. *Pet.*	5A **76**
Walton. *Powy.*	5E **59**
Walton. *Som.*	3H **21**
Walton. *Staf*	
nr. Eccleshall	3C **72**
nr. Stone	2C **72**
Walton. *Suff.*	2F **55**
Walton. *Telf.*	4H **71**
Walton. *Warw*	5G **61**
Walton. *W Yor*	
nr. Wakefield	3D **92**
nr. Wetherby	5G **99**
Walton Cardiff. *Glos.*	2E **49**
Walton East. *Pemb.*	2E **43**
Walton Elm. *Dors*	1C **14**
Walton Highway. *Norf.*	4D **77**
Walton in Gordano. *N Som.*	4H **33**
Walton-le-Dale. *Lanc.*	2D **90**
Walton-on-Thames. *Surr.*	4C **38**
Walton on the Hill. *Surr.*	5D **38**
Walton-on-the-Hill. *Staf.*	3D **72**
Walton-on-the-Naze. *Essx*	3F **55**
Walton on the Wolds. *Leics.*	4C **74**
Walton-on-Trent. *Derbs*	4G **73**
Walton West. *Pemb.*	3C **42**
Walwick. *Nmbd*	2C **114**
Walworth. *Darl.*	3F **105**
Walworth Gate. *Darl.*	2F **105**
Walwyn's Castle. *Pemb.*	3C **42**
Wambrook. *Som.*	2F **13**
Wampool. *Cumb*	4D **112**
Wanborough. *Surr.*	1A **26**
Wanborough. *Swin*	3H **35**
Wandel. *S Lan*	2B **118**
Wandsworth. *G Lon.*	3D **38**
Wangford. *Suff*	
nr. Lakenheath	2G **65**
nr. Southwold	3G **67**
Wanlip. *Leics.*	4C **74**
Wanlockhead. *Dum*	3A **118**
Wannock. *E Sus.*	5G **27**
Wansford. *E Yor*	4E **101**
Wansford. *Pet.*	1H **63**
Wanshurst Green. *Kent*	1B **28**
Wanstead. *G Lon*	2F **39**
Wanstrow. *Som*	2C **22**
Wanswell. *Glos.*	5B **48**
Wantage. *Oxon*	3C **36**
Wapley. *S Glo*	4C **34**
Wappenbury. *Warw*	4A **62**
Wappenham. *Nptn*	1E **51**
Warbleton. *E Sus.*	4H **27**
Warblington. *Hants*	2F **17**
Warborough. *Oxon.*	2D **36**
Warboys. *Cambs.*	2C **64**
Warbreck. *Bkpl*	1B **90**
Warbstow. *Corn.*	3C **10**
Warburton. *G Man*	2B **84**
Warcop. *Cumb.*	3A **104**
Warden. *Kent.*	3E **40**
Warden. *Nmbd*	3C **114**
Ward End. *W Mid*	2F **61**
Ward Green. *Suff.*	4C **66**
Ward Green Cross. *Lanc*	1E **91**
Wardhedges. *C Beds*	2A **52**
Wardhouse. *Abers*	5C **160**
Wardington. *Oxon*	1C **50**
Wardle. *Ches E*	5A **84**
Wardle. *G Man.*	3H **91**
Wardley. *Rut*	5F **75**
Wardley. *W Sus.*	4G **25**
Wardlow. *Derbs.*	3F **85**
Wardsend. *Ches E*	2D **84**
Wardy Hill. *Cambs*	2D **64**
Ware. *Herts.*	4D **52**
Ware. *Kent.*	4G **41**
Wareham. *Dors.*	4E **15**
Warehorne. *Kent.*	2D **28**
Warenford. *Nmbd*	2F **121**
Waren Mill. *Nmbd*	1F **121**
Warenton. *Nmbd.*	1F **121**
Wareside. *Herts.*	4D **53**
Waresley. *Cambs.*	5B **64**
Waresley. *Worc*	4C **60**
Warfield. *Brac*	4G **37**
Warfleet. *Devn*	3E **9**
Wargate. *Linc*	2B **76**
Wargrave. *Wok*	4F **37**
Warham. *Norf*	1B **78**
Wark. *Nmbd*	
nr. Coldstream	1C **120**
nr. Hexham	2B **114**
Warkleigh. *Devn*	4G **19**
Warkton. *Nptn*	3F **63**
Warkworth. *Nptn*	1C **50**
Warkworth. *Nmbd.*	4G **121**
Warlaby. *N Yor*	5A **106**
Warland. *W Yor*	2H **91**
Warleggan. *Corn.*	2F **7**
Warlingham. *Surr.*	5E **39**
Warmanbie. *Dum.*	3C **112**
Warmfield. *W Yor*	2D **93**
Warmingham. *Ches E*	4B **84**
Warminghurst. *W Sus.*	4C **26**
Warmington. *Nptn.*	1H **63**
Warmington. *Warw*	1C **50**
Warminster. *Wilts*	2D **23**
Warmley. *S Glo*	4B **34**
Warmsworth. *S Yor*	4F **93**
Warmwell. *Dors.*	4C **14**
Warndon. *Worc.*	5C **60**
Warners End. *Herts.*	5A **52**
Warnford. *Hants.*	4E **24**
Warnham. *W Sus*	2C **26**
Warren. *Ches E.*	3C **84**
Warren. *Pemb.*	5D **42**
Warrenby. *Red C.*	2C **106**
Warren Corner. *Hants*	
nr. Aldershot	2G **25**
nr. Petersfield	4F **25**
Warren Row. *Wind.*	3G **37**
Warren Street. *Kent.*	5D **40**
Warrington. *Mil.*	5F **63**
Warrington. *Warr.*	2A **84**
Warsash. *Hants.*	2C **16**
Warse. *High*	1F **169**
Warslow. *Staf.*	5E **85**
Warsop. *Notts*	4C **86**
Warsop Vale. *Notts*	4C **86**
Warter. *E Yor*	4C **100**
Warthermarske. *N Yor*	2E **98**
Warthill. *N Yor*	4A **100**
Wartling. *E Sus*	5A **28**
Wartnaby. *Leics.*	3E **74**
Warton. *Lanc*	
nr. Carnforth	2D **97**
nr. Freckleton	2C **90**
Warton. *Nmbd*	4E **121**
Warton. *Warw*	5G **73**
Warwick. *Warw*	4G **61**
Warwick Bridge. *Cumb*	4F **113**
Warwick-on-Eden. *Cumb.*	4F **113**
Warwick Wold. *Surr.*	5E **39**
Wasbister. *Orkn.*	4C **172**
Wasdale Head. *Cumb*	4C **102**
Wash. *Derbs.*	2E **85**
Washaway. *Corn.*	2E **7**
Washbourne. *Devn*	3D **9**
Washbrook. *Suff.*	1E **54**
Wash Common. *W Ber*	5C **36**
Washerwall. *Staf.*	1D **72**
Washfield. *Devn*	1C **12**
Washfold. *N Yor*	4D **104**
Washford. *Som.*	2D **20**
Washford Pyne. *Devn.*	1B **12**
Washingborough. *Linc.*	3H **87**
Washington. *Tyne.*	4G **115**
Washington. *W Sus.*	4C **26**
Washington Village. *Tyne.*	4G **115**
Waskerley. *Dur.*	5D **114**
Wasperton. *Warw*	5G **61**
Wasp Green. *Surr*	1E **27**
Wasps Nest. *Linc.*	4H **87**
Wass. *N Yor*	2H **99**
Watchet. *Som.*	2D **20**
Watchfield. *Oxon*	2H **35**
Watchgate. *Cumb.*	5G **103**
Watchhill. *Cumb*	5C **112**
Watcombe. *Torb*	2F **9**
Watendlath. *Cumb.*	3D **102**
Water. *Devn.*	4A **12**
Water. *Lanc.*	2G **91**
Waterbeach. *Cambs.*	4D **65**
Waterbeach. *W Sus.*	2G **17**
Waterbeck. *Dum.*	2D **112**
Waterditch. *Hants.*	3G **15**
Water End. *C Beds.*	2A **52**
Water End. *E Yor*	1A **94**
Water End. *Essx*	1F **53**
Water End. *Herts*	
nr. Hatfield	5C **52**
nr. Hemel Hempstead	4A **52**
Waterfall. *Staf.*	5E **85**
Waterfoot. *E Ren.*	4G **127**
Waterfoot. *Lanc.*	2G **91**
Waterford. *Herts.*	4D **52**
Water Fryston. *W Yor*	2E **93**
Waterhead. *Cumb.*	4E **103**
Waterhead. *E Ayr.*	3E **117**
Waterhead. *S Ayr.*	5C **116**
Waterheads. *Bord*	4F **129**
Waterhouses. *Dur.*	5E **115**
Waterhouses. *Staf.*	5E **85**
Wateringbury. *Kent.*	5A **40**
Waterlane. *Glos*	5E **49**
Waterlip. *Som.*	2B **22**
Waterloo. *Cphy*	3E **33**
Waterloo. *Corn.*	5B **10**
Waterloo. *Here.*	1G **47**
Waterloo. *High*	1E **147**
Waterloo. *Mers.*	1F **83**
Waterloo. *Norf*	4E **78**
Waterloo. *N Lan.*	4B **128**
Waterloo. *Pemb.*	4D **42**
Waterloo. *Per.*	5H **143**
Waterloo. *Pool*	3F **15**
Waterloo. *Shrp.*	2G **71**
Waterlooville. *Hants*	2E **17**
Watermead. *Buck.*	4G **51**
Watermillock. *Cumb*	2F **103**
Water Newton. *Cambs.*	1A **64**
Water Orton. *Warw*	1F **61**
Waterperry. *Oxon.*	5E **51**
Waterrow. *Som.*	4D **20**
Watersfield. *W Sus*	4B **26**
Waterside. *Buck*	5H **51**
Waterside. *Cambs*	3F **65**
Waterside. *Cumb.*	5D **112**
Waterside. *E Ayr*	
nr. Ayr	4D **116**
nr. Kilmarnock	5F **127**
Waterside. *E Dun*	2H **127**
Waterstein. *High*	4A **154**
Waterstock. *Oxon.*	5E **51**

Waterston. Pemb....................4D **42**
Water Stratford. Buck..............2E **51**
Waters Upton. Telf.................4A **72**
Water Yeat. Cumb...................1B **96**
Watford. Herts.................1C **38**
Watford. Nptn......................4D **62**
Wath. Cumb.........................4H **103**
Wath. N Yor
　nr. Pateley Bridge..............3D **98**
　nr. Ripon.......................2F **99**
Wath Brow. Cumb....................3B **102**
Wath upon Dearne. S Yor........4E **93**
Watlington. Norf...................4F **77**
Watlington. Oxon...................2E **37**
Watten. High.......................3E **169**
Wattisfield. Suff..................3C **66**
Wattisham. Suff....................5C **66**
Wattlesborough Heath. Shrp.........4F **71**
Watton. Dors.......................3H **13**
Watton. E Yor......................4E **101**
Watton. Norf.......................5B **78**
Watton at Stone. Herts.............4C **52**
Wattston. N Lan....................2A **128**
Wattstown. Rhon....................2D **32**
Wattsville. Cphy...................2F **33**
Wauldby. E Yor.....................2C **94**
Waulkmill. Abers...................4D **152**
Waun. Powy.........................4E **71**
Y Waun. Wrex.......................2E **71**
Waunarlwydd. Swan..................3F **31**
Waun Fawr. Cdgn....................2F **57**
Waunfawr. Gwyn.....................5E **81**
Waungilwen. Carm...................1H **43**
Waun-Lwyd. Blae....................5E **47**
Waun y Clyn. Carm..................5E **45**
Wavendon. Mil......................2H **51**
Waverbridge. Cumb..................5D **112**
Waverley. Surr.....................2G **25**
Waverton. Ches W...................4G **83**
Waverton. Cumb.....................5D **112**
Wavertree. Mers....................2F **83**
Wawne. E Yor.......................1D **94**
Waxham. Norf.......................3G **79**
Waxholme. E Yor....................2G **95**
Wayford. Som.......................2H **13**
Way Head. Cambs....................2D **65**
Waytown. Dors......................3H **13**
Way Village. Devn..................1B **12**
Wdig. Pemb.........................1D **42**
Wealdstone. G Lon..................2C **38**
Weardley. W Yor....................5E **99**
Weare. Som.........................1H **21**
Weare Giffard. Devn................4E **19**
Wearhead. Dur......................1B **104**
Wearne. Som........................4H **21**
Weasdale. Cumb.....................4H **103**
Weasenham All Saints. Norf.........3H **77**
Weasenham St Peter. Norf...........3A **78**
Weaverham. Ches W..................3A **84**
Weaverthorpe. N Yor................2D **100**
Webheath. Worc.....................4E **61**
Webton. Here.......................2H **47**
Wedderlairs. Abers.................5F **161**
Weddington. Warw...................1A **62**
Wedhampton. Wilts..................1F **23**
Wedmore. Som.......................2H **21**
Wednesbury. W Mid..................1D **61**
Wednesfield. W Mid.................5D **72**
Weecar. Notts......................4F **87**
Weedon. Buck.......................4G **51**
Weedon Bec. Nptn...................5D **62**
Weedon Lois. Nptn..................1E **50**
Weeford. Staf......................5F **73**
Week. Devn
　nr. Barnstaple..................4F **19**
　nr. Okehampton..................2G **11**
　nr. South Molton................1H **11**
　nr. Totnes......................2D **9**
Week. Som..........................3C **20**
Weeke. Devn........................2A **12**
Weeke. Hants.......................3C **24**
Week Green. Corn...................3C **10**
Weekley. Nptn......................2F **63**
Week St Mary. Corn.................3C **10**
Weel. E Yor........................1D **94**
Weeley. Essx.......................3E **55**
Weeley Heath. Essx.................3E **55**
Weem. Per..........................4F **143**
Weeping Cross. Staf................3D **72**
Weethly. Warw......................5E **61**
Weeting. Norf......................2G **65**
Weeton. E Yor......................2G **95**
Weeton. Lanc.......................1B **90**
Weeton. N Yor......................5E **99**
Weetwood Hall. Nmbd................2E **121**
Weir. Lanc.........................2G **91**
Welborne. Norf.....................4C **78**
Welburn. Linc......................5G **87**
Welburn. N Yor
　nr. Kirkbymoorside..............1A **100**
　nr. Malton......................3B **100**
Welbury. N Yor.....................4A **106**
Welby. Linc........................2G **75**
Welches Dam. Cambs.................2D **64**
Welcombe. Devn.....................1C **10**
Weld Bank. Lanc....................3D **90**
Weldon. Nptn.......................2G **63**
Weldon. Nmbd.......................5F **121**
Welford. Nptn......................2D **62**
Welford. W Ber.....................4C **36**
Welford-on-Avon. Warw..............5F **61**
Welham. Leics......................1E **63**
Welham. Notts......................2E **87**
Welham Green. Herts................5C **52**
Well. Hants........................2F **25**
Well. Linc.........................3D **88**
Well. N Yor........................1E **99**
Welland. Worc......................1C **48**
Wellbank. Ang......................5D **144**
Well Bottom. Dors..................1E **15**
Welldale. Dum......................3C **112**

Wellesbourne. Warw.................5G **61**
Well Hill. Kent....................4F **39**
Wellhouse. W Ber...................4D **36**
Welling. G Lon.....................3F **39**
Wellingborough. Nptn...........4F **63**
Wellingham. Norf...................3A **78**
Wellingore. Linc...................5G **87**
Wellington. Cumb...................4B **102**
Wellington. Here...................1H **47**
Wellington. Som................4E **21**
Wellington. Telf...................4A **72**
Wellington Heath. Here.............1C **48**
Wellow. Bath.......................1C **22**
Wellow. IOW........................4B **16**
Wellow. Notts......................4D **86**
Wellpond Green. Herts..............3E **53**
Wells. Som.....................2A **22**
Wellsborough. Leics................5A **74**
Wells Green. Ches E................5A **84**
Wells-next-the-Sea. Norf...........1B **78**
Wellswood. Torb....................2F **9**
Wellwood. Fife.....................1D **129**
Welney. Norf.......................1E **65**
Welsford. Devn.....................4C **18**
Welshampton. Shrp..................2G **71**
Welsh End. Shrp....................2H **71**
Welsh Frankton. Shrp...............2F **71**
Welsh Hook. Pemb...................2D **42**
Welsh Newton. Here.................4H **47**
Welsh Newton Common. Here..........4A **48**
Welshpool. Powy....................5E **70**
Welsh St Donats. V Glam............4D **32**
Welton. Bath.......................1B **22**
Welton. Cumb.......................5E **113**
Welton. E Yor......................2C **94**
Welton. Linc.......................2H **87**
Welton. Nptn.......................4C **62**
Welton Hill. Linc..................2H **87**
Welton le Marsh. Linc..............4D **88**
Welton le Wold. Linc...............2B **88**
Welwick. E Yor.....................2G **95**
Welwyn. Herts......................4C **52**
Welwyn Garden City. Herts......4C **52**
Wem. Shrp..........................3H **71**
Wembdon. Som.......................3F **21**
Wembley. G Lon..................2C **38**
Wembury. Devn......................4B **8**
Wembworthy. Devn...................2G **11**
Wemyss Bay. Inv....................2C **126**
Wenallt. Cdgn......................3F **57**
Wenallt. Gwyn......................1B **70**
Wendens Ambo. Essx.................2F **53**
Wendlebury. Oxon...................4D **50**
Wendling. Norf.....................4B **78**
Wendover. Buck.....................5G **51**
Wendron. Corn......................5A **6**
Wendy. Cambs.......................1D **52**
Wenfordbridge. Corn................5A **10**
Wenhaston. Suff....................3G **67**
Wennington. Cambs..................3B **64**
Wennington. G Lon..................2G **39**
Wennington. Lanc...................2F **97**
Wensley. Derbs.....................4G **85**
Wensley. N Yor.....................1C **98**
Wentbridge. W Yor..................3E **93**
Wentnor. Shrp......................1F **59**
Wentworth. Cambs...................3D **65**
Wentworth. S Yor...................1A **86**
Wenvoe. V Glam.....................4E **32**
Weobley. Here......................5G **59**
Weobley Marsh. Here................5G **59**
Wepham. W Sus......................5B **26**
Wereham. Norf......................5F **77**
Wergs. W Mid.......................5C **72**
Wern. Gwyn.........................1E **69**
Wern. Powy
　nr. Brecon......................4E **46**
　nr. Guilsfield..................4E **71**
　nr. Llangadfan..................4B **70**
　nr. Llanymynech.................3E **71**
Wernffrwd. Swan....................3E **31**
Wernyrheolydd. Mon.................4G **47**
Werrington. Corn...................4D **10**
Werrington. Pet....................5A **76**
Werrington. Staf...................1D **72**
Wervin. Ches W.....................3G **83**
Wesham. Lanc.......................1C **90**
Wessington. Derbs..................5A **86**
West Aberthaw. V Glam..............5D **32**
West Acre. Norf....................4G **77**
West Allerdean. Nmbd...............5F **131**
West Alvington. Devn...............4D **8**
West Amesbury. Wilts...............2G **23**
West Anstey. Devn..................4B **20**
West Appleton. N Yor...............5F **105**
West Ardsley. W Yor................2C **92**
West Arthurlie. E Ren..............4F **127**
West Ashby. Linc...................3B **88**
West Ashling. W Sus................2G **17**
West Ashton. Wilts.................1D **23**
West Auckland. Dur.................2E **105**
West Ayton. N Yor..................1D **101**
West Bagborough. Som...............3E **21**
West Bank. Hal.....................2H **83**
West Barkwith. Linc................2A **88**
West Barnby. N Yor.................3F **107**
West Barns. E Lot..................2C **130**
West Barsham. Norf.................2B **78**
West Bay. Dors.....................3H **13**
West Beckham. Norf.................2D **78**
West Bennan. N Ayr.................3D **123**
Westbere. Kent.....................4F **41**
West Bergholt. Essx................3C **54**
West Bexington. Dors...............4A **14**
West Bilney. Norf..................4G **77**
West Blackdene. Dur................1B **104**
West Blatchington. Brig............5D **27**
Westborough. Linc..................1F **75**
Westbourne. Bour...................3F **15**
Westbourne. W Sus..................2F **17**
West Bowling. W Yor................1B **92**

West Brabourne. Kent...............1E **29**
West Bradford. Lanc................5G **97**
West Bradley. Som..................3A **22**
West Bretton. W Yor................3C **92**
West Bridgford. Notts..........2C **74**
West Briggs. Norf..................4F **77**
West Bromwich. W Mid...........1E **61**
Westbrook. Here....................1F **47**
Westbrook. Kent....................3H **41**
Westbrook. Wilts...................5E **35**
West Buckland. Devn
　nr. Barnstaple..................3G **19**
　nr. Thurlestone.................4C **8**
West Buckland. Som.................4E **21**
West Burnside. Abers...............1G **145**
West Burrafirth. Shet..............6D **173**
West Burton. N Yor.................1C **98**
West Burton. W Sus.................4B **26**
Westbury. Buck.....................2E **50**
Westbury. Shrp.....................5F **71**
Westbury. Wilts................1D **22**
Westbury Leigh. Wilts..............1D **22**
Westbury-on-Severn. Glos...........4C **48**
Westbury on Trym. Bris.............4A **34**
Westbury-sub-Mendip. Som...........2A **22**
West Butsfield. Dur................5E **115**
West Butterwick. N Lin.............4B **94**
Westby. Linc.......................3G **75**
West Byfleet. Surr.................4B **38**
West Caister. Norf.................4H **79**
West Calder. W Lot.................3D **128**
West Camel. Som....................4A **22**
West Carr. N Lin...................4H **93**
West Chaldon. Dors.................4C **14**
West Challow. Oxon.................3B **36**
West Charleton. Devn...............4D **8**
West Chelborough. Dors.............2A **14**
West Chevington. Nmbd..............5G **121**
West Chiltington. W Sus............4B **26**
West Chiltington Common.
　　W Sus..........................4B **26**
West Chinnock. Som.................1H **13**
West Chisenbury. Wilts.............1G **23**
West Clandon. Surr.................5B **38**
West Cliffe. Kent..................1H **29**
Westcliff-on-Sea. S'end...........2C **40**
West Clyne. High...................3F **165**
West Coker. Som....................1A **14**
Westcombe. Som
　nr. Evercreech..................3B **22**
　nr. Somerton....................4H **21**
West Compton. Dors.................3A **14**
West Compton. Som..................2A **22**
West Cornforth. Dur................1A **106**
Westcot. Oxon......................3B **36**
Westcott. Buck.....................4F **51**
Westcott. Devn.....................2D **12**
Westcott. Surr.....................1C **26**
Westcott Barton. Oxon..............3C **50**
West Cowick. E Yor.................2G **93**
West Cranmore. Som.................2B **22**
West Croftmore. High...............2D **150**
West Cross. Swan...................4F **31**
West Cullerlie. Abers..............3E **153**
West Culvennan. Dum................3H **109**
West Curry. Corn...................3C **10**
West Curthwaite. Cumb..............5E **113**
West Dean. W Sus...................1G **17**
West Dean. Wilts...................4A **24**
Westdean. E Sus....................5G **27**
West Deeping. Linc.................5A **76**
West Derby. Mers...................1F **83**
West Dereham. Norf.................5F **77**
West Down. Devn....................2F **19**
Westdowns. Corn....................4A **10**
West Drayton. G Lon............3B **38**
West Drayton. Notts................3E **86**
West Dunnet. High..................1E **169**
West Ella. E Yor...................2D **94**
West End. Bed......................5G **63**
West End. Cambs....................1D **64**
West End. Dors.....................2E **15**
West End. E Yor
　nr. Kilham......................3E **101**
　nr. Preston.....................1E **95**
　nr. South Cove..................1C **94**
　nr. Ulrome......................4F **101**
West End. G Lon................2D **39**
West End. Hants....................1C **16**
West End. Herts....................5C **52**
West End. Kent.....................4F **41**
West End. Lanc.....................3D **96**
West End. Linc.....................1C **76**
West End. Norf.....................4H **79**
West End. N Som....................5H **33**
West End. N Yor....................4D **98**
West End. S Glo....................3C **34**
West End. S Lan....................5C **128**
West End. Surr.....................4A **38**
West End. Wilts....................4E **23**
West End. Wind.....................4G **37**
West End Green. Hants..............5E **37**
Wester Aberchalder. High...........2H **149**
Wester Balgedie. Per...............3D **136**
Wester Brae. High..................2A **158**
Wester Culbeuchly. Abers...........2D **160**
Westerdale. High...................3D **168**
Westerdale. N Yor..................4D **106**
Wester Dechmont. W Lot.............2D **128**
Wester Fearn. High.................5D **164**
Westerfield. Suff..................1E **55**
Westergate. W Sus..................5A **26**
Wester Galcantray. High............4C **158**
Wester Gruinards. High.............4C **164**
Westerham. Kent....................5F **39**
Westerleigh. S Glo.................4C **34**
Wester Mandally. High..............3E **149**
Wester Quarff. Shet................8F **173**
Wester Rarichie. High..............1C **158**

Wester Shian. Per..................5F **143**
Wester Skeld. Shet.................7D **173**
Westerton. Ang.....................3F **145**
Westerton. W Sus...................2G **17**
Westerton. Dur.....................1F **105**
Westerwick. Shet...................7D **173**
West Farleigh. Kent................5B **40**
West Felton. Shrp..................3F **71**
Westfield. Cumb....................2A **102**
Westfield. E Sus...................4C **28**
Westfield. High....................2C **168**
Westfield. Norf....................5B **78**
Westfield. N Lan...................2A **128**
Westfield. W Lot...................2C **128**
Westfields. Dors...................2C **14**
Westfields of Rattray. Per.........4A **144**
West Fleetham. Nmbd................2F **121**
Westford. Som......................4E **20**
West Garforth. W Yor...............1D **93**
Westgate. Dur......................1C **104**
Westgate. Norf.....................1B **78**
Westgate. N Lin....................4A **94**
Westgate on Sea. Kent..............3H **41**
West Ginge. Oxon...................3C **36**
West Grafton. Wilts................5H **35**
West Green. Hants..................1F **25**
West Grimstead. Wilts..............4H **23**
West Grinstead. W Sus..............3C **26**
West Haddlesey. N Yor..............2F **93**
West Haddon. Nptn..................3D **62**
West Hagbourne. Oxon...............3D **36**
West Hagley. Worc..................2D **60**
West Hall. Cumb....................3G **113**
Westhall. Suff.....................2G **67**
West Hallam. Derbs.................1B **74**
Westhall Terrace. Ang..............5D **144**
West Halton. N Lin.................2C **94**
West Ham. G Lon................2E **39**
Westham. Dors......................5B **14**
Westham. E Sus.....................5H **27**
Westham. Som.......................2H **21**
Westhampnett. W Sus................2G **17**
West Handley. Derbs................3A **86**
West Hanney. Oxon..................2C **36**
West Hanningfield. Essx............1B **40**
West Hardwick. W Yor...............3E **93**
West Harptree. Bath................1A **22**
West Harting. W Sus................4F **25**
West Harton. Tyne..................3G **115**
West Hatch. Som....................4F **21**
Westhay. Som.......................2H **21**
West Head. Norf....................5E **77**
Westhead. Lanc.....................4C **90**
West Heath. Hants
　nr. Basingstoke.................1D **24**
　nr. Farnborough.................1G **25**
West Helmsdale. High...............2H **165**
West Hendred. Oxon.................3C **36**
West Heogaland. Shet...............4D **173**
West Heslerton. N Yor..............2D **100**
West Hewish. N Som.................5G **33**
Westhide. Here.....................1A **48**
West Hill. Devn....................3D **12**
West Hill. E Yor...................3F **101**
West Hill. N Som...................4H **33**
West Hill. W Sus...................2E **27**
Westhill. Abers....................3F **153**
Westhill. High.....................4B **158**
West Hoathly. W Sus................2E **27**
West Holme. Dors...................4D **15**
Westhope. Here.....................5G **59**
Westhope. Shrp.....................2G **59**
West Horndon. Essx.................2H **39**
Westhorp. Nptn.....................5C **62**
Westhorpe. Linc....................2B **76**
Westhorpe. Suff....................4C **66**
West Horrington. Som...............2A **22**
West Horsley. Surr.................5B **38**
West Horton. Nmbd..................1E **121**
West Hougham. Kent.................1G **29**
Westhoughton. G Man............4E **91**
West Houlland. Shet................6D **173**
Westhouse. N Yor...................2F **97**
Westhouses. Derbs..................5B **86**
West Howe. Bour....................3F **15**
Westhumble. Surr...................5C **38**
West Huntspill. Som................2G **21**
West Hyde. Herts...................1B **38**
West Hynish. Arg...................5A **138**
West Hythe. Kent...................2F **29**
West Ilsley. W Ber.................3C **36**
Westing. Shet......................1G **173**
West Keal. Linc....................4C **88**
West Kennett. Wilts................5G **35**
West Kilbride. N Ayr...............5D **126**
West Kingsdown. Kent...............4G **39**
West Kington. Wilts................4D **34**
West Kirby. Mers...............2E **82**
West Knapton. N Yor................2C **100**
West Knighton. Dors................4C **14**
West Knoyle. Wilts.................3D **22**
West Kyloe. Nmbd...................5G **131**
Westlake. Devn.....................3C **8**
West Lambrook. Som.................1H **13**
West Langdon. Kent.................1H **29**
West Langwell. High................3D **164**
West Lavington. W Sus..............4G **25**
West Lavington. Wilts..............1F **23**
West Layton. N Yor.................4E **105**
West Leake. Notts..................3C **74**
West Learmouth. Nmbd...............1C **120**
West Leigh. Devn...................2G **11**
Westleigh. Devn
　nr. Bideford....................4E **19**
　nr. Tiverton....................1D **12**
Westleigh. G Man...................4E **91**
West Leith. Herts..................4H **51**
Westleton. Suff....................4G **67**
West Lexham. Norf..................4H **77**
Westley. Shrp......................5F **71**

Westley. Suff......................4H **65**
Westley Waterless. Cambs...........5F **65**
West Lilling. N Yor................3A **100**
West Lingo. Fife...................3G **137**
Westlington. Buck..................4F **51**
West Linton. Bord..................4E **129**
Westlinton. Cumb...................3E **113**
West Littleton. S Glo..............4C **34**
West Looe. Corn....................3G **7**
West Lulworth. Dors................4D **14**
West Lutton. N Yor.................3D **100**
West Lydford. Som..................3A **22**
West Lyng. Som.....................4G **21**
West Lynn. Norf....................4F **77**
West Mains. Per....................2B **136**
West Malling. Kent.................5A **40**
West Malvern. Worc.................1C **48**
Westmancote. Worc..................2E **49**
West Marden. W Sus.................1F **17**
West Markham. Notts................3E **86**
West Marsh. NE Lin.................4F **95**
Westmarsh. Kent....................4G **41**
West Marton. N Yor.................4A **98**
West Meon. Hants...................4E **25**
West Mersea. Essx..................4D **54**
Westmeston. E Sus..................4E **27**
Westmill. Herts
　nr. Buntingford.................3D **52**
　nr. Hitchin.....................2B **52**
West Milton. Dors..................3A **14**
Westminster. G Lon.............3D **39**
West Molesey. Surr.................4C **38**
West Monkton. Som..................4F **21**
Westmoor End. Cumb.................1B **102**
West Moors. Dors...................2F **15**
West Morden. Dors..................3E **15**
West Muir. Ang.....................2E **145**
Westmuir. Ang......................3C **144**
West Murkle. High..................2D **168**
West Ness. N Yor...................2A **100**
Westness. Orkn.....................5C **172**
West Newton. E Yor.................1E **95**
West Newton. N Yor.................3F **77**
West Newton. Som...................4F **21**
Westnewton. Cumb...................5C **112**
Westnewton. Nmbd...................1D **120**
West Norwood. G Lon................3E **39**
Westoe. Tyne.......................3G **115**
West Ogwell. Devn..................2E **9**
Weston. Bath.......................5C **34**
Weston. Ches E
　nr. Crewe.......................5B **84**
　nr. Macclesfield...............3C **84**
Weston. Devn
　nr. Honiton.....................2E **13**
　nr. Sidmouth....................4E **13**
Weston. Dors
　nr. Weymouth....................5B **14**
　nr. Yeovil......................2A **14**
Weston. Hal........................2H **83**
Weston. Hants......................4F **25**
Weston. Here.......................5F **59**
Weston. Herts......................2C **52**
Weston. Linc.......................3B **76**
Weston. Nptn.......................1D **50**
Weston. Notts......................4E **87**
Weston. Shrp
　nr. Bridgnorth..................1H **59**
　nr. Knighton....................3F **59**
　nr. Wem.........................3H **71**
Weston. S Lan......................5D **128**
Weston. Staf.......................3D **73**
Weston. Suff.......................2G **67**
Weston. W Ber......................4B **36**
Weston Bampfylde. Som..............4B **22**
Weston Beggard. Here...............1A **48**
Westonbirt. Glos...................3D **34**
Weston by Welland. Nptn............1E **63**
Weston Colville. Cambs.............5F **65**
Westoncommon. Shrp.................3G **71**
Weston Coyney. Stoke...............1D **72**
Weston Ditch. Suff.................3F **65**
Weston Favell. Nptn................4E **63**
Weston Green. Cambs................5F **65**
Weston Green. Norf.................4D **78**
Weston Heath. Shrp.................4B **72**
Weston Hills. Linc.................4B **76**
Weston in Arden. Warw..............2A **62**
Westoning. C Beds..................2A **52**
Weston in Gordano. N Som...........4H **33**
Weston Jones. Staf.................3B **72**
Weston Longville. Norf.............4D **78**
Weston Lullingfields. Shrp.........3G **71**
Weston-on-Avon. Warw...............5F **61**
Weston-on-the-Green. Oxon..........4D **50**
Weston-on-Trent. Derbs.............3B **74**
Weston Patrick. Hants..............2E **25**
Weston Rhyn. Shrp..................2E **71**
West Kirby. Mers...............2E **82**
West Knapton. N Yor................2C **100**
West Knighton. Dors................4C **14**
West Knoyle. Wilts.................3D **22**
West Kyloe. Nmbd...................5G **131**
Westlake. Devn.....................3C **8**
West Lambrook. Som.................1H **13**
West Langdon. Kent.................1H **29**
West Langwell. High................3D **164**
West Lavington. W Sus..............4G **25**
West Lavington. Wilts..............1F **23**
West Layton. N Yor.................4E **105**
West Leake. Notts..................3C **74**
West Learmouth. Nmbd...............1C **120**
West Leigh. Devn...................2G **11**
Weston-sub-Edge. Glos..............1G **49**
Weston-super-Mare. N Som.......5G **33**
Weston Town. Som...................2C **22**
Weston Turville. Buck..............4G **51**
Weston under Lizard. Staf..........4C **72**
Weston under Penyard. Here.........3B **48**
Weston under Wetherley.
　　Warw..........................4A **62**
Weston Underwood. Derbs............1G **73**
Weston Underwood. Mil..............5F **63**
Westonzoyland. Som.................3G **21**
West Orchard. Dors.................1D **14**
West Overton. Wilts................5G **35**
Westow. N Yor......................3B **100**
Westown. Per.......................1E **137**
West Panson. Devn..................3D **10**
West Park. Hart....................1B **106**
West Parley. Dors..................3F **15**
West Peckham. Kent.................5H **39**
West Pelton. Dur...................4F **115**
West Pennard. Som..................3A **22**
West Pentire. Corn.................2B **6**
West Perry. Cambs..............4A **64**

West Pitcorthie. Fife....3H 137
West Plean. Stir....1B 128
West Poringland. Norf....5E 79
West Porlock. Som....2B 20
Westport. Som....1G 13
West Putford. Devn....1D 10
West Quantoxhead. Som....2E 20
Westra. V Glam....4E 33
West Rainton. Dur....5G 115
West Rasen. Linc....2H 87
West Ravendale. NE Lin....1B 88
Westray Airport. Orkn....2D 172
West Raynham. Norf....3A 78
Westrigg. W Lot....3C 128
West Rounton. N Yor....4B 106
West Row. Suff....3F 65
West Rudham. Norf....3H 77
West Runton. Norf....1D 78
Westruther. Bord....4C 130
Westry. Cambs....1C 64
West Saltoun. E Lot....3A 130
West Sandford. Devn....2B 12
West Sandwick. Shet....3F 173
West Scrafton. N Yor....1C 98
Westside. Orkn....5C 172
West Sleekburn. Nmbd....1F 115
West Somerton. Norf....4G 79
West Stafford. Dors....4C 14
West Stockwith. Notts....1E 87
West Stoke. W Sus....2G 17
West Stonesdale. N Yor....4B 104
West Stoughton. Som....2H 21
West Stour. Dors....4C 22
West Stourmouth. Kent....4G 41
West Stow. Suff....3H 65
West Stowell. Wilts....5G 35
West Strathan. High....2F 167
West Stratton. Hants....2D 24
West Street. Kent....5D 40
West Tanfield. N Yor....2E 99
West Taphouse. Corn....2F 7
West Tarbert. Arg....3G 125
West Thirston. Nmbd....4F 121
West Thorney. W Sus....2F 17
West Thurrock. Thur....3G 39
West Tilbury. Thur....3A 40
West Tisted. Hants....4E 25
West Tofts. Norf....1H 65
West Torrington. Linc....2A 88
West Town. Bath....5A 34
West Town. Hants....3F 17
West Town. N Som....5H 33
West Tytherley. Hants....4A 24
West Tytherton. Wilts....4E 35
West View. Hart....1B 106
Westville. Notts....1C 74
West Walton. Norf....4D 76
Westward. Cumb....5D 112
Westward Ho!. Devn....4E 19
Westwell. Kent....1D 28
Westwell. Oxon....5H 49
Westwell Leacon. Kent....1D 28
West Wellow. Hants....1A 16
West Wemyss. Fife....4F 137
West Wick. N Som....5G 33
Westwick. Cambs....4D 64
Westwick. Dur....3D 104
Westwick. Norf....3E 79
West Wickham. Cambs....1G 53
West Wickham. G Lon....4E 39
West Williamston. Pemb....4E 43
West Willoughby. Linc....1G 75
West Winch. Norf....4F 77
West Winterslow. Wilts....3H 23
West Wittering. W Sus....3F 17
West Witton. N Yor....1C 98
Westwood. Devn....3D 12
Westwood. Kent....4H 41
Westwood. Pet....5A 76
Westwood. S Lan....4H 127
Westwood. Wilts....1D 22
West Woodburn. Nmbd....1B 114
West Woodhay. W Ber....5B 36
West Woodlands. Som....2C 22
Westwoodside. Cumb....5E 112
Westwoodside. N Lin....1E 87
West Worldham. Hants....3F 25
West Worlington. Devn....1A 12
West Worthing. W Sus....5C 26
West Wratting. Cambs....5F 65
West Wycombe. Buck....2G 37
West Wylam. Nmbd....3E 115
West Yatton. Wilts....4D 34
West Yell. Shet....3F 173
West Youlstone. Corn....1C 10
Wetheral. Cumb....4F 113
Wetherby. W Yor....5G 99
Wetherden. Suff....4C 66
Wetheringsett. Suff....4D 66
Wethersfield. Essx....2H 53
Wethersta. Shet....5E 173
Wetherup Street. Suff....4D 66
Wetley Rocks. Staf....1D 72
Wettenhall. Ches E....4A 84
Wetton. Staf....5F 85
Wetwang. E Yor....4D 100
Wetwood. Staf....2B 72
Wexcombe. Wilts....1A 24
Wexham Street. Buck....2A 38
Weybourne. Norf....1D 78
Weybourne. Surr....2G 25
Weybread. Suff....2E 67
Weybridge. Surr....4B 38
Weycroft. Devn....3G 13
Weydale. High....2D 168
Weyhill. Hants....2B 24
Weymouth. Dors....**215** (5B 14)
Weythel. Powy....5E 59
Whaddon. Buck....2G 51
Whaddon. Cambs....1D 52
Whaddon. Glos....4D 48

Whaddon. Wilts....4G 23
Whale. Cumb....2G 103
Whaley. Derbs....3C 86
Whaley Bridge. Derbs....2E 85
Whaley Thorns. Derbs....3C 86
Whalley. Lanc....1F 91
Whalton. Nmbd....1E 115
Whaplode. Linc....3C 76
Whaplode Drove. Linc....4C 76
Whaplode St Catherine. Linc....3C 76
Wharfe. N Yor....3G 97
Wharles. Lanc....1C 90
Wharley End. C Beds....1H 51
Wharncliffe Side. S Yor....1G 85
Wharram-le-Street. N Yor....3C 100
Wharton. Ches W....4A 84
Wharton. Here....5H 59
Whashton. N Yor....4E 105
Whasset. Cumb....1E 97
Whatcote. Warw....1B 50
Whateley. Warw....1G 61
Whatfield. Suff....1D 54
Whatley. Som
  nr. Chard....2G 13
  nr. Frome....2C 22
Whatlington. E Sus....4B 28
Whatmore. Shrp....3A 60
Whatstandwell. Derbs....5H 85
Whatton. Notts....2E 75
Whauphill. Dum....5B 110
Whaw. N Yor....4C 104
Wheatacre. Norf....1G 67
Wheatcroft. Derbs....5A 86
Wheathampstead. Herts....4B 52
Wheathill. Shrp....2A 60
Wheatley. Devn....3B 12
Wheatley. Hants....2F 25
Wheatley. Oxon....5E 50
Wheatley. S Yor....4F 93
Wheatley. W Yor....2A 92
Wheatley Hill. Dur....1A 106
Wheatley Lane. Lanc....1G 91
Wheatley Park. S Yor....4F 93
Wheaton Aston. Staf....4C 72
Wheatstone Park. Staf....5C 72
Wheddon Cross. Som....3C 20
Wheelerstreet. Surr....1A 26
Wheelock. Ches E....5B 84
Wheelock Heath. Ches E....5B 84
Wheelton. Lanc....2E 90
Wheldrake. York....5A 100
Whelford. Glos....2G 35
Whelpley Hill. Buck....5H 51
Whelpo. Cumb....1E 102
Whelston. Flin....3E 82
Whenby. N Yor....3A 100
Whepstead. Suff....5H 65
Wherstead. Suff....1E 55
Wherwell. Hants....2B 24
Wheston. Derbs....3F 85
Whetsted. Kent....1A 28
Whetstone. G Lon....1D 38
Whetstone. Leics....1C 62
Whicham. Cumb....1A 96
Whichford. Warw....2B 50
Whickham. Tyne....3F 115
Whiddon. Devn....2E 11
Whiddon Down. Devn....3G 11
Whigstreet. Ang....4D 145
Whilton. Nptn....4D 62
Whimble. Devn....2D 10
Whimple. Devn....3D 12
Whimpwell Green. Norf....3F 79
Whinburgh. Norf....5C 78
Whin Lane End. Lanc....5C 96
Whinney Hill. Stoc T....3A 106
Whinnyfold. Abers....5H 161
Whippingham. IOW....3D 16
Whipsnade. C Beds....4A 52
Whipton. Devn....3C 12
Whirlow. S Yor....2H 85
Whisby. Linc....4G 87
Whissendine. Rut....4F 75
Whissonsett. Norf....3B 78
Whisterfield. Ches E....3C 84
Whistley Green. Wok....4F 37
Whiston. Mers....1G 83
Whiston. Nptn....4F 63
Whiston. S Yor....1B 86
Whiston. Staf
  nr. Cheadle....1E 73
  nr. Penkridge....4C 72
Whiston Cross. Shrp....5B 72
Whiston Eaves. Staf....1E 73
Whitacre Heath. Warw....1G 61
Whitbeck. Cumb....1A 96
Whitbourne. Here....5B 60
Whitburn. Tyne....3H 115
Whitburn. W Lot....3C 128
Whitburn Colliery. Tyne....3H 115
Whitby. Ches W....3F 83
Whitby. N Yor....3F 107
Whitbyheath. Ches W....3F 83
Whitchester. Bord....4D 130
Whitchurch. Bath....5B 34
Whitchurch. Buck....3F 51
Whitchurch. Card....4E 33
Whitchurch. Devn....5E 11
Whitchurch. Hants....2C 24
Whitchurch. Here....4A 48
Whitchurch. Pemb....2B 42
Whitchurch. Shrp....1H 71
Whitchurch Canonicorum.
  Dors....3G 13
Whitchurch Hill. Oxon....4E 37
Whitchurch-on-Thames. Oxon....4E 37
Whitcombe. Dors....4C 14
Whitcot. Shrp....1F 59
Whitcott Keysett. Shrp....2E 59
Whiteash Green. Essx....2A 54
Whitebog. High....2B 158

Whitebridge. High....2G 149
Whitebrook. Mon....5A 48
Whitecairns. Abers....2G 153
Whitechapel. Lanc....5E 97
Whitechurch. Pemb....1F 43
White Colne. Essx....3B 54
White Coppice. Lanc....3E 90
White Corries. High....3G 141
Whitecraig. E Lot....2G 129
Whitecroft. Glos....5B 48
White Cross. Corn....4D 5
Whitecross. Corn....1D 6
Whitecross. Falk....2C 128
White End. Worc....2C 48
Whiteface. High....5E 164
Whitefarland. N Ayr....5G 125
Whitefaulds. S Ayr....4B 116
Whitefield. Dors....3E 15
Whitefield. G Man....4G 91
Whitefield. Som....4D 20
Whiteford. Abers....1E 152
Whitegate. Ches W....4A 84
Whitehall. Devn....1E 12
Whitehall. Hants....1F 25
Whitehall. Orkn....5F 172
Whitehall. W Sus....3C 26
Whitehaven. Cumb....3A 102
Whitehaven. Shrp....3E 71
Whitehill. Hants....3F 25
Whitehill. N Ayr....4D 126
Whitehills. Abers....2D 160
Whitehills. Ang....3D 144
White Horse Common. Norf....3F 79
Whitehough. Derbs....2E 85
Whitehouse. Abers....2D 152
Whitehouse. Arg....3G 125
Whiteinch. Glas....3G 127
Whitekirk. E Lot....1B 130
White Kirkley. Dur....1D 104
White Lackington. Dors....3C 14
Whitelackington. Som....1G 13
White Ladies Aston. Worc....5D 60
White Lee. W Yor....2C 92
Whiteley. Hants....2D 16
Whiteley Bank. IOW....4D 16
Whiteley Village. Surr....4B 38
Whitemans Green. W Sus....3E 27
White Mill. Carm....3E 45
Whitemire. Mor....3D 159
Whitemoor. Corn....3D 6
Whitenap. Hants....4B 24
Whiteness. Shet....7F 173
White Notley. Essx....4A 54
Whiteoak Green. Oxon....4B 50
Whiteparish. Wilts....4H 23
White Pit. Linc....3C 88
Whiterashes. Abers....1F 153
White Rocks. Here....3H 47
White Roding. Essx....4F 53
Whiterow. High....4F 169
Whiterow. Mor....3E 159
Whiteshill. Glos....5D 48
Whiteside. Nmbd....3A 114
Whiteside. W Lot....3C 128
Whitesmith. E Sus....4G 27
Whitestaunton. Som....1F 13
White Stone. Here....1A 48
Whitestone. Abers....4D 152
Whitestone. Devn....3B 12
Whitestones. Abers....3F 161
Whitestreet Green. Suff....2C 54
Whitewall Corner. N Yor....2B 100
White Waltham. Wind....4G 37
Whiteway. Glos....4E 49
Whitewell. Lanc....5F 97
Whitewell Bottom. Lanc....2G 91
Whiteworks. Devn....5G 11
Whitewreath. Mor....3G 159
Whitfield. D'dee....5D 144
Whitfield. Kent....1H 29
Whitfield. Nptn....2E 50
Whitfield. Nmbd....4A 114
Whitfield. S Glo....2B 34
Whitford. Devn....3F 13
Whitford. Flin....3D 82
Whitgift. E Yor....2B 94
Whitgreave. Staf....3C 72
Whithorn. Dum....5B 110
Whiting Bay. N Ayr....3E 123
Whitkirk. W Yor....1D 92
Whitland. Carm....3G 43
Whitleigh. Plym....3A 8
Whitletts. S Ayr....2C 116
Whitley. N Yor....2F 93
Whitley. Wilts....5D 35
Whitley Bay. Tyne....2G 115
Whitley Chapel. Nmbd....4C 114
Whitley Heath. Staf....3C 72
Whitley Lower. W Yor....3C 92
Whitley Thorpe. N Yor....2F 93
Whitlock's End. W Mid....3F 61
Whitminster. Glos....5C 48
Whitmore. Dors....2F 15
Whitmore. Staf....1C 72
Whitnage. Devn....1D 12
Whitnash. Warw....4H 61
Whitney. Here....1F 47
Whitrigg. Cumb
  nr. Kirkbride....4D 112
  nr. Torpenhow....1D 102
Whitsbury. Hants....1G 15
Whitsome. Bord....4E 131
Whitson. Newp....3G 33
Whitstable. Kent....4F 41
Whitstone. Corn....3C 10
Whittingham. Nmbd....3E 121
Whittingslow. Shrp....2G 59
Whittington. Derbs....3B 86
Whittington. Glos....3F 49
Whittington. Lanc....2F 97
Whittington. Norf....1G 65

Whittington. Shrp....2F 71
Whittington. Staf
  nr. Kinver....2C 60
  nr. Lichfield....5F 73
Whittington. Warw....1G 61
Whittington. Worc....5C 60
Whittington Barracks. Staf....5F 73
Whittlebury. Nptn....1E 50
Whittleford. Warw....1H 61
Whittle-le-Woods. Lanc....2D 90
Whittlesey. Cambs....1B 64
Whittlesford. Cambs....1E 53
Whittlestone Head. Bkbn....3F 91
Whitton. N Lin....2C 94
Whitton. Nmbd....4E 121
Whitton. Powy....4E 59
Whitton. Bord....2B 120
Whitton. Shrp....3H 59
Whitton. Stoc T....2A 106
Whittonditch. Wilts....4A 36
Whittonstall. Nmbd....4D 114
Whitway. Hants....1C 24
Whitwell. Derbs....3C 86
Whitwell. Herts....3B 52
Whitwell. IOW....5D 16
Whitwell. N Yor....5F 105
Whitwell. Rut....5G 75
Whitwell-on-the-Hill. N Yor....3B 100
Whitwick. Leics....4B 74
Whitwood. W Yor....2E 93
Whitworth. Lanc....3G 91
Whixall. Shrp....2H 71
Whixley. N Yor....4G 99
Whoberley. W Mid....3H 61
Whorlton. Dur....3E 105
Whorlton. N Yor....4B 106
Whygate. Nmbd....2A 114
Whyle. Here....4H 59
Whyteleafe. Surr....5E 39
Wibdon. Glos....2A 34
Wibtoft. Warw....2B 62
Wichenford. Worc....4B 60
Wichling. Kent....5D 40
Wick. Bour....3G 15
Wick. Devn....2E 13
Wick. High....3F 169
Wick. Shet
  on Mainland....8F 173
  on Unst....1G 173
Wick. Som
  nr. Bridgwater....2F 21
  nr. Burnham-on-Sea....1G 21
  nr. Somerton....4H 21
Wick. S Glo....4C 34
Wick. V Glam....4C 32
Wick. W Sus....5B 26
Wick. Wilts....4G 23
Wick. Worc....1E 49
Wick Airport. High....3F 169
Wicken. Cambs....3E 65
Wicken. Nptn....2F 51
Wicken Bonhunt. Essx....2E 53
Wickenby. Linc....2H 87
Wicken Green Village. Norf....2H 77
Wickersley. S Yor....1B 86
Wicker Street Green. Suff....1C 54
Wickford. Essx....1B 40
Wickham. Hants....1D 16
Wickham. W Ber....4B 36
Wickham Bishops. Essx....4B 54
Wickhambreaux. Kent....5G 41
Wickhambrook. Suff....5G 65
Wickhamford. Worc....1F 49
Wickham Green. Suff....4C 66
Wickham Heath. W Ber....5C 36
Wickham Market. Suff....5F 67
Wickhampton. Norf....5G 79
Wickham St Paul. Essx....2B 54
Wickham Skeith. Suff....4C 66
Wickham Street. Suff....4C 66
Wick Hill. Wok....5F 37
Wicklewood. Norf....5C 78
Wickmere. Norf....2D 78
Wick St Lawrence. N Som....5G 33
Wickwar. S Glo....3C 34
Widdington. Essx....2F 53
Widdrington. Nmbd....5G 121
Widdrington Station. Nmbd....5G 121
Widecombe in the Moor. Devn....5H 11
Widegates. Corn....3G 7
Widemouth Bay. Corn....2C 10
Wide Open. Tyne....2F 115
Widewall. Orkn....8D 172
Widford. Essx....5G 53
Widford. Herts....4E 53
Widham. Wilts....3F 35
Widmer End. Buck....2G 37
Widmerpool. Notts....3D 74
Widnes. Hal....2H 83
Widworthy. Devn....3F 13
Wigan. G Man....4D 90
Wigbeth. Dors....2F 15
Wigborough. Som....1H 13
Wiggaton. Devn....3E 12
Wiggenhall St Germans. Norf....4E 77
Wiggenhall St Mary Magdalen.
  Norf....4E 77
Wiggenhall St Mary the Virgin.
  Norf....4E 77
Wiggenhall St Peter. Norf....4F 77
Wiggens Green. Essx....1G 53
Wigginton. Herts....4H 51
Wigginton. Oxon....2B 50
Wigginton. Staf....5G 73
Wigginton. York....4H 99
Wigglesworth. N Yor....4H 97
Wiggonby. Cumb....4D 112
Wiggonholt. W Sus....4B 26
Wighill. N Yor....5G 99
Wighton. Norf....1B 78
Wightwick. W Mid....1C 60

Wigley. Hants....1B 16
Wigmore. Here....4G 59
Wigmore. Medw....4B 40
Wigsley. Notts....3F 87
Wigsthorpe. Nptn....2H 63
Wigston. Leics....1D 62
Wigtoft. Linc....2B 76
Wigton. Cumb....5D 112
Wigtown. Dum....4B 110
Wike. W Yor....5F 99
Wilbarston. Nptn....2F 63
Wilberfoss. E Yor....4B 100
Wilburton. Cambs....3D 65
Wilby. Norf....2C 66
Wilby. Nptn....4F 63
Wilby. Suff....3E 67
Wilcot. Wilts....5G 35
Wilcott. Shrp....4F 71
Wilcove. Corn....3A 8
Wildboarclough. Ches E....4D 85
Wilden. Bed....5H 63
Wilden. Worc....3C 60
Wildern. Hants....1C 16
Wilderspool. Warr....2A 84
Wilde Street. Suff....3G 65
Wildhern. Hants....1B 24
Wildmanbridge. S Lan....4B 128
Wildmoor. Worc....3D 60
Wildsworth. Linc....1F 87
Wildwood. Staf....3D 72
Wilford. Nott....2C 74
Wilkesley. Ches E....1A 72
Wilkhaven. High....5G 165
Wilkieston. W Lot....3E 129
Wilksby. Linc....4B 88
Willand. Devn....1D 12
Willaston. Ches E....5A 84
Willaston. Ches W....3F 83
Willaston. IOM....4C 108
Willen. Mil....1G 51
Willenhall. W Mid
  nr. Coventry....3A 62
  nr. Wolverhampton....1D 60
Willerby. E Yor....1D 94
Willerby. N Yor....2E 101
Willersey. Glos....2G 49
Willersley. Here....1G 47
Willesborough. Kent....1E 28
Willesborough Lees. Kent....1E 29
Willesden. G Lon....2D 38
Willesley. Wilts....3D 34
Willett. Som....3E 20
Willey. Shrp....1A 60
Willey. Warw....2B 62
Willey Green. Surr....5A 38
Williamscot. Oxon....1C 50
Williamsetter. Shet....9E 173
Willian. Herts....2C 52
Willingale. Essx....5F 53
Willingdon. E Sus....5G 27
Willingham. Cambs....3D 64
Willingham by Stow. Linc....2F 87
Willingham Green. Cambs....5F 65
Willington. Bed....1B 52
Willington. Derbs....3G 73
Willington. Dur....1E 105
Willington. Tyne....3G 115
Willington. Warw....2A 50
Willington Corner. Ches W....4H 83
Willisham Tye. Suff....5C 66
Willitoft. E Yor....1H 93
Williton. Som....2D 20
Willoughbridge. Staf....1B 72
Willoughby. Linc....3D 88
Willoughby. Warw....4C 62
Willoughby-on-the-Wolds.
  Notts....3D 74
Willoughby Waterleys. Leics....1C 62
Willoughton. Linc....1G 87
Willow Green. Worc....5B 60
Willows Green. Essx....4H 53
Willsbridge. S Glo....4B 34
Willslock. Staf....2E 73
Wilmcote. Warw....5F 61
Wilmington. Bath....5B 34
Wilmington. Devn....3F 13
Wilmington. E Sus....5G 27
Wilmington. Kent....3G 39
Wilmslow. Ches E....2C 84
Wilnecote. Staf....5G 73
Wilney Green. Norf....2C 66
Wilpshire. Lanc....1E 91
Wilsden. W Yor....1A 92
Wilsford. Linc....1H 75
Wilsford. Wilts
  nr. Amesbury....3G 23
  nr. Devizes....1F 23
Wilsill. N Yor....3D 98
Wilsley Green. Kent....2B 28
Wilson. Here....3A 48
Wilson. Leics....3B 74
Wilsontown. S Lan....4C 128
Wilstead. Bed....1A 52
Wilsthorpe. E Yor....3F 101
Wilsthorpe. Linc....4H 75
Wilstone. Herts....4H 51
Wilton. Cumb....3B 102
Wilton. N Yor....1C 100
Wilton. Red C....3C 106
Wilton. Bord....3H 119
Wilton. Wilts
  nr. Marlborough....5A 36
  nr. Salisbury....3F 23
Wimbish. Essx....2F 53
Wimbish Green. Essx....2G 53
Wimblebury. Staf....4E 73
Wimbledon. G Lon....3D 38
Wimblington. Cambs....1D 64
Wimboldsley. Ches W....4A 84
Wimborne Minster. Dors....2F 15
Wimborne St Giles. Dors....1F 15

Wimbotsham – Wrekenton

Wimbotsham. *Norf* 5F 77
Wimpole. *Cambs* 1D 52
Wimpstone. *Warw* 1H 49
Wincanton. *Som* 4C 22
Winceby. *Linc* 4C 88
Wincham. *Ches W* 3A 84
Winchburgh. *W Lot* 2D 129
Winchcombe. *Glos* 3F 49
Winchelsea. *E Sus* 4D 28
Winchelsea Beach. *E Sus* 4D 28
Winchester. *Hants* 213 (4C 24)
Winchet Hill. *Kent* 1B 28
Winchfield. *Hants* 1F 25
Winchmore Hill. *Buck* 1A 38
Winchmore Hill. *G Lon* 1E 39
Wincle. *Ches E* 4D 84
Windermere. *Cumb* 5F 103
Winderton. *Warw* 1B 50
Windhill. *High* 4H 157
Windle Hill. *Ches W* 3F 83
Windlesham. *Surr* 4A 38
Windley. *Derbs* 1H 73
Windmill. *Derbs* 3F 85
Windmill Hill. *E Sus* 4H 27
Windmill Hill. *Som* 1G 13
Windrush. *Glos* 4G 49
Windsor. *Wind* 213 (3A 38)
Windsor Green. *Suff* 5A 66
Windyedge. *Abers* 4F 153
Windygates. *Fife* 3F 137
Windyharbour. *Ches E* 3C 84
Windyknowe. *W Lot* 3C 128
Wineham. *W Sus* 3D 26
Winestead. *E Yor* 2G 95
Winfarthing. *Norf* 2D 66
Winford. *IOW* 4D 16
Winford. *N Som* 5A 34
Winforton. *Here* 1F 47
Winfrith Newburgh. *Dors* 4D 14
Wing. *Buck* 3G 51
Wing. *Rut* 5F 75
Wingate. *Dur* 1B 106
Wingates. *G Man* 4E 91
Wingates. *Nmbd* 5F 121
Wingerworth. *Derbs* 4A 86
Wingfield. *C Beds* 3A 52
Wingfield. *Suff* 3E 67
Wingfield. *Wilts* 1D 22
Wingfield Park. *Derbs* 5A 86
Wingham. *Kent* 5G 41
Wingmore. *Kent* 1F 29
Wingrave. *Buck* 4G 51
Winkburn. *Notts* 5E 86
Winkfield. *Brac* 3A 38
Winkfield Row. *Brac* 4G 37
Winkhill. *Staf* 5E 85
Winklebury. *Hants* 1E 24
Winkleigh. *Devn* 2G 11
Winksley. *N Yor* 2E 99
Winkton. *Dors* 3G 15
Winlaton. *Tyne* 3E 115
Winlaton Mill. *Tyne* 3E 115
Winless. *High* 3F 169
Winmarleigh. *Lanc* 5D 96
Winnal Common. *Here* 2H 47
Winnard's Perch. *Corn* 2D 6
Winnersh. *Wok* 4F 37
Winnington. *Ches W* 3A 84
Winnington. *Staf* 2B 72
Winnothdale. *Staf* 1E 73
Winscales. *Cumb* 2B 102
Winscombe. *N Som* 1H 21
Winsford. *Ches W* 4A 84
Winsford. *Som* 3C 20
Winsham. *Devn* 3E 19
Winsham. *Som* 2G 13
Winshill. *Staf* 3G 73
Winsh-wen. *Swan* 3F 31
Winskill. *Cumb* 1G 103
Winslade. *Hants* 2E 25
Winsley. *Wilts* 5D 34
Winslow. *Buck* 3F 51
Winson. *Glos* 5F 49
Winson Green. *W Mid* 2E 61
Winsor. *Hants* 1B 16
Winster. *Cumb* 5F 103
Winster. *Derbs* 4G 85
Winston. *Dur* 3E 105
Winston. *Suff* 4D 66
Winstone. *Glos* 5E 49
Winswell. *Devn* 1E 11
Winterborne Clenston. *Dors* 2D 14
Winterborne Herringston. *Dors* 4B 14
Winterborne Houghton. *Dors* 2D 14
Winterborne Kingston. *Dors* 3D 14
Winterborne Monkton. *Dors* 4B 14
Winterborne St Martin. *Dors* 4B 14
Winterborne Stickland. *Dors* 2D 14
Winterborne Whitechurch. *Dors* 2D 14
Winterborne Zelston. *Dors* 3D 15
Winterbourne. *S Glo* 3B 34
Winterbourne. *W Ber* 4C 36
Winterbourne Abbas. *Dors* 3B 14
Winterbourne Bassett. *Wilts* 4G 35
Winterbourne Dauntsey. *Wilts* 3G 23
Winterbourne Earls. *Wilts* 3G 23
Winterbourne Gunner. *Wilts* 3G 23
Winterbourne Monkton. *Wilts* 4G 35
Winterbourne Steepleton. *Dors* 4B 14
Winterbourne Stoke. *Wilts* 2F 23
Winterbrook. *Oxon* 3E 36
Winterburn. *N Yor* 4B 98
Winter Gardens. *Essx* 2B 40
Winterhay Green. *Som* 1G 13
Winteringham. *N Lin* 2C 94
Winterley. *Ches E* 5B 84
Wintersett. *W Yor* 3D 93
Winterton. *N Lin* 3C 94
Winterton-on-Sea. *Norf* 4G 79
Winthorpe. *Linc* 4E 89
Winthorpe. *Notts* 5F 87
Winton. *Bour* 3F 15
Winton. *Cumb* 3A 104
Winton. *E Sus* 5G 27
Wintringham. *N Yor* 2C 100
Winwick. *Cambs* 2A 64
Winwick. *Nptn* 3D 62
Winwick. *Warr* 1A 84
Wirksworth. *Derbs* 5G 85
Wirswall. *Ches E* 1H 71
Wisbech. *Cambs* 4D 76
Wisbech St Mary. *Cambs* 5D 76
Wisborough Green. *W Sus* 3B 26
Wiseton. *Notts* 2E 86
Wishaw. *N Lan* 4A 128
Wishaw. *Warw* 1F 61
Wisley. *Surr* 5B 38
Wispington. *Linc* 3B 88
Wissenden. *Kent* 1D 28
Wissett. *Suff* 3F 67
Wistanstow. *Shrp* 2G 59
Wistanswick. *Shrp* 3A 72
Wistaston. *Ches E* 5A 84
Wiston. *Pemb* 3E 43
Wiston. *S Lan* 1B 118
Wiston. *W Sus* 4C 26
Wistow. *Cambs* 2B 64
Wistow. *N Yor* 1F 93
Wiswell. *Lanc* 1F 91
Witcham. *Cambs* 2D 64
Witchampton. *Dors* 2E 15
Witchford. *Cambs* 3E 65
Witham. *Essx* 4B 54
Witham Friary. *Som* 2C 22
Witham on the Hill. *Linc* 4H 75
Witham St Hughs. *Linc* 4F 87
Withcall. *Linc* 2B 88
Witherenden Hill. *E Sus* 3H 27
Withergate. *Norf* 3E 79
Witheridge. *Devn* 1B 12
Witheridge Hill. *Oxon* 3E 37
Witherley. *Leics* 1H 61
Withermarsh Green. *Suff* 2D 54
Withern. *Linc* 2D 88
Withernsea. *E Yor* 2G 95
Withernwick. *E Yor* 5F 101
Withersdale Street. *Suff* 2E 67
Withersfield. *Suff* 1G 53
Witherslack. *Cumb* 1D 96
Withiel. *Corn* 2D 6
Withiel Florey. *Som* 3C 20
Withington. *Glos* 4F 49
Withington. *G Man* 1C 84
Withington. *Here* 1A 48
Withington. *Shrp* 4H 71
Withington. *Staf* 2E 73
Withington Green. *Ches E* 3C 84
Withington Marsh. *Here* 1A 48
Withleigh. *Devn* 1C 12
Withnell. *Lanc* 2E 91
Withnell Fold. *Lanc* 2E 90
Withybrook. *Warw* 2B 62
Withycombe. *Som* 2D 20
Withycombe Raleigh. *Devn* 4D 12
Withyham. *E Sus* 2F 27
Withypool. *Som* 3B 20
Witley. *Surr* 1A 26
Witnesham. *Suff* 5D 66
Witney. *Oxon* 4B 50
Wittering. *Pet* 5H 75
Wittersham. *Kent* 3C 28
Witton. *Norf* 5F 79
Witton. *Worc* 4C 60
Witton Bridge. *Norf* 2F 79
Witton Gilbert. *Dur* 5F 115
Witton-le-Wear. *Dur* 1E 105
Witton Park. *Dur* 1E 105
Wiveliscombe. *Som* 4D 20
Wivelrod. *Hants* 3E 25
Wivelsfield. *E Sus* 3E 27
Wivelsfield Green. *E Sus* 4E 27
Wivenhoe. *Essx* 3D 54
Wiveton. *Norf* 1C 78
Wix. *Essx* 3E 55
Wixford. *Warw* 5E 61
Wixhill. *Shrp* 3H 71
Wixoe. *Suff* 1H 53
Woburn. *C Beds* 2H 51
Woburn Sands. *Mil* 2H 51
Woking. *Surr* 5B 38
Wokingham. *Wok* 5G 37
Wolborough. *Devn* 5B 12
Woldingham. *Surr* 5E 39
Wold Newton. *E Yor* 2E 101
Wold Newton. *NE Lin* 1B 88
Wolferlow. *Here* 4A 60
Wolferton. *Norf* 3F 77
Wolfhill. *Per* 5A 144
Wolf's Castle. *Pemb* 2D 42
Wolfsdale. *Pemb* 2D 42
Wolgarston. *Staf* 4D 72
Wollaston. *Nptn* 4G 63
Wollaston. *Shrp* 4F 71
Wollaston. *W Mid* 2C 60
Wollaton. *Nott* 1C 74
Wollerton. *Shrp* 2A 72
Wollescote. *W Mid* 2D 60
Wolseley Bridge. *Staf* 3E 73
Wolsingham. *Dur* 1D 105
Wolstanton. *Staf* 1C 72
Wolston. *Warw* 3B 62
Wolsty. *Cumb* 4C 112
Wolterton. *Norf* 2D 78
Wolvercote. *Oxon* 5C 50
Wolverhampton. *W Mid* 213 (1D 60)
Wolverley. *Shrp* 2G 71
Wolverley. *Worc* 3C 60
Wolverton. *Hants* 1D 24
Wolverton. *Mil* 1G 51
Wolverton. *Warw* 4G 61
Wolverton. *Wilts* 3C 22
Wolverton Common. *Hants* 1D 24
Wolvesnewton. *Mon* 2H 33
Wolvey. *Warw* 2B 62
Wolvey Heath. *Warw* 2B 62
Wolviston. *Stoc T* 2B 106
Womaston. *Powy* 4E 59
Wombleton. *N Yor* 1A 100
Wombourne. *Staf* 1C 60
Wombwell. *S Yor* 4D 93
Womenswold. *Kent* 5G 41
Womersley. *N Yor* 3F 93
Wonersh. *Surr* 1B 26
Wonson. *Devn* 4G 11
Wonston. *Dors* 2C 14
Wonston. *Hants* 3C 24
Wooburn. *Buck* 2A 38
Wooburn Green. *Buck* 2A 38
Wood. *Pemb* 2C 42
Woodacott. *Devn* 2D 11
Woodale. *N Yor* 2C 98
Woodall. *S Yor* 2B 86
Woodbank. *Ches W* 3F 83
Woodbastwick. *Norf* 4F 79
Woodbeck. *Notts* 3E 87
Woodborough. *Notts* 1D 74
Woodborough. *Wilts* 1G 23
Woodbridge. *Devn* 3E 13
Woodbridge. *Dors* 1C 14
Woodbridge. *Suff* 1F 55
Wood Burcote. *Nptn* 1E 51
Woodbury. *Devn* 4D 12
Woodbury Salterton. *Devn* 4D 12
Woodchester. *Glos* 5D 48
Woodchurch. *Kent* 2D 28
Woodchurch. *Mers* 2E 83
Woodcock Heath. *Staf* 3E 73
Woodcombe. *Som* 2C 20
Woodcote. *Oxon* 3E 37
Woodcote Green. *Worc* 3D 60
Woodcott. *Hants* 1C 24
Woodcroft. *Glos* 2A 34
Woodcutts. *Dors* 1E 15
Wood Dalling. *Norf* 3C 78
Woodditton. *Cambs* 5F 65
Wood Eaton. *Staf* 4C 72
Woodeaton. *Oxon* 4D 50
Wood End. *Bed* 4H 63
Wood End. *Herts* 3D 52
Wood End. *Warw*
nr. Bedworth 2G 61
nr. Dordon 1G 61
nr. Tanworth-in-Arden 3F 61
Woodend. *Cumb* 5C 102
Woodend. *Nptn* 1E 50
Woodend. *Staf* 3F 73
Woodend. *W Sus* 2G 17
Wood Enderby. *Linc* 4B 88
Woodend Green. *Essx* 3F 53
Woodfalls. *Wilts* 4G 23
Woodfield. *Oxon* 3D 50
Woodfields. *Lanc* 1E 91
Woodford. *Corn* 1C 10
Woodford. *Devn* 3D 9
Woodford. *Glos* 2B 34
Woodford. *G Lon* 1E 39
Woodford. *G Man* 2C 84
Woodford. *Nptn* 3G 63
Woodford. *Plym* 3B 8
Woodford Green. *G Lon* 1F 39
Woodford Halse. *Nptn* 5C 62
Woodgate. *Norf* 4C 78
Woodgate. *W Mid* 2D 61
Woodgate. *W Sus* 5A 26
Woodgate. *Worc* 4D 60
Wood Green. *G Lon* 1D 39
Woodgreen. *Hants* 1G 15
Woodgreen. *Oxon* 4B 50
Woodhall. *Inv* 2E 127
Woodhall. *Linc* 4B 88
Woodhall. *N Yor* 5C 104
Woodhall Spa. *Linc* 4A 88
Woodham. *Surr* 4B 38
Woodham Ferrers. *Essx* 1B 40
Woodham Mortimer. *Essx* 5B 54
Woodham Walter. *Essx* 5B 54
Woodhaven. *Fife* 1G 137
Wood Hayes. *W Mid* 5D 72
Woodhead. *Abers*
nr. Fraserburgh 2G 161
nr. Fyvie 5E 161
Woodhill. *N Som* 4H 33
Woodhill. *Shrp* 2B 60
Woodhill. *Som* 4G 21
Woodhorn. *Nmbd* 1F 115
Woodhouse. *Leics* 4C 74
Woodhouse. *S Yor* 2B 86
Woodhouse. *W Yor*
nr. Leeds 1C 92
nr. Normanton 2D 93
Woodhouse Eaves. *Leics* 4C 74
Woodhouses. *Ches W* 3H 83
Woodhouses. *G Man*
nr. Failsworth 4H 91
nr. Sale 1B 84
Woodhouses. *Staf* 4F 73
Woodhuish. *Devn* 3F 9
Woodhurst. *Cambs* 3C 64
Woodingdean. *Brig* 5E 27
Woodland. *Devn* 2D 9
Woodland. *Dur* 2D 104
Woodland Head. *Devn* 3A 12
Woodlands. *Abers* 4E 153
Woodlands. *Dors* 2F 15
Woodlands. *Hants* 1B 16
Woodlands. *Kent* 4G 39
Woodlands. *N Yor* 4F 99
Woodlands. *S Yor* 4F 93
Woodlands Park. *Wind* 4G 37
Woodlands St Mary. *W Ber* 4B 36
Woodlane. *Shrp* 3A 72
Woodlane. *Staf* 3F 73
Woodleigh. *Devn* 4D 8
Woodlesford. *W Yor* 2D 92
Woodley. *G Man* 1D 84
Woodley. *Wok* 4F 37
Woodmancote. *Glos*
nr. Cheltenham 3E 49
nr. Cirencester 5F 49
Woodmancote. *W Sus*
nr. Chichester 2F 17
nr. Henfield 4D 26
Woodmancote. *Worc* 1E 49
Woodmancott. *Hants* 2D 24
Woodmansey. *E Yor* 1D 94
Woodmansgreen. *W Sus* 4G 25
Woodmansterne. *Surr* 5D 38
Woodmanton. *Devn* 4D 12
Woodmill. *Staf* 3F 73
Woodminton. *Wilts* 4F 23
Woodnesborough. *Kent* 5H 41
Woodnewton. *Nptn* 1H 63
Woodnook. *Linc* 2G 75
Wood Norton. *Norf* 3C 78
Woodplumpton. *Lanc* 1D 90
Woodrising. *Norf* 5B 78
Wood Row. *W Yor* 2D 93
Woodrow. *Cumb* 5D 112
Woodrow. *Dors*
nr. Fifehead Neville 1C 14
nr. Hazelbury Bryan 2C 14
Woods Eaves. *Here* 1F 47
Woodseaves. *Shrp* 2A 72
Woodseaves. *Staf* 3C 72
Woodsend. *Wilts* 4H 35
Woodsetts. *S Yor* 2C 86
Woodsford. *Dors* 3C 14
Wood's Green. *E Sus* 2H 27
Woodshaw. *Wilts* 3F 35
Woodside. *Aber* 3G 153
Woodside. *Brac* 3A 38
Woodside. *Derbs* 1A 74
Woodside. *Dum* 2B 112
Woodside. *Dur* 2E 105
Woodside. *Fife* 3G 137
Woodside. *Herts* 5C 52
Woodside. *Per* 5B 144
Wood Stanway. *Glos* 2F 49
Woodstock. *Oxon* 4C 50
Woodstock Slop. *Pemb* 2E 43
Woodston. *Pet* 1A 64
Wood Street. *Norf* 3F 79
Wood Street Village. *Surr* 5A 38
Woodthorpe. *Derbs* 3B 86
Woodthorpe. *Leics* 4C 74
Woodthorpe. *Linc* 2D 88
Woodthorpe. *Notts* 1C 74
Woodthorpe. *York* 5H 99
Woodton. *Norf* 1E 67
Woodtown. *Devn*
nr. Bideford 4E 19
nr. Littleham 4E 19
Woodvale. *Mers* 3B 90
Woodville. *Derbs* 4H 73
Woodwalton. *Cambs* 2B 64
Woodwick. *Orkn* 5C 172
Woodyates. *Dors* 1F 15
Woody Bay. *Devn* 2G 19
Woofferton. *Shrp* 4H 59
Wookey. *Som* 2A 22
Wookey Hole. *Som* 2A 22
Wool. *Dors* 4D 14
Woolacombe. *Devn* 2E 19
Woolage Green. *Kent* 1G 29
Woolage Village. *Kent* 5G 41
Woolaston. *Glos* 2A 34
Woolavington. *Som* 2G 21
Woolbeding. *W Sus* 4G 25
Woolcotts. *Som* 3C 20
Wooldale. *W Yor* 4B 92
Wooler. *Nmbd* 2D 121
Woolfardisworthy. *Devn*
nr. Bideford 4D 18
nr. Crediton 2B 12
Woolfords. *S Lan* 4D 128
Woolgarston. *Dors* 4E 15
Woolhampton. *W Ber* 5D 36
Woolhope. *Here* 2B 48
Woolland. *Dors* 2C 14
Woollard. *Bath* 5B 34
Woolley. *Bath* 5C 34
Woolley. *Cambs* 3A 64
Woolley. *Corn* 1C 10
Woolley. *Derbs* 4A 86
Woolley. *W Yor* 3D 92
Woolley Green. *Wilts* 5D 34
Woolmere Green. *Worc* 4D 60
Woolmer Green. *Herts* 4C 52
Woolminstone. *Som* 2H 13
Woolpit. *Suff* 4B 66
Woolridge. *Glos* 3D 48
Woolscott. *Warw* 4B 62
Woolsery. *Devn* 4D 18
Woolsington. *Tyne* 3E 115
Woolstaston. *Shrp* 1G 59
Woolsthorpe By Belvoir. *Linc* 2F 75
Woolsthorpe-by-Colsterworth. *Linc* 3G 75
Woolston. *Devn* 4D 8
Woolston. *Shrp*
nr. Church Stretton 2G 59
nr. Oswestry 3F 71
Woolston. *Som* 4B 22
Woolston. *Sotn* 1C 16
Woolston. *Warr* 2A 84
Woolstone. *Glos* 2E 49
Woolstone. *Oxon* 3A 36
Woolston Green. *Devn* 2D 9
Woolton. *Mers* 2G 83
Woolton Hill. *Hants* 5C 36
Woolverstone. *Suff* 2E 55
Woolverton. *Som* 1C 22
Woolwell. *Devn* 2B 8
Woolwich. *G Lon* 3F 39
Woonton. *Here*
nr. Kington 5F 59
nr. Leominster 4H 59
Wooperton. *Nmbd* 2E 121
Woore. *Shrp* 1B 72
Wooth. *Dors* 3H 13
Wooton. *Shrp* 2B 60
Wootton. *Bed* 1A 52
Wootton. *Hants* 3H 15
Wootton. *IOW* 3D 16
Wootton. *Kent* 1G 29
Wootton. *Nptn* 5E 63
Wootton. *N Lin* 3D 94
Wootton. *Oxon*
nr. Abingdon 5C 50
nr. Woodstock 4C 50
Wootton. *Shrp*
nr. Ludlow 3G 59
nr. Oswestry 3F 71
Wootton. *Staf*
nr. Eccleshall 3C 72
nr. Ellastone 1F 73
Wootton Bassett, Royal. *Wilts* 3F 35
Wootton Bridge. *IOW* 3D 16
Wootton Common. *IOW* 3D 16
Wootton Courtenay. *Som* 2C 20
Wootton Fitzpaine. *Dors* 3G 13
Wootton Rivers. *Wilts* 5G 35
Wootton St Lawrence. *Hants* 1D 24
Wootton Wawen. *Warw* 4F 61
Worcester. *Worc* 214 (5C 60)
Worcester Park. *G Lon* 4D 38
Wordsley. *W Mid* 2C 60
Worfield. *Shrp* 1B 60
Work. *Orkn* 6D 172
Workhouse Green. *Suff* 2C 54
Workington. *Cumb* 2A 102
Worksop. *Notts* 3C 86
Worlaby. *N Lin* 3D 94
World's End. *W Ber* 4C 36
World's End. *W Sus* 4E 27
Worlds End. *Hants* 1E 17
Worlds End. *W Mid* 2F 61
Worldsend. *Shrp* 1G 59
Worle. *N Som* 5G 33
Worleston. *Ches E* 5A 84
Worlingham. *Suff* 2G 67
Worlington. *Suff* 3F 65
Worlingworth. *Suff* 4E 67
Wormbridge. *Here* 2H 47
Wormegay. *Norf* 4F 77
Wormelow Tump. *Here* 2H 47
Wormhill. *Derbs* 3F 85
Wormingford. *Essx* 2C 54
Worminghall. *Buck* 5E 51
Wormington. *Glos* 2F 49
Worminster. *Som* 2A 22
Wormit. *Fife* 1F 137
Wormleighton. *Warw* 5B 62
Wormley. *Herts* 5D 52
Wormley. *Surr* 2A 26
Wormshill. *Kent* 5C 40
Wormsley. *Here* 1H 47
Worplesdon. *Surr* 5A 38
Worrall. *S Yor* 1H 85
Worsbrough. *S Yor* 4D 92
Worsley. *G Man* 4F 91
Worstead. *Norf* 3F 79
Worsthorne. *Lanc* 1G 91
Worston. *Lanc* 5G 97
Worth. *Kent* 5H 41
Worth. *W Sus* 2D 27
Wortham. *Suff* 3C 66
Worthen. *Shrp* 5F 71
Worthenbury. *Wrex* 1G 71
Worthing. *Norf* 4B 78
Worthing. *W Sus* 5C 26
Worthington. *Leics* 3B 74
Worth Matravers. *Dors* 5E 15
Worting. *Hants* 1E 24
Wortley. *Glos* 2C 34
Wortley. *S Yor* 1H 85
Wortley. *W Yor* 1C 92
Worton. *N Yor* 1B 98
Worton. *Wilts* 1E 23
Wortwell. *Norf* 2E 67
Wotherton. *Shrp* 5E 71
Wothorpe. *Pet* 5H 75
Wotter. *Devn* 2B 8
Wotton. *Glos* 4D 48
Wotton. *Surr* 1C 26
Wotton-under-Edge. *Glos* 2C 34
Wotton Underwood. *Buck* 4E 51
Wouldham. *Kent* 4B 40
Wrabness. *Essx* 2E 55
Wrafton. *Devn* 3E 19
Wragby. *Linc* 3A 88
Wragby. *W Yor* 3E 93
Wramplingham. *Norf* 5D 78
Wrangbrook. *W Yor* 3E 93
Wrangle. *Linc* 5D 88
Wrangle Lowgate. *Linc* 5D 88
Wrangway. *Som* 1E 13
Wrantage. *Som* 4G 21
Wrawby. *N Lin* 4D 94
Wraxall. *N Som* 4H 33
Wraxall. *Som* 3B 22
Wray. *Lanc* 3F 97
Wraysbury. *Wind* 3B 38
Wrayton. *Lanc* 2F 97
Wrea Green. *Lanc* 1B 90
Wreay. *Cumb*
nr. Carlisle 5F 113
nr. Penrith 2F 103
Wrecclesham. *Surr* 2G 25
Wrecsam. *Wrex* **Wrexham** 214 (5F 83)
Wrekenton. *Tyne* 4F 115

Wrelton. *N Yor* 1B **100**
Wrenbury. *Ches E* 1H **71**
Wreningham. *Norf* 1D **66**
Wrentham. *Suff* 2G **67**
Wrenthorpe. *W Yor* 2D **92**
Wrentnall. *Shrp* 5G **71**
Wressle. *E Yor* 1H **93**
Wressle. *N Lin* 4C **94**
Wrestlingworth. *C Beds* 1C **52**
Wretton. *Norf* 1F **65**
Wrexham. *Wrex* **214** (5F **83**)
Wreyland. *Devn* 4A **12**
Wrickton. *Shrp* 2A **60**
Wrightington Bar. *Lanc* 3D **90**
Wright's Green. *Essx* 4F **53**
Wrinehill. *Staf* 1B **72**
Wrington. *N Som* 5H **33**
Writtle. *Essx* 5G **53**
Wrockwardine. *Telf* 4A **72**
Wroot. *N Lin* 4H **93**
Wrotham. *Kent* 5H **39**
Wrotham Heath. *Kent* 5H **39**
Wroughton. *Swin* 3G **35**
Wroxall. *IOW* 4D **16**
Wroxall. *Warw* 3G **61**
Wroxeter. *Shrp* 5H **71**
Wroxham. *Norf* 4F **79**
Wroxton. *Oxon* 1C **50**
Wyaston. *Derbs* 1F **73**
Wyatt's Green. *Essx* 1G **39**
Wybers Wood. *NE Lin* 4F **95**
Wyberton. *Linc* 1C **76**
Wyboston. *Bed* 5A **64**
Wybunbury. *Ches E* 1A **72**
Wychbold. *Worc* 4D **60**
Wych Cross. *E Sus* 2F **27**
Wychnor. *Staf* 4F **73**
Wychnor Bridges. *Staf* 4F **73**
Wyck. *Hants* 3F **25**
Wyck Hill. *Glos* 3G **49**
Wyck Rissington. *Glos* 3G **49**
Wycliffe. *Dur* 3E **105**
Wycombe Marsh. *Buck* 2G **37**
Yr Wyddgrug. *Flin* 4E **83**
Wyddial. *Herts* 2D **52**
Wye. *Kent* 1E **29**
Wyesham. *Mon* 4A **48**
Wyfold. *Oxon* 3E **37**
Wyfordby. *Leics* 4E **75**

The Wyke. *Shrp* 5B **72**
Wyke. *Devn* 3B **12**
Wyke. *Dors* 4C **22**
Wyke. *Shrp* 5A **72**
Wyke. *Surr* 5A **38**
Wyke. *W Yor* 2B **92**
Wyke Champflower. *Som* 3B **22**
Wykeham. *Linc* 3B **76**
Wykeham. *N Yor*
   nr. Malton 2C **100**
   nr. Scarborough 1D **100**
Wyken. *Shrp* 1B **60**
Wyken. *W Mid* 2A **62**
Wyke Regis. *Dors* 5B **14**
Wykey. *Shrp* 3F **71**
Wykin. *Leics* 1B **62**
Wylam. *Nmbd* 3E **115**
Wylde Green. *W Mid* 1F **61**
Wylye. *Wilts* 3F **23**
Wymering. *Port* 2E **17**
Wymeswold. *Leics* 3D **74**
Wymington. *Bed* 4G **63**
Wymondham. *Leics* 4F **75**
Wymondham. *Norf* 5D **78**
Wynbunbury. *B'end* 2C **32**
Wynford Eagle. *Dors* 3A **14**
Wyng. *Orkn* 8C **172**
Wynyard Village. *Stoc T* 2B **106**
Wyre Piddle. *Worc* 1E **49**
Wysall. *Notts* 3D **74**
Wyson. *Here* 4H **59**
Wythall. *Worc* 3E **61**
Wytham. *Oxon* 5C **50**
Wythenshawe. *G Man* 2C **84**
Wythop Mill. *Cumb* 2C **102**
Wyton. *Cambs* 3B **64**
Wyton. *E Yor* 1E **95**
Wyverstone. *Suff* 4C **66**
Wyverstone Street. *Suff* 4C **66**
Wyville. *Linc* 3F **75**
Wyvis Lodge. *High* 1G **157**

Y

Yaddlethorpe. *N Lin* 4B **94**
Yafford. *IOW* 4C **16**
Yafforth. *N Yor* 5A **106**
Yalding. *Kent* 5A **40**

Yanley. *N Som* 5A **34**
Yanwath. *Cumb* 2G **103**
Yanworth. *Glos* 4F **49**
Yapham. *E Yor* 4B **100**
Yapton. *W Sus* 5A **26**
Yarburgh. *Linc* 1C **88**
Yarcombe. *Devn* 2F **13**
Yarde. *Som* 3D **20**
Yardley. *W Mid* 2F **61**
Yardley Gobion. *Nptn* 1F **51**
Yardley Hastings. *Nptn* 5F **63**
Yardley Wood. *W Mid* 2F **61**
Yardro. *Powy* 5E **59**
Yarhampton. *Worc* 4B **60**
Yarkhill. *Here* 1B **48**
Yarlet. *Staf* 3D **72**
Yarley. *Som* 2A **22**
Yarlington. *Som* 4B **22**
Yarm. *Stoc T* 3B **106**
Yarmouth. *IOW* 4B **16**
Yarnbrook. *Wilts* 1D **22**
Yarnfield. *Staf* 2C **72**
Yarnscombe. *Devn* 4F **19**
Yarnton. *Oxon* 4C **50**
Yarpole. *Here* 4G **59**
Yarrow. *Nmbd* 1A **114**
Yarrow. *Bord* 2F **119**
Yarrow. *Som* 2G **21**
Yarrow Feus. *Bord* 2F **119**
Yarrow Ford. *Bord* 1G **119**
Yarsop. *Here* 1H **47**
Yarwell. *Nptn* 1H **63**
Yate. *S Glo* 3C **34**
Yatesbury. *Wilts* 4F **35**
Yattendon. *W Ber* 4D **36**
Yatton. *Here*
   nr. Leominster 4G **59**
   nr. Ross-on-Wye 2B **48**
Yatton. *N Som* 5H **33**
Yatton Keynell. *Wilts* 4D **34**
Yaverland. *IOW* 4E **16**
Yawl. *Devn* 3G **13**
Yaxham. *Norf* 4C **78**
Yaxley. *Cambs* 1A **64**
Yaxley. *Suff* 3D **66**
Yazor. *Here* 1H **47**
Yeading. *G Lon* 2C **38**
Yeadon. *W Yor* 5E **98**

Yealand Conyers. *Lanc* 2E **97**
Yealand Redmayne.
   Lanc 2E **97**
Yealand Storrs. *Lanc* 2D **97**
Yealmpton. *Devn* 3B **8**
Yearby. *Red C* 2D **106**
Yearngill. *Cumb* 5C **112**
Yearsett. *Here* 5B **60**
Yearsley. *N Yor* 2H **99**
Yeaton. *Shrp* 4G **71**
Yeaveley. *Derbs* 1F **73**
Yeavering. *Nmbd* 1D **120**
Yedingham. *N Yor* 2C **100**
Yeldersley Hollies. *Derbs* 1G **73**
Yelford. *Oxon* 5B **50**
Yelland. *Devn* 3E **19**
Yelling. *Cambs* 4B **64**
Yelsted. *Kent* 4C **40**
Yelvertoft. *Nptn* 3C **62**
Yelverton. *Devn* 2B **8**
Yelverton. *Norf* 5E **79**
Yenston. *Som* 4C **22**
Yeoford. *Devn* 3A **12**
Yeolmbridge. *Corn* 4D **10**
Yeo Mill. *Devn* 4B **20**
Yeovil. *Som* 1A **14**
Yeovil Marsh. *Som* 1A **14**
Yeovilton. *Som* 4A **22**
Yerbeston. *Pemb* 4E **43**
Yesnaby. *Orkn* 6B **172**
Yetlington. *Nmbd* 4E **121**
Yetminster. *Dors* 1A **14**
Yett. *N Lan* 4A **128**
Yett. *S Ayr* 2D **116**
Yettington. *Devn* 4D **12**
Yetts o' Muckhart. *Clac* 3C **136**
Yielden. *Bed* 4H **63**
Yieldshields. *S Lan* 4B **128**
Yiewsley. *G Lon* 2B **38**
Yinstay. *Orkn* 6E **172**
Ynysboeth. *Rhon* 2D **32**
Ynysddu. *Cphy* 2E **33**
Ynysforgan. *Swan* 3F **31**
Ynyshir. *Rhon* 2D **32**
Ynyslas. *Cdgn* 1F **57**
Ynysmaerdy. *Rhon* 3D **32**
Ynysmeudwy. *Neat* 5H **45**
Ynystawe. *Swan* 5G **45**
Ynys-wen. *Rhon* 2C **32**

Ynyswen. *Powy* 4B **46**
Ynys y Barri. *V Glam* 5E **32**
Ynysybwl. *Rhon* 2D **32**
Ynysymaerdy. *Neat* 3G **31**
Yockenthwaite. *N Yor* 2B **98**
Yockleton. *Shrp* 4G **71**
Yokefleet. *E Yor* 2B **94**
Yoker. *Glas* 3G **127**
Yonder Bognie. *Abers* 4C **160**
Yonderton. *Abers* 5G **161**
York. *York* **214** (4A **100**)
Yorkletts. *Kent* 4E **41**
Yorkley. *Glos* 5B **48**
Yorton. *Shrp* 3H **71**
Yorton Heath. *Shrp* 3H **71**
Youlgreave. *Derbs* 4G **85**
Youlthorpe. *E Yor* 4B **100**
Youlton. *N Yor* 3G **99**
Young's End. *Essx* 4H **53**
Young Wood. *Linc* 3A **88**
Yoxall. *Staf* 4F **73**
Yoxford. *Suff* 4F **67**
Ysbyty Cynfyn. *Cdgn* 3G **57**
Ysbyty Ifan. *Cnwy* 1H **69**
Ysbyty Ystwyth. *Cdgn* 3G **57**
Ysceifiog. *Flin* 3D **82**
Yspitty. *Carm* 3E **31**
Ystalyfera. *Neat* 5A **46**
Ystrad. *Rhon* 2C **32**
Ystrad Aeron. *Cdgn* 5E **57**
Ystradfellte. *Powy* 4C **46**
Ystradffin. *Carm* 1A **46**
Ystradgynlais. *Powy* 4A **46**
Ystradmeurig. *Cdgn* 4G **57**
Ystrad Mynach. *Cphy* 2E **33**
Ystradowen. *Carm* 4A **46**
Ystradowen. *V Glam* 4D **32**
Ystumtuen. *Cdgn* 3G **57**
Ythanbank. *Abers* 5G **161**
Ythanwells. *Abers* 5D **160**

Z

Zeal Monachorum. *Devn* 2H **11**
Zeals. *Wilts* 3C **22**
Zelah. *Corn* 3C **6**
Zennor. *Corn* 3B **4**
Zouch. *Notts* 3C **74**

Published by Geographers' A-Z Map Company Limited
An imprint of HarperCollins Publishers
Westerhill Road
Bishopbriggs
Glasgow
G64 2QT

www.az.co.uk
a-z.maps@harpercollins.co.uk

HarperCollinsPublishers
1st Floor, Watermarque Building, Ringsend Road, Dublin 4, Ireland

30th edition 2022

© Collins Bartholomew Ltd 2022

This product uses map data licenced from Ordnance Survey
© Crown copyright and database rights 2020 OS 100018598

AZ, A-Z and AtoZ are registered trademarks of Geographers' A-Z Map Company Limited

Base relief by Geo-Innovations, © www.geoinnovations.co.uk

The Shopmobility logo is a registered symbol of The National Federation of Shopmobility

A catalogue record for this book is available from the British Library.

ISBN 978-0-00-852872-0

10 9 8 7 6 5 4 3 2 1

Printed in Poland

INDEX TO SELECTED PLACES OF INTEREST

(1) A strict alphabetical order is used e.g. Benmore Botanic Gdn. follows Ben Macdui but precedes Ben Nevis.

(2) Places of Interest which fall on City and Town Centre maps are referenced first to the detailed map page, followed by the main map page if appropriate.
The name of the map is included if it is not clear from the index entry.
e.g. Ashmolean Mus. of Art & Archaeology (OX1 2PH)........ **Oxford 207** (5D **50**)

(3) Entries in italics are not named on the map but are shown with a symbol only.
e.g. *Aberdour Castle (KY3 0XA)* *1E* ***129***

SAT NAV POSTCODES

Postcodes are shown to assist Sat Nav users and are included on this basis.
It should be noted that postcodes have been selected by their proximity to the Place of Interest and that they may not form part of the actual postal address.
Drivers should follow the Tourist Brown Signs when available.

ABBREVIATIONS USED IN THIS INDEX

Centre : Cen. Garden : Gdn. Gardens : Gdns. Museum : Mus. National : Nat. Park : Pk.

A

Abbeydale Industrial Hamlet (S7 2QW) 2H 85
Abbey House Mus. (LS5 3EH) 1C 92
Abbot Hall Art Gallery. (LA9 5AL) 5G 103
Abbotsbury Subtropical Gdns. (DT3 4LA) 4A 14
Abbotsbury Swannery (DT3 4JG) 4A 14
Abbotsford (TD6 9BQ) 1H 119
Aberdeen Maritime Mus. (AB11 5BY) 187 (3G 153)
Aberdour Castle. (KY3 0XA) 1E 129
Aberdulais Falls (SA10 8EU) 5A 46
Aberglasney Gdns. (SA32 8QH) 3F 45
Abernethy Round Tower (PH2 9RT) 2D 136
Aberystwyth Castle (SY23 1DZ) 187 (2E 57)
Acorn Bank Gdn. & Watermill (CA10 1SP) 2H 103
Acton Burnell Castle. (SY5 7PF) 5H 71
Acton Scott Historic Working Farm (SY6 6QN) 2G 59
Adlington Hall (SK10 4LF) 2D 84
Africa Alive! (NR33 7TF) 2H 67
Aintree Racecourse (L9 5AS) 1F 83
Aira Force (CA11 0JX) 2F 103
A la Ronde (EX8 5BD) 4D 12
Alby Gdns. (NR11 7QE) 2E 78
Aldeburgh Mus. (IP15 5DS) 5G 67
Alfred Corry Mus. (IP18 6NB) 3H 67
Alfriston Clergy House (BN26 5TL) 5G 27
Alloa Tower (FK10 1PP) 4A 136
Alnwick Castle. (NE66 1NQ) 3F 121
Alnwick Gdn. (NE66 1YU) 3F 121
Althorp (NN7 4HQ) 4D 62
Alton Towers (ST10 4DB) 1E 73
Amberley Mus. & Heritage Cen. (BN18 9LT) 4B 26
The American Mus. in Britain (BA2 7BD) 5C 34
Angel of the North (NE9 6PG) 4F 115
Anglesey Abbey & Lode Mill (CB25 9EJ) 4E 65
Anne Hathaway's Cottage (CV37 9HH) 5F 61
Antonine Wall, Rough Castle (FK4 2AA) 2B 128
Antony (PL11 2QA) 3A 8
Appuldurcombe House (PO38 3EW) 4D 16
Arbeia Roman Fort & Mus. (NE33 2BB) 3G 115
Arbroath Abbey. (DD11 1JQ) 4F 145
Arbury Hall (CV10 7PT) 2H 61
Arbuthnott House Gdn. (AB30 1PA) 1G 145
Ardkinglas Woodland Gdns. (PA26 8BG) 2A 134
Ardnamurchan Point (PH36 4LN) 2E 139
Arduaine Gdn. (PA34 4XQ) 2E 133
Ardwell Gdns. (DG9 9LY) 5G 109
Argyll's Lodging (FK8 1EG) Stirling 211 (4G 135)
Arley Hall & Gdns. (CW9 6NA) 2A 84
Arlington Court (EX31 4LP) 3G 19
Arlington Row (GL7 5NJ) 5G 49
Armadale Castle Gdns. (IV45 8RS) 3E 147
Arniston House (EH23 4RY) 4G 129
Arundel Castle. (BN18 9AB) 5B 26
Arundel Wetland Cen. (BN18 9PB) 5B 26
Ascot Racecourse (SL5 7JX) 4A 38
Ascott (LU7 0PT) 3G 51
Ashby-de-la-Zouch Castle. (LE65 1BR) 4A 74
Ashdown Forest (TN7 4EU) 2F 27
Ashdown House (RG17 8RE) 3A 36
Ashmolean Mus. of Art & Archaeology (OX1 2PH) Oxford 207 (5D 50)
Astley Hall Mus. & Art Gallery. (PR7 1NP) 3D 90
Athelhampton House & Gdns. (DT2 7LG) 3C 14
Attingham Pk. (SY4 4TP) 5H 71
Auchingarrich Wildlife Cen. (PH6 2JE) 2G 135
Auckland Castle. (DL14 7NP) 1F 105
Audley End House & Gdns. (CB11 4JF) 2F 53
Avebury (SN8 1RE) 4G 35
Avoncroft Mus. of Historic Buildings (B60 4JR) 4D 60
Avon Valley Adventure & Wildlife Pk. (BS31 1TP) 5B 34
Avon Valley Railway (BS30 6HD) 4B 34
Aydon Castle (NE45 5PJ) 3C 114
Ayr Racecourse (KA8 0JE) 187 (2C 116)
Ayscoughfee Hall Mus. & Gdns. (PE11 2RA) 3B 76
Aysgarth Falls (DL8 3SR) 1C 98
Ayton Castle (Eyemouth). (TD14 5RD) 3F 131

B

Bachelors' Club (KA5 5RB) 2D 116
Baconsthorpe Castle. (NR25 6PS) 2D 78
Baddesley Clinton (B93 0DQ) 3F 61
Bala Lake Railway (LL23 7DD) 2A 70
Ballindalloch Castle (AB37 9AX) 5F 159
Balmoral Castle (AB35 5TB) 4G 151
Balvaird Castle (PH2 9PY) 2D 136
Balvenie Castle (AB55 4DH) 4H 159
Bamburgh Castle. (NE69 7DF) 1F 121
Bangor Cathedral. (LL57 1DN) 3E 81
Banham Zoo (NR16 2HE) 2C 66
Bannockburn Battle Site (FK7 0PL) 4G 135
Barbara Hepworth Mus. & Sculpture Gdn. (TR26 1AD) 2C 4
Barnard Castle. (DL12 8PR) 3D 104
Barnsdale Gdns. (LE15 8AH) 4G 75
Barrington Court (TA19 0NQ) 1G 13
Basildon Pk. (RG8 9NR) 4E 36
Basing House (RG24 8AE) 1E 25
Basingwerk Abbey (CH8 7GH) 3D 82
Bateman's (TN19 7DS) 3A 28
Bath Abbey (BA1 1LT) 187 (5C 34)
Bath Assembly Rooms (BA1 2QH) 187
Battle Abbey (TN33 0AD) 4B 28
The Battlefield Line Railway (CV13 0BS) 5A 74
The Battle of Britain Memorial (CT18 7JJ) 2G 29
Battle of Britain Memorial Flight Visitors Cen. (LN4 4SY) 5B 88
Battle of Hastings Site (TN33 0AD) 4B 28
Bayham Abbey (TN3 8BG) 2H 27
Beachy Head (BN20 7YA) 5G 27
Beamish (DH9 0RG) 4F 115
The Beatles Story (L3 4AD) Liverpool 200
Beaulieu Abbey (SO42 7ZN) 2B 16
Beauly Priory (IV4 7BL) 4H 157
Beaumaris Castle. (LL58 8AP) 3F 81
Beck Isle Mus. (YO18 8DU) 1B 100
Bedgebury National Pinetum (TN17 2SL) 2B 28
Bedruthan Steps (PL27 7UW) 2C 6
Beeston Castle & Woodland Pk. (CW6 9TX) 5H 83
Bekonscot Model Village & Railway (HP9 2PL) 1A 38
Belgrave Hall Mus. & Gdns. (LE4 5PE) 5C 74
Belmont House & Gdns. (ME13 0HH) 5D 40
Belsay Hall, Castle & Gdns. (NE20 0DX) 2D 115
Belton House (NG32 2LS) 2G 75
Belvoir Castle (NG32 1PD) 2F 75
Beningbrough Hall & Gdns. (YO30 1DD) 4H 99
Benington Lordship Gdns. (SG2 7BS) 3C 52
Ben Lawers (PH15 2PA) 4D 142
Ben Lomond (FK8 3TR) 3C 134
Ben Macdui (PH22 1RB) 4D 151
Benmore Botanic Gdn. (PA23 8QU) 1C 126
Ben Nevis (PH33 6SY) 1F 141
Benthall Hall (TF12 5RX) 5A 72
Berkeley Castle (GL13 9BQ) 2B 34
Berkhamsted Castle (HP4 1LJ) 5H 51
Berney Arms Windmill (NR31 9HU) 5G 79
Berrington Hall (HR6 0DW) 4H 59
Berry Pomeroy Castle (TQ9 6LJ) 2E 9
Bessie Surtees House (NE1 3JF) Newcastle upon Tyne 205
Beverley Minster (HU17 0DP) 1D 94
Bicton Gdns. (EX9 7BJ) 4D 12
Biddulph Grange Gdn. (ST8 7SD) 5C 84
Big Ben (SW1A 2PW) London 203
Bignor Roman Villa (RH20 1PH) 4A 26
Big Pit National Coal Mus. (NP4 9XP) 5F 47
Binham Priory (NR21 0DJ) 1B 78
Birmingham Mus. & Art Gallery (B3 3DH) 188
Bishop's Waltham Palace (SO32 1DP) 1D 16
Black Country Living Mus. (DY1 4SQ) 1D 60
Blackgang Chine (PO38 2HN) 5C 16
Blackhouse (HS2 9DB) 3F 171
Blackness Castle (EH49 7NH) 1D 128
Blackpool Pleasure Beach (FY4 1EZ) 1B 90
Blackpool Zoo (FY3 8PP) 1B 90
The Blackwell Arts & Crafts House (LA23 3JR) 5F 103
Blaenavon Ironworks (NP4 9RJ) 5F 47
Blaenavon World Heritage Cen. (NP4 9AS) 5F 47
Blair Castle (PH18 5TL) 2F 143
Blair Drummond Safari & Adventure Pk. (FK9 4UR) 4G 135
Blakeney Point (NR25 7SA) 1C 78
Blakesley Hall (B25 8RN) 2F 61
Blenheim Palace (OX20 1PX) 4C 50
Bletchley Pk. (MK3 6EB) 2G 51
Blickling Estate (NR11 6NF) 3D 78
Blists Hill Victorian Town (TF7 5DS) 5A 72
Bluebell Railway (TN22 3QL) 3E 27
Blue John Cavern (S33 8WP) 2F 85
Blue Reef Aquarium, Newquay (TR7 1DU) 2C 6
Blue Reef Aquarium, Hastings (TN34 3DW) 5C 28
Blue Reef Aquarium, Portsmouth (PO5 3PB) 209 (3E 17)
Blue Reef Aquarium, Tynemouth (NE30 4JF) 2G 115
Boath Doocot (IV12 5TD) 3D 158
Bodelwyddan Castle (LL18 5YA) 3B 82
Bodiam Castle. (TN32 5UA) 3B 28
Bodleian Library (OX1 3BG) Oxford 207
Bodmin & Wenford Railway (PL31 1AQ) 2E 7
Bodmin Moor (PL15 7TN) 5B 10
Bodnant Gdn. (LL28 5RE) 3H 81
Bodrhyddan Hall (LL18 5SB) 3C 82
Bolingbroke Castle (PE23 4HH) 4C 88
Bolsover Castle. (S44 6PR) 3B 86
Bolton Castle (DL8 4ET) 5D 104
Bolton Priory (BD23 6AL) 4C 98
Bonawe Historic Iron Furnace (PA35 1JQ) 5E 141
Bo'ness & Kinneil Railway (EH51 9AQ) 1C 128
Booth Mus. of Natural History (BN1 5AA) Brighton & Hove 189 (5D 27)
Borde Hill Gdn. (RH16 1XP) 3E 27
Borth Wild Animal Kingdom (SY24 5NA) 2F 57
Boscobel House (ST19 9AR) 5C 72
Boston Stump. (PE21 6NQ) 1C 76
Bosworth Field Battle Site (CV13 0AB) 5A 74
Bothwell Castle (G71 8BL) 4H 127
Boughton House (NN14 1BJ) 2G 63
Bowes Castle. (DL12 9LE) 3C 104
Bowes Mus. (DL12 8NP) 3D 104
Bowhill House & Country Estate (TD7 5ET) 2G 119
Bowood House & Gdns. (SN11 0LZ) 5E 35
Box Hill (KT20 7LF) 5C 38
Braemar Castle (AB35 5XR) 4F 151
Bramall Hall (SK7 3NX) 2C 84
Bramber Castle. (BN44 3FJ) 4C 26
Bramham Pk. (LS23 6ND) 5G 99
Brands Hatch (DA3 8NG) 4G 39
Brantwood (LA21 8AD) 5E 102
Breamore House (SP6 2DF) 1G 15
Brean Down (TA8 2RS) 1F 21
Brecon Beacons Nat. Pk. (CF44 9JG) 3C 46
Brecon Mountain Railway (CF48 2UP) 4D 46
Bressingham Steam & Gdns. (IP22 2AB) 2C 66
Brimham Rocks (HG3 4DW) 3E 98
Brindley Mill & The James Brindley Mus. (ST13 8FA) 5D 85
Brinkburn Priory (NE65 8AR) 5F 121
Bristol Aquarium (BS1 5TT) 189
Bristol Cathedral (BS1 5TJ) 189 (4A 34)
Bristol Zoo Gdns. (BS8 3HA) 189 (4A 34)
Britannia Bridge (LL61 5YH) 3E 81
British Airways i360 (BN1 2LN) Brighton & Hove 189 (5E 27)
British Golf Mus. (KY16 9AB) St Andrews 209 (2H 137)
British in India Mus. (BB9 8AD) 1G 91
British Library (NW1 2DB) London 203
British Motor Mus. (CV35 0BJ) 5A 62
British Mus. (WC1B 3DG) London 203
Broadlands (SO51 9ZD) 4B 24
Broads Nat. Pk. (NR3 1BJ) 5G 79
Broadway Tower (WR12 7LB) 2G 49
Brobury House Gdns. (HR3 6BS) 1G 47
Brockhampton Estate (WR6 5TB) 5A 60
Brockhole, Lake District Visitor Cen. (LA23 1LJ) 4E 103
Brodick Castle & Gdn. (KA27 8HY) 2E 123
Brodie Castle (IV36 2TE) 3D 159
Brodsworth Hall & Gdns. (DN5 7XJ) 4F 93
Brogdale (ME13 8XU) 5E 40
Bronllys Castle (LD3 0HL) 2E 47
Brontë Parsonage Mus. (BD22 8DR) 1A 92
Broseley Pipeworks. (TF12 5LX) 5A 72
Brougham Castle. (CA10 2AA) 2G 103
Brough Castle. (CA17 4EJ) 3A 104
Broughton Castle (OX15 5EB) 2C 50
Broughton House & Gdn. (DG6 4JX) 4D 111
Brownsea Island (BH13 7EE) 4F 15
Bruce's Stone (DG7 3SQ) 2C 110
Brunel's SS Great Britain (BS1 6TY) Bristol 189
Bubblecar Mus. (PE22 7AW) 1B 76
Buckfast Abbey (TQ11 0EE) 2D 8
Buckingham Palace (SW1A 1AA) London 202
Buckland Abbey (PL20 6EY) 2A 8
Buckler's Hard Maritime Mus. (SO42 7XB) 3C 16
Buildwas Abbey (TF8 7BW) 5A 72
Bungay Castle. (NR35 1DD) 2F 67
Bure Valley Railway (NR11 6BW) 3E 79
Burford House Gdns. (WR15 8HQ) 4H 59
Burghley (PE9 3JY) 5H 75
Burleigh Castle (KY13 9TD) 3D 136
Burnby Hall Gdns. & Mus. (YO42 2QF) 5C 100
Burns House Mus. (KA5 5BZ) 2D 117
Burton Agnes Hall (YO25 4ND) 3F 101
Burton Constable Hall (HU11 4LN) 1E 95
Buscot Pk. (SN7 8BU) 2H 35
Butser Ancient Farm (PO8 0QF) 1F 17
The Buttertubs (DL11 6DR) 5B 104
Buxton Pavilion Gdns. (SK17 6XN) 3E 85
Byland Abbey (YO61 4BD) 2H 99

C

Cadair Idris (LL40 1TN) 4F 69
Cadbury World (B30 1JR) 2E 61
Caerlaverock Castle (DG1 4RU) 3B 112
Caerleon Roman Fortress (NP18 1AY) 2G 33
Caernarfon Castle (LL55 2AY) 190 (4D 81)
Caerphilly Castle. (CF83 1JD) 3E 33
Cairngorms Nat. Pk. (PH26 3HG) 3D 151
Cairnpapple Hill (EH48 4NW) 2C 128
Caister Castle (NR30 5SN) 4H 79
Calanais Standing Stones (HS2 9DY) 4E 171
Caldey Island (SA70 7UH) 5F 43
Caldicot Castle. (NP26 5JB) 3H 33
Caledonian Railway (DD9 7AF) 3F 145
Calke Abbey (DE73 7LE) 3A 74
Calshot Castle. (SO45 1BR) 2C 16
Camber Castle (TN31 7TB) 4D 28
Cambo Gdns. (KY16 8QD) 2H 137
Cambridge University Botanic Gdn. (CB2 1JE) 191 (5D 64)
Camperdown Wildlife Cen. (DD2 4TF) 5C 144
Canal Mus. (NN12 7SE) 5E 63
Cannock Chase (WS12 4PW) 4D 73
Cannon Hall Mus. (S75 4AT) 4C 92
Canons Ashby House (NN11 3SD) 5C 62
Canterbury Cathedral (CT1 2EH) 190 (5F 41)
Capesthorne Hall (SK11 9JY) 3C 84
Cape Wrath (IV27 4QQ) 1C 166
Captain Cook Schoolroom Mus. (TS9 6NB) 3C 106
Cardiff Castle (CF10 3RB) 191 (4E 33)
Cardoness Castle (DG7 2EH) 4C 110
Carew Castle. (SA70 8SL) 4E 43
Carisbrooke Castle & Mus. (PO30 1XY) 4C 16
Carlisle Castle (CA3 8UR) 192 (4E 113)
Carlisle Cathedral (CA3 8TZ) 192 (4E 113)
Carlyle's Birthplace (DG11 3DG) 2C 112
Carnasserie Castle (PA31 8RQ) 3F 133
Carn Euny Ancient Village (TR20 8RB) 4B 4
Carreg Cennen Castle & Farm (SA19 6UA) 4G 45
Carsluith Castle (DG8 7DY) 4B 110
Cartmel Priory (LA11 6QQ) 2C 96
Castell Coch. (CF15 7JQ) 3E 33
Castell Dinas Bran (LL20 8DY) 1E 70
Castell y Bere (LL36 9TP) 5F 69
Castle Acre Castle. (PE32 2XB) 4H 77
Castle Acre Priory (PE32 2AA) 4H 77
Castle & Gdns. of Mey (KW14 8XH) 1E 169
Castle Campbell & Gdn. (FK14 7PP) 4B 136
Castle Drogo (EX6 6PB) 3H 11
Castle Fraser (AB51 7LD) 2E 152
Castle Howard (YO60 7DA) 2B 100
Castle Kennedy Gdns. (DG9 8SJ) 3G 109
Castle Leod (IV14 9AA) 3G 157
Castle Menzies (PH15 2JD) 4F 143
Castlerigg Stone Circle (CA12 4RN) 2D 102
Castle Rising Castle. (PE31 6AH) 3F 77
Catalyst Science Discovery Cen. (WA8 0DF) 2H 83
Cawdor Castle. (IV12 5RD) 4C 158
Cerne Giant (DT2 7TS) 2B 14
Chanonry Point (IV10 8SD) 3B 158
Charlecote Pk. (CV35 9ER) 5G 61
Charleston (BN8 6LL) 5F 27
Chartwell (TN16 1PS) 5F 39
Chastleton House (GL56 0SU) 3H 49
Chatsworth House (DE45 1PP) 3G 85
Chavenage House (GL8 8XP) 2D 34
Cheddar Gorge (BS40 7XT) 1H 21
Chedworth Roman Villa (GL54 3LJ) 4F 49
Cheltenham Racecourse (GL50 4SH) 3E 49
Chenies Manor House & Gdns. (WD3 6ER) 1B 38
Chepstow Castle (NP16 5EZ) 2A 34
Chepstow Racecourse (NP16 6EG) 2A 34
Chesil Beach (DT3 4ED) 4B 14
Chessington World of Adventures (KT9 2NE) 4C 38
Chester Cathedral (CH1 2HU) 192 (4G 83)
Chester Roman Amphitheatre (CH1 1RF) 192
Chesters Roman Fort & Mus. (NE46 4EU) 2C 114
Chester Zoo (CH2 1LH) 3G 83
Chichester Cathedral. (PO19 1PX) 2G 17
Chiddingstone Castle (TN8 7AD) 1F 27
Chillingham Castle. (NE66 5NJ) 2E 121
Chillingham Wild Cattle (NE66 5NJ) 2E 121
Chillington Hall (WV8 1RE) 5C 72
Chiltern Hills (RG9 6DR) 3E 37
Chiltern Open Air Mus. (HP8 4AB) 1B 38
Chirk Castle (LL14 5AF) 2E 71
Cholmondeley Castle Gdns. (SY14 8AH) 5H 83
Christchurch Castle & Norman House (BH23 1BW) 3G 15
Churnet Valley Railway (ST13 7EE) 5D 85
Chysauster Ancient Village (TR20 8XA) 3B 4
Cilgerran Castle. (SA43 2SF) 1B 44
Cissbury Ring (BN14 0SQ) 5C 26
Clandon Pk. (GU4 7RQ) 5B 38
Claremont Landscape Gdn. (KT10 9JG) 4C 38
Claydon (MK18 2EY) 3F 51
Clearwell Caves (GL16 8JR) 5A 48
Cleeve Abbey (TA23 0PS) 2D 20
Clevedon Court (BS21 6QU) 4H 33
Clifford's Tower (YO1 9SA) York 214 (4A 100)
Clifton Suspension Bridge (BS8 3PA) Bristol 189
Cliveden (SL6 0JA) 2A 38
Clouds Hill (BH20 7NQ) 3D 14
Clumber Pk. (S80 3BX) 3D 86
Clun Castle. (SY7 8JR) 2E 59
Clyde Muirshiel Regional Pk. (PA10 2PZ) 3D 126
Coalbrookdale Mus. of Iron (TF8 7DQ) 5A 72
Coalport China Mus. (TF8 7HT) 5A 72
Coed y Brenin Visitor Cen. (LL40 2HZ) 3G 69
Coggeshall Grange Barn (CO6 1RE) 3B 54
Coity Castle. (CF35 6AU) 3C 32
Colby Woodland Gdn. (SA67 8PP) 4F 43
Colchester Castle Mus. (CO1 1TJ) 3D 54
Colchester Zoo (CO3 0SL) 3C 54
Coleridge Cottage (TA5 1NQ) 3E 21
Coleton Fishacre (TQ6 0EQ) 3F 9
Colour Experience (BD1 2PW) Bradford 190
Colzium Walled Gdn. (G65 0PY) 2A 128
Combe Martin Wildlife & Dinosaur Pk. (EX34 0NG) 2F 19
Compton Acres (BH13 7ES) 4F 15
Compton Castle. (TQ3 1TA) 2E 9
Compton Verney (CV35 9HZ) 5H 61
Conisbrough Castle. (DN12 3BU) 1C 86
Conishead Priory (LA12 9QQ) 2C 96
Conkers (DE12 6GA) 4H 73
Constable Burton Hall Gdns. (DL8 5LJ) 5E 105
Conwy Castle. (LL32 8LD) 3G 81
Coombes & Churnet Nature Reserve. (ST13 7NN) 5E 85
Corbridge Roman Town (NE45 5NT) 3C 114
Corfe Castle (BH20 5EZ) 4E 15
Corgarff Castle (AB36 8YP) 3G 151
Corinium Mus. (GL7 2BX) 5F 49
Cornish Seal Sanctuary (TR12 6UG) 4E 5
Corrieshalloch Gorge (IV23 2PJ) 1E 156
Corsham Court (SN13 0BZ) 4D 35
Cotehele (PL12 6TA) 2A 8
Coton Manor Gdn. (NN6 8RQ) 3D 62
Cotswold Farm Pk. (GL54 5UG) 3G 49
Cotswold Hills (GL8 8NU) 2E 35
Cotswold Water Pk. (GL7 5TL) 2F 35
Cottesbrooke Hall & Gdns. (NN6 8PF) 3E 62
Cotton Mechanical Music Mus. (IP14 4QN) 4C 66
Coughton Court (B49 5JA) 4E 61
The Courts Gdn. (BA14 6RR) 5D 34
Coventry Cathedral (CV1 5AB) 192 (3H 61)
Coventry Transport Mus. (CV1 1JD) 192 (3H 61)
Cowdray House (GU29 9AL) 4G 25
Cragside (NE65 7PX) 4E 121
Craigievar Castle (AB33 8JF) 3C 152
Craigmillar Castle. (EH16 4SY) 2F 129
Craignethan Castle (ML11 9PL) 5B 128
Craigston Castle (AB53 5PX) 3E 161
Cranborne Manor Gdns. (BH21 5PS) 1F 15
Cranwell Aviation Heritage Cen. (NG34 8QR) 1H 75
Crarae Gdn. (PA32 8YA) 4G 133
Crathes Castle, Gdn. & Estate (AB31 5QJ) 4E 153
Creswell Crags (S80 3LH) 3C 86
Crewe Heritage Cen. (CW1 2DD) 5B 84
Criccieth Castle. (LL52 0DP) 2D 69
Crichton Castle (EH37 5XA) 3G 129
Crich Tramway Village (DE4 5DP) 5H 85
Croft Castle (HR6 9PW) 4G 59
Croft Circuit (DL2 2PL) 4F 105
Cromford Mill (DE4 3RQ) 5G 85

270 A-Z Great Britain Road Atlas

Cromwell Mus. (PE29 3LF)................3B 64
Crookston Castle (G53 5RR)................3G 127
Croome (WR8 9JS)................1D 49
Crossraguel Abbey (KA19 8HQ)................4B 116
Croxden Abbey ST14 5JG)................2E 73
Croxteth (LL12 0HB)................1G 83
Cruachan Power Station (PA33 1AN)................1H 133
Culloden Battlefield Visitor Cen. (IV2 5EU)................4B 158
Culloden Battle Site (IV2 5EU)................4B 158
Culross Palace (KY12 8JH)................1C 128
Culzean Wildlife Pk. (KA19 8LE)................3B 116
Curraghs Wildlife Pk. (IM7 5EA)................2C 108
Cusworth Hall. (DN5 7TU)................4F 93
Cymer Abbey (LL40 2HE)................4G 69

D

Dalemain (CA11 0HB)................2F 103
Dales Countryside Mus. (DL8 3NT)................5B 104
Dallas Dhu Historic Distillery (IV36 2RR)................3E 159
Dalmeny House (EH30 9TQ)................2E 129
Darby Houses (TF8 7DQ)................5A 72
Dartington Crystal (EX38 7AN)................1E 11
Dartington Hall Gdns. (TQ9 6EL)................2E 9
Dartmoor Nat. Pk. (TQ13 9JQ)................4F 11
Dartmoor Zoo (PL7 5DG)................3B 8
Dartmouth Castle (TQ6 0JN)................3E 9
Dartmouth Steam Railway (TQ4 6AF)................3E 9
Dawyck Botanic Gdn. (EH45 9JU)................1D 118
Deal Castle. (CT14 7BA)................5H 41
Dean Castle (KA3 1XB)................1D 116
Dean Forest Railway (GL15 4ET)................5B 48
Deene Pk. (NN17 3EW)................1G 63
The Deep (HU1 4DP)................Kingston upon Hull 199 (2E 94)
Deep Sea World (KY11 1JR)................1E 129
Delamere Forest Pk. (CW8 2JD)................3H 83
Delgatie Castle (AB53 5TD)................3E 161
The Den & The Glen (AB12 5FT)................4F 153
Denbigh Castle. (LL16 3NB)................4C 82
Devil's Dyke (BN45 7DE)................4D 26
Devil's Punch Bowl (GU26 6AB)................3G 25
Dewa Roman Experience (CH1 1NL)................Chester 192
DH Lawrence Birthplace Mus. (NG16 3AW)................1B 74
Dickens House Mus. (CT10 1QS)................4H 41
Didcot Railway Cen. (OX11 7NJ)................2D 36
Dinefwr Castle (SA19 6PF)................3G 45
Dinefwr Pk. (SA19 6RT)................3G 45
Dinorwig Power Station (LL55 4UR)................5E 81
Dinosaur Adventure (NR9 5JW)................4D 78
The Dinosaur Mus. (DT1 1EN)................3B 14
Dirleton Castle & Gdn. (EH39 5ER)................1B 130
Discovery Mus. (NE1 4JA)................Newcastle upon Tyne 205 (3F 115)
Discovery Point, Dundee (DD1 4XA)................194
Dock Mus. (LA14 2PW)................3A 96
Doddington Hall & Gdns. (LN6 4RU)................3F 87
Doddington Place Gdns. (ME9 0BB)................5D 40
Dolaucothi Gold Mines (SA19 8RR)................2G 45
Dolbadarn Castle (LL55 4SU)................5E 81
Dolforwyn Castle (SY15 6JH)................1D 58
Dolwyddelan Castle. (LL25 0JD)................5G 81
Doncaster Racecourse (DN2 6BB)................4G 93
Donington Pk. (DE74 2RP)................3B 74
Donnington Castle. (RG14 2LE)................5C 36
Dorfold Hall (CW5 8LD)................5A 84
Dorothy Clive Gdn. (TF9 4EU)................2B 72
Doune Castle. (FK16 6EA)................3G 135
Dove Cottage (LA22 9SH)................4E 103
Dovedale (DE6 1NL)................5F 85
Dover Castle (CT16 1HU)................193 (1H 29)
Down House (BR6 7JT)................4F 39
Dozmary Pool (PL15 7TP)................5C 6
Drayton Manor Theme Pk. (B78 3TW)................5F 73
Drum Castle & Gdn. (AB31 5EY)................3E 153
Drumlanrig Castle (DG3 4AQ)................5A 118
Drummond Gdns. (PH5 2AA)................2H 135
Drusillas (BN26 5QS)................5G 27
Dryburgh Abbey (TD6 0RQ)................1H 119
Dryslwyn Castle. (SA32 8JQ)................3F 45
Duart Castle (PA64 6AP)................5B 140
Dudmaston Estate (WV15 6QN)................2B 60
Duff House Country Gallery (AB45 3SX)................2D 160
Duffus Castle (IV30 5RH)................2E 159
The Dukeries (S80 3BT)................3D 86
Dumbarton Castle (G82 1JJ)................2F 127
Dunblane Cathedral. (FK15 0AQ)................3G 135
Dun Carloway (HS2 9AZ)................3D 171
Duncombe Pk. (YO62 5EB)................1A 100
Dundonald Castle. (KA2 9HD)................1C 116
Dundrennan Abbey (DG6 4QH)................5E 111
Dunfermline Abbey. (KY12 7PE)................1D 129
Dungeon Ghyll Force (LA22 9JY)................4D 102
Dunge Valley Rhododendron Gdns. (SK23 7RF)................3D 85
Dunham Massey (WA14 4SJ)................2B 84
Dunkeld Cathedral. (PH8 0AW)................4H 143
Dunkery Beacon (TA24 7AT)................2B 20
Dunnet Head (KW14 8XS)................1E 169
Dunninald (DD10 9TD)................5F 153
Dunnottar Castle (AB39 2TL)................5F 153
Dunrobin Castle (KW10 6SF)................3F 165
Dunstaffnage Castle (PA37 1PZ)................5C 140
Dunstanburgh Castle (NE66 3TG)................2G 121
Dunster Castle. (TA24 6SL)................2C 20
Dunvegan Castle (IV55 8WF)................4B 154
Durdle Door (BH20 5PU)................4D 14
Durham Cathedral (DH1 3EH)................194 (5F 115)
Dyffryn Gdns. (CF5 6SU)................4D 32
Dylan Thomas Boathouse (SA33 4SD)................3H 43
Dynamic Earth (EH8 8AS)................Edinburgh 194
Dyrham Pk., Gloucestershire (SN14 8ER)................4C 34

E

Eagle Heights Wildlife Pk. (DA4 0JB)................4G 39
Easby Abbey (DL10 7JU)................4E 105
East Anglian Railway Mus. (CO6 2DS)................3B 54
East Bergholt Place Gdn. (CO7 6UP)................2D 54
East Kent Railway (CT15 7PD)................1G 29
East Lambrook Manor Gdns. (TA13 5HH)................1H 13
East Lancashire Railway (BB4 6AG)................4G 91
Eastnor Castle (HR8 1RD)................2C 48
East Pool Mine (TR15 3NP)................4A 6
East Riddlesden Hall (BD20 5EL)................5C 98
East Somerset Railway (BA4 4QP)................2B 22

Eden Project (PL24 2SG)................3E 7
Edinburgh Castle (EH1 2NG)................194 (2F 129)
Edinburgh St Giles' Cathedral (EH1 1RE)................194 (2F 129)
Edinburgh Zoo. (EH12 6TS)................2F 129
Edzell Castle & Gdn. (DD9 7UE)................2E 145
Egglestone Abbey (DL12 9TN)................3D 104
Eilean Donan Castle (IV40 8DX)................1A 148
Elcho Castle. (PH2 8QQ)................1D 136
Electric Mountain (LL55 4UR)................4E 81
Elgar's Birthplace (WR2 6RH)................5C 60
Elgin Cathedral. (IV30 1EL)................2G 159
Eltham Palace & Gdns. (SE9 5QE)................3F 39
Elton Hall House & Gdns. (PE8 6SH)................1H 63
Ely Cathedral. (CB7 4DL)................2E 65
Embsay & Bolton Abbey Steam Railway (BD23 6AF)................4C 98
Emmetts Gdn. (TN14 6BA)................5F 39
Enginuity (TF8 7DQ)................5A 72
Epping Ongar Railway (CM5 9BN)................5F 53
Epsom Downs Racecourse (KT18 5LQ)................5D 38
Erddig (LL13 0YT)................1F 71
Etal Castle. (TD12 4TN)................1D 120
Eureka! The National Children's Mus. (HX1 2NE)................2A 92
Euston Hall (IP24 2QW)................3A 66
Ewloe Castle. (CH5 3BZ)................4E 83
Exbury Gdns. (SO45 1AZ)................2C 16
Exeter Cathedral (EX1 1HS)................195 (3C 12)
Exmoor Nat. Pk. (TA22 9HL)................3B 20
Eyam Hall (S32 5QW)................3G 85
Eye Castle. (IP23 7AP)................3D 66
Eynsford Castle. (DA4 0AA)................4G 39

F

Fairbourne Steam Railway (LL38 2PZ)................4F 69
Fairhaven Woodland & Water Gdn. (NR13 6DZ)................4F 79
Falkirk Wheel (FK1 4RS)................1B 128
Falkland Palace (KY15 7BU)................3E 137
Falls of Glomach (IV40 8DS)................1C 148
Farleigh Hungerford Castle. (BA2 7RS)................1C 22
Farmland Mus. & Denny Abbey (CB25 9PQ)................4D 65
Farnborough Hall (OX17 1DU)................1C 50
Farne Islands (NE68 7SY)................1G 121
Farnham Castle Keep. (GU9 0AE)................2G 25
Felbrigg Hall (NR11 8PR)................2D 78
Fell Foot Pk. (LA12 8NN)................1C 96
Ferniehirst Castle (TD8 6NX)................3A 120
Festiniog Railway (LL49 9NF)................1F 69
Fiddleford Manor (DT10 2BU)................1D 14
Finchale Priory (DH1 5SH)................5F 115
Finch Foundry (EX20 2NW)................3G 11
Fingal's Cave (PA73 6NA)................5E 138
Finlaystone Country Estate (PA14 6TJ)................2E 127
Firle Place (BN8 6LP)................5F 27
The Firs (WR2 6RH)................5C 60
Fishbourne Roman Palace & Gdns. (PO19 3QR)................2G 17
Fitzwilliam Mus. (CB2 1RB)................Cambridge 191 (5D 64)
Five Sisters of Kintail (IV40 8HQ)................2B 148
Flambards (TR13 0QA)................4D 4
Flamingo Land (YO17 6UX)................2B 100
Fleet Air Arm Mus. (BA22 8HT)................4A 22
Flint Castle. (CH6 5PE)................3E 83
Fonmon Castle. (CF62 3ZN)................5D 32
Forde Abbey & Gdns. (TA20 4LU)................2G 13
Ford Green Hall. (ST6 1NG)................5C 84
Forest of Dean (GL15 4SL)................5B 48
Fort George (IV2 7TD)................3B 158
Forth Bridge (EH30 9TB)................1E 129
Fort Nelson (Royal Armouries) (PO17 6AN)................2E 16
Fountains Abbey & Studley Royal Water Gdn. (HG4 3DY)................3E 99
Foxfield Steam Railway (ST11 9BG)................1D 72
Foxton Locks (LE16 7RA)................2D 62
Framlingham Castle. (IP13 9BP)................4E 67
Froghall Wharf (ST10 2HH)................1E 73
Furness Abbey (LA13 0PG)................2A 96
Furzey Gdns. (SO43 7EL)................1A 16
Fyne Court (TA5 2EQ)................3F 21
Fyvie Castle. (AB53 8JS)................5E 161

G

Gainsborough Old Hall (DN21 2NB)................1F 87
Gainsborough's House (CO10 2EU)................1B 54
Gallery of Modern Art, Glasgow (G1 3AH)................196
Galloway Forest Pk. (DG8 6TA)................1B 110
Galloway House Gdns. (DG8 8HF)................5B 110
The Gdn. House (PL20 7LQ)................2A 8
Gawsworth Hall (SK11 9RN)................4C 84
Gawthorpe Hall (BB12 8UA)................1G 91
Geevor Tin Mine Mus. (TR19 7EW)................3A 4
George Stephenson's Birthplace (NE41 8BP)................3E 115
The Georgian House (EH2 4DR)................Edinburgh 194
Gibside (NE16 6BG)................4E 115
Gilbert White's House (GU34 3JH)................3F 25
Gisborough Priory (TS14 6BU)................3D 106
Gladstone Pottery Mus. (ST3 1PQ)................1D 72
Gladstone's Land (EH1 2NT)................Edinburgh 194
Glamis Castle (DD8 1QJ)................4C 144
Glasgow St Mary's Episcopal Cathedral. (G4 9JB)................3G 127
Glastonbury Abbey (BA6 9EL)................3A 22
Glastonbury Tor (BA6 8BG)................3A 22
Glenarn (G84 8LL)................1D 126
Glenbuchat Castle (AB38 8TN)................2A 152
Glencoe Gorge (PH50 4SG)................3F 141
Glendurgan Gdn. (TR11 5JZ)................4E 5
Glenfinnan Monument (PH37 4LT)................5B 148
Glenluce Abbey (DG8 0LW)................4G 109
Glenmore Forest Pk. (PH22 1QT)................2D 151
Glenwhan Gdns. (DG8 0PH)................4G 109
Gloucester Cathedral (GL1 2LR)................196 (4D 48)
Gloucestershire Warwickshire Steam Railway (GL54 5DT)................2F 49
Gloucester Waterways Mus. (GL1 2EH)................196 (4D 48)
Glynde Place (BN8 6SX)................5F 27
Godinton House & Gdns. (TN23 3BP)................1D 28
Godolphin (TR13 9RE)................3D 4

Goodnestone Pk. Gdns. (CT3 1PL)................5G 41
Goodrich Castle. (HR9 6HY)................3A 48
Goodwood House (PO18 0PX)................2G 17
Goodwood Racecourse (PO18 0PS)................1G 17
Gordale Scar (BD23 4DL)................3B 98
Grampian Transport Mus. (AB33 8AE)................2C 152
The Grange at Northington (SO24 9TG)................3D 24
Graves Gallery (S1 1XZ)................Sheffield 210 (2A 86)
Graythwaite Hall Gdns. (LA12 8BA)................5E 103
Great Central Railway (LE11 1RW)................4C 74
Great Central Railway (Nottingham) (NG1 6NX)................2C 74
Great Chalfield Manor & Gdn. (SN12 8NH)................5D 34
Great Comp Gdn. (TN15 8QS)................5H 39
Great Dixter (TN31 6PH)................3C 28
Great North Mus.: Hancock (NE2 4PT)................Newcastle upon Tyne 205
Greenbank House & Gdn. (G76 8RB)................4G 127
Greenknowe Tower (TD3 6JL)................5C 130
Greenway (TQ5 0ES)................3E 9
Gretna Green Famous Blacksmith's Shop (DG16 5EA)................3E 112
Grey Mare's Tail Waterfall, Moffat (DG10 9LH)................3D 118
Greys Court (RG9 4PG)................3F 37
Grimes Graves (IP26 5DE)................1H 65
Grimsby Fishing Heritage Cen. (DN31 1UZ)................4F 95
Grimspound (PL20 6TB)................4H 11
Grimsthorpe Castle (PE10 0LZ)................3H 75
Grizedale Forest (LA22 0QJ)................5E 103
Groombridge Place Gdns. (TN3 9QG)................2G 27
Grove Mus. (IM8 3UA)................2D 108
Guildhall, Lavenham (CO10 9QZ)................1C 54
Gulliver's Kingdom, Matlock Bath. (DE4 3PG)................5G 85
Gulliver's Land, Milton Keynes (MK15 0DT)................204 (2G 51)
Gulliver's World, Warrington (WA5 9YZ)................1H 83
Gunby Hall (PE23 5SS)................4D 88
Gwydir Castle (LL26 0PN)................4H 81

H

Haddo House (AB41 7EQ)................5F 161
Haddon Hall (DE45 1LA)................4G 85
Hadleigh Castle (SS7 2AP)................2C 40
Hadrian's Wall, Winshields (NE47 7AW)................3A 114
Hailes Abbey (GL54 5PB)................3F 49
Hailes Castle (EH41 3SB)................2B 130
Hall i' th' Wood Mus. (BL1 8UA)................3F 91
Hall Place & Gdns. (DA5 1PQ)................3G 39
Hamerton Zoo Pk. (PE28 5RE)................2A 64
Ham House & Gdns. (TW10 7RS)................3C 38
Hammerwood Pk. (RH19 3QE)................2F 27
Hampden Pk. (G42 9AY)................3G 127
Hampton Court Castle & Gdns. (HR6 0PN)................5H 59
Hampton Court Palace & Gdns. (KT8 9AU)................4C 38
Hanbury Hall (WR9 7EA)................4D 60
Hardknott Roman Fort (LA20 6EQ)................4D 102
Hardwick Hall (S44 5QJ)................4B 86
Hardy Monument (DT2 9HY)................4B 14
Hardy's Cottage (DT2 8QJ)................3C 14
Hare Hill (SK10 4QA)................3C 84
Harewood House (LS17 9LG)................5F 99
Harley Gallery (S80 3LW)................3C 86
Hartland Abbey & Gdns. (EX39 6DT)................4C 18
Harvington Hall (DY10 4LR)................3C 60
Harwich Redoubt (CO12 3NL)................2F 55
Hatchlands Pk. (GU4 7RT)................5B 38
Hatfield House (AL9 5NQ)................5C 52
Haughley Abbey (SY4 4RW)................4H 71
Haverfordwest Castle. (SA61 2BW)................3D 42
Haverfordwest Priory. (SA61 1RN)................3D 42
Hawk Conservancy Trust (SP11 8DY)................2B 24
Haydock Pk. Racecourse (WA12 0HQ)................1H 83
Head of Steam - Darlington Railway Mus. (DL3 6ST)................3F 105
Heale Gdns. (SP4 6NT)................3G 23
Heaton Hall (M25 2SW)................4G 91
Hedingham Castle (CO9 3DJ)................2A 54
Heights of Abraham (DE4 3PB)................5G 85
Hellens (HR8 2LY)................2B 48
Helmingham Hall Gdns. (IP14 6EF)................5D 66
Helmshore Mills Textile Mus. (BB4 4NP)................2F 91
Helmsley Castle. (YO62 5AB)................1A 100
Helvellyn (CA12 4TP)................3E 103
Heptonstall Mus. (HX7 7PL)................2H 91
Hereford Cathedral (HR1 2NG)................197 (2A 48)
Hereford Cider Mus. (HR4 0LW)................197 (2A 48)
Hergest Croft Gdns. (HR5 3EG)................5E 59
Hermitage Castle (TD9 0LU)................5H 119
Herstmonceux Castle & Gdns. (BN27 1RN)................4H 27
Hestercombe (TA2 8LG)................4F 21
Hever Castle & Gdns. (TN8 7NG)................1F 27
Hexham Abbey (NE46 3NB)................3C 114
Hidcote (GL55 6LR)................1G 49
High Beeches Gdns. (RH17 6HQ)................2D 27
Highclere Castle (RG20 9RN)................1C 24
Highland Folk Mus. (PH20 1LA)................4B 150
Highland Wildlife Pk. (PH21 1NL)................1D 126
Hill of Tarvit Mansionhouse & Gdns. (KY15 5PB)................2F 137
Hill Top (LA22 0LF)................5E 103
Hinton Ampner. (SO24 0LA)................4D 24
Hirsel (TD12 4LP)................5E 131
The Historic Dockyard Chatham (ME4 4TZ)................Medway Towns 204 (4B 40)
HMS Victory (PO1 3LJ)................Portsmouth 209
HMS Warrior 1860 (PO1 3QX)................Portsmouth 209
Hodnet Hall Gdns. (TF9 3NN)................3A 72
Hoghton Tower (PR5 0SH)................2E 90
Hog's Back (GU3 1AQ)................1A 26
The Holburne Mus. (BA2 4DB)................Bath 187 (5C 34)
Holdenby House Gdns. & Falconry Cen. (NN6 8DJ)................4D 62
Holehird Gdns. (LA23 1NP)................4F 103
Holker Hall & Gdns. (LA11 7PL)................2C 96
Holkham Hall (NR23 1AB)................1A 78
Hollycombe Steam in the Country (GU30 7LP)................4G 25
Holst Birthplace Mus. (GL52 2AY)................Cheltenham 192 (3E 49)

Holy Jesus Hospital (NE1 2AS)................Newcastle upon Tyne 205
Holyrood Abbey (EH8 8DX)................Edinburgh 194 (2F 129)
Holyroodhouse (EH8 8DG)................2D 129
Hop Farm Family Pk. (TN12 6PY)................1A 28
Houghton Hall (PE31 6TZ)................3G 77
Houghton House (MK45 2EZ)................2A 52
Houghton Lodge Gdns. (SO20 6LQ)................3B 24
House of Dun (DD10 9LG)................3F 145
House of Manannan Mus. (IM5 1TA)................3B 108
House of the Binns (EH49 7NA)................1D 128
Houses of Parliament (SW1A 0RS)................London 203
Housesteads Roman Fort & Mus. (NE47 6NN)................3A 114
Hoveton Hall Gdns. (NR12 8RJ)................3F 79
Hovingham Hall (YO62 4LU)................2A 100
Howick Hall Gdns. (NE66 3LB)................3G 121
Howletts Wild Animal Pk. (CT4 5EL)................5F 41
Hughenden Manor (HP14 4LA)................2G 37
Hugh Miller Mus. & Birthplace Cottage (IV11 8XA)................2B 158
Hunstanton Sea Life Sanctuary (PE36 5BH)................1F 77
Hunterian Mus. & Art Gallery. (G12 8QQ)................3G 127
Huntingtower Castle (PH1 3JL)................1C 136
Huntly Castle (AB54 4SH)................4C 160
Hurst Castle (SO41 0TP)................4B 16
Hutton-in-the-Forest (CA11 9TH)................1F 103
Hylands House & Gdns. (CM2 8WQ)................5G 53

I

Ickworth (IP29 5QE)................4H 65
Iford Manor (Peto Gdn.) (BA15 2BA)................1D 22
Ightham Mote (TN15 0NT)................5G 39
Ilam Pk. (DE6 2AZ)................5F 85
Ilfracombe Aquarium (EX34 9EQ)................2F 19
Imperial War Mus. Duxford (CB22 4QR)................1E 53
Imperial War Mus. London, Main Mus. (SE1 6HZ)................203
Imperial War Mus. North. (M17 1TZ)................1C 84
Inchcolm Abbey (KY3 0XR)................1E 129
Inchmahome Priory (FK8 3RD)................3E 135
Ingatestone Hall (CM4 9NS)................1A 40
International Bomber Command Cen. (LN4 2HQ)................4G 87
International Cen. for Birds of Prey (GL18 1JJ)................3C 48
Inveraray Castle (PA32 8XE)................3H 133
Inveresk Lodge Gdn. (EH21 7TE)................2G 129
Invererwe Gdn. (IV22 2LG)................5C 162
Inverlochy Castle (PH33 6TQ)................1F 141
Inverness Mus. & Art Gallery (IV2 3EB)................198 (4A 158)
Iona (PA76 6SP)................2A 132
Iron Bridge. (TF8 7JP)................5A 72
Isel Hall (CA13 0QG)................1C 102
Isle of Man Steam Railway (IM1 4LL)................4C 108
Isle of Wight Steam Railway (PO33 4DS)................4D 16
Ivinghoe Beacon (LU6 2EG)................4H 51
Izaak Walton's Cottage (ST15 0PA)................3C 72

J

Jane Austen's House Mus. (GU34 1SD)................3F 25
Jarlshof Prehistoric & Norse Settlement (ZE3 9JN)................10E 173
Jedburgh Abbey (TD8 6JQ)................3A 120
Jervaulx Abbey (HG4 4PH)................1D 98
JM Barrie's Birthplace (DD8 4BX)................3C 144
Jodrell Bank Discovery Cen. (SK11 9DL)................3B 84
Jorvik Viking Cen. (YO1 9WT)................York 214 (4A 100)

K

Kedleston Hall (DE22 5JH)................1H 73
Keighley & Worth Valley Railway (BD22 8NJ)................1A 92
Kelburn Castle & Country Cen. (KA29 0BE)................4D 126
Keld Chapel (CA10 3QF)................3G 103
Kelham Island Mus. (S3 8RY)................Sheffield 210
Kellie Castle & Gdn. (KY10 2RF)................3H 137
Kelmarsh Hall & Gdns. (NN6 9LY)................3E 63
Kelmscott Manor (GL7 3HJ)................2A 36
Kelso Abbey (TD5 7BB)................1B 120
Kelvingrove Art Gallery & Mus. (G3 8AG)................3G 127
Kempton Pk. Racecourse (TW16 5AE)................3C 38
Kenilworth Castle. (CV8 1NE)................3G 61
Kent & East Sussex Railway (TN30 6HE)................3C 28
Kentwell (CO10 9BA)................1C 54
Kenwood House (NW3 7JR)................2D 38
Keswick Mus. & Gallery. (CA12 4NF)................2D 102
Kew Palace (TW9 3AB)................3C 38
Kidwelly Castle. (SA17 5BQ)................5E 45
Kielder Water & Forest Pk. (NE48 1QZ)................1H 113
Kiftsgate Court Gdns. (GL55 6LN)................1G 49
Kilchurn Castle (PA33 1AF)................1A 134
Kildrummy Castle (AB33 8RA)................2B 152
Killerton (EX5 3LE)................2C 12
Kilmartin Glen Prehistoric Sites (PA31 8RQ)................4F 133
Kilmartin House Mus. (PA31 8RQ)................4F 133
Kinder Scout (S33 7ZJ)................2E 85
King's College Chapel (CB2 1TN)................Cambridge 191 (5D 64)
Kingston Bagpuize House (OX13 5AX)................2C 36
Kingston Lacy (BH21 4EA)................2E 15
Kingston Maurward Gdns. & Animal Pk. (DT2 8PY)................3C 14
Kinnersley Castle (HR3 6QF)................1G 47
Kiplin Hall (DL10 6AT)................5F 105
Kirby Hall (NN17 3EN)................1G 63
Kirby Muxloe Castle. (LE9 2DH)................5C 74
Kirkham Priory (YO60 7JS)................3B 100
Kirklees Light Railway (HD8 9XJ)................3C 92
Kirkstall Abbey (LS5 3EH)................1C 92
Kirkwall Cathedral. (KW15 1JF)................6D 172
Knaresborough Castle. (HG5 8BB)................4F 99
Knebworth House (SG3 6PY)................3C 52
Knightshayes (EX16 7RQ)................1C 12
Knockhill Motor Circuit (KY12 9TF)................4C 136
Knole (TN15 0RP)................5G 39
Knoll Gdns. (BH21 7ND)................2F 15
Knowsley Safari Pk. (L34 4AN)................1G 83

Lacock Abbey – Royal Yacht Britannia

L

Lacock Abbey (SN15 2LG) 5E **35**
*Lady Lever Art Gallery. (CH62 5EQ) 2F **83***
The Lady of the North (NE23 8AU) 2F **115**
Laing Art Gallery (NE1 8AG) **Newcastle upon Tyne 205**
Lake District Nat. Pk. (LA9 7RL) 3E **103**
Lakeside & Haverthwaite Railway (LA12 8AL) 1C **96**
Lamb House (TN31 7ES) 3D **28**
Lamphey Bishop's Palace (SA71 5NT) 4E **43**
Lamport Hall & Gdns. (NN6 9HD) 3E **63**
*Lancaster Castle. (LA1 1YJ) 3D **96***
Landmark Forest Adventure Pk. (PH23 3AJ) 1D **150**
Land's End (TR19 7AA) 4A **4**
Lanercost Priory (CA8 2HQ) 3G **113**
Langdale Pikes (LA22 9JY) 4D **102**
Langley Chapel (SY5 7HU) 1H **59**
Lanhydrock (PL30 5AD) 2E **7**
Lappa Valley Steam Railway (TR8 5LX) 3C **6**
Larmer Tree Gdns. (SP5 5PZ) 1E **15**
*Laugharne Castle. (SA33 4SA) 3H **43***
*Launceston Castle. (PL15 7DR) 4D **10***
Launceston Steam Railway (PL15 8DA) 4D **10**
Lauriston Castle (EH4 5QD) 2F **129**
Laxey Wheel (IM4 7NL) 3D **108**
Layer Marney Tower (CO5 9US) 4C **54**
Leeds Castle (ME17 1PL) 5C **40**
Leeds City Mus. (LS1 3AA) **199**
Legoland (SL4 4AY) 3A **38**
Leighton Buzzard Railway (LU7 4TN) 3H **51**
Leighton Hall (LA5 9ST) 2E **97**
Leiston Abbey (IP16 4TD) 4G **67**
Leith Hall (AB54 4NQ) 1C **152**
Leith Hill (RH5 6LX) 1C **26**
Lennoxlove House (EH41 4NZ) 2B **130**
Leonardslee Gdns. (RH13 6PP) 3D **26**
Levant Mine & Beam Engine (TR19 7SX) 3A **4**
Levens Hall (LA8 0PD) 1D **97**
*Lewes Castle. (BN7 1YE) 4F **27***
*Lichfield Cathedral. (WS13 7LD) 4F **73***
Life (NE1 4EP) **Newcastle upon Tyne 205**
Lightwater Valley (HG4 3HT) 2E **99**
Lilleshall Abbey (TF10 9HW) 4B **72**
Lincoln Castle (LN1 3AA) **198** (3G **87**)
Lincoln Cathedral (LN2 1PZ) **198** (3G **87**)
Lincolnshire Road Transport Mus. (LN6 3QT) 4G **87**
Lindisfarne (TD15 2SF) 5H **131**
Lindisfarne Castle (TD15 2SH) 5H **131**
Lindisfarne Priory (TD15 2RX) 5H **131**
Linlithgow Palace (EH49 7AL) 2D **128**
Linton Zoo (CB21 4XN) 1F **53**
Little Clarendon (SP3 5DZ) 3F **23**
Little Malvern Court (WR14 4JN) 1C **48**
Little Moreton Hall (CW12 4SD) 5C **84**
*Liverpool Cathedral Church of Christ. (L1 7AZ) 2F **83***
Liverpool Metropolitan RC Cathedral of Christ the King (L3 5TQ) **200** (1F **83**)
Lizard Point (TR12 7NU) 5E **5**
Llanberis Lake Railway (LL55 3HB) 4E **81**
Llanerchaeron (SA48 8DG) 4D **57**
Llangollen Railway (LL20 7AJ) 1D **70**
*Llansteffan Castle. (SA33 5JX) 4D **44***
*Llawhaden Castle. (SA67 8HL) 3E **43***
Llechwedd Slate Caverns (LL41 3NB) 1G **69**
Llywernog Silver-Lead Mine (SY23 3AB) 2G **57**
Lochalsh Woodland Gdn. (IV40 8DN) 1F **147**
Loch Doon Castle (KA6 7QE) 5D **117**
Lochleven Castle (KY13 8ET) 3D **136**
Loch Lomond (G83 8PA) 4C **134**
Loch Lomond & The Trossachs Nat. Pk. (FK8 3UA) 2D **134**
*Lochmaben Castle. (DG11 1JE) 1B **112***
Loch Ness Cen. & Exhibition (IV63 6TU) 5H **157**
Locomotion (DL4 1PQ) 2F **105**
The Lodge Nature Reserve (SG19 2DL) 1B **52**
Lodge Pk. (GL54 3PP) 4G **49**
Logan Botanic Gdn. (DG9 9ND) 5F **109**
Logan Fish Pond & Marine Life Cen. (DG9 9NF) 5F **109**
London Dungeon (SE1 2SZ) **203**
London Eye (SE1 7PB) **203**
London Film Mus. (WC2E 7BN) **203**
London Zoo (NW1 4RY) **202** (2D **39**)
Long Cross Victorian Gdns. (PL29 3TF) 1D **6**
Longleat Safari & Adventure Pk. (BA12 7NW) 2D **22**
Long Mynd (SY7 8BH) 1G **59**
Longthorpe Tower (PE3 6SU) 1A **64**
*Longtown Castle. (HR2 0LE) 3G **47***
*Lord Leycester Hospital & The Master's Gdn. (CV34 4BH) 4G **61***
Loseley Pk. (GU3 1HS) 1A **26**
The Lost Gdns. of Heligan (PL26 6EN) 4D **6**
Lotherton Hall (LS25 3EB) 1E **93**
Loughwood Meeting House (EX13 7DU) 3F **13**
*Ludgershall Castle. (SP11 9QS) 1A **24***
*Ludlow Castle. (SY8 1AY) 3H **59***
Lullingstone Castle & World Gdn. (DA4 0JA) 4G **39**
Lullingstone Roman Villa (DA4 0JA) 4G **39**
Lulworth Castle & Pk. (BH20 5QS) 4D **14**
Lundy Island (EX39 2LY) 2B **18**
Lyddington Bede House (LE15 9LZ) 1F **63**
*Lydford Castle & Saxon Town. (EX20 4BH) 4F **11***
Lydford Gorge (EX20 4BH) 4F **11**
Lydiard House & Pk. (SN5 3PA) 3G **35**
Lydney Pk. Gdns. (GL15 6BU) 5B **48**
Lyme Pk. (SK12 2NX) 2D **84**
Lytes Cary Manor (TA11 7HU) 4A **22**
Lyveden New Bield (PE8 5AT) 2G **63**

M

Macclesfield Silk Mus. (SK11 6PD) 3D **84**
Macduff Marine Aquarium (AB44 1SL) 2E **160**
MacLellan's Castle (DG6 4JD) 4D **111**
Madame Tussaud's (NW1 5LR) **London 202**
Maeshowe Chambered Cairn (KW16 3HQ) 6C **172**
Magna Science Adventure Cen. (S60 1DX) 1B **86**
Maiden Castle (DT2 9PP) 4B **14**
The Major Oak, Sherwood Forest Country Pk. (NG21 9HN) 4D **86**
Malham Cove (BD23 4DJ) 3A **98**
Malham Tarn (BD24 9PU) 3A **98**
Malleny Gdn. (EH14 7AF) 3E **129**
*Malton Mus. (YO17 7LP) 2B **100***
Malvern Hills (HR8 1EN) 2C **48**
Manchester Art Gallery (M2 3JL) **201**
Manderston (TD11 3PP) 4E **130**
Mannington Gdns. (NR11 7BB) 2D **78**
*Manorbier Castle. (SA70 7SY) 5E **43***
Manx Electric Railway (IM2 4NR) 2D **108**
Manx Mus. (IM1 3LY) 4C **108**
Mapledurham House (RG4 7TR) 4E **37**
Marble Hill House (TW1 2NL) 3C **38**
Markenfield Hall (HG4 3AD) 3E **99**
*Mar Lodge Estate. (AB35 5YJ) 5E **151***
Martin Mere Wetland Cen. (L40 0TA) 3C **90**
Marwell Wildlife (SO21 1JH) 4D **24**
Marwood Hill Gdns. (EX31 4EB) 3F **19**
Mary Arden's Farm (CV37 9UN) 5F **61**
Mary, Queen of Scots' Visitor Cen. (TD8 6EN) 2A **120**
Mary Rose Mus. (PO1 3LJ) **Portsmouth 209**
Max Gate (DT1 2AB) 3C **14**
M&D's Scotland Theme Pk. (ML1 3RT) 4A **128**
The Medieval Bishop's Palace (LN2 1PU) **Lincoln 198**
Megginch Castle Gdns. (PH2 7SW) 1E **137**
Melbourne Hall & Gdns. (DE73 8EN) 3A **74**
Melford Hall (CO10 9AA) 1B **54**
Mellerstain House (TD3 6LG) 1A **120**
*Melrose Abbey. (TD6 9LG) 1H **119***
Menai Suspension Bridge (LL59 5HH) 3E **81**
Mendip Hills (BS40 7XS) 1H **21**
Merriments Gdns. (TN19 7RA) 3B **28**
Merseyside Maritime Mus. (L3 4AQ) **Liverpool 200** (2F **83**)
Mertoun Gdns. (TD6 0EA) 1A **120**
Michelham Priory (BN27 3QS) 5G **27**
*Middleham Castle, Middleham. (DL8 4QR) 1D **98***
Midland Railway Cen. (DE5 3QZ) 5B **86**
Mid-Norfolk Railway (NR19 1DF) 5C **78**
Millennium Coastal Pk. (SA15 2LG) 3D **31**
Milton Manor House (OX14 4EN) 2C **36**
Milton's Cottage (HP8 4JH) 1A **38**
Minack Theatre (TR19 6JU) 4A **4**
Minsmere (IP17 3BY) 4G **67**
Minterne House & Gdns. (DT2 7AU) 2B **14**
Mirehouse (CA12 4QE) 2D **102**
Misarden Pk. Gdns. (GL6 7JA) 5E **49**
Mr Straw's House (S81 0JG) 2C **86**
Mistley Towers (CO11 1ET) 2E **54**
Mompesson House (SP1 2EL) **Salisbury 210** (4G **23**)
Monk Bretton Priory (S71 5QE) 4D **93**
Monkey Forest at Trentham (ST4 8AY) 2C **72**
Monkey Sanctuary (PL13 1NZ) 3G **7**
Monkey World (BH20 6HH) 4D **14**
Monk's House (BN7 3HF) 5F **27**
Montacute House (TA15 6XP) 1H **13**
Monteviot House (TD8 6UH) 2A **120**
*Montgomery Castle. (SY15 6HN) 1E **58***
*Moreton Corbet Castle. (SY4 4DW) 3H **71***
Morwellham Quay (PL19 8JL) 2A **8**
*Moseley Old Hall. (WV10 7HY) 5D **72***
Mother Shipton's Cave (HG5 8DD) 4F **99**
Mottisfont (SO51 0LP) 4B **24**
Mount Edgcumbe House (PL10 1HZ) 3A **8**
Mount Ephraim Gdns. (ME13 9TX) 4E **41**
Mountfitchet Castle (CM24 8SP) 3F **53**
Mount Grace Priory (DL6 3JG) 5B **106**
*Mount Stuart. (PA20 9LR) 4C **126***
Muchelney Abbey (TA10 0DQ) 4H **21**
Muchelney Priest's House (TA10 0DQ) 4H **21**
Mull of Kintyre (PA28 6RU) 5A **122**
Muncaster Castle (CA18 1RQ) 5C **102**
Mus. of Army Flying (SO20 8DY) 3B **24**
Mus. of East Anglian Life (IP14 1DL) 5C **66**
*Mus. of Lakeland Life & Industry. (LA9 5AL) 5G **103***
Mus. of Lincolnshire Life (LN1 3LY) **Lincoln 198** (3G **87**)
Mus. of London (EC2Y 5HN) **203**
Mus. of Royal Worcester (WR1 2ND) **214** (5C **60**)
Mus. of Scottish Lighthouses (AB43 9DU) 2G **161**
Mus. of The Gorge (TF8 7NH) 5A **72**
Mus. of the Isles (IV45 8RS) 3E **147**
Mus. of the Jewellery Quarter (B18 6HA) **Birmingham 188**

N

National Botanic Gdn. of Wales (SA32 8HG) 4F **45**
National Coal Mining Mus. for England (WF4 4RH) 3C **92**
National Coracle Cen. (SA38 9JL) 1C **44**
National Exhibition Cen. (NEC) (B40 1NT) 2F **61**
National Football Mus. (M4 3BG) **Manchester 201**
The National Forest (DE12 6HZ) 4H **73**
National Gallery (WC2N 5DN) **London 203**
National Glass Cen. (SR6 0GL) 4H **115**
National Heritage Cen. for Horseracing & Sporting Art (CB8 8JL) 4F **65**
National Marine Aquarium (PL4 0LF) **Plymouth 208**
*National Maritime Mus. (SE10 9NF) 3E **39***
*National Maritime Mus. Cornwall. (TR11 3QY) 5C **6***
National Memorial Arboretum (DE13 7AR) 4F **73**
National Mining Mus. Scotland (EH22 4QN) 3G **129**
National Motorcycle Mus. (B92 0EJ) 2G **61**
The National Motor Mus. (SO42 7ZN) 2B **16**
National Mus. Cardiff (CF10 3NP) **191** (4E **33**)
National Mus. of Flight (EH39 5LF) 2B **130**
National Mus. of Rural Life Scotland (G76 9HR) 4H **127**
National Mus. of Scotland (EH1 1JF) **Edinburgh 194** (2F **129**)
National Mus. of the Royal Navy (PO1 3NH) **Portsmouth 209**
National Portrait Gallery (WC2H 0HE) **London 203**
National Railway Mus., York (YO26 4XJ) **214** (4H **99**)
*National Roman Legion Mus. (NP18 1AE) 2G **33***
National Science & Media Mus. (BD1 1NQ) **Bradford 190** (1B **92**)
National Sea Life Cen. (B1 2HL) **Birmingham 188**
National Showcaves Cen. for Wales (SA9 1GJ) 4B **46**
National Slate Mus. (LL55 4TY) 4E **81**
National Space Cen. (LE4 5NS) 5C **74**
National Waterfront Mus. (SA1 3RD) **Swansea 212** (3F **31**)
National Waterways Mus. (CH65 4FW) 3G **83**
National Wool Mus. (SA44 5UP) 2D **44**
Natural History Mus., London (SW7 5BD) **202**
Natural History Mus. at Tring (HP23 6AP) 4H **51**
Neath Abbey (SA10 7DW) 3G **31**
The Needles (PO39 0JH) 4A **16**
Nene Valley Railway (PE8 6LR) 1A **64**
Ness Botanic Gdns. (CH64 4AY) 3F **83**
Nessieland (IV63 6TU) 5H **157**
Nether Winchendon House (HP18 0DY) 4F **51**
Netley Abbey (SO31 5HB) 2C **16**
New Abbey Corn Mill (DG2 8DX) 3A **112**
Newark Air Mus. (NG24 2NY) 5F **87**
Newark Castle, Port Glasgow (PA14 5NG) 2E **127**
*Newark Castle, Newark-on-Trent. (NG24 1BN) 5E **87***
Newark Pk. (GL12 7PZ) 2C **34**
*The New Art Gallery Walsall. (WS2 8LG) 1E **61***
Newburgh Priory (YO61 4AS) 2H **99**
Newbury Racecourse (RG14 7NZ) 5C **36**
Newby Hall & Gdns. (HG4 5AE) 3F **99**
*Newcastle Castle, Bridgend. (CF31 4JW) 3B **32***
Newcastle Upon Tyne Castle Keep (NE1 1RQ) **205**
New Forest Nat. Pk. (SO43 7BD) 1H **15**
New Lanark World Heritage Site (ML11 9DB) 5B **128**
*Newmarket Racecourse. (CB8 0TG) 4F **65***
*Newquay Zoo. (TR7 2LZ) 2C **6***
Newstead Abbey (NG15 8NA) 5C **86**
Nine Ladies Stone Circle (DE4 2LF) 4G **85**
Norfolk Broads Nat. Pk. (NR3 1BJ) 5G **79**
Norfolk Lavender (PE31 7JE) 2F **77**
*Norham Castle. (TD15 2LL) 5F **131***
Normanby Hall Mus. (DN15 9HU) 3B **94**
North Downs (GU10 5QE) 5C **38**
North Norfolk Railway (NR26 8RA) 1D **78**
Northumberlandia, the Lady of the North (NE23 8AU) 2F **115**
Northumberland Nat. Pk. (NE46 1BS) 5C **120**
North York Moors Nat. Pk. (YO18 8RN) 5D **107**
North Yorkshire Moors Railway (YO18 7AJ) 1C **100**
Norton Conyers (HG4 5EQ) 2F **99**
Norton Priory Mus. & Gdns. (WA7 1SX) 2H **83**
Norwich Castle Mus. & Art Gallery (NR1 3JU) **205** (5E **79**)
Norwich Cathedral (NR1 4DH) **205** (5E **79**)
Nostell Priory (WF4 1QE) 3E **93**
Nuffield Place (RG9 5RX) 3E **37**
*Nunney Castle. (BA11 4LN) 2C **22***
Nunnington Hall (YO62 5UY) 2A **100**
Nymans (RH17 6EB) 3D **26**

O

Oakham Castle (LE15 6DR) 5F **75**
*Oakwell Hall. (WF17 9LG) 2C **92***
Oakwood Theme Pk. (SA67 8DE) 3E **43**
The Observatory Science Cen. (BN27 1RN) 4A **28**
Oceanarium (BH2 5AA) **Bournemouth 190**
Offa's Dyke, Brockweir (NP16 7NQ) 5A **48**
*Okehampton Castle. (EX20 1JA) 3F **11***
Old Beaupre Castle (CF71 7LT) 4D **32**
Old Gorhambury House (AL3 6AH) 5B **52**
Old Oswestry Hill Fort (SY10 7AA) 2E **71**
Old Sarum (SP1 3SD) 3G **23**
Old Wardour Castle (SP3 6RR) 4E **23**
Old Winchester Hill Hill Fort (GU32 1HN) 4E **25**
*Orford Castle & Mus. (IP12 2NF) 1H **55***
Orford Ness (IP12 2NU) 1H **55**
Ormesby Hall (TS7 9AS) 3C **106**
Osborne House (PO32 6JX) 3D **16**
*Osterley Pk. & House. (TW7 4RB) 3C **38***
Oulton Pk. Circuit (CW6 9BW) 4H **83**
Overbeck's (TQ8 8LW) 5D **8**
Owletts (DA12 3AP) 4A **40**
Oxburgh Hall (PE33 9PS) 5G **77**
Oxford Christ Church Cathedral (OX1 4JF) **207** (5D **50**)
*Oxwich Castle. (SA3 1LU) 4D **31***
Oystermouth Castle (SA3 5TA) 4F **31**

P

Packwood House (B94 6AT) 3F **61**
Paignton Zoo (TQ4 7EU) 3E **9**
Painshill Pk. (KT11 1JE) 5B **38**
Painswick Rococo Gdn. (GL6 6TH) 4D **48**
Palace of Holyroodhouse (EH8 8DX) **Edinburgh 194** (2F **129**)
Papplewick Pumping Station (NG15 9AJ) 5C **86**
Paradise Pk. Wildlife Sanctuary (TR27 4HB) 3C **4**
Paradise Wildlife Pk. (EN10 7QZ) 5D **52**
Parcevall Hall Gdns. (BD23 6DE) 3C **98**
Parham (RH20 4HS) 4B **26**
Pashley Manor Gdns. (TN5 7HE) 3B **28**
Paultons Pk. (SO51 6AL) 1B **16**
*Paxton House. (TD15 1SZ) 4F **131***
Paycocke's House & Gdn. (CO6 1NS) 3B **54**
Peak Cavern (S33 8WS) 2F **85**
Peak District Nat. Pk. (DE45 1AE) 2F **85**
Peak Rail (DE4 3NA) 4G **85**
Peckover House & Gdn. (PE13 1JR) 5D **76**
*Peel Castle. (IM5 1AB) 3B **108***
*Pembroke Castle. (SA71 4LA) 4D **43***
Pembrokeshire Coast Nat. Pk. (SA41 3XD) 4C **42**
Pencarrow (PL30 3AG) 5A **10**
Pendennis Castle (TR11 4LP) 5C **6**
Penrhyn Castle (LL57 4HN) 3F **81**
*Penrith Castle. (CA11 7JB) 2G **103***
Penshurst Place & Gdns. (TN11 8DG) 1G **27**
Peover Hall (WA16 9HW) 3B **84**
Perth Mus. & Art Gallery (PH1 5LB) **207**
Peterborough St Peter's Cathedral (PE1 1XZ) **208** (1A **64**)
Petworth House & Pk. (GU28 0AE) 3A **26**
*Pevensey Castle. (BN24 5LE) 5H **27***
Peveril Castle (S33 8WQ) 2F **85**
Pickering Castle (YO18 7AX) 1C **100**
Picton Castle (SA62 4AS) 3E **43**
Piel Castle (LA13 0QN) 3B **96**
Pistyll Rhaeadr (SY10 0BZ) 3C **70**
Pitmedden Gdn. (AB41 7PD) 1F **153**
Pitt Rivers Mus. (OX1 3PP) **Oxford 207** (5D **50**)
Plantasia, Swansea (SA1 2AL) **212**
Plas Brondanw Gdns. (LL48 6SW) 1F **69**
Plas Newydd, Llangollen (LL20 8AW) 1E **70**
Plas Newydd, Llanfair Pwllgwyngyll (LL61 6DQ) 4E **81**
Plas yn Rhiw (LL53 8AB) 3B **68**
Pleasurewood Hills (NR32 5DZ) 1H **67**
Poldark Mine (TR13 0ES) 5A **6**
Polesden Lacey (RH5 6BD) 5C **38**
Pollok House (G43 1AT) 3G **127**
Pontcysyllte Aqueduct (LL20 7YS) 1E **71**
*Portchester Castle. (PO16 9QW) 2E **17***
Portland Castle (DT5 1AZ) 5B **14**
Port Lympne Reserve (CT21 4PD) 2F **29**
Portsmouth Historic Dockyard (PO1 3LJ) **209** (2E **17**)
The Potteries Mus. & Art Gallery (ST1 3DW) **211**
*Powderham Castle. (EX6 8JQ) 4C **12***
Powis Castle & Gdn. (SY21 8RF) 5E **70**
The Prebendal Manor House (PE8 6QG) 1H **63**
Prestongrange Mus. (EH32 9RX) 2G **129**
*Preston Manor. (BN1 6SD) 5E **27***
Preston Mill & Phantassie Doocot (EH40 3DS) 2B **130**
Preston Tower, Prestonpans (EH32 9NN) 2G **129**
Preston Tower, Chathill (NE67 5DH) 2F **121**
Prideaux Place (PL28 8RP) 1D **6**
Principality Stadium (CF10 1NS) **Cardiff 191**
Prior Pk. Landscape Gdn. (BA2 5AH) 5C **34**
Provan Hall (G34 9NJ) 3H **127**
Prudhoe Castle (NE42 6NA) 3D **115**

Q

Quantock Hills (TA4 4AP) 3E **21**
Quarry Bank Mill (SK9 4LA) 2C **84**
Quebec House (TN16 1TD) 5F **39**
Queen Elizabeth Country Pk. (PO8 0QE) 1F **17**
Queen Elizabeth Forest Pk. (FK8 3UZ) 4D **134**
Queen Elizabeth Olympic Pk. (E20 2ST) 2E **39**
Quex House & Gdns. (CT7 0BH) 4H **41**

R

Raby Castle (DL2 3AH) 2E **105**
RAF Holmpton (HU19 2RG) 2G **95**
RAF Mus. Cosford (TF11 8UP) 5B **72**
RAF Mus. London (NW9 5LL) 1D **38**
Raglan Castle (NP15 2BT) 5H **47**
Ragley (B49 5NJ) 5E **61**
Ramsey Island (SA62 6SA) 2A **42**
Ravenglass & Eskdale Railway (CA18 1SW) 5C **102**
Raveningham Gdns. (NR14 6NS) 1F **67**
Ravenscraig Castle (KY1 2AZ) 4E **137**
Reculver Towers (CT6 6SX) 4G **41**
Red House (DA6 8JF) 3F **39**
Renishaw Hall & Gdns. (S21 3WB) 3B **86**
Restoration House, Rochester (ME1 1RF) **Medway Towns 204**
Restormel Castle (PL22 0HN) 2F **7**
Revolution House (S41 9LA) 3A **86**
Rheged Cen. (CA11 0DQ) 2F **103**
Rheidol Power Station (SY23 3NF) 3G **57**
Rhossili Bay (SA3 1PR) 4D **30**
RHS Gdn. Harlow Carr (HG3 1QB) 4E **99**
RHS Gdn. Hyde Hall (CM3 8ET) 1B **40**
RHS Gdn. Rosemoor (EX38 8PH) 1F **11**
RHS Gdn. Wisley (GU23 6QB) 5B **38**
*Rhuddlan Castle. (LL18 5AD) 3C **82***
Ribchester Roman Mus. (PR3 3XS) 1E **91**
*Richmond Castle. (DL10 4QW) 4E **105***
Rievaulx Abbey (YO62 5LB) 1H **99**
Rievaulx Terrace (YO62 5LJ) 1H **99**
Ripley Castle (HG3 3AY) 3E **99**
*Ripon Cathedral. (HG4 1QT) 2F **99***
River & Rowing Mus. (RG9 1BF) 3F **37**
*Riverside Mus., Mus. of Transport & Travel. (G3 8RS) 3G **127***
Robert Burns Birthplace Mus. (KA7 4PY) 3C **116**
Robert Burns House (DG1 2PS) **Dumfries 193** (2A **112**)
Roche Abbey (S66 8NW) 2C **86**
Rochester Castle (ME1 1SW) **Medway Towns 204** (4B **40**)
Rochester Cathedral (ME1 1SX) **Medway Towns 204** (4B **40**)
Rockbourne Roman Villa (SP6 3PG) 1G **15**
Rockingham Castle (LE16 8TH) 1F **63**
Rockingham Motor Speedway (NN17 5AF) 1G **63**
Rocks by Rail (LE15 7BX) 4F **75**
Rode Hall & Gdns. (ST7 3QP) 5C **84**
Rodmarton Manor (GL7 6PF) 2E **35**
Rokeby Pk. (DL12 9RZ) 3D **105**
Rollright Stones (OX7 5QB) 2A **50**
Roman Army Mus. (CA8 7JB) 3H **113**
Roman Baths (BA1 1LZ) **Bath 187** (5C **34**)
The Roman Painted House (CT17 9AJ) **Dover 193**
Roman Vindolanda (NE47 7JN) 3A **114**
Romney, Hythe & Dymchurch Railway (TN28 8PL) 3E **29**
Roseberry Topping (TS9 6QX) 3C **106**
*Rothesay Castle. (PA20 0DA) 3B **126***
Rothiemurchus Cen. (PH22 1QH) 2D **150**
Rousham House & Gdns. (OX25 4QX) 3C **50**
Royal Academy of Arts (Burlington House) (W1J 0BD) **London 202**
*Royal Albert Bridge. (PL12 4GT) 3A **8***
The Royal Armouries Mus. (LS10 1LT) **Leeds 199**
Royal Botanic Gdn. (EH3 5LR) 2F **129**
Royal Botanic Gdns., Kew (TW9 3AB) 3C **38**
Royal Cornwall Mus. (TR1 2SJ) 4C **6**
Royal Crown Derby Mus. (DE23 8JZ) **193** (2A **74**)
Royal Mint Mus. (CF72 8YT) 3D **32**
Royal Navy Submarine Mus. (PO12 2AS) 3E **16**
Royal Pavilion (BN1 1EE) **Brighton & Hove 189** (5E **27**)
Royal Pump Room Mus. (HG1 2RY) **Harrogate 197** (4E **99**)
Royal Yacht Britannia (EH6 6JJ) 2F **129**

Ruddington Framework Knitters Mus.
(NG11 6HE) 2C **74**
Rufford Abbey (NG22 9DF) 4D **86**
Rufford Old Hall (L40 1SG) 3C **90**
Rufus Stone (SO43 7HN) 1A **16**
Rushton Triangular Lodge (NN14 1RP) 2F **63**
Russell-Cotes Art Gallery & Mus.
(BH1 3AA) ....**Bournemouth 190** (3F **15**)
Rutland County Mus. (LE15 6HW) 5F **75**
Rydal Mount & Gdns. (LA22 9LU) 4E **103**
Ryedale Folk Mus. (YO62 6UA) 5E **107**
Ryton Gdns. (CV8 3LG) 3B **62**

S

Saatchi Gallery (SW3 4RY) ....**London 202**
Sainsbury Cen. for Visual Arts (NR4 7TJ) 5D **78**
St Abb's Head (TD14 5QF) 3F **131**
St Albans Cathedral. (AL1 1BY) 5B **52**
St Andrews Aquarium (KY16 9AS) **209** (2H **137**)
St Andrews Cathedral (KY16 9QL) **209** (2H **137**)
St Augustine's Abbey, Canterbury
(CT1 1PF) **190** (5F **41**)
St David's Cathedral. (SA62 6RD) 2B **42**
St Dogmaels Abbey (SA43 3JH) 1B **44**
St Edmunds Abbey, Bury St Edmunds
(IP33 1RS) 4A **66**
St Fagans National Mus. of History
(CF5 6XB) 4E **32**
St John's Jerusalem (DA4 9HQ) 3G **39**
St Mary's House & Gdns. (BN44 3WE) 4C **26**
St Mawes Castle (TR2 5DE) 5C **6**
St Michael's Mount (TR17 0HS) 4C **4**
St Paul's Cathedral (EC4M 8AE) ....**London 203**
Salford Mus. & Art Gallery
(M5 4WU) ....**Manchester 201** (1C **84**)
Salisbury Cathedral (SP1 2EG) **210** (4G **23**)
Saltaire World Heritage Village. (BD18 4PL) ...1B **92**
Saltram (PL7 1UH) 3B **8**
Samlesbury Hall (PR5 0UP) 1E **90**
Sandford Orcas Manor House (DT9 4SB) 4B **22**
Sandham Memorial Chapel (RG20 9JT) 5C **36**
Sandown Pk. Racecourse (KT10 9AJ) 4C **38**
Sandringham (PE35 6EP) 3F **77**
Sandwich Wildlife Pk. (CT13 0DD) 5H **41**
Sarehole Mill (B13 0BD) 2E **61**
The Savill Gdn. (SL4 2HT) 3A **38**
Sawley Abbey (BB7 4LE) 5G **97**
Saxtead Green Post Mill (IP13 9QQ) 4E **67**
Scafell Pike (CA20 1EX) 4D **102**
Scampston Hall (YO17 8NG) 2C **100**
Scarborough Castle. (YO11 1HY) 1E **101**
Science & Industry Mus.
(M3 4FP) ....**Manchester 201**
Science Mus. (SW7 2DD) ....**London 202**
Scone Palace (PH2 6BD) 1D **136**
Scotch Whisky Experience
(EH1 2NE) ....**Edinburgh 194**
Scotney Castle (TN3 8JN) 2A **28**
Scotstarvit Tower (KY15 5PA) 2F **137**
Scottish Deer Cen. (KY15 4NQ) 2F **137**
Scottish Exhibition & Conference Cen.
(G3 8YW) ....**Glasgow 196**
Scottish Fisheries Mus. (KY10 3AB) 3H **137**
Scottish Industrial Railway Cen.
(KA6 7JF) 4D **116**
Scottish Maritime Mus. (KA12 8QE) 1C **116**
Scottish National Gallery
(EH2 2EL) ....**Edinburgh 194**
Scottish National Gallery of Modern Art.
(EH4 3DR) 2F **129**
Scottish National Portrait Gallery
(EH2 1JD) ....**Edinburgh 194**
Scottish Parliament (EH99 1SP) ....**Edinburgh 194**
Scottish Sea Life Sanctuary (PA37 1SE) 4D **140**
Sea Life, Blackpool (FY1 5AA) **188**
Sea Life, Brighton
(BN2 1TB) **189** (5E **27**)
Sea Life, Weymouth (DT4 7SX) 4B **14**
Sea Life, London (SE1 7PB) **203**
Sea Life, Great Yarmouth
(NR30 3AH) **196** (5H **79**)
Sea Life, Scarborough (YO12 6RP) 5H **107**
Sea Life, Southend-on-Sea (SS1 2ER) 2C **40**
Sea Life, Loch Lomond (Glasgow)
(G83 8QL) 1E **127**
SeaQuarium, Rhyl (LL18 3AF) 2C **82**
SeaQuarium, Weston (BS23 1BE) 5G **33**
Seaton Delaval Hall (NE26 4QR) 2G **115**
Seaton Tramway (EX12 2NQ) 3F **13**
Selby Abbey (YO8 4PF) 1G **93**
Selly Manor (B30 2AD) 2E **61**
Severn Bridge (BS35 4BL) 2A **34**
Severn Valley Railway (DY12 1BE) 2B **60**
Sewerby Hall & Gdns. (YO15 1EA) 3G **101**
Sezincote (GL56 9AW) 2G **49**
Shaftesbury Abbey Mus. & Gdns.
(SP7 8JR) 4D **22**
Shakespeare's Birthplace
(CV37 6QW) ....**Stratford 212**
Shandy Hall (YO61 4AD) 2H **99**
Shap Abbey (CA10 3NB) 3G **103**
Shaw's Corner (AL6 9BX) 4B **52**
Sheffield Pk. & Gdn. (TN22 3QX) 3F **27**
Shepreth Wildlife Pk. (SG8 6PZ) 1D **53**
Sherborne Castle (DT9 5NR) 1B **14**
Sherborne Old Castle (DT9 3SA) 1B **14**

Sherwood Forest (NG21 9HN) 5C **86**
Shibden Hall. (HX3 6XG) 2B **92**
Shipton Hall (TF13 6JZ) 1H **59**
Shoe Mus. (BA16 0EQ) 3H **21**
Shrewsbury Castle (SY1 2AT) **210** (4G **71**)
Shugborough (ST17 0XB) 3D **73**
Shute Barton (EX13 7PT) 3F **13**
The Shuttleworth Collection (SG18 9EP) 1G **52**
Silbury Hill (SN8 1QH) 5G **35**
Silverstone Circuit (NN12 8TN) 1E **51**
Sir Harold Hillier Gdns. (SO51 0QA) 4B **24**
Sir Walter Scott's Courtroom (TD7 4BT) 2G **119**
Sissinghurst Castle Gdn. (TN17 2AB) 2C **28**
Sizergh Castle & Gdn. (LA8 8AE) 1D **97**
Skara Brae Prehistoric Village
(KW16 3LR) 6B **172**
Skenfrith Castle. (NP7 8UH) 3H **47**
Skiddaw (CA12 4QE) 2D **102**
Skipness Castle (PA29 6XU) 4H **125**
Skipton Castle. (BD23 1AW) 4B **98**
Skokholm Island (SA62 3BL) 4B **42**
Skomer Island (SA62 3BL) 4B **42**
Sledmere House (YO25 3XG) 3D **100**
Slimbridge Wetland Cen. (GL2 7BT) 5C **48**
Smailholm Tower (TD5 7PG) 1A **120**
Smallhythe Place (TN30 7NG) 3D **28**
Snaefell Mountain Railway (IM4 7NL) 3D **108**
Snowdonia Nat. Pk. (LL48 6LF) 2G **69**
Snowdon Mountain Railway (LL55 4TY) 5F **81**
Snowdon Summit (LL55 4UL) 5F **81**
Snowshill Manor & Gdn. (WR12 7JU) 2F **49**
Somerleyton Hall (NR32 5QQ) 1G **67**
Somerset Heritage Cen. (TA2 6SF) 4F **21**
Souter Lighthouse (SR6 7NH) 3H **115**
South Devon Railway (TQ11 0DZ) 5D **8**
South Downs Nat. Pk. (GU29 9SB) 5D **26**
South Tynedale Railway (CA9 3JB) 5A **114**
Southwell Minster (NG25 0HD) 5E **86**
Spa Valley Railway (TN2 5QY) 2G **27**
Speedwell Cavern (S33 8WA) 2F **85**
Speke Hall Gdn. & Estate (L24 1XD) 2G **83**
Spetchley Pk. Gdns. (WR5 1RR) 5C **60**
Spinnaker Tower
(PO1 3TN) ....**Portsmouth 209** (3E **17**)
Spinners Gdn. (SO41 5QE) 3B **16**
Spofforth Castle (HG3 1DA) 4F **99**
Sprivers Gdn. (TN12 8DR) 1A **28**
Spurn Head (HU12 0UG) 3H **95**
Spynie Palace (IV30 5QG) 2G **159**
Squerryes (TN16 1SJ) 5F **39**
Stafford Castle. (ST16 1DJ) 3D **72**
Stagshaw Gdns. (LA22 0HE) 4E **103**
Stanage Edge (S33 0AD) 2G **85**
Standen (RH19 4NE) 2E **27**
Stanford Hall (LE17 6DH) 3C **62**
Stansted Pk. (PO9 6DX) 2F **17**
Stanway House & Fountain (GL54 5PQ) 2F **49**
Staunton Harold Church (LE65 1RT) 3A **74**
STEAM Mus. of the Great Western Railway
(SN2 2EY) 3G **35**
Stirling Castle (FK8 1EJ) **211** (4G **135**)
Stoke Pk. Pavilions (NN12 7RZ) 1F **51**
Stokesay Castle. (SY7 9AH) 2G **59**
Stoke-sub-Hamdon Priory (TA14 6QP) 1H **13**
Stoneacre (ME15 8RS) 5C **40**
Stonehenge (SP4 7DE) 2G **23**
Stoneleigh Abbey (CV8 2LF) 3H **61**
Stonor (RG9 6HF) 3F **37**
Stott Pk. Bobbin Mill (LA12 8AX) 1C **96**
Stourhead (BA12 6QD) 3C **22**
Stowe House (MK18 5EH) 2E **51**
Stowe Landscape Gdns. (MK18 5EH) 2E **51**
Strata Florida Abbey (SY25 6BJ) 4G **57**
Stratfield Saye House (RG7 2BZ) 5E **37**
Strathaven Castle. (ML10 6QS) 5A **128**
Strathspey Railway (PH22 1PY) 2D **150**
Strawberry Hill (TW1 4ST) 3G **38**
Strome Castle (IV54 8YJ) 5A **156**
Sudbury Hall (DE6 5HT) 2F **73**
Sudeley Castle (GL54 5JD) 3F **49**
Sufton Court (HR1 4LU) 2A **48**
Sulgrave Manor (OX17 2SD) 1D **50**
Summerlee Mus. of Scottish Industrial Life
(ML5 1QD) 3A **128**
Sundown Adventureland (DN22 0HX) 3E **87**
Sutton Hoo (IP12 3DJ) 1F **55**
Sutton Pk. (YO61 1DP) 3H **99**
Sutton Scarsdale Hall (S44 5UT) 4B **86**
Sutton Valence Castle. (ME17 3DA) 1C **28**
Swaledale Mus. (DL11 6QT) 5D **104**
Swallow Falls (LL24 0DH) 1G **69**
Swansea RC Cathedral (SA1 2BX) **212** (3F **31**)
Sweetheart Abbey (DG2 8BU) 3A **112**
Swindon & Cricklade Railway (SN25 2DA) 2G **35**
The Swiss Gdn. (SG18 9ER) 1B **52**
Syon Pk. (TW8 8JF) 3C **38**

T

Tabley House (WA16 0HB) 3B **84**
Talley Abbey (SA19 7AX) 2G **45**
Talyllyn Railway (LL36 9EY) 5F **69**
Tamworth Castle. (B79 7NA) 5G **73**
Tank Mus. (BH20 6JG) 4D **14**
Tantallon Castle (EH39 5PN) 1B **130**
Tarn Hows (LA22 0PR) 5E **103**
Tar Tunnel (TF8 7HS) 5A **72**

Tate Britain (SW1P 4RG) ....**London 203**
Tate Liverpool (L3 4BB) **200** (2F **83**)
Tate Modern (SE1 9TG) ....**London 203**
Tate St Ives (TR26 1TG) 2C **4**
Tattershall Castle (LN4 4NR) 5B **88**
Tatton Pk. (WA16 6QN) 2B **84**
Tay Forest Pk. (PH17 2QG) 3C **142**
Teifi Valley Railway (SA44 5TD) 1D **44**
Temple Newsam House (LS15 0AE) 1D **92**
Tenby Castle. (SA70 7BP) 4F **43**
Thames Barrier (SE18 5NJ) 3F **39**
Thetford Forest Pk. (IP26 5DB) 1A **66**
Thetford Priory (IP24 1AZ) 2A **66**
Thirlestane Castle (TD2 6RU) 5B **130**
Thoresby Gallery (NG22 9EP) 3D **86**
Thornham Walled Gdn. (IP23 8HH) 3D **66**
Thornton Abbey & Gatehouse (DN39 6TU) 3E **94**
Thorpe Pk. (KT16 8PN) 4B **38**
Thorp Perrow Arboretum (DL8 2PR) 1E **99**
Threave Castle (DG7 2AB) 3E **111**
Threave Gdn. (DG7 1RX) 3E **111**
Thrigby Hall Wildlife Gdns. (NR29 3DR) 4G **79**
Thruxton Circuit (SP11 8PW) 2A **24**
Thursford Collection (NR21 0AS) 2B **78**
Tilbury Fort (RM18 7NR) 3H **39**
Tintagel Castle (PL34 0HE) 4A **10**
Tintagel Visitor Cen. (PL34 0AJ) 4A **10**
Tintern Abbey (NP16 6SH) 5A **48**
Tintinhull Gdn. (BA22 8QL) 4A **22**
Titchfield Abbey (PO15 5RA) 2D **16**
Tiverton Castle. (EX16 6RP) 1C **12**
Tolpuddle Martyrs Mus. (DT2 7EH) 3C **14**
Tolquhon Castle (AB41 7LP) 1F **153**
Torridon Countryside Cen. (IV22 2EW) 3B **156**
Totnes Castle. (TQ9 5NU) 2E **9**
Tower Bridge (SE1 2UP) ....**London 203**
The Tower of London (EC3N 4AB) **203**
Towneley Hall (Art Gallery & Mus.)
(BB11 3RQ) 1G **91**
Townend (LA23 1LB) 4F **103**
Traquair House (EH44 6PW) 1F **119**
Treasurer's House, Martock (TA12 6JL) 1H **13**
Treasurer's House, York (YO1 7JL) **214**
Trebah Gdn. (TR11 5JZ) 4E **5**
Tredegar House (NP10 8YW) 4F **33**
Tregrehan Gdn. (PL24 2SJ) 3E **7**
Trelissick Gdn. (TR3 6QL) 5C **6**
Trengwainton Gdn. (TR20 8RZ) 3B **4**
Trentham Gdns. (ST4 8NF) 1C **72**
Trerice (TR8 4PG) 3C **6**
Tresco Abbey Gdns. (TR24 0QQ) 1A **4**
Tretower Castle. (NP8 1RF) 3E **47**
Trewithen (TR4 0DD) 4D **6**
Tropical Birdland (LE9 9GN) 5B **74**
The Trossachs (FK17 8HZ) 3E **135**
Tudor Merchant's House (SA70 7BX) 4F **43**
Tudor World (CV37 6EE) ....**Stratford 212**
Turner Contemporary (CT9 1HG) 3H **41**
Turton Tower (BL7 0HG) 3F **91**
Tutbury Castle (DE13 9JF) 3G **73**
Twycross Zoo (CV9 3PX) 5H **73**
Ty Mawr Wybrnant (LL25 0HJ) 5G **81**
Tynemouth Castle. (NE30 4BZ) 3G **115**
Tyntesfield (BS48 1NT) 4A **34**

U

Uffington White Horse (SN7 7QJ) 3B **36**
Ugbrooke (TQ13 0AD) 5B **12**
Upnor Castle (ME2 4XG) 3B **40**
Uppark (GU31 5QR) 1F **17**
Upton Castle Gdns. (SA72 4SE) 4E **43**
Upton House & Gdns. (OX15 6HT) 1B **50**
Urquhart Castle (IV63 6XJ) 1H **149**
Usher Gallery (LN2 1NN) ....**Lincoln 198**
Usk Castle. (NP15 1SD) 5G **47**

V

Vale of Rheidol Railway (SY23 1PG) 3F **57**
Valle Crucis Abbey (LL20 8DT) 1E **70**
The Valley Gdns. (SL4 2HT) 3A **38**
V&A Mus. of Design, Dundee
(DD1 4QB) **194** (1G **137**)
Veddw House Gdn. (NP16 6PH) 2H **33**
Verulamium Mus. (AL3 4SW) 5B **52**
Victoria & Albert Mus. (SW7 2RL) ....**London 202**
The Vyne (RG24 9HL) 1E **25**

W

Waddesdon Manor (HP18 0JH) 4F **51**
Wakehurst Place (RH17 6TN) 2E **27**
Walker Art Gallery (L3 8EL) ....**Liverpool 200** (1F **83**)
Wallington (NE61 4AR) 1D **114**
Wallsend Roman Fort (CT14 7LJ) 1H **29**
Walsingham Abbey (NR22 6BL) 2B **78**
Warkworth Castle. (NE65 0UJ) 4G **121**
Warwick Castle. (CV34 4QX) 4G **61**
Washington Old Hall. (NE38 7LE) 4G **115**
Watercress Line (SO24 9JG) 3E **25**
Watermouth Castle (EX34 9SL) 2F **19**
Waterperry Gdns. (OX33 1JZ) 5E **51**
Watersmeet (EX35 6NT) 2H **19**

Weald & Downland Living Mus.
(PO18 0EU) 1G **17**
Weaver Hall Mus. & Workhouse (CW9 8AB) 3A **84**
Weaver's Cottage (PA10 2JG) 3E **127**
Wedgwood Visitor Cen. (ST12 9ER) 2C **72**
The Weir (HR4 7QF) 1H **47**
Wells & Walsingham Light Railway
(NR23 1QB) 1B **78**
Wells Cathedral. (BA5 2UE) 2A **22**
Welney Wetland Cen. (PE14 9TN) 1E **65**
Welsh Highland Heritage Railway
(LL49 9DY) 2E **69**
Welsh Highland Railway
(LL54 5UP) ....**Caernarfon 190** (5E **81**)
Welsh Mountain Zoo (LL28 5UY) 3H **81**
Welshpool & Llanfair Light Railway
(SY21 0SF) 5D **70**
Wembley Stadium (HA9 0WS) 2C **38**
Wenlock Edge (SY7 9JH) 2G **59**
Wenlock Priory (TF13 6HS) 5A **72**
Wentworth Castle Gdns. (S75 3ET) 4D **92**
Weobley Castle (SA3 1HB) 3D **31**
Wesley Cottage (PL15 7TG) 4C **10**
Westbury Court Gdn. (GL14 1PD) 4C **48**
West Green House Gdns. (RG27 8JB) 1F **25**
West Highland Mus. (PH33 6AJ) 1F **141**
West Midland Safari & Leisure Pk.
(DY12 1LF) 3C **60**
Westminster Abbey (SW1P 3PA) ....**London 203**
Westminster RC Cathedral
(SW1P 1QH) ....**London 202**
Westonbirt National Arboretum (GL8 8QS) 3D **34**
Weston Pk. (TF11 8LE) 4C **72**
West Somerset Railway (TA24 5BG) 4E **21**
Westwood Manor (BA15 2AF) 1D **22**
West Wycombe Pk. (HP14 3AJ) 2G **37**
Wetlands Animal Pk. (DN22 8SB) 2D **86**
Whalley Abbey (BB7 9TN) 1F **91**
Wheal Martyn (PL26 8XG) 3E **6**
Whipsnade Tree Cathedral (LU6 2LL) 4A **52**
Whipsnade Zoo (LU6 2LF) 4A **52**
Whitby Abbey (YO22 4JT) 3G **107**
White Castle (NP7 8UD) 4G **47**
White Horse Hill (SN7 7QJ) 3B **36**
White Scar Cave (LA6 3AW) 2G **97**
Whithorn Priory & Mus. (DG8 8PY) 5B **110**
Whitworth Art Gallery. (M15 6ER) 1C **84**
Wicken Fen National Nature Reserve
(CB7 5YG) 3E **65**
Wicksteed Pk. (NN15 6NJ) 3F **63**
Wightwick Manor & Gdns. (WV6 8EE) 1C **60**
Wigmore Castle. (HR6 9UJ) 4G **59**
Wilberforce House Mus.
(HU1 1NE) ....**Kingston upon Hull 199** (2E **94**)
Wilderhope Manor (TF13 6EG) 1H **59**
Wildwood Escot (EX11 1LU) 3D **12**
Wilton House (SP2 0BJ) 3F **23**
Wimbledon Lawn Tennis Mus. (SW19 5HP) 3D **38**
Wimpole Hall & Gdns. (SG8 0BW) 5C **64**
Winchester Cathedral (SO23 9LS) **213** (4C **24**)
Windmill Hill Neolithic Camp (SN4 9NW) 4F **35**
Windsor Castle (SL4 1NJ) **213** (3A **38**)
Wingfield Manor (DE55 7NH) 5A **86**
Winkworth Arboretum (GU8 4AD) 1A **26**
Winter Gdn. (S1 2PP) ....**Sheffield 210**
Witley Court & Gdns. (WR6 6JT) 4B **60**
Woburn Abbey (MK17 9WA) 2H **51**
Woburn Safari Pk. (MK17 9QN) 2H **51**
The Wolds, Yorkshire (YO25 9EN) 4D **100**
The Wolds, Lincolnshire (LN8 6BL) 1B **88**
Wolfeton House (DT2 9QN) 3B **14**
Wollaton Hall (NG8 2AE) 2C **74**
The Wolseley Cen. (ST17 0WT) 3E **73**
Wolvesey Castle (SO23 9NB) ....**Winchester 213**
Woodchester Mansion (GL10 3TS) 5D **48**
Woodhenge (SP4 7AR) 2G **23**
Woolsthorpe Manor (NG33 5PD) 3G **75**
Wookey Hole (BA5 1BB) 2A **22**
Worcester Cathedral (WR1 2LH) **214** (5C **60**)
Worcestershire County Mus. (DY11 7XZ) 3C **60**
Wordsworth House (CA13 9RX) 1C **102**
The Wordsworth Mus. & Art Gallery
(LA22 9SH) 4E **103**
Wotton House Landscape Gdns.
(HP18 0SB) 4E **51**
Wrest Pk. (MK45 4HR) 2A **52**
Wrexham RC Cathedral (LL11 1RB) **214** (5F **83**)
Wroxeter Roman City (SY5 6PH) 5H **71**
Wroxton Abbey Gdns. (OX15 6PX) 1C **50**
Wylfa Visitor Cen. (LL67 0DH) 1C **80**
Wyre Forest (DY14 9UH) 3C **60**
Wythenshawe Hall. (M23 0AB) 2C **84**

Y

Yarmouth Castle (PO41 0PB) 4B **16**
York Art Gallery (YO1 7EW) **214**
York Castle Mus. (YO1 9RY) **214** (4A **100**)
York Minster (YO1 7JN) **214** (4A **100**)
York Racecourse (YO23 1EX) 5H **99**
Yorkshire Dales Nat. Pk. (BD23 5LB) 2H **97**
Yorkshire Mus. (YO30 7DR) **214**
Yorkshire Sculpture Pk. (WF4 1LG) 3C **92**

Limited Interchange Motorway Junctions are shown on the mapping pages by red junction indicators [2]

Junction M1

2	Northbound	No exit, access from A1 only
	Southbound	No access, exit to A1 only
4	Northbound	No exit, access from A41 only
	Southbound	No access, exit to A41 only
6a	Northbound	No exit, access from M25 only
	Southbound	No access, exit to M25 only
17	Northbound	No access, exit to M45 only
	Southbound	No access, exit to M45 only
19	Northbound	Exit to M6 only, access from A14 only
	Southbound	Access from M6 only, exit to A14 only
21a	Northbound	No access, exit to A46 only
	Southbound	No exit, access from A46 only
24a	Northbound	No exit
	Southbound	Access from A50 only
35a	Northbound	No access, exit to A616 only
	Southbound	No exit, access from A616 only
43	Northbound	Exit to M621 only
	Southbound	Access from M621 only
48	Eastbound	Exit to A1(M) northbound only
	Westbound	Access from A1(M) southbound only

Junction M2

1	Eastbound	Access from A2 eastbound only
	Westbound	Exit to A2 westbound only

Junction M3

8	Eastbound	No exit, access from A303 only
	Westbound	No access, exit to A303 only
10	Northbound	No access from A31
	Southbound	No exit to A31
13	Southbound	No access from A335 to M3 leading to M27 Eastbound

Junction M4

1	Eastbound	Exit to A4 eastbound only
	Westbound	Access from A4 westbound only
21	Eastbound	No exit to M48
	Westbound	No access from M48
23	Eastbound	No access from M48
	Westbound	No exit to M48
25	Eastbound	No exit
	Westbound	No access
25a	Eastbound	No exit
	Westbound	No access
29	Eastbound	No exit, access from A48(M) only
	Westbound	No access, exit to A48(M) only
38	Westbound	No exit, access to A48 only
39	Eastbound	No access or exit
	Westbound	No exit, access from A48 only
42	Eastbound	No access from A48
	Westbound	No exit to A48

Junction M5

10	Northbound	No exit, access from A4019 only
	Southbound	No access, exit to A4019 only
11a	Southbound	No exit to A417 westbound
18a	Northbound	No access from M49
	Southbound	No exit to M49

Junction M6

3a	Eastbound	No exit to M6 Toll
	Westbound	No access from M6 Toll
4	Northbound	No exit to M42 northbound
		No access from M42 southbound
	Southbound	No exit to M42
		No access from M42 southbound
4a	Northbound	No exit, access from M42 southbound only
	Southbound	No access, exit to M42 only
5	Northbound	No access, exit to A452 only
	Southbound	No exit, access from A452 only
10a	Northbound	No access, exit to M54 only
	Southbound	No exit, access from M54 only
11a	Northbound	No exit to M6 Toll
	Southbound	No access from M6 Toll
20	Northbound	No exit to M56 eastbound
	Southbound	No access from M56 westbound
24	Northbound	No exit, access from A58 only
	Southbound	No access, exit to A58 only
25	Northbound	No access, exit to A49 only
	Southbound	No exit, access from A49 only
30	Northbound	No exit, access from M61 northbound only
	Southbound	No access, exit to M61 southbound only
31a	Northbound	No access, exit to B6242 only
	Southbound	No exit, access from B6242 only
45	Northbound	No access onto A74(M)
	Southbound	No exit from A74(M)

Junction M6 Toll

T1	Northbound	No exit
	Southbound	No access
T2	Northbound	No access or exit
	Southbound	No access
T5	Northbound	No exit
	Southbound	No access
T7	Northbound	No access from A5
	Southbound	No exit
T8	Northbound	No exit to A460 northbound
	Southbound	No exit

Junction M8

6	Eastbound	No exit, access only
	Westbound	No access, exit only
6a	Eastbound	No exit, access only
	Westbound	No access, exit only
7	Eastbound	No exit, access only
	Westbound	No exit, access only
7a	Eastbound	No exit, access from A725 Northbound only
	Westbound	No access, exit to A725 Southbound only
8	Eastbound	No exit to M73 northbound
	Westbound	No access from M73 southbound
9	Eastbound	No exit, access only
	Westbound	No access, exit only
13	Eastbound	No access from M80 southbound
	Westbound	No exit to M80 northbound
14	Eastbound	No exit, access only
	Westbound	No access, exit only
16	Eastbound	No exit, access only
	Westbound	No access, exit only
17	Eastbound	No exit, access from A82 only
	Westbound	No access, exit to A82 only
18	Westbound	No exit, access only
19	Eastbound	No exit to A814 eastbound
	Westbound	No access from A814 westbound
20	Eastbound	No exit, access only
	Westbound	No access, exit only
21	Eastbound	No exit, access only
	Westbound	No access, exit only
22	Eastbound	No exit, access from M77 only
	Westbound	No access, exit to M77 only
23	Eastbound	No exit, access from B768 only
	Westbound	No access, exit to B768 only
25	Eastbound & Westbound	Access from A739 southbound only
		Exit to A739 northbound only
25a	Eastbound	Access only
	Westbound	Exit only
28	Eastbound	No exit, access from airport only
	Westbound	No access, exit to airport only
29a	Eastbound	No exit, access only
	Westbound	No access, exit only

Junction M9

2	Northbound	No exit, access from B8046 only
	Southbound	No access, exit to B8046 only
3	Northbound	No exit, access to A803 only
	Southbound	No exit, access from A803 only
6	Northbound	No exit, access only
	Southbound	No access, exit to A905 only
8	Northbound	No exit, access to M876 only
	Southbound	No access, exit from M876 only

Junction M11

4	Northbound	No access, exit to A406 eastbound only
	Southbound	No exit, access from A406 westbound only
5	Northbound	No access, exit to A1168 only
	Southbound	No exit, access from A1168 only
8a	Northbound	No access, exit only
	Southbound	No exit, access only
9	Northbound	No access, exit only
	Southbound	No exit, access only
13	Northbound	No access, exit only
	Southbound	No exit, access only
14	Northbound	No access from A428 eastbound
		No exit to A428 westbound
	Southbound	No exit, access from A428 eastbound only

Junction M20

2	Eastbound	No exit, access to A20 only (access via M26 Junction 2a)
	Westbound	No exit, access only(exit via M26 Jun.2a)
3	Eastbound	No access from M26 eastbound only
	Westbound	No access, exit to M26 westbound only
10	Eastbound	No exit, access only
	Westbound	No exit, access only
11a	Eastbound	No access from Channel Tunnel
	Westbound	No exit to Channel Tunnel

Junction M23

7	Northbound	No exit to A23 southbound
	Southbound	No access from A23 northbound

Junction M25

5	Clockwise	No exit to M26 eastbound
	Anti-clockwise	No access from M26 westbound
Spur to A21	Northbound	No exit to M26 eastbound
	Southbound	No access from M26 westbound
19	Clockwise	No exit, access only
	Anti-clockwise	No exit, access only
21	Clockwise & Anti-clockwise	No exit to M1 southbound
		No access from M1 northbound
31	Northbound	No access, exit only (access via Jun.30)
	Southbound	No exit, access only (exit via Jun.30)

M26

Junction with M25 (M25 Jun.5)

Eastbound	No access from M25 clockwise or spur from A21 northbound
West bound	No exit to M25 anti-clockwise or spur to A21 southbound

Junction with M20 (M20 Jun.3)

Eastbound	No exit to M20 westbound
Westbound	No access from M20 eastbound

Junction M27

4	Eastbound & Westbound	No exit to A33 southbound (Southampton)
		No access from A33 northbound
10	Eastbound	No exit, access from A32 only
	Westbound	No access, exit to A32 only

Junction M40

3	North-Westbound	No access, exit to A40 only
	South-Eastbound	No exit, access from A40 only
7	N.W bound	No access, exit only
	S.E bound	No access, exit only
13	N.W bound	No access, exit only
	S.E bound	No access, exit only
14	N.W bound	No access, exit only
	S.E bound	No access, exit only
16	N.W bound	No access, exit only
	S.E bound	No access, exit only

Junction M42

1	Eastbound	No exit
	Westbound	No access
7	Northbound	No access, exit to M6 only
	Southbound	No exit, access from M6 northbound only
8	Northbound	No exit, access from M6 southbound only
	Southbound	Exit to M6 northbound only
		Access from M6 southbound only

M45

Junction with M1 (M1 Jun.17)

Eastbound	No exit to M1 northbound
Westbound	No access from M1 southbound

Junction with A45 east of Dunchurch

Eastbound	No access, exit to A45 only
Westbound	No exit, access from A45 northbound only

M48

Junction with M4 (M4 Jun.21)

Eastbound	No exit to M4 westbound
Westbound	No access from M4 eastbound

Junction with M4 (M4 Jun.23)

Eastbound	No access from M4 westbound
Westbound	No exit to M4 eastbound

Junction M53

11	Northbound & Southbound	No access from M56 eastbound, no exit to M56 westbound

Junction M56

1	Eastbound	No exit to M60 N.W bound
		No exit to A34 southbound
	S.E bound	No access from A34 northbound
	Westbound	No access from M60
2	Eastbound	No exit, access from A560 only
	Westbound	No access, exit to A560 only
3	Eastbound	No access, exit only
	Westbound	No exit, access only
4	Eastbound	No exit, access only
	Westbound	No access, exit only
7	Westbound	No access, exit only
8	Eastbound	No access or exit
	Westbound	No exit, access from A556 only
9	Eastbound	No access from M6 northbound
	Westbound	No exit to M60 southbound
10a	Northbound	No exit, access only
	Southbound	No access, exit only
15	Eastbound	No exit to M53
	Westbound	No access from M53

Junction M57

3	Northbound	No exit, access only
	Southbound	No access, exit only
5	Northbound	No exit, access from A580 westbound only
	Southbound	No access, exit to A580 eastbound only

Junction M60

2	N.E bound	No access, exit to A560 only
	S.W bound	No exit, access from A560 only
3	Eastbound	No access from A34 southbound
	Westbound	No exit to A34 northbound
4	Eastbound	No exit to M56 S.W bound
		No exit to A34 northbound
	Westbound	No access from A34 southbound
		No access from M56 eastbound
5	N.W bound	No access from or exit to A5103 southbound
	S.E bound	No access from or exit to A5103 northbound
14	Eastbound	No exit to A580
		No access from A580 westbound
	Westbound	No exit to A580 eastbound
		No access from A580
16	Eastbound	No exit, access from A666 only
	Westbound	No access, exit to A666 only
20	Eastbound	No access from A664
	Westbound	No exit to A664
22	Westbound	No access from A62
25	S.W bound	No access from A560 / A6017
26	N.E bound	No access or exit
27	N.E bound	No access, exit only
	S.W bound	No exit, access only

Junction M61

2&3	N.W bound	No access from A580 eastbound
	S.E bound	No exit to A580 westbound

Junction with M6 (M6 Jun.30)
	N.W bound	No exit to M6 southbound
	S.E bound	No access from M6 northbound

Junction M62

23	Eastbound	No access, exit to A640 only
	Westbound	No exit, access from A640 only

Junction M65

9	N.E bound	No access, exit to A679 only
	S.W bound	No exit, access from A679 only
11	N.E bound	No access, access only
	S.W bound	No access, exit only

Junction M66

1	Northbound	No access, exit to A56 only
	Southbound	No exit, access from A56 only

Junction M67

1	Eastbound	Access from A57 eastbound only
	Westbound	Exit to A57 westbound only
1a	Eastbound	No exit, access to A6017 only
	Westbound	No exit, access from A6017 only
2	Eastbound	No exit, access from A57 only
	Westbound	No access, exit to A57 only

Junction M69

2	N.E bound	No exit, access from B4669 only
	S.W bound	No access, exit to B4669 only

Junction M73

1	Southbound	No exit to A721 eastbound
2	Northbound	No access from M8 eastbound
		No exit to A89 eastbound
	Southbound	No exit to M8 westbound
		No access from A89 westbound
3	Northbound	No exit to A80 S.W bound
	Southbound	No access from A80 N.E bound

Junction M74

1	Eastbound	No access from M8 Westbound
	Westbound	No exit to M8 Westbound
3	Eastbound	No exit
	Westbound	No access
7	Northbound	No exit, access from A72 only
	Southbound	No access, exit to A72 only
9	Northbound	No access or exit
	Southbound	No access, exit to B7078 only
10	Southbound	No access, access from B7078 only
11	Northbound	No exit, access from B7078 only
	Southbound	No access, exit to B7078 only
12	Northbound	No access, exit to A70 only
	Southbound	No exit, access from A70 only

Junction M77

Junction with M8 (M8 Jun.22)
	Northbound	No exit to M8 westbound
	Southbound	No access from M8 eastbound
4	Northbound	No exit
	Southbound	No access
6	Northbound	No exit to A77
	Southbound	No access from A77
7	Northbound	No access from A77
		No exit to A77

Junction M80

1	Northbound	No access from M8 westbound
	Southbound	No exit to M8 eastbound
4a	Northbound	No access
	Southbound	No exit
6a	Northbound	No exit
	Southbound	No access
8	Northbound	No access from M876
	Southbound	No exit to M876

Junction M90

1	Northbound	No exit
	Southbound	No access from A90
2a	Northbound	No access, exit to A92 only
	Southbound	No exit, access from A92 only
7	Northbound	No exit, access from A91 only
	Southbound	No access, exit to A91 only
8	Northbound	No access, exit to A91 only
	Southbound	No exit, access from A91 only
10	Northbound	No access from A912
		Exit to A912 northbound only
	Southbound	No exit to A912
		Access from A912 southbound only

Junction M180

1	Eastbound	No access, exit only
	Westbound	No exit, access from A18 only

Junction M606

2	Northbound	No access, exit only

Junction M621

2a	Eastbound	No exit, access only
	Westbound	No access, exit only
4	Southbound	No exit
5	Northbound	No access, exit to A61 only
	Southbound	No exit, access from A61 only
6	Northbound	No access, exit only
	Southbound	No exit, access only
7	Eastbound	No access, exit only
	Westbound	No exit, access only
8	Northbound	No exit, access only
	Southbound	No exit, access only

Junction M876

Junction with M80 (M80 Jun.5)
	N.E bound	No access from M80 southbound
	S.W bound	No exit to M80 northbound

Junction with M9 (M9 Jun.8)
	N.E bound	No exit to M9 northbound
	S.W bound	No access from M9 southbound

Junction A1(M)

Hertfordshire Section
2	Northbound	No access, exit only
	Southbound	No exit, access to A1001 only
3	Southbound	No access, exit only
5	Northbound	No exit, access only
	Southbound	No access or exit

Cambridgeshire Section
14	Northbound	No access, exit only
	Southbound	No exit, access only

Leeds Section
40	Southbound	Exit to A1 southbound only
43	Northbound	Access from M1 eastbound only
	Southbound	Exit to M1 westbound only

Durham Section
57	Northbound	No access, exit to A66(M) only
	Southbound	No exit, access from A66(M)
65	Northbound	Exit to A1 N.W bound and to A194(M) only
	Southbound	Access from A1 S.E bound and from A194(M) only

Junction A3(M)

4	Northbound	No access, exit only
	Southbound	No exit, access only

Aston Expressway A38(M)

Junction with Victoria Road, Aston
	Northbound	No exit, access only
	Southbound	No access, exit only

Junction A48(M)

Junction with M4 (M4 Jun.29)
	N.E bound	Exit to M4 eastbound only
	S.W bound	Access from M4 westbound only
29a	N.E bound	Access from A48 eastbound only
	S.W bound	Exit to A48 westbound only

Mancunian Way A57(M)

Junction with A34 Brook Street, Manchester
	Eastbound	No access, exit to A34 Brook Street, southbound only
	Westbound	No exit, access only

Leeds Inner Ring Road A58(M)

Junction with Park Lane / Westgate
	Southbound	No access, exit only

Leeds Inner Ring Road A64(M) (continuation of A58(M))

Junction with A58 Clay Pit Lane
	Eastbound	No access
	Westbound	No exit

A66(M)

Junction with A1(M) (A1(M) Jun.57)
	N.E bound	Access from A1(M) northbound only
	S.W bound	Exit to A1(M) southbound only

Junction A74(M)

18	Northbound	No access
	Southbound	No exit

Newcastle Central Motorway A167(M)

Junction with Camden Street
	Northbound	No exit, access only
	Southbound	No access or exit

A194(M)

Junction with A1(M) (A1(M) Jun.65) and A1 Gateshead Western By-Pass
	Northbound	Access from A1(M) only
	Southbound	Exit to A1(M) only

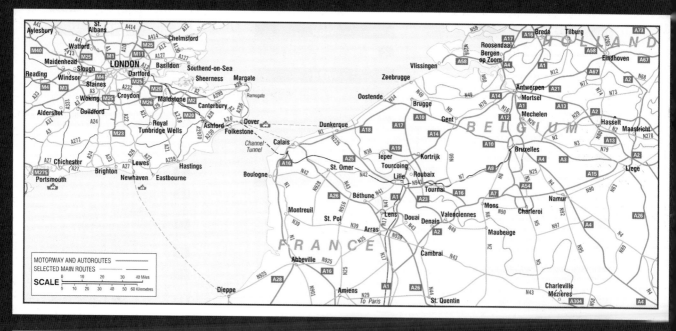

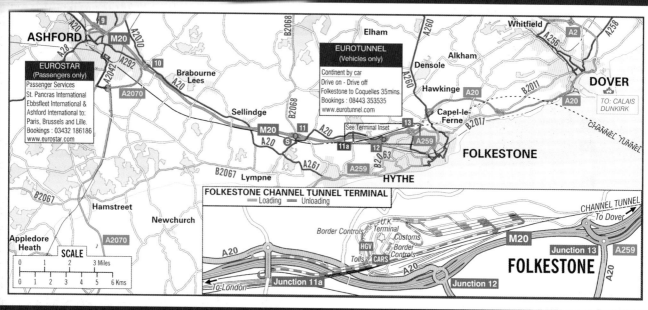

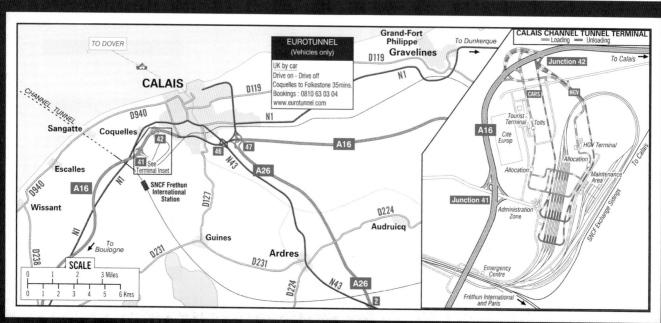